W9-ADY-309

The Legal Writing Handbook

How to use your Connected Casebook

Step 1: Go to **www.CasebookConnect.com** and redeem your access code to get started.

Access Code:

Step 2: Go to your **BOOKSHELF** and select your Connected Casebook to start reading, highlighting, and taking notes in the margins of your e-book.

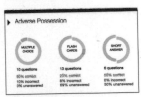

Step 3: Select the **STUDY** tab in your toolbar to access a variety of practice materials designed to help you master the course material. These materials may include explanations, videos, multiple-choice questions, flashcards, short answer, essays, and issue spotting.

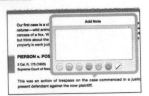

Step 4: Select the **OUTLINE** tab in your toolbar to access chapter outlines that automatically incorporate your highlights and annotations from the e-book. Use the My Notes area for copying, pasting, and editing your book notes or creating new notes.

Step 5: If your professor has enrolled your class, you can select the **CLASS INSIGHTS** tab and compare your own study center results against the average of your classmates.

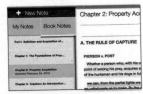

PIN: 9111149539

22236

Aspen Coursebook Series

The Legal Writing Handbook

Analysis, Research, and Writing

Sixth Edition

Laurel Currie Oates
Professor of Law
Seattle University School of Law

Anne Enquist
Director, Legal Writing Program
Professor of Lawyering Skills
Seattle University School of Law

 Wolters Kluwer
Law & Business

Published by Wolters Kluwer Law & Business in New York.

Wolters Kluwer Law & Business serves customers worldwide with CCH, Aspen Publishers, and Kluwer Law International products. (www.wolterskluwerlb.com)

To contact Customer Service, e-mail customer.service@wolterskluwer.com, call 1-800-234-1660, fax 1-800-901-9075, or mail correspondence to:

Wolters Kluwer Law & Business
Attn: Order Department
PO Box 990
Frederick, MD 21705

Printed in the United States of America.

1 2 3 4 5 6 7 8 9 0

ISBN 978-1-4548-4155-5

Oates, Laurel Currie, 1951- author.
 The legal writing handbook : analysis, research, and writing / Laurel Currie Oates, Professor of Law, Seattle University School of Law; Anne Enquist, Director, Legal Writing Program Professor of Lawyering Skills, Seattle University School of Law. -- Sixth Edition.
     pages cm
 Includes bibliographical references and index.
  ISBN 978-1-4548-4155-5 (alk. paper)
 1. Legal composition. 2. Legal research--United States. I. Enquist, Anne, 1950- author. II. Title.
 KF250.O18 2014
  808.06'634--dc23
                                                                2013049507

About Wolters Kluwer Law & Business

Wolters Kluwer Law & Business is a leading global provider of intelligent information and digital solutions for legal and business professionals in key specialty areas, and respected educational resources for professors and law students. Wolters Kluwer Law & Business connects legal and business professionals as well as those in the education market with timely, specialized authoritative content and information-enabled solutions to support success through productivity, accuracy and mobility.

Serving customers worldwide, Wolters Kluwer Law & Business products include those under the Aspen Publishers, CCH, Kluwer Law International, Loislaw, ftwilliam.com and MediRegs family of products.

CCH products have been a trusted resource since 1913, and are highly regarded resources for legal, securities, antitrust and trade regulation, government contracting, banking, pension, payroll, employment and labor, and healthcare reimbursement and compliance professionals.

Aspen Publishers products provide essential information to attorneys, business professionals and law students. Written by preeminent authorities, the product line offers analytical and practical information in a range of specialty practice areas from securities law and intellectual property to mergers and acquisitions and pension/benefits. Aspen's trusted legal education resources provide professors and students with high-quality, up-to-date and effective resources for successful instruction and study in all areas of the law.

Kluwer Law International products provide the global business community with reliable international legal information in English. Legal practitioners, corporate counsel and business executives around the world rely on Kluwer Law journals, looseleafs, books, and electronic products for comprehensive information in many areas of international legal practice.

Loislaw is a comprehensive online legal research product providing legal content to law firm practitioners of various specializations. Loislaw provides attorneys with the ability to quickly and efficiently find the necessary legal information they need, when and where they need it, by facilitating access to primary law as well as state-specific law, records, forms and treatises.

ftwilliam.com offers employee benefits professionals the highest quality plan documents (retirement, welfare and non-qualified) and government forms (5500/PBGC, 1099 and IRS) software at highly competitive prices.

MediRegs products provide integrated health care compliance content and software solutions for professionals in healthcare, higher education and life sciences, including professionals in accounting, law and consulting.

Wolters Kluwer Law & Business, a division of Wolters Kluwer, is headquartered in New York. Wolters Kluwer is a market-leading global information services company focused on professionals.

To my family, Terry Oates, Julia, Michael, and Milla Fishler, and
Michael Oates and Michelle Aragon.
Thank you for everything.

To my family, Steve, Matt, Mary, Natalie and
Jeff Enquist and Ilana Stern,
for their love and support.

Summary of Contents

Contents xi
List of Electronic Supplement Sections xxxiii
Preface xxxvii
Acknowledgments xxxix

Book 1: Introduction to Legal Writing 1

Chapter 1: Making the Transition 3
Chapter 2: The United States Legal System 15
Chapter 3: Reading and Analyzing Statutes and Cases 31

Book 2: Legal Research 41

Chapter 4: Researching Issues Governed by State Statutes
and Regulations 43
Chapter 5: Researching Plan for Issues Governed by Federal
Statutes and Regulations 57
Chapter 6: Researching Issues Governed by City or County
Ordinances 71
Chapter 7: Researching Issues Governed by Common Law 77
Chapter 8: Researching Constitutional Issues 89
Chapter 9: Researching Issues Governed by Federal, State, or
Local Court Rules 97
Chapter 10: Citators 105

**Book 3: Objective Memoranda, E-Memos, Opinion Letters,
and Email and Text Messages** 109

Chapter 11: Drafting Memos 111
Chapter 12: Drafting Memo 1 131
Chapter 13: Drafting Memo 2 209
Chapter 14: Drafting Memos Requiring Other Types of Analysis 247
Chapter 15: Drafting E-Memos, Email, and Text Messages 263
Chapter 16: Drafting Letters 283

Book 4: Briefs and Oral Argument 299

Chapter 17: Writing a Motion Brief 301
Chapter 18: Writing an Appellate Brief 381

Chapter 19: Oral Advocacy   509

Book 5: A Guide to Effective Writing   527

Chapter 20: Effective Writing — The Whole Paper   529
Chapter 21: Connections Between Paragraphs   551
Chapter 22: Effective Paragraphs   557
Chapter 23: Connections Between Sentences   573
Chapter 24: Effective Sentences   589
Chapter 25: Effective Words   615
Chapter 26: Eloquence   663

Book 6: A Guide to Correct Writing   677

Chapter 27: Grammar   679
Chapter 28: Punctuation   721
Chapter 29: Mechanics   769
Chapter 30: Before You Practice   789

Book 7: A Guide to Legal Writing for English-as-a-Second-Language Writers   809

Chapter 31: Legal Writing for English-as-a-Second-Language
             Writers   811

Glossary of Usage   859
Glossary of Terms   867
Index   883

Contents

List of Electronic Supplement Sections xxxiii
Preface xxxvii
Acknowledgments xxxix

Book 1:   Introduction to Legal Writing   1

Chapter 1:   Making the Transition   3

§ 1.1   Understanding the Purpose of a Piece of Legal Writing   4
§ 1.2   Writing for Legal Readers   6
§ 1.3   Understanding Your Role as a Legal Writer   9
§ 1.4   Learning the Conventions of Legal Writing   10
§ 1.5   Advice for Specific Groups   11
   § 1.5.1   English Majors   11
   § 1.5.2   Philosophy Majors   12
   § 1.5.3   Journalism Majors and Journalists   12
   § 1.5.4   Science Majors and Scientists   13
   § 1.5.5   Writers from Other Cultures   14

Chapter 2:   The United States Legal System   15

§ 2.1   The Three Branches of Government   16
   § 2.1.1   The Executive Branch   16
   § 2.1.2   The Legislative Branch   16
   § 2.1.3   The Judicial Branch   17
      a.   The Hierarchical Nature of the Court System   17
      b.   The Federal Courts   19
      c.   State Courts   22
      d.   Other Courts   23
§ 2.2   The Relationship Between the Federal and State Governments   23
   § 2.2.1   A Short History   23
   § 2.2.2   The Relationship Between Laws Enacted by Congress and Those Enacted by the State Legislatures   23
   § 2.2.3   The Relationship Between Federal and State Courts   24
   § 2.2.4   The Relationship Among Federal, State, and Local Prosecutors   25

§ 2.3   Deciding How Much Weight to Give to a Particular
           Authority   25
           § 2.3.1   Which Jurisdiction's Law Applies?   26
           § 2.3.2   What "Law" Will Be Binding on the Court?   26

Chapter 3:   Reading and Analyzing Statutes and Cases   31

§ 3.1   Good Lawyers Are Good Readers   32
§ 3.2   Good Legal Readers Read and Reread Material
           Until They Are Sure That They Understand It   33
§ 3.3   Good Legal Readers Engage in Both Analysis and
           Synthesis   34
§ 3.4   Good Legal Readers Place the Statutes and Cases
           They Read into Their Historical, Social, Economic,
           Political, and Legal Contexts   36
§ 3.5   Good Legal Readers "Judge" the Statutes and Cases
           They Read   37
§ 3.6   Good Legal Readers Read for a Specific Purpose   38
§ 3.7   Good Legal Readers Understand That Statutes and
           Cases Can Be Read in More Than One Way   38

Book 2:   Legal Research   41

**Chapter 4:   Researching Issues Governed by State Statutes
                and Regulations   43**

§ 4.1   Research Plan for an Issue Governed by State Statutes   43
§ 4.2   Sources for State Statutory Research   44
           § 4.2.1   Sources for Background Reading   44
                       a.   Practice Manuals and Practice Books   45
                       b.   Hornbooks and Nutshells   46
                       c.   The Internet   46
           § 4.2.2   Sources for Statutes   47
                       a.   Session Laws   47
                       b.   Unannotated Codes   47
                       c.   Annotated Codes   48
           § 4.2.3   Sources for State Regulations   49
           § 4.2.4   Locating Cases That Have Interpreted or
                       Applied a State Statute   49
                       a.   Notes of Decision/Case Notes   49
                       b.   Reporters   51
           § 4.2.5   Sources for Secondary Materials   53
                       a.   State Attorney General Opinions   53
                       b.   American Law Reports   53
                       c.   Law Reviews and Journals   54
§ 4.3   Using the Research Plan to Research an Issue Governed
           by State Statutes   54

**Chapter 5:   Researching Plan for Issues Governed by
Federal Statutes and Regulations   57**

§ 5.1   Research Plan for Issues Governed by Federal Statutes
and Regulations   58
§ 5.2   Sources for Federal Statutory Research   58
    § 5.2.1   Sources for Background Reading   58
        a.   The Internet   58
        b.   Practice Manuals   60
        c.   Hornbooks and Nutshells   60
        d.   Legal Encyclopedias   60
    § 5.2.2   Sources for Federal Statutes and Regulations 61
        a.   Sessions Laws   61
        b.   Unannotated Codes   61
        c.   Annotated Codes   62
        d.   Federal Regulations   62
    § 5.2.3   Sources for Cases That Have Interpreted or
               Applied a Federal Statute or Regulation   63
        a.   Finding Tools   63
        b.   Reporters   65
    § 5.2.4   Sources for Additional Secondary Authority   67
        a.   Law Reviews and Law Journals   67
        b.   *American Law Reports*, Federal   67
        c.   Looseleaf Services   67
§ 5.3   Using the Research Plan to Research an Issue Governed
by Federal Statutes and Regulations   68

**Chapter 6:   Researching Issues Governed by
City or County Ordinances   71**

§ 6.1   An Introduction to City and County Government   72
§ 6.2   Research Plans for Issues Governed by City or County
Ordinances   72
§ 6.3   Sources for Researching Issues Governed by City
or County Ordinances   73
    § 6.3.1   Charters   73
    § 6.3.2   Ordinances   74
    § 6.3.3   Other City or County Documents   75
§ 6.4   Using the Research Plan to Research an Issue Governed
by City or County Ordinances   75

Chapter 7:   Researching Issues Governed by Common Law   77

§ 7.1   Are All Cases the Same?   77
§ 7.2   Modifying the Generic Research Plan for Issues
That Are Governed by Common Law   79
§ 7.3   Sources for Researching Problems Governed by
State Common Law   80
    § 7.3.1   Background Reading   80
        a.   The Internet   80
        b.   Practice Manuals and Books   80

		c.	Hornbooks and Nutshells	81
		d.	Legal Encyclopedias	82
	§ 7.3.2		Finding Tools	82
		a.	Practice Manuals and Books	82
		b.	Digests	83
		c.	Fee-Based Services	83
		d.	Free Websites	84
	§ 7.3.3		Cases	84
	§ 7.3.4		Other Authorities	85
		a.	American Law Reports	85
		b.	Law Reviews and Journals	86

§ 7.4   Using the Research Plan to Research an Issue Governed by Common Law   86

Chapter 8:   Researching Constitutional Issues   89

§ 8.1   Research Plan for Constitutional Issues   89
§ 8.2   Sources for Researching Constitutional Issues   90
    § 8.2.1   Background Reading   90
    § 8.2.2   Primary Authority   92
        a.   United States Constitution   92
        b.   Federal Cases Interpreting and Applying the United States Constitution   92
        c.   State Constitutions   93
        d.   Cases Interpreting and Applying a State Constitution   93
    § 8.2.3   Finding Tools   94
    § 8.2.4   Briefs   95
§ 8.3   Using the Research Plan to Research a Constitutional Issue   95

Chapter 9:   Researching Issues Governed by Federal, State, or Local Court Rules   97

§ 9.1   Research Plans for Projects Involving Federal, State, or Local Court Rules   98
§ 9.2   Sources for Federal Rules   99
    § 9.2.1   *United States Code, United States Code Annotated,* and *United States Code Service*   99
    § 9.2.2   Specialized Books   99
    § 9.2.3   Free Internet Sites   100
    § 9.2.4   Fee-Based, Online Services   100
§ 9.3   Sources for State Rules   101
    § 9.3.1   State Codes   101
    § 9.3.2   Specialized Books   101
    § 9.3.3   Free Internet Sites   101
    § 9.3.4   Fee-Based, Online Services   101
§ 9.4   Sources for Local Rules   102
    § 9.4.1   Books   102
    § 9.4.2   Free Internet Sites   102
    § 9.4.3   Fee-Based, Online Services   103

§ 9.4.4   Telephone Calls and Emails   103
§ 9.5   Using the Research Plan to Research an Issue Governed
by Federal, State, or Local Court Rules   103

Chapter 10: Citators   105

§ 10.1   Introduction to Citators   106
§ 10.2   Types of Citators   106
§ 10.3   Cite Checking Using *Shepard's*, KeyCite, and BCite 107

Book 3: Objective Memoranda, E-Memos, Opinion Letters,
and Email and Text Messages   109

Chapter 11: Drafting Memos   111

§ 11.1   Audience   112
§ 11.2   Purpose   112
§ 11.3   Conventions   112
§ 11.4   Sample Memos   113
          § 11.4.1   Sample Memo 1   113
          § 11.4.2   Sample Memo 2   119
          § 11.4.3   Sample E-Memo   125
          § 11.4.4   Sample E-Memo   126
          § 11.4.5   Sample E-Memo   127

Chapter 12: Drafting Memo 1   131

§ 12.1   The Assignment   131
§ 12.2   Researching the Law   133
§ 12.3   Understanding What You Have Found   137
          § 12.3.1   Make Sure You Understand the Big Picture 137
          § 12.3.2   Make Sure You Understand the Statute   137
          § 12.3.3   Make Sure You Understand the General and
                      Specific Rules   128
§ 12.4   Drafting the Heading   140
§ 12.5   Drafting the Statement of Facts   141
          § 12.5.1   Decide What Facts to Include   141
                      a.   Legally Significant Facts   141
                      b.   Emotionally Significant Facts   143
                      c.   Background Facts   143
                      d.   Unknown Facts   144
          § 12.5.2   Select an Organizational Scheme   144
          § 12.5.3   Present the Facts Clearly and Concisely 146
          § 12.5.4   Present the Facts Accurately and Objectively 146
          § 12.5.5   Checklist for Critiquing the Statement of Facts 147
                      a.   Content   147
                      b.   Organization   147
                      c.   Writing   147
§ 12.6   Drafting the Issue Statement   148
          § 12.6.1   Select a Format: The "Under-Does-When"
                      Format   149

		a.	Reference to the Applicable Law	149
		b.	Statement of the Legal Question	149
		c.	The Key Facts	150
	§ 12.6.2	Make Sure that Your Issue Statement Is Easy to Read		152
	§ 12.6.3	Checklist for Critiquing the Issue Statement		153
		a.	Content	153
		b.	Format	153
		c.	Writing	153
§ 12.7	Drafting the Brief Answer			153
	§ 12.7.1	Select a Format		153
	§ 12.7.2	Set Out Your Conclusion and Reasoning		154
	§ 12.7.3	Checklist for Critiquing the Brief Answer		155
		a.	Content	155
		b.	Format	155
		c.	Writing	155
§ 12.8	Drafting the Discussion Section Using a Script Format			156
	§ 12.8.1	Modify the Template So That It Works for Your Issue		157
	§ 12.8.2	Draft the Introductory, or General Rule, Section		160
		a.	Decide What Information You Need to Include	160
		b.	Order the Information	160
		c.	Prepare the First Draft	161
		d.	Include a Citation to Authority for Each Rule	164
	§ 12.8.3	Draft the Discussion of the Undisputed Elements		164
		a.	Decide Where to Put Your Discussion of the Undisputed Elements	165
		b.	Prepare the First Draft of Your Discussion of the Undisputed Elements	166
	§ 12.8.4	Draft the Discussion of the Disputed Elements		167
		a.	Set Out the Specific Rules	167
		b.	Describe the Analogous Cases	168
		c.	Draft the Arguments	178
		d.	Predict How the Court Will Decide the Element	189
	§ 12.8.5	Checklist for Critiquing a Discussion Section Written Using a Script Format		190
		a.	Content	190
		b.	Large-Scale Organization	191
		c.	Writing	191
§ 12.9	Drafting the Formal Conclusion			191
	§ 12.9.1	Summarize Your Conclusions		192
	§ 12.9.2	Present Your Advice		192
	§ 12.9.3	Checklist for Formal Conclusion		193
		a.	Content	193
		b.	Organization	193

		c.	Writing	193

§ 12.10   Revising, Editing, and Proofreading the Memo   194

    § 12.10.1   Revise Your Draft   194

        a.   Check Content   194

        b.   Check to Make Sure That the Information Is Presented Accurately   194

        c.   Check to Make Sure That the Discussion Section Is Well Organized   194

        d.   Check to Make Sure That the Connections Are Explicit   194

            1.   Roadmaps   195

            2.   Topic Sentences, Signposts, and Transitions   196

            3.   Dovetailing   197

    § 12.10.2   Edit Your Draft   199

        a.   Writing Effective Sentences   199

            1.   Use the Actor as the Subject of Most Sentences   199

            2.   Keep the Subject and Verb Close Together   203

            3.   Put Old Information at the Beginning of the Sentence and New Information at the End   203

            4.   Vary Sentence Length and Pattern   204

        b.   Writing Correctly   205

    § 12.10.3   Proofreading   205

    § 12.10.4   Citations   206

Chapter 13:   Drafting Memo 2   **209**

§ 13.1   The Assignment   209

§ 13.2   Researching the Law   211

§ 13.3   Understanding What You Have Found   211

    § 13.3.1   Organize Your Research Notes   211

    § 13.3.2   Make Sure You Understand the Big Picture   214

    § 13.3.3   Make Sure You Understand the Common Law Rule and Any Applicable Statutes   214

    § 13.3.4   Make Sure You Understand the Burden of Proof   215

    § 13.3.5   Make Sure You Understand the Specific Rules and the Cases That Have Applied Those Rules   215

§ 13.4   Drafting the Heading   217

§ 13.5   Drafting the Statement of Facts   217

    § 13.5.1   Decide What Facts to Include   217

    § 13.5.2   Select an Organizational Scheme   218

    § 13.5.3   Present the Facts Accurately and Objectively   220

    § 13.5.4   Checklist for Critiquing the Statement of Facts   220

        a.   Content   220

		b.	Organization	220
		c.	Writing	221
§ 13.6	Drafting the Issue Statement			221
	§ 13.6.1	Select a Format: The "Whether" Format		221
	§ 13.6.2	Make Sure Your Issue Statement Is Easy to Read		222
	§ 13.6.3	Checklist for Critiquing the Issue Statement		224
		a.	Content	224
		b.	Format	224
		c.	Writing	224
§ 13.7	Drafting the Brief Answer			224
	§ 13.7.1	Use One of the Conventional Formats		224
	§ 13.7.2	Checklist for Critiquing the Brief Answer		225
		a.	Content	225
		b.	Format	225
		c.	Writing	225
§ 13.8	Drafting the Discussion Section Using an Integrated Format			225
	§ 13.8.1	Draft the Specific Rule Section		228
	§ 13.8.2	Draft the Analogous Case Section		229
	§ 13.8.3	Draft the Mini-Conclusion		230
	§ 13.8.4	Draft the Arguments		232
	§ 13.8.5	Avoid the Common Problems		234
		a.	Give Appropriate Weight to Each Side's Arguments	234
		b.	Write Sentences That Are Easy to Read	234
	§ 13.8.6	Checklist for Discussion Section Written Using an Integrated Format		237
		a.	Content	237
		b.	Large-Scale Organization	238
		c.	Writing	238
§ 13.9	Draft the Conclusion			239
§ 13.10	Revising and Editing Your Draft			240
	§ 13.10.1	Revise for Content and Organization		240
	§ 13.10.2	Edit Your Draft		241
		a.	Write Concisely	241
		b.	Write Precisely	242
		1.	Select the Correct Term	242
		2.	Use Terms Consistently	243
		3.	Make Sure the Subjects and Verbs Go Together	243
		4.	Compare or Contrast Like Things	244
	§ 13.10.3	Proofread the Final Draft		245

Chapter 14:   Drafting Memos Requiring Other Types of Analysis   247

| § 14.1 | Factor Analysis | | 247 |
| | § 14.1.1 | Templates for Issues Involving a Factor Analysis | 247 |

§ 14.1.2   Draft the Introductory or General Rule
            Section   251
§ 14.1.3   Draft the Discussion of the Undisputed
            Factors   252
§ 14.1.4   Draft the Discussion of the Disputed Factors   252
§ 14.1.5   Draft the Paragraph or Block of Paragraphs
            in Which You Weigh the Factors   253
§ 14.2   Balancing of Competing Interests   254
§ 14.2.1   Templates for Issues Requiring the
            Balancing of Competing Interests   254
§ 14.2.2   Draft the Introductory or General Rule
            Section   256
§ 14.2.3   Draft the Discussion of the Competing
            Interests   256
§ 14.3   Issue of First Impression   257
§ 14.3.1   Circuit Split   258
§ 14.3.2   The Statute Is Ambiguous, and There Are No
            Regulations or Cases That Have Interpreted
            That Statute   260
§ 14.3.3   Arguments Based on Agency Decisions   260
§ 14.3.4   Policy Arguments   261

Chapter 15: Drafting E-Memos, Email, and Text Messages   263

§ 15.1   E-Memos   263
§ 15.1.1   Audience   263
§ 15.1.2   Purpose   264
§ 15.1.3   Conventional Formats for E-Memos   264
            a.   Introductory Sentence or Paragraph   265
            b.   Summary of the Applicable Law   266
            c.   Application of the Law to the Key Facts   268
§ 15.1.4   Writing Style   269
§ 15.1.5   Client Confidentially   270
§ 15.1.6   Checklist for Critiquing E-Memos   270
§ 15.1.7   Sample E-Memos   271
§ 15.2   Email   275
§ 15.3   Text Messages   279

Chapter 16: Drafting Letters   283

§ 16.1   The Assignment   283
§ 16.2   Know Your Audience and Your Purpose   284
§ 16.2.1   The Audience for an Opinion Letter   284
§ 16.2.2   The Purpose of an Opinion Letter   284
§ 16.3   Prepare the First Draft of the Letter   285
§ 16.3.1   The Introductory Paragraph   286
§ 16.3.2   Statement of the Issue   287
§ 16.3.3   Opinion   287
§ 16.3.4   Summary of the Facts   288
§ 16.3.5   Explanation   288
§ 16.3.6   Advice   289

§ 16.3.7   Concluding Paragraph   289
§ 16.3.8   Warnings   289
§ 16.4   Revising, Editing, and Proofreading the Opinion Letter   289
§ 16.4.1   Drafting a Well-Written Letter   289
§ 16.4.2   Using an Appropriate Tone   290
§ 16.4.3   Checklist for Critiquing the Opinion Letter   291
§ 16.5   Sample Client Letters   292

Book 4: Briefs and Oral Argument   299

Chapter 17: Writing a Motion Brief   301

§ 17.1   Motion Briefs   301
§ 17.1.1   Audience   301
§ 17.1.2   Purpose   303
§ 17.1.3   Conventions   303
§ 17.2   *State v. Patterson*   303
§ 17.3   Constructing a "Theory of the Case"   304
§ 17.4   The Caption   305
§ 17.5   Introductory Paragraph/Prayer for Relief   305
§ 17.6   The Statement of Facts   306
§ 17.6.1   Select the Facts   307
        a.   Background Facts   307
        b.   Legally Significant Facts   307
        c.   Emotionally Significant Facts   307
§ 17.6.2   Select an Organizational Scheme   307
§ 17.6.3   Present the Facts in a Light Favorable to
            Your Client   308
        a.   Create a Favorable Context   308
        b.   Tell the Story from the Client's Point
              of View   310
        c.   Emphasize the Facts That Support Your
              Theory of the Case, and De-emphasize
              Those That Do Not   310
            1.   Airtime   311
            2.   Detail   311
            3.   Positions of Emphasis   312
            4.   Sentence Length   313
            5.   Active and Passive Voice   314
            6.   Dependent and Main Clauses   314
        d.   Select Words Both for Their Denotation
              and Their Connotation   315
§ 17.6.4   Checklist for Critiquing the Statement
            of Facts   316
§ 17.7   Drafting the Issue Statement   317
§ 17.7.1   Select the Lens   317
§ 17.7.2   Select a Format   317
§ 17.7.3   Make Your Issue Statement Subtly Persuasive   318
§ 17.7.4   Checklist for Critiquing the Issue Statement   320
§ 17.8   Ordering the Issues and Arguments   321

§ 17.8.1   Present the Issues and Arguments in a
           Logical Order   321
§ 17.8.2   Decide Which Issues and Arguments Should
           Be Presented First   321

§ 17.9   Drafting the Argumentative Headings   322
§ 17.9.1   Use Your Argumentative Headings to Define
           the Structure of the Argument   322
§ 17.9.2   Use Your Argumentative Headings to Persuade   323
§ 17.9.3   Make Your Headings Readable   324
§ 17.9.4   Follow the Conventions: Number, Placement,
           and Typefaces   325
§ 17.9.5   Checklist for Critiquing the Argumentative
           Headings   326

§ 17.10   Drafting the Arguments   326
§ 17.10.1 Identify Your Assertions and Your Support
           for Those Assertions   327
       a. Setting Out Your Assertion   327
       b. Supporting Your Assertion   327
§ 17.10.2 Select an Organizational Scheme   329
§ 17.10.3 Present the Rules in the Light Most
           Favorable to Your Client   332
§ 17.10.4 Present the Cases in the Light Most
           Favorable to Your Client   336
§ 17.10.5 Present the Arguments in the Light Most
           Favorable to Your Client   337
       a. Present Your Own Arguments First   337
       b. Give the Most Airtime to Your Own
           Arguments   338
       c. Use Language That Strengthens Your
           Arguments and Undermines the Other
           Side's Arguments   338
       d. Use the Same Persuasive Techniques
           You Used in Setting Out the Facts,
           Issues, Rules, and Analogous Cases   339
§ 17.10.6 Checklist for Critiquing the Argument   339

§ 17.11   The Prayer for Relief   340
§ 17.12   Signing the Brief   341
§ 17.13   Sample Briefs   342

Chapter 18: Writing an Appellate Brief   381

§ 18.1   Practicing Before an Appellate Court   381
§ 18.1.1   Types of Appellate Review   381
§ 18.1.2   Time Limits for Filing the Notice of Appeal
           or Petition for Discretionary Review   383
§ 18.1.3   The Notice of Appeal or Notice for
           Discretionary Review   383
§ 18.1.4   Scope of Review   384
§ 18.1.5   The Record on Appeal   384
§ 18.1.6   Types of Briefs   385

§ 18.2   Understanding Your Audience, Your Purpose, and the
           Conventions   385
           § 18.2.1   Audience   385
           § 18.2.2   Purpose   387
           § 18.2.3   Conventions   387
§ 18.3   Getting the Case: *United States v. Josephy*   391
§ 18.4   Preparing to Write the Brief   393
           § 18.4.1   Reviewing the Record for Error   393
           § 18.4.2   Selecting the Issues on Appeal   395
                       a.   Was There an Error?   395
                       b.   Was the Error Preserved?   395
                       c.   What Is the Standard of Review?   394
                       d.   Was the Error Harmless?   395
           § 18.4.3   Preparing an Abstract of the Record   399
           § 18.4.4   Preparing the Record on Appeal   399
§ 18.5   Researching the Issues on Appeal   399
§ 18.6   Planning the Brief   400
           § 18.6.1   Analyzing the Facts and the Law   400
           § 18.6.2   Developing a Theory of the Case   402
           § 18.6.3   Selecting an Organizational Scheme   403
                       a.   Deciding on the Number of Issues
                            and Headings   403
                       b.   Ordering the Issues and Arguments   407
§ 18.7   Preparing the Cover   409
§ 18.8   Preparing the Table of Contents   409
§ 18.9   Preparing the Table of Authorities   409
§ 18.10   Drafting the Jurisdictional Statement   410
§ 18.11   Drafting the Statement of Issues Presented for Review   410
           § 18.11.1   Select a Format   411
           § 18.11.2   Make the Issue Statement Subtly Persuasive   412
                       a.   State the Question So That It Suggests
                            the Conclusion You Want the Court
                            to Reach   411
                       b.   Emphasize the Facts That Support
                            Your Theory of the Case   413
                       c.   Emphasize or De-emphasize the
                            Burden of Proof and Standard of Review   414
           § 18.11.3   Make Sure the Issue Statement Is Readable   414
§ 18.12   Drafting the Statement of the Case   415
           § 18.12.1   Check the Rules   415
           § 18.12.2   Draft the Statement of the Case   415
           § 18.12.3   Select the Facts   416
                       a.   Legally Significant Facts   416
                       b.   Emotionally Significant Facts   416
                       c.   Background Facts   417
           § 18.12.4   Select an Organizational Scheme   417
           § 18.12.5   Present the Facts in the Light Most Favorable
                       to the Client   418
                       a.   Create a Favorable Context   418

	b.	Tell the Story from the Client's Point of View	420
	c.	Emphasize Those Facts That Support Your Theory of the Case and De-emphasize Those That Do Not	422
		1. Airtime	422
		2. Detail	423
		3. Positions of Emphasis	425
		4. Sentence and Paragraph Length	426
		5. Sentence Construction	427
		6. Active and Passive Voice	428
	d.	Choose Words Carefully	428
	e.	Be Subtly Persuasive	429

§ 18.13　Drafting the Summary of the Argument 430

§ 18.14　Drafting the Argumentative Headings 431

§ 18.14.1　Use the Argumentative Headings to Outline the Arguments for the Court 431

§ 18.14.2　Use the Argumentative Headings to Persuade 431

　　　　　a. Make a Positive Assertion 432

　　　　　b. Provide Support for Your Assertions 433

　　　　　c. Make Sure That Your Headings Are Neither Too Specific nor Too General 434

　　　　　d. Make Your Headings Readable 435

　　　　　e. Use the Same Persuasive Techniques You Used in Drafting the Issue Statements and Statement of Facts 436

§ 18.14.3　Use the Conventional Formats for Headings 437

§ 18.15　Drafting the Arguments 438

§ 18.15.1　Knowing What You Need, and Want, to Argue 438

§ 18.15.2　Selecting an Organizational Scheme 439

§ 18.15.3　Presenting the Rules, Descriptions of Analogous Cases, and Arguments in the Light Most Favorable to Your Client 443

　　　　　a. Presenting the Rules 443

　　　　　b. Presenting the Cases 445

　　　　　c. Constructing and Presenting the Arguments 451

　　　　　d. Using Quotations 453

　　　　　e. Responding to the Other Side's Arguments 455

　　　　　f. Avoiding the Common Problem of Neglecting to Make Explicit Connections 458

　　　　　g. Avoiding the Common Problem of Not Dealing with Weaknesses 459

　　　　　h. Avoiding the Mistake of Overlooking Good Arguments 460

§ 18.16　Drafting the Conclusion or Prayer for Relief 461

§ 18.17　Preparing the Signature Block 462

§ 18.18　Preparing the Appendix 462

§ 18.19   Revising, Editing, and Proofreading   461
§ 18.20   Sample Briefs   464

Chapter 19: Oral Advocacy   509

§ 19.1   Audience   509
§ 19.2   Purpose   510
§ 19.3   Preparing for Oral Argument   510
    § 19.3.1   Deciding What to Argue   510
    § 19.3.2   Preparing an Outline   511
    § 19.3.3   Practicing the Argument   511
    § 19.3.4   Reviewing the Facts and the Law   511
    § 19.3.5   Organizing Your Materials   511
        a.   Notes or Outline   512
        b.   The Briefs   512
        c.   The Record   512
        d.   The Law   512
§ 19.4   Courtroom Procedures and Etiquette   512
    § 19.4.1   Seating   512
    § 19.4.2   Before the Case Is Called   512
    § 19.4.3   Courtroom Etiquette   513
    § 19.4.4   Appropriate Dress   513
§ 19.5   Making the Argument   513
    § 19.5.1   Introductions   514
    § 19.5.2   Opening   514
    § 19.5.3   Statement of the Issues   514
        a.   The Moving Party   514
        b.   The Responding Party   515
    § 19.5.4   Summary of Facts   515
        a.   The Moving Party   515
        b.   The Responding Party   516
    § 19.5.5   The Argument   516
    § 19.5.6   Answering Questions   517
    § 19.5.7   The Closing   518
    § 19.5.8   Rebuttal   518
§ 19.6   Delivering the Argument   519
    § 19.6.1   Breathe   519
    § 19.6.2   Do Not Read Your Argument   519
    § 19.6.3   Maintain Eye Contact   519
    § 19.6.4   Do Not Slouch, Rock, or Put Your Hands
          in Your Pockets   519
    § 19.6.5   Limit Your Gestures and Avoid Distracting
          Mannerisms   520
    § 19.6.6   Speak So That You Can Be Easily Understood   520
§ 19.7   Making Your Argument Persuasive   520
§ 19.8   Handling the Problems   520
    § 19.8.1   Counsel Has Misstated Facts or Law   521
    § 19.8.2   You Make a Mistake   521
    § 19.8.3   You Don't Have Enough Time   521
    § 19.8.4   You Have Too Much Time   521

§ 19.8.5   You Don't Know the Answer to a Question   521
§ 19.8.6   You Don't Understand the Question   522
§ 19.8.7   You Become Flustered or Draw a Blank   522
§ 19.8.8   You're Asked to Concede a Point   522
§ 19.9   A Final Note   522
§ 19.9.1   Checklist for Critiquing the Oral Argument   523

Book 5: A Guide to Effective Writing   527

Chapter 20: Effective Writing — The Whole Paper   529

§ 20.1   The Psychology of Writing   529
§ 20.2   Outlines, Writing Plans, and Ordered Lists   531
§ 20.2.1   Read It All; Mull It Over   531
§ 20.2.2   Don't Overlook Obvious Ways to Organize   531
§ 20.2.3   Find Order Using a Three-Column Chart   532
§ 20.2.4   Talk to a Colleague   532
§ 20.2.5   Try a New Analogy or Format   533
§ 20.2.6   Create a Dining Room Table, Bedroom
            Floor, or Multiple Monitor Outline   533
§ 20.2.7   Consider Your Reader and Purpose and
            How You View the Case   535
§ 20.3   Drafting the Document   535
§ 20.3.1   Give Yourself Optimum Writing Conditions   535
§ 20.3.2   Trick Yourself into Getting Started   536
§ 20.3.3   Write What You Know Best First   536
§ 20.3.4   "Get the Juices Flowing"   536
§ 20.3.5   Take It One Step at a Time   536
§ 20.3.6   Stay Focused   537
§ 20.3.7   Tackle and Conquer the Procrastination Habit   537
§ 20.3.8   Manage the Multi-Tasking Habit   538
§ 20.3.9   Reward Yourself   542
§ 20.4   Revising   542
§ 20.4.1   Develop a Revision Checklist   542
§ 20.4.2   Write an After-the-Fact Outline   543
§ 20.4.3   Do a Self-Critique   543
§ 20.4.4   Check for Unity and Coherence   544
§ 20.5   Editing   544
§ 20.6   Proofreading   545
§ 20.7   Myths About Writing   546

Chapter 21: Connections Between Paragraphs   551

§ 21.1   Headings   551
§ 21.2   Roadmaps and Signposts   553
§ 21.2.1   Roadmaps   553
§ 21.2.2   Signposts   555

Chapter 22: Effective Paragraphs   557

§ 22.1   The Function of a Paragraph   557

§ 22.2   Paragraph Patterns   558
§ 22.3   Unity and Coherence in Paragraphs   559
            § 22.3.1   Paragraph Unity   559
            § 22.3.2   Paragraph Coherence   560
                        a.   Using Familiar Organizational Patterns 560
                        b.   Using Key Terms   561
                        c.   Using Sentence Structure and Other
                              Coherence Devices   561
§ 22.4   Paragraph Length   562
§ 22.5   Topic and Concluding Sentences   563
            § 22.5.1   Stated Topic Sentences   564
            § 22.5.2   Implied Topic Sentences   567
            § 22.5.3   Concluding Sentences   567
§ 22.6   Paragraph Blocks   569

Chapter 23:   Connections Between Sentences   573

§ 23.1   Generic Transitions   573
            § 23.1.1   Using Generic Transitions   573
            § 23.1.2   Problems with Generic Transitions   576
§ 23.2   Orienting Transitions   578
§ 23.3   Substantive Transitions   579
            § 23.3.1   The Structure of Substantive Transitions   580
                        Dovetailing   580
            § 23.3.2   The Content of Substantive Transitions   584
                        a.   Bridging the Gap Between Law and
                              Application   585
                        b.   Applying Another Court's Rationale   585
                        c.   Gathering Together Several Facts   586
                        d.   Bridging the Gap Between Sections
                              of a Document   586

Chapter 24:   Effective Sentences   589

§ 24.1   Active and Passive Voice   589
            § 24.1.1   Identifying Active and Passive Voice   589
            § 24.1.2   Effective Use of Active Voice   591
            § 24.1.3   Effective Use of Passive Voice   592
§ 24.2   Concrete Subjects   593
§ 24.3   Action Verbs   595
§ 24.4   Distance Between Subjects and Verbs   597
§ 24.5   Sentence Length   599
            § 24.5.1   The Reader   599
            § 24.5.2   The Context   601
            § 24.5.3   The Power of the Short Sentence   602
§ 24.6   Emphasis   602
            § 24.6.1   Telling the Reader What Is Important   603
            § 24.6.2   Underlining   604
            § 24.6.3   Using Positions of Emphasis   604
            § 24.6.4   Using Punctuation for Emphasis   606
            § 24.6.5   Using Single-Word Emphasizers   607

§ 24.6.6   Changing the Normal Word Order   608
§ 24.6.7   Repeating Key Words   609
§ 24.6.8   Setting Up a Pattern   609
§ 24.6.9   Variation: Deliberately Breaking a Pattern   610
§ 24.7   Sentence Structures That Highlight Similarities or
          Differences   610

Chapter 25: Effective Words   **615**

§ 25.1   Diction and Precision   615
          § 25.1.1   Colloquial Language   617
          § 25.1.2   Reader Expectations and Idioms   617
          § 25.1.3   Not-Really-Synonymous Synonyms   618
          § 25.1.4   The Same Term for the Same Idea   620
          § 25.1.5   Precise Comparisons   620
          § 25.1.6   Subject-Verb-Object Mismatch   621
          § 25.1.7   Grammatical Ambiguities   626
§ 25.2   Conciseness   626
          § 25.2.1   Don't State the Obvious   627
          § 25.2.2   Don't Start Too Far Back   628
          § 25.2.3   Do Not Overuse Quotations   628
          § 25.2.4   Create a Strong Subject-Verb Unit   630
          § 25.2.5   Avoid Throat-Clearing Expressions   631
          § 25.2.6   Do Not Use Pompous Language   633
          § 25.2.7   Do Not Repeat Yourself Needlessly   634
          § 25.2.8   Clean Out the Clutter   636
          § 25.2.9   Focus and Combine   637
          § 25.2.10   Avoid Excessive Conciseness   641
§ 25.3   Plain English vs. Legalese   642
          § 25.3.1   Archaic Word Choice   644
          § 25.3.2   Foreign Phrases   645
          § 25.3.3   Use of Terms of Art and Argot   647
          § 25.3.4   Use of "Said" and "Such" as Adjectives   648
          § 25.3.5   Omission of the Article "The"   648
          § 25.3.6   Absence of First- and Second-Person
                      Pronouns   649
§ 25.4   Gender-Neutral Language   651
          § 25.4.1   Generic Use of "Man"   651
          § 25.4.2   Generic Use of "He"   652
                      a.   Revise the Sentence So That the
                           Antecedent and Its Pronoun Are Plural   652
                      b.   Revise the Sentence So That a Pronoun
                           Is Not Needed   652
                      c.   Replace the Masculine Noun and
                           Pronoun with "One," "Your," or "He"
                           or "She," as Appropriate   652
                      d.   Alternate Male and Female Examples
                           and Expressions   653
                      e.   Repeat the Noun Rather Than Use an
                           Inappropriate Masculine Pronoun   653

§ 25.4.3   Gender-Neutral Job Titles   653
§ 25.4.4   Sexist Modifiers   654
§ 25.4.5   Other Sexist Language   654
§ 25.5   Bias-Free Language   655
§ 25.5.1   Avoid Irrelevant Minority References   656
§ 25.5.2   Stay Abreast of the Preferred Terminology   656
      a.   Prefer Self-Chosen Labels   657
      b.   Choose Precise, Accurate Terms   658
      c.   Whenever Possible, Prefer the Specific
           Term over the General Term   659
      d.   Prefer Terms That Describe What
           People Are Rather Than What They
           Are Not   659
      e.   Notice That a Term's Connotations
           May Change as the Part of Speech
           Changes   660
      f.   In Selecting Terms, Emphasize the
           Person over the Difference   660
      g.   Avoid Terms That Are Patronizing or
           Overly Euphemistic or That Paint
           People as Victims   661

Chapter 26: Eloquence   663

§ 26.1   Purple Prose   664
§ 26.2   Common Features of Eloquent Writing   665
§ 26.2.1   Alliteration and Assonance   665
§ 26.2.2   Cadence   667
§ 26.2.3   Variety in Sentence Length   669
§ 26.2.4   Variety in Sentence Openers   670
§ 26.2.5   Parallelism   671
§ 26.2.6   Onomatopoeia   673
§ 26.2.7   Simile and Metaphor   674
§ 26.2.8   Personification   675

Book 6: A Guide to Correct Writing   677

Chapter 27: Grammar   679

§ 27.1   Basic Sentence Grammar   679
§ 27.1.1   Sentence Patterns   679
§ 27.1.2   Single-Word Modifiers   682
§ 27.1.3   Phrases   682
      a.   Gerunds   683
      b.   Participles   683
      c.   Infinitives   684
      d.   Absolutes   684
§ 27.1.4   Clauses   684
§ 27.1.5   Appositives   685

§ 27.1.6   Connecting Words   686
                 a.   Coordinating Conjunctions   686
                 b.   Correlative Conjunctions   687
                 c.   Conjunctive Adverbs   687
§ 27.2   Fragments   687
         § 27.2.1   Missing Main Verb   688
         § 27.2.2   Subordinate Clauses Trying to Pose as
                     Sentences   688
         § 27.2.3   Permissible Uses of Incomplete Sentences   690
                 a.   In Issue Statements Beginning with
                        "Whether"   690
                 b.   As Answers to Questions   690
                 c.   In Exclamations   691
                 d.   For Stylistic Effect   691
                 e.   As Transitions   691
§ 27.3   Verb Tense and Mood   692
         § 27.3.1   Tense   692
         § 27.3.2   Mood   696
§ 27.4   Agreement   697
         § 27.4.1   Subject-Verb Agreement   698
         § 27.4.2   Pronoun-Antecedent Agreement   703
§ 27.5   Pronoun Reference   706
         § 27.5.1   Each Pronoun Should Clearly Refer Back
                     to Its Antecedent   707
         § 27.5.2   Avoid the Use of "It," "That," "Such,"
                     and "Which" to Refer Broadly to a
                     General Idea in a Preceding Sentence   707
         § 27.5.3   Pronouns Should Refer Back to Nouns,
                     Adjectives   709
§ 27.6   Modifiers   710
         § 27.6.1   Misplaced Modifiers   710
         § 27.6.2   Dangling Modifiers   712
         § 27.6.3   Squinting Modifiers   714
§ 27.7   Parallelism   714

Chapter 28: Punctuation   721

§ 28.1   The Comma   721
         § 28.1.1   Critical Commas: Those That Affect Meaning
                     and Clarity   723
         § 28.1.2   Basic Commas: Those That Educated Readers
                     Expect   730
         § 28.1.4   Unnecessary Commas: Those That Should Be
                     Omitted   739
§ 28.2   The Semicolon   743
         § 28.2.1   Use of the Semicolon with "Yet" or "So"   746
         § 28.2.2   Use of the Semicolon with Coordinating
                     Conjunctions   746
§ 28.3   The Colon   747
§ 28.4   The Apostrophe   749

§ 28.5   Other Marks of Punctuation   752
          § 28.5.1   Quotation Marks   752
                      a.   Identification of Another's Written or
                            Spoken Words   752
                      b.   Block Quotations   753
                      c.   Effective Lead-ins for Quotations   753
                      d.   Quotations Within Quotations   754
                      e.   Quotation Marks with Other Marks of
                            Punctuation   755
                      f.   Other Uses for Quotation Marks   755
          § 28.5.2   Ellipses   756
          § 28.5.3   Brackets   758
          § 28.5.4   Parentheses   759
                      a.   To Enclose Short Explanations of Cases
                            Within Citations   760
                      b.   To Refer Readers to Attached or
                            Appended Documents   760
                      c.   To Confirm Numbers   760
                      d.   To Enclose Numerals that Introduce
                            the Individual Items in a List   760
                      e.   To Announce Changes to a Quotation
                            That Cannot Be Shown by Ellipses or
                            Brackets   761
                      f.   To Introduce Abbreviations After a Full
                            Name Is Given   761
          § 28.5.5   The Hyphen   761
          § 28.5.6   The Dash   764
§ 28.6   Comma Splices and Fused Sentences   766
          § 28.6.1   Comma Splices   766
          § 28.6.2   Fused Sentences   768

Chapter 29: Mechanics   769

§ 29.1   Spelling   769
§ 29.2   Capitalization   770
          § 29.2.1   General Rules   770
                      a.   Beginning of a Sentence   770
                            1.   Quotations   771
                            2.   Sentences Following a Colon   771
                      b.   Proper Nouns and Adjectives   772
          § 29.2.2   Miscellaneous Rules for Capitalization   777
§ 29.3   Abbreviations and Symbols   779
          § 29.3.1   General Rules for Abbreviations   779
          § 29.3.2   Miscellaneous Rules for Abbreviation   780
          § 29.3.3   Inappropriate Abbreviations   782
          § 29.3.4   General Rules for Symbols   783
§ 29.4   Italics   783
§ 29.5   Conventions of Formal Writing   786
          § 29.5.1   Use of First-Person Pronouns   786
          § 29.5.2   Use of Contractions   786

§ 29.5.3   Use of Numbers   786
§ 29.5.4   Use of Questions and Exclamations   786

Chapter 30: Before You Practice   789

§ 30.1   Usage   789
§ 30.2   Punctuation   795
§ 30.3   Grammar   799
§ 30.4   Revising, Editing, and Proofreading   800
§ 30.5   Defeating Procrastination   806

Book 7: A Guide to Legal Writing for English-as-a-Second-Language Writers   809

Chapter 31: Legal Writing for English-as-a-Second-Language Writers   811

§ 31.1   Grammar Rules for Non-Native Speakers of English   811
   § 31.1.1   Articles   811
      a.   "A" and "An"   812
      b.   "The"   816
      c.   No Article   820
   § 31.1.2   Verbs   822
      a.   Verbs with Auxiliary, or Helping, Verbs   822
      b.   Verb Tense in Conditional Sentences   825
      c.   Verb Tense in Speculative Sentences   826
      d.   Verbs + Gerunds, Infinitives, or Objects   826
      e.   Two- or Three-Word Verbs   832
   § 31.1.3   Prepositions   833
      a.   Prepositions That Follow Verbs Commonly Used in Law   834
      b.   Prepositions That Follow Adjectives Commonly Used in Law   835
      c.   Prepositions That Follow Nouns Commonly Used in Law   835
      d.   Prepositions in Idioms   836
§ 31.2   Rhetorical Preferences in Writing   836
   § 31.2.1   Cultural Assumptions About Readers and the Purposes for Writing   837
      a.   Assumptions and Expectations in the United States and in the U.S. Legal Culture   838
         1.   The Reader's Time Is Valuable   838
         2.   The Reader Wants to Know What You Are Thinking: Be Direct and Explicit   839
         3.   The Writing Has to Get a Job Done   840
         4.   The Writer Should State and Support a Position   840

5.   Writing Is Like Personal Property:
Avoid Plagiarism   841
b.   Assumptions and Expectations in Other
Cultures   843
§ 31.2.2   Culturally Determined Patterns in Writing   845
a.   Preferences in the United States   845
b.   Preferences in Other Cultures   846
§ 31.2.3   Conciseness vs. Repetition   847
a.   Preferences in the United States   847
b.   Preferences in Other Cultures   848
§ 31.2.4   Some Final Thoughts   856

Glossary of Usage   859
Glossary of Terms   867
Index   883

List of Electronic Supplement Sections

See http://www.aspenlawschool.com/books/oates_legalwritinghandbook/.

Chapter 4: Researching Issues Governed by State Statutes and Regulations
§ 4.3.1 The Assignment
§ 4.3.2 Researching an Issue Governed by State Statutes and Regulations Using Free Websites
§ 4.3.3 Researching an Issue Governed by State Statutes and Regulations Using Lexis Advance®
§ 4.3.4 Researching an Issue Governed by State Statutes and Regulations Using WestlawNext™
§ 4.3.5 Researching an Issue Governed by State Statutes and Regulations Using Bloomberg Law
§ 4.3.6 Researching an Issue Governed by State Statutes and Regulations Using Lexis.com®
§ 4.3.7 Researching an Issue Governed by State Statutes and Regulations Using Westlaw® Classic

Chapter 5: Researching Issues Governed by Federal Statutes and Regulations
§ 5.3.1 The Assignment
§ 5.3.2 Researching an Issue Governed by Federal Statutes and Regulations Using Free Websites
§ 5.3.3 Researching an Issue Governed by Federal Statutes and Regulations Using Lexis Advance®
§ 5.3.4 Researching an Issue Governed by Federal Statutes and Regulations Using WestlawNext™
§ 5.3.5 Researching an Issue Governed by Federal Statutes and Regulations Using Bloomberg Law
§ 5.3.6 Researching an Issue Governed by Federal Statutes and Regulations Using Lexis.com®
§ 5.3.7 Researching an Issue Governed by Federal Statutes and Regulations Using Westlaw® Classic

Chapter 6: Researching Issues Governed by City or County Ordinances

§ 6. 4.1 The Assignment

§ 6.4.2 Researching an Issue Governed by City or County Ordinances Using Free Websites

§ 6.4.3 Researching an Issue Governed by City or County Ordinances Using Lexis Advance®

§ 6.4.4 Researching an Issue Governed by City or County Ordinances Using WestlawNext™

§ 6.4.5 Researching an Issue Governed by City or County Ordinances Using Bloomberg Law

§ 6.4.6 Researching an Issue Governed by City or County Ordinances Using Lexis.com®

§ 6.4.7 Researching an Issue Governed by City or County Ordinances Using Westlaw® Classic

Chapter 7: Researching Issues Governed by Common Law

§ 7.4.1 The Assignment

§ 7.4.2 Researching an Issue Governed by Common Law Using Free Websites

§ 7.4.3 Researching an Issue Governed by Common Law Using Lexis Advance®

§ 7.4.4 Researching an Issue Governed by Common Law Using WestlawNext™

§ 7.4.5 Researching an Issue Governed by Common Law Using Bloomberg Law

§ 7.4.6 Researching an Issue Governed by Common Law Using Lexis.com®

§ 7.4.7 Researching an Issue Governed by Common Law Using Westlaw® Classic

Chapter 8: Researching Constitutional Issues

§ 8.3.1 The Assignment

§ 8.3.2 Researching Constitutional Issues Using Free Websites

§ 8.3.3 Researching Constitutional Issues Using Lexis Advance®

§ 8.3.4 Researching Constitutional Issues Using WestlawNext™

§ 8.3.5 Researching Constitutional Issues Using Bloomberg Law

§ 8.3.6 Researching Constitutional Issues Using Lexis.com®

§ 8.3.7 Researching Constitutional Issues Using Westlaw® Classic

Chapter 9: Researching Issues Governed by Federal, State, or Local Court Rules

§ 9.5.1 The Assignment

§ 9.5.2 Researching an Issue Governed by Federal, State, or Local Court Rules Using Free Websites

§ 9.5.3 Researching an Issue Governed by Federal, State, or Local Court Rules Using Lexis Advance®

§ 9.5.4 Researching an Issue Governed by Federal, State, or Local Court Rules Using WestlawNext™

§ 9.5.5 Researching an Issue Governed by Federal, State, or Local Court Rules Using Bloomberg Law

§ 9.5.6   Researching an Issue Governed by Federal, State, or Local Court
          Rules Using Lexis.com®
§ 9.5.7   Researching an Issue Governed by Federal, State, or Local Court
          Rules Using Westlaw® Classic

Chapter 10: Citators
§ 10.3.1 Cite Checking Using *Shepard's*®
§ 10.3.2 Cite Checking Using KeyCite®
§ 10.3.3 Cite Checking Using BCite
§ 10.3.4 Cite Checking Using Free Websites

Chapter 11: Doing Federal and State Legislative Histories
§ 11.6.1 The Assignment
§ 11.6.2 Doing a Legislative History Using Free Websites
§ 11.6.3 Doing a Legislative History Using Lexis Advance®
§ 11.6.4 Doing a Legislative History Using WestlawNext™
§ 11.6.5 Doing a Legislative History Using Bloomberg Law
§ 11.6.6 Doing a Legislative History Using Lexis.com®
§ 11.6.7 Doing a Legislative History Using Westlaw® Classic

Chapter 12: Locating Forms
§ 12.5.1 The Assignment
§ 12.5.2 Locating Forms Using Free Websites
§ 12.5.3 Locating Forms Using Lexis Advance®
§ 12.5.4 Locating Forms Using WestlawNext™
§ 12.5.5 Locating Forms Using Bloomberg Law
§ 12.5.6 Locating Forms Using Lexis.com®
§ 12.5.7 Locating Forms Using Westlaw® Classic

**Chapter 13: Researching Judges, Law Firms, People, Companies, and
Things**
§ 13.8.1 The Assignment
§ 13.8.2 Researching Judges, Law Firms, People, Companies, and Things
          Using Free Websites
§ 13.8.3 Researching Judges, Law Firms, People, Companies, and Things
          Using Lexis Advance®
§ 13.8.4 Researching Judges, Law Firms, People, Companies, and Things
          Using WestlawNext™
§ 13.8.5 Researching Judges, Law Firms, People, Companies, and Things
          Using Bloomberg Law
§ 13.8.6 Researching Judges, Law Firms, People, Companies, and Things
          Using Lexis.com®
§ 13.8.7 Researching Judges, Law Firms, People, Companies, and Things
          Using Westlaw® Classic

Preface

One of the first things that you learn as a first-year law student is that law school textbooks are big. The casebooks for your doctrinal courses are big, and this book, your legal writing textbook, is also big. While we will let your other professors explain why their casebooks are so big, we want to take a moment to explain the size of this book.

This book is big because it's really seven books in one. Think of that as a bargain and not a burden. Book 1, designed to be read during orientation, introduces you to law school, to the U.S. legal system, and to what you will spend most of your time doing in law school: legal reading. Book 2 introduces legal research, providing you with research plans and describing many of the sources that you will be reading. The electronic supplement then shows you how to use those plans and sources to research a variety of different types of legal issues. The electronic supplement is available at *http://www.aspenlawschool .com/books/oates_legalwritinghandbook.* Your access number is on the card that came with your book.

The next two books walk you through the process of drafting, revising, and editing some of the most common types of legal documents: Book 3 moves you, step by step, through the process of writing objective memoranda, e-memos, and opinion letters, and Book 4 does the same for motion briefs and appellate briefs. In addition, Book 4 covers making oral arguments before a court. We then turn to writing in general. Books 5 and 6 contain information about writing effectively and correctly, and Book 7 addresses the grammatical and rhetorical writing issues that English-as-a-Second-Language law students and lawyers face. In other words, once you add your citation book, this book and its website for legal research contain everything you need for learning legal research, analysis, and writing.

If your school has a one-year legal writing program, you probably will not have enough time to cover some of the chapters in these books, but we hope you will be glad to have them at your fingertips when you graduate and start to practice. If your school has a three- or four-semester legal writing program, you will probably use the material in Books 1, 2, and 3 in your first year of law school and the material in Book 4 in your second year. Think of Books 5 and 6, which have all the general writing chapters, as a reference book that you will use both in law school and in practice.

This book is big because it contains numerous examples. Our experience as professors who teach legal writing has taught us that most students find models and examples important keys to learning legal writing. So, instead of just telling you what to do, this book shows you what to do.

Think of this approach as a kind of apprenticeship. Imagine that you are sitting next to an expert legal writer and researcher and learning by observing how he or she does things. For example, in Book 3 we walk you through the process of writing several different types of memos and an opinion letter, and in Book 4, we walk you through the process of writing motion and appellate briefs, and we explain how to do an oral argument. Similarly, in Books 5 and 6, we provide you with numerous examples, often showing you how to revise a draft to make the writing more effective or to correct errors in grammar or punctuation.

Finally, this book is big because becoming a good legal writer is a complex process involving skills that can take years to master. Although many students entering law school are good writers, few are good legal writers. Therefore, even though you are able to write an effective term paper, business letter, or report without additional instruction, you are going to need help to write a strong objective memo or appellate brief: help in learning how to do legal research; help in learning to read and analyze the information that you find in doing that research; help in learning the conventional formats for memos, letters, and briefs; and help in learning how to present complex ideas and arguments clearly and concisely and without any mistakes in grammar or punctuation.

Our hope is that this book will provide you with more than a weightlifting program. Yes, it is big and a bit heavy, so you may actually develop a few muscles carrying it around. The muscles we care about, though, are the mental ones that will make you a successful attorney. It is to that end that we hope you will see this book as just what you need — the perfect exercise for the well-built legal mind.

Laurel Currie Oates
Anne Enquist
January 2014

Acknowledgments

Now that this book is in its 6th edition, we are humbled by the number of people who are using the book in law schools throughout the United States and in legal education programs around the world. In any given day, we receive emails from users in South Africa, Qatar, Belarus, across the United States, and across town at the other law school in Seattle. We wish we could name and thank each one because they have all given us comments and suggestions that have improved this book. Thank you to all of you who have used our books over the years and have shared with us what you think works and doesn't.

We also want to say a special thanks to some colleagues and friends who were particularly instrumental in the early years when we were first writing. Mary Beth Harney was critical to the book's development in the early stages. She helped conceptualize the book and allowed us to use many examples of her own writing. Our friend and colleague, Marilyn Berger, introduced us to the people at Little, Brown (now Wolters Kluwer) and encouraged us to persevere. At Little, Brown and then at Aspen and now at Wolters Kluwer, we have been fortunate to have wonderful editors, Betsy Kenny, Peter Skagestad, and Dana Wilson.

Four law school deans have been significant supporters of this project. Former Dean Fred Tausend gave us the "green light" in the early years; former Dean Jim Bond provided institutional support and personal encouragement; former Dean Kellye Testy and our current dean, Dean Annette Clark, have continued that support and encouragement.

We have been fortunate throughout this process to have had the critiques and counsel of numerous colleagues who have taught legal writing. A heartfelt thank you to our longtime colleagues Lori Bannai, Janet Dickson, Connie Krontz, Susan McClellan, Chris Rideout, and Mimi Samuel, Mary Bowman, Lucas Cupps, and Deirdre Bowen. We would also like to give a special thanks to our friend and colleague from Maine, Jessie Grearson.

Special thanks to Connie Krontz, our colleague and co-author for the second edition of *Just Briefs*, for allowing us to use the chapter on writing appellate briefs that the three of us wrote for *Just Briefs* in this edition of *The Legal Writing Handbook*, to Denis Stearns for allowing us to use examples based on the problem that he developed for our Legal Writing II students; to Merryn DeBenedetti for her help on drafting the section on e-memos; and to Anne's niece, Peggy Graham, who gave us helpful feedback on the chapter about drafting email and text messages.

In addition, we have benefited from the knowledge and advice of many other faculty members at the Seattle University School of Law: Janet Ainsworth, Melinda Branscomb, Annette Clark, Sid DeLong, Paula Lustbader, John Mitchell, Mark Reutlinger, John Strait, John Weaver, Carmen Gonzalez,

Maggie Chon, Dean Spade, and Natasha Martin. In addition, we would like to give a special thanks to our former co-author and law librarian, Kelly Kunsch, for his continued research assistance.

Perhaps the most important collaborators in this project have been our students. Their writing appears throughout the book, and they were our first readers. So many made recommendations and allowed us to use their writing that we cannot mention them all, but we want them to know how much we appreciate their part in what we think of as "their book."

Some students made substantial contributions and deserve special recognition. Thank you to Ahmad Kahil for his tireless work in helping us update the electronic supplement; to Carmen Butler for her research on procrastination; and to Megan Coluccio for her research on multi-tasking. We would also like to thank former students Susan McClellan, Annette Clark, Luanne Coachman, Mary Lobdell, Eileen Peterson, Lance Palmer, Edwina Martin-Arnold, Vonda Sargent, Melissa May, Kevin Dougherty, Cindy Burdue, Amy Blume, Chris Fredrikson, Daryl Wareham, Elaine Conway, and Monique Redford.

The chapter on "Legal Writing for English-as-a-Second Language Law Students" would not have been possible without the help of several colleagues and students. Thanks to Donn R. Callaway for his guidance as we first began to explore this topic; to Dana Yaffee, Linda Chu, and Megan Coluccio for their excellent research; and to Jessie Grearson and Jeffrey Gore for their comments and suggestions on early drafts. Thanks too to our many ESL law students who inspired us with their dedication and hard work. We are particularly grateful to Stephanie Ko, Neli Espe, Nicolay Kvasnyuk, Masha Fartoutchnaia, Linda Chu, Meihuei Hu, and Julian Lin for allowing us to use their writing as examples and for reading early drafts of the chapter and suggesting changes.

The diagnostic test that is available with this edition has also been a collaborative effort. Special thanks to Connie Krontz and Judi Maier for their help with early versions of the test, to all the Seattle University School of Law legal writing faculty in 2001-02 for helping us iron out the kinks.

We also want to thank our administrative assistant, Lori Lamb, who was an instrumental part of the earlier editions of the book and who helped assemble this edition and Steve Burnett, who helped us think about and develop a website for this book.

The Legal Writing Handbook

Introduction to Legal Writing

Making the Transition

Everyone comes to law school with some writing experience. Whether you were an undergraduate or graduate student at a university, a business person, scientist, poet, paralegal, student, or attorney from a country other than the United States, you have come to a U.S. law school with a range of writing skills and experience that shape who you are as a writer.

For example, if you are coming to law school immediately after receiving your undergraduate degree, you have undoubtedly been shaped as a writer by the expectations of your undergraduate professors, particularly those in your major. Consciously or subconsciously, you have absorbed some of the customs and conventions of academic writing and the specific conventions of your major's discipline.

Similarly, if your most recent writing experiences have been from work, whether it be as a businessperson, social worker, police officer, or other professional, you too have absorbed the writing conventions of your field. The various writing projects and reports you wrote and read for work have shaped your beliefs about what is "good writing" and how it is done.

Even if you wrote for a living—as a novelist, journalist, poet, technical writer—or perhaps we should say, especially if you wrote for a living, you have been shaped as a writer by the work you did before law school. As a writer, you are more likely to be consciously aware of the conventions of the genre in which you were writing before entering law school, and you have undoubtedly honed the writing skills necessary to write successfully in that genre. The challenge, of course, will be to adapt those writing strengths to a new genre, legal writing, and to new readers, lawyers and judges in the U.S. legal community.

Whatever you were doing before law school, you were part of a specific culture — whether it be the world of health care, the world of school children, the world of wildlife biologists — and the writing that was done in those cultures was tailored for specific purposes and specific readers. The change to legal writing will require an adjustment.

Those of you who are coming to a U.S. law school from another country may have a more obvious cultural adjustment to make when it comes to writing. In some cases it will include the challenge of learning the writing conventions of another language, but even in cases in which the language of your home country is English, there will undoubtedly be cultural differences in what your new readers will expect from your written work.

In short, everyone coming to law school is making a transition from the writing he or she did before law school to the writing of the U.S. legal community. The trick will be to figure out what are the obvious and subtle similarities and differences between the writing culture you are coming from and the writing culture you are joining. Even if you were a paralegal before law school, you will have to figure out what was specific to the firm or legal setting in which you worked and what is generally true about writing for the larger, more generic legal community. At the very least, your specific role as a writer will have changed from paralegal to attorney, and that change alone will make a difference in the expectations your readers will have for your writing.

This chapter is designed to help law students make the transition to legal writing as smoothly and painlessly as possible. Several concepts are the keys to a successful transition: (1) understand the purpose of the new type of writing you are learning; (2) know what your new readers want and need from what you write; (3) understand your role as the writer in this genre; and (4) learn the specific conventions of the new type of writing you are adding to your writing repertoire.

§ 1.1   Understanding the Purpose of a Piece of Legal Writing

Here's an important truth that will help you make effective choices as you work as a writer: Once you understand what a piece of writing is supposed to accomplish — its purpose — you will have a sound basis for the many decisions you as the writer will make in creating a document. Put another way, you have about 90 percent of the information you need for creating a document once you know

- why you are writing something,
- what the document is supposed to do, and
- what the reader hopes to achieve by reading it.

Like other types of writing, legal writing exists to communicate. Lawyers write because they want to communicate information to their readers. But the broad term "communicate" is not specific enough to be particularly helpful as you transition to the new genre of legal writing.

Most legal writing exists for one or more of these three specific reasons:

1. to explain,
2. to persuade,
3. to memorialize.

Whether you are writing a letter to a client, an office memo for a senior partner, or a brief for a judge, you will undoubtedly have as one of your primary purposes the goal of explaining. You might be explaining to the client that the law is on her side and therefore she is likely to be successful if she sues her employer. You might be explaining to a partner how the courts have interpreted a statute and why that interpretation means the firm's biggest client should not include a particular term in a contract. You might be explaining to a judge why an application of the law to your client's facts would lead to a just result.

If clear explanation is the first goal of most legal writing, then the goal of effective persuasion is not far behind. Sometimes the persuasion is subtle. In writing an opinion letter, you may be persuading a client to see the strengths and weaknesses of his or her legal position. You may also be subtly persuading that client to see not only the limitations of his or her options but also the wisdom of adopting one particular option.

Persuasion is also part of legal memoranda. Although you will see in Chapters 11-14 that an office memorandum should be an objective assessment of the law and its application to a case, a good office memo also includes persuasion in the sense that it anticipates the arguments each side is likely to make and, in doing so, showcases which ones will be more or less persuasive.

The goal of persuasion is most obvious, and important, in brief writing. When writing to a court, you will be working to get a judge or justice to see the law, precedent, the facts, and the arguments from your side's point of view. You will want that judge or justice to view the case from your perspective so he or she will rule in your favor. When you write for a court, you will have clear-cut evidence of whether you succeeded or failed in your goal to persuade, and that will be what the court decides as a result of reading your writing.

The third goal of most legal writing — to memorialize — is especially evident in documents like contracts and wills. The document exists as a statement of what the contracting parties agreed to or how the deceased person wanted his or her assets distributed. Opinion letters, office memos, and briefs also have a goal of memorializing the work an attorney has done. Because the work is preserved in writing, the client can go back over a letter and review the advice. An office memo written for one client's case may be used by other attorneys in the office working on that case. Undoubtedly, it will be filed for future consideration, and it might be reviewed and used again, at least in part, if the client has a similar problem or even if another client has a similar problem. In litigation, a brief written in support of or opposition to a pretrial motion can become part of the record on appeal, recording what the parties did, or did not argue, to the trial court.

Before leaving the topic of purpose in legal writing, let's think again about the transition most new law students are making from writing they did before they came to law school to writing they will do as lawyers. Note how different the purposes of student writing are from the purposes of "real world" legal writing. Student writers write to prove that they have learned something. They write to demonstrate knowledge and mastery of a subject, and quite frankly, to get a good grade. As a general rule, readers of student writing (professors) do not read student essays, reports, and research papers to gain information or learn anything new. Because professors are already experts in the subject matter, their purpose in reading is to evaluate how well the writer has learned the material. This difference between student writing and real world writing is actually a rather profound one, and one that accounts for many of the other differences between writing that is done for class and writing that is done for professional reasons.

Keep in mind, then, as you work on the assignments for your legal writing and research classes that, even though the assignments are part of a law class, in almost every case, the writing tasks are intended to simulate real world practice situations. In other words, you are not supposed to be writing like you are a student with the purposes of a student writer. You are supposed to be writing as if you are a practicing lawyer with one or more of the real world goals of explaining, persuading, and memorializing. Even though you are still a student learning how to write like a lawyer (and hoping for a good grade), stay focused on key concept number 1: Know your purpose for writing.

> **COMMON MISTAKE 1**   Some students in legal writing courses mistakenly assume that their legal writing professors will be reading and evaluating their papers as though they, the professors, are the real readers. Consequently, these students leave things out of the writing on the assumption that "my professor already knows that." While it is true that your professor undoubtedly researched the problem and knows the analysis inside out, he or she will be evaluating your writing from the point of view of a "real world" reader—someone who is depending on the writer's research and analysis and who was not in class and participating in the class discussions on the issues.

> **COMMON MISTAKE 2**   Some new legal writers make the "undergraduate mistake" when they are writing their first office memos: They want to make sure their legal writing professor or their supervising attorney knows how much work they did and how thoroughly they researched the problem. Consequently, they include far more cases than are necessary to understand the analysis or make the arguments. This mistake often comes directly from their undergraduate experience. As undergraduates, many of us were rewarded for writing papers that showed how much work we had done. Length often translated into high grades. Law school and law firm writing is different. Legal writers should adopt the real world reader's point of view about length, which is "I'm busy. Tell me what I need to know and then stop writing."

§ 1.2   Writing for Legal Readers

Closely related to understanding your purpose in writing is understanding who your reader or readers are. In legal writing, the goal is not just to explain or persuade in the abstract. Instead, you are writing to real readers, readers who need your writing with all of its research, analysis, arguments, citations, conclusions, and insights in order to do their jobs.

Real legal readers include both lawyers and nonlawyers. When writing for a reader who is not a lawyer, keep in mind how much or how little experience that person may have with law and legal matters. For example, clients who are not lawyers and are not experienced in matters related to law may need explanations in lay terms. Other nonlawyer readers may have a sophisticated understanding of law and their legal issues and would find a watered down explanation condescending. The point, of course, is that an effective writer will adjust his or her approach accordingly.

To some extent, you may have to make similar adjustments for readers who are lawyers.[1] All lawyers do not have the same background or practice experience. In some situations, a senior partner who is the reader for a given memo about a tax issue may be the firm's tax expert. In such a situation, the writer can assume much more knowledge and start the discussion further into the law and analysis. Writing a memo for a different reader, maybe someone who hasn't looked at tax law since law school, would require an adjustment. In this second situation, the smart writer will give a quick refresher and enough background to get that kind of reader up to speed quickly so that he or she is ready to follow the analysis.

Anticipating your reader's knowledge base is only the beginning of writing for legal readers. Most legal readers, whether they are senior partners or judges, tend to have a few common characteristics, and these characteristics have shaped their notions of what is good legal writing. First, they tend to be very busy. Consequently, they appreciate writing that gets to the point quickly and lays out information clearly. They don't want writers to take them down every blind alley the writer had to explore before figuring out that information was irrelevant. They don't give extra credit for discussing additional cases or extra arguments if those cases or arguments aren't needed. They are annoyed, not impressed, if they think the writer is padding the document. Therefore, before including something in a piece of legal writing, ask yourself, "does my reader need to know this?" Notice that this question is different from "did I need to know this in order to analyze the problem?" Legal readers will expect legal writers to be selective about what they include in the document and to synthesize the relevant material. They will expect legal writers to understand that their time is valuable and to write, and edit, with that in mind.

Second, legal readers appreciate — actually demand — clear organization. They want the information they need laid out in a well-structured, easy-to-follow fashion. They appreciate roadmaps that give them an overview of the analysis and signposts that guide them through it, all the while focusing their attention on "where the fight is." They like transitions that help them see the connections between ideas and follow the writer's line of reasoning. They appreciate mini-conclusions that summarize a section and macro conclusions that summarize all the main pieces of a large document. In short, it is hard to over-emphasize how important a clear and explicit organization is to most legal readers.

---

1. The generalizations in this section about legal readers refer to U.S. legal readers.

The fact that experienced, sophisticated attorneys want such explicit organization and analysis may come as a surprise to some new legal writers. After all, not all cultures value explicitness in the same way the U.S. legal culture does. In fact, leaving things unsaid and for readers to figure out is a mark of sophisticated writing in some academic cultures and in some Asian and Middle Eastern cultures. Stating one's point so directly may be considered not just unsophisticated but also brash and even rude. For writers coming from these backgrounds, it may feel unnatural at first to spell out points so clearly and explicitly, but over time it will become second nature as these writers better understand how writing works in the U.S. legal culture.

Third, because legal readers need the writing they read in order to do their jobs well, they insist on the highest levels of professionalism. This means that accuracy and precision are critical virtues in legal writing — no playing loose with the facts or the law. Legal readers depend on their writers to get the facts and law right and to be strictly accurate in how they are represented.

The emphasis on professionalism also means that mistakes such as poor citation form; the misspelling, especially of a name; and grammar, punctuation, and proofreading errors matter more than they do in other kinds of writing. Being accurate, precise, and polished in written documents are all critical parts of being professional that legal readers expect.

If accuracy, brevity, clarity, precision, and professionalism are high priorities for legal readers, then the next obvious question is what isn't such a high priority for them? Unlike a great deal of undergraduate writing, legal writing places less emphasis on creativity. While the professor reader in an undergraduate course in poetry or creative writing might reward an unusual approach to a topic or a novel twist in a plot, readers of legal writing tend to prefer writing that is far more conventional. Creativity is nice, especially if a creative argument turns out to be a winning argument, but remember that legal readers are not reading to be entertained. The writing is all about work and getting a job done, so creative introductions or unusual analytical approaches take a back seat to accuracy, brevity, and clarity for legal readers.

Similarly, legal readers resent unnecessary complexity. Consequently, when it comes to things like sentence structure and word choice, the acronym KISS for "keep it simple stupid" is useful advice. Legal readers do not want to puzzle over a sentence or word. For them, the sign of a well-written sentence is one that can be understood the first time they read it. For them, the well-chosen word is, more often than not, one they already know. If an unfamiliar word is required in a given instance, they expect the writer to define it immediately within the writing. Legal writers don't need to worry that they are "dumbing down" the writing when they present information as simply as possible. For legal readers, clear communication is the goal; they don't want to be dazzled by the writer's vocabulary or convoluted syntax.

Does this mean that legal readers are incapable of handling complexity or that they have weak vocabularies? Certainly not. The appreciation for simplicity goes back to the initial point about how busy legal readers are. The legal issues are often so inherently complex that no one wants added unnecessary complexity that will simply take up time and attention.

| COMMON MISTAKE 3 | Some new legal writers make the mistake of "dressing up their ideas." They fear that if they state things simply they will seem unsophisticated. Here again, the mistake may be the result |

of an undergraduate writing experience that rewarded students for making simple ideas seem complex. The opposite is true in legal writing: You will be rewarded and appreciated if you can make complex ideas seem simple.

§ 1.3 Understanding Your Role as a Legal Writer

When a junior associate or a legal intern is assigned to research and write a client letter, office memo, or brief, the expectation is that the associate or intern will spend many hours researching and analyzing the legal problem and then write up that work in a document that will take the client, assigning attorney, or judge approximately fifteen minutes to read and understand.

An underlying assumption of the U.S. legal culture, then, is that the reader's time is more valuable than the writer's time. Legal readers, including supervising attorneys, partners in law firms, and judges, tend to have positions of authority over the writers of legal memos. Consequently, writers are expected to expend their time and energy writing clearly so that readers do not have to spend extra time and energy understanding what they are reading.

This does not mean, then, that the writer's role is unimportant—far from it. As the writer, your role is to become the expert on a given case. Through careful study of the facts and thorough research, you will be the one who knows what law is the controlling law and which cases are the key cases. In addition, after reading the arguments set out in the cases and the courts' evaluation of those arguments, you will be the one who is in the best position to predict what each side will argue and how the court will view those arguments.

Ultimately, your role as the writer of a client letter is to be the one who advises the client about what he or she should do next and why. Your role as the writer of an office memo is to give your educated opinion about what the court is likely to do in the current case and be clear about how you reached that opinion. Your role as the writer of a brief is to figure out what approach and arguments will persuade the court to rule in your client's favor. In short, your role is to exercise expert judgment, and in fact, that is exactly what you are paid to do when you are assigned to write a client letter, office memorandum, or brief.

You need to exercise judgment

- about what are the legally significant facts,
- about what statute(s) or common law doctrine will govern,
- about which cases are the key analogous cases, and
- about which arguments the court will find persuasive.

As new attorneys or law students, many find the legal writer's role a bit intimidating. It can be hard enough to be confident that you have found the right law and key cases without trying to create brand new, never-seen-before arguments, or worse, predicting what a court will do or convincing a court what it should do. Take heart, though. Many of the arguments will be variations of ones you see in the cases (no one is expecting you to make this all up from scratch), and law school is exactly the right place to learn and practice these skills.

A key part of your role as well will be to cite authority (at least in office memos and briefs) to support each of the points you make. The citations show that you have the support of the law, other courts, and other legal minds behind your analysis. Furthermore, by including the source for the facts and correctly citing the record, statutes, cases, books, law review articles, and other secondary sources, you create a document in which everything about the case comes together. Thus, one major aspect of your role as a legal writer is to be the synthesizer—the one who brings all the relevant material together and presents it in a way that gets the job done.

One final point about your role as a legal writer: Every piece of writing you create in your role as a lawyer reflects on your professionalism. Words are the tools of your trade, so how you use words represents how seriously you take your work. In the heat of the moment or in the thick of an argument, it can be tempting to slip into a sarcastic or denigrating tone. Resist the temptation. Be particularly careful to maintain a professional tone in all the writing you do. As a lawyer, your writing, including the tone you use, is a big part of how you are representing your client and yourself.

§ 1.4   Learning the Conventions of Legal Writing

In the earlier discussion of the purposes of legal writing, legal readers, and the writer's role, a number of the common practices and conventions of legal writing have already been mentioned:

1. a high priority on clarity, brevity, precision, and organization
2. an appreciation for explicit roadmaps, signposts, topic sentences, and transitions
3. an expectation for easy-to-read sentences and paragraphs, but not bullet points or charts
4. a requirement for citations to authority
5. an expectation about professional tone.

In addition, new legal writers may be struck by a number of other conventions of legal writing. For example, specific formats are often expected and sometimes required in legal writing. Legal readers expect an office memo to have an issue statement, sometimes called a Question Presented, which seems to be an artifact from an earlier time. Briefs have required cover pages, tables of authorities, argumentative headings, and page and paragraph numbering systems. Therefore, when you are assigned a new type of legal writing, check to see whether there are court rules governing the format and review some samples or models of that type of writing. Knowing format requirements before starting to write is more efficient than spending a lot of time creating a format only to find it does not meet expectations.

Less surprising is the convention to set out a rule before applying it to the facts or making an argument using the rule. Also not surprising, at least for some, is the custom of setting out general rules before more specific rules. In fact, throughout legal writing the convention is to organize material from general to specific.

Writers of academic prose may be immediately comfortable with other conventions, such as the tendency not to use contractions or the use of the third person rather than the first person "I" or "we" or the second person "you." The practice of staying in the third person means that language such as "I think," "I believe," or "I feel" is not typically used in legal writing. Rather than write "I think the court is unlikely to find," most lawyers write "the court is unlikely to find." Some firms do make an exception and use the first person "our" when referring to "our client" or "our case," but others maintain the more formal "the client" or the client's name when referring to the case.

§ 1.5   Advice for Specific Groups

Even though it can be a bit risky to generalize about the customs and conventions of any given community of writers, knowing about some patterns in different writing cultures can ease a writer's transition into legal writing. Making that knowledge more explicit can help a writer look at his or her assumptions about "good writing" and see which assumptions apply and which do not apply to legal writing.

Below is a list of different communities of writers and some of the common assumptions those communities have about writing and how those assumptions are similar to or different from the underlying assumptions that shape legal writing. In creating this list, however, we do not mean to suggest that legal writing is somehow "right" in its assumptions about what makes good writing and these other fields or cultures are somehow "wrong." In fact, we would argue that the differences make sense given the differences in readers, purpose, and culture. Nor do we mean to suggest that writers need to erase and replace what they know about how to write for the communities they were part of before joining the legal community. Instead we would suggest that writers think of the experience of learning to do legal writing as adding a new category or genre of writing to their writing repertoire.

One final point: Although we cannot discuss every undergraduate major, previous profession, or culture, we hope that the insights about how different disciplines and cultures view writing will help you make a smooth transition into legal writing.

§ 1.5.1   English Majors

Most English majors come to law school believing that they will do exceptionally well in their legal writing classes. In most cases, this proves to be true, but their success tends to happen more toward the end of the course rather than at the beginning. Early in the course, English majors may resist what they consider the formulaic and restrictive nature of legal writing. They complain that it "stifles their creativity," and they are frustrated because they cannot show off their vocabularies and sophisticated writing style. Once they accept the idea that they are learning a new genre, in much the way a poet would adapt when learning to write screenplays, they stop resisting, start adapting, and then gradually see how they can channel some of their earlier skills into legal writing. Their storytelling ability helps them write the facts; they apply their creativity to constructing arguments; and they bring the close reading skills they developed for literature and poetry to their reading of statutes and rules.

§ 1.5.2   Philosophy Majors

Like English majors, philosophy majors are likely to feel that their creativity is stifled and their analytic ability tightly restricted by the standard modes of legal analysis. In their doctrinal courses, they may be initially surprised by the heavy emphasis on precedent and the layers of doctrine, as well as disappointed by what may appear to them to be the law's emphasis on rhetoric.

As they learn to write office memos, philosophy majors are likely to find the construction of rules paragraphs to be arbitrary; their natural instinct will be to think about the validity of the rules rather than simply lay them out for the readers. Once they get to the arguments, philosophy majors are likely to feel at home, and it is here that their background in logic can give them an edge.

§ 1.5.3   Journalism Majors and Journalists

Like their "cousins" the English majors, journalism students and journalists bring an interesting combination of advantages and disadvantages to legal writing. Perhaps most important is the simple fact that they have fresh writing skills. They come to law school and the practice of law with their writing skills honed by lots of practice. In addition, journalists are already well schooled in the concept of writing for a specific audience. Many of them have learned to adjust their style to the varying demands of straight news reporting to the specific conventions of the sports page, the op-ed page, the lifestyle and feature sections, or a blog. Initially some journalists may resent having to tone down their style a bit for legal writing, particularly if they have grown accustomed to writing "zinger" sentences or writing with vivid language and extended metaphors for the sports page.

Yet another advantage that journalists bring to legal writing is their thoroughness and accuracy with the facts. They are used to answering the questions "who," "what," "when," "where," and "how," and they are also used to being required to state the source for the facts.

Organization and paragraph length are usually the two areas in which journalists will have to adjust. The typical journalism piece is written in an inverted-pyramid, front-loaded style so the editors can cut the piece from the end to fit space limitations and, if a reader loses interest and stops reading midway in a story, he or she still will have gotten the key ideas in the opening sentences. While much of legal writing also puts key points (rules, the best cases, and arguments) up front, the organizational structure is shaped by very different considerations and reader expectations. A threshold issue will almost always be treated first, even if it is relatively easy to resolve. Even though legal readers are busy, most will read a memo through to the end and not treat the last pages or lines as optional. For the most part, true paragraphs do not exist in journalism. Because of the narrow width of many newspaper columns, the convention in journalism is to write mostly one-sentence paragraphs. Journalists transitioning into writing about law have to learn to write longer paragraphs.

Finally, most journalists have learned to be extraordinarily careful with spelling, particularly the spelling of proper names, which is an asset that carries over nicely into legal writing. Punctuation, however, may be a different matter. Journalism prefers "open punctuation," which means using as little punctuation as the rules will allow; legal writing, by contrast, tends to used "closed punctuation," which means that lawyers lean in the other direction and use commas when the rules give them the option to do so. The serial comma, for example, is generally omitted in journalism (no comma before the "and" in "red, white and blue") but is included in legal writing ("red, white, and blue").

§ 1.5.4   Science Majors and Scientists

Science majors and scientists bring a strong set of skills in critical thinking and formal analysis that individuals in many other professions or disciplines may lack. The ability to evaluate evidence, make logical connections, and draw plausible conclusions forms the very basis of substantive legal analysis. However, legal writing diverges from scientific writing in several ways that may prove challenging or even frustrating.

In terms of writing style, legal writing favors active voice sentences, not the passive voice sentences used as the professional standard in scientific writing. Formal organization of various legal writing projects requires a different organizational structure than scientific writing (e.g., title, hypothesis, materials, methods, observations, results, conclusion), although experience working with any formal structure will be of help in legal writing.

In terms of substantive analysis, deriving governing rules and tests from case law precedent or statutory language is similar to formulating the hypothesis and methods sections of a scientific paper. However, on a practical level jurisprudence has little in common with scientific laws and validity studies. Science majors and scientists may find their experience similar to the frustration experienced by philosophy students. "Law" is not created by systematic application of the scientific method in order to discover logically necessary, objective truths with universal application that can be repeated and verified by any scientist in a variety of conditions. Rather, "law" is created by a combination of individual circumstances, public policies, concepts of fairness, tradition, emotion, credibility, economic realities, political considerations, and persuasive argument, among other factors.

In fact, legal reasoning and persuasive argument may represent the greatest challenges to science majors and scientists engaged in legal writing. Although persuasive argument skills have a subtle use in the results and conclusion parts of a scientific paper, the rhetorical strategies and skills necessary for legal writing will likely draw on a legal writer's experience in non-scientific areas of life. Consequently, science majors and scientists transitioning into writing about law should be prepared to merge an "objective" approach with a more subjective "relational" approach.

§ 1.5.5   Writers from Other Cultures

Each of us absorbs the writing preferences of our first language and our native culture. Those preferences are often so deeply embedded in the many aspects of writing that they are hard to see and even harder to articulate. Often we are unaware that different cultures (and different professions) have different ideas about what makes something "good writing."

The U.S. culture, and specifically the U.S. legal culture, is no different from any other professional culture. It has expectations and preferences that have developed over time about how something should be written. Students who come to U.S. law schools wanting to learn U.S. legal writing may find it useful to begin by examining the cultural preferences related to writing from their native cultures and languages and then compare those preferences with those of the U.S. legal culture.

Chapter 31 at the end of this book is designed specifically for English-as-a-second-language law students who want to learn about the subtle and not-so-subtle differences between their native cultures and languages and the U.S. legal culture and its use of English. Although the first half of the chapter focuses on grammatical challenges for ESL law students, the second half explores the rhetorical preferences in a wide variety of cultures and compares those preferences with those of the U.S. legal culture. Exhibit 31.5 in Chapter 31 shows the contrasting rhetorical preferences of the U.S. legal culture and of a number of different languages, including Chinese, Japanese, Korean, French, Spanish, Arabic, and Russian.

The United States Legal System

The United States system of government. For some, it is the secret to democracy, the power to elect one's leaders and the right to speak freely. For others, it is a horrendous bureaucracy, a maze through which one must struggle to obtain a benefit, to change a law, or to get a day in court. For still others, it is more abstract—a chart in an eighth-grade civics book describing the three branches of government and explaining the system of checks and balances.

For lawyers, the United States system of government is all of these things and more. It is the foundation for their knowledge of the law, the stage on which they play out their professional roles, the arena for the very serious game of law.

No matter which metaphor you prefer—foundation, stage, arena—the point is the same. To be an effective researcher, you must understand the system. You must know the framework before you can work well within it.

Like most complex systems, the United States system of government can be analyzed in a number of different ways. You can focus on its three branches—the executive branch, the legislative branch, and the judicial branch—or you can focus on the system's two parts, the federal government and the state governments.

In this chapter we do both. We look first at the three branches, examining both their individual functions and their interrelationships. We then examine the relationship between state and federal government, again with an eye toward their individual functions and powers.

§ 2.1   The Three Branches of Government

Just as the medical student must understand both the various organs that make up the human body and their relationship to each other, the law student must understand both the three branches of government and the relationships among them.

§ 2.1.1   The Executive Branch

The first of the three branches is the executive branch. In the federal system, the executive power is vested in the President; in the states, it is vested in the governor. (See Article II, Section 1 of the United States Constitution and the constitutions of the various states.) In general, the executive branch has the power to implement and enforce laws. It oversees public projects, administers public benefit programs, and controls law enforcement agencies.

The executive branch also has powers that directly affect our system of law. For example, the President (or a governor) can control the law-making function of the legislative branch by exercising his or her power to convene and adjourn the Congress (or state legislature) or by vetoing legislation. Similarly, the President (or a governor) can shape the decisions of the courts through his or her judicial nominations or by directing the attorney general to enforce or not to enforce certain laws.

§ 2.1.2   The Legislative Branch

The second branch is the legislative branch. Congress's powers are enumerated in Article I, Section 8, of the United States Constitution, which gives Congress, among other things, the power to lay and collect taxes, borrow money, regulate commerce with foreign nations and among the states, establish uniform naturalization and bankruptcy laws, promote the progress of science and the useful arts by creating copyright laws, and punish counterfeiting. Powers not granted Congress are given to the states or left to the people. (See the Tenth Amendment to the United States Constitution.) The state constitutions enumerate the powers given to the state legislatures.

Like the executive branch, the legislative branch exercises power over the other two branches. It can check the actions of the executive branch by enacting or refusing to enact legislation requested by the executive, by controlling the budget and, at least at the federal level, by consenting or refusing to consent to nominations made by the executive.

The legislative branch's power over the judicial branch is less obvious. At one level, it can control the judiciary through its power to establish courts (Article I, Section 8, grants Congress the power to establish inferior federal courts) and its power to consent to or reject the executive branch's judicial nominations. However, the most obvious control it has over the judiciary is its power to enact legislation that supersedes, or replaces, a common law or court-made doctrine or rule.

The legislative branch also shares its law-making power with the executive branch. In enacting legislation, it sometimes gives the executive branch the power to promulgate the regulations needed to implement or enforce the legislation. For example, although Congress (the legislative branch) enacted the Internal Revenue Code, the Internal Revenue Service (part of the executive branch) promulgates the regulations needed to implement that code.

§ 2.1.3 The Judicial Branch

The third branch is the judicial branch. Article III, Section 1, of the United States Constitution vests the judicial power of the United States in one supreme court and in such inferior courts as Congress may establish. The state constitutions establish and grant power to the state courts.

a. The Hierarchical Nature of the Court System

Both the federal and the state court systems are hierarchical. At the lowest level are the trial courts, whose primary function is fact-finding. The judge or jury hears the evidence and enters a judgment.

At the next level are the intermediate courts of appeals. These courts hear the majority of appeals, deciding (1) whether the trial court applied the right law and (2) whether there is sufficient evidence to support the jury's verdict or the trial judge's findings of fact and conclusions of law. Unlike the trial courts, these courts do not conduct trials. There are no witnesses, and the only exhibits are the exhibits that were admitted during trial. The decisions of the appellate courts are based solely on the written trial record and the attorneys' arguments.

At the top level are the states' highest courts and the Supreme Court of the United States. The primary function of these courts is to make law. They hear only those cases that involve issues of great public import or cases in which different divisions or circuits have adopted or applied conflicting rules of law. Like the intermediate courts of appeals, these courts do not hear evidence; they only review the trial court record. See Exhibit 2.1.

An example illustrates the role each court plays. In *State v. Strong*, a criminal case, the defendant, Mr. Strong, was charged with possession of a controlled substance. At the trial court level, both the State and the defendant presented witnesses and physical evidence. On the basis of this evidence, the trial court decided the case on its merits, with the trial judge deciding the questions of law (whether the evidence should be suppressed) and the jury deciding the questions of fact (whether the State had proved all of the elements of the crime beyond a reasonable doubt).

Both issues were decided against the defendant: The trial court judge ruled that the evidence was admissible, and the jury found that the State had met its burden of proof. Disagreeing with both determinations, the defendant filed an appeal with the intermediate court of appeals.

In deciding this appeal, the appellate court could consider only two issues: whether the trial court judge erred when he denied the defendant's motion to suppress and whether there was sufficient evidence to support the jury's verdict.

Because the first issue raised a question of law, the appellate court could review the issue de novo. The court did not need to defer to the judgment of the trial court judge. Instead, the appellate court could exercise its own independent judgment to decide the issue on its merits.

The appellate court had much less latitude with respect to the second issue. Because the second issue raised a question of fact rather than law, the appellate court could not substitute its judgment for that of the jury. It could only review the jury's findings to make sure that they were supported by the evidence. When the question is one of fact, the appellate court may decide only (1) whether there is sufficient evidence to support the jury's verdict or (2) whether the jury's verdict is clearly erroneous. It may not substitute its judgment for the judgment of the jury.

Exhibit 2.1	The Roles of the Trial, Intermediate, and Supreme Courts

Trial Court

- The trial court hears witnesses and views evidence.
- The trial court judge decides issues of law; the jury decides questions of fact. (When there is no jury, the trial court judge decides both the questions of law and the questions of fact.)

Intermediate Court of Appeals

- The intermediate court of appeals reviews the written record and exhibits from the trial court.
- When an issue raises a question of law, the intermediate court of appeals may substitute its judgment for the judgment of the trial court judge; when an issue raises a question of fact, the appellate court must defer to the decision of the finder of fact (the jury or, if there was no jury, the trial judge).

Supreme, or Highest, Court

- Like the intermediate court of appeals, it reviews the written record and exhibits from the trial court.
- Like the intermediate court of appeals, it has broad powers to review questions of law: It determines whether the trial court and intermediate court of appeals applied the right law correctly. Its power to review factual issues is, however, very limited. Like the intermediate court of appeals, it can determine only whether there is sufficient evidence to support the decision of the jury or, if there was no jury, the decision of the trial court judge.

Regardless of the type of issue (fact or law), the appellate court must base its decision on the written trial court record and exhibits and the attorneys' arguments. Consequently, in *Strong*, the intermediate court of appeals did not see or hear any of the witnesses. The only people present when the appeal was argued were the appellate court judges assigned to hear the case and Strong's and the State's attorneys. Not even the defendant, Mr. Strong, was present.

If Mr. Strong lost his first appeal, he could petition the state supreme court (through a petition for discretionary review) and ask that court to review the intermediate court of appeals' decision. If the state supreme court granted the petition, its review, like that of the intermediate court of appeals, would be limited. Although the supreme court would review the issue of law de novo, it would have to defer to the jury's decision on the questions of fact.

Most of the cases that appear in law school casebooks are appellate court decisions, for example, decisions of the United States Court of Appeals or the United States Supreme Court or decisions from state appellate courts. These cases, however, represent only a small, and perhaps not representative, percentage of the disputes that lawyers see during the course of their practice.

Accordingly, as you read the cases in the casebooks, remember that you are seeing only the proverbial tip of the iceberg. For a case to reach the United States Supreme Court, the parties must have had the financial means to pursue it, and the Court must have found that the issue raised was significant enough to grant review.

> **PRACTICE POINTER**
>
> As you will learn in Civil Procedure, to hear a case a court must have both subject matter jurisdiction and personal jurisdiction. Stated very simply, a court has subject matter jurisdiction when it has power to hear a particular type of case. For example, the federal courts have subject matter jurisdiction to hear cases involving the United States Constitution and United States statutes, state courts of general jurisdiction have subject matter jurisdiction to hear cases involving the state constitution and state statutes, and municipal courts have subject matter jurisdiction to hear cases involving city ordinances. It is not, though, enough that a court has subject matter jurisdiction. The court must also have personal jurisdiction or the power to hear and decide cases involving the parties to the case or controversy.

b. The Federal Courts

In the federal system, most cases are heard initially in the federal district courts, the primary trial courts in that system. These courts have original jurisdiction over most federal questions and have the power to review the decisions of some administrative agencies. Each state has at least one district court, and many have several. For example, Indiana has the District Court for Northern Indiana and the District Court for Southern Indiana. Cases that are not heard in the district court are usually heard in one of several specialized courts, for example, the United States Tax Court, the United States Court of Federal Claims, or the United States Court of International Trade.

In the federal system, the intermediate court of appeals is the United States Court of Appeals. There are currently thirteen circuits: eleven numbered circuits, the District of Columbia Circuit, and the Federal Circuit. See Exhibit 2.2. The Federal Circuit, which was created in 1982, reviews the decisions of the United States Court of Federal Claims and the United States Court of International Trade, as well as some administrative decisions.

> **PRACTICE POINTER**
>
> For an electronic copy of a map showing the federal circuits, see *http://www.uscourts.gov/ court_locator.aspx*

Exhibit 2.2   The Thirteen Federal Judicial Circuits

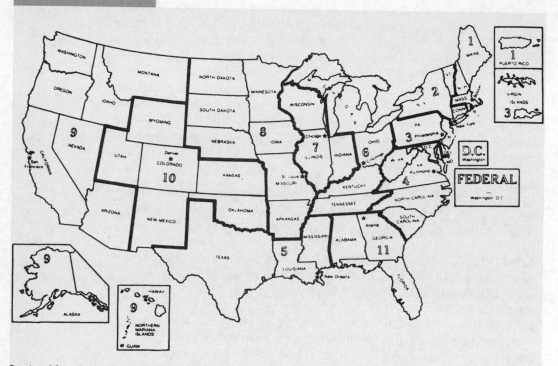

Reprinted from *Federal Reporter* (West's National Reporter System) with permission of West, a Thomson Reuters business.

The highest federal court is the United States Supreme Court. Although many people believe that the Supreme Court is all-powerful, in fact it is not. As with other courts, there are limits on the Supreme Court's powers. It can play only one of two roles.

In one role, the United States Supreme Court is similar to the state supreme courts. In the federal system, the United States Supreme Court is the highest court, the court of last resort. In contrast, in its other role, it is the final arbiter of federal constitutional law, interpreting the United States Constitution and determining whether the federal government or a state has violated rights granted under the United States Constitution.

Thus, although people often assert that they will take their case all the way to the Supreme Court, they may not be able to. As a general rule, the Supreme Court may hear a case only if it involves a question of federal constitutional law or a federal statute. The Supreme Court does not have the power to hear cases involving only questions of state law. For example, although the United States Supreme Court has the power to determine whether a state's marriage dissolution statutes are constitutional, the Court does not have the power to hear purely factual questions, such as whether it would be in the best interests of a child for custody to be granted to the father or whether child support should be set at $300 rather than $400 per month.

Each year the United States Supreme Court receives more than 7,000 requests for review (writs of certiorari). Of the approximately 100 cases that the Court actually hears, the overwhelming majority are appeals from the federal courts.

Exhibit 2.3 illustrates the relationships among the various federal courts.

Because the United States District Courts and Courts of Appeals hear so many cases, not all of their decisions are "published." When they are published, decisions from the United States District Courts are published in either the *Federal Supplement*, or *Federal Rules Decisions*, and decisions from the United States Courts of Appeals are published in the *Federal Reporter*. (Decisions from the specialized courts are published in specialized reporters.

> **PRACTICE POINTER**
>
> A "published" decision is a decision that is published in a set of books called a "reporter." (For more about reporters, see §4.2.4b.) Thus, decisions that appear on Lexis Advance®, WestlawNext™, Bloomberg Law, or a free website but that are not in a reporter are not published decisions. They are unpublished, or unreported, decisions. In some jurisdictions, you cannot cite to an unpublished decision in a brief to that jurisdiction's courts. To find out whether you can cite to an unpublished decision, see your local court rules.

All United States Supreme Court decisions are published. The official reporter is *United States Reports*, and the two unofficial reporters are *Supreme Court Reporter* and *United States Supreme Court Reports, Lawyers' Edition*.

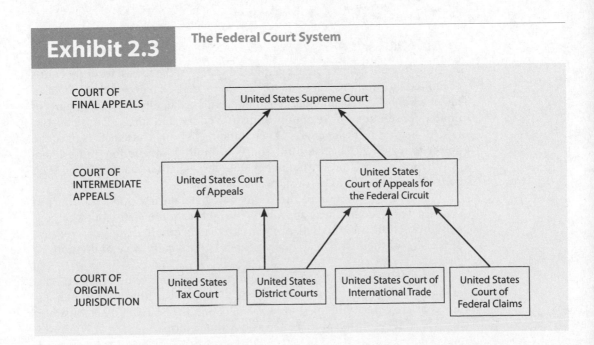

Exhibit 2.3   The Federal Court System

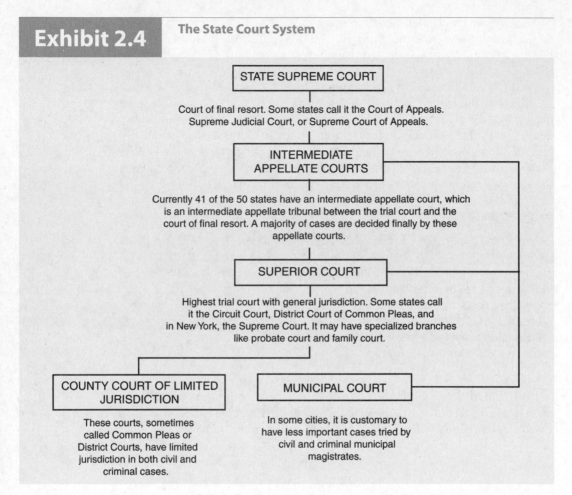

Exhibit 2.4   **The State Court System**

c.   State Courts

A number of courts operate within the states. At the lowest level are courts of limited jurisdiction. These courts hear only certain types of cases or cases involving only limited amounts of money. Municipal or city courts are courts of limited jurisdiction, as are county or district courts and small claims courts.

At the next level are courts of general jurisdiction. These courts have the power to review the decisions of courts of limited jurisdiction and original jurisdiction over claims arising under state law, whether that law is the state constitution, state statutes, or state common law.

About three-quarters of the states now have an intermediate court of appeals. These courts hear appeals as of right from the state courts of general jurisdiction, and the bulk of their caseload is criminal appeals. Because of the size of their workload, many of these courts have several divisions or districts.

Every state has a state "supreme" court. These courts review the decisions of the state trial courts and courts of appeals and are the final arbiters of questions of state constitutional, statutory, and common law. Exhibit 2.4 illustrates the typical relationship among the various state courts.

PRACTICE POINTER	Not all states call their highest court the supreme court. For example, in New York, the highest court is called the Court of Appeals, and the trial courts are called the supreme courts.

Decisions of state trial courts are not usually published. In addition, because of the volume, not all decisions of intermediate state courts of appeals are published. Those that are, and all decisions of the state supreme court, appear in one of West Publishing Company's regional reporters and, if the state has one, the state's official reporter.

d.   Other Courts

There are also several other court systems. As sovereign entities, many Native American tribes have their own judicial systems, as does the United States military.

§ 2.2   The Relationship Between the Federal and State Governments

It is not enough, however, to look at our system of government only from the perspective of its three branches. To understand the system, you must also understand the relationship between the federal and state governments.

§ 2.2.1   A Short History

Like most things, our system of government is the product of our history. From the early 1600s until 1781, the "united states" were not united. Instead, the "country" was composed of independent colonies, all operating under different charters and each having its own laws and legal system. Although the colonies traded with each other, the relationship among the colonies was no closer than the relationship among the European countries prior to 1992. It was not until the Articles of Confederation were adopted in 1781 that the "states" ceded any of their rights to a federal government.

Even though the states ceded more rights when the Constitution became effective in 1789, they preserved most of their own law. Each state retained its own executive, its own legislature and laws, and its own court system.

Thus, our system of government is really two systems, a federal system and the fifty state systems, with the United States Constitution brokering the relationship between the two.

§ 2.2.2   The Relationship Between Laws Enacted by Congress and Those Enacted by the State Legislatures

As citizens of the United States, we are subject to two sets of laws: federal law and the law of the state in which we are citizens (or in which we act).

Most of the time, there is no conflict between these two sets of laws: federal law governs some conduct; state law, other conduct. For example, federal law governs bankruptcy proceedings, and state law governs divorce.

Occasionally, however, both Congress and a state legislature enact laws governing the same conduct. Sometimes these laws coexist. For example, both Congress and the states have enacted drug laws. Acting under the powers granted to it under the Commerce Clause, Congress has made it illegal to import controlled substances or to transport them across state lines. The states, acting consistently with the powers reserved to them, have made illegal the possession or sale of controlled substances within the state. In such instances, citizens are subject to both laws. A defendant may be charged under federal law with transporting a drug across state lines and under state law with possession.

There are times, however, when federal and state law do not complement each other and cannot coexist. An act can be legal under federal law but illegal under state law. In such instances, federal law preempts state law, provided that the federal law is constitutional. As provided in the Supremacy Clause, laws enacted by Congress under the powers granted to it under the Constitution are the "supreme Law of the Land; and the Judges in every State shall be bound thereby . . . ."

The issue is different when the conflicting laws are from different states. Although there are more and more uniform laws (the Uniform Child Custody Act, the Uniform Commercial Code), an activity that is legal in one state may be illegal in another state. For instance, although prostitution is legal in Nevada as a local option, it is illegal in other states.

§ 2.2.3   The Relationship Between Federal and State Courts

The relationship between the federal and state court systems is complex. Although each system is autonomous, in certain circumstances the state courts may hear cases brought under federal law, and the federal courts may hear cases brought under state law.

For example, although the majority of cases heard in state courts are brought under state law, state courts also have jurisdiction when a case is brought under a provision of the United States Constitution, a treaty, and certain federal statutes. Similarly, although the majority of cases heard in the federal courts involve questions of federal law, the federal courts have jurisdiction over cases involving questions of state law when the parties are from different states (diversity jurisdiction).

The appellate jurisdiction of the courts is somewhat simpler. In the federal system, the United States Court of Appeals has appellate jurisdiction to review the decisions of the United States District Courts and certain administrative agencies, and the United States Supreme Court is the court of last resort, having the power to review the decisions of the lower federal courts. Similarly, if a state has an intermediate court of appeals, that court has the power to review the decisions of the lower courts within its geographic jurisdiction, and the state's highest, or supreme court, is the court of last resort.

§ 2.2.4   **The Relationship Among Federal, State, and Local Prosecutors**

The power to prosecute cases arising under the United States Constitution and federal statutes is vested in the Department of Justice, which is headed by the Attorney General of the United States, a presidential appointee. Assisting the United States Attorney General are the United States Attorneys for each federal judicial district. The individual United States Attorneys' offices have two divisions: a civil division and a criminal division. The civil division handles civil cases arising under federal law, and the criminal division handles cases involving alleged violations of federal criminal statutes.

At the state level, the system is slightly different. In most states, the attorney for the state is the state attorney general, usually an elected official. Working for the state attorney general are a number of assistant attorneys general. However, unlike the United States attorneys, most state attorneys general do not handle criminal cases. Their clients are the various state agencies. For example, an assistant attorney general may be assigned to a state's department of social and health services, the department of licensing, the consumer protection bureau, or the department of workers' compensation, providing advice to the agency and representing the agency in civil litigation.

Criminal prosecutions are handled by county and city prosecutors. Each county has its own prosecutor's office, which has both a civil and a criminal division. Attorneys working for the civil division play much the same role as state assistant attorneys general. They represent the county and its agencies, providing both advice and representation. In contrast, the attorneys assigned to the criminal division are responsible for prosecutions under the state's criminal code. The county prosecutor's office decides whom to charge and then tries the cases.

Like the counties, cities have their own city attorney's office, which, at least in large cities, has civil and criminal divisions. Attorneys working in the civil division advise city departments and agencies and represent the city in civil litigation; attorneys in the criminal division prosecute criminal cases brought under city ordinances. State, county, and city prosecutors do not represent federal departments or agencies, nor do they handle cases brought under federal law.

§ 2.3   Deciding How Much Weight to Give to a Particular Authority

Not all enacted and common law is given equal weight. In deciding which law to apply, courts distinguish between mandatory and persuasive authority.

Mandatory authority is law that is binding on the court deciding the case. The court must apply that law. In contrast, persuasive authority is law that is not binding. Although the court may look to that law for guidance, it need not apply it.

Determining whether a particular statute or case is mandatory or persuasive authority is a two-step process. You must first determine which jurisdiction's law applies (that is, whether federal or state law applies and, if state law applies, which state's law); you must then determine which of that jurisdiction's statutes and cases are binding on the court that will be deciding the case.

§ 2.3.1   Which Jurisdiction's Law Applies?

Sometimes determining which jurisdiction's law applies is easy. For example, common knowledge (and common sense) tells you that federal law probably governs whether a federal PLUS loan constitutes income for federal income tax purposes. Similarly, you would probably guess that a will executed in California by a California resident would be governed by California state law. At other times, though, the determination is much more difficult. You probably would not know which jurisdiction's law governs a real estate contract between a resident of New York and a resident of Pennsylvania for a piece of property located in Florida.

Although the rules governing the determination of which jurisdiction's law applies are beyond the scope of this book (they are studied in Civil Procedure, Federal Courts, and Conflicts), keep two things in mind.

First, remember that in our legal system, federal law almost always preempts, or takes precedence over, state law. Consequently, if there is both a federal and a state statute on the same topic, the federal statute will preempt the state statute to the extent that the two are inconsistent. For example, if a federal statute makes it illegal to discriminate on the basis of familial status when renting an apartment but under a state statute such discrimination is lawful, the federal statute governs — it is illegal to discriminate on the basis of familial status. There are a few instances, however, when a state constitutional provision or a state statute will govern. If the state constitution gives a criminal defendant more rights than does the federal constitution, the state constitution applies. While states can grant an individual more protection, they cannot take away or restrict rights granted by the federal constitution or a federal statute.

Second, in the federal system there is not the same body of common law that there is in the states. Unlike the state systems, in the federal system there are no common law rules governing adverse possession or intentional torts such as assault and battery, false imprisonment, or the intentional infliction of emotional distress. As a consequence, if the cause of action is based on a common law doctrine, the case is probably governed by state and not federal law.

§ 2.3.2   What "Law" Will Be Binding on the Court?

Within each jurisdiction, the authorities are ranked. The United States Constitution is the highest authority, binding both state and federal courts. Other federal and state law is under the United States Constitution.

In the federal system, the highest authority is the Constitution. Under the Constitution are the federal statutes and regulations, and under the federal statutes and regulations are the cases interpreting and applying them.

In the state system, the ranking is similar. The highest authority is the state constitution, followed by state statutes and regulations and the cases interpreting and applying those statutes and regulations and state common law.

In addition, the cases themselves are ranked. In both the federal and state systems, decisions of the United States Supreme Court carry the most weight: When deciding a case involving the same law and similar facts, both the courts of appeals and the trial courts are bound by the decisions of the supreme, or highest, state courts. Decisions of intermediate courts of appeals come next; the trial courts under the jurisdiction of the intermediate courts of appeals are bound by the courts of appeals' decisions. At the bottom are the trial courts. Trial court decisions are binding only on the parties involved in the particular case.

Statutes and cases are also ranked by date. More recent statutes supersede earlier versions, and more recent common law rules supersede early rules by the same level court. Courts are bound by the highest court's most recent decision. For example, if there is a 1967 state intermediate court of appeals decision that makes an activity legal and a 1986 state supreme court decision that makes it illegal, in the absence of a statute, the 1986 supreme court decision governs. The 1986 decision would be mandatory authority, and all the courts within that jurisdiction would be bound by that decision.

Exercise 2A	Mandatory and Persuasive Authority

1. In 1930, in Case A, the Supreme Court of your state set out a common law rule. In 1956, in Case B, the Supreme Court of your state changed that rule. In your state, which case would be binding on a trial court: Case A or Case B?

2. Same facts as in Question 1 except that in 1981, in Case C, the Supreme Court of your state modified the rule set out in Case B, adding a requirement. In your state, which test would a trial court use: the test set out in Case A, the test set out in Case B, or the test set out in Case C?

Case A	State Supreme Court	1930
Case B	State Supreme Court	1956
Case C	State Supreme Court	1981

3. Same facts as in Question 2 except that in 1983 your state legislature enacted a statute that completely changed the common law rule. What is now binding on the trial court: the cases or the statute?

Case A	State Supreme Court	1930
Case B	State Supreme Court	1956
Case C	State Supreme Court	1981
State Statute		1983

4. Same facts as in Question 3 except that in 1985, in Case D, a case involving the application of the 1983 statute, the Court of Appeals of your state gives one of the words in the statute a broad interpretation. (The word was not defined in the statute.) In applying the statute, which courts are bound by the Court of Appeals' decision in Case D: a trial court within the Court of Appeals' geographic jurisdiction? A trial court outside the Court of Appeals' geographic jurisdiction? The division of the Court of Appeals that decided Case D? A division of the Court of Appeals other than the division that decided Case D? Your state's Supreme Court?

State Statute	1983
Case D	1985

5. In 1995, in Case E, a different division of the Court of Appeals applies the 1983 statute. In reaching its decision, the court declines to follow the decision in Case D. Instead of interpreting the word broadly, the court interprets it narrowly. The losing party disagrees with this decision and files an appeal with your state's Supreme Court. In deciding the appeal, is the Supreme Court bound by the Court of Appeals' decision in Case D? The Court of Appeals' decision in Case E?

State Statute		1983
Case D	Court of Appeals	1985
Case E	Court of Appeals	1995

6. Same facts as in Question 5 except that in 1999 the state legislature amends that statute, explicitly defining the word that was the subject of debate in Cases D and E. The legislature elects to give the word a very narrow meaning. In Case F, which is brought before a state trial court in 2008, what would be controlling: the 1983 version of the statute? The 1985 decision in Case D? The 1995 decision in Case E? The amended version of the statute?

   Note: In Case E, the Supreme Court reversed the Court of Appeals and interpreted the term broadly.

State Statute		1983
Case D	Court of Appeals	1985
Case E	Court of Appeals	1995
Case E	Supreme Court	1996
Amended State Statute		1999

Chapter 2 Quiz

Draft answers for each of the following questions. Make your points clearly and concisely, and write sentences that are easy to read and that are grammatical and correctly punctuated.

1. Which branch of the federal government has the power to enact statutes?
2. Which branch of the federal government is responsible for enforcing federal statutes?
3. Which branch of the federal government has the power to determine whether a federal statute is constitutional?
4. What is the difference between a statute and a regulation?
5. At trial, what is the role of the judge? The role of the jury?
6. What role do the appellate courts play?
   a. Do they hear testimony?
   b. Do they decide issues of fact?
   c. Do they determine whether there was sufficient evidence to support the trial court's judgment?
   d. Do they determine whether the trial court applied the right law and applied that law correctly?
7. In the federal system, what is the name of the trial court? The intermediate court of appeals? What courts operate in your state? (To find this information, you will need to do an Internet search.)
8. What do lawyers and judges mean when they say that a federal statute "preempts" a state statute?

9. What do lawyers and judges mean when they say that a court has "jurisdiction" to hear a particular type of case?

10. Are all of the court decisions that appear on the Internet (for example, on Lexis Advance and WestlawNext) "published" decisions? What makes a decision a "published opinion"?

Reading and Analyzing Statutes and Cases

When you think about becoming a lawyer, what image comes to mind? Do you see yourself cross-examining a witness? Making an impassioned argument to a jury? Hugging your client when the jury returns the verdict in his or her favor?

Although some lawyers do these things, these are more likely the images of TV lawyering than they are of real lawyering. Real lawyers spend much of their time reading and writing. Consider the following quotation from an associate at a major law firm.

> My view of lawyering has changed dramatically since I entered law school. In my first year of law school, I saw myself as a trial lawyer. I thought that most of my time would be spent either preparing for trial or in trial. The truth of the matter is that I have been inside the courthouse only three or four times during the last year and that was to look through court files. Instead, most of my time is spent reading and preparing documents, doing legal research, and writing memos and briefs. Don't get me wrong. The work that I do is extremely interesting. It is just that I never saw myself spending seven or eight hours a day reading and writing.
>
> —*Second-year associate at a large law firm*

The way in which lawyers read is not, however, the way in which most individuals read. Therefore, part of learning how to think like a lawyer is learning how to read like a lawyer. In this chapter, we describe some of the strategies that lawyers use in reading statutes and cases.

§ 3.1   Good Lawyers Are Good Readers

Good lawyers are good readers. When they read a document, statute, or case, they read exactly what is on the page. They do not skip words, read in words, or misread words. In addition, they have good vocabularies. They recognize and understand most of the words that they read, and the ones they do not recognize or understand they look up in a dictionary.

PRACTICE POINTER	There are a number of good, free dictionaries online. For example, Merriam-Webster Online dictionary is at *http://www.m-w.com*; JURIST's legal dictionaries are at *http://jurist.law.pitt*

.edu/dictionary.htm; and FindLaw's® legal dictionary is at *http://dictionary .lp.findlaw.com*.

Poor reading skills can significantly affect your ability to understand what it is that you are reading. For instance, in Example 1, which is taken from the transcript of a law student reading a case aloud, Jackie, a first-year student, mispronounced and apparently did not recognize the word "palatial."

EXAMPLE 1	**Transcript of a Student, Jackie, Reading a Case Aloud**

Some months prior to the alleged imprisonment, the plaintiff, while in *Jaffa*, announced her intention to leave the sect. The defendant, with the help of the plaintiff's husband, persuaded the plaintiff to return to the United States aboard the sect's platial [sic] yacht, the Kingdom.

James, another student who read the same case, misread the following sentence. Example 2 shows how the sentence appears in the casebook. Example 3 shows how James read it when he read the sentence aloud.[1]

EXAMPLE 2	**Sentence as It Appears in the Casebook**

According to the uncontradicted evidence, at no time did anyone physically restrain the plaintiff except for the defendant's refusal once the plaintiff announced her decision to quit the yacht to let the plaintiff use a small boat to take herself, her children and her belongings ashore.

EXAMPLE 3	**How James Read the Sentence**

According to the uncontradicted evidence, at no time did anyone physically restrain the plaintiff except for the defendant's [pause] defendant's refusal once [pause] defendant's refusal once [pause] the plaintiff announced her decision to the quit the yacht to let the plaintiff use a small boat to take herself, her children, and her belongings ashore.

---

1. The examples in this section come from the following article: Laurel Currie Oates, *Beating the Odds, Reading Strategies of Law Students Admitted Through Special Admissions Programs*, 83 Iowa L. Rev. 139 (1997).

When questioned about what the court was saying in this sentence, James stated that the defendant had, on one occasion, refused to let the plaintiff take the boat. In fact, the court said that the refusal came once the defendant announced her decision to quit the yacht.

Although at first these errors may seem insignificant, in each instance they resulted in the student misunderstanding the case and thus the rules and the court's reasoning. In addition, in both instances, the errors were a harbinger of things to come. Both students ended up doing poorly on their exams. At the end of the first year, Jackie was in the bottom 20 percent of her class, and James had flunked out.

To determine whether you may be misreading cases, make two copies of one of the cases in your casebook. Keep one copy for yourself and give the other to a trusted classmate or teaching assistant. Then read aloud from your copy while your partner follows along on his or her copy, highlighting any words or phrases that you misread and any words that you mispronounce or do not appear to understand. After you have finished your reading of the case, compare your understanding of the case with your partner's. Did you both read the case in essentially the same way? If your partner noted more than one or two problems or if your understanding of the case is substantially different from your partner's understanding of it, try the following. First, try reading more slowly. You may be trying to read the material too quickly. Second, take the time to look up any words that you do not recognize or are not sure that you understand. Third, if the problems appear to be serious, ask your school's learning center if it can provide you with a more thorough evaluation of your reading skills.

§ 3.2   Good Legal Readers Read and Reread Material Until They Are Sure That They Understand It

While in some types of reading you can skip sections that you do not completely understand, such a strategy does not work when you are doing legal reading. If the document, statute, or case is one that is relevant to your problem, you need to read and reread it until you are sure that you understand it.

Example 1 shows how a student, William, stayed with a case until he was sure that he understood it. The material in the regular typeface is the text of the case. The material in italics is what William said after he had read that section of the text.

| EXAMPLE 1 | **Transcript of a Student, William, Reading a Case Aloud** |

Whittaker v. Sanford
110 Me. 77, 88 S. 399 (1912)

Savage, J. Action for false imprisonment. The plaintiff recovered a verdict for $1100. The case comes up on defendant's exceptions and a motion for a new trial.

So the defendant is the appellant and is appealing the verdict of $1100.

The plaintiff had been a member of a religious sect which had colonies in Maine and in Jaffa, Syria, and of which the defendant was a leader. Some months prior to the alleged imprisonment, the plaintiff, while in Jaffa, announced her intention to leave the sect.

> *I need to reread this again. [Rereads sentence.] So just prior to the alleged imprisonment the plaintiff was in Jaffa and expressed an intention to leave the sect. At this point, I am a bit confused about who the parties are. I need to reread this to make sure that I have the facts straight. [Rereads from the beginning.] OK. This is an action for false imprisonment. The plaintiff recovered a verdict for $1100. The case came up on the defendant's exceptions. The plaintiff is a member of the sect and the defendant is the head of the sect so Whittaker is the member of the sect and Sanford is its leader.*

Although it took William more time to read the case than it took some of the other students who read the case, the payoff was substantial. Although his undergraduate GPA and LSAT placed William in the bottom 10 percent of his entering law school class, at the end of his first year, he was in the top 10 percent.

There are several things that you can do to make sure that you understand the cases that you are reading. First, see if you can diagram the action. At the trial court level, who sued whom and what was the cause of action? Who "won" at trial, who filed the appeal, and what is the issue on appeal?

> **PRACTICE POINTER**
>
> In some instances, you may be able to compare your chart showing the case's prior and subsequent history with the chart that is on KeyCite® under "Direct History (Graphical View)." For more information about this KeyCite feature, see section 10.3.2 in the electronic supplement.

Second, do not underestimate the value of preparing your own case briefs. While it may be faster and easier to highlight sections of a statute or case, highlighting does not ensure that you understand the material you are reading. In fact, there is some evidence that students who highlight remember less than students who do not highlight: In highlighting a section, some students focus their attention on the process of highlighting and not on the material they are highlighting. As a result, when they are asked to recall what it is that they just highlighted, they are unable to do so.

Finally, after reading a section, test yourself to make sure that you understood what it is that you have just read. After you have finished reading a statute or case, close the book or your computer and summarize what the statute or case said.

§ 3.3   Good Legal Readers Engage in Both Analysis and Synthesis

In addition to reading accurately and until they understand the materials, good legal readers analyze and synthesize the material that they read.

Analysis is the process of taking a statute or case apart. In reading statutes, you analyze each section and subsection, making sure that you understand each. In reading cases, you identify the issue that was before the court, the rule or rules that the court applied in deciding that issue, the facts that the court considered in applying those rules, and the court's reasoning or rationale. When you "brief" a statute or case, you are engaging in analysis.

In contrast, synthesis is the process of putting the pieces together. You take each of the statutory sections and cases you have read and try to make sense of them. Are they consistent? What are the steps in the analysis? How do they fit into your existing conceptual frameworks?

Example 1 shows how a law professor engaged in both analysis and synthesis. Note both how she analyzes the case she is currently reading and how she tries to reconcile what the court says in that case with the Restatement section that set out the elements of false imprisonment. The text is set out in regular type and the professor's comments are in italics.

EXAMPLE 1	**Transcript of a Professor Reading a Case Aloud**

There was evidence that the plaintiff had been ashore a number of times, had been on numerous outings and had been treated as a guest during her stay aboard the yacht. According to the uncontradicted evidence, at no time did anyone physically restrain the plaintiff except for the defendant's refusal, once the plaintiff announced her decision to quit the yacht, to let the plaintiff use a small boat to take herself, her children, and her belongings ashore.

I'm sort of getting a visual image of the boat that she was in and out of . . . uhm . . . the plaintiff had been ashore. I'm thinking about the elements that I just read [a reference to the Restatement section that had been set out immediately before the case] *and I'm trying to see how, I guess, frankly how I would decide the case on a certain level before I even want to know what Judge Savage thought.* [Pause.] *I need to look at the Restatement section.* [Looks back at the Restatement section.] *Is the defendant acting to or with the intent to confine the plaintiff? She got off the boat. That kind of bothers me. That results directly or indirectly in confinement. Maybe that's relevant here. The other is conscious of the confinement or is harmed by it. Given the facts, that bothers me too.*

Doing analysis and synthesis is both time-consuming and hard work. You are no longer reading just for information. Instead, as you are reading, you are either placing new information into existing conceptual frameworks or constructing completely new frameworks.

If you are like most law students, at some point you will argue that law school would be a lot easier if your professors put the pieces together for you, if they just gave you their conceptual frameworks. If you had come to law school just to learn the law, you would be right. It would be easier for both you and your professors if they just gave you the law. There is, however, a lot more to law school than just learning the law. Although you will learn some law while you are in law school, the real reason that you came to law school was to learn to think like a lawyer. Accordingly, the primary skills that you will need to teach yourself while you are in law school are how to do legal analysis and synthesis. You need to be able to look at a statute and a group of cases and determine what the law is and how it might be applied in a particular situation.

§ 3.4   Good Legal Readers Place the Statutes and Cases They Read into Their Historical, Social, Economic, Political, and Legal Contexts

Good legal readers understand that statutes are usually enacted to solve a problem or to promote certain interests and that judicial decisions reflect, at least in part, the time and place in which they were written. As a consequence, in reading statutes and cases, good legal readers place them in their historical, social, economic, political, and legal contexts. They note the date that the statute was enacted and amended and the year in which the case was decided. They think about the social and economic conditions during those periods and about the political issues that were in the headlines when the statute was enacted or the case was decided. Finally, they place the case in its larger legal context. They determine how the particular issue fits into the broader area of law, they note whether the decision is from an intermediate court of appeals or the highest court in the jurisdiction, and they read the court's decision in light of the standard of review that the court applied. Was the court deciding the issue de novo, or was it simply looking to see whether there was sufficient evidence to support the jury's verdict?

PRACTICE POINTER	If you do not know what the phrase *"de novo"* means, look it up in a book or online dictionary.

In reading the case that was described earlier in this chapter, the professor placed the case in its historical, social, and political context. First, she noted that the case was an old one. It was decided by the Supreme Court of Maine in 1912. Second, she noted that in 1912, $1,100 would have been a substantial sum of money. Third, she considered the social climate in 1912: the role of women and their rights and the public's attitudes about "religious cults." She knew that in 1912 women had far fewer rights. For instance, it was often the husband who determined where the couple lived and what religion they practiced. What she did not know is how religious cults were viewed. In 1912 did people view religious cults in the same way that most people view them today? Were cults seen as a problem? How did these factors influence the court's decision and the way the judge wrote the opinion?

You need to think about the cases that you read in similar ways. When you are reading cases, pay close attention to the dates of the decisions and the courts that issued them. If you read the cases in chronological order, can you discern a trend? Over the last fifty, twenty-five, or five years, have the rules or the ways the courts apply those rules changed? If the answer is yes, what social, economic, or political events might account for those changes? In contrast, if you arrange the decisions by jurisdiction, does a pattern appear? For example, do industrial states tend to take one approach and more rural states another? Are some jurisdictions more conservative while others are more liberal? As you read between the lines, what do you think motivated the judges and persuaded them to decide the case in one way rather than another?

§ 3.5   Good Legal Readers "Judge" the Statutes and Cases They Read

As a beginning law student, you may be tempted to accept everything you read. Who are you to judge the soundness of a Supreme Court Justice's analysis or Congress's choice of a particular word or phrase? Do not give in to this temptation. If you are going to be a good legal reader, you need to question and evaluate everything you read.

In judging the cases you read, make sure you do more than evaluate the facts. Although in Example 1 William engages in some evaluation, it is the evaluation of a nonlawyer. William evaluates the witness's testimony, not the court's choice of rule, application of the rules to the facts, or reasoning. Once again, the text of the case is set out in a regular typeface and William's comments are in italics.

EXAMPLE 1   **Transcript of a Student, William, Reading a Case Aloud**

There was evidence that the plaintiff had been ashore a number of times, had been on numerous outings and had been treated as a guest during her stay aboard the yacht.

So at this point I'm getting a picture of what happened. . . . I'm not sure though: There is evidence that the plaintiff had been ashore so at this point I'm thinking was she really held against her will? So I have doubts, doubts about the plaintiff's story at this point.

According to the uncontradicted evidence, at no time did anyone physically restrain the plaintiff except for the defendant's refusal, once the plaintiff announced her decision to quit the yacht, to let the plaintiff use a small boat to take herself, her children, and her belongings ashore.

Well, . . . the defendant by this point isn't really stopping the plaintiff from leaving.

Throughout the entire episode the plaintiff's husband was with her and repeatedly tried to persuade her to change her mind and remain with the sect.

At this point, mentally, I think, . . . I don't think the plaintiff's story doesn't hold water, . . . that's what I am thinking. Because her husband was there so maybe you, there's in my mind that her story doesn't hold water. So I am thinking at this point that the court might end up reversing her position.

In contrast, the professor evaluated the court's conclusion and reasoning. After she finished reading the case, the professor made the following comments. Note how the professor talks about the elements of the tort and how she poses a hypothetical.

EXAMPLE 2   **Transcript of Professor's Comments**

I'm not sure that the plaintiff proved all of the elements of false imprisonment. For example, I'm not sure that the plaintiff proved that the defendant intended to confine the plaintiff. If I remember correctly, [pause] on a number of occasions he allowed her to go ashore. He just wouldn't let her use the small boat to take her children and their things ashore. It would have been interesting to know what would have happened if a boat had come to get the plaintiff. Would the defendant have let her go? If he would have, there wouldn't have been false imprisonment. [Pause.] The facts may, however, support a finding that the defendant's actions resulted in confinement. In those days, the plaintiff may not have had a way to contact anyone on shore to ask them to come get her. Although the court may have reached the right result, I wish that Judge Savage had done more analysis. [Pause.] I get the feeling that he had made up his mind, maybe he didn't like cults, and then just tried to justify his conclusion.

§ 3.6   Good Legal Readers Read for a Specific Purpose

The reading that you do for your law school classes is very different from the reading you will do in practice. In law school, you read so that you will be prepared for class. Consider the following comment made by James.

> When I read cases, I usually read them not for briefing cases per se, but more out of fear of being called on in class. I don't want to look like a fool so I just want to know the basic principles.

In contrast, in practice you will read for a specific purpose. For example, you will read to keep up to date in an area of law, to find the answer to a question that a client has posed, to find statutes or cases to support your client's position, or to find holes in your opponent's arguments.

In reading the statutes and cases for your legal writing assignments, read not as a student, but as a lawyer. Initially, read to find out what the law is. Analyze the statutes and cases that you have found, and then put the pieces together. Then read the cases as the parties and the court would read them. Begin by putting yourself in your client's position. How can your client use the statutes and cases to support its position? Put yourself in the other side's shoes. How could the opponent use the same statutes and cases to support his or her position? Finally, put yourself in the court's position. If you were the judge, how would you read the statutes and cases?

§ 3.7   Good Legal Readers Understand That Statutes and Cases Can Be Read in More Than One Way

Different people have different beliefs about text. While some people believe that there is a right way to read each statute or case, others believe that most statutes and cases can be read in more than one way. For those in the first group, the meaning of a particular text is fixed. For those in the second group, the meaning of a particular text is "constructed" by juries and judges and by the attorneys who talk to them.

As a general rule, the students who seem to have the easiest time in their first year of law school are those who believe that statutes and cases can be read in more than one way, that the meaning of a particular text is socially constructed. These students have an easier time seeing how each side might interpret a particular statute and stating a rule so that it favors their client's position. When they talk about a court's holding, they refer to it as "a holding," not "the holding."

If you are a student who believes that meaning is fixed, be aware of how your belief system affects the way in which you read statutes and cases and the way in which you make arguments. In reading cases, can you see how both the plaintiff and the defendant might be able to use the same case to support their arguments? In making arguments, are you able to see what the other side might argue and how you might be able to respond to those arguments? Are you spending too much time looking for the correct answer and not enough time creating that answer? In contrast, if you are a student who believes that meaning is socially constructed, be careful that you do not become cynical or only a hired gun. Although there may be many ways of reading a particular statute or case, not all of those readings will lead to a "just" result.

Reading and thinking like a lawyer are not skills that you can learn overnight. There are no crash courses, shortcuts, or magic wands. Instead, you will learn to read and think like a lawyer through trial and error and by observing how real lawyers, not TV lawyers, read and think about statutes and cases.

Legal Research

Researching Issues Governed by State Statutes and Regulations

L earning to research issues governed by state statutes and regulations is a lot like learning to play chess. Although you can learn the names of the pieces and the standard moves relatively quickly, it takes a long time to become an expert. This chapter should, however, help you develop that expertise a bit more rapidly.

Before you begin reading this chapter, note that it has several components: (1) the text, which sets out basic information; (2) exercises, which ask you to apply what you have just read; (3) a quiz that tests the materials set out in the chapter; and (4) an electronic supplement, which shows you how to research an issue governed by a state statute using free sources, Lexis Advance®, WestlawNext™, Bloomberg Law, Lexis.com®, and Westlaw® Classic. To access the supplement, go to *http://www.aspenlawschool.com/books/oates_legalwriting handbook/*. Your access code to the website is on the card that came with the book. In the ebook, instructions for getting an access code are on the page immediately following the cover page.

§ 4.1 Research Plan for an Issue Governed by State Statutes

The research plan for issues governed by state statutes and regulations has four steps: (1) do background reading to familiarize yourself with the area of law; (2) locate and read primary sources; (3) cite check your primary sources to make sure that they are still good law; and (4) if appropriate, look for cases from other jurisdictions, law review articles, or other commentaries.

Research Plan for an Issue Governed by State Statutes

Jurisdiction: [Enter the name of the applicable state.]

Type of Law: Enacted law

Preliminary Issue

Statement: [Put your first draft of the issue statement here.]

Step 1:   If you are unfamiliar with the area of law, spend thirty to sixty minutes doing background reading.

Step 2:   Locate the governing statutes and regulations and the cases that have interpreted and applied those statutes and regulations.

Step 3:   Cite check the cases that you plan to use to make sure that they are still good law.

Step 4:   If appropriate, locate cases from other jurisdictions, law review articles, or other commentaries that might be on point.

§ 4.2   Sources for State Statutory Research

The first step is to learn what sources are available. Table 4.1 lists some, but not all, of the sources that you can use in researching an issue governed by state statutes and regulations. Note that because the names of the sources vary by state, we have listed the sources using generic labels rather than specific names. (For a list of the names of the sources in a particular state, see the listing for that state in Appendix 1 of the *ALWD Citation Manual* or Table 1 in *The Bluebook*.) Also note that not all states will have all the sources listed. For example, not all states have both an unannotated and an annotated code. Finally, note that many of the sources are available in book form, on free websites, and on fee-based services. In practice, you will need to decide which option is the best option.

§ 4.2.1   Sources for Background Reading

If you are familiar with the area of law that you have been asked to research, you can skip this step. If, however, the area is one that is new to you, begin your research by spending a few minutes doing background reading.

PRACTICE POINTER   In some situations, you will not need to do background reading. For example, if all you need is the text of the statute or a list of cases that have discussed the statute, you will not need to do background reading. Don't make the research harder than it needs to be. If, however, you are not sure which statute applies or even whether there is a governing statute, doing background reading will usually save you time and help you do more sophisticated analysis.

Table 4.1	Sources of State Law	
	State Law	
Background Reading	▪ State practice manuals ▪ Hornbooks ▪ *Nutshells* ▪ The Internet	
State Session Laws (stat-utes in order enacted)	▪ State session laws	
State Codes (statutes organized by topic)	▪ Unannotated code ▪ Annotated code	
State Regulations	▪ Administrative code	
Cases Interpreting and Applying Statutes	▪ State reporter setting out decisions from the state's highest appellate court ▪ State reporter setting out decisions from the state's intermediate appellate courts ▪ West regional reporter that contains decisions from the state's highest appellate court and the state's intermediate appellate courts and decisions from other courts in the same region.	
Cite Checking	▪ KeyCite® ▪ *Shepard's*® ▪ BCite	
Secondary Authorities	▪ Attorney general opinions ▪ *American Law Reports* (for example, A.L.R.4th, A.L.R.5th, and A.L.R.6th) ▪ Law review articles	

a. Practice Manuals and Practice Books

For issues governed by state law, the best source for background reading is almost always a state practice manual. In most states, these manuals are written by practitioners and provide the reader with an overview of the area of law and citations to key statutes, regulations, and cases. In addition, some practice manuals set out sample forms and practice pointers. Although most practice manuals are updated regularly, some are not. Therefore, always check to see when the manual that you are using was last updated.

Historically, most practice manuals were available only in book form. Today, however, many of these manuals are available on fee-based services. For example, practice manuals published by West, a Thomson Reuters business, are available on Westlaw Classic and WestlawNext, and some of the practice manuals are available on Lexis.com and Lexis Advance.

To find the book version of a practice manual, use your library's electronic card catalog and do key word searches using the name of the state and one or more of the following words: "practice," "procedure," and "manual." To find out what practice manuals are available on a particular fee-based service, check that service's list of databases or ask a colleague or your service's sales representative.

Exercise 4A	**State Practice Manuals**

Using your library's electronic card catalog, locate the names and call numbers for practice manuals for one of the following states:

1. California
2. Maine
3. Texas
4. The state in which your law school is located

---

b. Hornbooks and *Nutshells*

If the practice manuals do not discuss the issue that you have been asked to research, look for a hornbook or a *Nutshell*. Hornbooks are one-volume hardbound books that provide the reader with an overview of an area of law, for example, civil procedure, contract law, property law, or tort law. *Nutshells* are shorter one-volume paperbacks designed primarily as a study tool for law students. Like hornbooks, *Nutshells* deal with broad areas of law. Although hornbooks and *Nutshells* will not tell you what the law is in your state, they can provide you with general information about the area of law. To find copies of hornbooks and *Nutshells*, use your library's electronic card catalog. For example, to find a *Nutshell*, do a title or key word search using the word "Nutshell" and a word or phrase describing the area of law.

Exercise 4B	**Hornbooks and *Nutshells***

Using your library's electronic card catalog, locate the names and call numbers for hornbooks and *Nutshells* that discuss one of the following areas of law:

1. Civil Procedure
2. Property
3. Contracts
4. The area of law that you would like to practice

---

c. The Internet

Increasingly, the Internet is a good source for doing background reading related to state statutes. To locate a website that discusses a particular statute, either use the citation to the statute as a search term or enter terms that relate to the area of law. If your search retrieves a number of websites, look first at government-sponsored sites (.gov), educational sites (.edu), and sites sponsored by reliable organizations (.org).

Exercise 4C   Bing and Google

Using either Bing or Google, locate and record the URL for one or more websites that provide background information about landlord-tenant law in one of the following states:

1. California
2. New York
3. Texas
4. The state in which your law school is located

§ 4.2.2   Sources for Statutes

Most state statutes come in three forms: in the state's session laws, in unannotated codes, and in annotated codes.

> **PRACTICE POINTER**   Although the session laws of some states can only be found in book form, you can find the *Statutes at Large* (the session laws for federal statutes) and unannotated and annotated versions of state and federal codes in both book and electronic formats.

a.   Session Laws

Session laws are the statutes published in the order in which they were enacted. At the end of a legislative session, the statutes enacted during that session are collected and arranged, not by topic, but by date. For instance, statutes enacted during the 2009 legislative session will be set out in date order in one volume, the statutes enacted during the 2010 legislative session will be set out in date order in another volume, and so on. To find a session law, you need to know when the statute was enacted and its number. In most state codes, that number is found at the end of the statute: The information set out in the "CREDIT(S)" section tells you when the statute was enacted and amended, and the chapter and section numbers tell you where you can find the original version of the statute and any amendments.

The only time that you will use session laws is when you are doing a legislative history. (See Chapter 11 in this book.) For other types of statutory research, use an unannotated or annotated code.

b.   Unannotated Codes

Statutes are "codified" when they are arranged, not in the order in which they were enacted, but by topic. Thus, in a code, all the statutes relating to a particular topic will be placed together. For instance, all the statutes relating to criminal law will be placed under one "title" or subject heading, all the statutes relating to marriage will be placed under another title or subject heading, and all the statutes relating to commercial transactions will be placed under yet another title or subject heading. The decision about where to place a particular statute is made not by the legislative body itself but by attorneys who work for the state as "code revisers."

Most unannotated codes set out only the text of the statutes, the credits, and historical notes. Therefore, think about using an unannotated code when all you want is the text of the statute. In particular, use an unannotated code when your issue is governed by several different statutory sections: Because there will not be any cross-references or Notes of Decisions between the sections, it will be easier to see how the various sections work together.

An unannotated code may be a state's official code or its unofficial code. Most unannotated codes are available both in book form and on both fee-based and free websites. For instance, if the unannotated code is the state's official code, you should be able to find a copy on the state's website.

> **PRACTICE POINTER**   As a practicing attorney, you will probably use your state's official website frequently. It is, therefore, a good idea to spend some time exploring that site to see what is and is not there. In addition, think about adding your state's website to your list of favorites.

c. Annotated Codes

As you may have guessed, an annotated code is a code that has been annotated. In addition to setting out the text of the statutes, the credits, and historical notes, an annotated code also sets out cross-references to other sources published by the same publisher and Notes of Decisions (Westlaw Classic and WestlawNext) or Case Notes (Lexis.com and Lexis Advance), which are one-paragraph descriptions of cases that have cited the statute. Consequently, an annotated code is both primary authority[1] because it sets out the law itself and a finding tool because you can use it to find other primary authority, in this instance cases that have interpreted and applied the statute.

In the past, most states published their own unannotated codes, and private publishing companies published the annotated codes. Some states have stopped publishing the unannotated version of their state codes, however, and have entered into contracts with private publishing companies to make the publishing company's annotated code their official state code. For example, both Maine and New Jersey use the West versions of the code as their official codes. Annotated codes are available both in books and on Lexis.com, Lexis Advance, Westlaw Classic, and WestlawNext.

You should use an annotated code when you are interested not only in the text of the statute but also in how the courts have interpreted and applied the statute. Read the statute; determine which elements, or requirements, are likely to be in dispute; and then locate cases that have discussed those elements, or requirements, using the Notes of Decisions or Case Notes.

---

1. For a definition of the terms "primary authority," "secondary authority," and "finding tools," see Chapter 3 or the Glossary at the end of the book.

PRACTICE POINTER	Most citation systems require you to cite to the official rather than unofficial version of the code unless the material that you are citing appears in only the unofficial version. See Rule 14.1 in the

ALWD Citation Manual and Rule 12.2.1(a) in The Bluebook.

Exercise 4D — State Statutes: The Names of State Codes

Using the *ALWD Citation Manual* or *The Bluebook,* record the names of the unannotated codes and annotated codes that are published for the following states:

1. California
2. New York
3. Texas
4. The state in which your law school is located

§ 4.2.3   Sources for State Regulations

In enacting a state statute, the state legislature may grant a state administrative agency the power to promulgate regulations. When the proper procedures have been followed, those regulations have the effect of law and are, therefore, primary authority.

Although the process varies from state to state, in most states proposed regulations are first published in a state register and then in the state's administrative code. In most states, the register and the administrative code are available in both book form and on the state's website. In addition, the regulations are on fee-based and other free websites.

Exercise 4E — State Regulations: The Names of State Administrative Codes

Using the *ALWD Citation Manual* or *The Bluebook,* record the name of the administrative code for one of the following states:

1. California
2. New York
3. Texas
4. The state in which your law school is located

§ 4.2.4   Locating Cases That Have Interpreted or Applied a State Statute

a.   Notes of Decisions/Case Notes

When the statutory language, by itself, answers your question, you do not need to look for cases that have interpreted or applied the statute. However, when the statutory language is ambiguous, you will need to look for cases that have interpreted the statute. One of the easiest ways to find these cases is to use an annotated code.

As soon as they release an opinion, most courts send an electronic copy of their opinion to the publishing companies. When the Thomson West attorneys receive an opinion, they draft a one-sentence summary for each point of law set out in the opinion. When the summary appears at the beginning of an opinion, it is called a "headnote." When it appears after the text of a statute, it is called a "Note of Decision." LexisNexis uses a slightly different approach. Instead of drafting one-sentence summaries, the LexisNexis attorneys identify the key language and quote that key language at the beginning of the opinion in headnotes or, if the language relates to a statute, in Case Notes following the text of the statute.

If there are relatively few cases that have discussed a particular statute, these Notes of Decisions and Case Notes will be listed together after the statute. If, though, there are a number of cases that have discussed a particular statute, the Notes of Decisions and Case Notes will be organized by subtopics. Your job as a legal researcher is to read through the relevant Notes of Decisions and Case Notes and then locate and read the cases that appear to have the types of information that you need.

PRACTICE POINTER	As a general rule, decisions from higher courts will be listed before decisions from lower courts and, if there is more than one decision from a particular court, newer cases will be listed before older cases.

Although Notes of Decisions and Case Notes set out points of law, the notes are only finding tools and not something that you can rely on or cite to in a memo or a brief. Thus, use the Notes of Decisions and Case Notes as finding tools and not as authority.

Exercise 4F   Locating State Statutes

1. In the law library, locate the annotated code for one of the following states:

   a. Indiana
   b. Kentucky
   c. Massachusetts
   d. The state in which your law school is located

   Using the index, locate the statutory section or sections in your state's code that deal with security deposits for residential rentals. Once you have found the applicable statutory section or sections, list the types of information that follow the text of one of the sections. For example, are there historical notes? Cross-references to other sources? Notes of Decisions or Case Notes?

2. Read section 4.3.3 or 4.3.4 in the electronic supplement. For your state, how would you find the statutory section or sections dealing with security deposits for residential rentals? Once you

have found the applicable statutory section or sections, examine the information following the text of the statute. Is it the same information that you found in the book? Why or why not?

b. Reporters

A "reporter" is a set of books in which court decisions are reported. In many states, the decisions of a state's highest court are placed in one reporter, and the decisions of a state's intermediate court of appeals are placed in a different reporter. For example, in Georgia, copies of the Supreme Court of Georgia's opinions are published in *Georgia Reports*, and copies of the Georgia Court of Appeals' decisions are published in *Georgia Appeals Reports*. In addition, both Georgia Supreme Court and Georgia Court of Appeals decisions are published in a regional reporter, the *South Eastern Reporter*, which is published by West and is part of West's National Reporter System. For a map showing which states' opinions are published in which regional reporter, see *http://lawschool.westlaw .com/federalcourt/NationalReporterPage.asp*.

When the decisions of a particular court are published in more than one reporter, one of those reporters will be designated as the official reporter, and the other reporter(s) will be designated as the unofficial reporter(s). For example, in Georgia, *Georgia Reports* and *Georgia Appeals Reports* are the official reporters and *South Eastern Reporter* is the unofficial reporter.

In other states, the decisions of both the state's highest court and intermediate court of appeals are published in the same state reporter. For instance, in New Mexico, the decisions of both the New Mexico Supreme Court and the New Mexico Court of Appeals are published in *New Mexico Reports*. In addition, the decisions of both the New Mexico Supreme Court and the New Mexico Court of Appeals are published in the *Pacific Reporter*, which is another one of West's regional reporters.

Still other states have stopped publishing their own reporters. In these states, the state's decisions can only be found in the regional reporter. For instance, since 1968, Iowa decisions have been published in only the *North Western Reporter*.

PRACTICE POINTER	To find the names of the reporters in which a particular court's decisions are published, see Appendix 1 in the *ALWD Citation Manual* or Table 1 of *The Bluebook*.

Exercise 4G   **The Names of State Reporters**

Using the *ALWD Citation Manual* or *The Bluebook,* identify the names of reporters in which current decisions of the following courts are published.

1. Current decisions of the Idaho Supreme Court are published in _____
    _____.

2. Current decisions of the Massachusetts Supreme Judicial Court are published in _____
    _____.

3. Current decisions of New Mexico Court of Appeals are published in _____
    _____.

Like session laws (see section 4.2.2.a), reporters are organized chronologically. Cases decided in 1995 appear before cases that were decided in 2000, and cases that were decided in 2009 appear before cases that were decided in 2013. In addition, a case that was decided on May 20 will appear before one that was decided on May 21.

> **PRACTICE POINTER**   When two cases are published in the same reporter, you can use the citation to determine which case is the most recent: The case with the highest volume number is the most recent case. Similarly, if the cases appear not only in the same reporter but also in the same volume of that reporter, the case with the highest page number will be the most recent case.

To find a case in the book version of a reporter, you need three pieces of information: (1) the name of the reporter, (2) the volume in which the case appears, and (3) the page on which the case begins. This information is buried in the citation that appears at the end of each Note of Decision/Case Note. Look, for example, at the following citation, which is taken from the Notes of Decisions following section 48.031 of the *Florida Statutes Annotated*, a West publication.

Busman v. State, Dept. of Revenue, App. 3 Dist., 905 So. 2d 956 (2005).

Although this citation is not in the form specified by either the *ALWD Citation Manual* or *The Bluebook*, it does give you the information that you need to find the case. This citation tells you that the court's opinion in *Busman v. State, Dept. of Revenue* can be found in volume 905 of the *Southern Reporter, Second Series*, beginning on page 956. In addition, the citation tells you that the opinion was issued in 2005 and that the case was heard and decided by the Third District Appellate Court. Because the citation appears in the annotation to the Florida statutes, you can infer that the case is a Florida case.

> **PRACTICE POINTER**   It is not uncommon for a publishing company to use its own citation rules and not the citation rules in the *ALWD Citation Manual* or *The Bluebook*. If, however, you are citing the case in a memo or brief, you need to use the citation rules used in your jurisdiction and not the publishing company's rules. In other words, do not just copy and paste the citation into your memo or brief without first making sure that the citation complies with your jurisdiction's citation rules.

You can find a copy of a published decision in a number of places: (1) if the state publishes its own reporter, in that reporter; (2) in the applicable regional reporter; (3) on fee-based services, for example, Lexis.com, Lexis Advance,

Westlaw Classic, WestlawNext, and Bloomberg Law; and (4) on free websites, for example, Google® Scholar.

Exercise 4H	Locating Cases

Select one of the following cases, and then locate a copy of the case in the official reporter (a book), in the regional reporter (a book), and on Lexis Advance, WestlawNext, and Google Scholar. Compare the text of the opinions. Are they the same or different? Compare the "editorial features." Are the headnotes the same or different? For instructions on how to locate cases using Google Scholar, Lexis Advance, and WestlawNext, see 4.3.2, 4.3.3, and 4.3.4 in the electronic supplement.

1. *State v. Lambert*, 175 Vt. 275, 830 A.2d 9 (2003).
2. *People v. Bell*, 264 Mich. App. 58, 689 N.W.2d 732 (2004).
3. A case selected by your professor.

---

§ 4.2.5   Sources for Secondary Materials

When the statute, regulations, and in-state cases do not answer the question that you were asked to research, you may need to look at cases from other jurisdictions or at secondary sources.

a.   State Attorney General Opinions

As we explained in Chapter 2, the state attorney general is the state's attorney. As the attorney for the governor, the legislature, and state agencies, the state attorney general will sometimes prepare written opinions that analyze, explain, or evaluate a state statute or regulation. While these opinions do not have the effect of law, they do provide insight into how the state believes the statute or regulation should be interpreted and applied.

In most states, the state attorney general opinions are available on the state's website.

b.   American Law Reports

American Law Reports (A.L.R.) was first published in 1919 to compete with West's National Reporter System. However, instead of publishing every state and federal opinion, A.L.R. was selective and published only those cases that it deemed to be "significant." For each of these significant cases, it included an annotation that collected and discussed other cases that dealt with the issue raised in the significant case.

Today, researchers use A.L.R. not as a source for the text of an opinion but for its annotations. In particular, researchers use A.L.R. as a finding tool to locate summaries of cases from around the country that deal with a particular issue of law.

Like other reporters, A.L.R. is arranged chronologically. Annotations dealing with state issues are set out in A.L.R., A.L.R.2d, A.L.R.3d, A.L.R.4th, A.L.R.5th, and A.L.R.6th. Annotations dealing with federal issues are set out in A.L.R. Fed. or A.L.R. Fed. 2d.

A.L.R.	1919-1948
A.L.R.2d	1948-1965
A.L.R.3d	1965-1980
A.L.R.4th	1980-1991
A.L.R.5th	1992-2005
A.L.R.6th	2005-current
A.L.R. Fed.	1969-2005
A.L.R. Fed. 2d	2005-current

A.L.R. is available both in book form and on Lexis.com, Lexis Advance, Westlaw Classic, and WestlawNext. The books have subject indexes.

> **PRACTICE POINTER**   Because you want the most current information, look first for annotations published in A.L.R.5th and A.L.R.6th. In addition, if you are using the book version, be sure to check the "pocket parts," that is, the inserts at the back of the book, for more recent cases.

c. Law Reviews and Journals

Law reviews and journals publish articles written by law school professors, judges, practitioners, and law students. While most law reviews and journals are published by law schools, some are published by organizations.

Occasionally, you will find a law review article that analyzes the state statute that governs your case or that analyzes one of the cases that has interpreted and applied that statute. In addition, occasionally you will find a law review article that analyzes an identically or similarly worded statute from another state. In these instances, the law review article can provide you with an analysis of the statute, the history of the statute, and possible arguments.

Some law review articles are now available for free. To look for articles, see the American Bar Association's website (*http://www.americanbar.org/groups/ departments_offices/legal_technology_resources/resources/free_journal_ search.html*), SSRN (*http://papers.ssrn.com/sol3/DisplayAbstractSearch.cfm*), or Google Scholar (*http://scholar.google.com/schhp?hl=en&as_sdt=0,48*).

In addition, you can find copies of law review articles using Lexis.com, Lexis Advance, Westlaw Classic, or WestlawNext. If your search retrieves more than one document, look first at the articles published in law reviews or journals from your state's law schools. Most of the articles that deal with a specific state statute are published in the law reviews and journals of that state's law schools.

§ 4.3   Using the Research Plan to Research an Issue Governed by State Statutes

In researching an issue governed by a state statute, you will usually use a combination of free sources and fee-based services. For example, if all you need is the text of a statute, you should locate the text of that statute using the state's legislature's website. If, however, you also need to find cases that have interpreted and applied that statute, you may want to use the Case Notes that are on Lexis Advance or the Notes of Decision that are on WestlawNext. You can, however, then download and read the cases for free using Google Scholar.

The bottom line is that to be an effective researcher you need to know how to use a variety of tools. Thus, before you go into practice you should familiarize yourself with the free websites and the fee-based services that are currently available, comparing and contrasting the advantages and disadvantages of each.

> **PRACTICE POINTER**   You should be able to do most statutory research using free sources: State and federal statutes are available on free government websites that are both reliable and up-to-date. In addition, you can find the text of cases that have cited a statute using free websites. You may, though, want to use an annotated code to find cases, which means that you will need to use Lexis Advance, WestlawNext, Lexis.com, or Westlaw Classic. (At this point, Bloomberg Law does not have an annotated code.) In addition, you will need to cite check any cases that you use from *Shepard's*, KeyCite, or BCite, which is on Bloomberg Law.

To learn more about using free and fee-based services to research issues governed by state statutes, see the electronic supplement at http://www.aspen lawschool.com/books/oates_legalwritinghandbook/.

§ 4.3.1 The Assignment
§ 4.3.2 Researching an Issue Governed by State Statutes and Regulations Using Free Websites
§ 4.3.3 Researching an Issue Governed by State Statutes and Regulations Using Lexis Advance
§ 4.3.4 Researching an Issue Governed by State Statutes and Regulations Using WestlawNext
§ 4.3.5 Researching an Issue Governed by State Statutes and Regulations Using Bloomberg Law
§ 4.3.6 Researching an Issue Governed by State Statutes and Regulations Using Lexis.com
§ 4.3.7 Researching an Issue Governed by State Statutes and Regulations Using Westlaw Classic

Chapter 4 Quiz

Draft answers for each of the following questions. Make your points clearly and concisely, and write sentences that are easy to read and that are grammatical and correctly punctuated.

1. What are practice manuals? Are practice manuals primary or secondary authority?
2. What are session laws? Are session laws law primary or secondary authority?

3. What does it mean to say the statutes have been "codified"?
4. What type of information does an unannotated code contain? An annotated code?
5. Under what circumstances can a state agency promulgate regulations?
6. What is one way to find cases that discuss a particular statute?
7. Can you cite to Notes of Decision? Who writes the Notes of Decision?
8. What is a reporter?
9. Are all court decisions published decisions?
10. What is an attorney general's opinion? Is an attorney general's opinion primary or secondary authority?

Researching Issues Governed by Federal Statutes and Regulations

The commentators are right. There is almost no area of the law or, for that matter, our lives, that is not regulated, at least in part, by federal statutes. Federal statutes regulate our food supply, the vehicles we drive, the schools we attend, and our working conditions. Thus, no matter what type of law you practice, you need to know how to research federal statutes and regulations.

In this chapter, you will learn how to modify the research plan presented in Chapter 1 so that it works for issues governed by federal statutes and regulations. In particular, you will learn about secondary sources that you can use to familiarize yourself with a particular federal act; how you can find the governing federal statutes and regulations and the cases that have applied those statutes and regulations; how you can determine whether the statutes, regulations, and cases you have found are still good law; and which secondary sources you can consult to gain a more sophisticated understanding of the issue you were asked to research.

Like the prior chapter, this chapter has several components: (1) the text, which sets out basic information; (2) exercises, which ask you to apply what you have just read; (3) a quiz that tests the materials set out in the chapter; and (4) an electronic supplement, which shows you how to research an issue governed by federal statutes and regulations using free sources, Lexis Advance®, WestlawNext™, Bloomberg Law, Lexis.com®, and Westlaw® Classic. To access the supplement, go to *http://www.aspenlawschool.com/books/oates_legalwrit inghandbook/*. Your access code to the website is on the card that came with the book. In the ebook, instructions for getting an access code are on the page immediately following the cover page.

§ 5.1   Research Plan for Issues Governed by Federal Statutes and Regulations

Like the research plan for issues governed by state statutes and regulations, the research plan for issues governed by federal statutes and regulations has four steps.

Research Plan for an Issue Governed by Federal Statutes and Regulations

Jurisdiction: Federal

Type of Law: Enacted law

Preliminary Issue
Statement: [Put your first draft of the issue statement here.]

Step 1:   If you are unfamiliar with the area of law, spend thirty to sixty minutes familiarizing yourself with the area of law by looking for information on the Internet, in a practice manual, in a hornbook, in a *Nutshell*, in a legal encyclopedia, or in another secondary source.

Step 2:   Locate, read, and analyze the applicable *United States Code* sections, the applicable *Code of Federal Regulations* sections, and cases that have interpreted or applied the applicable statutory sections and regulations.

Step 3:   Cite check the statutes, regulations, and cases to make sure they are still good law.

Step 4:   If appropriate, locate and read additional primary and secondary authorities.

§ 5.2   Sources for Federal Statutory Research

Before you begin researching a problem, you need to know what sources are available. Table 5.1 lists some of the sources that you can use in researching an issue governed by federal statutes and regulations. As you look at this list, note that some of these sources are available in book form; on fee-based services such as Lexis Advance, WestlawNext, and Bloomberg Law; and on free websites.

§ 5.2.1   Sources for Background Reading

a.   The Internet

For many issues governed by federal statutes, the best place to do your background reading is on the Internet. If you know the name of the act, select

Table 5.1	Sources of Federal Law
	FEDERAL LAW
Background Reading	▦ Internet ▦ Practice manuals ▦ Hornbooks ▦ *Nutshells* ▦ Legal encyclopedias
Session Laws (statutes in order enacted)	▦ *Statutes at Large* ▦ *United States Code* (U.S.C.)
Codes (statutes organized by topics)	▦ *United States Code Annotated* (U.S.C.A.) ▦ *United States Code Service* (U.S.C.S.)
Regulations	▦ *Code of Federal Regulations* (C.F.R.) ▦ *Federal Register* (Fed. Reg.)
Cases Interpreting and Applying Statutes	▦ *Federal Supplement* (F. Supp. or F. Supp. 2d) (decisions from the United States District Courts) ▦ *Federal Reporter* (F., F.2d, or F.3d) (decisions from the United States Courts of Appeals) ▦ *United States Reports* (U.S.) (decisions from the United States Supreme Court) ▦ *Supreme Court Reporter* (S. Ct.) (decisions from the United States Supreme Court) ▦ *United States Supreme Court Reports, Lawyers' Edition* (L. Ed. or L. Ed. 2d) (decisions from the United States Supreme Court)
Cite Checking	▦ KeyCite ▦ *Shepard's* ▦ BCite
Secondary Authorities	▦ Law review articles ▦ Treatises ▦ Looseleaf services ▦ *American Law Reports, Federal* (A.L.R. Fed. or A.L.R. Fed. 2d)

a search engine, and search for reliable websites that discuss that act. For example, if you are looking for information about the Americans with Disabilities Act, go to Bing, Google, or a similar search engine, and search for websites that contain the phrase "Americans with Disabilities Act." When the list appears, quickly review it, looking for websites that summarize the Americans with Disabilities Act. As a general rule, select government websites (.gov) over commercial websites (.com).

PRACTICE POINTER	If you do not know the name of the act, type in a word or words that describe your topic.

b. Practice Manuals

Although most law firms, agencies, and courts have copies of their state's practice manuals in book form, they may not have federal practice manuals. Instead, they may purchase looseleaf services for the areas of law in which they practice and rely on fee-based services such as Lexis Advance, WestlawNext, or Bloomberg Law for their other needs. For example, a tax attorney might purchase the *CCH Standard Federal Tax Reporter*® and rely on fee-based services for everything else.

c. Hornbooks and *Nutshells*

Hornbooks and *Nutshells* are one-volume books that provide the reader with an overview of an area of law. For example, the hornbook *Intellectual Property: The Law of Copyrights, Patents, and Trademarks* provides an overview of the various topics in intellectual property law. Similarly, the shorter, one-volume *Intellectual Property: Unfair Competition in a Nutshell* provides an overview of the law relating to unfair competition.

Note that most hornbooks and *Nutshells* deal with areas of law and not with specific federal acts. Therefore, as a general rule, use a hornbook or a *Nutshell* when you want to do background reading on an area of law, and use the Internet when you want to do background reading on a specific act.

PRACTICE POINTER	You can use your library's electronic card catalog to find hornbooks and *Nutshells*. You can also ask the law librarian and practitioners for recommendations.

d. Legal Encyclopedias

At one point, the book versions of legal encyclopedias were the source of choice for background reading. When asked to research an issue in an unfamiliar area of law, attorneys would go to one of the two legal encyclopedias, *American Jurisprudence* (Am. Jur.) or *Corpus Juris Secundum* (C.J.S.), and read the summary of the law.

Like the book versions of other more general encyclopedias, the book versions of Am. Jur. and C.J.S. are being used less and less often; the books are expensive to buy and update and take lots of space to store. Consequently, if the office in which you work has one of these encyclopedias, by all means use it. If, however, your office does not have Am. Jur. or C.J.S., another good source is WEX, a free online dictionary and legal encyclopedia sponsored and hosted by the Legal Information Institute at Cornell Law School. See *http://www.law.cornell.edu/wex/*.

Exercise 5A	Sources That Can Be Used to Find Background Reading

1. Using Bing or Google, locate a government website that provides background information about the Clean Air Act of 1990. Make a screenshot of the page that provides readers with an overview of the Act.

2. Using Lexis Advance or WestlawNext, locate a practice manual that provides an overview of the Clean Air Act. Record the citation for the source and provide a one- or two-sentence description of the practice manual.
3. Using your library's electronic card catalog, locate an environmental law hornbook or Nutshell that provides background information about the Clean Air Act. Record the call number and write a one- or two-sentence description of the hornbook or *Nutshell*.
4. Look up "Clean Air Act" and "Environmental Law" in either the book or electronic version of Am. Jur. 2d or C.J.S. What do you find?

---

§ 5.2.2   Sources for Federal Statutes and Regulations

Federal statutes come in three forms. You can find the text of a particular federal act in the session laws, in the unannotated code, and in two annotated codes.

a.   Session Laws

Statutes at Large sets out federal statutes in the order in which they were enacted. At the end of each Congress, the statutes enacted during that Congress are collected and arranged, not by topic, but by date. For instance, statutes enacted during the 106th Congress will be printed in date order in one set of volumes, the statutes enacted during the 107th Congress will be printed in date order in another set of volumes, and the statutes enacted during the 108th Congress will be printed in yet another set of volumes. Therefore, to find a session law, you need to know the Congress during which the statute was enacted and the public law number.

PRACTICE POINTER	The only time that you will use session laws is when you are doing a legislative history. For other types of statutory research, use an unannotated or annotated code.

b.   Unannotated Codes

Statutes are "codified" when they are arranged, not in chronological order, but by topic. For instance, in a federal code, all the federal statutes relating to interstate highways are placed under one title, all the statutes relating to veterans' benefits are placed under a different title, and all the statutes relating to Social Security benefits are placed under yet another title. The decision about where to place a particular statute is made not by Congress itself but by attorneys who work for the Office of the Law Revision Counsel.

The unannotated code for federal statutes is the *United States Code* (U.S.C.). It is published by the United States Printing Office, and it is the official version of the United States statutes. You can find the *United States Code* in book form in most law libraries and larger public libraries. In addition, you can also find free copies on a number of websites, including the following:

> *http://www.loc.gov/law/help/guide/federal/uscode.php*
> *http://uscode.house.gov*
> *www.gpoaccess.gov/uscode/index.html*
> *http://lp.findlaw.com*

Use an unannotated code when all you need is the text of the particular statute or when you want to see several different sections.

c. Annotated Codes

An annotated code is a code that contains not only the text of the statutes but also historical notes, cross-references to other sources published by the same publisher, and Notes of Decisions/Case Notes. Thus, an annotated code is both a primary authority because it sets out the law itself and a finding tool because you can use it to find other primary and secondary authorities.

For federal statutes, there are two annotated codes. *The United States Code Annotated* (U.S.C.A.) is published by West, a Thomson Reuters business, and is available both in books and on Westlaw Classic and WestlawNext. The *United States Code Service* (U.S.C.S.) is published by LexisNexis and is available both in books and on Lexis.com and Lexis Advance. You should use an annotated code when you are interested not only in the text of the statute but also in how the courts have interpreted and applied the statute.

> **PRACTICE POINTER** All your citations to federal statutes should be to the U.S.C. and not to the U.S.C.A. or the U.S.C.S. Cite to the U.S.C.A. or the U.S.C.S. only when the material appears in one of those sources but not in the U.S.C. See Rule 14.1 in the *ALWD Citation Manual* and Rule 12.2.1 in *The Bluebook*.

Exercise 5B   Federal Statutes

For this exercise, select one of the following statutory sections:

a. 17 U.S.C. § 1201 (2012)
b. 18 U.S.C. § 228 (2012)
c. 12 U.S.C. § 1811 (2012)

Locate the text of your statutory section in each of the following:

1. The book version of the *United States Code*
2. The book version of the *United States Code Annotated*
3. The book version of the *United States Code Service*
4. http://law.justia.com/us/codes/
5. Lexis Advance or WestlawNext

Is the text of the statute the same in each source? In each source, what types of information are set out after the text of the statute?

d. Federal Regulations

In enacting a statute, Congress often grants an administrative agency the power to promulgate regulations. When agencies follow the proper procedures for promulgating these regulations, the regulations have the effect of law and are, therefore, primary authority.

For most agencies, the procedures for promulgating regulations are set out in the Administrative Procedure Act. This Act, which is codified at 5 U.S.C. § 551 and the sections that follow, require (1) that notice of a proposed regulation be published in the *Federal Register*, (2) that there be time for comment and hearings, and (3) that the final version of the regulation be published initially in the *Federal Register* and permanently in the *Code of Federal Regulations*.

You can find the book version of the *Code of Federal Regulations* (C.F.R.) in most law libraries and in larger public libraries. In addition, you can find copies of the C.F.R. on a number of free websites. For instance, you can find the entire text of the C.F.R. on the Government Printing Office's website, *http://www.gpoaccess.gov/cfr*, and on FindLaw for Professionals, *http://lp.findlaw.com*. You can also find selected C.F.R. sections on agency websites. For example, you can find the regulations that relate to the Social Security Act on the Social Security Administration's website (*http://ssa.gov/regulations*), and you can find the regulations that relate to U.S. national parks on the National Park Service's website (*http://home.nps.gov/applications/npspolicy/getregs.cfm*).

There are also a number of sites that provide access to all or part of the *Federal Register*. You can find the complete text of the *Federal Register* on the Government Printing Office's website, www.gpoaccess.gov/fr and on www.regulations.gov, which not only lists proposed regulations but also provides a vehicle for commenting on those proposed regulations. Another site that can be used to comment on proposed regulations is http://www.regulations.gov/#!home.

To find regulations that have been promulgated pursuant to a particular section of the *United States Code*, use one of the tables that provides cross-references. See, for example, see the tables that are available at *http://www.gpo.gov/help/parallel_table.pdf*.

Exercise 5C   **Federal Regulations**

For this exercise, select one of the following regulations:

a. 25 C.F.R. § 309.1
b. 34 C.F.R. § 636.10
c. 45 C.F.R. § 144.101

Locate your statutory section in each of the following sources:

1. *Code of Federal Regulations*
2. *www.gpoaccess.gov/cfr/*
3. Lexis.com, Lexis Advance, Westlaw Classic, or WestlawNext

For each source, briefly summarize the types of information that you find. Does each source set out the same information? If not, describe the types of information in each source.

---

§ 5.2.3   Sources for Cases That Have Interpreted or Applied a Federal Statute or Regulation

a.   Finding Tools

When the statute and any applicable regulations answer your question, you do not need to look for cases that have interpreted or applied that statute.

However, when the statute and its applicable regulations are ambiguous, you do. One of the easiest ways to find these cases is to use the Notes of Decisions/Case Notes following the statutory section.

PRACTICE POINTER	Not all statutes have corresponding regulations. For example, there are no regulations for criminal statutes.

As soon as they issue a decision, the federal courts send an electronic copy of the decision to the publishing companies (for example, LexisNexis and Thomson West), and these companies create a Note of Decision or Case Note of each point of law addressed in the decision. In addition to placing these "summaries" as headnotes at the beginning of the case, if the summary relates to a particular statute, the publishing company places that summary after the text of the statute.

If there are relatively few cases that have discussed a particular statute, the Notes of Decisions/Case Notes will be listed by court and date after the statute. (Notes of Decisions/Case Notes from higher courts will be listed before Notes of Decisions/Case Notes from lower courts, and Notes of Decisions/Case Notes from more recent cases will be listed before Notes of Decisions/Case Notes from older cases.) If, however, there are a number of cases that have discussed a particular statute, the Notes of Decisions/Case Notes will be organized by subtopics and then, within those topics, by court and date. Your job as a legal researcher is to select the topics that appear to be on point and then to read through the Notes of Decisions/Case Notes under those topics, identifying the cases that appear to be most on point. Once you identify the cases that appear to be most on point, locate and read the relevant portions of those cases.

PRACTICE POINTER	Because the Notes of Decisions/Case Notes are created by the publishing companies, the notes are finding tools and are not something you can cite to in a memo or a brief.

You can also find cases using the citations that you found during the course of your background reading, by using a federal digest or by doing a search on Lexis.com, Lexis Advance, Westlaw Classic, WestlawNext, Bloomberg Law, or a free Internet site.

Exercise 5D   Notes of Decisions/Case Notes

1. Using the book version of the *United States Code Annotated,* find the most recent case listed under 29 U.S.C. § 2611 that has discussed the length of employment requirements. Record the name and citation for the case.
2. Using Lexis Advance and WestlawNext, find the most recent case listed under 29 U.S.C. § 2611 that has discussed the length of employment/requisite hours of service requirements. Is the case that you found using the book version of the *United States Code Annotated* the same case that you found using Lexis Advance and WestlawNext? If it isn't, why did you find different cases?

b.   Reporters

Federal cases are published in a number of reporters, which are sets of books that publish the text of court decisions, not by topic, but in the order in which the cases were decided. Table 5.2 shows the reporters in which decisions from the United States Supreme Court, the United States Courts of Appeals, and the United States District Courts are published.

Table 5.2	List of Federal Reporters		
COURT	**NAME OF REPORTER**	**ABBREVIATION**	**COVERAGE DATES**
United States Supreme Court (appellate court)	*United States Reports*	U.S.	1789 to date
	Supreme Court Reporter	S. Ct.	1882 to date
	United States Supreme Court Reports, Lawyers' Edition	L. Ed.	1879 to 1956
	United States Supreme Court Reports, Lawyers' Edition, Second Series	L. Ed. 2d	1956 to date
United States Courts of Appeals (appellate court)	*Federal Reporter*	F.	1889 to 1924
	Federal Reporter, Second Series	F.2d	1924 to 1993
	Federal Reporter, Third Series	F.3d	1993 to date
United States District Courts (trial court)	*Federal Supplement*	F. Supp.	1932 to 1998
	Federal Supplement, Second Series	F. Supp. 2d	1998 to date
	Federal Rules Decisions (contains district court decisions interpreting and applying the Federal Rules of Civil Procedure)	F.R.D.	1938 to date

PRACTICE POINTER   Although all United States Supreme Court opinions are reported, or published, not all United States District Court and United States Court of Appeals opinions are reported in the book versions of the official federal reporters. While historically you could not cite unreported cases, that rule changed in 2006 when the United States Supreme Court announced that unpublished opinions decided after January 1, 2007, could be cited. See Federal Rule of Appellate Procedure 32.1, available at *http:// www.law.cornell.edu/rules/frap/rules.html.*

To find a federal case in a book or electronic source, use the case citation. In particular, use the volume number, the abbreviation for the reporter, and the page number. Look for a moment at the following citation, which is the full citation for the United States Supreme Court's decision in *Brown v. Board of Education*.

> *Brown v. Board of Education*, 347 U.S. 483, 74 S. Ct. 686, 98 L. Ed. 873 (1954).

This citation tells you that you can find a copy of the Court's decision in *Brown v. Board of Education* in three different reporters: volume 347 of the *United States Reports* beginning on page 483; volume 74 of the *Supreme Court Reporter* beginning on page 686; and volume 98 of the *United States Supreme Court Reports, Lawyers' Edition*, beginning on page 873. The first citation, the citation to the *United States Reports*, is the official citation. The citations to the *Supreme Court Reporter* and the *United States Supreme Court Reports, Lawyers' Edition*, are parallel citations.

Both the *Supreme Court Reporter* and the *United States Supreme Court Reports, Lawyers' Edition*, are unofficial reporters published by private publishing companies. (The *Supreme Court Reporter* is published by West, a Thomson Reuters business, and the *United States Supreme Court Reports, Lawyers' Edition*, is published by LexisNexis.) While the text of the opinion will be the same in all three reporters, the headnotes and other editorial enhancements will be different.

Although some law firms have their state reporters in book form, fewer have the book versions of the federal reporters. As a consequence, to find the text of a federal case, you will usually have to use an online source. You can do so using a fee-based service, such as Lexis Advance or WestlawNext, or on a free website. For example, most federal cases are now on Google® Scholar.

Exercise 5E   Sources for United States Supreme Court Decisions

Locate the text of *Bush v. Gore*, 531 U.S. 98, 121 S. Ct. 525, 148 L. Ed. 2d 388 (2000), in each of the following sources:

a. The *United States Reports* (U.S.).
b. The *Supreme Court Reporter* (S. Ct.)
c. The *United States Supreme Court Reports, Lawyers' Edition, Second Series* (L. Ed. 2d)
d. Google Scholar
e. *http://www.supremecourtus.gov/opinions/opinions.html*

For each of the sources above, answer the following questions:

1. Is there a "summary" or "syllabus" before the text of the opinion?
2. Are there headnotes?
3. Are the summaries and headnotes the same in each source? If they are not the same, why aren't they the same?

§ 5.2.4   Sources for Additional Secondary Authority

a.   Law Reviews and Law Journals

Law reviews and law journals publish articles about the law. Some of these journals are general in nature, publishing articles on a wide range of topics. (See, for example, the *Maine Law Review* and the *Stanford Law Review*.) Others deal with specific areas of the law, for instance, environmental law or international law. (See, for example, *Journal of Environmental Law and Litigation* and *Harvard International Law Journal*.) In addition, some organizations and groups also publish law reviews. While most law review articles are written by law school professors, law reviews also publish articles written by judges and practitioners, and notes and comments written by law students.

Use law reviews when you are looking for information about a new area of law or a new issue in an established area of law. You can find law review articles in the book version of the individual law reviews themselves and online on Lexis.com, Lexis Advance, Westlaw Classic, or WestlawNext. In addition, a few law schools have begun putting their law reviews on their websites, and some journals are available for free. See the American Bar Association's website (*http://www.americanbar.org/groups/departments_offices/legal_technology_resources/resources/free_journal_search.html*), SSRN (*http://papers.ssrn.com/sol3/DisplayAbstractSearch.cfm*), or Google Scholar (*http://scholar.google.com/schhp?hl=en&as_sdt=0,48*).

b.   *American Law Reports,* Federal

American Law Reports (A.L.R.) was first published in 1919 to compete with West's National Reporter System. However, unlike West's National Reporter System, which publishes every reported state and federal decision, A.L.R. is selective, publishing only "significant" cases and annotations that discuss the issues raised in those cases. These annotations, which are researched and written by attorneys, collect and summarize cases that have discussed a particular issue. The annotations that deal with federal issues are set out in A.L.R. Fed. and A.L.R. Fed. 2d.

You can find the A.L.R. in your law library or online on Lexis.com, Lexis Advance, Westlaw Classic, or WestlawNext. In the book, you can find annotations using the subject index; online, you can find annotations using a terms and connectors search or doing a natural language search.

c.   Looseleaf Services

Historically, looseleaf services were what their name suggests: a service that provided information in "looseleaf" notebooks, which were updated by taking out a page and replacing that page with a new page. Today, most looseleaf services are available both in book form and on fee-based services such as Lexis.com, Lexis Advance, Westlaw Classic, or WestlawNext.

Although each looseleaf service is different, most deal with specialized areas of law: There are looseleaf services that deal with federal tax issues, with federal benefits issues (for example, Social Security), and with other federal issues (for example, environmental issues). Most looseleaf services provide a wide range of up-to-date information about these specialized areas. For example, many of them provide the text of the applicable statutes and regulations, the text of proposed legislation and regulations, and summaries of relevant court and administrative decisions.

To determine which looseleaf services are in your library, check your library's electronic card catalog or ask a law librarian. To determine which looseleaf services are available on a particular fee-based service, check the service's database directory or ask your service's representative.

> **PRACTICE POINTER**
>
> Because looseleaf services are expensive, they may not be included in the basic Lexis.com, Lexis Advance, Westlaw Classic, or WestlawNext service package. You can, however, access them for an additional fee.

Exercise 5F   Sources for Law Review Articles

Locate one of the following law review articles both in book form in the library and on either Lexis Advance or WestlawNext:

1. John B. Kirkwood, The Robinson-Patman Act and Consumer Welfare: Has Volvo Reconciled Them? 30 Seattle U. L. Rev. 349 (2007).
2. Lorraine K. Bannai, Taking the Stand: The Lessons of Three Men Who Took the Japanese American Internment to Court, 4 Seattle J. Soc. Just. 1 (2005).
3. Michael Ashley Stein, Same Struggle, Different Difference: ADA Accommodations as Antidiscrimination, 153 U. Pa. L. Rev. 579 (2004).

Copy the first page of the print version, and print out the first page from Lexis.com, Lexis Advance, Westlaw Classic, or WestlawNext.

§ 5.3   Using the Research Plan to Research an Issue Governed by Federal Statutes and Regulations

To research issues governed by federal statutes and regulations, you have a number of options: You can research the issue using books; fee-based services like Westlaw Classic, WestlawNext, Lexis.com, Lexis Advance, Bloomberg Law; or free websites. While in practice you will seldom use a single tool, in this section we walk you through the process of researching an issue governed by federal statutes and regulations in six ways. While you do not need to go through each section, do go through several, comparing and contrasting the advantages and disadvantages of each.

To learn more about using free and fee-based services to research issues governed by federal statutes or regulations, see the electronic supplement.

> **PRACTICE POINTER**   You should be able to do most statutory research using free sources: State and federal statutes are available on free government websites that are both reliable and up-to-date. In addition, you can find the text of cases that have cited a statute using free websites, for instance, the "Selected courts" options on Google Scholar. You may, though, want to use an annotated code to find cases, which means that you will need to use Lexis Advance, WestlawNext, Lexis.com, or Westlaw Classic. (At this point, Bloomberg Law does not have an annotated code.) In addition, you will need to cite check any cases that you use using *Shepard's*®, KeyCite®, or BCite, which is on Bloomberg Law.

§ 5.3.1   The Assignment

§ 5.3.2   Researching an Issue Governed by Federal Statutes and Regulations Using Free Websites

§ 5.3.3   Researching an Issue Governed by Federal Statutes and Regulations Using Lexis Advance

§ 5.3.4   Researching an Issue Governed by Federal Statutes and Regulations Using WestlawNext

§ 5.3.5   Researching an Issue Governed by Federal Statutes and Regulations using Bloomberg Law

§ 5.3.6   Researching an Issue Governed by Federal Statutes and Regulations Using Lexis.com

§ 5.3.7   Researching an Issue Governed by Federal Statutes and Regulations Using Westlaw Classic

Chapter 5 Quiz

Draft answers for each of the following questions. Make your points clearly and concisely, and write sentences that are easy to read and that are grammatical and correctly punctuated.

1. As a general rule, where is the best place to do background reading about a federal statute? For example, where would be the best place to do background reading on disability benefits under the Social Security Act?
2. How is the organizational scheme that is used in the *Statutes at Large* different from the organizational scheme that is used in the *United States Code*?
3. What is the difference between an unannotated code and an annotated code?
4. When would you cite to the *United States Code Annotated*?
5. How can you determine whether there are federal regulations that relate to a particular section of the *United States Code*?
6. What is a Note of Decision? A Case Note?
7. What is a reporter?
8. What is a parallel cite?

9. Where can you find a free copy of United States District Court decisions?

10. What type of information is in A.L.R. Fed. 2d?

Researching Issues Governed by City or County Ordinances

I f you are like many law students, when you applied to law school you
envisioned yourself working on the big issues: prosecuting or defend-
ing individuals charged with felonies, investigating major corporate
scandals, or working to enforce treaties protecting the environment or
basic human rights.

Although you may end up working on high-profile cases or issues of national
or international importance, it is also likely that you will work on smaller, more
local cases, cases that are governed not by federal or state statutes or international treaties but by city or county ordinances. While these cases may not
make the front page of anything other than your local newspaper, they involve
important issues. For it is often city or county ordinances that determine what
can and cannot be built in our neighborhoods, what our local businesses can
and cannot do, and what does and does not constitute a nuisance.

Like Chapters 4 and 5, this chapter has several components: (1) the text,
which sets out basic information; (2) exercises, which ask you to apply what
you have just read; (3) a quiz that tests the materials set out in the chapter;
and (4) an electronic supplement, which shows you how to research an issue
governed by local law using free sources, Lexis Advance®, WestlawNext™,
Bloomberg Law, Lexis.com®, and Westlaw® Classic. To access the supplement,
go to *http://www.aspenlawschool.com/books/oates_legalwritinghandbook/*.
Your access code to the website is on the card that came with the book. In the
ebook, instructions for getting an access code are on the page immediately
following the cover page.

§6.1 An Introduction to City and County Government

In many ways, city and county governments are analogous to state governments. Just as the state constitutions define a state's powers and responsibilities, charters define a county's or city's powers and responsibilities. In addition, just as the federal and state governments have three branches, so do counties and cities. Cities and counties have a legislative branch (for example, a city or county council) that enacts legislation; an executive branch (for example, a county executive, mayor, or city manager) that enforces that legislation; and a court system (for example, a district or municipal court) that has limited jurisdiction.

§6.2 Research Plans for Issues Governed by City or County Ordinances

Because many cases involving city or county ordinances involve small amounts of money or are brought by individuals with limited resources, you will often need to research issues involving ordinances quickly and inexpensively. Accordingly, the first research plan is designed to help you answer relatively simple questions in just an hour or two, using free sources. There will, of course, be other cases in which you need to do more thorough research. The second research plan is designed to help you research those issues.

Plan No. 1:

Research Plan for Quickly and Inexpensively Researching an Issue Governed by a City or County Ordinance

Jurisdiction: [Enter the name of the city or county.]

Type of Law: Enacted law

Preliminary Issue
Statement: [Put your first draft of the issue statement here.]

Step 1: Locate your city or county ordinances on the city or county website or on a free website that provides links to city and county websites, for example, *http://www.municode.com* or *http://www.statelocalgov.net*.

Step 2: Read and analyze the applicable section or sections and then apply the plain language of those sections to the facts of your case.

Plan No. 2:

Research Plan for Doing More Thorough Research of an Issue Governed by a City or County Ordinance

Jurisdiction: [Enter the name of the city or county.]

Type of Law: Enacted law

Preliminary Issue
Statement: [Put your first draft of the issue statement here.]

Step 1:   Locate your city or county ordinances on the city or county website or on a free website that provides links to city and county websites, for example, *http://www.municode.com* or *http://www.statelocalgov.net*.

Step 2:   Read and analyze the applicable sections, determining whether the ordinance is constitutional and identifying the elements and determining which elements appear to be in dispute. If none of the elements is likely to be in dispute, stop researching. If, however, one or more of the elements are likely to be in dispute, research the disputed elements using Steps 3–6.

Step 3:   Using free websites, look for articles that discuss the area of law. Using those articles, identify cases that may be on point.

Step 4:   Using free websites, for example, Google® Scholar, or fee-based sites such as Lexis.com, Lexis Advance, Westlaw Classic, or WestlawNext, locate copies of cases that are on point.

Step 5:   Before deciding to use a case, cite check the case to determine (1) whether the case is still good law and (2) whether there are any additional cases that discuss the same point. Look up and, if appropriate, cite check any additional cases you locate.

Step 6:   If appropriate, locate law review articles and other commentaries that might be on point.

§ 6.3   Sources for Researching Issues Governed by City or Ordinances

In researching issues governed by city or county ordinances, you will usually be looking for one or more of the following documents.

§ 6.3.1   Charters

In most instances, you will not need to find a copy of the city or county charter. For example, you will not need to find a copy of the charter when common sense tells you that the city or county had the power to enact a particular ordinance or do a particular act.

However, when you do need to find a copy of the charter, look first on the city or county website. To do this, use a search engine such as Bing or Google, and type in the name of the city, the name of the state, and the word "charter." In the alternative, look for a website that collects and publishes charters for the counties or cities in your state, or contact your county or city offices and ask the clerk to email you an electronic copy of the charter.

Exercise 6A	City Charters

Find the city charter for one of the following cities using Bing or Google. Record the URL for the page that contains a copy of the charter.

   a. San Diego, California
   b. Tampa, Florida
   c. Seattle, Washington
   d. Bangor, Maine
   e. The city in which your law school is located

§ 6.3.2   Ordinances

Charters give cities and counties the power to enact certain types of legislation. For example, as a general rule, cities and counties have the power to enact legislation governing activities such as the use of property, the operation of businesses, and the creation and governance of parks when these activities are within the city's or county's boundaries. These pieces of legislation, which are similar to statutes, are called ordinances. Like state and federal statutes, ordinances are enacted by the legislative branch (for example, the city council) and enforced by the executive branch (for example, the city agencies and the city police).

Many cities and counties post copies of their ordinances on their official city or county websites. In addition, some free websites collect or provide links to city and county ordinances—for example, *http://www.statelocalgov .net* and *http://www.municode.com*. As a last resort, you can usually obtain a paper copy of the ordinances from either the city or county clerk or at the local public library.

Because not all counties and cities update their materials regularly, always check to make sure the ordinances you find are the ordinances that govern. If the cause of action arose in the past, make sure you have the ordinances that were in effect at the time the cause of action arose. In contrast, if you are advising a client about what it can or cannot do in the future, make sure you know what the ordinances currently say and what changes have been proposed.

Exercise 6B	Municipal Ordinances

Find the municipal ordinances for one of the following cities using Bing or Google. Record the URL for the page that contains a copy of the ordinances.

   a. San Diego, California
   b. Tampa, Florida
   c. Seattle, Washington
   d. Bangor, Maine
   e. Your city

§ 6.3.3   Other City or County Documents

Sometimes you will need to find copies of other city or county documents. For example, you may want to find the minutes of a city or county council meeting to find out what the council intended when it adopted a particular ordinance; you may want to find the decisions of a city or county commission, department, or agency; or you might want to find a record that was filed with a city or county. Although you may be able to find some of this information on the city's, county's, commission's, or department's website, more likely than not you will have to obtain that information from the city or county itself.

§ 6.4   Using the Research Plan to Research an Issue Governed by City or County Ordinances

To research issues governed by city or county ordinances, you have a number of options: You can research the issue using books and fee-based services such as WestlawNext, Lexis Advance, or Bloomberg Law. However, in almost all instances, the best option is free websites.

To learn more about using free and fee-based services to research issues governed by city or county ordinances, see the electronic supplement, especially section 6.4.2.

§ 6.4.1   The Assignment

§ 6.4.2   Researching an Issue Governed by City or County Ordinances Using Free Websites

§ 6.4.3   Researching an Issue Governed by City or County Ordinances Using Lexis Advance

§ 6.4.4   Researching an Issue Governed by City or County Ordinances Using WestlawNext

§ 6.4.5   Researching an Issue Governed by City or County Ordinances Using Bloomberg Law

§ 6.4.6   Researching an Issue Governed by City or County Ordinances Using Lexis.com

§ 6.4.7   Researching an Issue Governed by City or County Ordinances Using Westlaw Classic

Chapter 6 Quiz

Draft answers for each of the following questions. Make your points clearly and concisely, and write sentences that are easy to read and that are grammatical and correctly punctuated.

1. What function(s) does a city charter serve?
2. Where can you find a copy of a city's or county's charter?
3. What is an ordinance?

4. Where can you find a copy of city ordinances that are currently in effect?

5. What entities typically function as the executive and legislative branches of a city or county?

Researching Issues Governed by Common Law

W hile common law problems are no longer so common, there are still some issues that are governed by common law. As a result, you need to know how to find the cases that set out and apply common law rules.

Like the prior chapters, this chapter has several components: (1) the text, which sets out basic information; (2) exercises, which ask you to apply what you have just read; (3) a quiz that tests the materials set out in the chapter; and (4) and electronic supplement, which shows you how to research an issue governed by common law using free sources, Lexis Advance®, WestlawNext™, Bloomberg Law, Lexis.com®, and Westlaw® Classic. To access the supplement, go to *http://www.aspenlawschool.com/books/oates_legalwriting handbook/*. Your access code to the website is on the card that came with the book. In the ebook, instructions for getting an access code are on the page immediately following the cover page.

§ 7.1   Are All Cases the Same?

The answer to this question is no. In fact, cases fall into two categories. In one category are the cases that set out, interpret, and apply the common law, and in the other category are the cases that interpret and apply enacted law.

The following example shows how common law rules are created and the relationship between common law rules, enacted law, and the cases that interpret and apply enacted law.

Assume for the moment a blank slate. You are in a state with no common law rules and no statutes, ordinances, or regulations. The first case that your state's courts hear is *In re Marriage of Adamson*.

In *Adamson*, a mother asks the court to grant her custody of her two children, a 2-year-old son and a 4-year-old daughter. Because the slate is blank, the court must make its own law. After considering the community's norms and the facts of the case, the court grants the mother's request for custody on the grounds that young children should be with their mother.

Not long after the court decides *Adamson*, another mother requests custody of her children, a 4-year-old son and a 14-year-old daughter. Unlike the situation in *Adamson*, in this situation the slate is not blank. There is now precedent. In deciding *Brown*, the court will be guided by the court's decision in *Adamson*. The reasoning in *Adamson* (that young children should be with their mother) is now a common law rule that the court applies in *Brown*.

Applying that common law rule, the court grants the mother custody of her 4-year-old son. There is, however, no rule that deals with 14-year-old daughters. Consequently, the court is once again in the position of creating a common law rule. This time, the court rules that teenage daughters should remain with their mother and grants the mother custody of her daughter.

In the next case, *In re Marriage of Carey*, a mother with a history of abusing alcohol asks the court to grant her custody of her two daughters, who are 5 and 13. In deciding this case, the court applies both the common law rule set out in *Adamson*—that young children should be with their mother—and the common law rule set out in *Brown*—that teenage daughters should remain with their mother—and grants the mother custody of both daughters. In granting the mother custody, the court interprets the rules set out in *Adamson* and *Brown*, deciding that those common law rules apply even if the mother has a history of abusing alcohol.

As *Adamson*, *Brown*, and *Carey* illustrate, in a common law system, the court's reasoning in one case becomes a common law rule that is applied in the next case. Of course, not all the rules announced in earlier cases are applied in all subsequent cases. For instance, if Case 4, *In re Marriage of Davidson*, involves the custody of a 1-year-old girl whose mother does not have a history of alcohol abuse, the court would apply only the rule announced in *Adamson*; it would not need to consider the additional common law rules set out in *Brown* and *Carey*. Nor does each case need to add to the existing law. The court could decide *Davidson* without creating any new rules.

Continuing with our example, presume that a few years after the court decided *In re Marriage of Davidson*, the legislature enacts a statute that sets out the rules for determining child custody issues. In enacting this statute, the legislature can do one of two things: It can enact or "codify" the common law rule, or it can abolish the common law rule and create its own statute-based rule. If the legislature enacts or codifies the common law rule, the cases that were decided before the statute was enacted are still good law, and the courts can use them in deciding how to interpret and apply the statute. If, however, the legislature abolishes the common law rule, the cases that were decided before the statute was enacted are, most likely, no longer good law.

In our example, the legislature decides to abolish the common law rules that favor awarding custody to the mother. Under the statute, the courts must grant custody "in accordance with the best interests of the children." In determining what is in the best interests of the children, the courts must consider a variety of factors including "the parents' wishes; the children's wishes; the interaction and inter-relationship of the child with parents and siblings; the child's adjustment to his or her home, school, and community; and the mental and physical health of all of the individuals involved." Because this statute abolished the common law rules set out in *Adamson*, *Brown*, and *Carey*, these cases are, to the extent that they are inconsistent with the statute, no longer good law. Accordingly, when Case 5, *In re Marriage of Edwards*, comes before the court, the court applies the statute and not the rules from *Adamson*, *Brown*, and *Carey*.

The application of a statute is not, however, always clear. For example, assume that in *Edwards*, the mother contends that she should be given custody, not because the children are young, but because she has always been their primary caregiver. Although the statute does not specifically address this argument, the court agrees with the mother, reasoning that because the mother has always been the primary caregiver, it would be in the children's best interest to remain with her.

Because the court's reasoning in *Edwards* (that it is in the best interests of the children to remain with the parent who has been their primary caregiver) is not inconsistent with the statute, that reasoning can be used by the courts in subsequent cases. In deciding Case 6, *In re Marriage of Forino*, the court will apply not just the statute, but also the reasoning announced in *Edwards*. Similarly, in deciding Case 7, *In re Marriage of Gonzales*, the court will consider not only the statute and the reasoning from *Edwards*, but also the reasoning from *Forino*. Although the "rules" created in *Edwards* and *Forino* create precedent, these cases do not, at least technically, fall into the category of cases that we call the common law. Instead, they fall into a second category: They are simply cases that interpret and apply enacted law.

§ 7.2   Modifying the Generic Research Plan for Issues That Are Governed by Common Law

Before electronic research became common, the tools that attorneys used to research issues governed by state and federal statutes were very different from the tools that they used to research common law issues. When they researched an issue that was governed by a statute, attorneys used an annotated code to find the cases that had interpreted and applied the statute. (See Chapters 4 and 5.) In contrast, when they researched a common law issue, attorneys used a digest to find both the common law rule and the cases that had interpreted and applied that common law rule. While digests are still an excellent finding tool, today many lawyers use fee-based services such as Lexis Advance, WestlawNext and Bloomberg Law or free Internet sites to find the cases setting out and applying common law doctrines.

Research Plan for an Issue Governed by Common Law

Jurisdiction: [Enter the name of the applicable state.]

Type of Law: Common law

Preliminary Issue
Statement: [Put your first draft of the issue statement here.]

Step 1:   If you are unfamiliar with the area of law, spend thirty to sixty minutes doing background reading on the Internet, in a state practice manual or book, a hornbook or *Nutshell*, or a legal encyclopedia.

Step 2:   Locate the cases from your jurisdiction that set out and apply the common law rules.

Step 3:   Cite check the cases that you plan to use to make sure that they are still good law.

Step 4:   If appropriate, locate cases from other jurisdictions, law review articles, or other commentaries that might be on point.

§ 7.3 Sources for Researching Problems Governed by State Common Law

Table 7.1 lists some, but not all, of the sources you can use in researching an issue governed by common law. Because the names of the sources vary by state, we have listed the sources using generic labels and not specific names. You can, however, find the names of your state's practice books using your library's electronic card catalog, and you can find the names of your state's reporters using Appendix 1 of the *ALWD Citation Manual* or Table 1 in *The Bluebook*. Finally, note that not all states will have all the sources listed.

§ 7.3.1 Background Reading

a. The Internet

As you learned in Chapter 5, sometimes you can do your background reading on the Internet. For example, in some states, there are law firms that post plain language explanations of common law doctrines. One of the easiest ways to find these types of websites is to use Bing or Google, or another search engine. Simply type in the name of your state and terms that describe the doctrine. Remember, though, that information on free websites may not be accurate or up-to-date. Accordingly, use the websites to familiarize yourself with the doctrine but not as authority.

b. Practice Manuals and Books

Although sometimes you can find good information about a common law doctrine on a free website, most of the time the best source is a state practice

Table 7.1	State Law Research Tools

	State Law
Background Reading	▪ The Internet ▪ State practice manuals and practice books ▪ Hornbooks ▪ *Nutshells* ▪ Legal encyclopedias
Finding Tools	▪ State practice manuals and practice books ▪ State digests ▪ Regional digests ▪ Fee-based services, such as Lexis.com, Lexis Advance, Westlaw Classic, and WestlawNext ▪ Free websites such as Google Scholar, FindLaw, Justia.com, lexisONE®, or a state government website
Cases	▪ State reporter containing decisions from the state's highest appellate court ▪ State reporter containing decisions from the state's intermediate appellate court ▪ West regional reporter containing decisions from the state's highest appellate court and the state's intermediate appellate court ▪ Fee-based services, such as Lexis.com, Lexis Advance, Westlaw Classic, and WestlawNext ▪ Free websites, such as Google Scholar, FindLaw, Justia.com, lexisONE, or a state government website
Cite Checking	▪ KeyCite ▪ *Shepard's* ▪ BCite
Secondary Authorities	▪ *American Law Reports* (for example, A.L.R.4th, A.L.R.5th, and A.L.R.6th) ▪ Law review articles

manual or book. These manuals usually provide a short history of the common law rule or doctrine, the general rules, and citations to key cases. In addition, if there are any statutes that affect the common law doctrine, the manuals usually provide you with cross-references to those statutes. Some examples of state practice manuals are *Trawick's Florida Practice and Procedure, Illinois Law and Practice,* and *Washington Practice.* While some practice books are available only in book form, increasingly they are being added to fee-based services. For instance, the Thomson West practice books are on Westlaw Classic and WestlawNext, and many state bar publications are on Loislaw.

c.   Hornbooks and *Nutshells*

Hornbooks and *Nutshells* are also a good source for background reading. Like practice manuals, these books provide you with a short history of the common law rule and with the general rules. In addition, they usually include descriptions and citations to cases. However, unlike a state practice manual, which lists cases from a single state, hornbooks set out citations to cases from a variety of states.

Most hornbooks are available only in book form. To find them in your library, use your library's electronic card catalog or ask a librarian.

d. Legal Encyclopedias

If one is available, you can also do background reading in a legal encyclopedia. While a few states have their own legal encyclopedia, most states do not. As a result, you will need to use a more general encyclopedia, for example, *American Jurisprudence, Second Series* (Am. Jur. 2d) or *Corpus Juris Secundum* (C.J.S.). You can find legal encyclopedias in book form in your law library or on fee-based services such as Lexis Advance and WestlawNext. In addition, the Legal Information Institute at Cornell Law School sponsors and hosts a free online dictionary and legal encyclopedia. This dictionary and encyclopedia, which is called WEX, is available at *http://www.law.cornell.edu/wex/*.

Exercise 7A   **Background Reading**

1. Using your law school's electronic card catalog, locate a hornbook that discusses adverse possession. Record the name of the hornbook, its call number, and the chapter or sections that discuss adverse possession.
2. Does WEX, the free online dictionary and legal encyclopedia sponsored and hosted by the Legal Information Institute at Cornell Law School, discuss adverse possession? See *http://www.law.cornell.edu/wex/*. If yes, is the information helpful? Why or why not?
3. Using Bing or Google, look for websites that provide an overview of the law relating to adverse possession. What are the pros and cons of using free Internet sites?

---

§ 7.3.2   Finding Tools

While at one point digests were the best way to find cases setting out and applying common law rules, today there are a number of other good ways to find cases.

a. Practice Manuals and Books

If you do your background reading in a practice manual or book, you can use that practice manual to find cases. More likely than not, the practice manual will cite cases that set out the common law rule and explain who has the burden of proof and what that burden is. You can find these cases in a number of ways:

- Use the citation to locate the cases in the book version of a state, regional, or federal reporter;
- Use the citation to find the case on Google® Scholar, Justia.com, or FindLaw®;
- Use the "Find by citation" option to find the cases on a Lexis.com or Westlaw Classic; or
- Type the citation into the search window on Lexis Advance, WestlawNext, or Bloomberg Law.

b. Digests

Digests are subject indexes for both common law cases and cases that interpret and apply enacted law. Each digest is divided into a number of topics, with those topics divided into subtopics and, sometimes, sub-subtopics. Under these topic headings are Notes of Decisions from cases that have discussed the particular point of law.

West publishes a number of digests, including state digests, which contain headnotes from the cases published in the corresponding state reporters; regional digests, which contain headnotes from the cases published in the corresponding regional reporter; and federal digests, which can be used to find cases published in the *Supreme Court Reporter*, the first, second, and third series of the *Federal Reporter*, and the first and second series of the *Federal Supplement*. In addition, West publishes a number of specialty digests, for example, the *Bankruptcy Digest*, the *Military Justice Digest*, and the *Education Law Digest*.

Digests published by West use the West Key Number System®, which works as follows. Through the years, West has created a series of topics and within those topics, "Key Numbers" for each point of law. This set of topics and Key Numbers is the West Key Number System.

When a court publishes an opinion, it sends a copy of its opinion to West, which assigns the case to an editor. The editor, who is an attorney, identifies each point of law discussed in the court's opinion, writes a single sentence, summarizing that point of law, and then assigns that summary a topic and Key Number. These summaries are used in three ways. First, West uses them as headnotes for the case. Second, if the summary relates to a statute, the summary is placed in the Notes of Decision following the applicable statute. Third, these summaries are placed in the appropriate digests under their assigned topic and Key Number.

> **PRACTICE POINTER**   Because the headnotes are written by the company that publishes the reporter and not by the court, you can never cite to a headnote as authority. Instead, you must cite to that part of the court's opinion from which the publishing company took the point of law summarized in the headnote. Similarly, you cannot cite the Notes of Decisions set out following a statute in an annotated code or presented in a digest. Instead, you must read and cite the case from which the Note of Decision was drawn.

c. Fee-Based Services

There are a number of ways to find cases using Lexis.com, Lexis Advance, Westlaw Classic, WestlawNext, and Bloomberg Law. If, during your background reading, you located a case that is on point, you can use that case to find additional cases. For example, if you are using Westlaw Classic or WestlawNext, you can identify the headnotes that are on point and then use either the Key Numbers associated with those cases to do a Key Number search or use the "Most Frequently Cited Cases" option.

In the alternative, you can select your state's case law database (use a database that contains all your state's published decisions) and then construct a Boolean (terms and connectors) search that includes a word or phrase that describes the common law doctrine (for instance, "false imprisonment," "battery," or "nuisance") and a word that the courts are likely to have used in setting out the general rules or burden of proof (for example, "prove," "establish," "elements," or "factors"). Once you have found and analyzed the general rules, you can then run additional searches for cases that have interpreted or applied a specific element or factor. See the electronic supplement for more information about running searches in the particular services.

d. Free Websites

While historically cases were not available on free websites, most cases are now available on Google Scholar. In addition, you can find cases on FindLaw (*http://lp.findlaw.com*) and Justia.com (*http://www.justia.com*).

Exercise 7B   Finding Tools

1. Using your library's electronic card catalog, locate a digest. Which volume contains information about adverse possession? What type of information is in the volume? How is the information organized?
2. Go to Google Scholar and select "Legal Documents" and then, on the next screen, your state's courts. Run a search and note the first ten cases that your search retrieves. Next, go to Lexis Advance, WestlawNext, or Bloomberg Law. Using the various "filters," limit your search to cases from your jurisdiction and then run the same search that you ran on Google Scholar. Does this search retrieve the same ten cases that your Google Scholar search retrieved? Why or why not?

---

§ 7.3.3   Cases

The cases setting out, interpreting, and applying common law rules are in the same reporters as the cases that interpret and apply enacted law. In publishing a case, neither the courts nor the publishing companies distinguish between the two categories of cases. Instead, all the cases are grouped together, organized not by type of case or by topic but by the date of the decision.

In some states, decisions are published in both the state's reporter or reporters and in a regional reporter. For example, you can find the Virginia Supreme Court's decisions in both *Virginia Reports* (Va.) and in *South Eastern Reporter* (S.E., S.E.2d) and the Virginia Court of Appeals' decisions in both the *Virginia Court of Appeals Reports* (Va. App.) and *South Eastern Reporter* (S.E., S.E.2d). By contrast, in Maine, recent decisions of the Maine Supreme Court are published only in the *Atlantic Reporter* (A. or A.2d). Maine does not have its own official or state reporter.

Exercise 7C	Reporters

1. Using Appendix 1 in the *ALWD Citation Manual* or Table 1 in *The Bluebook*, determine the names of reporters for each of the following states. Record the name of the reporter, the types of decisions that are included in the reporter, and the coverage dates.

   a. Indiana
   b. North Dakota
   c. Wisconsin
   d. The state in which your law school is located

2. Locate the reporters for your state's court and select a case from a recent volume. Is there a summary at the beginning of the case? Are there headnotes? If there are headnotes, which publishing company prepared the headnotes?

§ 7.3.4   Other Authorities

Although most of the time you will be able to answer a client's question using your state's cases, occasionally you will need or want to go beyond those cases and look at cases from other states, or see what others have said about the issue that you have been asked to research. For example, you may want to do this additional type of research if your case involves an issue that has not been dealt with in your state, if different divisions within your state's intermediate appellate court have taken different approaches, or if the case is particularly complex or important.

a.   *American Law Reports*

One of the easiest ways to find cases from other states is to use *American Law Reports* (A.L.R.). While originally A.L.R. served as a reporter, today most researchers use it for its annotations. Each annotation deals with a specific topic and lists cases by result and by jurisdiction.

Annotations dealing with state issues are found in A.L.R., A.L.R.2d, A.L.R.3d, A.L.R.4th, A.L.R.5th, and A.L.R.6th. Annotations dealing with federal issues are found in A.L.R. Fed. or A.L.R. Fed. 2d.

A.L.R.	1919-1948
A.L.R.2d	1948-1965
A.L.R.3d	1965-1980
A.L.R.4th	1980-1991
A.L.R.5th	1992-2005
A.L.R.6th	2005 to present
A.L.R. Fed.	1969-2005
A.L.R. Fed. 2d	2005 to present

A.L.R. is available both in book form and on Lexis.com, Lexis Advance, Westlaw Classic, and WestlawNext. Both the book and the electronic versions have indexes.

> **PRACTICE POINTER**   Because you want the most current information, look first for annotations published in A.L.R.5th, A.L.R.6th, and A.L.R. Fed. 2d. In addition, if you are using the book version, be sure to check the pocket parts for more recent cases.

b.   Law Reviews and Journals

If you are looking for an in-depth discussion of a particular common law issue or for a critique of a case that has set out, interpreted, or applied a common law rule, consider looking for a law review article. While most law reviews and journals are published by law schools, some are published by organizations.

You can now access some law review articles for free. For a list of law reviews that are currently available, see *http://www.americanbar.org/groups/depart ments_offices/legal_technology_resources/resources/free_journal_search.html*. In addition, you can find articles using Google Scholar and SSRN.com. Law review articles are also available on Lexis.com, Lexis Advance, Westlaw Classic, and WestlawNext.

§ 7.4   Using the Research Plan to Research an Issue Governed by Common Law

To research issues governed by common law, you have a number of options: You can research the issue using books, free sources, and fee-based services such as Lexis Advance, WestlawNext, and Bloomberg Law. While you do not need to master all of the ways in which you can research common law problems, you should learn to use a number of different tools.

To learn more about using free and fee-based services to research issues governed by common law, see the electronic supplement at *http://www.aspen lawschool.com/books/oates_legalwritinghandbook/*.

§ 7.4.1   The Assignment
§ 7.4.2   Researching an Issue Governed by Common Law Using Free Websites
§ 7.4.3   Researching an Issue Governed by Common Law Using Lexis Advance
§ 7.4.4   Researching an Issue Governed by Common Law Using WestlawNext
§ 7.4.5   Researching an Issue Governed by Common Law Using Bloomberg Law
§ 7.4.6   Researching an Issue Governed by Common Law Using Lexis .com
§ 7.4.7   Researching an Issue Governed by Common Law Using Westlaw Classic

Chapter 7 Quiz

Draft answers for each of the following questions. Make your points clearly and concisely, and write sentences that are easy to read and that are grammatical and correctly punctuated.

1. You have been asked to research a common law issue that involves an area of law that you did not study in law school. Where should you start your research?
2. Your supervising attorney has asked you to get her copies of some of the cases cited in opposing counsel's brief. Where can you get copies of those cases for free?
3. You are doing your research on WestlawNext and have found a case that is on point. How can you use the West Key Number System to find other cases that discuss the same point?
4. When might you use A.L.R.?
5. When might you look for a law review article?

Researching Constitutional Issues

C onstitutional issues can be some of the most interesting, and most time-consuming, issues to research and analyze. Why? Because when you research constitutional issues, you are researching not just the law but also our country's historical underpinnings and ever-changing values.

Like the prior chapters, this chapter has several components: (1) the text, which sets out basic information; (2) exercises, which ask you to apply what you have just read; (3) a quiz that tests the materials set out in the chapter; and (4) an electronic supplement, which shows you how to research a constitutional issue using free sources, Lexis Advance®, WestlawNext™, Bloomberg Law, Lexis.com®, and Westlaw® Classic. To access the supplement, go to *http://www .aspenlawschool.com/books/oates_legalwritinghandbook/*. Your access code to the website is on the card that came with the book. In the ebook, instructions for getting an access code are on the page immediately following the cover page.

§ 8.1   Research Plan for Constitutional Issues

The research plan for constitutional issues is, at its core, the same as the generic research plan set out in Chapter 1: background reading in a secondary source, followed by a search for primary sources; cite checking the primary sources; and, finally, when appropriate, reading additional primary and secondary authorities.

Research Plan for Constitutional Issues

Jurisdiction: Federal or State

Type of Law: Constitutional

Issue: [Set out your issue here.]

Step 1:   If you are unfamiliar with the area of law, spend 30 to 120 minutes doing background reading in a secondary source.

Step 2:   Locate, read, and analyze the applicable constitutional provisions and the cases interpreting and applying those provisions.

Step 3:   Cite check the cases to make sure that they are still good law.

Step 4:   If appropriate, locate and read primary and secondary authorities.

§ 8.2 Sources for Researching Constitutional Issues

§ 8.2.1 Background Reading

Where to start? While the answer to this question is relatively straightforward for most types of research, when you are talking about constitutional issues, there is not an easy answer. For some issues one source might work well; for other issues looking at that source would be a waste of time.

To figure out what source might work best, ask yourself the following questions.

Question 1: Does My Issue Involve Federal Constitutional Law, State Constitutional Law, or Both?

If the issue involves federal constitutional law, your best source for background reading will probably be a hornbook or a law review article. If, however, the issue is governed by state constitutional law, a state practice manual or a law review article published in one of your state's law reviews may be the better choice. If your issue involves both federal and state constitutional law, you may need to look in a hornbook, a state practice manual, and law reviews.

Question 2: Does My Issue Involve an Established or an Emerging Area of Law?

The second question is whether the issue involves an established area of law — for example, a doctrine that you studied in your Constitutional Law class—or a "cutting-edge" or emerging issue. If the issue involves an established area of law, the best source for background reading will probably be a hornbook. For example, see the fifth edition of the *Treatise on Constitutional Law: Substance and Procedure* by Ronald D. Rotunda and John E. Nowak; *American Constitutional Law* by Laurence H. Tribe; or the second edition of *Modern Constitutional Law* by James Antieau. To find these books in your law school library, use your library's online card catalog.

> ## PRACTICE POINTER
>
> Some issues involve new twists in established areas. When you are asked to research one of these issues, start by reading about the established area of law in a hornbook, and then look for law review articles about your specific issue. The hornbooks will give you the conceptual framework, and the law review articles will discuss the new twist.

Question 3:   Have I Been Asked to Determine Whether a Particular Federal or State Statute Is Constitutional?

If your task includes determining whether a particular federal or state statute is constitutional, you have three options: (1) start by reading about the tests the courts use to determine whether a statute is constitutional; (2) start by reading about the statute; or (3) skip the background reading and begin by cite checking the statute, looking for cases that have discussed whether the statute is constitutional.

Option 1

If you decide to start your research by reading about the tests the courts use in determining whether a statute is constitutional, your best source is a hornbook. Using the hornbook's index, look up the doctrines. For example, look up the words "overbreadth" and "vagueness."

Option 2

If the statute you have been asked to research is a federal statute, the best place to read about the statute is probably the Internet. (See Chapter 5, which describes how to research federal statutes.) Go on Bing, Google, or another search engine, and type in both the full name of the act and, if it has one, its acronym.

Option 3

If the statute has been in effect for more than a few years, think about starting with the statute. In particular, use *Shepard's®*, KeyCite®, or BCite to determine whether any existing cases have discussed the constitutionality of the statute. If there are cases, locate and read the cases.

Exercise 8A   **Background Reading**

If you were assigned to research the following issues, where would you start your research? By doing background reading in a hornbook? By looking for a law review article? By looking for cases that have discussed the statute? Explain your answer.

1. You have been asked to determine whether the local police violated your client's rights when officers searched, without a warrant, a garbage can that he placed on the curb in front of his house.
2. You have been asked to determine whether your client, a high school basketball coach, is a private or a public figure as those terms have been defined by the United States Supreme Court.
3. You have been asked to determine whether a section of the USA PATRIOT Act is constitutional.

§ 8.2.2   Primary Authority

For issues governed by the United States Constitution, your primary authorities will be the United States Constitution itself and the cases that have interpreted and applied it. For issues governed by a state constitution, your primary authorities will be the state constitution itself and state cases interpreting the state constitution.

a.   United States Constitution

The easiest place to find a copy of the United States Constitution is the Internet. For instance, go to Bing, Google, or another search engine, and type in the phrase "United States Constitution." This search will take you to a number of reliable websites, including *http://www.archives.gov/exhibits/charters/constitution_transcript.html*. You can also find the text of the United States Constitution in the first volume of the *United States Code*, the *United States Code Annotated*, the *United States Code Service*, and in most state codes.

b.   Federal Cases Interpreting and Applying the United States Constitution

In looking for cases that have interpreted or applied the United States Constitution, look first for United States Supreme Court decisions; second, for published United States Courts of Appeals decisions from your circuit; third, for published United States Courts of Appeals decisions from other circuits; and finally, for published United States District Court decisions. The following list sets out the abbreviations for the reporters in which each court's decisions can be found.

United States Supreme Court: U.S. (official reporter)
S. Ct. (unofficial reporter)
L. Ed. (unofficial reporter) (1790–1955)
L. Ed. 2d (unofficial) (1956–present)

United States Courts of Appeals: F. (1880–1924)
                                  F.2d (1924–1993)
                                  F.3d (1993–present)
United States District Court: F. Supp. (1933–1998)
                                  F. Supp. 2d (1998–present)

Reporters are available in both book and electronic formats. To find the cases in book form, find where the reporter is located in your library, and then, using the citation, look up the case in the appropriate volume. Similarly, you can use the citation to find copies of the cases on fee-based services such as Lexis Advance, WestlawNext, and Bloomberg Law. Each of these services has the full text of United States Supreme Court decisions, United States Courts of Appeals decisions, and United States District Court decisions.

Increasingly, federal cases are available on free websites, including Google® Scholar and sites maintained by the courts. The following is a list of some of the reliable free websites:

- Google Scholar
- The United States Supreme Court website (*http://www.supremecourtus .gov/opinions/opinions.html*)
- Cornell University Legal Information Institute website (*http://www .law.cornell.edu/supct*)
- Justia.com
- FindLaw®

c. State Constitutions

Most state constitutions are available on a number of websites. Two of the easiest ways to find copies of a state's constitution are to go on to Bing or Google and search for websites that contain the name of the state and the word "constitution." For example, search for the phrase "Colorado constitution." In addition, you can find links to state constitutions on the Cornell Legal Information Institute site (*http://www.law.cornell.edu/states/listing.html*) and on FindLaw.

d. Cases Interpreting and Applying a State Constitution

The cases interpreting and applying a particular state's constitution can be found in that state's reporters. Look first for decisions from the state's highest appellate court and then for decisions from the state's intermediate court of appeals. To find the names of the reporters in which a particular state's decisions are reported, see Appendix 1 in the *ALWD Citation Manual* and Table 1 in *The Bluebook*.

Exercise 8B	Primary Authority

You have been asked to determine whether a website that sets out "wanted posters" containing the names and addresses of doctors who perform abortions is speech that is protected by the First Amendment or is a "true threat," which is not protected by the First Amendment.

1. Locate a copy of the First Amendment using two of the following sources. Create a screenshot of each of your selected sources that shows the text of the First Amendment.
    a. *http://www.archives.gov/exhibits/charters/constitution.html*
    b. *http://www.house.gov/house/Educate.shtml*
    c. *http://www.law.cornell.edu/constitution/constitution.overview.html*
    d. *http://supreme.justia.com/constitution/*
2. Using each of the following sources, locate a United States Supreme Court case that discusses "true threats."
    a. Lexis.com or Lexis Advance
    b. Westlaw Classic or WestlawNext
    c. Google Scholar
    Describe the process you used to find a case and include a screenshot showing the case you located.
3. Select one of the following states and then locate a website that sets out that state's constitution. Include a screenshot showing the first page of the state's constitution. In addition, indicate whether the online source is searchable and whether it contains citations to cases that have interpreted or applied a particular constitutional provision.
    a. Colorado
    b. New Mexico
    c. Mississippi
    d. The state in which your law school is located

§ 8.2.3   Finding Tools

There are a number of ways to find cases that have interpreted and applied a particular constitutional provision.

- You can find cases by using the citations found in a hornbook, practice manual, or law review article.
- You can find cases by using the Notes of Decisions/Case Notes in an annotated version of a constitution or, if the question is whether a statute is constitutional, in an annotated version of a code.
- You can find cases by using a digest.
- You can find cases by using a fee-based service such as Lexis.com, Lexis Advance, Westlaw Classic, or WestlawNext.
- You can find cases by using *American Law Reports* (A.L.R.).

Exercise 8C	Finding Tools

Examine each of the following sources, determining whether they contain citations to cases that discuss the "true threats" doctrine.

1. Locate a constitutional law hornbook. Is there a section in the hornbook that discusses the difference between speech that is protected under the First Amendment and true threats, which are not protected under the First Amendment?
    a. What is the name of the hornbook you consulted?
    b. What chapter or section discusses the First Amendment?
    c. Is there a discussion of true threats?

    d. If there is a discussion of true threats, what cases are cited?
2. Using West's Practice Digest Fourth, locate the topic and key number that discusses true threats.
    a. What is the topic and key number?
    b. Are the cases that are listed the same cases that were listed in the hornbook?
3. Using Lexis Advance or WestlawNext, look for a law review article that discusses the difference between speech that is protected by the First Amendment and true threats, which are not protected by the First Amendment. What is the title of a law review article that is on point? (Include a screenshot of the first page of the article.)

§ 8.2.4 Briefs

In recent years, fee-based services such as Lexis Advance and WestlawNext have added the parties' briefs to their databases. As a result, in addition to finding the text of a court's decision, you may also be able to find copies of briefs that the court considered before writing its opinion. You can use these briefs to find out what each party argued, what authorities each party used to support its arguments, and how each party organized its brief.

Exercise 8D   Briefs

1. Using Lexis Advance or WestlawNext, locate the petitioner's brief in *N.A.A.C.P. v. Claiborne Hardware Co.*, 458 U.S. 886 (1982). Include a screenshot showing the first page of the brief.
2. Using Lexis.com, Lexis Advance, Westlaw Classic, or WestlawNext, find the Brief of Plaintiffs-Appellees (Jan. 4, 2000) in *Planned Parenthood v. American Coalition of Life Activists*, 290 F.3d 1058 (9th Cir. 2002).

---

§ 8.3   Using the Research Plan to Research a Constitutional Issue

Just as there are a number of ways to research issues governed by common law, there are also a number of ways to research constitutional issues. Because no one tool is always the best tool, we recommend that you learn to use a number of different tools: free websites and one or more fee-based services.

To learn more about using free and fee-based services to research constitutional issues, see the electronic supplement.

§ 8.3.1   The Assignment
§ 8.3.2   Researching Constitutional Issues Using Free Websites
§ 8.3.3   Researching Constitutional Issues Using Lexis Advance
§ 8.3.4   Researching Constitutional Issues Using WestlawNext
§ 8.3.5   Researching Constitutional Issues Using Bloomberg Law
§ 8.3.6   Researching Constitutional Issues Using Lexis.com
§ 8.3.7   Researching Constitutional Issues Using Westlaw Classic

Chapter 8 Quiz

Draft answers for each of the following questions. Make your points clearly and concisely, and write sentences that are easy to read and that are grammatical and correctly punctuated.

1. Your supervising attorney wants to know whether a court has ruled on the constitutionality of a federal statute. Where should you start your research?
2. If you are arguing a case before the Ninth Circuit Court of Appeals, what would be mandatory authority?
3. How might you use parties' briefs?

Researching Issues Governed by Federal, State, or Local Court Rules

Congratulations! It is your first day at a summer clerkship at the law firm of your dreams.

Before you have settled in at your desk, one of the partners stops by and tells you that she needs you to find a copy of the Northern District of New York's local rules. She is writing a brief in support of a motion for summary judgment, and she does not know what format the court requires. Thus, she asks you to locate a copy of the applicable local court rule.

As the first partner is walking away from your desk, another partner approaches and tells you that he needs your help. He is representing a man charged with residential burglary and wants you to research ER 609.

You sigh. Although you know how to research issues governed by federal and state statutes and by common law, you haven't a clue about how to research an issue governed by federal or state court rules.

Like the prior chapters, this chapter has several components: (1) the text, which sets out basic information; (2) exercises, which ask you to apply what you have just read; (3) a quiz that tests the materials set out in the chapter; and (4) an electronic supplement, which shows you how to research an issue governed by court rules using free sources, Lexis Advance®, WestlawNext™, Bloomberg Law, Lexis.com®, and Westlaw® Classic. To access the supplement, go to *http://www.aspenlawschool.com/books/oates_legalwritinghandbook/*. Your access code to the website is on the card that came with the book. In the ebook, instructions for getting an access code are on the page immediately following the cover page.

§ 9.1   Research Plans for Projects Involving Federal, State, or Local Court Rules

Most rules questions fall into one of two categories: simple or difficult. The simple questions are usually how, what, and where questions. How many days do I have to file my notice? What should be included in that notice? Where do I file that notice? In contrast, the difficult questions are the questions involving a party's rights. Was the defendant denied his right to a speedy trial? Is a piece of evidence more probative than prejudicial? Is a party entitled to judgment as a matter of law?

When the question falls into the first category, the research is simple. All you need to find is the applicable rule. When, however, the question is a more difficult one, you will need to find not only the rule but the cases that have interpreted and applied that rule. The research plans for these two categories of questions are set out below.

Research Plan for a Simple Rules Question

Jurisdiction: Federal, state, or local

Type of Law: Enacted or court-made

Preliminary Issue
Statement: [Put your first draft of the issue statement here.]

Step 1:   Locate, read, and apply the applicable federal, state, and local rules.

Research Plan for a Difficult Rules Question

Jurisdiction: Federal, state, or local

Type of Law: Enacted or court-made

Preliminary Issue
Statement: [Put your first draft of the issue statement here.]

Step 1:   If you are unfamiliar with the rule in question, spend ten to sixty minutes familiarizing yourself with the rule by reading about the rule in a secondary source.

Step 2:   Locate, read, and analyze the applicable federal, state, or local rules, any comments accompanying the rules, and the cases that have interpreted and applied the rules.

Step 3:   Cite check any cases that you plan to use to make sure they are still good law.

Step 4:   If appropriate, locate and read additional primary and secondary authorities.

§ 9.2   Sources for Federal Rules

"Enacting" federal rules is not an easy process. Proposals for new rules or amendments to existing rules must be submitted to the Judicial Conference, which refers the proposed rule or amendment to the Standing Committee, which refers the proposed rule or amendment to one of five subcommittees. If the subcommittee that receives the proposal believes that the proposal has merit, it sends the proposed rule or amendment out for comment and holds public hearings. If, after these hearings, the subcommittee recommends adoption of the proposed rule or amendment, it refers the proposal back to the Standing Committee, which, if it approves the proposal, sends the proposed rule or amendment to the United States Supreme Court. If the United States Supreme Court approves the rule or amendment, it sends the rule to Congress, which has seven months to approve or reject it. See 28 U.S.C. §§ 2072-2075. Not surprisingly, it usually takes two or three years to enact a new rule or to amend an existing one.

You can find copies of the rules that are eventually "enacted" in a number of sources, including the *United States Code*, the *United States Code Annotated*, the *United States Code Service*; specialized books; a number of free websites; and fee-based, online services (for example, Lexis Advance, WestlawNext, and Bloomberg Law).

§ 9.2.1   *United States Code, United States Code Annotated,* **and** *United States Code Service*

Because the federal rules are "enacted" by Congress, they are listed in the *United States Code*. For example, the bankruptcy rules are listed in Title 11 of the *United States Code*; the Federal Rules of Criminal Procedure for the United States District Courts are listed in Title 18; and the Federal Rules of Civil Procedure for the United States District Courts are listed in Title 28. While the *United States Code* has just the text of the rules, the *United States Code Annotated* and the *United States Code Service* have the text of the rules, historical notes, cross-references, and notes of decisions.

> **PRACTICE POINTER** Unlike the other parts of the *United States Code*, the rules do not have section numbers. Instead, they have rule numbers. For instance, in the Federal Rules of Civil Procedure, the rule governing summary judgment is called FRCP 56 and, in the Rules of Evidence, the hearsay rule is Rule 802.

§ 9.2.2   Specialized Books

A number of publishing companies publish paperback books containing all or some of the federal rules. For example, LegalPub.com publishes the *Federal Civil Rules Booklet*, which contains not only the Federal Rules of Civil Procedure but also the Federal Rules of Evidence and selected portions of Title 28 of the *United States Code*. Similarly, the National Institute for Trial Advocacy

(NITA) publishes *Federal Rules of Criminal Procedure* and *Federal Rules of Evidence*. Most of these books are replaced or supplemented each year.

There are also a number of books and treatises that provide the text of the rules, in-depth explanations of those rules, and references to key cases. A partial list is set out below. To see what books and treatises are in your library, check your library's electronic card catalog.

Federal Civil Rules Handbook by Baicker-McKee, Janssen & Corr.
> A one-volume book that provides the text of each rule; the authors' commentary, which includes a description of the rule, the rule's purpose and scope, and the core concepts; and citations to key cases.

Moore's Federal Practice (Third Edition).
> A multi-volume treatise that discusses in detail the Rules of Civil Procedure, the Rules of Criminal Procedure, and the United States Courts of Appeals and Supreme Court rules.

Federal Practice and Procedure by Wright, Miller & Kane.
> A multi-volume treatise that discusses the federal rules in detail.

Federal Rules of Evidence Manual (Ninth Edition) by Stephen Saltzberg, Michael M. Martin & Daniel J. Capra.
> A multi-volume treatise that provides the text of each rule; commentary, which includes definitions, an explanation of the rules, and a discussion of the standard of review; and an annotated list of cases.

PRACTICE POINTER Because most states have modeled their rules after the federal rules, you can use sources such as *Moore's Federal Practice* and *Federal Practice and Procedure* to research both federal and state rules. Just remember to make sure that your state rule is the same as the federal rule.

---

§ 9.2.3   Free Internet Sites

Two of the better free Internet sites for researching rules are LLRX.com, which is at *http://www.llrx.com*, and Cornell's Legal Information Institute (LII) website, which is at *http://www.law.cornell.edu./rules*.

Another good site is the uscourts.gov site. To find a copy of the rules, click on "Rules and Policies," then on "Federal Rules of Practice and Procedure," and lastly on "Current Rules of Practice and Procedure." See *http://www.uscourts .gov/RulesAndPolicies/rules/current-rules.aspx*. Although the U.S. Courts site does not provide links to cases, it does provide you with the text of the rules, summaries of recent changes to the rules, proposed changes to the rules, and links to the federal courts websites, which set out local rules. For more on finding local rules, see section 9.4.

§ 9.2.4   Fee-Based, Online Services

All the fee-based services that have the *United States Code* also have the federal rules. If you know the rule number, you can find the rule by typing the citation into the search box. If you do not know the rule number, you can find the rule by searching for key words.

Exercise 9A   **Federal Rules**

1. Locate the text of Fed. R. Civ. P. 56 on one of the following websites:
   a. *http://www.law.cornell.edu/rules/frcp/*
   b. *http://www.uscourts.gov/uscourts/rules/civil-procedure.pdf.*
   Create a screenshot of the first page that discusses Fed. R. Civ. P. 56.
2. Find a copy of Fed. R. Civ. P. 56 on both Lexis Advance and WestlawNext and examine the material that follows the text of the rule. What material follows the text of the rule on Lexis Advance? What material follows the text of the rule on WestlawNext? Why is there a difference?

---

§ 9.3   Sources for State Rules

Like the federal rules, state rules are published in a variety of sources.

§ 9.3.1   State Codes

In many states, the state's rules are published in a separate volume of the state's code or integrated into the state's code. If a state has both an unannotated code and an annotated code, the unannotated code will have just the text of the rules, while the annotated code will have the text of the rules, historical notes and cross-references, and Notes of Decisions or Case Notes.

§ 9.3.2   Specialized Books

In most states, either the state or a private publishing company publishes a book setting out all or most of the state's rules. In some instances, these books have just the text of the rules. In other instances, the books have not only the text of the rules but also notes that describe cases that have interpreted or applied the rules. For a list of books for your state, check your law library's electronic catalog or ask a reference librarian.

§ 9.3.3   Free Internet Sites

In most states, you can find a copy of the state's rules using the state courts' home page. Alternatively, go to Bing or Google and type in the name of the state and the word "rules."

§ 9.3.4   Fee-Based, Online Services

If a state's rules are part of its state code, you can find copies of the rules on fee-based, online services, such as Lexis Advance, WestlawNext, or Bloomberg Law. If the state's rules are not part of the state code, you may or may not be able to find copies of the rules on the fee-based services. To find out if the rules are on your service, either do a database search or call your representative or the service's help number.

Exercise 9B	**State Rules**

Look for your state's summary judgment rule in each of the following sources. In most states, this will be Civil Rule 56.

  a Your state's website or another free website. Create a screenshot showing the URL and the rule.

  b. Either Lexis Advance or WestlawNext. Create a screenshot showing the rule.

---

§ 9.4   Sources for Local Rules

Most of the federal and state rules allow the courts within their jurisdiction to adopt their own local rules. Generally, these rules establish the procedures and timelines for filing various papers with the court and the formats that the judges want parties to use. In addition, in many jurisdictions, the local rules include sample forms.

PRACTICE POINTER	No matter what source you use, always make sure that the local rules you have located are the rules that are currently in effect.

§ 9.4.1   Books

Sometimes you can find a copy of a court's local rules in a book. For instance, *Federal Local Courts Rules* is a multivolume set published by West, a Thomson Reuters business, that provides the local rules for the United States federal courts. Some circuits also have their own books. For example, in *Federal Ninth Circuit Civil Appellate Practice*, author Christopher A. Goelz walks you through the process of filing and arguing an appeal in the Ninth Circuit Court of Appeals.

§ 9.4.2   Free Internet Sites

The easiest place to find a copy of a court's local rules is on a free Internet site. You can, for instance, find the local rules for federal courts using the links on the United States Courts' website: Go to *http://www.uscourts.gov/Court_Locator/CourtWebsites.aspx* and select the appropriate court. Alternatively, use the links on *http://www.llrx.com/courtrules*.

Similarly, to find the local rules for a state court, select a search engine and, using the advanced search option, insert the name of the court and the word "rules."

§ 9.4.3　Fee-Based, Online Services

You can also find local rules on fee-based, online services, such as Lexis Advance, WestlawNext, and Bloomberg Law.

§ 9.4.4　Telephone Calls and Emails

If you cannot find a copy of the local rules in a book, on a free Internet site, or on a fee-based service, call or email the court clerk.

PRACTICE POINTER	As a practicing attorney, keep abreast of proposed changes to the rules by regularly reading your local bar bulletin or checking the local bar's web page and the court's web page.

Exercise 9C　　Local Rules

Locate the United States District Court for the Northern District of California's local rules governing the notice requirements for motions for summary judgment using one of the following sources:

a. A free website. For example, can you find a copy of the local rule using the links on http://www .uscourts.gov/Court_Locator/CourtWebsites.aspx? Create a screenshot showing the applicable rule.

b. A fee-based service (Lexis Advance or WestlawNext). Create a screenshot showing the applicable rule.

§ 9.5　Using the Research Plan to Research an Issue Governed by Federal, State, or Local Court Rules

In researching issues governed by federal, state, or local rules, you have a number of options: You can research the issue using books and fee-based services like WestlawNext, Lexis Advance, or Bloomberg Law. However, in almost all instances, the best option is a free website.

To learn more about using free and fee-based services to research issues governed by court rules, see the electronic supplement, especially section 9.5.2.

§ 9.5.1　The Assignment

§ 9.5.2　Researching an Issue Governed by Federal, State, or Local Court Rules Using Free Websites

§ 9.5.3　Researching an Issue Governed by Federal, State, or Local Court Rules Using Lexis Advance

§ 9.5.4　Researching an Issue Governed by Federal, State, or Local Court Rules Using WestlawNext

§ 9.5.5   Researching an Issue Governed by Federal, State, or Local Court
          Rules Using Bloomberg Law
§ 9.5.6   Researching an Issue Governed by Federal, State, or Local Court
          Rules Using Lexis.com
§ 9.5.7   Researching an Issue Governed by Federal, State, or Local Court
          Rules Using Westlaw Classic

Chapter 9 Quiz

Draft answers for each of the following questions. Make your points clearly and concisely, and write sentences that are easy to read and that are grammatical and correctly punctuated.

1. Where can you find a copy of the Federal Rules of Civil Procedure and Notes of Decisions/Case Notes for cases that have discussed those rules?
2. Where can you find an in-depth discussion of the Federal Rules of Civil Procedure?
3. Where is the easiest place to find copies of the local rules for the United States Courts of Appeals?

Citators

One of the most embarrassing things that can happen to you as an attorney is to discover that the case you are relying on was either reversed on appeal or overruled in a subsequent case. The conversation usually goes something like this:

Attorney: Your Honor, our case is almost identical to *State v. Smith*, a 2013 Court of Appeals decision. In that case, . . .
Judge (interrupting the attorney): Counsel, are you aware that that decision was reversed by the Supreme Court earlier this month?
Attorney: (long pause) No, your Honor. I was not.

To make sure you do not find yourself in this position, cite check every case that you include in your memos and briefs. In addition, cite check every case that your opponent relies on in its brief. One of the easiest ways to win a case is to show that the authority on which the other side has relied is no longer good law.

Like the earlier chapters, this chapter has several components: (1) the text, which sets out basic information; (2) exercises, which ask you to apply what you have just read; (3) a quiz that tests the materials set out in the chapter; and (4) an electronic supplement, which shows you how to cite check using *Shepard's*®, KeyCite®, and BCite, which is on Bloomberg Law. To access the supplement, go to *http://www.aspenlawschool.com/books/oates_legalwriting handbook/*. Your access code to the website is on the card that came with the book. In the ebook, instructions for getting an access code are on the page immediately following the cover page.

§ 10.1   Introduction to Citators

Citators serve two purposes. First, they are used to determine whether a particular authority, for example, a case, is still good law. Second, they are used to find other authorities that have cited to a particular case, statute, regulation, law review article, or other authority.

Case citators work as follows. Each time a court publishes a decision, an attorney who works for the company that produces the citator reads the case and determines whether the case reverses or overrules an earlier decision. A decision is reversed when, in the same case, a higher court reverses the decision of a lower court. In contrast, a case is overruled when, in a different case, a court determines that, in an earlier decision, the court applied the wrong rule of law.

After determining whether the case reverses or overrules an earlier decision, the attorney who works for the company that publishes the citator examines each of the cases that are cited in the new case, determining how, in that new case, the court treats the cases that it cites. Does the court apply the rule or rules set out in the case, distinguish the case, criticize the court's reasoning, or do something else (for example, simply cite the case)? This information is then collected and placed in the citator. For example, if in Case D, the court distinguishes Case A, that fact will be indicated in the citator under Case A. Similarly, if Case D follows Case B, that fact will be indicated in the citator under Case B.

In addition to cite checking cases, you can also cite check a variety of other sources. For example, if you want to find cases that have cited to a particular statute, you can cite check that statute. Similarly, if you want to find cases that have cited to a particular restatement section or to a particular law review article, you can cite check those sources.

§ 10.2   Types of Citators

Although historically attorneys checked their citations using the book version of one of *Shepard's* Citators, today most attorneys do their cite checking online using the online version of *Shepard's*, which is on Lexis.com® and Lexis Advance®; or KeyCite®, which is on Westlaw® Classic and WestlawNext™; or BCite, which is on Bloomberg Law. The online versions of *Shepard's*, KeyCite, and BCite provide the attorney with more up-to-date information than the book version of *Shepard's* and are easier to use.

> **PRACTICE POINTER**   Just as individuals who ask you to Xerox a case are not asking you to copy a case using a machine sold by Xerox, attorneys who ask you to *Shepardize* a case are not asking you to cite check the case using *Shepard's*. They are simply asking you to check the case to make sure that it is still good law, and you can do that using *Shepard's*, KeyCite, or BCite.

Because determining whether a source is still good law must be done source by source by someone trained in the law, to date there are no free sources that provide all of the information contained in *Shepard's*, KeyCite, or BCite. While the "How cited" option that is on Google® Scholar lists citing cases, it does not provide you with the subsequent history or tell you how later cases treated the case that you are cite checking.

§ 10.3   Cite Checking Using *Shepard's*, KeyCite, and BCite

To learn more about using free and fee-based services to cite check, see the electronic supplement.

§ 10.3.1 Cite Checking Using *Shepard's*
§ 10.3.2 Cite Checking Using KeyCite
§ 10.3.3 Cite Checking Using BCite
§ 10.3.4 Cite Checking Using Free Websites

Exercise 10A   *Shepard's*

1. Is *Harbert v. Healthcare Services Group, Inc.*, 391 F.3d 1140 (10th Cir. 2004), still good law?
2. What is the name of a Third Circuit Court of Appeals decision that cited *Harbert* for the point of law set out in headnote 8 in *Harbert*?

Exercise 10B   KeyCite

1. Is *Harbert v. Healthcare Services Group, Inc.*, 391 F.3d 1140 (10th Cir. 2004), still good law?
2. Is the point of law set out in headnote 8 in the Lexis Advance version of the case the same as the point of the law set out in headnote 8 in the WestlawNext version of the case?
3. Did the United States Supreme Court accept review?

Exercise 10C   BCite

1. Is *Harbert v. Healthcare Services Group, Inc.*, 391 F.3d 1140 (10th Cir. 2004), still good law?
2. Is the point of law set out in headnote 8 in the Bloomberg Law version of the case the same as the point of law set out in headnote 8 in either the Lexis Advance version of the case or in headnote 8 in the WestlawNext version of the case?
3. Can you determine which cases have cited Harbert for a particular headnote?

Chapter 10 Quiz

Draft answers for each of the following questions. Make your points clearly and concisely, and write sentences that are easy to read and that are grammatical and correctly punctuated.

1. If an attorney asks you to *Shepardize* a case, what is the attorney asking you to do?
2. What are the two ways in which citators can be used?
3. What does it mean when someone says that a court's decision was reversed? That a court's decision was overruled?

Objective Memoranda, E-Memos, Opinion Letters, and Email and Text Messages

Drafting Memos

More likely than not, one of your first assignments as an intern, extern, or associate will be to research a legal issue and prepare a memo for your supervising attorney. Sometimes, your supervising attorney will give you several days to complete the assignment and will want you to prepare a formal memo; at other times, the attorney needs the answer "now," and wants not a formal memo but just an email in which you set out your analysis and conclusion.

So that you are ready for practice, this chapter and the following four chapters walk you through the process of writing both formal memos and shorter memos, which we call e-memos. Because they are an effective tool for teaching you to think like a lawyer, we begin by showing you how to write a formal memo: In Chapter 12, we show you how to write a formal memo using a "script" format, in Chapter 13 we show you how to write a formal memo using an "integrated" format, and in Chapter 14 we talk about other types of formal memos. Then, in Chapter 15, we explain how you can use what you have learned to write shorter, less formal e-memos.

| PRACTICE POINTER | So how difficult can it be to write a memo? Unfortunately, if the memo is a legal memo, it can be very difficult. To write an effective memo, you need to know how to do legal research; how to analyze and synthesize statutes, regulations, and cases; how to construct arguments; how to evaluate the relative merits of different arguments; and how to write about complex issues clearly and concisely. |

§ 11.1   Audience

For an objective, or office, memo, your primary audience is other attorneys in your office. In most instances, a more experienced attorney asks a law student or newer attorney to research an issue and write a memo setting out not only the law but also how that law applies to a particular situation, for example, how the law might apply in a particular client's case. While sometimes a copy of the memo will be sent to the client, memos are, if appropriate precautions are taken, attorney work product and are not, therefore, discoverable. Consequently, neither an opposing party nor the courts have a right to see these memos.

§ 11.2   Purpose

Your primary purpose in writing an office memo is to give the attorneys in your law office the information they need to evaluate a case, advise a client, or draft another document, for example, a complaint, brief, or contract. Thus, your memo needs to be objective. In drafting the statement of facts, include both the facts that favor your client and the facts that favor the other side. In addition, make sure that your issue statement, your summaries of the general and specific rules, and your descriptions of the analogous cases are neutral. Most importantly, in setting out the arguments, give appropriate weight to each side's arguments and, in setting out your conclusions, be candid.

§ 11.3   Conventions

Because objective memos are in-house documents, there are no rules governing their format. As a result, the format used for a memo varies from office to office and even from lawyer to lawyer. In addition, the practice of law is changing. While historically lawyers wanted longer, more formal memos, today many lawyers prefer shorter memos that are either imbedded in or attached to an email. These less formal memos save supervising lawyers time and save clients money, both important efficiencies in today's law firm.

Therefore, before writing a memo, ask the attorney who is assigning the project the following questions:

1. Should I prepare a formal memo or a less formal, shorter "e-memo"?
2. About how much time should I spend on this project?
3. What research resources may I use (e.g., can I use LexisAdvance® and Westlaw Next™)?

> **PRACTICE POINTER**
> As an intern or clerk, you also need to know what types of questions you should not ask. Do not, for example, ask how many cases you should include in the memo. Writing a memo is not a school assignment. If the attorney knew how many cases were relevant, he or she would not have asked you to do the research and write the memo.

§ 11.4   Sample Memos

In the first two examples set out below, we show the final drafts of the memos that we discuss in Chapters 12 and 13. While both examples involve a single issue that requires an elements analysis, the examples differ in two ways. In the first example, the writer sets out the facts before the issue statement and brief answer and organizes the discussion section using what we call a script format. In contrast, in the second example, the writer sets out the issue statement first, does not include a brief answer, and organizes the discussion section using an integrated format. (For more on organizing the discussion section using a script format, see Chapter 12. For more on organizing the discussion section using an integrated format, see Chapter 13. For a discussion of other types of memos, see Chapter 14.)

The third, fourth, and fifth examples are e-memos that provide the attorney with a "quick" answer to his or her question. Once again, the format varies: Because e-memos are in-house memos, there are no rules governing the format. You do, however, want to present the information in the order in which the attorney expects to see it: rules before examples of how those rules have been applied in analogous cases and rules and analogous cases before your analysis and conclusion.

The first time that you read the examples, focus on the content. What is the issue? What is the law? How does that law apply in the client's situation? The second time that you read the examples, focus on organization. How is the memo organized? How is each subsection organized? The last time that you read the examples, focus on the writing. Have the writers used what is commonly known as legalese? If they haven't, how would you describe the tone and the writing style?

PRACTICE POINTER	More likely than not, once you begin applying for jobs, you will need a writing sample. Because some employers allow first-year students to use a memo that they prepared as part of a class, you may be

able to use one of your legal writing memos as a writing sample. Accordingly, make sure that you understand what information needs to go into a memo and why that information needs to be presented in a particular order and in particular ways. In addition, make sure that your analysis is sophisticated and that your writing is clear, concise, and correct.

§ 11.4.1   Sample Formal Memo 1

For a description of the process involved in writing this memo,[1] see Chapter 12.

---

1. Because this memo was written for a Florida attorney and involves an issue of Florida law, it uses the Florida citation rules. See Fla. R. Civ. P. 9.800, *available at* http://www.floridasupreme court.org/decisions/barrules.shtml.

To: Christina Galeano

From: Legal Intern

Date: September 9, 2013

Re: Elaine Olsen, Case No. 13-478
           Service of Process, Usual Place of Abode; Notification of
           Contents

Statement of Facts

Elaine Olsen has contacted our office asking for assistance in over-turning an order terminating her parental rights. You have asked me to determine whether the service of process was valid.

On February 1, 2013, Ms. Olsen entered an inpatient drug treatment program in Miami, Florida. She remained in the program until March 27, 2013, when she moved into a residential treatment house for recovering addicts.

During April, May, and June 2013, Ms. Olsen was a full-time resident at the residential treatment house. She had a bedroom in the house, ate her meals there, and had some of her possessions there. In addition, when she applied for jobs, she listed the treatment house address as her address.

Beginning in July 2013, Ms. Olsen began spending less time at the treatment house and more time with her sister, Elizabeth Webster, who is 32. Both Ms. Olsen's sister and the manager of the halfway house will testify that, during July and August 2013, Ms. Olsen spent weeknights at the treatment house and Friday, Saturday, and Sunday nights at her sister's house. Because she was spending time at her sister's house, Ms. Olsen moved some of her clothing and personal effects into her sister's house.

On Wednesday, July 24, 2013, a process server went to Ms. Webster's house and asked for Elaine Olsen. When Ms. Webster told the process server that "Elaine isn't here today," the process server handed the summons to Ms. Webster and told her that Ms. Olsen "needed to go to court."

Ms. Webster will testify that she never gave the summons to her sister. Because she thought that the papers related to some of Ms. Olsen's unpaid bills, she simply put the summons in a shoebox in the kitchen with a stack of Ms. Olsen's other mail. Ms. Olsen says she never received the summons and, as a result, did not respond. The return of service is regular on its face.

Ms. Olsen has been employed since August 1, 2013, and she has lived in her own apartment since September 1, 2013. She has her sister's address on her driver's license.

There is nothing in the record that indicates whether the State tried to personally serve Ms. Olsen or whether it tried to serve her at the halfway house.

Issue

Under Florida's service of process statute, was Ms. Olsen properly served when (1) during the month when service was made, Ms. Olsen spent weeknights at a residential treatment house where she had a room, ate meals, and kept belongings, and spent Friday, Saturday, and Sunday nights at her sister's house, where she had some belongings; (2) Ms. Olsen listed the treatment house address on job applications but her sister's address on her driver's license; (3) service was made on Ms. Olsen's 32-year-old sister on a Wednesday at Ms. Olsen's sister's house; (4) the process server told Ms. Olsen's sister that Ms. Olsen needed to go to court; and (5) Ms. Olsen's sister did not give the summons and petition to Ms. Olsen, and Ms. Olsen states that she did not receive notice?

Brief Answer

Probably not. Because the return is regular on its face, Ms. Olsen has the burden of proving that she was not properly served. Because the petition was left with Ms. Olsen's 32-year-old sister at the sister's house, Ms. Olsen will have to concede that service was made on a person 15 years or older who was living at the house at which the service was made. In addition, because the process server told Ms. Olsen's sister that Ms. Olsen needed to go to court, more likely than not the court will decide that the person served was informed of the contents of the documents. However, because Ms. Olsen can present evidence that establishes that she was staying at the residential treatment house on the day that service was made, the court may decide that the petition was not left at Ms. Olsen's usual place of abode.

Discussion

The Florida courts have repeatedly stated that the fundamental purpose of service of process is to give defendants notice of claims that have been filed against them and to provide them with an opportunity to defend their rights. *E.g., Shurman v. Atl. Mortg. & Inv. Corp.*, 795 So. 2d 952, 953-54 (Fla. 2001). Because these rights are so important, the courts strictly construe and enforce statutes governing service of process. *Id.* at 954.

In the present case, the relevant portion of the statute reads as follows:

> (1)(a) Service of original process is made by delivering a copy of it to the person to be served with a copy of the complaint, petition, or other initial pleading or paper or by leaving the copies at his or her usual place of abode with any person residing therein who is 15 years of age or older and informing the person of their contents. . . .

§ 48.031(1)(a), Fla. Stat. (2013).

Although the party seeking to invoke the jurisdiction of the court has the burden of proving that service was proper, if the return is regular on its face, the courts presume that the service was valid. *Busman v. State, Dep't of Revenue*, 905 So. 2d 956, 958 (Fla. 3d DCA 2005); *Thompson v. State,*

Dep't of Revenue, 867 So. 2d 603, 605 (Fla. 1st DCA 2004). In such instances, the party challenging the service has the burden of presenting clear and convincing evidence that the service was invalid. *Id.*

In this case, Ms. Olsen may be able to present clear and convincing evidence that the petition was not left at her usual place of abode. However, if the court decides that the petition was left at her usual place of abode, Ms. Olsen will have to concede that the summons was left with a person 15 years or older who was residing at the house where service was made. In addition, although Ms. Olsen can argue that her sister was not informed of the contents of the documents, it is unlikely that she can meet her burden of proof.

A. Usual Place of Abode

Although the statute does not define the phrase "usual place of abode," the courts have said that a defendant's usual place of abode is the place "where the defendant was actually living at the time of service." *E.g., Shurman v. Atl. Mortg. & Inv. Corp.*, 795 So. 2d 952, 953-54 (Fla. 2001); *Busman v. State, Dep't of Revenue*, 905 So. 2d 956, 957 (Fla. 3d DCA 2005).

In an early case, and one of the few published decisions in which the court concluded that the defendant had been served at his usual place of abode, the court emphasizes that, at the time of service, defendant's wife and children were living at the apartment where service was made. *State ex rel. Merritt v. Heffernan*, 195 So. 145, 146-47 (Fla. 1940). In that case, the defendant had relocated his family to Florida two months before service was made and had twice visited them while they were in Florida, the second time leaving the apartment to return to Minnesota just an hour before service was made. *Id.* Although the defendant argued that his usual place of abode was Minnesota, where he had an office, paid taxes, and voted, the court disagreed, stating that "[w]e do not hold the view that Florida was the permanent residence of the defendant, but we do feel that in the circumstance reflected in the record, it was his usual place of abode . . . ." *Id.* at 148.

In contrast, in the more recent cases, the courts have emphasized that it is not enough that the complaint or petition is left with a relative. *See, e.g., Busman*, 905 So. 2d at 947; *Torres v. Arnco Const., Inc.*, 867 So. 2d 583 (Fla. 5th DCA 2004). For example, in *Busman*, the court concluded that service of process was not valid even though the summons and complaint had been left with the defendant's half brother. *Id.* at 958. Similarly, in *Torres*, the court concluded that service had not been made at the defendant's usual place of abode when, after trying unsuccessfully to serve the defendant at his New York apartment, the plaintiff served the defendant's mother at her home in Florida. *Id.* at 585, 587. Although the defendant's mother told the process server that her son "would be home soon," the court decided that this statement was, at best, ambiguous. *Id.* at 585; *accord Portfolio Recovery Assocs., LLC v. Gonzalez*, 951 So. 2d 1037, 1038 (Fla. 3d DCA 2007) (service was not made at the defendants' usual place of abode when the summons and complaint were left with a woman who was the mother of one defendant and the mother-in-law of the other defendant, but the defendants had not lived at the residence for five years).

Ms. Olsen can make three arguments to support her assertion that her sister's house was not her usual place of abode. First, Ms. Olsen will argue that, under the plain language of the statute, her sister's house was not her usual place of abode. As the courts have stated, service must be made at the place where the defendant was actually living at the time the summons and complaint were served. In this case, the summons and complaint were served on a weekday, and on weekdays Ms. Olsen was actually living at the residential treatment house.

Second, Ms. Olsen will argue that the facts in her case are more like the facts in *Busman* and *Torres* than the facts in *Heffernan*. Like Mr. Busman, who produced a lease that corroborated his testimony that he was not living with his half brother on the day that the summons and complaint were served, Ms. Olsen can produce evidence that establishes that on the day she was served she was living at the residential treatment house. Both Ms. Olsen's sister and the manager of the residential treatment house have said they will testify that during June and July Ms. Olsen lived at the treatment house during the week and stayed with her sister only on weekends. In the alternative, Ms. Olsen can argue that the facts in her case are even stronger than the facts in *Torres*. While Mr. Torres's mother's statement that Mr. Torres "would be home soon" suggested that Mr. Torres would be returning to his mother's house that day, Ms. Olsen's sister told the process server that Ms. Olsen "isn't here today." In addition, Ms. Olsen can distinguish *Heffernan*: Although Mr. Heffernan had been at his family's apartment only an hour before the summons and complaint were served, Ms. Olsen had not been at her sister's house for several days.

Finally, Ms. Olsen can argue that, as a matter of public policy, the court should decide that the summons and petition were not left at her usual place of abode. The courts have stated that the statute should be narrowly construed, and this policy is particularly important in cases in which the State is seeking to terminate a mother's parental rights. In addition, this is not a case in which the State tried but could not locate Ms. Olsen: There is no evidence that the State tried to serve Ms. Olsen at the residential treatment house.

In response, the State will argue that Ms. Olsen was served at one of her usual places of abode. The courts have not required that the plaintiff be living at the house where the summons and complaint are served on the day on which the service is made. Therefore, while Ms. Olsen may not have been at her sister's house on the day that the summons and complaint were served, she had been there the previous weekend, and she was there the following weekend. In addition, Ms. Olsen had possessions at her sister's house.

Thus, the State will argue that the facts in this case are much stronger than the facts in *Heffernan*. While in *Heffernan*, Mr. Heffernan visited his family only "twice during the season," Ms. Olsen lived at her sister's house on weekends. In addition, while Mr. Heffernan had another permanent residence, Ms. Olsen was staying at a halfway house, which, by definition, is only a temporary residence. Finally, while in *Heffernan* there was no indication that Mr. Heffernan listed the Florida address on any documents, Ms. Olsen listed her sister's address on her driver's license, and there is evidence indicating that Ms. Olsen received other types of mail at her sister's house.

The State will use these same facts to distinguish *Torres*. While in *Torres*, Mr. Torres presented evidence establishing that his permanent residence was in New York, in the present case, Ms. Olsen did not have a permanent residence. In the five months before service, she had been an inpatient in a treatment facility, she had lived at the halfway house, and she had lived with her sister. The plaintiff can also distinguish *Shurman* and *Busman*. While in *Shurman* and *Busman* the record indicated that the defendants had not lived at the house where service had been made for months or years, in this case, Ms. Olsen admits that she stayed at her sister's house on the weekend before her sister was served.

Finally, the State will argue that, because the return was regular on its face, Ms. Olsen has the burden of proving, by clear and convincing evidence, that her sister's house was not her usual place of abode. In this instance, Ms. Olsen has not met that burden. When there is evidence that the defendant was in fact living at the house where service was made, the courts should not require plaintiffs to determine which house the defendant was living at on any particular day.

While both sides have strong arguments, the court will probably conclude that the summons and petition were not left at Ms. Olsen's usual place of abode. In the more recent cases, the courts have emphasized that it is not enough that service is made on a relative and concluded that the service was invalid when the defendant presented evidence establishing that he or she was not actually living at the place where the summons and complaint were left. Therefore, we can argue that it is not enough that the summons and petition were left with Ms. Olsen's sister: Service was invalid because, on the day that service was made, Ms. Olsen was not actually living with her sister. The problem, of course, is that Ms. Olsen stayed with her sister the weekend preceding and following service. Although these facts make this case weaker than the analogous cases, the court may be persuaded by the fact that this case involves termination of parental rights, that there is no evidence that the State tried to serve Ms. Olsen personally or at the treatment house, and that Ms. Olsen did not have actual notice.

B. Person 15 Years Old or Older Residing Therein

In addition to leaving the summons at the defendant's usual place of abode, the process server must leave the summons with a person 15 years old or older residing therein. Because Ms. Webster is 32 and lives at the house where the summons and complaint were left, Ms. Olsen will have to concede that the summons was left with a person residing therein who is at least 15 years old.

C. Informed of Contents

[Not shown]

Conclusion

Because of the strong public policy in favor of ensuring that defendants receive notice of actions that have been filed against them, the court will probably decide that the substituted service of process was not valid and vacate the judgment terminating Ms. Olsen's parental rights.

Ms. Olsen will have to concede that her sister, Ms. Webster, is a person of suitable age and that Ms. Webster was residing at the house where the service was made. In addition, because the process server told Ms. Webster that Ms. Olsen needed to go to court, it seems unlikely that Ms. Olsen will be able prove that Ms. Webster was not informed of the contents.

Ms. Olsen may, however, be able to prove that the summons and complaint were not served at her usual place of abode. In the more recent cases, the courts have concluded that service made on a relative was invalid when the defendants produced evidence establishing that they were not actually living with that relative on the day that service was made. While in most of these cases the defendants had not lived at the house where service was made for several months or several years, in the present case the court may be swayed by three facts: This case involves the termination of Ms. Olsen's parental rights; there is no evidence that the State tried to personally serve Ms. Olsen or that it tried to serve Ms. Olsen at the treatment house; and Ms. Olsen states that she did not receive notice.

§ 11.4.2 Sample Formal Memo 2

For a description of the process involved in writing this memo,[2] see Chapter 13.

To:	Julia Fishler
From:	Legal Intern
Date:	November 1, 2013
Re:	Michael Garcia Adverse possession; Washington law

Issue

Whether Doctors and Nurses Who Care (DNWC) has obtained a right to Mr. Garcia's land through adverse possession when (1) it has used Mr.

---

2. Because this memo was written for a Washington attorney and involves an issue of Washington law, it uses the Washington citation rules. *See* Wash. Courts, Style Sheet (Dec. 28, 2010), *available at* http://www.courts.wa.gov/appellate_trial_courts/supreme/?fa=atc_supreme.style.

Garcia's land for campouts several nights a week for eight weeks each summer since 1997; (2) to facilitate these campouts, DNWC has maintained the campsites, fire area, outhouse, and dock; (3) in 2001, DNWC sent a letter to Mr. Garcia asking him whether it could continue using the land for campouts, but Mr. Garcia did not respond to the letter; and (4) Mr. Garcia has paid the taxes but did not visit the land from 1999 until August 2013.

Statement of Facts

Michael Garcia has contacted our office regarding property that he owns in Washington State. Mr. Garcia is concerned that the organization that owns the property next to his, Doctors and Nurses Who Care (DNWC), may be able to claim title to his property through adverse possession.

Mr. Garcia's property is on Lake Chelan, which is in the eastern part of Washington State. Mr. Garcia's grandfather, Eduardo Montoya, purchased the two-acre waterfront parcel in 1958, and the Montoya family used the land every summer from 1958 until Eduardo Montoya became ill in the early 1990s. When it used the land, the family would camp on the site and use a small dock for swimming, fishing, and boating. In 1999, Mr. Garcia's grandfather died and left the property to Mr. Garcia. Although Mr. Garcia spent one weekend at the property in fall of 1999, he moved to California in 2000 and did not visit the property until last August. He has, however, continued to pay all of the taxes and assessments.

In 1996, DNWC purchased the five-acre parcel that adjoins Mr. Garcia's property. Since 1997, DNWC has used its land as a summer camp for children with serious illnesses or disabilities. In a typical summer, the DNWC runs two one-week camps for children with cancer, two one-week camps for children who are blind, two one-week camps for children with autism, and two one-week camps for children with diabetes.

Most of the time the children stay in cabins located on the DNWC property. However, DNWC uses Mr. Garcia's property for "campouts." On one night, one group of about 10 children will camp out in tents on Mr. Garcia's property, the next night another group of 10 will camp out on the property, and so on. Thus, DNWC has been using the Garcia property four or five nights a week for eight weeks each summer since 1997. During these campouts, the children pitch and stay in tents, cook over a fire, and use the dock. To facilitate these campouts, DNWC has maintained the campsite, the fire area, the outhouse, and the dock.

In February 2001, DNWC sent Mr. Garcia a letter asking him whether it could continue using his land for campouts. Mr. Garcia was busy and did not respond to the letter. Sometime during the summer of 2001, DNWC posted a no trespassing sign on the dock, and the sign is still there.

Last August, Mr. Garcia visited the property with the intent of spending a few days camping on the lake. When he got there, he discovered the children and their counselors on the property.

After discovering the children on his land, Mr. Garcia went to the DNWC camp headquarters and talked to the director, Dr. Liu, who told Mr. Garcia that it was his understanding that the land belonged to DNWC. Although Mr. Garcia did not spend that night at the property, he did spend the next night there after the children left. DNWC did not ask him to leave.

Although over the years the land around the lake has become more and more developed, the area in which the camp is located is still relatively undeveloped. Most of the property owners use their land only during the summer.

Discussion

The doctrine of adverse possession was developed to assure maximum use of the land, to encourage the rejection of stale claims, and to quiet titles. *Chaplin v. Sanders*, 100 Wn.2d 853, 859-60, 676 P.2d 431 (1984); *see also* William B. Stoebuck, *The Law of Adverse Possession in Washington*, 35 Wash. L. Rev. 53, 53 (1960).

To establish title through adverse possession, the claimant must prove that its possession was (1) exclusive, (2) actual and uninterrupted, (3) open and notorious, and (4) hostile for the statutory period. *ITT Rayonier, Inc. v. Bell*, 112 Wn.2d 754, 757, 774 P.2d 6 (1989); *Chaplin v. Sanders*, 100 Wn.2d 853, 857, 676 P.2d 431 (1984). In this case, the statutory period is 10 years. RCW 4.16.020(1).

Adverse possession is a mixed question of law and fact. *Chaplin*, 100 Wn.2d at 863. Whether the essential facts exist is for the trier of fact to decide; but whether the facts, as found, constitute adverse possession is for the court to determine as a matter of law. *Id.*

In this case, DNWC can easily prove that its possession was open and notorious and exclusive. In addition, it can probably prove that its possession is actual and uninterrupted. The only element that it may not be able to prove is that its possession was hostile.

A. Open and Notorious

A claimant can satisfy the open and notorious element by showing either (1) that the title owner had actual notice of the adverse use throughout the statutory period or (2) that the claimant used the land such that any reasonable person would have thought that the claimant owned it. *Riley v. Andres*, 107 Wn.2d 391, 396, 27 P.3d 618 (2001).

In this case, DNWC can prove both that Mr. Garcia had actual notice of its adverse use and that any reasonable person would have thought that DNWC owned the land. To prove that Mr. Garcia had actual knowledge of DNWC's use of the land, DNWC can offer the letter that it sent to Mr. Garcia in 2001 asking for continuing permission to use his land for campouts. To prove that a reasonable person would have thought that DNWC owned the land, DNWC will point out that it not only used the land for campouts but also maintained the campsites, fire area, outhouse, and dock and posted a no trespassing sign.

B. Actual and Uninterrupted

Although the Washington courts have not set out a test for actual possession, the cases illustrate the types of acts that are needed to establish actual possession. 17 *Wash. Prac., Real Estate: Property Law* § 8.10 (2d ed.).

The courts have held that the claimants had actual possession of rural land when the claimants built a fence and cultivated or pastured up to it, *Faubion v. Elder*, 49 Wn.2d 300, 301 P.2d 153 (1956); cleared the land, constructed and occupied buildings, and planted orchards, *Metro. Bldg. Co. v. Fitzgerald*, 122 Wash. 514, 210 P. 770 (1922); or cleared and fenced the land, planted an orchard, and built a road, *Davies v. Wickstrom*, 56 Wash. 154, 105 P. 454 (1909). In contrast, the courts have held that the claimants did not have actual possession of rural land when they maintained a fence intended to be a cattle fence and not a line fence, *Roy v. Goerz*, 26 Wn. App. 807, 614 P.2d 1308 (1980); erected two signboards and a mailbox and ploughed weeds, *Slater v. Murphy*, 55 Wn.2d 892, 339 P.2d 457 (1959); or occasionally used the land for gardening, piling wood, and mowing hay, *Smith v. Chambers*, 112 Wash. 600, 192 P. 891 (1920). *See generally* 17 *Wash. Prac., Real Estate: Property Law* § 8.10 (2d ed.).

If DNWC had used the land only for occasional campouts, it would have been difficult for it to prove that it had actual possession. However, in addition to using the land for campouts, DNWC maintained the campsites, the fire area, the outhouse, and the dock, and it posted a no trespassing sign. Because DNWC maintained permanent structures and posted the no trespassing sign, more likely than not a court will hold that it had actual possession.

In addition, DNWC's use and maintenance of the campsites, fire area, outhouse, and dock are probably enough to establish that its possession was uninterrupted. In all of the cases in which the claimants maintained and used permanent structures, the courts have held that the use was uninterrupted. For instance, in *Howard v. Kunto*, 3 Wn. App. 393, 477 P.2d 210 (1970), the court held that the claimants' use was continuous even though the claimants used the property only during the summer. As the court noted in that case, "the requisite possession requires such possession and dominion 'as ordinarily marks the conduct of owners in general in holding, managing, and caring for property of like nature and condition.'" *Id.* at 397. Consequently, while Mr. Garcia might be able to argue that DNWC's use of the land was not uninterrupted because it used the land only during the summer months, this argument is a weak one. Because the land is recreational land, DNWC's use of the land only in summer is consistent with how the owners of similar land hold, manage, and care for their property.

C. Exclusive

To establish that its possession was exclusive, the claimant must show that its possession was "of a type that would be expected of an owner . . . ." *ITT Rayonier*, 112 Wn.2d 754, 758, 774 P.2d 6 (1989). Therefore, while sharing possession of the land with the true owner will prevent a claimant from establishing that its possession was exclusive, sharing possession with a tenant or allowing occasional use by a neighbor does not. *Id.*

In this case, Mr. Garcia has stated that he did not visit the property between 1999 and 2013. Thus, during that period, DNWC did not share the property with the true owner. Although DNWC "shared" its use of Mr. Garcia's land with its campers, this fact should not prevent a court from finding that its possession was exclusive. Because the campers used the Garcia land under the supervision of DNWC, they are analogous to tenants.

D. Hostile

While before 1984 the Washington courts considered the claimant's subjective intent in determining whether its use of the land was hostile, since 1984 the claimant's subjective intent has been irrelevant. *Chaplin*, 100 Wn.2d at 860-61 (overruling cases in which the courts had considered the claimant's subjective intent). Accordingly, under current Washington law, the claimant must prove only that it used the land as if it were its own for the statutory period. *Id.; Miller v. Anderson*, 91 Wn. App. 822, 828, 964 P.2d 365 (1998). If the claimant proves that it used the land as if it were its own, the use was hostile unless the true owner can prove that it gave the claimant permission to use the land. *Id.*

Permission can be express or implied. *Miller*, 91 Wn. App. at 829 (case dealt with a prescriptive easement and not adverse possession). The courts infer that the use was permissive if, under the circumstances, it is reasonable to assume that the use was permitted. *Id.* If there was permission, the party claiming adverse possession bears the burden of proving that permission terminated because either (1) the servient estate changed hands through death or alienation or (2) the claimant has asserted a hostile right. *Id.*

In deciding whether a claimant was using the land as if it were its own, the courts consider whether the claimant made improvements to the land, whether the claimant maintained the property, and whether the claimant used the land on a regular basis. *See, e.g., Chaplin*, 100 Wn.2d at 855-56; *Timberlane Homeowners Ass'n, Inc. v. Brame*, 79 Wn. App, 303, 310-11, 901 P.2d 1074 (1995). For example, in *Chaplin*, the court held that the claimants were using the land as if it were their own when the claimants built a road across the disputed land, cleared and maintained the disputed land, installed utility lines, and used the area for recreational activities. *Id.* at 855-56. Similarly, in *Timberlane*, the court held that claimants had used land belonging to the homeowners' association as if it was their own when they built and maintained a fence and a concrete patio and the claimants' children played on the land. *Id.* at 310-11.

In deciding whether the claimants' use was permissive, the courts consider whether the parties are related or have a friendly relationship, whether the improvements benefited both the claimants' and the title owners' property, and whether the title owners allowed the claimants to use the land as a neighborly accommodation. *See, e.g., Granston v. Callahan*, 52 Wn. App. 288, 294-95, 759 P.2d 462 (1988); *Miller v. Jarman*, 2 Wn. App.

994, 471 P.2d 704 (1970). For instance, in *Granston*, the court held that the claimants' use was permissive because the original owners of the two parcels were brothers who worked together to build driveways, walkways, and other improvements that benefited both properties. *Id.* at 294-95. Likewise, in *Miller*, the court held that the use was permissive because the title owners had allowed the claimants, who were their neighbors, to use their driveway as a neighborly accommodation. *Id.* at 998. In contrast, in *Lingvall v. Bartmess*, 97 Wn. App. 245, 256, 982 P.2d 690 (1999), the court held that the antagonistic relationship between two brothers negated a finding that the claimant's use of the land was permissive.

In the Garcia case, the court will probably conclude that DNWC's use of Mr. Garcia's land was hostile.

First, the court will probably conclude that DNWC used Mr. Garcia's land as if it were the true owner. Although DNWC did not build any new structures on Mr. Garcia's land, it maintained the campsites, the fire area, the outhouse, and the dock. In addition, although DNWC did not use the property year-round, it did use the property during the summer, which is how a typical owner would have used the land. As a result, this case is similar to *Chaplin* and *Timberlane,* in which the claimants maintained and used the disputed land as a true owner would have used the land. While in *Chaplin* and *Timberlane* the claimants built new structures (in *Chaplin*, the claimants built a road, and in *Timberlane*, they built a fence and a patio), the courts have held that the claimant does not have to do everything that a title owner might do.

Second, the court will probably conclude that DNWC's use of Mr. Garcia's land was not permissive. Unlike *Granston*, in which the parties were related and had a close relationship, there is no evidence that the members of DNWC are related to Mr. Garcia. In addition, unlike *Miller*, in which the title owners allowed their neighbors to use their driveway as a neighborly accommodation, the typical owner of recreational land does not allow a neighboring property owner to use its land several days a week during the peak season.

While Mr. Garcia can argue that the letter that DNWC sent to him establishes that DNWC's use of the land was permissive, the court will probably reject this argument. More likely than not, the court will conclude that, if Mr. Garcia's grandfather gave DNWC permission to use his land, that permission terminated when his grandfather died. In addition, the court will probably conclude that even if DNWC used Mr. Garcia's land with Mr. Garcia's implied permission from the time of his grandfather's death until it sent the letter in February of 2001, that permission terminated in the summer of 2001 when DNWC posted the no trespassing sign and continued to use the property as its own.

Conclusion

More likely than not, DNWC will be able to establish title to Mr. Garcia's land through adverse possession.

To prove that its possession was open and notorious, DNWC needs to show only that Mr. Garcia had actual notice of its use of his land throughout the statutory period or that it used his land in such a way that any reasonable person would have thought that it owned this land. In this case, DNWC can use the letter that it sent to Mr. Garcia to prove that he had actual notice, and it can show that its use of the land for campouts was such that any reasonable person would have thought that DNWC owned the land.

To prove that its possession was actual and uninterrupted, DNWC needs to show only that it actually used the land and that its use was consistent with how the true owner might have used the land. The case law suggests that DNWC's maintenance of the campsites, fire area, outhouse, and dock were sufficient to establish actual possession. In addition, although DNWC used the land only during the summer months, the court is likely to find that such use was uninterrupted because most owners of recreational land use their land only during certain seasons.

To prove that its use of the land was exclusive, DNWC will have to show that it did not share the land with anyone else. Although we could try to argue that DNWC's use was not exclusive because it allowed campers to use the land, this argument is weak because the campers used the land under DNWC's supervision.

Finally, to prove that its use was hostile, DNWC will have to prove that it used the land as if it were its own and that it did not do so with Mr. Garcia's permission. DNWC's maintenance and use of the property is probably sufficient to establish that it used Mr. Garcia's land as if it were its own. In addition, DNWC will be able to prove that its use was not permissive. Even if DNWC's initial use of the property was with Mr. Garcia's grandfather's permission, that permission terminated when Mr. Garcia's grandfather died. In addition, although in its 2001 letter DNWC asked Mr. Garcia for permission to continue using the land, DNWC has a strong argument that it did a hostile act that terminated permission when, even after Mr. Garcia did not respond, it continued maintaining and using the property and it posted the no trespassing sign.

Because all of these elements have been met for the statutory period, which is 10 years, it is likely that a court will decide that DNWC has established a right to title to the land through adverse possession.

§ 11.4.3 Sample E-Memo (For more on e-memos, see Chapter 15)

You asked me to research Illinois law and determine what the statute of limitations is on actions to recover damages to personal property. The applicable statute is 735 ILCS 5/13-205, which states that the statute of limitations is five years:

> [A]ctions on unwritten contracts, expressed or implied, or on awards of arbitration, or *to recover damages for an injury done to property, real or personal*, or to recover the possession of personal property or damages for the detention

or conversion thereof, and all civil actions not otherwise provided for, shall be commenced within 5 years next after the cause of action accrued.

(Emphasis added.)

If you need additional research, please let me know.

§ 11.4.4 Sample E-Memo (For more on e-memos, see Chapter 15)

You have asked me to determine whether KOSLaw LLP, must provide one of its employees, Melissa Karimi, with parental leave under the Family and Medical Leave Act (FMLA.) Specifically, the issue is whether Ms. Karimi's worksite is the firm's Des Moines insourcing office,[3] which has 12 employees, or the firm's Chicago office, which has approximately 175 employees. If Ms. Karimi's worksite is Des Moines, she would not be entitled to leave under the FMLA; if her worksite is Chicago, she is entitled to FMLA leave.

To be entitled to leave under the FMLA, an employee must work for an employer that has 50 or more employees working at worksites that are within a 75-mile radius of one another (50/75 rule). 29 U.S.C. § 2611(2)(B)(ii) (2012) According to the Act's legislative history, Congress included the 50/75 rule to protect employers who might not have enough employees within a particular geographic area to cover FMLA leaves. *See Harbert v. Healthcare Serv. Grp., Inc.*, 391 F.3d 1140, 1149 (10th Cir. 2004).

As a general rule, an employee's worksite is the site to which employee reports to *or*, if the employee does not report to a particular site, the site from which the employee's work is assigned. 29 C.F.R. § 825.111(a) (2013). However, the regulations set out a different test for employees who work from home or who telecommute. In those situations, the employee's worksite is the office where the employee reports *and* from which assignments are given. *Id.* § 825.111(a)(2).

In our case, it is not clear which test applies. Although Ms. Karimi works from home the majority of the time, she does go into the Des Moines office once or twice a week to use the Des Moines office's conferencing technology, to review sensitive documents, or to receive assistance from the IT staff. However, her supervising attorney is in the Chicago office, and she receives her assignment from that attorney and sends her completed work to that attorney, usually via email.

In other cases in which the employee had a connection to more than one worksite, the courts have held that the location of the employee's worksite was a question of fact. *See, e.g., Podkovich v. Glazer's Distrib. of Iowa, Inc.*, 446 F. Supp. 2d 982, 1000-02 (N.D. Iowa 2006) (concluding that there was an issue of fact when a traveling saleswoman physically

---

3. Insourcing is similar to outsourcing. However, instead of sending work to individuals in a different country, the work is sent to individuals who live in another part of the United States.

reported to one worksite but received her assignments from another site); *Collinsworth v. Earthlink/Onemain, Inc.*, CIV.A. 03-2299GTV, 2003 WL 22916461, at *4 (D. Kan. Dec. 4, 2003) (concluding that there was an issue of fact when the plaintiff worked from home, sometimes used a branch office with fewer than 50 people within 75 miles, yet received and delivered her work product to the main office with more than 50 people within 75 miles).

Given the courts' decision in the above cases, if Ms. Karimi files a lawsuit, it is unlikely that a court would grant KOSLaw summary judgment. Instead, the case would have to go to trial, and a jury would have to decide whether the Des Moines or the Chicago office is Ms. Karimi's worksite. If the jury decides that Ms. Karimi reports to the Des Moines office because that is the office that she sometimes uses, that office would be her worksite, and she would not be entitled to FMLA leave. If, however, the jury decides that Ms. Karimi reports to the Chicago office because that it is the office from which she receives her assignments, then she would be entitled to FMLA leave. The result is more uncertain if the jury decides that Ms. Karimi works from home. In that situation, Ms. Karimi's worksite would be the place where she reports to *and* from which she receives her assignments.

Although a jury might find that the Des Moines office is Ms. Karimi's worksite because she "reports" to that office once or twice a week, I recommend that the firm grant Ms. Karimi the leave she has requested. Litigation is expensive, the type of leave that Ms. Karimi is requesting is unpaid leave, and the policy underlying the rule does not apply in this case. Because the Des Moines office is an insourcing office, the work does not need to be done by someone in Des Moines. It can be done by someone in the Chicago office or in any of the firm's other offices.

Please let me know whether you have any more questions or need additional research.

§ 11.4.5   Sample E-Memo (For more on e-memos, see Chapter 15)

TO: Supervising Attorney

FROM: Jessica Burns, Intern

RE: Amanda Nickerson, Admissibility of Prior Convictions for Purpose of Impeachment

You have asked me to determine whether any of Ms. Nickerson's prior convictions can be used to impeach her credibility as a witness in our upcoming products liability trial. I have determined that Ms. Nickerson's conviction for the possession of stolen property is admissible for purposes of impeachment.

The Washington Rules of Evidence state that, for the purpose of attacking the credibility of a witness in a civil case, evidence of a prior criminal conviction can be used to impeach the credibility of a witness if the information is elicited from the witness or established by public record during examination of the witness. ER 609(a). However, evidence of a prior conviction can be used for the purpose of impeachment *only if*

> the crime (1) was punishable by death or imprisonment in excess of 1 year under the law under which the witness was convicted, and the court determines that the probative value of admitting this evidence outweighs the prejudice to the party against whom the evidence is offered, or (2) involved dishonesty or false statement, regardless of the punishment.

ER 609(a)(1)-(2).

The Washington Rules of Evidence have also imposed a time limit on the admissibility of criminal convictions for the purposes of impeachment of a witness:

> [E]vidence of a conviction under this rule is not admissible if a period of more than 10 years has elapsed since the date of the conviction or of the release of the witness from the confinement imposed for that conviction, whichever is the later date, unless the court determines, in the interests of justice, that the probative value of the conviction supported by specific facts and circumstances substantially outweighs its prejudicial effect.

ER 609(b).

1. Assault Charge

Ms. Nickerson's assault charge was an offense punishable by more than one year: Assault in the second degree is punishable by no more than 10 years in prison, RCW 9A.36.021. However, because Ms. Nickerson's assault conviction is more than 10 years old, evidence of the conviction is not admissible unless the court determines that the probative value of the conviction *substantially* outweighs the prejudicial effect of admitting the evidence.

In this case, a products liability case, the prior conviction has no probative value. The fact that Ms. Nickerson committed an assault is not relevant to whether she was injured by a defective product. In addition, the admission of the conviction could be prejudicial because if the jury hears about the conviction, it may view Ms. Nickerson in a less favorable light. Consequently, because the probative value does not outweigh the prejudicial effect, the court is unlikely to admit evidence of the assault conviction.

2. DUI Conviction

The courts have held that a DUI conviction is not admissible for the purposes of impeachment. *State v. Kilgore*, 107 Wn. App. 160, 186, 26 P.3d 308 (2001), *aff'd*, 147 Wn.2d 288 (2002).

3. Possession of Stolen Property

Ms. Nickerson's conviction for possession of stolen property in 2009 could be used to impeach her credibility. Although Ms. Nickerson's conviction for possession of stolen property was not punishable by more than one year in jail, the courts have held that possession of stolen property is admissible because it is a crime of dishonesty. *State v. McKinsey*, 116 Wn.2d 911, 912, 801 P.2d 908 (1991).

In conclusion, it is unlikely that a court would allow the defendant to use either Ms. Nickerson's assault charge or DUI charge to impeach Ms. Nickerson. However, the court could admit Ms. Nickerson's conviction for possession of stolen property.

Please let me know whether you have any additional questions or concerns.

Drafting Memo 1

A lthough you are still a first-year law student, you have just gotten a part-time job at a local law firm. On your first day, your supervising attorney stops by your desk and asks you to help her with one of her cases.

§ 12.1   The Assignment

Assignments come in different shapes and sizes. While sometimes the attorney will give you the facts orally, at other times you may need to find the facts, pulling them from documents in the client's file or from other sources. In this instance, however, the attorney has set out the facts, and the issue that she wants you to research, in the following memo.

To: Legal Intern

From: Christina Galeano

Date: September 9, 2013

Re: Elaine Olsen, Case No. 13-478

Elaine Olsen has requested our help in overturning an order terminating her parental rights.

- Ms. Olsen says she never received the summons and, as a result, did not respond.
- On Wednesday, July 24, 2013, a process server went to Ms. Webster's house and asked for Elaine Olsen. (Ms. Webster is Ms. Olsen's sister.) When Ms. Webster told the process server that "Elaine isn't here today," the process server handed what was probably a summons and complaint to Ms. Webster and told Ms. Webster that Ms. Olsen "needed to go to court."
- On February 1, 2013, Ms. Olsen entered an inpatient drug treatment program in Miami, Florida. She remained in the program until March 27, 2013, when she moved into a "halfway" house. The residential treatment house was a four-bedroom house in a residential neighborhood. Up to eight women live in the house for three to twelve months while they make the transition from inpatient treatment to living on their own. The house is staffed 24/7; staff members provide counseling; enforce house rules, including no drug or alcohol use; and handle administrative duties.
- During April, May, and June, Ms. Olsen was a full-time resident at the residential treatment house. She had a bedroom in the house, ate her meals there, and had some of her possessions there.
- Beginning in July 2013, Ms. Olsen began spending less time at the residential treatment house and more time with her sister, Elizabeth Webster. During July and August 2013, Ms. Olsen usually spent weeknights at the residential treatment house and Friday, Saturday, and Sunday nights at her sister's house. Because she was spending time at her sister's house, Ms. Olsen moved some of her clothing and personal effects into her sister's house.
- Ms. Webster is 32. She will testify that she never gave the summons to her sister. Because she thought that the papers related to some of Ms. Olsen's unpaid bills, she simply put them in a shoebox in the kitchen with a stack of Ms. Olsen's other mail.
- During April and May 2013, Ms. Olsen put the residential treatment house address on employment applications. However, her driver's license showed her sister's address as her address.
- On September 1, 2013, Ms. Olsen moved into her own apartment. Since August 1, 2013, she has worked part-time.
- I looked at the return on the service of process and everything appears to be in order. Thus, please assume that the return of service is regular on its face.
- There is nothing in the record that indicates whether the State tried to personally serve Ms. Olsen or whether it tried to serve her at the residential treatment house.

As the first step, I need to determine whether the service of process is valid under the applicable Florida statute or statutes. Therefore, please research the rules relating to substituted service of process in Florida, and prepare an objective memo in which you set out the applicable rules and apply those rules to the facts of this case.

§ 12.2   Researching the Law

After reading, and rereading, the assignment, your next step is to do the research. Because service of process is governed by a Florida statute, use the research plan set out in Chapter 4 of this book: Researching Issues Governed by State Statutes and Regulations. In addition, see the electronic supplement for step-by-step instructions on how to research an issue governed by a state statute using free sources, Lexis Advance®, WestlawNext™, Bloomberg Law, Lexis.com®, and Westlaw® Classic. You can access the electronic supplement by going to *http://www.aspenlawschool.com/books/oates_legalwritinghandbook/* and clicking on the Chapter 4 links.

> **PRACTICE POINTER**
> You can often research an issue governed by a state statute using free sources: You can find a copy of the applicable statutory sections on the state legislature's website, and you can find copies of cases on Google® Scholar. You will, however, need to cite check using *Shepard's*®, KeyCite®, or BCite. Before doing other research on a fee-based service, get permission from your supervising attorney.

Do not, however, treat research as a separate stage in the process. As you research, read and analyze the statutes and cases that you find, determining whether they help answer the question or questions that you were asked to research. In addition, as soon as possible, begin creating a research log in which you record and organize the information that you find during your research. This log will help guide your research, reminding you of what types of information you need to find, and will serve as an outline for the discussion section of your memo. See the sample set out in Example 1 below.

> **PRACTICE POINTER**
> In your log, be clear about what material is quoted directly and what is paraphrased. Record cites, including pinpoint cites. Finally, come up with a system that tells you when you have cited checked a case. For more on cite checking, see Chapter 10.

| EXAMPLE 1 | **Research Log** |

I. General Rules

A. What are the policies underlying the statute?

The purpose of service of process is to advise the defendant that an action has been commenced and to warn the defendant that he or she must appear in a timely manner to state such defenses as are available.

■ *Torres v. Arnco Constr., Inc.*, 867 So. 2d 583, 586 (Fla. 5th DCA 2004). (Cite checked; still good law.)

It is well settled that the fundamental purpose of service is "to give proper notice to the defendant in the case that he is answerable to the claim of plaintiff and, therefore, to vest jurisdiction in the court entertaining the controversy.

■ *Shurman v. Atl. Mortg. & Inv. Corp.*, 795 So. 2d 952, 953-54 (Fla. 2001) (citing *State ex rel. Merritt v. Heffernan*, 142 Fla. 496, 195 So. 145, 147 (1940)). (Cite checked; still good law.)

B. What is the applicable statute?

Service of original process is made by delivering a copy of it to the person to be served with a copy of the complaint, petition, or other initial pleading or paper or by leaving the copies at his or her usual place of abode with any person residing therein who is 15 years of age or older and informing the person of their contents. . . .

§ 48.031(1)(a), Fla. Stat. (2013). (Cite checked; this is the applicable version of the statute.)

C. What are the elements?

a. the usual place of abode of the person being served
b. with any person residing therein
c. who is 15 years of age or older and
d. informing the person of their contents.

D. Who has the burden of proof?

(1) Excerpt from page 605 in *Thompson v. State, Dep't of Revenue*, 867 So. 2d 603 (Fla. 1st DCA 2004). (Cite checked; still good law.)

"The burden of proof to sustain the validity of service of process is upon the person who seeks to invoke the jurisdiction of the court and, without proper service of process, the court lacks personal jurisdiction over the defendant." *M.J.W. v. Department of Children and Families*, 825 So. 2d 1038, 1041 (Fla. 1st DCA 2002).

[4] [5] "[A] process server's return of service on a defendant which is regular on its face is presumed to be valid absent clear and convincing evidence presented to the contrary." *Telf Corp. v. Gomez*, 671 So. 2d 818 (Fla. 3d DCA 1996). Although simple denial of service is not sufficient, *id.* at 819, Thompson's motion and affidavit are based on the fact that the service did not comply with section 48.031 and was therefore legally deficient. *National Safety Associates, Inc. v. Allstate Insurance Co.*, 799 So. 2d 316, 317 (Fla. 2d DCA 2001). Thompson's affidavit makes a *prima facie* showing that he was not served at his usual place of abode by valid substituted service. . . . Having raised the issue of personal jurisdiction, Thompson's motion and accompanying affidavit placed the burden on the Department to establish the validity of service of process. M.J.W., 825 So. 2d at 1041.

(2) Excerpt from page 958 in *Busman v. State, Dep't of Revenue*, 905 So. 2d 956, 958 (Fla. 3d DCA 2005). (Cite checked; still good law.)

Although the sheriff's return of service, which is regular on its face, is presumptively valid, [footnote omitted] see *Department of Revenue v. Wright*, 813 So. 2d 989, 992 (Fla. 2d DCA 2002); *Fla. Natl. Bank v. Halphen*, 641 So. 2d 495, 496 (Fla. 3d DCA 1994), Busman presented clear, convincing and uncontradicted evidence that the 327 N.W. 4th Avenue address was not his "usual place of abode."

E. Other general rules

"The statutes regulating service of process are to be strictly construed to assure that a defendant is notified of the proceedings." Torres, 867 So. 2d at 586. "Indeed, because statutes authorizing substituted service are exceptions to the general rule requiring a defendant to be served personally, due process requires strict compliance with their statutory requirements." *Id.*

II. Elements

A. Usual place of abode (in dispute)

1. Specific rules (what test do the courts use in determining whether a particular place is a person's usual place of abode?)

(1) Excerpt from page 605 in *Thompson v. State, Dep't of Revenue*, 867 So. 2d 603 (Fla. 1st DCA 2004). (Cite checked; still good law.)

Turning to the merits, "[s]ection 48.031 expressly requires that substituted service be at the person's usual place of abode." *Shurman v. Atl. Mortg. & Inv. Corp.*, 795 So. 2d 952, 954 (Fla. 2001). The requirement "usual place of abode" means "the place where the defendant is actually living at the time of service." *Id., citing State ex rel. Merritt v. Heffernan*, 142 Fla. 496, 195 So. 145, 147 (1940).

(2) Excerpt from page 586 in *Torres v. Arnco Const., Inc.*, 867 So. 2d 583 (Fla. 5th DCA 2004). (Cite checked; still good law.)

In *State ex rel. Merritt v. Heffernan*, 142 Fla. 496, 195 So. 145, 147 (1940), the Florida Supreme Court defined the term "usual place of abode" as the place where the defendant "is actually living at the time of service." The word "abode" means "one's fixed place of residence for the time being when service is made." *Id.* If a person has more than one residence, he must be served at the residence in which he is actually living at the time of service. *Id.*

(3) Excerpt from page 954 in Shurman v. Atl. Mortg. & Inv. Corp., 795 So. 2d 952 (Fla. 2001). (Cite checked; still good law.)

Going one step further, "usual place of abode" is the place where the defendant is actually living at the time of the service. The word abode means one's fixed place of residence for the time being when the service is made. Thus, if a person has several residences, he must be served at the residence in which he is actually living at the time service is made.

2. Analogous cases

■ *State ex rel. Merritt v. Heffernan*, 142 Fla. 496, 195 So. 145, 147 (1940).

Facts are set out on pages 147-48. (Cite checked; still good law.)

The summons was left with the defendant's wife at the family's apartment in Florida an hour after the defendant boarded a train to Minnesota. Although the defendant argued that his usual place of abode was Minnesota, where he had an office, paid taxes, and voted, the court disagreed, noting that the defendant had moved his family to the Florida apartment two months before his wife was served, that the defendant had visited his family at the apartment twice "during the season," and that the defendant's family had remained in Florida for some time after he was served. As the court stated, "We do not hold the view that Florida was the permanent residence of the defendant, but we do feel that in the circumstance reflected in the record, it was his usual place of abode . . . ." *Id.* at 148.

■ *Busman v. State, Dep't of Revenue*, 905 So. 2d 956 (Fla. 3d DCA 2005).

(Facts are on page 958. Cite checked; still good law.)

In a paternity action, service was made on the defendant' half-brother on July 16, 2003. Defendant testified that he had moved out of his half-brother's house on July 1, 2002, and presented lease and landlord's testimony. Although the return of service was regular on its face, the court held that Busman had presented clear, convincing, and uncontradicted evidence that service was not made at his usual place of abode. The court stated that the statute must be strictly construed.

■ *Thompson v. State, Dep't of Revenue*, 867 So. 2d 603 (Fla. 1st DCA 2004).

(Facts are set out at page 605. Cite checked; still good law.)

In a child support case service was made with the defendant's wife. The defendant filed an affidavit stating that he had been separated from his wife for three years and that he not lived at the address where service was made. The court reversed and remanded for an evidentiary hearing.

■ *Torres v. Arnco Const., Inc.*, 867 So. 2d 583 (Fla. 5th DCA 2004).

(Facts are set out at page 587. Cited checked; still good law.)

NY process server tried to serve the defendant at his NY address, where he had lived for 12 years. Although NY neighbors told process server that the defendant lived at the house, they also said that he traveled a lot. Service was then made on the defendant's mother, who lived in Florida. When process server left the papers with defendant's mother, mother said that the defendant "would be home soon, and she would see to it that he received the papers." Majority concluded that the plaintiff had not met its burden of proof and that the mother's statement was ambiguous. The dissent argued that if the defendant spent substantial amounts of time visiting family in Florida the Florida house was his usual place of abode at the time service was made.

3. Ms. Olsen's arguments:

■ On the day that service was made, Ms. Olsen was living not at her sister's house but at the residential treatment house.
■ Service on a relative is not sufficient.
■ Her more permanent address was the residential treatment house address. She had a room, etc., at the residential treatment house.
■ *Heffernan* is an old case.
■ In *Torres*, the court held that the defendant's mother's house was not the defendant's usual place of abode even though the mother indicated that the defendant would be home later.

4. The State's arguments:

■ Ms. Olsen stayed at her sister's house three nights a week.
■ Ms. Olsen apparently received mail at her sister's house—the shoebox.
■ Ms. Olsen listed her sister's address on her driver's license.
■ In *Heffernan*, the court held that the apartment was the defendant's usual place of abode even though the defendant had left the apartment and was on a train back to his permanent residence.
■ In *Torres*, the defendant had a permanent residence where he had lived for 12 years. He was just visiting his mother.

B. Any person residing therein (not in dispute)

■ Service was left with Ms. Webster, who is a person, at Ms. Webster's house.

C. 15 years old or older (not in dispute)

■ Ms. Webster is 32.

D. Informing the person of their contents (in dispute)

1. Specific rules (what test do the courts use in determining whether the process server informed the person being served of the contents of the documents?)
2. Analogous cases
3. Ms. Olsen's arguments
4. State's arguments

§ 12.3   Understanding What You Have Found

§ 12.3.1   Make Sure You Understand the Big Picture

Your first step should be a step back. Can you place the issue that you were asked to research into the bigger picture? For instance, in the Olsen case, do you understand how service of process relates to jurisdiction and how jurisdiction relates to whether the court had the power to enter a default judgment? If you don't, don't panic. The law is complicated, and neither professors nor employers expect first-, second-, or even third-year students to have a complete understanding of how the system works. However, both professors and employers expect students to look for answers and, if they can't find them, to ask questions.

§ 12.3.2 Make Sure You Understand the Statute

Once you understand the big picture, make sure you understand the statute. In particular, make sure you understand the requirements, or elements, and that you have looked for statutory sections that explain the statute's purpose and that define terms used in the statute. In addition, if the statute is a complicated one, take the time to diagram the statute.

In the example problem, the applicable statute is Fla. Stat. § 48.031(a)(1) (2013), which reads as follows:

> Service of original process is made by delivering a copy of it to the person to be served with a copy of the complaint, petition, or other initial pleading or paper or by leaving the copies at his or her usual place of abode with any person residing therein who is 15 years of age or older and informing the person of their contents. . . .

A close reading of the statute reveals that service can be accomplished in either of two ways: (1) by delivering a copy of the summons, complaint, petition, or other initial pleading or paper to the person to be served or (2) by leaving a copy of those documents at the person's usual place of abode with a person who resides there who is 15 years old or older and by informing the person with whom the documents are left of their contents.

Note that in this instance there is an "or" between the (1) and the (2) but that there is an "and" between the "c" and the "d." While you can accomplish service of process either by delivering the summons to the person being served or by leaving it at his or her usual place of abode, if you leave it at the person's usual place of abode, you must leave the summons with a person who is residing therein, that person must be 15 years old or older, and you must inform the person with whom you leave the documents of their contents.

Also note that, in some instances, the statutory language will be ambiguous. Some of these ambiguities are the result of poor drafting; some may, however, be intentional. To get enough votes to enact the legislation, the drafters may have intentionally used vague language. Don't despair. You will often be able to use these ambiguities to make an argument on behalf of your client.

> **PRACTICE POINTER** There is often more than one way to list the elements. For example, you can list "any person residing therein" and "who is 15 years of age or older" as separate elements, or you can combine these two elements and treat them as one: "any person residing therein who is 15 years of age or older." In deciding whether to combine elements, look at how the cases have listed the elements (do they separate or combine them?) and think about whether, in your memo, it make more sense to treat the requirements as separate elements or one element.

§ 12.3.3   Make Sure You Understand the General and Specific Rules

In addition to reading the statute carefully, read carefully those portions of the cases that are relevant to the issue you were asked to research. For more on legal reading, see Chapter 3.

Begin by focusing on the cases that have set out general rules, that is, the cases that have listed the elements, the cases that have set out the rules relating to the burden of proof, and the cases that have explained the policies underlying the statute. For example, in researching the sample problem, we found several cases that set out the rules relating to the burden of proof.

If all of the cases set out the same rule, all you need to do is make sure that you understand that rule. If, however, different cases set out different rules, you need to determine which of those rules governs. To do this, begin by cite checking the cases. If one or more of the cases have been reversed or overruled on the point of law for which you are looking at the case, do not use those cases. They are no longer good law.

If the remaining cases, that is, the cases that are still good law, set out the same rule, use that rule. If, though, there is still a discrepancy, try to resolve that discrepancy by looking to see if different rules apply in different types of cases (for example, is there a different rule in child custody cases than there is in contract cases?); whether different divisions apply different rules (for example, does the 1st DCA apply one rule and the 3d DCA apply a different rule?); or whether the rule seems to be evolving.

In our example case, all of the cases seem to set out the same rule of law. Although it takes some careful reading to determine what that rule is, the rule seems to be as follows:

1. The party who is seeking to invoke the jurisdiction of the court (the plaintiff) has the burden of proving that the service was valid.
2. If, however, the "return of service" is regular on its face, service is presumed to be valid.
3. Thus, if the "return of service" is regular on its face, the party challenging the validity of the service (the defendant) must present clear and convincing evidence that the service is invalid.

> **PRACTICE POINTER**
>
> When you are not sure what a particular word or phrase means, take a few minutes to look up the definition. For example, if you are not sure what the phrase "return of service" means, look up that phrase. If you are online, the easiest way to find a definition is to go to Bing or Google and type in the word "definition" and the phrase "return of service." When you do, you will be taken to a site like thefreedictionary.com, which provides plain English definitions for legal terms. In this instance, the website sets out the following definition for "return of service": "n. Written confirmation from a process server under oath that declares that the legal documents were served (such as a summons and complaint)." Although you should not cite to this type of dictionary in a memo or brief, you can use this type of dictionary to help you understand terms used in a statute or case.

Accordingly, in our example problem, because the return is regular on its face, Ms. Olsen would have to present clear and convincing evidence that the service was not valid.

> **PRACTICE POINTER**
>
> If several cases set out the same rule, you will usually want to cite a recent case from the jurisdiction's highest court as authority for that rule. For instance, in our sample case, you would want to cite to a recent Florida Supreme Court case. If there is not a recent case from the jurisdiction's highest court, you can cite to an older case from the jurisdiction's highest court and then to a more recent decision from an intermediate court of appeals. The exception to this "rule" is when the rule is known by the name of the case that announced it. For example, if you are setting out the *Miranda* rule, cite to *Miranda v. Arizona*, 384 U.S. 436 (1966), and not to a more recent United States Supreme Court case.

Once you understand the general rules, turn your attention to the specific rules, that is, the rules that the courts apply in determining whether a particular element, or requirement, is met. For instance, in the Olsen case, look at the rules that the courts apply in determining whether the service was made at the defendant's usual place of abode. Do all of the cases set out the same rule? If they do not set out the same rule, are some of the cases no longer good law?

If all of the cases are still good law, is there a way of reconciling the various rules?

Once you understand the big picture and have a good understanding of both the general and specific rules, it is time to start writing. As you do this writing, keep two things in mind. First, writing a memo is usually a multi-step process. If you want to do a good job, you will need to do a first draft, a second draft, and maybe even a third or fourth draft. As a consequence, do not put off writing the first draft until the night before the final draft is due. Second, most of the time drafting a memo involves more than recording completely formed ideas and arguments. Most law students and attorneys find that they rethink their analysis and synthesis as they write. Consequently, do not be surprised if, part way through writing the first draft, you have one of those "aha!" moments in which you see the issue, the law, or an argument in a different light.

The rest of this chapter walks you through the process of writing the memo. Although we discuss the sections in the order in which they appear in a formal memo, you do not have to write the sections in order. For example, many law students and attorneys find that it works better to write the first draft of the discussion section before they write the first draft of the statement of facts, issue statement, and brief answer.

Chapter 12 Quiz No. 1

Draft answers for each of the following questions. Make your points clearly and concisely, and write sentences that are easy to read and that are grammatical and correctly punctuated.

1. How will keeping a research log like the one set out in Example 1 on page 134 help you research and write a memo?
2. What is an element?
3. What is the difference between burden of proof and standard of review?
4. What is the difference between a general rule and a specific rule?
5. If more than one case sets out the applicable rule, what factors should you consider in deciding which case or cases to cite as authority for that rule?

§ 12.4   Drafting the Heading

The heading is the easiest section to write. It consists of only four entries: the name of the person to whom the memo is addressed, the name of the person who wrote the memo, the date, and an entry identifying the client and the issue or issues discussed in the memo. Although the first three entries are self-explanatory, the fourth needs some explanation.

In some firms, the memo is filed only in the client's file. For such firms, the "Re:" entry can be quite general.

EXAMPLE 1   **Sample Heading**

To: Christina Galeano

From: Legal Intern

Date: September 9, 2013

Re: Elaine Olsen, Case No. 13-478

In other firms, the memo is filed not only in the client's file but also in a "memo bank"—that is, a computer or paper file in which all memos are filed by topic. In these offices, the "Re:" section serves two purposes: (1) within the client's file, it distinguishes the memo from other memos that have been or will be written, and (2) in the memo bank, it provides either the database for a word search or topic categories under which the memo will be filed. To serve this last purpose, the heading should include the key terms.

EXAMPLE 2   **Sample Heading**

To: Christina Galeano

From: Legal Intern

Date: September 9, 2013

Re: Elaine Olsen, Case No. 13-478
          Service of Process, Usual Place of Abode; Notification of Contents

---

§ 12.5   Drafting the Statement of Facts

Just as every case starts with a story, so does every memo. Therefore, in most instances, begin your memo by telling your supervising attorney who did what when.

§ 12.5.1   Decide What Facts to Include

In a typical statement of facts, there are three types of facts: the legally significant facts, the emotionally significant facts, and the background facts. In addition, in some instances you will want to identify the facts that are not yet known.

a.   Legally Significant Facts

A legally significant fact is a fact that a court would consider in deciding whether a statute or rule is applicable or that a court would use in applying that statute or rule. For instance, in the Olsen case, the legally significant facts are those facts that the court would consider in determining whether service of process was valid. More specifically, the legally significant facts are the facts that the court would consider in determining (1) whether the summons was left at the defendant's usual place of abode, (2) whether the summons was left with a person residing therein who is 15 years old or older, and (3) whether the process server notified the person being served of the contents of the documents. Because a change in one of the legally significant facts could change your analysis and prediction, you should include all of the legally significant facts in your statement of facts.

You can use either of two techniques to determine whether a fact is legally significant. Before you write the discussion section, you can prepare a two-column chart in which you list the elements in the first column and the facts that relate to those elements in the second column. See Exhibit 12.1.

Exhibit 12.1	Determining Which Facts Are Legally Significant
Element	**Facts Related to Element**
Usual Place of Abode	Ms. Webster told the process server that "Elaine isn't here today." On February 1, 2013, Ms. Olsen entered an inpatient drug treatment program in Miami. She remained in the program until March 27, 2013, when she moved into a residential treatment house for recovering addicts. During April, May, and June 2013, Ms. Olsen was a full-time resident at the residential treatment house. She had a bedroom in the house, ate her meals there, and had some of her possessions there. Beginning in July 2013, Ms. Olsen began spending less time at the residential treatment house and more time with her sister, Elizabeth Webster. During July and August 2013, Ms. Olsen spent weeknights at the residential treatment house and Friday, Saturday, and Sunday nights at her sister's house. Because she was spending time at her sister's house, she moved some of her clothing and personal effects into her sister's house. During April and May 2013, Ms. Olsen put the residential treatment house address on employment applications. However, her driver's license showed her sister's address as her address. On September 1, 2013, Ms. Olsen moved into her own apartment.

Element	Facts Related to Element
	The return on the service of process appears to be in order.
	The service was made on Wednesday, July 24, 2013.
	At this point there is no evidence indicating that the state tried to serve Ms. Olsen at the treatment house.
Person Residing Therein Who Is 15 Years Old or Older	Ms. Webster lives in the house where the summons was left.
	Ms. Webster is 32.
Element	**Facts Related to Element**
Informing Person of Contents	The process server handed what was probably a summons and complaint to Ms. Webster and told Ms. Webster that Ms. Olsen "needed to go to court."

The second technique is used after the discussion section has been completed. To ensure that you have included all of the legally significant facts in your statement of facts, go through your discussion section, checking to make sure that each of the facts that you used in setting out the arguments is in your statement of facts. If you used a fact in the analysis, that fact is legally significant and should be included in the statement of facts.

PRACTICE POINTER	Remember, writing a memo is a recursive process. Even though you may write the statement of facts first, you may need to revise it after you have completed the discussion section.

b. Emotionally Significant Facts

An emotionally significant fact is one that, while not legally significant, may affect the way the judge or jury decides the case.

For example, in the Olsen case, while it is not legally significant that Ms. Olsen was in a drug treatment program, that fact may color the way the judge views her. Therefore, this fact is an emotionally significant fact and should be included in the statement of facts. In addition, while it is not legally significant that Ms. Olsen got a job, that fact may also color the way in which the judge views her and should, therefore, be included in the statement of facts.

c. Background Facts

In addition to including the legally and emotionally significant facts, also include those facts that are needed to tell the story and that provide the context for the legally and emotionally significant facts.

d.   Unknown Facts

Sometimes you are not given all of the facts needed to analyze an issue. For instance, because the attorney did not know the law, he or she may not have asked the right questions, or the documents containing the unknown facts are in the possession of the opposing party. If the unknown facts are legally significant and you can obtain them, try to do so before writing the memo. If, however, the unknown facts are not legally significant or if you cannot obtain them, write the memo, but tell the attorney, either in the statement of facts, the discussion section, or the conclusion what facts are unknown.

| **PRACTICE POINTER** | You may not realize a fact is unknown until you have read the cases. For instance, in the example problem, at the time that she interviewed Ms. Olsen, the attorney did not ask Ms. Olsen whether |

the process server had tried to serve her at the residential treatment house or on any other occasions. However, after doing the research, you know that these facts may be legally significant.

§ 12.5.2   Select an Organizational Scheme

As a general rule, begin your statement of facts with an introductory sentence or paragraph that identifies the parties and the issue. Then present the facts using one of three organizational schemes: a chronological organizational scheme, a topical organizational scheme, or a combination of the two, for example, a scheme in which you organize the facts by topic and then, within each topic, you set out the facts in chronological order.

Most of the time, the facts dictate which organizational scheme will work best. If the case involves a series of events related by date, then the facts should be presented chronologically. If, however, there are a number of facts that are not related by date (for example, the description of several different pieces of property) or a number of unrelated events that occurred during the same time period (for example, four unrelated crimes committed by the defendant over the same two-day period), the facts should be organized by topic.

Sometimes, though, the facts can be presented in more than one way. For example, in the Olsen case, the facts can be presented using either a scheme that is primarily chronological or a scheme that is primarily topical. See Examples 1 and 2.

| **EXAMPLE 1** | **Statement of Facts with Facts Presented in Chronological Order** |

Elaine Olsen has contacted our office asking for assistance in overturning a judgment terminating her parental rights. You have asked me to determine whether the service of process was valid.

On February 1, 2013, Ms. Olsen entered an inpatient drug treatment program in Miami, Florida. She remained in the program until March 27, 2013, when she moved into a residential treatment house for recovering addicts.

During April, May, and June 2013, Ms. Olsen was a full-time resident at the treatment house. She had a bedroom in the house, ate her meals there, and had some of her possessions there. In addition, when she applied for jobs, she listed the treatment house address as her address.

Beginning in July 2013, Ms. Olsen began spending less time at the treatment house and more time with her sister, Elizabeth Webster, who is 32. Both Ms. Olsen's sister and the manager of the residential treatment house will testify that, during July and August 2013, Ms. Olsen spent weeknights at the residential treatment house and Friday, Saturday, and Sunday nights at her sister's house. Because she was spending time at her sister's house, Ms. Olsen moved some of her clothing and personal effects into her sister's house.

On Wednesday, July 24, 2013, a process server went to Ms. Webster's house and asked for Elaine Olsen. When Ms. Webster told the process server that "Elaine isn't here today," the process server handed the summons to Ms. Webster and told her that Ms. Olsen "needed to go to court."

Ms. Webster will testify that she never gave the summons to her sister. Because she thought that the papers related to some of Ms. Olsen's unpaid bills, she simply put the summons in a shoebox in the kitchen with a stack of Ms. Olsen's other mail. Ms. Olsen says she never received the summons and, as a result, did not respond. The return of service is regular on its face.

Ms. Olsen has been employed since August 1, 2013, and she has lived in her own apartment since September 1, 2013. She has her sister's address on her driver's license.

There is nothing in the record that indicates whether the State tried to personally serve Ms. Olsen or whether it tried to serve her at the residential treatment house.

| EXAMPLE 2 | **Statement of Facts with Facts Organized by Topic** |

You have asked me to determine whether the service of process on one of our clients, Elaine Olsen, is valid.

During the past six months, Ms. Olsen has lived in three places. From February 1, 2013, until March 27, 2013, Ms. Olsen was a patient in an in-patient drug treatment program in Miami, Florida. On March 27, 2013, she moved into a residential treatment house for recovering addicts. During April, May, and June, Ms. Olsen was a full-time resident at the treatment house. She had a bedroom in the house, ate her meals there, and had some of her possessions there. In addition, Ms. Olsen listed the treatment house address on job applications. Beginning in July 2013, Ms. Olsen began spending more time at her sister's house. During July and August 2013, Ms. Olsen spent weeknights at the treatment house and Friday, Saturday, and Sunday nights at her sister's house. Because she was spending time at her sister's house, Ms. Olsen moved some of her clothing and personal effects into her sister's house. Ms. Olsen has her sister's address on her driver's license.

On Wednesday, July 24, 2013, a process server went to Ms. Olsen's sister's house and asked for Elaine Olsen. When Ms. Olsen's sister, Ms. Webster, told the process server that "Elaine isn't here today," the process server handed the summons to Ms. Webster and told her that Ms. Olsen "needed to go to court."

Ms. Webster, who is 32, will testify that she never gave the summons to her sister. Because she thought that the papers related to some of Ms. Olsen's unpaid bills, she simply put the summons in a shoebox in the kitchen with a stack of Ms. Olsen's other mail. Ms. Olsen says she never received the summons and complaint, and as a result, she did not respond.

You have asked me to presume that the return of service is regular on its face. There is nothing in the record that indicates whether the State tried to personally serve Ms. Olsen or whether it tried to serve her at the residential treatment house.

PRACTICE POINTER	If you are using a chronological organizational scheme, you can signal that fact to your readers by starting the sentence that follows your introduction with a date. In contrast, if you are using a topical organizational scheme, try to use topic sentences that identify the topics. Do not, however, include law or argue the facts in the statement of facts; save that material for the discussion section.

§ 12.5.3   Present the Facts Clearly and Concisely

Most attorneys prefer statements of facts that are short and to the point. This does not, however, mean that they want the facts set out using bullet points. While bullet points are common in some types of business writing, most attorneys want the facts presented in easy-to-read sentences in well-constructed paragraphs. (For more on writing effective sentences and paragraphs, see Chapters 22, 23, and 24.)

Well-written sentences and paragraphs have several advantages over bullet points. First, most readers have an easier time understanding what happened when the facts are presented in the form of a "story." The narrative quality of a story helps readers understand who the actors are and the sequence of events. Second, setting out the facts in story form makes it easier to use the statement of facts in the memo to write the summary of facts for a letter to the client or the statement of the case for a brief.

§ 12.5.4   Present the Facts Accurately and Objectively

In writing the statement of facts for an objective memorandum, present the facts accurately and objectively. Do not include facts that are not in your file, and do not set out legal conclusions, misstate facts, leave out facts that are legally significant, or present the facts so that they favor one side over the other. In Example 3, the writer has violated all of these "rules."

PRACTICE POINTER	You set out a legal conclusion when you set out as a fact that one of the elements or rules is met or is not met. Whether an element or rule is or is not met is a legal conclusion and not a fact.

EXAMPLE 3	**Writer Has Not Presented the Facts Accurately and Objectively**

Hoping to obtain a default judgment against Ms. Olsen, the plaintiff had the sheriff serve the summons and petition at Ms. Olsen's sister's house and not at the residential treatment house where Ms. Olsen was actually living. Although Ms. Olsen occasionally visited her sister at her sister's house, she did not keep any of her personal belongings at her sister's house.

In the first sentence, the writer violates the first two rules. First, she sets out facts that are not in the record when she states that the plaintiff hoped to get a default judgment and when she states that the plaintiff had a sheriff serve Ms. Olsen at her sister's house and not at the residential treatment house. Second, she sets out legal conclusions when she states that the defendant was actually living at the residential treatment house. Because a person's usual place of abode is the place where the defendant is actually living, in the context of this case, the statement that the defendant was actually living in the residential treatment house is a legal conclusion.

In the second sentence, the writer violates the last three rules. The writer misstates the facts when she states that Ms. Olsen did not keep any personal belongings at her sister's house; she leaves out legally significant facts when she does not include the fact that Ms. Olsen had her sister's address on her driver's license; and she presents the facts in a light favorable to her client when she states that Ms. Olsen visited her sister only occasionally.

> **PRACTICE POINTER**
>
> As a general rule, do not refer to individuals by their first names only. Instead, use the appropriate title and family name. For instance, instead of referring to Elaine Olsen as "Elaine," use "Elaine Olsen" or "Ms. Olsen." For information on bias-free language, see section 25.4.

§ 12.5.5　Checklist for Critiquing the Statement of Facts

a.　Content

- The writer has included all of the legally significant facts.
- When appropriate, the writer included emotionally significant facts.
- The writer included enough background facts that a person not familiar with the case can understand what happened.
- The writer has identified the unknown facts.
- The writer presented the facts accurately.
- The writer presented the facts objectively.
- The writer has not included legal conclusions in the statement of facts.

b.　Organization

- The writer has included an introductory sentence or paragraph that identifies the parties and the nature of the dispute.
- The writer has used one of the conventional organizational schemes: chronological, topical, or a combination of chronological and topical.

c.　Writing

- The attorney can understand the facts of the case after reading the statement of facts once.
- The paragraph divisions are logical, and the paragraphs are neither too long nor too short. See Chapter 22.

- Transitions and dovetailing have been used to make the connection between ideas clear. See Chapter 23.
- In most sentences, the writer has used the actor as the subject of the sentence, and the subject and verb are close together. See sections 24.1 through 24.5.
- The writer has varied the length of the sentences and the sentence patterns so that each sentence flows smoothly from the prior sentence. See section 24.5.
- The writing is concise and precise. See sections 25.1 and 25.2.
- The writing is grammatically correct and correctly punctuated. See Chapters 27 and 28.
- The statement of facts has been proofread.

§ 12.6   Drafting the Issue Statement

It is not unusual for students to ask whether they really need to include an issue statement in their memo. Doesn't the attorney know the issue? The answer to both questions is yes. However, even though your supervising attorney told you what issue to research, you should include an issue statement.

You should include an issue statement, or question presented, because, by convention, formal memos have an issue statement. While at first it may seem as if writing a formal statement of the issue is a waste of time, the opposite is often true. Writing an issue statement provides you the opportunity to do more sophisticated analysis: Given your research, what is the applicable law? What is the legal question? What are the most important facts?

As a general rule, you should have the same number of issue statements as you have "parts" to the discussion section. Accordingly, if you have three issue statements — (1) whether service of process was valid, (2) whether the statute of limitations has run, and (3) whether the defendant is entitled to judgment as a matter of law — you should also have three parts to the discussion section, one corresponding to each of the three issues. If, however, you have only one issue statement, for example, whether service of process is valid, your discussion section will have only one part.

> **PRACTICE POINTER**   As a general rule, do not treat each element as a separate issue. For example, if the issue is whether the service of process was valid, do not treat the first element, usual place of abode, as one issue; the second element, person residing therein who is 15 or older, as a second issue; and the third element, informing about the contents, as a third issue.

Convention also dictates that in a multi-issue memo you list the issues in the same order in which you discuss those issues in the discussion section. The first issue statement will correspond to the first part of the discussion section, the second will correspond to the second part, and so on.

In this chapter we describe how to write an issue statement using the "under-does-when" format. In the next chapter, we describe the "whether" format.

§ 12.6.1 Select a Format: The "Under-Does-When" Format

The under-does-when format is easy to use because the format forces you to include all of the essential information. After the "under," insert a reference to the applicable law; after the verb (for example, "does," "is," or "may"), insert the legal question; and after "when," insert the most important of the legally significant facts. Because the format is written as a question, place a question mark at the end.

Under [insert reference to applicable law]
does/is/may [insert legal question]
when [insert the key facts]?

a. Reference to the Applicable Law

To be useful to the reader, the reference to the rule of law cannot be too specific or too general. For example, a reference to "Florida law" is too broad; hundreds of cases are filed each year in which the issue is governed by Florida law.

EXAMPLE 1   **Reference to the Rule of Law Too General**

Under Florida law, . . .

EXAMPLE 2   **Appropriate References**

Under Florida's service of process statute, . . .
Under Florida's service of process statute, § 48.031 Fla. Stat. (2013), . . .

If you identify the statute in your statement of the legal question, you can refer to the statute by number in your reference to the rule of law. For example, in some instances, the following format works well: "Under § 48.031 Fla. Stat. (2013), was service of process valid when . . . ."

b. Statement of the Legal Question

After identifying the applicable law, set out the legal question. In doing so, make sure that your statement of the legal question is neither too narrow nor too broad. If stated too narrowly, your statement of the legal question will not cover all of the issues and subissues; if stated too broadly, the question does not serve its function of focusing the reader's attention on the real issue.

PRACTICE POINTER	Although we refer to this format as the "under-does-when" format, you do not need to use "does" as the verb. As the following examples illustrate, a number of different verbs can work.

EXAMPLE 3   Legal Questions That Are Too Narrow

■ Was the summons left at Ms. Olsen's usual place of abode when . . . ?
■ Was the summons left at the place where Ms. Olsen was actually living when . . . ?
■ Did the process server inform Ms. Webster about the contents of the summons when . . . ?

EXAMPLE 4   Legal Questions That Are Too Broad

■ Did the court properly terminate Ms. Olsen's parental rights when . . . ?
■ Were Ms. Olsen's rights violated when . . . ?

EXAMPLE 5   Legal Questions That Are Properly Framed

■ Was service valid when . . . ?
■ Was Ms. Olsen properly served when . . . ?
■ Was service at Ms. Olsen's sister's house valid when . . . ?
■ Was the substituted service on the defendant's sister at the sister's house valid when . . . ?

---

c.   The Key Facts

Unless the issue that you have been asked to research involves only a question of law, end your issue statement by setting out the key facts. How will the court apply the rule of law to the facts in your client's case?

How many facts you include depends on how many facts are legally significant. If there are only a few legally significant facts, you will usually want to include all of them. If, however, there are a large number of legally significant facts, be selective. Either list only the most important of the legally significant facts, or list only the facts that relate to the disputed element or elements.

In Example 6, the writer has not included enough facts: While he has included the facts that the court would consider in deciding whether the process server informed the person served of the contents of the documents, he has not included facts that the court would consider in deciding whether the summons was left at Ms. Olsen's usual place of abode with a person 15 years or older residing therein.

EXAMPLE 6   Writer Has Not Included Enough Facts

Under Florida's service of process statute, § 48.031, Fla. Stat. (2013), was the service valid when the process server told Ms. Webster that Ms. Olsen "needed to go to court"?

In contrast, in Example 7, the writer has included too many facts. As a result, the issue statement is so long that some attorneys would not read it.

EXAMPLE 7　　**Writer Has Included Too Many Facts**

Under Florida's service of process statute, was substituted service on Ms. Olsen's sister at the sister's house valid when (1) Ms. Olsen was a patient in an inpatient drug treatment program in Miami from February 1, 2013, until March 27, 2013; (2) Ms. Olsen moved into a residential treatment house for recovering addicts on March 27, 2013; (3) during April, May, and June 2013, Ms. Olsen was a full-time resident at the residential treatment house, where she had a bedroom, where she ate her meals, and where she had some possessions; (4) during April and May 2013, Ms. Olsen listed the residential treatment house address on job applications; (5) beginning in July 2013, Ms. Olsen began spending less time at the residential treatment house and more time with her sister, Ms. Webster; (6) during July and August 2013, Ms. Olsen usually spent weeknights at the residential treatment house and Friday, Saturday, and Sunday nights at her sister's house; (7) on July 24, 2013, a process server went to Ms. Webster's house and asked for Elaine Olsen; (8) when Ms. Webster told the process server that "Elaine isn't here today," the process server handed the summons to Ms. Webster and told her that Ms. Olsen "needed to go to court"; and (9) Ms. Webster is 32 years old and lives at the house where she received the summons?

Examples 8 and 9 are better: They include the key facts without going into too much detail.

EXAMPLE 8　　**Better Example**

Under Florida's service of process statute, was Ms. Olsen properly served when (1) during the month when service was made, Ms. Olsen spent weeknights at a residential treatment house and spent Friday, Saturday, and Sunday nights at her sister's house; (2) Ms. Olsen listed the address of the residential treatment house on job applications but her sister's address on her driver's license; (3) service was made on Ms. Olsen's 32-year-old sister on a Wednesday at Ms. Olsen's sister's house; (4) the process server told Ms. Olsen's sister that Ms. Olsen needed to go to court; and (5) Ms. Olsen's sister did not give the summons to Ms. Olsen, and Ms. Olsen states that she did not receive notice?

EXAMPLE 9　　**Better Example**

Under Florida's statute authorizing substituted service of process, was service on the defendant's adult sister at the sister's house valid when the defendant spent weeknights at a residential treatment house and weekends at her sister's house; when the service was made on a weekday; when the process server told the defendant's sister that the defendant "needed to go to court"; and when the defendant states that she did not receive notice?

PRACTICE POINTER　　While some attorneys will want you to "personal-ize" your issue statements by using the parties' names, other attorneys will want you to write issue statements that are more generic. Compare Example 8 in which the writer used Ms. Olsen's name with Example 9 in which the writer uses the words, "the defendant."

In setting out the facts, make sure you set out facts and not legal conclusions. While what is a fact and what is a legal conclusion will vary from case to case, saying or implying that an element is or is not met will always be a legal conclusion. In Example 10, the writer has set out legal conclusions. Instead of setting out the facts that the court would consider in deciding whether an element is met, she has simply listed the elements.

EXAMPLE 10   **Writer Has Incorrectly Set Out Legal Conclusions Rather Than Facts**

Under Florida's statute authorizing substituted service of process, was the service valid when the process server left the summons with a person of suitable age and discretion at one of the defendant's usual places of abode and told the person about the contents of the notice?

Finally, make sure that you set out the facts accurately and objectively. Do not misstate a fact, and do not include only those facts that favor your client. While in a brief to a court you will want to present the facts in the light most favorable to your client, in an office memo you need to be objective.

EXAMPLE 11   **Writer Has Not Set Out Facts Accurately and Objectively**

Under Florida's service of process statute, was the service invalid when (1) at the time that service was made, Ms. Olsen's permanent residence was a residential treatment house where she had a room, ate meals, and kept belongings; (2) Ms. Olsen listed the residential treatment house address on job applications; (3) the process server did not tell Ms. Olsen's sister that the State was planning to terminate Ms. Olsen's parental rights; and (4) Ms. Olsen's sister did not give the summons to Ms. Olsen, and Ms. Olsen states that she did not receive notice?

---

§ 12.6.2 Make Sure That Your Issue Statement Is Easy to Read

It is not enough to include the right information in your issue statement. You must also present that information in such a way that your issue statement is easy to read.

The "under-does-when" format helps you write a readable issue statement by forcing you to use the three slots in a sentence: the reference to the rule of law goes into the introductory phrase or clause, the legal question goes into the main clause, and the key facts go into a list of "when" clauses at the end of the sentence.

_____,_____ _____?

introductory phrase or clause,   main clause   "when" clauses

You can also make your issue statement easier to read by using the active voice and concrete subjects and action verbs. See sections 24.1 through 24.4.

Finally, in listing the key facts, use parallel constructions for each item in the list and, when appropriate, use enumeration. See section 27.7.

PRACTICE POINTER	End issue statements written using the "under-does-when" format with a question mark. End issue statements written using the "whether" format, which is discussed in Chapter 13, with a period.

§ 12.6.3 Checklist for Critiquing the Issue Statement

a. Content

- The reference to the rule of law is neither too broad nor too narrow.
- The legal question is properly focused.
- The most significant of the legally significant facts have been included.
- Legal conclusions have not been set out as facts.

b. Format

- The writer has used one of the conventional formats, for example, the "under-does-when" format or the "whether" format.

c. Writing

- The issue statement is easy to read and understand.
- In setting out the legal question, the writer has used a concrete subject and an action verb. See sections 24.1 through 24.3.
- In listing the facts, the writer has used parallel constructions for all of the items in the list. See section 27.7.
- If the list of facts is long, the writer has used enumeration or has repeated key structural cues, for example, words like "when" and "that."

§ 12.7   Drafting the Brief Answer

The brief answer serves a purpose similar to that served by the formal conclusion: it tells the attorney how you think a court will decide an issue and why. The brief answer is not, however, as detailed as the formal conclusion.

§ 12.7.1 Select a Format

Convention dictates that, in a formal memo, you should include a separate brief answer for each issue statement. In addition, convention dictates that you should start each of your brief answers with a one- or two-word short answer. The words that are typically used are "probably," and "probably not." After this one- or two-word answer, briefly explain your answer.

§ 12.7.2 Set Out Your Conclusion and Reasoning

In writing your brief answers, keep a couple of things in mind. First, remember your audience and purpose. You are writing to an attorney who needs an objective evaluation of the client's case. Second, make sure that you answer the question you set out in your issue statement and that you match the style you used in your issue statement. For example, if you used the parties' names in your issue statement, also use them in your brief answer. Third, be specific. Tell the attorney which elements you or the other side will or will not be able to prove. Finally, make sure that you get the burden of proof right. If you have personalized your issue statement and your client has the burden of proof, talk about what your client can and cannot prove. If, however, the other side has the burden of proof, talk about what it can and cannot prove. In contrast, if you wrote a more generic issue statement, talk about what the court will do.

EXAMPLE 1   **Issue Statement and Brief Answer in Which the Writer Uses the Parties' Names**

Issue

Under Florida's service of process statute, was Ms. Olsen properly served when (1) during the month when service was made, Ms. Olsen spent weeknights at a residential treatment house and spent Friday, Saturday, and Sunday nights at her sister's house; (2) Ms. Olsen listed the address of the residential treatment house on job applications but her sister's address on her driver's license; (3) service was made on Ms. Olsen's 32-year-old sister on a Wednesday at Ms. Olsen's sister's house; (4) the process server told Ms. Olsen's sister that Ms. Olsen needed to go to court; and (5) Ms. Olsen's sister did not give the summons to Ms. Olsen, and Ms. Olsen states that she did not receive notice?

Brief Answer

Probably not. Because the return is regular on its face, Ms. Olsen has the burden of proving that she was not properly served. Because the summons and petition were left with Ms. Olsen's 32-year-old sister at the sister's house, Ms. Olsen will have to concede that service was made on a person 15 years or older who was living at the house at which the service was made. In addition, because the process server told Ms. Olsen's sister that Ms. Olsen needed to go to court, more likely than not the court will decide that the person served was informed of the contents of the documents. However, because Ms. Olsen can present evidence that establishes that she was staying at the residential treatment house on the day that service was made, the court may decide that the summons and petition were not left at Ms. Olsen's usual place of abode.

EXAMPLE 2   **Issue Statement and Brief Answer in Which the Writer Does Not Use the Parties' Names**

Issue

Under Florida's statute authorizing substituted service of process, was service at the defendant's adult sister's house valid when the defendant spent weeknights at a residential treatment house and weekends at her sister's house; the service was made on a Wednesday; the process server told the defendant's sister that the defendant "needed to go to court"; and the defendant states that she did not receive notice?

Brief Answer

Probably not. The court will conclude that the service was made on a person 15 years old or older living at the place where service was made and that the process server informed the person served of the contents of the documents. However, the court will probably conclude that the service was not made at the defendant's usual place of abode because the defendant was not actually living at her sister's house on the day service was made.

---

§ 12.7.3   Checklist for Critiquing the Brief Answer

a.   Content

- The writer has predicted but not guaranteed how the issue will be decided.
- The writer has briefly explained his or her prediction, for example, the writer has explained which elements will be easy to prove and which will be more difficult and why.

b.   Format

- The writer has included a separate brief answer for each issue statement.
- The answer begins with a one- or two-word short answer. This one- or two-word short answer is then followed by a short explanation.

c.   Writing

- The brief answer is easy to read and understand.
- Most of the sentences have concrete subjects and action verbs. See sections 25.1 through 25.4.
- There are no grammatical or punctuation errors. See Chapters 27 and 28.

Chapter 12 Quiz No. 2

Draft answers for each of the following questions. Make your points clearly and concisely, and write sentences that are easy to read and that are grammatical and correctly punctuated.

1. What is a legally significant fact?
2. Why should you include all of the legally significant facts in a statement of facts?
3. How can you determine whether a fact is legally significant?
4. What is a legal conclusion? Why is there a "rule" against including legal conclusions in your statement of facts?
5. Given that your supervising attorney gave you the issue, why should you include an issue statement in a formal memo?

§ 12.8   Drafting the Discussion Section Using a Script Format

Expectations. We all have them, and we have them about a variety of things. If we go to the symphony, we expect to be handed a program, have an usher show us to our seats, wait until the hall is darkened, hear the orchestra members tuning their instruments, and then applaud the conductor as he or she takes the podium. We expect these things to be in a certain order, and there is a sense of satisfaction when our expectations are met.

We even have expectations about the organization of the most mundane things in our lives. If you walk into a house, you expect to see certain types of rooms (kitchen, bedrooms, bathroom, living or family room), and you expect those rooms to be in specific places. Dining rooms should be near kitchens; bathrooms should be near bedrooms, and so on. We even expect certain things to be in each room. Stoves should be in kitchens, not in dining rooms, and desks are usually in bedrooms, offices, or studies, not in bathrooms.

The same is true of discussion sections. When attorneys read a discussion section, they expect to see specific types of information. For example, in a formal memo, the attorney expects to see the applicable rules, examples of how those rules have been applied in analogous cases, each side's arguments, and a conclusion. In addition, the attorney expects to see each of those types of information in specific places. In most instances, the rules should be before, and not after, the descriptions of the analogous cases, and the descriptions of analogous cases should be before, and not after, the arguments. Finally, the attorney expects to see specific things in each section. Just as you would be surprised to see a dining table in a bedroom, an attorney would be surprised to see arguments in the rules section.

These expectations are not born of whim. Instead, they reflect the way attorneys in the United States think about legal questions. In most instances, attorneys begin their analysis by identifying the applicable statute or common law rule and by determining who has the burden of proof and what that burden is. If this "general rule" sets out a list of elements, most attorneys then go through those elements one by one, determining which elements the party with the burden of proof can easily prove and which elements will be more difficult to prove.

In most situations, the attorney gives relatively little space to the elements that the party with the burden of proof can easily prove: For these "undisputed elements," the attorney simply applies the law to the facts. Instead, the attorney focuses on the elements that will be more difficult to prove. For each of these "disputed elements," the attorney looks at the definitions or tests the courts use in determining whether the element is met, at examples of how those definitions or tests have been applied in analogous cases, and at each side's arguments. What factual arguments will the parties make? How will each side use the analogous cases? Given the purpose and policies underlying the statute or rule, what types of policy arguments might each side make? Finally, most attorneys make a prediction. Given the facts, rules, cases, and arguments, how will a court decide each element?

The discussion section reflects this process. It contains the same components—rules, analogous cases, arguments, and mini-conclusions—in the same order. At its simplest, and at its best, the discussion section analyzes the problem, walking the attorney step by step through the statute, cases, and arguments to the writer's prediction.

§ 12.8.1   Modify the Template So That It Works for Your Issue

Just as different people prefer different styles of houses, some attorneys prefer different styles of discussion sections: some prefer discussion sections written using what we call the script format, and others prefer discussion sections written using a more integrated format. Although neither format is inherently better than the other, the script format tends to be a bit easier to use. Thus, in this chapter we show you how to write a discussion section using that format. Then, once you have mastered the script format, turn to the next chapter for a description of how to write a discussion section using a more integrated format.

In studying Example 1 below, note how the template reflects the way attorneys think about problems involving an elements analysis. The first section is an introductory section in which the writer introduces and sets out the applicable statute or common law rule, the burden of proof, and any other general rules. At the end of this introductory section, most writers provide the attorney with a roadmap that tells the attorney which elements the party with the burden of proof can easily prove and which elements will be more difficult to prove. The writer then walks the attorney through the elements one by one. For the elements that the party with the burden of proof can easily prove, the writer simply sets out the specific rules for that element and applies them to the client's case. For the elements that will be more difficult to prove, the writer sets out the specific rules for those elements, provides the attorney with descriptions of analogous cases in which those rules have been applied, and then writes the "script" for the arguments related to that element. If that element were litigated, what would the party with the burden of proof argue? What would the other side argue? How would the court decide the question?

EXAMPLE 1   **Template for Discussion Section Written Using a Script Format**

Discussion

Introductory section *(Note: Do not include this subheading in the memo.)*

- If one or both sides will make a policy argument, describe the policies underlying the statute or rule.
- Introduce and set out the applicable statute(s) or common law rule.
- Explain which side has the burden of proof and what that burden is.
- Set out any other rules that apply to all of the elements.
- End by providing the attorney with a roadmap for the rest of the discussion.

A. First Element *(Note: Include a subheading that identifies the element.)*

- If the first element is not likely to be in dispute, simply set out and apply applicable rule.
- If, however, the first element will be in dispute, set out the following information:
  1. Specific rules for the first element
  2. Examples showing how the specific rules have been applied in analogous cases
  3. Arguments
  4. Mini-conclusion for the first element

B. Second Element *(Note: Include a subheading that identifies the element.)*

- If the second element is not likely to be in dispute, simply set out and apply applicable rule.
- If, however, the second element will be in dispute, set out the following information:
  1. Specific rules for second element
  2. Examples of how specific rules have been applied in analogous cases
  3. Arguments
  4. Mini-conclusion for the second element

C. Third Element *(Note: Include a subheading that identifies the element.)*

- If the third element is not likely to be in dispute, simply set out and apply applicable rule.
- If, however, the third element will be in dispute, set out the following information:
  1. Specific rules for the third element
  2. Examples of how specific rules have been applied in analogous cases
  3. Arguments
  4. Mini-conclusion for the third element

D. Fourth Element *(Note: Include a subheading that identifies the element.)*

- If the fourth element is not likely to be in dispute, simply set out and apply applicable rule.
- If, however, the fourth element will be in dispute, set out the following information:
  1. Specific rules for fourth element
  2. Examples of how specific rules have been applied in analogous cases
  3. Arguments
  4. Mini-conclusion for the fourth element

The template set out in Example 1 is, however, only a template. Just as a builder may need to modify a standard blueprint so that the house fits on the lot and satisfies the buyer's preferences, you may need to modify the template set out below in Example 2 so that it works for your issue. For example, if the applicable statute or rule has only two elements, you would need to modify the template so that it has only two subsections. Similarly, if the statute has five elements, you would need to modify the template so that it has five subsections.

In the Olsen case, the statute sets out three elements: (1) the complaint or petition must be left at the usual place of abode of the person being served, (2) the complaint or petition must be left with a person who is 15 years old or older who resides therein; and (3) the process server must inform the person served of the contents. Therefore, we modify the template so that it has three subsections. See Example 2.

PRACTICE POINTER	In the Olsen case, we decided to combine the discussion of "residing therein" and "15 years or older." These two elements are closely related, and neither is in dispute.

EXAMPLE 2   **Revised Template**

Discussion

Introductory section:

Set out policies underlying § 48.031, Fla. Stat. (2013).

- Introduce and set out § 48.031, Fla. Stat. (2013).
- Explain which side has the burden of proof and what that burden is.
- Set out any other rules that apply to all of the elements.
- End with a roadmap that tells the attorney that the State can easily prove the second element but that it may not be able to prove the first and third elements.

A. Usual Place of Abode *(disputed element)*

1. Specific rules
2. Examples of how specific rules have been applied in analogous cases
3. Arguments
    - Ms. Olsen's arguments
    - The State's arguments
4. Mini-conclusion

B. Age and Residing Therein *(undisputed element)*

1. Set out applicable rules
2. Apply applicable rules

C. Informing of Contents *(disputed element)*

1. Specific rules
2. Examples of how specific rules have been applied in analogous cases
3. Arguments
    - Ms. Olsen's arguments
    - The State's arguments
4. Mini-conclusion

PRACTICE POINTER	As a general rule, set out the party who has the burden of proof's arguments first. In the sample problem, Ms. Olsen has the burden of proof because the return of service is regular on its face.

§ 12.8.2 Draft the Introductory, or General Rule, Section

Drafting the introductory, or general rule, section is a three-step process. Decide what information to include, order that information, and draft the section.

a. Decide What Information You Need to Include

The first step is to list the information that you want to include in your introductory section. In preparing this list, keep two things in mind. First, remember your audience. If the attorney for whom you are preparing the memo knows little or nothing about the area of law, provide the attorney with an overview of the area of law, distinguishing closely related doctrines and defining key terms. If, however, the attorney knows the area of law, do not include this type of information. Second, distinguish between general rules — that is, rules that apply to all of the elements — and specific rules — that is, rules that apply to only one element. Include only general rules in your introductory section. Save the specific rules for the discussion of the element to which they apply.

In the sample problem, you can presume that the attorney will have taken civil procedure as a law student and will, therefore, know the basics. Accordingly, in drafting the introductory section, you do not need to explain the difference between personal service and substituted service or define those terms. You do, though, need to set out the applicable portion of the statute and the rules relating to the burden of proof. In addition, you should set out two other "rules" that apply to all of the elements. First, because Ms. Olsen can make a policy argument, set out the policies underlying the statute. Second, tell your supervising attorney that the courts have said that the statute should be narrowly construed to assure due process. Finally, include a roadmap, which is what the name suggests: a map for the rest of the discussion.

b. Order the Information

The next step is to order the items on the list. Most of the time, you will want to set out more general information before more specific information. Therefore, in drafting the introductory section, you will usually want to use an inverted pyramid: broad rules first, narrower rules next, and exceptions last. (For more on this paragraph pattern, see section 23.2.)

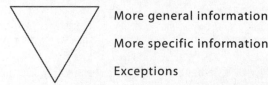

More general information

More specific information

Exceptions

Most attorneys would agree that the policies that underlie the statute are the most general piece of information, that the applicable portion of the statute is the next most general piece of information, and that the rules relating to the burden of proof are the most specific. Consequently, in our sample problem, you would want to set out the policies underlying the statute first, the applicable portions of the statute next, and the rules relating to the burden of proof last.

PRACTICE POINTER	If you are not sure which rules are the more general rules and which rules are the more specific rules, look at the cases. In most instances, the courts set out more general rules before more specific rules.

The approach is similar when there is more than one applicable statutory section: Instead of setting out the statutes in the order in which they appear in the code, set out the more general statutory sections first. For example, set out the section that explains the statute's purpose before the section that sets out the rule, and set out the section that contains the rule before the section that contains the definitions.

c. Prepare the First Draft

In preparing the first draft, do not do what the writer did in Example 3: String together a series of quotes, some of which set out the same rules using slightly different language.

EXAMPLE 3	**Poor Draft: Writer Has Simply Strung Together a Series of Quotes**

Discussion

"The purpose of service of process is to advise the defendant that an action has been commenced and to warn the defendant that he or she must appear in a timely manner to state such defenses as are available." *Torres v. Arnco Constr., Inc.*, 867 So. 2d 583 (Fla. 5th DCA 2004). It is well settled that the fundamental purpose of service is "to give proper notice to the defendant in the case that he is answerable to the claim of plaintiff and, therefore, to vest jurisdiction in the court entertaining the controversy." *Shurman v. Atl. Mortg. & Inv. Corp.*, 795 So. 2d 952, 953-54 (Fla. 2001) (citing *State ex rel. Merritt v. Heffernan*, 142 Fla. 496, 195 So. 145, 147 (1940)). Therefore, "a judgment entered without due service of process is void." *Torres*, 867 So. 2d at 586.

The statute specifically states:

Service of original process is made by delivering a copy of it to the person to be served with a copy of the complaint, petition, or other initial pleading or paper or by leaving the copies at his or her usual place of abode with any person residing therein who is 15 years of age or older and informing the person of their contents. Minors who are or have been married shall be served as provided in this section.

§ 48.031(1)(a), Fla. Stat. (2013).

"The statutes regulating service of process are to be strictly construed to assure that a defendant is notified of the proceedings." *Torres*, 867 So. 2d at 586. "Indeed, because statutes authorizing substituted service are exceptions to the general rule requiring a defendant to be served personally, due process requires strict compliance with their statutory requirements." *Id.*

Thus, because Ms. Olsen is challenging the validity of the service, she will have the burden of proof. Ms. Olsen will concede that the summons was left with a person who is 15 years old or older residing therein. In addition, she will probably concede that her sister was informed of the contents of the documents. She may, however, be able to prove that the summons was not left at her usual place of abode.

Instead of just cutting and pasting the rules from your research notes into your first draft, take the time to read, analyze, and synthesize the rules. Once you understand the rules, determine which rules apply to your case, and then set out each of the applicable rules once and only once.

> **PRACTICE POINTER** Almost all attorneys will want you to quote the relevant portions of statutes. However, when it comes to other rules, for example, common law rules or rules that the courts have set out, different attorneys prefer different things. While some attorneys will want you to quote all of the rules, others find a series of quotes annoying and prefer that you set out close paraphrases of the rules. Therefore, before you do your first draft, check with your supervising attorney to see which style he or she prefers.

EXAMPLE 4   **Better Draft: Writer Has Set Out Each Rule Only Once**

Discussion

The fundamental purpose of service of process is to give defendants notice of claims that have been filed against them and to provide them with an opportunity to defend their rights. *Shurman v. Atl. Mortg. & Inv. Corp.*, 795 So. 2d 952, 953-54 (Fla. 2001). Because it is important that litigants receive notice of actions against them, courts strictly construe and enforce statutes governing service of process. *Id.* at 954.

In this case, the applicable section of the statute reads as follows:

Service of original process is made by delivering a copy of it to the person to be served with a copy of the complaint, petition, or other initial pleading or paper or by leaving the copies at his or her usual place of abode with any person residing therein who is 15 years of age or older and informing the person of their contents. Minors who are or have been married shall be served as provided in this section.

§ 48.031(a)(1), Fla. Stat. (2013).

Although the party seeking to invoke the jurisdiction of the court has the burden of proving that service was proper, if the return is regular on its face, the courts presume that the service was valid. *Busman v. State, Dep't of Revenue*, 905 So. 2d 956, 958 (Fla. 3d DCA 2005); *Thompson v. State, Dep't of Revenue*, 867 So. 2d 603, 605 (Fla. 1st DCA 2004). In such instances, the party challenging the service has the burden of presenting clear and convincing evidence that the service was invalid. *Id.*

In this case, Ms. Olsen will have to concede that the summons was left with a person 15 years or older who was residing at the house where the summons and complaint were served. In addition, it is unlikely that Ms. Olsen will be able to prove that her sister was not informed of the contents of the documents. Ms. Olsen may, however, be able to present clear and convincing evidence that the summons was not left at her usual place of abode.

You do not, however, have to quote the entire statute. If only part of the statute is applicable, you can set out only that part.

EXAMPLE 5   **Better Draft: Writer Has Quoted Only the Applicable Portion of the Statute**

Discussion

The Florida courts have repeatedly stated that the fundamental purpose of service of process is to give defendants notice of claims that have been filed against them and to provide defendants with an opportunity to defend their rights. *E.g., Shurman v. Atl. Mortg. & Inv. Corp.*, 795 So. 2d 952, 953-54 (Fla. 2001). Because these rights are so important, the courts strictly construe and enforce statutes governing service of process. *Id.* at 954.

In the present case, the relevant portion of the statute reads as follows:

> (1)(a) Service of original process is made by delivering a copy of it to the person to be served with a copy of the complaint, petition, or other initial pleading or paper or by leaving the copies at his or her usual place of abode with any person residing therein who is 15 years of age or older and informing the person of their contents. . . .

§ 48.031(a)(1), Fla. Stat. (2013).

Although the party seeking to invoke the jurisdiction of the court has the burden of proving that service was proper, if the return is regular on its face, the courts presume that the service was valid. *Busman v. State, Dep't of Revenue*, 905 So. 2d 956, 958 (Fla. 3d DCA 2005); *Thompson v. State, Dep't of Revenue*, 867 So. 2d 603, 605 (Fla. 1st DCA 2004). In such instances, the party challenging the service has the burden of presenting clear and convincing evidence that the service was invalid. *Id.*

In this case, Ms. Olsen may be able to present clear and convincing evidence that the summons was not left at her usual place of abode. However, if the court decides that the summons was left at her usual place of abode, Ms. Olsen will have to concede that the summons was left with a person 15 years or older who was residing at the house where the summons and complaint were served. In addition, although Ms. Olsen can argue that her sister was not informed of the contents of the summons and complaint, it is unlikely that she can meet her burden of proof.

PRACTICE POINTER

If your quotation has fifty words or more, you need to set it out as a block quote, indenting five spaces on the left and five spaces on the right and omitting the quotation marks. In contrast, if the quote has fewer than fifty words, you can include it in the text of your sentence. See Rule 38 in the *ALWD Guide to Legal Citation* and Rule 5.1 in *The Bluebook*.

| PRACTICE POINTER | Read other lawyers' memos, briefs, wills, contracts, and other documents to learn how experienced attorneys organize their arguments and craft their writing. Do not just copy those documents, |

however: What worked in one situation may not work in another situation. Instead, adapt the examples so that they reflect the law that applies in your case.

d.   Include a Citation to Authority for Each Rule

You must include a citation to authority for each rule that you set out in your memo. This authority may be a constitutional provision, a statute, a regulation, a court rule, or a case.

| PRACTICE POINTER | In drafting your memo, use the applicable citation rules. For example, if you are writing a memo to a Florida attorney about an issue governed by Florida law, use the Florida citation rules. |

In choosing a citation for a rule, always choose mandatory, or binding, authority over persuasive authority. See section 2.3. For example, in choosing a case, always choose cases from your jurisdiction over cases from other jurisdictions. In addition, as a general rule, choose decisions from higher courts over decisions from lower courts and more recent decisions over older decisions. The exception might be when the decisions of the jurisdiction's highest court, for example, your state's highest court, are quite old and there are more recent decisions from your state's intermediate court of appeals. If the decisions from both your state's highest court and intermediate court are mandatory authority, you can choose to cite the more recent decision from the state intermediate court of appeals. Although there may be times when you want to list more than one case to show the attorney that the rule is well established, avoid long string cites, that is, listing more than two or three cases.

| PRACTICE POINTER | As a general rule, do not cite unpublished or unreported decisions as authority for a rule. Instead, cite a published decision, for example, the case or cases that the unpublished or unreported decision |

cited as authority for the rule.

§ 12.8.3   Draft the Discussion of the Undisputed Elements

More likely than not, one or more of the elements will not be in dispute. Although you cannot ignore these undisputed elements, you do not need to devote much space to them.

a.   Decide Where to Put Your Discussion of the Undisputed Elements

While some attorneys choose to raise and dismiss the undisputed elements at the end of their introductory section, others choose to discuss all of the elements in order. Compare the following examples. In Example 6, the writer has raised and dismissed the undisputed element in her roadmap at the end of her introductory section. In contrast, in Example 7, the writer has raised and dismissed the undisputed elements in their own subsections.

EXAMPLE 6   **Undisputed Elements Raised and Dismissed at the End of the Introductory Section**

[Note: The text of the first part of the introductory section is not shown.]

In this case, Ms. Olsen may be able to present clear and convincing evidence that the petition was not left at her usual place of abode. However, if the court decides that the petition was left at her usual place of abode, Ms. Olsen will have to concede that the summons was left with a person 15 years or older who was residing at the house where service was made. In addition, although Ms. Olsen can argue that her sister was not informed of the contents of the documents, it is unlikely that she can meet her burden of proof.

EXAMPLE 7   **Undisputed Elements Raised in Separate Subsections**

Introductory section

[Note: The first part of the introductory section is not shown.]

In this case, the second element is not in dispute: The summons was left with Ms. Webster at her home, and Ms. Webster is over the age of 15. In addition, more likely than not, a court would conclude that the process server told Ms. Webster about the contents of the document. Ms. Olsen may be able to prove, however, that service was not made at her usual place of abode.

A. Usual Place of Abode

[Disputed element; text not included in this example.]

B. Person 15 Years Old or Older Residing Therein

In addition to leaving the complaint or petition at the defendant's usual place of abode, the process server must leave the complaint or petition with a person 15 years old or older residing therein. If the court concludes that Ms. Olsen's sister's house was Ms. Olsen's usual place of abode, Ms. Olsen will have to concede that the petition was left with a person residing therein who is at least 15 years old: Ms. Webster is 32 years old, and the petition was left with her at her house.

C. Notified of Contents

[Disputed element; text not included in this example]

To see the full text of this example, see the memo set out in section 11.4.1.

---

b.   Prepare the First Draft of Your Discussion of the Undisputed Elements

In most instances, your discussion of an undisputed element will be very short: Identify the element, set out any applicable specific rules, and apply those rules to the facts of your case. While in some instances you will need to include brief case descriptions, in most instances such descriptions are not necessary. Compare the following examples.

PRACTICE POINTER	As a general rule, in a criminal case a defendant does not "concede" that an element is met. He or she makes the government prove each element of the crime. Accordingly, in a criminal case, do not state that the defendant will concede that an element is met. Instead, frame the sentence in terms of what the government can prove.

EXAMPLE 8   **Poor Draft of Undisputed Element: Writer Has Set Out Conclusion Without Setting Out Facts That Support That Conclusion**

Ms. Olsen should concede that the second element, that the complaint or petition be left with a person 15 years or older residing therein, is met.

EXAMPLE 9   **Poor Draft of Undisputed Element: Writer Has Gone into Too Much Depth on Undisputed Element**

For substitute service of process to be valid at a defendant's "usual place of abode," the complaint or petition must be left with a person residing therein who is 15 years of age or older. § 48.031, Fla. Stat. (2013). Although the statute does not specify the period of time an individual must occupy a home to be regarded as "residing therein," the courts do not require extended habitation. *Compare Magazine v. Bedoya*, 475 So. 2d 1035 (Fla. 3d DCA 1985) (six-week stay long enough to establish residency), *with Gamboa v. Jones*, 455 So. 2d 613 (Fla. 3d DCA 1985) (ten-day visit not sufficient to establish residency). Because she is 32, Ms. Webster satisfies the age requirement. From the facts given, it is unclear how long Ms. Webster has lived at the home in question; however, the memo indicated that she was served at "her house." Consequently, unless other facts are presented, Ms. Webster appears to be the owner and a resident of the house, and she has lived there long enough to establish residency. Therefore, the residing therein requirement is met.

EXAMPLE 10   **Better Draft of Undisputed Element**

In addition to leaving the complaint or petition at the defendant's usual place of abode, the process server must leave the documents with a person 15 years old or older residing therein. If the court concludes that Ms. Olsen's sister's house was Ms. Olsen's usual place of abode, Ms. Olsen will have to concede that the summons was left with a person residing therein who is at least 15 years old: Ms. Webster is 32 years old, and the summons and complaint were left with her at her house.

| **EXAMPLE 11** | **Better Draft of Undisputed Element** |

A court will find that the second element is met. Because the summons and complaint were left with Ms. Olsen's 32-year-old sister, the age requirement is met. In addition, because Ms. Olsen's sister lives at the house where the summons and complaint were left, the residing therein requirement is met.

PRACTICE POINTER

While some elements are clearly not in dispute and some are clearly in dispute, there will be elements that fall somewhere in between these two categories.

_____X_____
              Not in dispute   In dispute

When you have an element that falls into this "in between" category, you will usually do more than raise and dismiss the element but less than a full analysis. Alert the attorney to the fact that one side might have a weak argument, set out that argument, explain why the argument is weak, and then move on.

§ 12.8.4   Draft the Discussion of the Disputed Elements

You will usually want to create a separate subsection for each disputed element. Include a subheading that identifies the element and then set out, in paragraph form, the following information:

a. the specific rules for that element;
b. cases that illustrate how those specific rules have been applied;
c. each side's arguments; and
d. your prediction about how the court is likely to decide the element.

a.   Set Out the Specific Rules

Begin your discussion of a disputed element by setting out the rules that relate to that element. For example, if the courts apply a particular test in determining whether the element is met, set out that test. Similarly, if the courts have defined any terms, set out those definitions.

In drafting your specific rule paragraphs, use the same process that you used in drafting the introductory section. Begin by listing all of the information that you want to include in your specific rule paragraph, and then order that information, setting out more general information before more specific information. Finally, draft the specific rule paragraph or paragraphs.

In drafting these paragraphs, keep the following in mind. First, include only those rules that apply to the element that you are currently discussing. Do not repeat general rules that you set out in your introductory section, and do not set out rules that apply to other elements. Second, do not simply cut and paste the rules from your research notes into your draft. Instead, determine what the rules are, and then set out each rule once, and only once, using clear and concise language. Finally, remember to include a citation to authority for each rule that you set out. Compare Examples 12 and 13, both of which are examples of the specific rule paragraph for the usual place of abode element.

EXAMPLE 12   **Poor Draft: Writer Has Simply Cut and Pasted Rules from Research Notes into Draft**

The Florida courts have defined "usual place of abode" as "the fixed place of residence for the time being when the service is made." *Shurman v. Atl. Mortg. & Inv. Corp.*, 795 So. 2d 952, 953-54 (Fla. 2001). "If a person has more than one residence, a summons must be served at the residence at which the defendant is actually living at the time of service." *Id.* at 954. As the Florida Supreme Court noted in *Torres v. Arnco Const., Inc.*, 867 So. 2d 583, 586 (Fla. 5th DCA 2004), "the courts have frequently invalidated substituted service of process in cases where the defendant was not actually living at the place where service was made, even though process might have been delivered to a relative."

EXAMPLE 13   **Better Draft: Writer Has Identified the Rules and Then Set Out Each Rule Once, Using Language That Is Clear and Concise**

Although the statute does not define the phrase "usual place of abode," the courts have said that a defendant's usual place of abode is the place "where the defendant was actually living at the time of service." *E.g., Shurman v. Atl. Mortg. & Inv. Corp.*, 795 So. 2d 952, 953-54 (Fla. 2001); *Busman v. State, Dep't of Revenue*, 905 So. 2d 956, 957 (Fla. 3d DCA 2005).

---

b. Describe the Analogous Cases

When an element is in dispute, most attorneys want to see not only the specific rules but also examples of how those specific rules have been applied in analogous cases. Therefore, if an element is in dispute and there are analogous cases, you will usually want to describe at least some of those cases.

In drafting the analogous case section, always keep in mind why you are including cases. Do not include analogous case descriptions just to show your supervising attorney that you found and read cases. The analogous case section is not there so that you can prove that you did a lot of work. Instead, include analogous case descriptions because the case descriptions will help the attorney understand the rules or because either your side or the other side is likely to use the cases to support its position.

Step 1: Identify the Analogous Cases

The first step is to go back through your research notes and identify the cases in which the court discussed the disputed element. In the Olsen case, there are about a dozen cases that discuss usual place of abode. (For a list of the Florida cases that discuss usual place of abode, see subheading 9 in the notes of decision following section 48.031 in Florida Statutes Annotated.)

> **PRACTICE POINTER**
>
> In looking for analogous cases, look first for cases from your jurisdiction. If you do not find any, you can then look for analogous cases from other jurisdictions. However, before deciding to use an out-of-state case, make sure that the other state's specific rules are the same as your state's specific rules.

Step 2: Sort the Analogous Cases

Once you have identified the analogous cases, sort those cases. Put the cases in which the court held that the element was met in one stack and the cases in which the court held that the element was not met in another stack.

EXAMPLE 14   Chart Listing Cases

Cases in Which Element Was Not Met	Cases in Which Element Was Met
• *Shurman v. Atl. Mortg. & Inv. Corp.*, 795 So. 2d 952 (Fla. 2001) • *Heck v. Bank Liberty*, 86 So. 3d 1281) (Fla. 1st DCA 2012) • *Portfolio Recovery Assocs., LLC v. Gonzalez*, 951 So. 2d 1037 (Fla. 3d DCA 2007) • *Cordova v. Jolcover*, 942 So. 2d 1045 (Fla. 2d DCA 2006) • *Gilbert v. Storey*, 920 So. 2d 1173 (Fla. 3d DCA 2006) • *Busman v. State, Dep't of Revenue*, 905 So. 2d 956 (Fla. 3d DCA 2005) • *Thompson v. State, Dep't of Revenue*, 867 So. 2d 603 (Fla. 1st DCA 2004) • *Torres v. Arnco Const., Inc.*, 867 So. 2d 583 (Fla. 5th DCA 2004) [other entries not included]	• *State ex rel. Merritt v. Heffernan*, 195 So. 145 (Fla. 1940) • *Johnston v. Hudlett*, 32 So. 3d 700 (Fla. 4th DCA 2010)

Step 3: Analyze and Synthesize the Cases

It is at this step that the real work begins. Because you want to do more than provide the attorney with "book reports" on the cases that you have read, you need to analyze each of the cases and then synthesize the group of cases.

Analysis requires you to read the cases carefully and critically, identifying the issue that was before the court, the standard of review that the court applied, the facts that the court considered, the court's holding, and the court's reasoning. For more on reading and analyzing cases, see Chapter 3.

PRACTICE POINTER The standard of review is the standard that an appellate court uses in reviewing a trial court's decision. If the standard of review is *de novo,* the appellate court does not defer to the trial court. Instead, the appellate court reviews the issue on the merits and can substitute its judgment for the judgment of the trial court. In contrast, if the standard of review is abuse of discretion, the appellate court defers to the trial court. When the standard of review is abuse of discretion, the appellate court will overturn the trial court only when the trial court abused its discretion.

In general, the standard of review is *de novo* when the issue is an issue of law—for example, whether the trial court properly instructed the jury. In contrast, the standard of review is usually abuse of discretion if the issue is an issue of fact—for example, whether a particular expert is qualified. For more on the *de novo* standard of review and some of the other standards of review, see Chapter 18.

If there is more than one case, you also need to do synthesis. When the cases are read as a group, what principle or principles can you draw from them? For example, in the Olsen case, what principle or principles can you draw from the group of cases in which the courts have held that the summons was not left at the defendant's usual place of abode?

One way of doing this analysis and synthesis is to prepare a chart in which, for each case, you identify the court, the date of the decision, the key facts, and the court's reasoning. Note that in Examples 15 and 16 there is not a column for the holding. This column is not necessary because the cases are grouped based on their holdings. Example 15 analyzes the cases in which the element was met, and Example 16 is an excerpt from the chart that analyzes cases in which the element was not met.

PRACTICE POINTER There is more than one way to list the cases: You can list them in chronological order; in reverse chronological order; by court; or within a court, by district or division. In Example 15, we set out decisions from the Florida Supreme Court first. We then list the decisions from the Court of Appeals in reverse chronological order.

EXAMPLE 15   **Excerpt from Chart Analyzing Cases in Which the Court Held That Service Was Not Made at the Defendant's Usual Place of Abode**

Case	Court	Date	Facts	Reasoning
Shurman v. Atl. Mortg. & Inv. Corp.	Florida Supreme Court	2001	• Mortgage foreclosure action • Service left with D's wife. • D had been incarcerated for at least 9 months.	• D was actually living in the prison. • Substituted service, being in derogation of the common law, must be strictly construed. • In general, the courts presume that the defendant will receive notice of process if the summons is left with a competent member of his household who lives in his house. This presumption is not, however, valid when the head of the household is in prison.
Portfolio Recovery Assocs., LLC v. Gonzalez	Fla. 3d DCA	2007	• Summons left with the woman who was mother of one D and mother-in-law of the other D. • Undisputed affidavit established that neither D had lived at residence for five years.	• DCA affirmed trial court because undisputed affidavit established that neither defendant had lived at residence for five years. Thus, residence was not their usual place of abode. • It does not describe the underlying cause of action.
Cordova v. Jolcover	Fla. 2d DCA	2006	• P sued D to enforce real estate contract. Summons was left with D's estranged wife, who told process server that the D was not in the country. D submitted his passport and police report that showed that he was living in Peru. Estranged wife also submitted affidavit saying that she and husband were estranged and that process server did not notify her of content.	• DCA reversed trial court because defendant presented clear and convincing evidence that service was not left at the defendant's usual place of abode. The return of service raised doubts and the defendant submitted proof that he was living in Peru.
Busman v. State, Dep't of Revenue	Fla. 3d DCA	2005	• Action to establish paternity. • Service was left with the defendant's half brother on July 16, 2003 • D testified that he had moved out of half brother's house on July 1, 2003, and presented lease and landlord's testimony.	• Although the sheriff's return of service was regular on its face, Busman presented clear, convincing, and uncontradicted evidence that the summons was not left at his "usual place of abode." • Statute must be strictly construed.

Case	Court	Date	Facts	Reasoning
Thompson v. State, Dep't of Revenue	Fla. 1st DCA	2004	• Child support action. • Summons left with wife. • D filed affidavit stating that he had been separated from wife for three years, that he had not lived at the address where the summons was left for three years, and he did not authorize anyone to accept service on his behalf.	• DCA reversed and remanded for an evidentiary hearing. • Thompson's motion and affidavit are based on the fact that the service did not comply with §48.031 and was, therefore, legally deficient.
Torres v. Arnco Const., Inc.	Fla. 5th DCA	2004	• Summons left with D's mother. • D had resided in NY for 57 years and at NY address for 12 years. • NY neighbors verified that D lived in house but that he traveled a lot. • Mother said that D would be home soon.	• Although standard of review is gross abuse of discretion, no live testimony. • P has the burden of proof. • P did not meet burden. • Mother's statement was ambiguous. • Dissent argues that D had burden of proof and that his statements were not sufficient. If D were visiting his family in Florida for substantial periods of time, the Florida house was his "usual abode" when he was served in Florida. It would also be consistent with the affidavit of the Florida process server who said that D's mother remarked that Torres "would be home soon, and she would see to it that he received the papers."
Alvarez v. State Farm	Fla. 3d DCA	1994	• Service was left with D's cousin at cousin's residence. • Affidavits, telephone bill, and marriage license established that D was not living with cousin at time of service and that D had not lived there for some time.	• Uncontradicted evidence established that D was not living at that address on the date of service or for some time before. Therefore, service of process was ineffective as a matter of law.

| EXAMPLE 16 | **Case in Which the Court Held That Service Was Made at the Defendant's Usual Place of Abode** |

Case	Court	Date	Facts	Reasoning
State ex rel. Merritt v. Heffernan, 195 So. 145 (Fla. 1940)	Florida Supreme Court	1940	• Wife served one hour after D left to go back to Minnesota. • D had an office, voted, and paid taxes in Minnesota. • D had moved family to Florida two months earlier. • D had visited family twice "during season." • Summons was left with D's wife and, apparently, D received actual notice.	• Ct acknowledges that D's permanent residence was in Minnesota. • However, ct seems to think that it was more important that his family was in Florida, that D was on a train and not in Minnesota at the time of service, and that the evidence suggested that D intended to return to Minnesota.

> **PRACTICE POINTER**
>
> Just as it is unlikely that anyone other than you will see your research notes, it is also unlikely that anyone other than you will see your charts. Therefore, use the format and abbreviations that make sense to you. Do not waste time creating charts that "look nice."

In creating and examining your chart, you might discover that the cases in which the element was met (or not met) have one of the following in common:

- that all of the cases in which the element is met (or not met) have a particular fact or set of facts in common;
- that in all of the cases in which the element is met (or not met) the courts seem to focus on a particular policy underlying the rule;
- that different courts or different divisions of the same court seem to take a particular approach;
- that the rules seem to be evolving; or
- that the decisions seem to be result oriented.

When you determine what the cases have in common, or that they do not have anything in common, you have done synthesis.

Step 4: Write the Sentences Introducing Your Description of the Analogous Cases

Do not make your supervising attorney guess about how a case or group of cases contributes to the overall analysis. Instead, use topic sentences to introduce each case or group of cases. The language you use will depend on a number of factors, including the number of analogous cases and what you discovered in analyzing and synthesizing those cases.

In the Olsen case, the writer wants to illustrate how the courts have interpreted the phrase "usual place of abode" by providing her supervising attorney with examples of the types of fact situations in which the courts have concluded that service was made at the defendant's usual place of abode and with examples of the types of fact situations in which the courts have held that the service was not made at the defendant's usual place of abode. While the writer could introduce the first case with a sentence that says, "In State ex rel. Merritt v. Heffernan, 195 So. 145, 146 (Fla. 1940), service was made on the defendant's wife at the defendant's apartment in Florida," most attorneys expect more. They want to know why the case is important and why you included the case in your memo.

In charting the first group of cases, the writer discovered that there was only one analogous case, one from 1940, in which the court held that the service was made at the defendant's usual place of abode. In addition, in analyzing and synthesizing both the 1940 case and the more recent cases, the writer concluded that, although the 1940 case had never been overruled, in the more recent cases the courts have changed the way in which they view service on a relative. As a consequence, the writer begins her description of the 1940 case by placing the old case in its historical context, by telling the attorney that the case is one of the few published decisions, and by setting out the court's conclusion. See Example 17.

EXAMPLE 17   **Sentence Introducing Analogous Cases**

In an early case, and one of the few published decisions in which the court concluded that the defendant had been served at his usual place of abode, the court reasoned that, at the time of service, defendant's wife and children were living at the apartment where service was made. *State ex rel. Merritt v. Heffernan*, 195 So. 145, 146-47 (Fla. 1940). In that case, the defendant had relocated his family to Florida two months before service was made and had twice visited them while they were in Florida, the second time leaving the apartment to return to Minnesota just an hour before service was made. *Id.* Although the defendant argued that his usual place of abode was Minnesota, where he had an office, paid taxes, and voted, the court disagreed, stating that "[w]e do not hold the view that Florida was the permanent residence of the defendant, but we do feel that in the circumstance reflected in the record, it was his usual place of abode . . . ." *Id.* at 148.

However, when there is more than one analogous case, you want to do more than just tell your readers that there are two, three, or four cases. In these instances, draft a principle-based topic sentence.

A principle-based topic sentence is a sentence that tells your reader what "principle" you are using the cases to illustrate. Sometimes, the courts set out these principles. For instance, in our sample problem the courts have explicitly said that the phrase "usual place of abode" should be narrowly construed and, in fact, in their decisions they do construe the language narrowly. At other times, you will "discover" the principle while synthesizing the cases. In charting the cases, you may discover (1) that all or most of cases have a particular set of facts in common; (2) that in all or most of the cases the courts seem to focus on a particular policy underlying the rule; (3) that different courts or different divisions of the same court seem to take a particular approach; (4) that the rules seem to be evolving; or (5) that the decisions seem to be result oriented.

While in some situations the case law is so consistent that everyone who reads a group of cases draws the same principle or principles from those cases, in other situations there is more than one way to read the cases or, depending on the arguments that you think the parties are likely to make, you may want to emphasize different points. See Examples 18, 19, and 20. In each example, the principle-based topic sentence is in bold.

EXAMPLE 18   Principle-Based Topic Sentence Used to Introduce a Group of Analogous Cases

In contrast, in the more recent cases, the courts have emphasized that it is not enough that the complaint or petition is left with a relative. *See, e.g., Busman*, 905 So. 2d at 947; *Torres v. Arnco Const., Inc.*, 867 So. 2d 583 (Fla. 5th DCA 2004). For example, in *Busman*, the court concluded that service of process was not valid even though the summons and complaint had been left with the defendant's half brother. *Id.* at 958. Similarly, in *Torres*, the court concluded that service had not been made at the defendant's usual place of abode when, after trying unsuccessfully to serve the defendant at his New York apartment, the plaintiff served the defendant's mother at her home in Florida. *Id.* at 585, 587. Although the defendant's mother told the process server that her son "would be home soon," the court decided that this statement was, at best, ambiguous. *Id.* at 585; *accord Portfolio Recovery Assocs., LLC v. Gonzalez*, 951 So. 2d 1037, 1038 (Fla. 3d DCA 2007) (service was not made at the defendants' usual place of abode when the summons and complaint were left with a woman who was the mother of one defendant and the mother-in-law of the other defendant, but the defendants had not lived at the residence for five years).

EXAMPLE 19   Principle-Based Topic Sentence Used to Introduce a Group of Analogous Cases

In the most recent cases, the courts have held that the service was invalid or remanded the case for an evidentiary hearing when the defendant presented evidence that he was not actually living at the house where service was made. *See, e.g., Busman*, 905 So. 2d at 958; *Thompson*, 867 So. 2d at 605. For example, in *Busman*, the Third District Court of Appeals held that service was invalid when the defendant presented a lease agreement that corroborated his testimony that he had moved out of his half brother's house two and one-half months before his half brother was served. Likewise, in *Thompson*, the First District Court of Appeals reversed and remanded the case for an evidentiary hearing when the defendant submitted an affidavit in which he stated that he was separated from his wife, that he had not resided at that address for over three years, and that he did not authorize anyone to accept service of process on his behalf. *Id.* at 605.

EXAMPLE 20   Principle-Based Topic Sentence Used to Introduce a Group of Analogous Cases

In most of the cases in which the courts have held that the summons was not left at the defendant's usual place of abode, the defendant had not lived at the house where service was made for a substantial period of time. *See, e.g., Shurman v. Atl. Mortg. & Inv. Corp.*, 795 So. 2d 952 (Fla. 2001); *Portfolio Recovery Assocs. LLC v. Gonzalez*, 951 So. 2d 1037 (Fla. 3d DCA 2007). For instance, in *Shurman*, the defendant was incarcerated and had not lived at the family home for at least nine months, 795 So. 2d at 953, and in *Portfolio Recovery Assocs.*, the defendants had not lived at the house where service was made for five years, 951 So. 2d at 1038.

PRACTICE POINTER   When you have difficulty coming up with a good topic sentence (and there will be times when you do), try asking yourself the following questions:

1. Why am I including these cases in my memo?
2. What is the common thread that runs through this group of cases?
3. If the client's case is litigated, how will each side use these cases?

Step 5: Draft Your Descriptions of the Cases

Once you have drafted the topic sentence, the next step is to draft the case descriptions.

If there are only two or three analogous cases, you can describe all of them. If, however, there are a number of cases, describe only the "best" cases. In selecting these cases, use the following criteria:

- Select cases from your jurisdiction over cases from other jurisdictions.
- Select cases with published decisions over cases with unpublished, or unreported, decisions.
- Select more recent cases over older cases.
- Select cases from higher courts over cases from lower courts.

In addition, most of the time you will be using the cases to see where your case falls along the continuum of decided cases. Is your case more like the cases in which the court held that the element was met or more like the cases in which the court held that the element was not met? Accordingly, select cases that are more factually analogous over cases that are less factually analogous.

$$??\leftarrow\text{my case}\rightarrow??$$

Cases in which element met	Cases in which element not met

How much you say about a case will depend on the point that you are using the case to illustrate. If you are using the case to illustrate a small point, then a sentence or even a clause, phrase, or word may be enough. In contrast, if you expect that one or both sides will rely heavily on the case, your description will be longer. The bottom line is that you need to include only that information that is relevant to the principle that you are using the case to illustrate and to set up the arguments based on that case.

Compare Examples 21, 22, and 23. In Example 21, the case descriptions are very short because the writer is using the cases to illustrate a small point. In contrast, in Example 22, the case description is longer because the writer wants to use the case to illustrate several points and because the writer expects that both sides will use the case. In Example 23, the writer sets out two medium-length case descriptions.

| EXAMPLE 21 | Short Descriptions of Two Cases |

Although the statute does not specify how long the person who received the service must have been "residing therein," the courts do not require extended habitation. While in *Gamboa*, the court determined that a ten-day visit was not sufficient to establish residency, *id.* at 614, in *Magazine*, the court determined that a six-week stay was sufficient, *id.* at 1035.

| EXAMPLE 22 | Longer Description in Which the Writer Sets Out Facts and the Court's Holding and Reasoning |

In an early case, and one of the few published decisions in which the court concluded that the defendant had been served at his usual place of abode, the summons was left with the defendant's wife at the family's apartment in Florida an hour after the defendant boarded a train to Minnesota. *State ex rel. Merritt v. Heffernan*, 195 So. 145, 146 (Fla. 1940). Although the defendant argued that his usual place of abode was Minnesota, where he had an office, paid taxes, and voted, the court disagreed, noting that the defendant had moved his family to the Florida apartment two months before his wife was served, that the defendant had visited his family at the apartment twice "during the season," and that the defendant's family had remained in Florida for some time after the defendant was served. *Id.* at 147. As the court stated, "We do not hold the view that Florida was the permanent residence of the defendant, but we do feel that in the circumstance reflected in the record, it was his usual place of abode . . . ." *Id.* at 148.

| EXAMPLE 23 | Two Descriptions in Which the Writer Sets Out Facts and the Courts' Holdings and Reasoning |

In recent cases, the courts have either held that the service was invalid or remanded the case for an evidentiary hearing when the defendant produced evidence establishing that he was not actually living at the house where the summons was served. *See, e.g., Busman*, 905 So. 2d at 958; *Thompson*, 867 So. 2d at 605. For example, in *Busman*, the Third District Court of Appeals held that the service was not valid when the defendant presented a lease agreement that corroborated his testimony that he had moved out of his half brother's house two and one-half months before his half brother was served. *Id.* at 958. Likewise, in *Thompson*, the First District Court of Appeals reversed and remanded the case for an evidentiary hearing when the defendant submitted an affidavit in which he stated that he was separated from his wife, that he had not resided at that address for over three years, and that he did not authorize anyone to accept service of process on his behalf. *Id.* at 605.

Occasionally, you will not need to include a full description of an analogous case. For instance, you may not need to include a full description of a case if you are using the case to illustrate a single point or if you have already given full descriptions of one or two cases but want to tell the attorney about a third or fourth case, or when you simply want to illustrate one aspect of a rule. In these situations you can use parentheticals.

EXAMPLE 24   **Cases Described in Parentheticals**

Although the statute does not specify the period of time an individual must occupy a home to be regarded as "residing therein," the courts do not require extended habitation. *Compare Magazine v. Bedoya*, 475 So. 2d 1035 (Fla. 3d DCA 1985) (six-week stay sufficient to establish residency), *with Gamboa v. Jones*, 455 So. 2d 613 (Fla. 3d DCA 1985) (ten-day visit not sufficient to establish residency).

EXAMPLE 25   **Additional Cases Described in Parentheticals**

In contrast, in the more recent cases, the courts have emphasized that it is not enough that the complaint or petition is left with a relative. *See, e.g., Busman*, 905 So. 2d at 947; *Torres v. Arnco Const., Inc.*, 867 So. 2d 583 (Fla. 5th DCA 2004). For example, in *Busman*, the court concluded that service of process was not valid even though the summons and complaint had been left with the defendant's half brother. *Id.* at 958. Similarly, in *Torres*, the court concluded that service had not been made at the defendant's usual place of abode when, after trying unsuccessfully to serve the defendant at his New York apartment, the plaintiff served the defendant's mother at her home in Florida. *Id.* at 585, 587. Although the defendant's mother told the process server that her son "would be home soon," the court decided that this statement was, at best, ambiguous. *Id.* at 585; *accord Portfolio Recovery Assocs., LLC v. Gonzalez*, 951 So. 2d 1037, 1038 (Fla. 3d DCA 2007) (service was not made at the defendants' usual place of abode when the summons and complaint were left with a woman who was the mother of one defendant and the mother-in-law of the other defendant, but the defendants had not lived at the residence for five years).

> **PRACTICE POINTER**
>
> In most instances, when you refer to a case by only one party's name, you should use the plaintiff's name. For example, when you refer to *Thompson v. State, Dep't of Revenue*, you would say "in *Thompson*," and when you refer to *Cordova v. Jolcover*, you would say, "in *Cordova*." There are, however, some exceptions to this general rule. When the plaintiff is the state, you will refer to the case using the defendant's name: "*State v. Smith*" becomes "*Smith*," and "*Commonwealth v. Jones*" becomes "*Jones*." In addition, if the courts typically refer to a case using the defendant's name, you should use that name. For more on short cites, see Rule 12.19 in the *ALWD Guide to Legal Citation* and Rule 10.9 in *The Bluebook*.

c.   Draft the Arguments

At this point your role changes dramatically. No longer are you just a "reporter" telling the attorney what you found in doing your research. To do a good job presenting each side's arguments, you must become an advocate, using your training, intellectual abilities, and creativity to construct the arguments each side is likely to make. You must think like the plaintiff's attorney and then like the defendant's attorney.

When you use the script format, you are, in effect, writing a "script" for the oral arguments on the issue. You begin by putting yourself in the shoes of the party with the burden of proof, setting out the arguments that side might make. You then step into the other side's shoes and set out that side's arguments. Finally, you assume the role of the judge, predicting how the court would decide the element and how it would justify its decision.

| **EXAMPLE 26** | **"Script" for Arguments** |

- ■ Party with the burden of proof's arguments
- ■ Responding party's arguments
- ■ Party with the burden of proof's rebuttal (optional)
- ■ Court's decision + rationale

Step 1: Identify Each Side's Arguments

The first step is to identify each side's arguments. If you wrote down possible arguments as you did your research, start with that list.

| **EXAMPLE 27** | **List of Arguments from Research Notes** |

Ms. Olsen's arguments

- ■ On the day that she was served, Ms. Olsen was living at the residential treatment house.
- ■ Service on a relative is not sufficient.
- ■ Her more permanent address was the residential treatment house address. She had a room, etc., at the residential treatment house.
- ■ *Heffernan* is an old case.
- ■ In *Torres*, the court held that the defendant's mother's house was not the defendant's usual place of abode even though the mother indicated that the defendant would be home later.
- ■ There is no indication that the State tried to serve Ms. Olsen at the residential treatment house.

The State's arguments

- ■ Ms. Olsen stayed at her sister's house three nights a week.
- ■ Ms. Olsen apparently received mail at her sister's house—the shoebox.
- ■ Ms. Olsen listed her sister's address on her driver's license.
- ■ In *Heffernan*, the court held that the apartment was the defendant's usual place of abode even though the defendant had left the apartment and was on a train back to his permanent residence.
- ■ In *Torres*, the defendant had a permanent residence where he had lived for twelve years. He was just visiting his mother.

Do not, however, stop with the list that you came up with while researching the issue. Push yourself further, asking yourself whether the parties can make any of the other standard types of arguments. For example, can one or both of the parties make plain language arguments, arguments based on the analogous cases, or policy arguments?

1. Plain Language Arguments

A plain language argument is an argument in which you apply the plain language of a statute or rule to the facts of your case. For instance, in the service of process problem, you would make a plain language argument if you argued that, under the plain language of the statute, the service was not made at Ms. Olsen's "usual" place of abode because her sister's house was not the place where she "usually" stayed. During the month in which service was made, Ms. Olsen spent four nights a week at the residential treatment house and only three nights a week at her sister's house. Similarly, you would be making a plain language argument if you argued that, under the plain language of the rule that the courts have set out, Ms. Olsen was not "actually living" at her sister's house because the summons and complaint were served on a weekday and, during the week, Ms. Olsen "actually lived" at the residential treatment house. Note that a plain language argument has two components: a word or phrase from the statute or rule and facts that show that that element is or is not met.

> **PRACTICE POINTER**   To make sure that you have considered all the plain language arguments, do two things. First, think about each word or phrase in the applicable part of the statute and/or rules, asking yourself what the plain meaning of that word or phrase requires. Second, go through each of your facts, asking yourself how each side might be able to use that fact.

2. Analogous Case Arguments

Under our system of law, judges usually decide like cases in a like manner. Therefore, if the analogous cases support the conclusion that you want the court to reach, you need to argue, first, that your case is like the analogous cases and, second, because your case is like the analogous cases, the court should reach the same result as the courts reached in those decisions. In contrast, if the analogous cases do not support the conclusion that you want the court to reach, you need to distinguish those cases. For example, in Ms. Olsen's case, she will want to argue that her case is like *Busman* and *Torres*, and she will want to distinguish *Heffernan*. Conversely, the State will want to distinguish *Busman* and *Torres* and argue that its case is more like *Heffernan*.

To make sure that you have considered all analogous case arguments, think about rules and the principles you drew from the cases and how the parties might be able to use those rules and principles to support their respective positions. In addition, go through the analogous cases one by one, thinking about how each side might be able to use that case.

> **PRACTICE POINTER**   In constructing analogous case arguments, ask yourself the following questions:
>
> - In what ways is the analogous case similar to my case?
> - In what ways is it different?
> - Is the case a relatively old case? If it is, how can each side use that fact?
> - Is the case from an intermediate court of appeals or from the state's highest court? How can each side use that fact?
> - Is the case well reasoned or poorly reasoned? How can each side use that fact?
> - How have other cases used or distinguished the case?

3. Policy Arguments

In making a policy argument, look at the reasons why the legislature enacted a particular statute or a court adopted a particular rule and use those underlying reasons to support your client's position. For example, in the Olsen case you could use the policy behind the service of process statutes—to ensure that defendants have notice of actions filed against them—to argue that service was invalid because Ms. Olsen did not receive notice.

When your issue is one that is governed by a statute, you may be able to find the policies underlying the statute in a "finding" or "purpose" section of the act of which your statute is a part, or a legislative history may tell you what the legislature intended when it enacted the statute. In addition, in applying a statute, the courts frequently set out what they believe are the policies underlying the statutes. Therefore, to come up with policy arguments, look at the text of the statute, the statute's legislative history, and those parts of other courts' decisions that discuss the policies underlying the statute. Once you identify the various policies, determine how each side might be able to use those policies to support its position.

In situations in which the underlying reason for the statute is not explicitly laid out in the act, in its legislative history, or in court decisions, use common sense to determine why the statute was enacted. Ask yourself "what good was the legislature trying to promote" or "what harm was the legislature trying to prevent" when it enacted the statute.

> **PRACTICE POINTER** At this initial stage, list all of the arguments (plain language, analogous case, and policy), no matter how weak they may seem. Later, you can go through these arguments, weeding out those that don't pass "the giggle test," that is, those that you could not make to a court without laughing.

You can use a chart like the one set out in Example 28 to keep track of the arguments that each side makes.

EXAMPLE 28   **List of Arguments**

Element	Olsen's Arguments	State's Arguments
Usual Place of Abode (in dispute)	Plain language arguments:	Plain language arguments:
	Analogous case arguments:	Analogous case arguments:
	Policy arguments:	Policy arguments:

Element	Olsen's Arguments	State's Arguments
Age and Residing Therein (not in dispute)		
Informing of Contents (in dispute)	Plain language arguments: Analogous case arguments: Policy arguments:	Plain language arguments: Analogous case arguments: Policy arguments

> **PRACTICE POINTER**
>
> If you find yourself staring at your computer screen unable to come up with more than one or two arguments, find an empty room and then stand up and make Ms. Olsen's arguments. After you have made all of her arguments, take a few steps to your right and make the State's arguments. In most instances, this process will trigger more ideas about what each side can argue. Thus, keep going to back and forth, making and then countering each side's arguments and "answering" questions that you think that a judge might ask you. While at first this exercise may feel a little silly, it will help you come up with additional arguments and it will help you develop the oral skills that you will need as a lawyer.

Step 2: Present the Arguments

After you have identified each side's arguments, you are ready to move to the second step: deciding how you want to present those arguments. Once again, you have some choices. For instance, you can do what we do in this chapter and set out the arguments using a script format, or you can do what we do in the next chapter and set out the rules using an integrated format.

Even under the script format, you have choices. One way to organize the arguments is by type of argument. If you choose this organizational scheme, set out the party with the burden of proof's plain language arguments in one paragraph, its analogous cases arguments in another paragraph or block of paragraphs, and its policy arguments in a third paragraph. Then set out the other side's arguments: Set out the other side's plain language arguments in one paragraph, its analogous case arguments in another paragraph or block of paragraphs, and its policy arguments in a third paragraph.

PRACTICE
POINTER

If you organize your arguments around types of
arguments, you will usually want to set out the
plain language arguments first, analogous cases
arguments second, and policy arguments third.
This ordering reflects the weight that courts typically give to the different
types of arguments. If a court can decide an issue by applying the plain language of the statute or common law to the facts of the case, it will usually
do so. If, however, the court cannot decide the issue based on the plain language, it will look to the cases to see how the cases have applied the rules.
If the cases do not resolve the issue, the court will then look to the policies
underlying the statute.

In the alternative, organize the arguments around the principles that you
identified when you analyzed and synthesized the cases. For example, if you
determined that all of the cases have three facts in common, you could organize
your arguments around those three facts. In setting out the party with the burden
of proof's arguments, you would discuss the first fact in one paragraph or block
of paragraphs, the second fact in a second paragraph or block of paragraphs, and
the third fact in a third paragraph or block of paragraphs. Similarly, in setting
out the other side's arguments, you would discuss the first fact in one paragraph
or block of paragraphs, the second fact in a second paragraph or block of paragraphs, and the third fact in a third paragraph or block of paragraphs. Within
the paragraphs discussing these facts, you would set out any plain language,
analogous case, and/or policy arguments that relate to that fact.

A third, and more sophisticated, approach is to organize your arguments
around "lines of argument." For example, if you have a burden of proof argument and an argument on the merits, you could organize the arguments around
these two lines of argument. In setting out your arguments, set out the party
with the burden of proof's arguments relating to the first line of argument in
one paragraph or block of paragraphs and its arguments relating to the second
line of argument in a second paragraph or block of paragraphs. Then set out
the other side's arguments, putting the other side's points relating to the first
line of argument in one paragraph and its points relating to the second line of
argument in a second paragraph or block of paragraphs. In setting out these
lines of argument, include the plain language, analogous case, or policy arguments that relate to that line of argument.

PRACTICE
POINTER

If you use the second option—organizing your
arguments around the principles you identified
when you analyzed and synthesized the cases—
you will usually want to discuss the principles in
the same order that you set them out and illustrated them in your analogous
case section. If you use the third approach—organizing your arguments
around "lines of argument"—you should discuss threshold arguments first.
In other words, if one argument builds upon another argument, set out the
foundational argument first.

Example 29 illustrates the differences between these three organizational schemes.

EXAMPLE 29   **Three Ways of Organizing the Arguments**

Arguments Organized by Type of Argument	Arguments Organized by Principles	Arguments Organized by Lines of Argument
Party with burden of proof's arguments	**Party with burden of proof's arguments**	**Party with burden of proof's arguments**
• Plain language arguments	• Arguments relating to first principle (include any plain language, analogous case, and policy arguments)	• First line of argument (include any plain language, analogous case, and policy arguments)
• Analogous case arguments	• Arguments relating to second principle (include any plain language, analogous case, and policy arguments)	• Second line of argument (include any plain language, analogous case, and policy arguments)
• Policy arguments	• Arguments relating to third principle (include any plain language, analogous case, and policy arguments)	
Responding party's arguments	**Responding party's arguments**	**Responding party's arguments**
• Plain language arguments	• Arguments relating to first principle (include any plain language, analogous case, and policy arguments)	• First line of argument (include any plain language, analogous case, and policy arguments)
• Analogous case arguments	• Arguments relating to second principle (include any plain language, analogous case, and policy arguments)	• Second line of argument (include any plain language, analogous case, and policy arguments)
• Policy arguments	• Arguments relating to third principle (include any plain language, analogous case, and policy arguments)	

Step 3: Draft the Arguments

In most instances, you should start your discussion of each side's arguments by setting out that side's general assertion. For example, in the Olsen case, start the usual place of abode arguments by setting out Ms. Olsen's general assertion: that her sister's house was not her usual place of abode. Similarly, start your discussion of the State's arguments by setting out the State's assertion: Ms. Olsen's sister's house was Ms. Olsen's usual place of abode or it was one of her usual places of abode. In addition, if you are going to make a number of different arguments, you may want to alert the attorney to that fact.

EXAMPLE 30　**Three Ways of Setting Out Ms. Olsen's General Assertion Relating to Usual Place of Abode**

1. Ms. Olsen will argue that her sister's house was not her usual place of abode.
2. Ms. Olsen will argue that she was not actually living at Ms. Webster's house and that, therefore, Ms. Webster's house was not her usual place of abode.
3. Ms. Olsen can make three arguments to support her assertion that her sister's house was not her usual place of abode. First, ...

EXAMPLE 31　**Three Ways of Setting Out the State's General Assertion Relating to Usual Place of Abode**

1. In response, the State will argue that Ms. Webster's house was Ms. Olsen's usual place of abode.
2. The State will counter by arguing that Ms. Olsen was actually living at her sister's house.
3. The State can make three arguments to support its assertion that the service was made at Ms. Olsen's usual place of abode.

In addition to setting out each side's general assertion, you should also introduce and set out each side's subassertions. For example, if you have decided to organize the arguments around types of arguments, introduce each of these types of arguments, asserting that the plain language, the analogous cases, and the policies underlying the statute or rule support your general assertion. Likewise, if you are organizing your arguments around lines of arguments, include a sentence introducing each line of argument.

EXAMPLE 32　**Sentences Introducing Subassertions**

- First, Ms. Olsen can argue that under the plain language of the statute her sister's house was not her usual place of abode.
- Second, Ms. Olsen can argue that her case is more like [case names] than it is like [case names].
- Third, Ms. Olsen can argue that, as a matter of public policy, the court should hold that service was not left at Ms. Olsen's usual place of abode.

It is not, however, enough to just set out general assertions and subassertions. You also need to show the attorney how each side will support those assertions. One way to do this is to picture yourself standing in front of a judge. If you are making a plain language argument, what facts would you use, and how would you characterize those facts? If you are making an analogous case argument, what cases would you use, and how would you characterize and use those cases? If you are making a policy argument, what policies would you rely on, and how would you use those policies? Similarly, picture the other side presenting its arguments. How would its attorney use the facts, cases, and policies to support its position?

The following example, Example 33, is ineffective because the writer has not supported her assertions. For instance, in the first paragraph, the writer asserts that Ms. Olsen's sister's house was not Ms. Olsen's usual place of abode because the residential treatment house was her usual place of abode. The writer does not, however, back up this assertion with facts: She does not point out that Ms. Olsen had been a full-time resident of the residential treatment house for several months and that she was still spending four nights a week there. Similarly, although the writer asserts that Ms. Olsen's case is more like *Busman* and *Torres* than it is like *Heffernan*, she does not support this assertion by comparing and contrasting the facts in those cases to the facts in the Olsen case. Finally, although the writer sets out a rule relating to the burden of proof, she does not explain why or how that rule will produce a just result.

> **PRACTICE POINTER**   While almost every attorney wants citations to authority in the rule and analogous case sections of memos, not all attorneys want them in the argument sections. Thus, before you draft your memo, determine which approach the attorney that you are working for prefers. (In the following examples, citations are not included in the argument section.)

EXAMPLE 33   **Poor Example: The Writer Has Set Out Assertions but Has Not Supported Those Assertions**

General assertion
First subassertion

Second subassertion
Third subassertion

General assertion
First subassertion
Second subassertion

Third subassertion

In this case, Ms. Olsen can make three arguments to support her assertion that the summons and complaint were not left at her usual place of abode. First, she can argue that her sister's house was not her usual place of abode because the residential treatment house was her usual place of abode. Second, she can use the cases to support her position: her case is more like *Busman* and *Torres* than *Heffernan*. Finally, she can argue that as a matter of public policy the party seeking to invoke the jurisdiction of the court has the burden of proving that the service was valid.

In response, the State will argue that the summons and complaint were left at Ms. Olsen's usual place of abode. The facts establish that Ms. Olsen was, in fact, living at her sister's house at the time the summons and complaint were served. Accordingly, this case is like *Heffernan*. In addition, the State will distinguish *Busman* and *Torres* on the basis that, in those cases, the defendant was not spending any time at the house where the service was made. Finally, the State can argue that the service was valid because the defendant's sister's house was the place where she was most likely to receive notice.

Example 34, while not perfect, is much better. In addition to setting out his assertions, the writer has supported those assertions.

EXAMPLE 34   **Better Example: The Writer Has Set Out Assertions and Support for Those Assertions**

Ms. Olsen can make three arguments to support her assertion that her sister's house was not her usual place of abode. First, Ms. Olsen will argue that, under the plain language of the statute, her sister's house was not her usual place of abode. As the courts have stated, service must be made at the place where the defendant was actually living at the time service is made. In this case, the summons and petition were served on a weekday, and on weekdays Ms. Olsen was actually living at the residential treatment house.

Second, Ms. Olsen will argue that the facts in her case are more like the facts in *Busman* and *Torres* than the facts in *Heffernan*. Like Mr. Busman, who produced a lease that corroborated his testimony that he was not living with his half brother on the day that the summons and complaint were served, Ms. Olsen can produce evidence that establishes that on the day she was served she was living at the residential treatment house. Both Ms. Olsen's sister and the manager of the residential treatment house have said that they will testify that, during June and July, Ms. Olsen lived at the treatment house during the week and only visited her sister on weekends. In the alternative, Ms. Olsen can argue that the facts in her case are even stronger than the facts in *Torres*. While Mr. Torres's mother's statement that Mr. Torres "would be home soon" suggested that Mr. Torres would be returning to his mother's house that day, Ms. Olsen's sister told the process server that Ms. Olsen "isn't here today." In addition, Ms. Olsen can distinguish *Heffernan*: Although Mr. Heffernan had been at his family's apartment only an hour before the summons and complaint were served, Ms. Olsen had not been at her sister's house for several days.

Finally, Ms. Olsen can argue that, as a matter of public policy, the court should decide that the summons and petition were not left at her usual place of abode. The courts have stated that the statute should be narrowly construed, and this policy is particularly important in cases in which the State is seeking to terminate a mother's parental rights. In addition, this is not a case in which the State tried but could not locate Ms. Olsen: There is no evidence that the State tried to serve Ms. Olsen at the residential treatment house.

In response, the State will argue that Ms. Olsen was served at one of her usual places of abode.

The courts have not required that the plaintiff be living at the house where the summons and complaint are served on the day on which the service is made. Therefore, while Ms. Olsen may not have been at her sister's house on the day that the summons and complaint were served, she had been there the previous weekend, and she was there the following weekend. In addition, Ms. Olsen had possessions at her sister's house.

Therefore, the State will argue that the facts in this case are much stronger than the facts in *Heffernan*. While in *Heffernan*, Mr. Heffernan visited his family only "twice during the season," Ms. Olsen lived at her sister's house on weekends. In addition, while Mr. Heffernan had another permanent residence, Ms. Olsen was staying at a halfway house, which, by definition, is only a temporary residence. Finally, while in *Heffernan* there was no indication that Mr. Heffernan listed the Florida address on any documents, Ms. Olsen listed her sister's address on her driver's license, and there is evidence indicating that Ms. Olsen received other types of mail at her sister's house.

Marginal notes:

Ms. Olsen's general assertion
Ms. Olsen's first subassertion
Facts that support Ms. Olsen's first subassertion
Ms. Olsen's second subassertion
Explanation of how cases support Ms. Olsen's second subassertion

Ms. Olsen's third subassertion
Policies supporting Ms. Olsen's third subassertion

State's main assertion

State's first subassertion
Facts that support State's first subassertion

State's second subassertion
Cases that support State's second subassertion

Cases that support State's second subassertion

The State will use these same facts to distinguish *Torres*. While in *Torres*, Mr. Torres presented evidence establishing that his permanent residence was in New York, in the present case, Ms. Olsen did not have a permanent residence. In the five months before service, she had been an inpatient in a treatment facility, she had lived at the treatment house, and she had lived with her sister. The State can also distinguish *Busman*. While in *Busman* the record indicated that the defendant had not lived at the house where service had been for several weeks, Ms. Olsen admits that she stayed at her sister's house on the weekend before her sister was served.

State's third subassertion

Policies supporting State's third subassertion

Finally, the State will argue that, because the return was regular on its face, Ms. Olsen has the burden of proving, by clear and convincing evidence, that her sister's house was not her usual place of abode. In this instance, Ms. Olsen has not met that burden. When there is evidence that the defendant was in fact living at the house where service was made, the courts should not require plaintiffs to determine which house the defendant was living at on any particular day.

While in the prior example, the writer organized the arguments by type of argument, in the following example, the writer organized the arguments by lines of argument. Once again, the writer has not included pinpoint citations.

EXAMPLE 35   **Arguments Organized Around Lines of Argument**

Ms. Olsen's strongest argument is that service was not made at the place where she was actually living. Although Ms. Olsen stayed at her sister's house on weekends, on the day that service was made, she was actually living at the residential treatment center. Consequently, this case is more like *Busman* and *Torres* than it is like *Heffernan*. Like Mr. Busman, who was not actually living with his half brother on the day that the summons and complaint were served, Ms. Olsen was not living with her sister on July 24. Both Ms. Olsen's sister and the manager of the residential treatment house have said that they will testify that, during June and July, Ms. Olsen lived at the treatment house during the week and visited her sister only on weekends. This testimony makes this case stronger than *Torres*, in which the defendant's mother's statement that Mr. Torres "would be home soon" suggested that Mr. Torres would be returning to his mother's house that day. Ms. Olsen can also distinguish *Heffernan*: While Mr. Heffernan had been at his family's apartment only an hour before the summons and complaint were served, Ms. Olsen had not been at her sister's house for several days.

Ms. Olsen also has strong policy arguments. The courts have repeatedly said that the purpose of the statute is to ensure that defendants receive notice and that, to that end, the statute should be narrowly construed. In this case, the defendant will testify that she did not receive notice. Her sister states that instead of giving the summons to Ms. Olsen, she put the summons in a shoebox in the kitchen. Moreover, Ms. Olsen can argue that in cases involving the termination of parental rights, the courts should err on the side of ensuring that the parent receives notice. At a minimum, the State should have tried to serve Ms. Olsen at the residential treatment house.

The State can counter this policy argument with its own policy argument. When a defendant has two or more places of abode, the State should not have to determine which one the defendant is staying at on the day that service is actually made. Service can be made at any of the defendant's usual places of abode.

The State can also argue that Ms. Olsen has not met her burden of proving by clear and convincing evidence that she was not actually living at her sister's house on the day when service was made. Unlike

Mr. Busman, who had proof that he had moved out of his half brother's house three weeks before service was attempted, Ms. Olsen had not moved out of her sister's house. In fact, she stayed at her sister's house both on the weekend before and the weekend after service was made. The State can also distinguish *Torres*. As the majority in that case noted, the mother's statement was ambiguous; in addition, there was nothing in Mr. Torres's affidavit that established where he was living on the date service was made. In contrast, in this case Ms. Olsen does not deny that she was living at her sister's house three nights a week during the month of July, the month during which service was made. Finally, the State can argue that this case is similar to *Heffernan* in that, as in that case, Ms. Olsen was moving back and forth between two residences. While in *Heffernan* there was no indication that Mr. Heffernan planned to return to the family home the next weekend, in this case Ms. Olsen did, in fact, go back to her sister's house.

d.   Predict How the Court Will Decide the Element

The final piece of information you need to include is your prediction about how a court is likely to decide the element. Is it more likely that the court will find that the element is met, or is it more likely that the court will decide that the element is not met?

In writing this section, you must once again change roles. Instead of playing the role of the reporter describing the rules and analogous cases or of the advocate making each side's arguments, you must play the role of judge. You must put yourself in the position of the particular court that will decide the issue — trial court, appellate court, state court, federal court — and decide how that court is likely to decide that element.

At least initially, you may be uncomfortable making such predictions. How can you predict what a court might do? The good news is that with time, and experience, you will get better and better at making predictions. In the meantime, read the statutes and cases carefully, and critically evaluate each side's arguments. Careful reading and careful consideration of arguments — plus common sense — will help you make reliable predictions. Remember, too, that you are predicting, not guaranteeing, an outcome.

In drafting your mini-conclusion, do two things: First, set out your prediction. Second, briefly explain why you believe the court will decide the element as you have predicted. As a general rule, do not include phrases like "I think" or "in my opinion."

In Example 36, the writer has set out his prediction but not his reasoning. As a consequence, the reader has to guess about why the writer reached the conclusion that he reached. Example 37 is better: In it, the writer has set out both his prediction and his reasoning.

EXAMPLE 36   **Poor Draft: The Writer Has Set Out the Prediction but Not the Reasoning**

While both sides have strong arguments, the court will probably conclude that the summons was not left at Ms. Olsen's usual place of abode.

EXAMPLE 37	**Better Draft: The Writer Has Set Out Both the Prediction and Reasoning**

While both sides have strong arguments, the court will probably conclude that the summons was not left at Ms. Olsen's usual place of abode. In the more recent cases, the courts have strictly construed the statute, holding that the service was not made at the defendant's usual place of abode when the defendant had a more permanent place of abode. Thus, because the residential treatment house was Ms. Olsen's more permanent residence, the court will probably conclude that it was Ms. Olsen's usual place of abode. In addition, the court may be influenced by two key facts: The record does not indicate that the State tried to serve Ms. Olsen at the residential treatment house, and Ms. Olsen states that she did not receive notice.

§ 12.8.5   Checklist for Critiquing a Discussion Section Written Using a Script Format

a.   Content

Introduction

■ The writer has included a sentence or paragraph introducing the governing statute or common law rule.
■ The writer has set out the general rule, quoting the applicable statutory sections and quoting or paraphrasing the common law rule.
■ The writer has set out any other general rules.
■ When appropriate, the writer has briefly described the policies underlying the statute or common law rule.
■ The writer has included a roadmap.
■ The writer has not included rules or information that the attorney does not need.
■ The rules are stated accurately and objectively.
■ For each rule stated, the writer has included a citation to authority.

Discussion of Undisputed Elements

■ The writer has identified the element and, when there are specific rules, set out those specific rules.
■ The writer has applied the rules to the facts of the client's case, explaining why the element is not in dispute.

Discussion of Disputed Elements

■ For each disputed element, the writer has set out the specific rules, described cases that have interpreted and applied those rules, set out each side's arguments, and predicted how the court will decide the element.
■ The writer has included all of the applicable specific rules and set out those rules accurately and objectively.
■ The writer has introduced each group of analogous cases, telling the attorney what rule or principle the cases illustrate.

- The case descriptions illustrate the rule or principle and are accurate and objective.
- In setting out the arguments, the writer has set out both assertions and support for those assertions.
- The analysis is sophisticated: the writer has set out more than the obvious arguments.
- The writer has predicted how each element will be decided and given reasons to support those predictions.

b. Large-Scale Organization

- The writer has presented the information in the order in which the attorney expects to see it. For example, the writer begins the discussion section with an introductory section in which he or she sets out the general rules. The writer then walks the attorney through each of the elements, raising and dismissing the undisputed elements and doing a more complete analysis of the disputed elements.

c.   Writing

- The attorney can understand the discussion with just one reading.
- The paragraph divisions are logical, and the paragraphs are neither too long nor too short. See Chapter 22.
- Transitions and dovetailing have been used to make the connection between ideas clear. See Chapter 23.
- In most sentences, the writer has used the actor as the subject of the sentence, and the subject and verb are close together. See sections 24.1 through 24.5.
- The writer has varied the length of the sentences and the sentence patterns so that each sentence flows smoothly from the prior sentence. See section 24.5.
- The writing is concise and precise. See sections 25.1 and 25.2.
- The writing is grammatically correct and correctly punctuated. See Chapters 27 and 28.
- The discussion section has been proofread.

§ 12.9   Drafting the Formal Conclusion

You are not doing anything wrong. In drafting a formal memo, you do set out your conclusions in more than one place. If you included a brief answer, you set out your conclusion there. In addition, if your problem required an elements analysis, you set out mini-conclusions for each disputed element. And yes, you will now, once again, set out your conclusion, this time in a formal conclusion.

While some attorneys think that the typical memo has too many conclusions, other attorneys believe that each conclusion serves a useful purpose. The brief answer is exactly that: a brief answer. If the client is on the phone and the attorney has not had time to read the full memo, he or she can read the brief answer. The mini-conclusions serve a different purpose. They are part of the analysis and help the attorney understand which elements will be easy to prove and which may be more difficult to prove. The formal conclusion serves still a different purpose. It is the place where you pull all of the pieces together.

§ 12.9.1   Summarize Your Conclusions

In a one-issue memo, the formal conclusion is used to summarize the analysis of that one issue. For example, in the Olsen memo, you would use the formal conclusion to tell the attorney whether you think Ms. Olsen was properly served. In Example 1 below, the writer begins by answering the question set out in the issue statement. The writer does not, however, stop there. In addition to answering the question, she goes through the elements, element by element. In the second paragraph, the writer tells the attorney that Ms. Olsen will have to concede that the summons was left with a person of suitable age and discretion and that, more likely than not, the court will conclude that the process server told Ms. Olsen's sister about the contents. In the third paragraph, the writer discusses usual place of abode, briefly explaining why she thinks that Ms. Olsen can prove that the summons was not left at her usual place of abode.

Notice that in Example 1, the writer has not included citations to authority. Most legal readers do not expect citations in a formal conclusion.

EXAMPLE 1   **Formal Conclusion**

Conclusion

Because of the strong public policy in favor of ensuring that defendants receive notice of actions that have been filed against them, the court will probably decide that the substituted service of process was not valid and vacate the judgment terminating Ms. Olsen's parental rights.

Ms. Olsen will have to concede that her sister, Ms. Webster, is a person of suitable age and that Ms. Webster was residing at the house where the service was made. In addition, because the process server told Ms. Webster that Ms. Olsen needed to go to court, it seems unlikely that Ms. Olsen will be able to prove that Ms. Webster was not informed of the contents.

Ms. Olsen may, however, be able to prove that the summons and complaint were not served at her usual place of abode. In the more recent cases, the courts have concluded that service made on a relative was invalid when the defendants produced evidence establishing that they were not actually living with that relative on the day that service was made. While in most of these cases the defendants had not lived at the house where service was made for several months or several years, in the Olsen case the court may be swayed by three facts: This case involves the termination of Ms. Olsen's parental rights; there is no evidence that the State tried to personally serve Ms. Olsen or that it tried to serve Ms. Olsen at the residential treatment house; and Ms. Olsen states that she did not receive notice.

---

§ 12.9.2   Present Your Advice

While some attorneys just want conclusions, others may want you to go one step further and offer advice. What are the client's options? What action should the attorney take next? Is this the type of case that the firm should, or wants to, handle? When you are asked to include this type of information in the conclusion, add a paragraph like the one in Example 2.

EXAMPLE 2	**Paragraph Setting Out Advice**

Because Ms. Olsen has some strong arguments, I recommend that we move to quash the service of process and vacate the order terminating her parental rights.

---

§ 12.9.3 Checklist for Formal Conclusion

a.   Content

■ In a one-issue memorandum, the conclusion is used to predict how the issue will be decided and to summarize the reasons supporting that prediction.
■ When appropriate, the writer includes not only the conclusion but also strategic advice.

b.   Organization

■ The information is organized logically.

c.   Writing

■ The attorney can understand the conclusion with just one reading.
■ The paragraph divisions are logical, and the paragraphs are neither too long nor too short. See Chapter 22.
■ Transitions and dovetailing have been used to make the connection between ideas clear. See Chapter 23.
■ In most sentences, the writer has used the actor as the subject of the sentence, and the subject and verb are close together. See sections 24.1 through 24.5.
■ The writer has varied the length of the sentences and the sentence patterns so that each sentence flows smoothly from the prior sentence. See section 24.5.
■ The writing is concise and precise. See sections 25.1 and 25.2.
■ The writing is grammatically correct and correctly punctuated. See Chapters 27 and 28.
■ The conclusion has been proofread.

Chapter 12 Quiz No. 3

Draft answers for each of the following questions. Make your points clearly and concisely, and write sentences that are easy to read and that are grammatical and correctly punctuated.

1. What is the difference between a disputed element and an undisputed element?
2. When should you include descriptions of analogous cases?
3. Why should you begin your descriptions of a group of analogous cases with a principle-based topic sentence?

4. In drafting the analogous case section, when might you use a parenthetical?
5. What distinguishes a good argument section from a weak one?

§ 12.10 Revising, Editing, and Proofreading the Memo

Yes, there are occasions when, because of time or money constraints, you will have to turn in a first draft of an in-house memo. You should not, however, get in the habit of submitting first drafts to your supervising attorney, and you should never submit a first draft to a court, to opposing counsel, or to your client. Unlike speech, which disappears as soon as the words are spoken, written words remain: While well-written documents can enhance your reputation, poorly written ones can damage it

As a consequence, whenever possible, do what we do in this section, and treat revising, editing, and proofreading as three separate processes.

§ 12.10.1 Revise Your Draft

Revising is the process of "re-visioning" what you have drafted. During this re-visioning process, step back from your draft, and look at it through the eyes of your reader. Have you given the attorney all of the information that he or she needs? Have you presented that information in the order that the attorney expects to see it?

During the revising stage, you need to be willing to make major changes. If, in revising the draft, you realize that you did not need to include one part of your discussion, delete that part, no matter how many hours you spent drafting it. Similarly, if in revising the draft, you realize that you did not research or discuss a major point, go back and do that research, analysis, and writing. Finally, if in revising your draft, you realize that your organizational scheme just does not work, start over, reorganizing one section or even the entire statement of facts or discussion section.

PRACTICE POINTER	Many writers do a better job revising when they print out a draft and lay out the pages side by side.

a.   Check Content

In revising a draft, look first at its content. If there are problems with content, solving those problems must be your first priority.

In checking content, the first question to ask yourself is whether you have given the attorney the information that he or she requested. Did you research the assigned issue or issues? Did you locate all of the applicable statutes and cases? Did you identify and present the arguments that each side is likely to make? Did you evaluate those arguments and predict how the court is likely to rule?

b.　Check to Make Sure That the Information Is Presented Accurately

In law, small errors can have serious consequences. The failure to cite check to make sure that a case is still good law, an omitted "not," or an "or" that should have been "and" can make the difference between winning and losing, between competent lawyering and malpractice.

Consequently, in writing the memo, exercise care. Because the attorney is relying on you, your research must be thorough. Make sure that you have located the applicable statutes and cases and that you have checked to make sure that those statutes and cases are still good law. In addition, make sure your analysis is sound. Did you read the statutes and cases carefully? Is the way in which you have put the pieces together sound? Finally, make sure you have presented the statutes and cases accurately and fairly. Did you correctly identify the issue in the analogous cases? Did you take a rule out of context? Did you misrepresent the facts or omit a key fact? Unless the attorney reads the statutes and cases you cite, he may not see an error until it is too late.

c.　Check to Make Sure That the Discussion Section Is Well Organized

The next step is to check the discussion section's large-scale organization. Has the information been presented in the order that the attorney expects to see it?

One way to check large-scale organization is to prepare an after-the-fact outline. This is done either by labeling the subject matter of each paragraph and then listing those labels in outline form or by summarizing what each paragraph says. See section 21.4.2.

d.　Check to Make Sure That the Connections Are Explicit

Once you have revised for content and organization, look at your use of roadmaps, signposts, topic sentences, and transitions.

1. Roadmaps

A roadmap is just what the term implies: a "map" providing the reader with an overview of the document. For example, in our sample problem, the writer put a roadmap at the end of the introductory section that tells readers which elements will be easy to prove and which elements will be more difficult to prove.

EXAMPLE 1　　　**Roadmap Telling the Attorney Which Elements Will Be in Dispute and Which Elements Will Not Be in Dispute**

In this case, Ms. Olsen will have to concede that the summons was left with a person 15 years or older who was residing at the house where the summons and complaint were served. In addition, it is unlikely that Ms. Olsen will be able to prove that her sister was not informed of the contents of the documents. Ms. Olsen may, however, be able to present clear and convincing evidence that the summons was not left at her usual place of abode.

Note that in Example 1 above, the roadmap is substantive in nature. Instead of saying, "First I will discuss this and then I will discuss that," the writer has talked about what Ms. Olsen can and cannot prove. For more on roadmaps, see section 22.2.1.

2. Topic Sentences, Signposts, and Transitions

Topic sentences, signposts, and transitions serve the same function that directional signs serve on a freeway. They tell readers where they are, what to expect, and how the pieces are connected. See Chapter 24 and sections 21.2.2 and 22.5. While these directional signs may not be particularly important in some types of writing, they are essential in legal writing. Without them, the connections between paragraphs and between sentences may not be clear, making the analysis difficult to follow.

Similarly,   In contrast,   In addition,

Compare Example 2 below, in which the writer has not included topic sentences, signposts, or transitions, with Example 3. In Example 3, the topic sentences, signposts, and transitions are in boldface type.

EXAMPLE 2   **The Writer Has Not Included Topic Sentences, Signposts, or Transitions**

When a defendant has more than one residence, the service must be made at the place where the defendant was actually living at the time the summons and complaint were served. Ms. Olsen had more than one residence: During the week she lived at the treatment house, and on weekends she visited her sister. Because the summons and complaint were served on a Wednesday, a weekday, the service was not made at the place where Ms. Olsen was actually living.

Like Mr. Torres, who only visited his mother and who was not at his mother's house when service was made, Ms. Olsen only visited her sister and was not at her sister's house when the summons and complaint were served. While Mr. Torres's mother's statement that Mr. Torres "would be home soon" suggested that Mr. Torres would be returning to his mother's house that day, Ms. Olsen's sister told the process server that Ms. Olsen "isn't here today." While the plaintiff in *Torres* had tried on a number of occasions to serve Mr. Torres at his New York house, we do not know whether the defendant tried to serve Ms. Olsen personally or at the treatment house. While Mr. Heffernan had been at his family's apartment only an hour before the summons and complaint were served, Ms. Olsen had not been at her sister's house for several days and, while in *Heffernan* the summons and complaint were served on the defendant's wife, in the present case the summons and complaint were served on Ms. Olsen's sister. Since *Heffernan*, the courts have interpreted the service process statutes more narrowly.

The courts have repeatedly held that the service of process statutes should be strictly construed and that service on a relative is not, by itself, enough. *Shurman v. Atl. Mortg. & Inv. Corp.*, 795 So. 2d 952, 953-54 (Fla. 2001). Ms. Olsen did not receive notice.

EXAMPLE 3   The Writer Has Included Topic Sentences,
Signposts, and Transitions

Ms. Olsen can make three arguments to support her assertion that her sister's house was not her usual place of abode. First, Ms. Olsen will argue that, under the plain language of the statute, her sister's house was not her usual place of abode. As the courts have stated, service must be made at the place where the defendant was actually living at the time the summons and complaint were served. **In this case,** the summons and complaint were served on a weekday, and on weekdays Ms. Olsen was actually living at the residential treatment house.

Second, Ms. Olsen will argue that the facts in her case are more like the facts in *Busman* and *Torres* than the facts in *Heffernan*. Like Mr. Busman, who produced a lease that corroborated his testimony that he was not living with his half brother on the day that the summons and complaint were served, Ms. Olsen can produce evidence that establishes that on the day she was served she was living at the residential treatment house. Both Ms. Olsen's sister and the manager of the residential treatment house have said they will testify that during June and July Ms. Olsen lived at the treatment house during the week and only stayed with her sister on weekends. **In the alternative,** Ms. Olsen can argue that the facts in her case are even stronger than the facts in *Torres*. While Mr. Torres's mother's statement that Mr. Torres "would be home soon" suggested that Mr. Torres would be returning to his mother's house that day, Ms. Olsen's sister told the process server that Ms. Olsen "isn't here today." **In addition,** Ms. Olsen can distinguish *Heffernan*: Although Mr. Heffernan had been at his family's apartment only an hour before the summons and complaint were served, Ms. Olsen had not been at her sister's house for several days.

Finally, Ms. Olsen can argue that, as a matter of public policy, the court should decide that the summons and petition were not left at her usual place of abode. The courts have stated that the statute should be narrowly construed, and this policy is particularly important in cases in which the State is seeking to terminate a mother's parental rights. **In addition,** this is not a case in which the State tried but could not locate Ms. Olsen: There is no evidence that the State tried to serve Ms. Olsen at the residential treatment house.

---

3. Dovetailing

Another technique that you can use to make the connections between ideas clear is dovetailing. You use dovetailing when you refer back to a point made in the prior sentence or paragraph.

A   B   Reference to B   C

_____   _____

In Examples 4 and 5, the writer has used dovetailing to make clear the connections between the first and second sentences. The language that is in bold is the dovetail.

EXAMPLE 4   Dovetailing Used to Connect First and
Second Sentences

During April, May, and June 2013, Ms. Olsen usually spent weeknights at the treatment house and Friday, Saturday, and Sunday nights at her **sister's house. Because she was spending time at her sister's house,** she moved some of her clothing and personal effects into her sister's house.

EXAMPLE 5	Dovetailing Used to Connect First and Second Sentences

Although the party seeking to invoke the jurisdiction of the court has the burden of proving that service was proper, if the return is regular on its face, the courts presume that the service was valid. *Busman v. State, Dep't of Revenue*, 905 So. 2d 956, 958 (Fla. 3d DCA 2005); *Thompson v. State, Dep't of Revenue*, 867 So. 2d 603, 605 (Fla. 1st DCA 2004). **In such instances,** the party challenging the service has the burden of presenting clear and convincing evidence that the service was invalid. *Id.*

While in Examples 4 and 5 dovetailing was used to make clear the connections between sentences, in Example 6 it is used to make clear the connections between paragraphs. The first sentence in the second paragraph refers back to the information at the end of the first paragraph.

EXAMPLE 6	Dovetailing Used to Connect Paragraphs

Thus, the plaintiff will argue that the facts in this case are much stronger than the facts in *Heffernan*. While in *Heffernan*, Mr. Heffernan visited his family only "twice during the season," Ms. Olsen lived at her sister's house three days a week. In addition, while Mr. Heffernan had another permanent residence, Ms. Olsen was staying at a treatment house, which by definition, is only a temporary residence. Finally, while in *Heffernan* there was no indication that Mr. Heffernan listed the Florida address on any documents, Ms. Olsen listed her sister's address on her driver's license.

The plaintiff will use these same facts to distinguish *Torres*. While in *Torres*, Mr. Torres presented evidence establishing that his permanent residence was in New York, in our case, Ms. Olsen did not have a permanent residence. In the five months prior to service, she had been an . . .

For more on dovetailing, see section 23.3.

PRACTICE POINTER	While roadmaps, topic sentences, signposts, transitions, and dovetailing are more important in legal writing than in many other types of writing, do not overuse them. For example, do not use dovetailing to connect all of your sentences or all of your paragraphs.

The work is now almost done. When you step back from the memo and look at it through the attorney's eyes, you are pleased with its content and organization. You do, however, still need to edit and proofread your memo.

Although some writers mistakenly believe that revising, editing, and proofreading are the same, they are not. While during the revision process you "revision" your creation, during the editing process you make that vision clearer, more concise, more precise, and more accessible. Proofreading is different yet again. It is the search for errors. When you proofread, you are not asking yourself, "Is there a better way of saying this?" Instead, you are looking to see if what you intended to have on the page is in fact there.

Although the lines between revising and editing and between editing and proofreading blur at times, the distinctions among these three skills are important to keep in mind, if for no other reason than to remind you that there are three distinct ways of making changes to a draft and that the best written documents undergo all three types of changes.

§ 12.10.2 Edit Your Draft

Like revising, editing requires that you look at your work through fresh eyes. At this stage, however, the focus is not on the larger issues of content and organization but on sentence structure, precision and conciseness, grammar, and punctuation. The goal is to produce a professional product that is easy to read and understand. In this chapter, we focus on writing effective sentences and writing correctly; in Chapter 13, we focus on writing precisely and concisely.

a.   Writing Effective Sentences

Most writers can substantially improve their sentences by following four simple pieces of advice about writing:

1. Use the actor as the subject of most sentences.
2. Keep the subject and verb close together.
3. Put old information at the beginning of the sentence and new information at the end.
4. Vary sentence length and pattern.

1. Use the Actor as the Subject of Most Sentences

By using the actor as the subject of most of your sentences, you can eliminate many of the constructions that make legal writing hard to understand: overuse of the passive voice, most nominalizations, expletive constructions, and many misplaced modifiers.

(a) Passive Constructions

In a passive construction, the actor appears in the object rather than the subject slot of the sentence, or it is not named at all. For instance, in Example 7, although the jury is the actor, the word "jury" is used as the object of the preposition "by" rather than the subject of the sentence.

EXAMPLE 7   **Passive Voice**

A verdict was reached by the jury.

In the following example, the actor, "jury," is not named at all.

EXAMPLE 8   **Passive Voice**

A verdict was reached.

To use the active voice, simply identify the actor (in this case, the jury) and use it as the subject of the sentence.

EXAMPLE 9   Active Voice

The jury reached a verdict.

Now read each of the sentences in Example 10, marking the subject and verb and deciding whether the writer used the actor as the subject of the sentence. If the writer did not use the actor as the subject of the sentence, decide whether the sentence should be rewritten. As a general rule, the active voice is better unless the passive voice improves the flow of sentences or the writer wants to de-emphasize what the actor did. For more on the effective use of the active and passive voices, see section 24.1.

> If the return is regular on its face, there is a presumption that the service was valid. *Thompson v. State, Dep't of Revenue*, 867 So. 2d 603, 605 (Fla. 1st DCA 2004); *Magazine v. Bedoya*, 475 So. 2d 1035, 1035 (Fla. 3d DCA 1985). In such instances, the defendant must prove that the service was invalid. *Thompson*, 867 So. 2d at 605; *Magazine*, 475 So. 2d at 1035.

Sentence 1

If the return is regular on its face, <u>there</u> <u>is</u> a presumption that the service was valid.

In writing Sentence 1, the writer used the passive voice. Instead of using the actor (the court) as the subject of the sentence, the writer has used an expletive construction: "there is." Because the writer did not have a good reason for using the passive voice, we have rewritten the sentence using the active voice.

EXAMPLE 10   Rewrite Using the Active Voice

However, if the return is regular on its face, the <u>courts</u> <u>presume</u> that the service was valid.

Sentence 2

In such instances, the <u>burden</u> of presenting clear and convincing evidence that the service was invalid is on the defendant.

Sentence 2 is also written in the passive voice. Instead of using the actor (the defendant) as the subject of the sentence, the writer has placed the actor in a prepositional phrase. Because the writer did not have a good reason for using the passive voice, we have shown three ways to rewrite the sentence.

EXAMPLE 11	**Edits Using the Active Voice**

In such instances, the <u>party</u> challenging the service <u>has</u> the burden of presenting clear and convincing evidence that the service was invalid.

In such instances, the <u>party</u> challenging the service <u>must</u> <u>prove</u> that the service was invalid by clear and convincing evidence.

In such instances, the <u>party</u> challenging the service <u>must prove</u>, by clear and convincing evidence, that the service was invalid.

PRACTICE POINTER	Be sure to distinguish between the passive voice and past tense. A sentence written in the past tense may or may not use the passive voice.

For more on the active and passive voice, see section 24.1.

(b) Nominalizations

You create a nominalization when you turn a verb or an adjective into a noun.

Verb		Nominalization
apply	→	application
conclude	→	conclusion
decide	→	decision

Although there are times when you will want to use a nominalization, overusing nominalizations can make your writing harder to read and understand. In the following sentence, "presumption" is a nominalization.

EXAMPLE 12	**Nominalization**

If the return is regular on its face, there is a <u>presumption</u> that the service is valid.

To make this sentence better, identify the real actor (in this instance, the court) and then, in the verb, specifically state what action that actor has taken or will take. Note that "presumption" becomes "presume."

EXAMPLE 13	**Edit Without Nominalization**

If the return is regular on its face, the courts <u>presume</u> that the service is valid.

(c) Expletive Constructions

In an expletive construction, phrases such as "it is" or "there are" are used as the subject and verb of the sentence. Although it is sometimes necessary to use such a construction (note the use of an expletive construction in this sentence), such a construction gives the reader almost no information. Therefore, when possible, use a concrete subject and verb—that is, a subject and verb that describe something the reader can "see" in his or her mind. See also sections 24.2 and 25.2.4.

EXAMPLE 14   **Expletive Constructions**

However, if the return is regular on its face, <u>there is a</u> presumption that the service was valid.

<u>It is</u> Ms. Olsen's argument that . . .

EXAMPLE 15   **Edits Without Expletive Constructions**

If the return is regular on its face, the <u>courts presume</u> that the service was valid.

<u>Ms. Olsen will argue</u> that . . .

PRACTICE POINTER   Note that expletive constructions and nominalizations often go hand in hand. Because you use a expletive construction, you are forced into using a nominalization:

If the return is regular on its face, <u>there is</u> a <u>presumption</u> that the service is valid.

(d) Dangling Modifiers

A dangling modifier is a modifier that does not reasonably modify anything in the sentence. For example, in the following sentence, the modifying phrase "Applying this test" does not reasonably modify anything in the sentence. It is not "it was held" that is doing the applying.

EXAMPLE 16   **Dangling Modifier**

Applying this test, it was held that the summons and complaint were not left at the defendant's usual place of abode.

The dangling modifier can be eliminated if the actor is used as the subject of the sentence.

EXAMPLE 17   **Edit Without Dangling Modifier**

Applying this test, the **court** held that the summons and complaint were not left at the defendant's usual place of abode.

Now the phrase "Applying this test" modifies something in the sentence: the court. For more on dangling modifiers, see section 27.6.2.

> **PRACTICE POINTER** When you see a word ending in "ing" (a participle) in a phrase or clause near the beginning of a sentence, ask yourself who is doing the action. For example, in the preceding sentence, ask who is doing the "applying." Then look at the subject of the sentence. If the subject does not identify who is doing the action, then you have a dangling modifier.

2. Keep the Subject and Verb Close Together

Researchers have established that readers cannot understand a sentence until they have located both the subject and the verb. In addition, readers have difficulty remembering the subject if it is separated from the verb by more than seven or eight words: If there are more than seven or eight words, after finding the verb, many readers must go back and relocate the subject.

The lesson to be learned from this research is that, as a writer, you should try to keep your subject and verb close together. In Examples 18 and 19, the subject and verb are underlined.

EXAMPLE 18   **Subject and Verb Too Far Apart**

In such instances, the <u>burden</u> of presenting clear and convincing evidence that the service was invalid <u>is</u> on the party challenging the service.

EXAMPLE 19   **Edits with Subject and Verb Closer Together**

In such instances, the <u>party</u> challenging the service <u>has</u> the burden of presenting clear and convincing evidence that the service was invalid.

In such instances, the <u>defendant must prove</u> by clear and convincing evidence that the service was invalid.

For more on subject-verb distance, see section 24.4.

3. Put Old Information at the Beginning of the Sentence and New Information at the End

Sentences, and the paragraphs they create, make more sense when the old information is placed at the beginning and the new information is placed at the end. When this pattern is used, the development progresses naturally from left to right without unnecessary backtracking.

EXAMPLE 20   **Old Information Is at the Beginning of the Sentence, and New Information Is at the End**

The only Florida case in which the summons was left with a relative with whom the defendant was visiting is _Torres_. _Id._ at 585. <u>In that case, the plaintiff tried for more than a month to serve Mr. Torres at the New York apartment where Mr. Torres had lived for 12 years.</u> _Id._ Although all attempts at service were unsuccessful, the New York process server indicated in his affidavit that he had "verified" with a neighbor that "Mr. Torres lived at the New York address, but that he was often out of town, and was expected to return in two weeks." *Id.* Because it could not serve the defendant in New York, the plaintiff served Mr. Torres's mother at her residence in Florida. In his affidavit, the Florida process server stated that Mr. Torres mother told him that "he (presumably Mr. Torres) would be home soon." *Id.* Mr. Torres stated that he never received notice. In holding that the service was not valid, the court noted that while the standard of review was gross abuse of discretion, the trial court had not heard live testimony and the plaintiff had the burden of establishing that the service was valid. *Id.* at 587. It then went on to note that the evidence tended to support Mr. Torres's position that his usual place of abode was in New York and that Mr. Torres's mother's statement that Mr. Torres would be home soon was, at best, ambiguous. *Id.*

In the paragraph set out above, the first sentence, which is in bold, acts as a topic sentence, telling the attorney that there is only one Florida case that has facts similar to the facts in the client's case. That first sentence ends with a reference to the new information, which is the name of the case: *"Torres."* In the second sentence, the name of the case is now the old information, and the second sentence begins with a reference back to that old information. The second sentence then ends with the new information: that the plaintiff had tried, on a number of occasions, to serve the defendant in New York. In the third sentence, the old information is that the plaintiff had tried to serve the defendant in New York. Thus, the author uses this old information to start the third sentence, putting the new information, that the neighbor had told the process server that the defendant was out of town, at the end of the third sentence.

PRACTICE POINTER	Note how putting "old" information at the beginning of the sentence allows you to use dovetailing.

4. Vary Sentence Length and Pattern

Even if writing is technically correct, it is not considered good if it is not pleasing to the ear. Read Example 21 aloud.

EXAMPLE 21	All the Sentences Are About the Same Length and Use the Same Pattern

A process server went to Ms. Webster's house on Wednesday, July 24, 2013. The process server asked for Elaine Olsen. Ms. Webster told the process server that "Elaine isn't here today." The process server then handed the summons and complaint to Ms. Webster. The process server told Ms. Webster that Ms. Olsen "needed to go to court."

In Example 21, the writing is not pleasing because the sentences are similar in length and all follow the same pattern. Although short, uncomplicated sentences are usually better than long, complicated ones, the use of too many short sentences results in writing that sounds choppy and sophomoric. As Example 22 illustrates, the passage is much better when the writer varies sentence length and pattern.

EXAMPLE 22   **The Writer Has Varied the Length of the Sentences and the Sentence Pattern**

On Wednesday, July 24, 2013, a process server went to Ms. Webster's house and asked for Elaine Olsen. When Ms. Webster told the process server that "Elaine isn't here today," the process server handed the summons to Ms. Webster and told her that Ms. Olsen "needed to go to court."

For more on sentence construction, see Chapter 24.

b.   Writing Correctly

For a moment, imagine that you have received the following letter from a local law firm.

EXAMPLE 23   **Sample Letter**

Dear Student:

Thank you for submitting an application for a position as a law clerk with are firm. Your grades in law school are very good, however, at this time we do not have any positions available. Its possible, however, that we may have a opening next summer and we therefore urge you to reapply with us then.

Sincerely,

Senior Partner

No matter how bad the market is, most students would not want to be associated with a firm that sends out a three-line letter containing three major errors and several minor ones. Unfortunately, the reverse is also true. No matter how short-handed they are, most law firms do not want to hire someone who has not mastered the basic rules of grammar and punctuation. Most firms cannot afford an employee who makes careless errors or one who lacks basic writing skills.

Consequently, at the editing stage you need to go back through your draft, correcting errors. Look first for the errors that potentially affect meaning (misplaced modifiers, incorrect use of "which" and "that") and for errors that educated readers are likely to notice (incomplete sentences, comma splices, incorrect use of the possessive, lack of parallelism). Then look for the errors that you know from past experience that you are likely to make.

§ 12.10.3 Proofreading

Most writers learn the importance of proofreading the hard way. A letter, brief, or contract goes out with the client's name misspelled, with an "or" where there should have been an "and," or without an essential "not." At a minimum, these errors cause embarrassment; at worst, they result in a lawsuit.

To avoid such errors, treat proofreading as a separate step in the revising process. After you have finished revising and editing, go back through your draft, looking not at content, organization, or sentence style, but for errors.

Proofreading is most effective when it is done on hard copy several days (or, when that is not feasible, several hours) after you have finished editing. Force yourself to read slowly, focusing not on the sentences but on the individual words in the sentences. Is a word missing? Is a word repeated? Are letters transposed? You can force yourself to read slowly by using a clean piece of paper to cover up all but the line you are reading, by reading from right to left, or by reading from the bottom of the page to the top.

Also, force yourself to begin your proofreading by looking at the sections that caused you the most difficulty or that you wrote last. Because you were concentrating on content or were tired, these sections probably contain the most errors.

Finally, when you get into practice, don't rely on just your spelling and grammar checkers. Instead, make it a habit to have a second person proofread your work. Not only will someone else see errors that you missed, he or she is also less likely than you to "read in" missing words.

§ 12.10.4 Citations

As a legal writer, you have an extra burden. In addition to editing and proofreading the text, you must also edit and proofread your citations to legal authorities.

At the editing stage, focus on selection and placement of citations. Is the authority you cited the best authority? Did you avoid string cites (the citing of multiple cases for the same point)? Have you included a citation to authority for every rule stated? Did you include the appropriate signal? Have you over- or under-emphasized the citation? (You emphasize a citation by placing it in the text of a sentence; you de-emphasize it by placing it in a separate citation sentence.)

In contrast, at the proofreading stage, focus on the citation itself. Are the volume and page numbers correct? Are the pinpoint cites accurate? Have you included the year of the decision and any subsequent history? Is the spacing correct?

Chapter 12 Quiz No. 4

Draft answers for each of the following questions. Make your points clearly and concisely, and write sentences that are easy to read and that are grammatical and correctly punctuated.

1. What is the difference between revising, editing, and proofreading?
2. In the following sentences, has the writer used dovetailing? If your answer is yes, what is the dovetail?

> The State will use these same facts to distinguish *Torres*. While in *Torres*, Mr. Torres presented evidence establishing that his permanent residence was in New York, in the present case, Ms. Olsen did not have a permanent residence.

3. Rewrite the following sentence using the active voice.

> There are three arguments that the State can make to support its assertion.

4. Rewrite the following sentence eliminating the nominalization.

   The court's conclusion was that the plaintiff had not met its burden of proof.

5. Rewrite the following sentence eliminating the dangling modifier.

   Weighing these arguments, it is likely that the court will conclude that Ms. Olsen has met her burden of proving that service was not made at her usual place of abode.

CHAPTER

13

Drafting Memo 2

F or the purposes of this memo, presume that you are spending the summer working for a law firm in San Francisco. Although it is only your first week at the firm, your supervising attorney has given you the following assignment.

§ 13.1   The Assignment

To:	Legal Intern
From:	Supervising Attorney
Date:	October 13, 2013
Re:	Michael Garcia; Adverse Possession of Property in Washington State

- One of our longtime clients, Michael Garcia, has contacted our office regarding property that he owns in Washington State. Mr. Garcia is worried that an organization may have obtained title to this property through adverse possession.
- Mr. Garcia inherited the Washington property from his grandfather, Eduardo Montoya, in 1999.

- Mr. Montoya purchased the land in 1958. He and his family used the land every summer from 1958 until the early 1990s, when he became ill.

- When Mr. Montoya's family used the property, family members camped on the site and used a small dock for swimming, fishing, and boating.

- Mr. Garcia visited the property in the fall of 1999 but moved to California not long after that visit. He did not visit the property from 2000 until last August.

- The group that has been using Mr. Garcia's land since 1997 is called Doctors and Nurses Who Care (DNWC).

- DNWC has owned the five-acre parcel that is just to the north of Mr. Garcia's property since 1996. DNWC uses its property for summer camps for children who suffer from serious illnesses and disabilities. In a typical summer, DNWC runs two one-week camps for children with cancer, two one-week camps for children who are blind, two one-week camps for children with autism, and two one-week camps for children with diabetes.

- DNWC maintains and uses the campsites, the fire area, the outhouse, and the dock, all of which are on Mr. Garcia's property.

- During the summer of 2001, DNWC posted a no trespassing sign on the dock, and the sign is still there.

- Most of the time the children stay in cabins located on the DNWC property. However, DNWC uses Mr. Garcia's property for "campouts." One night each week, one group of about 10 children will camp out in tents on Mr. Garcia's property, the next night another group of 10 will camp out on his property, and so on. Thus, DNWC uses Mr. Garcia's land four or five nights a week for eight weeks each summer.

- During these campouts, the children pitch and stay in tents and cook over a fire.

- Mr. Garcia has paid all of the taxes and assessments.

- In about February 2001, Mr. Garcia received a letter from DNWC asking whether it could continue using his land for campouts. Mr. Garcia was busy and never responded to the letter.

- Last August, Mr. Garcia visited the property with the intent of spending a few days camping on the lake. When he got there, he discovered that there were children and their counselors on the property.

- Mr. Garcia went to the camp's headquarters and talked to the director, Dr. Liu, who was very nice. However, Dr. Liu told Mr. Garcia that it was his understanding that the land belonged to DNWC.

- Mr. Garcia did not spend the night at the property that night, but he did spend the next night there after the children left. No one from DNWC asked him to leave.

- Although over the years the land around the lake has become more and more developed, the area on which the camp is located

is still relatively undeveloped. Most of the property owners use
their land only during the summer.

Because I am not familiar with Washington State law, can you please
research this issue for me? Under Washington State law, can DNWC claim
title to Mr. Garcia's land through adverse possession?

§ 13.2   Researching the Law

Unlike the first memo, which involved an issue governed by a state statute,
this problem is governed by common law. For a discussion of how to research
this type of issue, see Chapter 7. To see how to research this problem using
free sources, Lexis Advance®, WestlawNext™, Bloomberg Law, Lexis.com®,
or Westlaw® Classic, go to *http://www.aspenlawschool.com/books/oates_legal-
writinghandbook/* and click on the links.

§ 13.3   Understanding What You Have Found

A word to the wise: Do not put off analyzing and synthesizing the cases
until you "finish" your research. Although in this book we talk about research,
analysis, and writing in separate chapters, in practice they are part of a single,
and often recursive, process.

§ 13.3.1   Organize Your Research Notes

Although there are many ways to organize your research notes, one way
that works well is to record your findings using a research log like the one set
out in Example 1. Although you can cut and paste the general and specific rules
from the cases into your log, take the time to write your own "case briefs" for
the cases you think you want to use as analogous cases. In addition, as you
think of them, write down arguments that each side might make.

EXAMPLE 1   **Research Log for Memo 2**

Issue: Whether DNWC has obtained a right to Mr. Garcia's land through adverse possession?
Type of Law: State common law and statutes
Jurisdiction: Washington

Introductory Section

General Rules

- **ITT Rayonier, Inc. v. Bell, 112 Wn.2d 754, 774 P.2d 6 (1989) (cite checked; still good law)**

Quote from pages 757-58:
"In order to establish a claim of adverse possession, there must be possession that is: (1) open and notorious, (2) actual and uninterrupted, (3) exclusive, and (4) hostile. *Chaplin v. Sanders*, 100 Wash.2d 853, 857, 676 P.2d 431 (1984). Possession of the property with each of the necessary concurrent elements must exist for the statutorily prescribed period of 10 years. RCW 4.16.020."

- **Chaplin v. Sanders, 100 Wn.2d 853, 676 P.2d 431 (1984) (cite checked; still good law)**

Quote from page 857:
"In order to establish a claim of adverse possession, the possession must be: 1) exclusive, 2) actual and uninterrupted, 3) open and notorious and 4) hostile and under a claim of right made in good faith."

- **Riley v. Andres, 107 Wn. App. 391, 27 P.3d 618 (2001) (cite checked; still good law)**

Quote from page 395:
"To claim title to property by adverse possession, a party must possess the property for 10 years in a manner that is actual, uninterrupted, open and notorious, exclusive, and hostile."

- **RCW 4.16.020.** *Actions to be commenced within 10 years—Exception* **(cite checked; this is the applicable version of the statute)**

"The period prescribed for the commencement of actions shall be as follows:
Within 10 years:
(1) For actions for the recovery of real property, or for the recovery of the possession thereof; and no action shall be maintained for such recovery unless it appears that the plaintiff, his or her ancestor, predecessor or grantor was seized or possessed of the premises in question within ten years before the commencement of the action."

Burden of Proof

- **ITT Rayonier, Inc. v. Bell, 112 Wn.2d 754, 774 P.2d 6 (1989) (cite checked; still good law)**

Quote from pages 757-58:
"As the presumption of possession is in the holder of legal title, *Peeples v. Port of Bellingham*, 93 Wash.2d 766, 773, 613 P.2d 1128 (1980), *overruled on other grounds, Chaplin v. Sanders, supra,* the party claiming to have adversely possessed the property has the burden of establishing the existence of each element. ***758** Skansi v. Novak*, 84 Wash. 39, 44, 146 P. 160 (1915), *overruled on other grounds, Chaplin v. Sanders, supra.*"

Other General Rules

- **Chaplin v. Sanders, 100 Wn.2d 853, 676 P.2d 431 (1984) (cite checked; still good law)**

Quote from page 863:
"[A]dverse possession is a mixed question of law and fact. Whether the essential facts exist is for the trier of fact; but whether the facts, as found, constitute adverse possession is for the court to determine as a matter of law." *Peeples v. Port of Bellingham, supra* at 771, 613 P.2d 1128.

Policies Underlying Doctrine

■ *Chaplin v. Sanders, 100 Wn.2d 853, 676 P.2d 431 (1984)* **(cite checked; still good law)**

Quote from pages 859-60:

"The doctrine of adverse possession was formulated at law for the purpose of, among others, assuring maximum utilization of land, encouraging the rejection of stale claims and, most importantly, quieting titles. 7 R. Powell, *Real Property* ¶ 1012[3] (1982); C. Callahan, *Adverse Possession* 91-94 (1961). Because the doctrine was formulated at law and not at equity, it was originally intended to protect both those who knowingly appropriated the land of others and those who honestly entered and held possession in full belief that the land was their own. R. Powell, at ¶ 1013 [2]; C. Callahan, at 49-50; 3 Am.Jur.2d *Advancements* § 104 (1962). Thus, when the original purpose of the adverse possession doctrine is considered, it becomes apparent that the claimant's motive in possessing the land is irrelevant and no inquiry should be made into his guilt or innocence. *Accord Springer v. Durette*, 217 Or. 196, 342 P.2d 132 (1959); *Agers v. Reynolds*, 306 S.W.2d 506 (Mo.1957); *Fulton v. Rapp*, 59 Ohio Law Abs. 105, 98 N.E.2d 430 (1950); *see also* Stoebuck, *The Law of Adverse Possession in Washington*, 35 Wash. L. Rev. 53, 76-80 (1960)."

1. Open and Notorious

A.   Specific Rules

Riley v. Andres, **107 Wn. App. 391, 27 P.3d 618 (2001) (cite checked; still good law)**

Quote from page 396:

"A claimant can satisfy the open and notorious element by showing either (1) that the title owner had actual notice of the adverse use throughout the statutory period or (2) that the claimant used the land such that any reasonable person would have thought he owned it."

Anderson v. Hudak, **80 Wn. App. 398, 907 P.2d 305 (1995) (cite checked; still good law)**

Quote from pages 404-05:

"The open and notorious requirement is met if (1) the true owner has actual notice of the adverse use throughout the statutory period, or (2) the claimant uses the land so any reasonable person would assume that the claimant is the owner."

B.   Analogous Cases

Element Met:

Riley v. Andres, **107 Wn. App. 391, 397, 27 P.3d 618 (2001) (cite checked; still good law)**

Facts:

The claimants planted trees and shrubs and maintained land up to the point where the title owners' landscaping began. In particular, the claimants watered and pruned the plants, spread beauty bark, and pulled weeds.

Holding:

Although the court set out the two-part test listed above, it applied a slightly different test. It began by stating that a party who claims adverse possession must show that its use is that of a true owner. It then states that the landscaping was the typical use of land of that character.

Element Not Met:

Anderson v. Hudak, **80 Wn. App. 398, 907 P.2d 305 (1995) (cite checked; still good law)**

Facts:

The claimant (Anderson) planted a row of trees on a fifteen-foot strip of land that she thought belonged to her. There was, however, no evidence establishing that she did anything else on the land.

Holding:

The court stated that there was no evidence establishing that any of the true owners had actual notice of her possession of the trees. In addition, the court stated that the evidence was insufficient to establish that Anderson had used the land so that any reasonable person would assume that the claimant was the owner. Thus, the appellate court held that there was insufficient evidence to support the trial court's finding that Anderson's possession was open and notorious. *Id.* at 405.

C.   DNWC's Arguments

Letter provided Mr. Garcia with actual knowledge that DNWC was using his land.

The way in which DNWC used the land would have led any reasonable person to assume that it owned the land. In fact, the DNWC director seemed to think that DNWC owns the land.

Our case is more like *Riley* than *Anderson*. DNWC did more with the land than the Rileys did, and the court held that the Rileys' use of the land was sufficient to establish that their use was open and notorious.

D.   Garcia's Arguments

It does not appear as if Garcia has an argument on actual notice. A court would probably find that the letter gave Mr. Garcia actual notice. However, even if the letter is not enough to establish actual notice, DNWC's acts are probably enough to establish that a reasonable person would have thought that DNWC owned the land.

2. Actual and Uninterrupted

A.   Specific Rules

[The rest of the log is not shown.]

---

§ 13.3.2   Make Sure You Understand the Big Picture

Before you start to write, take a step back and make sure that you see the big picture. For instance, in Garcia's case, do you understand the policies underlying the doctrine of adverse possession? Historically, why did the courts create the doctrine? Why have most state legislatures left the common law rules intact, only enacting statutes that set out the time period for which the common law elements must be met?

§ 13.3.3   Make Sure You Understand the Common Law Rule and Any Applicable Statutes

In addition to making sure that you understand the big picture, make sure that you understand the common law rule. If the common law rule is complicated, diagram it using the same techniques that you would use to diagram a complicated statute. If the common law rule is not complicated, simply read the rule carefully, making sure that you know how many elements there are and whether those elements are connected by an "and" or an "or." Finally, make sure that you understand the relationship between the common law rule and any statutes that might apply. For example, in the Garcia case, make sure that you understand the relationship between the common law rule, which lists the elements, and the statutes, which list the time periods for which the elements must be met.

§ 13.3.4   Make Sure You Understand the Burden of Proof

In many cases, the determinative factor is the burden of proof. Therefore, make sure that you know which side has the burden of proof and what that burden is.

While in most civil cases the plaintiff has the burden of proof, that is not true in adverse possession cases. In adverse possession cases, the party claiming the property through adverse possession has the burden of proof regardless of whether it filed the action claiming title to the land through adverse possession or whether it was the true owner who filed an action to quiet title. There is only one exception: If the claimant proves that it used the land as if the land were its own, then the true owner has the burden of proving that that use was permissive.

§ 13.3.5   Make Sure You Understand the Specific Rules and the Cases That Have Applied Those Rules

Finally, make sure you understand the law. Sometimes, this part of the process is easy: The courts have set out, clearly and concisely, the rules that they apply in determining whether a particular element is met, and the courts apply those rules consistently. Unfortunately, however, this is not always the case. Sometimes the rules are complicated, sometimes the courts set out what seem to be conflicting rules, and sometimes the courts set out one rule but seem to apply a different one. In addition, in some situations, it can be difficult to distinguish between the test for one element and the test for another element. An example of this type of situation is adverse possession: In many states, the tests for actual possession, open and notorious, and hostile are very similar.

To make sure that you understand the specific rules and the cases that have interpreted and applied them, look first at that section of your research log in which you have set out the specific rules for a particular element. In discussing that element, do all of the courts set out the same rule? If they do, you have the rule. If, though, different courts seem to be setting out different rules, your job is more difficult. Begin by rereading the specific rules. Are the courts setting out the same rule using different language, or are they setting out different rules? If the courts are setting out the same rules using different language, you have the rule.

If, though, the courts are setting out different rules, you need to try to reconcile the courts' statements. Are the courts doing what the Washington Supreme Court did in *Chaplin v. Sanders* and overruling or abandoning one rule and adopting a new one? If they are, you need to determine which rule applies in your client's case. In the alternative, do different divisions of the same court apply different rules, or do the courts apply different rules in different types of situations? For instance, does Division I of the Washington Court of Appeals apply one rule and Division II a different rule, or do all of the divisions apply one rule when the land is in a rural area and another rule when the land is in an urban area?

Once you have figured out the specific rules, look at how the courts have applied the rules in the analogous cases. Do the courts apply the rules they set out? If they do not, what is the difference between the rules they set out and the rules they apply? Also look at the issue that was before the court. Was the issue whether the trial court erred in granting summary judgment? If it was, the appellate court will review the issue de novo and apply the same test that the trial court applied in deciding whether to grant or deny the motion. Keep in mind, though, that a decision that the trial court erred does not mean that the other side wins; instead, in most instances, it means that the appellate court will remand the case for a trial on the merits. In contrast, if the issue is whether there was sufficient evidence to support the jury's verdict, then the appellate court's review is much more limited. If there is sufficient evidence to support the jury's verdict, the appellate court cannot substitute its judgment for the judgment of the jury.

After you have analyzed all of the elements, compare them, making sure that you understand the difference between the specific rules for each of the elements. An easy way to do this part of the analysis is to make a chart in which you compare the specific rule for each element. See Example 2.

EXAMPLE 2   **Chart Comparing Specific Rules**

Open and Notorious	Actual and Uninterrupted	Exclusive	Hostile
The open and notorious requirement is met if (1) the true owner has actual notice of the adverse use throughout the statutory period, <u>or</u> (2) the claimant uses the land so any reasonable person would assume that the claimant is the owner. *Riley v. Andres*, 107 Wn. App. 391, 396, 27 P.3d 618 (2001).	The Washington courts have not set out a test for actual possession. 17 *Wash. Prac., Real Estate: Property Law* § 8.10 (2d ed.) In discussing "uninterrupted," the courts have held that the claimants' use was "continuous" even though they used the property only during the summer. The requisite possession requires such possession and dominion as ordinarily marks the conduct of owners in general in holding, managing, and caring for property of a like nature and condition. *Howard v. Kunto,* 3 Wn. App. 393, 477 P.2d 210 (1970).	"While possession of property by a party seeking to establish ownership of it by adverse possession need not be absolutely exclusive," "the possession must be of a type that would be expected of an owner. . . ." *ITT Rayonier*, 112 Wn.2d 754, 758, 774 P.2d 6 (1989).	"The 'hostility/claim of right' element of adverse possession requires only that the claimant treat the land as his own as against the world throughout the statutory period. The nature of his possession will be determined solely on the basis of the manner in which he treats the property. His subjective belief regarding his true interest in the land and his intent to dispossess or not dispossess another is irrelevant to this determination. Under this analysis, permission to occupy the land, given by the true title owner to the claimant or his predecessors in interest, will still operate to negate the element of hostility. The traditional presumptions still apply to the extent that they are not inconsistent with this ruling."

> **PRACTICE POINTER** If you have trouble distinguishing the test used for one element from the test used for another element, look for a case, a law review article, or a practice book that explains how the elements are the same and how they are different.

§ 13.4   Drafting the Heading

As you discovered in drafting your first memo, drafting the heading is easy: Just complete the "To," "From," "Date," and "Re" blocks. If the memo will only be filed in the client's file, the "Re" entry can be quite general. If, however, the memo will be filed not only in the client's file but also in a "memo bank," include words that will allow other people in your office who are researching similar issues to find your memo.

EXAMPLE 1   **Example 1   Sample Heading**

To: Supervising Attorney

From: Your name

Date: November 2, 2013

Re: Michael Garcia
          Adverse Possession; Washington Law

---

§ 13.5   Drafting the Statement of Facts

In drafting the statement of facts for this chapter's sample memo, use the same process that we used in drafting the statement of facts for Memo 1, which is set out in Chapter 12: (1) identify the legally significant, emotionally significant, background, and unknown facts; (2) select an organizational scheme; and (3) present the facts accurately and objectively.

§ 13.5.1   Decide What Facts to Include

To identify the legally significant facts, create a chart similar to the one set out below. In the first column, list the elements, and in the second column list the facts that the court would consider in determining whether those elements are met. For more on identifying the legally significant facts, see section 12.5.1a.

EXAMPLE 1	**Chart Listing Elements and the Facts That the Court Would Consider in Deciding Whether the Element Is Met**

Elements	Facts That the Court Would Consider in Deciding Whether the Element Is Met
Open and Notorious	
Actual and Uninterrupted	
Exclusive	
Hostile	

To identify the emotionally significant facts, think about which facts might influence a judge's or a jury's decision. In Garcia's case, is the fact that the claimant is a group of doctors and nurses that is running a camp for ill and disabled children likely to influence the jury's or the judge's decision? If it is, then you should include that fact in the statement of facts. Similarly, is the fact that the land has been in Mr. Garcia's family for more than fifty years something that will influence the judge's or the jury's decision? If it is, you should include that fact in your statement of facts. For more on identifying the emotionally significant facts, see section 12.5.1b

Finally, identify the facts that you need to tell the story and the unknown facts. If you cannot analyze the issue without the unknown facts, ask your supervising attorney for permission to obtain those facts. If, however, you can analyze the issue without the unknown facts, do so. For more on identifying background and unknown facts, see section 12.5.1c and d.

§ 13.5.2   Select an Organizational Scheme

Once you have decided which facts need to be included, select an organizational scheme. As you learned in Chapter 12, the two most common organizational schemes are chronological and topical.

If you use a chronological organizational scheme, set out the facts in date order: Start the story with Mr. Garcia's grandfather giving the land to Mr. Garcia, and end with Mr. Garcia's visit to the property. In contrast, if you use a topical organizational scheme, set out the facts relating to the Garcia property in one paragraph or block of paragraphs, the facts relating to DNWC's property and DNWC's use of the Garcia property in a second paragraph or block of paragraphs, and the facts relating to the dispute in a third paragraph or block of paragraphs. In all instances, start the statement of facts with a paragraph in which you identify the parties and the issue. For more on paragraphs and paragraph blocks, see Chapter 22.

| EXAMPLE 2 | **Statement of Facts Written Using a Chronological Organizational Scheme** |

Michael Garcia has contacted our office regarding property that he owns in Washington State. Mr. Garcia is concerned that the organization that owns the property next to his, Doctors and Nurses Who Care (DNWC), may be able to claim title to his property through adverse possession.

Mr. Garcia's property is on Lake Chelan in eastern Washington. Mr. Garcia's grandfather, Eduardo Montoya, purchased the two-acre waterfront parcel in 1958, and the family used the land every summer from 1958 until Eduardo Montoya became ill in the early 1990s. When they used the land, the family would camp on the site and use a small dock for swimming, fishing, and boating.

In 1996, DNWC purchased the five-acre parcel that adjoins Mr. Montoya's property. Since 1997, DNWC has used its land as a summer camp for children with serious illnesses or disabilities. In a typical summer, DNWC runs two one-week camps for children with cancer, two one-week camps for children who are blind, two one-week camps for children with autism, and two one-week camps for children with diabetes.

Most of the time the children stay in cabins located on DNWC property. However, DNWC uses the Garcia property for "campouts." One night each week, one group of about 10 children will camp out in tents on Mr. Garcia's property; the next night another group of 10 will camp out on his property, and so on. Thus, DNWC has been using the Garcia property four or five nights a week for eight weeks each summer since 1997. During these campouts, the children pitch and stay in tents, cook over a fire, and use the dock. To facilitate these campouts, DNWC has maintained the campsite, the fire area, the outhouse, and the dock.

In 1999, Mr. Garcia's grandfather died and left the property to him. Although Mr. Garcia spent one weekend at the property in the fall of 1999, he moved to California in 2000 and did not visit the property again until last August. He has, however, continued to pay all of the taxes and assessments.

In February 2001, DNWC sent Mr. Garcia a letter asking him whether it could continue using his land for campouts. Mr. Garcia was busy and did not respond to the letter. Sometime during the summer of 2001, DNWC posted a no trespassing sign on the dock, and the sign is still there.

Last August Mr. Garcia visited the property with the intention of spending a few days camping on the lake. When he got there, he discovered children and their counselors on the property.

After discovering the children on his land, Mr. Garcia went to DNWC's camp headquarters and talked to the director, Dr. Liu, who told Mr. Garcia that it was his understanding that the land belonged to DNWC. Although Mr. Garcia did not spend that night on the property, he did spend the next night there after the children left. DNWC did not ask him to leave.

Although over the years the land around the lake has become more and more developed, the area in which the camp is located is still relatively undeveloped. Most of the property owners use their land only during the summer.

| EXAMPLE 3 | **Statement of Facts Written Using a Topical Organizational Scheme** |

Michael Garcia has contacted our office regarding property that he owns in Washington State. Mr. Garcia is concerned that the organization that owns the property next to his, Doctors and Nurses Who Care (DNWC), may be able to claim title to his property through adverse possession.

Mr. Garcia's property is located on Lake Chelan in eastern Washington. Mr. Garcia's grandfather, Eduardo Montoya, purchased the two-acre waterfront parcel in 1958. From 1958 until Eduardo Montoya became ill in the early 1990s, the family used the land every summer. The family would camp on the site and use a small dock for swimming, fishing, and boating. In 1999, Mr. Garcia's grandfather died and left the property to Mr. Garcia. Although Mr. Garcia spent one weekend on the property in 1999, he moved to California in 2000 and did not visit the property from 1999 until last August. He has, however, continued to pay all of the taxes and assessments.

DNWC purchased the five-acre parcel that is to the north of Mr. Garcia's property in 1996. Since 1997, DNWC has used its land for a summer camp for children who suffer from serious illnesses and disabilities. In a typical summer, DNWC runs two one-week camps for children with cancer, two one-week camps for children who are blind, two one-week camps for children with autism, and two one-week camps for children with diabetes. While normally the children stay in cabins located on DNWC property, DNWC uses Mr. Garcia's property for "campouts." For example, on one night of the week, one group of about 10 children will camp out in tents on Mr. Garcia's property, the next night another group of 10 will camp out on his property, and so on. During these campouts, the children pitch and stay in tents and cook over a fire. To facilitate these campouts, DNWC has maintained the campsites, the fire area, the outhouse, and the dock. In the summer of 2001, DNWC posted a no trespassing sign on the dock, and the sign is still there.

In February 2001, DNWC sent a letter to Mr. Garcia asking him if it could continue using his land for campouts. Mr. Garcia was busy and never responded to the letter.

Late last August, Mr. Garcia visited the property with the intention of spending a few days camping on the lake. When he got there, he discovered children and their counselors on the property. Upon making this discovery, Mr. Garcia went to DNWC's camp headquarters and talked to the director, Dr. Liu, who was very nice. However, Dr. Liu told Mr. Garcia that the land belonged to DNWC. Although Mr. Garcia did not spend that night on his property, he did spend the next night there after the children had gone. DNWC did not ask him to leave.

While the land around the lake has become more and more developed, the area in which the camp is located is still relatively undeveloped. Most of the property owners only use their land during the summer.

---

§ 13.5.3   Present the Facts Accurately and Objectively

Finally, in writing the statement of facts, make sure that you present the facts accurately and objectively. Do not set out facts that are not in your case file; do not set out legal conclusions; and do not present the facts in a light that favors your client or the other side.

§ 13.5.4   Checklist for Critiquing the Statement of Facts

a.   Content

- ■ The writer has included all of the legally significant facts.
- ■ When appropriate, the writer has included emotionally significant facts.
- ■ The writer has included enough background facts that a person not familiar with the case can understand what happened.
- ■ The writer has identified the unknown facts.
- ■ The writer has presented the facts accurately.
- ■ The writer has presented the facts objectively.
- ■ The writer has not included legal conclusions in the statement of facts.

b.   Organization

- ■ The writer has included an introductory sentence or paragraph that identifies the parties and the nature of the dispute.

- The writer has used one of the conventional organizational schemes: chronological, topical, or a combination of chronological and topical.

c. Writing

- The attorney can understand the facts of the case after reading the statement of facts once.
- The paragraph divisions are logical, and the paragraphs are neither too long nor too short. See Chapter 22.
- Transitions and dovetailing have been used to make the connection between ideas clear. See Chapter 23.
- In most sentences, the writer has used the actor as the subject of the sentence, and the subject and verb are close together. See sections 24.1 and 24.4.
- The writer has varied the length of the sentences and the sentence patterns so that each sentence flows smoothly from the prior sentence. See section 24.5.
- The writing is concise and precise. See sections 25.1 and 25.2.
- The writing is grammatically correct and correctly punctuated. See Chapters 27 and 28.
- The statement of facts has been proofread.

§ 13.6 Drafting the Issue Statement

§ 13.6.1 Select a Format: The "Whether" Format

Although the "under-does-when" format is the easiest format to use, some attorneys prefer the more traditional "whether" format. When you use the "whether" format, begin your issue statement with the word "whether" and then set out the legal question and the key facts. Although you do not need to include a reference to the rule of law, you may incorporate one into your statement of the legal question.

Compare the following examples. In Example 1 the writer uses the "under-does-when" format, and in Examples 2 and 3 the writers use the "whether" format. While in Examples 1 and 2 the writers use the parties' names, in Example 3 the writer uses more generic labels.

EXAMPLE 1   **Issue Statement Written Using the "Under-Does-When" Format, the Parties' Names, and Enumeration**

Issue

Under Washington common law, has Doctors and Nurses Who Care (DNWC) obtained a right to Mr. Garcia's land through adverse possession when (1) DNWC has used the land for campouts several nights a week for eight weeks each summer since 1997; (2) to facilitate these campouts, DNWC has maintained the campsites, fire area, outhouse, and dock; (3) in 2001, DNWC sent a letter to Mr. Garcia asking him if it could continue using the land for campouts, but Mr. Garcia did not respond to the letter; and (4) Mr. Garcia has paid the taxes but did not visit the land from 1999 until August 2013?

EXAMPLE 2	**Issue Statement Written Using the "Whether" Format, the Parties' Names, and Enumeration**

Issue

Whether Doctors and Nurses Who Care (DNWC) has obtained a right to Mr. Garcia's land through adverse possession when (1) DNWC has used the land for campouts several nights a week for eight weeks each summer since 1997; (2) to facilitate these campouts, DNWC has maintained the campsites, fire area, outhouse, and dock; (3) in 2001, DNWC sent a letter to Mr. Garcia asking him if it could continue using the land for campouts, but Mr. Garcia did not respond to the letter; and (4) Mr. Garcia has paid the taxes but did not visit the land from 1999 until August 2013.

EXAMPLE 3	**Issue Statement Written Using the "Whether" Format But Not the Names of the Parties or Enumeration**

Issue

Whether a claimant may obtain a right to land through adverse possession when the claimant used the disputed land for campouts several nights a week for eight weeks each summer since 1997; when the claimant has maintained the campsites, fire area, outhouse, and dock; when the claimant sent a letter to the title owner asking him if it could continue using the land for campouts but the title owner did not respond to the letter; and when the title owner has paid the taxes but did not visit the land for more than 10 years.

§ 13.6.2 Make Sure Your Issue Statement Is Easy to Read

As we stated in section 12.6.2, it is not enough to include the right information in your issue statement. You must also present that information in a way that is easy to read.

One key to making an issue statement easy to read is to use the subject, verb, and object slots in the issue statement for the legal question.

Look again at Examples 1, 2, and 3 set out above.

EXAMPLE 4	**Subject-Verb-Object for Examples 1 and 2**

DNWC	has obtained	a right
subject	*verb*	*object*

EXAMPLE 5	**Subject-Verb-Object for Example 3**

claimant	has obtained	a right
subject	*verb*	*object*

In addition, in listing the key facts, remember to use parallel constructions for all of the items in the list. If you are not sure whether the items in the list are parallel, try setting them out in a vertical list. See Example 6.

EXAMPLE 6   **Key Facts Set Out in a Vertical List**

Whether Doctors and Nurses Who Care (DNWC) has obtained a right to Mr. Garcia's land through adverse possession when

(1) DNWC has used the land for campouts several nights a week for eight weeks each summer since 1994;

(2) to facilitate these campouts, DNWC has maintained the campsites, fire area, outhouse, and dock;

(3) in 2001, DNWC sent a letter to Mr. Garcia asking him if it could continue using the land for campouts, but Mr. Garcia did not respond to the letter; and

(4) Mr. Garcia has paid the taxes but did not visit the land from 1999 until August 2013.

Once you have created the list, compare the items. Do all of the items have the same grammatical structure? For instance, in the example, can each item stand by itself as a complete sentence? For more on parallelism, see section 27.7.

Finally, check your punctuation. First, as a general rule, do not include a colon unless the material before the colon is grammatically complete, that is, it has a subject, verb, and object. For more on the correct use of the colon, see section 28.3. Second, if the items in your list are long or have internal commas, use semicolons to separate the items, including the next to the last and the last items in your list. For more on the correct use of semicolons to separate items in a list, see Rule 2 in section 28.2.

EXAMPLE 7   **Issue Statement That Is Punctuated Correctly**

Whether Doctors and Nurses Who Care (DNWC) has obtained a right to Mr. Garcia's land through adverse possession when (1) DNWC has used the land for campouts several nights a week for eight weeks each summer since 1997; (2) to facilitate these campouts, DNWC has maintained the campsites, fire area, outhouse, and dock; (3) in 2001, DNWC sent a letter to Mr. Garcia asking him if it could continue using the land for campouts, but Mr. Garcia did not respond to the letter; and (4) Mr. Garcia has paid the taxes but did not visit the land from 1999 until August 2013.

PRACTICE POINTER   At first, some writers are bothered by the fact that issue statements written using the "whether" format are incomplete sentences. If you are one of those writers, remember that the "whether" is shorthand for "The question is whether . . ." Because a "whether" issue statement is a statement and not a question, put a period and not a question mark at the end.

§ 13.6.3 Checklist for Critiquing the Issue Statement

a. Content

- The reference to the rule of law is neither too broad nor too narrow.
- The legal question is properly focused.
- The most significant of the legally significant facts have been included.
- Legal conclusions have not been set out as facts.

b. Format

- The writer has used one of the conventional formats, for example, the "under-does-when" format or the "whether" format.

c. Writing

- The issue statement is easy to read and understand.
- In setting out the legal question, the writer has used a concrete subject and an action verb. See sections 24.1 through 24.3.
- In listing the facts, the writer has used parallel constructions for all of the items in the list. See section 27.7.
- If the list of facts is long, the writer has used enumeration or has repeated key structural cues, for examples, words like "when" and "that."

§ 13.7   Drafting the Brief Answer

§ 13.7.1 Use One of the Conventional Formats

As we explained in Chapter 12, the brief answer answers the question asked in the issue statement. By convention, most brief answers begin with a one- or two-word answer, which is followed by a one-, two-, or three-sentence explanation.

In writing the brief answer, think about what you would tell the attorney if he or she stopped you in the hallway and asked you for a quick answer.

Attorney: Has DNWC obtained a right to Mr. Garcia's property through adverse possession?

You: It looks as if it may have. DNWC can easily prove that its possession was open and notorious, actual and uninterrupted, and exclusive. In addition, it looks like DNWC can prove that its possession was hostile. It has been using the property as if it were its own and, because Mr. Garcia did not respond to the letter asking for permission, DNWC has a good argument that its use was not permissive.

EXAMPLE 1   **Example 1   Brief Answer**

Brief Answer

Probably. DNWC can easily prove that its possession was open and notorious, actual and uninterrupted, and exclusive. In addition, DNWC can probably prove that its possession was hostile: It used the land as a true owner would have used it and, although initially it may have been using the property with either the permission of Mr. Garcia's grandfather or Mr. Garcia, it appears that it has been using the property without permission since 1999. Because all of the elements are met for the statutory period, which is 10 years, DNWC has a right to the land through adverse possession.

PRACTICE POINTER	Before you include a brief answer, check with your supervising attorney to see whether he or she wants one in the memo.

§ 13.7.2   Checklist for Critiquing the Brief Answer

a.   Content

- The writer has predicted but not guaranteed how the issue will be decided.
- The writer has briefly explained his or her prediction, for example, the writer has explained which elements will be easy to prove and which will be more difficult and why.

b.   Format

- A separate brief answer has been included for each issue statement.
- The answer begins with a one- or two-word short answer. This one- or two-word short answer is then followed by a short explanation.

c.   Writing

- The brief answer is easy to read and understand.
- Most of the sentences have concrete subjects and action verbs. See sections 24.2 and 24.3.
- There are no grammatical or punctuation errors. See Chapters 27 and 28.

§ 13.8   Drafting the Discussion Section Using an Integrated Format

Sometimes novice legal writers ask which is better to use: the script format used in the memo in Chapter 12 or the more integrated format used in the memo in this chapter. Like so much else in law, the answer is "it depends." While some attorneys prefer the script format because it is easy to see what each side will argue, other attorneys prefer a more integrated format because memos written using an integrated format are shorter. Consequently, as a law clerk or new attorney, you need to know how to organize a memo using both formats.

The script and integrated formats have much in common. For example, when the problem involves an elements analysis, the large-scale organization is the same. Regardless of whether you use a script or integrated format, you will begin the discussion section with an introductory section in which you set out the general rule. In addition, regardless of which format you use, you will then walk the attorney through the elements one by one, spending less time on those that are not in dispute and more time on those that are. Finally, your discussion of the disputed elements will include the same types of information: rules, descriptions of analogous cases, arguments or analysis, and conclusions.

In fact, the script and integrated format differ from each other in only two ways. The first difference is a difference in the way that you organize your analysis of the disputed elements. When you use the script format, you present the information using inductive reasoning. You set out the specific rules, illustrate how those rules have been applied in analogous cases, set out each side's arguments, and end by setting out your conclusion. In contrast, when you use an integrated format, you use deductive reasoning and set out your conclusion before your reasoning. See Example 1.

| **EXAMPLE 1**   **Inductive vs. Deductive Reasoning** |

Script Format **Inductive Reasoning** **(specific to general)**	**Integrated Format** **Deductive Reasoning** **(general to specific)**
Specific Rules	Specific Rules
Descriptions of Analogous Cases	Descriptions of Analogous Cases
Party with Burden of Proof's Arguments	Mini-Conclusion/Prediction
■ First Argument ■ Second Argument ■ Third Argument	Reasoning
	■ First Reason (Summarize and evaluate each side's arguments)
Responding Party's Arguments	■ Second Reason (Summarize and evaluate each side's arguments)
■ First Argument ■ Second Argument ■ Third Argument	■ Third Reason (Summarize and evaluate each side's arguments)
Rebuttal (if any)	
Mini-Conclusion/Prediction	

The second difference is a difference in perspective. When you use a script format, your role is similar to that of a writer setting out the script for an oral argument. In contrast, when you write a memo using a more integrated format, you assume a perspective that is similar to that of a judge drafting an opinion. After setting out the specific rules and analogous cases, you set out your conclusion and then your reasoning. In doing so, you do what most judges do. You summarize each side's arguments and then explain why one side's arguments are more persuasive than the other side's.

Example 2 illustrates the ways in which the script and integrated formats are the same and different.

EXAMPLE 2	Same Discussion Using the Script and an Integrated Format

Script Format	Integrated Format
Introductory Section	**Introductory Section**
■ If one or both sides will make a policy argument, describe the policies underlying the statute or rule. ■ Introduce and set out the applicable statute(s) or common law rule. ■ Explain which side has the burden of proof and what that burden is. ■ Set out any other rules that apply to all of the elements. ■ End the introduction by providing the attorney with a roadmap for the rest of the discussion.	■ If one or both sides will make a policy argument, describe the policies underlying the statute or rule. ■ Introduce and set out the applicable statute(s) or common law rule. ■ Explain which side has the burden of proof and what that burden is. ■ Set out any other rules that apply to all of the elements. ■ End the introduction by providing the attorney with a roadmap for the rest of the discussion.
A. First Element (not in dispute)	**A. First Element (not in dispute)**
■ Set out and apply applicable rule.	■ Set out and apply the applicable rule.
B. Second Element (in dispute)	**B. Second Element (in dispute)**
■ Specific rules for second element ■ Examples of how specific rules have been applied in analogous cases ■ Arguments 　■ Party with burden of proof's arguments 　■ Responding party's arguments ■ Mini-conclusion for second element	■ Specific rules for second element ■ Examples of how specific rules have been applied in analogous cases ■ Mini-conclusion/prediction ■ Reasoning Note: Instead of setting out the cases in a separate section, you can integrate them into the reasoning.
C. Third Element (in dispute)	**C. Third Element (in dispute)**
■ Specific rules for third element ■ Examples of how specific rules have been applied in analogous cases ■ Arguments 　■ Party with burden of proof's arguments 　■ Responding party's arguments ■ Mini-conclusion for third element	■ Specific rules for third element ■ Examples of how specific rules have been applied in analogous cases ■ Mini-conclusion/prediction ■ Reasoning Note: Instead of setting out the cases in a separate section, you can integrate them into the reasoning.

PRACTICE POINTER The discussion of a disputed element written using the integrated format should contain the same information as a discussion of that element written using the script format. If you are leaving out information, you are doing something wrong.

§ 13.8.1   Draft the Specific Rule Section

The specific rule section is the same regardless of whether you use the script or the integrated format. Set out more general rules before more specific rules and exceptions, do more than just string together a series of quotes, and include a citation to authority for each rule that you set out. For more on drafting the specific rule section, see section 12.8.4a.

EXAMPLE 3 — **Specific Rule Section for a Discussion Section Written Using the Script Format and for a Discussion Section Written Using an Integrated Format**

Specific Rules—Script Format	Specific Rules—Integrated Format
D. Hostile	**D. Hostile**
Since 1984, the claimant's subjective intent has been irrelevant. *Chaplin v. Sanders*, 100 Wn.2d 853, 860-61, 676 P.2d 431 (1984) (overruling cases in which the courts considered the claimant's subjective intent). Thus, under current Washington law, the claimant must prove only that it used the land as if it were its own for the statutory period. *Id.; Miller v. Anderson*, 91 Wn. App. 822, 828, 964 P.2d 365 (1998). If the claimant proves that it used the land as if it were its own, the use was hostile unless the true owner can prove that it gave the claimant permission to use the land. *Id.*	Since 1984, the claimant's subjective intent has been irrelevant. *Chaplin v. Sanders*, 100 Wn.2d 853, 860-61, 676 P.2d 431 (1984) (overruling cases in which the courts considered the claimant's subjective intent). Thus, under current Washington law, the claimant must prove only that it used the land as if it were its own for the statutory period. *Id.; Miller v. Anderson*, 91 Wn. App. 822, 828, 964 P.2d 365 (1998). If the claimant proves that it used the land as if it were its own, the use was hostile unless the true owner can prove that it gave the claimant permission to use the land. *Id.*
Permission can be express or implied. *Miller v. Anderson*, 91 Wn. App. at 829, *citing Granston v. Callahan*, 52 Wn. App. 288, 759 P.2d 462 (1988) (case involved a prescriptive easement and not adverse possession). The courts infer that the use was permissive when, under the circumstances, it is reasonable to assume that the use was permitted. *Id.* If there was permission, the party claiming adverse possession bears the burden of proving that permission terminated either because (1) the servient estate changed hands through death or alienation or (2) the claimant has asserted a hostile right. *Id.*	Permission can be express or implied. *Miller v. Anderson*, 91 Wn. App. at 829, *citing Granston v. Callahan*, 52 Wn. App. 288, 759 P.2d 462 (1988) (case involved a prescriptive easement and not adverse possession). The courts infer that the use was permissive when, under the circumstances, it is reasonable to assume that the use was permitted. *Id.* If there was permission, the party claiming adverse possession bears the burden of proving that permission terminated either because (1) the servient estate changed hands through death or alienation or (2) the claimant has asserted a hostile right. *Id.*

PRACTICE POINTER   In setting out citations to authority, you can use parentheticals to provide the attorney with additional information about the cases. For instance, in the preceding example, the writer used a parenthetical to tell the attorney that, in *Chaplin*, the Washington Supreme Court overruled those cases in which the courts had considered the claimant's subjective intent in determining whether the claimant's use was hostile. Similarly, the writer used a parenthetical to tell the attorney that, while the *Miller* court cited *Granston* as authority, *Granston* involved a prescriptive easement and not adverse possession.

§ 13.8.2　Draft the Analogous Case Section

The specific rules section is not the only section that is the same under the script and integrated formats. If you set out the descriptions of analogous cases in a separate analogous case section, that section will be the same regardless of whether you use a script or an integrated format.

In drafting the analogous case section, remember why you are including descriptions of analogous cases. You are not including them to prove that you read cases. Instead, you are including them to provide the attorney with examples of how the specific rules have been applied in cases that are factually similar to your case. As a consequence, to write the analogous case section for a discussion section written using an integrated format, you need to go through the same process that you went through in drafting the analogous case section for a discussion section using a script format: (a) identify the analogous cases; (b) sort the analogous cases, putting the cases in which the element was met in one stack and the cases in which the element was not met in another stack; (c) go through the cases in both stacks, analyzing each case and then synthesizing each group of cases; (d) draft a sentence introducing each group of cases; and (e) draft your case descriptions. For more on each of these steps, see section 12.8.4b.

EXAMPLE 4　　**Analogous Case Section for a Discussion Section Written Using the Script Format and for a Discussion Section Written Using an Integrated Format**

Analogous Case Section Script Format	Analogous Case Section Integrated Format
In deciding whether the claimant was using the land as if it were its own, the courts consider whether the claimant made improvements to the land, whether the claimant maintained the property, and whether the claimant used the land on a regular basis. *See, e.g., Chaplin*, 100 Wn.2d at 855-56; *Timberlane*, 79 Wn. App. at 310-11. For example, in *Chaplin*, the court held that the claimants were using the land as if it were their own when the claimants built a road across the disputed land, cleared and maintained the disputed land, installed utility lines, and used the area for recreational activities. *Id.* at 855-56. Similarly, in *Timberlane*, the court held that claimants had used land belonging to the homeowners' association as if it were their own when they built and maintained a fence and a concrete patio and the claimants' children played on the land. *Id.* at 310-11.	In deciding whether the claimant was using the land as if it were its own, the courts consider whether the claimant made improvements to the land, whether the claimant maintained the property, and whether the claimant used the land on a regular basis. *See, e.g., Chaplin*, 100 Wn.2d at 855-56; *Timberlane*, 79 Wn. App. at 310-11. For example, in *Chaplin*, the court held that the claimants were using the land as if it were their own when the claimants built a road across the disputed land, cleared and maintained the disputed land, installed utility lines, and used the area for recreational activities. *Id.* at 855-56. Similarly, in *Timberlane*, the court held that claimants had used land belonging to the homeowners' association as if it were their own when they built and maintained a fence and a concrete patio and the claimants' children played on the land. *Id.* at 310-11.

> **PRACTICE POINTER**
>
> Remember to use a principle-based topic sentence to introduce each group of cases. For example, include a topic sentence that tells the attorney what principle you are using a group of cases to illustrate. In addition, use a transition to tell the attorney whether a second case illustrates the same or different point from the first case.

While most of the time you will want to set out the cases in a separate analogous case section, if the case descriptions are very short, you may want to integrate the case descriptions into your reasoning. See Example 5.

EXAMPLE 5　　**Case Description Integrated into Reasoning**

In addition, the court will probably conclude that DNWC's use of the property was uninterrupted. Although DNWC only used the property during the summer, in other cases the courts have held that such use was sufficient. For example, in *Howard v. Kunto*, 3 Wn. App. 393, 397, 477 P.2d 210 (1970), the court held that the claimants' use was continuous even though the claimants only used the beach house during the summer. As the court noted in that case, "the requisite possession requires such possession and dominion 'as ordinarily marks the conduct of owners in general in holding, managing, and caring for property of like nature and condition.'" Therefore, because the land is recreational land, DNWC's use of the land only in summer is consistent with how the owners of similar land hold, manage, and care for their property.

---

§ 13.8.3　Draft the Mini-Conclusion

The first subsection that is different is the mini-conclusion. While in the script format the mini-conclusion goes after the argument, in an integrated format your mini-conclusion goes before your reasoning. Example 6 illustrates the differences.

EXAMPLE 6　　**Mini-Conclusion for a Discussion Section Written Using the Script Format and for a Discussion Section Written Using an Integrated Format**

Mini-Conclusion Script Format	Mini-Conclusion Integrated Format
D. Hostile Specific Rules [not shown]	**D. Hostile** Specific Rules [not shown]

Mini-Conclusion Script Format	Mini-Conclusion Integrated Format
Analogous Cases [not shown]	Analogous Cases [not shown]
Arguments [not shown]	Mini-Conclusion
DNWC's arguments [not shown]	In this case, the court will probably conclude that DNWC has met its burden of proving that its use of the Garcia land was hostile.
	First, the court will probably conclude that DNWC has met its burden of proving that it used the land as if it were its own. [Rest of reason 1 goes here.]
Mr. Garcia's arguments [not shown]	Second, the court will probably conclude that DNWC's use of the Garcia land was not permissive. [Rest of reason 2 goes here.]
Mini-Conclusion	Finally, the court will probably conclude that Mr. Garcia did not allow DNWC to use his land as a neighborly accommodation. [Rest of reason 3 goes here.]
In this case, DNWC appears to have the stronger arguments. First, although DNWC has the burden of proof, it will probably be able to prove that it used Mr. Garcia's land as if it were its own when it maintained and used the campsites, the fire area, the outhouse, and the dock during the peak season. Second, DNWC will probably be able to prove that its use was not permissive. Although it is possible that initially DNWC was using the land with Mr. Garcia's grandfather's permission, that permission terminated when Mr. Garcia's grandfather died and left the property to Mr. Garcia. In addition, even though DNWC asked for permission to continue using the property, Mr. Garcia never responded to that request, and DNWC did an act that indicated its hostile intent when it posted the no trespassing sign and continued to use the property as its own. Third, it seems unlikely that a court would conclude that Mr. Garcia allowed DNWC to use his land as a neighborly accommodation. Although it may not be uncommon for farmers to allow a neighbor to use a driveway, it is uncommon for an owner of recreational land to allow a neighbor to use his land through the peak season. Thus, because DNWC used the property as its own and did an act that would have terminated the permission, the court will probably hold that it has proven that its use was hostile.	

PRACTICE POINTER	When you use an integrated format, you can use your mini-conclusion both to set out your conclusion and as a roadmap for the paragraphs setting out your reasoning.

EXAMPLE 7   **Mini-Conclusion Also Acts as a Roadmap for the Reasoning**

In this case, the court will probably conclude that DNWC's use of Mr. Garcia's land was hostile for two reasons: (1) DNWC was using the land as if it were its own, and (2) DNWC's use of Mr. Garcia's land was not permissive.

First, the court will probably conclude that DNWC has met its burden of proving that it used the land as if it were its own. [Rest of the analysis goes here.]

Second, the court will probably conclude that DNWC's use of Mr. Garcia's land was not permissive. [Rest of the analysis goes here.]

---

§ 13.8.4   Draft the Arguments

When you set out the arguments using the script format, you organize the arguments by party. You set out the party with the burden of proof's arguments and then the responding party's arguments. In contrast, when you use an integrated format, you organize the arguments, or analysis, around "reasons." You set out the mini-conclusion and then the first reason, the second reason, and so on.

EXAMPLE 8   **Outline Showing Organizational Scheme for Arguments Presented Using the Script Format and Using an Integrated Format**

Script Format (Arguments organized by party)	Integrated Format (Arguments organized by reasons)
Party with Burden of Proof's Arguments ■ Party with burden of proof's general assertion ■ Party with burden of proof's first subassertion and support for that subassertion ■ Party with burden of proof's second subassertion and support for that subassertion Responding Party's Arguments ■ Responding party's first subassertion and support for that subassertion ■ Responding party's second subassertion and support for that subassertion	Mini-Conclusion Reason 1 ■ Integrated discussion of moving and responding parties' arguments Reason 2 ■ Integrated discussion of moving and responding parties' arguments Reason 3 ■ Integrated discussion of moving and responding parties' arguments

EXAMPLE 9   **"Argument Section" for a Discussion Section Written Using the Script Format and for a Discussion Section Written Using an Integrated Format**

Arguments Script Format	Conclusions and Reasoning Integrated Format
DNWC can argue that its use of Mr. Garcia's land was hostile because (1) it has treated Mr. Garcia's land as its own and (2) since 1999, it has not had either express or implied permission to use the land. DNWC will begin by arguing that it used the land as if the land were its own. Like the claimants in *Chaplin* and *Timberlane*, DNWC maintained the disputed land: Not only did it maintain the campsites and fire area, but it also maintained the outhouse and the dock. In addition, like the claimants in *Chaplin* and *Timberlane*, DNWC used the property on a regular basis by holding campouts on the land several nights a week for eight weeks every summer. DNWC will also argue that its use was not permissive. Unlike *Granston*, in which the parties were related, in this case there are no facts indicating that any of DNWC's members are related to Mr. Garcia. In addition, unlike the title owners in *Miller* who allowed their neighbors to use their driveway, owners of recreational property do not typically allow their neighbors to use their land throughout the summer months. In contrast, Mr. Garcia can argue that DNWC was not using the property as if it were its own or, even if it was, it was using the land with his implied permission. Mr. Garcia will argue that the facts do not support a conclusion that DNWC was using the land as if it were its own. Although DNWC maintained the campsites, fire area, outhouse, and dock, it did not build any new structures. In addition, although it used the land, it did so for only a few days a week during the summer. Therefore, the facts in this case can be distinguished from the facts in *Chaplin* and *Timberlane*. While in both of those cases, the claimants made substantial improvements to the land, for example, building a road or building a fence and a patio, in this case DNWC did not build anything new. In the alternative, Mr. Garcia can argue that even if DNWC was using the land as if it were its own, it was doing so with his permission. In its 20017 letter to Mr. Garcia, DNWC acknowledged that it was using the land with Mr. Garcia's permission, and it requested permission to continue using the land. Because Mr. Garcia did not revoke his permission, it is reasonable to assume that DNWC used the land with Mr. Garcia's implied permission. Consequently, this case is	The court will probably conclude that DNWC's use of Mr. Garcia's land was hostile. First, the court will probably conclude that DNWC used Mr. Garcia's land as if it were the true owner. Although DNWC did not build any new structures on Mr. Garcia's land, it maintained the campsites, the fire area, the outhouse, and the dock. In addition, although DNWC did not use the property year round, it did use the property during the summer, which is how a typical owner would have used the land. Thus, this case is similar to *Chaplin* and *Timberlane*, in which the claimants maintained and used the disputed land as a true owner would have used it. While in *Chaplin* and *Timberlane* the claimants built new structures (in *Chaplin*, the claimants built a road and, in *Timberlane*, they built a fence and a patio), the courts have held that the claimant does not have to do everything that a title owner might do. Second, the court will probably conclude that DNWC's use of Mr. Garcia's land was not permissive. Unlike *Granston*, in which the parties were related and had a close relationship, there is no evidence that the members of DNWC are related to Mr. Garcia. In addition, unlike *Miller*, in which the title owners allowed the claimants, their neighbors, to use their driveway, the typical owners of recreational land do not allow a neighboring property owner to use their land several days a week during the peak season. While Mr. Garcia can argue that the letter that DNWC sent to him establishes that DNWC's use of the land was permissive, the court will probably reject this argument. First, the court will conclude that if Mr. Garcia's grandfather gave DNWC permission to use his land, that permission terminated when his grandfather died. In addition, the court will probably conclude that even if DNWC used Mr. Garcia's land with Mr. Garcia's implied permission from the time of his grandfather's death until it sent the letter in February of 2001, that permission terminated in the summer of 2001 when the DNWC posted the no trespassing sign and continued to use the property as its own.

Arguments Script Format	Conclusions and Reasoning Integrated Format
more like *Miller* than it is *Lingvall*. Like the title owners in *Miller*, who allowed the claimants to use their driveway as a neighborly accommodation, Mr. Garcia allowed DNWC to use his land as a neighborly accommodation. In addition, unlike *Lingvall* in which there was an antagonistic relationship between the parties, in this case there was not. In response, DNWC can argue that even if its initial use was permissive, that permission would have terminated when Mr. Garcia's grandfather died. See *Granston*, 52 Wn. App. at 294-95. Likewise, even if DNWC had Mr. Garcia's implied permission to use the land, that permissive use ended in 2001 when, after not receiving a response from Mr. Garcia, the DNWC posted a no trespassing sign on the dock and continued to use the property as if it were its own.	

§ 13.8.5   Avoid the Common Problems

The two most common problems that writers encounter when using an integrated format are (a) that they do not give appropriate weight to each side's arguments and (b) that, in trying to give appropriate weight to each side's arguments, they write sentences that are hard to read.

a.   Give Appropriate Weight to Each Side's Arguments

While the script format forces writers to give appropriate weight to each side's arguments, the integrated format does not. As a consequence, as the writer, you need to make a special effort to tell the attorney what each side is likely to argue and why one set of arguments is more persuasive than another set. Compare Examples 10 and 11.

EXAMPLE 10   **Poor Example: The Writer Sets Out Only the Arguments That Support Her Conclusion**

First, the court will probably conclude that DNWC used Mr. Garcia's land as if it were the true owner. DNWC maintained the campsites, the fire area, the outhouse, and the dock. In addition, DNWC used the land for eight weeks each summer, which would be typical for that type of property. Consequently, this case is similar to *Chaplin* and *Timberlane*, in which the claimants maintained and used the disputed land as if it were their own.

EXAMPLE 11   **Better Example: The Writer Sets Out Both Sides' Arguments**

First, the court will probably conclude that DNWC used Mr. Garcia's land as if it were the true owner. Although DNWC did not build any new structures on Mr. Garcia's land, it maintained the campsites, the fire area, the outhouse, and the dock. In addition, although DNWC did not use the property year round, it did use the property during the summer, which is how a typical owner would have used the land. Therefore, this case is similar to *Chaplin* and *Timberlane*, in which the claimants maintained and used the disputed land as a true owner would have used the land. While in *Chaplin* and *Timberlane* the claimants built new structures (in *Chaplin*, the claimants built a road and in *Timberlane*, they built a fence and a patio), the courts have held that the claimant does not have to do everything that a title owner might do.

PRACTICE POINTER	In switching from the script format to an integrated format, you should not lose any content.

b.   Write Sentences That Are Easy to Read

Writing sentences that give appropriate weight to each side's arguments can be difficult. If you are having trouble with a sentence, try one of the following strategies.

Strategy 1:   Put the Weaker Argument in a Dependent Clause and the Stronger Argument in the Main Clause

One of the easiest ways to give appropriate weight to each side's argument is to put the weaker argument in a dependent clause and the stronger argument in the main clause.

Although [weaker argument], [stronger argument].

In Example 12, the dependent clauses are underlined, and the main clauses are in bold.

EXAMPLE 12	Weaker Argument in the Dependent Clause and Stronger Argument in the Main Clause

Although DNWC did not build any new structures on Mr. Garcia's land, **it maintained not only the campsites and the fire area but also the outhouse and the dock.** In addition, although DNWC did not use the property year round, **it did use the property during the summer, which is how a typical owner would have used the land.**

The problem, of course, is that if you use this construction too often your writing becomes monotonous. Sometimes you can solve the problem by changing the word that you use to introduce the dependent clause. Instead of using "although," you can use "even though," or "while." At other times, though, you will need to break the pattern by using another strategy.

P R A C T I C E P O I N T E R	Many attorneys think that the word "though" is too informal for use in a formal memo or a brief. Instead, use the more formal "although" or "even though."

Strategy 2:   Use a "This and Not That" Sentence Structure

Another strategy that can work well is a "this and not that" sentence. When you use this strategy, remember to include a sentence that explains why your case is more like Case A than it is Case B.

EXAMPLE 13   **"This But Not That" Sentence Structure**

Thus, this case is more like Case A than it is Case B. Unlike Case B, in which . . . , in this case, . . . Instead, as in Case A, . . .

Strategy 3:   Set Out One Side's Argument in One Sentence or Set of Sentences and the Other Side's Argument in a Second Sentence or Set of Sentences

When you use an integrated format, you do not need to set out both side's arguments in a single sentence. When the arguments are complicated, set out one side's arguments in one sentence or set of sentences and the other side's arguments in a separate sentence or set of sentences. Note that it is often a good idea to start the other side's argument with a transitional word or phrase.

EXAMPLE 14   **Each Side's Arguments Set Out in Separate Sentences**

(Mr. Garcia's argument is underlined, and DNWC's argument is in bold.)

Mr. Garcia has paid all of the taxes and assessments on the disputed piece of property. **Nevertheless, the courts have consistently found that payment of taxes and assessments is not enough to defeat an adverse possession claim.**

EXAMPLE 15   **Each Side's Arguments Set Out in Separate Sentences**

(Mr. Garcia's arguments are underlined, and DNWC's arguments are in boldface type.)

Some actions taken by DNWC and Mr. Garcia suggest that both sides knew the property was his. In about February 2001, DNWC wrote Mr. Garcia, asking whether it could continue using his land for campouts. In addition, in August of 2013, Mr. Garcia visited the property with the intent of spending a few days camping on the lake. Arguably, both of these actions suggest that Mr. Garcia was asserting his rights as an owner. **Other actions, however, suggest that DNWC was successfully asserting its adverse claim. First, when Mr. Garcia did not respond to the DNWC letter, DNWC put up a no trespassing sign. There is no evidence that Mr. Garcia had ever put up a no trespassing sign, nor is there evidence that he removed DNWC's no trespassing sign. Second, when Mr. Garcia found children and counselors on the property, he did not tell them to leave. Instead he was the one who left, returning only the following evening after they had gone.**

Strategy 4:   Use the "Plaintiff Will Argue, Defendant Will Argue" Language

It is also not wrong to include an occasional "the plaintiff will argue" or "the defendant will respond." Just make sure to organize the arguments around the lines of argument and not each side's arguments.

EXAMPLE 16   **Using the Phrase "the Plaintiff Will Argue" and "the Defendant Will Respond" to Set Out the Arguments**

We can argue that the letter that DNWC sent to Mr. Garcia establishes that DNWC's use of the land was permissive. However, the court will probably reject this argument on the ground that even though Mr. Garcia did not respond, DNWC continued using his land for more than 10 years.

PRACTICE POINTER   In reading cases, pay attention to the ways in which the courts present each side's arguments. In particular, note which types of sentences are easy to read and understand and which are more difficult. You can then use some of the easy-to-read sentence patterns in your own writing.

§ 13.8.6   Checklist for Discussion Section Written Using an Integrated Format

a.   Content

Introduction

■ The writer has included a sentence or paragraph introducing the governing statute or common law rule.
■ The writer has set out the general rule, quoting the applicable statutory sections and quoting or paraphrasing the common law rule.
■ The writer has set out any other general rules.
■ When appropriate, the writer has briefly described the policies underlying the statute or common law rule.
■ The writer has included a roadmap.
■ The writer has not included rules or information that the attorney does not need.

■ The rules are stated accurately and objectively.

■ For each rule stated, the writer has included a citation to authority.

Discussion of Undisputed Elements

■ The writer has identified the element and, when there are specific rules, set out those specific rules.

■ The writer has applied the rules to the facts of the client's case, explaining why the element is not in dispute.

Discussion of Disputed Elements

■ For each disputed element, the writer has set out the specific rules, described cases that have interpreted and applied those rules, stated her conclusion or prediction, and summarized her reasoning.

■ The writer has included all of the applicable specific rules and set out those rules accurately and objectively.

■ The writer has introduced each group of analogous cases, telling the attorney what rule or principle the cases illustrate.

■ The case descriptions illustrate the rule or principle and are accurate and objective.

■ In setting out the reasoning, the writer has given appropriate weight to each side's arguments.

■ The analysis is sophisticated.

b.   Large-Scale Organization

■ The writer has presented the information in the order in which the attorney expects to see it. For example, the writer begins the discussion section with an introductory section in which she sets out the general rules. The writer then walks the attorney through each of the elements, raising and dismissing the undisputed elements and doing a more complete analysis of the disputed elements.

c.   Writing

■ The attorney can understand the discussion with just one reading.

■ The paragraph divisions are logical, and the paragraphs are neither too long nor too short. See Chapter 22.

■ Transitions and dovetailing have been used to make the connection between ideas clear. See Chapter 23.

■ In most sentences, the writer has used the actor as the subject of the sentence, and the subject and verb are close together. See sections 24.1 and 24.4.

■ The writer has varied the length of the sentences and the sentence patterns so that each sentence flows smoothly from the prior sentence. See section 24.5.

■ The writing is concise and precise. See sections 25.1 and 25.2.

■ The writing is grammatically correct and correctly punctuated. See Chapters 27 and 28.

■ The discussion section has been proofread.

§ 13.9   Draft the Conclusion

The last section of the memo is the formal conclusion. In a one-issue memo, use your formal conclusion to summarize your analysis of that issue. Set out your conclusion and then summarize your analysis. In Example 1, the writer sets out his conclusion in the first sentence and then, in the following paragraphs, summarizes his analysis of the elements.

EXAMPLE 1   Conclusion

Conclusion

More likely than not, DNWC will be able to establish title to Mr. Garcia's land through adverse possession.

To prove that its possession was open and notorious, DNWC only needs to show that Mr. Garcia had actual notice of its use of his land throughout the statutory period or that it used his land in such a way that any reasonable person would have thought that it owned this land. In this case, DNWC can use the letter that it sent to Mr. Garcia to prove that he had actual notice, and it can show that its use of the land for campouts was such that any reasonable person would have thought that DNWC owned the land.

To prove that its possession was actual and uninterrupted, DNWC need only show that it actually used the land and that its use was consistent with how the true owner might have used the land. The case law suggests that DNWC's maintenance of the campsites, fire area, outhouse, and dock were sufficient to establish actual possession. In addition, although DNWC only used the land during the summer months, the court is likely to find that such use was uninterrupted because most owners of recreational land only use their land during certain seasons.

To prove that its use of the land was exclusive, DNWC will have to show that it did not share the land with anyone else. Although we could try to argue that DNWC's use was not exclusive because it allowed campers to use the land, this argument is weak because the campers used the land under DNWC's supervision.

Finally, to prove that its use was hostile, DNWC will have to prove that it used the land as if it were its own and that it did not do so with Mr. Garcia's permission. DNWC's maintenance and use of the property is probably sufficient to establish that it used Mr. Garcia's land as if it were its own. In addition, DNWC will be able to prove that its use was not permissive. Even if DNWC's initial use of the property was with Mr. Garcia's grandfather's permission, that permission terminated when Mr. Garcia's grandfather died. In addition, although in its 2001 letter DNWC asked Mr. Garcia for permission to continue using the property, DNWC has a strong argument that it did a hostile act that terminated permission when, even after Mr. Garcia did not respond, it continued maintaining and using the property and it posted the no trespassing sign.

Because all of these elements have been met for the statutory period, which is 10 years, DNWC has established a right to title to the land through adverse possession.

In contrast, if your memo discusses more than one issue, use your conclusion to summarize your analysis of each issue and to explain the interrelationships among those issues.

Chapter 13 Quiz No. 1

Draft answers for each of the following questions. Make your points clearly and concisely, and write sentences that are easy to read and that are grammatical and correctly punctuated.

1. In reading a discussion of a disputed element, what types of information does an attorney expect to see? What information does the attorney expect to see first? Second? Third? Fourth?
2. What is the difference between inductive and deductive reasoning?
3. Why should you discuss the elements one at a time rather than as a group?
4. What is the relationship between the IRAC formula that is used to brief a case or draft an exam answer and the IRAC formula that is used to discuss a disputed element?
5. How is the discussion of a disputed element written using an integrated format the same as and different from the discussion of a disputed element written using the script format?

§ 13.10 Revising and Editing Your Draft

As you learned in writing your first memo, your first draft should not be your last draft. Because so much is as stake for the client, for the firm, and for you, make the time to revise, edit, and proofread your memo.

§ 13.10.1 Revise for Content and Organization

In revising the draft, focus first on content and organization. Begin by checking the memo's content. Have you given the attorney the information that he or she needs to evaluate the case? If you did not, add that information. Did you include information that the attorney does not need? If you did, delete that information. Did you present the information accurately and objectively? If you have misstated a rule or misrepresented a case, correct those errors.

Next, check the large-scale organization. Did you present the information in the order that the attorney expects to see it? For example, did you start with an introductory section and then walk the attorney through the elements one by one? In walking the attorney through the disputed elements, did you use one of the standard organizational schemes—for example, did you use the script format or an integrated format? In setting out the specific rules, did you set out more general rules before more specific rules and exceptions? If you did not do all of these things, stop and make the necessary revisions.

Finally, check your small-scale organization. Have you used roadmaps, signposts, topic sentences, and transitions? One way to check the small-scale organization is to look at the first sentence of each paragraph. Does that sentence accurately identify the topic of that paragraph? Is there a transition that tells the attorney how that paragraph is related to the prior paragraphs?

Also check to make sure that the discussion of the various elements is "coherent." For example, make sure that you have repeated key terms and phrases. What terms and phrases are in the specific rules? Do those same terms and phrases appear in the descriptions of the analogous cases? In the arguments? In the mini-conclusion? In Example 1, note how the writer has repeated the key terms and phrases, which are "actual notice" and "used the land such that any reasonable person would have thought that the claimant owned it." The references to "actual notice" are in bold, and the references to "used the land such that any reasonable person would have thought that the claimant owned it" are underlined.

EXAMPLE 1   **Good Example: The Writer Has Repeated Key Terms**

A claimant can satisfy the open and notorious element by showing either (1) that the title owner had **actual notice** of the adverse use throughout the statutory period or (2) that the claimant <u>used the land such that any reasonable person would have thought that the claimant owned it</u>. *Riley v. Andres*, 107 Wn. App. 391, 396, 27 P.3d 618 (2001).

In this case, DNWC can prove both that Mr. Garcia had **actual notice** of its adverse use and <u>that any reasonable person would have thought that DNWC owned the land</u>. To prove that Mr. Garcia had **actual notice** of DNWC's use of the land, DNWC can point to the letter that it sent to Mr. Garcia in 1998 asking for continuing permission to use his land for campouts. To prove that <u>a reasonable person would have thought that DNWC owned the land</u>, DNWC will point out that it not only used the land for campouts but also maintained the campsites, fire area, outhouse, and dock. In addition, it posted a no trespassing sign.

---

§ 13.10.2 Edit Your Draft

In section 12.10.2, we set out four pieces of advice that will help you to write effective sentences: (1) use the actor as the subject of most of your sentences; (2) keep your subjects and verbs close together, (3) put old information at the beginning of the paragraph and new information at the end, and (4) vary sentence length and patterns. You should apply that same advice to this second memo. In particular, pay particular attention to the sentences that tend to be more difficult to write: the sentence setting out the issue, the sentences setting out complex rules, and, when you use an integrated format, the sentences in which you set out the parties' arguments and your evaluation of those arguments.

In this chapter, we add two more recommendations: (a) make sure that your writing is concise and (b) make sure that your writing is precise.

a.   Write Concisely

Although writing sentences with strong subject-verb units eliminates much unnecessary language, you also need to edit out such throat-clearing expressions as "it is expected that . . ." and "it is generally recognized that . . ." and redundancies like "combined together" and "depreciate in value" (see sections 25.2.5 and 25.2.7). In Example 2, without the citation, the first draft has 73 words, and the revised draft has 54 words.

| EXAMPLE 2 | **Example 2 Delete Unnecessary Words and Phrases** |

First Draft (73 Words)

It is generally recognized that a claimant can satisfy the open and notorious element by showing one of two things. The claimant can show either (1) that the title owner had real and actual notice of the adverse use of the claimant's land throughout the statutory period or (2) that the claimant used the land in such a way that any reasonable person would have thought or believed that the claimant owned it. *Riley v. Andres*, 107 Wn. App. 391, 396, 27 P.3d 618 (2001).

Revised Draft (54 Words)

A claimant can prove that its possession was open and notorious by showing either (1) that the title owner had actual notice of the adverse use throughout the statutory period or (2) that the claimant used the land in such a way that any reasonable person would have thought that the claimant owned it. *Riley v. Andres*, 107 Wn. App. 391, 396, 27 P.3d 618 (2001).

In Example 2, the writer reduced the number of words by 25 percent by doing some simple editing. Writers using the same technique throughout a draft can get a ten-page draft down to seven and one-half pages. For more on writing concisely, see section 25.2.

b.   Write Precisely

If conciseness is the first hallmark of excellent legal writing, precision is the second. Make sure that you use correct terms, that you use those terms consistently, that subjects and verbs are paired correctly, and that in making your arguments you compare or contrast like things.

1.   *Select the Correct Term*

In the law, many words have specific meanings. For example, the words "held," "found," and "ruled" have very different meanings. In most instances, use "held" when you are setting out the appellate court's answer to the issue raised on appeal. In contrast, use "found" to refer to the trial court's or jury's findings of fact, and "ruled" when talking about the court's ruling on a motion or objection.

Compare the following examples. In Example 3, the writer used "held" incorrectly. Because the writer is not setting out the court's holding, "held' is incorrect. In contrast, in Example 4, the writer has used "held' correctly. Similarly, in Examples 5 and 6, the writer uses "found" and "ruled" correctly.

| EXAMPLE 3 | **"Held" Used Incorrectly** |

For example, in *Chaplin*, the court **held** that the claimants had built a road across the disputed land, cleared and maintained the disputed land, installed utility lines, and used the disputed land for recreational activities.

EXAMPLE 4   "Held" Used Correctly

For example, in *Chaplin*, the court **held** that the claimants had proven that their use of the property was hostile when they built a road across the disputed land, cleared and maintained the disputed land, installed utility lines, and used the disputed land for recreational activities. *Id.* at 864.

EXAMPLE 5   "Found" Used Correctly

For example, in *Chaplin*, the trial court **found** that the claimants had built a road across the disputed land, cleared and maintained the disputed land, installed utility lines, and used the disputed land for recreational activities.

EXAMPLE 6   "Ruled" Used Correctly

The court **ruled** that the evidence was inadmissible.

---

2. Use Terms Consistently

In addition to making sure that you use the correct term, also make sure that you use terms consistently. If something is an "element," continue referring to it as an element. Do not switch and suddenly start calling it a "factor" or a "requirement."

EXAMPLE 7   Poor Example: Inconsistent Use of Terms

To prove adverse possession, the claimant must prove four **elements:** that its possession was (1) exclusive, (2) actual and uninterrupted, (3) open and notorious, and (4) hostile for the statutory period. *ITT Rayonier, Inc. v. Bell*, 112 Wn.2d 754, 757, 774 P.2d 6 (1989); *Chaplin v. Sanders*, 100 Wn.2d 853, 857, 676 P.2d 431 (1984). In this case, the statutory period is 10 years. RCW 4.16.020(1). Whether a particular **factor** is met is a mixed question of law and fact. *Chaplin*, 100 Wn.2d at 863. Whether the essential facts exist is for the trier of fact to decide; but whether the facts, as found, satisfy the **requirement** is for the court to determine as a matter of law. *Id.*

EXAMPLE 8   Good Example: Consistent Use of Terms

To prove adverse possession, the claimant must prove four **elements:** that its possession was (1) exclusive, (2) actual and uninterrupted, (3) open and notorious, and (4) hostile for the statutory period. *ITT Rayonier, Inc. v. Bell*, 112 Wn.2d 754, 757, 774 P.2d 6 (1989); *Chaplin v. Sanders*, 100 Wn.2d 853, 857, 676 P.2d 431 (1984). In this case, the statutory period is 10 years. RCW 4.16.020(1). Whether a particular **element** is met is a mixed question of law and fact. *Chaplin*, 100 Wn.2d at 863. Whether the essential facts exist is for the trier of fact to decide, but whether the facts, as found, satisfy the **element** is for the court to determine as a matter of law. *Id.*

---

3. Make Sure the Subjects and Verbs Go Together

In addition to making sure that you have selected the right word and used it consistently, also make sure that the subjects of your sentences go with the verbs and objects. For instance, while courts "state," "find," "rule," and "hold," they do not "argue." It is the parties who present arguments. See section 25.1.6. Thus, in Example 9, the subject and verb do not go together.

EXAMPLE 9	Poor Example: Subject and Verb Mismatch

While a **court** can **argue** that DNWC was not using the land as if it were its own, this argument is not a strong one.

EXAMPLE 10	Good Example: Subject and Verb Go Together

While **Mr. Garcia** can **argue** that DNWC was not using the land as if it were its own, this argument is not a strong one.

PRACTICE POINTER	You can, however, say that the dissent argued.

4. Compare or Contrast Like Things

In setting out the arguments, you will often want to show how your case is similar to or different from other cases. For instance, you will want to compare or contrast the facts in your case to the facts in another case. In making these comparisons, make sure that you are comparing apples with apples and oranges with oranges. For example, do not compare a case name to a party or a party to a fact.

In Example 11, the writer has not compared similar things. She compared a case (*Crites*) to a person (Mr. Garcia).

EXAMPLE 11	Poor Example: The Writer Has Not Compared Similar Things

Unlike **Crites**, in which the title owner allowed the claimants to use his land as a neighborly accommodation, **Mr. Garcia** did not allow DNWC to use his land as a neighborly accommodation.

EXAMPLE 12	Good Example: The Writer Has Compared Similar Things

Unlike **Crites**, in which the title owner allowed the claimants to use his land as a neighborly accommodation, **in this case,** Mr. Garcia did not allow DNWC to use his land as a neighborly accommodation.

> **PRACTICE POINTER** Remember that when a name is italicized, the reference is to the court's decision. When the name is not italicized, the reference is to a person. Thus, in the following sentence, *"Crites"* is a reference to the court's decision in *Crites v. Koch*, and the reference to "Crites" is a reference to the plaintiff, Mr. Crites.
>
> In *Crites*, the court held that Koch allowed Crites to use his land as a neighborly accommodation.

For more on writing precisely, see section 25.1.

§ 13.10.3 Proofread the Final Draft

The final step in the process is to proofread your draft, checking for spelling errors, grammatical and punctuation errors, typographical errors, and citation errors. The easiest way to proofread is to print out a copy of your memo and read through it word by word, spending the most time on the sections that you worked on last or when you were the most tired.

For a copy of the completed memo, see section 11.4.2.

Chapter 13 Quiz No. 2

Draft answers for each of the following questions. Make your points clearly and concisely, and write sentences that are easy to read and that are grammatical and correctly punctuated.

1. What technique can you use to make your discussion of an element more coherent?
2. How might you revise the following paragraph to make the same points more concisely?

   > Second, more likely than not it will probably be the court's conclusion that DNWC's use of the land belonging to Garcia was not permissive. In reaching this conclusion, it is likely that the court will probably point out that, unlike the court in *Granston*, in which the parties were related and had a close relationship, in the case before the court there is no evidence that the members of DNWC are related to Mr. Garcia in any way. In addition, unlike the court's decision in *Miller*, in which the owners of the land allowed the claimants, who were their neighbors, to use their driveway, it is more typical that owners of recreational land are not so generous as to allow a neighboring property owner to use their land several days a week during the peak seasons of the year, which in this case the summer months. [146 words]

3. What is the difference between an element and a factor?
4. In the following example, has the writer compared like things? If not, how could you rewrite the sentences?

   > Unlike *Chaplin* and *Timberlane* in which the claimants built new structures, DNWC did not do anything other than maintain existing improvements.

5. Does the following paragraph contain any errors? If yes, how would correct those errors?

In deciding whether the claimant was using the land as if it were its own, the primary consideration appears to be whether the plaintiff made any improvements to the land, the type of maintenance, and how much the claimant used the land. [citations omitted.] For example, in *Chaplin*, the court ruled that the claimants' were using the land as if it were there own when the claimants built a road across the disputed land, cleared and maintained the disputed land, installed utility lines and used the area for recreation.

Drafting Memos Requiring Other Types of Analysis

I n Chapters 12 and 13, we showed you one of the most common types of legal analysis, an elements analysis. There are, however, other types of analysis, and this chapter provides you with templates for three of those types: section 14.1 provides you with a template for issues that require the analysis of a set of factors; section 14.2, with a template for issues that require the balancing of competing interests, and section 14.3, with templates for issues of first impression.

§ 14.1   Factor Analysis

While in an elements analysis the party with the burden of proof must prove all of the elements, in a factor analysis no one factor is determinative. The court can find for a party even when one or more of the factors favor the other side. For example, in most states, the legislature has set out a list of factors that the courts must consider in deciding child custody cases. Although the statutes may state that a particular factor, or set of factors, should be given the most weight, the courts can find for a parent even when the majority of the factors favor the other parent.

§ 14.1.1   Templates for Issues Involving a Factor Analysis

The templates for issues involving a factor analysis are very similar to the templates for issues involving an elements analysis. In both instances, you begin the discussion section with an introductory section, and in both instances you then walk your reader through the analysis step by step: In an elements analysis you walk the reader through the elements, and in a factor analysis you walk the reader through the factors. The primary difference is that, in a factor analysis, you need to add a section in which you weigh the factors. Taken as a group, do the factors weigh in favor of the plaintiff, or do they weigh in favor of the defendant?

In the following examples, Example 1 sets out the templates for an elements and factor analysis using the script format, and Example 2 sets out the templates for an elements and factor analysis using a more integrated format. For the purposes of both examples, presume that, for the issue involving an elements analysis, there are three elements, one of which is not likely to be in dispute and two that will be in dispute. Likewise, for the issue involving a factors analysis, presume that there are three factors: Even though the first factor is not "in dispute," the second and third factors are.

> **PRACTICE POINTER**   When you use a script format, you use inductive reasoning and organize the analysis around the parties' arguments: You set out all of one side's arguments and then all of the other side's arguments. On the other hand, when you use a more integrated format, you use deductive reasoning: You set out your conclusion and then your reasoning. For more on the script and integrated formats, see section 13.7.

EXAMPLE 1   **Templates for an Elements and Factor Analysis Using a Script Format**

Elements Analysis	Factor Analysis
Discussion	**Discussion**
Introductory Section	**Introductory Section**
■ If one or both sides will make a policy argument, describe the policies underlying the statute, common law rule, or court rule. ■ Introduce and set out the applicable statute, common law rule, or court rule. ■ If one of the parties has the burden of proof, explain which side has the burden of proof and what that burden is. ■ Set out any other rules that apply to all of the elements. ■ End the introductory section by providing the attorney with a roadmap for the rest of the discussion.	■ If one or both sides will make a policy argument, describe the policies underlying the statute, common law rule, or court rule. ■ Introduce and set out the applicable statute, common law rule, or court rule. ■ If one of the parties has the burden of proof, explain which side has the burden of proof and what that burden is. ■ Set out any other rules that apply to all of the factors. ■ End the introductory section by providing the attorney with a roadmap for the rest of the discussion.

Elements Analysis	Factor Analysis
A. First Element (not in dispute)	**A. First Factor (not in dispute)**
■ Set out and apply the applicable rule and/or definitions.	■ Set out and apply the applicable rule and/or definitions.
B. Second Element (in dispute)	**B. Second Factor (in dispute)**
■ Set out the specific rules or definitions for the second element. ■ If there are analogous cases that discuss the second element and descriptions of those analogous cases would help your supervising attorney understand how the courts have interpreted this element, include descriptions of analogous cases. ■ Set out arguments: 　■ Party with burden of proof's arguments 　■ Responding party's arguments. ■ Evaluate each side's arguments and set out mini-conclusion for the second element.	■ Set out the specific rules or definitions for the second factor. ■ If there are analogous cases that discuss the second factor and descriptions of those analogous cases would help your supervising attorney understand how the courts have interpreted this factor, include descriptions of analogous cases. ■ Set out arguments: 　■ Party with burden of proof's arguments 　■ Responding party's arguments. ■ Evaluate each side's arguments and set out mini-conclusion for the factor.
C. Third Element (in dispute)	**C. Third Factor (in dispute)**
■ Set out the specific rules or definitions for the third element. ■ If there are analogous cases that discuss the second element and descriptions of those analogous cases would help your supervising attorney understand how the courts have interpreted this element, include descriptions of analogous cases. ■ Set out each side's arguments: 　■ Party with burden of proof's arguments 　■ Responding party's arguments. ■ Evaluate each side's arguments and set out mini-conclusion for the third element.	■ Set out the specific rules or definitions for the third factor. ■ If there are analogous cases that discuss the second factor and descriptions of those analogous cases would help your supervising attorney understand how the courts have interpreted this factor, include descriptions of analogous cases. ■ Set out each side's arguments: 　■ Party with burden of proof's arguments 　■ Responding party's arguments. ■ Evaluate each side's arguments and set out mini-conclusion for the third factor.
Conclusion	**Evaluation of Factors**
■ Set out your conclusion and advice.	■ Using either a script or an integrated format, weigh the factors and set out your mini-conclusion. Note: if doing so would help your reader, describe how the courts have weighed the factors in analogous cases, and then show how the parties would use those cases to support their arguments (script format) or how the court might use those cases in making its decision (integrated format).
	Conclusion
	■ Set out your conclusion and advice.

EXAMPLE 2	**Templates for an Elements and Factor Analysis Using a More Integrated Format**

Elements Analysis	**Factor Analysis**
Discussion	**Discussion**

Introductory Section

- If one or both sides will make a policy argument, describe the policies underlying the statute, common law rule, or court rule.
- Introduce and set out the applicable statute, common law rule, or court rule.
- If one of the parties has the burden of proof, explain which side has the burden of proof and what that burden is.
- Set out any other rules that apply to all of the elements.
- End the introductory section by providing the attorney with a roadmap for the rest of the discussion.

A. First Element (not in dispute)

- Set out and apply the applicable rule and/or definitions.

B. Second Element (in dispute)

- Set out the specific rules or definitions for the second element.
- If there are analogous cases that discuss the second element and descriptions of those analogous cases would help your supervising attorney understand how the courts have interpreted this element, include descriptions of analogous cases.
- Set out your conclusion.
- Set out your reasoning, summarizing and evaluating each side's arguments.

C. Third Element (in dispute)

- Set out the specific rules or definitions for the third element.
- If there are analogous cases that discuss the third element and descriptions of those analogous cases would help your supervising attorney understand how the courts have interpreted this element, include descriptions of analogous cases.
- Set out your conclusion.
- Set out your reasoning, summarizing and evaluating each side's arguments.

Introductory Section

- If one or both sides will make a policy argument, describe the policies underlying the statute, common law rule, or court rule.
- Introduce and set out the applicable statute, common law rule, or court rule.
- If one of the parties has the burden of proof, explain which side has the burden of proof and what that burden is.
- Set out any other rules that apply to all of the factors.
- End the introductory section by providing the attorney with a roadmap for the rest of the discussion.

A. First Factor (not in dispute)

- Set out and apply the applicable rule and/or definitions.

B. Second Factor (in dispute)

- Set out the specific rules or definitions for the second factor.
- If there are analogous cases that discuss the second factor and descriptions of those analogous cases would help your supervising attorney understand how the courts have interpreted this factor, include descriptions of analogous cases.
- Set out your conclusion.
- Set out your reasoning, summarizing and evaluating each side's arguments.

C. Third Factor (in dispute)

- Set out the specific rules or definitions for the third factor.
- If there are analogous cases that discuss the third factor and descriptions of those analogous cases would help your supervising attorney understand how the courts have interpreted this factor, include descriptions of analogous cases.
- Set out your conclusion.
- Set out your reasoning, summarizing and evaluating each side's arguments.

Elements Analysis	Factor Analysis
Conclusion	**Evaluation of Factors**
■ Set out your conclusion and advice.	Using an integrated format, weigh the factors and set out your mini-conclusion. Note: if doing so would help your reader, describe how the courts have weighed the factors in analogous cases, and then show how the court might use those cases in making its decision.
	Conclusion
	Set out your conclusion and advice.

You must, of course, modify the templates so that they work for your issue and your readers. For instance, if there are four and not three factors, discuss each of those four factors. However, if there are more than three or four factors, think about whether you need a separate subsection for each factor. Can you raise and dismiss some of the factors at the end of your introductory section? If some of the factors are closely related, can you combine your discussions of the related factors?

In addition, modify your template so that it is consistent with your supervising attorney's preferences. While some attorneys love subheadings and will want you to use lots of them, others don't. Likewise, while in a factor analysis some attorneys will want you to include both a section in which you weigh the factors and a formal conclusion, others will say that the formal conclusion is repetitive and that you can either (1) delete the formal conclusion or (2) keep the formal conclusion but move the weighing of the factors out of the discussion section and into that formal conclusion. When in doubt, use common sense or ask your supervising attorney what he or she prefers.

§ 14.1.2　Draft the Introductory or General Rule Section

In both a memo involving an elements analysis and a memo involving a factor analysis, the introductory section serves the same function. It places the issue in context, it sets out the general rules, and it provides the reader with a roadmap for the rest of the discussion.

In deciding what to include in your introductory section, think about how much your supervising attorney knows about the area of law. If the area is one that she knows well, the section can be short. In most instances, include only the following information:

■ a sentence introducing the applicable law;
■ the applicable law, for example, the applicable portions of the statute, common law rule, or court rule;
■ any other rules that apply to all of the factors; and
■ a roadmap that tells your supervising attorney which factors appear to be in dispute and which factors are not in dispute.

If, however, the area of law is not one that your supervising attorney knows, you will usually want to include at least some background information. Depending on the issue and the types of arguments that you expect that the parties may make, explain how the law developed, the policies underlying the law, and the rules relating to the burden of proof.

PRACTICE POINTER	While most attorneys will want you to quote the applicable portions of statutes and regulations, you can paraphrase common law and other rules.

As a general rule, set out more general rules before more specific rules. Thus, set out the policies underlying the rules before the rules themselves and the rules before the exceptions to the rules. Also remember to include a citation to authority for each rule that you set out. Finally, in most instances, keep the focus on the rule by putting the citation not at the beginning of the sentence, but in a separate citation sentence after the rule.

§14.1.3   Draft the Discussion of the Undisputed Factors

Most likely, not all of the factors will be in dispute. Sometimes the factor will favor one side but not the other side; at other times, the factor helps — or hurts — both sides equally.

For these undisputed factors, you have a choice. You can either raise and dismiss these factors at the end of the introductory section, or you can discuss them in separate, but very short, subsections. For example, if you are working on a child custody case and both parents want custody of their 3-year-old child, you could raise and dismiss the factor that relates to the parents' and child's preferences either at the end of the general rule section or in a separate subsection.

PRACTICE POINTER	Even if the factor is not in dispute, you need to discuss it, both initially and in the section where you weigh the various factors.

§ 14.1.4   Draft the Discussion of the Disputed Factors

Just as disputed elements require more analysis, so do disputed factors. In some instances, the dispute will be a purely factual dispute. For example, in a custody case, the mother might argue that she has the more flexible work schedule while the father argues that his schedule is the more flexible schedule. In this situation, you do not need to include descriptions of the analogous cases. Simply set out the facts and each side's arguments based on those facts using either a script or integrated format.

There will, of course, be times when you will need to do more than just set out the factual arguments. If the rules are ambiguous and there are analogous cases, set out the rules, provide the attorney with the examples of how those rules have been applied in analogous cases, and then set out each side's arguments and your mini-conclusion using either a script or an integrated format. For more on drafting the descriptions of analogous cases, and in particular, drafting the description of analogous cases using a principle-based analysis, see sections 12.8.4b and 13.8.2.

§ 14.1.5　Draft the Paragraph or Block of Paragraphs in Which You Weigh the Factors

Unlike an elements analysis in which your discussion section is done once you have discussed each of the elements, in a factor analysis you need to go one step further. You need to weigh the factors.

There are several ways to organize this part of the discussion section. If you use a script format, set out the rules first, the descriptions of any analogous cases second, the plaintiff's arguments third, the defendant's arguments fourth, and your mini-conclusion at the end. If you use a more integrated format, begin by setting out the rules, then set out the description of any analogous cases, and end by setting out your conclusion and reasoning.

EXAMPLE 3　　**Organizational Schemes for Section Weighing the Factors**

Script Format	Integrated Format
■ Set out the rules or tests that the courts use in weighing the factors. ■ If there are analogous cases that illustrate how the courts have weighed the factors in situations that are analogous to your situation, include descriptions of those analogous cases. ■ Set out each side's arguments: 　■ Party with burden of proof's arguments 　■ Responding party's arguments. ■ Evaluate each side's arguments and set out your conclusion.	■ Set out the rules or tests that the courts use in weighing the factors. ■ If there are analogous cases that illustrate how the courts have weighed the factors in situations that are analogous to your situation, include descriptions of those analogous cases. ■ Set out your conclusion. ■ Set out your reasoning, summarizing and evaluating each side's arguments.

Whichever organizational scheme you choose, take the time to think critically and carefully about each side's arguments and about how a court might view those arguments. If there is a statute, begin by reviewing the statute. Has the legislature stated that one factor or one set of factors should be given the most weight? Similarly, if the issue is governed by a common law or court rule, review the cases. Do the courts give one factor or set of factors more weight? In creating and applying the rules, what policies have the courts emphasized or tried to promote?

Do not, however, stop there. Push yourself to construct each side's story. For example, in a custody case, how will the mother use the factors to tell her story and persuade the court that it would be in the best interests of the children to grant her custody? How will the father use the factors to construct his story? Then ask yourself which story a court is likely to find most compelling.

EXAMPLE 4	**Block of Paragraphs in Which the Writer Weighs the Factors**

In this case, even though three of the four factors favor Ms. Morris, the court will probably find in favor of Ms. Springer. The three factors that favor Ms. Morris are position of authority, susceptibility, and the public nature of the comment. As Ms. Morris's basketball coach, Ms. Springer was in a position of authority over Ms. Morris, and given that Ms. Morris cried during her meeting with Ms. Springer, Ms. Springer knew that Ms. Morris was susceptible to statements about her weight. In addition, Ms. Springer made the comments about Ms. Morris's weight publicly on the basketball court in front of players, parents, and scouts.

The factor that favors Ms. Springer is that the case involves a single statement. Given that there are no cases in which the courts have held that a single statement by a defendant constituted extreme and outrageous conduct, the court is likely to find that Ms. Springer's comment, although inappropriate behavior for a coach, does not rise to the level of extreme and outrageous conduct. Other factors that are likely to contribute to the decision that the conduct was not extreme and outrageous are that the statement was made at the end of an emotionally charged basketball game between two elite teams, no racial slurs were involved, and Ms. Morris was almost 18 and not a young child.

§ 14.2   Balancing of Competing Interests

Another common type of analysis is an analysis that requires the balancing of competing interests. For example, in a criminal case, the trial court will balance the probative value of admitting particular evidence against the prejudicial value of allowing the jury to view that evidence, and in a nuisance case, the court will balance one individual's right to use his or her land against the rights of adjoining landowners.

§ 14.2.1   Templates for Issues Requiring the Balancing of Competing Interests

As with an elements analysis and factor analysis, there is more than one way to organize the discussion of an issue that requires the balancing of competing interests. However, regardless of which organizational scheme you choose to use, you need to do two things: identify the competing interests, and do the balancing.

Example 1 sets out two templates: The template in the left-hand column shows how to organize the discussion section using a script format while the template in the right-hand column shows how to organize the discussion section using a more integrated format. As you look at these templates, note that there is no one "right place" for the descriptions of analogous cases. While sometimes it will make more sense to put the descriptions of the analogous cases in a separate section, at other times it will make more sense to integrate them into the parties' arguments or into your reasoning.

In making the decision about where to put the cases, think about how you are going to use the cases. If you are going to use a case or set of cases extensively, showing how both sides would use the cases or how the court would treat the cases, it will probably make more sense, and be more efficient, to put the descriptions of those cases in a separate analogous case section. If, however, you are using the case to illustrate only a small point, it will probably make more sense to integrate your description of the case into your discussion of that point. For more on drafting the descriptions of analogous cases, and in particular, drafting the description of analogous cases using a principle-based analysis, see sections 12.8.4b and 13.8.2.

EXAMPLE 1	Templates for an Issue Requiring the Balancing of Competing Interests

Script Format	Integrated Format
Discussion	**Discussion**
Introductory Section	**Introductory Section**
■ If one or both sides will make a policy argument, describe the policies underlying the general rule (constitutional provision, statute, common law rule, or court rule). ■ Introduce and set out the general rule, identifying the competing interests and explaining the burden of proof. ■ Set out any other general rules or exceptions.	■ If one or both sides will make a policy argument, describe the policies underlying the general rule (constitutional provision, statute, common law rule, or court rule). ■ Introduce and set out the general rule, identifying the competing interests and explaining the burden of proof. ■ Set out any other general rules or exceptions.
[If appropriate, descriptions of analogous cases]	**[If appropriate, descriptions of analogous cases]**
Plaintiff's or Moving Party's Arguments	**Conclusion**
■ Set out the plaintiff's or moving party's assertion. ■ Summarize the plaintiff's arguments, including any plain language, analogous case, and policy arguments.	■ Set out your conclusion. (In this case, which interest outweighs the other interest?)
Defendant's or Responding Party's Arguments	**Reasoning**
■ Set out the defendant's or responding party's assertion. ■ Summarize the defendant's or responding party's arguments, including any plain language, analogous case, and policy arguments. ■ Set out your mini-conclusion (in this case, which interest outweighs the other interest?) and explain your reasoning.	■ Set out your first reason, incorporating and evaluating each side's arguments. (Often this will be a discussion of the first interest.) ■ Set out your second reason, incorporating and evaluating each side's arguments. (Often, this will be a discussion of the second interest.) ■ Set out your third reason, incorporating and evaluating each side's arguments. (Often, this will be where you balance the competing interests.)
Conclusion	**Conclusion**
[Put your formal conclusion here. In this conclusion, explain why one party's interests outweigh the other party's interests.]	**[Put your formal conclusion here.]**

§ 14.2.2   Draft the Introductory or General Rule Section

In a memo involving the balancing of competing interests, the introductory section serves the same function that the introductory section serves in memos involving other types of analysis. It introduces and sets out the applicable law, and it provides the reader with a roadmap for the rest of the discussion.

However, for issues involving the balancing of competing interests, the introductory section serves an additional function. While there are always exceptions, in most instances, you will want to use the introductory section to explain the competing interests and describe the policies that underlie them. How much you say will, of course, depend on the issue and what your supervising attorney knows about that issue. At one end of the continuum are those instances in which your supervising attorney knows the area of law and the application of the law to your client's facts is relatively easy. In these situations, your description of the competing interests and the underlying policies can be very short. At the other end of the continuum are cases in which your supervising attorney is not familiar with the area of law, the rules are evolving, the application of the law to the facts of your case is nuanced, and/or a lot is at stake. While you never want to turn a memo into a law review article, in these situations, your descriptions of the interests and the underlying policies needs to be more thorough.

> **PRACTICE POINTER**   Remember to include a citation to authority for each rule that you set out. In addition, when possible, cite to mandatory authority.

§ 14.2.3   Draft the Discussion of the Competing Interests

In most instances, your discussion of the competing interests will have three components: an analysis of each interest; an analysis of how a court, or other decision maker, is likely to balance those competing interests; and a conclusion. How you organize those components depends on whether you use a script format or a more integrated format.

If you use the script format, begin by setting out one side's arguments in a paragraph or, more likely, a block of paragraphs. For more on paragraph blocks, see section 22.6. In setting out your client's arguments, begin by setting out your assertion, which will usually consist of a statement that your client's interests outweigh the other side's interests. Then set out your support for your assertion, showing your supervising attorney how you can use the facts, analogous cases, and underlying policies to support that assertion. While sometimes you will want to organize these arguments by type of argument—for example, putting your plain language arguments first, your analogous case arguments second, and your policy arguments last—it is usually better to organize the arguments around lines of argument, showing your supervising attorney how you can weave together the facts, analogous cases, and policies to make a particular point. After you have set out your client's arguments, then set out the other side's arguments using the same format: Set out the other side's assertion and the arguments that it can make to support that assertion. Finish by setting out your prediction and your reasoning. How do you think the court will balance the competing interests? What reasons do you think that the court will give for finding that one party's interests are stronger than the other party's interests?

> **PRACTICE POINTER** Sometimes there are more than two competing interests. For instance, in a land use case, the court, or another decision maker, may not only have to balance the interests of two parties but also the interests of the public at large. In such situations, discuss and balance all of the competing interests.

If you use a more integrated format, begin by setting out your conclusion. How do you think that the court will balance the competing interests? Then, in a paragraph or block of paragraphs, walk your supervising attorney through your reasoning. If you have several reasons, you will usually want to start your discussion of each reason by setting out a subassertion that builds on a rule, the cases interpreting that rule, or one of the underlying policies. You will then want to set out your reasoning in much the same way that a court might discuss its reasoning in a judicial decision. Just make sure that you do not omit or give short shrift to the losing side's arguments. To do her job well, your supervising attorney needs thorough analysis of each side's potential arguments.

> **PRACTICE POINTER** In moving from a script to an integrated format, you should not lose any arguments. For more on strategies that you can use in constructing sentences that keep each side's arguments and give each side's arguments appropriate weight, see section 13.8.2.

Depending on the format that you use, your supervising attorney's preferences, and whether your memo discusses just one issue or several issues, you may or may not need a formal conclusion. If you are analyzing a single issue using a script format, you may be able to use your mini-conclusion, that is, the paragraph or block of paragraphs in which you predict how the court will balance the interests and how it will explain its decision, as your formal conclusion. On the other hand, if your memo has more than one issue statement and, thus, more than one part to the discussion section, include a formal conclusion.

§ 14.3   Issue of First Impression

Some of the most interesting, and most challenging, issues that you will work on are issues of first impression, that is, issues that have not been decided by the courts in your jurisdictions.

Issues of first impression have two things in common: They require you to predict what rule the court is likely to apply, and they require you to apply that rule, and in some instances, alternative rules, to the facts of your case.

Unfortunately, though, that is about all that issues of first impression have in common. You will, therefore, need to use the following templates as starting, and not ending, points for determining what types of information you need to include in your discussion section and the best way of organizing that information.

§ 14.3.1 Circuit Split

One of the most common scenarios is one in which there is a "circuit split." In the federal system, a circuit split occurs when one or more of the federal circuits adopt one rule or approach while one or more of the other circuits adopt a different rule or approach. In the state systems, a "split" occurs when one or more of the divisions of a state's intermediate court of appeals adopt one rule or approach and one or more of the other divisions adopt a different rule or approach. Until the United States Supreme Court or the state's highest court resolves the split, other circuits or divisions are free to adopt whichever rule or approach that they choose.

In discussing an issue in which there is a circuit split, you need to do the following:

- You need to tell your supervising attorney that your jurisdiction has not decided the issue and that there is a circuit split, with other circuits taking two or more different approaches.
- You need to describe the different approaches, telling your supervising attorney which circuits have taken which approach and the reasons that the courts have given for selecting one approach over other approaches. If different courts have adopted the same approach for different reasons, make that point clear.
- You need to evaluate the different approaches, predict which approach your jurisdiction is likely to take, and explain your reasoning.
- You need to apply the rules to the facts of your case. If you are confident that your jurisdiction will adopt a particular rule, just apply that rule to the facts of your case. If, however, it is not clear which rule your jurisdiction will adopt, you should do an alternative analysis, applying the various rules to the facts of your case.

Example 1 shows two templates for organizing this information.

EXAMPLE 1	Templates for Organizing a Discussion of First Impression Involving a Circuit Split Using the Script and a More Integrated Format

Script Format	Integrated Format
Introductory Section ■ Introduce the issue and explain (1) that in your jurisdiction the issue is an issue of first impression and (2) that in other jurisdictions the courts have adopted different rules or taken different approaches. **Majority Rule** ■ If the majority of jurisdictions have adopted a particular rule or approach, begin by introducing that rule or approach, telling your supervising attorney which jurisdictions have adopted that rule or approach, and summarizing the courts' reasons for adopting that rule or approach. **Minority Rule** ■ Set out the minority rule, telling your readers which jurisdiction or jurisdictions have adopted that rule or approach and explaining the court's or courts' reasons for adopting that rule or approach. **Arguments** ■ Set out the plaintiff's or moving party's assertion about which rule or approach the court should adopt and the arguments that the plaintiff or moving party is likely to make. ■ Set out the defendant's or responding party's assertion about which rule or approach the court should adopt and the arguments that the defendant or responding party is likely to make. **Conclusion and Reasoning** ■ Tell your supervising attorney which rule you think the court is likely to adopt and why you think that the court will adopt that rule. **Application of Rule or Approach to Facts** ■ Apply the rule or approach that you predict the court will adopt to the facts of your case. If the application of the rule or approach will be in dispute, set out the	**Introductory Section** ■ Introduce the issue and explain (1) that in your jurisdiction the issue is an issue of first impression and (2) that in other jurisdictions the courts have adopted different rules or taken different approaches. **Majority Rule** ■ If the majority of jurisdictions have adopted a particular rule or approach, begin by introducing that rule or approach, telling your supervising attorney which jurisdictions have adopted that rule or approach, and summarizing the courts' reasons for adopting that rule or approach. **Minority Rule** ■ Set out the minority rule, telling your readers which jurisdiction or jurisdictions have adopted that rule or approach and explaining the court's or courts' reasons for adopting that rule or approach. **Conclusion and Reasoning** ■ Tell your supervising attorney which rule or approach you think the court is likely to adopt. ■ Set out your reasoning, incorporating into your reasoning a discussion and evaluation of each side's arguments. **Application of Rule or Approach to Facts** ■ Apply the rule or approach that you predict the court will adopt to the facts of your case. If the application of the rule will be in dispute, set out the plaintiff's or moving party's assertion and arguments, the defendant's or responding party's assertion and arguments, and your mini-conclusion using either a script or integrated format. Note: If that rule or approach requires an elements analysis, a factor analysis, or the balancing of competing interests, do that analysis using the templates set out in Chapters 12 and 13 and sections 14.1 and 14.2.

Script Format	Integrated Format
plaintiff or moving party's assertion and arguments, the defendant's or responding party's assertion and arguments, and your mini-conclusion. Note: If that rule or approach requires an elements analysis, a factor analysis, or the balancing of competing interests, do that analysis using the templates set out in Chapters 12 and 13 and sections 14.1 and 14.2. ■ If you think that there is a possibility that the court will adopt a different rule or approach, do an alternative analysis. If the application of the other rule or approach will be in dispute, set out the plaintiff's or moving party's assertion and arguments, the defendant's or responding party's arguments, and your mini-conclusion. Note: If that rule or approach requires an elements analysis, a factor analysis, or the balancing of competing interests, do that analysis using the templates set out in Chapters 12 and 13 and sections 14.1 and 14.2.	■ If you think that there is a possibility that the court will adopt a different rule or approach, apply that different rule or approach to the facts of your case. If the application of the rule will be in dispute, set out the plaintiff or moving party's assertion and arguments, the defendant's or responding party's assertion and arguments, and your mini-conclusion using a script or an integrated format. Note: If that rule or approach requires an elements analysis, a factor analysis, or the balancing of competing interests, do that analysis using the templates set out in Chapters 12 and 13 and sections 14.1 and 14.2.

§ 14.3.2   The Statute Is Ambiguous, and There Are No Regulations or Cases That Have Interpreted That Statute

Another common scenario is one in which the statute is ambiguous and there are no regulations or cases that have resolved that ambiguity.

In this situation, you will usually want to start your discussion section by introducing and quoting the relevant statutory language, identifying the ambiguity, and telling your supervising attorney that there are no regulations or cases that have resolved the ambiguity. What else you include, and how you order that other information, will depend on what you found in doing your research and what arguments you think the parties are likely to make.

§ 14.3.3   Arguments Based on Agency Decisions

If, in doing your research, you located administrative memos or decisions that interpret the statute, you will need to do a *Chevron* analysis[1] to determine

---

1. In *Chevron U.S.A., Inc. v. Natural Resources Defense Council, Inc.*, 67 U.S. 837 (1984), the United States Supreme Court set out a two-part test to determine whether courts should defer to an administrative agency's interpretation of a statute. Under the first part of this test, the courts look to see whether the statute is ambiguous or whether there is a "gap" in the statute that Congress intended the agency to fill. If the statute is ambiguous, the courts then look to see whether the agency's interpretation of the statute is reasonable. If the agency's decision is reasonable, the courts will defer to the agency; if the agency's decision is not reasonable, the courts will substitute their judgment for the agency's. In more recent cases, some courts have added a "Step Zero," in which they look to see if an agency's interpretation has the force of law, for example, whether the agency followed the notice and comment provisions of § 553 of the Administrative Procedure Act. See Cass R. Sunstein, *Chevron Step Zero*, 92 Va. L. Rev. 187 (2006). While the courts do not have to defer to

whether the courts will defer to the agency's interpretation. Because the courts sometimes do the Step Zero analysis first and sometimes they do it last, Example 2 shows two ways of organizing a *Chevron* analysis.

| EXAMPLE 2 | Templates for Doing a *Chevron* Analysis |

Option 1	Option 2
A. *Chevron* Analysis	**A. *Chevron* Analysis**
■ Explain *Chevron*, including a brief description of the two-part test. ■ Do a *Chevron* Step Zero analysis, using a script or integrated format to discuss whether the agency's decision has the force of law. ■ Do a *Chevron* Step One analysis, discussing whether the statutory language is, in fact, ambiguous. (If this step of the analysis is not in dispute, you can simply raise and dismiss this issue.) ■ Do a *Chevron* Step Two analysis, using a script or integrated format to discuss whether the agency's interpretation of the statute is reasonable.	■ Explain *Chevron*, including a brief description of the two-part test. ■ Do a *Chevron* Step One analysis, discussing whether the statutory language is, in fact, ambiguous. (If this step of the analysis is not in dispute, you can simply raise and dismiss this issue.) ■ Do a *Chevron* Step Two analysis, using a script or integrated format to discuss whether the agency's interpretation of the statute is reasonable. ■ If, given your facts, there is an issue about whether the agency's decision has the force of law, do a *Chevron* Step Zero analysis.

§ 14.3.4   Policy Arguments

If there are no agency decisions interpreting a statute, or if you believe that the courts will find that an agency's decision is unreasonable or does not have the force of law, think policy. In doing your research, did you locate a "findings" or "purpose" section in which Congress or the state legislature explained why it enacted the statute and/or what its purpose or goal was in enacting that statute? (These sections are often set out in a separate section or sections at the beginning of the act or of the chapter in which your statute has been placed.) If there isn't a findings or purpose section, is there anything in the legislative history that the parties might use to support their assertions about how the statute should be interpreted? Last, but certainly not least, take a step back. Given the facts of your case, and the larger social, political, and economic context in which that case is being decided, what will each side argue is the "right" or "just" way to interpret the statute?

If there is a finding and/or purposes section, make those arguments first. Then move to any arguments based on the legislative history and, if you think the parties will use them, any broader policy arguments. See Example 3.

---

agency interpretations that do not have the force of law, the courts often give these interpretations substantial weight.

<table>
<tr><td>PRACTICE POINTER</td><td>If you did a legislative history but did not find any relevant information, include that fact in your discussion section.</td></tr>
</table>

EXAMPLE 3   **Templates for Organizing Policy and Legislative History Arguments Using the Script and a More Integrated Format**

Script Format	Integrated Format
B. Policy Arguments If you are going to include more than one type of policy argument, include a roadmap that alerts your supervising attorney to that fact. 1. Arguments based on a findings and/or purpose section ■ Introduce and quote the relevant portions of any findings or purpose sections. ■ Set out the plaintiff's or moving party's assertion and support for those assertions. ■ Set out the defendant's or responding party's assertion and support for those assertions. ■ Set out your mini-conclusion. 2. Arguments based on legislative history ■ Describe and, if appropriate, quote, relevant portions of legislative history. ■ Set out the plaintiff's or moving party's assertions and support for those assertions. ■ Set out the defendant's or responding party's assertion and support for those assertions. ■ Set out your mini-conclusion. 3. Broader policy arguments ■ Set out the plaintiff's or moving party's assertions and support for those assertions. ■ Set out the defendant's or responding party's assertion and support for those assertions. ■ Set out your mini-conclusion.	**B. Policy Arguments** If you are going to include more than one type of policy argument, include a roadmap that alerts your supervising attorney to that fact. 1. Arguments based on a findings and/or purpose section ■ Introduce and quote the relevant portions of any findings or purpose sections. ■ Set out your prediction. ■ Set out your first reason, summarizing and evaluating the arguments that each side is likely to make. ■ If you have additional reasons, set out those additional reasons, summarizing and evaluating the arguments that each side is likely to make. 2. Arguments based on legislative history ■ Describe and, if appropriate, quote, relevant portions of legislative history. ■ Set out your conclusion ■ Set out your first reason, summarizing and evaluating the arguments that each side is likely to make. ■ If you have additional reasons, set out those additional reasons, summarizing and evaluating the arguments that each side is likely to make. 3. Broader policy arguments ■ Set out your conclusion. ■ Set out your first reason, summarizing and evaluating the arguments that each side is likely to make. ■ If you have additional reasons, set out those additional reasons, summarizing and evaluating the arguments that each side is likely to make.

Drafting E-Memos, Email, and Text Messages

On the one hand, the practice of law seems timeless. No matter what the era, clients ask their lawyers questions, and lawyers—often with the help of an intern or a newer associate—answer those questions. On the other hand, the practice of law is constantly changing. Instead of going to the library to do their research, most attorneys turn to their computers, using free and fee-based websites to find the information that they need. In addition, shorter, less formal memos are becoming more common, and instead of letters, sometimes attorneys send emails or, occasionally, text messages.

In this chapter, we focus on these last three changes in practice, providing you examples of e-memos and reminders about email and text messages.

§ 15.1   E-Memos

While some attorneys still want the types of formal memos described in Chapters 11 through 14, other attorneys want what we call an e-memo: a shorter, less formal memo that is often, but not always, sent by email. This section explains the audience, purpose, and conventional formats for such memos and, at the end, sets out three samples.

§ 15.1.1   Audience

Like more formal memos, the primary audience for an e-memo is another attorney in the same firm or office: A more senior attorney asks an intern or a newer attorney to research and analyze an issue. In addition, like more formal memos, e-memos may be sent to the client. As a consequence, make sure that your writing is clear, concise, and correct and that you follow the conventions of formal writing. For example, as a general rule, do not use contractions, colloquialisms, or abbreviations. Be professional.

§ 15.1.2   Purpose

As with more formal memos, your primary purpose in writing an e-memo is to provide other attorneys in your office with the information that they need to evaluate a case, advise a client, or draft another document, for instance, a complaint, an answer, a motion, a brief, or a contract. To meet this purpose, the e-memo must be objective: You must set out the law objectively, you must give appropriate weight to each side's arguments, and your advice must be candid.

§ 15.1.3   Conventional Formats for E-Memos

Just as the format of more formal memos varies from law firm to law firm and attorney to attorney, so does the format of e-memos.

At one end of the continuum are e-memos in which the attorney asks a question for which there is an easy answer, for example, the attorney asks what the statute of limitations is in Illinois for actions to recover damages to personal property. In such instances, simply set out the question and the applicable law.

EXAMPLE 1   **Short E-Memo**

You asked me to research Illinois law and determine what the statute of limitations is on actions to recover damages to personal property. The applicable statute is 735 ILCS 5/13-205, which states that the statute of limitations is five years:

> [A]ctions on unwritten contracts, expressed or implied, or on awards of arbitration, or *to recover damages for an injury done to property, real or personal,* or to recover the possession of personal property or damages for the detention or conversion thereof, and all civil actions not otherwise provided for, *shall be commenced within 5 years next after the cause of action accrued.*

(Emphasis added.)
If you need additional research, please let me know.

At the other end of the continuum are the more formal memos that we described in Chapters 11 through 14: The only difference is that instead of handing your supervising attorney a paper copy of the memo, you email a copy of the memo, usually as an attachment. For examples of more formal memos, see section 11.4.

Many e-memos fall somewhere in between the short memo set out above and the more formal memo described in Chapters 11 through 14. In most instances, these memos deal with a relatively narrow issue. For example, instead of discussing all of the elements of a cause of action, they discuss only one element. While these e-memos will be shorter than more formal memos, the analysis still needs to be sophisticated.

Although the format and content of e-memos vary depending on the office and the issue, most e-memos have the following information.

    a. Introductory sentence or paragraph
    b. Summary of the applicable law
    c. Application of the law to the key facts

a.   Introductory Sentence or Paragraph

Unlike a more formal memo, shorter e-memos do not have a formal statement of facts, a formal statement of the issue, or a separate section setting out a brief answer. Instead, the writer begins the e-memo with a sentence, paragraph, or block of paragraphs that identifies the client, the writer's task, the issue, and the key fact or facts. In addition, in most instances, the writer sets out his or her conclusion, the issue, and, sometimes, the key fact or facts. Compare the following examples.

EXAMPLE 2   **Introductory Sentence in Which the Writer Identifies the Client and the Issue**

You have asked me to research whether our client, Pacific Oil Company, LLC (Pacific), properly terminated a franchise under the Petroleum Marketing Practices Act (PMPA) after the franchisee frequently ran out of various grades of motor fuel.

EXAMPLE 3   **Introductory Paragraph in Which the Writer Identifies the Client, the Issue, and the Key Facts and Sets Out His Conclusion**

You have asked me to determine whether our client, Ms. Dunn, can state a valid claim under the Consumer Protection Act (CPA) when she contracted Salmonella from a burrito she purchased from a food truck. Specifically, you have asked whether we can use the amount that Ms. Dunn paid for the burrito or the amount that she spent for medical care to establish an injury to business or property. Given the current case law, the answer to both questions is no.

Note that in many e-memos, the "statement of facts" is much shorter: The number and type of facts depends on the question asked and who will be reading the memo. If the question is a legal question and the intended audience for the memo is the partner who has spent the last year working on the case, just set out the facts that are relevant to the issue that you were asked to research. Do not include background facts. If, however, the question is a factual question and you know that the e-memo will go to several attorneys, some of whom are not familiar with the case, set out the relevant facts and put those facts in context.

To see how writers set out the relevant facts, compare the three e-memos set out in section 15.1.7 below. In Example 8, the writer includes only a few facts, and she integrates those facts into her statement of the issue. Similarly, in Example 9, the writer includes only a few facts. However, unlike Example 8 in which the facts were at the beginning of the e-memo, in Example 9 the facts are near the end of the memo in the paragraph in which the writer applies the law to the facts. The e-memo in Example 10 is very different. Because the issue required an analysis of the specific facts of the case, the writer goes into detail in setting out the facts.

b.   Summary of the Applicable Law

In most e-memos, the next "section" is the summary of the applicable law: Depending on the issue, this section may be a single sentence or several paragraphs.

The key to writing this section is to give your readers just the information that they need, no more and no less. To do this, you need to have a sophisticated understanding of the applicable law and the issue that you were asked to research. For example, you need to understand the steps in the analysis, you need to be able to determine which rules apply at each step and which of those rules your readers need to know, and you need to make good decisions about when to include descriptions of analogous cases and what to include in those descriptions.

1. Steps in the Analysis

If there are several steps in the analysis, walk your reader through those steps in order. For example, if there is a two-part test, tell your reader that the courts use a two-part test and then discuss the two parts in order. Similarly, if there are different legal theories, identify those theories and then discuss each in turn. See, for example, the e-memo in Example 10, which is set out at the end of this section.

2. The Rules

As in a more formal memo, you need to set out the applicable rules, and you need to include a citation to authority for each of those rules. The primary difference is in focus: In an e-memo, the focus is usually narrower and sharper. As a practical matter, this means that you will be more selective in quoting statutes and regulations and in discussing the rules set out in cases. While you do not want to mislead your readers by leaving out relevant rules, do not give your readers more than they need.

In setting out the rules, remember the principles discussed in sections 12.8.2 and 12.8.4. First, set out more general rules before more specific rules and exceptions. Second, keep the focus on the rules by putting the citations to authority for those rules in a separate citation sentence following your statement of the rule and not in the sentence setting out the rule. Finally, set out the rules clearly and concisely and avoid overquoting.

3. The Analogous Cases

Do not include case descriptions just to include case descriptions. Instead, think about what your readers need. Do your readers need case descriptions to understand how the courts are applying a particular rule or to understand a line of argument? If they do, include the case descriptions. If, however, your readers can understand the rule and arguments without case descriptions, move directly from your discussion of the rules to your application of those rules to the facts of your client's case.

While the case descriptions in e-memos are similar to the case descriptions in more formal memos, they are usually shorter, and parentheticals are more common. In some instances, it may be enough to set out a rule and then, following the citation to the case or cases, parentheticals setting out the key facts.

EXAMPLE 4   **Rule Followed by Citations to Authority with Parentheticals Setting Out Key Facts**

Although the statute does not specify the period of time an individual must occupy a home to be regarded as "residing therein," the courts do not require extended habitation. *Compare Magazine v. Bedoya*, 475 So. 2d 1035 (Fla. Dist. Ct. App. 1985) (six-week stay sufficient to establish residency), with *Gamboa v. Jones*, 455 So. 2d 613 (Fla. Dist. Ct. App. 1985) (ten-day visit not sufficient to establish residency).

EXAMPLE 5   **Rule Followed by Citations to Authority with Parentheticals Setting Out Key Facts**

In other cases in which the employee had a connection to more than one worksite, the courts have held that the location of the employee's worksite was a question of fact. *See, e.g., Podkovich v. Glazer's Distrib. of Iowa, Inc.*, 446 F. Supp. 2d 982, 1000-02 (N.D. Iowa 2006) (concluding that there was an issue of fact when a traveling saleswoman physically reported to one worksite but received her assignments from another site); *Collinsworth v. Earthlink/Onemain, Inc.*, CIV.A. 03-2299GTV, 2003 WL 22916461, at *4 (D. Kan. Dec. 4, 2003) (concluding that there was an issue of fact when the plaintiff worked from home, sometimes used a branch office with fewer than 50 people within 75 miles, yet received and delivered her work product to the main office with more than 50 people within 75 miles.)

PRACTICE POINTER   The rules about citing unpublished decisions are different for memos than they are for other legal documents, such as appellate briefs. While some attorneys will instruct you not to cite to an unpublished decision in an in-house memo, other attorneys will instruct you to cite to an unpublished decision if the decision is directly on point and no other equally applicable published decision is available. In addition, some attorneys will want you to include a citation to an unpublished decision when the judge who wrote the decision is the judge who has been assigned to hear the client's case. The bottom line is that you should ask your supervising attorney whether he or she wants you to include citations to unpublished decisions.

If you need to provide your readers with more information about a case or a group of cases, go through the same steps that you went through to draft the analogous case section for a more formal memo: (1) identify the analogous cases, (2) sort the analogous cases, (3) analyze and synthesize the analogous cases, (4) draft the sentence introducing the analogous cases, and (5) draft your case descriptions. See section 12.8.4. While making sure that you do not misrepresent the facts of the case or the court's holding or reasoning, keep your case descriptions as focused and as short as possible.

EXAMPLE 6   **Sentence Introducing Analogous Cases and Short, Focused Case Descriptions**

In recent cases, the courts have either held that the service was invalid or remanded the case for an evidentiary hearing when the defendant produced evidence establishing that he was not living at the house where the summons was served. *See, e.g., Busman v. State, Dep't of Revenue*, 905 So. 2d 956, 958 (Fla. 3d DCA 2005); *Thompson v. State, Dep't of Revenue*, 867 So. 2d 603, 605 (Fla. 1st DCA 2004). For example, in *Busman*, the Third District Court of Appeals held that the service was not valid when the defendant presented a lease agreement that corroborated his testimony that he had moved out of his half brother's house two and one-half months before his half brother was served. 905 So. 2d at 958. Likewise, in *Thompson*, the First District Court of Appeals reversed and remanded the case for an evidentiary hearing when the defendant submitted an affidavit in which he stated that he was separated from his wife, that he had not resided at that address for more than three years, and that he did not authorize anyone to accept service of process on his behalf. 867 So. 2d at 605.

For more examples of how to discuss analogous cases, see Examples 8 through 10 set out at the end of this section.

c.   Application of the Law to the Key Facts

In an e-memo, you can either "apply the law as you go" or you can set out your summary of the applicable law and then, in a separate paragraph or block of paragraphs, apply that law to the key facts. While there are always exceptions, as a general rule, apply the law as you go when the analysis uses a number of steps and each step builds on the prior one. If, however, the analysis uses only one step or if your readers need to see the "big picture" before you begin your discussion of the individual pieces, summarize and then apply the law. In other situations, use your judgment about what will work best for your particular reader or readers.

You also have a choice about where to put your conclusion. As noted above, sometimes you can put your conclusion at the end of your introductory paragraph. Set out the question that you were asked to research and then answer that question. At other times, you will want to save the conclusion for your application section. When you put your conclusion in your application section, you can use either deductive or inductive reasoning: If you use deductive reasoning, set out your conclusion and then your reasoning; if you use inductive reasoning, set out your reasoning and then your conclusion. Neither approach is inherently better: Some attorneys prefer one approach, and others prefer the other approach. Thus, write for your particular audience.

Regardless of which approach you use, your analysis must be objective, focused, and sophisticated. Because e-memos are objective memos, make sure that your analysis is not one-sided. Your readers need to know both what they can argue on behalf of your client and what the other side is likely to argue. Do not, though, lose your focus. Save the discussion of related issues, arguments, or strategies for the very end of your e-memo or for another conversation or memo. Finally, remember that even if your discussion of an issue is short, your analysis needs to be sophisticated. While it is hard to define "sophisticated," e-memos with sophisticated analysis have the following characteristics:

- The analysis indicates that the writer understands the legal system and the area of law.
- The writer identifies the determinative issue or the key question and gets to that issue or question quickly.
- The writer is specific in applying language from the applicable statute to the facts of the client's case.
- The writer sees not only the obvious arguments but also the less obvious ones and uses good judgment in choosing which arguments to present.
- The writer uses the rules and cases that he or she set out earlier in the memo, using terms consistently and making connections.
- The conclusions that the writer sets out are candid and follow logically from the analysis.
- In setting out advice, the writer considers not only the law but also the client's practical needs and the larger context.

§ 15.1.4 Writing Style

While e-memos are less formal than the memos discussed in Chapters 11 through 14, they still need to be professional in appearance and in register, that is, in the level of formality. Therefore, pause before hitting "send" and view what you have written through the eyes of your supervising attorney and, if the e-memo may go to the client, through that client's eyes. Does the memo look like and read like it was prepared by a knowledgeable and careful individual who communicates clearly and concisely? If your memo meets this standard, send it; if it doesn't, make the necessary changes.

> **PRACTICE POINTER**
>
> The rules that apply to writing effective and correct formal memos also apply to writing e-memos. Consequently, make sure that your paragraph divisions are logical and that your paragraphs are neither too short nor too long; use roadmaps, signposts, and transitions to explain the connections between paragraphs and sentences; write most of your sentences using the active voice and concrete subjects and action verbs; be precise and concise; and proofread your e-memo to make sure it does not contain any grammar, punctuation, or citation errors.

§ 15.1.5 Client Confidentiality

In-house memos are part of an attorney's work product and are, therefore, protected if you take the necessary precautions: Include a statement in the email that the attached document represents your work product and is confidential; when possible use encryption; and check and double check the email addresses to which you are sending the e-memo. In addition, make sure that you know your local rules relating to the use of email.

EXAMPLE 7   **Statement That Email Contains Confidential Information**

This electronic message contains information from the law firm of Jones and Jones, LLP. The contents are privileged and confidential and are intended for the use of the intended addressee(s) only. If you are not an intended addressee, note that any disclosure, copying, distribution, or use of the contents of this message is prohibited. If you have received this email in error, please contact me at _____.

PRACTICE POINTER   Attorneys do, however, need to warn clients, that emails received on or sent from employer-owned devices may not be protected. See ABA Comm. on Ethics & Prof'l Responsibility, Formal Op. 11-459 (2011), *available at* http://www.americanbar.org/content/dam/aba/adminis trative/professional_responsibility/11_459_nm_formal_opinion.authcheck dam.pdf.

§ 15.1.6 Checklist for Critiquing E-Memos

I. Organization

- The information has been presented in a logical order: In most e-memos, an introductory paragraph is followed by a summary of the applicable law and the application of that law to the facts of the client's case.

II. Content

- The writer has made good decisions about what information to include in the e-memo.
  - The writer includes an introductory sentence or paragraph that identifies the client and the issue that the writer was asked to research.
  - The writer includes only the relevant facts.
  - The writer includes descriptions of analogous cases only when the cases will help the attorney understand how the courts have applied the rules or understand a line of argument.
  - The writer includes a section applying the law to fact.
- The statement of the research question is accurate and appropriately focused.
- The facts are set out accurately and objectively.

- The rules are supported by appropriate citations to authority.
- The descriptions of the analogous cases are accurate and objective.
- The analysis is objective and sophisticated.

III. Writing

- The attorney can understand the e-memo with just one reading.
- The paragraph divisions are logical, and the paragraphs are neither too long nor too short. (See Chapter 22.)
- Transitions and dovetailing are used to make the connection between ideas clear. (See Chapters 21 and 23.)
- In most sentences, the actor is the subject, and the subject and verb are close together. (See sections 24.1 through 24.4.)
- The writer varies the length of the sentences and the sentence patterns so that each sentence flows smoothly from the prior sentence. (See section 24.5.)
- The writing is concise and precise. (See sections 25.1 and 25.2.)
- The writing is grammatically correct and correctly punctuated. (See Chapters 27, 28, and 29.)
- The discussion section has been proofread. (See section 20.6.)

§ 15.1.7　Sample E-Memos

EXAMPLE 8	E-Memo to Attorney Familiar with the Underlying Law and the Facts of the Case

To:　　Supervising Attorney
From:　Intern
Date:　January 30, 2014
Re:　　Dunn CPA Claim: Can we use amount paid for medical care or for the burrito to prove an injury to business or property?

You have asked me to determine whether our client, Ms. Dunn, can state a valid claim under the Consumer Protection Act (CPA) when she contracted Salmonella from a burrito she purchased at a food truck. Specifically, you have asked whether we can use the amount that Ms. Dunn paid for medical care or the amount she paid for the burrito to establish the requirement under RCW 19.86.090 that the plaintiff prove an injury to business or property. Given the current case law, the answer to both questions is no.

The Washington courts have consistently stated that plaintiffs cannot use the amounts paid for medical care to establish an injury to business or property. *See, e.g., Stevens v. Hyde Athletic Indus.*, 54 Wn. App. 366, 370, 773 P.2d 871 (1989). For example, in *Stevens*, a case in which the plaintiff sued the store that sold her defective softball cleats, the court rejected Stevens's argument that her medical expenses constituted an injury to property, stating that actions for personal injury do not fall within the coverage of the CPA. *Id.*

In a more recent case in which the plaintiff sued the surgeon who had operated on her shoulder, the court restated the rule set out in *Stevens* and concluded that the plaintiff could not use the amount she paid for subsequent medical care to establish an injury to business or property. *Ambach v. French*, 167 Wn. 2d 167, 179, 216 P.3d 405 (2009). In addition, the court did not allow the plaintiff to use the amount that she had paid for the original surgery to establish an injury to business or property. *Id.* According to the court, "[w]here plaintiffs are both physically and economically injured by one act, courts generally refuse to find injury to 'business or property.'" *Id.* at 174.

Given the courts' decisions in *Stevens* and *Ambach*, we will not be able to establish an injury to business or property. In both *Stevens* and *Ambach*, the courts stated that the plaintiffs could not use medical bills to establish injuries to business or property. In addition, because the *Ambach* court did not allow the plaintiff to use the amount she paid for the original surgery to establish an injury to business or property, it is unlikely that we can persuade a court to use the amount Ms. Dunn paid for the burrito. Finally, like the claims in *Stevens* and *Ambach*, our claim is, at its core, a personal injury claim, and the courts have held that the CPA does not apply to such claims.

If you have any questions or would like me to do additional research, please let me know.

EXAMPLE 9	**E-Memo to an Experienced Attorney About an Issue of Law**

You have asked me to research the scope of 11 U.S.C. § 1301 to determine whether the co-debtor stay applies not only to consumer debt but also to commercial debt. Specifically, you have asked me to determine whether, once the other debtor has filed for a Chapter 13 bankruptcy, a creditor is stayed from enforcing a judgment against a co-debtor on a personal guaranty that arose out of a commercial debt. In short, section 1301 applies only to consumer debts; thus, a creditor should be able to enforce a judgment arising out of a commercial debt against a co-debtor even after the other debtor has filed his/her bankruptcy petition.

Under 11 U.S.C. § 1301, "after the order for relief under this chapter [has been filed], a creditor may not act, or commence or continue any civil action, to collect all or any part of a *consumer* debt of the debtor from an individual that is liable on such debt with the debtor, or that secured such debt, unless such individual became liable on or secured such debt in the ordinary course of such individual's business." 11 U.S.C. § 1301(a)(1) (emphasis added). "The automatic stay under [11 U.S.C. § 1301] pertains only to collection of a *consumer* debt." S. Rep. No. 95-989, at 138 (1978) (emphasis added). Consumer debt means "debt incurred by an individual *primarily* for a personal, family, or household purpose." 11 U.S.C. § 108 (emphasis added.) Thus, "not all debts owed by a Chapter 13 debtor will be subject to the stay of the codebtor, particularly those business debts incurred by an individual with regular income, as defined by section 101[(30)] of this title, engaged in business, that is permitted by virtue of section 109(b) and section 1304 to obtain chapter 13 relief." S. Rep. No. 95-989, at 138.

Accordingly, the automatic stay under 11 U.S.C. § 1301 is inapplicable to commercial debt. *See, e.g., In re Demaree*, 27 B.R. 1 (Bankr. D. Or. 1982) (holding that since it was admitted that the primary reason for the loan was for a business purpose and funds were, in fact, primarily used for a business purpose, loan was not a consumer debt and co-debtor stay was inapplicable); *In re Chrisman*, 27 B.R. 648 (Bankr. S.D. Ohio 1982) (holding that the automatic stay of section 1301 was inapplicable because the proceeds of the loan were used for training for a business opportunity and thus did not constitute consumer debt). Moreover, debts incurred with a profit motive generally are not consumer debts. 8 *Collier on Bankruptcy* 1301.03 (Mathew Bender 15th ed. rev.) (citing *In re Booth*, 858 F.2d 1051 (5th Cir. 1988)).

In this case, the debt was not incurred for personal, family, or household purposes; instead, the debt was incurred for commercial or business purposes. Furthermore, the co-debtor became liable on the debt in the ordinary course of the company's business: The personal guaranty was entered into to benefit the company. Thus, because the debt is not a consumer debt, the creditor may proceed with enforcing its judgment against the co-debtor without moving for relief from the stay.

Please let me know if you have any questions.

EXAMPLE 10	Example 10 Longer E-Memo

To: Supervising Attorney
From: Associate
Date: April 10, 2013
Re: Pacific Oil Co., LLC: Termination of Franchise Agreement

You have asked me to research whether our client, Pacific Oil Company, LLC (Pacific), properly terminated a franchise under the Petroleum Marketing Practices Act (PMPA) after the franchisee frequently ran out of various grades of motor fuel. A court is likely to conclude that Pacific properly terminated the franchise relationship with ABC under all three statutory grounds enumerated in the PMPA.

ABC, Inc. (ABC) operated Forest Service Station (Forest), a service station, from 1998 to November 23, 2012. ABC leased the premises from Pacific pursuant to a Retail Facility Lease (the Lease). ABC sold Pacific-branded motor fuel at the premises pursuant to a Retail Sales Agreement with Pacific (the Sales Agreement).

Under the Sales Agreement, ABC agreed that Pacific could terminate ABC's franchise if ABC failed to "comply with any provision of th[e] Agreement, which provision is both reasonable and of material significance to the relationship under this Agreement" **or** if ABC "failed to maintain a sufficient amount of all grades of Products for resale at Retailer's station, or Retailer's failure to operate Retailer's Station, for . . . such lesser period [than 7 consecutive days] which under the facts and circumstances constitutes an unreasonable period of time." Sales Agreement, ¶ 22.

Similarly, the Lease permitted Pacific to terminate ABC's franchise if ABC failed "to operate the Premises for 7 consecutive days, or such lesser period which under the facts and circumstances constitutes an unreasonable period of time," or because of "termination of the [Retail Sales Agreement]," **or** upon "[a]ny other ground for which termination is provided for in this Lease or is otherwise allowed by the PMPA or other applicable law." Lease, ¶ 18(a).

ABC began a pattern of running out of one or more grades of motor fuel. In response to ABC's habitual fuel outages, Pacific sent ABC three notices of violation. In these notices, Pacific outlined the outages at Forest and warned ABC that ongoing product outages or returned drafts would result in termination of the franchise agreements and the franchise relationship "pursuant to provisions of the supply agreement, lease (if applicable) and the [PMPA]." Ignoring these warnings, ABC continued to run out of various grades of motor fuel at its service station.

Pacific sent ABC a "Notice of Termination" pursuant to the Sales Agreement, the Lease, and the PMPA and stated that it would take possession of the retail premises. In the Notice of Termination, Pacific noted ten instances from April 25, 2012, through August 11, 2012, in which Forest had run out of various grades of motor fuel for time periods ranging from 11 hours to 96 hours in duration. ABC failed to take any action with respect to Pacific's Notice of Termination, except to file a Complaint on November 22, 2012.

A franchisor may terminate a franchise when the franchisor has a statutory basis for termination, and the franchisor's notice of termination comports with the requirements of the PMPA. *E.g., Zipper v. Sun Co.*, 947 F. Supp. 62, 67 (E.D.N.Y. 1996). In this case, Pacific has three bases for terminating ABC's franchise based upon fuel outages under the PMPA. These bases are not mutually exclusive. *See Lyons v. Mobil Oil Corp.*, 884 F.2d 1546, 1548 (2d Cir. 1989).

Pacific properly terminated ABC's franchise based upon 15 U.S.C. § 2802(b)(2)(A). This statutory provision permits Pacific to terminate a franchise if a franchisee fails "to comply with any provision of the franchise, [a provision] which . . . is both reasonable and of material significance to the franchise relationship." *See N.I. Petroleum Ventures Corp. v. Gles, Inc.*, 333 F. Supp. 2d 251, 256-57 (D. Del. 2004). Although the PMPA does not define what types of provisions of the franchise are of "material significance to the franchise relationship," a "failure" is not one that is "technical or unimportant to the franchise relationship," "beyond the reasonable control of the franchisee," or invalid under state law grounds. 15 U.S.C. § 2801(13).

The first issue is whether the franchise provision that required ABC to "maintain a sufficient amount of all grades of Products for resale" is reasonable. A court defers to the franchisor's "legitimate business judgment" when it reviews franchise provisions. *Gruber v. Mobil Oil Corp.*, 570 F. Supp. 1088, 1093 (E.D. Mich. 1983) (Mobil's legitimate business judgment entitled to considerable weight so long as decision made in good faith and in the normal course of business); *Crown Central Petroleum Corp. v. Waldman*, 515 F. Supp. 477, 483 (M.D. Pa. 1981), *aff'd,* 676 F.2d 684 (3d Cir. 1982) (court's role is not to discern the economic advisability of a particular term if there exists a reasonable basis for it). A provision is reasonable if it is "not absurd, ridiculous, extreme, or excessive[.]" *See, e.g., Texaco Ref. & Mktg. Inc. v. Davis*, 835 F. Supp. 1223, 1228 (D. Or. 1993) (citation omitted). However, in some jurisdictions, courts apply an objective standard. *See, e.g., Doebereiner v. Sohio Oil Co.*, 880 F.2d 329, 334 (11th Cir. 1989) (reasonableness determined from standpoint of neutral observer).

Under either the subjective or objective standard, the franchise provision that required ABC to "maintain a sufficient amount of all grades of Products for resale" likely is reasonable. Sales Agreement, ¶ 22. Not only does the provision satisfy legitimate business needs of Pacific, *i.e.,* to provide all grades of motor fuel at all times to the motoring public, which is the purpose of a gas station, but it is also neutrally rational to require a franchisee to carry all grades of motor fuel at all times. A court would be unlikely to characterize this term as "absurd, ridiculous, extreme, or excessive," especially in light of a recent opinion from a District Court in California, in which the court observed, " [i]t is difficult to imagine a contractual requirement more material to the franchise than requiring the franchise to actually sell . . . gasoline." *Harara v. ConocoPhillips Co.*, 377 F. Supp. 2d 779, 791 (N.D. Cal. 2005).

The second issue is whether the franchise provision that required ABC to "maintain a sufficient amount of all grades of Products for resale" is material. With respect to whether fuel outages are material, the *N.I. Petroleum Ventures* court stated that "[t]he frequency with which fuel run outs occurred is relevant to whether plaintiff's breach was material. A single run out, for example, may only be a technical breach and not a basis for nonrenewal." 333 F. Supp. 2d at 261 n.18. In this case, the number of fuel outages significantly exceeded a single run out because ABC ran out of a particular grade of motor fuel on at least 21 occasions preceding the notice. A court may find this fact persuasive and determine that Pacific properly terminated ABC's franchise under 15 U.S.C. § 2802(b)(2)(A).

Pacific also properly terminated ABC's franchise under section 2802(b)(2)(B). The PMPA also permits a franchisor to terminate a franchise when a franchisee fails "to exert good faith efforts to carry out the provisions of the franchise if . . . the franchisee was apprised by the franchisor in writing of such failure and was afforded a reasonable opportunity to exert good faith efforts to carry out such provisions." 15 U.S.C. § 2802(b)(2)(B).

The Sales Agreement required ABC "to maintain a sufficient amount of all grades of Products for resale[.]" Sales Agreement, ¶ 22. On at least 21 occasions in the 120 days preceding Pacific's Notice of Termination, ABC ran out of at least one grade of motor fuel. On two previous occasions prior to the termination, Pacific notified ABC in writing that ABC's conduct lacked "good faith efforts in complying with the terms of the supply agreement." Indeed, the February 2, 2005, "Final Notice of Violation" cited to "PMPA Section 2802(b)(2)(B) and provided that "termination would also be justified based upon Retailer's failure to exert good faith efforts to carry out the provisions of the franchise."

Pacific also properly terminated ABC under 15 U.S.C. § 2802(b)(2)(C) and (c)(9). Subsection (b)(2)(C) permits Pacific to terminate a franchise relationship should one of the enumerated, but not exclusive, events in section 2802(c) occur. One such event is the "failure of the franchisee to operate the marketing premises . . . for such lesser period [than 7 consecutive days] which under the facts and circumstances constitutes an unreasonable period of time." 15 U.S.C. § 2802(c)(9). Importantly, at least one court has found that only those run outs occurring in the 120 days preceding the notice may be evidence of failure to operate. *N.I. Petroleum Ventures Corp.*, 333 F. Supp. 2d at 261 (refusing to grant summary judgment where disputed issues as to whether plaintiff maintained adequate supplies of fuel).

In our case, ABC ran out of fuel on at least 21 occasions in the 120-day time period preceding the Notice of Termination. Therefore, the question is whether these run outs constituted an "unreasonable period of time" under section 2802(c)(9)(B). While the procedural posture of *N.I. Petroleum Ventures Corp.* limits its usefulness with respect to that question, three other cases may inform a court's analysis in this case.

In one of these cases, *Harara v. ConocoPhillips Co.*, the plaintiff ran out of 89 and 91 octane gasoline in January or February of 2004. 377 F. Supp. 2d at 784. The plaintiff argued that the defendant oil company constructively terminated his franchise by "making untimely and late deliveries of gasoline" and "canceling his credit privileges and putting him on 'Cash in Advance' status," among other reasons. *Id.* at 790 n.11. The defendant oil company "specified three reasons for termination: (1) plaintiff's failure to stock 76-branded motor fuel, (2) plaintiff's failure to pay $13,163.18 in rent and other charges, and (3) plaintiff's failure to take reasonable steps to control the operations of the station." *Id.* at 791. While it is unclear how many days prior to the notice of termination that the plaintiff ran out gasoline, the court remarked, "[i]t is difficult to imagine a contractual requirement more material to the franchise than requiring the franchise to actually sell 76-branded gasoline." *Id.; see also Rodgers v. Sun Ref. & Mktg. Co.*, 772 F.2d 1154, 1155 (3d Cir. 1985) (concluding that franchisor was entitled to terminate the franchise under section 2802(b)(2)(C) when the franchisee ran out of one or more grades of gasoline products at least 20 times over an approximately two-year period due to cash flow problems); *Crown Cent. Petroleum Corp.*, 515 F. Supp. at 486 (concluding that franchisor was entitled to terminate the franchise under the PMPA where franchisee failed to operate franchise for 10 out of 60 days after repeated warnings even though franchisee did not fail to operate franchise for 7 consecutive days).

The risk if we rely on *N.I Petroleum Ventures* is that some commentators suggest that the case stands for the proposition that fuel outages equate to a failure to operate and must be brought under section 2802(c)(9), rather than brought under section 2802(b)(2)(A). 333 F. Supp. 2d at 260-61; 2 *Franch. and Dist. Law & Prac.* § 15.7. However, our case is distinguishable because the Sales Agreement contains a provision directed at the failure to stock all grades of motor fuel, unlike the provision upon which the defendant oil company in *N.I. Petroleum Ventures* relied, which involved only operations. *Id.* (paragraph 14(j) of the agreement required franchisee to operate business for 24 hours a day, 7 days a week). Thus, the provision at issue in this case imposes a duty on the franchisee to both operate the service station and maintain sufficient amounts of all grades of motor fuel. A court may find this fact dispositive and distinguish our case from *N.I. Petroleum Ventures*.

There are few cases that directly address 15 U.S.C. § 2802(c)(9)(B) and delineate how many fuel outages constitute an unreasonable number so that a franchisor can terminate a franchise under that section. However, Pacific likely will prevail on at least one of the three enumerated grounds for termination set forth in its Notice of Termination to ABC.

Please let me know if you would like additional research on any of these points.

---

§ 15.2   Email[1]

Most attorneys have an email horror story. A client who is a manager sends another manager an email suggesting that the company could save money by forcing all of the employees who are over the age of 60 to retire. Another client unthinkingly hits "Reply All" and sends a message to more than a dozen people in which she essentially admits that she committed a crime. A new associate

---

1. The material about email first appeared in an article written by Anne Enquist and Laurel Oates, *You've Sent Mail*, 15 Perspectives 127 (Winter 2007).

attaches the wrong file to an email, accidentally sending opposing counsel a copy of an office memo that outlines the firm's trial strategy.

The horror stories confirm what most of us know: Email is both a blessing and a curse. It has made communication easier and faster, but like most new tools, email has a learning curve. Most people are still figuring out how to use it appropriately in professional settings, and in the meantime, many lawyers are discovering that careless or ineffective use can cause serious problems.

Many of the serious and not so serious email problems can be avoided by using a little common sense. Below are several tips that many professionals, particularly lawyers, find helpful for their work-related emails.

Tip 1: Do Not Include Anything in an Email That You Would Not Want Read Aloud in Court

No matter what types of statements about confidentiality that you insert in your email, there are no guarantees that your email will remain confidential. Although the ABA has stated that there is a reasonable expectation of privacy in emails, emails (and text messages, for that matter) may be discoverable. Consequently, the safest policy is not to include anything in an email that you do not want shared with the rest of the world.

When you do include confidential information in an email, consider the following precautions. First, consider obtaining client consent that it is acceptable to communicate confidential information via email. Second, always include a confidentiality in your emails. Third, draft emails with sensitive information in a Word document first. Once you are satisfied with the document, you can cut and paste it into the email. This process will prevent discovery of metadata (edits made to a document that are deleted). Fourth, be sure that your office's encryption programs are up to date.

Tip 2: Use the Same Professional Language That You Would Use in an Office Memo, an Opinion Letter, or a Business Letter

Sending an office email is not the same thing as text messaging a friend. No matter how well you know the person to whom you are writing a work-related email, use the same language that you would use drafting an office memo, an opinion letter, or a business letter. Do not use abbreviations, code words, slang, or emoticons such as ☺.

EXAMPLE 1   **Example 1   Inappropriate Language**

BTW, if you have questions, feel free to call me 24-7.

Edited: Appropriate Language

Finally, if you have questions, please feel free to call me.

Tip 3: Make Sure That the Tone of the Email Is the Tone That You Intend

"Flaming" in email is the equivalent of shouting at a person. Messages written in all caps, boldface, or other attention-getting fonts should be used with extreme care.

EXAMPLE 2   **Inappropriate Tone**

I got your request for the meeting with Chong. ARE YOU SERIOUS ABOUT WANTING AN HOUR WITH HIM?

Edited: Appropriate Tone

I got your request for the meeting with Chong. An hour meeting seems excessive. Would a shorter meeting work for you?

Notice, too, that while some people view very short emails as efficient, others may read in a curt or rude tone. In addition, it is often a good idea to follow up a request for information with a quick note of thanks so that colleagues and employees know you have received their emails and that their follow-up was appreciated.

EXAMPLE 3   **Tone May Be Interpreted as Curt or Rude**

Original Email

Do you want to review the draft before I submit it to O'Brien?

Answer

No.

Original Email

Do you want to review the draft before I submit it to O'Brien?

Edited Answer

No, that won't be necessary. Thanks for your hard work on this project.

In addition, in drafting an email, keep cultural differences in mind. If you are emailing a person from a culture where it is customary to begin a conversation with an exchange of pleasantries, include the same kind of opening pleasantries in an email to that person.

Tip 4: Before Hitting "Send" or "Reply," Reread Your Email, Including the Address Lines

Although it takes a bit of extra time, rereading an email before sending it is time well spent. Before sending an email, take a few minutes to proofread the email and to double check the address lines. While many people are forgiving of small typos in emails, others are not. In addition, some typos can lead to serious miscommunication. Remember, too, that if you are using a tablet or smart phone that tries to predict what word you intend as you type, you may end up sending gibberish if you do not proofread your messages before sending them.

Tip 5: Do Not Misuse the "High Importance" or the "Read Receipt" Functions

Marking every email as being of high importance is a bit like calling "wolf" every time you hear a noise in the bushes. At some point, no one pays any attention to emails that come from you with the high importance mark. Therefore, limit your use of the mark to those emails that are, in fact, of high importance.

In addition, do not ask for a read receipt for every email you send. At best, most individuals find the process annoying; at worst, it sends the message that you do not trust the individual to whom you are sending the email. If you would like a response, you can ask for such a response in the text of your email. If you need proof that someone received information, use one of the more traditional methods: Send the information through a delivery service or by some type of registered mail.

Tip 6: Be Selective in Attaching Large Files to an Email

If you know that someone uses a tablet or smart phone to retrieve email, do not attach large files without first checking with the recipient to make sure that he or she will be able to receive and open the file. Similarly, if the person to whom you are sending the email is traveling in a country where email access is limited, do not send large files without first checking with that individual.

Tip 7: Make Sure the Subject Line Accurately Reflects the Topic or Topics Discussed in the Email

If, in sending email back and forth, the topic changes, change the subject line so that it matches the topic or topics discussed in the email. Also try to select labels that will increase the chance that the recipient will open the email and that will allow you and the recipient to store the email in appropriate folders or easily retrieve the email.

Tip 8: As a General Rule, Do Not Copy or Forward an Email Message or Attachment Without the Author's Permission, But Be Aware That Others May Forward Your Emails Without Asking Your Permission

In most instances, ask for the original author's permission before forwarding an email or an attachment to an email. Asking for permission demonstrates your personal integrity and can help prevent misunderstandings. Do, however, use common sense. You do not, for example, need to ask for permission to forward an email to a colleague who is working on the same project.

Remember, too, that when you forward an email, the recipient may read the whole string of exchanged emails in the message, not just the last message that was sent.

Unfortunately, though, not all recipients of your emails will return the favor and ask your permission before forwarding an email you have written. Some may do so without any malicious intent. They just assume that it is fine to pass along the information. If you have concerns about an email you are writing getting forwarded, you may want to begin the email with a strong request asking the recipient not to forward the email to others, or you may want to reconsider whether email is the best way to communicate the message.

Tip 9: There Is No Such Thing as "Delete"

Many people mistakenly assume that they can eliminate the paper trail they have created through email by simply deleting old messages. While computer experts may have the necessary skills to permanently delete old emails, they also have the skills to recover emails that the typical user believes he or she has deleted.

Tip 10: When in Doubt, Sleep on It or Get a Second Opinion Before Hitting "Send"

Emails allow us to respond to someone else's ideas or comments almost instantaneously. Sometimes in the heat of a situation, that is not a good thing. Use the speed and convenience of email to your advantage, but remember that in some situations, it may be to your advantage to take a breath, slow down, and not respond immediately.

§ 15.3   Text Messages

If email is the modern update for snail mail, then text messaging is the modern update for the phone call. Although phone calls and voice mail are still commonplace in all work settings, text messages are growing in popularity, and with that growth has come a number of issues regarding effective use.

Because text messages have a fair amount in common with emails, many of the tips and cautions about use of email in section 15.2 apply to text messages as well. And just like email, text messages have both advantages and disadvantages.

The principal advantages of text messages over phone calls are that they can be less intrusive and more efficient. Text messages can be sent and read when it is convenient for both sender and receiver, and messages can be sent and read silently, without interrupting another meeting with all the sounds attendant to a phone call.

Text messages also tend to be shorter and thus more efficient than phone calls. Probably because the screen size is small, most recipients expect text messages to be short, even cryptic. In addition, incomplete sentences are not uncommon. Consequently, there is less of a chance that a short text message will be interpreted as curt or rude.

An additional advantage of text messages over phone calls may be cost, especially for international communications. While international phone calls can be very expensive, text messages are not.

Capitalizing on the advantages of text messaging, then, a lawyer might well use a text message for short communications, such as changing a meeting location. The message can be sent and received with minimal interruption, and the recipient can be in transit and still receive it. While a phone call might have a more personal touch, a phone call will inevitably be more of an interruption and take longer to convey the message. Note, though, that the assumption is that the recipient of the communications not only has a cell phone that is set up to receive text messages but also that he or she would prefer a text message over a call.

The main disadvantage of text messages is that most people consider them to be an informal form of communication that works best among family members and close friends. Indeed because so many people use text messaging for their personal lives, there is a tendency to bring an inappropriate level of informality to text messages in the work place. The sort of shorthand phrasing or spelling such as "R U coming?" or "Thx" that is commonplace in text messaging close friends may be inappropriate with colleagues at work and certainly with clients.

One additional consideration is that some cell phone users have not set up password protection for their text messages so confidential information sent in a text message may be read by anyone who answers the phone.

Chapter 15 Quiz

Draft answers for each of the following questions. Make your points clearly and concisely, and write sentences that are easy to read and that are grammatical and correctly punctuated.

1. How are e-memos the same as more formal memos? How are they different?
2. In writing an e-memo, when should you include descriptions of analogous cases?

3. What are some of the characteristics of a memo in which the analysis is sophisticated?
4. Are emails confidential?
5. What is the appropriate "tone" for an email or text message?

Drafting Letters

Some clients love their attorney and recommend him or her to their business associates, friends, relatives, and people they meet at the gym and on the golf course. Unfortunately, other clients do not give their attorneys the same rave reviews. As a new attorney, how do you make it more likely that you fall into the first and not the second category? While "by winning" seems like the obvious answer, it is not the only answer. Even though clients tend to like attorneys who win or who tell the clients what they want to hear better than attorneys who lose or who have to give them bad news, many clients are looking for more: They want an attorney who listens to them, who explains the law to them in language they can understand, who gives them good advice, and who does not make promises that are not kept. In addition, they want an attorney who is professional. They want someone who dresses professionally, who has a professional demeanor, and who creates professional documents.

Thus, in writing a letter to a client, keep in mind that you are doing more than just telling the client what the law is or what you think your client should do. You are establishing a relationship with your client and building, or destroying, your professional reputation.

§ 16.1   The Assignment

As an attorney, you will write many different types of letters to clients. You will, for example, write letters confirming that you have agreed to represent a particular individual, letters updating your client about the status of his or her case, demand letters, and letters like the ones that we describe in this chapter: opinion letters that explain the law and your client's options.

PRACTICE POINTER	Before you write your first demand letter, read Bret Rappaport's article, *A Shot Across the Bow: How to Write an Effective Demand Letter,* 5 JALWD 32 (2008).

For the purposes of this chapter, assume that you are an attorney in Austin, Texas, and that you represent Mary Corner, who has just purchased a restaurant in a historic building in the Austin Historic District. On September 13, 2013, Ms. Corner filed an application for a permit to install two six-foot by four-foot painted signs on the front of her new restaurant, the Corner Café, which is located in the corner of a building that has been designated as a Historic Landmark. One sign would be on the north side of the building, and the other sign would be on the west side of the building. Each sign would extend eighteen inches above the roof line and would have a beige background and green lettering. At night, the signs would be lit by a small light installed under the signs. On October 1, 2013, the Historic Landmark Commission denied Ms. Corner's application and gave her fourteen days to appeal its decision. Ms. Corner is thinking about appealing and has asked for our advice.

§ 16.2   Know Your Audience and Your Purpose

Before you begin writing, ask yourself two questions: Who is my audience? What is my purpose?

§ 16.2.1   The Audience for an Opinion Letter

Although the primary audience for an opinion letter is the client, there may be a secondary audience. The letter may be read not only by the client but also by an interested third party. Consequently, in writing the letter, write both for the client and for anyone else who may read the letter.

In the Corner Café sign case, the primary audience for your opinion letter will be Mary Corner. Ms. Corner may, however, show the letter to another small business owner, to friends and relatives, or even to a city official.

§16.2.2   The Purpose of an Opinion Letter

Assume for a moment that the audience is the client and no one else. In writing to that client, what is your purpose? Is it to inform? To persuade? To justify your bill? Should you be giving the client only your conclusions, or should you include the information that the client needs to reach his or her own conclusions?

Your role is determined, at least in part, by your state's Rules of Professional Conduct. For example, in Texas attorneys are bound by the following rule and comments.

| EXAMPLE 1 | **Texas Disciplinary Rules of Professional Conduct** |

1.03 Communication

(a) A lawyer shall keep a client reasonably informed about the status of a matter and promptly comply with reasonable requests for information.

(b) A lawyer shall explain a matter to the extent reasonably necessary to permit the client to make informed decisions regarding the representation.

Comment:

1. The client should have sufficient information to participate intelligently in decisions concerning the objectives of the representation and the means by which they are to be pursued, to the extent the client is willing and able to do so. For example, a lawyer negotiating on behalf of a client should provide the client with facts relevant to the matter, inform the client of communications from another party and take other reasonable steps to permit the client to make a decision regarding a serious offer from another party. A lawyer who receives from opposing counsel either an offer of settlement in a civil controversy or a proffered plea bargain in a criminal case should promptly inform the client of its substance unless prior discussions with the client have left it clear that the proposal will be unacceptable. See Comment 2 to Rule 1.02.

2. Adequacy of communication depends in part on the kind of advice or assistance involved. For example, in negotiations where there is time to explain a proposal the lawyer should review all important provisions with the client before proceeding to an agreement. In litigation a lawyer should explain the general strategy and prospects of success and ordinarily should consult the client on tactics that might injure or coerce others. . . .The guiding principle is that the lawyer should reasonably fulfill client expectations for information consistent with the duty to act in the client's best interests, and the client's overall requirements as to the character of representation.

Accordingly, under the Texas rules, your primary purpose in writing the letter would be to give Ms. Corner the information that she needs to make an informed decision about whether to appeal the Historic Landmark Commission's decision.

§ 16.3   Prepare the First Draft of the Letter

Just as convention dictates the content and form of the objective memorandum, convention also dictates the content and form of the opinion letter. Most opinion letters have (1) an introductory paragraph identifying the issue and, most often, the attorney's opinion; (2) a summary of the facts on which the opinion is based; (3) an explanation of the law; (4) the attorney's advice; and (5) a closing sentence or paragraph. Note the similarities between a formal memorandum and the opinion letter.

Objective Memorandum	**Opinion Letter**
Heading	Name
	Address
	File
	Reference
	Salutation
Question presented	Introductory paragraph
Brief answer	Opinion
Statement of facts	Summary of facts on which opinion is based
Discussion section	Explanation
Conclusion	Advice
	Closing

§ 16.3.1   The Introductory Paragraph

In writing the introductory paragraph, you have two objectives: to establish the appropriate relationship with your client and to define the issue or goal. In addition, you will often include substantive information. For example, when the news is favorable, you will usually set out your opinion in the introductory paragraph.

Because the introductory paragraph is so important, avoid "canned" opening sentences. For instance, do not begin all of your letters with "This letter is in response to your inquiry of . . ." or "As you requested . . . ." Instead of beginning with platitudes, begin by identifying the issue or goal. Compare Examples 1, 2, and 3.

EXAMPLE 1   **Canned Opening Sentence**

This letter is in response to your inquiry of October 3, 2013. The information that you requested is set out below.

EXAMPLE 2   **Better Opening Sentence**

After our meeting yesterday, I researched the Austin ordinances governing signs in the Austin Historic Districts.

EXAMPLE 3   **Even Better Opening Sentence**

During our meeting yesterday, you asked me whether you should appeal the Historic Landmark Commission's decision denying your request for a permit to install two signs above the entrance to your new restaurant, the Corner Café. To answer your question, I have reviewed the facts and the Austin ordinances on signs in Historic Landmark Districts.

Because Example 1 could be used to open almost any letter, it subtly suggests to the reader that he or she is just one more client to whom the attorney is cranking out a response. Consequently, most successful attorneys avoid opening sentences like the one in Example 1 and, like the authors of Examples 2 and 3, personalize their openings.

§ 16.3.2 Statement of the Issue

Although you need to identify the issue, you do not want to include a formal issue statement. In most instances, the "under-does-when" and the "whether" formats used in formal memos are inappropriate in an opinion letter.

In deciding how to present the issue, keep in mind your purpose, both in including a statement of the issue and in writing the letter itself. In most letters, your purpose is twofold: You want the client to know that you understand the issue, and you want to protect yourself. Consequently, you include a statement of the issue for both rhetorical and practical reasons. You use it to establish a relationship with the client and to limit your liability.

In the Corner Café sign case, there are a number of different ways and places to set out the issue: You can incorporate your issue statement into your introductory paragraph; you can combine your statement of the issue with your statement of your opinion; or you can set out the issue at the beginning of your explanation of the law.

EXAMPLE 4   **Issue Statement Incorporated into the Introductory Paragraph**

During our meeting on Tuesday, you asked whether you should appeal the City's decision denying your request to install two signs above the entrance to your new restaurant, the Corner Café.

EXAMPLE 5   **Issue Statement Combined with Your Opinion**

I have completed my review of the ordinances governing business signs in the Austin Historic Districts. Based on this review, I recommend that you appeal the City's decision denying your request to install two signs above the entrance to your new restaurant, the Corner Café.

EXAMPLE 6   **Issue Used to Introduce Explanation of the Law**

[Introductory paragraph and facts go here.]
Before deciding whether to appeal the City's denial of your application for a permit to install two signs above the entrance to your new restaurant, you should consider the following ordinances and the procedures and costs that are involved in appealing a decision. [Explanation of the law goes here.]

---

§ 16.3.3 Opinion

When the client has asked for your opinion, set out your opinion in the letter. When the news is good, you will usually put your opinion in the introductory paragraph; having had his or her question answered, the client can then concentrate on the explanation. You may, however, want to use a different strategy when the news is bad. Instead of putting your opinion "up front," you may choose to put it at the end, in the hope that having read the explanation, the client will better understand your opinion.

Whatever your opinion, present it as your opinion. Because you are in the business of making predictions and not guarantees, never tell clients that they will or will not win. Instead, present your opinion in terms of probabilities: "It is unlikely that you would win on appeal." "It is unlikely that the City Council will overturn the decision of the Historic Landmark Commission and grant your application for a permit."

§ 16.3.4 Summary of the Facts

There are two reasons for including a summary of the facts. As with the statement of the issue, the first is rhetorical. You want the client to know that you heard his or her story. The second is practical. You want to protect yourself. Your client needs to know that your opinion is based on a particular set of facts and that, if the facts turn out to be different, your opinion might also be different.

Just as you do not include all of the facts in the statement of facts written for an objective memorandum, you do not include all of the facts in an opinion letter. Include only those facts that are legally significant or that are important to the client. Because the letter itself should be short, keep your summary of facts as short as possible. For instance, in the Corner Café sign case, your statement of facts might look like this.

EXAMPLE 7   Summary of Facts

You submitted your original application on September 13, 2013. In that application, you requested a permit that would have allowed you to install two six-foot by four-foot painted wood signs on the front of your building. One of the signs would have been installed on the north side of the building, and the other would have been installed on the west side of the building. Both signs would extend about eighteen inches above the top of the building and would be beige with green lettering. At night, the signs would be lit by a light installed under the signs. The Historic Landmark Commission denied your application on October 1, 2013, giving you fourteen days to appeal its decision to the City Council.

---

§ 16.3.5 Explanation

Under the rules of professional responsibility, you must give the client the information that he or she needs to make an informed decision. It is essential, therefore, that you give not only your opinion but also the basis for your opinion. The explanation section is not, however, just a repeat of the discussion section from an objective memorandum. It is usually much shorter and much more client-specific.

When the explanation requires a discussion of more than one or two issues, you will usually want to include a roadmap. See Section 21.2.1. Having outlined the steps, you can then discuss each step in more detail. The amount of detail will depend on the question, the subject matter, and the client. Although there are exceptions, as a general rule, do not set out the text of ordinances or statutes or include references to specific cases. Instead, just tell the client what the ordinances, statutes, and cases say, without citations to authority.

After explaining the law, apply the law to the facts of your client's case. If a particular point is not in dispute, explain why it is not in dispute; if it is in dispute, summarize each side's arguments. The difference between the analysis in an objective memorandum and in an opinion letter is a difference in degree, not kind. In each instance, give the reader what he or she needs — nothing more and nothing less. For examples of explanations, see the sample letters set out at the end of this chapter.

§ 16.3.6   Advice

When there is more than one possible course of action, include an advice section in which you describe and evaluate each option. For example, if there are several ways in which your client could change its business operations to avoid liability, describe and evaluate each of those options. Similarly, if your client could choose negotiation over arbitration or arbitration over litigation, describe and evaluate each option. Having described the options, you can then advise the client as to which option you think would be in his or her best interest.

§ 16.3.7   Concluding Paragraph

Just as you should avoid canned openings, also avoid canned closings. Instead of using stock sentences, use the concluding paragraph to cement the relationship that you have established with the client and to confirm what, if anything, is to happen next. What is the next step and who is to take it?

§ 16.3.8   Warnings

Some firms will want you to include explicit warnings. They will want you to tell the client that your opinion is based on current law and on the facts currently available and that your opinion might be different if the facts turn out to be different. Other firms believe that these warnings, when set out explicitly, set the wrong tone. Because practice varies, determine which approach your firm takes before writing the letter.

In writing your letter, you can use any of the standard formats for business letters. For examples of accepted formats, see the sample letters at the end of this chapter.

§ 16.4   Revising, Editing, and Proofreading the Opinion Letter

It is not enough that the law be stated correctly and that your advice be sound. Your letter must be well written and the tone must be the one that you intend.

§ 16.4.1   Drafting a Well-Written Letter

Like other types of writing, a well-written letter is well organized. As a general rule, present the information in the order listed above: an introductory paragraph in which you identify the issue and give your opinion followed by a summary of the facts, an explanation of the law, your advice, and a concluding sentence or paragraph. You will also want to structure each paragraph carefully, identifying the topic in the first sentence and making sure that each sentence builds on the prior one.

In addition, take care in constructing your sentences. You can make the law more understandable by using concrete subjects and action verbs and relatively short sentences. When longer sentences are needed, manage those sentences by using punctuation to divide the sentences into shorter units of meaning.

Finally, remember that you will be judged by the letter you write. Although clients may not know whether you have the law right, they will know whether you have spelled their names correctly. In addition, many will notice other mistakes in grammar, punctuation, or spelling. If you want to be known as a competent lawyer, make sure that your letters provide the proof.

§ 16.4.2   Using an Appropriate Tone

In addition to selling competence, you are selling an image. As you read each of the following letters, picture the attorney who wrote it.

EXAMPLE 1

Dear Mr. and Mrs. McDonald:

This letter is to acknowledge receipt of your letter of February 17, 2013, concerning your prospects as potential adoptive parents. The information that you provided about yourselves will need to be verified through appropriate documentation. Furthermore, I am sure that you are cognizant of the fact that there are considerably more prospective adoptive placements than there are available adoptees to fill those placement slots.

Nonetheless, I will be authorizing my legal assistant to keep your correspondence on file. One can never know when an opportunity may present itself and, in fact, a child becomes unexpectedly available for placement. If such an opportunity should arise, please know that I would be in immediate contact with you.

Very sincerely yours,

Kenneth Q. Washburn III
Attorney at Law

EXAMPLE 2

Dear Bill and Mary,

Just wanted you to know that I got your letter asking about adopting a baby. I can already tell that you two would make great parents. But, as you probably know, there are far more "would be" parents out there than there are babies.

But I don't want you to lose hope. You might be surprised. Your future little one may be available sooner than you think. It has happened before! And you can be sure that I'll call you the minute I hear of something. Until then, I'll have Marge set up a file for you.

All the best,

Ken Washburn

EXAMPLE 3

Dear Mr. and Mrs. McDonald:

Your letter about the possibility of adopting a baby arrived in my office yesterday. Although the information in your letter indicates that you would be ideal adoptive parents, I am sure that you realize that there are more couples who wish to adopt than there are adoptable babies. For this reason, you may have to wait for some time for your future son or daughter.

Even so, occasionally an infant becomes available for adoption on short notice. For this reason, I will ask my legal assistant to open a file for you so that we can react quickly if necessary. Because we do not know exactly when an infant will become available, I recommend that we begin putting together the appropriate documentation as soon as possible. In the meantime, please know that I will call you immediately if I learn of an available infant who would be a good match for you.

Sincerely,

Kenneth Washburn

---

§ 16.4.3 Checklist for Critiquing the Opinion Letter

I. Organization

- ■ The information has been presented in a logical order: The letter begins with an introductory sentence or paragraph that is followed, in most instances, by the attorney's opinion, a summary of the facts, an explanation, the attorney's advice, and a concluding paragraph.

II. Content

- ■ The introductory sentence identifies the topic and establishes the appropriate relationship with the client.
- ■ The attorney's opinion is sound and is stated in terms of probabilities.
- ■ The summary of the facts is accurate and includes both the legally significant facts and the facts that are important to the client.
- ■ The explanation gives the client the information that he or she needs to make an informed decision.
- ■ The options are described and evaluated.
- ■ The concluding paragraph states who will do what next and sets an appropriate tone.

III. Writing

- ■ The client can understand the letter after reading it once.
- ■ The paragraph divisions are logical, and the paragraphs are neither too long nor too short. See Chapter 22.
- ■ Transitions and dovetailing have been used to make the connections between ideas clear. See Chapter 23.
- ■ In most sentences, the writer has used the actor as the subject of the sentence, and the subject and verb are close together. See sections 24.1 and 24.4.
- ■ The writer has varied the length of the sentences and the sentence patterns so that each sentence flows smoothly from the prior sentence. See section 24.5.

- The writing is concise and precise. See sections 25.1 and 25.2.
- The writing is grammatically correct and correctly punctuated. See Chapters 27 and 28.
- The letter has been proofread.

Chapter 16 Quiz

Draft answers for each of the following questions. Make your points clearly and concisely, and write sentences that are easy to read and that are grammatical and correctly punctuated.

1. In writing an opinion letter, what is your purpose?
2. As a general rule, what types of information should be included in an opinion letter and in what order should that information be presented?
3. In general, what is the appropriate tone for an opinion letter?

§ 16.5   Sample Client Letters

EXAMPLE 1   **Sample Client Letter**

Confidential
Attorney-Client Communication

Mary Corner
101 Main Street
Austin, Texas 73344

Dear Ms. Corner:

During our meeting yesterday, you asked me whether you should appeal the Historic Landmark Commission's decision denying your request for a permit to install two signs above the entrance to your new restaurant, the Corner Café. To answer your question, I have reviewed the facts and the Austin ordinances on signs in Historic Landmark Districts.

You submitted your original application on September 13, 2013. In that application, you requested a permit that would have allowed you to install two six-foot by four-foot painted wood signs on the front of your building. One of the signs would have been installed on the north side of the building, and the other would have been installed on the west side of the building. Both signs would extend about eighteen inches above the top of the building and would be beige with green lettering. At night, the signs would be lit by a light installed under the signs. The Historic Landmark Commission denied your application on October 1, 2013, giving you fourteen days to appeal its decision to the City Council.

City of Austin ordinances prohibit certain types of signs in Historic Landmark Districts. For example, the ordinances specifically prohibit roof signs and any sign, or any portion of a sign, that rotates. Although your signs would not rotate, they might fall within the definition of a roof sign, which is defined as a sign that is "installed over or on the roof of a building." In determining whether to grant a permit for other types of signs, the Historic Landmark Commission considers a number of other factors, including the following:

(1.)　the proposed size, color, and lighting of the sign;

(2.)　the material from which the sign is to be constructed;

(3.)　the proliferation of signs on a building or lot;

(4.)　the proposed orientation of the sign with respect to structures; and

(5.)　other factors that are consistent with the Historic Landmark Preservation Plan, the character of the National Historic Register District, and the purpose of historic landmark regulations.

If the Commission denied your application for a permit because your proposed signs fall within the definition of a roof sign, it is unlikely that the City Council would overturn the Commission's decision. Our only hope would be to persuade the City Council that a sign that extends above the top of the building does not fall within the definition of a roof sign.

If, however, the Commission denied the permit for some other reason, the City Council might overturn the Commission's decision, particularly if your proposed signs are consistent in size, color, lighting, and material with other signs in the area and if there are not already a number of other signs on the building.

To preserve your right to appeal, I recommend that you file a notice of appeal within the time limits set out in the letter that you received from the Commission. I would then schedule a meeting with a member of the Commission to determine the reason that the Commission denied your application. If the Commission denied your application because your signs would extend beyond the roof line, the Commission may be willing to approve your application for a permit if you agree to change the size and/or locations of your signs so that they do not extend beyond the roof line. Similarly, if the Commission denied your application because of the signs' size, color, or lighting, you may be able to work with the Commission to modify your application so that your proposed signs meet the Commission's criteria. If, however, you cannot find out from the Commission why it denied your application or you cannot reach an agreement with the Commission about an application that would meet its criteria, you can then proceed with your appeal to the City Council.

Although you do not need an attorney to file an appeal with the City Council or to schedule meetings with the Commission, I would be glad to assist you with either or both actions. If you would like me to act on your behalf, please call me by Wednesday, October 9, 2013, so that I can submit the appeal before the deadline. If you would like to file the appeal without my assistance, please see the instructions that are set out in the letter that you received from the Commission. In addition, you can request an appointment with a Commissioner by calling the following number: (512) 974-2680. If you have any further questions or concerns, please feel free to call me. Please keep in mind that you must file your appeal no later than Monday, October 14, 2013.

Very truly yours,

Your name

EXAMPLE 2	**Sample Client Letter**

Confidential
Attorney-Client Communication

September 30, 2013

Ms. Marian Walter
1234 Main Street
Wichita, KS 67218

File No. 0192002

Dear Ms. Walter:

Thank you for contacting me about whether you can vacate your current location before the expiration of your lease. After researching the issues, I have determined that, if you decide to move out before the end of your lease and your landlord, Valley Antiques, files a lawsuit to collect the unpaid rent, you can probably win the lawsuit. You should, however, consider some of your other options.

Because my opinion is based on the following facts, please contact me if I have left out a fact or misstated a fact.

In June 2012, you received a brochure advertising an "elegant antiques mall" that was certain to attract "the most discriminating clients." When you met with the leasing agent, Joann Carter, she told you that the mall would house antique stores and that the mall was designed to attract adults, not children. In August 2012, you signed a five-year lease. The lease stated that the remaining spaces would be rented to antique stores or other retail businesses.

Between August 2012 and November 2012, five other upscale antique stores moved into the mall. The landlord was, however, unable to rent the remaining eight spaces to antique dealers. As a result, between February and April 2013, the landlord leased four of the remaining spaces to other types of businesses. It leased one of the spaces to a video arcade and three others to secondhand stores. Since these stores moved into the mall, there have been children with skateboards in the mall area, and you have experienced a 20 percent decrease in profits. In addition to making oral complaints, on April 30, 2013, you sent a letter to the landlord notifying it that you believe that it violated the terms of your lease when it leased spaces in the mall to the video arcade and secondhand stores.

If you vacate the premises and default on the lease, Valley Antiques may file a lawsuit against you to recover the rent due for the remaining months of the lease. If this happens, you can argue that Valley Antiques "constructively evicted" you when it leased to the arcade and secondhand stores. A constructive eviction is different from an actual eviction: While an actual eviction occurs when the landlord literally takes the premises away from the tenant, a constructive eviction occurs when the landlord interferes with a tenant's right to use the premises for their intended purpose. It would be up to the jury to decide whether the circumstances surrounding your case constitute constructive eviction.

To establish that you have been constructively evicted, you will need to prove four things. First, you must prove that Valley Antiques violated the lease agreement. Valley Antiques will argue that, under the lease, it had the right to lease to retail stores and that an arcade and thrift shops are retail stores. Although the lease does allow Valley Antiques to lease to retail stores, you can argue that both parties understood the language in the lease to mean that Valley Antiques could lease to antique stores and other "upscale" retail establishments, for example, an upscale jewelry store or restaurant. Based on the language in the brochure and the statements made by the leasing agent, a jury should conclude that the landlord violated the lease by leasing the other spaces to the video arcade and secondhand stores.

Second, you must prove that when Valley Antiques leased the vacant spaces to a video arcade and secondhand stores it substantially interfered with your ability to use your leased space. Although there have been cases in which the courts have found that a landlord substantially interfered with a tenant's use of its leased space when the landlord rented to an incompatible business, there are other cases in which the court found that the landlord did not substantially interfere. The key seems to be whether the landlord's act caused a loss of profits. As a consequence, to prove substantial interference, we will have to show that Valley Antiques caused your loss of profits when it leased the vacant spaces to the arcade and the secondhand stores. Even though we should be able to do this, Valley Antiques will try to prove that your losses are the result of other factors, such as the seasonal nature of your business, the current economic climate, or your own business practices.

Third, you must prove that you gave Valley Antiques notice of the problem and an opportunity to correct it. You should be able to meet this requirement: in addition to making oral complaints, you also sent a letter, and you have given Valley Antiques several months to correct the problem.

Finally, you must prove that you vacated the premises within a reasonable amount of time after complaining to the landlord. If you vacate the premises by November 1, 2013, the jury will most likely find that you have met this requirement.

Although you should be able to prove that you have been constructively evicted, litigation is expensive and stressful, and there are no guarantees. As a result, you should consider some of your other options.

One option is to stay and pay rent. Although this option avoids the expense and stress of litigation, you may lose your right to claim that you have been constructively evicted. As I indicated earlier in this letter, one of the requirements for constructive eviction is that you move out within a reasonable time. In addition, if your loss in profits continues, it may be impractical to stay in business.

A second option would be to try to sublease your space to another business. Even though your lease requires that you obtain Valley Antiques' approval before you sublet your space, the courts have said that a landlord cannot withhold approval except for good cause. The risk associated with this option is that you may be liable for unpaid rents if the new tenant fails to make payments.

A third option is to try to negotiate an early termination of the lease on the grounds that Valley Antiques has violated the lease by leasing to the arcade and secondhand stores. I can do this for you or, if you want to minimize your costs, you can do it on your own.

A fourth option would be to file a lawsuit against Valley Antiques for breach of contract. Although you should be able to win this lawsuit and recover your lost profits, such a lawsuit would be expensive and, once again, there are no guarantees.

Unfortunately, none of these options is very good. As a result, you need to balance your desire to move out of the mall against the potential costs. Although there is a good chance that your landlord will not sue you, under our state's statute of limitations it has six years to file a lawsuit. Therefore, you would have to live under the cloud of potential litigation for a number of years.

Please contact my office to schedule an appointment to talk in more detail about your options. I look forward to meeting with you.

Sincerely,

Name
Attorney at Law

EXAMPLE 3	Sample Client Letter

Confidential
Attorney-Client Communication

September 20, 2013

Onlinebooks.com
6524 Industrial Parkway South
Tampa Bay, Florida 33607

Dear Mr. Brooks:

You have asked if Onlinebooks may ask job applicants whether they have back problems or have used more than five days of sick leave during the past year. My research indicates that the Americans with Disabilities Act (ADA) prohibits the asking of such questions. You can, however, ask questions that will help you determine whether an applicant can perform the essential job requirements. Because my opinion is based on current law and my understanding of the facts, I have set out those facts so that you can review them for accuracy. Please note that a change in the facts might change my opinion.

Onlinebooks employs "pickers," that is, individuals who pick books off shelves, place them in a box, and then place the box on a conveyor belt. Pickers must be able to climb, reach, and lift boxes weighing up to thirty pounds. In the past, some of the individuals you have hired as pickers have not been able to do all parts of the job or have used substantial amounts of sick leave for back or other health problems. Thus, you want to ask job applicants about whether they have back problems and about how they use sick leave.

The ADA prohibits employers from discriminating against qualified job applicants who are disabled. More specifically, the ADA prohibits employers from asking applicants questions that are designed to "weed out" individuals who have a disability or who suffer from a chronic illness. As a result, Onlinebooks cannot ask job applicants about whether they have back problems or about their use of sick leave.

The ADA does not, however, prohibit an employer from asking job applicants whether they can, with or without reasonable accommodations, perform the essential functions of the job for which they are applying. Therefore, Onlinebooks may describe the essential functions of the job and then ask applicants whether they can perform those functions. For example, you may tell applicants that pickers must be able to climb, reach, and lift thirty-pound boxes and then ask them whether they can perform each of these tasks. In addition, Onlinebooks may ask applicants to demonstrate that they can do each of these tasks.

If an applicant asks for a reasonable accommodation, Onlinebooks must grant that accommodation unless doing so would impose an unreasonable burden on Onlinebooks. For example, if an applicant asks to be allowed to wear a back support or to use a handcart to move heavy boxes longer distances, you should grant the request unless doing so would create an unreasonable burden on the company. You would not, however, need to grant an employee's request to be exempted from carrying boxes weighing over, for example, ten pounds.

In addition, the ADA does not prohibit employers from asking applicants about their work histories. Consequently, although you may not ask applicants how much sick leave they used in the last year, you may ask them about their attendance records. In doing so, you just need to make sure that the questions are designed to collect information about the applicants' work records, not to determine whether the individual is disabled or suffers from a chronic illness.

To summarize then, although you may not ask applicants whether they have back problems, you may ask them whether they can, with or without reasonable accommodations, perform the essential functions of the job. In addition, although you may not ask applicants about their use of sick leave, you may ask them about their attendance records as long as your questions are not designed to collect information about whether the person is disabled or suffers from a chronic illness.

   If you have any additional questions, please feel free to contact me.

                                               Sincerely,

                                               Name
                                               Attorney at Law

Briefs and Oral Argument

Writing a Motion Brief

§ 17.1   Motion Briefs

Much of litigation is motions practice. For example, as a trial attorney, you may file motions for temporary relief, to compel discovery, to suppress evidence, to dismiss, or for summary judgment. Although not all of these motions will be supported by briefs, many will.

> **PRACTICE POINTER**   The names of these briefs vary from jurisdiction to jurisdiction. In some jurisdictions, they are called "briefs in support of a motion" or "motion briefs," while in other jurisdictions they are called "memoranda of law," "memoranda of points of authority" or , for short, "P and A memos." Check your court rules and with local attorneys to see what these briefs are called in your jurisdiction.

§ 17.1.1   Audience

In writing a brief in support of or in opposition to a motion, your primary audience is the trial judge.

Sometimes you will know which judge will read your brief. Either the brief has been requested by a specific judge, or you know which judge will hear the motion. At other times, though, you will not know who the judge will be. The brief will be read by whichever judge is hearing motions on the day that your motion is argued.

If you know which judge will read your brief, write your brief for that judge. Learn as much as you can about that judge, and then craft a brief that he or she will find persuasive. If you do not know which judge will read your brief, write a brief that will work for any of the judges who might hear your motion.

In whichever situation you find yourself, keep the judge's schedule in mind. It is not uncommon for a judge hearing civil motions to hear twenty motions in a single day. If in each of these cases each party has filed a twenty-page brief, the judge would have 800 pages to read. Given this workload, it is not surprising that for most judges the best brief is the short brief. Know what you need and want to argue, make your argument, and then stop.

PRACTICE POINTER	Check your court rules to determine whether those rules impose a page limit. If they do, make sure that you comply with those limits.

Also keep in mind the constraints placed on trial judges. Because trial judges must apply mandatory authority, they need to know what the law is, not what you think it should be. Whenever possible, make the easy argument: Set out and apply existing law.

§ 17.1.2 Purpose

In writing to a trial judge, you have two goals: to educate and to persuade. You are a teacher who teaches the judge both the applicable law and the facts of the case. You are not, however, *just* a teacher; you are also an advocate. As you teach, you will be trying to persuade the court to take a particular action.

§ 17.1.3 Conventions

The format of a particular brief will vary from jurisdiction to jurisdiction and, even within a jurisdiction, from court to court. Consequently, check both the general and the local rules. Is there a rule that prescribes the types of information that should be included in the brief, the order in which that information should be presented, and the particular format? If there is, follow that rule. If there is no rule, check with other attorneys or with the court clerk to see if there is a format that is typically used.

§ 17.2   *State v. Patterson*

In this chapter, the example case is *State v. Patterson*, a criminal case in which the defendant has filed a motion to suppress the identifications obtained at a show-up held shortly after an assault and at a line-up held one day later. The facts of the case are as follows. At about 4:00 p.m. on Monday, August 12, 2013, Beatrice Martinez left her apartment and began walking down residential streets to her place of employment, a restaurant located about one mile from her apartment. As she was walking, Ms. Martinez noticed an older model red station wagon with a chrome luggage rack as it drove by her. A few minutes later, the same car drove by once again. This time, the driver pulled in front of Martinez, blocking the sidewalk. The driver then got out of the car, walked toward Martinez, and, when he was about five feet from Martinez, pulled a gun from his coat pocket and pointed it at her.

At about 4:15 p.m. Chester Clipse was walking home when he saw a man in a red station wagon driving slowly down the street. Because it appeared that the car was going to pull into Mr. Clipse's private parking spot, it drew his attention. As a result, Clipse was watching when the driver got out of the station wagon and pulled a gun. As soon as he saw the gun, Clipse shouted, "Hey!" Startled, the man turned and went back to his car, got in it, and drove away. Crying, Martincz ran across the street.

Clipse then took Martinez, who was visibly shaken, to his landlady's apartment, where they called the police. While the landlady comforted Martinez, Clipse went back out to the street to wait for the police, where he saw a parking enforcement officer. Clipse told the parking enforcement officer what had happened and gave him a description of the vehicle. After getting the description, the parking enforcement officer left to look for the vehicle.

A few minutes later, Officer Yuen and Officer Cox arrived at Clipse's apartment building and interviewed Clipse. Because he had been down the street when the incident occurred, Clipse was able to tell the officers only that the man was a white man in his late thirties or early forties and that he was of average height and weight. While the officers were talking to Clipse, the parking enforcement officer radioed, stating that he had found a red station wagon with a chrome luggage rack parked on a nearby street. At this point, Officer Cox drove Clipse in his police car to see whether Clipse could identify the car. Meanwhile, Officer Yuen went inside to interview Martinez.

Martinez told Officer Yuen that her assailant was a white male who was about 5′7″ tall; that he weighed between 165 and 170 pounds; that he had wavy blondish-brown hair; that he appeared to be in his early forties; and that at the time of the assault, he was wearing a dark jacket and glasses. Neither Clipse nor Martinez had been able to give the license plate numbers on the man's vehicle.

After completing the interview, Officer Yuen asked Martinez if she wanted a ride home or to work. Martinez accepted the offer of a ride home and got into the back seat of Officer Yuen's vehicle. About four blocks later, Officer Yuen asked Martinez whether a man who was on the sidewalk in front of them looked like her assailant. Because she could not see the man's face, Martinez did not rcspond. As the police car drew nearer, Officer Yuen again asked Martinez whether the man looked like her assailant. This time, Martinez answered, "Yes, I think so." On hcaring this response, Officer Yuen pulled up next to the man, got out of his vehicle, and talked to the man, who was wearing a green jacket and glasses.

As Officer Yuen was questioning the man, Officer Cox drove up with Clipse. While Martinez and Clipse watched, Officers Cox and Yuen continued to question the man. Officer Cox then returned to Martinez and Clipse and walked them back to Clipse's apartment. While he did so, Officer Yuen arrested the man, who was identified as Dean E. Patterson, for assault with a deadly weapon. Later that day, the police searched Mr. Patterson's apartment and found a gun issued to Patterson by his employer. At a line-up held the next day, Martinez identified Patterson as the man who assaulted her. Clipse was not able to make an identification.

In his statement to the police, twenty-two-year-old Dean Patterson stated that, on the day in question, he finished his shift as a security guard at 7:30 a.m. and walked to his apartment. After having breakfast with his wife, Patterson went to bed and slept until about 1:00 p.m. At about 2:30 p.m., Patterson's wife received a phone call asking her to cover for a co-worker, a nurse who was ill. After about 3:00 p.m., Patterson drove his wife the three-quarters of a mile to the hospital. When he returned home, Patterson could not find a parking place close to his apartment and had to park several blocks away.

At about 3:30 p.m., Patterson called his wife to find out how long she would have to work. They had plans to go to a movie that evening, and he wanted to know whether he should change those plans. At about 3:50 p.m., Patterson took a load of laundry to the apartment complex's laundry room. When he returned to his apartment, Patterson watched part of an old movie. At about 4:15 p.m., Patterson went back to the laundry room to put the clothes in the dryer. On his way back to his apartment, Patterson saw a parking place in front of his apartment and moved his car. By this time, it was 4:30 p.m., and Patterson decided to phone his wife again. He arranged to meet her at 5:15 p.m. for her dinner break. Patterson picked up the laundry and then left the apartment a little before 5:00 p.m. to meet his wife.

While Patterson was walking to the hospital, a police car pulled up behind him, and a police officer got out of his car and began questioning him. Patterson was then arrested and charged with assault with a deadly weapon.

Patterson has no prior convictions and has volunteered to take a lie detector test.

§ 17.3   Constructing a "Theory of the Case"

While different people use different labels, all good advocates understand the importance of having a theory of the case. For some, constructing the "theory of the case" means selecting the lens through which you want the court to view your client's case. There is almost always more than one way to view the law and the facts.

For others, constructing a theory of the case means selecting a theme, which might or might not be summed up in a single sentence or phrase. For instance, in the example problem, defense counsel might select the theme, "wrong place, wrong time." Mr. Patterson just happened to be at the wrong place at the wrong time.

No matter which label resonates for you, keep in mind that, to be a good advocate, it is not enough that you know the facts and the law. You must also be a good storyteller. Your statement of facts should read like a well-written short story and, in your arguments, you must do more than just mechanically set out the law and apply that law to the facts of your case. Instead, you must weave the law and facts together in such a way that you present legally sound arguments that appeal both to the judge's head and heart.

There are at least two ways of coming up with a good theory of the case. The first is to look at the case through your client's eyes. According to your client, what happened? Why did the other people involved do what they did? Why did your client act as he or she did? Why does your client think that what he or she did was legally right? Justified? Is there law that supports your client's view of what happened?

The second way is to look at the cases involving the same issue in which the court reached the result that you want the court to reach in your case. In those cases, what was the winning party's theory of the case? What legal arguments did that party make? How did it characterize what happened? What was the court's reaction? Did the trial court "buy" the winning party's theory of the case or come up with its own theory of the case?

In the example case, Patterson says that he did not commit the crime. He was simply at the wrong place at the wrong time. At the time the crime was committed, Patterson was doing laundry, moving his car, and getting ready to meet his wife for dinner. Although Ms. Martinez has identified him as her assailant, she did so only because police pointed him out to her and suggested to her that he was the man who had assaulted her. In addition, Patterson does not match Ms. Martinez's and Clipse's descriptions of the assailant. Although both Ms. Martinez and Clipse told the police that the assailant was in his late thirties or early forties, Patterson is only twenty-two.

In contrast, the State says that Patterson is the person who assaulted Ms. Martinez. Ms. Martinez has identified Patterson as her assailant, his car matches the one that Ms. Martinez and Clipse have described, and a gun was found in his apartment.

§ 17.4   The Caption

While in some jurisdictions, motion briefs are printed on pleading, or numbered, paper, in other jurisdictions they are printed on regular paper. In addition, the rules about where the caption is placed and what information should be included varies from jurisdiction to jurisdiction. In the example case, we have used the Washington rules: The caption is set out on the first page beginning on about line 5. The parties' names are set out on the left-hand side, and the case number and the title of the document are set out on the right-hand side. See the sample briefs at the end of this chapter.

> **PRACTICE POINTER**   Many jurisdictions now allow, or even require, that the parties file their pleadings and briefs electronically. Therefore, before filing your brief, check your local rules.

§ 17.5   Introductory Paragraph/Prayer for Relief

In many, but not all, jurisdictions the first paragraph after the caption is an introductory paragraph. Most of the time, these paragraphs are very "matter of fact." The attorney simply identifies the motion and sets out the relief that he or she is requesting. At other times, the attorney uses the introductory paragraph in the same way that a motion picture company uses a trailer. In such instances, the attorney uses the introductory paragraph to engage the judge, enticing him or her to read further. In deciding which approach to take, consider the conventional practices in your jurisdiction, the nature and importance of your case, and your own personal style.

EXAMPLE 1   **Introductory Paragraph from Defendant's Brief**

Mr. Patterson asks the Court to suppress Martinez's show-up and line-up identifications and to prohibit both Martinez and Clipse from making in-court identifications. The show-up was impermissibly suggestive and, because she viewed her assailant for only a few seconds, Martinez's identifications are unreliable. Mr. Patterson was simply at the wrong place at the wrong time.

EXAMPLE 2   **State's Introductory Paragraph/Prayer for Relief**

The State asks the Court to deny the defendant's motion to suppress the victim's show-up and line-up identifications and to allow both the victim and the witness to make in-court identifications. The show-up was not suggestive, and the victim's and the witness's identifications are reliable.

EXAMPLE 3   **Alternative Introductory Paragraph from Defendant's Brief**

August 12, 2013, started out as a normal day for Dean Patterson. After finishing his shift as a security guard, he slept, had breakfast with his wife, and then, after his wife left for work, watched a movie and did the laundry. Everything changed, however, when Mr. Patterson decided to walk to the hospital where his wife worked to have dinner with her. As he was walking down the street, Mr. Patterson saw a police car pull up behind him, and, while a young woman who had been assaulted watched, the police officer got out of the police car and questioned Mr. Patterson. Although Mr. Patterson was twenty years younger than the man the victim said had assaulted her, the police arrested Mr. Patterson and charged him with the assault. Because Mr. Patterson's only "crime" was being at the wrong place at the wrong time, Mr. Patterson respectfully requests that the Court grant his motion to suppress.

PRACTICE POINTER   Capitalize "court" when referring to the court to which your brief is addressed or the United States Supreme Court or when you are setting out the full name of the court. In all other instances, do not capitalize "court."

§ 17.6   The Statement of Facts

Never underestimate the importance of the facts. Particularly at the trial court level, it is usually the facts that determine the outcome.

§ 17.6.1   Select the Facts

In drafting your statement of facts, you will, typically, include three types of facts: background facts, legally significant facts, and emotionally significant facts.

a.   Background Facts

Background facts play a different role in persuasive writing than they do in objective writing. In an objective statement of facts, the writer includes only those background facts that are needed for the story to make sense. In contrast, in drafting a persuasive statement of facts, you can also use background facts to create a favorable context. See section 17.6.3(a).

b.   Legally Significant Facts

Because most courts require that the statement of facts be "fair," in writing the statement of facts you must include all of the legally significant facts, both favorable and unfavorable. Thus, in the example case, both the State and the defendant must include all of the facts that will be relevant in determining whether the identifications obtained at the show-up and at the line-up should be suppressed and whether Martinez and Clipse should be allowed to make in-court identifications.

c.   Emotionally Significant Facts

While you must include all of the legally significant facts, you do not need to include all of the facts that are emotionally significant. Although as a defensive move you may sometimes include an emotionally significant fact that is unfavorable, recharacterizing it or minimizing its significance, most of the time you will not. It is more common to include only those emotionally significant facts that favor your client.

The harder question is how to handle emotionally significant facts that are unfavorable to the other side. Should you sling mud, or should you take a higher road and omit any reference to those facts? The answer is that it depends: It depends on the case and on the attorney. If the fact's connection to the case is tenuous, most attorneys will not include it. If, though, the case is weak and the fact's connection is closer, many attorneys will include it, some using it as a sword, others using it much more subtly.

§ 17.6.2   Select an Organizational Scheme

In selecting an organizational scheme, consider two factors. First, decide which organizational scheme makes the most sense. Does it make more sense to use a chronological organizational scheme, a topical organizational scheme, or a topical organizational scheme with the facts within each topic set out in chronological order? Second, decide which organizational scheme will allow you to set out the facts in such a way that you are able to present your story and your theory of the case most effectively.

In the example case, it makes sense to set out the facts in chronological order. In deciding whether to suppress the evidence, the trial judge will want to know what happened first, second, and third. A chronological organizational scheme will also allow each side to tell its story. The only difference will be that Patterson will start his story with his activities on the day in question, while the State will start its story where it started for the victim: with the assault.

> **PRACTICE POINTER**
>
> If your statement of facts is long or if you are setting out the facts for two unrelated issues, think about adding subheadings. While the argumentative headings should be in the form of positive assertions (see section 17.8.2), the subheading in the statement of facts can be in the form of labels.

§ 17.6.3 Present the Facts in a Light Favorable to Your Client

In writing the statement of facts for an objective memo, you set out the facts accurately and objectively. You did not present the facts in the light most favorable to your client.

In writing the statement of facts for a motion brief, you still need to set out the facts accurately. One of the fastest ways to lose a case is to leave out legally significant facts or to misrepresent either the legally significant or emotionally significant facts. Being accurate does not mean, however, that you need to set out the facts objectively. You are permitted and, in fact, are expected to present the facts in such a way that they support your theory of the case.

In presenting the facts, attorneys use a number of different techniques. They create a favorable context, they tell the story from their client's point of view, they emphasize the facts that support their theory of the case and de-emphasize those that do not, and they select their words correctly.

> **Techniques for Presenting the Facts in a
> Light Favorable to Your Client**
>
> a. Create a favorable context
> b. Tell the story from your client's point of view
> c. Emphasize favorable facts and de-emphasize unfavorable facts
>   i.   Airtime
>   ii. Detail
>   iii. Positions of emphasis
>   iv. Short sentences
>   v.   Main and dependent clauses
> d. Select facts both for their denotation and their connotation

a. Create a Favorable Context

People tend to view a fact differently depending on the context in which that fact is presented. Judges are no different.

One way to create a favorable context is to start the story where it favors your client. Look for instance at Example 1 below. Instead of starting the statement of facts with the assault or Patterson's arrest, defense counsel starts it by describing what Patterson was doing on the day of the assault. By starting with these facts, she is able to start the story with facts that support her theory of the case: Patterson is an innocent pedestrian who happened to be in the wrong place at the wrong time. Note how defense counsel works in the fact that Patterson is married, that he has a job, and that he does nice things, for instance, he takes his wife to work, does the laundry, and arranges to meet his wife during her dinner break.

EXAMPLE 1   **The First Three Paragraphs of the Defendant's Statement of Facts**

At 7:30 on Monday morning, August 12, 2013, twenty-two-year-old Dean Patterson finished his shift as a security guard and walked to his apartment. After having breakfast with his wife, Mr. Patterson went to bed and slept until about 1:00 p.m. At about 2:30 p.m., Mr. Patterson's wife received a phone call asking her to work at the local hospital, where she is employed as a nurse. She got ready, and Mr. Patterson dropped her off at the hospital at about 3:10 p.m. When he returned, Mr. Patterson could not find a parking place close to his apartment and had to park several blocks away.

At about 3:30 p.m., Mr. Patterson called his wife to find out how long she would have to work. They had plans to go to a movie that evening, and he wanted to know whether he should change those plans. At about 3:50 p.m., Mr. Patterson took a load of laundry to the apartment complex's laundry room. When he returned to his apartment, Mr. Patterson watched part of an old movie. At about 4:15 p.m., Mr. Patterson went back to the laundry room to put the clothes in the dryer. On his way back, he saw a parking spot in front of his apartment and moved his car—an older model red station wagon—to that spot. After parking his car, Mr. Patterson got out of the car and, because the driver's side door does not lock from the outside, walked to the passenger side to lock the doors. As he did so, he nodded to a parking enforcement officer who was driving by.

By this time, it was 4:30 p.m., and Mr. Patterson decided to phone his wife again. He arranged to meet her at 5:15 p.m. for her dinner break. Mr. Patterson picked up the laundry and then left the apartment a little before 5:00 p.m. to meet his wife.

The State also creates a favorable context. However, instead of starting its statement of facts by describing Patterson's actions, it begins the story where it started for the victim. In the first paragraph of its statement of facts, the State describes the assault and then the show-up and line-up.

EXAMPLE 2   **The First Paragraph of the State's Statement of Facts**

On Monday, August 12, 2013, Beatrice Martinez was assaulted with a deadly weapon. At a show-up held thirty to forty minutes after the attack, Ms. Martinez positively identified the defendant, Dean E. Patterson, as her assailant. Four days after the assault, Ms. Martinez picked Patterson out of a line-up, once again positively identifying him as her assailant.

---

b. Tell the Story from the Client's Point of View

One of the most powerful persuasive devices is point of view. In many cases, you will want to tell the story as your client would tell it.

One way of telling the story from your client's point of view is to make your client the "actor" in most of your sentences. Note how in the defendant's statement of facts, the writer has made Patterson or his wife the subject in most of the main clauses, while in the State's statement of facts, the writer has made Martinez the subject in most of the main clauses.

In the following examples, the subject of each sentence is in bold.

EXAMPLE 3   **Excerpt from Defendant's Statement of Facts**

At 7:30 on Monday morning, August 12, 2013, twenty-two-year-old **Dean Patterson** finished his shift as a security guard and walked to his apartment. After having breakfast with his wife, **Mr. Patterson** went to bed and slept until about 1:00 p.m. At about 2:30 p.m., **Mr. Patterson's wife** received a phone call asking her to work at the local hospital where she is employed as a nurse. She got ready, and **Mr. Patterson** dropped her off at the hospital at about 3:10 p.m. When he returned, **Mr. Patterson** could not find a parking place close to his apartment and had to park several blocks away.

At about 3:30 p.m., **Mr. Patterson** called his wife to find out how long she would have to work. **They** had plans to go to a movie that evening, and **he** wanted to know whether he should change those plans. At about 3:50 p.m., **Mr. Patterson** took a load of laundry to the apartment complex's laundry room. When he returned to his apartment, **Mr. Patterson** watched part of an old movie. At about 4:15 p.m., **Mr. Patterson** went back to the laundry room to put the clothes in the dryer. On his way back, he saw a parking spot in front of his apartment and moved his car, an older model red station wagon, to that spot. After parking his car, **Mr. Patterson** got out of the car and, because the driver's side door does not lock from the outside, walked to the passenger side to lock the doors. As he did so, **he** nodded to a parking enforcement officer who was driving by.

By this time, **it** was 4:30 p.m., and **Mr. Patterson** decided to phone his wife again. **He** arranged to meet her at 5:15 p.m. for her dinner break. **Mr. Patterson** picked up the laundry and then left the apartment a little before 5:00 p.m. to meet his wife.

EXAMPLE 4   **Excerpt from the State's Statement of Facts**

On Monday, August 12, 2013, **Beatrice Martinez** was assaulted with a deadly weapon. At a show-up held thirty to forty minutes after the attack, **Ms. Martinez** positively identified the defendant, Dean E. Patterson, as her assailant. Four days after the assault, **Ms. Martinez** picked Patterson out of a line-up, once again positively identifying him as her assailant.

---

c. Emphasize the Facts That Support Your Theory of the Case, and De-emphasize Those That Do Not

In addition to presenting the facts from the client's point of view, good advocates emphasize those facts that support their theory of the case and de-emphasize those that do not. They do this by using one or more of the following techniques.

1. Airtime

Just as listeners remember best the songs that get the most airtime, readers remember best the facts that get the most words. Consequently, favorable facts should be given considerable "airtime," and unfavorable ones should be given little or no "play." In the example case, if Patterson is going to persuade the court that the identifications are unreliable, he needs to de-emphasize the fact that Martinez saw the car twice. Although he cannot omit this fact, he does not need to give it very much airtime. In contrast, if the State is going to persuade the court that Martinez's identifications are reliable, it needs to emphasize the fact that she did see the car twice. Consequently, the State wants to give this fact as much airtime as possible. In the following examples, the relevant facts are in bold.

EXAMPLE 5　　**Excerpt from the Defendant's Statement of Facts**

Martinez has stated that she was walking down Belmont **when a car that had driven by earlier** pulled in front of her. The man got out of his car, took one or two steps toward Martinez and then pulled a gun from his pocket. As soon as she spotted the gun, Martinez screamed, looked away, and then, crying, ran across the street. The entire encounter was over in a second or two.

EXAMPLE 6　　**Excerpt from the State's Statement of Facts**

As she was walking north on Belmont, Ms. Martinez observed an older model red station wagon with a chrome luggage rack as it passed slowly by her. Moments later, the same car came down the street again. This time, the driver pulled his car in front of Ms. Martinez, stopping his car so that it blocked her path. As Ms. Martinez watched, the driver got out of his car and walked toward her. The man then took a gun from his coat pocket and pointed it at Ms. Martinez. Ms. Martinez looked at the gun, looked back up at her assailant, and then, crying, ran back across the street to safety.

---

2. Detail

Just as readers tend to remember best those facts that get the most airtime, they also tend to remember best those facts that are described in the most detail. The more detail, the more vivid the picture; the more vivid the picture, the more likely it is that the reader will remember the particular facts. Thus, airtime and detail work hand in hand. In contrast, to de-emphasize unfavorable facts, good advocates describe them in general terms.

Look again at the following examples, this time comparing the way in which the defendant and the State describe the assailant's car. By leaving out the description of the car, is the defendant setting out all of the legally significant facts? What inference does the State want the judge to draw from the fact that Ms. Martinez provided the police with a detailed description of her assailant's car?

| EXAMPLE 7 | Excerpt from the Defendant's Statement of Facts |

Martinez has stated that she was walking down Belmont when **a car** that had driven by earlier pulled in front of her. The man got out of his car, took one or two steps toward Martinez, and then pulled a gun from his pocket. As soon as she spotted the gun, Martinez screamed, looked away, and then, crying, ran across the street. The entire encounter was over in a second or two.

| EXAMPLE 8 | Excerpt from the State's Statement of Facts |

As she was walking north on Belmont, Ms. Martinez observed **an older model red station wagon with a chrome luggage rack as it passed slowly by her. Moments later, the same car came down the street again**. This time, the driver pulled his car in front of Ms. Martinez, stopping his car so that it blocked her path. As Ms. Martinez watched, the driver got out of his car and walked toward her. The man then took a gun from his coat pocket and pointed it at Ms. Martinez. Ms. Martinez looked at the gun, looked back up at her assailant, and then, crying, ran back across the street to safety.

3.   Positions of Emphasis

Because readers tend to remember best information that is placed in a position of emphasis (the beginning or end of a section, the beginning or end of a paragraph, and the beginning or end of a sentence), whenever possible, place the facts that you want to emphasize in one of these positions. Conversely, if you want to de-emphasize a fact, bury it in the middle — in the middle of a sentence, in the middle of a paragraph, or in the middle of a section.

In the following examples, the defendant wants to emphasize that Ms. Martinez told the police that her assailant was in his early forties. As a consequence, defense counsel places that fact near the end of the paragraph. In contrast, because the State wants to de-emphasize that fact, it places it in the middle of a sentence in the middle of a paragraph.

| EXAMPLE 9 | Excerpt from the Defendant's Statement of Facts |

Because she was upset, Martinez was able to give the police only a general description of her assailant. She described him as being a short, white male with blondish-brown hair who was wearing glasses and a dark jacket. In addition, **she told the police that her assailant was in his early forties. Mr. Patterson is twenty-two**.

| EXAMPLE 10 | Excerpt from the State's Statement of Facts |

Ms. Martinez told the police that her assailant was a white male who was about 5′7″ tall; that her assailant had wavy blondish-brown hair; **that her assailant appeared to be in his early forties**; and that at the time of the assault, her assailant was wearing a dark jacket and glasses.

In the next set of examples, the defendant wants to de-emphasize that he owns an older model red station wagon, while the State wants to emphasize that fact. In addition, because the State wants to de-emphasize that the gun found in Patterson's apartment was issued to him by his employer, it has placed that fact in the middle of a paragraph.

| **EXAMPLE 11** | **Excerpt from the Defendant's Statement of Facts** |

At about 3:50 p.m., Mr. Patterson took a load of laundry to the apartment complex's laundry room. When he returned to his apartment, Mr. Patterson watched part of an old movie. At about 4:15 p.m., Mr. Patterson went back to the laundry room to put the clothes in the dryer. On his way back, he saw a parking spot in front of his apartment and moved his car, **an older model red station wagon**, to that spot. After parking his car, Mr. Patterson got out of the car and, because the driver's side door does not lock from the outside, he walked to the passenger side to lock the doors. As he did so, he nodded to a parking enforcement officer who was driving by.

| **EXAMPLE 12** | **Excerpt from the State's Statement of Facts** |

Later that day, **the police searched Patterson's car—an older model red station wagon with a chrome luggage rack—and his apartment**. In the apartment, the police found the gun issued to Patterson by his employer. Four days later, the police held a line-up. Although Mr. Clipse did not identify Patterson, Ms. Martinez identified Patterson as the man who had approached her.

---

4. Sentence Length

Just as airtime and detail work together, so do positions of emphasis and sentence length. Because readers tend to remember information placed in shorter sentences better than information placed in longer sentences, good advocates place favorable facts in short sentences in a position of emphasis. For instance, in Example 13, not only did defense counsel place the favorable fact in a position of emphasis, but she also put that fact in a short sentence. In Example 14, the State not only buried the unfavorable fact in the middle of the paragraph, it also placed that fact in the middle of a long sentence.

| **EXAMPLE 13** | **Excerpt from the Defendant's Statement of Facts** |

Because she was upset, Martinez was able to give the police only a general description of her assailant. She described him as being a short, white male with blondish-brown hair who was wearing glasses and a dark jacket. In addition, she told police that her assailant was in his early forties. **Mr. Patterson is twenty-two**.

| **EXAMPLE 14** | **Excerpt from the State's Statement of Facts** |

Ms. Martinez told the police that her assailant was a white male who was about 5'7" tall; that her assailant had wavy blondish-brown hair; **that her assailant appeared to be in his early forties**; and that at the time of the assault, her assailant was wearing a dark jacket and glasses.

> **PRACTICE POINTER**
>
> Another way to emphasize a favorable fact is by highlighting discrepancies. For instance, in Example 13, defense counsel places the fact that the defendant is twenty-two next to the fact that Ms. Martinez told police that her assailant appeared to be in his early forties. By juxtaposing these two facts, defense counsel is able to highlight the discrepancies. In contrast, the prosecutor creates space between these two facts by putting the fact that Mr. Patterson is twenty-two in one paragraph and the fact that Ms. Martinez told police that her assailant was in his early forties in a different paragraph.

5.   Active and Passive Voice

Good advocates use the active voice when they want to emphasize what the actor did and the passive voice when they want to draw the reader's attention away from the actor's actions. Consider the following examples.

EXAMPLE 15   **Active Voice**

Patterson assaulted Martinez.

EXAMPLE 16   **Passive Voice**

Martinez was assaulted.

Because the State wants to emphasize that it was Patterson who assaulted Ms. Martinez, the prosecutor would use the language in Example 15. In contrast, because defense counsel states that Patterson is not the person who assaulted Ms. Martinez, she would use the language set out in Example 16. For more on the active and passive voice, see section 24.1.

6.   Dependent and Main Clauses

Another technique is to put favorable facts in the main clause and unfavorable facts in a dependent clause. While the defendant wants to emphasize the fact that the bystander, Clipse, was unable to make an identification and de-emphasize the fact that Martinez was able to make an identification, the State wants to do the opposite. Compare the following examples.

EXAMPLE 17   **Excerpt from the Defendant's Brief**

Later that day, the police searched Mr. Patterson's car and apartment. In the apartment, the police found the gun issued to Mr. Patterson by his employer. Four days later, the police held a line-up at the police station. **Although Martinez identified Mr. Patterson as the man who had approached her, Clipse did not pick Mr. Patterson out of the line-up.**

EXAMPLE 18　　**Excerpt from the State's Brief**

A line-up was held four days later. **Although Mr. Clipse was unable to identify the man who had assaulted Ms. Martinez, Ms. Martinez identified Patterson as her assailant.**

---

d.　Select Words Both for Their Denotation and Their Connotation

Words are powerful. Not only do they convey information (denotation), but they also create images (connotation). Consider, for example, the labels that might be used to describe Mr. Patterson:

> Mr. Dean Patterson
> Mr. Patterson
> Dean Patterson
> Patterson
> Dean
> the suspect
> the accused
> the defendant

While defense counsel would probably want to use "Mr. Patterson," "Dean Patterson," or "Patterson" in referring to her client, the prosecutor might use "the defendant." By using his name, defense counsel reminds the judge that her client is a real person. The title "Mr. Patterson" makes Patterson seem less like a person charged with a felony and more like an average, respectable citizen. In contrast, by using the label "the defendant," the State suggests that Patterson is guilty.

> **PRACTICE POINTER**　　Because legal proceedings are formal proceedings, as a general rule, do not refer to parties or to witnesses by just their first names. The only times that you might want to break this "rule" are when referring to a child (for example, the child in a juvenile case), or when there are two or more individuals with the same last name.

Other word choices can also subtly persuade the court. For instance, in the following paragraph the defendant wants to set up his argument that Officer Yuen's actions tainted the identifications. Accordingly, he uses "agreed" to suggest that Martinez's identification was prompted by Officer Yuen's questions, "questioned" to suggest that the officers' actions would have indicated to Martinez and Clipse that Patterson was guilty, and "watched" to remind the court that Martinez and Clipse may have been influenced by the officers' actions.

EXAMPLE 19　　**Excerpt from the State's Statement of Facts**

Even though Ms. Martinez was unable to see the man's face, she **agreed** with the officer that the man looked like her assailant. At this point, Officer Yuen stopped the car, got out, and approached Patterson. As Officer Yuen was **questioning** Patterson, Officer Cox drove up with the witness, Clipse.

While Ms. Martinez and Mr. Clipse **watched**, Officers Cox and Yuen **continued questioning** Patterson. Officer Cox then returned to Ms. Martinez and Mr. Clipse and walked them back to Clipse's apartment. While Officer Cox did so, Officer Yuen placed Patterson under arrest.

§ 17.6.4   Checklist for Critiquing the Statement of Facts

I. Organization

- The facts have been presented in a logical order (chronologically or topically or a combination of the two).
- When possible, the facts have been presented in an order that favors the client.

II. Content

- All of the legally significant facts have been included.
- The emotionally significant facts that favor the client have been included.
- An appropriate number of background facts have been included.

III. Persuasiveness

- The writer has presented the facts so that they support the writer's theory of the case.
- The writer has presented the facts in a favorable context.
- The writer has presented the facts from the point of view that favors the client. (In telling the client's story, the writer has used the client as the subject of most sentences.)
- The writer has emphasized favorable facts and de-emphasized unfavorable ones.
  - Favorable facts have been given more airtime than unfavorable facts.
  - Favorable facts have been described in detail; unfavorable facts have been described more generally.
  - The positions of emphasis have been used effectively. When possible, favorable facts have been placed at the beginning or end of the statement of facts, at the beginning or end of a paragraph, and at the beginning or end of a sentence.
  - Short sentences and short paragraphs have been used to emphasize favorable facts; unfavorable facts have been placed in longer sentences in longer paragraphs.
  - Active and passive voices have been used effectively.
  - Favorable information has been emphasized by placing it in the main, or independent, clause; unfavorable facts have been placed in dependent, or subordinate, clauses.
  - Words have been selected not only for their denotation but also for their connotation.
  - The writing is grammatically correct, correctly punctuated, and proofread.

§ 17.7   Drafting the Issue Statement

While you may not include an issue statement in all of your briefs, when you do include one, think carefully about how you want to frame the legal question. By asking the right question, you improve your chances of getting the result that your client wants.

§ 17.7.1   Select the Lens

The issue statement is the lens through which the judge views the case. Select the correct lens, and you improve your chances that the court will see the case as you see it and decide the motion in your client's favor. The difficulty, of course, is in selecting that lens. How do you select just the right one? Unfortunately, there is no easy answer. Because selecting the lens is, at least in part, a creative act, there is no foolproof formula.

There are, however, some strategies that you can use. First, think about your theory of the case. Given your theory, how should you frame the issue? Second, look at how the court framed the issues in cases that are similar to yours. In the cases in which the courts suppressed the evidence, how did the court frame the issue? Then look at the cases in which the courts did not suppress the evidence.

Finally, brainstorm. From what other angles can you view the case? What other labels can you attach? Think outside the box.

§ 17.7.2   Select a Format

Most courts do not prescribe a format for an issue statement. Although you should have the same number of issue statements as you have main argumentative headings, you can state the issue using the under-does-when format, the whether format, or the multi-sentence format. For more on the "under-does-when" format, see section 12.6.1; for more on the "whether" format, see section 13.6.1. In addition, in some jurisdictions and for some types of briefs, you can just set out the legal or factual question that you want the court to decide.

EXAMPLE 1   **"Under-Does-When" Format**

Under the Fourteenth Amendment, should the Court grant Mr. Patterson's motion to suppress Martinez's show-up and line-up identifications and both Martinez's and Clipse's in-court identifications when (1) a police officer pointed out Mr. Patterson to Martinez, repeatedly asking the shaken Martinez whether Mr. Patterson looked like her assailant; (2) the police questioned Mr. Patterson in front of Martinez and Clipse; (3) during the second or two that Martinez had to view her assailant, her attention was focused on his gun and not his face; and (4) Martinez told police that her assailant was in his forties, and Mr. Patterson is twenty-two?

EXAMPLE 2   **"Whether" Format**

Whether the Court should grant Mr. Patterson's motion to suppress Martinez's show-up and line-up investigations and both Martinez's and Clipse's in-court identifications when (1) a police officer pointed out Mr. Patterson to Martinez, repeatedly asking the shaken Martinez whether Mr. Patterson looked like her assailant; (2) the police questioned Mr. Patterson in front of Martinez and Clipse; (3) during the second or two that Martinez had to view her assailant, her attention was focused on his gun and not his face; and (4) Martinez told police that her assailant was in his forties, and Mr. Patterson is twenty-two.

EXAMPLE 3	Multi-Sentence Format

On August 12, 2013, a man jumped out of his car, approached Martinez, and pointed a gun at her. As soon as she saw the gun, Martinez screamed and, crying, ran across the street. Shortly after the assault, a police officer twice asked Martinez whether a pedestrian looked like her assailant. Although Martinez could not see the pedestrian's face, she agreed. The police then questioned the pedestrian, Mr. Dean Patterson, while Martinez and another witness watched. Both Martinez and the witness told the police that Martinez's assailant was in his late thirties or early forties. Mr. Patterson is twenty-two. Under these circumstances, should the Court suppress Martinez's show-up and line-up identifications and prevent Martinez and Clipse from making in-court identifications?

EXAMPLE 4	Issue Statement That Just Sets Out the Legal Question

Whether the Court should suppress Ms. Martinez's show-up and line-up identifications and prevent Martinez and Clipse from making in-court identifications.

EXAMPLE 5	Issue Statement That Just Sets Out the Legal Question

Should the court grant Mr. Patterson's motion to suppress?

PRACTICE POINTER

Once you select a format, use that format for each of your issue statements. Do not write one issue statement using the under-does-when format, a second issue statement using the whether format, and a third using the multi-sentence format. Also remember that you are not bound by opposing counsel's choices. You do not need to use the same format that he or she used, and you do not need to have the same number of issue statements. Do not let your opponent dictate your strategy.

§ 17.7.3   Make Your Issue Statement Subtly Persuasive

Your issue statement should be subtly persuasive. After reading it, the judge should be inclined to rule in your client's favor.

There are two techniques that you can use to make your issue statements persuasive. First, state the legal question so that it suggests the conclusion you want the court to reach. For example, if you want the court to grant the motion, ask whether the court should grant the motion. In contrast, if you want the court to deny the motion, ask whether the court should deny the motion. Second, when you include facts, present those facts in the light most favorable to your client.

For instance, in the example case, the defendant wants to state the legal question so that it suggests that the court should grant his motion to suppress. In contrast, the State wants to frame the question so that it suggests that the court should deny the defendant's motion.

EXAMPLE 6   **The Defendant's Statement of the Legal Question**

"Whether the Court should grant the motion to suppress when . . . ."

EXAMPLE 7   **The State's Statement of the Legal Question**

"Whether the Court should deny the motion to suppress when . . . ."

The defendant also wants to set out the facts so that they suggest that the police procedures were unnecessarily suggestive and that Martinez's identifications are unreliable. Accordingly, the defendant wants to set out the facts that establish that the procedure was suggestive. (Instead of allowing Martinez to identify Patterson independently, a police officer pointed out Patterson and repeatedly asked the shaken Martinez whether he looked like her assailant.) In addition, the defendant wants to set out facts that establish that Martinez had a limited opportunity to view her assailant and that her description was inaccurate. Note that in both instances the writers set out the facts related to the first part of the test first and then the facts related to the second part of the test.

EXAMPLE 8   **The Defendant's Issue Statement**

Under the Fourteenth Amendment, should the Court grant Mr. Patterson's motion to suppress Martinez's show-up identification (1) when a police officer pointed out Mr. Patterson to Martinez, repeatedly asking the shaken Martinez whether Ms. Patterson looked like her assailant; (2) when, during the second or two that Martinez had to view her assailant, her attention was focused on his gun and not his face; and (3) when Martinez told the police that her assailant was in his early forties, and Mr. Patterson is only twenty-two years old?

While the defendant wants to set out the facts that indicate that the police procedures were unnecessarily suggestive and that Martinez's identifications are unreliable, the State wants to downplay the police officer's questions and emphasize instead that Martinez had a good opportunity to view her assailant.

EXAMPLE 9   **The State's Issue Statement**

Should the Court deny the defendant's motion to suppress when the police merely asked the victim whether a pedestrian looked like her assailant and when the victim observed her assailant on two occasions for several seconds in broad daylight?

Thus, writing a persuasive issue statement is a three-step process. You must select the appropriate lens, choose a format, and then craft your issue statement so that it is subtly persuasive.

§17.7.4   Checklist for Critiquing the Issue Statement

I. Format

- There are the same number of issue statements as there are main argumentative headings.
- The writer has used one of the conventional formats: for example, the under-does-when format, the whether format, or the multi-sentence format.
- The same format has been used for each issue statement.

II. Content

- The issue statement states the legal question and includes references to the legally significant facts. In addition, when appropriate, it also includes a reference to the rule of law.
- The legal questions have been framed so that they support the writer's theory of the case.

III. Persuasiveness

- The legal question has been framed so that it suggests an answer favorable to the client.
- Favorable facts have been emphasized, and unfavorable ones de-emphasized.
- Words have been selected for both their denotation and their connotation.

IV. Writing

- The judge can understand the issue statement after reading it through once.
- Punctuation has been used to divide the issue statement into manageable units of meaning.
- When appropriate, parallel constructions have been used.
- In both the main and subordinate clauses, the subjects and verbs are close together.
- The issue statement is grammatically correct, correctly punctuated, and proofread.

Chapter 17 Quiz No. 1

Draft answers for each of the following questions. Make your points clearly and concisely, and write sentences that are easy to read and that are grammatical and correctly punctuated.

1. How is the statement of facts for a motion brief the same as the statement of facts for a formal memo? How is it different?
2. How is an issue statement for a motion brief the same as an issue statement in a formal memo? How is it different?

3. What is one way to give favorable facts more airtime?
4. In an issue statement, what are the positions of emphasis?
5. In selecting a word, what should you consider?

§ 17.8 Ordering the Issues and Arguments

§ 17.8.1 Present the Issues and Arguments in a Logical Order

In many cases, logic dictates the order of both the issues and, under each issue, the arguments. Threshold questions (for example, issues relating to whether the court has jurisdiction or to the statute of limitations) must be discussed before questions relating to the merits of the case. Similarly, the parts of a test must be discussed in the correct order and, when one argument builds on another, the foundation argument must be presented first.

Although in the example case there is only one issue — whether the court should grant the defendant's motion to suppress — under that issue are several subissues. The court must decide (1) whether to suppress Martinez's show-up identification, (2) whether to suppress Martinez's line-up identification, and (3) whether to suppress any in-court identifications that Martinez or Clipse might make.

Logic dictates, at least in part, the order in which these three subissues should be discussed. Because an impermissibly suggestive show-up would taint the line-up and in-court identifications, the attorneys would discuss the show-up before the line-up and both the show-up and the line-up before the in-court identifications.

Logic also dictates the order of the arguments. Before it can suppress an identification, the court must find (1) that the police procedures were impermissibly suggestive and (2) that, under the totality of the circumstances, the resulting identifications are unreliable. Consequently, the defendant must discuss suggestiveness first.

In deciding whether an identification is reliable, the court considers five factors: (1) the witness's opportunity to see her assailant, (2) the witness's degree of attention, (3) the accuracy of the witness's description, (4) the witness's level of certainty, and (5) the length of time between the crime and the confrontation. Does logic dictate that these factors be discussed in any particular order?

§ 17.8.2 Decide Which Issues and Arguments Should Be Presented First

First impressions count. As a consequence, when logic does not dictate the order of your issues or arguments, put your strongest issues and your strongest arguments first. In addition, some attorneys like to end their brief with a strong argument. Although this strategy allows you to take advantage of the positions of emphasis, it also creates a risk. If the judge does not finish your brief or starts skimming, he or she might not see one of your strongest arguments.

§ 17.9   Drafting the Argumentative Headings

§ 17.9.1 Use Your Argumentative Headings to Define the Structure of the Argument

Just as posts and beams define the form of a building, argumentative headings define the form of the argument. When drafted properly, they provide the judge with an outline of the argument.

EXAMPLE 1   **Defendant's Argumentative Headings**

I. THE COURT SHOULD GRANT MR. PATTERSON'S MOTION TO SUPPRESS MARTINEZ'S SHOW-UP AND LINE-UP IDENTIFICATIONS AND MARTINEZ'S AND CLIPSE'S IN-COURT IDENTIFICATIONS.

> [Put general rules here.]

A. Martinez's show-up identification should be suppressed because the police procedures were impermissibly suggestive and because Martinez's identification is unreliable.

> [Set out the two-part test.]

  1. The police procedures were impermissibly suggestive because the police officer repeatedly asked Martinez whether Mr. Patterson looked like her assailant and because the officers questioned Mr. Patterson in Martinez's presence.

> [Set out argument.]

  2. Martinez's identification is unreliable because Martinez was able to view her assailant for only a few seconds, her attention was focused on the gun and not his face, and her description of her assailant does not match the description of Mr. Patterson.

> [Set out argument.]

B. Martinez's line-up identification should be suppressed because it was tainted by the show-up.

> [Set out argument.]

C. Martinez and Clipse should not be permitted to make in-court identification because those identificants would be tainted by the impermissibly suggestive show-up and the line-up.

> [Set out argument.]

In addition to defining the structure of the argument, argumentative headings also act as locators. By using the headings and subheadings, a judge can locate a particular argument.

> **PRACTICE POINTER**   Argumentative headings also help the writer. As a practicing attorney, you will seldom have large blocks of time available for writing. Instead, you will have to squeeze in an hour here and two hours there. If you prepare your argumentative headings first, you can use those blocks to write a section at a time.

§ 17.9.2 Use Your Argumentative Headings to Persuade

In addition to using argumentative headings to define the structure of your argument, use the headings to persuade.

Begin your heading by setting out a positive assertion. If you want the court to grant your motion to suppress, make that assertion: "The Court should grant the motion to suppress . . . ." In contrast, if you want the court to deny the motion to suppress, make that assertion: "The Court should deny the motion to suppress . . . ."

EXAMPLE 2   **Not Effective: Not a Positive Assertion**

The Court should not grant the motion to suppress . . . .

The Court should not suppress Martinez's show-up identification . . . .

EXAMPLE 3   **Effective: Positive Assertion**

The Court should deny the motion to suppress . . . .

The Court should admit Martinez's show-up identification . . . .

After setting out your assertion, you will usually want to set out the facts or reasons that support your assertion. The most common format is as follows:

Assertion	because	facts or reasons that support your assertion
Martinez's line-up identification should be suppressed	because	it was tainted by the impermissibly suggestive show-up.

In those instances in which you do not set out the reasons in your heading, use subheadings or sub-subheadings to set out the reasons. Look again at the headings and subheadings in the defendant's argumentative headings. Although the writer has not included a "because" clause in the main heading, she has included them in the subheadings and sub-subheadings.

EXAMPLE 4   **Defendant's Argumentative Headings**

I. THE COURT SHOULD GRANT MR. PATTERSON'S MOTION TO SUPPRESS MARTINEZ'S SHOW-UP AND LINE-UP IDENTIFICATIONS AND MARTINEZ'S AND CLIPSE'S IN-COURT IDENTIFICATIONS.

[Put general rules here.]

A. <u>Martinez's show-up identification should be suppressed because the police procedures were impermissibly suggestive and because Martinez's identification is unreliable.</u>

[Set out two-part test.]

1. The police procedures were impermissibly suggestive because the police officer repeatedly asked Martinez whether Patterson looked like her assailant and because the officers questioned Patterson in Martinez's presence.

   [Set out argument.]

2. Martinez's identification is unreliable because Martinez was able to view her assailant for only a few seconds, her attention was focused on the gun and not his face, and her description of her assailant does not match the description of Mr. Patterson.

   [Set out argument.]

B. <u>Martinez's line-up identification should be suppressed because it was tainted by the show-up.</u>

   [Set out argument.]

C. <u>Martinez should not be permitted to make an in-court identification because such an identification would be tainted by the impermissibly suggestive show-up and the line-up.</u>

   [Set out argument.]

§ 17.9.3   Make Your Headings Readable

If the judge does not read your headings, they do not serve either of their functions: They do not provide the judge with an outline of your argument, and they do not persuade. To make sure that your headings are read by the judge, keep them short and make them easy to read. As a general rule, your headings should be no more than three typed lines.

In the following example, the writer has tried to put too much information in her heading. As a result, the heading is too long, and the sentence is difficult to understand.

EXAMPLE 5   **Heading Is Too Long**

A. <u>The police procedures were impermissibly suggestive because the witness viewed only one person, the police repeatedly asked the witness whether that person looked like her assailant, and the police questioned the person in front of the witness, and because the person was simply walking down the street and not trying to escape, and the witness was not likely to die or disappear, there was no reason to conduct a one-person show-up.</u>

The following heading is much better. Instead of trying to put her entire argument into her heading, the writer has included only her most important points.

EXAMPLE 6   **Heading Is Shorter and Easier To Understand**

A. <u>The police procedures were impermissibly suggestive because the police officer repeatedly asked Martinez whether Mr. Patterson looked like her assailant and because the officers questioned Mr. Patterson in Martinez's and Clipse's presence.</u>

§ 17.9.4 Follow the Conventions: Number, Placement, and Typefaces

By convention, you should have one, and only one, main argumentative heading for each issue statement. You set out the question in your issue statement and answer the question in the corresponding main heading. Although subheadings and sub-subheadings are optional, if you include one, you should have at least two. You might or might not elect to include text between the main heading and the first subheading or between a subheading and the first sub-subheading.

> **PRACTICE POINTER**
>
> Historically, only three typefaces were used. When briefs were prepared using typewriters, the main headings were set out using all capital letters, the subheadings were underlined, and the sub-subheadings were set out using regular typeface. Although many attorneys still use this system, others have adopted different systems, for example, setting out the main headings in bold rather than all capitals. Check with your local court and firm to see what is commonly done in your jurisdiction.

EXAMPLE 7   **Typefaces for Main Heading, Subheadings, and Sub-Subheadings**

I.   FIRST MAIN HEADING [Answers question set out in first issue statement.]
     [If appropriate, set out introductory paragraph and general rules here.]

     A.   <u>First subheading</u>
          [If appropriate, set out test here.]
          1.   First sub-subheading
               [Set out argument here.]
          2.   Second sub-subheading
               [Set out argument here.]
     B.   <u>Second subheading</u>
          [Set out argument here.]

II. SECOND MAIN HEADING [If you had two issue statements, answers question set out in the second issue statement.]
     A.   <u>First subheading</u>
          [Set out argument here.]
     B.   <u>Second subheading</u>
          [Set out argument here.]
     C.   <u>Third subheading</u>
          [Set out argument here.]

§ 17.9.5   Checklist for Critiquing the Argumentative Headings

I. Content

- When read together, the headings provide the judge with an outline of the argument.

II. Persuasiveness

- Each heading is in the form of a positive assertion.
- Each assertion is supported, either in the main heading or through the use of subheadings.
- The headings are case-specific — that is, they include references to the parties and the facts of the case.
- Favorable facts are emphasized, and unfavorable facts are de-emphasized or omitted if not legally significant.
- Favorable facts have been placed in the positions of emphasis.
- Favorable facts have been given more airtime than unfavorable facts.
- Words have been selected both for their denotation and their connotation.

III. Conventions

- The writer has used different typefaces for main headings, subheadings, and sub-subheadings.
- There is never just one subheading or just one sub-subheading.

IV. Writing

- The judge can understand the heading after reading it through once. (As a general rule, headings are not more than three lines long.)
- Punctuation has been used to divide the heading into manageable units of meaning.
- When appropriate, parallel constructions have been used.
- In both the main and subordinate clauses, the subject and verb are close together.
- The headings are grammatically correct, correctly punctuated, and proofread.

§ 17.10   Drafting the Arguments

Most of us have had arguments. As children, we fought with our parents over cleaning our rooms or over how late we could stay out. As adults, we have fought with friends, roommates, spouses, and partners over household chores, budgets, and world events.

Although most of us have had arguments, very few of us have been taught how to make arguments. We know how to express our anger and frustration; we do not know how to set out an assertion and then systematically walk our listener through our "proof." Even fewer of us have been taught how to set out our proofs persuasively.

It is, however, exactly these skills — the ability to set out an assertion, to walk your reader through your proof, and to present that proof persuasively — that you will need to develop if you are going to write an effective brief. Good advocates have the mental discipline of a mathematician. They think linearly, identifying each of the steps in the analysis, and then walk the judge through those steps in a logical order. They also have the creativity and insight of an advertising executive. They know their "market," and they know both the image they want to create and how to use language to create it. In short, they have mastered both the science and the art of advocacy.

§ 17.10.1 Identify Your Assertions and Your Support for Those Assertions

An argument has two parts: an assertion and the support for that assertion.

a. Setting Out Your Assertion

An assertion can take one of two forms. It can be procedural — setting out the procedural act you want the court to take — or it can be substantive — setting out the legal conclusion you want the court to reach.

EXAMPLE 1   **Types of Assertions**

Procedural

The Court should grant the motion to suppress.

The Court should deny the motion to suppress.

Substantive

The police procedures were impermissibly suggestive.

The witness's identification is reliable.

---

b. Supporting Your Assertion

Although your assertion is an essential part of your argument, it is not, by itself, an argument. How many judges would be persuaded by the following exchange?

Defense counsel:	Your Honor, the Court should grant Mr. Patterson's motion to suppress.
Prosecutor:	Your Honor, we respectfully disagree. The Court should deny the motion.
Defense counsel:	No, Your Honor, the Court should grant the motion.
Prosecutor:	No. The Court should deny the motion.

An exchange in which the defendant asserts that the police procedures were impermissibly suggestive and the prosecutor asserts that they were not is equally unpersuasive. Standing alone, assertions do not persuade. They must be supported.

In law, that support can take one of several forms. You can support an assertion by citing to the constitution; by applying a statute or common law rule to the facts of your case; by comparing or contrasting the facts in your case to the facts in analogous cases; or by explaining why, as a matter of public policy, the court should rule in your client's favor.

In Example 2 below, defense counsel supports her assertion by applying the rule to the facts of Mr. Patterson's case. In Example 3, the defense counsel supports her assertion by comparing the facts in Mr. Patterson's case to the facts in the analogous cases, and in Example 4, she supports her assertion by using public policy.

| EXAMPLE 2 | **Defendant Supports His Assertion by Applying the Rules to the Facts of His Case** |

Assertion: The police procedures were impermissibly suggestive.

Support: Rule: One-person show-ups are inherently suggestive. *See Neil v. Biggers*, 409 U.S. 188, 199, 93 S. Ct. 375, 34 L. Ed. 2d 401 (1972).[1] When the police present the witness with a single suspect, the witness usually infers that the police believe that the person being presented committed the crime. *Id.*

Application: In this case, the police presented Martinez with a single suspect: Dean Patterson. In doing so, the police suggested to Martinez that Mr. Patterson was the man who had assaulted her.

| EXAMPLE 3 | **Defendant Supports His Assertion by Comparing the Facts in His Case with the Facts in an Analogous Case** |

Assertion: The police procedures were impermissibly suggestive.

Support: Analogous case: *In State v. Booth*, 36 Wn. App. 66, 67-68, 671 P.2d 1218 (1983), the police brought the witness to the scene of the arrest and showed him a single suspect, who was sitting with his back to the witness in the back seat of the police car. The court held that the police procedures were impermissibly suggestive. *Id.* at 70.

Application: As in *Booth*, in our case the police showed the witness a single suspect and asked her to identify him before she had an opportunity to see his face. The only difference between the two cases is the identity of the person in the police car. While in *Booth* it was the suspect who was in the car, in our case it was the witness.

---

1. Because the briefs will be filed in a Washington court, the attorneys have used Washington's citation rules. See http://www.courts.wa.gov/appellate_trial_courts/supreme/?fa=atc_supreme .style.

EXAMPLE 4	Example 4 The Defendant Supports His Assertion by Using Public Policy

Assertion: The police procedures were impermissibly suggestive.

Support: Policy: To protect the rights of defendants, the courts should suppress unreliable identifications.

Application: Because Martinez's identifications are unreliable, Mr. Patterson will be denied his right to a fair trial if Martinez's show-up and line-up identifications are admitted.

If there is only one argument that supports your assertion, make that argument. If, however, you can make several different arguments, think about whether you want to include all of those arguments. Will your brief be more persuasive if you set out only one strong argument, or will it be more persuasive if you set out three, four, or five arguments? Identifying the arguments is the science; deciding which arguments to include is the art.

§ 17.10.2 Select an Organizational Scheme

In making their arguments, most advocates use one of two types of reasoning: deductive or inductive. When you use deductive reasoning, you set out your assertion and then the support for that assertion. In contrast, when you use inductive reasoning, you set out your support first, and then walk the judge through your support to your conclusion.

EXAMPLE 5	Deductive Reasoning

Assertion: The identification is not reliable.

Support: The identification is not reliable because Martinez viewed her assailant for only three or four seconds.

The identification is not reliable because Martinez's attention was focused on the gun and not on her assailant's face.

The identification is not reliable because Martinez's description of her assailant was inaccurate.

The identification is not reliable because, at least initially, Martinez was not certain that Mr. Patterson was her assailant.

EXAMPLE 6	Inductive Reasoning

Support: Martinez viewed her assailant for only three or four seconds.

Martinez's attention was focused on the gun and not on her assailant's face.

Martinez's description of her assailant was inaccurate.

At least initially, Martinez was not certain that Mr. Patterson was her assailant.

Conclusion: Because Martinez viewed her assailant for only three or four seconds, because her attention was focused on the gun and not on her assailant's face, because her description of her assailant was inaccurate, and because, at least initially, she was not certain that Mr. Patterson was her assailant, Martinez's identification is not reliable.

If you use deductive reasoning, you will usually use a version of the following template. Note the similarities between this template and the templates that you use to organize the discussion section in an objective memo. Also note that the following example shows two different ways of setting out the arguments. Under the first subheading, the assertion is set out first. Under the second subheading, the assertion is set out after the rules and the descriptions of the cases. You should use whichever format is, in your case, most likely to be effective.

EXAMPLE 7   **Template for an Argument Using Deductive Reasoning**

I. MAIN HEADING
    [Test set out in the light most favorable to your client.]

    A. First subheading
        1. Assertion
        2. Rules set out in the light most favorable to your client
        3. Descriptions of the analogous cases
        4. Your arguments
        5. Your response to your opponent's arguments

    B. Second subheading
        1. Rules set out in the light most favorable to your client
        2. Descriptions of the analogous cases
        3. Assertion
        4. Your arguments
        5. Your response to your opponent's arguments

When you use inductive reasoning, you will usually integrate the rules, the descriptions of the cases, and your response to the other side's arguments into each of your arguments.

EXAMPLE 8   **Template for an Argument Using Inductive Reasoning**

I. MAIN HEADING

    A. First subheading
        1. First argument
        2. Second argument
        3. Third argument
        4. Fourth argument
        5. Conclusion

　　B.　Second subheading
　　　　1.　First argument
　　　　2.　Second argument
　　　　3.　Third argument
　　　　4.　Conclusion

There are also several other organizational schemes that you may use. For example, if in your case the facts are your best argument, start by setting out the facts. Then show how those facts are similar to the facts in cases in which the court reached the conclusion you want the court to reach.

EXAMPLE 9　　**Facts Set Out First**

　I.　MAIN HEADING
　　　[Test set out in the light most favorable to your client.]

　　A.　First subheading
　　　　1.　Facts of your case
　　　　2.　Comparison of the facts in your case to the facts in analogous cases
　　　　3.　Courts' holdings in analogous cases
　　　　4.　Response to other side's arguments
　　　　5.　Conclusion

In the following example, defense counsel used the "facts-first" strategy in arguing that the show-up was impermissibly suggestive. Because none of the cases supported her position, defense counsel began her argument by setting out her assertion and the facts that support that assertion.

EXAMPLE 10　　**Excerpt from the Defendant's Brief**

　　A.　<u>The police procedures were unnecessarily suggestive because the police showed Martinez a single suspect, asked Martinez whether the suspect looked like her assailant, and questioned the suspect in front of Martinez.</u>

In this case, Officer Yuen's actions suggested to Martinez that he believed Mr. Patterson was her assailant.

While driving Martinez home, Officer Yuen pulled up behind Mr. Patterson and asked Martinez whether Mr. Patterson looked like her assailant. When Martinez did not respond, Officer Yuen repeated his question, asking "Does that look like your assailant?"

Although Martinez could not see Mr. Patterson's face, after hesitating, she agreed with Officer Yuen that Mr. Patterson looked like her assailant. At that point, Officer Yuen pulled up behind Mr. Patterson, got out of the police car, and began questioning him. A few minutes later, Officer Cox and Clipse arrived, and both Officer Yuen and Officer Cox questioned Mr. Patterson while Martinez and Clipse watched.

Thus, this case can be distinguished from *State v. Kraus*, 21 Wn. App. at 392, in which the show-up identification occurred during a prompt search for the robber. In this case the show-up did not occur while the police were searching for Martinez's assailant. Instead, it occurred while the officer was driving Martinez home. In addition, unlike *Stovall*, 388 U.S. at 302, in which the police held the show-up because they were concerned that the suspect might die, in this case, there were no exigent circumstances. In fact, because the police had located a car that matched the description of the one driven by the assailant, they could have identified the owner of the car and any individuals who had driven it and placed them in a line-up.

In contrast, if your best argument is an argument based on an analogous case, start by describing that case.

EXAMPLE 11	**Excerpt from the State's Brief**

A. <u>Merely asking the victim whether a pedestrian looks like her assailant does not make a permissible show-up impermissibly suggestive.</u>

There are no published Washington cases in which the courts have held that a show-up was impermissibly suggestive. Instead, in a Division I case, the court held that the show-up was not impermissibly suggestive when the police picked up the witness at a tavern and told him that they wanted to take him back to his apartment to see if he could identify his assailant. *State v. Rogers*, 44 Wn. App. 510, 515-16, 722 P.2d 1249 (1986). When the witness, an elderly individual who was not wearing his glasses, arrived back at his apartment, he identified the defendant when the defendant came out of the building. *Id.* There was a uniformed police officer in front of the defendant and another uniformed police officer following behind him. *Id.*

Similarly, in *State v. Booth*, 36 Wn. App. 66, 70-71, 671 P.2d 1218 (1983), the court held that the show-up was not impermissibly suggestive when the police asked the witness to accompany them to the place where the defendant had been arrested, and the witness identified the defendant after seeing him in the back of a police car. *Id.* at 67-68; *accord State v. Guzman-Cuellar*, 47 Wn.2d 326, 734 P.2d 966 (1987) (show-up not impermissibly suggestive when the defendant was shown to three of the four eyewitnesses while he was in handcuffs standing next to a police car).

Although you want to set out the pieces of your argument in the order that the judge expects to see them, you also want to emphasize your best arguments. Therefore, instead of using a format mechanically, use it creatively to accomplish your purpose.

PRACTICE POINTER	Initially, you may be frustrated by the fact that there are no rules for selecting issues or arguments or set formats for organizing your arguments. However, with time, you will learn to enjoy exercising your judgment and creativity.

§17.10.3 Present the Rules in the Light Most Favorable to Your Client

Although the structure of the argument section is similar to the structure of the discussion section, the way in which you present the rules is very different. While in an objective memo you set out the rules objectively, in a brief you set them out in the light most favorable to your client. Without misrepresenting the rules, you want to "package" them so that they support your assertion.

To set out the rules in the light most favorable to your client, use one or more of the techniques set out in the following box.

Techniques for Presenting the
Rules in a Light Favorable to Your Client

A. Create a favorable context.
B. State favorable rules as broadly as possible and unfavorable rules as narrowly as possible.
C. Emphasize favorable rules and de-emphasize unfavorable rules.
   1. Emphasize the burden of proof if the other side has the burden; de-emphasize the burden of proof if you have the burden.
   2. Give favorable rules more airtime and unfavorable rules less airtime.
   3. Place favorable rules in a position of emphasis and bury unfavorable ones.
   4. Place favorable rules in short sentences or in the main clause, and place unfavorable rules in longer sentences or in dependent clauses.
D. Select your words carefully.

Compare the following examples, identifying the techniques that the writers used.

EXAMPLE 12   **Objective Statement of the Rule**

In deciding whether identification testimony is admissible, the courts apply a two-part test. Under the first part of the test, the defendant must prove that the police procedures were impermissibly suggestive. If the court finds that the procedure was impermissibly suggestive, the State then has the burden of showing that, under the totality of the circumstances, the reliability of the identification outweighs the suggestive police procedure. *Manson v. Braithwaite*, 432 U.S. 98, 108, 97 S. Ct. 2243, 53 L. Ed. 2d 140 (1977).

EXAMPLE 13   **Rules Stated in the Light Most Favorable to the Defendant**

The United States Supreme Court has developed a two-part test to ensure a criminal defendant the procedural due process guaranteed to every individual by the Fourteenth Amendment. *Manson v. Braithwaite*, 432 U.S. 98, 108, 97 S. Ct. 2243, 53 L. Ed. 2d 140 (1977).

Under the first part of the test, the defendant need show only that the identification that he seeks to suppress was obtained through the use of unnecessarily suggestive police procedures. *Id.* Once this has been established, the onus shifts to the State to prove that, under the totality of the circumstances, the witness's identification is so reliable that it should be admitted even though it was obtained through unnecessarily suggestive means. *Id.*

EXAMPLE 14	Rules Stated in the Light Most Favorable to the State

Identifications should not be kept from the jury unless the procedures used in obtaining the identifications were so suggestive and unreliable that a substantial likelihood of irreparable misidentification exists. *Perry v. New Hampshire*, __ U.S. ___, 132 S. Ct. 716, 720, 181 L. Ed. 2d 694 (2012); *Simmons v. United States*, 390 U.S. 377, 384, 89 S. Ct. 1127, 22 L. Ed. 2d 402 (1969).

In deciding whether identification evidence is admissible, the courts employ a two-part test. Under the first part of the test, the defendant has the burden of proving that the identification evidence that he or she seeks to suppress was obtained through impermissibly suggestive procedures. *Manson v. Braithwaite*, 432 U.S. 98, 113, 97 S. Ct. 2243, 53 L. Ed. 2d 140 (1977). Only if the defendant satisfies this substantial burden is the second part of the test applied. *Id.*

Even if the court determines that the police procedures were impermissibly suggestive, the evidence is admissible if, under the totality of the circumstances, the identifications are reliable. *Perry v. New Hampshire*, 132 S. Ct. at 720; *Simmons v. United States*, 390 U.S. at 384. Due process does not compel the exclusion of an identification if it is reliable. *Id.* Identifications should not be kept from the jury unless the procedures used in obtaining the identifications were so suggestive and unreliable that a substantial likelihood of irreparable misidentification exists. *Simmons v. United States*, 390 U.S. at 384.

Let's begin by comparing the opening sentences of all three examples. In Example 15, the writer simply states that the court applies a two-part test. There is no attempt to create a favorable context.

EXAMPLE 15	Objective Statement of the Rule

In deciding whether identification testimony is admissible, the courts apply a two-part test.

In contrast, in Examples 16 and 17, the writers package the rule, using policy to create a context that favors their respective clients. The key language is in boldface type.

EXAMPLE 16	Rules Stated in the Light Most Favorable to the Defendant

The United States Supreme Court has developed a two-part test to ensure a criminal **defendant the procedural due process guaranteed to every individual by the Fourteenth Amendment**.

EXAMPLE 17	Rules Stated in the Light Most Favorable to the State

Identifications should not be kept from the jury unless the procedures used in obtaining the identifications were so suggestive and unreliable that a substantial likelihood of irreparable misidentification exists.

In addition to creating a favorable context, the parties have emphasized or de-emphasized the burden of proof depending on whether they have the burden or the other side has the burden. Compare the highlighted passages.

EXAMPLE 18   **Objective Statement of the Rule**

Under the first part of the test, **the defendant must prove** that the police procedures were impermissibly suggestive.

EXAMPLE 19   **Rules Stated in the Light Most Favorable to the Defendant**

Under the first part of the test, **the defendant need show** only that the identification that he seeks to suppress was obtained through the use of unnecessarily suggestive police procedures.

EXAMPLE 20   **Rules Stated in the Light Most Favorable to the State**

Under the first part of the test, **the defendant has the burden of proving** that the identification evidence he seeks to suppress was obtained through impermissibly suggestive procedures.

Similarly, both sides try to lead the court to the desired conclusions. Defense counsel presumes that the defendant will meet his burden; the State presents the second part of the test as an alternative. Even if the State loses on the first part of the test, it wins on the second. Once again, in excerpts from earlier Examples 16 and 17 the key language is in boldface type.

EXAMPLE 21   **Rules Stated in the Light Most Favorable to the Defendant**

Once this has been established, the onus shifts to the State to prove that, under the totality of the circumstances, the witness's identification is so reliable that it should be admitted even though it was obtained through unnecessarily suggestive means.

EXAMPLE 22   **Rules Stated in the Light Most Favorable to the State**

In deciding whether identification evidence is admissible, the courts employ a two-part test. Under the first part of the test, the defendant has the burden of proving that the identification evidence that he or she seeks to suppress was obtained through impermissibly suggestive procedures. *Manson v. Braithwaite*, 432 U.S. 98, 113, 97 S. Ct. 2243, 53 L. Ed. 2d 140. **Only if the defendant satisfies this substantial burden is the second part of the test applied**. *Id.*

Even if the court determines that the police procedures were impermissibly suggestive, the evidence is admissible if, under the totality of the circumstances, the identifications are reliable. *Simmons v. United States*, 390 U.S. at 384. Due process does not compel the exclusion of an identification if it is reliable. *Id.*

Finally, look at the words that each side uses:

Defendant	State
ensure	so suggestive
guaranteed	burden
onus shifts	substantial burden
so reliable	compel

Instead of using the language they saw in the cases or the first word that came to mind, each side selected its words carefully, with the goal of subtly influencing the decision-making process.

> **PRACTICE POINTER**
> If you are having a hard time coming up with just the right word, look for alternative words using the thesaurus that is on your computer.

§ 17.10.4 Present the Cases in the Light Most Favorable to Your Client

When you use analogous cases to support your argument, present those cases in the light most favorable to your client. If a case supports your position, emphasize the similarities between the facts in the analogous case and the facts in your case. On the other hand, if a case does not support your position, emphasize the differences.

In the example case, both sides use *State v. Booth*, 36 Wn. App. 66, 671 P.2d 1218 (1983), a case in which the court held that the identification was reliable. The relevant portion of the court's opinion is set out in Example 23.

EXAMPLE 23   **Excerpt From *State v. Booth***

"The facts provide several indicia of reliability. Ms. Thomas was driving slowly, it was a clear day, and she observed Booth for approximately forty-five seconds. Her attention was greater than average because he had money in his hands and was running. In addition, her attention was particularly drawn to the car with Missouri plates because she had lived in Missouri. Finally, the identification took place thirty to forty minutes later and was unequivocal. On the basis of these facts we find that reliability outweighed the harm of suggestiveness and the identification was properly admitted."

Because the court found that the identification was reliable, the defendant wants to distinguish *Booth*. As a consequence, in discussing opportunity to view, the defendant wants to emphasize that in *Booth* the witness viewed the defendant for almost a minute, while in our case the witness viewed her assailant for only a few seconds.

EXAMPLE 24   **Excerpt From The Defendant's Brief**

An identification will not be found to be reliable unless the witness had an adequate opportunity to view the defendant. This was the situation in *Booth*. In that case, a bystander was able to view the defendant for almost a minute. *Id.* at 70. Because she was able to view the defendant for an extended period of time under good conditions, the court concluded that her identification was reliable. *Id.* In contrast, in our case Martinez viewed her assailant for only three or four seconds.

Conversely, the State wants to emphasize the similarities between the facts in its case and the facts in *Booth*. Thus, it tries to minimize the amount of time that the witness had to view the defendant.

EXAMPLE 25   **Excerpt from the State's Brief**

The courts do not require that the witness have viewed the defendant for an extended period of time. For example, in *Booth*, the court found the witness's identification was reliable even though the witness had viewed the defendant for less than a minute. *Id.* at 70.

---

§ 17.10.5 Present the Arguments in the Light Most Favorable to Your Client

In addition to presenting the rules and analogous cases in the light most favorable to your client, you also want to set out the arguments in the light most favorable to your client. As a general rule, set out your own arguments first, give your own arguments the most airtime, and use language that strengthens your arguments and undermines the other side's arguments.

a.   Present Your Own Arguments First

You should almost always set out your own arguments first. By doing so, you can take advantage of the position of emphasis, emphasizing your argument and de-emphasizing the other side's arguments.

The following example shows what you do *not* want to do. By setting out the defendant's assertions, the State gives the defendant's arguments extra airtime. The court gets to read the defendant's argument in the defendant's brief and then again in the State's brief.

EXAMPLE 26   **Excerpt from the State's Brief: Ineffective**

The defendant argues that the police procedures were impermissibly suggestive because the police showed Martinez a single suspect, Patterson, and because they asked Martinez whether Patterson looked like her assailant.

It is our contention that the police procedures were not impermissibly suggestive. One-person show-ups are not per se impermissibly suggestive; if the show-up occurs shortly after the commission of the crime during a search for the suspect, it is permissible. *See State v. Booth*, 36 Wn. App. 66, 70-71, 671 P.2d 1218 (1983).

The following example is substantially better. Instead of starting its arguments by setting out the defendant's assertions, the State starts by setting out a favorable statement of the rule. It then sets out its own argument, integrating its responses to the defendant's arguments into its own arguments.

| EXAMPLE 27 | Excerpt from the State's Brief: More Effective |

One-person show-ups are not per se impermissibly suggestive: A show-up is permissible if it occurs shortly after the commission of a crime during a search for the suspect. *See State v. Booth*, 36 Wn. App. 66, 70-71, 671 P.2d 1218 (1983).

In this case, the show-up occurred within forty-five minutes of the assault. It also occurred before the police officers had completed their investigation: Officer Yuen saw Patterson as he was leaving the crime scene to take Ms. Martinez home.

Under these circumstances, Officer Yuen would not have been doing his job if, upon seeing a man who matched the assailant's description, he had not asked Ms. Martinez whether the man looked like her assailant. The officer's question, "Is that the man?" was not enough to turn a permissible show-up into one that was impermissibly suggestive.

b.   Give the Most Airtime to Your Own Arguments

Most of the time, you will want to give more airtime to your own arguments than you do to the other side's arguments. Your goal is to respond to or counter the other side's arguments without giving them too much airtime. Compare the following examples. In the first example, the State gives too much airtime to the defendant's age. In the second, the State counters the defendant's arguments without overemphasizing them.

| EXAMPLE 28 | Excerpt from the State's Brief: Ineffective |

On the whole, Ms. Martinez's description was accurate. When she was interviewed, Ms. Martinez told the police that her assailant was a white male, that he was approximately 5'7" tall, that he weighed between 165 and 170 pounds, that he had blondish-brown hair, that he was wearing a dark jacket, and **that he appeared to be in his early forties. In fact, the defendant is twenty-two.**

This discrepancy in age is insignificant. It is often difficult to guess a person's age: Some people appear older than they are, and others appear younger. Thus, the court should give little weight to the fact that Ms. Martinez misjudged the defendant's age. On the basis of the other information Ms. Martinez gave to the police, the police were able to identify the defendant as the assailant.

| EXAMPLE 29 | Excerpt from the State's Brief: More Effective |

Ms. Martinez was able to give the police a detailed description of her assailant. When she was interviewed, she told the police that her assailant was a white male with blondish-brown hair, that he was approximately 5'7" tall and weighed between 165 and 170 pounds, **that he appeared to be in his early forties**, and that he was wearing a dark green jacket.

This description is accurate in all but one respect. **Although Ms. Martinez misjudged the defendant's age**, she accurately described his hair, his height and weight, and his clothing.

c.   Use Language That Strengthens Your Arguments and Undermines the Other Side's Arguments

In setting out your own arguments, do not use phrases such as "We contend that . . . ," "It is our argument that . . . ," "We believe that . . . ," or "We feel that . . ." Just set out your assertions. The following examples from the defendant's brief demonstrate this.

EXAMPLE 30   **Excerpt from the Defendant's Brief**

Ineffective

It is our contention that the police procedures were impermissibly suggestive.

More Effective

The police procedures were impermissibly suggestive.

On the other hand, when it is necessary to set out the other side's argument, use an introductory phrase that reminds the court that the statement is just the other side's assertion or argument.

EXAMPLE 31   **Excerpt from the Defendant's Brief**

Although the State contends that Martinez's identification is reliable, Martinez had only a second or two to view her assailant.

---

d.   Use the Same Persuasive Techniques You Used in Setting Out the Facts, Issues, Rules, and Analogous Cases

Finally, when appropriate, use the same persuasive techniques that you used in writing the other parts of your brief. For instance, use the positions of emphasis to your best advantage. Place your best points at the beginning or end of a section or paragraph. In addition, whenever possible, put your strong points in short sentences or, in a longer sentence, in the main clause. Finally, select your words carefully. Choose words that convey not only the right denotation but also the right connotation.

Also remember that persuasive arguments are not written; they are crafted. In first drafts, concentrate on content and organization; in subsequent drafts, work on writing persuasively.

§ 17.10.6 Checklist for Critiquing the Argument

I. Content

- Has the writer set out his or her assertions?
- Has the writer supported his or her assertions?
    - If appropriate, has the writer applied the constitutional provision, applicable statute, or common law rule to the facts of his or her case?
    - If appropriate, has the writer compared and contrasted the facts in the analogous cases to the facts in his or her case?
    - If appropriate, has the writer explained why, as a matter of public policy, the court should rule in his or her client's favor?

- Has the writer cited to the key relevant authorities?
- Are the writer's statements of the rules and descriptions of the cases accurate?

II. Organization

- Has the writer used one of the conventional organizational schemes — for example, deductive or inductive reasoning?
- Has the writer used an organizational scheme that allows him or her to emphasize the strongest parts of his or her arguments?

III. Persuasiveness

Rules
- Has the writer presented the rules in the light most favorable to his or her client?
  - Did the writer create a favorable context?
  - Did the writer state favorable rules as broadly as possible and unfavorable rules as narrowly as possible?
  - Did the writer emphasize favorable rules and de-emphasize unfavorable ones?
  - Did the writer select words both for their denotation and for their connotation?

Analogous Cases
- Has the writer presented the cases in the light most favorable to his or her client?
  - Did the writer create a favorable context?
  - Did the writer state favorable holdings as broadly as possible and unfavorable holdings as narrowly as possible?
  - Did the writer emphasize favorable facts and de-emphasize unfavorable ones?
  - Did the writer select words both for their denotation and for their connotation?

Arguments
- Did the writer present his or her own arguments first?
- Did the writer give his or her own arguments the most airtime?
- Did the writer use language that strengthens his or her arguments and weakens his or her opponent's arguments?

§ 17.11 The Prayer for Relief

The final section of the brief is the prayer for relief or the conclusion. In some jurisdictions, the prayer for relief is very short. The attorney simply sets out the relief that he or she wants.

EXAMPLE 1	**Excerpt from the Defendant's Brief**

Prayer for Relief

For the reasons set out above, Mr. Patterson respectfully requests that the Court grant his motion and suppress Martinez's show-up and line-up identifications and any in-court identifications that Martinez or Clipse might make.

In other jurisdictions, the attorney sets out the relief that he or she is requesting and summarizes the arguments.

EXAMPLE 2	**Excerpt from the Defendant's Brief**

Conclusion

The Court should suppress Martinez's show-up identification because the police officer's questions were impermissibly suggestive and because, given Martinez's limited opportunity to view her assailant and the inaccuracies in her description, her identification is unreliable.

The Court should also suppress Martinez's line-up identification and any in-court identifications that Martinez or Clipse might make. Both the line-up and the in-court identifications have been tainted by the impermissibly suggestive show-up.

---

§ 17.12 Signing the Brief

Before the brief is submitted to the court, it must be signed by an attorney licensed to practice law in the state. The following format is used in many jurisdictions.

EXAMPLE 3	**Standard Format for Dating and Signing a Brief**

Submitted this _____ day of _____, 20 _____.

_____

Attorney for the Defendant

Chapter 17 Quiz No. 2

Draft answers for each of the following questions. Make your points clearly and concisely, and write sentences that are easy to read and that are grammatical and correctly punctuated.

1. What are the characteristics of an effective argumentative heading?
2. What techniques can you use to present the rules in a light favorable to your client?

3. What techniques can you use to present analogous cases in a light favorable to your client?
4. When might you want to set out factual arguments first?
5. What is a good way of countering one of your opponent's argument?

§17.13 Sample Briefs

In this section, we set out two sets of briefs: the briefs from the *Patterson* case, which is used as the example case in this chapter, and the briefs from a civil case in which defense counsel has asked the court to grant defendant's Motion for Partial Summary Judgment. Because the briefs are written for a Washington trial court, the attorneys use the Washington court rules and the Washington citation rules.

The King County Rules, which govern both sets of briefs, are as follows:

(B) Form of Motion and of Responsive Pleadings. The motion shall be combined with the memorandum of authorities into a single document, and shall conform to the following format:

(i) Relief Requested. The specific relief the court is requested to grant or deny.

(ii) Statement of Facts. A succinct statement of the facts contended to be material.

(iii) Statement of Issues. A concise statement of the issue or issues of law upon which the Court is requested to rule.

(iv) Evidence Relied Upon. The evidence on which the motion or opposition is based must be specified with particularity. Deposition testimony, discovery pleadings, and documentary evidence relied upon must be quoted verbatim or a photocopy of relevant pages must be attached to an affidavit identifying the documents. Parties should highlight those parts upon which they place substantial reliance. Copies of cases shall not be attached to original pleadings. Responsive pleadings shall conform to this format.

(v) Authority. Any legal authority relied upon must be cited. Copies of all cited non-Washington authorities upon which parties place substantial reliance shall be provided to the hearing Judge and to counsel or parties, but shall not be filed with the Clerk.

(vi) Page Limits. The initial motion and opposing memorandum shall not exceed 12 pages without authorization of the court; reply memoranda shall not exceed five pages without the authority of the court.

LCR 7(b)(5)(B).

EXAMPLE 1	**Defendant's Brief in Support of Motion to Suppress**

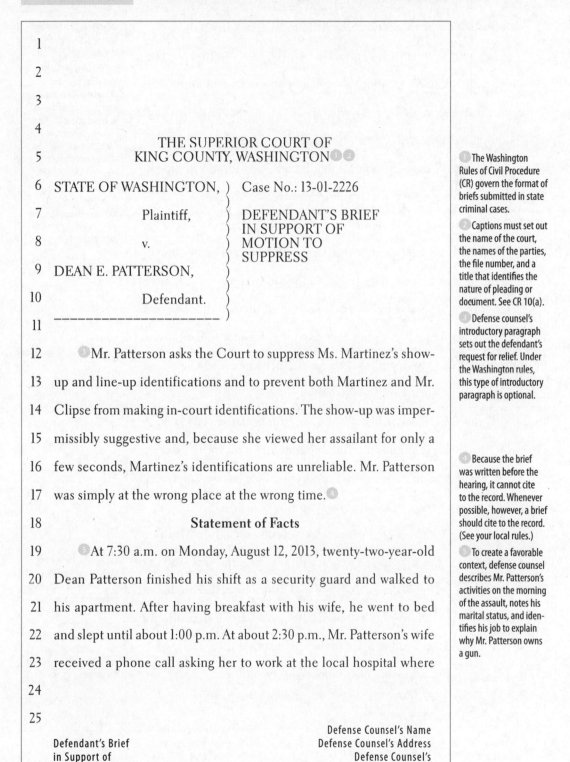

1

2

3

4

5   THE SUPERIOR COURT OF
     KING COUNTY, WASHINGTON ① ②

6   STATE OF WASHINGTON,)   Case No.: 13-01-2226
)

7   Plaintiff,   )   DEFENDANT'S BRIEF
)   IN SUPPORT OF

8   v.   )   MOTION TO
)   SUPPRESS

9   DEAN E. PATTERSON,   )
)

10   Defendant.   )

11   —————————————)

12   ③ Mr. Patterson asks the Court to suppress Ms. Martinez's show-

13 up and line-up identifications and to prevent both Martinez and Mr.

14 Clipse from making in-court identifications. The show-up was imper-

15 missibly suggestive and, because she viewed her assailant for only a

16 few seconds, Martinez's identifications are unreliable. Mr. Patterson

17 was simply at the wrong place at the wrong time. ④

18   **Statement of Facts**

19   ⑤ At 7:30 a.m. on Monday, August 12, 2013, twenty-two-year-old

20 Dean Patterson finished his shift as a security guard and walked to

21 his apartment. After having breakfast with his wife, he went to bed

22 and slept until about 1:00 p.m. At about 2:30 p.m., Mr. Patterson's wife

23 received a phone call asking her to work at the local hospital where

24

25

Defendant's Brief
in Support of
Motion to Suppress - 1

           Defense Counsel's Name
           Defense Counsel's Address
           Defense Counsel's
           Phone Number

① The Washington Rules of Civil Procedure (CR) govern the format of briefs submitted in state criminal cases.

② Captions must set out the name of the court, the names of the parties, the file number, and a title that identifies the nature of pleading or document. See CR 10(a).

③ Defense counsel's introductory paragraph sets out the defendant's request for relief. Under the Washington rules, this type of introductory paragraph is optional.

④ Because the brief was written before the hearing, it cannot cite to the record. Whenever possible, however, a brief should cite to the record. (See your local rules.)

⑤ To create a favorable context, defense counsel describes Mr. Patterson's activities on the morning of the assault, notes his marital status, and identifies his job to explain why Mr. Patterson owns a gun.

1   she is employed as a nurse. Mr. Patterson's wife got ready, and Mr.

2   Patterson ⑥ dropped her off at the hospital at about 3:10 p.m.

3   At about 3:30 p.m., Mr. Patterson called his wife to find out how

4   long she would have to work ⑦; they had plans to go to a movie that

5   evening, and he wanted to know whether he should change those plans.

6   At about 3:50 p.m., Mr. Patterson took a load of laundry to the apart-

7   ment complex's laundry room. When he returned to his apartment,

8   Mr. Patterson watched part of an old movie. At about 4:15 p.m., ⑧

9   Mr. Patterson went back to the laundry room to put the clothes in the

10 dryer. On his way back, he saw a parking spot in front of his apartment

11 and moved his car, an older model red station wagon, to that spot.

12 After parking his car, Mr. Patterson got out of the car and, because

13 the driver's side door does not lock from the outside, walked to the

14 passenger side to lock the doors. As he did so, he nodded to a parking

15 enforcement officer who was driving by.

16   By this time, it was 4:30 p.m., and Mr. Patterson decided to phone

17 his wife again. He arranged to meet her at 5:15 p.m. for her dinner

18 break. Mr. Patterson retrieved the laundry and then left the apartment

19 a little before 5:00 p.m. to meet his wife.

20   At about 4:30 p.m. on the same day, seventeen-year-old Beatrice

21 Martinez left her apartment to walk to work. As she was walking

22 southbound on Belmont, a car ⑨ that had driven by earlier pulled in

23 front of her. The man got out of his car, took one or two steps toward

24 Martinez, and then pulled a gun from his pocket. As soon as she spot-

25 ted the gun, Martinez screamed, looked away, and then, crying, ran

26

⑥ Mr. Patterson or his wife is the subject of most sentences. This technique tells the story from the client's point of view.

⑦ The facts in this paragraph paint the defendant in a favorable light by explaining what he was doing at the time of the assault and why the parking enforcement officer saw him near his car shortly after the assault.

⑧ Because the facts appear in chronological order, time references are used frequently.

⑨ Because Mr. Patterson owns a car that matches the description of the car that the assailant drove, defense counsel describes the car using a generic term: "car." In addition, she minimizes the fact that the car drove by twice.

Defendant's Brief
in Support of
Motion to Suppress - 2

Defense Counsel's Name
Defense Counsel's Address
Defense Counsel's
Phone Number

1   across the street. ⑩ The entire encounter was over in three or four

2   seconds.

3   The assault was witnessed by Chester Clipse, who was walking

4   home when he saw a man in a red station wagon driving slowly down

5   the street. When the man pulled into Clipse's parking space, Clipse

6   began walking toward him to tell him that he could not park there.

7   As he did so, Clipse saw the man get out of his car and walk toward a

8   woman who was on the sidewalk. He then heard the woman scream,

9   and as she screamed, Clipse saw that the man had a gun. Clipse yelled

10 "Hey," and the man turned and ran to his car, putting the gun under

11 his coat. As the woman ran across the street, the man got back into

12 his car, backed out, and drove away. ⑪

13   A few seconds later, a parking enforcement officer drove down

14 the street. Clipse flagged him down, told him what had happened,

15 and described the car and the man. The parking enforcement officer

16 called 911 and then left to try to locate the car. Because the woman

17 was still crying, Clipse took her to his landlady's apartment. He then

18 went back outside and waited for the police.

19   When the police arrived, ⑫ Clipse told Officers Yuen and Cox

20 what had happened. Clipse told the police that the man was white,

21 about 5'10" tall, and about 180 to 185 pounds. He also told the officers

22 that the man was wearing a green outfit and that he was in his late

23 thirties or early forties. ⑬

24   While Clipse was talking to the police, Officer Cox received a

25 radio message indicating that the parking enforcement officer had

26

⑩ Because she wants to argue that Martinez's identification is not reliable, defense counsel uses language that suggests that Martinez did not have a good opportunity to view her assailant. Putting the facts in short clauses in a single sentence creates the impression that events happened quickly.

⑪ Again, putting the facts in short clauses in a single sentence creates the impression that events happened quickly.

⑫ Dovetailing is used to make clear the connection between the information in this paragraph and the information in the prior paragraph.

⑬ Defense counsel places a favorable fact, that Clipse said the assailant was in his late thirties or early forties, in a position of emphasis.

Defendant's Brief
in Support of
Motion to Suppress - 3

Defense Counsel's Name
Defense Counsel's Address
Defense Counsel's
Phone Number

1   located a car that matched the one Clipse had described. While

2   Officer Cox took Clipse in his car to see if Clipse could identify the

3   car, Officer Yuen went inside to interview Martinez.

4   Because she was still upset, Martinez was able to give Officer Yuen

5   only a general description of her assailant. She described him as being

6   a short, white male with blondish-brown hair who was wearing glasses

7   and a dark jacket. 🔴 In addition, she told police that her assailant was

8   in his early forties. Mr. Patterson is twenty-two. 🔴

9   After interviewing Martinez, Officer Yuen took the still-shaken

10   Martinez to his car to take her home. When they had traveled less

11   than a block, Officer Yuen noticed a white male wearing a dark jacket.

12   As he drove up behind him, Yuen asked Martinez, "Is that the man?"

13   When Martinez did not immediately answer, Yuen asked the question

14   again: "Is that the man who assaulted you?" 🔴

15   Even though Martinez was unable to see the man's face, 🔴 she

16   agreed with the officer that the man looked like her assailant. At this

17   point, Officer Yuen stopped the car, got out, and approached Mr. Pat-

18   terson. As he was questioning Mr. Patterson, Officer Cox drove up with

19   Clipse. While Martinez and Clipse watched, Officers Cox and Yuen

20   continued questioning🔴 Mr. Patterson. Officer Cox then returned

21   to Martinez and Clipse and walked them back to Clipse's apartment.

22   While he did so, Yuen placed Mr. Patterson under arrest.

23   Later that day, the police searched Mr. Patterson's car and

24   apartment. In the apartment, the police found the gun issued to Mr.

25   Patterson by his employer. 🔴 Four days later, the police held a line-

26

🔴 Unfavorable facts—those parts of Martinez's description that are accurate—are placed in the middle of the paragraph. A favorable fact—Martinez's statement that her assailant was in his forties—appears in a position of emphasis, juxtaposed with Mr. Patterson's age of twenty-two.

🔴 A favorable fact is placed in a position of emphasis in a short sentence.

🔴 Quotations emphasize that the officer's language suggested to Martinez that Mr. Patterson was the person who had assaulted her. Note how the second quote is in a position of emphasis.

🔴 Another favorable fact—that Martinez was not able to see Patterson's face—is placed in a position of emphasis.

🔴 Word choice matters. The word "questioning" suggests that the officer was treating Mr. Patterson as if he had committed a crime.

🔴 Defense counsel has tried to convert an unfavorable fact to a favorable one by emphasizing that Mr. Patterson's employer had issued him the gun.

Defendant's Brief
in Support of
Motion to Suppress - 4

Defense Counsel's Name
Defense Counsel's Address
Defense Counsel's
Phone Number

1   up. Although Martinez identified Mr. Patterson as the man who had

2   approached her, Clipse did not identify Mr. Patterson. [20]

3   **Issue**

4   Under the Fourteenth Amendment, should the Court grant Mr.

5   Patterson's motion to suppress [21] Martinez's show-up and line-up iden-

6   tifications and Martinez's and Clipse's in-court identification when

7   (1) a police officer pointed out Mr. Patterson to Martinez, repeatedly

8   asking the shaken Martinez whether Mr. Patterson looked like her

9   assailant; (2) the police questioned Mr. Patterson in front of Martinez

10   and Clipse; (3) during the second or two that Martinez had to view her

11   assailant, her attention was focused on his gun and not his face; and

12   (4) both Martinez's and Clipse's descriptions were inaccurate? [22]

13   **Argument**

14   I.   THE COURT SHOULD GRANT MR. PATTERSON'S

15   MOTION TO SUPPRESS MARTINEZ'S SHOW-UP AND
LINE-UP IDENTIFICATIONS AND MARTINEZ'S AND

16   CLIPSE'S IN-COURT IDENTIFICATIONS. [23]

17   The United States Supreme Court has developed a two-part test

18   to ensure a criminal defendant the procedural due process guaranteed

19   to every individual by the Fourteenth Amendment. *Manson v. Braith-*

20   *waite,* [24] 432 U.S. 98, 113, 97 S. Ct. 2243, 53 L. Ed. 2d 140 (1977).

21   Under the first part of the test, [25] the defendant need show

22   only [26] that the identification that he seeks to suppress was obtained

23   through the use of unnecessarily suggestive police procedures. *Id.*

24   Once the defendant has established that the procedure was sugges-

25   tive, [27] the onus shifts to the State to prove that, under the totality of

26

Defendant's Brief
in Support of
Motion to Suppress - 5

Defense Counsel's Name
Defense Counsel's Address
Defense Counsel's
Phone Number

---

[20] The favorable fact that Clipse did not identify Patterson as the assailant appears in the main clause in the position of emphasis. The unfavorable fact that Martinez did identify Patterson appears in the dependent clause.

[21] The question is phrased to suggest defense counsel's desired conclusion.

[22] Defense counsel sets out the key facts in a light favorable to her client. The facts that go to the first part of the test (whether the show-up was suggestive) appear first; the facts that go to the second part of the test (whether the identifications were reliable) appear second.

[23] This heading answers the question in the issue statement, and the subheadings set out defense counsel's support. (Although a "because" clause is an effective persuasive tool, here it would have made the main heading too long.)

[24] The argument starts with the general rules most favorable to Patterson.

[25] This transition prepares readers for the first part of a two-part test.

[26] This language minimizes Patterson's burden.

[27] This language suggests that Patterson can meet his burden.

1 the circumstances, the witness's identification is so reliable that it

2 should be admitted even though it was obtained through suggestive

3 means.㉘ *Id.*

4   In this case, the Court should suppress Martinez's show-up

5 identification both because the police procedures were impermissi-

6 bly suggestive and because, under the totality of the circumstances,

7 Martinez's identification is not reliable. In addition, the Court should

8 suppress Martinez's line-up identification because that line-up was

9 tainted by the show-up. Finally, the Court should rule that neither

10 Martinez nor Clipse should be allowed to make in-court identifica-

11 tions: Like Martinez's line-up identification, any in-court identifica-

12 tions would be tainted by the show-up.㉙

13   A. <u>Martinez's show-up identification should be suppressed</u>

14   <u>because the police procedures were impermissibly suggestive</u>
         <u>and Martinez's identification is not reliable.</u>㉚

15

16   The courts have repeatedly condemned the practice of show-

17 ing a witness a single suspect.㉛ *See, e.g., Stovall v. Denno*, 388 U.S.

18 293, 302, 87 S. Ct. 1967, 18 L. Ed. 2d 1199 (1967); *State v. Rogers*, 44

19 Wn. App. 510, 515, 722 P.2d 1349 (1986); *State v. Kraus*, 21 Wn. App.

20 388, 391-92, 584 P.2d 946 (1978).㉜ Although such show-ups are not

21 per se impermissibly suggestive,㉝ identifications following such a

22 show-up should be admitted only if the show-up occurs during the

23 prompt search for the suspect and if the State proves that the witness's

24 identification is reliable.㉞ *State v. Rogers*, 44 Wn. App. at 515.

25

26

Defendant's Brief
in Support of
Motion to Suppress - 6

Defense Counsel's Name
Defense Counsel's Address
Defense Counsel's
Phone Number

㉘ This language suggests that the State's burden is high.

㉙ After setting out the general rules, defense counsel sets out a roadmap for the rest of her arguments.

㉚ This "traditional" format for an argumentative heading sets out the assertion and then a "because" clause. This "because" clause is very general; the sub-subheadings provide the facts that support defense counsel's assertions.

㉛ This rule is phrased in a light favorable to Patterson.

㉜ This effective use of a string cite shows that courts have condemned the practice of showing witnesses a single suspect. Use string cites sparingly.

㉝ An unfavorable rule is placed in a dependent clause in the middle of a paragraph.

㉞ A favorable rule is placed in the main clause at the end of the paragraph, a position of emphasis. In addition, the word "only" states the rule narrowly.

1.   <u>The police procedures were unnecessarily suggestive because the police showed Martinez one suspect, asked Martinez whether that suspect looked like her assailant, and questioned the suspect in front of Martinez.</u> ⑤

In this case, ㊱ Officer Yuen's actions suggested to Martinez that he believed that Mr. Patterson was her assailant. While driving Martinez home, Officer Yuen pulled up behind Mr. Patterson and asked Martinez whether Mr. Patterson looked like her assailant. When Martinez did not respond, Officer Yuen repeated his question, asking "Is that the man who assaulted you?" ㊲ Although Martinez could not see Mr. Patterson's face, after hesitating, she agreed ㊳ with Officer Yuen that Mr. Patterson looked like her assailant. At that point, Officer Yuen pulled up behind Mr. Patterson, got out of the police car, and began questioning him. A few minutes later, Officer Cox and Clipse arrived, and both Officer Yuen and Officer Cox questioned Mr. Patterson while Martinez and Clipse watched.

Thus, this case can be distinguished from *State v. Kraus*, 21 Wn. App. at 392, in which the show-up identification occurred during a prompt search for the robber. ㊴㊵ In this case, the show-up did not occur while the police were searching for Martinez's assailant. Instead, it occurred while the officer was driving Martinez home. In addition, unlike *Stovall*, 388 U.S. at 302, in which the police held the show-up because they were concerned that the suspect might die, in this case there were no exigent circumstances. In fact, because the police had located a car that matched the description of the one driven by the assailant, they could have identified the owner of the car and any individuals who had driven it and placed them in a line-up. ㊶

Defendant's Brief
in Support of
Motion to Suppress - 7

Defense Counsel's Name
Defense Counsel's Address
Defense Counsel's
Phone Number

㉟ Defense counsel sets out her assertion (that the police procedures were unnecessarily suggestive) and then includes a "because" clause in which she sets out the facts that support this assertion.

㊱ While usually the applicable rules are set out before the facts, here the order is reversed. This strategy is effective when, as here, the best argument is a factual one. As a general rule, place your strongest elements first, but make sure that the argument is easy to follow.

㊲ Defense counsel emphasizes this favorable fact by using a quotation.

㊳ Once again, defense counsel selects words that carry not only the right denotation but also the right connotation. In particular, note the words "agreed," "watched," and "questioned."

㊴ Instead of setting out the other side's argument—e.g., by saying that the State will argue that this case is like Kraus—defense counsel sets out her own positive assertion, which is that Patterson's case can be distinguished from Kraus.

㊵ Defense counsel does not describe Kraus in detail; she sets out only the key fact.

㊶ This section ends with a strong argument: that the police had another way of locating the assailant.

1   2.   <u>Martinez's identification is unreliable because Martinez</u>
         <u>was able to view her assailant for only a few seconds, her</u>
2   <u>attention was focused on the gun and not his face, and her</u>
         <u>description of her assailant does not match the description</u>
3   <u>of Patterson.</u>⊙

4

5   ⊙The key inquiry in determining the admissibility of a witness's

6   identification is its reliability. *Manson v. Braithwaite*, 432 U.S. 98, 114,

7   97 S. Ct. 2243, 53 L. Ed. 2d 140 (1977). In determining whether an

8   identification is reliable,⊙ the courts consider the witness's opportu-

9   nity to view the person who committed the crime, the witness's degree

10   of attention, the time between the crime and the confrontation, the

11   witness's level of certainty, and the accuracy of the witness's prior

12   description. *Neil v. Biggers*, 409 U.S. 188, 93 S. Ct. 375, 34 L. Ed. 2d

13   401 (1972); *State v. Birch*, 151 Wn. App. 505, 514, 213 P.3d 63 (2009).

14   ⊙First, in this case, Martinez did not have a good opportunity to

15   view her assailant. Unlike⊙ the witness in Rogers, who was with his

16   assailant for almost twenty minutes, and the witness in *Booth*, who

17   observed the robber for at least forty-five seconds, Martinez was able

18   to view her assailant for only a few seconds. Martinez told the police

19   that she had seen her assailant for three or four seconds before she

20   turned and ran. In addition, although Martinez testified that she had

21   noticed the car on a prior occasion,⊙ she did not testify that she had

22   noticed the driver. In a similar case, the court held that the witness

23   had not had a good opportunity to view the robber when the witness

24   was with the robber for five to six minutes and viewed him for two

25

26

Defendant's Brief   Defense Counsel's Name
in Support of   Defense Counsel's Address
Motion to Suppress - 8   Defense Counsel's
                                                   Phone Number

⊙ This sub-subheading uses the same format as the prior one: assertion and then supporting facts.

⊙ This subsection uses the more traditional format: specific rules and then application of these rules to the facts.

⊙ Defense counsel reorders the list of factors to place the two most favorable ones in positions of emphasis.

⊙ Defense counsel makes effective use of signposts and topic sentences. For example, she starts this paragraph with "First" and then makes her assertion (that Martinez did not have a good opportunity to view her assailant).

⊙ Defense counsel uses the cases to support her assertion. She sets out the key facts from each of the cases and then distinguishes those cases.

⊙ Defense counsel anticipates and responds to an argument that she believes the State will make. Note that she does not set out the State's argument. She simply sets out her own argument. Also note that the unfavorable fact that Martinez testified that she had noticed the car on a prior occasion is in a dependent clause in the middle of the paragraph. Finally, note defense counsel's word choices (e.g., Martinez had "noticed" the car).

1   or three minutes. *State v. McDonald*, 40 Wn. App. 743, 747, 700 P.2d

2   327 (1985).

3   Second, Martinez's attention was not focused on her assailant.[48]

4   Unlike the witness in *Booth*, whose attention was focused on the robber

5   because he was running and carrying money and got into a car with

6   license plates from the witness's home state, Martinez's attention was

7   focused on the car and then on the gun that her assailant was holding.

8   As Martinez told police, she looked at the gun, glanced at the man

9   holding it, and then ran.[49]

10   Third, although the show-up occurred within about forty-five

11 minutes of the assault, Martinez's level of certainty was low. The first

12 time that Officer Yuen asked Martinez whether Mr. Patterson looked

13 like the man who had assaulted her, she did not respond.[50] In addi-

14 tion, the second time that Officer Yuen asked her the same question,

15 she said only that Mr. Patterson looked like him. She did not say, "Yes,

16 that is him."

17   Finally, Martinez's description was inaccurate. Although Martinez

18 told the police that her assailant was in his early forties, Mr. Patterson

19 is twenty-two.[51] While sometimes an individual will believe that an

20 individual is two, three, or even five years older than the individual

21 actually is, it is extremely uncommon for someone to be off by twenty

22 years.[52]

23   [53]In this case, Martinez identified Mr. Patterson as her assailant

24 only because Officer Yuen suggested to her that Mr. Patterson was

25 the man who had assaulted her. In addition, the State cannot prove

26

[48] Once again, defense counsel starts the paragraph with a signpost and a topic sentence that sets out her assertion.

[49] The favorable facts appear at the end of the paragraph in a position of emphasis.

[50] Because no relevant case law specifically discusses this factor, defense counsel uses the facts. Note how the paragraph ends: Sometimes what a party did not do or did not say will support an argument.

[51] While defense counsel would have liked to give this factor more airtime, she recognizes that she has no good way to accomplish that. Thus, she makes her point and moves on.

[52] While you will usually provide support for your assertions, sometimes you can make a "commonsense" argument.

[53] This paragraph (1) discusses the first part of the two-part test, arguing that the show-up was suggestive; (2) discusses the second part of the test, reminding the court that the State has the burden of proof, and then summarizes the arguments relating to the factors; and (3) returns to the general rule section, reminding the court of the constitutional issues.

Defendant's Brief   Defense Counsel's Name
in Support of   Defense Counsel's Address
Motion to Suppress - 9   Defense Counsel's
                                                     Phone Number

1   that Martinez's identification is reliable. Martinez did not have a good

2   opportunity to view her assailant, her attention was not focused on

3   her assailant, her identification was uncertain, and her description

4   was inaccurate. As a consequence, Mr. Patterson's due process rights

5   would be violated if Martinez's identification is admitted.

6   B.   <u>Martinez's line-up identification should be suppressed</u>
         <u>because it was tainted by the show-up.</u> 54

7

8   When the initial identification is obtained through impermis-

9   sibly suggestive procedures, subsequent identifications must also be

10 suppressed unless the State can prove that the subsequent identifica-

11 tions are reliable. 55 *State v. Birch*, 151 Wn. App. 505, 513-14, 213 P.3d

12 63 (2009); *State v. McDonald*, 56 40 Wn. App. 743, 747, 700 P.2d 327

13 (1985). In *McDonald*, the court reversed the defendant's conviction,

14 concluding that the procedures used at the line-up were impermis-

15 sibly suggestive and that the State had not proved that the witness's

16 subsequent in-court identification was reliable. *Id.* at 747-48.

17   Similarly, in this case the procedures were impermissibly sug-

18 gestive, and the State cannot prove that Martinez's subsequent iden-

19 tifications are reliable. See section 1A(2), *supra.* 57 Martinez picked

20 Patterson out of the line-up, not because she remembered him as her

21 assailant, but because the police had suggested to her that he was

22 her assailant. 58

23

24

25

26

Defendant's Brief   Defense Counsel's Name
in Support of   Defense Counsel's Address
Motion to Suppress - 10   Defense Counsel's
                                                     Phone Number

---

Side notes:

54 Defense counsel sets out her assertion and then a "because" clause in which she sets out her support for that assertion.

55 In setting out this rule, defense counsel emphasizes that the State has the burden of proof.

56 Defense counsel uses an analogous case to support her argument.

57 Instead of repeating this argument, defense counsel provides a cross-reference to an earlier section of the brief.

58 Arguments do not need to be long. Make your point and then move on.

1   C. <u>Martinez and Clipse should not be permitted to make an</u>
<u>in-court identification because such an identification would</u>
2   <u>be tainted by the impermissibly suggestive show-up and the</u>
3   <u>line-up.</u>

4   Just as Martinez's line-up identification was tainted by the imper-

5   missibly suggestive show-up, any in-court identification by Martinez

6   or Clipse would also be tainted. Although the police did not ask

7   Clipse whether Mr. Patterson looked liked the man who had assaulted

8   Martinez, Clipse watched as the police questioned Patterson. 59 In

9   addition, Patterson was with Martinez, who may have told him that

10   Officer Yuen believed that Patterson was her assailant.

11   **Prayer for Relief**

12   For the reasons set out above, Mr. Patterson respectfully requests

13   that the Court suppress Martinez's show-up and line-up identifica-

14   tions and that the Court not permit Martinez or Clipse to make an

15   in-court identification.

16   Dated this 23rd day of September, 2013.

17   Signature
                        Attorney for the Defendant
18   Name
                        Bar No. 00000
19

20

21

22

23

24

25

26

59 Defense counsel does not set out the State's argument. She simply counters that argument by setting out her own positive assertion.

Defendant's Brief
in Support of
Motion to Suppress - 11

Defense Counsel's Name
Defense Counsel's Address
Defense Counsel's
Phone Number

| **EXAMPLE 2** | **State's Brief in Opposition to Motion To Suppress** |

1

2

3

4

5   SUPERIOR COURT OF
                        KING COUNTY, WASHINGTON ❶

6   STATE OF WASHINGTON,)   Case No.: 13-01-2226
)
7   Plaintiff,   )   STATES'S BRIEF
)   IN OPPOSITION TO
8   v.   )   DEFENDANT'S
)   MOTION TO
9   DEAN E. PATTERSON,   )   SUPPRESS
)
10   Defendant.   )
    —————————————————————)
11

12   The State asks the Court to deny the defendant's motion to sup-

13   press the victim's show-up and line-up identifications and to allow

14   both the victim and the witness to make in-court identifications.

15   The show-up was not suggestive, and the victim's and the witness's

16   identifications are reliable. ❷

17   **Statement of Facts**

18   On Monday, August 12, 2013, Beatrice Martinez was assaulted

19   with a deadly weapon. ❸ At a show-up held thirty to forty minutes

20   after the attack, Ms. Martinez identified the defendant, Dean E.

21   Patterson, as her assailant. Four days after the assault, Ms. Martinez

22   picked Patterson out of a line-up, once again identifying him as her

23   assailant. ❹

24

25

State's Brief   Name of Prosecutor
in Opposition to   Deputy Prosecuting Attorney
Defendant's   for King County
Motion to Suppress - 1   Address of Prosecutor's Office

❶ Captions must set out the name of the court, the names of the parties, the file number, and a title that identifies the nature of the pleading or document. See CR 10(a).

❷ The prosecutor's introductory paragraph sets out his request for relief: Under the Washington rules, this type of introductory paragraph is optional.

❸ The prosecutor starts the story where it started for the victim: with the assault.

❹ Here, the prosecutor introduces his theory of the case: that Ms. Martinez repeatedly identified the defendant as her assailant.

1   Ms. Martinez left her apartment at about 4:30 p.m. to walk to work

2   at Angelo's, a restaurant. As she was walking north on Belmont, Ms.

3   Martinez observed an older model red station wagon with a chrome

4   luggage rack as it passed slowly by her.⑤ Moments later, the same

5   car came down the street again. This time, the driver pulled his car

6   in front of Ms. Martinez, stopping his car so that it blocked her path.

7   As Ms. Martinez watched,⑥ the driver got out of his car and walked

8   toward her. The man then took a gun from his coat pocket and pointed

9   it at Ms. Martinez. Ms. Martinez looked at the gun and then at her

10 assailant. Then, crying, she ran back across the street to safety.⑦

11   At about the same time,⑧ Chester Clipse was walking south on

12 Belmont. As he approached his apartment, Clipse saw a man in a

13 red station wagon pull into the area where he usually parked. Clipse

14 immediately started walking toward the man to tell him that he could

15 not park there. A moment later, Clipse saw the man get out of his car

16 and approach a young woman⑨ who had stopped suddenly. As Clipse

17 watched, the man pulled out a gun and pointed it at the woman.

18   Both Martinez and Clipse screamed, and the man turned and ran

19 to his car, putting the gun under his coat. As Ms. Martinez ran across

20 the street, the man got back into his car, backed out, and drove away,

21 traveling northbound on Belmont.

22   **Issue**

23   Should the Court deny the defendant's motion to suppress⑩

24 when the police merely asked the victim whether a pedestrian was her

25

26

State's Brief   Name of Prosecutor
in Opposition to   Deputy Prosecuting Attorney
Defendant's   for King County
Motion to Suppress - 2   Address of Prosecutor's Office

⑤ The prosecutor has described the facts related to the car and the victim's opportunity to view that car in detail, giving those facts considerable airtime. The inference that the prosecutor wants the court to make is that if the victim's description of the car is accurate, so is her description of the assailant.

⑥ The word "watched" suggests that Martinez had a good opportunity to view her assailant.

⑦ Setting out the facts in separate sentences "slows down time" and reinforces that Martinez had a good opportunity to view her assailant.

⑧ Note how the prosecutor puts the orienting transitions at the beginning of the sentence.

⑨ In choosing the words "a young woman" to describe Martinez, the prosecutor is balancing his desire to paint Martinez as a victim and his need to establish her reliability as a witness.

⑩ The prosecutor frames the legal question so that it suggests the conclusion that he wants the court to reach.

1   assailant and when the victim observed her assailant on two occasions

2   for several seconds in broad daylight?⑪

3   Argument

4   I. THE COURT SHOULD DENY THE DEFENDANT'S
    MOTION TO SUPPRESS BECAUSE THE POLICE
5   PROCEDURES WERE NOT IMPERMISSIBLY SUG-
    GESTIVE AND THE VICTIM'S IDENTIFICATION IS
6   RELIABLE.⑫

7

8   Identifications should not be kept from the jury unless the pro-

9   cedures used in obtaining the identifications were so suggestive and

10 unreliable that a substantial likelihood of irreparable misidentification

11 exists.⑬ *See Perry v. New Hampshire*, __ U.S. ___, 132 S. Ct. 716, 720,

12 181 L. Ed. 2d 694 (2012); *Simmons v. United States*, 390 U.S. 377, 384,

13 89 S. Ct. 1127, 22 L. Ed. 2d 402 (1969).⑭

14   In deciding whether identification evidence is admissible, the

15 courts employ a two-part test. Under the first part of the test, the

16 defendant has the burden of proving that the identification evidence

17 that he or she seeks to suppress was obtained through impermissibly

18 suggestive procedures. *Manson v. Braithwaite*, 432 U.S. 98, 113, 97 S.

19 Ct. 2243, 53 L. Ed. 2d 140 (1977). Only if the defendant satisfies this

20 substantial burden is the second part of the test applied. *Id.*⑮

21   Even if the court determines that the police procedures were

22 impermissibly suggestive, the evidence is admissible if, under the

23 totality of the circumstances, the identifications are reliable. *Simmons*

24 *v. United States*, 390 U.S. at 384. Due process does not compel the

25 exclusion of an identification if it is reliable. *Id.*⑯

26

State's Brief   Name of Prosecutor
in Opposition to   Deputy Prosecuting Attorney
Defendant's   for King County
Motion to Suppress - 3   Address of Prosecutor's Office

⑪ The prosecutor sets out a key fact related to the first part of the two-part test and then a fact related to the second part of the test. In doing so, the prosecutor presents those facts accurately but in a light favorable to the State.

⑫ If you have one issue statement, you should have one main heading. The issue statement sets out the question, and the heading answers that question. This heading uses the conventional format: the assertion first and then a "because" clause that provides support for that assertion.

⑬ The prosecutor starts his general rule section by creating a favorable context.

⑭ Because this brief is a brief to a Washington court, the prosecutor uses the Washington citation rules.

⑮ This language emphasizes that the burden of proving the first part of the test belongs to the defendant.

⑯ The prosecutor ends the general rule section by responding to Patterson's due process argument but without saying what Patterson argued.

1   A.   <u>Merely asking the victim whether a pedestrian was her</u>
2   <u>assailant does not make a permissible show-up impermissibly</u>
     <u>suggestive.</u> ⑰

3

4   There are no published Washington cases in which the courts

5   have held that a show-up was impermissibly suggestive. ⑱ *See, e.g.,*

6   *State v. Rogers*, 44 Wn. App. 510, 722 P.2d 1249 (1986); *State v. Booth*,

7   36 Wn. App. 66, 671 P.2d 1218 (1983). In *Rogers*, ⑲ the court held that

8   the show-up was not impermissibly suggestive even though the police

9   had picked up the witness at a tavern, told him that they wanted to

10   take him back to his apartment to see if he could identify his assailant,

11   and then presented the defendant to him while the defendant was

12   standing between two uniformed police officers. *Id.* at 511. Similarly, ⑳

13   in *Booth*, the court held that the show-up was not impermissibly sug-

14   gestive when the police asked the witness to accompany them to the

15   place where the defendant had been arrested and the witness identi-

16   fied the defendant after seeing him in the back of a police car. *Id.* at

17   67-68; *accord State v. Guzman-Cuellar*, 47 Wn.2d 326, 734 P.2d 966

18   (1987) (show-up not impermissibly suggestive when the defendant was

19   shown to three of the four eyewitnesses while in handcuffs standing

20   next to a police car).

21   In our case, ㉑ the show-up was not nearly as suggestive as the

22   show-ups in *Rogers*, *Booth*, or *Guzman-Cuellar*. ㉒ Unlike the officers

23   in *Rogers*, *Booth*, and *Guzman-Cuellar*, Officer Yuen did not ask Ms.

24   Martinez to go with him to identify her assailant. Instead, the show-

25   up occurred as he was taking Ms. Martinez home. In addition, when

26

State's Brief   Name of Prosecutor
in Opposition to   Deputy Prosecuting Attorney
Defendant's   for King County
Motion to Suppress - 4   Address of Prosecutor's Office

Margin notes:

⑰ This heading makes an assertion but does not use the conventional format.

⑱ The paragraph starts with a bold but accurate statement.

⑲ The prosecutor uses three cases to support his point: He discusses the first two cases in text and the third case in a parenthetical. Note that the case descriptions are short and to the point. The prosecutor sets out the court's holding and then sets out a short summary of the facts.

⑳ The prosecutor uses the transition to tell the court that he is moving to the next case and that case is another case that supports his assertion.

㉑ This transition signals a move from analogous cases to the prosecutor's own case.

㉒ Instead of discussing the cases one by one, the prosecutor discusses them as a group.

1   Ms. Martinez made her identification, the defendant was not flanked

2   by police officers, sitting in the back of a patrol car, or in handcuffs

3   standing next to a police car.㉓

4   If Officer Yuen had not asked Ms. Martinez whether the pedestrian

5   looked like her assailant, he would not have been doing his job.㉔ If

6   he was going to protect others, Officer Yuen needed to know whether

7   the pedestrian was Ms. Martinez's assailant. The officer's question,

8   "Is that the man?" was not enough to turn a permissible show-up into

9   one that was impermissibly suggestive.

10
11   B.   Ms. Martinez's identification was reliable: She had observed
          her assailant on two occasions; her attention was focused on
          her assailant; and, except for her statement about her assail-
12   ant's age, her description was accurate.㉕

13   Even if the police procedures were suggestive,㉖ the identification

14   is admissible unless㉗ the procedures are "so impermissibly suggestive

15   as to give rise to very substantial likelihood of irreparable misidentifi-

16   cations." *Simmons v. United States*, 390 U.S. 377, 384, 88 S. Ct. 967,

17   19 L. Ed. 2d 402 (1968); *accord Perry v. New Hampshire*, __ U.S. ___,

18   132 S. Ct. 716, 720, 181 L. Ed. 2d 694 (2012). In deciding whether the

19   identification is reliable, the courts consider the witness's opportunity

20   to view the criminal at the time of the crime, the witness's degree of

21   attention, the accuracy of the witness's description, the level of cer-

22   tainty demonstrated by the witness at the confrontation, and the length

23   of time between the crime and the confrontation. *Neil v. Biggers*, 409

24   U.S. 188, 199-200, 93 S. Ct. 375, 34 L. Ed. 2d 401 (1972).

25

26

State's Brief   Name of Prosecutor
in Opposition to   Deputy Prosecuting Attorney
Defendant's   for King County
Motion to Suppress - 5   Address of Prosecutor's Office

㉓ The prosecutor distinguishes the cases in the order that they are discussed in the preceding paragraph.

㉔ Here, the prosecutor makes a policy argument.

㉕ The prosecutor also uses an alternative format for this heading. Instead of using the word "because," he uses a colon. The statement that precedes the colon is the assertion, and the facts set out after the colon are the support for the assertion.

㉖ This language identifies the argument as an alternative argument.

㉗ The prosecutor sets out the rule broadly: "the identification is admissible unless…"

1   The courts do not require that the witness view the defendant

2   for an extended period of time. *State v. Booth*, 36 Wn. App. 66, 671

3   P.2d 1218 (1983). For example, in *Booth*, the court concluded that the

4   witness's identification was reliable when the witness had viewed the

5   defendant for less than a minute. *Id.* at 71. Because the witness's

6   attention had been drawn to the fleeing man and because she viewed

7   him in broad daylight, the court found that the identification was

8   reliable. *Id.* Similarly, in our case, Ms. Martinez's attention had been

9   drawn to her assailant. Shortly before the assault, Ms. Martinez

10   watched as her assailant drove slowly by her. Consequently, when

11   he drove by her again, her attention was focused on him. She watched

12   as he drove his car in front of her, blocking her path. In addition, she

13   watched as he got out of his car and walked toward her. Thus, although

14   she looked at him for only three or four seconds once he pulled out

15   the gun, before that time, she had a good opportunity to view him

16   and her attention had been focused on him.

17   The courts also do not require that the witness's description be

18   completely accurate. *State v. Kraus*, 21 Wn. App. 388, 584 P.2d 946

19   (1978). In *Kraus*, the court held that the witness's identification was

20   reliable despite the fact that the witness had stated that the robber was

21   wearing a dark jacket and the defendant was wearing a light-colored

22   jacket. *Id.* at 393. Similarly, in *State v. Maupin*, 63 Wn. App. 887, 822

23   P.2d 355 (1992), the court held that the witness's identification was reli-

24   able even though the witness was not able to tell the police the rapist's

25   race. *Id.* at 892. In this case, Ms. Martinez was able to give the police

26

State's Brief   Name of Prosecutor
in Opposition to   Deputy Prosecuting Attorney
Defendant's   for King County
Motion to Suppress - 6   Address of Prosecutor's Office

After listing the factors, the prosecutor goes through them one at a time.

In describing Booth, the prosecutor sets out only the key facts and the court's holding.

In comparing the facts in Booth to the facts in the case before the court, the prosecutor repeats key language from the case: "the witness's attention had been drawn."

The prosecutor selects words (e.g., "watched" and "focused") that suggest Martinez had a good opportunity to view her assailant.

The unfavorable fact appears in a dependent clause.

The prosecutor organizes the discussion of the second factor as he did the discussion of the first factor: (1) a topic sentence sets out the rule in a light favorable to the State; (2) cases illustrate how the courts have applied that rule, and these case descriptions include only the key facts, set out in a light favorable to the State; and (3) the rule is applied to the facts of this case.

1 a detailed description of her assailant. When she was interviewed, she

2 told the police that her assailant was a white male with blondish-brown

3 hair, that he was approximately 5'7" tall and weighed between 165 and

4 170 pounds, that he appeared to be in his early forties, and that he was

5 wearing a dark jacket. This description is accurate in all but one respect.

6 Although Ms. Martinez misjudged the defendant's age, she accurately

7 described his car, his hair, his height and weight, and his clothing.

8   In addition, Ms. Martinez's identification occurred shortly after the

9 assault, and Ms. Martinez was certain in her identification. Although

10 she did not answer Officer Yuen's question the first time that he asked

11 her, as soon as she got a better look at the defendant, Ms. Martinez

12 identified him as her assailant.㉞ As she stated during the suppression

13 hearing, "Once I got a good look at him I was sure it was him."㉟

14   Taken together, these facts establish that, even if the show-up was

15 suggestive, Ms. Martinez's identification was reliable.㊱ Ms. Martinez

16 had a good opportunity to view her assailant; her attention was focused

17 on her assailant; she accurately identified her assailant's build and

18 clothing; and once she got a good look at the defendant, she was certain

19 that he was her assailant. Accordingly, the Court should not suppress

20 Ms. Martinez's show-up identification.

21   C. <u>Because the show-up was not impermissibly suggestive, the
    Court should not suppress Ms. Martinez's line-up identifi-</u>
22   <u>cation or prevent Ms. Martinez or Mr. Clipse from making</u>
    <u>in-court identifications.</u>㊲
23

24   The Court should not suppress Ms. Martinez's line-up identifica-

25 tion, nor should it prevent Ms. Martinez or Mr. Clipse from making an

26

㉞ The prosecutor responds to defense counsel's argument that the officer's statement influenced Martinez's identification.

㉟ The prosecutor ends this section with a favorable quote.

㊱ The prosecutor ends this part of the argument by summarizing the points that he made.

㊲ This heading uses an alternative format: The "because" clause appears at the beginning rather than the end.

State's Brief
in Opposition to
Defendant's
Motion to Suppress - 7

Name of Prosecutor
Deputy Prosecuting Attorney
for King County
Address of Prosecutor's Office

1 in-court identification. ⊕ Because the show-up was not impermissibly

2 suggestive, see subsection IA, it did not taint either the line-up or any

3 potential in-court identifications.

4   Although Mr. Clipse may have seen the police talking with the

5 defendant, such an act by itself is not enough to make a show-up

6 impermissibly suggestive. ⊕ *See State v. Guzman-Cuellar*, 47 Wn.2d

7 326, 333, 734 P.2d 966 (1987); *State v. Rogers*, 44 Wn. App. 510, 512,

8 722 P.2d 1249 (1986); *State v. Booth*, 36 Wn. App. 66, 72, 671 P.2d 1218

9 (1983). In addition, like Ms. Martinez, Mr. Clipse had a good oppor-

10 tunity to view Ms. Martinez's assailant. His attention was drawn to

11 the assailant because the man was pulling into his parking spot, and,

12 except for his description of the assailant's age, Mr. Clipse's descrip-

13 tion was accurate.

14   **Prayer for Relief**

15   For the reasons set out above, the State respectfully requests

16 that the Court deny the defendant's motion to suppress and admit

17 Ms. Martinez's show-up and line-up identifications and permit Ms.

18 Martinez and Mr. Clipse to make in-court identifications.

19   Dated this 27th day of September, 2013.

20   _____

21   Assistant Prosecuting Attorney
                      Washington Bar No. 00000

22

23

24

25

26

State's Brief   Name of Prosecutor
in Opposition to   Deputy Prosecuting Attorney
Defendant's   for King County
Motion to Suppress - 8   Address of Prosecutor's Office

⊕ The prosecutor starts this section by setting out his assertion.

⊕ The prosecutor intentionally keeps this argument short. If he wins his first argument, he will also win this argument; if, however, he loses the first argument, he probably will lose this argument also.

EXAMPLE 3	**Defendant's Brief in Support of a Motion for Partial Summary Judgment**

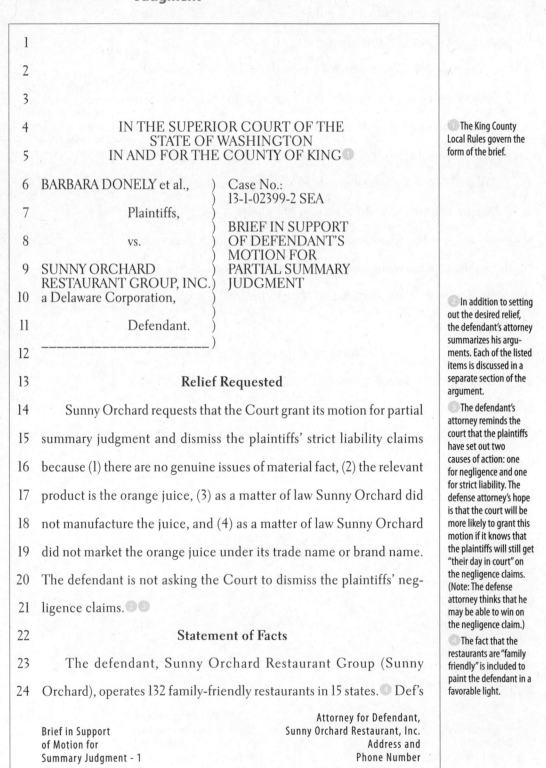

IN THE SUPERIOR COURT OF THE
STATE OF WASHINGTON
IN AND FOR THE COUNTY OF KING ❶

BARBARA DONELY et al.,   )   Case No.:
)   13-1-02399-2 SEA
            Plaintiffs,   )
)   BRIEF IN SUPPORT
      vs.   )   OF DEFENDANT'S
)   MOTION FOR
SUNNY ORCHARD   )   PARTIAL SUMMARY
RESTAURANT GROUP, INC.)   JUDGMENT
a Delaware Corporation,   )
)
            Defendant.   )
_____)

Relief Requested

Sunny Orchard requests that the Court grant its motion for partial summary judgment and dismiss the plaintiffs' strict liability claims because (1) there are no genuine issues of material fact, (2) the relevant product is the orange juice, (3) as a matter of law Sunny Orchard did not manufacture the juice, and (4) as a matter of law Sunny Orchard did not market the orange juice under its trade name or brand name. The defendant is not asking the Court to dismiss the plaintiffs' negligence claims. ❷❸

Statement of Facts

The defendant, Sunny Orchard Restaurant Group (Sunny Orchard), operates 132 family-friendly restaurants in 15 states. ❹ Def's

Brief in Support
of Motion for
Summary Judgment - 1

Attorney for Defendant,
Sunny Orchard Restaurant, Inc.
Address and
Phone Number

❶ The King County Local Rules govern the form of the brief.

❷ In addition to setting out the desired relief, the defendant's attorney summarizes his arguments. Each of the listed items is discussed in a separate section of the argument.

❸ The defendant's attorney reminds the court that the plaintiffs have set out two causes of action: one for negligence and one for strict liability. The defense attorney's hope is that the court will be more likely to grant this motion if it knows that the plaintiffs will still get "their day in court" on the negligence claims. (Note: The defense attorney thinks that he may be able to win on the negligence claim.)

❹ The fact that the restaurants are "family friendly" is included to paint the defendant in a favorable light.

1   Answer to 1st Amended Compl. ⑤ ¶ 1.3. One of the items that Sunny

2   Orchard⑥ serves at its restaurant is orange juice that it purchases from

3   the California Juice Company (California Juice). Def's Responses to

4   Pls' 1st Interr. No. 1.

5   ⑦California Juice delivers the juice in one-gallon containers to

6   Sunny Orchard's distribution center in Tukwila, Washington, which

7   then fill orders from individual restaurants. Def's Resp. to Pls' 1st Interr.

8   No. 3. When a restaurant receives the juice, it places the containers

9   containing the juice in a walk-in cooler. *Id.* As needed, the juice is

10 taken from the walk-in cooler and is poured into a juice dispenser from

11 which servers get the juice that they serve to customers. *Id.*

12   ⑧Sunny Orchard does not refer to the orange juice offered in

13 its restaurants as "Sunny Orchard juices," Def's Responses to Pls'

14 1st Interr. No. 10, and if asked whether the juice being served was

15 squeezed at the restaurant, the servers are assumed to answer truthfully

16 by saying, "No." Def's Responses to Pls' 1st Interr. No. 15. Although the

17 menu and servers describe the orange juice as "fresh" and "orchard-

18 squeezed,"⑨ any use of the name "Sunny Orchard" in conjunction

19 with a description of the juice refers only to the fact that the juice is

20 served within, at, or by a Sunny Orchard restaurant. Def's Responses

21 to Pls' 1st Interr. No. 11. The orange juice that is sold in the gift shop,

22 which is the same orange juice offered to Sunny Orchard customers,

23 is labeled with the California Juice name and not the Sunny Orchard

24 brand name.⑩ *Id.*

25

26

Brief in Support   Attorney for Defendant,
of Motion for   Sunny Orchard Restaurant, Inc.
Summary Judgment - 2   Address and
                                             Phone Number

⑤ The Washington Style Sheet does not prescribe the abbreviations that should be used in referring to documents filed with the court.

⑥ The defendant's attorney chooses to refer to his client as "Sunny Orchard" and to use the label "plaintiffs" for the opposing parties.

⑦ This matter-of-fact description of the distribution process establishes that the defendant, as simply a link in the distribution chain, does not alter or change the juice.

⑧ The defendant's attorney sets out the facts that he needs to respond to the plaintiffs' arguments. Note that paragraph is not in a position of emphasis.

⑨ This unfavorable fact appears in a dependent clause in the middle of a sentence that is in the middle of the paragraph.

⑩ The paragraph ends with a fact favorable to the defendant.

1   ⬤Sunny Orchard first offered the "Picnic Banquet Breakfast,"

2   which included orange juice in a souvenir glass, in 2005. Def's

3   Responses to Pls' 1st Interr. No. 13. While at first the glass was deco-

4   rated with the Sunny Orchard logo, the logo was removed four years

5   ago. Def's Responses to Pls' 1st Interr. No. 17. Since then, the glasses

6   have featured a seasonal design that changes four times a year. *Id.*

7   On May 12, 2013, the plaintiffs⬤ had breakfast at Sunny Orchard's

8   Seattle restaurant: All six plaintiffs ordered the Picnic Banquet Break-

9   fast, which comes with the orange juice that Sunny Orchard purchases

10   from California Juice. Complaint at ¶ 2.4. The juice was brought

11   to the table in a pitcher that had a kerchief tied on the handle and

12   poured into the decorative glasses, which had been garnished with a

13   slice of orange and a sprig of mint. Def's Responses to Pls' 1st Interr.

14   No. 16. Three days later, the Washington State Department of Com-

15   munity Health (WSDH) issued a warning to consumers not to drink

16   unpasteurized orange juice products distributed under the California

17   Juice brand name because the orange juice had the potential to be

18   contaminated with Salmonella. Complaint, ¶ 3.1. The plaintiffs allege,

19   Complaint, ¶ 5.4, and the defendant admits, that two of the plaintiffs,

20   Barbara Donely and Daniel Steddic, contracted Salmonella from the

21   juice that they drank at the Sunny Orchard restaurant. Requests for

22   Admission, Nos. 13, 14, 16. This has been the only confirmed claim of

23   a foodborne, illness-related injury at a Sunny Orchard restaurant in at

24   least five years. Def's Responses to Pls' 1st Interr. No. 20.⬤

25

26

Brief in Support
of Motion for
Summary Judgment - 3

⬤ This fact responds to the plaintiffs' argument that Sunny Orchard marketed the juice under its brand or trade name. The attorney puts the favorable facts at the end of the paragraph in a position of emphasis and the unfavorable fact in a dependent clause.

⬤ Word choice matters. The defendant's attorney deliberately identifies the opposing parties with a clinical-sounding term, "plaintiffs."

⬤ In this paragraph, the defendant's attorney minimizes the process that the servers used in serving the juice. See Example 4 to see how the plaintiffs' attorney presents these facts.

Because the facts set out in this paragraph do not favor California Restaurants, the defendant's attorney de-emphasizes them by placing them in a long paragraph.

Using chronological order highlights the fact that the restaurant did not know about the contamination until after it served the juice.

The fact that two of the plaintiffs became ill after drinking juice at a Sunny Orchard restaurant is given brief treatment. See Example 4 to see how the plaintiffs' attorney presented these facts.

Defense counsel ends this paragraph, and the statement of facts, with a favorable fact.

Note that the defendant's statement

1   **Statement of Issues**

2   Under the Washington Product Liability Act, RCW 7.72, is Sunny

3   Orchard entitled to judgment as a matter of law on the plaintiffs' strict

4   liability claim when (1) the plaintiffs became ill after drinking orange

5   juice at a Sunny Orchard restaurant; (2) Sunny Orchard purchased

6   the contaminated orange juice from California Juice; (3) all Sunny

7   Orchard did was pour the juice from the original containers into a

8   dispenser and then into a pitcher and garnished glasses; and (4) the

9   menu does not represent that Sunny Orchard made the juice and the

10   Sunny Orchard logo is not on the glasses?

11   **Evidence Relied Upon**

12   This motion is based on the First Amended Complaint for Prod-

13   uct Liability and Punitive Damages; Defendant's Answer to First

14   Amended Complaint for Product Liability and Punitive Damages;

15   Plaintiffs' First Requests for Admission and Defendant's Objections

16   and Responses to the Same; and Plaintiffs' First Interrogatories and

17   Requests for Production and Defendant's Objections and Responses

18   to the Same.

19   **Authority**

20   I.   THE COURT SHOULD GRANT SUNNY ORCHARD'S
          MOTION FOR PARTIAL SUMMARY JUDGMENT
21   BECAUSE THERE ARE NO ISSUES OF FACT AND,
          AS A MATTER OF LAW, SUNNY ORCHARD DID NOT
22   MANUFACTURE THE ORANGE JUICE OR MARKET
23   THE JUICE UNDER ITS BRAND NAME.

24   Summary judgment is appropriate when "the pleadings, deposi-

25   tions, answers to interrogatories, and admissions on file, together

26

Brief in Support   Attorney for Defendant,
of Motion for   Sunny Orchard Restaurant, Inc.
Summary Judgment - 4   Address and
                                                 Phone Number

---

of facts is much shorter than the plaintiffs'. The defendant's attorney wants to suggest that the facts in the case are not in dispute and that the only issues are legal ones.

The question is framed to suggest the conclusion that the defendant's attorney wants the court to reach.

In drafting this issue statement, the defendant's attorney had to decide whether to include the key facts, which makes for a long issue statement, or to set out legal conclusions. The attorney chose the first option.

Here the attorney had to decide whether to just set out his assertion or to include a "because" clause, which makes the issue statement much longer.

1 with the affidavits, if any, show that there is no genuine issue as to

2 any material fact and that the moving party is entitled to judgment as

3 a matter of law." CR 56(c). In making a decision, the courts must

4 consider all facts submitted and all reasonable inferences from them

5 in the light most favorable to the nonmoving party. *Sanders v. State*,

6 169 Wn.2d 827, 844, 240 P.3d 120 (2010). However, the nonmoving

7 party may not rely on speculation, argumentative assertions that unre-

8 solved factual issues remain, or on having its affidavits considered at

9 face value. *Seven Gables Corp. v. MGM/UA Entm't Co.*, 106 Wn.2d 1,

10 13, 721 P.2d 1 (1986). After the defendant submits adequate affidavits,

11 the burden shifts to the nonmoving party to provide specific facts

12 that sufficiently rebut the moving party's contentions and disclose

13 the existence of a material issue of fact. *Id.* A court should grant a

14 defendant's motion for summary judgment if there are no genuine

15 issues of material fact. *Sanders*, 169 Wn.2d at 844.

16   In this case, there are no genuine issues of material fact. Both

17 sides agree that the plaintiffs contracted Salmonella after drinking

18 the orange juice that the defendant purchased from California Juice.

19 Requests for Admission, Nos. 13, 14, 16. Because there are no genu-

20 ine issues of material fact, the questions before the Court are questions

21 of law. *See Almquist v. Finley Sch. Dist.*, 114 Wn. App. 395, 404, 57

22 P.3d 1191 (2002). In this case, as a matter of law, the relevant product is

23 the orange juice, and Sunny Orchard did not manufacture that orange

24 juice or market that orange juice under its trade or brand name.

25

26

Brief in Support
of Motion for
Summary Judgment - 5

Attorney for Defendant,
Sunny Orchard Restaurant, Inc.
Address and
Phone Number

The defendant's attorney starts the Authority section by setting out the general rules governing summary judgment. Because judges know the rules governing summary judgment, the attorney keeps this section brief but sets out the key rules in a light favorable to his client.

This paragraph begins with an assertion: that there are no genuine issues of material fact. Support for this assertion is given in the citation to the Requests for Admission.

At this point, the attorney does not know whether the plaintiffs will argue that there is a question of fact. If they do, he will respond to those arguments in a reply brief or in oral argument.

1   A.   <u>The relevant product is the orange juice because it was the</u>

2   <u>orange juice that gave rise to the product liability claim.</u>⑲

3   Under RCW 7.72.010(3), the relevant product is "that product or

4   its component part or parts, which gave rise to the product liability

5   claim."⑳ In this case, the plaintiffs allege that their injuries were

6   caused by the orange juice that they drank at one of Sunny Orchard's

7   restaurants. Complaint at ¶ 2.4. They do not allege that they were

8   harmed by the glass in which the orange juice was served, by the gar-

9   nishes that were placed on the glass, or by any of the other items that

10   were served as part of the Picnic Banquet Breakfast.㉑ *Id.* Therefore,

11   under the definition set out in the act, the relevant product is the

12   orange juice because it contained the Salmonella "which gave rise

13   to the product liability claim." RCW 7.72.010(3).

14   B.   <u>Sunny Orchard is not a "manufacturer" because all that it</u>

15   <u>did was serve orange juice that it purchased from California</u>

     <u>Juice.</u>

16

17   Although Sunny Orchard is a product seller, it is not a manufac-

18   turer. An entity is a manufacturer only if it "designs, produces, makes,

19   fabricates, constructs, or remanufactures the relevant product . . . ."

20   RCW 7.72.010(2).㉒

21   In the only Washington Products Liability Act case that discusses

22   whether a defendant who serves food falls within the definition of a

23   manufacturer, the defendant altered the food item that caused the

24   injury.㉓ *Almquist v. Finley Sch. Dist.*, 114 Wn. App. 395, 57 P.3d 1191

25   (2002). In *Almquist*, the defendant, the Finley School District (School

26

Brief in Support   Attorney for Defendant,
of Motion for   Sunny Orchard Restaurant, Inc.
Summary Judgment - 6   Address and
                                                             Phone Number

⑲ The attorney uses the conventional format for this argumentative heading. He sets out his assertion and then a "because" clause in which he provides support for that assertion.

⑳ In this brief, the attorney does not include a general rule section in which he provides the judge with an overview of the Washington Products Liability Act. Instead, he jumps right into the analysis. While this strategy would work well with judges who are familiar with the Act, it would not work for judges who are not. Consequently, unless the attorney knows that the judge is familiar with the ACT, he should add a general rule section.

㉑ Details emphasize what the plaintiffs have not alleged.

㉒ This subsection begins by setting out the specific rule in a light favorable to the defendant. Note the use of the word "only."

㉓ The discussion of the analogous case starts with a principle-based topic sentence.

1   District), did not just serve the tainted ground beef. *Id.* at 404. Instead,

2   it thawed the beef, cooked the beef, drained it, rinsed it, added season-

3   ings, and then added other ingredients to create tacos. *Id.* ㉔ In light

4   of these facts, the court concluded that the School District's cooking

5   process fell neatly into each of the definitions for "design," "produce,"

6   "make," "fabricate," and "construct": The District designed the school

7   lunch and, using the tainted meat, it produced, made, fabricated,

8   and constructed the taco lunch. *Id.* at 405. As the court noted in its

9   opinion, "[t]he reason for excluding nonmanufacturing retailers from

10   strict liability is to distinguish 'between those who have actual control

11   over the product and those who act as mere conduits in the chain of

12   distribution.'" ㉕ *Id.*

13   ㉖ Unlike the School District, which altered the frozen ground

14   beef, Sunny Orchard simply served juice that it purchased from Cali-

15   fornia Juice. It did not do anything to prepare the juice — for example,

16   it did not thaw frozen concentrate, and it did not add anything to the

17   orange juice. All it did was add an orange slice and a sprig of mint

18   to the glass. ㉗ The orange juice remained in exactly the same form

19   from the time Sunny Orchard purchased it from California Juice until

20   Sunny Orchard served it to its customers. Therefore, Sunny Orchard

21   acted as a mere conduit in the chain of distribution. ㉘

22   C.   The orange juice was marketed under California Juice's brand
              name and not Sunny Orchard's brand name.
23

24   Finally, Sunny Orchard did not market the orange juice under

25   its trade name or brand and, therefore, it is not a manufacturer under

26

Brief in Support   Attorney for Defendant,
of Motion for   Sunny Orchard Restaurant, Inc.
Summary Judgment - 7   Address and
                                                 Phone Number

㉔ Because he wants to distinguish *Almquist*, the defendant's attorney goes into detail in describing the process that the District used in preparing and mixing the tainted beef with other ingredients.

㉕ The defendant's attorney ends this paragraph with a quotation that supports his client's argument.

㉖ This paragraph distinguishes *Almquist*.

㉗ To emphasize his points, the attorney uses an example that is based on the facts in *Almquist*.

㉘ The attorney concludes this paragraph by repeating the quoted language from the preceding paragraph.
   Because most judges want short, concise briefs, the attorney makes his key points and then stops. If the plaintiffs make other arguments, he can respond to those arguments in a reply brief or during the oral arguments.

1   RCW 7.72.040(2)(e). The key case is *Johnson v. Recreational Equip-*

2   *ment, Inc.*, 159 Wn. App. 939, 247 P.3d 18 (2011), a case in which the

3   plaintiff brought a products liability action against the seller of an

4   allegedly defective carbon fiber fork that fractured and detached

5   from her bicycle. *Id.* at 943. Because both the bicycle and the car-

6   bon fiber fork were marketed under REI's brand name, "Novara," the

7   court held REI strictly liable for the injuries caused by the defective

8   product. *Id.*

9   Unlike REI, which marketed both the bicycle and the carbon fiber

10 fork under its brand name, Sunny Orchard did not market the juice

11 under its brand name. It did not advertise the juice as Sunny Orchard

12 juice and, on its menu it simply states that the juice is "sunny-fresh,

13 orchard-squeezed juice." Pls.' First Am. Compl. ¶ 3.12; Def.'s Resp.

14 to Pls.' Interrog. No. 11. In addition, the Sunny Orchard logo is not

15 on the pitcher or the glasses in which the juice is served. Finally, the

16 orange juice that is sold in the gift shop, which is the same orange

17 juice offered to Sunny Orchard customers, is labeled with the Cali-

18 fornia Juice brand name and not the Sunny Orchard brand name. *Id.*

19 Even if the court were to find that the Picnic Banquet Breakfast is

20 labeled under the Sunny Orchard name, the product that gave rise to

21 the product liability claim is the orange juice containing Salmonella

22 and, therefore, it is irrelevant whether the Picnic Banquet Breakfast

23 meets the trade name or brand name exception.

24

25

26

Attorney for Defendant,
Sunny Orchard Restaurant, Inc.
Brief in Support   Address and
of Motion for   Phone Number
Summary Judgment - 8

Side notes:

[29] This section begins by setting out the assertion and then introducing the key case.

[30] The attorney uses this paragraph to distinguish REI. In doing so, he sets out the facts that support his position.

[31] This sentence counters an argument that he expects the plaintiffs will make.

1   **Prayer for Relief**

2   For the reasons set out above, Sunny Orchard respectfully requests

3   that the Court grant its motion for partial summary judgment on the

4   plaintiffs' strict liability claims.

5

6   Respectfully submitted this 2nd
                                     day of October, 2013.
7

8   /s/
                                     Attorney's Name
9   Attorney for the defendant,
                                     Sunny Orchard Restaurant
10   Group, Inc.
11   Bar No.

12

13

14

15

16

17

18

19

20

21

22

23

24

25

26

Brief in Support   Attorney for Defendant,
of Motion for   Sunny Orchard Restaurant, Inc.
Summary Judgment - 9   Address and
                                                 Phone Number

EXAMPLE 4　　**Plaintiffs' Brief in Opposition to Motion for Partial Summary Judgment**

1

2

3

4　　　　IN THE SUPERIOR COURT OF THE
STATE OF WASHINGTON

5　　　IN AND FOR THE COUNTY OF KING

6　BARBARA DONELY et al.,　　　)　Case No.:

　　　　　　　　　　　　　　　　)　13-1-02399-2 SEA

7　　　　　　Plaintiffs,　　　　　)

　　　　　　　　　　　　　　　　)　BRIEF IN OPPOSITION TO

8　　　　v.　　　　　　　　　　　)　DEFENDANT'S MOTION

　　　　　　　　　　　　　　　　)　FOR PARTIAL SUMMARY

9　SUNNY ORCHARD　　　　　　　　)　JUDGMENT

10　RESTAURANT GROUP, INC.)

　　a Delaware Corporation,　　)

11　　　　　　　　　　　　　　　)

　　　　　　　Defendant.　　　　　)

12　　　　　　　　　　　　　　　　)

　　_____　　)

13

14　　　　　　**Relief Requested** ❶

15　　　The Plaintiffs ❷ request that the Court deny the Defendant's

16　Motion for Partial Summary Judgment on the Plaintiffs' strict liability

17　claims under the Washington Product Liability Act (Act) because there

18　are genuine issues of fact. In addition, even if there are no genuine

19　issues of fact, the Defendant is strictly liable both because it manu-

20　factured the relevant product and because it marketed the relevant

21　product under its brand or trade name.

22

23

24

Brief in Opposition to　　　　　　　　　Attorney for Plaintiffs
Defendant's Motion for　　　　　　　　　　　　Address and
Partial Summary Judgment - 1　　　　　　　　Phone Number

❶ The Washington Rules require a section in which the party submitting the brief sets out the relief that it is requesting. See LCR 7(b)(5)(B).

❷ Although the plaintiffs' attorney would prefer to call her clients by name, because the plaintiffs have different last names, she decides to use the more generic label.

1   **Statement of Facts**

2   1.   Exposure to Salmonella Typhimurium and Resulting

3   Injuries ⑤

4   ④ Plaintiffs Barbara and James Donely reside in Omaha, Nebraska.

5   Pls.' First Am. Compl. ¶ 1.1. Plaintiffs Michael and Beverly Steddic

6   reside in Seattle, Washington, and are the parents of Daniel and

7   Charlotte Steddic, the Donelys' grandchildren. Pls.' First Am. Compl.

8   ¶ 1.2. The Defendant, Sunny Orchard Restaurant Group, Inc., is a

9   Delaware public corporation headquartered in California. It operates

10   132 restaurants in fifteen states. Pls.' First Am. Compl. ¶ 1.3.

11   On Mother's Day, May 12, 2013, ⑤ the Plaintiffs visited one of

12   Sunny Orchard's Seattle restaurants where all six members of the fam-

13   ily ordered the "Picnic Banquet Breakfast," which the Defendant states

14   in its advertising and menu is like "having a family picnic in a sun-filled

15   orchard!" Def's Responses to Pls' 1st Interr. No. 12. The featured item

16   on the menu is a pitcher of "sunny-fresh, orchard-squeezed juice." Pls.'

17   First Am. Compl. ¶ 3.12; Def.'s Resp. to Pls.' Interrog. No. 11.

18   2.   Barbara Donely's Injuries and Medical Care

19   ⑥ Two days after eating at the Defendant's restaurant, Ms. Donely

20   became so ill that she had to be hospitalized for seven days. Pls.' First

21   Am. Compl. ¶ 3.14(a). During this time, Ms. Donely underwent a

22   series of tests: A stool culture confirmed the presence of Salmonella

23   Typhimurium. Pls.' First Am. Compl. ¶ 3.14(c); Def.'s Resp. to Pls.'

24   First Req. for Admis. No. 13.

25

26

Brief in Opposition to   Attorney for Plaintiffs
Defendant's Motion for   Address and
Partial Summary Judgment - 2   Phone Number

⑤ Because the statement of facts is long, it is divided into labeled subsections.

④ The statement of facts begins with a paragraph identifying the parties.

⑤ While the fact that the plaintiffs ate at the restaurant on Mother's Day is not legally significant, it helps the plaintiffs' attorney tell her clients' story.

⑥ While the defendant's attorney did not devote any space to the plaintiffs' injuries, the plaintiffs' attorney sets out those facts in detail. While these facts are not legally significant, they help the plaintiffs' attorney tell her clients' story.

1   3.   Daniel Steddic's Injuries and Medical Care

2   While at school on the Monday after he ate at the Defendant's

3 restaurant, nine-year-old Daniel Steddic developed abdominal

4 cramps and diarrhea. Pls.' First Am. Compl. ¶ 3.15. Because his symp-

5 toms worsened overnight, the next morning his parents took him to

6 the emergency room, where he was admitted with a temperature of

7 103 degrees. *Id.* Daniel was in the hospital for three days and was

8 diagnosed with gastroenteritis caused by Salmonella Typhimurium, a

9 condition called Salmonellosis. Pls.' First Am. Compl. ¶ 3.22; Def.'s

10 Resp. to Pls.' First Req. for Admis. No. 14.

11   4.   Salmonella Typhimurium Outbreak Investigation

12   During the week of May 12, 2013, the Washington State Depart-

13 ment of Community Health (WSDH) investigated nine Salmonella

14 infections that resulted from consumption of "fresh, orchard-squeezed"

15 orange juice at one of the Defendant's Seattle restaurants. Attach. No.

16 1 to Pls.' Interrogs. 2; Def.'s Resp. to Pls.' First Req. for Admis. No. 1.

17 One of the unopened gallon bottles of orange juice taken from the

18 Defendant's restaurant tested positive for Salmonella Typhimurium.

19 Def.'s Resp. to Pls.' First Req. for Admis. No. 15. Pulsed-field gel elec-

20 trophoresis (PFGE) testing concluded that the Salmonella bacteria

21 isolated from this unopened bottle was "a genetically indistinguish-

22 able match" to the Salmonella bacteria isolated from Ms. Donely's

23 and Daniel's stool cultures. Def.'s Resp. to Pls.' First Req. for Admis.

24 No. 16.

25

26

The plaintiffs' attorney emphasizes that one of the plaintiffs is a young child.

While parties are not generally referred to by their first names only, children are an exception.

Brief in Opposition to   Attorney for Plaintiffs
Defendant's Motion for   Address and
Partial Summary Judgment - 3   Phone Number

1   5.   Handling of "Sunny-Fresh, Orchard-Squeezed" Orange

2   Juice

3   The Defendant's Operations Manual sets out detailed instruc-

4   tions for the assembly and service of the "fresh, orchard-squeezed

5   juice" that is served as part of the Picnic Banquet Breakfast. Attach.

6   No. 2 to Pls.' Interrogs. 1. First, servers fill a pitcher with juice from the

7   refrigerated dispenser and tie a gingham kerchief around the handle

8   of the pitcher. Attach. No. 2 to Pls.' Interrogs. 2. Second, servers place

9   the pitcher on a tray and arrange "Sunny Orchard decorative glasses"

10   around the pitcher in a semi-circle. Attach. No. 2 to Pls.' Interrogs.

11   3. Third, servers garnish the glasses by placing a slice of orange on

12   the edge of the glass and tucking the stem of a mint sprig under the

13   fruit slice; at the table, a cherry is added to children's glasses. Attach.

14   No. 2 to Pls.' Interrogs. 4. In emphasizing the importance of these

15   garnishes, the Operations Manual states that "it would just not be

16   Sunny Orchard 'orchard-squeezed juice' without the proper 'picnic'

17   garnishes. Our guests expect and pay for these extra-steps [sic]."

18   Attach. No. 2 to Pls.' Interrogs. 4. Fourth, when they get to the table,

19   servers place a napkin with the Defendant's logo on it in front of each

20   guest and then place the glass on the napkin. Attach. No. 2 to Pls.'

21   Interrogs. 5, Def.'s Resp. to Pls.' Interrog. No. 14. Finally, servers pour

22   juice from the pitcher into each glass. As they do so, they say "I hope

23   that you enjoy our fresh, orchard-squeezed juice." Attach. No. 2 to

24   Pls.' Interrogs. 6.

25   Since introducing the Picnic Banquet Breakfast in 2005, the

26   Defendant has served the juice in "decorative glasses." While these

Unlike the defendant's attorney, the plaintiffs' attorney details the process that defendant uses in preparing and serving the juice. The use of "First," "Second," "Third," emphasizes the number of steps in the process.

This long paragraph highlights the fact that the process is long.

Plaintiffs' attorney ends the paragraph with a favorable fact, which she emphasizes by including a quotation.

Brief in Opposition to   Attorney for Plaintiffs
Defendant's Motion for   Address and
Partial Summary Judgment - 4   Phone Number

1　glasses now feature seasonal designs, originally the glasses had the

2　Defendant's logo printed on them. Def.'s Resp. to Pls.' Interrog.

3　No. 12. The Defendant advertises the glasses as "seasonal souvenir

4　glasses," and states that many customers collect the glasses by visiting

5　the Defendant's restaurants several times a year. Def.'s Resp. to Pls.'

6　Interrog. No. 12.

7　　　　　　　　　　　**Issue Statement**

8　　　Should the Court deny the Defendant's motion for partial sum-

9　mary judgment when the plaintiffs purchased the Picnic Banquet

10　Breakfast from the Defendant, and the featured product of that break-

11　fast, orange juice served from a pitcher with a kerchief tied around

12　the handle into decorative glasses garnished with an orange slice and

13　a sprig of mint, was contaminated with Salmonella?

14　　　　　　　　　　　**Evidence Relied Upon**

15　　　This Motion is based on Plaintiffs' First Requests for Admission

16　and Defendant's Responses Thereto, Plaintiffs' First Interrogatories

17　and Requests for Production and Defendant's Responses Thereto and

18　their attachments, and the pleadings on file with this Court.

19　　　　　　　　　　　**Argument**

20　　　I. THE COURT SHOULD DENY THE DEFENDANT'S
　　　　MOTION FOR PARTIAL SUMMARY JUDGMENT
21　　　BECAUSE THERE ARE GENUINE ISSUES OF MATE-
　　　　RIAL FACT AND THE DEFENDANT IS NOT ENTITLED
22　　　TO JUDGMENT AS A MATTER OF LAW.

23

24　　　A court should deny a motion for summary judgment unless it

25　concludes "that there is no genuine issue as to any material fact and

26　that the moving party is entitled to a judgment as a matter of law." CR

Brief in Opposition to　　　　　　　　　Attorney for Plaintiffs
Defendant's Motion for　　　　　　　　　　　Address and
Partial Summary Judgment - 5　　　　　　　Phone Number

The favorable fact appears in the main clause.

The plaintiffs' attorney frames the question so that it suggests the conclusion that she wants the court to reach.
　　Although these details make the issue statement longer, they are key facts.
　　Because she wants to remind the court that some of her clients became seriously ill, she puts the reference to Salmonella at the end of the sentence.

Because the plaintiffs' attorney has one issue statement, she has one main heading. The issue statement sets out the question, and the heading answers that question.

While the "because" clause makes the heading longer, the plaintiffs' attorney includes it to emphasize the issues of fact. Once she mentions the issues of fact, she needs to mention her alternative argument.

Because judges know the rules governing summary judgment, the plaintiffs' attorney briefly sets out the key rules, emphasizing those that favor her client.
　　Compare the way in which plaintiffs' attorney sets out the rules for summary judgment with the way that the defendant's attorney sets out the rules in Example 3.

1   56(c). In deciding the motion, the court considers the evidence and all

2   reasonable inferences drawn therefrom in the light most favorable to

3   the nonmoving party. *Seybold v. Neu*, 105 Wn. App. 666, 675, 19 P.3d

4   1068 (2001). It is the moving party—in this case, the defendant—that

5   bears the initial burden of showing that there is no genuine issue of

6   fact. *See id.*

7   A.   <u>There is a genuine issue of material fact.</u> ⑰

8   In this case, there is a genuine issue of material fact. Although the

9   defendant argues that the relevant product is the orange juice, ⑱ the

10 plaintiffs assert that the relevant product is the Picnic Banquet Break-

11 fast and that the component part giving rise to the plaintiffs' injuries

12 is the juice that was served, in accordance with detailed instructions,

13 from a pitcher with a kerchief on the handle into decorative glasses

14 garnished with a slice of orange and a sprig of mint. ⑲

15   *Almquist v. Finley School District*, 114 Wn. App. 395, 57 P.3d 1191

16 (2002), can be distinguished from this case. ⑳ While in that case the

17 plaintiffs argued that there was an issue of fact, the court noted that the

18 plaintiffs had not raised that issue at the trial court level and that, in

19 arguing the motion for summary judgment, the plaintiffs had referred

20 to the product as the tainted meat and not as the taco lunch. ㉑ *Id.* at

21 404. In contrast, in this case the plaintiffs have raised the issue. The

22 jury should be allowed to decide whether the relevant product is the

23 juice or whether it is the product that the Defendant sold and the

24 plaintiffs purchased: the Picnic Banquet Breakfast. ㉒

25

26

⑰ In this instance, the attorney sets out just her assertion. There is no concise way of setting out the facts.

⑱ To show that there is an issue of fact, the plaintiffs' attorney sets out each side's assertion. Note that the defendant's assertion is in the dependent clause and the plaintiffs' assertion is in the main clause.

⑲ The plaintiffs' attorney goes into detail in setting out the facts that support her assertion that the relevant product is the breakfast and that the component part is the juice as it was packaged and served.

⑳ Note the attorney's use of a strong topic sentence. However, when possible, avoid starting a paragraph and/or sentence with a full cite.

㉑ The plaintiffs' attorney responds to the defendant's argument without repeating that argument.

㉒ Unfortunately, there are no cases that say that the issue is an issue of fact. Thus, the plaintiffs' attorney must rely on assertions.

Brief in Opposition to   Attorney for Plaintiffs
Defendant's Motion for   Address and
Partial Summary Judgment - 6   Phone Number

1   B. <u>The Defendant is a Manufacturer.</u>

2   The Washington Product Liability Act (WPLA) imposes strict

3 liability on manufacturers of defective products. RCW 7.72.030(2).

4 The WPLA defines both "manufacturer" and "product": The term

5 manufacturer includes a "product seller who designs, produces,

6 makes, fabricates, constructs, or remanufactures the relevant product

7 or component part of a product before its sale," RCW 7.72.010(2),

8 and a product is "any object . . . produced for introduction into trade

9 or commerce." RCW 7.72.010(3). In addition, the WPLA defines the

10 term "relevant product." *Id.* The relevant product is "that product or its

11 component part or parts, which gave rise to the product liability claim."

12 *Id.* In discussing these definitions, the Almquist court emphasized that

13 the statute applies to all sellers who do "more than merely pass along,

14 unchanged, a previously packaged product." *Id.* at 401.

15   Because WPLA does not define the words "designs," "produces,"

16 "makes," "fabricates," "constructs," or "remanufactures," the courts

17 have used the dictionary definitions. *Id.* at 404-05. For example,

18 in *Almquist*, the court stated that the School District had a "design"

19 for cooking the meat: its recipe. In addition, the court held that the

20 District's cooking process fell within the definitions for "produce,"

21 "make," "fabricate," and "construct." *Id.* at 405.

22   Like the School District, the Defendant had a design for pre-

23 paring and serving the juice that was included in the Picnic Banquet

24 Breakfast: The Defendant's Operations Manual sets out in detail the

25 way in which the servers should prepare and serve the juice. The juice

26 is dispensed into a pitcher with a kerchief tied around the handle, the

Brief in Opposition to   Attorney for Plaintiffs
Defendant's Motion for   Address and
Partial Summary Judgment - 7   Phone Number

Margin notes: Again, the assertion appears without a "because" clause. Unlike the defendant's attorney, plaintiff's attorney starts her argument by setting out the applicable sections of the law. The plaintiffs' attorney ends this paragraph with a quote that supports her position. Note the attorney's use of a transition. The attorney starts this paragraph with an assertion: that this case is like *Almquist*. She then uses the facts from her case to support her assertion; at the end of the paragraph she compares the facts in *Almquist* to the facts in her client's case. In doing so, the attorney counters the arguments that defense counsel made in his brief and tries to create a new rule, that a manufacturer is someone who creates a new product.

1   glasses are garnished with a slice of orange and a sprig of mint, and

2   the servers are instructed not only on how to serve the juice but also

3   on what to say as they are serving it. Thus, just as the School District

4   produced and made a new product(28) when it combined the meat with

5   other ingredients, the Defendant produced and made a new product

6   when it combined juice, fruit slices, mint sprigs, cherries, and vari-

7   ous service items and breakfast foods to produce and make its Picnic

8   Banquet Breakfast. Because the Defendant designed, produced, and

9   made the relevant product, it is a manufacturer.

10   (29) The *Almquist* court also concluded that the School District

11   "was not merely a retailer" because it "did not simply resell frozen

12   ground beef, seasonings, and tortillas as a grocery store would." *Id.* at

13   405. Instead of simply reselling a product, the District took a product

14   and altered it. *Id.* at 405-06. (30) Similarly, in this case, the Defendant

15   did not act as a retailer, reselling juice, fruit slices, mint, cherries,

16   and the various service items and breakfast foods as separate goods.

17   Instead, it assembled and served these items in an elaborate way, as

18   evidenced by the multi-step procedure outlined in the Operations

19   Manual. The Operations Manual's own words — that restaurant "guests

20   expect and pay for these extra-steps [sic]" — show that the Defendant

21   transformed these items into a unique and valuable product, a product

22   that it manufactured.

23   C. <u>In the alternative, the Defendant marketed the Picnic Ban-</u>
         <u>quet Breakfast under its brand or trade name.</u>
24

25   Even if the Defendant is not deemed a manufacturer, it is still

26   strictly liable.(31) Under the Act, a non-manufacturing product seller

28 Note how the attorney repeats the phrase "produced and made a new product."

29 This paragraph sets out an additional/alternative argument, that *Almquist* supports that the defendant did more than resell a product.

30 To emphasize her point, the plaintiffs' attorney goes into detail in describing the facts.

31 The plaintiffs' attorney starts this subsection by setting out her assertion, making it clear that she is arguing in the alternative. She then sets out the specific rule.

Brief in Opposition to   Attorney for Plaintiffs
Defendant's Motion for   Address and
Partial Summary Judgment - 8   Phone Number

1 is strictly liable for a defective product when it markets that product

2 under its brand or trade name. RCW 7.72.040(2)(e).

3   In this case, the Defendant falls with the definition of a "product

4 seller" because it sells various food products to the public. See RCW

5 7.72.010(1). In addition, it marketed the Picnic Banquet Breakfast in

6 its advertising and on its menu, stating that the Picnic Banquet Break-

7 fast is [l]ike having a family picnic in a sun-filled orchard!" While the

8 Defendant has not done what REI did and created a special brand

9 name, see *Johnson v. Recreational Equip., Inc.*, 159 Wn. App. 939, 247

10 P.3d 18 (2011), it has done the equivalent. It has used a word from its

11 corporate name, "orchard," and put it in its advertising for the orange

12 juice (the juice is "sunny-fresh" and "orchard-squeezed"). In addition,

13 the Defendant serves the juice in decorative glasses that customers

14 associate with the Defendant's restaurants. Therefore, even if deemed

15 a non-manufacturing product seller, the Defendant is strictly liable

16 under Act.

17   **Prayer for Relief**

18   For the reasons set forth above, the Plaintiffs respectfully request

19 that the Court deny the Defendant's motion for partial summary judg-

20 ment on the Plaintiffs' strict liability claims.

21   Respectfully submitted this 11th day of
                    October, 2013.
22

23   /s/ _____

24   Attorney's name
                    Attorney for the plaintiffs

25

26

> In this sentence and the following sentence, plaintiffs' attorney counters the defendant's argument. Note that the attorney does not repeat the defendant's argument but simply sets out her own argument.

Brief in Opposition to   Attorney for Plaintiffs
Defendant's Motion for   Address and
Partial Summary Judgment - 9   Phone Number

Writing an Appellate Brief

I
t is the stuff of movies and childhood fantasies. You are standing before the United States Supreme Court making an impassioned argument. You are arguing that the votes should, or should not, be recounted in a presidential election; that the defendant was, or was not, the victim of racial profiling; or that the government should, or should not, require every citizen to purchase health care.

Although such high-stakes oral advocacy is exciting and dramatic, in many cases the brief is as important, if not more important. Although Hollywood and authors like John Grisham might be more inclined to write a scene depicting oral advocacy, in the real legal world it is frequently the written brief that makes the difference.

In this chapter, we continue our discussion of written advocacy, which was begun in the last chapter on motion briefs, and take it to the next level: the appellate brief. Much of what we discussed about writing a motion brief applies to appellate briefs. Thus, this chapter focuses on those parts of writing a brief that are unique to writing an appellate brief: finding and applying the rules on appeal, types of appeals, scope of review, standard of review, and harmless error. In Chapter 19 we discuss oral advocacy—specifically, how to prepare for and deliver an effective oral argument.

§ 18.1 Practicing Before an Appellate Court

In most jurisdictions, there are court rules that govern appellate practice. For example, appellate practice before the United States Supreme Court is governed by the Rules of the Supreme Court of the United States (Sup. Ct. R.), and appellate practice before the United States Courts of Appeal is governed by the Federal Rules of Appellate Procedure (Fed. R. App. P.). Similarly, states have rules that govern appellate practice within that state.

In addition to locating and reading the jurisdiction's or court's rules, also look for local rules. For example, if you are writing a brief in a case that will be heard by the Ninth Circuit Court of Appeals, look at both the Federal Rules of Appellate Procedure and the Ninth Circuit's rules. If you do not comply with both the general and local rules, the court might refuse to hear your appeal or petition for review or reject your brief.

> **PRACTICE POINTER**
>
> The easiest place to find a particular jurisdiction's or court's rules is the jurisdiction's or court's website. For example, you can find the Rules of the Supreme Court of the United States at http://www.supremecourt.gov/ctrules/2013RulesoftheCourt.pdf and the Ninth Circuit Court of Appeals rules at http://cdn.ca9.uscourts.gov/datastore/uploads/rules/frap.pdf

§ 18.1.1 Types of Appellate Review

In most jurisdictions, court rules provide for two types of appellate review: an appeal as of right (Fed. R. App. P. 4) and discretionary review (Fed. R. App. P. 5). For example, in both the federal and state systems, a defendant convicted of a crime has the right to appeal to an intermediate court of appeals or, if the state does not have an intermediate court of appeals, to the state's highest court. However, in the federal system and most states, review by the jurisdiction's highest court is discretionary. Consequently, a defendant seeking review of a decision of an intermediate court of appeals would have to file a petition for review or a writ of certiorari requesting such review. If the highest court grants review, the parties would then prepare briefs in which they argue the case on its merits. In determining whether to grant discretionary review, courts will generally look to whether the case involves a conflict between circuits or divisions, raises an important constitutional question, or raises an issue of great public import. For example, Supreme Court Rule 10 sets out the rules governing the Court's discretionary review on a writ of certiorari:

EXAMPLE 1   Supreme Court Rule 10

Review on a writ of certiorari is not a matter of right, but of judicial discretion. A petition for a writ or certiorari will be granted only for compelling reasons. The following, although neither controlling nor fully measuring the Court's discretion, indicate the character of the reasons the Court considers:

(a) a United States court of appeals has entered a decision in conflict with another United States court of appeals on the same important matter; has decided an important federal question in a way that conflicts with a decision by a state court of last resort; or has so far departed from the accepted and usual course of judicial proceedings, or sanctioned such a departure by a lower court, as to call for an exercise of this Court's supervisory power;

(b) a state court of last resort has decided an important federal question in a way that conflicts with the decision of another state court of last resort or of a United States court of appeals;

(c) a state court or a United States court of appeals has decided an important question of federal law that has not been, but should be, settled by this Court, or has decided an important federal question in a way that conflicts with relevant decisions of this Court.

A petition for a writ of certiorari is rarely granted when the asserted error consists of erroneous factual findings or the misapplication of a properly stated rule of law.

> **PRACTICE POINTER**   Different jurisdictions might use different labels to refer to the parties. For example, in cases involving an appeal as of right, the parties might be referred to as the appellant and appellee or as the appellant and respondent. In contrast, in a case involving discretionary review, the parties might be referred to as the petitioner and respondent. Therefore, before writing your brief, check the applicable rules to determine which labels apply.

§ 18.1.2   Time Limits for Filing the Notice of Appeal or Petition for Discretionary Review

In pursuing an appeal as of right or seeking discretionary review, a party must adhere to the timelines as set out in the applicable rules. For example, Fed. R. App. P. 4 sets out the time for filing an appeal as of right in a federal court of appeal, and the time limits differ depending on the nature of the case and the party seeking an appeal. In a civil case, the party filing the appeal must file its notice of appeal within thirty days of the date the judgment or order appealed was entered. Fed. R. App. P. (4)(a)(1)(A). However, if the United States, its officer, or its agency is a party, the party filing the appeal must file its notice of appeal within sixty days of the date the judgment or the order was entered. Fed. R. App. P. (4)(a)(1)(B).

In contrast, in a criminal case, the defendant must file his or her notice of appeal "within 10 days after the later of: (i) the entry of either the judgment or the order being appealed; or (ii) the filing of the government's notice of appeal." Fed. R. App. P. (4)(b)(1)(A). When the government is entitled to appeal, "its notice of appeal must be filed in the district court within 30 days after the later of: (i) the entry of the judgment or order being appealed; or (ii) the filing of the notice of appeal by any defendant." Fed. R. App. P. (4)(b)(1)(B).

If a party is seeking review by the United States Supreme Court, it must file its petition for review on certiorari within ninety days after the entry of judgment. Sup. Ct. R. 13.1.

§ 18.1.3   The Notice of Appeal or Notice for Discretionary Review

In addition, in most jurisdictions there is a court rule that sets out the procedure for filing a notice of appeal or a notice for discretionary review. For example, Fed. R. App. P. 3 sets out the rules for filing and serving the Notice of

Appeal when a party has an appeal as of right. A sample template for a notice of appeal is set out in Form 1 of the appendix to the Federal Rules of Appellate Procedure. Supreme Court Rule 12 sets out the method of seeking review on certiorari.

§ 18.1.4   Scope of Review

In determining the scope of review, the courts consider two factors. First, as a general rule, an appellate court will review only those issues or decisions listed in the notice of appeal or in the petition for discretionary review or writ of certiorari. Second, as a general rule, an appellate court will review only those errors that were raised, or preserved, at trial. This second rule gives the trial court the opportunity to rule on alleged errors in the first instance and helps ensure that attorneys will not stay silent, hoping for a favorable result at trial while using an appeal as a "fallback" position. There are, though, exceptions to this rule. In some jurisdictions, the requirement that issues be preserved for appeal by raising them at trial and exceptions to the requirement are developed through case law. *See, e.g.*, Ulrich, Kessler & Anger, P.C., et al., *Federal Appellate Practice: Ninth Circuit*, § 8.12 (West 2d ed. 1999), for a discussion of the Ninth Circuit's approach to these issues. In other jurisdictions, the rules and its exceptions are set out in a statute or a court rule. For example, in North Carolina, this rule and its exceptions are set out in a statute:

> (a) Except as provided in subsection (d), error may not be asserted upon appellate review unless the error has been brought to the attention of the trial court by appropriate and timely objection or motion. . . .
>
> (b) Failure to make an appropriate and timely motion or objection constitutes a waiver of the right to assert the alleged error on appeal, but the appellate court may review such errors affecting substantial rights in the interest of justice if it determines it is appropriate to do so.

N.C. Gen. Stat. Ann. § 15A-1446.

Some of the errors that can be raised on appeal, even absent an objection or motion, are a lack of jurisdiction, a failure of the pleading to state the essential elements of a violation, and insufficient evidence. N. C. Gen. Stat. A. § 15A-1446(d)(1), (4) and (5). In contrast, in Washington State, this rule and its exceptions are set out in the Rules of Appellate Procedure (RAP) 2.5.

§ 18.1.5   The Record on Appeal

After filing the notice of appeal or notice for discretionary review, the appellant or petitioner must then "designate the record on appeal," that is, select the portions of the trial record that the appellate court needs to decide the issues on appeal. Generally, the record consists of the original papers and exhibits filed in the trial court and transcripts of the proceedings that are relevant to the issues on review. While the appellant bears the burden of ensuring that the record is adequate for review of the issues raised, the responding party may supplement the record.

> **PRACTICE POINTER**
>
> Remember that there may be local rules that govern the record on appeal. For example, under a Ninth Circuit rule, if the appellant does not plan on ordering the entire transcript, either the parties have to agree on the portions that will be ordered, or the appellant must let the appellee know which portions it plans to order along with a statement of issues it plans to raise. Ninth Cir. R. 10-3.1(a).
>
> In addition, "Because all members of the panel assigned to hear the appeal ordinarily will not have the entire record (see Ninth Cir. R. 11-4.1), the parties must prepare excerpts of the record pursuant to Ninth Cir. R. 301. The purpose of the excerpts is to provide each member of the panel with those portions of the record necessary to reach a decision."

§ 18.1.6   Types of Briefs

The next step in the process is the preparation of the brief. As a general rule, the party seeking review (the appellant or petitioner) files an opening brief and serves a copy of that brief on the appellate court and the opposing party. After reading the appellant's (or petitioner's) brief, the opposing party (the appellee or respondent) prepares its brief, in which it addresses and responds to the issues and arguments raised in the appellant's (or petitioner's) brief. After the appellee (or respondent) has completed its brief, it serves it on both the court and the appellant (or petitioner). The appellant (or petitioner) then has the opportunity to file a reply brief, which answers arguments made in the appellee's (or respondent's) brief. In some jurisdictions, the court rules also permit the appellee (or respondent) to file a reply brief; the defendant in a criminal case to file a *pro se* brief; and interested parties to file an amicus brief, which is a brief submitted by a group or individual who has a strong interest in the subject matter of the case, but who is not a party.

§ 18.2   Understanding Your Audience, Your Purpose, and the Conventions

Just as it is important to understand the audience and purpose of an objective memorandum, opinion letter, and motion brief, it is also important to understand the audience and purpose of an appellate brief. If you understand your audience and your purpose in writing to that audience, you will be able to make sound decisions about what to include and exclude or about how to best present your arguments.

§ 18.2.1   Audience

The primary audience for an appellate brief is the panel of judges who will be deciding the appeal. This means that if you are seeking review in an intermediate court of appeals, you will usually be writing to a panel of three judges, and if you are seeking review in the United States Supreme Court, to nine justices. When you are writing for your intermediate court of appeals, you may or may not know who your judges will be: In the United States Courts of Appeal and in many state intermediate courts, there are more than three judges on the court, and you are not told which judges will be on your panel until all of the briefs are filed and your case has been set on the court's docket. In contrast, when you are writing to the United States Supreme Court or your state supreme court, you will know who will be hearing your case (although there may be instances in which a justice recuses himself or herself, or there could be an intervening election or appointment that changes the makeup of the court).

Even if you do not know which judges will be hearing your case, research your court before writing. You can do this research by reading recent decisions issued by the court or by talking with other attorneys who are familiar with the court. In addition, you can usually locate information about individual judges on the court's homepage or on other websites. Often these pages will provide a photograph of each judge and information about his or her education and legal experience.

The judges are not, however, your only audience. In most appellate courts, each appeal is assigned to a particular judge, who then assigns the case to one of his or her law clerks. After reading the briefs and independently researching the issues, the clerk prepares a memo to the judge (usually called a "bench memo" or a "prehearing memo") that summarizes the law and each side's arguments and, in some courts, recommends how the appeal should be decided. Because law clerks can shape how the judges view the appeal, they are some of your most significant readers.

In addition, you are writing for your client and for opposing counsel. You want to write your brief in such a way that your client feels that his or her story is being told and that opposing counsel knows that he or she is up against a well-prepared, thoughtful, and vigorous advocate.

As you write, you also need to keep in mind that most appellate judges have substantial workloads. Many intermediate appellate judges hear between 100 and 150 cases a year, and write opinions in approximately one-third of those cases. If each party submits a 30-page brief, each judge would have to read between 6,000 and 9,000 pages in the course of a year. Thus, although you might think that a longer brief is a better brief, most appellate judges would disagree. For most appellate judges, the best briefs are those that make their point clearly and concisely.

Also keep in mind that appellate judges must work within certain constraints, the most significant of which is the standard of review. Although in some cases the court's review is *de novo*, in most cases the review is more limited: Instead of deciding the case on its merits, the appellate court reviews only the trial court's decision to see if the trial judge abused his or her discretion or if there is substantial evidence to support the jury's verdict. (For more on standard of review, see section 18.4.2c in this book.)

Finally, in some cases the appellate court is itself bound by mandatory authority. State intermediate courts of appeal are bound by the decisions of the state's highest court, and both the state courts and the United States Courts of Appeal are bound by decisions of the United States Supreme Court interpreting and applying the United States Constitution.

§ 18.2.2   Purpose

In writing an appellate brief, you want to accomplish two things. You want to educate the judges about the facts of your case and the applicable law, and you want to persuade a majority of the judges to rule in your client's favor. Therefore, in addition to explaining the underlying facts, the relevant procedural history, and the law, you must also persuade the appellate court either that the decision of the trial court was correct and should be affirmed or that the trial court's decision was wrong and should be reversed or reversed and remanded.

§ 18.2.3   Conventions

Just as the process of bringing an appeal is governed by rules, so is the format of an appellate brief. These rules are usually quite specific, governing everything from the types of briefs that can be filed to the sections that must be included, the order of the required sections, and how to reference the parties and the record. The following excerpt from Fed. R. App. P. 28 is representative.

EXAMPLE 2   **Rule 28. Briefs**

(a) Appellant's Brief. The appellant's brief must contain, under appropriate headings and in the order indicated:
(1) a corporate disclosure statement if required by Rule 26.1;
(2) a table of contents, with page references;
(3) a table of authorities—cases (alphabetically arranged), statutes, and other authorities—with references to the pages of the brief where they are cited;
(4) a jurisdictional statement, including:
(A) the basis for the district court's or agency's subject matter jurisdiction, with citations to applicable statutory provisions and stating relevant facts establishing jurisdiction;
(B) the basis for the court of appeals' jurisdiction, with citations to applicable statutory provisions and stating relevant facts establishing jurisdiction;
(C) the filing dates establishing the timeliness of the appeal or petition for review; and
(D) an assertion that the appeal is from a final order or judgment that disposes of all parties' claims, or information establishing the court of appeals' jurisdiction on some other basis;
(5) a statement of the issues presented for review;
(6) a statement of the case briefly indicating the nature of the case, the course of proceedings, and the disposition below;
(7) a statement of facts relevant to the issues submitted for review with appropriate references to the record (see Rule 28(e));
(8) a summary of the argument, which must contain a succinct, clear, and accurate statement of the arguments made in the body of the brief, and which must not merely repeat the argument headings;

(9) the argument, which must contain:

(A) appellant's contentions and the reasons for them, with citations to the authorities and parts of the record on which the appellant relies; and

(B) for each issue, a concise statement of the applicable standard of review (which may appear in the discussion of the issue or under a separate heading placed before the discussion of the issues);

(10) a short conclusion stating the precise relief sought; and

(11) the certificate of compliance, if required by Rule 32(a)(7).

(b) Appellee's Brief. The appellee's brief must conform to the requirements of Rule 28(a)(1)–(9) and (11), except that none of the following need appear unless the appellee is dissatisfied with the appellant's statement:

(1) the jurisdictional statement;

(2) the statement of the issues;

(3) the statement of the case;

(4) the statement of the facts; and

(5) the statement of the standard of review.

(c) Reply Brief. The appellant may file a brief in reply to the appellee's brief. Unless the court permits, no further briefs may be filed. A reply brief must contain a table of contents, with page references, and a table of authorities—cases (alphabetically arranged), statutes, and other authorities—with references to the pages of the reply brief where they are cited.

(d) References to Parties. In briefs and at oral argument, counsel should minimize use of the terms "appellant" and "appellee." To make briefs clear, counsel should use the parties' actual names or the designations used in the lower court or agency proceeding, or such descriptive terms as "the employee," "the injured person," "the taxpayer," "the ship," "the stevedore."

(e) References to the Record. References to the parts of the record contained in the appendix filed with the appellant's brief must be to the pages of the appendix. If the appendix is prepared after the briefs are filed, a party referring to the record must follow one of the methods detailed in Rule 30(c). If the original record is used under Rule 30(f) and is not consecutively paginated, or if the brief refers to an unreproduced part of the record, any reference must be to the page of the original document. For example:

- Answer p. 7;
- Motion for Judgment p. 2;
- Transcript p. 231.

Only clear abbreviations may be used. A party referring to evidence whose admissibility is in controversy must cite the pages of the appendix or of the transcript at which the evidence was identified, offered, and received or rejected.

(f) Reproduction of Statutes, Rules, Regulations, etc. If the court's determination of the issues presented requires the study of statutes, rules, regulations, etc., the relevant parts must be set out in the brief or in an addendum at the end, or may be supplied to the court in pamphlet form.

(g) [Reserved]

(h) [Reserved]

(i) Briefs in a Case Involving Multiple Appellants or Appellees. In a case involving more than one appellant or appellee, including consolidated cases, any number of appellants or appellees may join in a brief, and any party may adopt by reference a part of another's brief. Parties may also join in reply briefs.

   (j)   Citation of Supplemental Authorities. If pertinent and significant authorities come to a party's attention after the party's brief has been filed—or after oral argument but before decision—a party may promptly advise the circuit clerk by letter, with a copy to all other parties, setting forth the citations. The letter must state the reasons for the supplemental citations, referring either to the page of the brief or to a point argued orally. The body of the letter must not exceed 350 words. Any response must be made promptly and must be similarly limited.

PRACTICE POINTER	Remember to check local rules. For example, in the Ninth Circuit, an appendix containing the record is not included with the brief. Instead, excerpts of the record are filed. *See* Ninth Cir. R. 10-2(b).

References to the excerpts of the record are referred to by "ER" followed by a page number.

   Also, a brief filed in the Ninth Circuit must contain a statement regarding the defendant's bail status, Ninth Cir. R. 28-2.4, and a statement of any known related cases pending before the court. Ninth Cir. R. 28-2.6. Moreover, the appellee cannot omit the jurisdictional statement section; an appellee must include either a statement of jurisdiction or a statement agreeing with the appellant's statement of jurisdiction. Ninth Cir. R. 28-2.2(c).

Although these rules are representative, some jurisdictions have other requirements. For example, in Washington State, the appellant must include assignments of error. RAP 10.3(g).

In addition to rules governing the content of briefs, there are rules governing the format of the briefs, including length, typeface, and paper size. For example, with the advent of word processing programs, the courts have enacted very specific rules as to length to avoid having attorneys try to skirt the length limits by changing typefaces, font sizes, and margins.

EXAMPLE 3	**Fed. R. App. P. 32 Form of Briefs, Appendices, and Other Papers**

(a) **Form of a Brief.**

. . .

   (2) Cover. Except for filings by unrepresented parties, the cover of the appellant's brief must be blue; the appellee's, red; an intervenor's or amicus curiae's, green; any reply brief, gray; and any supplemental brief, tan. The front cover of a brief must contain:
   (A) the number of the case centered at the top;
   (B) the name of the court;
   (C) the title of the case (see Rule 12(a));
   (D) the nature of the proceeding (e.g., Appeal, Petition for Review) and the name of the court, agency, or board below;

(E) the title of the brief, identifying the party or parties for whom the brief is filed; and

(F) the name, office address, and telephone number of counsel representing the party for whom the brief is filed.

(3) Binding. The brief must be bound in any manner that is secure, does not obscure the text, and permits the brief to lie reasonably flat when open.

(4) Paper Size, Line Spacing, and Margins. The brief must be on 8 1/2 by 11 inch paper. The text must be double-spaced, but quotations more than two lines long may be indented and single-spaced. Headings and footnotes may be single-spaced. Margins must be at least one inch on all four sides. Page numbers may be placed in the margins, but no text may appear there.

(5) Typeface. Either a proportionally spaced or a monospaced face may be used.

(A) A proportionally spaced face must include serifs, but sans-serif type may be used in headings and captions. A proportionally spaced face must be 14-point or larger.

(B) A monospaced face may not contain more than 10 1/2 characters per inch.

(6) Type Styles. A brief must be set in a plain, roman style, although italics or boldface may be used for emphasis. Case names must be italicized or underlined.

(7) Length.

(A) Page Limitation. A principal brief may not exceed 30 pages, or a reply brief 15 pages, unless it complies with Rule 32(a)(7)(B) and (C).

(B) Type-Volume Limitation.

(i) A principal brief is acceptable if:
- it contains no more than 14,000 words; or
- it uses a monospaced face and contains no more than 1,300 lines of text.

(ii) A reply brief is acceptable if it contains no more than half of the type volume specified in Rule 32(a)(7)(B)(i).

(iii) Headings, footnotes, and quotations count toward the word and line limitations. The corporate disclosure statement, table of contents, table of citations, statement with respect to oral argument, any addendum containing statutes, rules or regulations, and any certificates of counsel do not count toward the limitation.

(C) Certificate of Compliance.

(i) A brief submitted under Rules 28.1(e)(2) or 32(a)(7)(B) must include a certificate by the attorney, or an unrepresented party, that the brief complies with the type-volume limitation. The person preparing the certificate may rely on the word or line count of the word-processing system used to prepare the brief. The certificate must state either:
- the number of words in the brief; or
- the number of lines of monospaced type in the brief.

. . .

In addition to the rules, there might be other, unwritten conventions governing the format of the brief. For example, in some jurisdictions, attorneys may use a particular format for the table of authorities or for the questions presented, or there might be conventions regarding the capitalization of words like "court." Therefore, in addition to reading and following the rules, always check with the court clerk and other attorneys to find out what is expected.

§ 18.3   Getting the Case: *United States v. Josephy*

For the rest of this chapter, presume that it is your second year in law school and that you are working as an intern at the Office of the Federal Public Defender in Seattle, Washington. One of the cases the office is handling is *United States v. Josephy*. The facts of the case are as follows.

At about 9:30 a.m. on June 25, 2013, an individual placed a 911 call from a pay phone at the Bellis Fair Mall in Bellingham, Washington, which is about a five-minute drive from the Travel House Inn. The individual, who said that his name was Zachary Dillon, told the 911 operator that Peter Josephy was involved in drug trafficking between Canada and the United States and that Josephy was currently at the Travel House Inn, where he was going to sell a large amount of marijuana to a man named Oliver. Dillon also told the operator that police should go to the Travel House Inn right away because Josephy would only be there for another hour or two.

When the 911 operator asked Dillon to describe Josephy, Dillon stated that Josephy was a Native American, that Josephy had black hair, that Josephy was in his mid- to late twenties, and that Josephy was driving a blue Chevy Blazer. Dillon also told the operator that he did not know Oliver's last name but that Oliver was in his thirties, that he was six feet tall, and that he had brown hair and a beard. Dillon was not able to give the operator the license number of the Blazer, and he said that he did not know what the men were wearing. In addition, Dillon would not tell the operator where he lived or give the operator his home or cell phone number.

After the 911 operator conveyed the information from the phone call to a Bureau of Alcohol, Tobacco, and Firearms (ATF) agent, Agent Bhasin, the agent checked several databases, trying to locate a Zachary Dillon. Agent Bhasin was not, however, able to find anyone by that name in the greater Bellingham area.

At about 10:00 a.m., Agent Bhasin drove to the Travel House Inn to investigate. When he arrived at 10:15 a.m., Agent Bhasin located a blue Chevy Blazer parked in the parking lot. After running the license plate number and determining that the Blazer was registered to Peter Jason Josephy and that Josephy was registered at the motel, Agent Bhasin requested a K-9 unit (an agent and a dog trained to alert to the presence of drugs) as backup.

At about 10:45 a.m., Mr. Josephy and a man later identified as Oliver Preston walked out of one of the rooms and went into the office, where Mr. Josephy paid the bill. The two men left the office, talked for two or three minutes just outside the office, and then parted ways. Mr. Josephy walked to his car and got in. As Mr. Josephy started his car, Agent Bhasin pulled behind his car and another agent, Agent O'Brien, pulled in front.

Agent Bhasin then got out of his car, approached the driver's side of Mr. Josephy's car, and asked Mr. Josephy to get out of the car. Although Mr. Josephy complied with this request, he refused Agent Bhasin's request for permission to search the vehicle. Agent Bhasin then instructed the agent with the dog to walk the dog around the outside of the vehicle. After the dog alerted to the vehicle, Agent Bhasin searched the vehicle and located four kilos of marijuana in the wheel well. Agent Bhasin then arrested Mr. Josephy.

Before trial, Mr. Josephy moved to suppress the marijuana on the grounds that (1) a seizure occurred when Agent Bhasin pulled behind Mr. Josephy's car and Agent O'Brien pulled in front and (2) the tip was not sufficient to provide the agents with a reasonable suspicion that Mr. Josephy had possession of a controlled substance with intent to sell. Although the trial court agreed with Mr. Josephy that a seizure occurred when the agents blocked Mr. Josephy's car with their own vehicles, the trial court denied the motion to suppress on the grounds that the tip was sufficient to provide the agents with a reasonable suspicion that Mr. Josephy was in Unlawful Possession of a Controlled Substance with the Intent to Deliver in violation of 21 U.S.C. § 841(a)(1) (2012).

The case proceeded to trial, and during jury selection, the judge asked whether any jurors had concerns regarding their ability to serve as jurors for the duration of the trial. Juror No. 12, Mr. Williams, stated that his tribal council was scheduled to meet the following Thursday and Friday, that he would like to attend the meeting, but that he could skip the meeting if he needed to do so. Juror No. 2, Mr. Feldman, stated that he was flying to Africa on Saturday and that his boss was unhappy that he was missing work. However, Mr. Feldman stated that his boss would just have "to live with it." Juror No. 18, Mr. Woods, stated that his 87-year-old mother had had a massive heart attack, that she was given a 20% chance to live, and that he did not know whether he needed to go out of town the following week. No other jurors mentioned a problem regarding the trial schedule.

The prosecutor then asked whether anyone had had bad experiences with law enforcement officers. Juror No. 5, Ms. Whitefish, stated that she had been pulled aside for questions each time she crossed the border. Ms. Whitefish attributed the extra questioning to her age and her belief that college students are stopped more frequently than others. Juror No. 11, Mr. Martin, said that he had been stopped on a number of occasions for routine problems with his car — for example, a taillight that was not working. During further questioning Mr. Martin stated that the police stopped people with long hair more often than they did people with short hair and that he was bothered by the fact that the police tended to target people with long hair.

After the questioning ended, and both the prosecutor and the defense counsel accepted the panel for cause, the parties used their peremptory challenges. The prosecutor excused Juror No. 2, Mr. Feldman; Juror No. 5, Ms. Whitefish; and Juror No. 12, Mr. Williams.

Although the prosecutor then accepted the panel, defense counsel made a *Batson*[1] objection, arguing at sidebar that the Government's exclusion of

---

1. *Batson v. Kentucky*, 476 U.S. 79, 86-87 (1986). A *Batson* violation occurs when (1) the defendant establishes a prima facie case of purposeful discrimination in the government's use of peremptory challenges by showing that the challenged juror is a member of a cognizable class and that the circumstances raise an inference of discrimination; (2) the government fails to meet its burden to provide a race-neutral explanation for its strike; or (3) the government offers a race-neutral reason, but

Ms. Whitefish and Mr. Williams, the only two Native Americans on the panel, violated Mr. Josephy's right to equal protection.

The district court concluded that Mr. Josephy had made a prima facie case of discrimination regarding race and asked whether the prosecutor had race-neutral reasons for excluding Ms. Whitefish and Mr. Williams.

The prosecutor offered the following reasons: (1) He excused Ms. Whitefish because he believed that she would have difficulty being impartial given her personal experiences at the border, and (2) he excused Mr. Williams because he believed that Mr. Williams would have difficulty focusing on the facts of the case because he needed to attend the tribal council meeting the following Thursday and Friday. The trial court held that these reasons were neutral reasons.

Defense counsel then argued that, given the fact that the prosecutor had used his peremptory challenges to excuse the only Native Americans in the jury pool, the prosecutor's proffered reasons were pretexts for purposeful discrimination. The district court concluded that the prosecutor had not engaged in purposeful discrimination and denied Mr. Josephy's *Batson* challenge. At the close of trial, the jury found Mr. Josephy guilty.

Soon after the entry of judgment and sentence, Ms. Elder, Mr. Josephy's attorney, met with Mr. Josephy to explain his options. She described the appeals process, telling him how long he had to file an appeal, how long it would take for his case to be heard by the court of appeals, and the provisions for staying his sentence while his case was on appeal. In addition, she explained that if he did not appeal or if his appeal was denied, his current convictions might affect his sentence for any future crimes.

After considering his options, Mr. Josephy decided that he wanted to appeal. As a result, Ms. Elder filed a notice of appeal within the required time limits and ordered the relevant portions of the record.

§ 18.4　Preparing to Write the Brief

§ 18.4.1　Reviewing the Record for Error

Like many attorneys, Ms. Elder uses a four-step process to review the record for errors. First, she reviews her trial notes, writing down the errors that she had identified during the trial. Second, Ms. Elder goes through the record, document by document, page by page, and exhibit by exhibit, noting the following:

- Each motion that she made that was denied.
- Each motion that the prosecutor made that was granted.
- Each objection that she made that was overruled.
- Each objection that the prosecutor made that was granted.
- Each request for a jury instruction that she made that was denied.
- Each request for a jury instruction that the prosecutor made that was granted.

---

the defense meets its burden of showing that a review of all relevant circumstances shows purposeful discrimination. *Id.*; *see also Johnson v. California*, 545 U.S. 162, 169 (2005).

For example, during this step, Ms. Elder notes the following *Batson* objection, which the court overruled.

| **EXAMPLE 1** | **Excerpt from the Transcript of a Sidebar During Voir Dire** |

THE COURT: Does the defendant have an objection?

DEFENSE: Unfortunately, we do, Your Honor. As you know, Mr. Josephy is Native American, and the prosecutor improperly excluded both Juror No. 5, Ms. Whitefish, and Juror No. 12, Mr. Williams, the only two Native Americans on the panel.

THE COURT: Under *Batson*, the defendant is required, of course, to make a prima facie showing of purposeful discrimination based on race. Because the defendant has established a prima facie case, the prosecutor has the burden of showing that he had a neutral explanation for striking the juror. Can I hear from the prosecutor?

PROSECUTOR: Yes, Your Honor. I excused Ms. Whitefish because I think that her experiences at the border would make it difficult for her to judge this case fairly and impartially. I excused Mr. Williams because I think that his other obligation may make it difficult for him to focus on the trial. These are neutral reasons for excluding these people from this panel.

THE COURT: I agree. Defense Counsel, would you like to respond?

DEFENSE: The reasons stated are not neutral; they are only a mask for unconstitutional race discrimination. Mr. Williams said that it would not be a problem for him to be on the jury, and Ms. Whitefish indicated that she was not bothered by the fact that all college students seemed to be subjected to tighter screening. Given the pattern of strikes, the reasons that the prosecutor has given are pretexts.

THE COURT: Your objection is noted, Counsel, but the Court finds no purposeful discrimination here.

Third, Ms. Elder looks for the other, less obvious types of errors.

- Were Mr. Josephy's constitutional rights violated? (Was he read his *Miranda* rights? Was he represented by counsel at all significant stages in the process?)
- Was Mr. Josephy tried within the appropriate time period? Was he given the right to confront the witnesses against him? Is his sentence cruel and unusual?
- Is the statute under which Mr. Josephy was charged constitutional?
- Was there misconduct on the part of the judge, opposing counsel, or the jury?

Finally, Ms. Elder examines her own actions. Did she fail to raise a viable defense or fail to make an objection that she should have made? If she did, Mr. Josephy might be able to argue that he was denied effective assistance of counsel.

Having identified the potential errors, Ms. Elder moves to the next step in the process: researching the potential errors to determine which she should raise in her brief.

§ 18.4.2   Selecting the Issues on Appeal

As an appellate judge, whom would you find more credible: the attorney who alleges twenty-three errors or the one who alleges three?

Most appellate judges take the attorney who lists two, three, or four errors more seriously than the attorney who lists a dozen or more. Instead of describing the attorney who lists numerous errors as "thorough" or "conscientious," judges use terms such as "inexperienced," "unfocused," and "frivolous." When so many errors are listed, the appellate court is likely to think that the problem is the attorney bringing the appeal and not the trial court.

But how do you decide which errors to discuss in your brief? Once again, Ms. Elder uses a four-step process. She determines (1) whether there was in fact an error, (2) whether that error was preserved, (3) the standard of review, and (4) whether the error was harmless.

a.   Was There an Error?

The first question is whether there was in fact an error. Does the Constitution, a statute, or the case law allow you to make a credible argument that the trial court erred? To answer this question, you usually need to do some research. For example, in *United States v. Josephy*, Ms. Elder needs to do some preliminary research to determine whether she can make a good faith argument that the tip was not sufficient to establish a reasonable suspicion that Mr. Josephy was in possession of drugs with intent to sell them and whether she can make a good faith argument that the district court improperly overruled her *Batson* objection. Because her research indicates there are arguments to be made on both issues, she continues with her analysis. In contrast, the other research that Ms. Elder did is not as fruitful. For example, after doing some preliminary research, Ms. Elder determines that she cannot make a good faith argument that the district court erred in denying her objection to one of the statements that Agent Bhasin made during direct examination. As a result, Ms. Elder abandons that issue. Without a good faith basis for raising the issue, she risks, at a minimum, annoying the court and, at worst, a potential Rule 11 action for making a frivolous claim.

> **PRACTICE POINTER**   Under Fed. R. Civ. P. 11(b), an attorney signing a brief "certifies that to the best of the attorney's knowledge, information or belief, formed after an inquiry reasonable under the circumstances" that "the claims, defenses, and other legal contentions therein are warranted by existing law or by a nonfrivolous argument for the extension, modification, or reversal of existing law or the establishment of new law[.]" A violation of Rule 11 can lead to sanctions, including monetary sanctions, sufficient to deter the repetition of such conduct. Fed. R. Civ. P. 11(c).

b.   Was the Error Preserved?

It is not enough that there was an error. Unless the error involved an issue of constitutional magnitude, that error must have been preserved. Defense counsel must have objected or in some other manner brought the alleged error to the attention of the trial court and given the trial court the opportunity to correct the error. In some jurisdictions the rules regarding preservation of error for appeal are developed through case law; in others they are addressed explicitly in a statute or court rule.

In *United States v. Josephy*, both issues were preserved for appeal: Ms. Elder preserved the issue relating to the search incident to arrest through the motion to suppress and the issue relating to jury selection by making a *Batson* objection.

c.   What Is the Standard of Review?

The next step relates to the standard of review. In deciding whether there was an error, what standard will the appellate court apply? Will it review the issue *de novo*, making its own independent determination, or will it defer to the trial court, affirming the trial court unless, for example, the trial court's finding was clearly erroneous or the trial court judge abused his or her discretion.

As a general rule, an appellate court will review questions of law *de novo*. As a consequence, when the issue is whether the jury was properly instructed, the appellate court will make its own independent determination. The standard is different when the question is one of fact. In most circumstances, an appellate court will not disturb factual findings unless such findings are "clearly errone-ous" or "contrary to law." Similarly, an appellate court will give great deference to the trial court's evidentiary rulings and will not reverse the trial court unless the judge abused, or manifestly abused, his or her discretion. Because very few issues are pure questions of law or pure questions of fact, you might be able to argue the standard of review. While the appellant (or petitioner) will usually want to argue that the appellate court should review the question *de novo*, the appellee (or respondent) will usually want to argue that the appellate court should affirm unless the trial court's ruling was clearly erroneous or the trial court abused its discretion.

> **PRACTICE POINTER**   The standard of review can also be affected by the case's procedural posture. For example, the standard of review a federal circuit court uses in decid-ing a direct appeal will differ from the standard of review the court uses in deciding a case in which a party is seeking habeas relief from a state court ruling.

The rules set out above are general; for specific issues, you must research the standard of review. Sometimes this research will be easy. In one of its opin-ions, the court will set out the standard that is to be applied. At other times, the research is much more difficult. Although the court decides the issue, it does not explicitly state what standard it is applying. In such cases, read between the lines. Although the court does not explicitly state that it is reviewing the issue *de novo*, is that what the court has done? Also, look for helpful secondary sources. For example, if your appeal is in the Ninth Circuit, see http://www .ca9.uscourts.gov/content/view.php?pk_id=0000000368.

PRACTICE POINTER	One way to research the standard of review is to use one or more standards as a search term. For example, search for "de novo" or "abuse!" or "discretion."

d. Was the Error Harmless?

The final question that must be asked is whether an alleged error was harmless, that is, whether the error, even if established, would not warrant a reversal. As the courts have often said, an appellant is entitled to a fair trial, not a perfect one.

> The reversal of a conviction entails substantial social costs: it forces jurors, witnesses, courts, the prosecution, and the appellants to expend further time, energy, and other resources to repeat a trial that has already once taken place. . . . These societal costs of reversal and retrial are an acceptable and often necessary consequence when an error . . . has deprived the appellant of a fair determination of the issue of guilt or innocence. But the balance of interest tips decidedly the other way when the error has had no effect on the outcome of the trial.

William Rehnquist, *Harmless Error, Prosecutorial Misconduct, and Due Process: There's More to Due Process Than the Bottom Line*, 88 Colum. L. Rev. 1298, 1301 (1988).

As a consequence, as an advocate, you will usually not want to assign error to a decision that, although incorrect, was harmless. For instance, although the court might have acted improperly when it admitted a particular piece of evidence or testimony, that error might not be prejudicial if that same evidence or testimony was properly elicited from another witness.

In some instances, the court does not do a harmless error analysis; persuading the appellate court that a trial error occurred is all that is needed to obtain a reversal. For example, in *United States v. Josephy*, if Ms. Elder can persuade the Court of Appeals that the district court erred in denying her motion to suppress, reversal would be required because the conviction for possession of a controlled substance with intent to deliver cannot stand if the marijuana was inadmissible. Similarly, if she is able to persuade the Court of Appeals that the district court erred in overruling her *Batson* objection, the remedy would be a new trial (see *Gray v. Mississippi*, 481 U.S. 648, 668 (1987) (holding that there is no harmless error analysis when there has been a *Batson* violation).

Generally, however, you will need to consider whether the error was harmless. In so doing, keep in mind that the courts apply different tests for different types of errors. For example, as a general rule, the courts apply one test for nonconstitutional errors and a different, more stringent, test for constitutional errors. In addition, different jurisdictions can apply different tests: When reviewing a nonconstitutional error, some courts look to whether the error had a substantial and injurious effect on the verdict, while others look to whether, within reasonable probabilities, the outcome of the trial would have been materially affected had the error not occurred.

In contrast, when reviewing a constitutional error, most courts apply either the contribution test or the overwhelming untainted evidence test. Under the contribution test, the appellate court looks at the tainted evidence to determine whether that evidence could have contributed to the fact finder's determination of guilt. If it could have, reversal is required. The courts that apply the overwhelming untainted evidence test take a different approach. Instead of looking at the tainted evidence, they look at the untainted evidence. If the untainted evidence is sufficient to support a finding of guilt, reversal is not required. Note, however, that in a criminal case, the government has the burden of showing the error was harmless.

> **PRACTICE POINTER**   An argument that the erroneous admission or exclusion of evidence requires reversal necessarily rests on how the evidence related to the specific elements of the cause of action or charge. However, arguments can also be developed by looking to how the evidence was addressed in closing arguments: How much weight was it given? Was it emphasized, repeated, or touched on only briefly? Was it characterized as being a small piece in a larger puzzle or as being critical to the case?

Having gone through these four steps, Ms. Elder is ready to select the issues on appeal. She does, in fact, decide to challenge the district court's denial of her motion to suppress and the district court's decision to overrule her *Batson* objection. The first issue, whether the investigatory stop was supported by a reasonable, articulable suspicion, is a question of law; accordingly, review is *de novo*. However, for the second issue, whether the court correctly overruled the defense's *Batson* objection, the appellate court will give deference to the district court's finding that defense counsel did not establish unlawful discrimination in the prosecutor's use of peremptory challenges even though those findings relate to a constitutional issue.

§ 18.4.3   Preparing an Abstract of the Record

Before beginning to write, Ms. Elder does one last thing: She creates an abstract of the record by going through the trial transcript and taking notes on each piece of relevant testimony. For each piece of relevant testimony, she notes the name of the individual who gave the testimony, she writes down the page number on which the testimony appears, and she summarizes the testimony.

EXAMPLE 2   **Excerpt from Ms. Elder's Abstract of the Record**

Direct Examination of Gregory Bhasin.

P. 4:   Gregory Bhasin, ATF agent; several years experience investigating cross-border drug cases; 1-1/2 years in Blaine office.

P. 30-31:   At about 9:30 received a call from 911 operator in Bellingham. Man who said his name was Zachary Dillon had called and said that a man called Peter Josephy was involved in selling drugs that had been brought into the U.S. from Canada

P. 32-33:   Dillon says that Josephy will be at Travel House Inn for another hour or so. Gives physical description of Josephy's car, Josephy, and the man Josephy is selling the drugs to.

P. 32-35:   Dillon would not give 911 operator his address or a phone number. Records check does not indicate that anyone by the name of Zachary Dillon lives in the greater Bellingham area.

P. 42:   Agent Bhasin goes to the Travel House Inn and finds a blue Blazer in the parking lot. Checks license plate—car registered to Peter Josephy.

Although preparing such an abstract is time-consuming, the process forces Ms. Elder to go through the record carefully, identifying each piece of relevant testimony. It also makes brief writing and preparation for oral argument easier. Instead of having to search through the entire record looking for the testimony she needs, Ms. Elder can refer to her abstract.

§ 18.4.4 Preparing the Record on Appeal

After having determined which issues she will raise on appeal, Ms. Elder goes back through the trial record, identifying those parts that she wants included as the record on appeal. She selects pleadings and documents filed with the district court: the charging document, the Motion to Suppress, the Findings of Fact and Conclusions of Law and Order Denying the Motion to Suppress, the jury's Verdict Form, the Judgment and Sentence, and the Notice of Appeal. In addition, she includes the transcript of the evidentiary hearing on the motion to suppress and the transcript of voir dire.

Because she was not assigning error to anything that happened during the trial, Ms. Elder does not have the trial record transcribed. In addition, because there were no relevant exhibits, she does not include any of them in the record on appeal.

§ 18.5   Researching the Issues on Appeal

How an individual researches an issue depends in large part on that individual's familiarity with the area of law. For example, in this case, Ms. Elder is an experienced criminal defense lawyer with extensive trial experience who knows the law relating to a *Batson* analysis. As a consequence, when she starts her research, she already knows the names of the key cases—for example, *Batson v. Kentucky*, 476 U.S. 799 (1986), and *Johnson v. California*, 545 U.S. 162, 169 (2005). Ms. Elder rereads these and other cases and then cite checks the cases that are most on point to locate more recent cases. In contrast, attorneys who are less familiar with criminal law would have to take a different approach: They would need to begin their research by doing some background reading on a free website, in a hornbook, or in a federal practice book that discusses the analysis the Ninth Circuit uses to determine if a *Batson* violation has occurred. Using the citations that they obtain while doing this background reading, these attorneys would need to locate, read, and cite check the key cases. In addition, they might want to look for a law review or bar journal article that specifically discusses *Batson*.

For more on researching issues involving constitutional issues, see Chapter 8.

Chapter 18 Quiz No. 1

Draft answers for each of the following questions. Make your points clearly and concisely, and write sentences that are easy to read and that are grammatical and correctly punctuated.

1. What are the two types of appellate review?
2. What are the four questions that you should ask yourself before deciding whether to discuss an issue in your brief?
3. What does it mean to say that the error was harmless?

§ 18.6   Planning the Brief

Having researched the issues, Ms. Elder is ready to begin drafting the brief. She does not, however, start writing until she has spent several hours analyzing the facts and the law, developing a theory of the case, and selecting an organizational scheme.

§ 18.6.1   Analyzing the Facts and the Law

To write an effective brief, Ms. Elder must have mastered both the facts of the case and the law. For example, before she begins drafting the arguments relating to the motion to suppress, she needs to know what each witness said, and did not say, at the suppression hearing and every finding of fact and conclusion of law that the court entered. Likewise, before she begins drafting the arguments related to the *Batson* challenge, she needs to know what questions the potential jurors were asked during voir dire, needs to read carefully all of the relevant cases and think not only about how she might be able to use them to support her argument but also about how the government might use them in its arguments.

Ms. Elder also needs to think about what relief she wants and the various ways in which she might persuade the court to grant that relief. Here, ends–means reasoning often works well. In doing an ends–means analysis for the *Batson* issue, Ms. Elder starts with the conclusion that she wants the court to reach and then works backward through the steps in the analysis. Although the *Batson* analysis involves a three-step process, Ms. Elder does not address the first step in her ends–means analysis. She knows from her research of Ninth Circuit cases that the issue of whether defense counsel established a prima facie case of discrimination is moot because the government proffered reasons for the use of the peremptory challenges to excuse the two Native Americans. *See United States v. Esparza-Gonzalez*, 422 F.3d 897, 906 (9th Cir. 2012).

■ *Relief wanted:* conviction reversed.
↓

■ *How to have conviction reversed:* have the appellate court reverse the district court.
↓

■ *How to have the appellate court reverse the district court:* show the district court improperly overruled her *Batson* objection.
↓

■ *How to show that the district court erred:* show the prosecutor's reasons were not race neutral.
↓

■ *If the court determines the reasons were race neutral,* show that the district court erred in not finding that the reasons were a pretext for discrimination.
↓

■ *How to show the district court erred in not finding the reasons were a pretext for discrimination:*
↓

   ■ Show the reasons were not supported by the record.
   ■ Use a comparative analysis to show that the prosecutor did not use peremptory challenges to excuse similarly situated non-Native Americans by comparing the answers given by Native Americans with answers given by non-Native Americans.
   ■ Show the court failed to do the required analysis when it made a cursory ruling without setting out its reasons clearly on the record.

In contrast, the prosecutor's ends–means analysis for the *Batson* issue would look like this:

■ *Relief wanted:* jury verdict affirmed.
↓

■ *How to get the jury verdict affirmed:* show that the district court did not err when it overruled defense counsel's *Batson* objection.
↓

■ *How to show district court did not err:* show that the government met its burden of offering a race-neutral reason for excusing Mr. Williams and Ms. Whitefish and that the defendant did not carry his burden of showing discrimination.
↓

■ *How to show that the prosecution met its burden of offering a race-neutral reason for excusing Ms. Whitefish and Mr. Williams:* show that the reasons are not based on stereotypes about Native Americans, but are based on specific responses from Ms. Whitefish based on her experiences at the border and from Mr. Williams based on his outside obligations the following week.
↓

■ *How to show defense did not carry its burden of showing that the prosecutor's reasons were a pretext for discrimination:* dismissing only two jurors of the defendant's race does not, by itself, establish pretext.
↓

■ *How to show using peremptory challenges to excuse the two Native American jurors was not racially based in this case:* show that the defendant's comparative analysis does not satisfy his burden of showing the government's reasons were a pretext for discrimination.

↓

■ Show that the court did the required analysis on the record by specifically addressing each of the three steps.

Each side would do a similar ends–means analysis for each of the issues the parties will address.

§ 18.6.2   Developing a Theory of the Case

Having thoroughly mastered both the facts and the law, Ms. Elder is ready to develop her theory of the case. At its simplest, a theory of the case is the legal theory that the attorney relies on in arguing the case to the court. A good theory of the case, however, goes beyond a legal theory or legal argument. It becomes the lens through which the attorney and, if the attorney is effective, the court views the case. For more on theory of the case, see section 17.3 in this book.

Developing the legal theory is relatively easy: Simply research the points that you set out in your ends–means analysis and, based on that research, discard the weak arguments and keep the strong ones. When Ms. Elder did her ends–means analysis for the *Batson* issue, she thought that she could make alternative arguments based on the second and third parts of the *Batson* analysis. Under the second part of the analysis, she could argue that the district court erred when it concluded that the reasons the prosecutor gave for striking Mr. Williams and Ms. Whitefish were not neutral on their face and, under the third part of the analysis, she could argue that even if the reasons were neutral on their face, those reasons were a pretext for discrimination. However, in doing her research, Ms. Elder discovered that the argument based on the second part of the *Batson* analysis was very weak: After looking at the case law, Ms. Elder concluded that she had little or no chance of persuading the Ninth Circuit Court of Appeals that the reasons that the prosecutor gave were not neutral on their face. Therefore, Ms. Elder decided not to rely on this legal theory. There was, though, some good news. Based on her research, Ms. Elder concluded that the argument based on the third part of the *Batson* analysis was a strong argument. In doing her research, she found cases saying that the trial court must do a "sensitive analysis" and "set out its reasoning on the record." Because the district court's only statement was, "Your objection is noted, Counsel, but the Court finds no purposeful discrimination here," Ms. Elder thinks that she has a strong argument that the district court did not do the required analysis and, even if it did the required analysis, the record is not sufficient. Therefore, she decides to add this argument. Consequently, in arguing that the district court erred in denying her *Batson* challenge, Ms. Elder has two legal theories: She will argue that the district court erred in denying her *Batson* challenge (1) because the reasons that the government gave were a pretext for discrimination and (2) because the district court did not do the required "sensitive analysis."

Having identified her legal theories, Ms. Elder then thinks about the lens that she wants to use in arguing those legal theories. Does she want a narrow focus, emphasizing that Mr. Josephy's rights were violated when the government used a peremptory strike to excuse Ms. Whitefish and again when the government used a peremptory strike to excuse Mr. Williams? Or does she want a wider focus, emphasizing that this case is not just about Mr. Josephy but about the integrity of the jury system itself and Ms. Whitefish's and Mr. Williams's right not to be excluded from participation because they are Native Americans? Peremptory challenges serve an important function, but they cannot be a mask for discrimination.

In the end, Ms. Elder decides to keep the narrower focus, emphasizing the violation of Mr. Josephy's rights, rather than the integrity of the jury system as a whole. She believes this is her best approach for two reasons:. First, she will be arguing that Mr. Josephy's constitutional rights were violated both before trial when his suppression motion was denied, and in the jury selection at the start of trial. Second, the fact that both the struck jurors and Mr. Josephy are Native American makes the violation seem that much more egregious.

§ 18.6.3   Selecting an Organizational Scheme

Because there has to be a one-to-one correspondence between the issue statements and the argumentative headings (see sections 18.11 and 18.14.3), the last thing that Ms. Elder does before she begins writing is to select an organizational scheme. She needs to decide how many issue statements and, thus, how many main headings she wants to have, and she needs to decide how to order those issue statements and main headings.

a.   Deciding on the Number of Issues and Headings

In almost every brief, there is more than one way to organize the arguments. As a consequence, before you begin writing, you need to decide whether you want to set out only one issue statement and one main argumentative heading, or whether you want to set out several issue statements and a corresponding number of main argumentative headings. In addition, if you have more than one issue statement, you need to decide how to order those issues. Finally, you need to decide whether you want to use subheadings and, if you do, how many.

In *United States v. Josephy*, Ms. Elder decides to argue both that the district court erred when it denied her motion to suppress and that the district court erred in overruling her *Batson* objection. Because these two errors are not closely related, Ms. Elder decides to have at least one issue statement and one main argumentative heading that relate to the motion to suppress, and at least one issue statement and one main argumentative heading that relate to the *Batson* challenge. In deciding whether she should have one or more than one issue statement for each of these two errors, Ms. Elder thinks strategically: Which organizational scheme will allow her to set out her arguments clearly and concisely, and which organizational scheme will improve her chances of persuading the appellate court that the district court erred?

For example, in organizing her discussion of the first issue — the suppression issue — Ms. Elder has at least three options.

1. Ms. Elder could have three issue statements and three main argumentative headings.
2. Ms. Elder could have one issue statement, one main argumentative heading, and no subheadings.
3. Ms. Elder could have one issue statement, one main argumentative heading, and three subheadings.

The following examples illustrate these options.

EXAMPLE 1   **Option 1**

Three issue statements and three main headings. The first issue statement and main heading would relate to whether the tip was or was not anonymous, the second issue statement and main heading would relate to whether the tip had sufficient indicia of reliability, and the third issue statement and main heading would relate to whether the police corroborated more than innocuous details.

Issues

1. Did the ATF agents lack a particularized objective suspicion that Mr. Josephy was engaged in criminal activity when the tip came from an unknown informant who gave the 911 operator his name but refused to give his address or phone number?
2. Did the ATF agents lack a particularized objective suspicion that Mr. Josephy was engaged in criminal activity when the tip included only general physical descriptions of the people and vehicle, it omitted any description of clothing, and the only action it predicted was that Mr. Josephy would be leaving a motel shortly before checkout time?
3. Did the ATF agents have a particularized objective suspicion that Mr. Josephy was engaged in criminal activity when the police corroborated only innocuous details—for example, Mr. Josephy's physical appearance, his vehicle, and his departure from a motel shortly before checkout time?

Argument

A.   THE ATF AGENTS DID NOT HAVE A PARTICULARIZED OBJECTIVE SUSPICION THAT MR. JOSEPHY WAS ENGAGED IN CRIMINAL ACTIVITY BECAUSE THE TIP CAME FROM AN UNKNOWN INFORMANT AND, ALTHOUGH THE INFORMANT GAVE THE 911 OPERATOR HIS NAME, HE REFUSED TO GIVE HER HIS ADDRESS OR PHONE NUMBER.

[The law and arguments relating to this issue go here.]

B.   THE ATF AGENTS DID NOT HAVE A PARTICULARIZED OBJECTIVE SUSPICION THAT MR. JOSEPHY WAS ENGAGED IN CRIMINAL ACTIVITY BECAUSE THE TIP INCLUDED ONLY GENERAL PHYSICAL DESCRIPTIONS, IT OMITTED ANY DESCRIPTION OF CLOTHING, AND THE ONLY ACTION IT PREDICTED WAS THAT MR. JOSEPHY WOULD BE LEAVING A MOTEL SHORTLY BEFORE CHECKOUT TIME.

[The law and arguments relating to this issue go here.]

C.   THE ATF AGENTS DID NOT HAVE A PARTICULARIZED OBJECTIVE SUSPICION THAT MR. JOSE-PHY WAS ENGAGED IN CRIMINAL ACTIVITY BECAUSE THE POLICE CORROBORATED NO MORE THAN INNOCUOUS DETAILS—FOR EXAMPLE, MR. JOSEPHY'S PHYSICAL APPEARANCE, HIS VEHICLE, AND HIS DEPARTURE FROM A MOTEL SHORTLY BEFORE CHECKOUT TIME.

[The law and arguments relating to this issue go here.]

EXAMPLE 2   **Option 2**

One issue statement, one main heading, no subheadings.

Issue

Did the district court err in concluding that a telephone tip created an objective particularized suspicion when the informant declined to give more than his name; the informant called from a public pay phone and gave only a general physical description of Mr. Josephy, his vehicle, and his location; and the police merely corroborated that Mr. Josephy left a motel shortly before checkout time and got into his car?

Argument

A.   THE ATF AGENTS VIOLATED MR. JOSEPHY'S FOURTH AMENDMENT RIGHTS BECAUSE THEY DID NOT HAVE A PARTICULARIZED OBJECTIVE SUSPICION THAT MR. JOSEPHY WAS ENGAGED IN CRIMINAL ACTIVITY.

[Introductory paragraph and all of the law and arguments go here.]

EXAMPLE 3   **Option 3**

One issue statement, one main heading, and three subheadings. The first subheading relates to the argument that the tip should be treated as being anonymous, the second subheading relates to the argument that the tip lacked sufficient indicia of reliability, and the third subheading relates to the argument that the police failed to corroborate anything more than innocuous details.

Issue

Did the district court err in concluding that a telephone tip created an objective particularized suspicion when the informant declined to give more than his name; the informant called from a public pay phone and gave only a general physical description of Mr. Josephy, his car, and his location; and the police merely corroborated that Mr. Josephy left a motel shortly before checkout time and got into his car?

Argument

A.   THE ATF AGENTS VIOLATED MR. JOSEPHY'S FOURTH AMENDMENT RIGHTS BECAUSE THEY DID NOT HAVE A PARTICULARIZED OBJECTIVE SUSPICION THAT MR. JOSEPHY WAS ENGAGED IN CRIMINAL ACTIVITY.

[Introductory paragraphs go here.]

1.   The ATF agents did not have a particularized objective suspicion that Mr. Josephy was engaged in criminal activity because the tip came from an unknown informant: Although the informant gave the 911 operator his name, he refused to give his address or phone number.

[Arguments relating to first subheading go here.]

2.   The ATF agents did not have a particularized objective suspicion that Mr. Josephy was engaged in criminal activity because the tip included only general physical descriptions,

it omitted any description of clothing, and the only action it predicted was that Mr. Josephy would be leaving a motel shortly before checkout time.

[Arguments relating to second subheading go here.]

3.   The ATF agents did not have a particularized objective suspicion that Mr. Josephy was engaged in criminal activity because the police corroborated only innocuous details— for example, Mr. Josephy's physical appearance, his car, and his departure from a motel shortly before checkout time.

[Arguments relating to the third subheading go here.]

Although in *United States v. Josephy*, all three of these options could work, Ms. Elder chooses the third option. Ms. Elder rejects the first option (three issue statements and three main headings) because such an organizational scheme suggests that each of the issues and headings can stand on its own when, in fact, they cannot. Although the court will consider whether the tip came from a known or unknown informant, whether there are sufficient indicia of reliability, and whether law enforcement officers corroborated more than innocuous details, in the end the test is a totality of the circumstances test. In addition, under the first option, there is no place to set out the general rules, in this instance, the totality of the circumstances test and the factors that the courts consider. Finally, given that Ms. Elder plans to argue *Batson*, it will be easier for the appellate court to see that there are two different independent bases for reversal if the brief has one issue statement and one main heading relating to the motion to suppress and one issue statement and one main heading relating to the *Batson* objection.

Ms. Elder also rejects the second option (one issue statement and one main heading but no subheadings). The advantage of this second option is that it makes clear that the arguments relating to whether the tip came from a known or unknown informant, whether there are sufficient indicia of reliability, and whether law enforcement officers corroborated more than innocuous details are all related to the larger issue of whether the district court erred in denying Mr. Josephy's motion to suppress. The disadvantage of this second organizational scheme is that it does not allow Ms. Elder to emphasize that there are three reasons why the district court erred in denying Mr. Josephy's motion to suppress. Thus, while the government might want to use this organizational scheme to emphasize that the test is a totality of the circumstances test, Mr. Josephy does not.

The third option has all of the advantages with no disadvantages. By having a single issue statement and a single argumentative heading, Ms. Elder makes it clear that all of the pieces of her arguments are related to her main assertion: that the district court erred in denying Mr. Josephy's motion to suppress. In addition, by using three subheadings, Ms. Elder can emphasize that there are three reasons why the district court erred, and she can divide her argument into manageable chunks. Most importantly, though, the third option is consistent with Ms. Elder's theory of the case: The third option allows Ms. Elder to argue both of her legal theories through a narrow lens. For more on theory of the case, see section 18.6.2 in this book.

Like Ms. Elder, the government's attorney rejects the first option. Because the government wants the Court of Appeals to affirm the district court, it wants to limit and not expand the number of alleged errors. Deciding between the second and third options is more difficult. Although the second option allows the government to emphasize that the test is a totality of the circumstances test, the lack of subheadings means that the entire argument will need to be set out in one large chunk. On the flip side, although the third option allows the government to present its arguments in more manageable chunks, dividing the argument into three parts feeds into Ms. Elder's argument that any one reason is sufficient to support a conclusion that the district court erred. After weighing the pros and cons, the government's attorney settles on the second option because that option is more consistent with the government's theory of the case. He does, though, make presenting the government's argument concisely a high priority. See the appellee's brief set out at the end of this chapter.

b.   Ordering the Issues and Arguments

In many cases, logic dictates the order in which you set out the issues and the arguments related to those issues. Threshold questions — for example, issues relating to subject matter jurisdiction, service of process, and the statute of limitations — must be discussed before questions relating to the merits of the case. Similarly, the parts of a test should usually be discussed in order and, when one argument builds on another, the foundation argument should be set out first.

When logic does not dictate the order of the issues and arguments, you will usually want to start with your strongest argument. By doing so, you ensure that the judges will read your strongest argument, and your strongest argument is in a position of emphasis. You can then go through the rest of your issues and arguments in the order of their strength, or you can begin and end with strong issues and arguments, sandwiching your weaker arguments in the middle.

> **PRACTICE POINTER**   While the appellant files its brief first and the appellee needs to respond to the issues raised by the appellant, the appellee does not need to, and usually will not want to use, the appellant's organizational scheme. Instead, the appellee will usually want to select an organizational scheme that allows it to set out its strongest argument first.

In *United States v. Josephy*, both logic and strategy dictate the ordering of the issues and arguments related to those issues. If the appellate court determines that the evidence should have been suppressed, it will not reach the *Batson* issue. In addition, while a "win" on the *Batson* issue would result in a remand for a new trial, more likely than not a win on the suppression issue would end up with the charges being dismissed.

Having thoroughly analyzed the facts and the law, developed a theory of the case, and selected an organizational scheme, Ms. Elder is now ready to write. For the purpose of this chapter, we discuss the sections in the order in which they appear in the brief. You do not need to draft the sections in that order, however: Many attorneys start by drafting the arguments or the statement of the case. No matter how you decide to draft the brief, keep in mind that writing an appellate brief is a recursive process, with the completion of one section often requiring revision of another section. For example, once she drafts the arguments, Ms. Elder might find she needs to include additional facts in her statement of the facts or that she needs to revise her issue statements.

§ 18.7   Preparing the Cover

The first page of a brief is the title page, or cover. As in most other jurisdictions, in the federal courts there are rules that govern the cover. For instance, the rules prescribe the types of information that must be on the cover, the order of that information, and the color. *See* Fed. R. App. P. 32(2). The briefs at the end of the chapter comply with the rule for briefs submitted to the Ninth Circuit Court of Appeals.

§ 18.8.   Preparing the Table of Contents

The second page of the brief should be the table of contents. Once again, the rules specify the information that should be included and the format that should be used. *See* Fed. R. App. P. 28(a)(2) and the sample briefs at the end of this chapter.

> **PRACTICE POINTER**   If you are writing a brief to the United States Supreme Court, the questions presented would be set out, by themselves, on the page directly after the cover. *See* Sup. Ct. R. 24(1)(a).

§ 18.9   Preparing the Table of Authorities

Immediately following the table of contents is the table of authorities. In this section, list each of the cases, constitutional provisions, statutes, rules, and secondary authorities cited in the brief. As a general rule, cases are listed first, in alphabetical order, followed by constitutional provisions, statutes, court rules, and secondary authorities. *See* Fed. R. App. P. 28(a)(3).

In listing the authorities, use the citation form prescribed by your court rules (your jurisdiction might or might not have adopted the *ALWD Citation Manual* or *The Bluebook*) and include references to each page in the brief where the authority appears. Some of the fee-based services have programs that you can use to check your citations and prepare the table of authorities.

> **PRACTICE POINTER**   If you use a program to create your table of authorities, make sure that the table that the program generates is complete, accurate, and in compliance with the applicable rules. For example, some programs might not catch citations embedded in parentheticals, where one case cites to another case. In addition, make sure that the citations are in proper order (cases before secondary authorities) and in proper form (case

names in italics or underlined), and make sure that the table of authorities is easy to read: Use white space between each citation, and make sure that the citation does not run up against the page references. Finally, do not finalize your table of authorities until you have finished editing, revising, and proofreading the body of your brief so that the page references are accurate.

§ 18.10 Drafting the Jurisdictional Statement

Under Fed. R. App. P. 28(4), briefs filed in federal courts must have a jurisdictional statement setting out the following:

(A) the basis for the district court's or agency's subject matter jurisdiction, with citations to applicable statutory provisions and stating relevant facts establishing jurisdiction;

(B) the basis for the court of appeals' jurisdiction, with citations to applicable statutory provisions and stating relevant facts establishing jurisdiction;

(C) the filing dates establishing the timeliness of the appeal or petition for review; and

(D) an assertion that the appeal is from a final order or judgment that disposes of all parties' claims, or information establishing the court of appeals' jurisdiction on some other basis[.]

> **PRACTICE POINTER**   Under the federal rules, an appellee's brief need not include a jurisdictional statement unless the appellee disagrees with the appellant's jurisdictional statement. *See* Fed. R. App. P. 28(b)(1). However, in the Ninth Circuit, the appellee cannot omit the jurisdictional statement section; an appellee must include either a statement of jurisdiction or a statement agreeing with the appellant's statement of jurisdiction. Ninth Cir. R. 28-2.2(c).

§ 18.11 Drafting the Statement of Issues Presented for Review

The Federal Rules of Appellate Procedure require that the appellant include a statement of the issues presented for review. *See* Fed. R. App. P. 28(a)(5). The Federal Rules of Appellate Procedure do not require the appellee to include a statement of the issues. *See* Fed. R. App. P. 28(b)(2). However, in most instances, the appellee will want to set out the issues in such a way that they support its theory of the case.

Look, for example, at the following issue statements from *Hishon v. King & Spaulding*, a case in which the United States Supreme Court was asked to decide whether law firms were subject to federal civil rights laws prohibiting discrimination in employment on the basis of sex, race, religion, or national origin.

EXAMPLE 1   **Petitioner's Statement of the Issue**

Whether King and Spaulding and other large institutional law firms that are organized as partnerships are, for that reason alone, exempt from Title VII of the Civil Rights Act of 1964, and are free (a) to discriminate in the promotion of associate lawyers to partnership on the basis of sex, race or religion; and (b) to discharge those associates whom they do not admit to partnership based on reasons of sex, race or religion under an established "up-or-out" policy.

EXAMPLE 2   **Respondent's Statement of the Issues**

1.   Whether law partners organized for advocacy are entitled to constitutionally protected freedom of association.
2.   Whether Congress intended through Title VII of the Civil Rights Act of 1964 to give the Equal Employment Opportunity Commission, a politically appointed advocacy agency engaged in litigation, jurisdiction over invitations to join law firm partnerships.

The petitioner's issue statement sets out its theory of the case: According to the petitioner, the issue is whether law firms are free to discriminate on the basis of sex, race, religion, or national origin. Similarly, the respondent's issue statements set out its theory. To the respondent, this is not a case about discrimination. Instead, it is a case about whether the partners in a law firm are entitled to their constitutionally protected right of freedom of association and about whether members of a politically appointed advocacy agency have the right to determine who is invited to join a law firm.

§ 18.11.1 Select a Format

Most court rules do not prescribe the format that should be used for the issue statement. As a consequence, in writing your issue statement or statements, you can use the under-does-when format, the whether format, or a multisentence format. For a more in-depth discussion, *see* section 17.7.2.

EXAMPLE 3   **"Under-Does-When" Format**

Did the district court err in denying Mr. Josephy's *Batson* challenge when the prosecutor used his peremptory challenges to excuse both Mr. Williams and Ms. Whitefish, the only two Native Americans in the jury pool, and, in overruling the objection, the trial judge's only statement was, "Your objection is noted, Counsel, but the Court finds no purposeful discrimination here"?

EXAMPLE 4   **"Whether" Format**

Whether the district court erred in denying Mr. Josephy's *Batson* challenge when the prosecutor used his peremptory challenges to excuse both Mr. Williams and Ms. Whitefish, the only two Native

Americans in the jury pool, and, in overruling the objection, the court's only statement was, "Your objection is noted, Counsel, but the Court finds no purposeful discrimination here"?

EXAMPLE 5   **Multisentence Format**

The prosecutor excused a Native American juror who assured the court he could miss a scheduled meeting, but he did not excuse a white juror who might have had to leave town because the doctors had given his mother a 20 percent chance of living. In addition, the prosecutor excused a Native American juror who said she was not bothered by searches at the border that she attributed to her age, but he did not excuse a white juror with long hair who admitted being bothered by police officers who targeted individuals who had long hair. The judge's only ruling was, "Your objection is noted, Counsel, but the Court finds no purposeful discrimination here." Given the fact that Mr. Josephy is a Native American, did the district court err when it overruled Mr. Josephy's *Batson* objection?

Although you can use any format, once you select a format, use it for each of your issues. Do not write one issue using the "under-does-when" format and another using the "whether" format. Also, remember that you are not bound by opposing counsel's choices. You do not need to use the format that he or she used, and you do not need to have the same number of issues. Select the format and number of issues that work best for your client.

> **PRACTICE POINTER**   Some issues statements work equally well under any of the three formats; others do not. Consequently, although you might have a preferred format, if you have an issue that just does not work with that particular format, don't force it. Use the format that will work for all of the issues raised.

§ 18.11.2 Make the Issue Statement Subtly Persuasive

A good issue statement is subtly persuasive: Not only does your issue statement set out your theory of the case, but it also subtly suggests the conclusion you want the court to reach and provides support for that conclusion.

In writing the issue statements for an appellate brief, you can use three techniques to make your statements subtly persuasive: (1) You can state the question so that it suggests the conclusion you want the court to reach; (2) you can emphasize the facts that support your theory of the case; and (3) you can emphasize or de-emphasize the burden of proof or standard of review.

a.   State the Question So That It Suggests the Conclusion You Want the Court to Reach

Begin by framing the legal question so that it suggests the conclusion you want the court to reach. For instance, in writing the issue statement for *United States v. Josephy*, Ms. Elder frames the question so that it suggests that the district court erred in overruling her *Batson* objection, while the government frames the question so that it suggests that the district court acted properly when it overruled the objection.

EXAMPLE 6	**Appellant's Statement of the Legal Question**

Did the district court err in denying Mr. Josephy's *Batson* challenge . . . ?

EXAMPLE 7	**Appellee's Statement of the Legal Question**

Did the district court properly overrule the defendant's *Batson* objection . . . ?

Note that while the appellant uses "denying" and "*Batson* challenge," the appellee uses "overrule" and "*Batson* objection." Because some courts use one phrase and other courts use the other phrase, each side can select the phrase that is most favorable to its position. In this instance, the appellee uses "overrule" and "objection" because appellate courts usually defer to a trial court's decision to sustain or overrule an objection. In contrast, the appellant uses "denying" and "*Batson* challenge" because that phrase suggests that the case involves more than just a routine evidentiary issue.

Similarly, the attorneys think carefully about the language they will use in connection with the suppression issue. The appellee uses a general statement of the rule that courts apply: whether the officers had a reasonable suspicion that the defendant was involved in criminal activity. In contrast, Ms. Elder frames her argument using the more favorable language from Ninth Circuit cases, which define a reasonable suspicion as a "particularized and objective basis for suspecting the particular person stopped of criminal activity.".

PRACTICE POINTER	One way to see what phrase the courts use in a particular situation is to run a search for the possible alternative terms in a fee-based service like Lexis Advance®, WestlawNext™, Bloomberg Law, or a

free service that has copies of opinions, for example, Google Scholar.

There are, of course, other ways of framing the legal question.

EXAMPLE 8	**Other Ways That the Appellant Could Set Out the Legal Question That Suggest the Conclusion the Appellant Wants the Court to Reach**

Under the Equal Protection Clause, was Mr. Josephy denied his right to a jury trial when . . . ?

Were the reasons that the prosecutor gave for excusing the only two Native Americans in the jury pool a pretext for discrimination when . . . ?

Did the prosecutor violate Mr. Josephy's constitutional rights when . . . ?

EXAMPLE 9	Other Ways That the Appellee Could Set Out the Legal Question That Suggest the Conclusion the Appellee Wants the Court to Reach

Did the government properly exercise its right to use peremptory challenges when . . . ?

Did the defendant fail to prove purposeful discrimination when . . . ?

Given that the district court was in the best position to judge the prosecutor's action, did the district court properly overrule the *Batson* objection when . . . ?

b.　Emphasize the Facts That Support Your Theory of the Case

In addition to stating the question so that it suggests a favorable conclusion, also emphasize the facts that support your theory of the case. For instance, in the following example, Ms. Elder has emphasized the facts that suggest the prosecutor's proffered reasons were a pretext for discrimination by including the jurors' names and stating that these two jurors were the only two Native Americans in the jury pool. In addition, Ms. Elder has emphasized the facts that suggest that the district court did not do the required "sensitive analysis" by stating that the district court's ruling consisted of a single statement and quoting that statement.

EXAMPLE 10	Appellant's Use of Facts

Did the district court err in denying Mr. Josephy's *Batson* challenge when the prosecutor used his peremptory challenges to excuse both Mr. Williams and Ms. Whitefish, the only two Native Americans in the jury pool, and, in denying the challenge, the judge's only statement was, "Your objection is noted, Counsel, but the Court finds no purposeful discrimination here"?

In contrast, in drafting its issue statement, the government emphasizes the facts that support its theory of the case. In particular, in the first part of its issue statement, the government sets up its argument that it excused Ms. Whitefish because of her age and her experiences, and not because she is a Native American by including in its issue statement references to Ms. Whitefish's age and the problems that she encountered at the border. Similarly, the government sets up its argument that it did not engage in purposeful discrimination when it excused Mr. Williams by highlighting the fact that the government excused both a Native American and a white juror for similar reasons. Finally, note that while Ms. Elder refers to the jurors by name, which allows her to include a name that appears to be a Native American name (Ms. Whitefish) in her issue statement, the government does not refer to the jurors by name.

EXAMPLE 11	Appellee's Use of Facts

Whether Mr. Josephy failed to prove that the government engaged in purposeful discrimination when (1) the government excused a twenty-one-year-old Native American juror who volunteered that she had experienced problems each time she had crossed from the United States into Canada and (2) the government excused both a Native American juror who told the judge that he had a tribal council meeting the following week and a white juror who was worried about missing work.

c.   Emphasize or De-Emphasize the Burden of Proof and Standard of Review

Another way to make your issue statement subtly persuasive is to use the burden of proof and standard of review to your advantage. As a general rule, if the other side has the burden of proof, emphasize that fact. In contrast, if you have the burden of proof, de-emphasize that fact. Likewise, if the standard of review favors your client, include a reference to it in your issue statement; if it does not, do talk about the standard of review in the argument, but not in the issue statement.

EXAMPLE 12	**Because the Appellant Has the Burden of Proof, Ms. Elder Does Not Mention the Burden of Proof in Her Issue Statement**

Did the district court err in denying Mr. Josephy's *Batson* challenge when . . . ?

EXAMPLE 13	**Because the Appellant Has the Burden of Proof, the Government Emphasizes That Fact in Its Issue Statement**

Whether the defendant failed to prove that the government engaged in purposeful discrimination when . . . ,

> **PRACTICE POINTER**
>
> In some jurisdictions the courts or individual judges have stated that the parties should not be referred to as appellant/petitioner or appellee/respondent. Instead, the courts or judges have stated that the parties should be referred to by name, by a label that identifies their relationship to other parties (for example, employer and employee or doctor and patient), or by the label that describes their status at the trial court (for example, plaintiff and defendant). Thus, before deciding what to call the parties, check your local rules.

§ 18.11.3 Make Sure the Issue Statement Is Readable

An issue statement that is not readable is not persuasive. Therefore, during the revising process, check your issue statement to make sure a judge can understand it after reading it just once. First, look at length. If your issue statement is more than four or five lines long, try to shorten it. The longer the statement, the more difficult it becomes to read. Second, make sure that you have presented the information in manageable "chunks." One way to make a long issue statement easier to read is to use the three slots in a sentence:

_____ , _____ , _____ .
    introductory phrase   main clause   modifier(s)

Another way is to use enumeration: In listing the key facts, use numbers or letters to introduce each item in the list of facts.

Finally, make sure your statement of the issue does not contain any grammatical errors. In particular, make sure that your subject and verb agree and that, in listing the facts, you have used parallel constructions for all of the items in the list. For more on using parallel constructions, see sections 24.5.1 and 27.7.

See section 17.7.4 for a checklist for critiquing issue statements.

§ 18.12   Drafting the Statement of the Case

Over and over again, judges emphasize the importance of the facts. At both the trial and appellate court levels, judges want to know what the facts are and how the law should be applied to them.

Because the facts are so important, good advocates spend considerable time crafting their statement of the case. They think carefully about which facts they want to include, how those facts should be organized, and how the facts can be presented in the light most favorable to their client.

§ 18.12.1 Check the Rules

Just as there are rules governing the cover, tables, and statement of issues, most jurisdictions have rules that govern the statement of the case. Under the federal rules, an appellant's brief must contain the following:

Fed. R. App. P. 28(a)

     * * *

     (6)   a statement of the case briefly indicating the nature of the case, the course of proceedings, and the disposition below;
     (7)   a statement of facts relevant to the issues submitted for review with appropriate references to the record (see Rule 28(e))[.]

Although the rules do not require that an appellee include a statement of the case and statement of facts (_see_ Fed. R. App. P. 28(b)(3)-(4)), most attorneys include them so that they can set out the procedure and facts in a light favorable to their clients.

§ 18.12.2 Draft the Statement of the Case

Under the federal rules, the statement of the case precedes the statement of facts. _See_ Fed. R. App. P. 28(a)(6). In most instances, you will want to include the following facts in your statement of the case: (1) a statement describing the nature of the action, (2) a description of any relevant motions and their disposition, and (3) a statement telling the court whether the case was heard by a judge or by a jury. For example, in *United States v. Josephy*, the statement of the case would look something like this:

| EXAMPLE 1 | **Appellant's Statement of the Case** |

STATEMENT OF THE CASE

On June 25, 2013, Peter Jason Josephy was charged with one count of Unlawful Possession of a Controlled Substance with the Intent to Deliver under 21 U.S.C. § 841(a)(1) (2012). (CR 7). After an evidentiary hearing, the district court denied Mr. Josephy's motion to suppress evidence obtained during a warrantless search. (CR 26; ER 30).

The case proceeded to a jury trial, the Honorable Alesha J. Moore presiding. (CR 28). During voir dire, Mr. Josephy challenged the government's use of two of its peremptory challenges to excuse the only two Native Americans on the jury panel. (ER 123-24). The district court concluded that while Mr. Josephy had established a prima facie case of discrimination, the reasons given by the government were race neutral and that Mr. Josephy had not established purposeful discrimination. (ER 124). Based on this decision, the court denied Mr. Josephy's *Batson* challenge.

Notice that each statement is supported by a reference to the record. CR stands for Clerk's Record — that is, a document filed with the trial court; ER stands for Excerpt of Record — that is, those portions of the trial record filed in connection with the appeal.

§ 18.12.3 Select the Facts

Like the statement of facts in an objective memo and a motion brief, the statement of facts in an appellate brief contains three types of facts: legally significant facts, emotionally significant facts, and background facts.

a. Legally Significant Facts

Because the court rules require that the statement of the facts include the facts relevant to the issues being raised, in drafting the statement of facts include all of the legally significant facts, both favorable and unfavorable. For example, in *United States v. Josephy*, the parties must include all of the facts that will be relevant in determining whether ATF agents had a reasonable suspicion that Mr. Josephy was engaged in criminal activity and all of the facts that will be relevant in determining whether the district court erred in overruling Ms. Elder's *Batson* challenge. For example, in setting out the facts relating to the *Batson* challenge, Ms. Elder must include the fact that the prosecutor used one of his peremptory challenges to excuse a white juror who had scheduling problems, and the prosecutor must include the fact that he excused all of the Native Americans in the jury pool.

b. Emotionally Significant Facts

Although you must include all of the legally significant facts, you do not need to include all of the emotionally significant facts. While sometimes you might include an emotionally significant fact that is unfavorable, re-characterizing it or minimizing its significance, most of the time you will not. It is more common to include only those emotionally significant facts that favor your client.

The harder question is how to handle emotionally significant facts that are unfavorable to the other side. Should you sling mud, or should you take a higher road and omit any reference to those facts? The answer is that it depends: It depends on the fact, on the case, and on the attorney. If the case is strong and the fact's connection to the case is tenuous, most attorneys would not include the fact. If, however, the case is weak and the fact's connection is closer, many attorneys will include it — some using it as a sword, others using it much more subtly.

c.　Background Facts

Background facts play a different role in persuasive writing than they do in objective writing. In an objective statement of facts, the writer includes only those facts that are needed for the story to make sense. However, in drafting a persuasive statement of facts, you want to do more. You want to use background facts to create a favorable context. See section 18.12.5(a).

§ 18.12.4　Select an Organizational Scheme

After selecting the facts, the next step is to pick an organizational scheme. Should the facts be presented chronologically or topically, or would a scheme that combines topical and chronological organization work better?

Unlike an objective statement of facts in which the only selection criterion was logic, in writing a persuasive statement of facts there are three criteria: (1) You want to select a scheme that is logical, (2) you want to select a scheme that is consistent with the order in which you set out the arguments, and (3) you want to select a scheme that allows you to present the facts in a light favorable to your client.

In *United States v. Josephy*, logic dictates that Ms. Elder start with the facts relating to the seizure and not with the facts relating to the *Batson* challenge: The seizure occurred before the jury selection. In addition, starting with the facts relating to the search is consistent with the way in which Ms. Elder has decided to order the arguments: Because the court would probably dismiss the charges if it finds that the search was illegal, Ms. Elder has decided to discuss the search before she discusses the *Batson* challenge. Finally, starting with the facts that relate to the seizure allows Ms. Elder to present the facts in a light favorable to Mr. Josephy. Even though the facts relating to the *Batson* objection are more compelling than the facts relating to the search, Ms. Elder decides that, on balance, it works best to start with the facts relating to the search. However, instead of starting with the tip, she decides to start with the seizure, which favors her client.

In contrast, for the prosecutor, the best choice is to set the facts out in chronological order. Setting out the facts in chronological order is logical and consistent with the order in which the prosecutor plans to discuss the issues. In addition, setting out the facts in chronological order allows the prosecutor to start with the facts that are most favorable to the government: the fact that Zachary Dillon called and told the police that Mr. Josephy was involved in selling drugs that had been brought into the United States from Canada.

§ 18.12.5 Present the Facts in the Light Most Favorable to the Client

Although the statement of facts must be accurate, it need not be neutral. Therefore, as an advocate, you want to present the facts in the light most favorable to your client. In doing so, you can use the following strategies.

Strategies for Writing a Persuasive Statement of Facts

a. Create a favorable context.
b. Tell the story from the client's point of view.
c. Emphasize the facts that support your theory of the case and de-emphasize those that do not.
   1. Airtime
   2. Detail
   3. Positions of emphasis
   4. Sentence and paragraph length
   5. Main and dependent clauses
   6. Active and passive voice
d. Choose words carefully.
e. Be subtly persuasive.

PRACTICE POINTER   While the statement of the facts should be persuasive, do not misstate, mischaracterize, or overstate the facts. Because one of your greatest tools as an advocate is your professional reputation, do not do anything that might damage it or undermine your credibility.

a.   Create a Favorable Context

The opening paragraph or paragraphs of your statement of facts are like the opening scenes in a movie. They create both a context and a "mood" for the story that you are about to tell and for the arguments that you want to make. It is, therefore, important to think carefully about where you want to start the story and about the language that you want to use.

For instance, in the example problem set out in Chapter 17, Mr. Patterson's attorney wanted to start the story by creating a picture of Mr. Patterson and his activities on the day that the assault occurred. In doing so, the attorney hoped to present her client as a young and attentive husband who could not and would not have assaulted Ms. Martinez.

EXAMPLE 2   **Opening Paragraphs of the Defendant's Statement of Facts in *Patterson***

At 7:30 a.m. on Monday, August 12, 2013, twenty-two-year-old Dean Patterson finished his shift as a security guard and walked to his apartment. After having breakfast with his wife, Patterson went to bed and slept until about 1:00 p.m. At about 2:30 p.m., Mr. Patterson's wife received a phone call asking her to work at the local hospital where she is employed as a nurse. Mr. Patterson's wife got ready, and Mr. Patterson dropped her off at the hospital at about 3:10 p.m.

At about 3:30 p.m., Patterson called his wife to find how long she would have to work; they had plans to go to a movie that evening, and he wanted to know whether he should change those plans. At about 3:50 p.m., Patterson took a load of laundry to the apartment complex's laundry room. When he returned to his apartment, Patterson watched part of an old movie. At about 4:15 p.m., Patterson went back to the laundry room to put the clothes in the dryer. On his way back, he saw a parking spot in front of his apartment and moved his car, an older model red station wagon, to that spot. After parking his car, Mr. Patterson got out of the car and, because the driver's side door does not lock from the outside, walked to the passenger side to lock the doors. As he did so, he nodded to a parking enforcement officer who was driving by. By this time, it was 4:30 p.m., and Mr. Patterson decided to phone his wife again. He arranged to meet her at 5:15 p.m. for her dinner break. Mr. Patterson retrieved the laundry and then left the apartment a little before 5:00 p.m. to meet his wife.

In contrast, in *Patterson* the State started its statement of facts where the story started for the victim. In the first paragraph of its statement of facts, the State described the assault and then the show-up and line-up.

EXAMPLE 3   **Opening Paragraph of the State's Statement of Facts in *Patterson***

On Monday, August 12, 2013, Beatrice Martinez was assaulted with a deadly weapon. At a show-up held thirty to forty minutes after the attack, Martinez positively identified the defendant, Dean E. Patterson, as her assailant. One day after the assault, Martinez picked Patterson out of a line-up, once again positively identifying him as her assailant.

For more on the statement of facts in *Patterson*, see section 17.6.

Although the differences are more subtle, context is equally important in *United States v. Josephy*. For example, in drafting the opening paragraph, Ms. Elder wants to present Mr. Josephy in a favorable light by creating the impression that Mr. Josephy was engaged in a lawful activity when two ATF agents pulled behind and in front of his car. The following examples show two different ways in which Ms. Elder can create this favorable context.

EXAMPLE 4   **One Way of Starting the Statement of Facts in the Appellant's Brief**

On the evening of June 24, 2013, Peter Jason Josephy checked into the Travel House Inn in Bellingham, Washington. (ER 44). When he checked in, Mr. Josephy filled out a registration form on which he listed the make and model of his car and his license number. (ER 44).

The next morning, Mr. Josephy checked out a few minutes before the 11:00 a.m. check out time. (ER 22). After a brief conversation with an acquaintance, Oliver Preston, both men walked out of the hotel. Parting ways in front of the hotel, Mr. Preston walked toward his car and Josephy walked to his car and got in. (ER 43).

As Mr. Josephy started his car, AFT vehicles pulled in front of and behind Mr. Josephy's car. (ER 44). As a result, Mr. Josephy was not able to pull forward or back up. (ER 44).

EXAMPLE 5	Another Way of Starting the Statement of Facts in the Appellant's Brief

At 10:45 a.m. on June 25, 2013, Peter Josephy left his room at the Travel House Inn in Bellingham, checked out, and, after talking to a friend for three or four minutes, walked to his car and got in. (ER 22, 43). As Mr. Josephy started his car, one Alcohol, Tobacco, and Firearms (ATF) agent pulled behind Mr. Josephy's car, and another ATF agent pulled in front, preventing Mr. Josephy from leaving the parking lot. (ER 44).

In contrast, the government wants to start its statement of the facts by portraying Mr. Josephy as a drug dealer. The following examples show two ways of creating this favorable context for the prosecution.

EXAMPLE 6	One Way of Starting the Statement of Facts in the Appellee's Brief

At about 9:30 a.m. on June 25, 2013, Zachary Dillon called 911 and reported that Peter Josephy was involved in selling drugs that had been brought into the United States from Canada. (ER 30). Two hours later, Alcohol, Tobacco, and Firearms (ATF) agents searched Mr. Josephy's car and found four kilos of marijuana in the wheel well. (ER 49).

EXAMPLE 7	Another Way of Starting the Statement of Facts in the Appellee's Brief

At 9:30 a.m. on June 25, 2013, the Bellingham Police Department received a tip that Peter Josephy was involved in selling marijuana that had been brought into the United States from Canada. (ER 30). During the 911 call, which was recorded, the caller identified himself as Zachary Dillon. (ER 31). Although Mr. Dillon did not know where Josephy lived, he said that Josephy was currently at the Travel House Inn, a local motel. (ER 32).

PRACTICE POINTER	In the preceding *Patterson* examples, the authors did not include references to the record because, at the time that they drafted their briefs, there was no record. In contrast, in the Josephy examples, the authors did include references to the record because there was a record and the appellate rules required citations to that record.

b. Tell the Story from the Client's Point of View

One of the most powerful persuasive devices is point of view. Consequently, as a general rule, you will want to present the facts from your client's point of view: One way of doing this is to tell the story as your client would tell it, using your client's name as the subject in most sentences. Look again at the following examples. In Example 8, Mr. Josephy's name is used as the subject in five of the seven sentences. In contrast, in Example 10, Ms. Elder used Mr. Josephy as the subject in the first sentence but the ATF agents as the subjects in the second sentence. Although Ms. Elder wanted to emphasize that Mr. Josephy was engaged in lawful activities, she wanted to emphasize that Mr. Josephy was the victim of what she will argue were the agents' unlawful acts. Thus, in the second sentence, she puts the agents in the subject slots of the sentence and Mr. Josephy in the object slot.

In the following examples, the subjects are in boldface type.

EXAMPLE 8   **One Way of Starting the Statement of Facts in the Appellant's Brief**

On the evening of June 24, 2013, **Peter Jason Josephy** checked into the Travel House Inn in Bellingham, Washington. (ER 44). When he checked in, **Mr. Josephy** filled out a registration form on which he listed the make and model of his car and his license number. (ER 44).

The next morning, **Mr. Josephy** checked out a few minutes before the 11:00 a.m. check out time. (ER 22). After a brief conversation with an acquaintance, Oliver Preston, **both men** walked out of the hotel. Parting ways in front of the hotel, **Mr. Preston** walked toward his car, and **Mr. Josephy** walked to his car and got in. (ER 43).

As Mr. Josephy started his car, **AFT vehicles** pulled in front of and behind Mr. Josephy's car. (ER 44). As a result, **Mr. Josephy** was not able to pull forward or back up. (ER 44).

EXAMPLE 9   **Another Way of Starting the Statement of Facts in the Appellant's Brief**

At 10:45 a.m. on June 25, 2013, **Peter Josephy** left his room at the Travel House Inn in Bellingham, checked out, and, after talking to a friend for three or four minutes, walked to his car and got in. (ER 43). As Mr. Josephy started his car, **one Alcohol, Tobacco, and Firearms (ATF) agent** pulled behind Mr. Josephy's car, and **another ATF agent** pulled in front, preventing Mr. Josephy from leaving the parking lot. (ER 44).

While in a criminal case defense counsel usually tells the story from the client's point of view, the government has more options: If there is a victim, the government can tell the story from the victim's point of view or, if there is not a victim, it can tell the story from the point of view of government agents. In addition, when the defendant did something egregious, the prosecutor can use the defendant as the actor. In Example 10 below, the prosecutor uses the informant as the subject in the first sentence and the ATF agents as the subjects in the second sentence. In Example 11, the prosecutor has written the first sentence using the passive voice: "the Bellingham Police Department *received* a tip." By using the passive voice, the prosecutor is able to use the Police Department as the subject of the first sentence. The prosecutor then uses the "caller" and "he" as the subjects of the second and third sentences.

EXAMPLE 10   **One Way of Starting the Statement of Facts in the Appellee's Brief**

At about 9:30 a.m. on June 25, 2013, **Zachary Dillon** called 911 and reported that Peter Josephy was involved in selling drugs that had been brought into the United States from Canada. Two hours later, **ATF agents** searched Mr. Josephy's car and found four kilos of marijuana in the wheel well. (ER 49).

> **EXAMPLE 11**   **Another Way of Starting the Statement of Facts in the Appellee's Brief**
>
> At 10:00 a.m., **the Bellingham Police Department** received a tip that Peter Josephy was involved in selling marijuana that had been brought into the United States from Canada. (ER 30). During the 911 call, which was recorded, the **caller** identified himself as Zachary Dillon. (ER 31). Although Mr. Dillon did not know where Josephy lived, **he** said that Josephy was currently at the Travel House Inn, a local motel. (ER 32).

---

c.   Emphasize Those Facts That Support Your Theory of the Case and De-emphasize Those That Do Not

In addition to presenting the facts from the client's point of view, good advocates emphasize those facts that support their theory of the case and de-emphasize those that do not. They do this by using one or more of the following techniques.

1.   Airtime

Just as listeners remember best the songs that get the most airtime, readers remember best the facts that get the most words. Consequently, if you want the judges to remember a fact, give that fact as much airtime as possible.

For example, in *United States v. Josephy*, Ms. Elder wants to emphasize the facts that support her argument that the tip should be treated as an anonymous tip because the person called the 911 operator from a public pay telephone and, other than giving the operator a name, the person making the call did not provide the operator with information that the agents could use to locate the caller. The facts that Ms. Elder has emphasized by giving them airtime are in bold. In contrast, Ms. Elder wants to de-emphasize the fact that the caller told the 911 operator that Mr. Josephy was selling drugs that had been brought into the United States from Canada. Thus, Ms. Elder gives these facts, which are underlined, very little airtime.

> **EXAMPLE 12**   **Excerpt from the Appellant's Brief**
>
> Agent Bhasin had gone to the Travel House Inn after **receiving a phone call from a 911 operator who reported that she had received a call from a public pay telephone located in the Bellis Fair Mall**, which is about a five-minute drive from the Travel House Inn. (ER 30, 34). <u>The informant claimed that a Mr. Josephy was at the Travel House Inn to sell drugs to a man named Oliver</u>. (ER 30). In addition, the informant told that 911 operator that, if the police wanted to catch Mr. Josephy, they should go the Travel House Inn soon because Mr. Josephy would be there for only another hour or two. (ER 32-33).
>
> When asked to describe Mr. Josephy, the informant told the 911 operator that Mr. Josephy was a Native American with black hair in his mid- to late twenties and that he was driving a blue Chevy Blazer. (ER 32). When asked about Oliver's last name, the informant said that he did not know Oliver's last name. When pushed for a description, the informant told the 911 operator that Oliver was about six feet tall, that he had brown hair and a beard, and that he was in his thirties. (ER 32).
>
> **The 911 operator then asked the informant for his name, address, and a phone number so that the police or ATF agents could re-contact him. Although the informant told the 911 operator that his name was Zachary Dillon, he then became uncooperative and refused to**

give the 911 operator his address, his home telephone number, or a cell phone number. (ER 32, 35).

In contrast, the prosecutor wants to de-emphasize the fact that the 911 call came from a pay phone, that the caller did not provide the 911 operator with any information about himself other than his name, and that Agent Bhasin was not able to locate anyone by the name of Zachary Dillon in the databases that he checked. Therefore, the prosecutor gives these facts very little airtime. Instead, he gives airtime to the facts that support the government's position: that Mr. Dillon gave the operator his name, that he gave the 911 operator a description of both Mr. Josephy and Oliver, and that call was made from a phone that is very close to the Travel House Inn. The facts that the prosecutor has emphasized are in bold and the facts that he has de-emphasized are underlined.

EXAMPLE 13	**Excerpt from the Appellee's Brief**

During the 911 call, which was recorded, Mr. Dillon told the operator that Mr. Josephy was at the Travel House Inn to meet with, and deliver marijuana to, a man named Oliver. (ER 30-31). <u>While Mr. Dillon declined to give the 911 operator his address or phone number</u>, **Mr. Dillon did tell the 911 operator that Mr. Josephy was a Native American, that Josephy had black hair, and that Josephy was in his mid- to late twenties. (ER 32). Mr. Dillon also told the operator that Mr. Josephy owned and was driving a blue Chevy Blazer. (ER 32). Although Mr. Dillon did not know Oliver's last name, he described Oliver as being in his thirties, about six feet tall, and with brown hair and a beard. (ER 32). Finally, Mr. Dillon told the police not to wait too long because Mr. Josephy would be leaving the motel in the next hour or two. (ER 33).**

The 911 operator relayed the information from Mr. Dillon to Agent Bhasin, an ATF agent with more than ten years of service. (ER 4). <u>Not finding anyone by the name of Zachary Dillon in the ATF databases</u>, Agent Bhasin drove to the Travel House Inn in an unmarked car to determine whether there was a blue Chevy Blazer in the parking lot. (ER 35, 40). **When he arrived at the motel at approximately 10:15 a.m., Agent Bhasin located a blue Chevy Blazer in the parking lot; when he ran the license plates, he was told that the Blazer was registered to Peter Jason Josephy. (ER 43).**

2. Detail

Just as readers tend to remember best those facts that get the most airtime, they also tend to remember best those things that are described in detail. Consequently, one way to emphasize a favorable fact is to describe it in detail. Use concrete subjects, action verbs, adjectives, and adverbs to create vivid pictures. In contrast, if you want to de-emphasize a particular fact, use generic language in describing those facts. In the following examples, compare the ways in which the attorneys describe Ms. Whitefish's and Mr. Martin's statements during voir dire.

EXAMPLE 14	**Excerpt from the Appellant's Statement of Facts**

Later, the prosecutor asked if anyone had ever had negative experiences with law enforcement personnel. (ER 119). Ms. Whitefish, a Native American who was a junior majoring in history at Western Washington University, responded that each time she crossed the border she had been pulled over for questioning. (ER 119). When the prosecutor asked if this bothered her, Ms. Whitefish stated that the fact that she was pulled aside for additional questioning did not bother her because she knew that the border agents were more suspicious of younger people than they were of older individuals. (ER 119).

Similarly, Mr. Martin, a white man with long hair, told the prosecutor that he had had a number of negative experiences with police officers. (ER 119-20). For example, Mr. Martin told the prosecutor that on one occasion a police officer had stopped him because one of his taillights was out, but the police had not stopped other individuals who had one of their taillights out. (ER 120). In addition, Mr. Martin told the prosecutor that on two occasions he had been given tickets for jaywalking when other individuals on the same street who had short hair jaywalked but did not get tickets. (ER 120). When the prosecutor asked whether he was bothered by the police officers' actions, Mr. Martin said, "You bet I am." (ER 121).

EXAMPLE 15	**Excerpt from the Appellee's Statement of Facts**

During voir dire, the prosecutor asked the members of the jury panel whether anyone had had a negative experience with a law enforcement officer. (ER 119). Juror No. 5, a young Native American, responded that she had negative experiences each time she crossed the border between the United States and Canada. (ER 119). Although Juror No. 5 stated that she was not bothered by her experiences at the border, she also stated that she had been pulled aside for additional questioning every time that she had crossed the border. (ER 119).

In contrast, Juror No. 11, Mr. Martin, a white man in his forties with long hair, told the prosecutor that he had been stopped by the police on one occasion because he had a taillight out and on two other occasions because he was jaywalking. (ER 120). Although Mr. Martin said that he was bothered by the fact that he had been stopped by the police, he also said he felt that police officers tended to stop people with long hair more often than people with short hair. (ER 120).

Note that in her statement of facts, Ms. Elder goes into detail in describing Ms. Whitefish: Ms. Elder tells the court that Ms. Whitefish is a Native American, Ms. Elder refers to Ms. Whitefish by name and not by her jury number, and Ms. Elder tells the court that Ms. Whitefish is a junior majoring in history at Western Washington University. In contrast, the prosecutor refers to Ms. Whitefish by her jury number, Juror No. 5, and only tells the court that Juror No. 5 is a young Native American. Also note that while Ms. Elder goes into very little detail in describing Ms. Whitefish's experiences at the border, the prosecutor does just the opposite. Because Ms. Elder does not want to emphasize that Ms. Whitefish had negative experiences crossing the border, she is more general and concise about Ms. Whitefish's experiences. In contrast, the prosecutor emphasizes these facts, specifically stating that Juror No. 5 had been "pulled aside for additional questioning every time that she had crossed the border." Finally, note that although Ms. Elder goes into detail in describing Mr. Martin's negative experiences with the police, the prosecutor does not go into detail. Thus, although both Ms. Elder and the prosecutor have included all of the legally significant facts (for example, that Ms. Whitefish is a Native American and that Mr. Martin is white), when possible, they have described more favorable facts in more detail and less favorable facts in less detail.

3. Positions of Emphasis

Another technique that can be used to emphasize favorable facts is to place favorable facts in positions of emphasis. Because readers remember better those things that they read first and last, favorable facts should be placed at the beginning and end of the statement of facts, at the beginning and end of paragraphs, and at the beginning and end of sentences. Unfavorable facts should be "buried" in the middle: in the middle of the statement of facts, in the middle of a paragraph, and in the middle of a sentence.

Look again at the examples from *Patterson* set out in Chapter 17. In the first example, defense counsel wanted to emphasize that the victim, Beatrice Martinez, told the police that her assailant was in his forties but that Mr. Patterson was only twenty-two. Thus, she puts that fact at the end of the paragraph. In addition, defense counsel juxtaposes this fact with the fact that Mr. Patterson is twenty-two. In contrast, the prosecutor put the fact that Ms. Martinez told the police that her assailant was in his forties in the middle of a paragraph, burying the age between the other, more accurate, portions of Ms. Martinez's description.

EXAMPLE 16	**Excerpt from the Defendant's Brief in** *Patterson*

Because she was still upset, Martinez was able to give Officer Yuen only a general description of her assailant. She described him as being a short, white male with blondish-brown hair who was wearing glasses and a dark jacket. **In addition, she told police that her assailant was in his early forties. Mr. Patterson is twenty-two.**

EXAMPLE 17	**Excerpt from the State's Brief in** *Patterson*

When she [Ms. Martinez] was interviewed, she told the police that her assailant was a white male with blondish-brown hair, that he was approximately 5'7" tall and weighed between 165 and 170 pounds, that he **appeared to be in his early forties, and that he was wearing a dark jacket.**

In *United States v. Josephy*, the attorneys also use the positions of emphasis to emphasize favorable facts. For instance, Ms. Elder puts some of the facts that favor her client in the first paragraph of her statement of facts. In addition, in constructing that opening paragraph, she puts the most favorable fact, that the ATF agents pulled behind and in front of Mr. Josephy's car, preventing him from leaving, at the very end of the paragraph.

EXAMPLE 18	**Example from the Appellant's Brief**

At 10:45 a.m. on June 25, 2013, Peter Josephy left his room at the Travel House Inn in Bellingham, Washington; checked out; and, after talking to a friend for three or four minutes, walked to his car and got in. (ER 22, 43). As Mr. Josephy started his car, Agent Bhasin, an Alcohol, Tobacco, and Firearms (ATF) agent, pulled behind Mr. Josephy's car, and another ATF agent, Agent O'Brien, pulled in front. **As a result, Mr. Josephy was prevented from moving his car.** (ER 44).

The prosecutor does the same thing. He puts some of the facts that favor the government in the opening paragraph of his statement of facts, and he puts the most favorable fact from that group of facts—that the police found four kilos of marijuana in the wheel well of Mr. Josephy's car—in the last sentence.

EXAMPLE 19   **Excerpt from the Appellee's Brief**

At about 9:30 a.m. on June 25, 2013, Zachary Dillon called 911 and reported that Peter Josephy was involved in selling drugs that had been brought into the United States from Canada. (ER 30). Two hours later, Alcohol, Tobacco, and Firearms (ATF) agents searched Mr. Josephy's car **and found four kilos of marijuana in the wheel well**. (ER 49).

---

4.   Sentence and Paragraph Length

Because readers tend to remember information placed in shorter sentences better than information placed in longer sentences, good advocates place favorable facts in shorter sentences. Similarly, because readers tend to remember information placed in short paragraphs better than information placed in longer paragraphs, when they can, good advocates place their most favorable facts in short paragraphs. In contrast, when they can, good advocates try to bury unfavorable facts in longer sentences and in longer paragraphs.

In the next example, Ms. Elder places a favorable fact—that the agents parked their vehicles in such a way that Mr. Josephy could not move his car—in a short sentence in a position of emphasis. The favorable fact is in bold.

EXAMPLE 20   **Excerpt from Appellant's Brief**

At 10:45 a.m. on June 25, 2013, Peter Josephy left his room at the Travel House Inn in Bellingham, Washington; checked out; and, after talking to a friend for three or four minutes, walked to his car and got in. (ER 22, 43). As Mr. Josephy started his car, Agent Bhasin, an Alcohol, Tobacco, and Firearms (ATF) agent, pulled behind Mr. Josephy's car, and another ATF agent, Agent O'Brien, pulled in front. **As a result, Mr. Josephy could not move his car.** (ER 44).

In contrast, in the following example, the prosecutor buried an unfavorable fact—that Mr. Dillon would not give the 911 operator his address or phone number—in a long sentence in the middle of a long paragraph. The unfavorable fact is underlined.

EXAMPLE 21   **Excerpt from the Appellee's Brief**

During the 911 call, which was recorded, Mr. Dillon told the operator that Mr. Josephy was at the Travel House Inn to meet with, and deliver marijuana to, a man named Oliver. (ER 30-31). <u>While Mr. Dillon declined to give the 911 operator his address or phone number</u>, Mr. Dillon did tell the 911 operator that Mr. Josephy was a Native American, that Josephy had black hair, and that Josephy was in his mid- to late twenties. (ER 32). Mr. Dillon also told the operator that Mr. Josephy owned, and was driving, a blue Chevy Blazer. (ER 32). Although Mr. Dillon did not know Oliver's last name, he described Oliver as in his thirties, about six feet tall, and with brown hair and a beard. (ER 32). Finally, Mr. Dillon told the police not to wait too long because Mr. Josephy would be leaving the motel in the next hour or two. (ER 33).

5. *Sentence Construction*

Because information that is placed in a main, or independent clause, is more likely to be remembered than information that is placed in a dependent, or subordinate clause, try to put favorable facts in the main clause and unfavorable ones in a dependent clause. For example, in the next sample paragraph, Ms. Elder makes two points in the second sentence: (1) that the caller gave the 911 operator his name and (2) that the caller would not give the 911 operator his address or a telephone number. Because the fact that the caller gave the 911 operator his name is an unfavorable fact, Ms. Elder puts that fact in a dependent clause. In contrast, because the facts that the caller would not give the 911 operator his address or his phone number are favorable facts, Ms. Elder sets out those facts in the main clause and gives them a fair amount of airtime. Note also how Ms. Elder buries the unfavorable fact in the middle of the paragraph and how she uses airtime and detail to emphasize the favorable facts. The unfavorable facts are underlined and the favorable facts are in bold.

EXAMPLE 22	**Excerpt from the Appellant's Brief**

The 911 operator then asked the informant for his name, address, and a phone number so that the police or ATF agents could re-contact him. <u>Although the informant told the 911 operator that his name was Zachary Dillon</u>, **he then became uncooperative and refused to give the 911 operator his address, his home telephone number, or a cell phone number.** (ER 32, 35).

If the prosecutor wanted to make the same two points, he would flip the order, putting the fact that the caller did not give the operator his address or phone number in the dependent clause and the fact that he did give the operator his name in the main clause. Also note that the prosecutor would not set out the unfavorable facts in any detail and that he would choose his words carefully. Once again, the unfavorable facts are underlined and the favorable fact is in bold.

EXAMPLE 23	**How the Appellee Would Present the Same Facts**

<u>Although the caller did not give the 911 operator his address or phone number</u>, **he did give her his name.** (ER 32).

| **PRACTICE POINTER** | Putting favorable facts in the main clause often allows you to take advantage of the positions of emphasis: While the unfavorable fact is in a dependent clause in the middle of the paragraph, the favorable fact is in the main clause at the end of the paragraph. |

6. *Active and Passive Voice*

Good advocates use the active voice when they want to emphasize the actor and the passive voice when they want to draw the reader's attention away from who performed an action. For instance, in setting out the facts relating to the *Batson* challenge, Ms. Elder uses the active voice to describe the prosecutor's use of his peremptory challenges to strike the only Native Americans in the jury pool.

EXAMPLE 24   **Excerpt from the Appellant's Brief**

The government used two of its peremptory challenges to remove the only two Native Americans in the jury pool.

If the prosecutor were to make the same point, he would use the passive rather than the active voice.

EXAMPLE 25   **How the Prosecutor Might Make the Same Point**

Both Native Americans were excused.

Furthermore, more likely than not, the prosecutor would combine the use of the passive voice with another persuasive technique. For example, the prosecutor might put the fact that he used his peremptory challenges to excuse the only Native Americans in the jury pool in a dependent clause and the more favorable fact in the main clause. Note that in the following sentence the dependent clause is written using the passive voice, and the main clause is written using the active voice. The dependent clause, which uses the passive voice, is underlined, and the main clause, which uses the active voice, is in bold.

EXAMPLE 26   **How the Prosecutor Might Use the Active and Passive Voice in Conjunction With the Main and Dependent Clauses**

<u>Although both Native Americans were excused</u>, **the prosecutor also excused a white juror who had similar commitments.**

---

d. Choose Words Carefully

Because words create powerful images, select your words carefully. In addition to selecting the word that conveys the right meaning, select the word that creates the right image. Look, for example, at words that Ms. Elder uses in the following paragraphs.

| EXAMPLE 27 | **Excerpt from the Appellant's Brief** |

Agent Bhasin had gone to the Travel House Inn after receiving a phone call from a 911 operator who reported that she had received a call from a public pay telephone located in the Bellis Fair Mall, which is about a five-minute drive from the Travel House Inn. (ER 30, 34). The informant **claimed** that a Mr. Josephy was at the Travel House Inn to sell drugs to a man named Oliver. (ER 30). In addition, the informant told the 911 operator that, if the police wanted to catch Mr. Josephy, they should go to the Travel House soon because Mr. Josephy would be there for only another hour or two. (ER 32-33).

Instead of using "claimed," which suggests that the caller might be lying, Ms. Elder could have used "stated," which is neutral, or "advised," "informed," "notified," or "reported," which suggest that the caller was a credible source telling the truth. Likewise, in the following paragraph, the prosecutor chooses his words carefully. For example, while the prosecutor could have said that Mr. Dillon "refused" to give the operator his address or phone number, the prosecutor uses the word "declined," which has a softer feel and a more positive connotation.

| EXAMPLE 28 | **Excerpt from the Appellee's Brief** |

During the 911 call, which was recorded, Mr. Dillon told the operator that Mr. Josephy was at the Travel House Inn to meet with, and deliver marijuana to, a man named Oliver. (ER 30-31). While Mr. Dillon **declined** to give the 911 operator his address or phone number, Mr. Dillon did tell the 911 operator that Mr. Josephy was a Native American, that Josephy had black hair, and that Josephy was in his mid- to late twenties. (ER 32). Mr. Dillon also told the operator that Mr. Josephy owned, and was driving, a blue Chevy Blazer. (ER 32). Although Mr. Dillon did not know Oliver's last name, he described Oliver as being in his thirties, about six feet tall, and with brown hair and a beard. (ER 32). Finally, Mr. Dillon told the police not to wait too long because Mr. Josephy would be leaving the motel in the next hour or two. (ER 33).

| **PRACTICE POINTER** | If you are having trouble coming up with just the right word, use a thesaurus. Most popular word processing programs include an electronic thesaurus. |

e.   Be Subtly Persuasive

Most beginning attorneys make one of two mistakes. They either present the facts objectively or, in an attempt to be persuasive, they go over the line, including arguments in their statement of facts; setting out facts that are not supported by the record; or using "purple prose," that is, the use of flowery language that draws attention to itself.

| EXAMPLE 29 | **Excerpt from an Appellee's Brief With Novice Mistakes** |

Based on this reliable tip, Agent Bhasin drove to the Travel House Inn, where he immediately located a blue Chevy Blazer in the parking lot. (ER 40, 42). Not surprisingly, when Agent Bhasin ran the plates, he discovered that the Blazer belonged to Peter Josephy. (ER 42). Expecting trouble, Agent Bhasin immediately called for backup. (ER 43).

In this example, the writer makes a number of serious mistakes. First, in the opening sentence, the writer sets out a legal conclusion: that the tip was reliable. Although the writer might want to include this statement in his argument, he should not set out legal conclusions or arguments in the statement of facts. Second, in drafting the second sentence, the writer sets out his own "take" on the facts when he says "not surprisingly." Finally, in the last sentence, the writer misrepresents the testimony. There is nothing in the record that indicates that Agent Bhasin called for backup because he was "expecting trouble."

For a checklist for critiquing the statement of facts, see section 17.6.4.

Chapter 18 Quiz No. 2

Draft answers for each of the following questions. Make your points clearly and concisely, and write sentences that are easy to read and that are grammatical and correctly punctuated.

1. What is the relationship between the issue statements and the argumentative headings?
2. What are three techniques that you can use to present the issues in a light favorable to your client?
3. How can you use the positions of emphasis to your advantage?

§ 18.13 Drafting the Summary of the Argument

The summary of the argument is just what the title implies: a summary of the advocate's argument. Although some courts do not require a summary of the argument, the federal rules require "a summary of the argument, which must contain a succinct, clear, and accurate statement of the arguments made in the body of the brief, and which must not merely repeat the argument headings[.]" Fed. R. App. P. 28(a)(8).

However, even when the rules do not require a summary of the argument, consider including one. For those judges who read the entire brief, such a summary provides an overview of the arguments; for those judges who do not read everything, it sets out the key points.

You might want to write two drafts of your summary of the argument. By preparing a first draft before you write the argument section, you will force yourself to identify the most important points in your argument. If you truly understand your arguments, you should be able to set out each of them in a paragraph or two. If you can't, more thinking, charting, outlining, or writing is needed.

Preparing a second draft after you have written the argument section is equally useful. This version can serve as a check on your arguments: When read together, the opening sentences of your paragraphs or paragraph blocks should provide the judges with a summary of the argument. If they don't, it is the argument section itself, and not the summary, that needs work.

The most common problem attorneys have with the summary of the argument is length. They write too much. The summary of the argument should be no more than one or two pages long, with one or two paragraphs for each argument. Citations to authority should also be kept to a minimum. Although you might want to refer to key cases and statutes, the focus should be on the arguments, not the citations. Another common problem is that attorneys do not make clear the connections between their arguments. Use transitions to make clear when one argument is a continuation of another argument and when an argument is an alternative argument. For examples of summaries of the argument, see the sample briefs at the end of this chapter.

§ 18.14 Drafting the Argumentative Headings

Argumentative headings serve two functions in an appellate brief. They provide the court with an outline of the argument, and they help to persuade the judges.

§ 18.14.1 Use the Argumentative Headings to Outline the Argument for the Court

When properly drafted, the argumentative headings provide the court with an outline of the arguments. By reading the headings set out in the table of contents, the judges can see your assertions, your support for those assertions, and the relationships between your various assertions and arguments.

Argumentative headings also serve several other purposes. They help the judges by dividing the argument into manageable sections. In addition, they help the writer. Because attorneys like Ms. Elder seldom have large blocks of time available for writing, the brief must usually be written in sections. By drafting the headings first, an attorney can write one section or subsection at a time, putting the pieces together at the end.

> **PRACTICE POINTER** Although you might write your argumentative headings before the related arguments, do not let the headings lock you in to an analytical approach. The content of the arguments should drive the organization, and thus, the focus of the headings. Be willing to revise.

§ 18.14.2 Use the Argumentative Headings to Persuade

Good attorneys use argumentative headings in the same way good politicians use sound bites — to catch their reader's attention and to help their reader to see the issue as they see it.

Most good argumentative headings have four characteristics: (1) They are framed as positive assertions, (2) they set out both the assertion and the support for that assertion, (3) they are specific, and (4) they are easy to read and understand. In addition, in drafting the argumentative headings, the writer uses the same persuasive techniques that he or she used in drafting the issue statements and statement of facts.

a.   Make a Positive Assertion

In general, a heading is easier to understand and more persuasive if it is in the form of a positive assertion. For example, instead of writing, "The district court did not act properly when it denied Mr. Josephy's *Batson* challenge," Ms. Elder would write, "The district court erred when it denied Mr. Josephy's *Batson* challenge." The following example sets out the appellant's main headings and subheadings. Note first that each heading contains an assertion. Second, note that although Ms. Elder begins each of the subheadings relating to the motion to suppress with the same assertion, she does not use this technique in the subheadings relating to the *Batson* issue. Although the technique works for the first set of headings, it does not work for the second set. Third, note that Ms. Elder uses dovetailing to make it clear how the subheadings are related to the main headings. For example, she ends her first main heading with the phrase "did not have a particularized objective suspicion that Mr. Josephy was engaged in criminal activity" and then uses that same phrase in the assertion that begins each of the subheadings. For more on dovetailing, see section 23.3.1.

In the following examples, the assertions are in bold.

EXAMPLE 1   **Argumentative Headings from the Appellant's Brief**

A.   **THE ATF AGENTS VIOLATED MR. JOSEPHY'S FOURTH AMENDMENT RIGHTS** BECAUSE THEY DID NOT HAVE A PARTICULARIZED OBJECTIVE SUSPICION THAT MR. JOSEPHY WAS ENGAGED IN CRIMINAL ACTIVITY.

    1.   <u>**The ATF agents did not have a particularized objective suspicion that Mr. Josephy was engaged in criminal activity** because the tip came from an unknown informant: Although the informant gave the 911 operator his name, he refused to give her his address or phone number.</u>

    2.   <u>**The ATF agents did not have a particularized objective suspicion that Mr. Josephy was engaged in criminal activity** because the tip included only general physical descriptions, it omitted any description of clothing, and the only action it predicted was that Mr. Josephy would be leaving a motel shortly before checkout time.</u>

    3.   <u>**The ATF agents did not have a particularized objective suspicion that Mr. Josephy was engaged in criminal activity** because the police corroborated only innocuous details—for example, Mr. Josephy's physical appearance, his car, and his departure from a motel shortly before checkout time.</u>

B.   **THE DISTRICT COURT ERRED IN DENYING MR. JOSEPHY'S *BATSON* CHALLENGE** BECAUSE THE PROSECUTOR STRUCK THE ONLY TWO NATIVE AMERICANS IN THE JURY POOL, AND THE COURT'S ENTIRE RULING CONSISTED OF A SINGLE SENTENCE.

1. <u>**The reasons the prosecutor gave for striking the only two Native Americans in the jury pool were a pretext for discrimination** because they were not supported by the record and the prosecutor did not excuse white jurors who had similar obligations and experiences.</u>

2. In the alternative, **the district court erred by not conducting the required sensitive inquiry and by not stating its reasoning on the record.**

Likewise, the government sets out its positive assertions. The assertions are in bold.

EXAMPLE 2   **Argumentative Headings from the Appellee's Brief**

A. **THE *TERRY* STOP WAS PERMISSIBLE** BECAUSE THE ATF AGENTS HAD A REASONABLE SUSPICION THAT MR. JOSEPHY WAS INVOLVED IN CRIMINAL ACTIVITY.

B. **THE DISTRICT COURT PROPERLY EXERCISED ITS DISCRETION IN OVERRULING MR. JOSEPHY'S *BATSON* OBJECTION.**

1. <u>**Mr. Josephy has not met his burden of proving that the reasons that the prosecutor gave for the peremptory challenges were a pretext for purposeful discrimination.**</u>

2. <u>**The record establishes that the district court conducted the required sensitive inquiry because the court ensured that both parties had the opportunity to respond at each of the three steps in the *Batson* analysis.**</u>

---

b.   Provide Support for Your Assertions

By itself an assertion is not persuasive. Therefore, in most instances, you will want to support your assertions. One way to provide this support is to add a "because" clause.

Assertion   +   because   +   support for assertion

For example, instead of just stating that the ATF agents violated Mr. Josephy's Fourth Amendment rights, Ms. Elder should include the reason why. Similarly, instead of just saying that the *Terry* stop was permissible, the prosecutor needs to add the support for that assertion. In the following examples, the support for each assertion is set out in bold.

EXAMPLE 3   **Appellant's Assertion Followed by a "Because" Clause**

A. The ATF agents violated Mr. Josephy's fourth amendment rights **because they did not have a particularized objective suspicion that MR. JOSEPHY was engaged in criminal activity.**

1.   The ATF agents did not have a particularized objective suspicion that Mr. Josephy was engaged in criminal activity **because the tip came from an unknown informant: Although the informant gave the 911 operator his name, he refused to give his address or phone number.**

2.   The ATF agents did not have a particularized objective suspicion that Mr. Josephy was engaged in criminal activity **because the tip included only general physical descriptions, it omitted any description of clothing, and the only action it predicted was that Mr. Josephy would be leaving a motel shortly before checkout time.**

3.   The ATF agents did not have a particularized objective suspicion that Mr. Josephy was engaged in criminal activity **because the police corroborated only innocuous details—for example, Mr. Josephy's physical appearance, his car, and his departure from a motel shortly before checkout time.**

You do not, however, always need to include a "because" clause. In some instances, it might work better to set out your assertion in the main clause and then the support for that assertion in the subheadings. In other instances, it might work better to save the support for the argument. For instance, in the following example, look at the second subheading. Because Ms. Elder thought that emphasizing the fact that the argument was an alternative argument was more important than to set out the facts, she sets out her assertion without using a "because" clause.

EXAMPLE 4   **Headings from the Appellant's Brief**

B.   THE DISTRICT COURT ERRED IN DENYING MR. JOSEPHY'S *BATSON* CHALLENGE **BECAUSE THE PROSECUTOR STRUCK THE ONLY TWO NATIVE AMERICANS IN THE JURY POOL, AND THE COURT'S ENTIRE RULING CONSISTED OF A SINGLE SENTENCE.**

1.   The reasons the prosecutor gave for striking the only two Native Americans in the jury pool were a pretext for discrimination **because they were not supported by the record and the prosecutor did not excuse white jurors who had similar obligations and experiences.**

2.   In the alternative, the district court erred by not conducting the required sensitive inquiry and by not stating its reasoning on the record.

---

c.   Make Sure That Your Headings Are Neither Too Specific nor Too General

As a general rule, make your headings specific to the case at hand. Instead of writing statements that are so broad that they could apply to a number of different cases, write statements that talk specifically about the parties and facts in your case. Do not be so specific, though, that the headings are not broad enough to cover all of the points that you make in that section. Compare the following examples. The headings set out in Example 5 are too broad because they could apply equally to any number of cases. In contrast, the headings set out in Example 6 are too narrow because they cover only one of the government's two peremptory challenges.

EXAMPLE 5   **Headings Are Too General**

THE TRIAL COURT ERRED.

THE TRIAL COURT PROPERLY OVERRULED THE DEFENDANT'S *BATSON* OBJECTION.

EXAMPLE 6   **Headings Are Too Specific**

THE DISTRICT COURT ERRED WHEN IT DENIED THE DEFENDANT'S *BATSON* CHALLENGE BECAUSE THE PROSECUTOR DISMISSED A NATIVE AMERICAN JUROR WHO HAD HAD NEGATIVE EXPERIENCES WITH LAW ENFORCEMENT OFFICERS BUT NOT A WHITE JUROR WHO HAD SIMILAR EXPERIENCES.

THE DISTRICT COURT PROPERLY OVERRULED THE DEFENDANT'S *BATSON* OBJECTION BECAUSE THE GOVERNMENT EXCUSED BOTH A NATIVE AMERICAN JUROR AND A WHITE JUROR WHO HAD WORK COMMITMENTS.

---

d.   Make Your Headings Readable

A heading that is not readable is not persuasive. For example, even though the following heading is in the proper form, it is not persuasive because it is so long that very few judges would read it.

EXAMPLE 7   **Argumentative Heading That Is Difficult to Read**

A.   THE DISTRICT COURT ERRED IN DENYING MR. JOSEPHY'S *BATSON* CHALLENGE BECAUSE (1) THE PROSECUTOR EXCUSED A NATIVE AMERICAN JUROR WHO HAD HAD A NEGATIVE EXPERIENCE WITH LAW ENFORCEMENT OFFICERS BUT DID NOT EXCUSE A WHITE JUROR WHO HAD HAD SIMILAR NEGATIVE EXPERIENCES AND (2) THE PROSECUTOR EXCUSED A NATIVE AMERICAN JUROR WHO HAD A TRIBAL COUNCIL MEETING THE FOLLOWING WEEK BUT WHO WAS WILLING TO MISS THAT MEETING BUT DID NOT EXCUSE A WHITE JUROR WHO MIGHT HAVE TO GO OUT OF TOWN TO CARE FOR HIS MOTHER WHO HAD ONLY A 20 PERCENT CHANCE OF LIVING.

Thus, in drafting your headings, you need to balance two competing pieces of advice: making your headings fact specific and keeping your headings short. Ideally your headings would be both fact specific and short, but sometimes that is not possible, and you will have to choose between a longer, fact-specific heading and a shorter, more general heading. Compare the following two examples. In Example 8, Ms. Elder has chosen to write a longer heading that is fact specific. In contrast, in Example 9, the prosecutor has chosen to write a shorter heading that is more general.

EXAMPLE 8	Subheading from the Appellant's Brief That Is Longer But More Fact Specific

1. <u>The reasons the prosecutor gave for striking the only two Native Americans in the jury pool were a pretext for discrimination because they were not supported by the record and the prosecutor did not excuse white jurors who had similar obligations and experiences.</u>

EXAMPLE 9	Subheading from the Appellee's Brief That Is Shorter But More General

1. <u>Mr. Josephy has not met his burden of proving that the reasons that the prosecutor gave for the peremptory challenges were a pretext for purposeful discrimination.</u>

When you choose to write a longer heading, use sentence constructions that make the headings easier to read. Use parallel constructions (see sections 24.5.1 and 27.7) and, when appropriate, repeat the words that highlight the parallel structure (for example, "that" or "because"). Finally, when appropriate, use commas, semicolons, and colons to divide the sentence into more manageable units of meaning. See section 24.5.1.

e. Use the Same Persuasive Techniques You Used in Drafting the Issue Statements and Statement of Facts

In drafting argumentative headings, good advocates use many of the same persuasive techniques that they used in drafting their issue statements and statements of facts: When possible, they create a favorable context, set out the facts from the client's point of view, give more airtime to favorable facts than to unfavorable facts, describe favorable facts in more detail than unfavorable facts, take advantage of the positions of emphasis, and choose words carefully. In Example 10 that follows, the writer has set out her assertion and her support for that assertion, but she has not emphasized the favorable facts. In contrast, in Example 11, the writer has emphasized the favorable facts: She has added the word "only"; she has used the phrase "*Batson* challenge" rather than "*Batson* objection"; she has used the harsher word, "struck," rather than the softer word, "excused"; and instead of saying that the district court did not go into detail in explaining its reasoning, she states that the court's entire ruling consisted of a single sentence.

EXAMPLE 10	Appellant Has Not Used Persuasive Techniques

A.   THE DISTRICT COURT ERRED IN DENYING MR. JOSEPHY'S *BATSON* OBJECTION BECAUSE THE PROSECUTOR EXCUSED TWO NATIVE AMERICAN JURORS AND THE DISTRICT COURT DID NOT GO INTO DETAIL IN EXPLAINING ITS REASONING.

| EXAMPLE 11 | **Appellant Has Used Persuasive Techniques** |

A. THE DISTRICT COURT ERRED IN DENYING MR. JOSEPHY'S *BATSON* CHALLENGE BECAUSE THE PROSECUTOR STRUCK THE ONLY TWO NATIVE AMERICANS IN THE JURY POOL, AND THE COURT'S ENTIRE RULING CONSISTED OF A SINGLE SENTENCE.

§ 18.14.3 Use Conventional Formats for Headings

Although seldom set out in the court rules, in most jurisdictions there are conventions governing the number, type, and typeface for argumentative headings. For example, as we noted in section 17.9.4, convention dictates that you should have a main heading for each of your issue statements. Consequently, if you have one issue, you should have one main heading; if you have two issues, two main headings; and so on. The issue sets out the question, and the heading gives your answer to that question.

In addition to main headings, you can also use subheadings and sub-subheadings and, rarely, sub-sub-subheadings. There are, however, some things to keep in mind if you use additional headings. First, if you include one subheading, you need to have at least two headings at that same level. As a consequence, if you find that you have only one subheading in a section, either delete that heading or add at least one additional heading. Second, although you are not required to put text between the main heading and the first subheading, it is usually a good idea to do so: Use this space to set out the general rule and a roadmap for that section of your brief. Finally, keep in mind the typefaces that attorneys use for the various levels of headings. These typefaces provide judges with signals about where they are in the argument.

The following example shows one way of using headings. The main headings are set out using all capital letters, the subheadings are underlined, and the sub-subheadings are set out using regular typeface. (The sample briefs at the end of the chapter use a different scheme.).

| EXAMPLE 12 | **Conventional Formats for Argumentative Headings** |

Argument

A. FIRST MAIN HEADING [corresponds to first issue statement]
    [Introduce and set out the general rule.]
    [Provide your reader with a roadmap for your argument.]
   1. <u>First subheading</u>
      [Introduce and set out the specific rules.]
      a. First sub-subheading
         [Set out your argument.]
      b. Second sub-subheading
         [Set out your argument.]
   2. <u>Second subheading</u>
      [Set out your argument.]

3.   Third subheading
[Set out your argument.]
B.   SECOND MAIN HEADING [corresponds to second issue statement]
[Introduce and set out the general rule.]
[Provide your reader with a roadmap for your argument.]
1.   First subheading
[Set out your argument.]
2.   Second subheading
[Set out specific rules.]
a.   First sub-subheading
[Set out your argument.]
b.   Second sub-subheading
[Set out your argument.]

See section 17.9.5 for a checklist for critiquing the argumentative headings.

§ 18.15 Drafting the Arguments

Although it is relatively easy to tell someone how to draft the statement of the case, the statement of facts, the issue statements, and the argumentative headings, it is very difficult to tell someone how to draft the arguments. Although experienced attorneys can offer newer attorneys some general advice, by necessity, that advice is just that — general advice. Because the law and facts of each case are different, the arguments are also different, and there is no foolproof recipe for how to draft a persuasive argument.

At a minimum you must have mastered the facts of your case, you must have a solid understanding of the governing law, and you must be able to write clearly and concisely. However, this mastery, understanding, and ability are not enough. Writing a persuasive brief also requires some things that are much harder to describe and are impossible to teach: insight, creativity, and confidence. Thus, although this chapter can get you started, it cannot give you all of the answers. Instead, we will remind you of the overriding question when it comes to any argument: Is it persuasive? When in doubt, use that question as your touchstone for determining what is and is not an effective argument.

§ 18.15.1 Knowing What You Need, and Want, to Argue

One of the first steps in drafting an argument is knowing what you need, and want, to argue. You cannot just throw out a number of assertions, rules, and cases and hope that the court will make sense of them for you.

As a consequence, before you begin to write, determine what type of argument you are making. Are you arguing an issue of first impression — that is, are you asking the court to make new law by adopting a new rule or test — or are you arguing that the trial court improperly applied existing law? If you are arguing that the trial court improperly applied existing law, are you arguing that the trial court abused its discretion when it ruled on a motion or objection, or are you arguing that there is insufficient evidence to support the jury's verdict?

§ 18.15.2 Selecting an Organizational Scheme

Once you have determined what type of argument you want to make, select the organizational scheme that will work best for that argument.

If you are arguing an issue of first impression, you will usually use a version of the template set out in Example 1 below. You will start by establishing that there is no existing rule or test. You will then want to persuade the court that the rule or test you are proposing is "better" than the rule or test being proposed by your opponent. Finally, you will end by applying your proposed rule or test to the facts of your case. In addition, sometimes you will argue in the alternative: Even if the court adopts the rule or test being advocated by opposing counsel, you still win under that test.

EXAMPLE 1   **Organizational Scheme for Issues of First Impression**

A.   MAIN HEADING

Introduction establishing that the issue is one of first impression

1.   <u>Subheading setting out first assertion</u>

■ Paragraph setting out the rule that you want the court to adopt

■ Arguments relating to why the court should adopt your proposed rule rather than the rule being proposed by your opponent

■ Application of your proposed rule to the facts of your case

2.   <u>Subheading setting out additional or alternative argument(s)</u>

■ If appropriate, argue that even under the rule being proposed by your opponent your client wins

---

In contrast, if you are arguing that the trial court incorrectly applied the existing law, you have more options. For example, if your case involves an elements analysis or a multi-part test, you will usually want to include an introductory section in which you set out the general rules — that is, the standard of review and the applicable statutory language, the applicable regulations, the applicable court rule, or the applicable common law rule. However, once you begin your discussion of the elements or the multi-part test, you can start with an assertion, a statement of the rule, the facts of your case, or even an analogous case. The following examples show some of the options for an issue involving an elements analysis.

EXAMPLE 2   **Elements Analysis in Which the Author Begins the Discussion of Each Element with an Assertion**

A.   ARGUMENTATIVE HEADING

Paragraph setting out the standard of review, the applicable statutory language, regulations, court rule or rules, or common law, and listing or identifying the elements

1. <u>Argumentative heading for first element</u>
   - Assertion
   - Statement of the rule
   - Descriptions of analogous cases
   - Your argument, including your response to your opponent's arguments
   - Conclusion

2. <u>Argumentative heading for second element</u>
   - Assertion
   - Statement of the rule
   - Descriptions of analogous cases
   - Your argument, including your response to your opponent's arguments
   - Conclusion

3. <u>Argumentative heading for third element</u>
   - Assertion
   - Statement of the rule
   - Descriptions of analogous cases
   - Your argument, including your response to your opponent's arguments
   - Conclusion

EXAMPLE 3   **Elements Analysis in Which the Author Begins the Discussion with a Favorable Statement of the Rule**

A.   ARGUMENTATIVE HEADING

Paragraph setting out a favorable statement the standard of review and the applicable statutory language, regulations, court rule or rules, or common law rule, and listing or identifying the elements

1. <u>Argumentative heading for first element</u>
   - Statement of the rule
   - Descriptions of analogous cases
   - Your argument, including your response to your opponent's arguments
   - Conclusion

2. <u>Argumentative heading for second element</u>
   - Statement of the rule
   - Descriptions of analogous cases
   - Your argument, including your response to your opponent's arguments
   - Conclusion

3. <u>Argumentative heading for third element</u>
   - Statement of the rule
   - Descriptions of analogous cases
   - Your argument, including your response to your opponent's arguments
   - Conclusion

EXAMPLE 4	**Elements Analysis in Which the Author Starts the Discussion with a Favorable Statement of the Facts**

A.   ARGUMENTATIVE HEADING

Paragraph setting out the standard of review and the applicable statutory language, regulations, court rule or rules, or common law rule, and listing or identifying the elements

1.   <u>Argumentative heading for first element</u>
   - Statement of the facts
   - Statement of the rule
   - Descriptions of analogous cases
   - Your argument, including your response to your opponent's arguments
   - Conclusion

2.   <u>Argumentative heading for second element</u>
   - Statement of the facts
   - Statement of the rule
   - Descriptions of analogous cases
   - Your argument, including your response to your opponent's arguments
   - Conclusion

3.   <u>Argumentative heading for third element</u>
   - Statement of the facts
   - Statement of the rule
   - Descriptions of analogous cases
   - Your argument, including your response to your opponent's arguments
   - Conclusion

EXAMPLE 5	**Elements Analysis in Which the Author Starts the Discussion with a Favorable Statement of the Analogous Cases**

A.   ARGUMENTATIVE HEADING

Paragraph setting out the standard of review and the applicable statutory language, regulations, court rule or rules, or common law rule, and listing or identifying the elements.

1.   <u>Argumentative heading for first element</u>
   - Description of analogous cases
   - Statement of the rule
   - Your argument, including the application of the law to your facts and your response to your opponent's arguments
   - Conclusion

2.   <u>Argumentative heading for second element</u>
   - Description of analogous cases
   - Statement of the rule
   - Your argument, including an application of the law to your facts and your response to your opponent's arguments

     ■ Conclusion
3.   <u>Argumentative heading for third element</u>
     ■ Description of analogous cases
     ■ Statement of the rule
     ■ Descriptions of analogous cases
     ■ Your argument, including your response to your opponent's arguments
     ■ Conclusion

In selecting one of these organizational schemes, keep the following points in mind. First, you do not need to use the same organizational scheme for each element. For instance, it might work best to start your discussion of one element with an assertion, your discussion of another element with the facts, and your discussion of yet another element with a rule.

Second, in selecting an organizational scheme for a particular element, make sure that you pick a scheme that will work not only for you but also for the judges who will be reading your brief. Thus, select an organizational scheme that highlights your theory of the case and allows you to set out your points clearly and concisely.

Third, make sure that you don't get into a rut. Although there is always a temptation to use the organizational scheme with which you are most comfortable, as an advocate this is a temptation you need to resist. If you are to persuade the court, you need to pick the scheme that allows you to emphasize the strongest parts of your argument. For example, if the rule strongly favors your client, you will usually want to select an organizational scheme that allows you to put the rule at the beginning, in the position of emphasis. Conversely, if the facts are very favorable, you will usually want to use an organizational scheme that allows you to put them at the beginning. At other times, when there are a number of steps to the analysis, it works best to select an organizational scheme that allows you to begin your argument with your assertions, which can then act as a roadmap for the rest of the argument. Fourth, keep in mind that you are not bound by your opponent's organizational scheme. Instead, use the organizational scheme that allows you to make your points effectively.

Finally, make sure that you do not make one of the most common errors that attorneys make in writing briefs: setting out one case and then comparing the facts in that case to the facts in your case, setting out a second case and then comparing the facts in that second case to the facts in your case, and so on. Instead of organizing your arguments around individual cases, organize them around assertions.

   E X A M P L E 6   **Poor Way of Organizing the Arguments**

A.   ARGUMENTATIVE HEADING
      Statement of rule
         Description of Case A
           Comparison of the facts in your case to the facts in Case A

Description of Case B

    Comparison of the same facts in your case to the facts in Case B

Description of Case C

    Comparison of the same facts in your case to the facts in Case C

Description of Case D

    Comparison of the same facts in your case to the facts in Case D

Conclusion

EXAMPLE 7   **Better Way of Organizing the Arguments**

A.   ARGUMENTATIVE HEADING

Statement of rule

   Assertion 1

     ■ Principle

     ■ Description of Case A

     ■ Description of Case B

     ■ Argument using Case A and Case B

   Assertion 2

     ■ Principle

     ■ Description of Case C

     ■ Description of Case D

     ■ Argument using Case C and Case D

Conclusion

---

§ 18.15.3 Presenting the Rules, Descriptions of Analogous Cases, and Arguments in the Light Most Favorable to Your Client

Although the organizational schemes for the argument section in a brief are similar to the organizational schemes for the discussion section in an objective memorandum, the method of presentation is different. While in an objective memorandum you present the rules, cases, and arguments as objectively as possible, in a brief you present them persuasively.

a. Presenting the Rules

Good advocacy begins with a favorable statement of the rule. Although you do not want to misstate a rule, quote a rule out of context, or mislead the court, you do want to present the rule in such a way that it favors your client. There are a number of ways you can do this. You can present the rule in a favorable context, you can state the rule broadly or narrowly, you can state the rule so that it suggests the conclusion you want the court to reach, and you can emphasize who has the burden of proof.

The following example sets out an objective statement of a rule.

EXAMPLE 8	Objective Statement of the Rule

To determine if a *Batson* violation has occurred, the courts engage in a three-step analysis. First, the defendant must make out a prima facie case "by showing that the totality of the relevant facts gives rise to an inference of discriminatory purpose." *Batson v. Kentucky*, 476 U.S. 79, 93-94 (1986) (citing *Washington v. Davis*, 426 U.S. 229, 239-42 (1976)). Second, if the defendant has made out a prima facie case, the "burden shifts to the Government to explain adequately the racial exclusion" by offering permissible race-neutral justifications for the strikes. *Batson*, 476 U.S. at 93-94. Third, "[i]f a race-neutral explanation is tendered, the trial court must then decide . . . whether the opponent of the strike has proved purposeful racial discrimination." *Johnson v. California*, 545 U.S. 162, 168 (2005) (quoting *Purkett v. Elem*, 514 U.S. 765, 767 (1995)).

In the next example, Ms. Elder has rewritten the objective statement of the rule so that the rule is presented in a way that highlights her theory of the case and that is favorable to her client. Instead of beginning with the rule itself, she begins by creating a favorable context: In the first paragraph Ms. Elder reminds the court that the United States Supreme Court has "consistently and repeatedly . . . reaffirmed that racial discrimination by the State in jury selection offends the Equal Protection Clause." Then, in setting out the three-step test, Ms. Elder sets out the rules so that they suggest the conclusions that Ms. Elder wants the court to reach. For example, in setting out the test, Ms. Elder de-emphasizes the defendant's burden of proof and emphasizes the government's burden: "the defendant need only establish a prima facie case of purposeful discrimination," "the burden shifts to the government," and "the government must provide a race-neutral reason . . . ." In addition, Ms. Elder uses language that suggests that Mr. Josephy will be able to meet his burden: "once the defendant establishes a prima facie case." Finally, Ms. Elder sets up her "sensitive analysis" argument by using that language in the rule section.

EXAMPLE 9	Excerpt from the Appellant's Brief with Persuasive Presentation of the Rules

For more than a century, the United States Supreme Court has "consistently and repeatedly . . . reaffirmed that racial discrimination by the State in jury selection offends the Equal Protection Clause." *Miller-El v. Dretke*, 545 U.S. 231, 237 (quoting *Georgia v. McCollum*, 505 U.S. 42 (1992)). Racial discrimination in jury selection denies defendants their right to a jury trial, denies jurors the right to participate in public life, and undermines public confidence in the fairness of our justice system. *Batson v. Kentucky*, 476 U.S. 79, 86-87 (1986); *Williams v. Runnels*, 432 F.3d 1102, 1108 (9th Cir. 2006). Therefore, the "Constitution forbids striking even a single prospective juror for a discriminatory purpose." *United States v. Vasquez-Lopez*, 22 F.3d 900, 902 (9th Cir. 1992).

In *Batson*, the Court developed a three-step test to uncover discrimination masked by peremptory challenges. 476 U.S. at 96-97. Under the first step of the test, the defendant need only establish a prima facie case of purposeful discrimination by showing that the prosecutor has struck a member of a cognizable class and that the circumstances raise an inference of discrimination. *Id.* at 96. Once the defendant establishes a prima facie case, the burden shifts to the government: The government must provide a race-neutral explanation for striking a member of a cognizable class. *Id.* at 97. If the government does meet its burden, the court must do a sensitive analysis to determine whether the government has engaged in purposeful discrimination. *See Johnson v. California*, 545 U.S. 162, 169 (2005).

Similarly, the prosecutor has rewritten the neutral statement of the rule so that the rules are presented in a light that is more favorable to the government's position. In the following example, the prosecutor starts his statement of the rule by creating a favorable context: He reminds the court that peremptory challenges are an important tool available to both prosecutors and defense counsel. In the second sentence, the prosecutor de-emphasizes the United States Supreme Court's statements about the difficulty of balancing the need to protect constitutional rights with the proper use of peremptory challenges by placing that point in a dependent clause in the middle of a relatively long paragraph. The prosecutor then ends the paragraph with a favorable point: that the United States Supreme Court has not indicated a willingness to deprive parties of their right to use peremptory challenges or to change the *Batson* test.

EXAMPLE 10   **Excerpt from the Appellee's Brief with Persuasive Presentation of the Rules**

Peremptory challenges are an important trial tool that permits both parties' counsel to use their professional judgment and educated hunches about individual jurors to select a fair and impartial jury. *United States v. Bauer*, 84 F.3d 1549, 1555 (9th Cir. 1996). While the Supreme Court has acknowledged difficulties in balancing the need to protect constitutional rights with the proper use of peremptory challenges, the Court has not indicated a willingness to deprive the parties of their right to use peremptory challenges. *See Miller-El v. Dretke*, 545 U.S. 231, 239-40 (2005). Indeed, Justice Breyer's concurrence, in which he posited that the Court should reconsider the *Batson* test and the peremptory system as a whole, failed to garner a single co-signer. *Id.* at 266-67 (Breyer, J., concurring).

Thus, the courts continue to apply the three-step test set out in *Batson*. *Batson*, 476 U.S. at 89, 96-98. Under the test, a defendant's rights are not violated unless (1) the defendant establishes a prima facie case of purposeful discrimination in the government's use of peremptory challenges by showing that the challenged juror is a member of a cognizable class and that the circumstances raise an inference of discrimination; and (2) the government fails to meet its burden to provide a race-neutral explanation for its strike; or (3) the government offers a race-neutral reason, but the defendant meets his burden of showing that a review of all relevant circumstances shows purposeful discrimination. *See Johnson v. California*, 545 U.S. 162, 169 (2005); *Batson*, 476 U.S. at 89, 96-98.

For additional examples, see section 17.10.3.

b. Presenting the Cases

In drafting your brief, you will use cases in two ways: (1) as citations for rules — for example, a citation for a common law rule or rules that the courts have created in interpreting statutes, regulations, or court rules — and (2) as illustrations of how the courts have applied statutes, regulations, court rules, or common law rules in cases that are factually analogous to your case. What you do not want to do is to set out case descriptions just to set out case descriptions. Therefore, before you include a case description in your brief, ask yourself the following questions.

■ Does the case illustrate how the courts have applied a statute, regulation, court rule, or common law rule in a case that is factually analogous to my case?

■ Does the case or a group of cases illustrate how a particular rule has developed or is developing?

■ Do I need to distinguish the case because the other side has relied on it or is likely to rely on it?

■ As an officer of the court, am I obligated to bring the case to the court's attention?

Unless you have answered "yes" to one or more of these questions, do not include the case description in your brief.

PRACTICE POINTER	Remember that you can use a case as authority for a rule without setting out its facts, holdings, and rationale.

When you do include descriptions of analogous cases, be clear about why you have included those descriptions. One way to do this is to set out the principle that you are using the case or cases to illustrate and then to include the case description. The following example illustrates this type of "principle-based" analysis, that is, analysis in which the cases are used to illustrate how the courts have applied a rule or principle.

EXAMPLE 11   **Excerpt from Appellant's Brief Demonstrating Principle-Based Analysis**

2. <u>The ATF agents did not have a particularized objective suspicion that Mr. Josephy was engaged in criminal activity because the tip included only general physical descriptions, it omitted any description of clothing, and the only action it predicted was that Mr. Josephy would be leaving a motel.</u>

Subheading

A tip from an unknown informant that does no more than describe an individual's readily observable location and appearance does not have sufficient indicia of reliability to support a stop. *Florida v. J.L.*, 529 U.S. 266, 272 (2000). Although such a tip may help the police identify the person whom the informant means to accuse, such a tip does not establish that the informant has knowledge of concealed criminal activity. *Id.* at 272.

Rules

In the cases in which the courts have held that the tip lacked sufficient indicia of reliability, the tip lacked predictive information and included only a general description of the defendant and his location, and the informant did not explain how he had acquired the information. *See, e.g., Florida v. J.L.*, 529 U.S. at 272. For instance, in *J.L.*, an anonymous caller reported to police that "a young black male standing at a particular bus stop and wearing a plaid shirt was carrying a gun." *Id.* at 269. In concluding that this tip was not sufficient to establish a reasonable suspicion of criminal activity, the Court said that "[t]he anonymous call concerning J.L. provided no predictive information and therefore left the police without means to test the informant's knowledge or credibility." *Id.* at 270. The Court went on to say that the fact that the allegation about the gun turned out to be true did not establish a reasonable basis for suspecting J.L. of engaging in unlawful conduct:

Principle that Ms. Elder has drawn from the cases in which the courts have held the tips lacked sufficient indicia of reliability

Description of cases that illustrate the principle and illustrate the types of cases in which the courts have held that the tips lacked sufficient indicia of reliability

The reasonableness of official suspicion must be measured by what the officers knew before they conducted their search. All the police had to go on in this case was the bare report of an unknown, unaccountable informant who neither explained how he knew about the gun nor supplied any basis for believing he had inside information about J.L.

Id. at 271.

In contrast, in most of the cases in which the courts have held that the tips had sufficient indicia of reliability to support a *Terry* stop, the callers were reporting what they had recently seen or experienced, *see, e.g., United States v. Terry-Crespo*, 356 F.3d 1170, 1172 (9th Cir. 2004), or the callers provided the police with not only details about the defendant and his or her current location but also information about what the defendant was about to do, *see, e.g., United States v. Fernandez-Castillo*, 324 F.3d 1114, 1119 (9th Cir. 2003). For example, in *Terry-Crespo*, the court said that a 911 call contained sufficient indicia of reliability for four reasons: (1) The call was not anonymous because the caller provided the 911 operator with his name and the call was recorded; (2) the caller was the victim of a crime, and the police must be able to take seriously, and respond promptly to, emergency 911 calls; (3) the caller jeopardized any anonymity he might have had by calling 911 and providing his name to an operator during a recorded call; and (4) the caller was giving first-hand information about an event that had just occurred. *Id.* at 356 F.3d at 1172-77. Similarly, in *Fernandez-Castillo*, the court held that a tip had sufficient reliability because it came from a Montana Department of Transportation (MDOT) employee and there are relatively few MDOT employees; the MDOT employee who reported the erratic driving not only provided the dispatcher with the make and model of the car but also told the dispatcher that the car had North Dakota license plates; the MDOT employee made the report almost immediately after he observed the defendant driving erratically; and the report contained predictive information—that the car was driving eastbound near milepost 116. *Id.* at 1119.

Principle that Ms. Elder has drawn from the cases in which the courts have held that the tips had sufficient indicia of reliability followed by descriptions of cases that illustrate that principle

Although most of the time you will want to start your case description or descriptions by setting out the principle that you are using the case or cases to illustrate, there are times when it works to start with a citation to the case. For example, in the following excerpt, which is taken from the appellee's brief, the prosecutor starts the paragraph with a cite to *Alabama v. White*. In this instance, starting with a citation to a case is effective because it allows the prosecutor to emphasize that *Alabama v. White* is a United States Supreme Court case. When you use this technique, it usually works best to set out the court's holding in the topic sentence.

EXAMPLE 12   **Excerpt from Appellee's Brief in Which the Prosecutor Has Started a Paragraph with a Citation to a Case**

Similarly, in *Alabama v. White*, 496 U.S. 325, 330 (1990), the United States Supreme Court held that the police had a reasonable suspicion that the defendant, White, was engaged in criminal activity. In *White*, an anonymous caller phoned 911 and told the operator that Vanessa White would be leaving the Lynnwood Terrace Apartments at a particular time in a brown Plymouth station wagon with a broken taillight to go to Dobey's Motel. *Id.* at 327. In addition, the caller told the 911 operator that White would have about "an ounce of cocaine inside a brown attaché case." *Id.* Although the two police officers who went to the apartment complex saw White get into a brown Plymouth station wagon with a broken taillight, they did not see anything in White's hands. *Id.* Moreover, although White appeared to be driving to Dobey's Motel, the officers had a patrol unit stop the vehicle before it reached the motel. *Id.* The Court held that the officers had a reasonable suspicion despite failing to verify White's predicted destination.

Another way to make clear why you have included a particular case description is to state explicitly that the facts in the analogous case are similar to the facts in your case or to say that facts in the analogous case can be distinguished from the facts in your case. Example 13 shows how Ms. Elder sets up a case description by stating that the case be distinguished. In reading this example, also note the order in which Ms. Elder sets out information. Instead of putting the description of the analogous case between the rules and the arguments, Ms. Elder sets out the rules, her arguments based on those rules, and then the description of the case, which she then distinguishes.

EXAMPLE 13	**Excerpt from Appellant's Brief Demonstrating Distinguishing a Case**

1. The ATF agents did not have a particularized objective suspicion that Mr. Josephy   **Subheading**
    was engaged in criminal activity because the tip came from an unknown informant;
    Although the informant gave the 911 operator his name, he refused to give his
    address or phone number.

Where an informant declines to be identified, there is a risk the tip has been fabricated,   **Rules**
undercutting its reliability. *Florida v. J.L.*, 529 U.S. 266, 269-70, 272 (2000). The unknown
informant's reputation cannot be accessed, nor can the informant be held responsible for a
false accusation. *Id.* This possibility that the informant might be lying outweighs the value
of the information provided unless there are other factors that establish that the informant
is reliable—for example, the informant provides law enforcement officers with information
about the suspect's future actions, which law enforcement officers then independently verify.
United States v. Morales, 253 F.3d 1070, 1075 (9th Cir. 2001).

In *State v. Josephy*, the Court should treat the tip as a tip from an unknown informant.   **Argument**
Although the informant gave the 911 operator a name, "Zachary Dillon," he called from a
public pay phone in a large mall, and he refused to give the 911 operator his address or phone
number (ER 32, 35). In addition, when Agent Bhasin tried to locate an individual by the name
of Zachary Dillon in his databases, he was not able to find anyone by that name in the greater
Bellingham area (ER 42). Consequently, neither Agent Bhasin nor any other law enforcement
officer was able to contact Zachary Dillon to determine how he obtained the information
that he gave to the 911 operator or to hold him accountable if the statements that he made
turned out to be false.

Accordingly, the facts in this case can be distinguished from the facts in *United States v.*   **Case description**
Terry-Crespo, 356 F.3d 1170, 1172 (9th Cir. 2004), a case in which the court held that information
provided by an individual who had called 911 to report that the defendant had threatened him
with a firearm was sufficient to support a *Terry* stop even though the police were not able to
locate anyone by the caller's name in their databases. Unlike the caller in *Terry-Crespo*, who
was the victim of a crime, in this case the informant, "Dillon," was not the victim of a crime. In
addition, unlike the caller in *Terry-Crespo*, who made the call from the scene of the crime, in   **Argument**
this case "Dillon" made the call from a mall five minutes from the motel where the drug buy
was allegedly occurring. Finally, while in *Terry-Crespo* the caller did not give the 911 operator
his phone number because he did not know the number of the cell phone that he had borrowed to make the emergency call, in this case "Dillon" refused to give the operator his address,

home phone number, or a cell phone number. Consequently, while in *Terry-Crespo* the facts supported the court's conclusion that the caller was not trying to hide his identity, in this case the facts suggest just the opposite.

Thus, because "Dillon" appears to have taken steps to hide his identity, this Court should treat his tip as a tip from an unknown informant. However, even if this Court does not treat the tip as coming from an unknown informant, the tip is not reliable because it lacks sufficient indicia of reliability.

Conclusion

Just as there are a number of techniques that you can use to present a rule in a light favorable to your client, there are also a number of techniques you can use to present a case in a light favorable to your client. You can set out the court's holding more broadly in cases that support your client's position and more narrowly in cases that support the other side's position; you can emphasize or de-emphasize particular facts or rules through the use of airtime, detail, the positions of emphasis, sentence length, and sentence construction; and you can choose words not only for their denotation but also for their connotation.

For instance, in the following example, the prosecutor uses detail, the positions of emphasis, and word choices to set out his description of *United States v. Terry-Crespo* in a light favorable to the government.

EXAMPLE 14   **Excerpt from the Appellee's Brief Showing Favorable Presentation of a Case**

In determining whether a *Terry* stop was permissible, the courts do a *de novo* review, looking at the totality of the circumstances and considering all relevant factors, including those factors that "in a different context, might be entirely innocuous." *Florida v. J.L.*, 529 U.S. at 277-78; *accord United States v. Terry-Crespo*, 356 F.3d 1170, 1172 (9th Cir. 2004). For example, in *Terry-Crespo*, this Court held that the informant's preliminary phone call was, by itself, sufficient to establish a reasonable suspicion that the defendant, Terry-Crespo, was engaged in criminal activity. *Id.* at 1172. In doing so, this Court rejected Terry-Crespo's argument that the informant, Mr. Domingis, should be treated as an anonymous informant because he was not able to provide the 911 operator with the number of the phone from which he placed the call; he changed the subject when the operator asked him to provide another number; and, when asked for his location, he gave the operator a nonexistent intersection. *Id.* at 1174-75. As the court stated in its opinion,

> [d]uring the course of the 911 call, the operator asked Mr. Domingis for his telephone number. Mr. Domingis explained that he did not know the return number because he was calling from someone else's cellular telephone. When the operator asked if there was another number where she could reach him, he did not answer her question but returned to discussing the subject of the suspect's location. The operator asked Mr. Domingis for his location. Initially, he responded by providing a nonexistent intersection on Portland's grid system and then stammeringly told the operator that "I don't want . . . I

The prosecutor begins the paragraph by setting out the rule that he is using *Terry-Crespo* to illustrate.

The prosecutor uses the active voice and the phrase, "this Court" to emphasize that *Terry-Crespo* is a Ninth Circuit case. In addition, by using the phrase "this Court rejected Terry-Crespo's argument" the prosecutor suggests that the court should do the same thing in this case.

By setting out the facts in detail and using a quotation, the prosecutor emphasizes the facts in *Terry-Crespo*.

don't want . . . I don't want . . . ." Although not certain, it appears that Mr. Domingis did not want police contact.

Id. at 1172.

The court then went on to note that the police tried to locate Mr. Domingis in a number of different databases, including the Yahoo! databases, but that they were not able to locate anyone by that name. *Id.* However, the court concluded that the tip had sufficient indicia of reliability because Mr. Domingis was reporting that he had just been the victim of a crime and because Mr. Domingis risked any anonymity that he might have enjoyed by giving the 911 operator his name during a recorded call. *Id.* at 1174-76. As the court stated, "Merely calling 911 and having a recorded telephone conversation risks the possibility that the police could trace the call or identify Mr. Domingis by his voice." *Id.* at 1176. Thus, the court held that, under the totality of the circumstances, the tip was sufficient to support a finding that Terry-Crespo was engaged in criminal activity even though the police did not independently verify any of the information contained in the tip.

Instead of putting the fact that the police tried to locate Mr. Domingis in a number of different databases in the same paragraph as the quote, the prosecutor starts a new paragraph, which allows him to emphasize this fact by putting it in a position of emphasis.

The prosecutor buries an unfavorable fact, that Mr. Domingis was the victim of a crime, in the middle of the paragraph.

Although you will want to include full descriptions of the most important cases, avoid the temptation to describe all, or even most, of the cases that you found while researching the issue. By being selective, you will keep your brief shorter, something that will please almost every judge, and your preparation for oral argument will be easier. (Remember, for every case you cite, you need to know that case, inside and out, for oral argument.) When it is important to cite more than a few cases, set out the best case or cases in text and then reference the other cases using parentheticals.

EXAMPLE 15   **Excerpt from Appellant's Brief Demonstrating Full Case Description and Use of a Parenthetical**

Under this comparative analysis, a defendant meets his burden of proving the reason the prosecutor gave for striking a juror was a pretext for discrimination when the reason given applies equally to a juror of another race, but the prosecutor strikes only one of the jurors. *McClain v. Prunty*, 217 F.3d 1209, 1221 (9th Cir. 2000). For instance, in *McClain*, this Court concluded that the reason the prosecutor gave for striking a black juror was a pretext for discrimination when the reason given applied equally to a white juror, but the prosecutor did not strike the white juror. Although the prosecutor stated that he had struck a black juror because the juror lacked experience making decisions, the prosecutor did not strike a white juror who also lacked decision-making experience. As the court stated, the fact that the prosecutor did not treat jurors of different races in the same way "fatally undermine[d] the credibility of the prosecutor's stated justification." *Id.* at 1221-22; *see also United States v. Chinchilla*, 874 F.2d 695 (9th Cir. 1989) (reversing a conviction because the prosecutor's stated reason for striking a Hispanic juror—that the juror lived in La Mesa—applied equally to a juror who was not Hispanic and who was not struck).

Principle that Ms. Elder wants to illustrate

Full description of first case

Description of second case using a parenthetical

Finally, remember that if you describe a case you should use that case in your argument. Do not describe a case and then leave the judge to figure out why you included a description of that case in your brief.

> **PRACTICE POINTER**
>
> In choosing cases on which to rely, keep in mind your jurisdiction's rule on citing to unpublished opinions. In December 2006, the United States Supreme Court amended Fed. R. App. Proc. 32.1 to allow citation to unpublished federal opinions issued on or after January 1, 2007. However, some state jurisdictions still prohibit citation to unpublished cases. *See, e.g.,* Wash. R. App. P. 10.4(h).

c.   Constructing and Presenting the Arguments

For many attorneys, the most enjoyable part of drafting the brief is constructing and presenting the arguments: It is in constructing and presenting the arguments that attorneys get to use their insights and creativity to pull together, into a coherent and persuasive package, the facts, rules, and cases that they have set out in the earlier sections of their brief.

In constructing the arguments, think first about the standard types of arguments: factual arguments in which you apply the plain language of a statute, regulation, court rule, or common law rule to the facts of your case; analogous case arguments in which you compare and contrast the facts in your case to the facts in analogous cases; and policy arguments.

While factual arguments are very common in trial briefs, they are less common in appellate briefs. In most instances, the appellate courts defer to the trial court's findings of fact or the jury's verdict, only overturning a finding or the verdict if it is not supported by the evidence. There are, however, times when you can make an effective factual argument, either letting that factual argument stand by itself or combining it with an analogous case or policy argument. For example, in *United States v. Josephy*, Ms. Elder makes a factual argument that the tip is from an unknown rather than a known informant. In reading the following example, examine the way in which Ms. Elder uses the facts to support her assertion that the courts should treat the tip as a tip from an unknown informant. Ms. Elder puts unfavorable facts—for example, the fact that the informant gave the 911 operator a name—in a dependent clause, and she uses the phrase "gave the operator a name" rather than the phrase "gave the operator his name" to suggest that the informant might not have given the operator his real name. In addition, she places her strongest argument, that neither Agent Bhasin nor any other law enforcement officer was able to contact the informant to determine how he obtained the information or to hold him accountable if the statements turned out to be false, in a position of emphasis at the end of the paragraph.

EXAMPLE 16   **Excerpt from the Appellant's Brief Showing How to Present a Factual Argument**

When an informant declines to be identified, there is a risk the tip has been fabricated, undercut-   **Rules**
ting its reliability. *Florida v. J.L.*, 529 U.S. 266, 269-70, 272 (2000). The unknown informant's reputation cannot be assessed, nor can the informant be held responsible for a false accusation. *Id. In such*

situations, the possibility that the informant may be lying outweighs the value of the information provided unless there are other factors that establish that the informant is reliable—for example, the informant provides law enforcement officers with information about the suspect's future actions, which law enforcement officers then independently verify. *United States v. Morales,* 253 F.3d 1070, 1075 (9th Cir. 2001).

In this case, the Court should treat the tip as a tip from an unknown informant. Although the informant gave the 911 operator a name, "Zachary Dillon," he called from a public pay phone in a large mall, and he refused to give the 911 operator his address or phone number (ER 32, 35). In addition, when Agent Bhasin tried to locate an individual by the name of Zachary Dillon in his databases, he was not able to find anyone by that name in the greater Bellingham area (ER 42). Consequently, neither Agent Bhasin nor any other law enforcement officer was able to contact Zachary Dillon to determine how he obtained the information that he gave to the 911 operator or to hold him accountable if the statements that he made turned out to be false.

Assertion
Factual argument

If a factual argument is the least common type of argument in appellate briefs, the most common type is an analogous case argument—that is, an argument in which a party either compares its case to analogous cases or distinguishes its case from the cases that the other side says are analogous.

In constructing and presenting analogous case arguments, keep five things in mind. First, as a general rule, begin your argument by stating your assertion. Second, be explicit in making the comparisons. Third, in addition to making comparisons, explain why those comparisons are legally significant. Fourth, make sure that you compare like things; for example, make sure that you compare cases to cases, people to other people, and facts to facts. (See sections 24.7 and 25.1.) Finally, keep in mind that you can do more than just compare and contrast facts: You can also compare and contrast the arguments that the parties make and the courts' reasoning.

In the following excerpt from the appellant's brief, Ms. Elder begins her analogous case argument by setting out her assertion: Like the tip in *J.L.,* the tip in this case lacks the required indicia of reliability. Ms. Elder is then explicit in comparing the facts in *J.L.* to the facts in her case: "In *J.L.,* the informant called from a borrowed cell phone and did not give the 911 operator either his own phone number or his own address. Similarly, in this case 'Dillon' called from a public pay telephone and refused to give the operator his phone number or his address. (ER 30)." Ms. Elder does, however, do more than just tell the judge how the cases are similar. She also explains why that similarity is important: Because neither of the informants provided the 911 operator with contact information, law enforcement officers were not able to contact either informant to determine the basis for the allegations or to hold them accountable if the information that they provided turned out to be false. Finally, Ms. Elder compares like things. In the first sentence, she compares a tip to a tip, a case to a case, and facts to facts. In addition, in the second sentence, Ms. Elder compares a case to a case: *J.L.* to *United States v. Josephy.*

| EXAMPLE 17 | **Excerpt from the Appellant's Brief Showing an Analogous Case Argument** |

Like the tip in *J.L.,* the tip in this case lacked the required indicia of reliability. In *J.L.,* the informant called from a borrowed cell phone and did not give the 911 operator either his own phone number or his own address. Similarly, in this case "Dillon" called from a public pay telephone and refused to give the operator his phone number or his address. (ER 30). As a consequence, in both cases, law enforcement officers were not able to contact the informants to determine the basis for their allegations or to hold them accountable if the information that they provided turned out to be false.

> **PRACTICE POINTER**
>
> When you italicize a name, you are telling your reader that you are citing to a case. In contrast, when you do not italicize a name, you are telling your reader that you are referring to the party or person. "*J.L.*" is a reference to *Florida v. J.L.*, but "J.L." is a reference to the defendant, a juvenile with the initials J and L.

Although you might incorporate policy statements into your presentation of the rules and your descriptions of analogous cases on a fairly regular basis, typically you will not make a policy argument unless you are asking the court to modify an existing rule or adopt a new rule. Our example case, *United States v. Josephy*, illustrates this point. If Ms. Elder had argued that the court should eliminate peremptory challenges because they can mask discrimination, her primary argument would have been a policy argument, and the government's primary argument would have been a policy argument. Ms. Elder would have argued that, as a matter of public policy, the courts should eliminate peremptory challenges, and the government would have argued that, as a matter of public policy, the courts should not deprive parties of their right to use such challenges. However, given the fact that the United States Supreme Court rejected a request to eliminate peremptory challenges in a relatively recent opinion, *see Miller-El v. Dretke*, 545 U.S. 231, 239-40 (2005), Ms. Elder decided not to pursue this line of argument. As a consequence, although both Ms. Elder and the prosecutor refer to policy in their statements of the rules and their descriptions of the cases, neither Ms. Elder nor the prosecutor makes a policy argument in their brief.

d.   Using Quotations

While some attorneys and judges will tell you that you should not include quotations, and particularly long quotations, in your brief, other attorneys and judges will tell you that quotations are one of the advocate's most valuable tools. Both groups have legitimate points.

In drafting your brief, do not use quotations as a crutch. For example, do not use a quotation to cover up the fact that you do not understand a rule or a court's holding or reasoning. Instead, take the time to figure out the rule and the court's decision. Similarly, do not use a quotation because you lack confidence in your writing skills or because you do not want to take the time to construct your own language.

Do, however, use quotations in the following circumstances. First, as a general rule, quote the relevant portions of governing statutes, regulations, and court rules, and quote applicable sections of contracts, wills, and similar documents. Second, as a general rule, quote from the record when the specific language that the judge, attorney, witness, or juror used is important. In addition, feel free to use quotations to emphasize favorable facts, rules, and cases.

The following example illustrates an effective use of quotations from the record. Because Ms. Elder wants to emphasize that Ms. Whitefish was not bothered by the fact that she was subjected to additional scrutiny at the border but that Mr. Williams was bothered by the fact that police officers seemed to target him, Ms. Elder quotes from the record and places most of those quotations at the end of a paragraph in a position of emphasis.

EXAMPLE 18   **Excerpt from the Appellant's Brief Showing Use of Quotations from the Record to Emphasize Favorable Facts**

Later, the prosecutor asked if anyone had ever had negative experiences with law enforcement personnel. (ER 119). Ms. Whitefish, a Native American who was a junior majoring in history at Western Washington University, responded that each time she crossed the border she had been, "pulled aside for additional questions." (ER 119). However, when the prosecutor asked Ms. Whitefish whether she was bothered by the fact that she had been pulled over for additional questions, she stated, "Not particularly. I am a college student, and all of us have had similar experiences. They seem to stop young people more . . . ." (ER 119-20).

Similarly, Mr. Martin, a white man with long hair, told the prosecutor that he had had a number of negative experiences with police officers. (ER 120). For example, Mr. Martin told the prosecutor that on one occasion a police officer had stopped him because one of his taillights was out but that the police had not stopped other individuals who had one of their taillights out. (ER 120). In addition, Mr. Martin told the prosecutor that on two occasions he had been given tickets for jaywalking when other individuals on the same street who had short hair jaywalked but did not get tickets. (ER 120). When the prosecutor asked whether he was bothered by the police officers' actions, Mr. Martin said, "You bet I am." (ER 121).

When you are using quotations for emphasis, you will usually want to begin by making the point using your own language. You can then use the quotation to give that point more airtime or to give that point additional emphasis through the use of detail. The following example illustrates this use of a quotation. Ms. Elder makes her points using her own language, and then she emphasizes those points by quoting from the court's opinion. Although the quotation is longer than Ms. Elder would have liked, she uses the quotation because it was not possible to edit it without losing coherence and key content, and the point that she uses the quotation to illustrate is an important one.

EXAMPLE 19   **Excerpt from the Appellant's Brief Showing Use of a Quotation**

Even though the tip contained a number of details, the United States Supreme Court held that the tip was not, by itself, sufficient to justify a *Terry* stop. *White*, 496 U.S. at 329. According to the court, it became reasonable to think that the information was reliable only after the police verified not only easily obtained facts but also future actions that are not easily predicted. *Id.* at 332.

> We think it also important that, as in *Gates*, "the anonymous [tip] contained a range of details relating not just to easily obtained facts and conditions existing at the time of the tip, but to future actions of third parties ordinarily not easily predicted." [462 U.S. at 245.] The fact that the officers found a car precisely matching the caller's description in front of the 235

> building is an example of the former. Anyone could have "predicted" that fact because it was a condition presumably existing at the time of the call. What was important was the caller's ability to predict respondent's *future behavior*, because it demonstrated inside information—a special familiarity with respondent's affairs. The general public would have had no way of knowing that respondent would shortly leave the building, get in the described car, and drive the most direct route to Dobey's Motel. Because only a small number of people are generally privy to an individual's itinerary, it is reasonable for police to believe that a person with access to such information is likely to also have access to reliable information about that individual's illegal activities. *See ibid.* When significant aspects of the caller's predictions were verified, there was reason to believe not only that the caller was honest but also that he was well informed, at least well enough to justify the stop.

Id.

Although ultimately the court concluded that the anonymous tip, as corroborated, was sufficient to justify the *Terry* stop, the Court labeled the case as a "close case." *Id.*

> **PRACTICE POINTER**   Remember to include a citation to authority for every quotation. If the quotation is from the record, the citation to authority should be to the record; if the quotation is from a statute, the citation to authority should be the statute; and if the quotation is from a case, the citation should be to the case, including the specific page on which the quotation appears.

e. Responding to the Other Side's Arguments

In addition to setting out your own arguments, you need to respond to the other side's arguments. If you are the appellee, you do not have a choice about where to set out these responses: You need to set them out in your opening brief. However, when you are the appellant, you do have a choice: You can either anticipate what the appellee is going to argue and try to preempt its arguments by setting out your responses in your opening brief, or you can wait to see if the appellee makes the argument and then, if it does, set out your response in your reply brief. Even though there are pros and cons to both of these approaches, the conventional wisdom is that if you are relatively certain that the appellee will make an argument, you should anticipate and respond to that argument in your opening brief. In contrast, if there is a good possibility that the appellee will not make a particular point, you should wait for the appellee's brief.

The same considerations apply to deciding when to address cases on which the appellee relies. Although both parties have an ethical obligation to bring to the court's attention a case that is controlling, an appellant can choose to preempt a key, but not controlling, case the other side will likely rely on for support by distinguishing it in the opening brief. If the appellant is not sure the appellee will rely on the case, or the appellant believes the case is not critical to the analysis, the appellant might choose to wait until the reply brief to distinguish cases in the appellee's brief.

In responding to the other side's arguments, avoid repeating the other side's argument. Instead of repeating your opponent's arguments, make your own affirmative arguments.

Example 20 below sets out one of the appellant's arguments: that there was purposeful discrimination because the prosecutor excused Native Americans who had had a particular experience or commitment but did not excuse white jurors who had similar experiences or commitments. Example 21 is from a weak appellee's brief. By repeating the appellant's argument, the prosecutor gives the appellant's arguments additional airtime. In addition, instead of attacking the argument, the prosecutor attacks defense counsel when he states that she has misstated the law. Example 22 is a rewrite of Example 2, in which the prosecutor does a more effective job of responding to the appellant's argument without repeating the appellant's argument and without attacking defense counsel.

EXAMPLE 20   **Excerpt from the Appellant's Brief That Sets Up Argument to Which Appellee Must Respond**

Moreover, the government cannot lawfully exercise peremptory challenges "against potential jurors of one race unless potential jurors of another race with comparable characteristics are also challenged." *United States v. You*, 382 F.3d 958, 969 (9th Cir. 2004) (quoting *Turner*, 121 F.3d at 1252). Accordingly, a "comparative analysis of jurors struck and those remaining is a well-established tool for exploring the possibility that facially race-neutral reasons are a pretext for discrimination." *McClain v. Prunty*, 217 F.3d 1209, 1220-21 (9th Cir. 2000).

Under this comparative analysis, a defendant meets his burden of proving the reason the prosecutor gave for striking a juror was a pretext for discrimination when the reason given applies equally to a juror of another race, but the prosecutor strikes only one of the jurors. *McClain v. Prunty*, 217 F.3d 1209, 1221 (9th Cir. 2000). For instance, in *McClain*, this Court concluded that the reason the prosecutor gave for striking a black juror was a pretext for discrimination when the reason given applied equally to a white juror, but the prosecutor did not strike the white juror. Although the prosecutor stated that he had struck a black juror because the juror lacked experience making decisions, the prosecutor did not strike a white juror who also lacked decision-making experience. As the court stated, the fact that the prosecutor did not treat jurors of different races in the same way "fatally undermine[d] the credibility of the prosecutor's stated justification." *Id.* at 1221-22; *see also United States v. Chinchilla*, 874 F.2d 695 (9th Cir. 1989) (reversing a conviction because the prosecutor's stated reason for striking a Hispanic juror—that the juror lived in La Mesa—applied equally to a juror who was not Hispanic and who was not struck).

In *United States v. Josephy*, the reason the prosecutor gave for striking Mr. Williams, a Native American, was a pretext for discrimination because the reason applied equally to Mr. Woods, who is white. In explaining why he struck Mr. Williams, the prosecutor said that Mr. Williams would have difficulty focusing on the facts of the case because he had a meeting scheduled for the following week. (ER 125). However, the prosecutor did not strike Mr. Woods, who told the court that his mother was seriously ill, that the doctors were giving her a 20 percent chance to live, and that he might have to go out of town. (ER 117-18).

In addition, the reason that the prosecutor gave for striking Ms. Whitefish, a Native American, was a pretext for discrimination because the prosecutor did not strike a white juror who had had similar experiences with law enforcement personnel. When the judge asked the prosecutor why he had struck Ms. Whitefish, the prosecutor responded that he did not think Ms. Whitefish would be able "to judge this case fairly and impartially" based on her experiences crossing the border. (ER 125). However, although Ms. Whitefish stated that she had been "pulled aside for additional questions" (ER 19), when asked whether this bothered her, Ms. Whitefish replied, "Not particularly. I am a college student, and all of us have had similar experiences. They seem to stop young people more . . . ." (ER 119).

In contrast, Mr. Martin believed he had been targeted by police officers because he had long hair. (ER 120). He was stopped for having a taillight that was out; others were not. He was ticketed for jaywalking; others, who had short hair, were not. (ER 119-20). When asked whether he was bothered by his experiences with police officers, he said "You bet I am." (ER 121).

In a Ninth Circuit case, the court concluded that the subjective reasons prosecutors gave for excusing minority jurors were not pretextual even though prospective jurors of different races provided similar responses and one was excused while the other was not. *United States v. Burks*, 27 F.3d 1424, 1429 (9th Cir. 1994). In setting out its reasoning, the court noted, "While subjective factors may play a legitimate role in the exercise of challenges, reliance on such factors alone cannot overcome strong objective indicia of discrimination such as a clear and sustained pattern of strikes against minority jurors." *Id.*

In our case, there are objective indicia of discrimination stemming from a clear and sustained pattern of strikes against minority jurors. The prosecutor used two of his preemptory challenges to strike the only two Native American potential jurors. He struck Mr. Williams, who said he had a meeting scheduled after the trial was expected to end, despite the fact that Mr. Williams expressed willingness to serve even if it meant missing the meeting. In addition, he struck Ms. Whitefish based on her experiences at the border even though Ms. Whitefish assured the court that her experiences at the border did not bother her.

Because the prosecutor did not excuse white jurors who had similar experiences to the Native Americans whom he did strike, the district court erred in denying Mr. Josephy's *Batson* challenge. Such an erroneous denial is presumed to be prejudicial. *See Gray v. Mississippi*, 481 U.S. 648, 668 (1987). Therefore, this Court should reverse and remand the case for a new trial.

EXAMPLE 21   **Poor Response by the Appellee**

In her brief, defense counsel argues that a "comparative analysis of jurors struck and those remaining is a well-established tool for exploring the possibility that facially race-neutral reasons are a pretext for discrimination." *McClain v. Prunty*, 217 F.3d 1209, 1220-21 (9th Cir. 2000). In addition, defense counsel argues that a defendant meets his burden of proving the reason the prosecutor gave for striking a juror was a pretext for discrimination when the reason given applies equally to a juror of another race, but the prosecutor strikes only one of the jurors. *Id.* at 1221. Based on these rules, defense counsel argues that the appellant has met his burden of proving purposeful discrimination because the prosecutor excused Ms. Whitefish, a Native American, because she had problems crossing the border, but the prosecutor did not excuse Mr. Woods, who is white, even though Mr. Woods said that he believed that the police targeted him because he had long hair. In addition, defense counsel argues that the appellant has met his burden of proving purposeful discrimination because the prosecutor excused a Native American who had a tribal council meeting scheduled for the following week but did not excuse a white juror who said that he might have to go out of town to care for his mother, whom the doctors had given only a 20 percent chance of living.

Defense counsel misstates the law when she states that *Batson* is violated whenever prospective jurors of different races provide similar responses and one is excused while the other is not. *See Burks v. Borg*, 27 F.3d 1424, 1429 (9th Cir. 1994). For example, in *Burks*, this Court held that there was not purposeful discrimination in spite of the fact that a minority juror who was struck shared characteristics with a nonminority juror who was not struck. *Id.* The prosecutor told the court that he had stricken the minority jurors "because they were 'squishy' on the death penalty, expressed a reluctance to serve, and/ or lacked certain life experiences." *Id.* In concluding that there was no purposeful discrimination, the court reaffirmed that "[t]rial counsel is entitled to exercise his full professional judgment in pursuing his client's 'legitimate interest in using [peremptory] challenges . . . to secure a fair and impartial jury.'" *Id.* (quoting *J.E.B. v. Alabama ex rel. T.B.*, 511 U.S. 127, 137 (1994)). Thus, in using his or her peremptory challenges, trial counsel is entitled to take into account "tone, demeanor, facial expression, emphasis—all those factors that make the words uttered by the prospective juror convincing or not." *Burks*, 27 F.3d at 1429.

EXAMPLE 22   **Better Response by Appellee**

Furthermore, case law does not support the notion that *Batson* is violated whenever prospective jurors of different races provide similar responses and one is excused while the other is not. *Burks v. Borg*, 27 F.3d 1424, 1429 (9th Cir. 1994). For example, in *Burks*, this Court held that there was not purposeful discrimination in spite of the fact that a minority juror who was struck shared characteristics with a nonminority juror who was not struck. *Id.* The prosecutor told the court that he had stricken the minority jurors "because they were 'squishy' on the death penalty, expressed a reluctance to serve, and/or lacked certain life experiences." *Id.* In concluding that there was no purposeful discrimination, the court reaffirmed that "[t]rial counsel is entitled to exercise his full professional judgment in pursuing his client's 'legitimate interest in using [peremptory] challenges . . . to secure a fair and impartial jury.'" *Id.* (quoting *J.E.B. v. Alabama ex rel. T.B.*, 511 U.S. 127, 137 (1994)). Thus, in using his or her peremptory challenges, trial counsel is entitled to take into account "tone, demeanor, facial expression, emphasis—all those factors that make the words uttered by the prospective juror convincing or not." *Burks*, 27 F.3d at 1429.

---

f.   Avoiding the Common Problem of Neglecting to Make Explicit Connections

One of the most common mistakes that attorneys make in writing a brief is that they do not explicitly "connect" the parts of their argument. They set out an assertion but do not connect that assertion to a rule; they set out the rule but do not connect it to the descriptions of analogous cases; or they set out descriptions of analogous cases but do not connect the facts and holdings in those analogous cases to their case. For instance, in the following example, the attorney describes a case, *McClain*, but she does not make it clear that she is using the case to illustrate how the courts have applied the rule that she set out in the first sentence of the paragraph. In addition, although the attorney states that the facts in *McClain* are similar to the facts in her case, she does not explain how they are similar.

EXAMPLE 23   **Poor Example Because of Lack of Explicit Connections**

A court may conclude that the prosecutor's reasons are pretextual when the reason that the prosecutor gives for striking a juror applies equally to a juror of a different race who was not stricken. *McClain*, 217 F.3d at 1220. In McClain, the reason that the prosecutor gave for excusing a black juror was that she lacked decision-making experience. *Id.* at 1216. However, the prosecutor did not excuse a similar white juror. *Id.* at 1221. Thus, the court concluded that the prosecution's explanations were pretextual. *Id.* Similarly, in our case, the prosecutor excused Mr. Williams, a Native American, but she did not excuse Mr. Woods.

The following example is better because it uses a variety of ways to create connections and coherence. First, the author has gone into more detail in setting out the rules, the cases, and her arguments. The extra detail gives the author the raw material she needs to make the connections. Second, the author has used topic sentences to set up each paragraph. Third, the author has used transitions such as "for example" and "in addition" to make it clear how the information in one sentence is related to the information in the preceding or following sentence. Finally, to create coherence, the author has repeated key terms. For example, she has used the word "reason" and a version of the phrase "not supported by the record" in the statement of the rule, in the description of the analogous case, and in the argument. In the following example, the topic sentences are in all capital letters, the transitions are in large and small caps, the word "reason" is in bold, and the versions of the phrase "not supported by the record" are underlined.

EXAMPLE 24	**Better Example Because of Connections and Coherence**

WHEN THE **REASONS** THAT A PROSECUTOR GIVES FOR STRIKING A JUROR ARE <u>NOT SUPPORTED BY THE RECORD</u>, "SERIOUS QUESTIONS ABOUT THE LEGITIMACY OF A PROSECUTOR'S **REASONS** FOR EXERCISING PEREMPTORY CHALLENGES ARE RAISED." *McClain v. Prunty*, 217 F.3d 1209, 1221 (9th Cir. 2000). For example, in *McClain*, this Court determined that the first **reason** that the prosecutor gave for striking a black juror—that the juror mistrusted the system and had been treated unfairly—<u>was not supported by the record</u>. *Id.* at 1222. Instead of saying that she mistrusted the system and had been treated badly, the juror stated that she did not trust the public defender and, although she initially believed that her son had been treated unfairly, she had changed her mind. *Id.* at 1221. In addition, this Court determined that there was <u>nothing in the record to support</u> the prosecutor's second **reason**, that the juror must have lied about being a stewardess because she was heavyset. *Id.* The juror did not state that she was a stewardess; what she said was that she worked in airline maintenance. *Id.* Because the <u>record did not support</u> the **reasons** that the prosecutor gave, this Court held that the reasons that the prosecutor gave were a pretext for discrimination. *Id.*

As in *McClain*, in this case <u>the record does not support</u> the **reasons** that the prosecutor gave for excusing Mr. Williams and Ms. Whitefish. Although the prosecutor stated that he excused Mr. Williams because Mr. Williams would not be able to focus on the case because he had "other obligations next week" (ER 125), Mr. Williams told the court that he was willing to miss his tribal council meeting should the trial be extended. (ER 117). Similarly, although the prosecutor stated that he excused Ms. Whitefish because her experiences at the border would make it difficult for her "to judge this case fairly and impartially" (ER 125), Ms. Whitefish's response to the prosecutor's question about whether she was bothered by the fact that she had been "pulled aside for additional questions" was the following: "Not particularly. I am a college student, and all of us have had similar experiences. They seem to stop young people more . . . ." (ER 119).

Thus, just as the *McClain* court held that the trial court erred when it concluded that the **reasons** that the prosecutor gave were not a pretext for discrimination, this Court should decide that the district court erred when it concluded that the prosecutor's **reasons** were not a pretext for discrimination. "When there is **reason** to believe that there is a racial motivation for the challenge, [this Court is not] bound to accept at face value a list of neutral reasons that are either <u>unsupported in the record</u> or refuted by it. Any other approach leaves *Batson* a dead letter." *Johnson v. Vasquez*, 3 F.3d 1327, 1331 (9th Cir. 1993).

g.   Avoiding the Common Problem of Not Dealing with Weaknesses

Another error that attorneys commonly make is that they do not deal with the "weaknesses" in their argument. Although this strategy might work occasionally, more often it does not. Even if the opposing party does not notice the problems, the court will.

Look again at the last example. The writer does not deal with an important weakness: The courts do not always find it a pretext for discrimination when a prosecutor gives a reason for excusing a juror, prospective jurors of different races provide similar responses, and one is excused while the other is not. By not confronting contrary authority, the attorney allows the other side to make the following argument.

EXAMPLE 25   **Excerpt from Appellee's Brief Taking Advantage of an Unaddressed Weakness**

Furthermore, case law does not support the notion that *Batson* is violated whenever prospective jurors of different races provide similar responses and one is excused while the other is not. *Burks v. Borg*, 27 F.3d 1424, 1429 (9th Cir. 1994). For example, in *Burks*, this Court held that there was not purposeful discrimination in spite of the fact that a minority juror who was struck shared characteristics with a nonminority juror who was not struck. *Id.* The prosecutor told the court that he had stricken the minority jurors "because they were 'squishy' on the death penalty, expressed a reluctance to serve, and/or lacked certain life experiences." *Id.* In concluding that there was no purposeful discrimination, the court reaffirmed that "[t]rial counsel is entitled to exercise his full professional judgment in pursuing his client's 'legitimate interest in using [peremptory] challenges . . . to secure a fair and impartial jury.'" *Id.* (quoting *J.E.B. v. Alabama ex rel. T.B.*, 511 U.S. 127, 137 (1994)). Thus, in using his or her peremptory challenges, trial counsel is entitled to take into account "tone, demeanor, facial expression, emphasis—all those factors that make the words uttered by the prospective juror convincing or not." *Burks*, 27 F.3d at 1429.

Instead of ignoring problems, the better strategy is to anticipate and respond to arguments that you know the other side will make. In Example 26, Ms. Elder anticipated the government's argument and included the following paragraph.

EXAMPLE 26   **Excerpt from the Appellant's Brief Anticipating Opponent's Argument**

In *United States v. Burks*, 27 F.3d 1424, 1429 (9th Cir. 1994), the court concluded that the subjective reasons prosecutors gave for excusing minority jurors were not pretextual even though prospective jurors of different races provided similar responses and one was excused while the other was not. However, in doing so the court made the following statement: "While subjective factors may play a legitimate role in the exercise of challenges, reliance on such factors alone cannot overcome strong objective indicia of discrimination such as a clear and sustained pattern of strikes against minority jurors." *United States v. Burks*, 27 F.3d 1424, 1429 (9th Cir. 1994).

---

h.   Avoiding the Mistake of Overlooking Good Arguments

Finally, sometimes attorneys become so enthusiastic about one argument that they overlook other persuasive arguments. For example, in *United States v. Josephy*, Ms. Elder's strongest arguments are that the prosecutor's reasons are not supported by the record and that a comparative analysis of the Native American jurors who were struck and white jurors who were not reveals that the prosecutor's reasons were a pretext for discrimination. However, Ms. Elder can also argue that a *Batson* violation occurred because the district court failed to do the required sensitive inquiry before ruling on the *Batson* objection.

EXAMPLE 27   **Excerpt from the Appellant's Brief Showing an Additional Argument**

2.   <u>In addition, the district court erred by not conducting the required sensitive inquiry and by not stating its reasoning on the record.</u>

A trial court commits reversible error if it fails to do the required "sensitive inquiry" of the defendant's *Batson* challenge or if the trial court's decision is made in haste or is imprecise. *Jordan v. Lefevre*, 206 F.3d 196, 198 (2d Cir. 2006). *Jordan* provides an example. In that case, the trial judge attempted to save "an awful lot of time" by ruling on the defendant's *Batson* challenge without considering all of the facts and arguments and without setting out its analysis in the record. *Id.* at 199. As a result, the reviewing court concluded that the trial court had violated the defendant's right to equal protection by making a hasty decision and not stating on the record its analysis of why the reasons that the prosecutor gave for striking jurors were not a pretext for discrimination. *Id.*

As in *Jordan*, in this case the court made a hasty decision and did not state on the record why the reasons that the prosecutor gave were not a pretext for discrimination. In fact, the record consists of a single sentence: "Your objection is noted, Counsel, but the Court finds no purposeful discrimination here." (ER 126).

The "duty of assessing the credibility of the prosecutor's race-neutral reasons [embodies] the 'decisive question' in the *Batson* analysis." *Jordan*, 206 F.3d at 200. Although the lack of a reasoned analysis does not seem to stem from a blatant impatience with the proceedings as it did in *Jordan*, the result and the violation are the same: This Court is left with a record devoid of the reasoned credibility analysis regarding each challenged juror that due process requires.

Because the district court's erroneous denial of Mr. Josephy's *Batson* challenge is presumed to be prejudicial, *see Gray*, 481 U.S. at 668, this Court should reverse and remand the case for a new trial.

Although adding the additional argument makes the brief a bit longer, in this instance doing so was a good choice. Because both of her arguments are legally sound, Ms. Elder increases her chances of getting a reversal.

See section 17.10.6 for a checklist for critiquing the argument section.

§ 18.16 Drafting the Conclusion or Prayer for Relief

The final section of the brief is the conclusion or the prayer for relief. In most jurisdictions, this section is short. Unlike the conclusion in an objective memorandum, you do not summarize the arguments. Instead, simply set out the relief you are requesting. *See, e.g.,* Fed. R. App. P. 28 (a)(10). For example, as the appellant you usually ask the court to reverse or reverse and remand, and if you are the respondent you usually ask the court to affirm or remand. Sometimes you will ask for a single type of relief; at other times you will ask for different types of relief for different errors or for alternative forms of relief. To determine what type of relief you can request, read cases that have decided the same or similar issues and look to see what type of relief the parties requested and what type of relief the court granted.

In *United States v. Josephy*, Ms. Elder asks the court to reverse or, in the alternative, to remand the case for a new trial. Although it is possible that the court would reverse and dismiss, holding that the ATF agents did not have probable cause to arrest Mr. Josephy, the court could also remand the case and leave the decision to the prosecutor as to whether the case is to be retried without the suppressed evidence. Also, if the court reverses on the *Batson* issue, it would remand for a new trial. In contrast, the prosecution asks the appellate court to affirm the district court's decision.

EXAMPLE 1   **The Appellant's Conclusion**

The district court erred in denying Mr. Josephy's motion to suppress evidence obtained during a warrantless seizure unsupported by probable cause. Therefore, this Court should reverse his conviction.

In the alternative, the district court erred in denying Mr. Josephy's *Batson* challenge because the prosecution's reasons for striking the only two Native American jurors on the panel were a pretext for purposeful discrimination. Therefore, this Court should reverse his conviction and remand the case for a new trial.

---

§ 18.17 Preparing the Signature Block

Before submitting your brief to the court, you must sign it, listing your name and, in most jurisdictions, your bar number. The format typically used is as follows:

Dated: _____

                              Respectfully submitted,

                              _____
                              Name of attorney
                              Attorney for [Appellant or Respondent]
                              Address

§ 18.18 Preparing the Appendix

Most jurisdictions allow the parties to attach one or more appendices to their briefs. Such appendices should not be used to avoid the page limits. Instead, use appendices to set out information that a judge would find useful but that might not be readily available. For example, if you are arguing there was an instructional error, include a copy of the court's instructions to the jury. Likewise, if one of your issues requires the court to interpret the language in a particular statute or set of statutes, set out the text of the statute or statutes in an appendix.

Under Fed. App. P. 30(a)(l), an appendix containing specifically listed content is required. In contrast, under the Ninth Circuit local rules, an appendix need not be included, but excerpts of the record must be filed. Ninth Cir. R. 30-1.1(a).

§ 18.19 Revising, Editing, and Proofreading

It is impossible to state strongly enough the importance of revising, editing, and proofreading your brief. You do not want to waste a judge's time by making the judge read and reread a confusing sentence or by taking two pages to make a point that you could make in one page. In addition, you want the judges to focus on your arguments and not on grammar, punctuation, citation, or proofreading errors.

Because she wants to do the best that she can for her clients, Ms. Elder spends as much time revising, editing, and proofreading her brief as she does researching the issues and preparing the first draft. After completing the first draft, she sets it aside for a day or two while she works on other projects. When she comes back to the brief, she looks first at the arguments she has made, asking herself the following questions. Have I identified all of the issues? For each issue, have I made clear my position and what relief I am requesting? Have I provided the best support for each of my assertions? Have I included issues, arguments, or support that are unnecessary?

When she is happy with the content, Ms. Elder then rereads her brief, trying to read it as a judge would read it. Is the material presented in a logical order? Has she made clear the connections between arguments and parts of arguments? Is each argument, paragraph block, paragraph, and sentence easy to read and understand? At this stage, Ms. Elder also works more on writing persuasively. She checks to make sure that she has presented the rules, cases, and facts in a light favorable to her client and that she has used persuasive devices effectively.

Ms. Elder then tries to put the brief aside for at least a short period of time so that she can come back to it once again with "fresh eyes." This time, she works primarily on two things. She begins by looking at her writing style. Are there places where she could make her writing more eloquent? See Chapter 26. In particular, she looks for the types of mistakes that she knows she has a tendency to make. See Chapters 27, 28, and 29. Finally, she goes back through her brief, checking her citations and adding the page numbers to her table of contents and table of authorities.

Although this process is time-consuming, and thus expensive, Ms. Elder finds that the process pays off in a number of ways. First, and most important, she does a good job of representing her client. Because her briefs are well written, her clients get a fair hearing from the court. Second, because she has worked at it, through the years she has become both a better and a faster writer. Finally, she has protected and enhanced one of her most important assets: her reputation. Because her briefs are well written, judges tend to take them, and her, more seriously.

Chapter 18 Quiz No. 3

Draft answers for each of the following questions. Make your points clearly and concisely, and write sentences that are easy to read and that are grammatical and correctly punctuated.

1. What are the characteristics of a good summary of the argument?
2. What are the characteristics of an effective argumentative heading?
3. What are some of the techniques that you can use to present the rules in a light favorable to your client?
4. What are some of the techniques that you can use to present analogous cases in a light favorable to your client?
5. What are some of the common mistakes that you want to avoid in setting out the arguments?

§ 18.20 Sample Briefs

In this section we set out an appellant's brief and an appellee's brief.

EXAMPLE 1   **Appellant's Brief**

No. 13-12345

UNITED STATES COURT OF APPEALS

FOR THE NINTH CIRCUIT

UNITED STATES OF AMERICA,

Plaintiff-Appellee,

v.

PETER JASON JOSEPHY,

Defendant-Appellant.

On Appeal from the United States District Court
for the Western District of Washington

APPELLANT'S OPENING BRIEF

Susan Elder
Federal Public Defender
Westlake Center Office Tower
1601 Fifth Avenue, Suite 700
Seattle, WA 98101
Tel: (206) 555-4321
Counsel for Appellant

TABLE OF CONTENTS

I.   STATEMENT OF JURISDICTION 1

II.   BAIL STATUS 1

III.   STATEMENT OF THE ISSUES 1

IV.   STATEMENT OF THE CASE 1

V.   STATEMENT OF THE FACTS 2

VI.   SUMMARY OF THE ARGUMENT 5

VII.   ARGUMENT 7

        A.   THE ATF AGENTS VIOLATED MR. JOSEPHY'S FOURTH
                AMENDMENT RIGHTS BECAUSE THEY DID NOT HAVE
                A PARTICULARIZED OBJECTIVE SUSPICION THAT
                MR. JOSEPHY WAS ENGAGED IN CRIMINAL ACTIVITY 7

                1.   The ATF agents did not have a particularized objective
                        suspicion that Mr. Josephy was engaged in criminal
                        activity because the tip came from an unknown
                        informant; Although the informant gave the 911
                        operator his name, he refused to give his address or
                        phone number 7

                2.   The ATF agents did not have a particularized objective
                        suspicion that Mr. Josephy was engaged in criminal
                        activity because the tip included only general physical
                        descriptions, it omitted any description of clothing,
                        and the only action it predicted was that Mr. Josephy
                        would be leaving a motel shortly before checkout time 9

                3.   The ATF agents did not have a particularized objective
                        suspicion that Mr. Josephy was engaged in criminal
                        activity because the police corroborated only innocuous
                        details, for example, Mr. Josephy's physical appearance,
                        his vehicle, and his departure from a motel shortly
                        before checkout time 11

        B.   THE DISTRICT COURT ERRED IN DENYING MR. JOSEPHY'S
                BATSON CHALLENGE BECAUSE THE PROSECUTOR STRUCK
                THE ONLY TWO NATIVE AMERICANS IN THE JURY POOL,
                AND THE COURT'S ENTIRE RULING CONSISTED OF A
                SINGLE SENTENCE. 13

1. <u>The reasons the prosecutor gave for striking the only two Native Americans in the jury pool were a pretext for discrimination because they were not supported by the record and the prosecutor did not excuse white jurors who had similar obligations and experiences</u>.................................14

2. <u>In addition, the district court erred by not conducting the required sensitive inquiry and by not stating its reasoning on the record</u>. 18

VIII.   CONCLUSION...19

STATEMENT OF RELATED CASES.......................................20

TABLE OF AUTHORITIES

A. Table of Cases

Alabama v. White, 496 U.S. 325 (1990) 7, 11, 12, 13

Batson v. Kentucky, 476 U.S. 79 (1986) 1, 14, 15, 18

Burks v. Borg, 27 F.3d 1424 (9th Cir. 1994) 17

Florida v. J.L., 529 U.S. 266 (2000) 7, 9, 10, 11

Georgia v. McCollum, 505 U.S. 42 (1992) 13

Gray v. Mississippi, 481 U.S. 648 (1987) 18, 19

Hernandez v. New York, 500 U.S. 352 (1991) 18

Johnson v. California, 545 U.S. 162 (2005) 14

Johnson v. Vasquez, 3 F.3d 1327 (9th Cir. 1993) 14, 15

Jordan v. Lefevre, 206 F.3d 196 (2d Cir. 2000) 18

Illinois v. Gates, 462 U.S. 213 (1983) 7

McClain v. Prunty, 217 F.3d 1209 (9th Cir. 2000) 14, 15, 16

Miller-El v. Dretke, 545 U.S. 231 (2005) 13

Ornelos v. United States, 517 U.S. 690 (1996) 7

Turner v. Marshall, 121 F.3d 1248 (9th Cir. 1997) 16

United States v. Alanis, 335 F.3d 965 (9th Cir. 2003) 18

United States v. Chinchilla, 874 F.2d 695 (9th Cir. 1989) 16

United States v. Fernandez-Castillo, 324 F.3d 1114 (9th Cir. 2003) 7, 10

United States v. Jimenez-Medina, 173 F.3d 752 (9th Cir. 1999) 7

United States v. Morales, 252 F.3d 1070 (9th Cir. 2001) 8

United States v. Terry-Crespo, 356 F.3d 1170 (9th Cir. 2004) 8, 10, 11

United States v. Thomas, 211 F.3d 1186 (9th Cir. 1999) 7

United States v. Vasquez-Lopez, 22 F.3d 900 (9th Cir. 1992) 13, 14

United States v. Velazco-Durazo, 372 F. Supp. 2d 520 (D. Ariz. 2005) 13

United States v. You, 382 F.3d 958 (9th Cir. 2004) 16

Williams v. Runnels, 432 F.3d 1102 (9th Cir. 2006) 14

B. Constitutional Provisions

U.S. Const. amend. IV 7

U.S. Const. amend. XIV 13

C. Statutes

8 U.S.C. § 3231 (2012) 1

21 U.S.C. § 841(a)(1) (2012) 1

28 U.S.C. § 1291 (2012) 1

D. Rules

Fed. R. App. P. 4(b) 1

I. STATEMENT OF JURISDICTION

The appellant, Peter Jason Josephy, appeals his conviction and sentence on one count of unlawful possession of a controlled substance with the intent to deliver in violation of 21 U.S.C. § 841(a)(1) (2012). The district court asserted jurisdiction pursuant to 8 U.S.C. § 3231 (2012) and entered judgment and commitment on January 17, 2013. (CR 34; ER 205).[1] Mr. Josephy filed his notice of appeal on January 24, 2013, within the ten-day period set out in Fed. R. App. P. 4(b). (CR 35). Therefore, this Court has jurisdiction to review Mr. Josephy's final judgment pursuant to 28 U.S.C. § 1291 (2012).

II. BAIL STATUS

Mr. Josephy is currently serving his seventy-seven-month sentence at the Bureau of Prisons' Washington Correctional Institution.

III. STATEMENT OF THE ISSUES

A. Did the district court err in concluding that a telephone tip created an objective particularized suspicion when the informant declined to give more than his name; the informant called from a public pay phone and gave only a general physical description of Mr. Josephy, Mr. Josephy's vehicle, and Mr. Josephy's location; and the police merely corroborated that Mr. Josephy left a motel shortly before checkout time and got into his vehicle?

B. Did the district court err in denying Mr. Josephy's *Batson* challenge when the prosecutor used his peremptory challenges to excuse both Mr. Williams and Ms. Whitefish, the only two Native Americans in the jury pool and, in denying the challenge, the trial judge's only statement was "Your objection is noted, Counsel, but the Court finds no purposeful discrimination here"?

IV. STATEMENT OF THE CASE

On June 26, 2013, Peter Jason Josephy was charged with one count of Unlawful Possession of a Controlled Substance with the Intent to Deliver under 21 U.S.C. § 841(a)(1) (2012). (CR

7). After an evidentiary hearing, the district court denied Mr. Josephy's motion to suppress evidence obtained during a warrantless search. (CR 26; ER 52).

The case proceeded to jury trial, the Honorable Alesha J. Moore presiding. (CR 28). During voir dire, Mr. Josephy challenged the government's use of two of its peremptory challenges to excuse the only two Native Americans on the jury panel. (ER 123-24). The district court concluded that although Mr. Josephy had established a prima facie case of discrimination, the reasons given by the Government were race neutral and that Mr. Josephy had not established purposeful discrimination. (ER 124). Thus, the court denied Mr. Josephy's *Batson* challenge. (ER 125).

V. STATEMENT OF THE FACTS

<u>Motion to Suppress</u>

At 10:45 a.m. on June 25, 2013, Peter Josephy left his room at the Travel House Inn in Bellingham, Washington; checked out; and, after talking to a friend for three or four minutes, walked to his car and got in. (ER 22, 43). As Mr. Josephy started his car, Agent Bhasin, an Alcohol, Tobacco, and Firearms (ATF) agent, pulled behind Mr. Josephy's car, and another ATF agent, Agent O'Brien, pulled in front. As a result, Mr. Josephy could not move his car. (ER 44).

Agent Bhasin had gone to the Travel House Inn after receiving a phone call from a 911 operator who reported that she had received a call from a public pay telephone located in the Bellis Fair Mall, which is about a five-minute drive from the Travel House Inn. (ER 30, 34). The informant claimed that a Mr. Josephy was at the Travel House Inn to sell drugs to a man named Oliver. (ER 30). In addition, the informant told the 911 operator that, if the police wanted to catch Mr. Josephy, they should go to the Travel House Inn soon because Mr. Josephy would be there for only another hour or two. (ER 32-33).

When asked to describe Mr. Josephy, the informant told the 911 operator that Mr. Josephy was a Native American with black hair in his mid to late twenties and that he was driving a blue Chevy Blazer. (ER 32). When asked about Oliver's last name, the informant said that he did not know Oliver's last name. (ER 32) When pushed for a description, the informant told the 911 operator that Oliver was about six feet tall, that he had brown hair and a beard, and that he was in his thirties. (ER 32).

The 911 operator then asked the informant for his name, address, and a phone number so that the police or ATF agents could recontact him. Although the informant told the 911 operator that his name was Zachary Dillon, he then became uncooperative and refused to give the 911 operator his address, his home telephone number, or a cell phone number. (ER 32, 35).

Despite the fact that he was not able to find anyone by the name of Zachary Dillon in his databases, Agent Bhasin went to the Travel House Inn. (ER 42). When he arrived at the motel, Agent Bhasin searched the parking lot and located a blue Chevy Blazer registered to Peter Jason Josephy. (ER 42). After being told by the motel desk clerk that Mr. Josephy was a registered guest and that Josephy had given his vehicle's make, model, and license plate number when he registered, Agent Bhasin returned to his car and requested a backup unit with a dog from the K-9 unit. (ER 42-43).

At about 10:45 a.m. Agent O'Brien arrived with his dog. (ER 43). However, before Agent O'Brien could walk the dog around Mr. Josephy's vehicle, Mr. Josephy left his motel room with another man, went into the office and paid his bill, and walked to his car. (ER 43). As soon as Mr. Josephy got in his car and started it, Agent Bhasin pulled in front of Mr. Josephy's car and Agent O'Brien pulled in behind. (ER 44). Blocked, Mr. Josephy could not move his car. (ER 44).

After blocking Mr. Josephy's car, Agent Bhasin got out of his vehicle and approached the driver's side of Mr. Josephy's Blazer. (ER 45). When Agent Bhasin asked Mr. Josephy to step out of his vehicle, Mr. Josephy readily complied. (ER 46). Mr. Josephy did, however, decline Agent Bhasin's request to search the vehicle. (ER 46-47). In response, Agent O'Brien took his dog out of his car and walked the dog around the Blazer. (ER 47). When the dog alerted to the smell of marijuana, Agent Bhasin arrested Mr. Josephy. (ER 48). During a search incident to the arrest, Agent Bhasin found marijuana in the wheel well. (ER 49).

At the suppression hearing, the district court agreed with Mr. Josephy that a seizure occurred when the agents blocked Mr. Josephy's vehicle with their own vehicles. (CR 26; ER 52). However, the district court denied the motion to suppress on the grounds that, at the time they blocked Mr. Josephy's car, the agents had a reasonable suspicion that Mr. Josephy was engaged in criminal activity. (CR 26-27; ER 52).

Voir Dire

Mr. Josephy is a Native American. (ER 124). The government used two of its peremptory challenges to remove the only two Native Americans in the jury pool. (ER 123-24).

At the beginning of voir dire, a Monday, the trial judge told the jurors that the trial was scheduled to last for two or three days and asked the members of the venire whether this schedule would create a hardship. (ER 115). Two jurors responded. (ER 116). Juror No. 12, Mr. Williams, a Native American, told the judge that he had a tribal council meeting scheduled for the following week but that he could miss the meeting if necessary. (ER 117). Juror No. 18, Mr. Woods, who is white, told the judge that he might have to leave town the following week because his mother had suffered a massive heart attack and the doctors had given her a 20 percent chance of surviving. (ER 117-18).

Later, the prosecutor asked if anyone had ever had negative experiences with law enforcement personnel. (ER 119). Ms. Whitefish, a Native American who was a junior majoring in history at Western Washington University, responded that each time she crossed the border she had been "pulled aside for additional questions." (ER 119). However, when the prosecutor asked Ms. Whitefish whether she was bothered by the fact that she had been pulled over for additional questions, she stated, "Not particularly. I am a college student, and all of us have had similar experiences. They seem to stop young people more. . . ." (ER 119-20).

Similarly, Mr. Martin, a white man with long hair, told the prosecutor that he had had a number of negative experiences with police officers. (ER 120). For example, Mr. Martin told the prosecutor that on one occasion a police officer had stopped him because one of his taillights was out but that the police had not stopped other individuals who had one of their taillights out. (ER 120). In addition, Mr. Martin told the prosecutor that on two occasions he had been given tickets for jaywalking when other individuals on the same street who had short hair jaywalked but did not get tickets. (ER 120). When the prosecutor asked whether he was bothered by the police officers' actions, Mr. Martin said, "You bet I am." (ER 121).

At the end of voir dire, the government used two of its peremptory challenges to remove Mr. Williams and Ms. Whitefish. (ER 122). Because the prosecutor used his peremptory challenges to remove both Native Americans in the jury pool, Mr. Josephy made a *Batson* challenge to the exclusion of the two jurors based on race. (ER 123). Concluding that Mr. Josephy had established a prima facie case of discrimination, the judge asked the prosecutor to provide reasons for his strikes. The prosecutor stated that he struck Juror No. 5, Ms. Whitefish, because he believed that Ms. Whitefish would have difficulty being impartial given her personal experiences at the border, which could lead her to have negative feelings about law enforcement personnel in general. He said that he struck Mr. Williams because Mr. Williams would have difficulty focusing on the facts of the case given his meeting scheduled for the following week. (ER 125).

Mr. Josephy responded, stating that the reasons provided were not neutral and "are only a mask for unconstitutional race . . . discrimination." (ER 125). The trial judge's only statement was, "Your objection is noted, Counsel, but the Court finds no purposeful discrimination here." (ER 126).

VI. SUMMARY OF THE ARGUMENT

Mr. Josephy's conviction should be reversed for two reasons: (1) His Fourth Amendment rights were violated when the district court failed to suppress evidence obtained by police from an investigative detention unsupported by a reasonable suspicion of criminal activity, and (2) his constitutional right to equal protection was violated because the reasons that the prosecutor gave for using his peremptory challenges to excuse the only two Native Americans in the jury pool were a pretext for discrimination.

First, the district court erred in failing to suppress evidence obtained by police following an illegal seizure. At the time that the ATF agents seized Mr. Josephy by pulling their vehicles in front and behind his vehicle, the only information that the agents had came from a telephone tip made from a public pay telephone at a mall. Although the informant gave his name, the tip should be treated as being from an anonymous source: The informant gave no other identifying information, he ensured he could not be located by calling 911 from a public pay telephone at a shopping mall, and the police were unable to locate anyone by the name that he gave in the greater Bellingham area. Because there was no way to assess the caller's reputation or hold him responsible if the tip turned out to be a fabrication, the tip was less reliable than a tip from a known informant.

The tip also lacked sufficient indicia of reliability because it contained only a general description of Mr. Josephy, his location, and his vehicle. Although such information helped the police locate the person the caller accused, it did not show that the caller had information about hidden criminal activity. Moreover, police observations did no more than corroborate innocuous details, such as the time Mr. Josephy would check out of a motel. Because the agents did not have a reasonable suspicion of criminal activity, the investigatory detention was unconstitutional, and all evidence obtained should have been suppressed.

Second, Mr. Josephy's constitutional right to equal protection was violated when the prosecutor used his peremptory challenges to remove the only Native Americans from the jury pool. In denying Mr. Josephy's *Batson* challenge, the district court erred for two reasons. First, the reasons that the prosecutor gave for striking the only two Native Americans in the jury pool were a pretext for discrimination both because the reasons are not supported by the record and because a comparative analysis shows that the prosecutor did not excuse white jurors who had similar obligations and experiences. Second, the district court erred by not doing the "sensitive analysis required" under *Batson* and by not setting out its reasoning on the record. In fact, the trial judge's ruling on this crucial third step of the analysis consisted of only one statement: "Your objection is noted, Counsel, but the Court finds no purposeful discrimination here."

VII. ARGUMENT

A.   THE ATF AGENTS VIOLATED MR. JOSEPHY'S FOURTH AMENDMENT RIGHTS BECAUSE THEY DID NOT HAVE A PARTICULARIZED OBJECTIVE SUSPICION THAT MR. JOSEPHY WAS ENGAGED IN CRIMINAL ACTIVITY.

The district court erred in denying Mr. Josephy's motion to suppress because, at the time that the ATF agents seized Mr. Josephy, they did not have a particularized objective suspicion that Mr. Josephy was engaged in criminal activity. This Court reviews a district court's determination of reasonable suspicion *de novo*. *Ornelos v. United States*, 517 U.S. 690, 699 (1996); *United States v. Fernandez-Castillo*, 324 F.3d 1114, 1117 (9th Cir. 2003).

"The Fourth Amendment allows government officials to conduct an investigatory stop of a vehicle only upon a showing of reasonable suspicion: 'a particularized and objective basis for suspecting the particular person stopped of criminal activity.'" *United States v. Thomas*, 211 F.3d 1186, 1189 (9th Cir. 1999) (quoting *United States v. Jimenez-Medina*, 173 F.3d 752, 754 (9th Cir. 1999)); *see* U.S. Const. amend. IV. In determining whether the government officials had a reasonable suspicion, the courts look at the totality of the circumstances, including whether the informant was a known or unknown informant; whether the tip included sufficient indicia of reliability; and whether the law enforcement officer verified, through an independent investigation, details other than innocuous details. *See, e.g., Alabama v. White*, 496 U.S. 325, 330 (1990); *Illinois v. Gates*, 462 U.S. 213, 238-40 (1983).

1.   The ATF agents did not have a particularized objective suspicion that Mr. Josephy was engaged in criminal activity because the tip came from an unknown informant; although the informant gave the 911 operator his name, he refused to give his address or phone number.

Where an informant declines to be identified, there is a risk the tip has been fabricated, undercutting its reliability. *Florida v. J.L.*, 529 U.S. 266, 269-70, 272 (2000). The unknown informant's reputation cannot be accessed, nor can the informant be held responsible for a false accusation. *Id.* This possibility that the informant might be lying outweighs the value of the information provided unless there are other factors that establish that the informant is reliable, for example, the informant provides law enforcement officers with information

7

about the suspect's future actions, which law enforcement officers then independently verify. *United States v. Morales*, 253 F.3d 1070, 1075 (9th Cir. 2001).

In *United States v. Josephy*, the Court should treat the tip as a tip from an unknown informant. Although the informant gave the 911 operator a name, "Zachary Dillon," he called from a public pay phone in a large mall, and he refused to give the 911 operator his address or phone number. (ER 32, 35). In addition, when Agent Bhasin tried to locate an individual by the name of Zachary Dillon in his databases, he was not able to find anyone by that name in the greater Bellingham area. (ER 42). Consequently, neither Agent Bhasin nor any other law enforcement officer was able to contact Zachary Dillon to determine how he obtained the information that he gave to the 911 operator or to hold him accountable if the statements that he made turned out to be false.

Thus, the facts in this case can be distinguished from the facts in *United States v. Terry-Crespo*, 356 F.3d 1170, 1172 (9th Cir. 2004), a case in which the court held that information provided by an individual who had called 911 to report that the defendant had threatened him with a firearm was sufficient to support a *Terry* stop even though the police were not able to locate anyone by the caller's name in their databases. Unlike the caller in *Terry-Crespo*, who was the victim of a crime, *id.* at 1177, in this case the informant, "Dillon," was not the victim of a crime. In addition, unlike the caller in *Terry-Crespo*, who made the call from the scene of the crime, *id.* at 1176, in this case, "Dillon" made the call from a mall five minutes from the motel where the drug buy was allegedly occurring. Finally, in *Terry-Crespo* the caller did not give the 911 operator his phone number because he did not know the number of the cell phone that he had borrowed to make the emergency call, *id.*, but in this case "Dillon" refused to give the operator his address, home phone number, or a cell phone number. Consequently, in *Terry-Crespo* the facts supported the court's conclusion that the caller was not trying to hide his identity, but in this case the facts suggest just the opposite.

Thus, because "Dillon" appears to have taken steps to hide his identity, this Court should treat his tip as a tip from an unknown informant. However, even if this Court does not treat the tip as coming from an unknown informant, the tip is not reliable because it lacks sufficient indicia of reliability.

> 2. <u>The ATF agents did not have a particularized objective suspicion that Mr. Josephy was engaged in criminal activity because the tip included only general physical descriptions, it omitted any description of clothing, and the only action it predicted was that Mr. Josephy would be leaving a motel shortly before checkout time.</u>

A tip from an unknown informant that does no more than describe an individual's readily observable location and appearance does not have sufficient indicia of reliability to support a stop. *Florida v. J.L.*, 529 U.S. 266, 272 (2000). Although such a tip might help the police identify the person whom the informant means to accuse, such a tip does not establish that the informant has knowledge of concealed criminal activity. *Id.* at 272.

In the cases in which the courts have held that the tip lacked sufficient indicia of reliability, the tip lacked predictive information and included only a general description of the defendant and his location, and the informant did not explain how he had acquired the information. *See, e.g., Florida v. J.L.*, 529 U.S. at 272. For instance, in *J.L.*, an anonymous caller reported to police that "a young black male standing at a particular bus stop and wearing a plaid shirt was carrying a gun." *Id.* at 269. In concluding that this tip was not sufficient to establish a reasonable suspicion of criminal activity, the Court said that "[t]he anonymous call concerning J.L. provided no predictive information and therefore left the police without means to test the informant's knowledge or credibility." *Id.* at 270. The court went on to say that the fact that the allegation about the gun turned out to be true did not establish a reasonable basis for suspecting J.L. of engaging in unlawful conduct:

> The reasonableness of official suspicion must be measured by what the officers knew before they conducted their search. All the police had to go on in this case was the bare report of an unknown, unaccountable informant who neither explained how he knew about the gun nor supplied any basis for believing he had inside information about J.L.

Id. at 271.

In contrast, in most of the cases in which the courts have held that the tips had sufficient indicia of reliability to support a *Terry* stop, the callers were reporting what they had recently

9

seen or experienced, *see, e.g., United States v. Terry-Crespo*, 356 F.3d 1170, 1172 (9th Cir. 2004), or the callers provided the police with not only details about the defendant and his or her current location but also information about what the defendant was about to do, *see, e.g., United States v. Fernandez-Castillo*, 324 F.3d 1114, 1119 (9th Cir. 2003). For example, in *Terry-Crespo*, the court held that a 911 call contained sufficient indicia of reliability for three reasons: (1) The call was not anonymous because the caller provided the 911 operator with his name and the call was recorded; (2) the caller was the victim of a crime, and the police must be able to take seriously, and respond promptly to, emergency 911 calls; and (3) the caller was giving first-hand information about an event that had just occurred. *Terry-Crespo*, 356 F.3d at 1172-77. Similarly, in *Fernandez-Castillo*, the court held that a tip had sufficient reliability because it came from a Montana Department of Transportation (MDOT) employee and there are relatively few MDOT employees; the MDOT employee who reported the erratic driving not only provided the dispatcher with the make and model of the car but also told the dispatcher that the car had North Dakota license plates; the MDOT employee made the report almost immediately after he observed the defendant driving erratically; and the report contained predictive information: that the car was driving eastbound near milepost 116. *Fernandez-Castillo*, 324 F.3d at 1119.

In the case before this Court, the tip lacked the required indicia of reliability. Like the informant in *J.L.*, who called from a borrowed cell phone and did not give the 911 operator either his own phone number or his own address, Mr. Dillon called from a public pay telephone and refused to give the operator his phone number or his address. (ER 30). As a consequence, in both cases law enforcement officers were not able to contact the informants to determine the basis for their allegations or to hold them accountable if the information that they provided turned out to be false.

More important, though, Dillon's tip lacked sufficient indicia of reliability because he failed to give a description of Josephy's clothing, he failed to provide information based on first-hand observation, and he failed to give specific predictive information. First, in *J.L.*, the caller told the operator that the defendant was wearing a plaid jacket; in this case, Dillon did not describe either Mr. Josephy's or Oliver's clothing (ER 32), which suggests that Dillon had not seen Mr. Josephy or Oliver on the day of the call. Second, unlike *Terry-Crespo* and *Fernandez-Castillo*, in which it was clear that the callers were providing first-hand information, in this case, there is nothing to suggest that Dillon's statements were based on his own observations. At no time during the call did Dillon tell the operator how he knew that Mr. Josephy was at the motel or why he believed that Mr. Josephy was involved in illegal activity. (ER 30-35). Third, unlike *Fernandez-Castillo*, in which the caller provided the operator with specific predictive information about the defendant's location and direction of travel, in this case Dillon provided the operator with only general information: that Mr. Josephy was going to leave the motel shortly before checkout time. (ER 32-33). While predicting where a car will be at a given time provides evidence that the tip is reliable, predicting that a guest will check out of a motel at checkout time does not.

Thus, under the totality of the circumstances, the tip did not have the required indicia of reliability and was not, therefore, sufficient to support a *Terry* stop unless the police independently verified more than innocuous details.

3. <u>The ATF agents did not have a particularized objective suspicion that Mr. Josephy was engaged in criminal activity because the police corroborated only innocuous details, for example, Mr. Josephy's physical appearance, his vehicle, and his departure from a motel shortly before checkout time.</u>

When a tip lacks the required indicia of reliability, the tip is not sufficient to support a *Terry* stop unless law enforcement officers independently corroborate more than innocuous details. *See Alabama v. White*, 496 U.S. 325, 330 (1990). As the Court noted in *White*, when a tip has a relatively low degree of reliability, more information will be required to establish the requisite quantum of suspicion than would be required if the tip were more reliable. *Id.*

In *White*, the police received an anonymous tip in which the caller stated that "Vanessa White would be leaving 235-C Lynnwood Terrace Apartments at a particular time in a brown

Plymouth station wagon with the right taillight lens broken, that she would be going to Dobey's Motel, and that she would be in possession of about an ounce of cocaine inside a brown attaché case. *Id.* at 327. After receiving this tip, two police officers went to the Lynnwood Terrace Apartments, where they located a brown Plymouth station wagon with a broken right taillight in the parking lot in front of the 235 building. Id. As the police officers sat in their vehicle, they observed the defendant leave the 235 building, carrying nothing in her hands, and enter the station wagon. *Id.* The officers followed the vehicle as it drove the most direct route to Dobey's Motel. When the vehicle reached the Mobile Highway, on which Dobey's Motel is located, the officers had a patrol unit stop the vehicle. *Id.*

Even though the tip contained a number of details, the United States Supreme Court held that the tip was not, by itself, sufficient to justify a *Terry* stop. *White*, 496 U.S. at 329. According to the Court, it became reasonable to think that the information was reliable only after the police verified not only easily obtained facts but also future actions that are not easily predicted. *Id.* at 332.

> We think it also important that, as in *Gates*, "the anonymous [tip] contained a range of details relating not just to easily obtained facts and conditions existing at the time of the tip, but to future actions of third parties ordinarily not easily predicted." [462 U.S. at 245.] The fact that the officers found a car precisely matching the caller's description in front of the 235 building is an example of the former. Anyone could have "predicted" that fact because it was a condition presumably existing at the time of the call. What was important was the caller's ability to predict respondent's *future behavior*, because it demonstrated inside information — a special familiarity with respondent's affairs.

Id. (emphasis in original).

Although ultimately the Court concluded that the anonymous tip, as corroborated, was sufficient to justify the *Terry* stop, the Court labeled the case as a "close case." *Id.*

If *White* was a close case, this case is an easy case. First, in *White*, the informant provided the police with far more details than Dillon gave the 911 operator. For example, in *White*, the informant provided the police with the defendant's apartment number and the fact that the car had a broken taillight, but in this case Dillon did not provide anything more than the name of the motel and the make and model of the vehicle. (ER 32). Second, in *White*, the informant provided the police with information about the defendant's future actions that only someone who had a special familiarity with the defendant could know, but in this case, Dillon only predicted that Mr. Josephy would leave the motel shortly before checkout time. (ER 32-33). Finally, in *White*, the police independently verified most of the information that the informant had provided, including the fact that the defendant would leave the apartment at a particular time and drive to a particular motel; in this case, the police did not verify anything more than Mr. Josephy owned a vehicle and that he left the motel at checkout time. (ER 42-43).

Although in this case the *Terry* stop might have been justified if Dillon had told the 911 operator that Mr. Josephy would leave the motel and drive to a particular house or restaurant at a particular time, and the ATF agents had verified these facts through their own surveillance, those facts are not the facts of this case. Under the facts of this case, the stop was not justified for three reasons: (1) The tip was, for all practical purposes, an anonymous tip; (2) the tip did not contain sufficient indicia of reliability; and (3) the ATF agents were not able to verify, through their own independent investigation, facts that established a "particularized and objective basis" for suspecting Mr. Josephy of criminal wrongdoing. *See United States v. Velazco-Durazo*, 372 F. Supp. 2d 520, 528 (D. Ariz. 2005).

B. THE DISTRICT COURT ERRED IN DENYING MR. JOSEPHY'S *BATSON* CHALLENGE BECAUSE THE PROSECUTOR STRUCK THE ONLY TWO NATIVE AMERICANS IN THE JURY POOL, AND THE COURT'S ENTIRE RULING CONSISTED OF A SINGLE SENTENCE.

For more than a century, the United States Supreme Court has "consistently and repeatedly . . . reaffirmed that racial discrimination by the State in jury selection offends the Equal Protection Clause." *Miller-El v. Dretke*, 425 U.S. 231, 237 (2005) (quoting *Georgia v. McCollum*, 505 U.S. 42 (1992)); *see also* U.S. Const. amend. XIV. Racial discrimination in jury selection denies defendants their right to a jury trial, denies jurors the right to participate in public life, and undermines public confidence in the fairness of our justice system. *Batson v. Kentucky*, 476 U.S. 79, 86-87 (1986); *Williams v. Runnels*, 432 F.3d 1102, 1108 (9th Cir. 2006). Therefore, the "Constitution forbids striking even a single prospective juror for a discriminatory purpose." *United States v. Vasquez-Lopez*, 22 F.3d 900, 902 (9th Cir. 1992).

In *Batson*, the Court developed a three-step test to uncover discrimination masked by peremptory challenges. 476 U.S. at 96-97. Under the first step of the test, the defendant need only establish a prima facie case of purposeful discrimination by showing that the prosecutor has struck a member of a cognizable class and that the circumstances raise an inference of discrimination. *Id.* at 96. Once the defendant establishes a prima facie case, the burden shifts to the government: the government must provide a race-neutral explanation for striking a member of a cognizable class. *Id.* at 97. If the government does meet its burden, the court must do a sensitive analysis to determine whether the government has engaged in purposeful discrimination. *See Johnson v. California*, 545 U.S. 162, 169 (2005).

In this case, the district court erred when it denied Mr. Josephy's *Batson* challenge for two reasons. First, the district court erred when it concluded that the reasons that the prosecutor gave were not a pretext for discrimination. (ER 126). Second, the district court erred by not doing the "sensitive analysis required" under *Batson* and by not setting out its reasoning on the record. (ER 126).

1. <u>The reasons the prosecutor gave for striking the only two Native Americans in the jury pool were a pretext for discrimination because they were not supported by the record and the prosecutor did not excuse white jurors who had similar obligations and experiences.</u>

When the reasons that a prosecutor gives for striking a juror are not supported by the record, "serious questions about the legitimacy of a prosecutor's reasons for exercising peremptory challenges are raised." *McClain v. Prunty*, 217 F.3d 1209, 1221 (9th Cir. 2000). For example, in *McClain*, this Court determined that the first reason that the prosecutor gave for striking a black juror, that the juror mistrusted the system and had been treated unfairly, was not supported by the record. *Id.* at 1222. Instead of saying that she mistrusted the system and had been treated badly, the juror stated that she did not trust the public defender and, although she initially believed that her son had been treated unfairly, she had changed her mind. *Id.* at 1221. In addition, this Court determined that there was nothing in the record to support the prosecutor's second reason, that the juror must have lied about being a stewardess because she was heavyset. *Id.* The juror did not state that she was a stewardess; what she said was that she worked in airline maintenance. *Id.* Because the record did not support the reasons that the prosecutor gave, this Court held that the reasons that the prosecutor gave were a pretext for discrimination. *Id.*

As in *McClain*, in this case the record does not support the reasons that the prosecutor gave for excusing Mr. Williams and Ms. Whitefish. Although the prosecutor stated that he excused Mr. Williams because Mr. Williams would not be able to focus on the case because he had "other obligations next week," (ER 125), Mr. Williams told the court that he was willing to miss his tribal council meeting should the trial be extended. (ER 117). Similarly, although the prosecutor stated that he excused Ms. Whitefish because her experiences at the border would make it difficult for her "to judge this case fairly and impartially," (ER 125), Ms. Whitefish's response to the prosecutor's question about whether she was bothered by the fact that she had been "pulled aside for additional questions" was the following: "Not particularly. I am a college student, and all of us have had similar experiences. They seem to stop young people more . . . ." (ER 119).

Thus, just as the *McClain* court held that the trial court erred when it concluded that the reasons that the prosecutor gave were not a pretext for discrimination, this Court should decide that the district court erred when it concluded that the prosecutor's reasons were not a pretext for discrimination. "When there is reason to believe that there is a racial motivation for the challenge, [this Court is not] bound to accept at face value a list of neutral reasons that are either unsupported in the record or refuted by it. Any other approach leaves *Batson* a dead letter." *Johnson v. Vasquez*, 3 F.3d 1327, 1331 (9th Cir. 1993).

15

Moreover, the government cannot lawfully exercise peremptory challenges "against potential jurors of one race unless potential jurors of another race with comparable characteristics are also challenged." *United States v. You*, 382 F.3d 958, 969 (2004) (quoting *Turner v. Marshall*, 121 F.3d 1248, 1252 (9th Cir. 1997)). Accordingly, a "comparative analysis of jurors struck and those remaining is a well-established tool for exploring the possibility that facially race-neutral reasons are a pretext for discrimination." *McClain v. Prunty*, 217 F.3d 1209, 1220-21 (9th Cir. 2000).

Under this comparative analysis, a defendant meets his burden of proving the reason the prosecutor gave for striking a juror was a pretext for discrimination when the reason given applies equally to a juror of another race, but the prosecutor strikes only one of the jurors. *McClain v. Prunty*, 217 F.3d 1209, 1221 (9th Cir. 2000). For instance, in *McClain*, this Court concluded that the reason the prosecutor gave for striking a black juror was a pretext for discrimination when the reason given applied equally to a white juror, but the prosecutor did not strike the white juror. Although the prosecutor stated that he had struck a black juror because the juror lacked experience making decisions, the prosecutor did not strike a white juror who also lacked decision-making experience. *Id.* at 1221-22. As the court stated, the fact that the prosecutor did not treat jurors of different races in the same way "fatally undermine[d] the credibility of the prosecutor's stated justification." *Id.* at 1222; *see also United States v. Chinchilla*, 874 F.2d 695 (9th Cir. 1989) (reversing a conviction because the prosecutor's stated reason for striking a Hispanic juror—that the juror lived in La Mesa— applied equally to a juror who was not Hispanic and who was not struck).

In *United States v. Josephy*, the reason the prosecutor gave for striking Mr. Williams, a Native American, was a pretext for discrimination because the reason applied equally to Mr. Woods, who is white. In explaining why he struck Mr. Williams, the prosecutor said that Mr. Williams would have difficulty focusing on the facts of the case because he had a meeting scheduled for the following week. (ER 125). However, the prosecutor did not strike Mr.

16

Woods, who told the court that his mother was seriously ill, that the doctors were giving her a 20 percent chance to live, and that he might have to go out of town. (ER 117-18).

In addition, the reason that the prosecutor gave for striking Ms. Whitefish, a Native American, was a pretext for discrimination because the prosecutor did not strike a white juror who had had similar experiences with law enforcement personnel. When the judge asked the prosecutor why he had struck Ms. Whitefish, the prosecutor responded that he did not think Ms. Whitefish would be able "to judge this case fairly and impartially" based on her experiences crossing the border. (ER 125). However, although Ms. Whitefish stated that she had been "pulled aside for additional questions," (ER 19), when asked whether this bothered her, Ms. Whitefish replied, "Not particularly. I am a college student, and all of us have had similar experiences. They seem to stop young people more . . . ." (ER 119).

In contrast, Mr. Martin believed he had been targeted by police officers because he had long hair. (ER 120). He was stopped for having a taillight that was out; others were not. He was ticketed for jaywalking; others, who had short hair, were not. (ER 119-20). When asked whether he was bothered by his experiences with police officers, he said, "You bet I am." (ER 121).

Although in some cases the courts have concluded that the subjective reasons prosecutors gave for excusing minority jurors were not pretextual even though prospective jurors of different races provided similar responses and one was excused but the other was not, the Court noted, "While subjective factors may play a legitimate role in the exercise of challenges, reliance on such factors alone cannot overcome strong objective indicia of discrimination such as a clear and sustained pattern of strikes against minority jurors." *Burks v. Borg*, 27 F.3d 1424, 1429 (9th Cir. 1994).

In our case, there are objective indicia of discrimination stemming from a clear and sustained pattern of strikes against minority jurors. The prosecutor used two of his peremptory challenges to strike the only two Native American potential jurors. He struck Mr. Williams, who said he had a meeting scheduled after the trial was expected to end, despite his expressed willingness to serve, even if it meant missing the meeting. He struck Ms. Whitefish

17

based on her experiences at the border, even though Ms. Whitefish assured the Court that her experiences at the border did not bother her.

Because the prosecutor did not excuse white jurors who had similar experiences to the Native Americans whom he did strike, the district court erred in denying Mr. Josephy's *Batson* challenge. Such an erroneous denial is presumed to be prejudicial. *See Gray v. Mississippi*, 481 U.S. 648, 668 (1987). Therefore, this Court should reverse and remand the case for a new trial.

2. In addition, the district court erred by not conducting the required sensitive inquiry and by not stating its reasoning on the record.

A trial court commits an error if it fails to conduct "a sensitive inquiry into such circumstantial and direct evidence of intent as may be available," *Batson*, 476 U.S. at 93, or if it fails to show on the record that its decision was deliberate. *United States v. Alanis*, 335 F.3d 965, n.2 (9th Cir. 2003).

A trial court commits reversible error if it fails to do the required "sensitive inquiry" or if the trial court's decision is made in haste or is imprecise. *Jordan v. Lefevre*, 206 F.3d 196, 198 (2d Cir. 2006). In *Jordan*, the trial judge attempted to save "an awful lot of time" by ruling on the defendant's *Batson* challenge without considering all of the facts and arguments and without setting out its analysis in the record. *Id.* at 199. As a result, the reviewing court concluded that the trial court had violated the defendant's right to equal protection by making a hasty decision and not stating on the record its analysis of why the reasons that prosecutor gave for striking jurors were not a pretext for discrimination. *Id.*

As in *Jordan*, in this case the court made a hasty decision and did not state on the record its analysis of why the reasons that the prosecutor gave were not a pretext for discrimination. In fact, the record consists of a single sentence: "Your objection is noted, Counsel, but the Court finds no purposeful discrimination here." (ER 126).

The "duty of assessing the credibility of the prosecutor's race-neutral reasons [embodies] the 'decisive question' in the *Batson* analysis." *Jordan*, 206 F.3d at 200 (citing *Hernandez v. New York*, 500 U.S. 352, 365 (1991)). Although the lack of a reasoned analysis does not seem

18

to stem from a blatant impatience with the proceedings as it did in *Jordan*, the result and the violation are the same: This Court is left with a record devoid of the reasoned credibility analysis regarding each challenged juror that due process requires.

Because the district court's erroneous denial of Mr. Josephy's *Batson* challenge is presumed to be prejudicial, *see Gray*, 481 U.S. at 668, this Court should reverse and remand the case for a new trial.

VIII. CONCLUSION

The district court erred in denying Mr. Josephy's motion to suppress evidence obtained during an investigatory stop unsupported by a reasonable suspicion of criminal activity. Therefore, this Court should reverse his conviction.

In the alternative, the district court erred in denying Mr. Josephy's *Batson* challenge because the prosecutor's reasons for striking the only two Native American jurors on the panel were a pretext for purposeful discrimination and because the district court failed to conduct the required sensitive inquiry or state its reasoning. Therefore, this Court should reverse his conviction and remand the case for a new trial.

Dated: _____

                                        Respectfully submitted,

                                        _____
                                        Susan Elder
                                        Federal Public Defender
                                        Westlake Center Office Tower
                                        1601 Fifth Avenue, Suite 700
                                        Seattle, WA 98101

19

STATEMENT OF RELATED CASES

The appellant knows of no other related cases pending in this Court.

EXAMPLE 2   Appellee's Brief

No. 07-12345

UNITED STATES COURT OF APPEALS

FOR THE NINTH CIRCUIT

_____

UNITED STATES OF AMERICA,

Plaintiff-Appellee,

v.

PETER JASON JOSEPHY,

Defendant-Appellant.

_____

On Appeal from the United States District Court
for the Western District of Washington

_____

BRIEF OF APPELLEE

Andrew Froh
United States Attorney
Western District of Washington
James Jorgenson
Assistant United States Attorney
700 Stewart Street
Seattle, WA 98101
Tel: (206) 555-1234
Counsel for Appellee

TABLE OF CONTENTS

I.   STATEMENT OF JURISDICTION 1

II.   STATEMENT OF THE ISSUES 1

III.   STATEMENT OF THE FACTS 1

IV.   SUMMARY OF THE ARGUMENT 4

V.   ARGUMENT 6

    A.   THE *TERRY* STOP WAS PERMISSIBLE BECAUSE THE ATF
        AGENTS HAD A REASONABLE SUSPICION THAT MR.
        JOSEPHY WAS INVOLVED IN CRIMINAL ACTIVITY 6

    B.   THE DISTRICT COURT PROPERLY EXERCISED ITS
        DISCRETION IN OVERRULING MR. JOSEPHY'S *BATSON*
        OBJECTION 10

        1.   <u>Mr. Josephy has not met his burden of proving that the
            reasons that the prosecutor gave for the peremptory
            challenges were a pretext for purposeful discrimination.</u> 11

        2.   <u>The record establishes that the district court conducted
            the required sensitive inquiry because the court ensured
            that both parties had the opportunity to respond at each
            of the three steps of the *Batson* analysis.</u> 13

VI.   CONCLUSION 14

TABLE OF AUTHORITIES

A. Table of Cases

Alabama v. White, 496 U.S. 325 (1990) 7, 8, 9

Batson v. Kentucky, 476 U.S. 79 (1986) 10, 11

Burks v. Borg, 27 F.3d 1424 (9th Cir. 1994) 12, 13

Florida v. J.L., 529 U.S. 266 (2000) 6, 8

J.E.B. v. Alabama, 511 U.S. 127 (1994) 12

Johnson v. California, 545 U.S. 162 (2005) 11

Jordan v. Lefevre, 206 F.3d 196 (2d Cir. 2000) 13, 14

McClain v. Prunty, 217 F.3d 1209 (9th Cir. 2000) 11

Miller-El v. Dretke, 545 U.S. 231 (2005) 10

United States v. Bauer, 84 F.3d 1549 (9th Cir. 1996) 10, 11

United States v. Fernandez-Castillo, 324 F.3d 1114 (9th Cir. 2003) 6

United States v. Terry-Crespo, 356 F.3d 1170 (9th Cir. 2004) 6, 7, 9, 10

United States v. U.S. Gypsum Co., 333 U.S. 364 (1948) 11

B. Statutes

Wash. Rev. Code § 9A.76.175 (2012) 9

I. STATEMENT OF JURISDICTION

The appellee agrees with the appellant's statement of jurisdiction.

II. STATEMENT OF THE ISSUES

A. Whether police had a reasonable articulable suspicion that Mr. Josephy was engaged in criminal activity when (1) Zachary Dillon called 911 to report that Mr. Josephy was in possession of drugs he planned to sell; (2) Mr. Dillon provided the 911 operator with descriptions of Mr. Josephy, Mr. Josephy's car, and Mr. Josephy's companion; (3) Mr. Dillon told the 911 operator that Mr. Josephy and his companion were at the Travel House Inn and that Mr. Josephy would soon leave the motel in a blue Chevy Blazer; and (4) ATF agents verified that the blue Blazer in the motel parking lot was registered to Mr. Josephy and observed men matching the descriptions that Mr. Dillon had given leave the motel in the predicted time frame.

B. Whether Mr. Josephy failed to prove that the government engaged in purposeful discrimination when (1) the prosecutor excused a 21-year-old Native American juror who volunteered that she had experienced problems each time she had crossed from the United States into Canada and (2) the Government excused both a Native American juror who told the judge that he had a tribal council meeting the following week and a white juror who was worried about missing work.

III. STATEMENT OF THE FACTS

<u>Motion to Suppress</u>

At about 9:30 a.m. on June 25, 2013, Zachary Dillon called 911 and reported that Peter Josephy was involved in selling drugs that had been brought into the United States from Canada. (ER 30). Two hours later, Alcohol, Tobacco, and Firearms (ATF) agents searched Mr. Josephy's vehicle and found four kilos of marijuana in the wheel well. (ER 49).

During the 911 call, which was recorded, Mr. Dillon told the operator that Mr. Josephy was at the Travel House Inn to meet with, and deliver marijuana to, a man named Oliver. (ER 30-31). Although Mr. Dillon declined to give the 911 operator his address or phone

1

number, Mr. Dillon did tell the 911 operator that Mr. Josephy was a Native American, that Josephy had black hair, and that Josephy was in his mid to late twenties. (ER 32). Mr. Dillon also told the operator that Mr. Josephy owned, and was driving, a blue Chevy Blazer. (ER 32). Although Mr. Dillon did not know Oliver's last name, he described Oliver as being in his thirties, about six feet tall, and with brown hair and a beard. (ER 32). Finally, Mr. Dillon told the police not to wait too long because Mr. Josephy would be leaving the motel in the next hour or two. (ER 33).

The 911 operator relayed the information from Mr. Dillon to Agent Bhasin, an ATF agent with more than ten years of service. (ER 4). Not finding anyone by the name of Zachary Dillon in the ATF databases, Agent Bhasin drove to the Travel House Inn in an unmarked car to determine whether there was a blue Chevy Blazer in the parking lot. (ER 35, 40). When he arrived at the motel at approximately 10:15 a.m., Agent Bhasin located a blue Chevy Blazer in the parking lot; when he ran the license plates, he was told that the Blazer was registered to Peter Jason Josephy. (ER 42).

After confirming with the desk clerk not only that the blue Chevy Blazer in the parking lot was registered to Josephy but also that Josephy was a registered guest, Agent Bhasin called for backup and a K-9 unit. (ER 43).

Agent O'Brien arrived with his dog in an unmarked car at about 10:45 a.m. (ER 43). However, before Agent O'Brien could walk his dog around the Blazer, Agents Bhasin and O'Brien saw two men matching the descriptions of Josephy and Oliver come out of a motel room. (ER 43). The man matching Oliver's description walked out of the parking lot. (ER 44). The other man, who was later confirmed to be Peter Josephy, walked to the blue Blazer. (ER 43).

Based on Dillon's tip and his own observations, Agent Bhasin believed Mr. Josephy had possession of a controlled substance with intent to deliver. (ER 44). Therefore, when Mr. Josephy got into the Blazer and started the engine, Agent Bhasin pulled in front of Josephy's car, and Agent O'Brien pulled behind. (ER 44). Although Josephy complied with Agent Bhasin's request to get out of the Blazer, Josephy refused the request for permission to search the Blazer. (ER 46). As a consequence, Agent O'Brien walked his dog around the Blazer. (ER 46-7). After the dog alerted, Agent Bhasin arrested Mr. Josephy for possession of a controlled substance. (ER 49). During a search incident to the arrest, Agent Bhasin found the four kilos of marijuana. (ER 49).

After a pretrial hearing, the district court denied Mr. Josephy's motion to suppress, concluding that the *Terry* stop was justified because Agent Bhasin had a reasonable suspicion that Mr. Josephy was engaged in criminal conduct. (CR 26-27; ER 52).

Voir Dire

Out of a venire of twenty-four potential jurors, twelve jurors and one alternate were chosen by use of the Struck Jury Method. (ER 130). After Judge Moore explained the selection process to the jurors (ER 113-15), she asked whether serving on the jury would create a hardship. (ER 116). Juror No. 12, Mr. Williams, indicated that, although he could forego attending a tribal council meeting scheduled for Thursday and Friday, he would prefer not to. (ER 117). In addition, Juror No. 2, Mr. Feldman, told the judge that he was scheduled to go to Africa on the following Saturday and that his "boss would be unhappy if he did not finish some projects before he left." (ER 117). However, Mr. Feldman also told the judge that his boss would have to accept it if he was selected for the jury. (ER 117). Finally, Juror No. 18, Mr. Woods, revealed that his mother had recently had a heart attack, that the doctors had given her a 20 percent chance of surviving, and that he was unsure whether he would have to go out of town the next week to attend to her. (ER 117-18). None of these jurors were excused for cause. (ER 118).

During voir dire, the prosecutor asked the members of the jury panel whether anyone had had a negative experience with a law enforcement officer. (ER 119). Juror No. 5, a young Native American, responded that she had negative experiences each time she crossed the border between the United States and Canada. (ER 119). Although Juror No. 5 stated that she was not bothered by her experiences at the border, she also stated that she had been pulled aside for additional questioning every time that she had crossed the border. (ER 119).

3

In contrast, Juror No. 11, Mr. Martin, a white man in his forties with long hair, told the prosecutor that he had been stopped by the police on one occasion because he had a taillight out and on two other occasions because he was jaywalking. (ER 120). Although Mr. Martin said that he was bothered by the fact that he had been stopped by the police, he also said he felt that police officers tended to stop people with long hair more often than people with short hair. (ER 120).

After defense counsel questioned the jury, both the prosecutor and defense counsel were permitted to exercise their peremptory challenges. (ER 122). The prosecutor excused Mr. Feldman, Ms. Whitefish, and Mr. Williams. (ER 122).

At sidebar, defense counsel objected to the prosecutor's use of his peremptory challenges on the grounds that they were based on race, arguing that the prosecutor had excused Mr. Williams and Ms. Whitefish because they were Native Americans. (ER 123). After a hearing outside the presence of the jury, Judge Moore concluded that Mr. Josephy had established a prima facie case for racial discrimination and asked the prosecutor to explain why he had used his peremptory challenges to excuse Mr. Williams and Ms. Whitefish. (ER 124). The prosecutor explained that he excused both Mr. Feldman and Mr. Williams because he thought they would be unable to keep their minds on the case because of their other obligations — namely, Feldman's trip to Africa and Williams's tribal council meeting. (ER 125). The prosecutor then explained that he had excused Ms. Whitefish because her experiences at the border would make it difficult for her to remain impartial. (ER 125).

The judge ruled that these explanations were race neutral and that Josephy had not met his burden of proving that the reasons that the prosecutor had given were a pretext for discrimination. (ER 125). Thus, based on these facts and explanations, Judge Moore overruled the *Batson* objection. (ER 126).

IV. SUMMARY OF THE ARGUMENT

Mr. Josephy's conviction should be affirmed: The district court correctly concluded that the evidence obtained during an investigatory stop was admissible because Agent Bhasin had

4

a reasonable suspicion that Mr. Josephy was involved in criminal activity, and the district court properly exercised its discretion in finding that Mr. Josephy did not meet his burden of establishing that the reasons that the prosecutor gave for using two of his peremptory challenges to excuse Mr. Williams and Ms. Whitefish were a pretext for discrimination.

First, the district court correctly concluded that, under the totality circumstances, the *Terry* stop was permissible because Agent Bhasin had a reasonable suspicion that Mr. Josephy was engaged in criminal activity. The informant, Zachary Dillon, gave the 911 operator his name; Mr. Dillon's 911 call was recorded and transcribed; Mr. Dillon provided the 911 operator not only with a description of Mr. Josephy, Mr. Josephy's car, and Mr. Josephy's companion but also with the name of the motel where Mr. Josephy was staying; Mr. Dillon predicted when Mr. Josephy would leave the motel; and Agent Bhasin verified that Mr. Josephy was staying at the motel, that the vehicle found in the parking lot was registered to Mr. Josephy, and that men matching the descriptions given by Mr. Dillon left the motel during the time frame that Mr. Dillon had predicted.

Second, the district court properly exercised its discretion in denying Mr. Josephy's *Batson* objection based on a finding that Mr. Josephy failed to meet his burden of showing discrimination in the prosecutor's use of peremptory challenges. Peremptory challenges are an important trial tool that permits both parties' counsel to use their professional judgment and educated hunches about individual jurors to ensure a fair and impartial jury. As a result, a *Batson* violation is not established whenever prospective jurors of different races provide similar responses and one is excused but the other is not. Thus, in this case, the district court correctly found that the prosecutor's reasons for exercising peremptory challenges were not a pretext for discrimination. The prosecutor excused one juror because he was concerned that the juror would be distracted by his outside obligations, and the prosecutor excused the second juror because he was concerned that the juror's negative experiences when crossing the border would affect her ability to judge the Government's case fairly. In addition, the district court did the required analysis, and the record supports its conclusion that no *Batson* violation occurred. The court allowed Mr. Josephy to present his prima facie case and then asked the prosecutor to explain his reasons for excusing the jurors before stating that Mr. Josephy had not met his burden of proof.

V. ARGUMENT

A.   THE *TERRY* STOP WAS PERMISSIBLE BECAUSE THE ATF AGENTS HAD A REASONABLE SUSPICION THAT MR. JOSEPHY WAS INVOLVED IN CRIMINAL ACTIVITY.

Both the United States Supreme Court and this Court have repeatedly held that law enforcement officers have the authority to conduct an investigatory stop anytime they have a reasonable suspicion that a suspect is engaged in criminal activity. *See, e.g., Florida v. J.L.*, 529 U.S. 266, 272 (2000); *United States v. Fernandez-Castillo*, 324 F.3d 1114, 1119 (9th Cir. 2003). In addition, both the United States Supreme Court and this Court have repeatedly held that evidence obtained during a permissible *Terry* stop is admissible. *J.L.*, 529 U.S. at 272; *Fernandez-Castillo*, 324 F.3d at 119.

In determining whether a *Terry* stop was permissible, the courts do a de novo review, looking at the totality of the circumstances and considering all relevant factors, including those factors that "in a different context, might be entirely innocuous." *Florida v. J.L.*, 529 U.S. at 277-78; *accord United States v. Terry-Crespo*, 356 F.3d 1170, 1172 (9th Cir. 2004). For example, in *Terry-Crespo*, this Court held that the informant's preliminary phone call was, by itself, sufficient to establish a reasonable suspicion that the defendant, Terry-Crespo, was engaged in criminal activity. *Id.* at 1172. In doing so, this Court rejected Terry-Crespo's argument that the informant, Mr. Domingis, should be treated as an anonymous informant because he was not able to provide the 911 operator with the number of the phone from which he placed the call; he changed the subject when the operator asked him to provide another number; and, when asked for his location, he gave the operator a nonexistent intersection. *Id.* at 1174-75. As the court stated in its opinion,

> [d]uring the course of the 911 call, the operator asked Mr. Domingis for his telephone number. Mr. Domingis explained that he did not know the return number because

6

> he was calling from someone else's cellular telephone. When the operator asked if there was another number where she could reach him, he did not answer her question but returned to discussing the subject of the suspect's location. The operator asked Mr. Domingis for his location. Initially, he responded by providing a nonexistent intersection on Portland's grid system and then stammeringly told the operator that "I don't want . . . . I don't want . . . . I don't want . . . ." While not certain, it appears that Mr. Domingis did not want police contact.

Id. at 1172.

The Court then went on to note that, although the police tried to locate Mr. Domingis in a number of different databases, including the Yahoo! databases, they were not able to locate anyone by that name. *Id.* However, the Court concluded that the tip had sufficient indicia of reliability because Mr. Domingis was reporting that he had just been the victim of a crime and because Mr. Domingis risked any anonymity that he might have enjoyed by giving the 911 operator his name during a recorded call. *Id.* at 1174-76. As the Court stated, "Merely calling 911 and having a recorded telephone conversation risks the possibility that the police could trace the call or identify Mr. Domingis by his voice." *Id.* at 1176. Thus, even though the police did not independently verify any of the information contained in the tip, the court held that, under the totality of the circumstances, the tip was sufficient to support a finding that Terry-Crespo was engaged in criminal activity. *Id.* at 1177.

Similarly, in *Alabama v. White*, 496 U.S. 325, 330 (1990), the United States Supreme Court held that the police had a reasonable suspicion that the defendant, White, was engaged in criminal activity. In *White*, an anonymous caller phoned 911 and told the operator that Vanessa White would be leaving the Lynnwood Terrace Apartments at a particular time in a brown Plymouth station wagon with a broken taillight to go to Dobey's Motel. *Id.* at 327. In addition, the caller told the 911 operator that White would have about "an ounce of cocaine inside a brown attaché case." *Id.* Although the two police officers who went to the apartment complex saw White get into a brown Plymouth station wagon with a broken taillight, they did not see anything in White's hands. *Id.* Moreover, although White appeared to be driving to Dobey's Motel, the officers had a patrol unit stop the vehicle before it reached the motel. *Id.*

7

The Court held that the officers had a reasonable suspicion despite failing to verify White's predicted destination. *Id.* at 330.

In considering the totality of the circumstances, the Court noted that "the anonymous [tip] contained a range of details relating not just to easily obtained facts and conditions existing at the time of the tip, but to future actions of third parties ordinarily not easily predicted." As the Court stated,

> The general public would have had no way of knowing that respondent would shortly leave the building, get in the described car, and drive the most direct route to Dobey's Motel. Because only a small number of people are generally privy to an individual's itinerary, it is reasonable for police to believe that a person with access to such information is likely to also have access to reliable information about that individual's illegal activities. See ibid. When significant aspects of the caller's predictions were verified, there was reason to believe not only that the caller was honest but also that he was well informed, at least well enough to justify the stop.

Id. at 332.

In contrast, in *Florida v. J.L.*, the court held that the officers did not have a reasonable suspicion that the defendant, a minor, was engaged in criminal activity. *Id.* at 271. In *J.L.*, the only information the officers had at the time they stopped J.L. was a tip from an anonymous caller reporting that a "young black male standing at a particular bus stop and wearing a plaid shirt was carrying a gun." *Id.* at 269. Two officers were dispatched to the bus stop and, when they arrived, they saw three black males, one of whom was wearing a plaid shirt. *Id.* The officers did not, however, see a firearm, and J.L. made no threatening or otherwise unusual movements. *Id.* In concluding that, under the totality of the circumstances, the officers did not have a reasonable suspicion that J.L. was involved in criminal conduct, the Court considered three factors: (1) That the tip came from an individual who did not give his name; (2) that the call was not recorded; and (3) that the call did not contain any predictive information that would have allowed the police "to test the informant's knowledge or credibility." *Id.* at 270-72.

In contrast, in this case, under the totality of the circumstances, Agent Bhasin had a reasonable suspicion that Mr. Josephy was engaged in criminal activity.

First, like the caller in *Terry-Crespo*, in this case, the caller gave the 911 operator his name: Zachary Dillon. (ER 30). Although the ATF agents were not able to locate anyone by that name in their databases (ER 42), the same was true in *Terry-Crespo*, and in *Terry-Crespo*, the court concluded that a tip was not turned into an anonymous tip simply because the police officers were unable to find anyone by the informant's name in their databases.

Second, like the 911 call in *Terry-Crespo*, in this case the 911 call was recorded and transcribed. (ER 30). As a result, there is no risk that the tip was manufactured after the fact. *See id.* at 1175. In addition, the fact that Mr. Dillon gave his name in a recorded call subjected Mr. Dillon to the risk that the police could locate him and that, if he had provided false information, he would be subjected to criminal sanctions. Wash. Rev. Code § 9A.76.175 (2012).

Third, like the caller in *White*, in this case, Mr. Dillon provided the 911 operator with a number of details. For example, Mr. Dillon provided the operator not only with a physical description of Josephy, but also with a physical description of the man Josephy was meeting. (ER 32). Moreover, Mr. Dillon gave the operator the make, model, and color of Josephy's car and the name of the motel where Mr. Josephy was staying. (ER 30, 32). Although there may be a number of individuals who could provide the police with a description of a particular individual and his car, only a small number of people are generally privy to an individual's itinerary.

Fourth, as in *White*, in which the caller predicted that White would be leaving the apartment complex at a particular time, in this case, Mr. Dillon predicted that Josephy would be leaving the motel within an hour or two. (ER 33). That the time frame that Mr. Dillon provided coincides with the standard checkout time is not dispositive. Many motel guests check out long before the established checkout time, and many guests stay more than one night.

Finally, in this case the ATF agents verified all of the information that Mr. Dillon provided. As a consequence, the facts in this case are stronger than the facts in *Terry-Crespo*, in which the officers did not independently verify any of the information in the tip, and they are stronger than the facts in *White*, in which the officers did not see White carrying a brown attaché case and did not verify that she was in fact going to the motel.

9

Taken together, these factors establish that, under the totality of the circumstances, the tip was far more reliable than the tip in *J.L.*, in which the caller did not give his name, provided the police with only a general description of J.L., and did not provide the police with any predictive information. In fact, these factors establish that, under the totality of the circumstances, the tip is even more reliable than the tip in *Terry-Crespo*. In *Terry-Crespo*, Mr. Domingis reported that Terry-Crespo assaulted him, but the police did not independently verify this fact or any of the other information contained in the tip, and Mr. Domingis appears to have tried to hide from the police by changing the topic when asked for his phone number, by giving a nonexistent intersection as his location, and by making statements that suggested that he did not want the police to contact him. *Id.* 1172.

Because the totality of the circumstances establish that Agent Bhasin had a reasonable suspicion to believe that Mr. Josephy was engaged in criminal activity, the stop was permissible and the Court should affirm the district court's denial of Mr. Josephy's motion to suppress.

B.   THE DISTRICT COURT PROPERLY EXERCISED ITS DISCRETION IN OVER-
RULING MR. JOSEPHY'S *BATSON* OBJECTION.

Peremptory challenges are an important trial tool that permits both parties' counsel to use their professional judgment and educated hunches about individual jurors to select a fair and impartial jury. *United States v. Bauer*, 84 F.3d 1549, 1555 (9th Cir. 1996). While the Supreme Court has acknowledged difficulties in balancing the need to protect constitutional rights with the proper use of peremptory challenges, the Court has not indicated a willingness to deprive the parties of their right to use peremptory challenges. *See Miller-El v. Dretke*, 545 U.S. 231, 239-40 (2005). Indeed, Justice Breyer's concurrence, in which he posited that the Court should reconsider the *Batson* test and the peremptory system as a whole, failed to garner a single co-signer. *Id.* at 266-67 (Breyer, J., concurring).

Thus, the courts continue to apply the three-step test set out in *Batson*. *Batson*, 476 U.S. 79, 89, 96-98 (1986). Under the test, a defendant's rights are not violated unless (1) the defendant establishes a prima facie case of purposeful discrimination in the government's use of

10

peremptory challenges by showing that the challenged juror is a member of a cognizable class and that the circumstances raise an inference of discrimination; and (2) the government fails to meet its burden to provide a race-neutral explanation for its strike; or (3) the government offers a race-neutral reason, but the defendant meets his burden of showing that a review of all relevant circumstances shows purposeful discrimination. *See Johnson v. California*, 545 U.S. 162, 169 (2005); *Batson v. Kentucky*, 476 U.S. at 89, 96-98.

In the case before the court, Mr. Josephy has not argued that the district court erred in deciding that the reasons the prosecutor gave for exercising the peremptory challenges were not facially neutral. Thus, the only issues before this Court are whether the district court properly concluded that Mr. Josephy had not met his burden of proving that the reasons the prosecutor gave for exercising the peremptory challenges were a pretext for discrimination and whether the record is adequate.

1. Mr. Josephy has not met his burden of proving that the reasons that the prosecutor gave for the peremptory challenges were a pretext for purposeful discrimination.

In reviewing the third step in the *Batson* analysis, appellate courts give great deference to the trial court's determination and reverse a trial court only when the appellate court has a "definite and firm conviction" that a mistake has been made. *United States v. U.S. Gypsum Co.*, 333 U.S. 364, 395 (1948); *Bauer*, 84 F.3d 1555. While such a mistake occurs when the record contradicts the prosecutor's stated reasoning, *see, e.g., McClain v. Prunty*, 217 F.3d 1209, 1220-21 (9th Cir. 2000), in this case there is no such contradiction.

United States v. Josephy stands in stark contrast to *McClain*, where a review of the record revealed a clear contradiction in objectively verifiable facts. *Id.* In *McClain*, the first reason the prosecutor gave for excusing a black juror was that the juror had stated that she mistrusted the system and had been treated unfairly. *Id.* at 1221. In fact, what the juror said was that her son did not trust the public defender and that, although she initially believed that her son had been treated unfairly, this was no longer true. *Id.* In addition, the record contradicted the second reason the prosecutor gave for striking the juror. *Id.* Although the prosecutor stated that he was excusing the juror because she had lied about being a stewardess because she was heavyset, the juror had actually said she worked in airline maintenance. *Id.*

In contrast, in *United States v. Josephy*, the record supports the reasons that the prosecutor gave for excusing Mr. Williams and Ms. Whitefish. When asked why he had excused Mr. Williams, the prosecutor stated that he was concerned that, because Mr. Williams had a tribal council meeting scheduled for the following week, Mr. Williams might be distracted. (ER 125). The record supports this explanation: Mr. Williams told that court that although he could forego attending a tribal council meeting scheduled for the following week, he would prefer not to. (ER 117). Similarly, the prosecutor excused Ms. Whitefish because the prosecutor believed she would be unable "to judge this case fairly and impartially" based on her prior experiences crossing the border. (ER 125). The record supports the prosecutor's reason: Ms. Whitefish acknowledged that she had been subjected to additional questioning at the border. (ER 119).

Furthermore, case law does not support the notion that *Batson* is violated whenever prospective jurors of different races provide similar responses and one is excused but the other is not. *Burks v. Borg*, 27 F.3d 1424, 1429 (9th Cir. 1994). For example, in *Burks*, this Court held that there was not purposeful discrimination in spite of the fact that a minority juror who was struck shared characteristics with a nonminority juror who was not struck. *Id.* The prosecutor told the court that he had stricken the minority jurors "because they were 'squishy' on the death penalty, expressed a reluctance to serve, and/or lacked certain life experiences." *Id.* In concluding that there was no purposeful discrimination, this Court reaffirmed that "[t]rial counsel is entitled to exercise his full professional judgment in pursuing his client's 'legitimate interest in using [peremptory] challenges . . . to secure a fair and impartial jury.'" *Id.* (quoting *J.E.B. v. Alabama*, 511 U.S. 127 (1994)). Thus, in using his or her peremptory challenges, trial counsel is entitled to take into account "tone, demeanor, facial expression, emphasis — all those factors that make the words uttered by the prospective juror convincing or not." *Burks*, 27 F.3d at 1429.

12

In this case, such a comparison supports the district court's decision that there was no purposeful discrimination. For example, in response to the trial judge's question regarding other obligations, three jurors answered that they had conflicts the following week, and all stated a willingness to still serve on the jury. (ER 117-18). The prosecutor used two of his peremptory challenges against the two jurors who already had definite plans — one had a tribal council meeting and the other was going to Africa. (ER 117). In addition, the prosecutor provided the same neutral reason for both strikes — that the jurors would be too distracted to tend to the business of the jury. (ER 125). Therefore, the prosecutor acted consistently: He struck the two jurors who had definite plans for the following week, and he did not strike the one whose plans were not definite. Finally, in making his decision, the prosecutor was allowed to consider factors that are difficult to discern from a paper record, for example, the demeanor of each of the potential jurors.

Likewise, the district court did not err in concluding that the prosecutor had not engaged in purposeful discrimination when he excused Ms. Whitefish but not Mr. Martin. Although both Ms. Whitefish and Mr. Martin volunteered that they had negative experiences with law enforcement personnel, there may have been other factors that influenced the prosecutor in his decision about how to use his peremptory challenges. For example, the prosecutor may have taken into consideration Ms. Whitefish's young age or limited set of experiences. Because this type of judgment call is not based on race, it falls well within the purpose behind peremptory challenges of providing a "useful instrument for molding a more impartial jury." *See Burks*, 27 F.3d at 1429.

2. The record establishes that the district court conducted the required sensitive inquiry because the court ensured that both parties had the opportunity to respond at each of the three steps of the *Batson* analysis.

Mr. Josephy's reliance on *Jordan v. Lefevre*, 206 F.3d 196, 198 (2d Cir. 2000), is misplaced: In this case, the district court did the required analysis, and the record is sufficient.

In *Jordan*, the defendant objected to the prosecutor's use of his peremptory challenges to strike several black jurors. *Id.* at 199. However, before the defendant could even make

13

his prima facie case, the court cut him short "in order to save us an awful lot of time." *Id.* Instead, the trial court immediately asked the prosecutor for a "non-racial reason for exercising the challenges," prefacing the request with a statement that "I don't think it's necessary or required." *Id.*

The prosecutor gave neutral reasons, and the trial court summarily overruled the defendant's objection, stating only, "to the extent there is any application [on] the *Batson*, I'm denying it. It seems to me there is some rational basis for the exercise of the challenge." *Id.* When defense counsel later tried to create a record, the trial judge told him, "You've already made your record." *Id.* When defense counsel made a second objection, arguing that "the record is not complete," the judge replied "do it very succinctly, because I'm not going to be spending more time in here listening to you." *Id.* Given this specific set of facts, the Court of Appeals agreed with the defendant that "the district court's conclusory statement that the prosecutor's explanations were race neutral did not satisfy *Batson*'s third step." *Id.* at 200.

In contrast, in this case, the district court allowed Mr. Josephy to present his prima facie case and then asked the prosecutor to explain why he had excused Mr. Williams and why he had excused Ms. Whitefish. (ER 123-24). It was not until after the prosecutor had set out his reason that the district court judge stated that Mr. Josephy had not met his burden of proof. (ER 125-26). Therefore, in this case, the district court did the required analysis, and the record supports its conclusion.

VI. CONCLUSION

For the reasons set out above, the Government respectfully requests that the Court of Appeals affirm the district court. The district court properly denied the motion to suppress because the investigatory stop was supported by a reasonable suspicion that Mr. Josephy was involved in drug trafficking. In addition, the district court properly overruled the *Batson* objection because it properly found that Mr. Josephy failed to meet his burden of proving

purposeful discrimination.

Dated: _____   Respectfully submitted,

                                                   _____

                                                   Andrew Froh
                                                   United States Attorney
                                                   Western District of Washington
                                                   James Jorgenson
                                                   Assistant United States Attorney
                                                   700 Stewart Street
                                                   Seattle, WA 98101
                                                   Tel: (206) 555-1234
                                                   Counsel for Appellee

Oral Advocacy

Oral argument. For some, it is the part of practice they most enjoy; for others, it is the part they most dread.

Whichever group you fall into, oral argument is probably not what you expect. It is not a speech, a debate, or a performance. Instead, when done right, it is a dialogue between the attorneys and the judges. The attorneys explain the issues, facts, and law, and the judges ask questions, not because they want to badger the attorney or because they want to see how much he or she knows, but because they want to make the right decision.

§ 19.1   Audience

In making an oral argument, who is your audience? At the trial court level, the audience is the trial judge who is hearing the motion; at the appellate level, it is the panel of judges hearing the appeal. In both instances, the audience is extremely sophisticated. Although an eloquent oral argument is more persuasive than an oral argument that is not eloquent, form seldom wins out over substance. If you do not have anything to say, it does not matter how well you say it.

At oral argument, the court can be either "hot" or "cold." The court is hot when the judges come to the oral argument prepared. The judges have studied the briefs and, at least in some appellate courts, have met in a pre-oral argument conference to discuss the case. In contrast, a cold court is not as prepared. The judge or judges are not familiar with the case, and if they have read the briefs, they have done so only quickly.

As a general rule, hot courts are more active than cold courts. Because they have studied the briefs, they often have their own agenda. They want to know more about point A, or they are concerned about how the rule being advocated might be applied in other cases. As a consequence, they often take more control over the argument, directing counsel to discuss certain issues and asking a number of questions. A cold court is usually comparatively passive. Because the judges are not as familiar with the case, most of their questions are informational. They want counsel to clarify the issue, supply a fact, or explain in more detail how the law should be applied.

§ 19.2   Purpose

In making your oral argument, you have two goals: to educate and to persuade. You want to explain the law and the facts in such a way that the court rules in your client's favor.

§ 19.3   Preparing for Oral Argument

The key to a good oral argument is preparation. You must know what you must argue to win; you must know the facts of your case and the applicable constitutional provisions, statutes, regulations, and cases; and you must have practiced both the text of your argument and your responses to the questions the court can reasonably be expected to ask.

§ 19.3.1   Deciding What to Argue

In making your argument, you will have only a limited amount of time. Depending on the case and the court, you will be granted ten, fifteen, or thirty minutes to make your points; answer the judge or judges' questions; and, if you are the appellant, to make your rebuttal. Because time is so limited, you will not be able to make every argument that you made in your brief. You must be selective.

> **PRACTICE POINTER** In selecting the issues and arguments that you will make, choose those that are essential to your case. Do not spend your time on the easy argument if, to get the relief you want, you must win on the hard one. Make the arguments that you must make in order to win.

Also anticipate the arguments that the other side is likely to make. Although you do not want to make the other side's arguments for your opponent, try to integrate your responses to the other side's arguments into your argument. Similarly, anticipate the court's concerns and decide how they can best be handled.

§ 19.3.2 Preparing an Outline

Do not write out your argument. If you do, you will either read it or, perhaps worse yet, memorize and recite it. Neither is appropriate. A dialogue does not have a predetermined text. Instead, prepare either a list of the points you want to cover or create an outline.

Because it is difficult to predict how much of the oral argument time will be spent answering the court's questions, many advocates prepare two lists or outlines: a short version, in which they list only those points that they must make, and a long version, in which they list the points they would like to make if they have time. If the court is hot and asks a number of questions, they argue from the short list or outline; if the court is cold, they use the long one.

§ 19.3.3 Practicing the Argument

The next step is to practice, both by yourself and with colleagues. Working alone, practice your opening, your closing, your statements of the law, and the arguments themselves. Think carefully about the language you will use and about how you will move from one issue to the next and, within an issue, from argument to argument. Also list every question that you could reasonably expect a judge to ask and decide (1) how you will respond and (2) how you can move from the answer to another point in your argument.

Then, with colleagues, practice delivering the argument. Ask your colleagues to play the role of the judge, sometimes asking almost no questions and at other times asking many. As you deliver the argument, concentrate on "reading" the court, adjusting your argument to meet its concerns. You should also focus on responding to questions and on the transitions between issues and arguments. Before a major argument, you will want to go through your argument five to ten times, practicing in front of as many different people as you can.

§ 19.3.4 Reviewing the Facts and the Law

You will also want to review the facts of the case, the law, and both your brief and your opponent's brief. When you walk into the courtroom, you should know everything there is to know about your case.

> **PRACTICE POINTER** In practice, months might pass between the writing of an appellate brief and the oral argument. When this is the case, it is essential that you update your research, and, when appropriate, file a supplemental brief with the court.

§ 19.3.5 Organizing Your Materials

Part of the preparation is getting your materials organized. You do not want to be flipping through your notes or searching the record during oral argument.

a. Notes or Outline

To avoid the "flipping-pages syndrome," limit yourself to two pages of notes: a one-page short list or outline, and a one-page long list or outline, which you can staple to the inside of a manila folder. Use colored markers to highlight the key portions of the argument.

b. The Briefs

You will want to take a copy of your brief and your opponent's brief with you to the podium, placing them on the inside shelf. Make sure that you know both what is in the briefs and where that information is located.

c. The Record

In arguing an appeal, you will usually want to have the relevant portions of the record in the courtroom, either on the podium shelf or on counsel table. You should also be fully familiar with the record, as with the briefs, knowing both what is in the record and where particular information can be found. Many attorneys tab the record or prepare a quick index so that they can locate information quickly.

d. The Law

Although you do not need to have copies of all of law with you, you should be familiar with the constitutional provisions, statutes, regulations, cases, and court rules you cited in your brief and those on which your opponent's case is based. If you do bring cases with you, have them indexed and highlighted for quick reference.

§ 19.4   Courtroom Procedures and Etiquette

Like much of law, oral argument has its own set of conventions and procedures.

§ 19.4.1 Seating

In many jurisdictions, the appellant, or moving party, sits on the left (when facing the court) and the respondent, or responding party, sits on the right.

§ 19.4.2 Before the Case Is Called

If court is not in session, sit at counsel table, reviewing your notes or quietly conversing with co-counsel. If court is in session, sit in the audience until the prior case is completed. When your case is called, rise and move to counsel table.

§ 19.4.3 Courtroom Etiquette

Stand each time you are instructed to do so by the bailiff. For example, stand when the bailiff calls court into session and announces the judge or judges, and stand when court is recessed or adjourned. In the first instance, remain standing until the judges are seated, and in the latter instance, remain standing until the judges have left the courtroom.

Also stand each time you address the court, whether it be to tell the court that you are ready to proceed, to make your argument, or to respond to a question.

In addressing the court, you will want to use the phrases "Your Honor," "Your Honors," "this Court," "the Court," or, occasionally, the judge's name — for example, "Judge Brown" or "Justice Smith." Never use a judge's or justice's first name.

> **PRACTICE POINTER**　The title judge or justice can vary depending on your jurisdiction and on whether you are in an intermediate court or the jurisdiction's highest court. Make sure that you are using the correct title to address the members of the bench.

Finally, during the argument, do not speak directly to opposing counsel. Instead, address all of your statements to the court. Also remember that you are always "on." While opposing counsel is arguing, sit attentively at counsel table, listening and, if appropriate, taking notes.

§ 19.4.4 Appropriate Dress

As a sign of respect, both for the court and the client, most attorneys wear suits. Men wear conservative suits and ties, and women wear suit coats and matching pants or skirts. The key is to look professional but not severe. During oral argument, the judge's attention should be focused on your argument, not on your attire.

§ 19.5   Making the Argument

Like the brief, the oral argument has a prescribed format. The following example sets out the typical outline for an oral argument.

EXAMPLE 1　　**Outline of Oral Argument**

A. *Moving party* (party bringing the motion or, on appeal, the appellant)
  1. Introductions
  2. Opening
  3. Statement of the issue(s)

    4. Brief summary of the significant facts (when appropriate)

    5. Argument

    6. Conclusion and request for relief

B. *Responding party* (party opposing the motion or, on appeal, the respondent or appellee)

    1. Introductions

    2. Opening

    3. Statement of position

    4. Brief summary of significant facts (when appropriate)

    5. Argument

    6. Conclusion and request for relief

C. *Moving party's rebuttal*

D. *Sur-rebuttal* (when allowed)

§ 19.5.1   Introductions

Begin your oral argument by introducing yourself and your client. At the trial court level, the language is relatively informal. Most attorneys say, "Good morning, Your Honor," and then introduce themselves and the client. At the appellate level, the language is more formal. By convention, most attorneys begin by saying, "May it please the Court, my name is _____, and I represent the [appellant] [respondent], _____."

> **PRACTICE POINTER**
>
> In many courts, the introduction is also used to reserve rebuttal time. The attorney for the moving party reserves rebuttal either before introducing himself or herself or immediately afterwards: "Your Honor, at this time, I would like to reserve _____ minutes for rebuttal." If you do not reserve rebuttal time, the court might not allow you to present a rebuttal.

§ 19.5.2   Opening

The first minute of your argument should be memorable. The opening sentences should catch the judge's attention, making the case's importance clear, establishing the theme, and creating the appropriate context for the argument that follows.

> **PRACTICE POINTER**
>
> Do not, however, go too far. Few judges are persuaded by long, passionate calls for justice.

§ 19.5.3   Statement of the Issues

a. The Moving Party

If you are the moving party, you need to identify the issue or issues. Sometimes this is best done as part of the opening. From the issue statement alone, the case's importance is clear: "In this case, the appellant asks the Court to hold that the test set out in *Batson* is flawed." At other times, such a strategy is not effective. For example, few trial judges would find the following opening sentence memorable: "In this case, the defendant asks the Court to hold that the trial court erred in denying the defendant's motion to suppress." In such cases, the opening and the statement of the issues should not be combined. Come up with a more memorable opening sentence and then set out the issue or issues.

As a general rule, the statement of the issues should precede the summary of the facts. Before hearing the facts, the court needs a context. There are times, however, when it is more effective to set out the issues after the summary of the facts.

Whenever they are presented, the issue statements must be tailored to oral argument. What is effective in writing might not be effective when spoken. For example, although the under-does-when format works well in a brief, it does not work well orally. In oral argument, the issue needs to be presented more simply: "In this case, the court is asked to decide whether . . ." or "This case presents two issues: first, whether . . . and second, whether . . . ." An issue statement can be even stronger if it is stated as a positive assertion: "This court should reverse because Mr. Josephy's constitutional rights were violated by the admission of evidence obtained from an unlawful search and by the prosecutor's purposeful discrimination in the use of its peremptory challenges to remove Native Americans from the jury. The search was unlawful because . . . ."

Even though they are streamlined, the issues should be presented in the light most favorable to the client. The questions should be framed as they were in the brief, and the significant and emotionally favorable facts should be included. See sections 17.6 and 18.12.

b. The Responding Party

As a general rule, the responding party does not restate the issue or issues. Instead, it states its position, either as part of its opening or as a lead-in to its arguments: "The trial court did not err in denying Mr. Josephy's motion to suppress because the officers had a particularized objective suspicion that the defendant was engaged in criminal activity."

§ 19.5.4 Summary of the Facts

a. The Moving Party

When arguing to a cold court, you will want to spend one to three minutes on a summary of the facts, telling the court what the case is about. You might also want to include a summary of the facts when arguing to a hot court. If the facts are particularly important, you will want to summarize them, refresh the court's memory, and present the facts in the light most favorable to the client. There will, however, be times when a separate summary of the facts is not the best use of limited time. In those instances, instead of presenting the facts in a separate summary at the beginning, integrate them into the argument.

b.   The Responding Party

As the responding party, you do not want to use your time repeating what opposing counsel just said. Consequently, for you a summary of the facts is optional even if the court is cold. If opposing counsel has set out the facts accurately, the summary can be omitted. Just integrate the significant facts into the argument. You will, however, want to include a summary if opposing counsel has misstated key facts or has omitted facts that are important to your argument, or if you need to present the facts from your client's point of view.

> **PRACTICE POINTER**   In presenting the facts, you will not, as a matter of course, include references to the record. You must, however, be able to provide such references if asked to do so by the court or if you are correcting a misstatement made by opposing counsel.

§ 19.5.5   The Argument

Unless the issues and arguments build on each other, start with your strongest issue and, in discussing that issue, start with your strongest argument. This allows you to take advantage of the positions of emphasis and ensures that you will have the opportunity to make your best, or most crucial, arguments. In addition, it usually results in better continuity. Because the moving party's strongest issue is usually the responding party's weakest, the moving party's final issue will often be the responding party's first, providing the responding party with an easy opening for his or her argument.

Moving Party	*Responding Party*
Issue 1 → Issue 2	Issue 2 → Issue 1

In presenting the arguments, do what you did in your brief but in abbreviated form. If you are the moving party, begin by stating the rule, presenting that rule in the light most favorable to your client (see sections 17.10.3 and 18.15.3). Then argue that rule, explaining why the court should reach the result that you advocate. If you are the responding party, do not repeat the rule unless your opponent has misstated the rule or you are arguing for a different rule. Instead, use your time to make your own affirmative arguments and to counter the arguments that your opponent has made.

In both instances, you must support your assertions. You can do so by making plain language arguments, by arguing legislative intent, by using analogous cases, or by making policy arguments. When appropriate, cite to the relevant portions of a statute or to a common law rule and, when using analogous cases, be specific: Explain the rule that the court applied, the significant facts, and the court's reasoning. Although you should have the full case citations available, you do not need to include them in your argument. A reference to the case name is usually sufficient.

Although you want to cite to the relevant authorities, you do not, as a general rule, want to quote them or your own brief. Reading more than a line is seldom effective. If it is important that the court have specific language before it, refer the judge or judges to the appropriate page in the brief or, better yet, prepare a visual aid.

There are several other things that you need to keep in mind in making your argument. First, it is usually more difficult to follow an oral argument than a written one. As a result, it is important to include sufficient roadmaps, signposts, and transitions. Make both the structure of your argument and the connections between ideas explicit.

Second, you need to manage your time. Do not spend so much time on one issue or argument that you do not have time for the other issues or other arguments. Because it is difficult to predict how many questions the court will ask, practice both a short version and a long version of each argument.

Finally, remember that your goal is to persuade the judge to rule in your client's favor. Consequently, do not avoid the "hard" arguments. If you think that the judge already agrees with you on a point, move to your next point.

§ 19.5.6   Answering Questions

You should welcome the court's questions. They tell you what the court is thinking about your case, what the judges understand, and what they still question. If you are not getting questions, it is usually a bad sign. The judges have either already made up their minds or are not listening.

Questions from the bench fall into several categories. Some are mere requests for information. The judge wants to clarify a fact or your position on an issue, or wants to know more about the rule or how you think it should be applied.

Other questions are designed to elicit a particular response from you. For example, at the appellate level, Judge A might agree with your position and want you to pursue a particular line of argument for the benefit of Judge B, who is not yet persuaded. Still other questions are designed to test the merits of your argument. These questions may have as their focus your case or, at the appellate level, future cases. If the court applies rule A to your case, what does that mean for cases X, Y, and Z?

Whatever the type of question, when the judge begins to speak, you must stop. Although judges can interrupt you, you should not interrupt them. As the judge speaks, listen — not only to the question that is being asked, but also for clues about how the judge is perceiving the case.

The hardest part comes next. Before answering the judge, think through your answer. Although the second or two of silence might make you uncomfortable, the penalty for answering too quickly can be severe. Although few cases are won at oral argument, some are lost, usually because in answering a question an attorney concedes or asserts too much. The second or two of silence is by far better than an unfavorable ruling.

When you know what you want to say, answer. In most instances, you will want to begin by giving the judge a one-, two-, or three-word answer. "Yes." "No." "Yes, but . . . ," "No, but . . . ," or "In some cases, ..." Then explain or support your answer. In doing so, try to integrate key points from your list of bullet points or from your outline. Instead of thinking of questions as interruptions, think of them as another vehicle for making your argument.

There are a number of things that you should not do in responding to a question. First, do not tell the judge that you will answer the question later. It is you, not the judge, who must be flexible.

Second, do not argue with the judge. Answer all questions calmly and thoughtfully. Do not raise your voice, and even if you are frustrated, do not let it show. If one line of argument is not working and the point is essential to your case, try another, and if that line does not work, try still another. When the point is not important or you have given all the answers you have, answer, and then, without pausing, move as smoothly as you can into the next part of your argument.

Third, after answering the question, do not stop and wait for the judge's approval or permission to continue. Answer the question, and then, unless asked another question, move to the next part of your argument.

Finally, do not answer by asking the judge a question. In oral argument, it is inappropriate to question a judge.

§ 19.5.7   The Closing

The closing is as important as the opening. Because it is a position of emphasis, you want to end on a favorable point.

One way of doing this is to end with a summary of your arguments, reminding the court of your strongest points and requesting the appropriate relief. Although this is often effective, it can also be ineffective. Many judges stop listening when they hear the phrase "In conclusion" or "In summary." Consequently, when using a summary, avoid stock openers. Catch the court's attention by repeating a key phrase, weaving the pieces together, or returning to the points made in your opening.

Another way is to end on a strong point. If you are running out of time, it might be better to stop at the end of an argument or after answering a question than to rush through a prepared closing. Like a good comedian, a good advocate knows when to sit down.

§ 19.5.8   Rebuttal

Perhaps the hardest part of the oral argument is rebuttal. In one or two minutes you must identify the crucial issues and make your strongest argument or response.

If you try to make too many points in rebuttal, you dilute the power of each. Therefore, as a general rule, do not try to make more than one or two points. The points should be selected because of their importance to your case: Do not merely repeat what you said in the main portion of your argument or respond to trivial points made by opposing counsel. Instead, make your rebuttal a true rebuttal by responding to significant points made by opposing counsel or questions or concerns raised by the court during opposing counsel's argument.

Because time is so limited, most advocates begin their rebuttal by telling the court how many points they plan to make: "I would like to make two points." This introduction tells the court what to expect. The advocate then makes his or her first point and supports it and, unless interrupted by a question, moves to the second point. Most advocates close by quickly repeating their request for relief.

§ 19.6   Delivering the Argument

Every advocate has his or her own style. While some are soft-spoken, others are more theatrical; while some are plain-speaking, others strive for eloquence. As an advocate, you will need to develop your own style, building on your strengths and minimizing your weaknesses. Whatever your style, there are certain "rules" that you should follow.

§ 19.6.1   Breathe

Before you start speaking, take a deep breath. The breath will allow you to clear your mind, focus, and control your nerves. In addition, if at some point during your argument you lose your place or become flustered, look down at the podium and breathe.

§ 19.6.2   Do Not Read Your Argument

The first, and perhaps most important, rule is not to read your argument. Similarly, do not try to deliver a memorized speech. Know what you want to say and then talk to the court. You are a teacher, sharing information and answering the court's questions.

§ 19.6.3   Maintain Eye Contact

If you do not read, you will be able to maintain eye contact with the judge. This is important for several reasons. First, it helps you keep the judge's attention. It is very difficult not to listen to a person who is looking you in the eye. Second, it helps you "read" the court. By studying the judges, you can often determine (1) whether they already agree with you on a point and you can move to the next part of your argument, (2) whether they are confused, or (3) whether you have not yet persuaded them. Finally, eye contact is important because of what it says about you and your argument. An advocate who looks the judge in the eye is perceived as being more confident and more competent than one who does not.

PRACTICE POINTER	When you are arguing to an appellate court, maintain eye contact with all of the judges, even when you are answering a specific judge's question.

§ 19.6.4   Do Not Slouch, Rock, or Put Your Hands in Your Pockets

In delivering an oral argument to the court, stand erect, but not stiffly, behind the podium. Do not rock from foot to foot, and do not put your hands in your pockets.

Although it might be appropriate to move around the courtroom when arguing to a jury, you should not do so when arguing to the court.

§ 19.6.5   Limit Your Gestures and Avoid Distracting Mannerisms

Gestures are appropriate in an oral argument. They should, however, be natural and relatively constrained. If you talk with your hands, mentally put yourself inside a small telephone booth.

You also want to avoid distracting mannerisms. Do not play with a pen, the edge of your notes, or the keys in your pocket. In addition, do not repeatedly move hair out of your eyes or push your glasses back up on your nose.

§ 19.6.6   Speak So That You Can Be Easily Understood

In delivering your oral argument, speak loudly and clearly enough that you can be easily heard by the judges.

Also try to modulate your voice, varying both the pace and volume of your speech. If you want to emphasize a point, speak more slowly and either more softly or more loudly.

§ 19.7   Making Your Argument Persuasive

In delivering your oral argument, you will want to use many of the same techniques that you used in writing your brief. In stating the issue, frame the question so that it suggests the answer favorable to your client and, in presenting the facts, emphasize the favorable facts by placing them in positions of emphasis and by using detail and sentence structure to your advantage. See sections 17.6.3 and 18.12.5. Also, present the law in the light most favorable to your client. State favorable rules broadly, use cases to your advantage, and emphasize the policies that support your client's position. See sections 17.10.3 and 18.15.3.

You should also pick your words carefully. Select words both for their denotation and their connotation, and avoid words and phrases that undermine the persuasiveness of your argument. If you represent the defendant, do not say, "It is the defendant's position that the officers violated the defendant's Fourth Amendment rights when they searched his car." Instead, say, "The officers violated the defendant's Fourth Amendment rights when they searched his car." Similarly, do not say, "We feel that the State engaged in purposeful discrimination when it used its peremptory challenges to excuse the only two Native Americans in the jury pool." Say instead, "The State engaged in purposeful discrimination when it used its peremptory challenges to excuse the only two Native Americans in the jury pool."

§ 19.8   Handling the Problems

Because an oral argument is not scripted, you need to prepare for the unexpected and decide in advance how you will handle the problems that might arise.

§ 19.8.1   Counsel Has Misstated Facts or Law

If opposing counsel misstates an important fact or the governing law, you will usually want to bring the error to the attention of the court. You should, however, use care in correcting opposing counsel.

First, make sure you are right. If there is time, double-check the record, the statute, or the case. Second, make sure you are correcting a misstatement of fact or law, not the opposing party's interpretation of a fact, statute, or case. Third, correct the mistake, not opposing counsel. Instead of criticizing or attacking opposing counsel, simply provide the court with the correct information and, if possible, the citation to the record or the language of the statute or case.

EXAMPLE 1   **Correcting a Statement Made by Opposing Counsel**

"Ms. Martinez did not see the assailant three times. She testified that she saw him twice: once when he drove by slowly and then when he pulled in front of her."

Finally, correct only those errors that are significant.

§ 19.8.2   You Make a Mistake

If you make a significant mistake, correct it as soon as you can.

§ 19.8.3   You Do Not Have Enough Time

Despite the best planning, you will sometimes run out of time. You might have gotten more questions than you expected, leaving you little or no remaining time for your last issue or your final points. When this happens, you have two options. You can either quickly summarize the points that you would have made, or you can tell the court that, because you are out of time, you will rely on your brief for the issues and arguments that you did not cover.

What you do not want to do is exceed the time that you have been allotted. Unless the court gives you permission to continue, you must stop when your time is up.

§ 19.8.4   You Have Too Much Time

Having too much time is not a problem. You do not need to use all of your allotted time. When you have said what you need to say, thank the court and sit down.

§ 19.8.5   You Do Not Know the Answer to a Question

Occasionally, you will be asked a question that you cannot answer. If it is a question about the facts of your case or about the law, do not try to bluff. Instead, do one of the following: (1) if you can do so in a few seconds, look up the answer; (2) tell the judge that at this point you cannot answer the question but that you will be glad to provide the information after oral argument; or (3) give the best answer you can.

| **EXAMPLE 2** | **Statements That You Can Make When You Do Not Know the Answer** |

"So that I can answer correctly, let me quickly check the record."

"I'm not sure what the actual words were. I will check and provide you with that information after oral argument."

"As I recall, the police officer testified that he asked the question twice."

If the question raises an issue that you have not considered, the options are slightly different. You can either trust yourself and, on the spot, give your best answer or you can tell the court that you need to give the question some thought.

§ 19.8.6   You Do Not Understand a Question

If you do not understand a question, tell the judge and either ask him or her to repeat the question, or repeat the question in your own words, asking the judge whether you understood correctly: "I'm sorry, I'm not sure that I understand your question. Could you please rephrase it?" "If I am correct, you are asking whether . . . ."

§ 19.8.7   You Become Flustered or Draw a Blank

It happens, at some time or another, to almost everyone. You become flustered or draw a blank. When this happens, "buy" a few seconds by either taking a drink of water or taking a deep breath and looking down at your notes. If you still cannot continue with the point you were making, move to another one.

§ 19.8.8   You Are Asked to Concede a Point

Concessions can work both to your advantage and to your disadvantage. You will win points by conceding points that you cannot win or that are not important to your argument. You can, however, lose your case if you concede too much. Therefore, before you walk into court, decide what you can and cannot concede, concede when appropriate, and otherwise politely but firmly stand your ground. If the court presses for a concession, you can try to move the court past the issue: "Assuming, *arguendo*, that this Court decides that the trial court erred, the error was harmless because . . . ."

§ 19.9   A Final Note

No matter how much they dread it, initially most individuals end up enjoying oral argument for what it is, a stimulating dialogue among intelligent people.

§ 19.9.1   Checklist for Critiquing the Oral Argument

I. Preparation

- The advocate has anticipated and prepared rebuttals for the arguments the other side is likely to make.
- The advocate has anticipated and prepared responses to the questions the court is likely to ask.
- The advocate knows the law and the facts of the case.
- The advocate has determined what arguments he or she needs to make to win.
- The advocate has determined what points he or she can, or cannot, concede.
- The advocate has prepared two outlines: a long outline, which can be used if the court asks only a few questions, and a short outline, which can be used in case the court asks more questions.

II. Content and Organization

A. Introduction

- The advocate identifies himself or herself and the client.
- When appropriate, the advocate requests rebuttal time.

B. Opening and Statement of Issues or Position

- The advocate begins the argument with a sentence or phrase that catches the attention of the court and establishes the client's theory of the case.
- The advocate then presents the question or states his or her position.
- The question or statement of position is framed so that it supports the advocate's theory of the case and suggests an answer favorable to the client.
- The question or statement of position is presented using language that is easily understood.

C. Summary of Facts

- When appropriate, the advocate includes a short summary of the facts in which he or she explains the case and establishes an appropriate context. When a separate summary of the facts is not appropriate, the advocate weaves the facts into the argument.
- The facts are presented accurately but in the light most favorable to the client. The positions of emphasis and detail are used effectively, and words have been selected for both their denotation and their connotation.

D. Argument

- The advocate discusses the issues and makes the arguments needed to win.
- The argument is structured in such a way that it is easy to follow: (1) issues and arguments are discussed in a logical order and (2) sufficient roadmaps, signposts, and transitions are used.

■ The arguments are supported. The advocate uses the law, analogous cases, policy, and the facts to support each of his or her assertions.

■ The law, analogous cases, policies, and facts are presented accurately.

■ The law, analogous cases, policies, and facts are presented in the light most favorable to the client.

E. Questions from the Bench

■ When a judge asks a question, the advocate immediately stops talking and listens to the question.

■ The advocate thinks before answering.

■ As a general rule, the advocate begins his or her answer with a short response ("Yes," "No," "In this case") and then supports that answer.

■ After answering the question, the advocate moves back into his or her argument without pausing or waiting for the judge to give permission to continue.

■ The advocate sees questions not as an interruption, but as another opportunity to get his or her argument before the court.

■ As he or she listens to the questions, the advocate adjusts the argument to match the concerns and interests of the court.

F. Closing

■ The advocate ends the argument by summarizing the main points or on a strong point.

■ When appropriate, the advocate includes a request for relief.

G. Rebuttal

■ The advocate uses rebuttal to respond to the one or two most important points raised by opposing counsel or the court.

III. Delivery

■ The advocate treats the argument as a dialogue; he or she does not read or recite the argument.

■ The advocate maintains eye contact with all of the judges.

■ The advocate has good posture, uses gestures effectively, and speaks so that he or she can be easily understood.

■ The advocate does not use phrases like "I think," "We maintain," or "It is our position that . . ."

■ The advocate is composed and treats the court and opposing counsel with respect.

Chapter 19 Quiz

Draft answers for each of the following questions. Make your points clearly and concisely, and write sentences that are easy to read and that are grammatical and correctly punctuated.

1. In presenting your oral argument, what are your primary goals?

2. What should you do if a judge asks you to concede a point?

3 What should you do if, a minute or two into your argument, the judge asks a question that relates to a point that you were going to make at the end of your argument?

4. What should you do if opposing counsel misstates a fact?

5. What makes a good rebuttal?

A Guide to Effective Writing

This part of the book gives legal writers general recommendations and rules of thumb about what makes some legal writing effective. We believe what follows is good advice, but we also want to alert readers to three caveats about the notion of "effective legal writing."

First, effectiveness in legal writing is a relative thing. The same level of effectiveness is not needed in every situation. The trick, of course, is to make the writing effective enough so that it accomplishes its goal without laboring over it to the point that it consumes all of the working day and night. In short, some balance is appropriate.

Second, effectiveness in legal writing, and in all writing for that matter, always depends on the context. What will please and even delight one reader may irritate or anger another. An organizational scheme that is effective in one instance may be dead wrong in another. Even precision and conciseness, those most sought-after characteristics of effective legal writing, can be ineffective in some instances in which vagueness and verbosity accomplish the desired objective. In other words, writing that most readers would consider competent, stylistically pleasing, and even eloquent in the abstract but that does not work in a given context is, in that context, ineffective.

Finally, effectiveness is a fairly subjective notion. Again, we can give you the standard advice and some insights of our own about what is and is not effective legal writing, but ultimately you must determine whether you think something works. If, as you are writing a given piece, your instincts tell you it is working (or it is not working) and all the theory and advice tell you the opposite, we suggest that you look at it again. If your instincts and common sense still insist that the conventional wisdom about effective legal writing is not working here, trust your instincts.

20

Effective Writing — The Whole Paper

§ 20.1   The Psychology of Writing

Writing is not for the faint-hearted. It takes courage, perseverance, creativity, and flexibility, not to mention intelligence and a solid foundation of writing skills. A fair number of lawyers and judges profess to like writing and even say that they find the process satisfying. If you are in this fortunate group, this section is not addressed to you.

If you are among the less fortunate — those who have felt overwhelmed by the prospect of writing, who have struggled with writer's block, or who have found writing to be a difficult, perhaps even painful, process — there is hope. Writing, like most other skills, becomes more pleasurable with each successful experience. It also helps to know where the usual stumbling blocks are in the process and how to get past them.

Few legal writers have trouble getting started on the research phase of a writing project. Many encounter their first stumbling block when it is time to move from research to writing. A typical avoidance mechanism is to keep researching long past the point of need. Writers who have developed this pattern of approaching writing tasks usually postpone putting fingers to keyboard until the last possible moment. Then they write, almost out of desperation, and end up turning in as a final product something that is really a rough draft. By delaying the writing process, they make it virtually impossible to do any quality drafting, revising, editing, and proofreading. The result is yet another unsatisfying writing experience.

If this describes your typical writing process, you may be able to break this habit by developing a schedule for the completion of the entire document. In this schedule, allot a reasonable amount of time to complete the research but be firm about when you will begin writing. Give yourself mini-deadlines for completing an outline, producing a first draft, revising, editing, and proofreading. Allow breathing room in this timetable for problems such as a printer malfunction or a flat tire. If at all possible, plan as though your deadline is sooner than the real deadline. To do this, you may find it easier to write the schedule backwards, starting with the final deadline and allowing time for proofreading, then editing, all the way back to research.

Sample Schedule for a Two-Week Writing Project

Week 1   Research and organize research
Week 2   Day 1 brainstorm, create plan, outline
          Day 2 drafting
          Day 3 drafting
          Day 4 revising
          Day 5 editing, last-minute citation checks
          Day 6 proofreading
          Day 7 final product (ready a day early!)

For shorter time frames and quick turnarounds, a writing schedule is even more critical. In such cases, you will probably be working with half-day, quarter-day, or even hour units, but the principles are still the same. Figure out how much of the total time should be spent researching and how much should be spent writing. Create mini-deadlines for yourself. Start with your final deadline and work backwards as you plan.

Sample Schedule for a Two-Day Writing Project

Day 1   Research and organize research
Day 2   By 10:00 a.m. brainstorm, plan outline
          By 2:00 p.m. drafting
          By 3:00 p.m. revising
          By 4:00 p.m. editing
          By 4:30 p.m. proofreading
          By 5:00 p.m. final product completed (and in the partner's
            inbox!)

With practice, you may find that you don't need as much time for research and that you can begin to allow a larger percentage of your time for writing.

Schedules are invaluable, but many writers need more than a schedule to get them started writing. It is an enormous help if your research notes are organized in a way that will facilitate the writing process. Instead of organizing your research around cases, organize it around the law or the points you want to make. For example, once you have identified the steps in the analysis, create a template for your document and, as you research, place the information that you find under the appropriate heading or headings. In the alternative, you can color code either the electronic copies of the authorities or any photocopies you made of those authorities. Color coding helps during the drafting phase because it gives you a quick way to gather up all the information you have collected on a given point (grab all the yellow) and then physically order those sheets. The same sheets may have other colors on them, but while you are writing about the "yellow point" you can stay focused on the part of the notes and photocopied cases that concern that point. When it comes time to do the "blue point," the same sheets get picked up and ordered into the information about that point.

If color coding does not appeal to you, you may find that having separate file folders or a tabbed notebook works for you. The key is to develop files or sections of the notebook for the points you want to make in the whole document, not separate files or notebook sections for each analogous case. This means you may need two or more photocopies of the same page of a case so that it may be filed under each of the appropriate points.

§ 20.2   Outlines, Writing Plans, and Ordered Lists

For professional writers (and lawyers are professional writers) who must organize extensive and complex material, spending time creating an outline or writing plan or even just an ordered list almost always saves time in the end. Done properly, an outline or plan will keep you from backtracking, repeating yourself, missing a key point, or only discovering what it is you want to say after you have written the whole thing the wrong way.

But creating order in extensive and complex material is not easy; it takes the writer's complete attention. Consequently, the task deserves a distinct block of time for just that task. Don't fall into the trap of trying to create order at the same time you are drafting sentences and paragraphs. That approach is needlessly stressful because it forces you to keep track of several big tasks all at once.

Writing a good outline or plan may also mean that you have to change some of your preconceived ideas about outlines. First of all, the outline or plan is for you, the writer, not for a teacher. Roman numerals and capital A's and B's are not important. Use them if they help; discard them if they hinder. If you discard the roman numerals, letters, and numbers, keep the indentations. They will help you distinguish among main points, subpoints, sub-subpoints, and supporting details.

There are as many ways to go about creating an outline or writing plan as there are writers. The rest of this section describes some time-tested techniques that you may find helpful.

§ 20.2.1   Read It All; Mull It Over

Before beginning to write the outline or plan, read through all of your research. Let your mind mull it over while you do some mindless task such as mowing the lawn or taking a bath. While you are engaged in the mindless task, your mind will almost certainly begin organizing the ideas.

§ 20.2.2   Don't Overlook Obvious Ways to Organize

One obvious way of beginning to organize is to determine how the court will approach the problem. Are there any threshold questions the court will consider first? If so, place them first in your outline. What will the court look at and decide second, third, and so on? Your organizational scheme should mirror the process the court will follow.

Furthermore, in creating an organization for your document, do not assume that you always have to create a brand-new, never-seen-before organizational scheme. Most documents fit comfortably in one of the common organizational plans. Borrow freely from the bank of common knowledge about how to organize an elements analysis, a balancing test, or a discussion of the development of a trend, to name but a few. Many discussion sections follow an IRAC (issue, rule, analysis, conclusion) plan or use mini-IRACs in some of the sections.

§ 20.2.3   Find Order Using a Three-Column Chart

The three-column chart can be an effective way to find order in a document, particularly when the document does not immediately appear to fall into any of the typical organizational patterns. In the first column, make one giant list of everything you think the final document should include. Be as comprehensive as possible. Dump everything you have in your brain about the problem into this list. Do not worry about the order of the items.

Once Column One is complete, use Column Two to begin doing some preliminary ordering of the list in Column One. Column One will probably already contain some natural groupings of ideas. If so, place them together in Column Two at roughly the point in the document where you guess they will go.

Column Three is used to further refine the order of the list. This is the time to test out various places where the stray items may fit. Also check to see if anything was forgotten. Look for all the standard features of legal analysis (burden of proof, plain language arguments, policy arguments, and so on) and all the standard "moves" a lawyer makes (argument, counterargument, rebuttal, countervailing policy argument, and so on).

Working in this way, you will find that the secret to the three-column chart is that you focus on one main task with each column, and as you move through the columns, you get more and more control over the material until voilà! You have an outline.

§ 20.2.4   Talk to a Colleague

Whenever you are having trouble getting a large amount of material organized in your mind, try talking it over with a colleague. Approach the material like you are just going to explain the issues to your colleague. As you are talking, notice how you naturally organize the material. Jot down key words and phrases that come to mind as you are speaking. Don't be afraid to talk through the parts with which you are having the most difficulty. It may free you to address these areas if you begin by saying something like, "this is the part I'm having trouble with" or "this is the part that is still rough in my mind." Let your listener question you and provide his or her own insights.

If talking out the issues seemed helpful, sit down immediately afterwards and write out the organization you discovered as you were speaking. Then, if talking-before-writing becomes a valuable organizing technique for you, you may even want to record the talking-before-writing sessions.

§ 20.2.5 Try a New Analogy or Format

If you have a phobia about outlines, rename what it is you are doing when you develop the organization for a document. Some writers are more comfortable developing a "writing plan." Others like to think in terms of an "ordered list." You may need an entirely new analogy for what you are doing. Think instead of an architect creating a blueprint for a building or an engineer designing an aircraft.

Some people prefer horizontal flow charts to vertical outlines. There is nothing magical about organizing ideas from top to bottom in an outline. If working from left to right in a flow chart feels more comfortable to you, do it.

Others can find and better visualize an organizational scheme by using a technique called "clustering." To use clustering, simply begin by putting one main idea in a circle and then attach related subpoints. Exhibit 20.1 is an example of a basic cluster.

Once you have a basic cluster, begin a new circle for each main idea, each time attaching related subpoints. See Exhibit 20.2 for an expanded but not yet complete cluster for the same case. By continuing to expand the cluster diagram, you will end up with a map of how your mind is thinking about a legal problem.

Now look for clusters of ideas; these will usually become sections in the final document. You may even find that after doing the clustering diagram you can see that the material fits into one of the standard organizational plans. The final step is to translate the clustering diagram into a traditional outline.

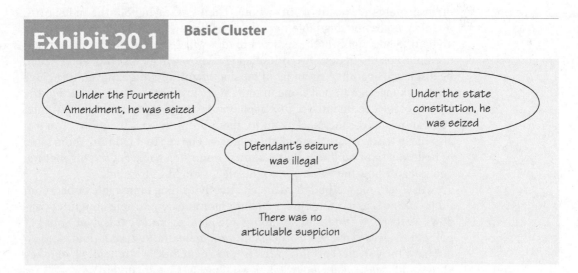

Exhibit 20.1   **Basic Cluster**

§ 20.2.6 Create a Dining Room Table, Bedroom Floor, or Multiple Monitor Outline

Many writers have difficulty developing a big picture perspective about the document they are trying to write. One way to get a big picture perspective is to create a "dining room table" (or "bedroom floor") outline. The process is simple: just jot each key point or idea that should appear in the document

Exhibit 20.2   Expanded Cluster

Officer accelerated as he drove toward Defendant

Defendant submitted to a show of authority

Spotlight was a show of authority

Defendant did not feel free to leave

Defendant stopped before ordered to do so

Under the Fourth Amendment, he was seized

Under the state constitution, he was seized

Defendant's seizure was illegal

State constitution provides more protection than U.S. Constitution

High crime area is not enough

There was no articulable suspicion

Area known for drugs is not enough

Defendant had cooperated, given his name, and answered questions

Defendant walked to the middle of the road, stopped, looked, and then walked back to the apartment complex

on a separate index card or sticky note. Then start laying out the index cards or sticky notes on a big table or counter or floor. Put related points together and put them roughly in the spot where they will appear in the document. For example, you might have two rules that you know will go together and need to be discussed near the beginning of the document; you might have three cases that work together to make one argument that will appear somewhere in the middle of the document. Because each point is on an index card or sticky note, you can maneuver the pieces and try them out in several locations. You can also begin to see where there might be holes. The key to the dining room table or bedroom floor outline is that it allows you to step back, get the big picture, and imagine how the various ways the pieces might fit together.

An electronic method to create an effective dining room table or bedroom floor outline is to use multiple computer monitors or multiple computer windows. In lieu of writing your key points and ideas on index cards, type your key points and ideas in one word processing document; the key points and ideas do not have to be in any specific order. After you are finished recording your key points and ideas, create a new blank word processing document.

If you are using two monitors, arrange the two documents so that one document is on one monitor, and the other document is on the other monitor. This can be done by clicking and dragging the title bar of the document into position. At this point, the documents should be side by side.

If you only have one monitor, you can arrange the documents to appear side by side in one monitor. Simply minimize the window for each document, sizing the windows so that each document takes up half the monitor. Then click and drag the title bar of one document to one side of your monitor, and click and drag the title bar for the other document to the other side of the monitor.

As you review your key points and ideas in one document, copy and paste each point or idea into the new blank document where you anticipate it will appear in the document. Just as if you were using index cards, you will want to put related points and ideas together. Sometimes, it helps to create a structural outline of headings in the blank document before copying and pasting your key points or ideas. For example, your new document might have headings for each element of a claim and you might copy and paste key points or ideas related to each element under those headings.

§ 20.2.7　Consider Your Reader and Purpose and How You View the Case

After spending hours doing research in the library or online—in the trenches, so to speak—it is a good idea to review the basics before composing a battle plan. For either a memo or a brief, ask yourself, for whom am I writing this document? What are that reader's purposes? What are my purposes? Above all, do not forget what legal question someone asked you to answer. Make sure your document answers that question.

For briefs, ask yourself, what is my overall theme? Is this a case about mistaken identity, inappropriate police procedures, self-defense, or freedom to assemble? The theme, or what some lawyers call "the theory of the case" in persuasive writing, should be evident in every section of the outline, from the statement of facts or statement of the case to the rule, discussion, or argument sections.

One final note before leaving the subject of outlines: Like the blueprint for a building or the design for an aircraft, outlines should be aids and not straitjackets for the writer. Don't be afraid to change an outline when it isn't working or when you get a better idea.

§ 20.3　Drafting the Document

If creating an outline is the first stumbling block for most writers, the second comes when it is time to start drafting. Some people develop "writer's block." Faced with what seems to be an overwhelming task, they freeze. Nothing seems like the perfect beginning, so nothing gets written.

If you tend to freeze when you must start writing, try some of the following techniques.

§ 20.3.1　Give Yourself Optimum Writing Conditions

Make writing as pleasant as possible. Start drafting at the time of day and in the place where you do your best thinking and writing. If you are a morning person, don't start drafting at 5:00 p.m. unless you absolutely must. If you prefer a legal pad to a computer, by all means use a legal pad. Treat yourself to a new fancy pen if that will make you feel better about writing.

§ 20.3.2   Trick Yourself into Getting Started

For many writers, the key to getting started drafting goes all the way back to the research phase. If, for example, as you read each case you stop afterwards and summarize in your own words the key point of the case and what it contributes to the analysis of the issue you are addressing, you will have started drafting. Keeping research notes in your own words or writing an outline will get you started before you even realize you are now writing a draft. By expanding outline labels into phrases, then clauses, then sentences, you begin developing the language that will appear in your draft. For some writers, this gradual "drift" into drafting helps them avoid writer's block.

§ 20.3.3   Write What You Know Best First

For some reason, many writers seem to think that they must write a document in order—the first sentence first, then the second sentence; the first paragraph before the second paragraph; and so on. This notion about writing is not a problem as long as the writer knows how to begin.

However, when you are not quite sure how to begin, it's often a good idea to start writing a draft at the point in the material where you are the most confident. Get the writing rolling and let your subconscious work through how to begin the document.

The same is true when you are hopelessly stuck in the middle of a document. Try skipping over the problem area for a time and write another section. With a bit of luck, you may figure out what to do about the problem area without letting it bring the project to a halt.

One caution, though: If you start in the middle of a document or if you skip over a problem area for the time being, you will have to come back and make sure the sections are logically and stylistically connected.

§ 20.3.4   "Get the Juices Flowing"

Athletes who are preparing to perform do warm-up and stretching exercises. Some writers find that freewriting has similar benefits when done before drafting. Others find that they can "get the writing juices flowing" by reading similar documents or rereading other documents that they have written.

§ 20.3.5   Take It One Step at a Time

Many writers are overwhelmed by the prospect of drafting twenty pages or more. Writing a page or even just a paragraph, however, seems relatively easy. The trick then is to give yourself only small parts of the whole document to do at any one time.

Your goal for the next hour, for example, may be to write the rule section. Before lunch you may want to complete a paragraph about the plaintiff's policy argument on the last element. By breaking the large task into several smaller tasks, you allow yourself to focus on one part at a time and direct all your energy toward writing that part well.

§ 20.3.6   Stay Focused

One of the biggest drafting challenges is staying focused on the writing project and not allowing yourself to get distracted. Avoiding distractions may mean shutting the office door, muting the phone, and, above all, turning off the Internet and email. Disciplined writers know that their computer, which is the very tool they need for writing, can also be their biggest source of interruptions and distractions. For some, it is the temptation to surf the Internet. For others, it is the little box that appears at the bottom corner of the screen indicating new emails from family, friends, and co-workers. Remember that Facebook and Twitter will still be there for you to check *after* your writing session. Rather than allow social networking sites to interrupt you, use checking them as a reward after you have completed a section or your writing goal for a set time period. The key to achieving focus is to manage distractions. It bears saying again; to stay focused you will probably have to log off the Internet.

§ 20.3.7   Tackle and Conquer the Procrastination Habit

It is no secret that procrastination can seriously interfere with a person's ability to write effectively. Putting off getting started is probably the easiest way to doom a writing project to mediocrity. Even though many writers have convinced themselves that they "write better under pressure," the reality is that the last-minute writer is almost certainly submitting something close to a first draft as his or her final project. Instead of being a slave to the procrastination habit, then, the smart writer tackles the problem head on.

Defeating procrastination is a two-step process. First, determine why you procrastinate about writing. Second, select strategies for defeating procrastination that are directed at the reason(s) why you procrastinate.

Some writers procrastinate because they are overly optimistic about how much time they have and they underestimate how much time the writing project will take. The experts call this type the "**relaxed procrastinators**"; they don't start working until they feel deadline pressure, and they often believe that they "do their best work under pressure."

If you are a relaxed procrastinator, your best strategy may be to follow the advice in this chapter and develop a writing schedule with mini-deadlines for completing your research, preparing an outline, completing a draft, doing an after-the-fact outline, editing, proofreading, and so on. If you are a "hardened" relaxed procrastinator, you may need to report in to someone who will hold you to those mini-deadlines.

Other people procrastinate because they lack confidence in their ability to do the project well. They don't believe that they are good writers, and they are anxious about whether their work will be good enough. Experts label these folks the "**anxious, tense procrastinators**."

If you are an anxious, tense procrastinator, you are more likely to respond to strategies that build your confidence about writing. It might be helpful to review any past written project that was a success. How did you go about getting it done? Can that process be replicated for the current project? Simply rereading a successful piece can help a person start a new project with a more positive frame of mind. In building a positive frame of mind, check the "self talk" you are engaging in related to the current project. Instead of "There's no way I can get this assignment done" try "Where should I start?" Instead of "I'll probably do this the wrong way" try "I'm likely to succeed if I . . ."

Related to the anxious, tense procrastinator is the "**perfectionist procrastinator.**" Perfectionists may feel they must research exhaustively before beginning to write; they may want the first sentence to be perfect before proceeding to the second sentence; if they are having trouble with one section, that problem may bring a whole project to a halt.

If you are a perfectionist procrastinator, good strategies are ones that help you keep perspective. Real clients can rarely pay for exhaustive research. It is important to know when you have done enough research and are ready to write. Once you start writing, try to focus on just a few big tasks, such as getting your ideas down and organizing them, on the first draft. Realize that you can come back to a less-than-perfect sentence and revise it later. Giving yourself permission to skip over a problem area for the time being and let your subconscious work on the problem while you keep writing another part can be key to maintaining some writing momentum.

§ 20.3.8 Manage the Multi-Tasking Habit

One simple truth about lawyers, law students, and really everyone who uses technology these days is that we have all become multi-taskers.[1] We are researching on Lexis Advance or WestlawNext while in the background the TV is tuned to the latest reality show. We are struggling to organize our ideas into an outline, while our favorite recording artist sings via ear bud and MP3 player into our ears. We are drafting a memo to a senior partner when our cell phone chirps — we have a new text message. We are writing a brief to the court and those little boxes with new emails pop up at the bottom of our computer screens, begging for our attention. And on top of all these techno competitors for our attention, we may be instant messaging with a few friends and checking out what they are doing on Facebook or saying on Twitter.

Is this smart? Is this efficient? Like so much else in law and law school, the answer is "it depends." For most of us, multi-tasking has become a habit (some say an addiction), but if we stop and take a little time to think about multi-tasking and how it works with our brains, we can figure out when the habit is helpful and when it undermines our productivity and effectiveness.

Recently there has been a fair amount of research about multi-tasking and its effect on various cognitive processes. The multi-tasking research builds on earlier research about the human brain, which showed that the typical brain has an estimated processing capacity of 126 bits per second and a short-term memory of 7 items at once.[2] Those biological facts haven't changed. Brain researchers tell us that it does not matter how much information from various sources hits our brain at a time; there is a limit to what we can process simultaneously.

---

1. This information on multi-tasking first appeared in an article written by Anne Enquist: *Multi-Tasking and Legal Writing*, 18 Perspectives 7-10 (Fall 2009).

2. Urs Gasser & John Palfrey, *Mastering Multitasking*, 66 Educ. Leadership 14, 15 (2009), *citing* G. A. Miller, *The Magical Number Seven, Plus or Minus Two: Some Limits on Our Capacity to Process Information*, 63 Psychol. Rev. 81 (1956).

The multi-tasking research makes a second important point, which is that there is a difference between parallel processing, which is when a person tries to do more than one thing at a time, and task switching, which is toggling between mental tasks.

In parallel processing, a person does two or more things simultaneously, but only one of the tasks requires a high degree of cognition and attention. The other task or tasks are usually routine, highly practiced skills, or motor skills that can be done almost without thinking. A good example of parallel processing is reading a case while eating a sandwich or while riding an exercise bike. The brain focuses on reading the case, and the other tasks are completed more or less on autopilot.

According to the research, parallel processing may increase efficiency. You can do two or more things at once if only one of them requires your attention.

In contrast, a good example of task switching is reading a case while responding to email or instant messages. Because both tasks require mental attention and focus, the brain cannot do them simultaneously. Instead, it switches back and forth.

Not surprisingly, then, task switching decreases efficiency.[3] Each time a person switches his or her attention from one mental task to another, the brain must activate different neural circuits.[4]

Unfortunately, time is lost at every step. Initially, the brain is focused on Task #1. Task #2 interrupts; now the brain must make a judgment call about which task to focus on. Researchers call this the "response selection bottleneck," which is another way of saying time is lost as the brain decides which task to perform. If the brain switches to Task #2, this switch involves different circuits; once Task #2 is complete, the brain must switch back to Task #1, trying to remember where it left off. And all of this assumes a disciplined task switch and not that Task #2 completely diverted the person to a third, fourth, or fifth distraction.

So, despite the myth that multi-taskers are somehow highly efficient and productive, study after study shows that task switching significantly increases the total amount of time needed to finish each task, sometimes even doubling the total time. In short, the harsh truth is that multi-taskers are deceiving themselves when they believe they are accomplishing more by multi-tasking. Task switching slows you down.

Perhaps the more important points about task switching, though, are not the ones about decreased efficiency. There are also serious questions being asked

---

3. The only efficiency advantage to task switching that the research has noted is that some students who find studying boring will stick with it longer if they have the pleasant distraction of social interventions (instant messaging, text messages, email) to keep them motivated. Note, however, that the added time studying in this scenario may not mean more is learned because task switching itself adds to the total time required.

4. The switching of attention from one task to another—toggling—occurs in a region right behind the forehead called Brodmann Area 10 in the brain's anterior prefrontal cortex, according to a functional magnetic resonance imaging (fMRI) study by a team headed by Jordan Grafman, chief of the cognitive neuroscience section at the National Institute of Neurological Disorders and Stroke, Bethesda, Md. Activity in an area of the brain shows up on MRI as increased flow of blood to this area. Ingrid Wickelgren, *System Overload*, 92 Current Sci. 4, 5 (2006); Claudia Wallis, *The Multitasking Generation*, 167 Time 48, 52 (2006); *see* Etienne Koechlin et al., *The Role of the Anterior Prefrontal Cortex in Human Cognition*, 399 Nature 148 (1999).

by brain researchers about (1) the increase in errors caused by multi-tasking and (2) how task switching affects a person's "cognitive style." In other words, when we are constantly juggling different mental tasks, do we make more mistakes and are we conditioning our brains to work less effectively?

Research has confirmed the increase in errors in many areas, such as in the number of accidents that occur when someone talks on the phone or sends a text message while driving. While no one has yet studied lawyers, it is reasonable to assume that lawyers who engage in multi-tasking might make more errors than lawyers who do not. For example, a lawyer who answers the phone while reading a draft of a contract might be more likely to overlook an important provision than the lawyer who gives the contract his or her undivided attention.

As to the second point about how multi-taskers are conditioning their brains, the studies that have focused on how multi-tasking affects cognitive style should raise concerns for lawyers and law students who want to enhance, not diminish, their capacity to do in-depth thinking and sophisticated legal work. For example, a study by Levine, Waite, and Bowman showed that "the amount of time that young people spent IMing was significantly related to higher ratings of distractibility for academic tasks . . . ."[5] Not surprisingly, the same study showed that the amount of time spent reading books was negatively related to distractibility. Another 2005 study concluded that "workers distracted by e-mail and phone calls suffer a fall in IQ more than twice that found in marijuana smokers."[6] Donald Roberts, a Stanford professor of communications commenting on the Kaiser Family Foundation 2005 survey of Americans, says that "habitual multi-tasking may condition their brain to an overexcited state, making it difficult to focus even when they want to."[7] Roberts notes that Stanford students "can't go the few minutes between . . . classes without talking on their cell phones. . . . [T]here is almost a discomfort with not being stimulated—a kind of 'I can't stand the silence.'"[8] Another researcher, David E. Meyer, director of the Brain, Cognition and Action Laboratory at the University of Michigan, agrees. His research suggests that habitual multi-taskers "lose the skill and the will to maintain concentration. . . . [T]hey get mental antsyness."[9]

While more research needs to be done on how multi-tasking and specifically task switching affects a person's cognitive style, the early findings suggest that habitual uncontrolled multi-tasking, especially in the form of task switching, can lead to what we might regard as a self-induced form of attention deficient disorder. Acquiring such a cognitive style would undoubtedly hamper the kind of in-depth thought and sophisticated analysis lawyers need to do.

Unfortunately, that is not all the bad news about multi-tasking and task switching. A related area of concern being explored by brain researchers is how task switching affects *how* we learn, specifically where in the brain we store new learning and how that affects our ability to use what we learned. One study

---

5. Laura E. Levine et al., *Electronic Media Use, Reading, and Academic Distractibility in College Youth*, 10 CyberPsych. & Behav. 560, 560 (2007).

6. Christine Rosen, *The Myth of Multitasking*, 20 New Atlantis 105, 106 (2008).

7. Wallis, *supra* note 4, at 54, *quoted in* Levine et al., *supra* note 5, at 561; see Victoria Rideout et al., *Generation M: Media in the Lives of 8-18 Year Olds* (Kaiser Family Foundation 2005).

8. Wallis, *supra* note 4, at 52.

9. Meyers is somewhat optimistic that the human brain can learn to task-switch more effectively, but his research uncovers still another negative finding: multi-tasking contributes to the release of stress hormones and adrenaline, which can cause long-term health problems if not controlled, and contribute to loss of short-term memory. *Id.* at 54.

showed that students could learn new information while distracted by a second task, but the distraction "decreased the degree to which the participants used declarative memory (which relies on a medial temporal lobe system), as opposed to habit learning (which relies on the striatum)."[10] Both types of memory systems support learning, but learning stored in the habit learning areas of the brain is "less flexible and more specialized so you cannot retrieve the information as easily."[11] Declarative memory is more flexible, so knowledge stored there (which is what happens when one studies in a focused, uninterrupted way) is more useful and transferable to new situations.

So what do we do with all this new information about multi-tasking, and how do we use it to ensure that our legal research, analysis, and writing processes are efficient and effective?

First, we have to be realistic. Most of us are unlikely to give up our multi-tasking habit completely. Instead, the better approach may be to use the research findings to shape and manage our multi-tasking habit to our best advantage. If we know, for example, that some forms of parallel processing work for us, such as experiencing the calming effect of listening to background music while we research online, then we should continue to use those forms of multi-tasking. If, on the other hand, we suspect that our task switching habits are making us inefficient or distracted or more prone to make mistakes, we should consider monitoring our task switching to determine how best to re-shape those habits so that we can be more effective.

How are a few ideas you may want to consider as you think about how to develop effective research, analysis, and writing processes:

1. Be intentional about your own attention:
   - Cultivate the art of paying attention.
   - Monitor your ability to shift attention.
   - Exercise judgment about what is worthy of your attention.
2. Consider adopting some simple strategies for managing distractions and maintaining focus:
   - When you know you need to focus, close your email or turn off the email alert function, close the instant message window, turn off the Internet, close your laptop, and/or turn off your phone.
   - To avoid other distractions coming over your computer, print out online materials before reading them.
   - Limit the number of websites, particularly social websites, you visit.
   - Create stronger divisions between your "work time" and your "social time."
3. Recognize that your readers may also be multi-taskers suffering from information overload and, when appropriate, adapt your written communications to them accordingly:
   - Simplify messages.
   - Shorten messages.
   - Use "reply all" with care.

---

10. Karin Foerde et al., *Modulation of Competing Memory Systems by Distraction*, 103 Proceedings of the Nat'l Acad. of Sci. of the U.S. 11778 (2006).

11. Rosen, *supra* note 6, at 107, *quoting* Professor Russell Poldrack, a UCLA professor, in *Cognitive Neuroscience of Human Learning and Memory*.

Finally, we may want to consider the virtues of "single tasking." We know that geniuses in many fields are often known for their ability to focus their attention in order to acquire a deep understanding of a problem or issue. Sir Isaac Newton, for example, attributed his genius "to patient attention more than any other skill." Rather than secretly congratulating ourselves when we try to do three things at once, perhaps we should pat ourselves on the back when we, at least occasionally, make one important person, project, or legal problem the sole focus of our attention.

> **PRACTICE POINTER** The habit of multi-tasking raises some interesting ethical questions about billing clients. If a lawyer is parallel processing (for example, traveling by plane for one client but simultaneously doing work on another client's case) can he or she bill both clients?[12] The ABA has said no and condemned this form of double billing.[13] If a lawyer is task switching (toggling between work for several clients), is he or she obligated to deduct the time lost by the task switching? To date this question has not been specifically addressed.

§ 20.3.9   Reward Yourself

As you complete small parts of the larger writing task and as you see yourself meeting deadlines in your personal timetable, reward yourself. Rewards can be something small like a coffee break or checking Facebook or something big like an evening off for a movie or a Saturday afternoon hike. What matters is that writing becomes a pleasurable task at which you feel successful.

§ 20.4   Revising

Revision, or re-vision, means "to see again." When you revise, you step back from the project and try to see it with fresh eyes. This is not an easy thing to do. Many writers have difficulty adopting a revisionist perspective. Most avoid rethinking the whole document and prefer the safety of tinkering with smaller editing issues such as sentence structure or word choice. To help make the shift from drafter to reviser, you may find one of the following techniques helpful.

§ 20.4.1   Develop a Revision Checklist

A revision checklist should focus on the large issues in writing. Below is a sample revision checklist that can be used for most documents.

---

12. *See* Dennis Curtis & Judith Resnick, *Teaching Billing: Metrics of Value in Law Firms and Law Schools*, 54 Stan. L. Rev. 1409, 1415-16 (2002).

13. *http://www.abanet.org/cpr/about/billing_practices.html*; ABA Comm. on Ethics & Prof'l Responsibility, Formal Op. 379 (1993), reprinted in ABA/BNA Lawyers' Manual on Professional Conduct: Ethics Opinions 1001: 209, 213. *But see* Douglass R. Richmond, *Professional Responsibilities of Law Firm Associates*, 45 Brandeis L.J. 199 (2007).

Revision Checklist

- Have I answered the question I was asked?
- Will this document meet the reader's needs?
- Is the tone right for this document and this reader?
- Is the document well organized?
- Are the ideas well developed?
- Is the analysis conclusory or superficial? What would make it more sophisticated?
- What else should be included?
    - A plain language argument?
    - An argument based on an analogous case?
    - A policy argument?
    - A countervailing policy argument?
    - A rebuttal to an argument?
- What can be omitted?
- Is the theme, or theory of the case, evident in all sections of the document?

On your own revision checklist, add any other habitual writing problems that have been pointed out to you by your legal writing professor, classmates, colleagues, or other readers.

§ 20.4.2   Write an After-the-Fact Outline

Of all the areas to rethink when you are revising, the most challenging is often the organization. One simple way to check the paper's organization is to create an after-the-fact outline. An after-the-fact outline is an outline of what you actually wrote, not a plan that precedes the writing.

To create an after-the-fact outline, read each of your paragraphs and try to sum up the point in that paragraph in a phrase, clause, or, at most, a sentence. (If you can't do this summarizing, that alone suggests that the paragraph needs revision.) Record the summarizing phrase, clause, or sentence on the outline, using indentations to distinguish main points, subpoints, and sub-subpoints.

Use after-the-fact outlines the way you would an aerial photograph of ground you just covered on a hike. Seen from this perspective, is the way you traveled through the material the most efficient one? Do you have any needless backtracking? Repetition? Did you miss anything along the way? If so, where can you easily add it? Is this the way you want your reader to move through the material?

Now that you have the "big picture" in mind, are there ways you can prepare your reader for the twists and turns your path will take? For example, are there insights you should add to your roadmap paragraph that will help your reader? What kinds of signposts will help the reader stay on track? (See section 21.2.2.)

§ 20.4.3   Do a Self-Critique

Leave the role of the writer and become a critical reader. Play the devil's advocate. Where can you punch holes in this thing? Where are its weaknesses? Where are its strengths? Using what you find, you can return to the role of the writer and improve the draft.

§ 20.4.4 Check for Unity and Coherence

For a draft to be well written, the entire document, as well as each paragraph and section, must have unity and coherence. Unity at the document level means that every part of the document contributes to the overall thesis. In a memo, the thesis is essentially the same as your conclusion.

Many writers, though, do not have a clear idea of what their thesis is until they have completed a draft. While drafting, however, they discover what it is they are trying to say. This way of arriving at a thesis, or controlling idea, is perfectly fine. What it means, though, is that now that the writer has discovered the thesis he or she must go back through the draft with that thesis in mind, making sure that all parts are working toward that goal.

The same process may be true at the paragraph level. The writer may begin drafting a paragraph without a clear idea of what point he or she is trying to make. After drafting the paragraph, however, the writer discovers what the point is and how it contributes to the larger whole. At this point, then, the writer should first add or revise the topic sentence and then go back through the paragraph making sure all the parts contribute to the paragraph's point. See section 22.3.1 for more about unity.

Like unity, coherence is also important at both the document and the paragraph level. Consequently, a good revision strategy is to check (at both the document and the paragraph level) to see if you are using the following common devices for creating coherence:

- Logical organization
  - Chronological, spatial, topical
  - General to specific, specific to general
  - IRAC: issues, rules, analysis, conclusion
- Roadmap paragraphs
- Topic sentences
- Signposts, dovetailing, and transitions
- Repetition of key terms
- Parallelism
- Pronouns

See section 22.3.2 for more about how these devices create coherence.

Two final points about revising: First, drafting and revising are not always distinct stages in the writing process; some revising occurs even as the first draft is being written. Second, if possible, do some revising on hard copy. Seeing your writing on just a computer screen can be misleading. Because you can see only a small portion of a whole document at a time, you may overlook problems with some of the larger issues in writing.

§ 20.5 Editing

Editing is an examination of the smaller issues in writing. As with revising, you must once again step out of the role of the drafter and look at the writing with a critical eye, but this time the critical eye is focused on smaller issues such as sentence structure and word choice.

When editing for sentence structure, writers should pay particular attention to the subjects and verbs of their sentences. If the subject-verb combination is effective, many other writing problems will clear up automatically. See Chapter 24.

Legal writers should also make an extra effort to edit for precision and conciseness. See sections 25.1 and 25.2. Sloppy word choice and added verbiage may be overlooked in other types of writing, but they are unforgivable in legal writing. In addition to editing for sentence structure and word choice, every writer should edit for his or her habitual problem areas.

If this seems like a lot to think about all at once, you are right. For this reason, many writers find it easier to edit for just one or two writing problems at a time. If, for example, your habitual problem is wordiness, do one reading with the single goal of editing out all unnecessary words.

A Few Editing Tips

1. Don't let yourself fall in love with a particular phrase or sentence. No matter how well crafted it might be, if it doesn't work with the whole paragraph, indeed the whole document, it is not an effective phrase or sentence.

2. Be selective about whom you ask for editing advice. Although you can sometimes get excellent editing advice from others, there are far too many instances of the blind leading the mildly nearsighted. What often works better is to notice the parts of the document your reader/editor pointed out as problems and figure out with that reader what threw him or her off track. This procedure is much less risky than the unquestioning use of an inexperienced editor's rewrites.

3. Read your writing aloud or, better yet, have a colleague read it aloud to you while you follow along on another copy. Mark any part that the reader misreads or stumbles over, or anything that just doesn't sound right. This technique may not tell you how to fix something, but it will give you a good idea of what needs to be fixed.

4. Spend the majority of your editing time on the section(s) of the document that you found hardest to write. No need to keep massaging the opening sentence long after you know it reads smoothly. Force yourself to focus your editing energy on the rockiest parts of the document.

5. As with revising, if at all possible, do some of your editing on hard copy. The same language looks slightly different on a page than it does on a computer screen. For some reason, that small change from screen to page allows you to see the writing with different, fresh eyes.

§ 20.6   Proofreading

Whether you or your secretary types your writing, you will be the one who is responsible for the final product. Any missed words, format problems, or typos are ultimately your missed words, format problems, or typos. Consequently, every lawyer, no matter how competent his or her support staff, needs to know a few simple proofreading strategies.

First of all, proofreading is a distinct skill. It is not the same as normal reading or revising or editing. It is reading for errors. Consequently, to proofread properly, you need to remember a few important things.

Slow down. Speed-reading and proofreading are mutually exclusive terms. Proofreading should be done at your slowest reading rate. One technique for slowing yourself down is to cover up with another sheet of paper all but the line you are proofreading. This technique also helps you to focus on the individual words on the page, so you will see transposed letters in the middle of words and notice missing words rather than mistakenly reading them in where they *should* be.

Consider proofreading the last third of your document first. Chances are there are more errors in the last sections simply because you and your typist were probably more tired and rushed when they were done. If that's true, then it makes sense to use the time when you are freshest on the part of the document that needs it most.

If at all possible, do your proofreading at a completely separate time — ideally, a day or more after you have completed drafting and revising. Even a small break in time allows you to see the document anew and bring fresh eyes to the pages.

Proofread all parts of the document, including headings, charts, appendices, captions, and page numbers. Double-check all dates and monetary figures and the spelling of every name.

Finally, do not be lulled into complacence by your word processor's spell checking tool. Even the best computer software does not know a "trail" from a "trial."

§ 20.7   Myths About Writing

No one seems to know exactly where they come from, but over the years a number of myths have developed about writing. Many of these myths have been repeated and even taught to several generations so that they now have an air of legitimacy. They seem to be part of the common knowledge about writing, although one never sees them repeated in reputable composition textbooks.

The most unfortunate consequence of these myths is the unnecessary constraints they place on sophisticated writers. A good writer, for example, may labor mightily to avoid splitting an infinitive only to find that all the other options are awkward or imprecise. Still, the myth hovers over the writer's head, creating uneasiness about using split infinitives.

What to do? Because at least some of the myths are treated as gospel by some readers, it is probably unwise to make split infinitives, or any of the other myths, a trademark of your writing style. When another, equally good construction is available, use it instead. But when the best thing to do is to split an infinitive or start the sentence with "but" (as this sentence does) or to violate any of these other non-rules, do so — and do so without guilt.

Myth: Never Split an Infinitive

Grammar historians tell us that we acquired this non-rule at the time grammarians attempted to force the English language into the Latin grammar system. In Latin, infinitives are one word; hence, Latin infinitives are never split. Without regard to either the obvious fact that infinitives are two words in English (to see, to argue, to determine) or the obvious fact that speakers of English regularly split infinitives with a modifier, the non-rule was created so that English grammar could conform to Latin grammar.

This all seems terribly silly until you remember that at the time English was considered an inferior, upstart, unruly language; and Latin was considered a superior, well-designed, systematic language. Moreover, devising a grammar that actually described the way English was used was unheard of at the time. The purpose of grammar, it was thought, was to bring order to a language raging out of control.

What should a legal writer do then about split infinitives? Because the split infinitive myth is entrenched in many educated readers' minds, it is not worth the possible negative reaction to a given split infinitive if there are reasonably good ways to change it.

However, when the split infinitive is the best, indeed the most precise, way to express a point, stand your ground and use it. Note, however, that infinitives should not be split by the word "not." The correct way to write the negative form of an infinitive is to place the "not" before the infinitive.

EXAMPLE 1　　　**Editing Split Infinitives**

Draft

The defendant explained that to not attend the meeting would have drawn undue attention to him.

Revised

The defendant explained that not to attend the meeting would have drawn undue attention to him.

OR

The defendant explained that not attending the meeting would have drawn undue attention to him.

Myth:　Never Start a Sentence with "And," "But," or "Or"

Although there is no real rule that you cannot start a sentence with "and," "but," or "or," it is often a good idea to choose a more specific transition. If using one of these three words is a hasty or lazy choice, it is probably a stylistically poor choice.

Occasionally, however, one of these three words is the perfect transition, especially because each is a one-syllable word that gets the next sentence started quickly. For this reason, it is usually not a good idea to start a sentence with "and," "but," or "or" and then follow the conjunction with a comma. When you do, you start the sentence up quickly only to immediately slow it down.

One final caveat about using "and," "but," or "or" at the beginnings of sentences: As transitions, these three words tend to sound informal.

Myth: Never Start a Sentence with "Because" or "However"

Legal writers often need to describe cause/effect relationships. In such cases, the best sentence structure is often "Because (fill in the cause), (fill in the effect)." This is an exceedingly useful sentence structure, and no rule prohibits its use.

Similarly, no rule prohibits beginning a sentence with "however." Stylistically, however, it is often a better idea to move the transition "however" further into the sentence so that it immediately precedes the point of contrast, as is the case in this sentence.

Myth: Never End a Sentence with a Preposition

Winston Churchill did more than anyone else to debunk this writing myth. Churchill pointed out the idiocy of this non-rule when he wrote the following marginal comment on a state document: "This is the sort of English up with which I will not put."

Notwithstanding Churchill's remark, many readers claim to be offended by sentences that end with prepositions. For this reason, it is not a good practice to end sentences with prepositions when they can be easily revised.

| EXAMPLE 2 | Editing Sentences That End with a Preposition |

Draft:

Winfield may be able to get title to the entire triangle, not just the part that the bathhouse is built on.

Revised:

Winfield may be able to get title to the entire triangle, not just the part on which the bathhouse is built.

Myth: Never Write a One-Sentence Paragraph

One-sentence paragraphs are not wrong per se, although they are often a sign of lack of development of the ideas in the writing. Numerous one-sentence paragraphs have the added drawback of making the writing seem unsophisticated.

For these reasons, use one-sentence paragraphs infrequently. Save them for occasions when the paragraph serves as a transition between two large sections of a document or when a shorter paragraph will give the reader a breather between two extremely long paragraphs. Notice too that a well-written one-sentence paragraph is usually made up of a fairly long sentence, although on rare occasions a one-sentence paragraph composed of a short sentence can be quite dramatic. See section 22.4 for more about paragraph length.

Chapter 20 Quiz

Draft answers for each of the following questions. Make your points clearly and concisely, and write sentences that are easy to read and that are grammatical and correctly punctuated.

1. What are some of the techniques writers use to get started on a writing project?
2. What are some of the techniques writers use to create organization?
3. What are some strategies for overcoming writer's block?
4. What are some techniques writers use to revise their work?
5. What are some approaches writers can use to edit their work?
6. What is probably the most important thing to remember about proofreading?
7. What are some of the techniques a writer can use to proofread effectively?

Connections Between Paragraphs

§ 21.1 Headings

Headings serve two purposes for the reader: They signal the overall organization, and they help the reader locate where he or she is in a document.

As indicators of organization, headings work a bit like a table of contents. They give the reader the framework within which to fit the ideas.

As locating devices, headings are invaluable to readers. A reader who does not have the time to read the whole document can use the headings to find the exact section he or she must read. For readers who have already read the whole document and later need to refer to a point, headings are a quick way to locate that point.[1]

For headings to be helpful, they must be written in parallel form (see section 27.7) and in a consistent format. If the document has headings and subheadings, the reader will be able to identify the different levels of headings if they use compatible but different formats. For example, the main headings may use Roman numerals and boldface while the subheadings may use capital letters and underlining.

---

1. Like all other headings, argumentative headings in briefs must be both indicators of overall organization and locating devices. In addition, they must persuade.

Even though headings in objective memos are somewhat less important to the overall document than argumentative headings are to a brief, they still must be well written. The best headings in memos are fairly short, not more than one typed line and usually less than half a line, and they capture the content in a nutshell.

EXAMPLE 1   **Headings Format**

I. Main Heading
   A. <u>Subheading</u>
   B. <u>Subheading</u>
II. Main Heading
   A. <u>Subheading</u>
   B. <u>Subheading</u>

When creating headings, remember the time-honored advice that "You can't have a 1 without a 2, and you can't have an A without a B." In other words, do not create a heading or a subheading unless there is at least one more heading or subheading at that same level.

Developing a good and consistent format for headings is simple. The bigger challenge is composing their content. To be useful finding devices, headings must capture the essence of the section with enough specificity to be meaningful and enough generality to encompass the entire section.

Often the law itself will suggest the content of various sections of the document and hence the headings. An elements analysis or a list of factors, for example, naturally suggests a document with the elements or factors as the headings.

But don't automatically assume that each element or factor deserves its own heading. Because undisputed elements will probably require minimal discussion, the document will appear chopped up if the writer uses a separate heading for each one. More importantly, the reader is not likely to need a heading for each undisputed element.

To compose good headings, find the key words and phrases that sum up the section. Sometimes the easiest way to write a heading is to reread the section and ask yourself, "In a nutshell, what is this section about?" The answer should be close to what would make a good heading. For example, if the answer is "the court's lack of jurisdiction in this matter," then the heading becomes "Lack of Jurisdiction."

But suppose you were writing an office memo for a case and your answer to the question "What is this section about?" was something like "whether or not the court will admit the eyewitnesses' line-up identifications." Although this clause may accurately sum up the section, consider how it will look as a heading.

EXAMPLE 2   **Weak Heading**

Whether or Not the Court Will Admit the Eyewitnesses'
Line-up Identifications

The example heading exceeds the one-line limit and includes some information that the reader can easily infer. Now consider the following four substitute headings for the same section.

EXAMPLE 3   **Substitute Headings**

1. The Line-up

2. Line-up Identifications

3. Admissibility of Line-up Identifications

4. Admissibility of Eyewitnesses' Line-up Identifications

Option 1 is probably too general. It is unlikely the following section will include everything about the line-up. Option 2 is better. Even so, if the focus of the following section is on the *admissibility* of the identifications, that key word in the heading will be helpful to the reader. Option 4 is also acceptable, but the word "eyewitnesses" can probably be inferred. Option 3 is the best. It sums up the section, it includes the key words and phrases, and it is short enough to be read at a glance.

One last thought about headings: Headings are for the reader, not the writer. The most common mistake legal writers make regarding headings is to use them as crutches for the writer. Headings should not be used as artificial bridges between two sections of the document. The connection between the sections should be made without the heading.

§ 21.2   Roadmaps and Signposts

§ 21.2.1 Roadmaps

Roadmaps are introductory paragraphs that give readers an overview of the entire document. They give readers the "big picture" perspective.

Like real roadmaps, roadmap paragraphs orient readers in several ways: They establish the overall structure of the discussion; they suggest what will be important and hence what deserves the readers' particular attention; and they create expectations for how the discussion will unfold and conclude.

Although not every objective memo needs a roadmap paragraph, those with several steps in the analysis are easier to read if the writer uses a roadmap to set the stage for what follows. For example, an attorney writing a memo on whether electromagnetic fields are a nuisance used the following roadmap to show the two steps in the court's analysis.

EXAMPLE 1   **Roadmap of the Analysis**

In deciding whether New Mexico will allow a cause of action in nuisance, the New Mexico courts will look first at whether EMFs constitute a public nuisance and then at whether they constitute a private nuisance.

A roadmap paragraph like the one that follows provides a helpful overview of how the court will analyze a particular issue.

EXAMPLE 2   **Overview Roadmap**

The McKibbins' claim is that, because there was no written contract, the oral contract is unenforceable under this state's version of the UCC Statute of Frauds. The first thing the court will have to determine, then, is whether the UCC applies at all. If the court finds that the UCC does govern the contract, the court will then have to decide whether the Statute of Frauds bars BCC's claim. Because BCC did not comply with the formal requirements of the Statute of Frauds, the court will find that the contract is unenforceable unless one of the exceptions included in the Statute applies. The only exception likely to apply is the specially manufactured goods exception.

A good roadmap paragraph also tells readers where to focus their attention. For example, if the applicable law includes several elements or factors, the reader will find it helpful to be told in the roadmap paragraph which elements or factors are critical to a case.

EXAMPLE 3   **Overview Roadmap with Focus**

To claim a prescriptive easement, the Oregon Wilderness Watchers (OWW) will have to satisfy four elements by clear and convincing evidence: (1) that its use was open and notorious; (2) that its use was continuous and uninterrupted; (3) that its use was adverse to the right of the owner; and (4) that its use of the property met each of the other requirements for over ten years. *See Thompson v. Scott*, 528 P.2d 509, 510 (Or. 1974). Although OWW should have no difficulty satisfying the first and fourth elements, the second element and especially the third element will be difficult to satisfy.

Roadmap paragraphs that use the "first, we will look at _____; then we will look at _____; and finally we will look at _____" approach tend to sound unsophisticated. Substituting "I" or "this memorandum" is no better. A better approach is to use the court as the actor.

Compare the following roadmap paragraphs. Notice how much more sophisticated Examples 5 and 6 sound.

EXAMPLE 4   **Unsophisticated Roadmap Paragraph**

In this memorandum, we will examine three issues. First, we will look at whether the statute applies. If we find that it does not, then we will look at whether the Oregon Wilderness Watchers had an easement. If we find that an easement was created, then we will examine the scope of the easement.

EXAMPLE 5   **Better Roadmap**

Our client would like to prevent or limit the use of a path across his property by the Oregon Wilderness Watchers (OWW). An Oregon statute exists that provides for public recreational use, while protecting the owner's interest in his land, and we will argue that it applies to this case. OWW will contend that the statute does not apply and that a prescriptive easement exists. If a prescriptive easement does exist, our client wants to limit the scope of its use.

EXAMPLE 6	**Better Roadmap**

In deciding this case, a court will consider three issues. First, a court will determine whether the statute applies. If it does not, the court will then determine whether the Oregon Wilderness Watchers had an easement. If the court determines that an easement had been created, the court will then decide the scope of the easement.

§ 21.2.2 Signposts

Signposts are those words and phrases that keep readers oriented as they progress through a piece of writing. They can be used as a connecting thread throughout a whole document or through a smaller section.

To be the most effective, a series of signposts needs to be signaled in advance. For example, a writer may signal a series of signposts by saying, "There are four exceptions to the Statute of Frauds." In the subsequent discussion, the writer can then use the words "first," "second," "third," "fourth" (or "final" or "last"), and "exception" to signal shifts to each new exception.

The following example is an excerpt from a memo about whether a contract is enforceable under the UCC Statute of Frauds. The set-up for the signpost series and the signposts are in boldface type.

EXAMPLE 7	**Roadmap Setting Up Signposts**

There are four exceptions to the Statute of Frauds, but three of them are not applicable. The first of these inapplicable exceptions, § 4-2-201(2), applies only to transactions "between merchants." In an earlier section, § 4-2-201(1), a merchant is defined as "a person who deals in goods of the kind or otherwise holds himself out as having knowledge or skill peculiar to the practices or goods involved in the transaction or to whom such knowledge or skill may be attributed by his employment of an agent or broker or other intermediary who by his occupation holds himself out as having such knowledge or skill." Because the McKibbins presumably had little or no experience in the carpeting business and because they hired no intermediary to negotiate the transaction for them, the court will probably not find that they are merchants. This exception, then, does not apply.

The second inapplicable exception, § 4-2-201(3)(b), provides that a contract that does not satisfy the requirements of subsection (1) is still enforceable if the party against whom enforcement is sought admits in his or her pleading, testimony, or otherwise in court that a contract for sale was made. Because we are not at the litigation stage of this case yet, this exception does not apply.

The third inapplicable exception, § 4-2-201(3)(c), provides that a contract is enforceable with respect to goods for which payment has been made and accepted or which have been received and accepted. The McKibbins made no payment for the rugs, and they never received the rugs, so this exception also does not apply.

The exception that may be applicable is the exception for specially manufactured goods . . . .

Notice that most signpost series use the ordinal numbers (first, second, third, and so on) before a noun such as "element," "exception," "factor," "issue," "part," "prong," "reason," "requirement," "question," or "section."

| EXAMPLE 8 | **Typical Signposts** |

three issues
the first issue, the second issue, the third issue

a two-part test
the first part of the test, the second part of the test

Once a signpost series is set up, do not change terminology. If there were "three questions" in the introduction to the series, it may confuse readers if the second question is suddenly relabeled "the second issue."

Chapter 21 Quiz

Draft answers for each of the following questions. Make your points clearly and concisely, and write sentences that are easy to read and that are grammatical and correctly punctuated.

1. What are the two purposes for headings?
2. What are the two requirements for writing a pair or group of headings?
3. What is the key to creating the best content for a heading?
4. What is a roadmap?
5. What are signposts? Give some examples.

22

Effective Paragraphs

§ 22.1   The Function of a Paragraph

Paragraphs exist for many reasons. First, they help writers organize what they are writing. Second, they help readers see and understand that organization. Third, they give readers a psychological, as well as a logical, break.

Writers need paragraphs to help them stay organized and in control of what they are writing. For writers, paragraphs are like tidy boxes in which to sort information. They make writing a manageable task.

Readers need paragraphs so that they can absorb information in manageable bits. If the typical legal reader must comprehend twenty hours' worth of research in the roughly twenty minutes it takes to study an eight-page memo, he or she will need some way to see significant groupings of ideas. That way is the paragraph.

But paragraphing is more than a matter of logic and organization. It is also a matter of reader comfort and aesthetics. After all, those "boxes" into which the writer is fitting ideas can be huge containers that are too heavy to lift or small cartons with barely enough room for half of an idea.

When paragraphs are too long, readers tend to become bewildered, even lost, or worse, lulled into inattention. Paragraphs that are too short, on the other hand, make the writing and the thinking seem skimpy and inconsequential. Readers need paragraphs that are the right size to comfortably follow what the writer is saying.

Paragraphs also change the look of a page. They create more white space, which can be a welcome relief. Anyone who has opened a book to see a solid mass of type on page one knows how intimidating overly long paragraphs can be. In contrast, the visual break at the beginning of a paragraph signals a brief mental breather.

As the first significant grouping of sentences, a paragraph becomes a kind of mini-composition all its own. It has a beginning, a middle, and an end.

The paragraph in Example 1, which is taken from the middle of an argument section of a brief in opposition to a motion to disclose the identity of a state informant, illustrates how a paragraph is a mini-composition.

EXAMPLE 1   **Paragraph as a Mini-Composition**

Beginning   The fact that the informant is present at the alleged drug transaction is not determinative of whether the testimony of that informant is relevant or necessary. *Lewandowski v. State*, 389 N.E.2d 706 (Ind. 1979). In *Lewandowski*, the Indiana Supreme Court held that "[m]ere presence of the informer when marijuana was sold to a police officer has been held to be insufficient to overcome the privilege

Middle   of nondisclosure." *Id.* at 710. The court made the same ruling on nearly identical facts in *Craig v. State*, 404 N.E.2d 580 (Ind. 1980) (informant introduced officer to defendant and was present during purchase of illegal drugs). In the present

Ending   case, the state's informant served mainly as a line of introduction and as such her testimony does not automatically become relevant or necessary to the defendant's case simply because she was present at the scene.

---

§ 22.2   Paragraph Patterns

Every paragraph needs a focus, a topic, a point to make. In addition, every paragraph needs a shape, a way of moving through sentences to make that point. The example paragraph in section 22.1 about the relevance of the informant's testimony has one of the most common shapes or patterns: that of a fat hourglass.

An hourglass paragraph begins with a general statement about the topic. This statement may take up one or more sentences. The paragraph then narrows to the specific support or elaboration or explanation the writer has for that general statement. The paragraph concludes with a more general sentence or two about the topic.

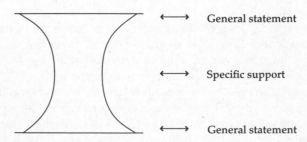

More common in legal writing is a variation of this pattern, the V-shaped paragraph. Like the hourglass paragraph, the V-shaped paragraph begins with a general discussion of the topic and then narrows to the specific support. The V-shaped paragraph does not return to a general statement.

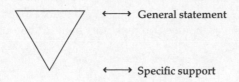

General statement

Specific support

EXAMPLE 1   **V-Shaped Paragraph**

Kraft Savings, one of three savings and loans represented on Kraft Island,   **General statement**
does a significant amount of the banking business on Kraft Island. As of 2009,
Kraft Savings had $3.2 million in deposits, $11.6 million in outstanding loans,   **Specific support**
and a large volume of business with the Kraft City Council. In 2009, Kraft
Savings handled $50 million in transactions for almost 1,900 customers in
about 2,400 accounts.

Both the hourglass and the V-shaped paragraph patterns work well in legal writing. Both use the opening sentence or sentences as an overview of what is to come and then proceed to support that generalization with specifics.

§ 22.3 Unity and Coherence in Paragraphs

§ 22.3.1 Paragraph Unity

To be a mini-composition, a paragraph must have its own topic, that is, its own point to make, and all parts in the paragraph must work together to make that point. When they do, the paragraph has unity.

Look again at the example in section 22.1 about the state informant.

EXAMPLE 1   **Unified Paragraph**

The fact that the informant is present at the alleged drug transaction is not determinative of whether the testimony of that informant is relevant or necessary. *Lewandowski v. State*, 389 N.E.2d 706, 710 (Ind. 1979); *accord Mays v. State*, 907 N.E.2d 128 (Ind. App. 2009). In *Lewandowski*, the Indiana Supreme Court held that the mere presence of the informer when marijuana was sold to a police officer is insufficient to overcome the privilege of nondisclosure. *Id.* The court reached the same conclusion on nearly identical facts in *Craig v. State*, 404 N.E.2d 580 (Ind. 1980) (informant introduced officer to defendant and was present during purchase of illegal drugs). In the present case, the State's informant served mainly as a line of introduction and as such her testimony does not automatically become relevant or necessary to the defendant's case simply because she was present at the scene.

All of the information is about one topic: The informant's testimony is not necessarily relevant or necessary simply because the informant was present at the drug transaction. This topic is introduced at the beginning of the paragraph by a topic sentence, developed and supported by two sentences in the middle of the paragraph, and then concluded by the last sentence.

What the paragraph does not do is stray from this topic. Even though the writer will need to refer to both *Lewandowski* and *Craig* later in the memo to support other points, he or she did not get sidetracked and try to do it here. The paragraph stays on course and makes its point. It has a clear focus; it has unity.

§ 22.3.2 Paragraph Coherence

When a paragraph is coherent, the various elements of the paragraph are connected in such a way that the reader can easily follow the writer's development of ideas. Coherence can be achieved in a number of ways: by using familiar organizational patterns, particularly those that are established patterns for legal writing; by establishing and then using key terms; and by using sentence structure and other coherence devices to reinforce the connections between ideas.

a.   Using Familiar Organizational Patterns

All readers expect certain patterns — cause/effect, problem/solution, chronological order — and when writers meet those expectations, the ideas are easy to follow. Legal readers have some additional patterns that they expect in legal writing. For example, once a rule, standard, or definition has been laid out, legal readers expect it to be applied. They expect a court's holding to be followed by its rationale. In office memos, arguments are almost always followed by counterarguments. In both office memos and briefs, the IRAC pattern (issue, rule, analysis/application, and conclusion) and all its variations are commonplace and expected.

Writers can also achieve coherence in paragraphs by creating reader expectations and then fulfilling them. For example, when a writer sets up a list of factors, elements, reasons, or issues, the reader expects the writing to follow up on that list, typically in the order in which the list was first set out. In Example 2, the writer uses this technique to create the expectation that the paragraph will set out the defendant's arguments.

EXAMPLE 2   **Paragraph Sets Up and Meets Expectations**

Ms. Johnson can make four arguments. First, she can argue that the consent element is not met because Elite did not tell her that all of her phone calls were being monitored. Elite only told Ms. Johnson that her calls would be monitored periodically. Second, Ms. Johnson can argue that, like the plaintiffs in *Campiti* and *Williams*, she did not know that her calls were being monitored. In the past, her phone calls had been monitored only in January, immediately before her annual performance review, and her supervisor had intercepted only two or three of her calls and had talked to her about those calls immediately afterwards. Third, Ms. Johnson can argue that Elite's statements and actions indicate that Elite did not believe that Ms. Johnson knew that her calls were being intercepted. Just as the Spears hoped to catch Deal in an admission tying her to a burglary, Elite hoped to catch Ms. Johnson in an admission tying her to an insurance fraud scheme. Finally, Ms. Johnson can argue that even if she did consent to the monitoring of her phone calls to determine whether she was providing good customer service, she did not consent to the monitoring of her personal calls. Thus, Elite should have stopped recording any personal calls of hers as soon as it recognized that the call was a personal call.

---

b.   Using Key Terms

Of the various methods writers have for creating coherence, repetition of key terms is the easiest and one of the most important. In the following example paragraph, we have used different typefaces for each of the key terms — informant or informer, **present** or **presence**, testimony, and RELEVANT OR NECESSARY — so you can see how the repetition of key terms gives the paragraph coherence. Together the key terms are part of a network of connecting threads that create a coherent theme for the paragraph.

EXAMPLE 3   **With Key Terms Highlighted**

The fact that the informant is present at the alleged drug transaction is not determinative of whether the testimony of that informant is RELEVANT OR NECESSARY. *Lewandowski v. State*, 389 N.E.2d 706 (Ind. 1979). In *Lewandowski*, the Indiana Supreme Court held that "[m]ere **presence** of the informer when marijuana was sold to a police officer has been held to be insufficient to overcome the privilege of nondisclosure." *Id.* at 710. The court made the same ruling on nearly identical facts in *Craig v. State*, 404 N.E.2d 580 (Ind. 1980) (informant introduced officer to defendant and was **present** during purchase of illegal drugs). In the present case, the state's informant served mainly as a line of introduction and as such her testimony does not automatically become RELEVANT OR NECESSARY to the defendant's case simply because she was **present** at the scene.

---

c.   Using Sentence Structure and Other Coherence Devices

Writers can also create coherence through sentence structure and through a number of other common coherence devices. "Dovetailing" (beginning a sentence with a reference to the preceding sentence) and other transitions create connections by establishing links between sentences. See section 23.3. Parallelism within a sentence or between sentences shows the reader which ideas should be considered together and which should be compared and contrasted. See section 27.7. Even pronouns in their own small way provide subtle links within the writing because they are a connection to the noun they replace.

For the paragraph in Example 4, notice how the writer uses the signposts "first," "second," "third," and "finally" followed by the parallel sentence openers "Ms. Johnson can argue that" to create coherence. Notice too how the parallel language "as the Spears hoped to catch Deal in an admission tying her to a burglary" and "Elite hoped to catch Ms. Johnson in an admission tying her to an insurance fraud scheme" create a coherent connection between these two points. Note too the dovetailing between sentences 3 and 4 ("Elite did not tell her all of her phone calls were being monitored" → "Elite only told Ms. Johnson that her calls would be monitored periodically"). Once again, pronouns also subtly provide coherence ("Ms. Johnson" → "she," "Elite" → "it").

EXAMPLE 4   **Creating Coherence in a Paragraph**

Ms. Johnson can make four arguments. First, she can argue that the consent element is not met because Elite did not tell her that all of her phone calls were being monitored. Elite only told Ms. Johnson that her calls would be monitored periodically. Second, Ms. Johnson can argue that, like the plaintiffs in *Campiti* and *Williams*, she did not know that her calls were being monitored. In the past, her phone calls had been monitored only in January, immediately before her annual performance review, and her supervisor had intercepted only two or three of her calls and had talked to her about those calls immediately afterwards. Third, Ms. Johnson can argue that Elite's statements and actions indicate that Elite did not believe that Ms. Johnson knew that her calls were being intercepted. Just as the Spears hoped to catch Deal in an admission tying her to a burglary, Elite hoped to catch Ms. Johnson in an admission tying her to an insurance fraud scheme. Finally, Ms. Johnson can argue that even if she did consent to the monitoring of her phone calls to determine whether she was providing good customer service, she did not consent to the monitoring of her personal calls. Thus, Elite should have stopped recording any personal calls of hers as soon as it recognized that the call was a personal call.

§ 22.4   Paragraph Length

First, the truth: Not all paragraphs are three to five sentences long. In fact, quite a few well-written paragraphs are as short as two sentences, and, yes, some well-written paragraphs contain only one sentence. One-sentence paragraphs are neither a goal to strive for nor a taboo to be feared. Writers simply need to know when they have finished what they set out to do in the paragraph.

Similarly, good paragraphs may run many sentences longer than five. It is not outrageous for a paragraph in legal writing to include seven or even eight sentences, as long as the writer needs that many to make the point. However, writers should keep in mind the reader's comfort and avoid seven- and eight-sentence paragraphs about complicated discussions of law. Remember too that an eight-sentence paragraph is likely to create a solid page of type, which has a negative psychological impact on readers.

The paragraphs in the following example are from a section in an appellate brief. Notice the number of sentences in and the length of each paragraph. (Citation sentences are not counted as substantive sentences.)

| **EXAMPLE 1** | **Variety in Paragraph Length** |

I. The Trial Court Erred in Holding That the Plaintiff Is a Public Figure as a Matter of Law

Two-sentence paragraph

The states have a legitimate interest in compensating plaintiffs for damage to reputation inflicted through defamatory publications. *Gertz v. Robert Welch, Inc.*, 418 U.S. 323, 341 (1974). While recognizing that "[s]ome tension necessarily exists between the need for a vigorous and uninhibited press and the legitimate interest in redressing wrongful injury," the U.S. Supreme Court has stressed that the plaintiff's right to the protection of his reputation must not be sacrificed when the court balances these two competing interests. *Id.*

Three-sentence paragraph

In an attempt to balance the interests of the media against the interests of plaintiffs injured by defamatory statements, the Court developed three classes of plaintiffs: public officials, public figures, and private figures. *Gertz*, 418 U.S. at 343; *Curtis Publ'g Co. v. Butts*, 388 U.S. 130 (1966); *N.Y. Times v. Sullivan*, 376 U.S. 254, 279 (1964). Because public figure plaintiffs are held to a higher standard of proof in defamation suits, the Court has made it clear that the public figure standard is to be construed narrowly. *Gertz*, 418 U.S. at 352. The Court will not lightly find a plaintiff to be a public figure. *Id.*

The first class of public figure defined by the Court in *Gertz* is the limited purpose public figure. To become a limited purpose public figure, a plaintiff must voluntarily inject himself or herself into a particular public controversy and attempt to influence its outcome. *Id.* at 351, 352. By doing so, the plaintiff invites public attention and comment on a limited range of issues relating to his or her involvement in the controversy. *Id.* at 351.

Three-sentence paragraph

The Court described the second class of public figure, the all-purpose public figure, as having "assumed roles of especial prominence in the affairs of society," or as occupying "positions of such persuasive power and influence," or as "achieving such pervasive fame or notoriety that he becomes a public figure for all purposes and in all contexts." *Id.* at 345, 351.

One-sentence paragraph

Under these narrow definitions laid down by the U.S. Supreme Court, Kraft Savings and Loan is neither a limited purpose public figure nor an all-purpose public figure. Therefore, the trial court erred in granting defendants' motion for partial summary judgment on the public figure issue. Furthermore, this error was prejudicial because it resulted in the plaintiffs being held to a higher standard of proof at trial. But because the standard of review is *de novo* when a partial summary judgment order is appealed, this Court is not bound by the erroneous trial court decision below. *Herron v. Tribune Publ'g Co.*, 108 Wn.2d 162, 169, 736 P.2d 249, 255 (1987); *Noel v. King County*, 48 Wn. App. 227, 231, 738 P.2d 692, 695 (1987). Rather, the Court should apply the *Gertz* public figure standard to the facts of this case and reach its own independent determination. Correct application of the standard will result in a holding that Kraft Savings and Loan is a private figure for purposes of this defamation suit.

Six-sentence paragraph

First, a few comments about the preceding example: Notice that the length of each paragraph is primarily determined by content. The writer wrote as few or as many sentences as she needed to make each point. The length of each paragraph is further determined by reader comfort and interest. Some variety in paragraph length helps keep the writing interesting. Short one- or two-sentence paragraphs tend to work in places where the reader needs a bit of a break before or after an unusually long paragraph. Too many short paragraphs, though, and the writing begins to seem choppy and undeveloped.

Short paragraphs can also be effective when the writer is making a major shift, change, or connection between ideas. Consequently, short paragraphs frequently serve as transitions between major sections and as introductions or conclusions to major sections.

An occasional long paragraph allows the writer to go into depth on a point. Too many long paragraphs, though, and the writing slows down to a plod and seems heavy and ponderous.

§ 22.5   Topic and Concluding Sentences

Again, the truth: Not all paragraphs have topic and concluding sentences. In fact, many well-written paragraphs have neither.

However, and this is a big "however," most well-written paragraphs do have topic sentences, and those that don't have an implied topic sentence that governs the paragraph as firmly as any written topic sentence. The truth about concluding sentences is that sometimes they are useful to the reader and sometimes they are not. You have to use your common sense about when to include one and when to leave one out. Readers are most likely to find concluding sentences helpful after longer, more complicated points. If, on the other hand, you are confident that the information in the concluding sentence would be painfully obvious, then leave it out.

The point then is to know what topic and concluding sentences do for a paragraph. Then you can decide whether a stated or an implied topic or concluding sentence works in a given situation.

§ 22.5.1   Stated Topic Sentences

The following examples demonstrate how the standard topic sentence works. Notice that the topic sentence has two functions: It introduces or names the topic and it asserts something about the topic.

EXAMPLE 1   **Standard Topic Sentence**

In determining whether service is proper under Fed. R. Civ. P. 4, courts consider several factors. First, the courts recognize that "each decision proceeds on its own facts." *Karlsson*, 318 F.2d at 668. Second, the courts consider whether the defendant will return to the place where service was left. *Id.* Third, the courts look at whether service was reasonably calculated to provide actual notice to the defendant. *Minnesota Mining & Mfg. Co. v. Kirkevold*, 87 F.R.D. 317, 323 (D. Minn. 1980).

EXAMPLE 2   **Standard Topic Sentence**

Defendants have successfully used the following articulated reasons to rebut a plaintiff's prima facie case. In *Kelly*, the defendant testified that the plaintiff was terminated because he was the least effective salesman. *Kelly*, 640 F.2d at 977 (*overruled on other grounds*). Similarly, in *Sakellar*, the defendant alleged that the plaintiff lacked the skills and experience for the position. *Sakellar*, 765 F.2d at 1456. And in *Sutton*, the defendant discharged the plaintiff for "intemperate and impolitic actions." *Sutton*, 646 F.2d at 410.

One common weakness of some novice legal writers is to write topic sentences that merely name the topic. These topic sentences fall under the category of "The next thing I'm going to talk about is . . ."

Compare the following two topic sentences. Which would a reader find more helpful?

EXAMPLE 3   **Poor Topic Sentence**

Another case that discussed actual malice is *Journal-Gazette Co., Inc. v. Bandido's Inc.*, 712 N.E.2d 446 (Ind. 1999).

EXAMPLE 4   **Improved Topic Sentence**

The court extended these protections in *Journal-Gazette Co., Inc. v. Bandidos, Inc.*, 712 N.E.2d 446 (Ind. 1999), holding that plaintiffs in a defamation action would have to prove actual malice if the published statements were of public or general interest. *Id.* at 452.

The topic sentence in Example 3 does little more than name a case. The topic sentence in Example 4 is far superior. In addition to naming the case, it sets up the point that the case contributes to the analysis, which is the point the paragraph will develop.

The topic sentence in Example 4 also demonstrates an excellent method for writing topic sentences that introduce a new case: It begins with a transition that relates the point from the new case to the previous discussion and then follows with a paraphrase of the holding. The following example shows how the writer completed the paragraph.

EXAMPLE 5   **Completed Paragraph**

The court extended these protections in *Journal-Gazette Co., Inc. v. Bandido's Inc.*, **712 N.E.2d 446 (Ind. 1999), holding that plaintiffs in a defamation action would have to prove actual malice if the published statements were of public or general interest.** *Id.* at 452. The court wrote, "If a matter is a subject of public or general interest, it cannot suddenly become less so merely because a private individual is involved, or because in some sense the individual did not 'voluntarily' choose to become involved." *Id.* (quoting *Rosenbloom v. Metromedia*, 403 U.S. 29, 43 (1971)).

The next two examples also show how to use a court's holding for the topic sentence. In Example 6, the writer develops the topic sentence by setting out the facts in the analogous case and then distinguishing them from the client's case. In Example 7, the writer develops the topic sentence by setting out the facts of the case and then returns to the holding.

EXAMPLE 6   **Holding for the Topic Sentence**

In *Messenger*, **the court determined that the trespassory slashing of trees was a permanent form of property damage.** *Messenger v. Frye*, 176 Wash. 291, 299, 28 P.2d 1023 (1934). However, the tree slashing in that case was extensive. *Id.* at 294. It was the extent of the injury, not the type of injury, that made the damage irreparable and therefore permanent. *See id.* at 294, 299. Unlike the slashed trees, the damage to the rosebushes in the Archers' case should not be considered extensive because only four out of twenty rosebushes were destroyed. The rosebushes can probably be replaced, thus restoring the Archers' property to its original condition. Therefore, the damage to the rosebushes and buds is temporary, and the Archers will recover only for the restoration cost of the rosebuds and bushes, as well as the diminished use value of their property.

EXAMPLE 7   **Holding for the Topic Sentence**

In an analogous Arizona case, **the court held that the trial court committed an error of constitutional magnitude when it allowed the prosecution to do exactly as the prosecution did in the present case.** *State v. Thomas*, 130 Ariz. 432, 636 P.2d 1217 (1981). In *Thomas*, the only pertinent evidence was the testimony of the defendant, who was accused of rape, and the testimony of the prosecuting witness. *Id.* at 434. During the trial, the prosecution questioned the witness about her religious beliefs and church-related activities, eliciting from her that she was a religious person. *Id.* In closing argument, the prosecutor told the jury that the ultimate issue was the credibility of the witnesses, and that before the jury could believe the defendant, it had to believe that the prosecuting witness, an "uprighteous, religious, moralistic type," was a liar. *Id.* The appellate court held that admission of the religious references was an error of constitutional magnitude. *Id.*

Writing strong topic sentences is critical to your analysis. Often the topic sentence is the spot where the writer synthesizes a group of analogous cases. Notice in Examples 8 and 9 how the topic sentences sum up the key features the writer has uncovered in a group of cases with the same holding.

EXAMPLE 8   **Topic Sentence Synthesizes Cases**

In deciding whether a claimant was using the land as if it were its own, the courts consider whether the claimant made improvements to the land, whether the claimant maintained the property, and whether the claimant used the land on a regular basis. *See, e.g., Chaplin*, 100 Wn.2d at 855-56; *Timberlane*, 79 Wn. App. at 310-11. For example, in *Chaplin*, the court held that the claimants were using the land as if it were their own when the claimants built a road across the disputed land, cleared and maintained the disputed land, installed utility lines, and used the area for recreational activities. *Id.* at 855-56. Similarly, in *Timberlane*, the court held that claimants had used land belonging to the homeowners' association as if it were their own when they built and maintained a fence and a concrete patio and the claimants' children played on the land. *Id.*

Another writer uses the same strategy for writing a topic sentence by synthesizing the cases when an element was not met.

EXAMPLE 9   **Topic Sentence Synthesizes Cases**

In most of the cases in which the courts have held that the summons was not left at the defendant's usual place of abode, the defendant had not lived at the house where service was made for a substantial period of time. *See, e.g., Shurman v. Atl. Mortgage & Inv. Corp.*, 795 So. 2d 952 (Fla. 2001); *Portfolio Recovery Assoc., LLC v. Gonzalez*, 951 So. 2d 1037 (Fla. 3d DCA 2007). For instance, in *Shurman*, the defendant was incarcerated and had not lived at the family home for at least nine months, *id.* at 953, and in *Portfolio Recovery Assoc.*, the defendants had not lived at the house where service was made for five years, *id.* at 1038.

As we have seen, the first sentence of a paragraph is usually the topic sentence. Topic sentences may, however, appear later in a paragraph, particularly if the opening sentence or sentences are used to provide a transition to or background for the topic.

The following example is taken from the beginning of the second argument in the same memorandum in opposition to the defendants' motion for partial summary judgment. Notice how sentence 1 serves as a transition between the two arguments and sentence 2 provides background for sentence 3, the topic sentence.

EXAMPLE 10   **Transition to and Background for Topic**

Transition	*Sullivan* and *Gertz* dealt with individual citizens who had been libeled and
Background	who had sought redress in the courts. The case before the court today is different;
	the plaintiff is a state chartered savings and loan, a business entity. The significance
Topic sentence	of the different status of a business entity and its reputation, as compared to a

private individual, has been recognized in several federal courts. In *Martin Marietta v. Evening Star Newspaper*, 417 F. Supp. 947, 955 (D.D.C. 1976), the court stated that "[t]he law of libel has long reflected the distinction between corporate and human plaintiffs" and that "a corporate libel action is not a basic [sic] of our constitutional system, and need not force the first amendment to yield as far as it would be in a private libel action." The *Marietta* court continued, "Corporations, which do not possess private lives to begin with, must similarly [to public figures] be denied full protection from libel." *Id.*

§ 22.5.2 Implied Topic Sentences

Many paragraphs with implied topic sentences occur in statements of fact. Although some statements of fact have paragraphs that are thematically organized and use traditional topic sentences, most have a chronological organization with implied topic sentences. Many use a mix of the two.

Practically all paragraphs in statements of fact depend on their narrative, or storytelling, quality to keep the writing organized. The organizing principle, or topic, of such paragraphs may be what happened in a given time period, what happened to a given person, or what facts make up a given part of the situation.

The following paragraph appeared in the statement of facts from a case about whether service of process was valid when it was left at a spouse's home. The paragraph prior to the one shown here explained that the defendant, Ms. Clay-Poole, has a job and residence in New York and that her husband has a job and residence in California. In the example paragraph, no topic sentence is stated, but one is certainly implied.

EXAMPLE 11   **No Stated Topic Sentence**

Ms. Clay-Poole and Mr. Poole usually see each other about once a month for three or four days. They split the traveling about equally, although Ms. Clay-Poole travels to San Diego somewhat more frequently than Mr. Poole travels to Albany. They are happy with this arrangement; consequently, they do not intend to move in together permanently.

The implied topic sentence of this paragraph is that Ms. Clay-Poole and Mr. Poole have a commuter marriage. The writer could have stated the topic sentence, but in this case it was sufficiently obvious to leave it implied.

§ 22.5.3 Concluding Sentences

To be worthwhile, concluding sentences need to do more than just restate the topic sentence. If they don't, then the paragraph will not have advanced the line of reasoning in the memo or brief. Look again at the paragraph about whether a drug informant's testimony is relevant. Notice how the topic and concluding sentences are not simply artful clones of each other.

EXAMPLE 12   **Concluding Sentence Advances Reasoning**

Topic sentence   The fact that the informant is present at the alleged drug transaction is
                            not determinative of whether the testimony of that informant is relevant or
Supporting   necessary. *Lewandowski v. State*, 389 N.E.2d 706 (Ind. 1979). In *Lewandowski*,
sentences   the Indiana Supreme Court held that "[m]ere presence of the informer when
                            marijuana was sold to a police officer has been held to be insufficient to
                            overcome the privilege of nondisclosure." *Id.* at 710. The court made the same
                            ruling on nearly identical facts in *Craig v. State*, 404 N.E.2d 580 (Ind. 1980)
                            (informant introduced officer to defendant and was present during purchase
Conclusion   of illegal drugs). The state's informant in the present case served mainly as a
                            line of introduction and does not as such automatically become relevant or
                            necessary to the defendant's case simply because she was present at the scene.

The concluding sentence advances the line of reasoning by taking that
topic, or that point, and applying it to the present case. It rather neatly argues
that the rationale in *Craig v. State* is applicable in the present case because
in both cases the informant "served mainly as a line of introduction." This
concluding sentence is not just extra baggage, the obligatory "Now I'm going
to tell you again what I told you before." It is a working sentence, perhaps the
most significant sentence in the paragraph.

Earlier we saw how a paraphrase of the holding often makes an excellent
topic sentence. Paraphrasing the holding can also be an effective way to conclude a paragraph about an analogous case.

EXAMPLE 13   **Concluding Sentence Paraphrases Holding**

The Georgia appellate court addressed the issue of consent in relation to the disposal of a stillborn
child. *See McCoy v. Georgia Baptist Hosp.*, 306 S.E.2d 746 (Ga. Ct. App. 1983). In that case, the mother
delivered a stillborn child in the defendant hospital. Both parents had signed a consent form authorizing
the hospital to dispose of the body "in any manner they deem advisable." *Id.* at 747. Thereafter, the mother
discovered that the body had been placed in a freezer and left there for approximately one month. The
court held that the parents released their quasi-property interests in the child's body to the defendant
hospital when they signed the consent form. *Id.*

Another effective technique for writing concluding sentences is to use a
particularly apt quotation.

EXAMPLE 14   **Concluding Sentence Uses Quotation**

The California Supreme Court has decided that an individual's property rights in his cells is not
absolute. *In Moore v. Regents of UCLA*, 271 Cal. Rptr. 146 (Cal. 1990), the appellant's diseased spleen was
removed by the appellee research hospital. Appellee subsequently discovered that Moore's spleen and
other bodily tissue contained cells with unique characteristics that could be used to develop substances
with potential commercial value. Moore was never told of appellee's discovery and continued to allow
appellee to extract cells from him under the auspices of continuing treatment. The state Supreme
Court held that once Moore's cells were removed, he did not retain ownership interest in them. *Id.* at

146-47. The court went on to say, "If the scientific users of human cells are to be held liable for failing to investigate the consensual pedigree of their raw materials, we believe the Legislature should make that decision." *Id.* at 147.

One word of caution, though: Many legal writers overuse quotations. For the technique of concluding with a quotation to be effective, it should be used only occasionally and only when the quotation is unusually well stated.

Remember, too, that every paragraph does not have to have a stated concluding sentence. As with implied topic sentences, implied concluding sentences are permissible as long as the reader can easily surmise the paragraph's conclusion.

§ 22.6   Paragraph Blocks

One reason many paragraphs may not have topic sentences or concluding sentences yet function well is that the paragraphs are part of a larger organizational element: a paragraph block. Like paragraphs, paragraph blocks are mini-compositions, only in this instance the beginning is likely to be a paragraph or two, the middle is usually several paragraphs, and the end is also a paragraph or more.

The beginning paragraph or paragraphs work like a topic sentence. They are general statements that introduce the topic of the paragraph block and assert something about that topic.

The middle paragraphs contain the subpoints — the specifics that support the topic paragraph. Ideally, each of the middle paragraphs will be organized like a mini-composition with its own topic sentence, supporting sentences, and concluding sentences.

The concluding paragraph or paragraphs work in the block the same way a concluding sentence works in a paragraph. They bring the discussion back to the broad general topic, but in a way that advances the line of reasoning.

The following example from an argument section in a brief demonstrates how a typical paragraph block works.

EXAMPLE 1   **Paragraph Block**

The court in *Coronado Credit Union v. KOAT Television, Inc.,* 99 N.M. 233, 656 P.2d 896 (1982), held that a financial institution was an all-purpose public figure; however, that case was decided incorrectly. In holding that a credit union was an all-purpose public figure, the New Mexico Court of Appeals extended and broadened the *Gertz* standard in a way the Supreme Court never intended. **Topic paragraph**

By ignoring the Court's mandate to construe the all-purpose public figure standard narrowly, the *Coronado* court extended this standard to include all credit unions. The court considered the following factors to reach this per se rule: (1) Credit unions are chartered by the state to serve the public; (2) Credit unions are regulated by the state through statutes; and (3) Credit unions' financial situation is of public concern. *Id.* at 242. **Supporting paragraph**

Supporting paragraph   The fatal flaw in the court's analysis is best illustrated by applying these three factors to the fact pattern in *Gertz*. In *Gertz*, the Supreme Court held that the plaintiff attorney was not an all-purpose public figure. 418 U.S. at 352. But if the *Coronado* analysis had been used, the opposite result would have been reached: (1) Attorneys must be licensed by the state to practice law and must meet certain state requirements to obtain that license; and (2) Attorneys are subject to regulation by the state through professional codes of conduct. In fact, lawyers are officers of the court, and as such, must seek the public good in the administration of justice.

Concluding paragraph   Thus, under the *Coronado* analysis, Mr. Gertz and indeed all attorneys would be classified as all-purpose public figures. Such a result is in direct opposition to the Court's holding in *Gertz*. Consequently, the rule applied in *Coronado* is far too broad and could not withstand constitutional scrutiny.

The following excerpt from a memo shows how two paragraph blocks work together to complete a section under the heading of "negligence." An elements analysis lends itself nicely to paragraph block writing. In the example, notice how the paragraph that concludes one paragraph block also serves as the topic paragraph for the second block.

EXAMPLE 2   **Paragraph Blocks**

Negligence

Topic paragraph   If Dennis's negligence created the emergency, then he cannot use the emergency doctrine. Negligence is defined as failing to act as a reasonable person. This general principle is best explained by way of illustration, and the courts provide numerous examples. *Martini ex rel. Dussault v. State*, 21 Wn. App. 150, 161, 89 P.3d (2004).

Topic sentence   Speed excessive to conditions can be negligent. For example, when a defendant's logging truck rounded a curve and was unable to stop within three hundred seventy-five feet, his speed

Supporting paragraph   was found to be negligent. *Sandberg v. Spoelstra*, 46 Wn.2d 766, 782, 285 P.2d 564 (1955). When early morning visibility was restricted to seventy-five feet by a heavy rainfall, the court held that a speed of fifty miles per hour could be negligent. *Pidduck v. Henson*, 2 Wn. App. 204, 206, 467 P.2d 322 (1970). Finally, when daylight visibility exceeding one hundred feet was restricted to about three car lengths at night because of the glare of a street light, the court held that a speed under the twenty-five miles per hour posted limit could be negligent. *Sonnenberg v. Remsing*, 65 Wn. 2d 553, 556, 398 P.2d 728 (1965).

Topic sentence   Failure to heed road hazard warnings can also be negligent. Thus, when a driver confronted a multiple car accident on the freeway, where patrol cars were present with flashing lights and other

Supporting paragraph   cars were parked along the shoulder and median, the driver was negligent for not slowing down. *Schlect v. Sorenson*, 13 Wn. App. 155, 157, 533 P.2d 1404 (1975). Likewise, when a driver was warned of a fog hazard, drove into a deteriorating fog bank, and collided with a stopped vehicle, the driver was negligent. *Hinkel v. Weyerhaeuser Co.*, 6 Wn. App. 548, 552-53, 494 P.2d 1008 (1972).

Topic sentence   Finally, violations of the rules of the road can be negligence per se. When the driver of a semi-trailer observed a car stalled in the road ahead of it, slowed, switched lanes, and passed to the rear of the automobile where it struck one of the occupants on the highway, the driver was

Supporting paragraph   negligent. The driver was negligent as a matter of law for failing to obey several rules of the road: (1) reducing speed when confronted with hazards, (2) sounding horn to warn pedestrians of danger, (3) changing lanes only when safe to do so, and (4) signaling a lane change for one hundred feet before turning. *Nesmith v. Bowden*, 17 Wn. App. 602, 607, 563 P.2d 1322 (1977).

Plaintiff is likely to employ all the above arguments. She will probably argue that Dennis was negligent because his speed was excessive, because he failed to heed road hazards, and because he violated the rules of the road.

Concluding paragraph/ topic paragraph

Dennis's speed was not excessive for the conditions he faced. Dennis can distinguish the conditions in *Pidduck* and *Sonnenberg* from the conditions that he faced. In both cases, visibility was restricted by unusual circumstances. Dennis faced no unusual circumstances. He was rounding a gradual curve under the speed limit, and there is no indication that the curve was so sharp that it required a reduced speed limit. Nor was there any indication that there was a lower speed limit for night driving as opposed to day driving. In *Sandberg*, the driver had three hundred seventy-five feet in which to stop, and there was no obstruction in his lane when the driver collided with a vehicle in the other lane. Although the exact distance is unknown in Dennis's case, apparently Dennis had much less space in which to stop. Also, he faced an obstruction in his own lane.

Topic sentence

Supporting paragraph

Dennis's situation is analogous to the situation in *Ryan v. Westgard*, 12 Wn. App. 500, 530 P.2d 687 (1975), in which the driver was found to be not negligent. There, the driver was following approximately one hundred feet behind another car. This car swerved into another lane, and the following driver confronted yet another car going extremely slowly. He attempted to stop, but collided with the slower vehicle. The court reasoned that the plaintiff was following the car in front of him at a proper speed until the moment that vehicle swerved out into the adjoining lane. Like the driver in *Ryan*, Dennis was travelling at a proper speed until the moment his vehicle encountered the stalled bus. Therefore, Dennis's speed was not excessive.

Topic sentence

Supporting paragraph

Concluding sentence

Plaintiff will also probably argue that Dennis was negligent for failing to slow when confronted with a road hazard. Again, Dennis can distinguish the warning that he had from the warnings given in *Schlect* and *Hinkel*. Dennis was not warned several miles in advance of the obstruction as was the driver in *Hinkel*. Nor did he confront a multiple car accident with flashing patrol car lights and cars parked along the highway as did the driver in *Schlect*.

Pair of topic sentences

Supporting paragraph

Dennis rounded a curve and confronted a bus with flashers on that was stopped in the left lane of the freeway at 11:30 p.m. His situation is more analogous to the cases in which drivers faced sudden and unexpected obstacles after little warning. *See Haynes v. Moore*, 14 Wn. App. 668, 545 P.2d 28 (1975); *Leach v. Weiss*, 2 Wn. App. 437, 467 P.2d 894 (1970). In *Haynes*, the driver confronted a car, which he first saw when fifty feet away, stopped on a bridge. *Id.* at 669-70. He braked, but collided with the car. *Id.* at 670. He was found to be not negligent. *Id.* Likewise, in *Leach*, the driver confronted a car stopped on a bridge, braked, crossed the center line, and collided with another vehicle. *Id.* at 443. The driver was not negligent. *Id.* Neither is Dennis negligent.

Topic sentence

Supporting paragraph

Concluding sentence

Finally, plaintiff will probably argue that Dennis was negligent for violating the rules of the road. Dennis was driving in the left-hand lane and was not passing or turning. This conduct violates RCW 46.61.100, which requires that a driver stay in the rightmost lane except when passing or turning. Under *Nesmith v. Bowden*, 17 Wn. App. 602, 608, 563 P.2d 1322 (1977), this violation creates a prima facie case of negligence. However, Dennis can argue that this conduct was not negligent because it did not endanger the class of persons that this rule was designed to protect. The purpose of RCW 46.61.100 is to protect vehicles traveling in the same direction by promoting safe passing. *Sadler v. Wagner*, 5 Wn. App. 77 81-82, 486 P.2d 330 (1971). Evert was not passing Dennis, and Dennis was not passing Evert. Thus, Evert does not fall within the class of persons this rule was designed to protect, and Dennis was not negligent.

Topic sentence

Supporting paragraph

Concluding sentence

Dennis was not negligent because of excessive speed, he was not negligent for failing to heed road hazard warnings, and he was not negligent for failing to obey the rules of the road. His conduct did not create the emergency. He can submit substantial evidence in support of this second element, even though he can expect opposing counsel to make this a difficult issue.

Concluding paragraph

Chapter 22 Quiz

Draft answers for each of the following questions. Make your points clearly and concisely, and write sentences that are easy to read and that are grammatical and correctly punctuated.

1. What do paragraphs do in a piece of writing?
2. How is a paragraph like a mini-composition?
3. What are the two common shapes of a paragraph, and what do these shapes represent?
4. What is paragraph unity?
5. What is paragraph coherence? What are some of the ways writers can achieve coherence in paragraphs?
6. Writers generally achieve coherence when they set up an expectation in the reader and then fulfill that expectation. What are some of the patterns used in legal writing that help achieve coherence by fulfilling a legal reader's expectations?
7. What are some of the common coherence devices?
8. What is the ideal length for a paragraph?
9. What are the two functions of a topic sentence?
10. What are paragraph blocks?

Connections Between Sentences

Transitions are the primary connectors between sentences. Used properly, transitions express the relationship between the ideas in the sentences they serve to connect and signal how the ideas are moving in a line of reasoning.

Three types of transitions connect sentences:

1. Generic transitions
2. Orienting transitions
3. Substantive transitions

Still other transitions, headings and signposts, are used to make connections between paragraphs and over a longer piece of writing. See Chapter 21.

§ 23.1   Generic Transitions

Generic transitions include those words and phrases that are used in every kind of writing. Exhibit 23.1 lists the most common generic transitions grouped by function.

§ 23.1.1   Using Generic Transitions

The first question writers have about generic transitions is when to use them. In theory, that seems simple. Because generic transitions signal those shifts or changes inherent in human thought, it would seem that all writers should have to do is insert an appropriate transition to signal each time they make such a shift in their writing.

Exhibit 23.1	**Generic Transitions**

A word of warning: This chart of generic transitions categorizes the transitions by function: for contrast, for comparison, for cause and effect, etc. The individual transitions and transitional phrases within any of the categories are not synonyms for each other. Each transition conveys distinct, sometimes subtle, differences in how ideas are connected. Consequently, it is crucial for writers to learn the meaning of any given transition in context in order to use it correctly in their own writing.

For Contrast

alternatively	except	on the other hand
although	however	rather
but	in place of	still
by (in) contrast	in spite of	that being said*
contrary to	instead (of)	though
conversely	nevertheless*	unlike
despite	nonetheless*	yet
even so*	notwithstanding	
even though	on the contrary	

For Difference

besides*	otherwise

For Comparison

analogously	in like manner	likewise
by the same token	in the same way	similarly
for the same reason	like	

For Cause and Effect or Result

accordingly*	consequently*	since[1]
(and) so	for	therefore*
as a consequence	for that reason	thus*
as a result	hence	
because (of)	now	

For What Is True in Most Cases

generally	generally speaking	in general

For Addition

additionally	besides*	moreover
also	further	(once) again
and	furthermore	(then) again
as well (as)	in addition	too

For Examples

for example	namely	that is*
for instance	specifically	to illustrate

1. Many usage experts discourage the use of "since" for cause and effect relationships and recommend that "since" be reserved as a transition to indicate time relationships.

For Emphasis

above all	clearly	rather
as a matter of fact	in fact	still*
certainly	indeed	

For Evaluation

allegedly	more important	unquestionably
arguably	surprisingly	
fortunately	unfortunately	

For Restatement

in other words	simply put	to put it differently
more simply	that is*	

For Concession

after all	granted	of course
all the same*	in any case/event	still*
at any rate	nevertheless*	that said
at the same time*	nonetheless*	to be sure

For Resumption After a Concession

all the same*	nevertheless*	still*
even so*	nonetheless*	that being said*

For Time

afterwards	formerly	shortly thereafter
at the same time*	in the meantime	simultaneously
at the time	initially	since
by the time	later	subsequently
earlier	meanwhile	then*
eventually	recently	until now

For Place

adjacent to	here	next to
beyond	nearby	opposite to

For Sequence or Enumeration

final	in the first place	primary, secondary
finally*	later	then*
first, second, third	last	to begin/start with
former, latter	next	

For Conclusion

all in all	in short	to conclude
consequently*	in sum	to (in) review
finally*	in summary	to sum up
in brief	therefore*	to summarize
in conclusion	thus*	

*Generic transition that falls under more than one category.

In practice, it is not so simple. For one thing, there are no hard and fast rules for when a transition is required. In fact, experienced writers do not always agree about when a transition is appropriate and when it is cumbersome. For beginning law students and new associates in a firm, such differences in opinion can be confusing; one reader wants more transitions added, and the next reader edits them out.

The truth is that, to some extent, the number and placement of generic transitions is a matter of personal style and preference. That being said, there is still a general consensus about when to use generic transitions. You can find that consensus and develop your own sense about when to use generic transitions in one or more of the following ways. First, observe how other writers, particularly professional writers, use generic transitions. For example, notice how they rarely omit transitions that signal contrast and ones that show movement up or down the ladder of abstraction. Observe the ways skilled legal writers use generic transitions to keep their readers on track.

Second, read your own writing aloud. Let your ear tell you when a new sentence starts with a jolt rather than a smooth connection.

Third, listen to someone else read your writing aloud. Try stopping that reader at several points along the way (particularly when there is no transition) and asking if he or she can guess what the next sentence will discuss. If the connections between the ideas are so obvious that the reader can anticipate where the writing is headed, then probably no transition is needed. Conversely, if your reader needs more guidance through your points, add the appropriate generic transitions as needed.

Fourth, and most important, when writing, constantly ask yourself what will help your reader. Keeping the reader's perspective and needs in mind will help you decide when a generic transition is a helpful guide and when it is extra baggage.

§ 23.1.2   Problems with Generic Transitions

Some legal writers have a tendency to write as though others can read their minds. These writers omit transitions because the connections between the ideas are obvious to them. They forget to consider whether these connections are obvious to the reader. For example, in the first pair of sentences that follow, notice how jarring the second sentence seems without the transition for contrast, and then notice how in the revised second sentence the reader easily adjusts once the generic transition for contrast is added.

EXAMPLE 1   **Missing Transition**

Mr. Wry, the owner of the Fitness Club, may claim that although Singh's restaurant has lost several customers, the majority of the customers will return. Mr. Singh may argue that the loss of several customers is significant to his business.

Revised

Mr. Wry, the owner of the Fitness Club, may claim that although Singh's restaurant has lost several customers, the majority of the customers will return. Mr. Singh, *on the other hand,* may argue that the loss of several customers is significant to his business.

Other writers omit transitions in hopes of being more concise, forgetting that being concise, although important, is a relative luxury compared to being clear.

Legal writers should also take great care to select the precise transition that best describes the relationship between the two ideas or sentences. In the following example, the writer mistakenly selected a transition for comparison rather than one for addition.

EXAMPLE 2   **Imprecise Transition**

Because some overt physical activity and noise are normally generated by fitness and aerobics classes, the Fitness Club's classes are not unreasonably noisy or offensive. *Similarly,* bathing suits are not unusual or unanticipated sights in a waterfront area.

Revised

Furthermore, bathing suits are not unusual or unanticipated sights in a waterfront area.

The need for precise transitions also means that it is not enough simply to select the right category of generic transition. Generic transitions within the same category often have distinct meanings and connotations. For example, two transitions for conclusion—"to sum up" and "finally"—have entirely different meanings. "To sum up" should signal a brief overview or general statement about the entire piece of writing; "finally" should signal that the last point is about to be made.

In some instances, generic transitions are similar in meaning but quite different in tone. For example, two transitions for cause and effect—"therefore" and "hence"—mean almost the same thing, but "therefore" creates a matter-of-fact tone while "hence" carries with it a feeling of heavy solemnity and old wisdom.

Of course, you will find that a few generic transitions in the same category are virtually synonymous. In such instances, you may find that the list offers some variety that may free you from using the same generic transition *ad nauseam*.

Some final advice about transitional expressions: First, because transitions show the connection between two ideas, it is best to place the transition right at the point of connection. In the following example, the transition showing the cause/effect relationship comes too late to help the reader very much.

EXAMPLE 3   **Late Transition**

Singh was made insecure in the use of his property when patrons threatened not to return. The Fitness Club and its activities constitute a nuisance *as a result.*

Revised

As a result, the Fitness Club and its activities constitute a nuisance.

Second, the break between paragraphs can also serve as a kind of transition. White space is a strong signal that the writing is moving to a new point.

§ 23.2   Orienting Transitions

Orienting transitions provide a context for the information that follows. They serve to locate—physically, logically, or chronologically—the ideas or points in the rest of the sentence.

Two of the most common orienting transitions in legal writing are those that include times and dates and those that refer to cases.

EXAMPLE 1   **Orientating Transitions for Times, Dates, and Cases**

At 2:00 a.m. on January 1, 2013, Jacob Stein was arrested and charged with reckless driving and driving while intoxicated.

In *Bugger*, the court found that the position of the driver was insignificant.

In the case at hand, there is no indication that the defendant intended to deceive the plaintiff about her rights under the contract.

Other orienting transitions create a context by directing the reader to adopt a certain point of view, by supplying the source of the information that follows, or by locating the information historically or chronologically.

EXAMPLE 2   **Orienting Transition for Point of View**

From the bank's perspective, granting a second loan would be ill advised and risky.

EXAMPLE 3   **Orienting Transition for Source of Information**

According to Dallas Police Department Officer James Richardson's report, Officers Richardson and Chon entered the warehouse at 12:30 a.m.

EXAMPLE 4   **Orienting Transitions for Historical Perspective**

In the 1990s, the court narrowed the scope of the "discretionary" category.

In a recent decision, the court upheld a conviction when the driver was asleep or passed out but remained in a position to control the vehicle's movement.

Over the last twenty years, courts have realized that some exceptions to the general principle were necessary.

EXAMPLE 5	**Orienting Transition to Suggest a Case's Importance**

In an often cited case, the court overturned a conviction for "actual physical control" when the motorist's vehicle was parked on the shoulder of the highway.

EXAMPLE 6	**Orienting Transition to Announce a Shift in Topic**

In regard to the prosecution's allegation that Mr. Hayes's original attorney thwarted the discovery process, Mr. Hayes will point out that he was unaware that his original attorney shredded the requested documents.

Some legal writers avoid the orienting transitions beginning with "as for," "as to," "in regard to," and "regarding" in sentences like the sentence in Example 6 on the grounds that these transitions are an abrupt, an ineffective, or a lazy way to make a significant shift in topic. These writers prefer that significant shifts in topics be introduced by full sentences.

EXAMPLE 7	**Shift in Topic Introduced by Full Sentence**

Edited

The prosecution's second allegation, that Mr. Hayes's original attorney thwarted the discovery process, should be directed at Mr. Hayes's original attorney, not at Mr. Hayes. Because Mr. Hayes was unaware that his original attorney shredded the requested document, he cannot be held responsible for the unsanctioned actions of his lawyer.

Orienting transitions frequently occur at the beginning of a section. In such positions, orienting transitions are not so much connections between points within the writing as they are connections between the writing and the mind of a reader first coming to the material.

Orienting transitions also occur at the beginning of paragraphs. From this position, they help readers adjust or "shift gears" as they mentally move along a line of reasoning within a larger idea. Of course, orienting transitions can occur within a paragraph, and when they do, they work like all other transitions to bridge the gap between sentences and between ideas.

§ 23.3   Substantive Transitions

Thus far, we have looked at generic transitions, which are like glue between sentences, and at orienting transitions, which are backdrops for information or sometimes windows through which information can be seen.

The third type of transition, substantive transitions, can best be compared to the interlocking links of a chain. Like the links of a chain, substantive transitions serve two functions: They make a connection and they provide content. In short, they live up to their name — they are both substantive and transitional.

EXAMPLE 1   **Substantive Transition**

Bugger and *Zavala* are the only cases in which a conviction was overturned when the motorist's vehicle was totally off the road. While these holdings could be helpful to Mr. Renko, the Montana court will still probably interpret the statute to include the shoulder of the highway.

Here, the substantive transition is "while these holdings could be helpful to Mr. Renko." It serves as a transition connecting the two sentences for two reasons: First, it is placed at or near the beginning of the following sentence, where it can help bridge the gap between the ideas; and second, it uses the phrase "these holdings" to refer back to the information in the previous sentence. In short, the transition looks both forward and back.

But, as we said before, a substantive transition does not serve merely as a transition; it also provides new content. It points out that "these holdings could be helpful to Mr. Renko" before going on to the main point of the sentence, that the court still is likely to interpret the statute as including the shoulder of the highway.

§ 23.3.1   The Structure of Substantive Transitions

Substantive transitions often employ a technique called "dovetailing" as the basis for their structure.

Dovetailing

A carpenter who wants a strong joint between two pieces of wood is likely to use the dovetail, a special joint characterized by the tight fit of interlocking pieces of wood. Similarly, a writer who wants a strong joint between two sentences uses a dovetail of words to connect the ideas. Through the dovetail, he or she interlocks ideas by creating an overlap of language. The overlap of language may be as simple as the repetition of terms from one sentence to the next or the use of pronouns to refer back to an earlier noun.

EXAMPLE 2   **Repetition of Terms Dovetail**

In *Esser*, four people agreed to share costs and build a road. After the road was built, each person used the road under a claim of right.

Sentence 1	*Sentence 2*
. . . four people . . . build a road.	After the road was built, each person used the road . . .

A slightly more complicated dovetail than the one in the previous example requires the writer to find a word or phrase to use in the second sentence that sums up the idea of the previous sentence.

EXAMPLE 3	**Summarizing Phrase Dovetail**

Searches and seizures are governed by the Fourth Amendment to the U.S. Constitution and Article I, Section 7 of the Washington Constitution. Both of these provisions have been interpreted as requiring that search warrants be valid and that searches and seizures be reasonable.

Sentence 1	*Sentence 2*
. . . Fourth Amendment . . . and Article I . . .	Both of these provisions . . .

Note that in both of these examples the words in the dovetail tend to be toward the end of the first sentence and toward the beginning of the second.

Often the summarizing noun or phrase will be preceded by a demonstrative pronoun, or "hook word," such as "this," "that," "these," "those," or "such."

EXAMPLE 4	**Hook and Summarizing Phrase**

Realizing that she would not be able to stop in time to avoid hitting the bus, Mrs. Long swerved her vehicle around the bus and into the parallel lane of traffic. This evasive action resulted in her sideswiping another vehicle in the oncoming lane.

Connecting idea	*Connecting idea*	
swerved . . . into . . . traffic	This (hook word)	evasive action (summarizing noun phrase)

To form an effective dovetail, then, a legal writer can use one or more of the following techniques:

1. Move the connecting idea to the end of the first sentence and to the beginning of the second sentence.
2. Repeat key words from the first sentence in the second sentence.
3. Use pronouns in the second sentence to refer back to nouns in the first sentence.
4. State the connecting idea in a specific form in the first sentence and then restate it in a summarizing noun or phrase in the second sentence.
5. Use hook words such as "this," "that," "these," "those," and "such" before a repeated key word or summarizing noun or phrase.

Nouns that tend to make useful summarizing nouns are shown in Exhibit 23.2.

Exhibit 23.2	Summarizing Nouns		
action(s)	concept	form	rationale
advantage	consequence(s)	idea	reason(ing)
angle	course [of action/to follow]	item	result
aspect	criterion(a)	motive	rule
attempt	disadvantage	outcome	stage
branch	drawback	period	step
category	end	plan	term
circumstance(s)	facet	principle	type
class	fact	problem	

Another way to think about dovetailing is to remember that most sentences are made up of two parts: old information and new information. The old information is what has already been named or discussed. It usually appears near the beginning of a sentence. The new information is the point the writer wants to add. It usually appears near the end of a sentence.

Sentence

old information   new information

A dovetail takes the new information from the end of one sentence and restates it as the now old information at the beginning of the subsequent sentence.

Sentence 1		*Sentence 2*	
A	B →	B	C
old	new	old	new
information	information	information	information

Obviously, though, it is unrealistic to assume that all sentences should follow a strict A+B, B+C, C+D pattern. In reality, and in good legal writing, the pattern is not followed rigidly. Quite often, for example, sentence three will start with old information B.

Sentence 1		*Sentence 2*		*Sentence 3*	
A	B	B	C	B	D
old	new	old	new	old	new

EXAMPLE 5   **Old → New Pattern in Sentences**

In 1983, the Montana legislature adopted new and stricter laws to deal with drunk drivers. This legislation extended law enforcement jurisdiction and generally provided for faster and stiffer penalties. Brendon J. Rohan, *Montana's Legislative Attempt to Deal with the Drinking Driver: The 1983 DUI Statutes,* 46 Mont. L. Rev. 309, 310 (1985). This legislation also demonstrates a definite trend in Montana towards greater liability for the individual and a preference toward upholding drunk driving convictions regardless of mitigating circumstances.

Another useful variation of the pattern is to begin a sentence with a combination of two earlier pieces of old information, as illustrated in Exhibit 23.3, sentence 3.

Exhibit 23.3	Variation on the Old → New Pattern				
Sentence 1		_Sentence 2_		_Sentence 3_	
A	B	B	C	B + C	D
old	new	old	new	old + old	new

EXAMPLE 6   **Sentences Using Variation on Old → New Pattern**

When the defendant entered his hotel room, he was surprised to find two men rummaging through his suitcase. One of the men turned toward him, drew his gun, and aimed it at the defendant. Under these circumstances, the defendant had every reason to believe that he was being robbed and that his life was in danger.

This pattern works well when the writer wants to point out the similarity in two or more cases just cited.

EXAMPLE 7   **Sentences Using Variation on Old → New Pattern**

Courts in both Arizona and Utah did not uphold convictions when the vehicle's motor was off. _State v. Zavalo_, 666 P.2d 456 (Ariz. 1983); _State v. Bugger_, 483 P.2d 442 (Utah 1971). These cases are significant because in both instances the engine was off and the vehicle was completely off the highway.

Some writers unconsciously reverse the old → new pattern. They begin a sentence with new information and tack on the old, connecting information at the end. The result is a halting, disjointed style.

EXAMPLE 8   **Sentences Reversing Old → New Pattern**

The defendant need not insure the plaintiff's safety; he need exercise only reasonable care. _Potter v. Madison Tavern_, 446 P.2d at 322. He has breached his duty to the plaintiff if he has not exercised reasonable care.

Revised

If he has not exercised reasonable care, he has breached his duty to the plaintiff.

Occasionally, however, it is awkward, if not impossible, to move the old information to the very beginning of a sentence and the new information to the very end. In such cases, remember that the old → new pattern is a general principle, not an absolute rule.

A final bit of advice about dovetailing: Avoid using hook words without repeating a key term or using a summarizing noun or phrase. See section 27.5.2 on broad pronoun reference.

EXAMPLE 9   **Hook Word Without Summarizing Phrase**

At common law, a duty is established when the defendant stands in a special relationship to the plaintiff. **This can exist** between a specific plaintiff and a specific defendant.

Revised

This **special relationship** can exist . . . .

---

§ 23.3.2   The Content of Substantive Transitions

The content in substantive transitions can be compared to half steps in a line of reasoning. Sometimes these half steps are articulated inferences that one can reasonably draw from the previous sentence or idea.

EXAMPLE 10   **Substantive Transition That States Inference**

The owners of the factory could agree to release the fumes only after certain hours at night or only under certain weather conditions. While these steps may ameliorate the situation, the question remains whether any emission of toxic fumes is reasonable.

In the preceding example, a thoughtful reader would surely be able to infer the content of the substantive transition — "while these steps may ameliorate the situation" — after reading the first sentence. Consequently, some may argue that it would be better to replace the substantive transition with a more concise generic transition such as "even so" or "still." Obviously, writers must exercise judgment and weigh the relative merit of completeness versus conciseness.

In the following two examples, notice how the generic transition, although more concise, is less persuasive for the Bells than the substantive transition.

EXAMPLE 11   **Generic Transition**

Generic Transition

The Bells' doctor, Peter Williams, advised them that future pregnancies had a 75 percent chance of ending in a stillbirth. Consequently, the Bells decided that Mr. Bell would have a vasectomy.

Substantive Transition

The Bells' doctor, Peter Williams, advised them that future pregnancies had a 75 percent chance of ending in a stillbirth. Relying on Dr. Williams's advice, the Bells decided that Mr. Bell would have a vasectomy.

Notice how the generic transition "consequently" seems fairly neutral. It suggests that the Bells' decision to have Mr. Bell undergo a vasectomy was the expected consequence of an unfavorable statistical probability. The substantive transition "relying on Dr. Williams's advice," on the other hand, stresses the Bells' dependence on their doctor's professional opinion. Mentioning the doctor again by name not only reminds the reader that the doctor was the source of the information but also emphasizes the role he played in the Bells' decision.

Although it would be impossible to illustrate the many ways substantive transitions are used in legal writing, there are a few common situations in which they are particularly effective.

a.   Bridging the Gap Between Law and Application

Perhaps the most common use of substantive transitions in legal writing occurs at junctures between law and application. Compare the following two examples and note how the substantive transition "under the rule announced in *Fire*" draws the rule and its application together better than a generic transition can.

EXAMPLE 12   **Generic Transition Between Law and Its Application**

When a juror could have been excused for cause, reversible error occurs when the accused is forced to exercise all of his or her peremptory challenges before the jury is finally selected. *State v. Fire*, 145 Wn.2d 152, 159, 34 P.3d 1218 (2001). In the case at hand, Chapman accepted the jury with one peremptory challenge unexercised. Thus, he was not forced to use all his peremptory challenges before the final selection of the jury. **Therefore**, the Court of Appeals' decision in finding harmless error is sustainable.

EXAMPLE 13   **Substantive Transition between Law and Its Application**

When a juror could have been excused for cause, reversible error occurs when the accused is forced to exercise all his peremptory challenges before the jury is finally selected. *State v. Fire*, 145 Wn.2d 152, 159, 34 P.3d 1218 (2001). In the case at hand, Chapman accepted the jury with one peremptory challenge unexercised. Thus, he was not forced to use all his peremptory challenges before the final selection of the jury. **Under the rule announced in *Fire***, the Court of Appeals' decision in finding harmless error is sustainable.

---

b.   Applying Another Court's Rationale

Similarly, substantive transitions are often used when the reasoning of one court has been laid out in detail and this reasoning will now be applied to the case at hand.

EXAMPLE 14   **Substantive Transition to Show Application of Another Court's Rationale**

Two Washington decisions have developed a more liberal definition of inadvertent. *State v. Henry*, 36 Wn. App. 530, 676 P.2d 521 (1984). In *Henry*, officers had learned from an informant that the defendant was heavily armed, and one officer testified that he was looking for guns as well as cocaine, which was specified in the warrant; yet, the court held that the guns were found inadvertently. *Id.* at 532-33. In doing so, the court relied on the definition of "inadvertent" provided in *State v. Callahan*, 31 Wn. App. 710, 644 P.2d 735, 736 (1982): "[T]he term 'inadvertent' in the context of the plain view doctrine, simply means that the officer discovered the evidence while in a position that does not infringe upon any reasonable expectation of privacy, and did not take any further unreasonable steps to find the evidence from that position." *Henry*, 36 Wn. App. at 533. The *Henry* court concluded that the officers were looking in places that were likely to contain drugs, that a person can harbor no reasonable expectation of privacy concerning a place that is likely to contain drugs, and that the officers took no further, unreasonable steps to find the guns. *Id.* Therefore, the discovery was inadvertent by the Washington definition. *Id.* The court added that there was no evidence that the drug search was a pretext for a gun search. *Id.*

The state's position in the instant case is stronger. At the time the officers received the search warrant for marijuana, they neither had knowledge nor expected that they might find incriminating photographic evidence of another crime. When he looked in the envelope, Morrison had no reason to believe that the photographs would be evidence of any crime.

Thus, **applying the *Henry* rationale to *Ehrlich***, the court would probably find that Morrison was looking in a place that was likely to conceal drugs (the envelope might have contained drugs as well as photographs), so Ehrlich had no reasonable expectation of privacy. After looking in the envelope, Morrison took no further unreasonable steps to find the photographs. Therefore, the discovery was inadvertent.

---

c.   Gathering Together Several Facts

Another juncture where substantive transitions can be used effectively occurs between a list of numerous individual facts and a statement about their collective significance.

In the following example, the substantive transition "based on these admissions" is essential. It is the one place where the point is made that three facts taken together were the basis for the court's action.

EXAMPLE 15   **Substantive Transition to Gather Several Facts**

In his deposition, Edwards acknowledged that the railroad tie had appeared wet and slippery before he stepped on it. He also stated that he had regularly delivered mail to the Bates's residence for two years and that he was familiar with the premises, including the railroad tie. Finally, Edwards acknowledged that he attended weekly postal safety meetings and knew about the hazards posed by wet surfaces. **Based on these admissions**, the trial court granted summary judgment in favor of Bates and dismissed Edwards's negligence action. *Id.* at 942.

---

d.   Bridging the Gap Between Sections of a Document

Substantive transitions are more effective than generic transitions at junctures between large sections of a paper. Even when headings are used for larger sections, substantive transitions are still needed to show the similarities or differences between the sections.

In the following example, the writer has just completed a long section on the Ninth Circuit's comments on the inappropriateness of bonuses for services rendered to a bankrupt estate. The following sentence begins the section under the heading Contingency Fees. The substantive transition — "unlike a bonus fee arrangement" — shows the connection between the sections.

| EXAMPLE 16 | **Substantive Transition to Connect Sections** |

Contingency Fees

Unlike a bonus fee arrangement, there is nothing that prevents a contingency fee agreement from being enforced in bankruptcy. *In re Yermahov*, 718 F.2d 1465, 1470 (9th Cir. 1983).

To sum up then, substantive transitions are those special points in writing where the writer pulls two or more thoughts together and, in doing so, creates a powerful bond between ideas. By overlapping the language and merging the ideas, the writer does more than just connect the points; he or she weaves them together.

Some final thoughts about transitions: Although the artificial division of transitions into separate categories makes it easier to understand their separate functions, it also masks the ways in which generic, orienting, and substantive transitions are similar. One can argue, for example, that all transitions, including generic transitions, provide some content or that all transitions orient the reader. Consequently, how you categorize a particular transition is not really important; what is important is that you are able to use all three categories of transitions to create connections in your own writing.

Chapter 23 Quiz

Draft answers for each of the following questions. Make your points clearly and concisely, and write sentences that are easy to read and that are grammatical and correctly punctuated.

1. What functions do writing transitions perform?
2. What are the three types of transitions?
3. Do all transitions in the same category have the exact same meaning?
4. What is the key to placing generic transitions?
5. What function do orienting writing transitions perform?
6. What are some of the common orienting transitions in legal writing?
7. What are the two main functions of substantive transitions?
8. What is another name for substantive transitions?
9. What are the ways to create a substantive transition?
10. How does the old → new pattern in sentence construction work to create flow in writing?

Effective Sentences

Effective sentence writing begins with the subject-verb unit. Those two key sentence positions should contain the crux of the sentence's message. If these two parts of the sentence are written well, then many of the other parts of the sentence will fall into place.

Consequently, our discussion of effective sentence writing begins with four points about the subject-verb unit: the use of active and passive voice, the use of concrete subjects, the use of action verbs, and the distance between subjects and verbs. The remainder of the chapter addresses points that concern the whole sentence: sentence length, emphasis, and sentence structures that highlight similarities or differences.

§ 24.1   Active and Passive Voice

The term "voice" when it is applied to the subject-verb unit refers to the relationship of the subject to the action expressed in the verb. This rather vague concept is easier to understand in terms of the difference between active and passive voice.

§ 24.1.1   Identifying Active and Passive Voice

In the active voice, the subject of the sentence is doing the action described by the verb.

The judge overruled the objection.
  (subject) (verb)   (direct object)

In the sentence above, the subject "judge" is doing the verb "overruled." Another way to look at it is to remember that in the active voice the subject is "active," or acting.

In the passive voice, the subject of the sentence is having the action of the verb done to it.

The objection was overruled by the judge.
  (subject)   (verb)

In this sentence, the subject "objection" is not doing the overruling; rather, the verb "was overruled" is being done to the subject. Another way to look at it is to remember that in the passive voice the subject is "passive." It is not acting; it is acted upon.

Notice that in the passive voice the person or thing doing the verb is either mentioned in a prepositional phrase ("by the judge," as in the previous example) or omitted, as in the example below.

The objection was overruled.
  (subject)   (verb)

Note that passive voice is different from past tense. Even though both concern the verb, past tense refers to the time of an action and passive voice refers to the relationship of an action to the subject of the sentence.

§ 24.1.2 Effective Use of Active Voice

Generally, the active voice is preferred over the passive voice for several reasons:

  1. It is more concise.

EXAMPLE 1   **Active Voice Is More Concise**

The marshal left the summons.

(active voice—5 words)

The summons was left by the marshal.

(passive voice—7 words)

---

2. It uses a more vigorous verb.

| EXAMPLE 2 | **Active Voice Uses a Vigorous Verb** |

The plaintiffs filed a complaint in the Superior Court of Chavez County, New Mexico.

(active voice—the verb "filed" is crisp and vigorous)

A complaint was filed by the plaintiffs in the Superior Court of Chavez County, New Mexico.

(passive voice—the verb "was filed" loses much of its vigor; the auxiliary verb "was" and the preposition "by" dilute the energy of "filed")

3. It allows information to be processed more readily.

| EXAMPLE 3 | **Readers Process Active Voice More Readily** |

The defendant's attorney must offer the deposition into evidence.

This active voice sentence is easy to process mentally. The reader can visualize the subject "defendant's attorney" doing the verb "must offer" to the object "deposition" as quickly as the words are read. The sentence suggests a mini-drama that readers can visualize in their minds.

| EXAMPLE 4 | **Passive Voice** |

The deposition must be offered into evidence by the defendant's attorney.

Although the information in this passive voice sentence is not difficult to process, readers must read the entire sentence before they can visualize the sentence in their minds. By the midpoint in the sentence, "The deposition must be introduced into evidence," the action has begun, but it is being done by unseen hands. The "actor" in the mini-drama does not come in until the end of the sentence.

In both objective and persuasive legal writing, active voice is usually preferred when you want to make a point that someone or something performed a particular action. Active voice emphasizes who or what is responsible for committing an act.

| EXAMPLE 5 | **Active Voice Affects Emphasis** |

The defendant embezzled over $1 million.

(active voice—emphasizes that the defendant is responsible for the act)

Over $1 million was embezzled by the defendant.

(passive voice—it is still clear that the defendant performed the act, but now the emphasis is on the amount of money)

Over $1 million was embezzled.

(passive voice—doer of the action is either unknown or left unsaid; emphasis is on the amount of money)

§ 24.1.3   Effective Use of Passive Voice

Although it is true that the active voice is generally preferable to the passive voice, there are several situations in which the passive voice is more effective.

1. Use passive voice when the person or thing performing the action is unknown or relatively unimportant.

EXAMPLE 6   **Passive Voice When Actor Is Unknown or Unimportant**

A portion of the tape was erased.

The safe's hinges must be examined before the manufacturer's liability can be determined.

2. Use passive voice when it is undesirable to disclose the identity of the person or thing performing the action.

EXAMPLE 7   **Passive Voice to Avoid Disclosing Actor**

The plaintiff's retirement benefits were discontinued.

Toxic fumes were ventilated out of the plant between 2:00 and 3:00 a.m.

3. Use passive voice when the deed, rather than the doer, should be emphasized.

EXAMPLE 8   **Passive Voice Keeps Emphasis on the Deed**

All four defendants were convicted of first degree murder.

4. Use passive voice when it allows the writer to keep the focus of the writing where it belongs, as in the following example from a paragraph about a mistake in a contract.

EXAMPLE 9   **Passive Voice to Maintain Focus**

A mistake can also be attributed to Lakeland Elementary School for believing the price of the playground equipment included installation.

5. Use passive voice when it provides a stronger link between preceding and subsequent sentences or clauses. See section 23.3 on dovetailing. This link is enhanced by moving the connecting ideas to the end of the first sentence (or clause) and then picking up on that point at the beginning of the second sentence (or clause).

$$\underline{\hspace{4cm}}.\qquad \underline{\hspace{4cm}}.$$

Sentence 1	*Sentence 2*
connecting idea	connecting idea

EXAMPLE 10   **Passive Voice to Create Dovetail**

Under the Revised Code of Washington, Title 62A, contracts for the sale of goods are regulated by the Uniform Commercial Code. The UCC outlines the requirements for a valid contract for the sale of goods and the various steps necessary to the contract's performance.

The first sentence uses passive voice so that "Uniform Commercial Code" will be at the end of the sentence. The second sentence begins with "The UCC" to provide a strong link between the sentences.

Sentence 1	*Sentence 2*
by the Uniform Commercial Code	The UCC

In persuasive writing, you will find that the passive voice allows you to downplay who performed certain actions. For example, counsel for the defendant may want to use the passive voice when admitting wrongdoing by the defendant.

EXAMPLE 11   **Passive Voice Downplays Actor**

A purse was taken from the plaintiff by the defendant.

Counsel for the plaintiff will use active voice to emphasize that it was the defendant who took the purse.

EXAMPLE 12   **Example 12   Active Voice Emphasizes Actor**

The defendant took the plaintiff's purse.

---

§ 24.2   Concrete Subjects

Effective subjects of sentences are concrete rather than abstract. They are real people and real things that readers can mentally visualize.

Unfortunately, in legal writing we are often forced to use abstractions as subjects of our sentences. The law and its application often require that we focus on ideas and concepts; consequently, we often end up placing these ideas and concepts in the subject position. Even so, legal readers appreciate having as many concrete subjects as possible to help bring the writing back down to earth.

To find the most effective concrete subject of a sentence, ask yourself, "Who (or what) is doing something in this sentence?" Then place that real person (or thing) in the subject position of the sentence.

EXAMPLE 1   **Finding the Concrete Subject**

Draft

> A <u>decision</u> <u>was made</u> by the district manager to eliminate all level four positions.
> *(subject)* *(verb)*

Revised

> The <u>district manager</u> <u>decided</u> to eliminate all level four positions.
>   *(subject)*   *(verb)*

Note that the preceding example illustrates a common problem in legal writing known as nominalization. Nominalization is the process of converting verbs into nouns (for example, "decide" → "decision"). The effect in the sentence is twofold: (1) the real action of the sentence is buried in a noun, making the sentence more ponderous and turgid, and (2) the verb becomes either a passive voice substitute or a *"to be"* verb substitute, making the sentence less energetic.

In many sentences, the real person or thing acting in the sentence has been buried in an abstraction or omitted altogether.

EXAMPLE 2   **Finding the Concrete Subject**

Draft

> The <u>awarding</u> of damages <u>will be left</u> to judicial discretion.
>   *(subject)*   *(verb)*

Revised

> The <u>judge</u> <u>will decide</u> whether to award damages.
>   *(subject)* *(verb)*

Often the subject position in the sentence is taken up by an almost meaningless abstraction such as "nature of," "kind of," "type of," or "area of." Notice how the sentence improves when these meaningless abstractions are omitted and real people and real things are placed in the subject position.

EXAMPLE 3	**Finding the Concrete Subject**

Draft

> The <u>nature</u> of the defendant's argument <u>was</u> that he was "temporarily insane."
>   *(subject)*   *(verb)*

Revised

> The <u>defendant</u> <u>argued</u> that he was "temporarily insane."
>   *(subject)* *(verb)*

Both the subject position and verb position are often taken up by the many weak subject-verb combinations that use the "it is _____ that" pattern.

> It is important to note that
> It is likely (unlikely) that
> It is obvious (clear) that
> It is essential that

To revise sentences with this weakness, look after the "that" for the real subject and verb.

EXAMPLE 4	**Editing Out "It Is _____ That" Openers**

Draft

> <u>It is</u> obvious that the defendant was read his rights.
> *(subject/verb)*

Revised

> The <u>defendant</u> <u>was read</u> his rights.
>   *(subject)*   *(verb)*

Draft

> <u>It is</u> unlikely that the defendant will plead guilty.
> *(subject/verb)*

Revised

> The <u>defendant</u> probably <u>will</u> not <u>plead</u> guilty.
>   *(subject)*   *(verb)*

---

§ 24.3   Action Verbs

Effective verbs show real action rather than vague action or state of being. To find the most effective verb for a sentence, ask yourself, "What is someone (or something) actually doing in the sentence?" Then place that action in the verb position.

Common Pitfalls to Avoid When Selecting a Verb

1. Avoid overusing a form of the verb "to be" ("am," "are," "is," "was," "were") as a main verb. Use forms of the verb "to be" only as the main verb when the point of the sentence is that something exists.

EXAMPLE 1   Using Action Verbs

Draft

The <u>owner</u> of the land <u>is</u> East Coast Properties, Inc.
   (subject)   *(verb)*

Revised

<u>East Coast Properties, Inc.</u> <u>owns</u> the land.
     (subject)   *(verb)*

Draft

There <u>are</u> four <u>elements</u> that must be proved to recover damages under the family car or
   (verb)   *(subject)*
purpose doctrine.

Revised

Four <u>elements</u> <u>must be proved</u> to recover damages under the family car or purpose doctrine.
     (subject)   *(verb)*

OR

Under the family car or purpose doctrine, the <u>plaintiff</u> <u>must prove</u> four elements.
          (subject) *(verb)*

Notice that the sentence openers "There is" or "There are" or "There was" or "There were" are weak unless the point of the sentence is that something exists. With these four sentence openers, the subject comes after the verb.

2. Avoid using vague verbs. Verbs such as "concerns," "involves," "deals (with)," and "reveals" tell the reader little about the real action in the sentence.

EXAMPLE 2   Using Action Verbs

Draft

Swanson <u>dealt</u> with a sales contract that contained an open item and that was signed by a
(subject) (verb)
homebuilder and a couple who were prospective buyers of a home.

Revised

> In *Swanson*, a <u>homebuilder</u> and a <u>couple</u> who were prospective buyers of a home <u>signed</u> a
>   *(subject)*   *(subject)*   *(verb)*
> contract that contained an open item.

3. Avoid nominalization, that is, burying the real action in a noun, and
   avoid burying the action in an adjective.

EXAMPLE 3   **Editing for Nominalization**

Draft

> The <u>corporate officers</u> <u>had</u> an informal meeting at an undisclosed location.
>   *(subject)*   *(verb)*

Revised

> The <u>corporate officers</u> <u>met</u> informally at an undisclosed location.
>   *(subject)*   *(verb)*

---

§ 24.4   Distance Between Subjects and Verbs

An effective sentence has its subject and verb close together. When they
are close together, the reader can identify the subject-verb unit quickly and
comprehend the entire sentence more easily. When they are separated by many
intervening words, the reader will find it much more difficult to understand
the sentence.

EXAMPLE 1   **Keeping Subjects and Verbs Close Together**

Draft

> <u>Information</u> about Mutual Trust Bank's standard operating procedures and about how the
>   *(subject)*
> contractor drew up his loan application <u>will be required</u> by the court.
>   *(verb)*

Revised

> The <u>court</u> <u>will require</u> information about Mutual Trust Bank's standard operating procedures
>   *(subject)* *(verb)*
> and about how the contractor drew up his loan application.

In some cases, the writer will have to rewrite one sentence as two sentences
to keep the subjects and verbs close together.

| EXAMPLE 2 | **Keeping Subjects and Verbs Close Together** |

Draft

> A <u>case</u> in which a section 11-902 charge was dropped because the driver was found lying in
> *(subject)*
> the highway near his truck <u>shows</u> that a driver's presence in the vehicle is a prerequisite for
>   *(verb)*
> finding him guilty.

Revised

> In one case, the <u>court</u> <u>dismissed</u> a section 11-902 charge because the driver was found lying
>   *(subject) (verb)*
> in the highway near his truck. The <u>court</u> <u>reasoned</u> that a driver's presence in a vehicle is a
>   *(subject) (verb)*
> prerequisite to finding the defendant guilty.

Another reason for keeping subjects and verbs close together is to reduce the chance that they will not agree in number. See section 27.4.1. In the following example, the writer has mistakenly made the verb agree with the singular noun "script" when the plural subject "quality and mutilation" requires the plural verb "are."

| EXAMPLE 3 | **Incorrect—Subject and Verb Do Not Agree** |

> Inferior <u>quality and mutilation</u> of the musical play *Not Enough Lovin'* as a result of Skylark
>   *(subject)*
> Productions' revisions of the script <u>is</u> hard to establish.
>   *(verb)*

Occasionally a writer must separate the subject and verb with quite a bit of information. In such cases, if the intervening information can be set off by punctuation, the reader will still be able to identify the subject-verb unit fairly easily.

| EXAMPLE 4 | **Using Intervening Punctuation** |

> The Lanham Trademark Act, a law primarily designed to prevent deceptive packaging of
>   *(subject)*
> goods in interstate commerce, <u>has been interpreted</u> to include false attribution and distortion
>   *(verb)*
> of literary and artistic works.

Remember too that keeping subjects and verbs close together is desirable but not absolutely required. There will be times in legal writing when it is all but impossible to keep subjects and verbs close together.

§ 24.5   Sentence Length

Whenever a legal writer asks "how long should my sentences be?" the only possible answer is "it depends." Obviously sentence length is primarily governed by what you are trying to say. In addition, decisions on sentence length should be made based on two other factors: the reader and the context.

§ 24.5.1   The Reader

Effective sentence length is that which the reader can handle comfortably. Educated readers — judges, attorneys, some clients — can comfortably read somewhat longer sentences than the general public. Consequently, legal writers can usually write sentences for their readers that average about twenty-two words per sentence, with only a rare sentence exceeding a thirty-five-word limit. For readers with less education, shorter sentences are usually more effective.

Notice how the overly long sentence in the following example creates a feeling in the reader of a mental overload. Several overly long sentences written one after another only compound this feeling.

EXAMPLE 1   **Overly Long Sentence**

The post-trial motion was supported by an affidavit by a juror that stated that a fellow juror discussed the case with a professional truck driver who was familiar with the accident scene and who told the juror that the accident could not have occurred as the plaintiff stated. (48 words)

There are several ways to revise overly long sentences so that they become more readable. One way is to break up the sentence into two or more separate sentences.

EXAMPLE 2   **Breaking Up an Overly Long Sentence**

Revised

The post-trial motion was supported by an affidavit by a juror. In his affidavit, the juror stated that a fellow juror discussed the case with a professional truck driver who was familiar with the accident scene. The truck driver told the juror that the accident could not have occurred as the plaintiff stated.

Another way to revise an overly long sentence is to create manageable units of meaning within the sentence. A writer can do this by identifying structural components within the sentence, especially phrases and clauses, and setting them off with appropriate punctuation.

Notice how much more readable the following example becomes when, in Revision 1, the "if" clause is moved to the front of the sentence, where it can be set off from the rest of the sentence by a comma.

EXAMPLE 3	Creating Units of Meaning Within a Long Sentence

The Reynoldses will be responsible for both the attacks on the Halversons' chickens and Mr. Halverson's medical bills resulting from the dog bite if the plaintiff can show that the Reynoldses should have known of their dog's viciousness. (38 words)

Revision 1

If the plaintiff can show that the Reynoldses should have known of their dog's viciousness, (15 words) then they will be responsible for both the attacks on the Halversons' chickens and Mr. Halverson's medical bills resulting from the dog bite. (23 words)

Other punctuation marks, such as the colon, can sometimes be added to create a break within a sentence.

EXAMPLE 4	Using Punctuation to Break Up Long Sentence

Revision 2

If the plaintiff can show that the Reynoldses should have known of their dog's viciousness, (15 words) then they will be responsible for the following: (8 words) the attacks on the Halversons' chickens and Mr. Halverson's medical bills resulting from the dog bite. (16 words)

This technique of arranging phrases and clauses so that they can be set off by punctuation is particularly helpful when writing issue statements.

EXAMPLE 5	Hard to Read Issue Statement

Under New Hampshire law did the trial court commit prejudicial error by refusing plaintiffs' motion for a new trial because of jury misconduct when the motion was supported by a juror affidavit stating that another juror discussed the case with an alleged expert outside the trial context and then related the information to the entire jury?

In Revision 1, the writer has broken up this same information into more readable units by using a comma to set off the introductory phrase and a conjunction between two main clauses. See section 28.1, Rules 1 and 2.

EXAMPLE 6	Using Punctuation in Issue Statement

Revision 1

Under New Hampshire law, (4 words) did the trial court commit prejudicial error by refusing plaintiffs' motion for a new trial because of jury misconduct when the motion was supported by a juror affidavit, (28 words) and that affidavit stated that another juror discussed the case with an alleged expert outside the trial context and then related the information to the entire jury? (27 words)

In Revision 2, the writer has used commas between a series of parallel clauses (here, the "when" clauses) to help break up the information into manageable units. See section 27.7. Even though the revised sentence is longer than the original, it is more readable because the reader gets the information in smaller, more manageable units.

EXAMPLE 7   **Using Parallelism in Issue Statement**

Revision 2

Under New Hampshire law, (4 words) did the trial court commit prejudicial error when it refused plaintiffs' motion for a new trial because of jury misconduct, (20 words) when the motion was supported by a juror affidavit, (9 words) and when that affidavit stated that another juror discussed the case with an alleged expert outside the trial context and then related information to the entire jury? (27 words)

Another way to solve sentence length problems is to eliminate wordiness. See section 25.2.

§ 24.5.2   The Context

Earlier we said that decisions about sentence length should be based on both the reader and the context. Readers rarely see a sentence in isolation. Most sentences are preceded by other sentences and followed by other sentences. Consequently, how readers respond to the length of any given sentence depends, in part, on the sentences that surround it.

For example, a forty-word sentence that is unwieldy in one context may work in another. A short, snappy sentence that drives a point home in one paragraph may seem trite and unsophisticated in another. Even a steady diet of medium-length sentences is unappetizing. Such writing tends to be monotonous and bland.

When it comes to sentence length, then, consistency is not a virtue. Effective sentences vary in length.

The following example from a statement of facts shows how lack of variety in sentence length makes the writing less interesting to read.

EXAMPLE 8   **Monotonous Sentence Length**

On December 15, 2013, Officers Jack Morrison and Wayne Garcia of the Phoenix Police Department searched Victor Ehrlich's apartment. (17 words) They had in their possession a valid search warrant for marijuana. (11 words) Marijuana was found in both the living room and the kitchen. (11 words) While searching the bedroom, Officer Morrison found a large manila envelope in one of the dresser drawers. (17 words) Photographs were protruding from the top of the envelope. (9 words) Morrison looked inside and found photographs of Ehrlich with three young girls sitting on his lap. (16 words) Ehrlich was wearing only boxer shorts, and the girls were nude from the waist up. (15 words) Considering the photographs to be perverse, Morrison showed them to Garcia, who agreed that they looked suspicious. (17 words) They seized the photographs as well as the marijuana. (9 words) The defendant, Victor Ehrlich, has now contested this seizure. (9 words) He has made a motion to suppress the photographic evidence as the result of an unconstitutional seizure. (17 words)

The following revised version is more interesting to read because sentence length now ranges from six words in the shortest sentence to twenty-nine words in the longest.

| EXAMPLE 9 | Variety in Sentence Length |

Revised

On December 15, 2013, Officers Jack Morrison and Wayne Garcia of the Phoenix Police Department searched Victor Ehrlich's apartment. (17 words) They had in their possession a valid search warrant for marijuana. (11 words) After finding marijuana in both the living room and the kitchen, they searched the bedroom, where Officer Morrison found a large manila envelope in one of the dresser drawers. (29 words) Seeing photographs protruding from the top of the envelope, Morrison looked inside and found photographs of Ehrlich with three young girls sitting on his lap. (25 words) Ehrlich was wearing only boxer shorts. (6 words) The girls were nude from the waist up. (8 words) Considering the photographs to be perverse, Morrison showed them to Garcia, who agreed that they looked suspicious. (17 words) They seized the photographs as well as the marijuana. (9 words) The defendant, Victor Ehrlich, has now contested this seizure and has made a motion to suppress the photographic evidence as the result of an unconstitutional seizure. (26 words)

Part of what makes the revised version effective is its use of short sentences. The four short sentences were all used to highlight particularly significant facts.

§ 24.5.3   The Power of the Short Sentence

Used sparingly, short sentences can energize writing. Not only can they provide relief to readers who have just labored through several long sentences, they also tend to highlight the information they contain.

Note how in the following example the short sentence serves both as a welcome break after two fairly long sentences and as a way to emphasize the significant point that individuals in both cases were possibly motivated by a reward.

| EXAMPLE 10 | Short Sentence for Variety and Emphasis |

In two older decisions, *United States v. Snowadzki*, 723 F.2d 1427 (9th Cir. 1984), and *United States v. Black*, 767 F.2d 1334 (9th Cir. 1985), individuals conducting unlawful searches were considered to have acted as private parties, not as government agents. In both cases, the individuals obtained the documents unlawfully and then turned them over to the government, which later submitted them as evidence at trial. In each instance, a reward was offered.

---

§ 24.6   Emphasis

Emphasis is a natural part of all writing. In objective writing, the writer uses emphasis to let the reader know where to focus his or her attention. In persuasive writing, emphasis allows the advocate to spotlight those points that favor the client and downplay those that hurt the client. It also allows the advocate to hammer home his or her theory of the case. In the previous section we saw how short sentences can be used to emphasize key points.

EXAMPLE 1   **Short Sentence for Emphasis**

Original

The defendant lied when she testified that she was in St. Paul, Minnesota, at the time of the robbery.

Revised

The defendant testified that she was in St. Paul, Minnesota, at the time of the robbery. She lied.

Besides short sentences, emphasis can be achieved in several other ways:

1. Telling the reader what is important
2. Underlining (or italics or boldface)
3. Using positions of emphasis
4. Using punctuation to highlight a point
5. Using single-word emphasizers
6. Changing the normal order in a sentence
7. Repeating key words
8. Setting up a pattern (and sometimes breaking it)

Of all these strategies, the most common and least sophisticated are the first two: simply telling the reader what is important and underlining. Some writers consider these first two strategies too obvious and overused to be effective. Others feel that they can be effective if used selectively.

§ 24.6.1   Telling the Reader What Is Important

Sentence openers such as "it is important to note that" or "above all" alert the reader to the importance of the point that follows. Used rarely, these sentence openers can help the reader identify which points deserve heightened emphasis. Used frequently, these same sentence openers bog down the writing and make it wordy.

EXAMPLE 2   **Sentence Openers for Emphasis**

Above all, the court should consider the defendant's past record as a good husband, model father, and leader in the community.

It is important to note that the check was postdated.

Notice that the last example may be even more emphatic when revised into a short sentence: "The check was postdated."

Expressions such as "especially," "particularly," and "most important" can work the same way when they are inserted right before the point to be emphasized.

EXAMPLE 3   **Expressions That Show Emphasis**

The court should consider the defendant's past record as a good husband, model father, and, most important, leader in the community.

---

§ 24.6.2 Underlining

Underlining is undoubtedly the simplest and least sophisticated strategy for emphasis. It requires no restructuring of the sentence and little, if any, planning. If you do decide to use underlining for emphasis, be extremely selective.

EXAMPLE 4   **Underlining for Emphasis**

The contract <u>permits</u> but does not <u>require</u> the tenant to add landscaping and similar outdoor improvements.

It is sometimes tempting to assume that readers will not detect subtle emphasis and must be told which words are crucial. Many writers would consider the underlining in the previous example unnecessary and possibly even condescending. The remaining strategies for emphasis are more subtle and therefore more suitable for sophisticated readers.

§ 24.6.3 Using Positions of Emphasis

When it comes to emphasis, all parts of the sentence are not created equal. That is, the beginning, middle, and end of a sentence are not equally emphatic.

In most sentences, writers place new information at the end of a sentence. Also, the end of the sentence is the point of climax. Everything in the sentence builds toward the words at the end. Consequently, in most sentences, the most emphatic position is at the end.

The next most emphatic position is usually at the beginning. Here the writer typically sets the stage for the rest of the sentence. The reader expects the beginning of the sentence to demonstrate how the new information in this sentence is connected with what has already been discussed.

The middle of the sentence is usually the least emphatic. Skillful advocates know that in this part of the sentence they can place information they do not wish to highlight.

SENTENCE

beginning	middle	end
somewhat emphatic	least emphatic	most emphatic

Examine the following two examples, either of which could appear in an objective memo. Example 5 places "are not attractive nuisances" in the end position, so this version should occur in a memo that emphasizes the point that natural streams are usually not attractive nuisances.

EXAMPLE 5　　**End Position for Emphasis**

Unless they are concealing some dangerous condition, natural streams that flow through the hatchery are not attractive nuisances.

Example 6 places "unless they are concealing some dangerous condition" in the end position, so this version is likely to occur in a memo that emphasizes that a concealed dangerous condition made a natural stream an attractive nuisance.

EXAMPLE 6　　**Changing Emphasis**

Natural streams that flow through the hatchery are not attractive nuisances, unless they are concealing some dangerous condition.

In the following example from a persuasive brief, note how the end position emphasizes that the error was harmless.

EXAMPLE 7　　**End Position for Emphasis**

Even if the trial court mischaracterized the property, the entire division was fair; thus, the error was harmless.

To emphasize that the entire division of property was fair, the same sentence can be revised.

EXAMPLE 8　　**Changing Emphasis**

Even if the trial court mischaracterized the property, the error was harmless because the entire division was fair.

As ethical members of the legal profession, legal writers must often include information that is unfavorable to their client. Rather than concede a point in a short sentence, which will highlight the unfavorable point, it is often better to include it with the favorable point and arrange the material so the reader ends with the point favorable to your client.

EXAMPLE 9　　**Controlling Emphasis**

Although Mr. Tucci admits that he raised his voice during the altercation with Mrs. Stein, he never threatened Mrs. Stein, as Mrs. Stein claims, but rather reminded her of his rights as a property owner.

Combining the End Position with Other Strategies for Emphasis

By using the emphatic end position in combination with another strategy for emphasis, legal writers can achieve even more emphasis.

Here the end position, combined with punctuation, is used for dramatic effect.

EXAMPLE 10   **End Position + Colon for Emphasis**

The courtroom fell silent in anticipation of the jury's verdict: guilty.

In the next example, the end position, combined with use of a phrase telling the reader what is important, is used to suggest a climax.

EXAMPLE 11   **End Position + Emphasizing Phrase**

Before awarding custody, the court must consider the mental and physical health of all individuals involved, the child's adjustment to home and school, the relationship of the child with his parents and siblings, the wishes of the parents, and, most important, the wishes of the child.

In the next example, the end position, combined with the technique of setting up a pattern and breaking it, is used to startle the reader.

EXAMPLE 12   **Creating Emphasis by Breaking a Pattern**

Daniel Klein was loyal to his parents, loyal to his wife, loyal to his friends, and disloyal to the company that had employed him for thirty years.

Two final points before leaving the topic of positions of emphasis: First, the positions of emphasis can also be applied at the paragraph and document levels; second, the characterization of most emphatic, somewhat emphatic, and least emphatic for the end, beginning, and middle of sentences is a general, not an absolute, principle. In the following subsections we will see how punctuation, single-word emphasizers, and changing normal word order can make the beginning and even the middle of sentences strong points of emphasis.

§ 24.6.4 Using Punctuation for Emphasis

Commas, colons, and dashes can all be used to set up a point in an appositive at the end of a sentence. An appositive is a restatement of an earlier word or group of words. It is often a more detailed substitute for the earlier word or group of words. In the following example "brother" is an appositive for "silent partner." Notice how the three different marks of punctuation cast a slightly different light on the words that follow them. The comma, as a rather commonplace punctuation mark, suggests in the first of these examples that there is nothing too surprising about the silent partner being his brother.

EXAMPLE 13   **Punctuation and Emphasis**

The construction contract included a silent partner, his brother.

The colon requires a longer pause; consequently the phrase "his brother" receives more emphasis in the example that follows. Colons also have an aura of formality that somehow suggests the seriousness of what follows them.

EXAMPLE 14   **Colon Increases Emphasis**

The construction contract included a silent partner: his brother.

The longer pause created by the dash gives even more emphasis to "his brother." The dash also suggests that it is rather surprising that the brother is the silent partner.

EXAMPLE 15   **Dash Increases Emphasis**

The construction contract included a silent partner—his brother.

One thing legal writers should consider before using dashes, however, is that some readers feel dashes also convey a sense of informality. Consequently, many legal writers avoid dashes in legal prose.

§ 24.6.5   Using Single-Word Emphasizers

Certain words in our language ("no," "not," "never," "only," "any," "still," "all," "every," "none") convey natural emphasis because they either dramatically change or intensify the meaning of the word they modify.

EXAMPLE 16   **Using Single-Word Emphasizers**

A change made to the contract must be approved by both parties.

Revision 1

Any change made to the contract must be approved by both parties.

Revision 2

A change may be made to the contract only if approved by both parties.

Note that the most effective way to use "not" for emphasis is to place a comma before it and use "not" as a contrasting element.

EXAMPLE 17   **"Not" for Emphasis**

It is the taxpayer, not the tax preparer, who is responsible for the accuracy of all information on the form.

Three other single-word emphasizers ("clearly," "obviously," and "very") are so overused that they have lost much of their ability to emphasize. Ironically, sentences that contain "clearly," "obviously," and "very" seem to have more impact when these words are omitted.

EXAMPLE 18   **Overused Emphasizers**

Weak

Clearly, the defendant knew she was committing a crime.

Revised

The defendant knew she was committing a crime.

---

§ 24.6.6   Changing the Normal Word Order

Readers expect the traditional subject-verb-object order in sentences. When a writer changes this expected order, the change draws attention to whatever words are out of the traditional order.

The most common change is from active voice to passive voice. See sections 24.1.1 to 24.1.3. Another fairly common change is to insert the words to be emphasized between either the subject and the verb or between the verb and its object.

EXAMPLE 19   **Inserting Words for Emphasis**

Martin Fuller, blinded by grief, lost his grip on reality and opened fire on the parking lot.

He shot—apparently at close range—both of the parents of Tim O'Connell.

Another, less frequent change is to delay the subject and verb and open the sentence with a part of the sentence that would normally come at the end.

EXAMPLE 20   **Delayed Subject and Verb**

Mrs. Shapiro rewrote her will only one week before she died.

Revised:

Only one week before she died, Mrs. Shapiro rewrote her will.

Notice that some of the preceding examples seem to contradict the earlier advice about keeping subjects and verbs close together and using the end position in sentences to achieve emphasis. None of the strategies for emphasis works as an absolute rule. The writer should use his or her judgment in selecting which strategy is effective in each instance.

§ 24.6.7   Repeating Key Words

Many writers mistakenly assume that repetition is a weakness. This assumption leads them to search desperately for synonyms of words that recur frequently in a given office memo or brief.

While it is true that needless repetition is ineffective, it is also true that deliberate repetition can be a powerful strategy for emphasis. Key terms and key points should reverberate throughout a piece of legal writing. Like the dominant color in a beautiful tapestry, key words and phrases should be woven throughout to create an overall impression that *this* is what the case is about.

Consider the following excerpt from the respondent's brief in a case where the appellant, a church, wants to operate a grade school without the special use permit required by the city's zoning ordinance for all schools in residential areas. Throughout the excerpt, three different words — "code," "use," and "school" — are deliberately repeated for emphasis. We have boldfaced these three words so you can see how frequently they appear.

EXAMPLE 21   **Repeating Key Words for Emphasis**

ARGUMENT

I. THE TRIAL COURT PROPERLY CONSTRUED AND APPLIED BOTH THE ZONING AND BUILDING **CODES** BECAUSE THE CHURCH HAS CHANGED THE **USE** OF ITS BUILDING BY OPERATING A FULLTIME GRADE **SCHOOL**.

The church must comply with the requirements of the zoning and building **codes** before it may legally operate its **school**. Each of these **codes** makes accommodation for **uses** that legally existed prior to enactment of the **codes**. However, the church never operated a **school** prior to the **codes'** enactment, so full compliance with the **codes** is required for the new **use** involved in operating a school.

---

§ 24.6.8   Setting up a Pattern

The earlier strategy of repeating key words is closely tied to another strategy for emphasis: setting up a pattern. In such cases a pattern is set up and key words are repeated within that pattern.

EXAMPLE 22   **Repetition for Emphasis**

Lieutenant Harris has been described by his superiors as an "exemplary officer"—exemplary in his demeanor and professionalism, exemplary in his management of subordinates, exemplary in his performance of duty, and exemplary in his loyalty to the service.

Both women were abducted in the same locale. Both women were abducted at night. Both women were abducted while alone. Both women were abducted by the same man: Edward Smith.

Note that to achieve a climactic effect, the writer usually used parallel structure (see section 27.7) to create the pattern and then arranged the material in an order of increasing importance.

§ 24.6.9   Variation: Deliberately Breaking a Pattern

A rather dramatic variation of the pattern strategy is to set up the pattern and then deliberately break it. The pattern and repetition of key words create a certain expectation in the reader. The reader's surprise when the pattern is broken creates heightened emphasis.

EXAMPLE 23   **Breaking a Pattern for Emphasis**

The defendant acted under a common scheme, for a common motive, but with uncommon results.

---

§ 24.7   Sentence Structures That Highlight Similarities or Differences

Legal writers often need to compare and contrast facts.[1] In arguing that a case is analogous to or distinguishable from the present case, writers must spell out exactly how the two sets of facts are similar or different. All too often, though, novice legal writers are tentative and vague when they set up these comparisons. Instead of making explicit factual comparisons, the novice writer is likely to start a comparison sentence with something such as "Like *Smith*, the defendant in our case . . . ."

This approach has at least two problems. First, the sentence has a basic precision problem. It is comparing a whole case, *Smith*, to a person, the defendant. See section 25.1.5. Second, it is very likely to send the reader scurrying back a page or two to where *Smith* was discussed. "Like *Smith*, the defendant in our case . . ." makes it the reader's responsibility to figure out what the factual similarity is between *Smith* and the present case. What exactly is it in *Smith* that is analogous to the present case?

The first problem can be easily solved by simply making sure that the comparison (or contrast) is apples to apples and oranges to oranges: "Like the <u>defendant</u> in *Smith*, the defendant in our case . . ." or "Unlike the <u>driver</u> in *Lee*, the driver in our case . . . ." That lining up of at least one fact (defendant to defendant or driver to driver) gives the reader a start at understanding the argument, but it is still just a start. The second problem can be solved by stating enough of the salient facts about the defendants or the drivers for the reader to see the similarities or differences.

---

1. The material and examples in this section first appeared in a column written by Anne Enquist, *Teaching Students to Make Explicit Factual Comparisons*, 12 Perspectives 147 (Spring 2004).

Step one, then, might be to create a table that sets out the parallel similarities or differences before beginning to write sentences.

analogous case	present case
defendants in *Smith*	defendants in our case (the Joneses)
allowed daughter's boyfriend	allowed family friend
to use the family car	to use the family car
to drive to a dance	to drive to work
boyfriend used car for a prank	friend used car for work-related errand
and got into an accident	and got into an accident

Holding	*Argument*
family car doctrine does not apply because	family car doctrine should not apply because
defendants' permission limited to driving to and from dance, not prank	defendants' permission limited to driving to and from work, not work-related errands
driver acted beyond scope of permission	driver acted beyond the scope of permission
defendants not liable	defendants should not be liable

Step two is to translate the table into sentences. The reader will readily see the comparison if the writer matches the sentence structure in the first and second parts of the sentence so that the information about the analogous case parallels the information about the present case. In the following example, the parallel parts are labeled A and A′, B and B′, and so on.

"Like the defendant in *Smith*, who allowed his daughter's boyfriend to use the family
          A   B

car to drive to a dance, the defendants in our case allowed their family friend to use
          C   A′   B′

the family car to drive to work. The *Smith* court held that the defendants were not
             C′   D

liable because the driver acted beyond the scope of the defendants' permission.
                   E

(cite) Their permission was limited to driving to and from the dance; it did not
                                      F

extend to using the car for a prank. (cite) Similarly, the Joneses should not be held
                 G   D′

liable because the driver acted beyond the scope of their permission. Their
                   E′

permission was limited to driving to and from work; it did not extend to work-
                      F′   G′

related errands."

Of course, writers do not have to rigidly and mindlessly repeat the exact sentence structure in the second part that they used in the first part, but notice that *some* repetition makes the comparison easier for the reader to follow.

Below are a few more examples of comparing or contrasting tables followed by "like" or "unlike" sentences. An "equals" sign (=) in the chart indicates similarities; an inequality sign (≠) indicates differences.

EXAMPLE 1	Comparing and Contrasting Cases

defendant in *Sheldon*	=	Ms. Olsen (the defendant in this case)
used parents' house	≠	used halfway house
for many activities	≠	for only a few activities
indicates	≠	does not indicate
center of domestic activity	=	center of domestic activity

"Unlike the defendant in *Sheldon*, who used her parents' home for many activities indicative of a center of domestic activity, Ms. Olsen used the halfway house for only a few activities indicative of a center of domestic activity."

EXAMPLE 2	Comparing and Contrasting Cases

driver in *Cook*, Whitner,	=	Ms. Foster (the driver in this case)
paid room and board	=	paid room and board
family's adult daughter	≠	family friend
lived with parents	≠	lived with Nguyens
since death of husband	≠	while attending university

"Like the driver in *Cook* who paid for room and board, Ms. Foster also paid for room and board; however, unlike Whitner, who was the family's adult daughter who had lived with her parents since the death of her husband, Ms. Foster was only a family friend who was living with the Nguyens while she attended the university."

When the facts in both the analogous and the present case are virtually identical on one or more points, writers often use a sentence structure such as the one below.

EXAMPLE 3	Sentence Structure When Facts Are Identical

"As in *Cook*, the driver in our case paid for room and board; however, unlike Whitner, who was the family's adult daughter who had lived with her parents since the death of her husband, Ms. Foster was only a family friend who was living with the Nguyens while she attended the university."

Note, however, that the "As in *case name*," sentence opening should be used with some care. Consider the example below.

EXAMPLE 4	Editing Sentences That Compare/Contrast

| *Chea* employee's stress | = | Officer Wu's stress (the employee in this case) |
| resulted from a series of incidents | = | resulted from three different incidents |

Incorrect

"As in *Chea*, Officer Wu's stress resulted from three different incidents: the Aurora Bridge accident, the City's failure to notify him about his exposure to HIV, and the WTO riots."

The sentence above incorrectly says the employee's stress in *Chea* also came from these same three incidents that caused Officer Wu's stress.

| **EXAMPLE 5** | **Editing Sentences That Compare/Contrast** |

Corrected

"Like *Chea*, in which the employee's stress resulted from a series of incidents, in this case, Officer Wu's stress resulted from three different incidents: the Aurora Bridge accident, the City's failure to notify him about his exposure to HIV, and the WTO riots."

In some situations, writers need to list many facts in order to compare or contrast cases, and doing so in one long sentence would affect readability. For those situations, companion sentences in which all of sentence 1 mirrors all of sentence 2 are often preferable.

| **EXAMPLE 6** | **Companion Sentences** |

Sentence 1

In *Cook*, because Ms. Whitner ate most meals with the family, had her own room in the family home, was assigned several family-related chores, and was included in the family holiday photo, the court held that she was "treated as a member of the family." (cite) Similarly, because Ms. Foster ate three to four times a week with the Nguyens, shared a room with their daughter, and vacationed in Oregon with them, the court should decide that she was treated as a member of the family.

Sentence 2

In *Cook*, the court noted numerous examples of how Ms. Whitner was treated as a member of the family: She ate most meals with the family, had her own room in the family home, was assigned several family-related chores, and was included in the family holiday photo. Similarly, in our case, Ms. Foster can also point to numerous examples of how she was treated as a member of the family: She ate three to four times a week with the Nguyens, shared a room with their daughter, and vacationed in Oregon with them.

Interestingly, however, distinguishing facts often works best through a series of sentences with juxtaposed parts.

| **EXAMPLE 7** | **Sentences with Juxtaposed Parts** |

Cook is easily distinguishable from our case. Ms. Whitner ate most meals with the family; Ms. Foster ate only three to four times a week with the Nguyens. Whitner had her own room in the family home; Foster shared a room with the Nguyens' daughter, but after October spent most nights at her boyfriend's apartment. Whitner was assigned several family-related chores, including cooking once a week and taking out the trash; Foster was never asked to perform any chores and was instead treated more as a guest. Whitner was included in the family holiday photo and wrote her own paragraph in the family Christmas letter; Foster was included in the Nguyens' Oregon vacation, but she paid for her own room, meals, and souvenirs. Therefore, although Ms. Foster was still living with the Nguyens at the time of the accident, the court is unlikely to find that Ms. Foster was treated as a member of the family.

The examples above are but a few of the many sentence structures for making factual comparisons. The key is to think through how the facts are similar or different and then consciously construct a sentence that highlights those similarities and differences.

Chapter 24 Quiz

Draft answers for each of the following questions. Make your points clearly and concisely, and write sentences that are easy to read and that are grammatical and correctly punctuated.

1. What is the difference between active and passive voice?
2. How is passive voice different from past tense?
3. Why is active voice generally preferred over passive voice?
4. When is it more effective to use passive voice?
5. What is nominalization? Why is a concrete subject often more effective than a nominalization as a subject?
6. What are some of the common pitfalls writers fall into when selecting a verb?
7. What are some of the ways to revise overly long sentences?
8. When is the best time to use a short sentence?
9. What are some of the ways writers can create emphasis?
10. In most sentences, what tends to be the positions of emphasis?

Effective Words

A powerful agent is the right word. Whenever we come upon one of
those intensely right words in a book or a newspaper the resulting
effect is physical as well as spiritual, and electrically prompt.

—Mark Twain,
Essay on William Dean Howells

§ 25.1   Diction and Precision

It is such a seemingly simple thing. Use the right word, Twain tells us, and
the effect is physical, spiritual, electric, prompt. But "right" is a relative thing,
isn't it? Some words are more right than others. Some words approach the
desired meaning; others capture it, embody it, nail it to the wall in a way that
leaves both the writer and reader satisfied, almost breathless.

Take the word "right," for example. Twain chose "right" to describe the
kind of word he meant, even though the thesaurus suggests that he might have
chosen any number of so-called synonyms. How about the "noble" word, the
"proper" word, the "suitable" word, the "exact" word, the "accurate" word, the
"correct" word, or even the "precise" word?

What is it about "right" that makes it the right choice?

First of all, denotation—that is, the word's definition. "Noble" is the wrong
choice because it has the wrong denotation. Webster tells us that "noble" means
"possessing outstanding qualities." The definition of "noble" also includes a tie
to some kind of superiority. Something is "noble" because it has a "superiority

of mind or character or ideals or morals." The kind of words Twain talks about do something different than possess outstanding qualities or superiority.

"Proper" seems to have the right denotation. "Proper" is defined as "marked by suitability, rightness, or appropriateness." Later in the definition we find "strictly accurate" and "correct." These meanings seem closer to Twain's intention. But wait a minute. Further still in the definition we see "respectable," "strictly decorous," and "genteel." But do we have to include all of the possible definitions of a word when we use it? Obviously not, but in the case of "proper," these later definitions are clues about the connotations, or associations, that the word carries.

The word "proper" has close ties with the word "propriety," which means "the quality or state of being proper." "Propriety" also means "the standard of what is socially acceptable." If "the proper thing to do" has overtones of decorum and civility, then "the proper word" might also suggest a bit of politeness in its selection. It's doubtful that Twain meant that a "polite word" is a powerful agent.

"Suitable" has similar denotation and connotation problems. Part of the definition of "suitable" is "adapted to a use or purpose." If "suitable words" are those that are adapted to a certain use or purpose, then it is unlikely anything with such a chameleon-like quality can ever be physical, spiritual, electric, or prompt.

"Exact" has the virtue of meaning in "strict, particular, and complete accordance with fact" and the minor flaw of connoting a kind of mathematical or scientific measurement. Still, it is a far better choice than "noble," "proper," or "suitable."

In fact, "exact," "accurate," "correct," "precise," and "right" all have what dictionaries call "the shared meaning element." They all mean "conforming to fact, truth, or a standard."

What is it then about the word "right" that makes it preferable to the other four words—that makes it just right? It has the right denotation and the right connotation, and it has the right sound.

Go back to the quotation at the beginning of the chapter. Try reading the first sentence aloud as it is. Now, one at a time, substitute the words "exact," "accurate," "correct," and "precise" for "right." Read each of these versions aloud. Notice how much harder it is to get the desired emphasis with the three-syllable "accurate." Even the two-syllable words dilute, albeit just a bit, the punch that we hear in the one syllable "right." Furthermore, "right" has a kind of honesty and simplicity that captures the spirit of Twain's insight.

Now what does all of this mean for a writer of legal briefs and memos? The same thing it means for any good writer. Finding the right word to express one's meaning is critical to clear communication. With anything other than the right word, you have sacrificed precision; you have sacrificed exact meaning.

In cases such as Twain's in which several words can express the intended meaning, the writer can then go beyond precision to eloquence to find the word with just the right sound. See Chapter 26. For now, though, we will focus just on diction and precision and the word choice problems that frequently occur in legal writing. (Three categories of word choice problems—legalese, gender-neutral language, and bias-free language—deserve special attention and are discussed in sections 25.3, 25.4, and 25.5, respectively.)

§ 25.1.1 Colloquial Language

Because legal writing is done for serious reasons and in a professional context, legal writers should select words that reflect seriousness and professionalism. Slang, colloquialisms, or informal expressions that are acceptable in everyday spoken language are usually out of place in legal writing.

EXAMPLE 1   **Editing for Informal Expressions**

Too Colloquial

The prosecutor noted that Mr. Webb is **hung up about** how clean his car is, what gas is used in it, and how it is driven.

Edited

The prosecutor noted that Mr. Webb is **obsessed** about how clean his car is, what gas is used in it, and how it is driven.

There is only one exception to the general ban on using slang, colloquialisms, and informal language in legal writing—when the writer is quoting. While a writer of a trial brief would be ill-advised to call the defendant "a bad dude," he or she may effectively use that expression, in quotation marks, if it appeared in the record.

§ 25.1.2 Reader Expectations and Idioms

A writer's choice among synonyms should also be governed by the reader's expectations. Legal readers, for example, expect to hear about "analogous" cases or "similar" cases, not "comparable" cases or "matching" cases.

Read the following example and see if any word is jarring for legal readers.

EXAMPLE 2   **Meeting Reader Expectations About Word Choice**

Draft

Beaver Custom Carpets will probably argue that there are significant **parallelisms** between its case and *Flowers*.

Edited

Beaver Custom Carpets will probably argue that there are significant **similarities** between its case and *Flowers*.

Similarly, some synonyms have the correct denotation and connotation, but their use is jarring because the reader expects certain idiomatic combinations.

Consider the following example. Which word doesn't seem quite right?

| **EXAMPLE 3** | **Word Choice Does Not Meet Reader Expectations** |

Corporations can elude liability by dissolution.

Although the thesaurus may list "elude" as a synonym for "avoid" and "escape," legal readers expect either the idiom "avoid liability" or the idiom "escape liability."

Numerous verbs have certain prepositions with which they commonly combine. In common usage, for example, one always "infers *from*" something. A client may "agree *to*" sign a contract, but she may "agree *with*" the way you are handling her case.

When in doubt about which idiom or preposition is appropriate, consult a reliable dictionary or a usage guidebook. Another strategy is to read the sentence aloud. Native speakers of English can usually "hear" which preposition is correct.

| **EXAMPLE 4** | **Wrong Preposition** |

Wrong Preposition

Publishers must be able to publish matters of public concern without fear **for** a lawsuit.

Edited

Publishers must be able to publish matters of public concern without fear **of** a lawsuit.

---

§ 25.1.3   Not-Really-Synonymous Synonyms

Of the many types of imprecision, the most common is the simple substitution of a not-really-synonymous "synonym." In the following example, the writer knew that there were several things he had to prove under the doctrine of adverse possession, but he forgot what to call those "things."

| **EXAMPLE 5** | **Imprecise Synonym** |

The adverse possessor must prove the **condition** of hostility.

"Condition" is not completely wrong; the reader can probably figure out what the writer intended. But "condition" is not precise. By using the precise term "element," the writer conveys the exact intended meaning, and he makes it clear that he is doing an elements analysis of the problem.

EXAMPLE 6	Precise Synonym

Edited

The adverse possessor must also prove the **element** of hostility.

Notice that in the above example the term "element" is used when there are indeed "elements" that must be proved. Some legal writers mistakenly use the terms "element" and "factor" as if they were synonyms. The term "element" refers to a requirement — something that must be proved or met. "Factors," on the other hand, refers to what a court must consider. For example, courts must examine several factors to determine which parent gets custody of a child.

Another group of problematic terms that some legal writers use imprecisely includes the words "part," "prong," and "step." If there is a two-part test, then both parts must be satisfied. If there are two prongs to a test, then the test can be satisfied in either of the two ways. If there is a two-step test, both steps must be satisfied in sequence.

Unfortunately, however, you may occasionally find that courts themselves sometimes use the terms "factor," "element," "part," "prong," and "step" imprecisely when describing a test. In such instances, you will probably want to adopt the court's word choice if you are writing to that same court. In writing for others, however, you will probably want to adopt the precise term.

Yet another precision problem occurs when writers try to dress up a simple idea in a fancy vocabulary word and end up instead with a word choice that misses the mark.

EXAMPLE 7	Imprecise Word Choice

Draft

The McKibbins may argue that rugs **are totally diverse** from closed circuit television camera security systems because few consumers have a need for such elaborate security systems.

Edited

The McKibbins may argue that rugs **differ** from closed circuit television camera security systems because few consumers have a need for such elaborate security systems.

The most serious type of "not-really-synonymous synonym" problem occurs when writers attempt to use words they are not quite sure of. Needless to say, it can be embarrassing to find that you have used a word that only sounds like the word you intended. Undoubtedly, the writers of the following examples intended to suggest that *Grimsby* was a "seminal" case and Mrs. Harris's point was "salient," not salty.

EXAMPLE 8	**Wrong Word**

The Seminole case that adopted the Restatement (Second) Torts § 46 in outrage tort claims is *Grimsby v. Samson*, 85 Wn.2d 52, 530 P.2d 291 (1975).

Mrs. Harris's most **saline** point is that Mr. Harris intends to move the children more than 250 miles away.

---

§ 25.1.4   The Same Term for the Same Idea

Another common precision problem in legal writing is the misuse of elegant variation. In other words, legal writers sometimes try to use synonyms for key terms in their writing in the mistaken belief that using the same term over and over again bores their readers.

What they have forgotten, though, is that their legal readers have been carefully trained to read statutes and, according to the rules of statutory construction, a different term signals a different idea. Many legal readers carry this rule over into their memo and brief reading. A change in a key term starts them wondering: "Does the writer mean the same thing as before, or is this really something new?"

Read the following example, and note how the writer uses the term "stability" and its variations consistently but floats back and forth among the terms "factor," "principle," and "element."

EXAMPLE 9	**Using Consistent Terms**

In determining custody, none of the **factors** listed in the statute are dispositive. *See, e.g., In re Marriage of Morales*, 159 P.3d 1183 (Or. App. 2007); *Matter of Marriage of Holcomb*, 888 P.2d 1046 (Or. App. 1995). However, in many cases, the courts have stressed the importance of the third **principle** and made every effort to maintain the continuity of relationships already established between a parent and a child. *E.g., Holcomb*, 888 P.2d at 1051. Another **element** appears, as in *Morales*, in which the court must decide whether a child's welfare is best served by separation from a sibling. *See id.* at 1189. This **factor** relates back to the first part of the statute, which deals with the emotional ties and interest and attitudes.

In cases such as the example above, the reader does not know whether to accuse the writer of sloppy writing or to try to make some fine distinction between "factor," "principle," and "element." In many cases, there is a legal distinction between "factor" and "element" or between "factor" and "principle." In those cases, substituting the terms for each other would be more than confusing; it would be legally inaccurate.

In short, then, legal readers appreciate appropriate variety, but they do not appreciate variety at the expense of clarity.

§ 25.1.5   Precise Comparisons

In the preceding sections, we saw how disconcerting it can be for readers when writers aren't careful about what they call something. Equally disconcerting for readers are situations in which writers are sloppy about the comparisons they make.

EXAMPLE 10   **Imprecise Comparison**

Draft

The facts of *Turner* are **similar to our case**.

Because a case includes more than just the facts, it is incongruous to compare just the facts of one case to another entire case.

EXAMPLE 11   **Precise Comparison**

Edited

The facts of *Turner* are **similar to the facts in our case**.

In the following examples, the writer has forgotten that the italic type signals the case, not the defendant.

EXAMPLE 12   **Imprecise Comparison**

Draft

Unlike *Callahan*, Richardson was not just a temporary visitor.

Edited

Unlike Callahan, Richardson was not just a temporary visitor.

EXAMPLE 13   **Creating Precise Comparisons**

Draft

Like *Collins*, Richardson had personal possessions on the premises.

Edited

Like the defendant in *Collins*, Richardson had personal possessions on the premises.

As in *Collins*, in our case, Richardson had personal possessions on the premises.

See section 24.7 for more on precise comparisons.

§ 25.1.6   Subject-Verb-Object Mismatch

Not all problems of precision are a matter of just one poorly chosen word. All too frequently, the problem is a poorly chosen combination of words. Read the following example from a case about a custody dispute and see if the subject, verb, and object go together.

EXAMPLE 14   **Imprecise Subject-Verb-Object Combinations**

Draft

Dr. Lopez's <u>occupation</u> as an obstetrician <u>has shown</u> a <u>diminished ability</u> to provide consistent
      (subject)   *(verb)*   *(object)*
care and guidance for her children.

Can an occupation show a diminished ability to do anything? Obviously not. What the writer wants to say is that Dr. Davis is an obstetrician and that people who are obstetricians often have demanding, irregular schedules and therefore less time and energy to give consistent care and guidance to their own children.

EXAMPLE 15   **Creating Precise Subject-Verb-Object Combinations**

Edited

Dr. Lopez's occupation, obstetrician, may impair her ability to provide consistent care and guidance for her children.

To determine whether this or any other subject-verb-object combination is mismatched, lift those three parts out of the sentence and see if they make sense as a unit.

> occupation   may impair   ability
> *(subject)*   *(verb)*   *(object)*

Does "occupation may impair ability" make sense? Most readers would say that it does; some, however, would argue against the personification of "occupation" and suggest that occupations cannot "impair" anything. Precision, as we said earlier, is a relative thing.

One common personification used in law that many readers consider imprecise is the use of a case in the subject position when the writer actually means the court that presided over that case.

EXAMPLE 16   **Imprecise Use of a Case as the Subject**

The case *Steele v. Neeman*, 206 P.3d 384 (Wyo. 2009), reversed the trial court's decision because the trial court inappropriately considered the relationship between father and child in calculating child support payments.

Using the "lift-out" strategy, we get the following combination:

> case   reversed   decision
> *(subject)*   *(verb)*   *(object)*

To be more precise, place the real actor, the appellate court, in the subject position.

Occasionally, legal writers mistakenly end up with a combination that essentially means "X equals X"; that is, the subject or beginning of the sentence and object or end of the sentence are the same.

EXAMPLE 17   **Imprecise Subject-Verb-Complement Combination**

The purpose of the legislation is compensatory intent.

purpose	is	intent
(subject)	*(verb)*	*(predicate nominative)*[1]

There is virtually no difference between "the purpose of the legislation" and "the intent of the legislation." More than likely, the writer intended to say that the purpose of the legislation was to compensate someone.

EXAMPLE 18   **Creating Precise Subject-Verb-Complement Combination**

Edited

The purpose of the legislation is to compensate victims of such crimes.

Part of matching the right subject with the right verb is understanding how the legal system works. Knowing exactly what courts, juries, parties to litigation, legislatures, and agencies do and don't do makes it easier to select appropriate verbs. Exhibit 25.1 lists some typical subject-verb-object combinations.

For example, "the court finds" is the right combination for describing the action a court takes in making a finding of fact. "The court held" is the right combination for describing the court's decision on a question of law. "The court ruled" is the right combination for describing the actions a court takes on a particular issue, such as a motion or an objection, in a particular case. Courts can also "deny motions" or "grant injunctions"; they can "take something under advisement."

Courts can "apply the law," they can "apply a standard," and they can "apply a test"; they never "apply the facts."

In cases in which the court is both the decider of law and the trier of fact, courts perform an additional set of duties. When no jury is present, the court will "find" the criminal defendant guilty or not guilty, and the court will "award" civil damages.

As both the decider of law and the trier of fact, the court may "make determinations" or simply "determine" something about the law or the facts. Even so, "determine" is more commonly used for findings of fact.

---

1. The term "predicate nominative" is used instead of "object" with linking verbs. See section 27.1.

Exhibit 25.1   Typical Subject-Verb-Object Combinations

the court found (findings of fact)
the court ruled (ruling on an objection or a motion)
the court held (law applied to facts of a specific case)
the court determined (or must determine)
the court granted an injunction
the court granted the motion
the court denied the motion
the court applied the law (the test, the rule, the standard)
the court adopted the test
the court ordered (psychological testing, discovery)

the court relied on
the court followed
the court concluded
the court examined
the court reasoned
the court stated
the court noted

the appellate court affirmed the trial court's decision
the appellate court modified the trial court's decision
the appellate court reversed the trial court's decision
the appellate court upheld the trial court's decision
the appellate court remanded the case

In *Smith*, the court criticized the court's holding in *Jones*.
In *Smith*, the court explained the court's holding in *Jones*.
In *Smith*, the court followed the court's holding in *Jones*.
In *Smith*, the court limited the court's holding in *Jones*.
In *Smith*, the court questioned the court's holding in *Jones*.
In *Smith*, the court expanded upon the court's holding in *Jones*.
In *Smith*, the court overruled *Jones*.

the jury found the defendant (guilty or not guilty)
the jury acquitted the defendant
the jury determined that the defendant was (was not) liable
the jury awarded damages

the defendant (or plaintiff, State, prosecutor, defense counsel) alleged, argued, asked, asserted, claimed, contended, countered, maintained, moved, rebutted, responded, stated
the defendant was arraigned, arrested, charged, convicted/found not guilty, tried

the legislature passed, enacted, amended
the legislature intended to (promote, encourage, prevent, protect)
the legislature wanted to (promote, encourage, prevent, protect)

the agency decided, determined
the agency ruled
the agency investigated, mediated, promulgated, proposed

For cases up on appeal, appellate courts have a variety of actions they can perform. They can "affirm," "modify," "reverse," or "remand" a case; they can also "criticize," "distinguish," "explain," "follow," "limit," "overrule," or "question" the decisions in another case.

The court never takes on the role of one of the parties to litigation. Consequently, as a general rule, the court does not "claim," "allege," "assert," "contend," or "argue." The court is in a position to "say," not to "claim."

Even though it is technically incorrect to say "the court claimed," "the court asserted," or "the court argued," there are a few times when these combinations may be strategic word choices. In instances in which the writer is disagreeing with another court, for example, a writer may deliberately use "the court claimed" as a pejorative attack on another court's reasoning. The effect, of course, is the subtle undermining of the court's authority.

Another instance in which it is appropriate to use a combination such as "the court argued" occurs when members of the same court differ. Consequently, a law professor or the author of a law review article may say "Justice X argued" to describe a position that a justice took when trying to persuade the other members of the same court.

Juries, on the other hand, are charged with different tasks from judges. They "find" that a defendant is guilty or not guilty, they "determine liability," and they "award damages," but they do not "rule" on the law. Consequently, "a jury found," "a jury determined," and "a jury awarded" are appropriate combinations. In a jury trial, the jury, not the judge, "renders a verdict," and the judge, not the jury, "enters a judgment" based on that verdict. In a bench trial, the judge "renders a verdict."

Defendants and plaintiffs perform certain acts as well. They "argue," "state," "ask," "claim," "contend," "allege," "assert," "respond," "rebut," and "counter," but they do not "apply" the law. That is for the court to do.

EXAMPLE 19   **Imprecise Combination**

Incorrect

Applying the majority rule, the defendant will argue that the benefit of having a healthy baby outweighs the burden.

Correct

The defendant **will argue** that the court should apply the majority rule and hold that having a healthy baby outweighs the burden.

Either party to litigation can make a preliminary motion. Although you often hear, for example, that "the plaintiff made a motion for summary judgment," it is more concise to say "the plaintiff moved for summary judgment."

Legislatures, of course, perform entirely different functions from judges, juries, and litigants. The legislature may "enact a statute," it may "amend a statute," and it may "pass a law." It does not "hold" or "find." When it comes to policy, it is appropriate to say that the legislature "intended," "wanted to promote," "wanted to encourage," "wanted to prevent," or "wanted to protect."

Like judges, agencies "make determinations" (or just "determine"), and they "decide" things. Rarely does an agency "hold"; save "hold" for the few times when an agency issues an opinion. Even then, it is more likely to "rule." And of course, agencies perform many other functions such as "promulgate," "investigate," "propose," and "decide."

Perhaps the most glaring errors in word choice made by novice legal writers are those that stem from confusion over criminal and civil cases. Use "accused," "prosecuted," and "charged" for criminal cases. The defendant in a civil suit may be "sued" or "an action may be filed" against him or her; a civil suit defendant is not "accused," "prosecuted," or "charged."

Similarly, defendants in civil suits are not found "guilty" or "not guilty"; they are found "liable" or "not liable."

The outcome of a trial is a "judgment," not a "settlement." Use "settlement" for those agreements reached by parties through negotiation, not litigation. Parties may "settle out of court." Exhibit 25.2 summarizes some of these distinctions.

Exhibit 25.2

Criminal Cases	Civil Cases
accused (verb)	sued
charged	action filed against
guilty	liable
not guilty	not liable
defendant	defendant
state (or commonwealth)	plaintiff
prosecutor	plaintiff's counsel

§ 25.1.7 Grammatical Ambiguities

Before leaving the topic of precision, we must consider those times when writing becomes ambiguous and imprecise because the writer has not paid close attention to the grammar of the sentence. Modifiers, in particular, can create unintended meanings because modifiers seem to be free-floating spirits that can find a home in many different spots in a sentence. See section 27.6 for more on modifiers.

§ 25.2 Conciseness

Imagine for a moment that you are at a great steak house. It's a special occasion, so you order the best steak on the menu. When your meal arrives, however, you find that the steak is surrounded by an inch of fat. Appealing? Hardly. The meat itself may be tender and juicy, but you find it hard to appreciate its flavor with all that fat staring up off the plate at you. Why, you wonder, didn't the chef trim off the fat before your meal was served to you?

Wordy writing is like a steak surrounded by fat. It may have great analysis and brilliant arguments, but if you haven't trimmed the fat, the reader is likely to find the writing unappealing.

The question for most legal writers is how to transform fatty writing into writing that is lean and appealing. What follows are numerous strategies for trimming excess verbiage.

§ 25.2.1   Don't State the Obvious

Judges, lawyers, and most clients are busy people. They don't want to spend time reading the legal equivalent of "the sky is blue" or "people breathe air," unless, of course, you have something new to say about what is obvious.

Wasting time with sentences such as "Now I am going to discuss the cases that are relevant to this issue" or "The appellate court will not reconsider factual issues" annoys legal readers. It is a given that an office memo will discuss cases that are relevant to the issue; it is old news that appellate courts don't retry a case on its facts.

Novice legal writers often state the obvious because it reminds them of the steps they must go through in legal analysis. For example, a writer who begins the discussion section of a memo with "To determine the answer to this question, we must first look at the rule that . . ." has not recognized that a legal reader would be shocked to find something other than the rule at this point in the memo.

Consider the following excerpt from a draft of a memo.

EXAMPLE 1   **Stating the Obvious**

Our client bears the burden of establishing that the action meets the federal removal requirements. *Abrego v. Dow Chem. Co.*, 443 F.3d 676 (9th Cir. 2006). Some of these requirements are more important than others, but all are required before removal may occur. *Id.* To understand these requirements, it is easiest to break down 28 U.S.C. § 1441(a) (1988) into its component parts and discuss each part separately.

Besides the wordiness that comes from the redundancy in the first two sentences — requirements are required — the last sentence is no more than an announcement that one should do the obvious: analyze the requirements.

Novice and experienced legal writers often fall into the "stating the obvious" trap when they are trying to compose topic and transitional sentences within a discussion or argument section.

Suppose, for example, that a writer has just completed a paragraph about the holding, rationale, and facts of an analogous case. The writer now wants to compare the facts of the analogous case with those of the present case. At first the writer may be tempted to begin with something such as "*Moore* and our client's case are factually similar." This announcement should be quickly obvious, however, and unworthy of mention. What the writer needs to discuss in this topic sentence is the nature of these similarities or why those similarities suggest a certain outcome.

§ 25.2.2   Don't Start Too Far Back

Some novice legal writers fall prey to a cousin of the "stating the obvious" problem — starting too far back. They forget that there is common knowledge among legal readers. Consequently, the writing problem is determining where to begin and what not to say.

Consider the following example of starting too far back from a draft of a memo about a case in which criminal charges had been filed against the client who had photocopied a dollar bill and, after a friendly bet, had tried it in a change machine.

EXAMPLE 2   **Too Much Unnecessary Background**

Counterfeiting has been classified as an offense affecting the administration of governmental functions because the power to coin money was expressly granted to Congress and denied to the states by the terms of the Constitution. See U.S. Const. art. I, § 8, cl. 5, 6. Hence, counterfeiting is a federal crime and the penalty for passing counterfeit money is found in the *United States Code*. 18 U.S.C. §§ 471-73 (2006). Congress has enacted statutes making counterfeiting a federal offense; the various counterfeiting crimes are defined by these statutes, and these statutes determine the essential elements of the respective crimes. 18 U.S.C. §§ 470-514 (2006).

The background information in the preceding example is unnecessary. The writer of this excerpt seems to have forgotten who the reader is and what that reader is likely to know.

Writers who have a tendency to start too far back often fill their writing with background information that *they* needed in order to focus their ideas or to clarify a point. Even if they needed the information to analyze the problem, that does not automatically mean that their reader will need it too.

For example, because of a lack of experience, the writer may have had to do a fair amount of spade work to fill in a skimpy background in a given area of law. Unless the writer believes the reader needs the same kind of review or preliminary discussion, it should be omitted from the reader's version.

Furthermore, writers are obliged to save their readers from at least some of the blind alleys they explored. Legal writers who were successful writers as undergraduates often have a difficult time realizing this. In law there is no extra credit for arguments that don't work.

Thus far, we have primarily discussed legal writing that starts too far back analytically. Occasionally legal writers start too far back historically. They give long, careful explanations of how a particular area of law has evolved when all the reader wants is a discussion of how the end result of that evolutionary process applies to the facts of a case at hand.

This is not to say that tracing the history of a statute or a judicial trend is never appropriate. The point is to consider your specific reader and the reader's purposes, and then ask yourself if it is appropriate in the document you are writing. Put another way, don't write a law review article when the senior partner has assigned you an office memo.

§ 25.2.3   Don't Overuse Quotations

When to quote and how much to quote — these are two tough questions for all legal writers. Like many other issues in legal writing, there is a range of opinion about when quoting is appropriate, even required, and when the writer should merely paraphrase and cite to authority.

Most legal readers agree that relevant portions of statutes should be quoted. The trick, of course, is to pare the quotation down to that which is relevant.

In the following example, the writer has mistakenly quoted more of the statute than her reader needs. The case she is working on does not have anything to do with obstruction of a highway or the closing of a channel, but rather with whether a noisy aerobics club with patrons in skimpy attire is a private nuisance.

EXAMPLE 3   **Overquoting a Statute**

In determining whether there is a cause of action for private nuisance, the court is guided by RCW § 7.48.010 (2004), which provides the following:

The obstruction of any highway or closing the channel of any stream used for boating or rafting logs, lumber or timber, or whatever is injurious to health or indecent or offensive to the senses, or an obstruction to the free use of property, so as to essentially interfere with the comfortable enjoyment of the life and property, is a nuisance and the subject of an action for damages and other and further relief.

First, edit out all of the statute that is extraneous to the case:

[t]he obstruction of any highway or closing the channel of any stream used for boating or rafting logs, lumber or timber, or whatever is injurious to health or indecent or offensive to the senses, or an obstruction to the free use of property, so as to essentially interfere with the comfortable enjoyment of the life and property, is a nuisance and the subject of an action for damages and other and further relief.

Appropriately pared down then, the quotation looks like this:

[W]hatever is . . . indecent or offensive to the senses, or an obstruction to the free use of property, so as to essentially interfere with the comfortable enjoyment of the life and property, is a nuisance . . . .

Note the use of ellipses to indicate words omitted in the middle and at the end of the quotation. The brackets, which are used to show that the "w" was not capitalized in the original, also show that the original did not begin at the word "whatever." See sections 28.5.2 and 28.5.3 for more on the use of ellipses and brackets in quotations.

Although there is a great deal of agreement about quoting relevant portions of statutes, there is some disagreement about whether common law should be set out verbatim. One rule of thumb is that if a specific phrase reappears in the cases, then that phrase has become the standard or familiar "rule" and should therefore be quoted.

Generally, it is best to paraphrase the holding and rationale and cite to authority. Occasionally, however, the particular language of the holding or court's reasoning is so apt or well stated that a quotation is effective. This tactic works best when used sparingly.

Never quote facts of a case, although you may want to quote the exact words of a person in a fact statement when those words suggest the person's attitude, motive, or intention.

When deciding how much to quote, consider as well what your purpose is. In persuasive writing, you will probably use fairly extensive quoting from the record to make points about errors and conflicting testimony. You might also use a few more quotations from analogous cases because they allow you to create emphasis and effective repetition. A well-written lead-in to a quotation, which makes your point, followed by a carefully selected quotation, which also makes your point, allows you to make that point twice without being tedious. The same tactic used in objective writing, however, would be tedious.

The cardinal rule of quotations can be summed up as follows: *Quote only when the language itself is worth attention.* The language of statutes is always worth our attention; the specific language of common law is sometimes worth our attention; and, occasionally, the language of a court stating its holding or expressing its rationale is so memorable that it should not escape our attention. In all three instances, quote; otherwise, don't.

§ 25.2.4   Create a Strong Subject-Verb Unit

The quickest way to achieve an energetic yet lean writing style is to make sure that the subject-verb unit carries the core of meaning in the sentence. In other words, put the real action in the verb; put the doer of that action in the subject.

All too frequently in ineffective legal writing, the real action of the sentence is buried in a noun. This practice of changing verbs to nouns, known as "nominalization," tends to make sentences wordy (see section 24.3). Because the real action in the sentence is somewhere other than the verb, the writer must find a substitute to fill the verb slot in the sentence, usually either a form of the verb "to be" or some other filler verb that expresses no real action.

EXAMPLE 4   **Revising for a Strong Subject-Verb Unit**

Draft

This case <u>is</u> an illustration of this point.
    (verb)

Edited

This case <u>illustrates</u> this point.
    (verb)

The examples in Exhibit 25.3 are but a few of the many ways legal writers can make their writing more concise by finding the real action in the sentence.

Exhibit 25.3

made the assumption	→ assumed
made a recommendation	→ recommended
made a statement	→ stated
perform a review	→ review
reached an agreement	→ agreed
supports an inference	→ infers

If the real doer of the action is somewhere other than in the subject, then the subject of the sentence is also inevitably wordy because the writer has had to manufacture some language to fill that slot in the sentence.

Sometimes writers fill the subject slot with wordy expletives such as "there is," "there are," "there was," "there were," "it is," or "it was." Avoid these expletive constructions unless the point of the sentence is that something exists.

EXAMPLE 5   Revising to Create a Strong Subject

Draft

It was his intention to return to Maryland.

Edited

He intended to return to Maryland.

When writers inadvertently slip into the passive voice (see section 24.1), they inevitably create a wordy sentence with a weak subject.

EXAMPLE 6   Revising to Create a Strong Subject

Draft

Authorization for the contract was given by the district manager.

Edited

The district manager authorized the contract.

§ 25.2.5   Avoid Throat-Clearing Expressions

Frequently legal writers create wordy sentences because they fill both the subject and verb slots with throat-clearing expressions that add little, if any, meaning to the sentence.

| EXAMPLE 7 | **Editing Out Throat-Clearing Expressions** |

Draft

It must be remembered that the statute requires that service be made at the dwelling house or usual place of abode.

Edited

The statute requires that service be made at the dwelling house or usual place of abode.

Most but not all of these throat-clearing expressions fall into the pattern "It is _____ that":

It is expected that
It is clear that
It is apparent that
It is generally recognized that
It has been determined that
It is significant that
It is a known fact that
It is obvious that
It is essential that
It is crucial that
It is conceivable that

Notice how in Exhibit 25.4 the following throat-clearing expressions may be reduced to one word or completely edited out.

Exhibit 25.4

It seems more likely than not that	→	probably
It can be presumed that	→	presumably
It may be argued that	→	arguably or say who may argue

A fair number of the throat-clearing expressions spend time saying that someone should take note of something.

It should also be noted that
It is interesting to note that
It should be noted that
It is worth noting that
It is crucial to note that
It is important to note that

If the writer can presume that the reader is already taking special note of all that is written, then such expressions are superfluous.

For an extended discussion on writing strong subject-verb units, see sections 24.2 and 24.3.

Two common-sense reminders: First, do not edit out every conceivable bit of wordiness from your writing. If you do, your writing will become sparse and lifeless. Second, do not focus on wordiness in the early stages of drafting. Being concerned about wordiness at that point is premature. First efforts and early drafts are, by nature, wordy and overwritten. In fact, at the beginning of the writing process, it may even be healthy for a writer to have an excess of words to work with. Thus, all the suggested strategies for conciseness in this section should be applied late in the writing process.

§ 25.2.6 Don't Use Pompous Language

A traveling geological formation acquires little vegetative growth. Translation: A rolling stone gathers no moss.

If only that were true. All too often, legal writers who are really "rolling" through an analysis begin gathering all kinds of moss in the form of stuffy, overly formal words. Instead of valuing their ideas for their clarity and simplicity, legal writers sometimes feel that they have to "dress them up" so that they look lawyerly and sound smart. They may have forgotten that their readers want to understand what they are saying, not be impressed by their vocabulary.

Exhibit 25.5 includes but a few of the many words and expressions that legal writers sometimes use to dress up an otherwise simple point. Resist the temptation. Keep it simple. Your readers will love you for it.

Exhibit 25.5

allocate	→	give, divide
ascertain	→	make sure
cease	→	stop
commence	→	begin
constitute	→	make up
emulate	→	copy
endeavor	→	try
finalize	→	complete, finish, end
implement	→	carry out, put into effect
initiate	→	begin
objective	→	goal, aim
originate	→	start
preclude	→	shut out, prevent
prior to	→	before
promulgate	→	issue, publish
pursuant	→	under
render	→	make, give
secure	→	get, take, obtain
subsequent	→	after
terminate	→	end, finish
utilize	→	use
verification	→	proof

§ 25.2.7 Don't Repeat Yourself Needlessly

Language seems to be inherently redundant. Start trying to string a few words together and fairly soon some of those words will start making the same point. No matter how hard we try, words just keep coming out at a faster rate than the ideas, so naturally some words double up and say the same thing.

Some of this doubling up seems to come from a lack of faith in the words themselves. For example, why does anyone ever say or write "close proximity"? Isn't proximity always close? How about "mutual cooperation"? When is cooperation not mutual?

What logic is there in the expression "sworn affidavit"? If an affidavit is a "sworn statement in writing," then is a "sworn affidavit" a "sworn sworn statement in writing"?

Exhibit 25.6 is a sampling of many common redundancies, adapted from a list called "Dog Puppies" compiled by writer and editor Yvonne Lewis Day.[2] A few extra redundant phrases have been added by the authors. The word or words in parentheses should be omitted.

Exhibit 25.6

3:00 a.m. (in the morning)	(advance) warning
11:00 p.m. (at night)	alongside (of)
red (in color)	(and) moreover
(a distance of) twenty feet	appreciate (in value)
(a period of) six months	(as) for example
(absolute) guarantee	ascend (up)
(absolutely) clear	ask (a question)
(actual) experience	(as to) whether
(advance) planning	(at a) later (date)
at (the) present (time)	emergency (situation)
(basic) fundamentals	(empty) space
belief (system)	(end) result
(but) however	eradicate (completely)
(but) nevertheless	(essential) element
(close) scrutiny	(established) pattern
combine (together)	estimated (roughly) at
(complete) monopoly	(false) pretenses
(completely) destroyed	few (in number)
consensus (of opinion)	(foreign) imports
crisis (situation)	(past) history
(current) trend	(past) records
daily (basis)	permeate (throughout)
depreciate (in value)	(personal) friendship
descend (down)	(plan) ahead

---

2. Adapted from "The Economics of Writing" by Yvonne Lewis Day, reprinted with permission from the August 1982 issue of *The Toastmaster*.

(different) kinds	postponed (until later)
(direct) confrontation	(pre-) planned
during (the course of)	probed (into)
during (the year of) 2012	protest (against)
each (and every)	(provision of) law
each (separate) incident	(rate of) speed
free (of charge)	recur (again)
(future) plans	refer (back)
(general) public	reflect (back)
healing (process)	reiterate (again)
(important) essentials	repeat (again)
indicted (on a charge)	reported (to the effect) that
(integral) part	revert (back)
is (now) pending	risk (factor)
join (together)	scrutinize (carefully)
(local) residents	(separate) entities
(major) breakthrough	shooting (incident)
(many) (different) ways	(specific) example
(mass) media	(State's) prosecutor
merged (together)	(subtle) nuance
my (own) opinion	(sudden) outburst
my (personal) opinion	(suddenly) exploded
never (at any time)	(temporary) reprieve
never (before)	(thorough) investigation
off (of)	(underlying) (basic) assumption
(over) exaggerate	(unexpected) surprise
(past) experience	(usual) custom

Many redundancies and wordy expressions have an "of" in them. Some legal writers find that they can spot many wordy constructions simply by searching for "of" and editing out about half of them.

The preceding list of redundancies includes those expressions that are common to writers in all disciplines. The language of law is much worse; it has made redundancy an art. In fact, to the average reader, the lawyer's motto seems to be: "When in doubt, say it twice."

One source of these redundancies, according to David Mellinkoff,[3] has been the law's tendency to draw on more than one language at a time to describe a single idea. Consequently, we get tautologies such as "null and void" when either "null" or "void" alone would be sufficient.

attorney (French) or lawyer (Old English)
buy (Old English) or purchase (French)
constable (French) or sheriff (Old English)
larceny (French) or theft or stealing (Old English)
minor (Latin) or child (Old English) or infant (French)

---

3. David Mellinkoff, *The Language of the Law* 58 (1963).

own (Old English) or possess (French)
property or chattels (French) or goods (Old English)
pardon (French) or forgive (Old English)
will (Old English) or testament (Latin)

Mellinkoff adds that other redundancies such as "aid and abet," "part and parcel," and "safe and sound" come from law's early oral tradition when the rhythm and sound of the words made them not only more memorable but also more powerful in the minds of the people.[4]

The question for modern legal writers, then, is whether doubling phrases serve any purpose for their readers. Is there some important distinction between "perform" and "discharge"? Is "cease and desist" more memorable or more emphatic than just "cease" or "desist" or "stop"?

If the answer to these questions is no, then what the writer has done by using doubling phrases is to double the words the reader must read. No new content, just more words — not exactly the way to win over a busy reader.

(Admittedly, some repetition in legal writing is done for effect. Used properly, repetition can be persuasive and even eloquent. Obviously, the discussion in this section refers to mindless, not deliberate, repetition.)

§ 25.2.8   Clean Out the Clutter

Clutter in writing takes several forms. One of the most common is the extraneous prepositional phrase. Notice how easily prepositional phrases can begin to grow and multiply.

EXAMPLE 8   **Editing Out Extra Prepositional Phrases**

Draft

At this point in time, we are in the process of filing a motion for summary judgment with the court.

Cutting Some Clutter

At this point in time, we are in the process of filing a motion for summary judgment.

Cutting More Clutter

We are in the process of filing a motion for summary judgment.

Cutting Still More Clutter

We are filing a motion for summary judgment.

Eight words have quickly grown to twenty, with no real gain in content.

As we saw in the earlier list of redundancies, the "of" preposition tends to be a frequent offender. Although we cannot write without *any* "of" phrases, in most people's writing about half of them can be eliminated.

---

4. *Id.* at 42-44.

| **EXAMPLE 9** | **Editing Out Extraneous "Of" Phrases** |

Draft

In the absence of any evidence of drugs on the premises, the police officers' actions can be given the interpretation of an invasion of privacy.

Edited

Without evidence of drugs on the premises, the police officers' actions were an invasion of privacy.

Notice in Exhibit 25.7 that the "of the" can be eliminated from some phrases and made into possessives in others.

Exhibit 25.7

all of the defendants	→	all defendants
none of the witnesses	→	no witness
the family of the victim	→	the victim's family
the reasoning of the court	→	the court's reasoning

Other modifiers besides prepositional phrases like to clutter up sentences. Adverbs, in particular, like to creep in legal writing sentences, often in the disguise of precision. You can usually (there's one!) spot adverbs by their *-ly* ending, but look out for "quite," "rather," "somewhat," and "very," too.

| **EXAMPLE 10** | **Adverb Clutter** |

Draft

Basically, the witness seemed quite relaxed as she carefully outlined the rather long list of extremely technical calculations she had made.

Edited

The witness seemed relaxed as she outlined the long list of technical calculations she had made.

One adverb that deserves special mention is "clearly." It is so overused in legal writing that one has to wonder if it has any meaning left. **Clearly**, it is time to think of a more sophisticated way to begin sentences.

§ 25.2.9 Focus and Combine

A clear focus will help you decide which sentences can be combined and, when combining, which parts to keep as the main subject and verb and which parts to subordinate. For example, two sentences can often be combined into one by changing one of the sentences into a relative clause beginning with "which," "who," "whom," "whose," or "that."[5]

EXAMPLE 11   **Combining for Conciseness**

Draft

The State's main witness was Arthur Hedges. Arthur Hedges agreed to testify after reaching a favorable plea bargain.

Combined

The State's main witness was Arthur Hedges, who agreed to testify after reaching a favorable plea bargain.

In some cases, these same relative clauses can be reduced to phrases by deleting unnecessary *whos*, *whichs*, and *thats*.

EXAMPLE 12   **Example 12   Editing for Conciseness**

Draft

The defendant lived in a room that was over the garage.

Edited

The defendant lived in a room over the garage.

Frequently, two sentences can be combined when one of them defines or identifies part of the other.

EXAMPLE 13   **Combining Sentences for Conciseness**

Draft

Upon entering the house, the police smelled phenyl-2-propanone. Phenyl-2-propanone is an organic chemical that is a necessary precursor ingredient of amphetamine.

Combined

Upon entering the house, the police smelled phenyl-2-propanone, an organic chemical that is a necessary precursor ingredient of amphetamine.

---

5. Use "who" for persons and the nominative case; use "whom" for the objective case; use "whose" when you need the possessive. Use "that" and "which" for things, but use "that" for restrictive clauses and "which" for nonrestrictive clauses. (See Glossary of Usage on "who/whom" and section 28.1.1, Rule 4, on "that" and "which.")

A colon can sometimes be used to combine two sentences when the first sentence introduces a list or an explanation that will be given in full in the second sentence.

EXAMPLE 14　　**Using a Colon to Combine a Sentence and List**

Draft

To assert the emergency doctrine, the defendant must be able to satisfy four elements. The four elements are (1) that he was suddenly confronted by an emergency; (2) that he did not cause the emergency by any negligence on his part; (3) that he was compelled to decide a course of action instantly; and (4) that he made such a choice as a reasonably careful person placed in such a position might have made.

Combined

To assert the emergency doctrine, the defendant must satisfy the following four elements: (1) he was suddenly confronted by an emergency; (2) he did not cause the emergency by any negligence on his part; (3) he was compelled to decide a course of action instantly; and (4) he made such a choice as a reasonably careful person placed in such a position might have made.

Occasionally, two or more sentences that have the same subject can be combined by using compound verbs or by changing one set of verbs into participles.

EXAMPLE 15　　**Combining Sentences for Conciseness**

Draft

The police officers discovered the laboratory used to make the amphetamine. The officers found a propane burner.

Combined (compound verbs)

The police officers discovered the laboratory used to make the amphetamine and found a propane burner.

To reduce phrases to words, be on the lookout for wordy constructions such as "the fact that," most phrases built around "regard," "of" prepositional phrases, and phrases that end in "that." Exhibit 25.8 sets out some examples of wordy constructions that frequently creep into legal writing.

Exhibit 25.8

Wordy		Edited
a number of	→	many
because of the fact that	→	because
by means of	→	by
by virtue of	→	by, under

despite the fact that	→ although, even though
due to the fact that	→ because
during the course of	→ during
except for the fact that	→ except for
for the purpose of	→ to
for the reason that	→ because
has the option of	→ may
in the absence of	→ without
in compliance with your request of	→ as requested, as you requested
in the course of	→ during
in the event that	→ if
in favor of	→ for
in light of the fact that	→ because, given that
in the neighborhood of	→ about, approximately
in point of fact	→ in fact
in regard(s) to	→ about, concerning
in spite of the fact that	→ although, even though
in view of the fact that	→ because, considering that
on the basis of	→ from
over the signature of	→ signed by
owing to the fact that	→ because
the fact that he asked	→ his question
with regard to	→ about, concerning

Legal writers are divided over whether (or not) to omit the "or not" in the expression "whether or not." Notice, for example, that the "or not" can be deleted from the preceding sentence with no loss in meaning. In such cases, it is better to delete it. Sometimes, however, the sentence becomes nonsensical if the "or not" is omitted. Usually, the "or not" can be omitted when the word "if" can substitute for "whether." Retain "or not" if the substitution of "if" for "whether" changes the meaning.

Exhibit 25.9 shows phrases that are deadwood and can be omitted or replaced with one word.

Exhibit 25.9

Wordy	Edited
at this point in time	→ omit or use "now"
at that point in time	→ omit or use "then"
in this day and age	→ omit or use "now," "nowadays"
in the case of	→ omit or use "in"
in reality	→ omit
in terms of	→ omit
in a very real sense	→ omit

§ 25.2.10 Avoid Excessive Conciseness

The question, of course, with the reducing and combining advocated in this section, is how much is too much? When does editing for conciseness improve the writing, and at what point does it hinder the readability of sentences?

Properly done, reducing and combining can make writing more focused and concise. Overdone, it can ruin writing by packing it too tightly and by creating overly long and overly complicated sentences.

One result of overdone combining is compound noun phrases, also known as noun strings. Like those Russian dolls that have a seemingly endless progression of smaller and smaller dolls inside each doll, compound noun phrases have a modifier modifying a modifier modifying a modifier to the point that the reader forgets where the whole thing began. Such overpacking in a sentence strains even the most cooperative reader.

EXAMPLE 16   **Editing Compound Noun Phrases**

Draft

Alabama's silent prayer statute's failure to satisfy "the purpose" prong of the *Lemon* test renders it unconstitutional.

Edited

Alabama's silent prayer statute fails to satisfy "the purpose" prong of the *Lemon* test; therefore, it is unconstitutional. *OR*

Alabama's statute on silent prayer fails . . . .

Notice that in the preceding example a nominalization, "failure," became the verb and the revision eliminated one of the possessives, "statute's." Because multiple possessives are always awkward, avoid them whenever possible.

Also remember that some nominalizations can be unpacked and improved by changing the noun into the participle, or adjective form, as is done with "exclusion" in the following example.

EXAMPLE 17   **Editing Compound Noun Phrases**

Draft

a broad prior conviction evidence exclusion rule

Edited

a broad rule excluding evidence of prior convictions

Like all tricks of the trade, then, editing for conciseness must be used with discretion and an eye toward what the reader will find easier to read and understand.

§ 25.3   Plain English v. Legalese

> Early in law school there seems to be an almost irresistible urge
> to clothe everything in the diction and style of the most
> incomprehensible insurance policy.
>
> —Norman Brand and John O. White[6]

> To communicate upon matters of technicality and complexity . . .
> is impossible with (and for) the nontechnical and simple person;
> and to use the language of simplicity in addressing a
> learned profession is to insult that profession.
>
> —Ray J. Aiken[7]

Above are but two samplings of the heated, ongoing debate over legalese. Proponents of the traditional style of legal writing argue that legalese is part of the specialized discourse of lawyers and that it serves worthwhile purposes for lawyers and their readers. Proponents of "plain English," on the other hand, argue that legalese is responsible for many of the ills that plague legal writing, not the least of which is that lay readers cannot readily comprehend what their attorneys are writing.

If you read the law journals, you may get the impression that the advocates for simplified, plain English are winning the debate. Article after article decries the use of such mainstays of legal writing as Latin phrases and legal argot. Perhaps a more significant indication that legalese is on the way out is that several state legislatures have passed legislation requiring "simple," "clear," "understandable" language that uses "words with common and everyday meanings" in consumer contracts and insurance policies.[8]

If you read the writing of most practicing attorneys, however, you might get the impression that the advocates for the traditional style of legal writing have won the day. Corporate lawyers rely heavily on boilerplate, and most practitioners seem to have absorbed the language of their law school casebooks. They may have heard that legalese is dead, but they don't write like they believe it.

And so the debate rages on, and although the plain English v. legalese issue has been before the collective "court" of legal professionals and their clients for some time now, we have yet to reach a verdict. The trend seems to be toward plain English, but the resistance is strong. In short, in the matter of Plain English v. Legalese, the jury is still out.

So what is a legal writer to do? While the profession continues to wrestle with this issue, we would like to offer a simple test for determining whether any given bit of legalese should be used or relegated to the dustbin.

---

6. *Legal Writing: The Strategy of Persuasion* 107 (1988).

7. *Let's Not Oversimplify Legal Language*, 32 Rocky Mtn. L. Rev. 364 (1960).

8. *See, e.g.*, Minn. Stat. § 325G31, N.Y. Gen. Oblig. Law § 5-702, N.J. Rev. Stat. § 56:12-2, Conn. Gen. Stat. § 38a-295, the Insurance Plain Language Act.

The Test

Given the document's reader, writer, purpose, and surrounding circumstances, does the legalese increase or decrease communication between writer and reader?

With the test as a backdrop, let's examine legalese and its characteristics.

First of all, there is no agreed-upon definition of "legalese." One law review author has defined a legalism as "a word or phrase that a lawyer might use in drafting a contract or a pleading but would not use in conversation with his wife."[9]

With a bit of editing, we can modify the definition to omit the sexism and to describe legalese: Historically, "legalese" is language a lawyer might use in drafting a contract or a pleading but would not use in ordinary conversation. In short, legalese is distinct from human talk; it is law talk.

What then are the characteristics that distinguish law talk from ordinary human talk?

Group 1

- long sentences, especially those with excessive modification and qualification
- abstractions as subjects — the real "doers" or actors are often omitted or relegated to a prepositional phrase
- weak verbs — both passive voice and nominalizations sap the sentences of their natural energy

Group 2

- archaic word choice
- foreign phrases
- terms of art and argot
- use of "said" and "such" as articles
- omission of articles, especially "the"
- use of "same" as a noun
- avoidance of the first and second person (I, we, you)
- doubling phrases

The first group of characteristics primarily involves sentence structure. These characteristics are discussed in the following sections: long sentences, section 24.5; abstractions as subjects, section 24.2; and weak verbs, sections 24.1 and 24.3.

The second group of characteristics occurs at the word level. Is it better to use a formal word, an unfamiliar word, a foreign word, or a simple word? When is a word or phrase an unnecessary legalism, and when is it a term of art? When is one word enough, and when should it be bolstered by one or more synonyms to cover every possible contingency?

These characteristics of legalese are the focus of this section.

---

9. George R. Smith, *A Primer of Opinion Writing, for Four New Judges*, 21 Ark. L. Rev. 197 (1967).

§ 25.3.1   Archaic Word Choice

Consider a story told by an attorney who is an advocate of plain English. Her client wanted her to draft a will. She drafted two versions: a plain English version and a traditional version. Although the attorney recommended the plain English version, the client selected the traditional version because it "sounded like a will." For this document and its purpose, the formality of "I hereby give, devise, and bequeath" was appropriate. It created the tone, the solemnity, and the timeless quality that the client wanted.

But what about client letters, office memoranda, and briefs to the court? Although these documents are formal in nature, do they require archaic language? Most authorities on legal language agree that they don't. In fact, research shows that appellate judges, who are the readers of the most formal of these documents, appellate briefs, strongly prefer plain English.[10]

The standard argument that "if I don't sound like a lawyer, I won't be believable" was strongly refuted in this research. In fact, the research showed that the judges were more likely to categorize writing in legalese as "poorly worded, unconvincing, vague, not concise, unpersuasive, uncreative, unscholarly, from a non-prestigious firm or an ineffective appellate advocate, unpowerful, incomprehensible and ambiguous."[11]

The legalese-ridden documents that the judges read included Old and Middle English words such as "thereby" and "herein." Exhibit 25.10 is a fairly comprehensive list of other Old and Middle English words and phrases that should be avoided in client letters, office memoranda, and briefs. In some cases, a more appropriate substitute word or phrase follows in italics.

Exhibit 25.10

Compound words that begin with *here-*, *there-*, and *where-*

hereafter	thereabout	whereas[12]
herebefore	thereafter	whereat
hereby	therefrom	whereby
herein	therein	wherefore
hereinabove → *above*	thereof	wheresoever
hereinafter	thereon	wherein → *there*
hereinunder → *below*	thereto	whereof
hereof	thereunto	whereon
heretofore → *before, up to this time*	therewith	whereupon
hereunder		
herewith (enclosed herewith → *enclosed*)		
aforementioned (omit or substitute *previously mentioned*)		
aforesaid (omit or substitute *above*)		

---

10.   Robert W. Benson & Joan B. Kessler, *Legalese v. Plain English: An Empirical Study of Persuasion and Credibility in Appellate Brief Writing*, 20 Loy. L.A. L. Rev. 301- (1987).

11.   *Id.* at 315.

12.   "Whereas" can often be eliminated or replaced with "because," "considering that," "while on the contrary," or "inasmuch as." At other times, it can be used but with care. Frequently, writers use it without seeming to know what it means. At times, "whereas" is the best choice; for example, using "whereas" is certainly better than the wordy "in view of the fact that."

behoove → *to be necessary, to be proper*
comes now the plaintiff
foregoing (for the foregoing reasons) → *for these reasons*
forthwith → *immediately*
henceforth[13]
hitherto → *until this time, up to now*
pursuant to → *under or according to*[14]
thence → *from there, from that place, time or source, for that reason*
thenceforth → *from that time on, after that*
thereafter → *from that time on*
to wit → *namely, that is to say*
whence → *from where*
whensoever → *whenever*

§ 25.3.2 Foreign Phrases

Many of the Latin phrases that appear in legal writing create a barrier between writer and reader. Only a student on the way home from Latin class (or possibly a lawyer specializing in property) will be comfortable with a phrase such as *Cujus est solum ejus est usque ad coelum et usque ad inferos.* The rest of us would do one of two things: use the context to try to figure out what the writer meant or reach for the *Unabridged Black's Law Dictionary.* In either case, the Latin has not aided communication. Even the conscientious consulter of the dictionary will understand the writer's meaning only by looking up the explanation the writer should have given the reader in the first place.

More often, the Latin is not so much confusing as it is unnecessary. Why say *"supra"* when "above" works just as well? Unnecessary Latin phrases make the writing appear stuffy and pretentious. When a simple English equivalent can be used without loss of meaning, use it. Exhibit 25.11 shows several Latin words and phrases that can be avoided and their plain English equivalents.

Exhibit 25.11

Latin Words or Phrases to Avoid		Plain English Substitutes
arguendo	→	for the sake of argument
et al.	→	and others
infra	→	below
inter alia	→	among other things
per curiam	→	by the court
seriatim	→	in turn, serially, one after another
sui generis	→	unique
supra	→	above
viz. (abbreviation for "videlicet")	→	namely, that is to say

---

13. Many would not object strenuously to "henceforth" but find it a bit dated. "From now on" is a satisfactory plain English substitute.

14. Sometimes "pursuant to" is a useful legalism that lawyers and judges find acceptable. Avoid using it, however, with nonlawyers.

Not all Latin should be replaced, however. Some Latin phrases ("gratis," "per diem") are sufficiently familiar to educated readers that their use does not impair communication. In fact, these phrases are often accepted as English.

Other Latin phrases (*"amicus curiae," "per se"*) are equally familiar to lawyers and judges and can be used for these readers without a second thought. They are the "shop talk" of law. The same phrases, though, may need substitutes or explanation for client readers.

A final group of Latin phrases (Exhibit 25.12) are so useful that few are willing to discard them. *"Respondeat superior,"* for example, sums up a whole doctrine in tort law; *"res judicata"* is a fundamental rule of Civil Procedure. While these phrases will probably need clarification for readers who are not lawyers, the average legal reader would find them not only familiar but indispensable.

Exhibit 25.12	**Latin Words or Phrases to Keep for Readers Who Are Lawyers**

ad hoc	*mens rea*
ad litem	*modus operandi*
amicus curiae	*nexus*
bona fide	*nolo contendere*
caveat emptor	*non sequitur*
certiorari	*penumbra*
consortium	*per diem*
corpus delicti	*per se*
de facto, de jure	*post mortem*
de novo	*prima facie*
dicta, dictum	*pro bono*
ex parte	*quorum*
ex post facto	*quid pro quo*
gratis	*res ipsa loquitur*
habeas corpus	*res judicata*
id. (abbreviation for idem)	*respondeat superior*
in limine	*scintilla*
in personam	*stare decisis*
ipso facto	*sua sponte*
mandamus	*supersedeas*

Of course, Latin is not the only foreign language that appears frequently in legal writing. Thanks to the Norman Conquest and its subsequent effect on the language of England, French plays an important role in the language of law.

The vast majority of the words derived from French are common terms that are already fully incorporated into English and as such pose few if any problems for readers ("assault," "defendant," "heir," "larceny," "mortgage," "plaintiff," "pleadings," "tort," "reprieve," and "verdict," to name just a few).

More likely troublemakers are those words and phrases that are Old French. For the French terms shown in Exhibit 25.13, use the suggested plain English substitutes.

Exhibit 25.13

Old French		Plain English Substitutes
alien or *aliene* (used as a verb)	→	to convey or to transfer
cestui que trust	→	beneficiary
cy-pres	→	as near as possible
en ventre sa mere	→	in its mother's womb
en vie	→	alive
feme covert	→	married woman
feme sole	→	single woman
save	→	except
seisin	→	possession or ownership

As we saw with Latin, though, there are French words and phrases that are terms of art for which we have no satisfactory plain English substitute. See Exhibit 25.14. Although they will almost certainly require explanation for readers who are not lawyers, they are indispensable vocabulary for a lawyer.

Exhibit 25.14   French Words and Phrases to Keep

estoppel	laches	voir dire

§ 25.3.3   Use of Terms of Art and Argot

Terms of art, by definition, do not have satisfactory substitutes. Even though one might be able to give a short explanation of a term of art's meaning, complete understanding would take an extensive explanation.

A term of art, according to David Mellinkoff, is "a technical word with a specific meaning."[15] In *Garner's Dictionary of Legal Usage*, "terms of art" are defined as "words having specific, precise significations in a given specialty."[16]

Given these requirements, it should not be surprising that there are relatively few terms of art in law. "Certiorari," for example, is a true term of art. Perhaps a satisfactory short explanation is that it refers to the order written by a higher court to a lower court requiring the lower court to produce a certified record of a certain case.

For a full understanding of "certiorari," however, one would have to lay out a much larger context: how discretionary review and the appellate process work in general and, specifically, how the Supreme Court of the United States chooses cases it wishes to hear.

Argot, by contrast, is legal jargon, or lawyers' shop talk. It is the shorthand of law, the quick-and-easy term or phrase that lawyers use among themselves.

---

15. David Mellinkoff, *The Language of the Law* 16 (1963) (quoting *Webster's New International Dictionary* (2d ed. 1934)).

16. Bryan A. Garner, *Garner's Dictionary of Legal Usage* 883 (3d ed. 2001).

For this reason, argot is inappropriate when communicating with nonlawyers. Used with discretion, it can be effective communication among lawyers.

"Case on all fours" is a classic example of argot. Other common examples include "adhesion contract," "attractive nuisance," "Blackacre," "case at bar," "case-in-chief," "clean hands," "cloud on title," "court below," "four corners of the document," "horse case," "instant case," "off the record," "pierce the corporate veil," "reasonable person," "*res ipsa loquitur*," "sidebar," and "Whiteacre."

In writing, avoid argot that has degenerated into slang. "Cert. denied" or "resipsey case" sounds cute rather than professional.

§ 25.3.4   Use of "Said" and "Such" as Adjectives

If you were a stand-up comic trying to make fun of the way lawyers write, all you would have to do is put "said" or "such" before almost every noun.

EXAMPLE 1   Avoiding "Said" and "Such" as Adjectives

It was snowing and icy on January 9, 2013, when Mr. Smith, the plaintiff, was driving home from work along a deserted highway in his 1995 Honda Accord with chains on said vehicle's tires. Suddenly said plaintiff felt said vehicle jerk violently, and then said plaintiff heard a loud clanging of metal. Such clanging continued until such time as said plaintiff was able to pull said vehicle over to the shoulder of said highway. Upon inspection of said vehicle, said plaintiff realized that such clanging was caused when said chains had broken and then wrapped around the axle of said plaintiff's said vehicle. "Oh, *!?/*!" said plaintiff.

In client letters, office memos, and briefs, rigorously avoid all use of "said" as an adjective. Replace with "the," "that," "this," or an appropriate, unambiguous pronoun.

"Such" can be used as an adjective with categories of persons, things, or concepts. For example, "such instances of neglect," "such witnesses as these," and "such an example of compassion" are not legalese. These phrases are good writing.

Do not, however, use "such" with singular nouns that are not categories of persons, things, or concepts but rather specific references to the same, previously mentioned singular noun. For example, "such payment" should be revised to "this payment"; "such stock certificate" should be changed to "the stock certificate."

§ 25.3.5   Omission of the Article "The"

Occasionally, one sees legal writing that has the sound of a police report.

EXAMPLE 2   Omitted Article

Draft

Defendant denies that she hit victim.

This rather terse style is achieved by omitting the article "the." The reason for omitting "unnecessary" articles in police reports may be that information needs to be recorded on forms. Happily, lawyers do not have such requirements, so they do not have to sacrifice a fluid writing style.

| **EXAMPLE 3** | **Adding Omitted Article** |

Edited

The defendant denies that she hit the victim.

---

§ 25.3.6 Absence of First- and Second-person Pronouns

By convention, legal writers rarely use the pronouns "I," "me," "we," "us," "you" and "your." Occasionally, in a client letter, a lawyer might write "I recommend" or, more commonly, "in my opinion." Much less frequent would be the phrase "I think" or (horrors!) "I feel" (the common explanation for the horrified reaction being that lawyers are paid to think, not to feel) in an office memorandum. Pity the naive attorney, though, who writes in a brief "you should rule" or "you must determine."

To get around the *I*'s and *you*'s in legal writing—because after all it is I, the writer, who is recommending and thinking, and it is you, the judge and reader, who is ruling and determining—legal writers resort to all sorts of linguistic gymnastics. Before discussing which of these gymnastic moves work and which lead to new problems, let's examine why the first- and second-person pronouns are *persona non grata* in legal writing.

First of all, remember the long-standing tradition of avoiding first and second person pronouns in any formal writing. While the recommendations about this issue have relaxed considerably for undergraduate research papers and the like, the original rationale applies to most legal writing. The facts and the application of law to those facts are the focus of attention for both writer and reader. As such, they should occupy center stage.

Second, the use of "I" and "you" often creates an inappropriately informal tone. While a bit of informality and familiarity may be appropriate in some client letters and an occasional office memo, generally these documents should be formal and professional in tone. (Remember, though, formal does not mean stilted.)

Third, indiscreet use of "you" in client letters and especially in briefs may make the writer appear arrogant, pushy, and disrespectful. Readers rarely like to be ordered around. Not surprisingly, "you must" or "you should" language often backfires. Rather than encouraging the reader to act as the writer wants, such language sets the stage for resistance to the writer's recommendations and arguments.

In the following example, the inclusion of "my," "I," and "you" is both distracting and inappropriate. The first-person references incorrectly place the emphasis on the writer, and the second-person references may even anger the judge.

EXAMPLE 4	Editing for Personal Pronouns

Draft

In my research, I found that you must apply Washington Rule of Evidence 609(a) to determine the admissibility of evidence of a criminal defendant's prior convictions.

Edited

In Washington, the admissibility of evidence of a criminal defendant's prior convictions is governed by Washington Rule of Evidence 609(a). *OR*

Washington Rule of Evidence 609(a) governs the admissibility of evidence of a criminal defendant's prior convictions.

The first revision of the example illustrates one of the common gymnastic moves that legal writers use to avoid the first- and second- person pronouns: using the passive voice. While the passive voice is a good choice in some instances (see section 24.1.3), it can easily lead to dull, lifeless writing. Use it with care.

Some legal writers use the pronoun "one" to get around using "you." This tactic works reasonably well as long as the writer does not use "one" several times and then shift—incorrectly—from "one" to the third-person pronoun "he," "she," "him," "her," "it," "they," or "them."

EXAMPLE 5	Incorrect Shifting Pronouns

Incorrect

One should avoid first-person pronouns in his or her legal writing.

Edited

One should avoid first-person pronouns in one's legal writing.

Better

Avoid first-person pronouns in legal writing.

In office memos, some writers slip into a *we-they* style as they describe the various arguments the two sides can make: "They will argue . . . and we will rebut this argument by showing . . ." This practice is accepted in some firms. Other firms simply name the parties: "Smith will argue . . . and Jones will rebut this argument."

Frequently, a writer of an office memo is tempted to use "we" in the following situation. The writer has just explained the law or just described an analogous case to the reader. Now the writer wants the reader to follow along as he or she applies that law or case.

The writer might begin by saying "If we apply the plain meaning of statute X to our facts, we can see that the photocopy is a similitude" or "If we compare the actions of the defendant in *Smith v. Jones* to the actions of Brown, we can see that Brown, unlike Jones, knew he was lying to the F.B.I." This is not a serious writing sin, of course, but it can be easily avoided.

Unfortunately, some writers try to write around the "we" in such instances and end up with a dangling modifier. See section 27.6.2.

There is a better way. The writer does want the reader to follow along as he or she makes the next logical connection, but the writer also wants to suggest that the court must see the same logical connection. Therefore, it makes good sense, both in terms of writing style and strategy, to say "If the court applies the plain meaning of statute X to our facts, it will find . . ." or "Applying the plain meaning of statute X to our facts, the court will find . . . ."

One final note about first- and second-person pronouns: Because these pronouns have gained acceptance in some other types of formal writing, they are likely to gain increasing acceptance in all but the most formal documents in legal writing. Watch the trend, and you will be able to adjust accordingly.

§ 25.4   Gender-Neutral Language

The language of law, while a bit slower to change than the language in other fields, is moving in the direction of gender-neutral word choices. Numerous states now require gender-neutral language in their legislation. Increasingly, legislators, practitioners, and jurists are realizing that some language they previously considered to be inclusive has just the opposite effect: It excludes.

For legal writers, there are at least four good reasons for making the effort to use gender-neutral language: fairness, clarity, precision, and reader reaction. These reasons more than justify the effort it takes to master the five problem areas legal writers face when trying to use gender-neutral language.

§ 25.4.1   Generic Use of "Man"

Avoid using the term "man" to mean all people or all of humanity. Similarly, avoid using expressions and other derivatives built on this broad use of the term "*man.*" Exhibit 25.15 sets out numerous examples of gender-neutral substitutes.

Exhibit 25.15

Sexist Terms	Gender-Neutral Substitutes
man (noun) or mankind	people, humanity, human race, human beings, human population, homo sapiens
man (verb) as in "man the office"	staff, operate, run, work
a man who . . .	an individual who . . . , a person who . . . , one who . . . , someone who . . .
the common man, the average man, the man in the street	the common individual, the average citizen, the person in the street, ordinary people
man-made	hand-crafted, handmade, manufactured, machine-made, fabricated, synthetic, created
manpower	human energy, human resources, work force, personnel, staff

§ 25.4.2 Generic Use of "He"

It used to be standard practice for grammar and writing texts to advise writers to use masculine pronouns when the gender of the antecedent noun or pronoun could be either male or female. Now most grammar and writing texts advise writers to avoid the generic use of "he." Unfortunately, though, we have been unable to agree on a gender-neutral singular pronoun as a substitute. Until we do, we will need to use one or more of several approaches for avoiding the generic use of the masculine pronouns.

a.   Revise the Sentence So That the Antecedent and Its Pronoun Are Plural

EXAMPLE 6

Draft

The holding suggests that a defendant waives his constitutional rights only through an affirmative or overt act.

Edited

The holding suggests that defendants waive their constitutional rights only through affirmative or overt acts.

b.   Revise the Sentence So That a Pronoun Is Not Needed

EXAMPLE 7

Draft

As a general rule, an employer is not liable for the work performed by his independent contractors.

Edited

As a general rule, an employer is not liable for the work performed by independent contractors.

c.   Replace the Masculine Noun and Pronoun with "One," "Your," or "He" or "She," as Appropriate

EXAMPLE 8

Draft

Every man has a right to defend his home.

Edited

One has a right to defend one's home.

You have a right to defend your home.

Everyone has a right to defend his or her home.

d.   Alternate Male and Female Examples and Expressions

EXAMPLE 9

Draft

If a student enrolls at a university with the promise that he will receive an athletic scholarship and he later finds out that his scholarship has been revoked, he can sue the university for breach of contract. If, on the other hand, a student enrolls at a university with the promise that he will receive an athletic scholarship and he later refuses to play the sport, the university can sue him for breach of contract.

Edited

If a student enrolls at a university with the promise that she will receive an athletic scholarship and she later finds out that her school scholarship has been revoked, she can sue the university for breach of contract. If, on the other hand, a student enrolls at a university with the promise that he will receive an athletic scholarship and he later refuses to play the sport, the university can sue him for breach of contract.

e.   Repeat the Noun Rather Than Use an Inappropriate Masculine Pronoun

EXAMPLE 10

Draft

Joinder of counts should not be used to embarrass or prejudice a defendant or to deny him a substantial right.

Edited

Joinder of counts should not be used to embarrass or prejudice a defendant or to deny a defendant a substantial right.

One approach that is occasionally recommended for avoiding the generic "he" is to use the plural pronouns "they" and "their" for singular nouns and indefinite pronouns, such as "everyone" or "anybody." While using this approach may arguably solve the sexism problem, it still leaves the writer with an error in pronoun agreement (see section 27.4.2) as well as with more than a few logical inconsistencies, for example, "Everyone is entitled to their opinion." Rather than trade one problem for another, use one of the other five strategies outlined above for avoiding the generic "he."

§ 25.4.3   Gender-Neutral Job Titles

Avoid job titles that suggest it is nonstandard for women to hold the position. Exhibit 25.16 sets out numerous gender-neutral substitutes for sexist job titles.

Exhibit 25.16

Sexist Terms	Gender-Neutral Substitutes
businessman, chairman	business executive, manager coordinator, presiding officer, head, chair
Congressman	Representative, member of Congress, congressional representative, Senator
councilman	council member
fireman	firefighter
foreman (as the head of a group of workers)	supervisor, head worker, section chief
foreman (as the head of a jury)	foreperson
insuranceman	insurance agent
juryman	juror
landlord	owner, manager, lessor
mailman, postman	postal carrier, postal worker, mail carrier
middleman	negotiator, liaison, intermediary
newspaperman	reporter, editor
policeman	police officer
salesman	sales associate, sales representative
spokesman	representative, spokesperson
steward, stewardess	flight attendant
waitress	waiter
watchman	guard, security officer

§ 25.4.4   Sexist Modifiers

Unconsciously, writers sometimes assign needless sexist modifiers to words. Avoid modifiers that suggest that it is unusual for either a woman or a man to occupy a certain position. Exhibit 25.17 sets out several examples.

Exhibit 25.17

Sexist Modifier	Revised
female judge	judge
lady lawyer	lawyer
male nurse	nurse
male model	model
woman attorney	attorney

§ 25.4.5   Other Sexist Language

Avoid feminizing a word with a suffix, for example, "actress," "executrix," "testatrix." Such endings suggest that it is nonstandard for women to fill certain roles.

Avoid terms with connotations of youth (girl), decorum (lady), or informality (gal) unless the comparable terms for males (boy, gentleman, guy) are also appropriate.

When using titles (Miss, Mrs., Ms.) before women's names, follow the particular woman's preference, if known, or, if unknown, use no title. In professional contexts, professional titles take precedence over social titles for both women and men, for example, Justice Ruth Bader Ginsburg, not Mrs. Ginsburg. In salutations in letters, avoid using the outdated "Dear Sir" or "Gentlemen" when the gender of the receiver is unknown. Acceptable substitutes include "Dear Sir or Madam," "Ladies and Gentlemen," or the title of the receiver(s), as in "Dear Members of the Board." Some writers omit the salutation and use a reference line such as "To the Director of Operations" or "Re: Credit Department." Exhibit 25.18 gives numerous gender-neutral substitutes.

Exhibit 25.18

Sexist Term	Gender-Neutral Substitutes
coed	student
divorcee	divorced person
forefathers	ancestors, forerunners, forebears
girl or girls (when applied to adult females)	woman or women
househusband, housewife	homemaker
lady or ladies	woman or women (unless the equivalent "gentleman" or "gentlemen" is also used for men)
man and wife	man and woman, husband and wife
old wives' tale	superstitious belief or idea

§ 25.5   Bias-free Language

In addition to the concern that legal writers use gender-neutral language in their documents, there are related concerns that the language of law be free of bias against other groups, such as racial, religious, and ethnic minorities, homosexual persons, elderly people, poor people, and persons with disabilities.

Making bias-free language choices is not always easy, though, particularly when one realizes that the preferred terms are constantly changing and not all members of any given group have the same preferences. These challenges tempt some to ignore or just give up on the issue of bias-free language in law. The argument seems to go something like this: "Why should I bother when they can't decide what they want to be called?"

The temptation to avoid the issue is easier to resist, however, when one considers the power of language and its ability to shape perception. How we label something affects how we see it. Thus, language can serve to perpetuate stereotypes, or it can bring new insight and perspective. Choices in language can suggest that members of a group are inherently inferior or that they are valued members of society. In short, what we call ourselves or someone else matters. Naming, or labeling, is both an enormous power and an enormous responsibility, and like all legal writing, it should be done with a lot of thought and care.

§ 25.5.1   Avoid Irrelevant Minority References

Perhaps the most subtle and possibly the most insidious forms of prejudice in some legal writing are unnecessary references to race, ethnic origin, or other minority categories. In a case in which the description of an individual is necessary to the analysis (such as a case in which the police apprehended an individual based on the individual matching a victim's description), including the race of the individual is obviously appropriate. Unless a crime was racially motivated, however, it is probably inappropriate to include the race of a victim.

The same principle also applies to persons who are adopted. Include references to a person being adopted only when it is relevant.

§ 25.5.2   Stay Abreast of the Preferred Terminology

All language changes over time. Some parts of language tend to change more rapidly, however, because of rapid changes in sensibilities and society's collective thinking about certain issues.

Notice, for example, the changes in terminology for the following groups of people:

Colored People → Negro → Black → Black American[17] → African American or Afro-American
Indian → American Indian → Native American[18]
Oriental → Asian American
Mexican American → Chicano/Chicana or Hispanic or Latino/Latina
Handicapped → Disabled → Physically Challenged or Persons of Differing Abilities or Persons with Exceptionalities or Exceptional Persons
Mentally Retarded → Persons with Intellectual or Developmental Disabilities or Persons Who Are Cognitively Challenged
Elderly → Senior Citizens

Notice too that several of these progressions end with two or more choices, indicating a lack of consensus among the members of the group about the current preferred term.

---

17. While early forms of many terms that combined races or nationalities often had hyphens ("African-American," "Mexican-American," "Asian-American"), the current trend is toward omitting the hyphen. The argument for omitting the hyphen is that it conveys something less than full membership in both groups.

18. Note, however, that when the 1995 census asked members of this group for their preferences, 49.76% indicated that they preferred "American Indian," 37.35% preferred "Native American," 3.66% preferred "some other term," 3.51% preferred "Native Alaskan," and 5.72% had "no preference." Bureau of Labor Statistics, U.S. Census Bureau Survey, May 1995. The more recent censuses did not ask the same questions regarding preference regarding their identification.

How then does a legal writer decide what term to use? In addition to doing research to stay abreast of the preferred terminology,[19] legal writers can use the following general guidelines when deciding which words or labels will work best in any given situation:

a. Prefer self-chosen labels (and avoid terms that may offend members of that group);

b. Choose precise, accurate terms;

c. Whenever possible, prefer the specific term over the general term;

d. Prefer terms that describe what people are rather than what they are not;

e. Notice that a term's connotations may change as the part of speech changes (e.g., the same word that is offensive as a noun may be acceptable as an adjective);

f. In selecting terms, emphasize the person over the difference; and

g. Avoid terms that are patronizing or overly euphemistic or that paint people as victims.

a.   Prefer Self-Chosen Labels

While it may be difficult to determine what a whole group of individuals prefers to be called, it is often simple to determine what a given person wants to be called. One can just ask. If a client prefers to be labeled as "black" rather than "African American," for example, that preference should be honored. See Exhibit 25.19. If an individual describes herself as a "gay woman" rather than as a "homosexual" or "lesbian," the self-chosen term is the obvious choice.

If the applicable law uses a specific label for a group that differs from the individual's preferred term, the sensible solution is for the lawyer-writer to explain to the client why it might be preferable to use the term used in the law but then leave the final decision about word choice up to the client. For example, the law may refer to an "illegal alien" but an individual may prefer to be called an "undocumented worker." Each label carries with it strong connotations, which should also be considered before deciding which term to use.

Equally important to preferring self-chosen labels is to avoid offensive labels. Perhaps the best example of a term that members of a group find offensive is the label "Oriental" when used to refer to persons of Asian origin. The objections to the term are twofold. First, the word "Oriental," which means "eastern," identifies people from Asian countries in relationship to being east of Europe; hence the term smacks of a Eurocentric perspective. Second, and probably more important, the word "Oriental" has connotations of Asian countries as being "exotic" and the people being "inscrutable." As a result, many Asian Americans consider it nothing short of an ethnic slur to be called "Orientals." Using the word "Oriental" as an adjective in phrases such as "Oriental rug," "Oriental cuisine," or "Oriental medicine," however, is generally considered acceptable.[20]

---

19. For example, for updated information on terminology for the lesbian, gay, bisexual, transgender community, consult the NLGJA Stylebook Supplement, which can be found on the National Lesbian & Gay Journalists Association website at *http://www.nlgja.org/resources/stylebook*.

20. The term "retarded" is also considered offensive by many. Preferred terms are persons with an "intellectual disability" or who are "developmentally disabled." Recently the term "special needs"

Some whites, most notably the Irish, find it offensive to be labeled "Anglos." The alternate term "Caucasian" is still used in many police departments, but "Caucasian" is not generally a recommended term because it is based on an outmoded notion of a Caucasian race that is no longer accepted in the scientific community. The preferred term, "white," is also not without problems, not the least of which is that its parameters are ambiguous. The term obviously refers to skin color, and its generally accepted meaning is any white or light-skinned person of non-Latin extraction. In some cases, however, "white" includes Latinos and Latinas.

Exhibit 25.19   Honoring Personal Preferences[21]

The words used to describe African Americans have a history. The short way I explain it to my non-African American friends and my students is as follows:

My grandparents are **Colored**
My parents are **Negroes**
My siblings are **Black**
I was Black when I was born and now I am **African American**
My nieces and nephews are **People of Color** (and alternately **African American**)

Not surprisingly, my siblings still refer to themselves as Black. I refer to myself alternately as Black or African American. The point is that depending on the historical period you are discussing, any of the words in the above list is valid. You want to make sure that your audience is aware that you know the history of the words you are using. Your audience should also know that your present understanding is that the terms "African American" and "person of color" are current and acceptable.

I use exercises involving cases from the Civil Rights era all of the time, and I give the little talk that I outline above. It never fails to break the tension in the room so that we can get back to the lesson.

As for my personal preference, I do not like the term colored, and don't use "person of color" to refer to myself because it reminds me too much of colored. I do like Mark Wojik's "person with color,"[22] but I prefer Teri.[23]

---

b.   Choose Precise, Accurate Terms

Precision and accuracy are highly valued in all word choices in legal writing, and even more so when selecting words that describe race, ethnicity, national origin, and religion. For this reason it is important not to assume that terms are interchangeable. "Mexican American," for example, should be used only to refer to a person who is a United States citizen or permanent resident

---

has come under close scrutiny with some individuals noting that it may evoke unwanted sympathy and concerns about scarce resources, as well as contribute to exclusion and marginalization of the children so described. One possible replacement for "children with special needs" is "children with cognitive difficulties."

21. Included with permission from and thanks to Professor Teri McMurtry-Chubb, Mercer University School of Law in Macon, GA.

22. Mark Wojik is a Professor at the John Marshall Law School in Chicago, IL.

23. Professor McMurtry-Chubb's response was to the question "What word is proper?" asked on the Legal Writing Institute listserv, September 26, 2011.

with Mexican ancestry. "Spanish" refers to persons whose ancestors were from Spain. "Latino" and "Latina" are accurate terms only for persons who have Latin American ancestry.[24]

Similarly, the terms "Arab," "Middle Easterner," and "Muslim" are not synonyms; they refer to language, geography, and religion respectively. The term "Arab," for example, refers to persons who speak the Arabic language. The term "Middle Easterners," which focuses on geography, is obviously accurate only for those individuals from the Middle East and not for people from Algeria, Tunisia, Morocco, and Libya. Remember too that there are non-Arab countries — Iran, Turkey, and Israel — in the Middle East.

The term "Muslim" refers to a person who believes in the Islamic religion. Thus, not all Muslims are Arabs, nor are all Arabs Muslims. Likewise, not all Israelis are Jewish, nor are all Jewish people Israelis.

c. Whenever Possible, Prefer the Specific Term Over the General Term

Unnecessarily lumping groups of people with varying histories, cultures, and languages under a generic term can be interpreted as not making the effort to understand or respect the differences captured by the specific terms. Thus, while there are differences within the group over whether to use "American Indian" or "Native American" or even the newest term, "First American," what is consistently preferred is to use a more specific term, such as "Mohawk" or "Navajo," whenever possible rather than a generic term. This principle also applies to the term "Asian American." Although "Asian American" is appropriate when a generic term is needed, it is better to use a more specific term, such as "Japanese American," whenever possible. Note as well that many people who come from the republics that used to be part of the former Soviet Union are offended when they are lumped together and labeled "Russians." Here again, use specific terms such as "Armenians."

d. Prefer Terms That Describe What People Are Rather Than What They Are Not

Three terms that designate a person as a member of a group other than the majority white population — "nonwhite," "minority," and "person of color" — demonstrate the interplay of several principles related to bias in language. "Nonwhite" is often considered offensive because it classifies people by what they are not rather than by what they are. The term "minority" does not seem to create the same level of resentment as "nonwhite," although some members

---

24. In addition to accuracy, some terms are self-chosen and others are rejected because of their varying emphasis on geographic, historical, cultural roots, or political identity. For example, although "Hispanic" is an accurate term for people in the United States who trace their ancestry back to one or more Spanish-speaking countries, some Spanish-speaking persons resent the term, not only because it homogenizes so many diverse peoples but also because it came into common use by way of the government (particularly through the census), the media, and the public at large. Other people resent the term "Hispanic" because they associate it with Spanish colonialism and feel it overemphasizes Spanish ancestry and ignores the African and indigenous roots of Latino culture. "Latino," on the other hand, is preferred by many because it has both a Spanish sound and connotations of ethnic pride. Whether a given individual prefers to be called "Hispanic," "Latino," or "Chicano" may also depend on where the person resides in the United States or on the person's politics. "Hispanic" is the more popular choice in Florida and Texas; "Latino" is more commonly used in California; "Chicano" has connotations of political activism.

of minority communities that are not African American complain that the term "minority" is often treated as synonymous with the black community. All three terms have the disadvantage of grouping widely disparate peoples together and, at least in some instances, should be replaced by a specific reference. In some situations, long lists of specific references are impractical. In such cases, the generic term "person of color" is currently the preferred option.[25]

e. Notice That a Term's Connotations May Change as the Part of Speech Changes

Earlier we saw that while the term "Oriental" is considered offensive when used as a noun to label a person, it is acceptable as an adjective in such phrases as "Oriental rug" or "Oriental food." This same principle comes into play in the preferred terminology for sexual orientation, disability, and aging. "Homosexual," for example, is not considered offensive as an adjective in a phrase such as "homosexual relationship," but its use as a noun describing an individual is offensive to many members of this group. Those who object to the noun form cite its emphasis on the sexual life of an individual rather than on the broader cultural or social life of that person. The self-chosen terms are "gay man," "gay woman," or "lesbian." "Gay" by itself is not preferred as a noun.

Members of the disability community tend to prefer the adjective form of "disabled," as in "disabled persons," over the noun form, "the disabled." The adjective form of "elderly" as in "an elderly man" is less offensive than the noun form "the elderly." Members of this community tend to prefer the term "senior citizen."

f.   In Selecting Terms, Emphasize the Person Over the Difference

The disability community has endorsed what is known as the "person first" principle, which is selecting terms that put the person before the disability whenever possible. The idea is that the individual should be emphasized over the difference and that the difference should not be treated as the person's total identity. Consequently, although as we saw in the last section, members of the disability community prefer the adjective form of "disabled," as in "disabled persons," over the noun form, "the disabled," others further recommend "persons with disabilities" over "disabled persons" because it puts the person before the disability. Similarly, "person with epilepsy" is preferred over the term "epileptic," "person with an amputated leg" over "amputee," and "person with diabetes" over "diabetic." The same principle applies when discussing groups of people, so instead of "the demented," use "people with dementia"; instead of "the autistic," use "people with autism." Instead of "special needs children," use "children with special needs."

---

25. In custody disputes over the children of a lesbian couple, the choice in labels for each of the parents often foreshadows the legal arguments, for example, one side may use a term such as "co-mother" and the other use "non-biological mother."

g. Avoid Terms That Are Patronizing or Overly Euphemistic or That Paint People as Victims

While there is a temptation to move toward more euphemistic terms for persons who have physical and mental disabilities, that temptation should be tempered not only by the importance of communicating clearly but also by the realization that sugarcoated euphemisms can be patronizing. Some options also seem to be too long to be practical. Consider the progression shown in Exhibit 25.20.

Exhibit 25.20

Handicapped → Disabled → Physically challenged OR
Persons of differing abilities OR
Differently abled persons OR
Persons with exceptionalities OR
Exceptional persons

Well-meaning persons have tried to introduce terms such as "persons of differing abilities," "differently abled persons," "persons with exceptionalities," and "exceptional persons" to try to put a positive gloss on having a disability. Such euphemisms tend to fail because they are both imprecise and patronizing. The term "physically challenged" is more acceptable because it finds a balance between being sensitive to those described and being clear about the relevant condition.

Within the disability community, there is also a controversy over verbs that paint persons with disabilities as being weak and helpless victims. Some argue that writers should omit or replace the clichéd verbs in phrases such as "person *confined* to a wheelchair"—replace with "person in a wheelchair" or "person who uses a wheelchair"; "person *stricken* with multiple sclerosis"—replace with "person with multiple sclerosis"; "person *suffering* from arthritis"—replace with "person who has arthritis"; and "person *afflicted* with AIDS"—replace with "person with AIDS". In some instances, of course, a lawyer may feel that the "language of victimization" works to the client's advantage. The question, of course, is whether to use this kind of short-term "advantage" when it contributes to a particular cultural bias and stereotyping. As with so many decisions such as this, it may be appropriate to consult the described individual to determine his or her preference.

For an in-depth discussion of bias in legal language and argument, see Lorraine K. Bannai & Anne Enquist, *(Un)Examined Assumptions and (Un)Intended Messages: Teaching Students to Recognize Bias in Legal Analysis and Language*, 27 Seattle U. L. Rev. 1 (2003).

Chapter 25 Quiz

Draft answers for each of the following questions. Make your points clearly and concisely, and write sentences that are easy to read and that are grammatical and correctly punctuated.

1. Although informal, colloquial language is generally not acceptable in legal writing, when is the one time a legal writer might use such language?
2. Why should legal writers avoid using synonyms for key legal terms or terms of art?
3. What are the precise definitions of the noun "holding" and its companion verb "held" in legal writing?
4. What are some of the situations in which quoting is effective in legal writing?
5. Why should legal writers edit out "throat-clearing expressions"?
6. When a legal writer has the choice between using a simple word and a fancy word in a piece of legal writing, which is usually the better choice and why?
7. What is a good test for when and when not to use "legalese"?
8. What are "terms of art," and why should legal writers use legal terms of art carefully?
9. What are some of the reasons legal writers should use gender-neutral language?
10. What are the key principles in choosing bias-free language?

Eloquence

I
s it unrealistic for legal writing to be eloquent? After all, lawyers write
under enormous time pressure. Who has the time to massage language
to the point at which someone would call it "eloquent"?

Further, is it appropriate for legal writing to be eloquent? Should
an office memo sound like it was written by Shakespeare? What client is
willing to pay for a client letter that waxes poetic? Are judges more impressed
by arguments or by the language they are wrapped in?

All these good questions really boil down to one question: Should a lawyer
strive to write eloquently?

Yes, at least sometimes.

While it wouldn't hurt if every office memo and client letter were written
eloquently, the one area in which eloquence undoubtedly pays off is briefs.
An eloquent brief is a more persuasive brief. Of course the arguments must be
sound and persuasive in and of themselves, but one cannot divorce the content
of the argument from the form in which it is written. What one says and the
way one says it are inextricably linked.

One striking bit of evidence that eloquent briefs are persuasive is the frequency with which well-articulated arguments from briefs reappear in judicial
opinions. If imitation is the highest form of flattery, there can be nothing more
flattering to a brief writer than to have a judge "lift" a phrase or more from the
brief and incorporate it into the opinion.

But as we suggested before, eloquence is not something legal writers
can add as a kind of finishing touch. Eloquence is not a tuxedo or an evening
gown. A writer cannot "put on" eloquence any more than an artist can put on
originality.

Eloquence in legal writing and originality in art are there throughout the creative process, often at the point of conception, again through the drafting and revising, and yet again in the final polishing.

§ 26.1   Purple Prose

Like artists who try to force themselves to be original, legal writers who try to force themselves to be eloquent will probably end up creating something that is either absurd or monstrous.

The following excerpt is from the Statement of Facts in a case about whether racial slurs create a cause of action for the tort of outrage.

EXAMPLE 1   **Purple Prose**

Our client, Mr. Silvino Gomez, is a twenty-year-old of Mexican American descent. Mr. Gomez's prowess as a basketball player brought him to the delighted attention of enthusiastic recruiters from several private colleges. He ultimately accepted an athletic scholarship from the University of Newton, where he matriculated and began playing his chosen sport in September 2011. His maiden voyage into the waters of college life was off to a promising start: Barely out of the starting gate, he showed himself to be as talented in the classroom as on the court, and his grades reflected his academic acumen. His interests that fall also included the very beautiful Elizabeth Jaynes, former steady of the team's star guard, Michael Wilson.

Silvino's freshman year was not to be without troubles, however. Storm clouds gathered on the horizon as the season got underway. Gomez, playing well, sensed that Wilson considered him a threat, and tension between the two stirred the air as Wilson harassed Gomez on the court. Although there was no "name-calling" during October, the dust flew in November when Wilson thundered at Gomez, "You fucking spic!" At first, the insults were made only when the coaches were absent, but in late November Wilson hurled them like lightning bolts during several practices in the presence of the coaches. In December, even the fans at several games were listening as Wilson's insults fell like hailstones on Gomez.

Some call writing like the example above "purple prose." Instead of focusing the reader's attention on the point being made, it calls attention to itself. What's worse, the effort shows.

How does one prevent the purple prose syndrome? The best safeguard is the axiom "when in doubt, don't." If you think the writing may be "too much," it probably is. Err on the side of subtlety.

Or if you are fortunate enough to have a candid colleague, get a second opinion. If you fear that something you have written may be overdone, ask that colleague to read the writing and let you know if you have stepped over the invisible line and into the realm of purple prose.

You might also try watching out for some of the common features of purple prose, many of which appear in the example above.

- Excessive use of adjectives and adverbs: *delighted* attention, *enthusiastic* recruiters, *the very beautiful* Elizabeth Jaynes
- Cliché-ridden phrases and images: *the dust flew, hurled them like lightning bolts*

- Mixed metaphors: *maiden voyage* mixed with *out of the starting gate*
- Overdeveloped metaphors: the weather metaphor in the second paragraph
- Pretentious vocabulary: academic *acumen*

Other common features of purple prose not demonstrated in the previous example include the following:

- Too much of any one of the poetic devices (for example, excessive alliteration, or the "Peter Piper" effect)
- Heavy-handed use of stylistic devices
- Excessive use of underlining, boldface, and italics for emphasis

§ 26.2   Common Features of Eloquent Writing

Before writing can be considered eloquent, it must be clear, competent, and readable. Eloquent writing, however, goes a step beyond competence. The language is more than clear and energetic: It is memorable, striking, even poetic because the writer has paid attention to the sound, rhythm, and imagery of language.

Features of language that one may not have thought about since that last class in poetry—alliteration, assonance, cadence, stressed and unstressed syllables, onomatopoeia, simile, and metaphor—may be used, but they should not overwhelm eloquent legal writing. Rhetorical features you might have noticed in aphorisms—parallelism, balance, antithesis—may also be used, particularly at key points.

Other features, such as effective verbs (see section 24.3), occasional short sentences (see section 24.5), variety in sentence length and sentence openers, and subtle devices for creating emphasis (see section 24.6), are fairly common.

Best of all, all of this occurs naturally, apparently effortlessly, even though we know better. Like a pair of dancers who move as one body or a well-executed double play in baseball, eloquent writing is the perfect, harmonious matching of form and content. The reader feels satisfied, perhaps even uplifted, by the writing.

§ 26.2.1   Alliteration and Assonance

Eloquent writing begs to be read aloud. One wants to savor the language. Every word and phrase seems to be just the right choice. Quite simply, the writing sings.

Of the numerous features that affect the sound of a piece of writing, alliteration and assonance are probably the easiest to identify. Alliteration, or the repetition of consonant sounds, must be subtle or the writing will begin to sound like "Peter Piper picked a peck of pickled peppers." One way accomplished writers work in alliteration without overpowering the prose is to use it in the middle of words as well as at the beginning.

The following example demonstrates a subtle use of alliteration. The example is taken from the amicus brief for the United States in the landmark

Supreme Court case *Wallace v. Jaffree*, which concerned the constitutionality of a state statute authorizing public school teachers to allow a moment of silence at the beginning of the school day for "prayer or meditation."

EXAMPLE 1   **Subtle Alliteration**

Moment of silence statutes are libertarian in the precise spirit of the Bill of Rights: they accommodate those who believe that prayer should be an integral part of life's activities (including school), and do so in the most neutral and noncoercive spirit possible. The student may pray, but is equally free to meditate or daydream or doze. No one can even know what the other chooses to do: silence is precious because it creates the possibility of privacy within public occasions. To hold that the moment of silence is unconstitutional is to insist that any opportunity for religious practice, even in the unspoken thoughts of schoolchildren, be extirpated from the public sphere. It is to be censorial where the Religion Clauses are libertarian; it would make the very concept of religious accommodation constitutionally suspect.

The alliteration in this example is unobtrusive. In fact, most of us can read this passage and never consciously notice that it includes alliteration. Look again at these phrases:

the most <u>n</u>eutral and <u>n</u>oncoercive spirit possible
<u>d</u>ay<u>d</u>ream or <u>d</u>oze

The brief writer could have said "the most impartial and noncoercive spirit possible" or "the most objective and noncoercive spirit possible" or even "the most equitable and noncoercive spirit possible," but didn't. "Neutral," when coupled with "noncoercive," has both the right meaning and the right sound.

The same is true of "daydream and doze." Rather than select "doze," the writer could have easily said "nap," "rest," "sleep," or "snooze." All have similar meanings, but try substituting any one of the four in the original sentence to see what is gained by the alliterative "doze."

The brief writer saves the most subtle and arguably the most powerful alliteration for the clause "silence is precious because it creates the possibility of privacy within public occasions." This clause has two layers of alliteration. The more obvious is the repetition of the "p" sounds: "silence is <u>p</u>recious because it creates the <u>p</u>ossibility of <u>p</u>rivacy within <u>p</u>ublic occasions." The second layer is the repetition of "<u>s</u>" sounds, which is done by both the letters <u>s</u> and <u>c</u>: "<u>s</u>ilence is pre<u>c</u>iou<u>s</u> because it create<u>s</u> the po<u>ss</u>ibility of priva<u>c</u>y within public occasion<u>s</u>."

The soft "s" and "sh" sounds work perfectly in this context. They underscore the writer's meaning by gently, almost imperceptibly reminding the reader of the kind of quiet the writer wants the schoolchildren to have.

Assonance, or the repetition of vowel sounds, is similar to alliteration. In the following example, the brief writer repeated the "a" sound.

EXAMPLE 2   **Repetition of "a" Sound**

The absurdity of this implicit assumption is apparent when applied to the motivations of those responsible for the First Amendment itself.

Is the assonance overdone in the example above? Read it aloud to determine if it works.

§ 26.2.2 Cadence

Cadence is the rhythmic flow of the writing, what musicians might call "the beat." Unlike music, though, writing has no apparent time signature and few overt signals for where to place the emphasis. Even so, good writers control the pace and emphasis in their sentences by artful use of sentence structure, sentence length, punctuation, and stressed and unstressed syllables. Like good musicians, they "hear" what they are creating.

Read aloud the following example from the writing of Supreme Court Justice Louis Brandeis.

EXAMPLE 3   **Cadence in Justice Brandeis's Writing**

In a government of laws, existence of the government will be imperiled if it fails to observe the law scrupulously. Our Government is the potent, the omnipresent teacher. For good or for ill, it teaches the whole people by its example. Crime is contagious. If the Government becomes a lawbreaker, it breeds contempt for law; it invites every man to become a law unto himself; it invites anarchy. To declare that in the administration of the criminal law the end justifies the means—to declare that the Government may commit crimes in order to secure the conviction of a private criminal—would bring terrible retribution. Against that pernicious doctrine this Court should resolutely set its face.

This excerpt is rich with the features of eloquent prose, but for now let's look just at the rhythm in the language. Consider, for example, the phrase "the potent, the omnipresent teacher." The more common way to write two adjectives before a noun is "the potent, omnipresent teacher," without the extra "the." Why the extra "the" in the Brandeis version? Try scanning the phrase as you would a piece of poetry.

˘ / ˘ / ˘ / ˘ / ˘

the po-tent, om-ni-pres-ent teach-er

The unvarying unstressed, stressed, unstressed, stressed syllable pattern is flat and lifeless, particularly when it comes in two-syllable, sing-song units. It does not give "omnipresent" enough emphasis. Add the extra "the," however, and the rhythm is more interesting and, more important, more compatible with the desired emphasis.

Now look at the last sentence of this selection.

. . . this Court should resolutely set its face.

This clause is easy to read aloud. It is a grand, solemn conclusion. Why? Scan the last four words.

/ ˘ / ˘ / ˘ /

res-o-lute-ly set its face

The three one-syllable words "set its face" break up any sing-song effect. Further, notice where the stress falls — on "set" and "face." Thus, by ending the selection on a stressed syllable, a strong note, Justice Brandeis creates the sound of finality and conviction. Had Brandeis arranged the last clause so that it ended on "resolutely" (as he had the earlier one, "to observe the law scrupulously"), the unstressed syllable at the end of "resolutely" would have fought against the decisive closure he wanted.

/ ◡ /   / ◡ / ◡

set its face res-o-lute-ly

Does this mean Justice Brandeis scanned his prose for stressed and unstressed syllables as he was writing it? That's highly unlikely. What is likely is that he *heard* the sound he was creating and, perhaps through trial and error, manipulated the words until he achieved the aural effect he wanted.

The preceding examples show that an extra syllable here or there or changing a stressed to an unstressed syllable or vice versa can make a difference in how writing sounds. Adding or deleting an extra word or syllable also makes a difference in the pace of the writing. Such a change in pace is particularly obvious when the word added or omitted is a conjunction in a series.

A typical series reads like "red, white, and blue." Asyndeton, or the deliberate omissions of conjunctions in a series, quickens the pace. The same series without the conjunction — "red, white, blue" — sounds slightly rushed.

Polysyndeton, or the deliberate use of many conjunctions in a series, slows the pace and drags out the prose. Now the series takes more time: "red and white and blue."

Compare the following examples from a child custody case, in which the court looks at which of the parties was the child's primary caregiver. In an objective, neutral discussion of the father's care of the child, the following series may appear.

EXAMPLE 4   **Typical Series**

Mr. Lundquist had certain responsibilities regarding his daughter Anna's care: He drove her to school, checked her homework, and took her to medical appointments.

The attorney for Lundquist's former wife may use asyndeton to create the impression that Mr. Lundquist's care of his daughter was minimal.

EXAMPLE 5   **Omissions of "and" in a Series**

Mr. Lundquist had few responsibilities regarding his daughter Anna's care: He drove her to school, checked her homework, took her to medical appointments.

Mr. Lundquist, on the other hand, will probably want to create the impression that he was an involved parent who spent a great deal of time with his daughter. Notice how the use of polysyndeton, in combination with other persuasive devices such as characterizing the facts and adding detail, creates the desired effect.

EXAMPLE 6   **"And" Between All Items in a Series**

Mr. Lundquist had several significant responsibilities regarding his daughter Anna's care: He drove her to school each day and checked her homework every evening and took her to all regularly scheduled and emergency medical appointments.

---

§ 26.2.3 Variety in Sentence Length

In section 24.5, we said that legal readers can comfortably read sentences that average around twenty-two words in length. We also suggested that long sentences, thirty-five words or more, are difficult to read unless they are broken into manageable units of meaning. Finally, we briefly touched on the power of the short sentence. All of these points apply to eloquent writing.

Let's look again at the earlier example from Justice Brandeis.

EXAMPLE 7   **Sentence Length in Justice Brandeis's Writing**

In a government of laws, existence of the government will be imperiled if it fails to observe the law scrupulously. Our Government is the potent, the omnipresent teacher. For good or for ill, it teaches the whole people by its example. Crime is contagious. If the Government becomes a lawbreaker, it breeds contempt for law; it invites every man to become a law unto himself; it invites anarchy. To declare that in the administration of the criminal law the end justifies the means—to declare that the Government may commit crimes in order to secure the conviction of a private criminal—would bring terrible retribution. Against that pernicious doctrine this Court should resolutely set its face.

A reader's sense of how long a sentence is depends partly on the number of words in the sentence but also on the number of syllables in the sentence. Exhibit 26.1 shows how the sentences in the Brandeis excerpt break down, both in the number of words they contain and in the number of syllables.

Exhibit 26.1   Sentence Breakdown in Brandeis Excerpt

sentence 1	20 words	32 syllables
sentence 2	8 words	15 syllables
sentence 3	13 words	17 syllables
sentence 4	3 words	5 syllables
sentence 5	24 words	38 syllables
sentence 6	37 words	62 syllables
sentence 7	11 words	18 syllables

The variety in sentence length in this selection is remarkable — from three words to thirty-seven words. Having variety, though, is not an end in itself.

Notice how Brandeis uses sentence length. The one extremely short sentence, "Crime is contagious," is startling in its brevity. It hits the reader like a slap in the face. Its terseness creates the emphasis this point deserves.

The longest sentence in the selection has to be longer just to get across its points, but it also needs more words to create the effect of building to a climax. This sentence needs time to gather momentum. And even though it is fairly long — thirty-seven words or sixty-two syllables — this sentence is easy to read because it comes in manageable units of meaning: fifteen words, eighteen words, and four words.

Such variety in sentence length helps create an interesting and varied pace. Deliberately breaking the "rules" can be another effective way to create reader interest. In the following example from *Edwards v. Aguillard*, Justice Scalia uses a marathon sentence to help make a point.

EXAMPLE 8   **Extremely Long Sentence in Justice Scalia's Writing**

But the difficulty of knowing what vitiating purpose one is looking for is as nothing compared with the difficulty of knowing how or where to find it. For while it is possible to discern the objective "purpose" of a statute (*i.e.,* the public good at which its provisions appear to be directed), or even the formal motivation for a statute where that is explicitly set forth (as it was, to no avail, here), discerning the subjective motivation of those enacting the statute is, to be honest, almost always an impossible task. The number of possible motivations, to begin with, is not binary, or indeed even finite. In the present case, for example, a particular legislator need not have voted for the Act either because he wanted to foster religion or because he wanted to improve education. He may have thought the bill would provide jobs for his district, or may have wanted to make amends with a faction of his party he had alienated on another vote, or he may have been a close friend of the bill's sponsor, or he may have been repaying a favor he owed the Majority Leader, or he may have hoped the Governor would appreciate his vote and make a fundraising appearance for him, or he may have been pressured to vote for a bill he disliked by a wealthy contributor or by a flood of constituent mail, or he may have been seeking favorable publicity, or he may have been reluctant to hurt the feelings of a loyal staff member who worked on the bill, or he may have been settling an old score with a legislator who opposed the bill, or he may have been mad at his wife who opposed the bill, or he may have been intoxicated and utterly *un*motivated when the vote was called, or he may have accidentally voted "yes" instead of "no," or, of course, he may have had (and very likely did have) a combination of some of the above and many other motivations. To look for *the sole purpose* of even a single legislator is probably to look for something that does not exist.

The fifth sentence is a linguistic *tour de force*. At 202 words, it must set some kind of record for sentence length, yet the sentence is quite readable because it is broken up into manageable units that vary between 8 and 24 words.

But no one thinks Justice Scalia wrote this sentence to demonstrate that he can write a long sentence that is readable. Rather, in this rare instance, an extremely long sentence dramatically made his point that there is an extremely long list of reasons why any single legislator may vote for a bill.

§ 26.2.4 Variety in Sentence Openers

It is risky to suggest that legal writers should occasionally vary the openings of their sentences. In the hands of the wrong writer, this advice can lead to some clumsy prose.

For the most part, writers should follow the more traditional advice and begin the majority of their sentences with the subject. Writers who use all sorts of sentence openers other than the subject tend to write prose that sounds jumpy and disjointed. But writers who oversubscribe to the idea of starting sentences with the subject write incredibly boring prose.

The question then is when should a writer use something other than the subject to begin a sentence? Even in garden-variety prose, subjects are frequently preceded by phrases or clauses that establish a context or pick up on a previously established theme. (See sections 23.2 and 23.3.1 on orienting transitions and dovetailing.)

What is far more unusual and, when done well, more striking, is the inverted word order of some sentences. Such an inversion, known in classical rhetoric as "anastrophe," focuses particular attention on whatever words are out of their normal or expected order. The Brandeis excerpt ended with an example of inverted word order.

EXAMPLE 9   **Inverted Word Order in Sentence Opener**

Against that pernicious doctrine this Court should resolutely set its face.

As always, to understand the drama and power this arrangement creates, all one has to do is read the sentence in the normal, expected word order.

> This Court should resolutely set its face against that pernicious doctrine.

Here is another example from an amicus brief in *Wallace v. Jaffree*:

EXAMPLE 10   **Inverted Word Order in Sentence Opener**

The public schools serve as vehicles for "inculcating fundamental values," including "social, moral, or political" ones. *Bd. of Educ. v. Pico*, 102 S. Ct. 2799, 2806 (1982). Pointedly absent from this list are religious values. Education in those values is not, under the Constitution, the responsibility of the public schools; it is that of family and church.

The expected word order of the second sentence in the second example is "Religious values are pointedly absent from this list." Notice that by inverting the order, the brief writer not only places emphasis on what is out of order, "pointedly absent," but also strengthens the emphasis on "religious values" by moving it to the end of the sentence.

§ 26.2.5   Parallelism

Parallelism, or the use of similar grammatical structures in a pair or series of related words, phrases, or clauses, is required in some contexts. (See section 27.7.) Accomplished writers, however, treat parallelism not just as a grammatical requirement but as a stylistic opportunity. They use parallelism and its related forms to create special effects, emphasis, and euphony.

Here's an example from the appellants' brief in *Wallace v. Jaffree*:

EXAMPLE 11   **Using Parallelism to Improve Style**

This development is a tribute not only to the good sense of the American people, but also to the genius of the Framers of the body of the Constitution.

not only	to the good sense of the American people,
but also	to the genius of the Framers of the body of the Constitution

---

Look again at the Scalia excerpt. Justice Scalia uses a specialized version of parallelism called "isocolon" when he matches both the structure and the length of the parallel elements in the following sentence.

EXAMPLE 12   **Using Parallelism to Improve Style**

In the present case, for example, a particular legislator need not have voted for the Act either because he wanted to foster religion or because he wanted to improve education.

either	because he wanted to foster religion
or	because he wanted to improve education

The same excerpt from Justice Scalia includes examples of another specialized form of parallelism: balance. In the sentence below, notice how the first half of the sentence is balanced against the second half.

EXAMPLE 13   **Using Balance to Improve Style**

To look for the sole purpose of even a single legislator is probably to look for something that does not exist.

To look for	is	to look for
the sole purpose	probably	something that
of even a		does not exist.
single legislator		

Balance can also be created in a number of other ways. Here's an excerpt from Cardozo's opinion in *Hynes v. New York*:

EXAMPLE 14   **Using Balance to Improve Style**

The approximate and relative become the definite and absolute.

approximate	become	definite
and		and
relative		absolute

From the brief of the appellees in *Wallace*:

EXAMPLE 15   **Using Balance to Improve Style**

The First Amendment is as simple in its language as it is majestic in its purpose.

as simple	*as (it is) majestic*
in its language	*in its purpose*

Also fairly common in eloquent legal writing is a related form of parallelism known as "antithesis." Like balance, antithesis repeats similar parallel structures on both sides of the equation, but unlike balance, the ideas are in contrast.

The structure of antithesis is usually quite simple and falls into one of two patterns:

not _____ but _____
_____, not _____

Examples from the amicus brief of the United States in *Wallace*:

EXAMPLE 16   **Using Antithesis to Improve Style**

The touchstone is not secularism, but pluralism.

. . .

We believe that provision for a moment of silence in the public schools is not an establishment of religion, but rather a legitimate way for the government to provide an opportunity for both religious and nonreligious introspection in a setting where, experience has shown, many desire it. It is an instrument of toleration and pluralism, not of coercion or indoctrination.

Yet another variation of parallelism is the use of parallel openers. Parallel openers can start sentences, clauses, or phrases, and they often have the effect of building to a climax or suggesting that a point is well established.

From the Brandeis excerpt:

EXAMPLE 17   **Using Parallel Openers to Improve Style**

If the Government becomes a lawbreaker, it breeds contempt for law; **it invites** every man to become a law unto himself; **it invites** anarchy. **To declare that** in the administration of the criminal law the end justifies the means—**to declare that** the Government may commit crimes in order to secure the conviction of a private criminal—would bring terrible retribution.

---

§ 26.2.6   Onomatopoeia

"Snap," "crackle," and "pop"—these words are examples of onomatopoeia; that is, they sound like what they mean. So do "sizzle," "plop," "hiss," "click," "twang," "crinkle," and a host of others. These words sound like the natural sounds they represent.

Other words have an onomatopoetic quality even though the words don't represent a sound. Consider the word "weird." Not only does it sound weird, it is even spelled weirdly. The word "bizarre" works the same way; it looks and sounds bizarre. The list goes on. There is something grotesque in the look and sound of "grotesque," and it is hard to imagine a word that looks and sounds more unattractive than "ugly."

Consider the sound of words such as "sensual," "lascivious," and "licentious." Notice how the rolling "s" and "l" sounds combine in various ways to give the words a lazy, even erotic sound. "Sultry" works the same way.

The "slippery slope" one hears so much about in law puts the "s" and "l" together as a consonant blend and achieves a different effect. The words seem to *slide* off the tongue with slow ease. Like a judicial system that has started down that slippery slope, there are no natural brakes to stop these words once they are formed on the lips. Notice too that "slick," "slime," "slink," "slither," "slush," and "sludge" all somehow share this same slippery, even oily quality.

Should legal writers use onomatopoeia in their writing? Consider the following versions of essentially the same point.

EXAMPLE 18   **Using Onomatopoeia to Improve Style**

Harris suddenly took the keys and ran out the door.

Harris snatched the keys and ran out the door.

"Snatched" says in one word—even one syllable—what the first of the examples takes two words and four syllables to say. Its quickness mirrors the quickness in the action. It *sounds* like a quick grab at those keys.

§ 26.2.7 Simile and Metaphor

Similes are indirect comparisons.

EXAMPLE 19   **Using Simile to Improve Style**

Lowell's mental irresponsibility defense is like the toy gun he used in the robbery—spurious.

Metaphors are direct comparisons.

EXAMPLE 20   **Using Metaphor to Improve Style**

Our Government is the potent, the omnipresent teacher.

To be effective, similes and metaphors need to be fresh and insightful. Unfortunately, all too many metaphors used in legal writing are cliché-ridden.

How often must we hear that something or other is "woven into the fabric of our society"? When was the last time you actually thought about wolves and sheep when something or someone was described as a "wolf in sheep's clothing"?

Timeworn similes and metaphors suggest that the writer's thought processes are on autopilot, and no more than that will be expected of the reader. We can all mentally coast.

A fresh simile or metaphor makes demands of the reader. It asks the reader to bring to the new subject matter all the associations it has with the other half of the metaphor.

So powerful is metaphor that metaphors have become issues themselves. Consider, for example, the same landmark Supreme Court case from which we drew earlier examples, *Wallace v. Jaffree*, which involved the Alabama "silent meditation or prayer" in public schools statute. Throughout that case's history, both sides argued whether there was "an absolute wall of separation" between federal government and religion.

§ 26.2.8 Personification

Like so many of the suggestions in this chapter, personification, or giving human traits or abilities to abstractions or inanimate objects, must be used with a light hand if it is to be used at all in legal writing.

In the brief of the appellees in *Wallace v. Jaffree*, the writer used personification to make a point about the intent of the Alabama legislature.

EXAMPLE 21   **Using Personfication to Improve Style**

In 1982, in order to breathe religious life into its silent meditation statute, the Alabama legislature amended § 16-1-20 to expressly include "prayer" as the preferred activity in which the students and teachers may engage during the reverent moment of silence.

In his dissenting opinion in *Hoffa v. United States*, Chief Justice Warren uses personification to make a point about the government's actions and its witness.

EXAMPLE 22   **Using Personification to Improve Style**

Here the Government reaches into the jailhouse to employ a man who was himself facing indictments far more serious (and later including one for perjury) than the one confronting the man against whom he offered to inform.

Eloquent language does one of two things. It creates a satisfying sound or, as in the Warren excerpt above, it creates a memorable image. The best of the best does both. Such writing is memorable, even unforgettable. It grabs the reader's attention long enough to make the reader see something new or see something old in a new way.

Chapter 26 Quiz

Draft answers for each of the following questions. Make your points clearly and concisely, and write sentences that are easy to read and that are grammatical and correctly punctuated.

1. What is "purple prose"?
2. What are some ways in which writers can slip into purple prose?
3. What is the key to eloquent writing, and what are some of its common features?
4. What is onomatopoeia?
5. What are similes and metaphors? Give an example of each.
6. What are the two things mentioned in this chapter that eloquent writing does?

A Guide to Correct Writing

This section is a review of grammar and punctuation. While many legal writers have a good command of these aspects of writing, some complain that they never really understood how to use a semicolon or that they have heard about dangling modifiers but what in the world are they, anyway?

This section is designed to be a quick refresher and explanation for those who have forgotten some of the basic rules or who, for some reason, never learned some of them. Even those who have strong backgrounds in grammar and punctuation may find it helpful to review some of the chapters in this section simply because legal writing puts more demands on the writer than do most other types of writing. Consequently, it may make your writing more efficient and more effective if you have all the rules, and hence all the options, at your fingertips.

Finally, although this section is entitled "A Guide to Correct Writing," the term "correct" is slightly misleading because it may suggest that the choices outlined in these chapters are absolutely the "right" ones in all circumstances. This is not true. In informal language, for example, certain other usage choices are not only acceptable but preferred. In legal writing, however, standard English is the norm and therefore the "correct" choice.

Grammar

§ 27.1   Basic Sentence Grammar

Grammar, like law, is a system. Once you understand the basic workings of the system, you can begin to use the system effectively and efficiently.

Much of Book 5, A Guide to Effective Writing, and Book 6, A Guide to Correct Writing, depends on understanding the grammar of an English sentence. This section is a quick review of basic sentence structure and the various components of most English sentences.[1]

§ 27.1.1   Sentence Patterns

In law, as in most other writing, most sentences are statements. These statements name someone or something (the subject) and then describe an action that that someone or something is performing (the predicate).

Smith hit Jones.
(subject) *(predicate)*

Smith's car smashed into the railing.
 (subject)   *(predicate)*

---

1. Although modern grammarians have persuasively argued that structural and transformational grammars more accurately describe the English sentence, the authors have elected to use traditional grammar, partly because it is more familiar to most readers and partly because it is sufficient for our purposes.

Occasionally, the predicate describes the state in which the subject exists, or the subject's state of being.

Smith's car   is a total loss.
(subject)   *(predicate)*

At the heart of every subject is a noun or a pronoun. Nouns name persons (Supreme Court Justice Anthony Kennedy), places (Austin, Texas), things (savings bond), and concepts (negligence). Because pronouns are substitutes for nouns, they too can serve as subjects.

At the heart of every predicate is a verb. Some verbs express an action (argue, allege); others show a state of being (such as forms of the verb *to be*). Frequently, the main verb is preceded by other verbs known as auxiliary, or helping, verbs (*might have been* assaulted), which express time relationships and shades of meaning. See section 31.1.2.

Pattern 1: Subject + Verb

To write a sentence, you need at least one noun or pronoun for a subject and at least one verb for a predicate. This is the simplest sentence pattern.

subject   **predicate**
Lawyers   argue.
(noun)   *(verb)*

Pattern 2: Subject + Verb + Direct Object

Many verbs, however, cannot stand alone. They require a noun that will receive the action of the verb. We cannot, for example, simply say "lawyers make" and call that a sentence. "Make" what? To make sense, the verb needs a direct object. Notice that the direct object is part of the predicate.

subject   **predicate**
Lawyers   make arguments.
(noun)   *(verb)* *(noun)*
                        (direct object)

Another way of thinking about this point is to say that the subject performs the action of the verb, and the verb "is done to" the direct object.

You can often find the direct object in a sentence by simply asking the question "what?" after the verb. Make what? Make *arguments*.

Pattern 3: Subject + Linking Verb + Subject Complement

Similarly, state-of-being verbs, or linking verbs, need nouns (or sometimes adjectives) to complete the idea. Because these words do not directly receive the action of the verb in the same way as a direct object, they are not called direct objects. Instead, they are called "subject complements" because they complement the subject by renaming or describing it.

subject	predicate	
Lawyers	are	advocates.
(noun)	*(linking verb)*	*(noun)*
		(subject complement)

subject	predicate	
Lawyers	are	aggressive.
(noun)	*(linking verb)*	*(adjective)*
		(subject complement)

Note that some of the same words (am, is, are, was, were) function as linking verbs in some sentences and as auxiliary, or helping, verbs in other sentences. You can always tell whether one of these words is a linking verb or a helping verb by checking to see whether it is the only main verb in the sentence (then it is a linking verb) or whether it is followed by another main verb (then it is an auxiliary, or helping, verb).

EXAMPLE 1   **Linking Verb "Is"**

The judge is the trier of fact.

In the preceding example, "is" is the only verb; therefore, it is a linking verb.

EXAMPLE 2   **Helping Verb "Is"**

The judge is speaking to the jury.

In the preceding example, "is" is followed by another main verb, "speaking"; therefore, "is" is an auxiliary, or helping, verb in this example. Notice that the combination "is speaking" is an action verb.

Pattern 4: Subject + Verb + Indirect Object + Direct Object

In another common pattern, the verb is followed by two nouns. The second noun after the verb, the direct object, receives the action of the verb. The first noun after the verb, the indirect object, identifies to whom or for whom (or what) the action is performed.

subject	predicate		
Lawyers	tell	clients	their options.
	(verb)	*(noun)*	*(noun)*
		(indirect object)	*(direct object)*

Pattern 5: Subject + Verb + Direct Object + Object Complement

In this last pattern, we also have two nouns following the verb, but in this pattern, the first noun is the direct object and the second noun is an objective complement. An objective complement renames or describes the direct object.

subject	predicate		
Smith	called	Jones	a liar.
	(verb)	*(noun)*	*(noun)*
		(direct object)	*(objective complement)*

Using these basic sentence patterns, we can now begin adding all those extras that make sentences interesting and complex.

§ 27.1.2 Single-Word Modifiers

Modifiers change, limit, describe, or add detail. Words that modify nouns or pronouns are, by definition, adjectives (*illogical* argument, *bearded* suspect).

Words that modify verbs, adjectives, or adverbs are adverbs (*quickly* responded, finished *soon*, *extremely* angry, *very* recently). Notice that adverbs often end in "-ly."

Any of our basic sentences can be expanded by using adjectives and adverbs as modifiers.

EXAMPLE 3   **Adjective and Adverb Modifiers**

<u>Thoughtful</u> lawyers make <u>very</u> <u>persuasive</u> arguments.
(adjective)   *(adverb)(adjective)*

<u>Too</u> <u>many</u> lawyers are <u>overly</u> <u>aggressive</u>.
(adv.)(adj.)   *(adverb)(adjective)*

---

§ 27.1.3 Phrases

When expanding the basic sentence patterns, we are not limited to single-word modifiers. Groups of related words, or phrases, can also serve as modifiers. A phrase is easily distinguished from other groups of related words because a phrase always lacks a subject or a verb or both.

Probably the most common type of modifying phrase is the prepositional phrase, which is made up of a preposition (a word that shows a relationship between other words, such as "about," "at," "by," "for," "in," "of," "on," "to"), its object, and any modifiers.

Preposition	Modifiers	Object
at..........................	the same.......	time
for.......................	a new...........	trial
under.................	this..............	section

Prepositional phrases can modify nouns, verbs, adjectives, or adverbs.

EXAMPLE 4   **Prepositional Phrases**

<u>At 10:00 p.m. on April 5, 2012</u>, a two-truck collision occurred <u>in Delaware between a truck</u> driven <u>by Ms. Constance Ruiz</u> and a truck driven <u>by Mr. Fred Miller</u>.

Basic sentence patterns can also be expanded with verbals. Verbals are made from verbs, but they cannot serve as the main verb of a sentence. Instead, verbals are ways of using verb forms in other roles in a sentence. The three types of verbals — gerunds, infinitives, and participles — are described below. Notice that each can be expanded into a phrase.

a. Gerunds

Gerunds always act as nouns, so they are found in slots in the sentence that require nouns (subject, objects). They are formed by adding "-ing" to the base form of a verb.

EXAMPLE 5   **Gerunds in Sentences**

<u>Impeaching</u> his testimony will be difficult.
  (gerund)

Forgery includes <u>writing</u> a bad check.
          (gerund)

---

b. Participles

Participles act as adjectives. Present participles are formed by adding "ing" to the base form of the verb; past participles usually add "-d" or "-ed." Irregular verbs have a special past participle form (for example, *brought, drunk, stolen*).

EXAMPLE 6   **Participles in Sentences**

A laptop <u>wrapped</u> in a blanket was in the defendant's trunk.
     (participle)

<u>Applying</u> this rule, the New York Supreme Court held that the appellant's constitutional
(participle)
rights were not violated.

<u>Given</u> that forgery is not a crime of dishonesty, the court found that evidence of the
(participle)
prior conviction is inadmissible.

Notice that the only way to distinguish between a gerund and a present participle is to determine the role they perform in a sentence.

c.   Infinitives

Infinitives can act as nouns, adjectives, or adverbs. The infinitive form is always "to" plus the base form of the verb.

EXAMPLE 7   **Infinitives in Sentences**

To extend the all-purpose public figure standard to include all financial institutions ignores the Supreme Court's mandate to construe the standard narrowly.

---

d.   Absolutes

One additional type of phrase, the absolute phrase, can also be used to expand the basic sentence patterns. Absolute phrases do not modify any one word or phrase in a sentence; instead, they are whole-sentence modifiers. Absolute phrases are made up of a noun (or pronoun), a participle, and their modifiers.

attention		diverted
noun	+	*participle*

EXAMPLE 8   **Absolute in a Sentence**

His attention diverted by the fire, the witness is unlikely to have viewed the fleeing arsonist for more than a second.

---

§ 27.1.4 Clauses

A clause is a group of related words that has both a subject and a verb. There are two types of clauses: main (or independent) clauses and subordinate (or dependent) clauses. A main clause can stand alone as a sentence. A subordinate clause cannot stand alone as a sentence because a subordinate clause is introduced by a subordinating conjunction or relative pronoun.

Common Subordinating Conjunctions

after	if	though
although	if only	till
as	in order that	unless
as if	now that	until
as long as	once	when
as though	rather than	whenever
because	since	where
before	so that	whereas
even if	than	wherever
even though	that	while

Relative Pronouns

that	which	whom
what	who	whomever
whatever	whoever	whose

Notice that in subordinate clauses introduced by a relative pronoun, the subject of the clause is often the relative pronoun. ("Defendants *who do not take the stand* risk having jurors infer that they are guilty.")

EXAMPLE 9   **Clauses in Sentences**

Main Clauses:

Martin retained full possession of the stock.

The trial court abused its discretion.

It failed to consider the statutory factors.

Subordinate Clauses:

although Martin retained full possession of the stock

that the trial court abused its discretion

when it failed to consider the statutory factors

Subordinate Clauses Attached to Main Clauses:

Although Martin retained full possession of the stock, the trial court awarded the stock to Judith.

The appellate court found that the trial court abused its discretion when it failed to consider the statutory factors.

---

§ 27.1.5 Appositives

Appositives are words or groups of words that follow a noun and rename it. They may also further describe or identify the noun.

EXAMPLE 10   **Appositives**

Conrad Murray, <u>Michael Jackson's personal physician</u>, was found guilty of involuntary manslaughter.

In *Texas v. Johnson*, <u>a case about a state criminal statute forbidding "the desecration of a venerated object,"</u> the Supreme Court ruled that burning the American flag as an expression of political discontent is protected by the First Amendment.

Appositives are frequently introduced by phrases—*that is, such as, for example*.

EXAMPLE 11   **Phrases Introducing Appositives**

Evidence of some crimes, <u>such as fraud, embezzlement, and false pretense</u>, may be probative of a defendant's credibility as a witness.

---

§ 27.1.6 Connecting Words

The five basic sentence patterns can also be expanded by using connecting words that allow us to combine words or word groups of equal rank. For example, we can add one or more nouns to a subject to create a compound subject ("Smith and Wilson hit Jones"), or we can add one or more verbs to the predicate to create a compound predicate ("Smith hit and kicked Jones").

a.   Coordinating Conjunctions

The most common connecting words are the seven coordinating conjunctions.

and	nor	yet
but	for	so
or		

"And," "but," "or," and "nor" can connect any two (or more) of the same kind of word or word group. "For" and "so" connect main clauses.

EXAMPLE 12   **Connecting Words**

Connecting Two Nouns:

Crimes of dishonesty involve **fraud** <u>**or**</u> **deceit**.

Connecting Two Verbs:

The complaint stated that the defendants **had published** <u>but</u> not **retracted** a defamatory article about Vashon Savings and Loan.

Connecting Three Phrases:

Copies of the article were distributed to **subscribers, newsstands,** <u>**and**</u> **three civic groups**.

Connecting Two Subordinate Clauses:

Because there are only two witnesses <u>and</u> **because each witness has a different version of the facts**, the jury will have to choose which one to believe.

Connecting Two Main Clauses:

Vashon Savings and Loan has not assumed a role of special prominence in the affairs of society, <u>nor</u> **does it occupy a position of pervasive power or influence**.

---

b.   Correlative Conjunctions

Correlative conjunctions come in pairs.

both . . . and	either . . . or	whether . . . or
not . . . but	neither . . . nor	as . . . as
not only . . . but also		

EXAMPLE 13   **Correlative Conjunctions**

Plaintiff's contact with the community is <u>both</u> **conservative** <u>and</u> **low-key**.

The jury <u>either</u> **will not hear the defendant's testimony** <u>or</u> **will completely disregard it** if his prior convictions are admitted.

---

c.   Conjunctive Adverbs

Even though conjunctive adverbs do not connect parts of the sentence grammatically, they are useful because they show the relationship between two or more ideas.

The Most Common Conjunctive Adverbs

accordingly	further	likewise	similarly
also	furthermore	meanwhile	still
anyway	hence	moreover	then
besides	however	nevertheless	thereafter
certainly	incidentally	next	therefore
consequently	indeed	nonetheless	thus
finally	instead	otherwise	undoubtedly

EXAMPLE 14   **Conjunctive Adverbs in Sentences**

Mrs. Davis admits that her physician told her that she has a drinking problem. She refuses, <u>nevertheless</u>, to attend Alcoholics Anonymous. <u>Instead</u>, she claims that she drinks only an occasional glass of wine.

Mrs. Davis will have $63,872 a year to spend as she sees fit; <u>therefore</u>, she has no need for the dividend income from the stock.

---

§ 27.2   Fragments

Simply defined, a sentence fragment is an incomplete sentence. Theoretically, it may be missing its subject,[2] but more than likely it is missing a main verb, or it is a subordinate clause trying to pose as a sentence.

---

2. Imperative, or command, sentences such as "Sit down" or "Hang your coat in the cloakroom" may appear to have a missing subject, but the subject is always understood to be "you." Therefore, imperative sentences are not fragments even if they are only one word long, such as "Run!"

§ 27.2.1 Missing Main Verb

All verbals — gerunds, participles, and infinitives — are formed from verbs, but they cannot fill verb slots in a sentence. Consequently, they cannot serve as the main verb of a sentence. Some legal writers who are prone to writing fragments mistake verbals for main verbs. (See section 27.1.3 for definitions and explanations of verbals.)

EXAMPLE 1   **Fragment**

The attorney objecting to the line of questioning.

In the example above, "objecting" is not a verb; it is a participle modifying "attorney." Because the example has no main verb, it is a fragment, not a sentence. To make it a sentence, either add a main verb or change "objecting" from a participle to a main verb.

EXAMPLE 2   **Possible Revisions**

The attorney objecting to the line of questioning <u>rose</u> to her feet.

The attorney <u>objected</u> to the line of questioning.

The attorney <u>was objecting</u> to the line of questioning.

Notice that the same word, "objecting," can be a participle or, with an auxiliary verb added, a main verb.

§ 27.2.2 Subordinate Clauses Trying to Pose as Sentences

Take any main, or independent, clause and add a word such as "although," "until," or "when" in front of the word and it becomes a subordinate, or dependent, clause.

until + main clause = subordinate clause

EXAMPLE 3   **Example 3   Main → Subordinate Clause**

Main Clause:

The attorney objects to the line of questioning.

Subordinate Clause:

until the attorney objects to the line of questioning

Subordinate clauses must be attached to a main, or independent, clause.

| EXAMPLE 4 | Subordinate Clause Attached to Main Clause |

Until the attorney objects to the line of questioning, the judge will not rule.
(subordinate clause) *(main clause)*

"Although," "until," and "when" are not the only words, or subordinating conjunctions, that can change a main clause into a subordinate clause. Below is a fairly complete list of the most common subordinating conjunctions used in legal writing. Remember: If one of these words or phrases introduces a clause, that clause will be subordinate. It cannot stand alone.

Subordinating Conjunctions

after	before	now that	till
although	even if	once	unless
as	even though	provided	until
as if	if	rather than	when
as long as	if only	since	whenever
as soon as	in order that	so that	where
as though	in that	than	whereas
because	no matter how	that	wherever
		though	while

Notice, too, that subordinate clauses may follow a main clause. In fact, many fragments are written because the writer should have attached a subordinate clause to the preceding main clause.

| EXAMPLE 5 | Correcting a Fragment |

Fragment

Kaiser's statement acknowledging Sloan's ownership of the land may have no effect on the hostility of his claim. Because he never acted in subordination to the true owner.

Corrected

Kaiser's statement acknowledging Sloan's ownership of the land may have no effect on the hostility of his claim because Kaiser never acted in subordination to the true owner.

The relative pronouns — "who," "whoever," "whom," "whomever," "whose," "what," "whatever," "which," and "that" — also lure some writers into writing fragments.

| EXAMPLE 6 | Correcting a Fragment |

Fragment

The admission of a defendant's prior convictions may affect that defendant's decision to take the stand. Which would interfere with his right to testify freely on his own behalf.

Corrected

The admission of a defendant's prior convictions may affect that defendant's decision to take the stand. Therefore, admission of his prior convictions would interfere with his right to testify freely on his own behalf.

In short, to determine if you have written a sentence and not a fragment, (1) make sure you have a verb, (2) make sure you have a subject, and (3) make sure your subject and verb are not preceded by a subordinating conjunction or a relative pronoun.

§ 27.2.3   Permissible Uses of Incomplete Sentences

There are a handful of permissible uses for incomplete sentences in legal writing.

   a. In issue statements beginning with "whether"
   b. As answers to questions
   c. In exclamations
   d. For stylistic effect
   e. As transitions

a.   In Issue Statements Beginning with "Whether"

Many issue statements, or questions presented, begin with the word "whether."

EXAMPLE 7   **"Whether" Issue Statement**

Whether, under Washington tort law on wrongful death or conversion, the Hoffelmeirs may collect punitive damages for the destruction of their pet cat when the cat was impounded and when, after Mr. Janske of the Humane Society tried unsuccessfully to contact the Hoffelmeirs, the animal was destroyed before the time required by the Sequim city ordinance.

Although a grammarian would not consider the example above to be a complete sentence, most attorneys and judges find this format acceptable in legal writing. It is as though legal readers read in an elliptical "the issue is" before "whether."

b.   As Answers to Questions

Many office memos contain a brief answer section. Typically, a brief answer will begin with an incomplete sentence that is a short response to the legal question, such as "Probably not." This is an acceptable use of a fragment. The following example is the brief answer to the question presented in the preceding example.

EXAMPLE 8   **Acceptable Fragment in Brief Answer**

Probably not. In Washington, there is a strong policy against the award of punitive damages and, unless there is a statutory provision allowing for punitive damages, the courts will not award them. In this instance, there is no statutory provision allowing for punitive damages.

c. In Exclamations

Exclamations rarely occur in legal writing because they make the tone of the writing appear inflammatory, effusive, or sarcastic. The one place exclamations do appear in legal writing is in quoted dialogue. On such occasions, quote exactly what the speaker said and how he or she said it, including fragments.

d. For Stylistic Effect

Sophisticated writers who are well schooled in the rules of grammar can occasionally use an intentional fragment for stylistic effect. Most writers, however, should avoid writing any fragments.

EXAMPLE 9   **Acceptable Fragment for Stylistic Effect**

It may have been unavoidable, but it still took courage. <u>More courage than most of us would have had.</u>

---

e. As Transitions

As with fragments for stylistic effect, intentional fragments as transitions are a risk. Use them only if you are secure about and in complete control of your writing.

If you have already read sections 22.4 and 22.5 of this book, you may have noticed that the authors used two incomplete sentences as transitions to begin those sections.

EXAMPLE 10   **Acceptable Fragment as Transitions**

First, the truth.

Again, the truth.

Chapter 27 Quiz No. 1

Draft answers for each of the following questions. Make your points clearly and concisely, and write sentences that are easy to read and that are grammatical and correctly punctuated.

1. In English, what are the two basic components of a sentence?
2. What are the five basic patterns of English sentences?
3. What are modifiers? Name some examples of modifiers.
4. What are the three types of verbals in English?
5. What is a clause, and what are the two types of clauses in English?
6. What are the seven coordinating conjunctions, and what function to do they perform?
7. What are the seven pairs of correlative conjunctions?
8. What is a sentence fragment?

9. Although fragments are almost always grammatical errors, there are
a few instances in which they are permissible. What are some of the
permissible uses of a fragment?

§ 27.3   Verb Tense and Mood

§ 27.3.1 Tense

Verb tense does not pose problems for most legal writers who are native
speakers of English. Native speakers tend to "hear" when the verb is right or
wrong. Consequently, verb tense is one of those areas of writing that is best
left alone, unless a writer is having problems.

For those native and non-native speakers of English who are having problems with verb tense in legal writing, the following is a quick review of the
basic verb tense structure. (See Chapter 31 for more on verbs and verb tense,
particularly how auxiliary verbs create shades of meaning.)

Throughout this review of verb tense, we will use a capital "X" to indicate
the present on all time lines.

The term "tense" refers to the time in which the verb's action occurs in
relation to the time when the writer is writing. For example, present tense is used
for actions that occur in the present, that is, at the time the writer is writing.

EXAMPLE 1   **Present Tense**

The defendant <u>pleads</u> not guilty.

Time line:_____ X _____
the present
(the action is occurring
at the same time
the writer is writing)

Notice, however, that the "X" on the time line that represents "the present" may be as short as a fraction of a second or as long as several centuries,
depending on what time frame the writer sets up.

Past tense refers to actions that occurred before the writer is writing.

EXAMPLE 2   **Past Tense**

Two years ago, this same prosecutor <u>charged</u> the defendant with aggravated assault.

Time line: _____ X _____
←**the past**→

Legal writers usually use the past tense when describing analogous cases.

EXAMPLE 3   **Past Tense to Describe Analogous Case**

In *Colorado Carpet*, the court <u>rejected</u> the argument for the specially manufactured goods exception because the carpet <u>was</u> not <u>cut</u> to a room size.

Future tense refers to actions that will occur after the writer is writing.

EXAMPLE 4   **Future Tense**

The plaintiff <u>will call</u> an expert witness.

        Time line: _____ X _____
                              ←the future→

The simple tenses—present, past, and future—are just that: simple and easy to use. Only the present tense offers a few noteworthy wrinkles.

In addition to its common use for actions that occur in the present, present tense is also used to express general truths and to show habitual actions.

EXAMPLE 5   **Present Tense for General Truths/Habits**

Appellate courts <u>do</u> not <u>retry</u> a case on its facts.

The defendant <u>drinks</u> a six-pack of beer every Friday night.

Present tense can also be used to indicate the future when the sentence contains other words and phrases to signal a future time.

EXAMPLE 6   **Present Tense with Other "Future" Signals**

The court <u>hears</u> oral arguments later this afternoon.

The perfect tenses are a bit more complicated. Perfect tenses are designed to show that an action is completed before a certain time.

For example, the present perfect tense usually shows that an action is completed at the time of the statement. It is formed by using "have" or "has" before the past participle. In the sentence below, the present perfect "have tried" occurred before the present.

EXAMPLE 7   **Present Perfect Tense**

The plaintiffs <u>have tried</u> this strategy before, but it is not working this time.

Time line: _____ X _____

→

(action begun in the
past and completed
before the present)

The present perfect tense is also used when the action was begun in the past and it continues on into the present.

EXAMPLE 8   **Present Perfect Tense**

The prosecutor <u>has offered</u> Mr. Pemberque a plea bargain that would permit him to plead guilty to a gross misdemeanor and serve no jail time.

Time line: _____ X _____

→

(action begun in the
past and continues
on into the present)

In contrast, the past perfect tense is used when one past action was completed before another past action. For example, a legal writer may find it useful to use the past perfect to distinguish the time sequence of the facts of the case from the time sequence of a court's actions, both of which occurred in the past.

Note that the past perfect tense is formed by adding "had" before the past participle.

EXAMPLE 9   **Past Perfect Tense**

The court <u>noted</u> that the defendant <u>had known</u> about the defective brakes for three months.

Time line: _____ x _____ x _____ X _____
                           had   *noted*
                           known   *(simple*   *(present)*
                           (past   *past)*
                           perfect)

The past perfect tense is also useful when discussing court proceedings at different levels. For example, a writer may use the simple past tense to describe the decisions of an appellate court and the past perfect to describe the decisions of the trial court.

EXAMPLE 10   **Past Perfect Tense**

The Court of Appeals <u>affirmed</u> the trial court, which <u>had ruled</u> that the statute did not apply.
                    (simple past)   *(past perfect)*

The future perfect tense is used when an action that started in the past ends at a certain time in the future. It is formed by adding "will have" before the past participle.

EXAMPLE 11   **Future Perfect Tense**

By the time you finish dinner tonight, drunk drivers <u>will have claimed</u> five more victims on United States highways.

Time line: _____ X _____ x _____
           ——>
                                    will have
                                     claimed

Every verb can also be progressive, that is, it can show continuing action by adding "-ing."

Present progressive: is claiming
Past progressive: was claiming
Future progressive: will be claiming
Present perfect progressive: has been claiming
Past perfect progressive: had been claiming
Future perfect progressive: will have been claiming

One last word about verb tense: One common myth is that writers have to maintain a consistent verb tense. Although writers should avoid needless shifts in verb tense, shifts in verb tense are required when there is a shift in time. Such a shift in time may even occur within the same sentence.

EXAMPLE 12   **Acceptable Shifts in Verb Tense**

Her landlord <u>knows</u> that she <u>will be</u> unable to pay her rent.
          (present)   *(future)*

Although Mr. Henderson <u>built</u> the shed on the property in 2002, he <u>admits</u> that
                      (past)   *(present)*
Ms. Kyte <u>has owned</u> that corner since 1989.
        (present perfect)

Smith <u>will argue</u> that he <u>did</u> not knowingly or willingly <u>consent</u> to a search of his wallet.
     (future)   *(past)*   *(past)*

§ 27.3.2 Mood

In grammar, the term "mood" refers to the approach the writer gives the verb. English has three moods: indicative, imperative, and subjunctive. The indicative mood is used for statements of facts or questions.

EXAMPLE 13   **Indicative Mood**

The defendant <u>pleaded</u> "not guilty."

The imperative mood is used for sentences that are orders or commands. The subject of a sentence in the imperative mood is understood to be "you," the reader or listener.

EXAMPLE 14   **Imperative Mood**

<u>Plead</u> "not guilty."

The subjunctive mood is the only mood that is a bit tricky. Although grammarians are constantly discussing its demise, the subjunctive mood is still used in a variety of situations.

1. The subjunctive is used to express ideas contrary to fact.

EXAMPLE 15   **Subjunctive Mood**

If I <u>were</u> the defendant, I would plead "not guilty."

---

2. The subjunctive is used to express a requirement.

EXAMPLE 16   **Subjunctive Mood for a Requirement**

The law requires that contracts <u>be signed</u> willingly, not under duress.

---

3. The subjunctive is used to express a suggestion or recommendation.

EXAMPLE 17   **Subjunctive Mood for a Recommendation**

His attorney recommended that he <u>be allowed</u> to give his own closing argument.

---

4. The subjunctive is used to express a wish.

EXAMPLE 18   **Subjunctive Mood for a Request**

The clerk asked that the check <u>be postdated</u>.

Note that the contrary-to-fact clauses begin with "if"; the requirement, suggestion, recommendation, or wish clauses all begin with an expressed or elliptical "that."

The subjunctive mood is formed slightly differently depending on how it is used. For present conditions that are contrary to fact, it is formed from the past tense of the verb. For the verb "to be," it uses "were."

EXAMPLE 19   **Forming the Subjunctive**

If the government inspector <u>took</u> a reading on the toxic particles being emitted right now, it would show that the factory has completely disregarded EPA guidelines.

If she <u>were</u> to testify, the defendant's sister would corroborate his story.

For past conditions that are contrary to fact, the subjunctive mood is formed from the past perfect.

EXAMPLE 20   **Forming the Subjunctive**

<u>Had</u> the contract been signed, there would be no question that it is valid.

For requirements, recommendations, and suggestions, the subjunctive mood is formed from the infinitive form of the verb without the "to."

EXAMPLE 21   **Forming the Subjunctive**

The law requires that the adverse possessor <u>prove</u> that the possession was open and notorious.

Chapter 27 Quiz No. 2

Draft answers for each of the following questions. Make your points clearly and concisely, and write sentences that are easy to read and that are grammatical and correctly punctuated.

1. What is meant by "tense" in verb tense?
2. What are the three main verb tenses in English, and which of these tenses is primarily used when discussing past cases in legal writing?
3. What is a "perfect" tense used for, and what are the perfect tenses in English?
4. What does the progressive tense show about the time of the verb, and what is the ending that indicates progressive tense?
5. What are the three moods in English verbs?

§ 27.4   Agreement

Simply put, agreement is matching the form of one word to another. In legal writing, agreement can be a problem in two areas: (1) the agreement in number between a subject and verb and (2) the agreement in number between a pronoun and its antecedent.

§ 27.4.1 Subject-Verb Agreement

Singular subjects take singular verbs, and plural subjects take plural verbs. For most native speakers of English, this kind of subject–verb agreement comes almost as naturally as breathing, as long as the sentence is short and simple.

EXAMPLE 1   Subject-Verb Agreement

The law requires that all drivers wear seat belts.

singular subject = law
singular verb = requires

The immigration laws require that all workers provide proof of citizenship before starting a job.

plural subject = laws
plural verb = require

In English, we often think that adding "s" makes the plural form of words. This is true for nouns but not for verbs. We add an "s" to the singular form of present tense verbs (except the verb "to be") when they are matched with a singular noun or the pronouns "he," "she," or "it." For example, we say "a client maintains," "he rejects," "she alleges," or "it confirms."

In simple sentences, a writer can usually make subjects and verbs agree by listening to the way the sentences sound. The writer's ear tells him or her what matches and what doesn't. In longer, more complicated sentences, like those that often occur in legal writing, the ear is more likely to be misled. The following rules cover those situations.

Rule 1   A Subject and Its Verb Must Agree Even When They Are Separated by Other Words

---

When other words, particularly nouns, come between a subject and its verb, the writer may inadvertently match the verb to a word other than the subject.

EXAMPLE 2   Incorrect Agreement

Custom-made towels imprinted with the hotel's logo satisfies the requirement that the goods
          (subject)   (verb)
be specially manufactured.

The writer has mistakenly chosen the singular verb "satisfies" to match with the intervening noun "logo" when the verb should be the plural form "satisfy" to agree with the plural subject "towels." One way writers can check for this kind of agreement error is to read their subjects and verbs together without the intervening words. "Towels satisfy" will sound right to native speakers.

The number of the subject is not changed by adding intervening words that begin with expressions such as "accompanied by," "as well as," "in addition to," "with," "together with," or "along with." These expressions are considered prepositions and not coordinating conjunctions (see section 27.1), so they modify the subject. They do not change its number.

EXAMPLE 3   **Correct agreement**

The defendant's <u>statement</u> to the police, as well as her testimony at trial, <u>suggests</u> that her actions were premeditated.

Rule 2   Two or More Subjects Joined by "And" Usually Take a Plural Verb

Subjects joined by "and" are plural. This rule does not change even if one or all of the subjects are singular.

EXAMPLE 4   **Correct Agreement**

North Star Cinema and Highland Heights Theater question the validity of the admissions tax.

Unfortunately, writers sometimes hear only the second half of the subject with the verb and mistakenly select a singular verb ("Highland Heights Theater question<u>s</u>"). You may find it easier to mentally substitute the word "they" for plural subjects when using your hearing to find the correct form of the verb ("they question").

Exception

Occasionally two or more parts of the subject make up one idea or refer to one person or thing. In such cases, use a singular verb.

EXAMPLE 5   **Correct Agreement**

His wife and beneficiary was the only person mentioned in the will.

Rule 3   Subjects Joined by "Or" or "Nor" Take Verbs That Agree with the Part of the Subject Closest to the Verb

To check subject-verb agreement in sentences with subjects joined by "or" or "nor," simply read only the second half of the subject with the verb and let your ear help you select the correct verb form. In the following examples, read "Lazar Television is" and "her older sisters have."

EXAMPLE 6   **Correct Agreement**

Neither Horizon Telecommunications nor Lazar Television is the type of enterprise that the bulk sales statutes seek to regulate.

The child's mother or her older sisters have been caring for her after school.

In a verb phrase such as "have been caring" in the preceding example, the helping, or auxiliary, verbs are the ones that change.

singular: has been caring
plural: have been caring

Rule 4   **Most Indefinite Pronouns Take Singular Verbs**

Indefinite pronouns are ones that do not refer to any definite person or thing, or they do not specify definite limits. The following is a list of the most common indefinite pronouns:

all	each	everything	none
any	either	neither	somebody
anybody	everybody	nobody	someone
anyone	everyone	no one	something

Usually these pronouns refer to a single, indefinite person or thing, so they take singular verbs.

EXAMPLE 7   **Indefinite Pronoun with Singular Verb**

Everyone who ate in the restaurant is suffering the same symptoms.

A few indefinite pronouns — "none," "all," "most," "some," "any," and "half" — may take either a singular or a plural verb depending on the noun to which they refer.

EXAMPLE 8   **Correct Agreement**

All of the jewelry was recovered.

All of the rings were recovered.

| **Rule 5** | **Collective Nouns Take Singular Verbs When the Group Acts as One Unit; Collective Nouns Take Plural Verbs When the Members of the Group Act Separately** |

Although it may seem like a jury is a group of individuals, a jury acts as one unit. Therefore, "jury" is singular. Similarly, when a court acts, it acts as one unit, so "court" also requires a singular verb. The following is a list of the most common collective nouns in legal writing:

jury	committee	board
audience	team	majority
family	crowd	number
Supreme Court	appellate court	fractions (when
names of companies/		used as nouns)
corporations		

The following examples all use collective nouns that are acting as one unit, so the verbs are singular.

| EXAMPLE 9 | **Collective Nouns with Singular Verbs** |

The jury has reached its verdict.

The appellate court has affirmed the conviction.

Boeing is concerned about its liability.

| **Rule 6** | **Linking Verbs Agree with Their Subjects, Not Their Subject Complements** |

In the following example, the linking verb "was" agrees with "testimony," not the subject complement "contradictory and intentionally misleading."

| EXAMPLE 10 | **Correct Agreement** |

The defendant's testimony was contradictory and intentionally misleading.

In the next example, the linking verb "was" agrees with "reason," not "evaluations."

| EXAMPLE 11 | **Correct Agreement** |

The reason for firing Jones was his low evaluations.

Rule 7	Verbs Agree with Their Subjects Even When the Subjects Come After the Verb

Subjects follow verbs after expletive constructions such as "there is" and "there are."

EXAMPLE 12	Correct Agreement

There is a possibility that the defendant will plead "temporary insanity."

There are several options for ensuring that your loan is repaid.

Subjects may also follow verbs when normal word order is changed for emphasis.

EXAMPLE 13	Correct Agreement

At no time was Brown aware that his conversations were being tape recorded.

At no time were Brown and Smith aware that their conversations were being tape recorded.

Rule 8	The Title of a Work or a Word Used as a Word Takes a Singular Verb

EXAMPLE 14	Title Takes Singular Verb

Tactics in Legal Reasoning is an excellent resource for both law students and practitioners.

When a word is used as a word, it is often enclosed in quotation marks or preceded by "the word."

EXAMPLE 15	"Word" Takes Singular Verb

"Premises" has at least three different meanings: (1) the introductory propositions to a syllogism, (2) the area of land surrounding a building, or (3) a building or part of a building.

The word "premises" has three different meanings.

Compare the two previous examples, both of which used the singular verb "has," with the following example, which requires the plural verb form "have."

EXAMPLE 16	Correct Agreement

The premises have been searched by the police.

Rule 9	**Money, Distance, and Measurement Subjects Usually Take Singular Verbs**

EXAMPLE 17	**Correct Agreement**

Twenty thousand dollars is a reasonable fee for a case of this complexity.

---

§ 27.4.2 Pronoun-Antecedent Agreement

A pronoun must agree with its antecedent. The noun a pronoun refers to is known as its antecedent.

Pronouns are substitutes for nouns. They have no independent meanings. Consequently, they must refer to a noun and be consistent with that noun in gender, person, and number.

Legal writers usually do not have problems making their pronouns and antecedents agree in gender or person. Agreement in number, however, can be a bit more difficult.

Rule 1	**Singular Antecedents Require Singular Pronouns; Plural Antecedents Require Plural Pronouns**

EXAMPLE 18	**Correct Pronoun Agreement**

<u>William MacDonald</u> may claim that <u>his</u> constitutional rights were violated.
  (antecedent)   *(pronoun)*

<u>William MacDonald</u> and <u>Grace Yessler</u> may claim that <u>their</u> constitutional rights were violated.
  (antecedent)   *(antecedent)*   *(pronoun)*

This rule, although simple on the surface, becomes a little trickier when the pronoun substitutes for a generic noun that is singular. Because English does not have a singular generic pronoun to fit these situations, writers are left with less-than-ideal choices.

For example, in informal writing and oral language, you may frequently see or hear a plural pronoun used as a substitute for a singular generic noun, as in the ungrammatical example below. In formal writing, such as legal writing, this practice is unacceptable.

EXAMPLE 19	**Ungrammatical**

The <u>defendant</u> may claim that <u>their</u> constitutional rights were violated.
  (antecedent)   *(pronoun)*

Some writers try to solve the problem by resorting to the traditional masculine pronoun for all generic nouns. This practice is unacceptable to many modern writers who believe that language should be gender-neutral. (See section 25.4.)

EXAMPLE 20   **Masculine Pronoun**

The <u>defendant</u> may claim that <u>his</u> constitutional rights were violated.
  (antecedent)   *(pronoun)*

Occasionally, the problem can be solved by making the generic noun plural. Unfortunately, not all sentences will allow this quick fix.

EXAMPLE 21   **Plural Noun**

<u>Defendants</u> may claim that <u>their</u> constitutional rights were violated.
(antecedent)   *(pronoun)*

Even fewer sentences will allow a writer to remove the pronoun altogether without substantial revision or loss in meaning.

EXAMPLE 22   **Removed Pronoun**

A defendant may claim that constitutional rights were violated.

The example above avoids the grammatical problem but with a significant loss in meaning: The belief that one actually possesses constitutional rights is no longer included in the sentence's meaning.

What is left, then, is the option of using the slightly awkward "he or she," "his or her," "himself or herself."

EXAMPLE 23   **"His or Her" Option**

The <u>defendant</u> may claim that <u>his or her</u> constitutional rights were violated.
  (antecedent)   *(pronouns)*

While not perfect, this option seems to be the best choice, provided the writer doesn't put more than one "he or she," "his or her," or "himself or herself" in a sentence.

Exception to Rule 1

Occasionally the word "each" or "every" precedes one or more of the parts of a plural antecedent. In such cases, use a singular pronoun.

EXAMPLE 24   **Correct Pronoun Agreement**

Every girl and woman in the community feared for her safety.

Rule 2	When a Pronoun Refers to Two or More Antecedents Joined by "Or" or "Nor," the Pronoun Agrees with the Nearer Antecedent

EXAMPLE 25   Correct Pronoun Agreement

Either <u>David Wilson</u> or <u>Donald Wilson</u> left <u>his</u> keys in the car.
    (antecedent)   *(antecedent)*   *(pronoun)*

When a singular and a plural antecedent are joined by "or" or "nor," place the plural antecedent last so that the pronoun can be plural.

EXAMPLE 26   Correct Pronoun Agreement

Neither the <u>defendant</u> nor his <u>brothers</u> admit knowing where <u>their</u> neighbors keep items of value.

Rule 3	When an Indefinite Pronoun Is the Antecedent, Use the Singular Pronoun

Indefinite pronouns are ones that do not refer to any definite person or thing, or they do not specify definite limits. The most common indefinite pronouns are "all," "any," "anybody," "anyone," "each," "either," "everybody," "everyone," "everything," "neither," "nobody," "no one," "none," "somebody," "someone," and "something."

EXAMPLE 27   Example 27   Correct Pronoun Agreement

<u>Anyone</u> would have noticed that <u>his</u> or <u>her</u> license plate had been removed.

As with Rule 1, writers must take care not to use the informal and ungrammatical plural pronoun or the generic "he" as a pronoun substitute for an indefinite pronoun.

EXAMPLE 28   Correcting Pronoun Agreement

Ungrammatical

<u>Somebody</u> must have used <u>their</u> cell phone to call the police.

Masculine pronoun

<u>Somebody</u> must have used <u>his</u> cell phone to call the police.

Corrected

> Somebody must have used his or her cell phone to call the police.

OR

> Somebody must have used a cell phone to call the police.

Rule 4	When a Collective Noun Is the Antecedent, Use a Singular Pronoun When You Are Referring to the Group as One Unit and a Plural Pronoun When You Are Referring to the Individual Members of the Group

Some common collective nouns are "jury," "committee," "appellate court," "Supreme Court," "majority," "board," "team," "family," "audience," "crowd," "number," and the names of companies and corporations.

EXAMPLE 29   **Singular Collective Nouns**

> The jury must not be misled about Jason Richardson's credibility when it is considering his testimony.

> Shopping Haven discriminated against John Adams when it failed to issue him a new credit card for an existing account.

---

§ 27.5   Pronoun Reference

Pronouns are substitutes for nouns. Consequently, pronouns usually[3] refer back to a noun, and that noun is known as the antecedent.

EXAMPLE 1   **Pronoun and Its Antecedent**

> Marino moved for reconsideration, but her motion was denied.
> *(antecedent)*   *(pronoun)*

Legal writers tend to have two kinds of problems with pronouns and their antecedents: (1) they use plural pronouns to refer back to singular antecedents; and (2) they use pronouns that have unclear or ambiguous antecedents. The first problem is one of grammatical agreement, as discussed in the second half of section 27.4. The second problem is the focus of this section.

---

3. Indefinite pronouns such as "someone," "anybody," "everything," and "neither" do not refer back to nouns. Also, some pronouns that are parts of idioms ("it is likely that . . ." "it is clear that . . ." "it is raining") do not have antecedents.

§ 27.5.1   Each Pronoun Should Clearly Refer Back to Its Antecedent

Consider the following sentence:

EXAMPLE 2   **Ambiguous Pronoun**

Officer Robert O'Malley, who arrested Howard Davis, said that he was drunk at the time.

As it stands, the sentence has two possible readings because the pronoun "he" has two possible antecedents: Officer Robert O'Malley and Howard Davis. To clear up the ambiguity, do one of two things:

1. Repeat the noun rather than use a pronoun, or
2. Revise so that the pronoun is no longer ambiguous.

EXAMPLE 3   **Possible Revisions**

Officer Robert O'Malley, who arrested Howard Davis, said that Davis was drunk at the time.

Howard Davis was drunk when he was arrested by Officer O'Malley.

Officer O'Malley was drunk when he arrested Howard Davis.

According to the arresting officer, Robert O'Malley, Howard Davis was drunk at the time of the arrest.

Officer Robert O'Malley, who arrested Howard Davis, admitted being drunk at the time of the arrest.

---

§ 27.5.2   Avoid the Use of "It," "This," "That," "Such," and "Which" to Refer Broadly to a General Idea in a Preceding Sentence

Consider the following sentences:

EXAMPLE 4   **Incorrect Pronoun**

Even if Mr. Huang's testimony about possible embarrassment caused by Acme is adequate to justify a damage award, emotional harm is difficult to quantify. This makes it unlikely that Mr. Huang will receive any substantial recovery.

To what does "this" in the second sentence refer? Because "this" does not seem to refer back to any specific noun in the preceding sentence, the reader is left to guess exactly how much or how little of the preceding discussion "this" is supposed to encompass.

The solution to many broad pronoun reference problems is often a rather simple one: Add a summarizing noun after the pronoun to show the limits of the reference.

EXAMPLE 5	Corrected

<u>This difficulty</u> makes it unlikely that Mr. Huang will receive any substantial recovery.

The same technique often works well with "that" and "such."

EXAMPLE 6	Correcting Broad Pronoun

Mrs. Marquette has testified that Mr. Marquette has beaten her and their children on at least three occasions, that he has locked them out of their home twice, and that he has threatened to "cut their throats" if they told anyone. According to Mr. Marquette, that is a lie.

Corrected

Mrs. Marquette has testified that Mr. Marquette has beaten her and their children on at least three occasions, that he has locked them out of their home twice, and that he has threatened to "cut their throats" if they told anyone. According to Mr. Marquette, <u>that testimony</u> is a lie.

The use of the pronoun "which" to refer broadly to a preceding idea is a trickier problem to correct. Look at the following example and see if you can determine what the "which" stands for. Keep in mind the basic rule that a pronoun is a substitute for a noun.

EXAMPLE 7	Incorrect Pronoun

In *Boone v. Mullendore*, Dr. Mullendore failed to remove Mrs. Boone's fallopian tube, which resulted in the birth of a baby.

The only nouns that "which" could possibly refer to are the case name, "Dr. Mullendore," and "fallopian tube." Obviously none of these nouns resulted in the birth of a baby. Instead, the writer seems to suggest that "which" is a substitute for the following idea: Dr. Mullendore's failure to remove Mrs. Boone's fallopian tube. Notice that in expressing what the "which" referred to, we had to use the noun "failure" rather than the verb "failed." To correct the error, then, we must add the noun "failure" to the sentence.

EXAMPLE 8	Corrected

In *Bonne v. Mullendore*, Dr. Mullendore's failure to remove Mrs. Boone's fallopian tube resulted in the birth of a baby.

Be sure to distinguish between the incorrect use of "which" to refer broadly to a previously stated idea and the correct use of "which" to introduce nonrestrictive clauses. (See section 28.1.1, Rule 4.)

§ 27.5.3 Pronouns Should Refer Back to Nouns, Not Adjectives

Occasionally a word that appears to be a noun is actually an adjective because it modifies a noun.

EXAMPLE 9   **Adjective That Looks Like a Noun**

the <u>Rheams</u> <u>building</u>
   (adjective) (noun)

Often the possessive form of a noun is used as an adjective in a sentence.

EXAMPLE 10   **Adjective That Looks Like a Noun**

the <u>defendant's</u> <u>alibi</u>
   (adjective) (noun)

But because a pronoun must always refer to a noun, adjectives that are noun look-alikes cannot serve as antecedents for pronouns.

EXAMPLE 11   **Adjective That Looks Like a Noun**

Incorrect

The Rheams building has undergone as many facelifts as he has.

Corrected

The Rheams building has undergone as many facelifts as Rheams himself has.

Incorrect

After hearing the defendant's alibi, the jurors seemed to change their opinion of him.

Corrected

The jurors seemed to change their opinion of the defendant after they heard his alibi.

Admittedly, this rule is a grammatical technicality. Infractions rarely create ambiguity. Even so, because correctness and precision are required in legal writing, it is best to heed the rule.

Chapter 27 Quiz No. 3

Draft answers for each of the following questions. Make your points clearly and concisely, and write sentences that are easy to read and that are grammatical and correctly punctuated.

1. What is "agreement" in English sentences, and what are the two areas in which writers must have agreement?
2. When two or more subjects are joined by "and," what part of the subject must the verb agree with?
3. When two or more subjects are joined by "or," what part of the subject must the verb agree with?
4. Does a collective noun like "court" or "jury" take a singular or plural verb?
5. What is an "antecedent"?
6. It is grammatically incorrect to use a plural pronoun with a singular generic noun such as "defendant." What are some of the ways in which a writer can correct this error?
7. When two or more antecedents are joined by "or" or "nor," what part of the antecedent must the pronoun agree with?
8. Does a collective noun like "court" or "jury" use a singular or plural pronoun?
9. What are some ways to correct an error created by a pronoun's ambiguous antecedent?
10. What are some ways for correcting a broad pronoun reference error?

§ 27.6   Modifiers

Using modifiers correctly is simple. All one has to do is (1) remember to keep modifiers close to the word or words they modify and (2) make sure the words they modify are in the same sentence as the modifiers.

§ 27.6.1 Misplaced Modifiers

Forgetting to keep modifiers close to the word or words they modify leads to misplaced modifiers. Some words — "almost," "also," "even," "ever," "exactly," "hardly," "just," "merely," "nearly," "not," "only," "scarcely," "simply" — are particularly prone to being misplaced. Place these words immediately before the words they modify.

Notice, for example, how the placement of "only" changes the meaning in the following sentences.

EXAMPLE 1   **Placement of "Only" Changes Meaning**

<u>Only</u> the defendant thought that the car was rented.
No one but the defendant thought that.

The defendant <u>only</u> thought that the car was rented.
He did not know for sure.

The defendant thought <u>only</u> that the car was rented.
He thought one thing, nothing else.

The defendant thought that the <u>only</u> car was rented.
Only one car was available, and it was rented.

The defendant thought that the car was <u>only</u> rented.
He did not think it was leased or sold.

In speech, such single-word modifiers are often put before the verb even when the speaker does not intend them to modify the verb. Some authorities accept placing "only" immediately before the verb if it modifies the whole sentence.

> Speech: He only drove ten miles.
> Writing: He drove only ten miles.

Phrases, particularly prepositional phrases, can also be easily misplaced in sentences. The result can be imprecise writing, an awkward construction, and unintentional humor.

The writer of the following example was surprised to find out that because of a misplaced modifier he had inaccurately placed the brother instead of the cabin in New Hampshire.

EXAMPLE 2   **Misplaced Modifier**

The defendant owned a cabin with his brother in New Hampshire.

Corrected

The defendant and his brother owned a cabin in New Hampshire.

The misplaced modifier in the following example gave the writer a meaning she never intended.

EXAMPLE 3   **Misplaced Modifier**

The witness to the events may be unavailable after the accident.

Although there are contexts in which this sentence is correctly written, the writer intended to say, "The witness to the events after the accident may be unavailable." Her version makes it sound like an intentional "accident" was being planned for the specific purpose of making the witness "unavailable"!

Take care to place clauses that begin with "who," "which," and "that" immediately after the noun they modify.

EXAMPLE 4   **Misplaced Modifier**

The victim described her attacker as having a tattoo on his right buttock, which was shaped like a peace sign.

This sentence suggests that the attacker's right buttock, not his tattoo, was shaped like a peace sign.

EXAMPLE 5   **Corrected**

The victim described her attacker as having a tattoo that was shaped like a peace sign on his right buttock.

---

§ 27.6.2 Dangling Modifiers

Dangling modifiers are those modifiers that do not have a noun in the sentence that they can modify; hence, they are "dangling," or unattached to an appropriate noun. Legal writers tend to write dangling modifiers for one of two reasons: (1) the noun or pronoun the modifier is intended to modify is in the mind of the writer but inadvertently omitted from the sentence; or (2) the writer wanted to avoid the first person pronouns "I" or "we"[4] and, in doing so, left a modifier dangling.

EXAMPLE 6   **Dangling Modifier**

By calling attention to the defendant's post-arrest silence, the jury was allowed to make prejudicial and false inferences.

In the example above, the modifier "by calling attention to the defendant's post-arrest silence" should modify the noun "the prosecutor," which does not appear in the sentence. Unfortunately, it seems to be modifying the noun closest to it: "the jury."

EXAMPLE 7   **Corrected**

By calling attention to the defendant's post-arrest silence, the prosecutor encouraged the jury to make prejudicial and false inferences.

Notice how in the following example the dangling modifier can be corrected by including the pronoun it modifies, "we," or by revising the sentence so that the dangling modifier is no longer a modifier.

EXAMPLE 8   **Dangling Modifier**

Draft

In deciding whether to argue self-defense, more than the technical merits of the case have to be considered.

---

4. Many authorities in legal writing still advise legal writers to avoid using first-person references.

Corrected

In deciding whether to argue self-defense, we must consider more than the technical merits of the case. *OR*

A decision about whether to argue self-defense must be based on more than the technical merits of the case.

You can see that the majority of dangling modifiers occur at the beginnings of sentences. One way to avoid writing this type of dangling modifier is to remember to place the noun the modifier modifies right after the comma separating the modifier from the main clause.

Modifier,   Main Clause   .
(noun)
By calling attention . . . silence, the prosecutor . . . .

If you are having difficulty deciding what noun the modifier should modify, ask yourself who or what is doing the action described in that modifier. Then place the answer to that question right after the comma separating the modifier from the main clause.

In deciding . . . self-defense, we must consider . . . .

Some dangling modifiers can also be corrected by adding a subject to the modifier.

EXAMPLE 9   **Dangling Modifier**

Draft

While petitioning for a permit, zoning regulations in the area were changed.

Corrected

While the mental institution was petitioning for a permit, zoning regulations in the area were changed.

Subordinate clauses, such as the one in the revision above, are not dangling modifiers.

Dangling modifiers can also occur at the ends of sentences. Again, the problem is that the noun the modifier modifies does not appear in the sentence.

EXAMPLE 10   **Dangling Modifier**

This motion was denied in the interest of judicial economy, reasoning that there was evidence that raised a question regarding Anderson's knowledge of the relationship.

Who or what is doing the reasoning that there was evidence? Most certainly the court, but the noun "court" does not appear in the sentence.

EXAMPLE 11   **Corrected**

Reasoning that there was evidence that raised a question regarding Anderson's knowledge of the relationship, the court denied this motion in the interest of judicial economy.

It is also permissible to leave the modifier at the end of the sentence, as long as it modifies the subject of the sentence.

EXAMPLE 12   **Corrected**

The court denied this motion in the interest of judicial economy, reasoning that there was evidence that raised a question regarding Anderson's knowledge of the relationship.

---

§ 27.6.3 Squinting Modifiers

Squinting modifiers are labeled as such because they appear to be modifying both the word that precedes them and the word that follows them.

EXAMPLE 13   **Ambiguous Squinting Modifier**

The bridge inspection that was done frequently suggested that the drawbridge's electrical system was beginning to fail.

This sentence has two possible interpretations: Are the inspections themselves done frequently, or are there frequent suggestions throughout the inspection report?

EXAMPLE 14   **Corrected**

The bridge inspection that was frequently done suggested that the drawbridge's electrical system was beginning to fail. *OR*

The bridge inspection that was done suggested frequently that the drawbridge's electrical system was beginning to fail.

---

§ 27.7 Parallelism

Consider the following pairs of sentences. What is it about version B of each pair that makes it easier to read?

| **EXAMPLE 1** | **Correcting Errors in Parallelism** |

1A. The defendant claims that on the day of the murder he was at home alone washing his car, he mowed his lawn, and his dog needed a bath so he gave him one.

1B. The defendant claims that on the day of the murder he was at home alone washing his car, mowing his lawn, and bathing his dog.

2A. Dr. Stewart is a competent surgeon with over twenty years of experience and who is respected in the local medical community.

2B. Dr. Stewart is a competent surgeon who has over twenty years of experience and who is respected in the local medical community.

3A. The defendant claimed the evidence was prejudicial and that it lacked relevance.

3B. The defendant claimed the evidence was prejudicial and irrelevant.

In all the preceding pairs, the version A sentences lack parallelism and, as a result, are grammatically incorrect, as well as clumsy. The version B sentences do not change the content significantly; they simply use the structure of the sentence to make that content more apparent and more accessible. Specifically, they use parallelism.

In grammar, parallelism is defined as "the use of similar grammatical form for coordinated elements." This definition may seem overly abstract or vague until it is broken into its components.

"Coordinated elements" are parts of a sentence joined by conjunctions, such as "and," "but," "or," "nor," and "yet." Sometimes they are pairs, but often they are a series or a list.

"Similar grammatical form" simply means that a noun is matched with other nouns, verbs are matched with other verbs, prepositional phrases are matched with other prepositional phrases, and so on.

For example, look at the poorly coordinated elements in sentence 1A above.

washing his car,
he mowed his lawn, and
his dog needed a bath so he gave him one

Even without analyzing exactly what kind of phrase or clause each one of these elements is, we can see that they do not have similar grammatical form. Now look at the coordinated elements of sentence 1B. Note how the "ing" endings make the items parallel.

washing his car
mowing his lawn, and
bathing his dog

Matching endings of the first key word in each of the elements is one way to make elements parallel.

Now compare the coordinated elements in 2A and 2B.

2A. with over twenty years of experience and
     who is respected in the local medical community

2B. who has over twenty years of experience and
     who is respected in the local medical community

Again, without doing an analysis of the grammar of each element, we can see, or perhaps hear, that 2B is parallel, but this time the parallelism is signaled by using the same word, "who," to introduce each element.

In some cases, however, you will not be able to rely on matching endings to key words or matching introductory words; you will have to find the same grammatical form in order to make the elements parallel.

In 3A, for example, the writer has tried to match an adjective, "prejudicial," with a relative clause, "that it lacked relevance." The writer could have used the second tip — matching introductory words — and created the following parallel elements:

> that the evidence was prejudicial and
> that it lacked relevance

The more concise and better choice is to find the appropriate adjective to match "prejudicial."

> prejudicial and
> irrelevant

Because many sentences in legal writing are long and complicated, parallelism is critical for keeping the content and its presentation manageable. In the following sentence, for example, the defendant's two concessions are easier for the reader to see because they are set out using parallel constructions.

EXAMPLE 2   **Parallelism in Long Sentences**

Counsel for the defendant conceded that she did assault Coachman and that a trial would determine only the degree of the assault.

Notice too in both the preceding and subsequent examples that by repeating the introductory word "that," the writer has made the parallelism more obvious, which, in turn, makes the sentence easier to read.

EXAMPLE 3   **Repeating Introductory "That"**

When questioned at the parole hearing, Robinson claimed that it was wrong to tell only one side of the story, that he had not received permission but felt he had a right to write what he wanted, and that people had a right to hear the other side of the story.

Writing parallel elements is required for grammatical sentences; repeating an introductory word to heighten the parallelism is not required, but rather recommended for making the parallelism more obvious to the reader.

Issue statements can also become much more manageable when the legally significant facts are laid out using parallel construction. The following example uses "when" as the introductory word to each element. Notice too how the legally significant facts are not only written using parallel construction but also grouped according to those that favor the defendant and those that favor the plaintiff. The conjunction "but" helps the reader see the two groupings.

| EXAMPLE 4 | Parallelism in Issue Statements |

Under Federal Rule of Civil Procedure 4(d)(1), is service of process valid when process was left with defendant's husband at his home in California, when defendant and her husband maintain separate residences, when defendant intends to maintain a separate residence from her husband, but when defendant regularly visits her husband in California, when defendant keeps some personal belongings in the California house, when defendant receives some mail in California, and when defendant received actual notice when her husband mailed the summons and complaint to her?

when process was left with defendant's husband at his home in
    California
when defendant and her husband maintain separate residences
when defendant intends to maintain separate residence from her husband,
    BUT
when defendant regularly visits her husband in California
when the defendant keeps some personal belongings in the California
    house
when defendant receives some mail in California
when defendant received actual notice when her husband mailed the
    summons and complaint to her

Parallelism is also required when setting out lists.

| EXAMPLE 5 | Parallelism in Lists |

Wilson challenges the admission of three photographs, which he claims are gruesome: (1) the photograph of Melissa Reed as she appeared when discovered at the crime scene; (2) the photograph of Melinda Reed as she appeared when discovered at the crime scene; and (3) a photograph of Wilson wearing dental retractors to hold his lips back while exposing his teeth.

Lists require parallelism when they are incorporated into the writer's text, as in the example above, and when they are indented and tabulated, as in the example below.

| EXAMPLE 6 | Example 6   Parallelism in Lists |

The school district will probably be liable for the following:

1. the cost of restoring the Archers' rose bushes, as well as the lost use value of their property during restoration;
2. the cost of replacing Mr. Baker's windows and the market value of his vase; and
3. compensation to the Carlisles for the annoyance and inconvenience they have experienced.

To create parallelism, match the *key* words in each element; the parallelism is not destroyed if all the modifying words and phrases do not match exactly.

In the following examples, the key words "received" and "released" match, and the key words "for . . . harm" and "for . . . expenses" match.

EXAMPLE 7	Matching Key Words to Create Parallelism

In *Pepper*, the injured plaintiff <u>received</u> medical treatment and <u>released</u> the defendant from liability.

The Bells are seeking damages <u>for severe emotional and financial harm</u> and <u>for substantial medical expenses related to the pregnancy</u>.

Parallelism is also required for elements joined by correlative conjunctions, which are conjunctions that come in pairs. The most common correlative conjunctions are "either . . . or," "neither . . . nor," "not only . . . but also," "both . . . and," "whether . . . or," and "as . . . as."

To make the elements joined by one of these pairs parallel, simply match what follows the first half with what follows the second half.

either _____	either <u>similar</u>
or _____	or <u>identical</u>

EXAMPLE 8	Parallelism Required with "Either/Or"

Campbell's prior convictions are either similar or identical.

neither _____	neither <u>the photographs</u>
nor _____	nor <u>the testimony</u>

EXAMPLE 9	Parallelism Required with "Neither/Nor"

Neither the photographs nor the testimony can prove who actually committed the alleged assault.

not only _____	not only <u>verbally</u>
but also _____	but also <u>physically</u>

EXAMPLE 10	Parallelism Required with "Not Only/ But Also"

The defendant admits that she not only verbally but also physically abused her children.

Take care when using these pairs. All too frequently legal writers lose the parallelism in their sentences by misplacing one of the words in these pairs.

EXAMPLE 11	Lack of Parallelism

The purpose of the rule is to ensure that actual notice is provided either by personal or constructive service.

either _____   either <u>by personal</u>

or _____   or <u>constructive</u>

Note that "by personal" is not parallel with "constructive."

EXAMPLE 12   **Corrected**

The purpose of the rule is to ensure that actual notice is provided either by personal or by constructive service. *OR*

The purpose of the rule is to ensure that actual notice is provided by either personal or constructive service.

Parallelism is also required when elements are compared or contrasted. Many of the comparing and contrasting expressions use "than." Notice in each of the following pairs where the blanks are for the parallel elements.

more _____ than _____

less _____ than _____

_____ rather than _____

EXAMPLE 13   **Parallelism Required for Comparing/ Contrasting Elements**

Wilson's attention was centered more <u>on the assailant's gun</u> than <u>on his face</u>.

The court applied <u>the "clearly erroneous" standard</u> rather than <u>the arbitrary and capricious standard</u>.

Chapter 27 Quiz No. 4

Draft answers for each of the following questions. Make your points clearly and concisely, and write sentences that are easy to read and that are grammatical and correctly punctuated.

1. What is the key to correcting misplaced modifiers?
2. What is a dangling modifier?
3. Many dangling modifiers are *-ing* verbals at the beginning of a sentence. What is a good way to correct such dangling modifiers?
4. What is parallelism?
5. Parallelism is required for correlative conjunctions. What are some examples of correlative conjunctions?

Punctuation

§ 28.1   The Comma

Commas are everywhere. They are the most frequently used punctuation mark and, unfortunately, the most frequently misused punctuation mark. They give most legal writers fits. Few writers seem to be able to control the little buzzards, and most seem to be more than a bit controlled by them. Many fairly good legal writers admit that they punctuate by feel, especially when it comes to commas. They rely on the "rule" that one should use a comma whenever the reader should pause — advice that works only about 70 percent of the time.

It is no wonder that few legal writers know and apply all the rules for commas. There are too many of them. In this section, we have no fewer than twelve rules, all designed to govern one little punctuation mark. Even so, these twelve rules don't cover every conceivable use of the comma, just the high spots.

The good news, however, is that not all of these rules are equally important. Some are critical; misapplication of these rules will either miscue the reader or change the meaning of a sentence as significantly as a misplaced decimal can change the meaning of a number. The critical rules are listed under the heading "Critical Commas: Those That Affect Meaning and Clarity."

The next section, "Basic Commas: Those That Educated Readers Expect," includes all the commonly known comma rules. Using these rules incorrectly probably will not affect meaning, but it may distract the reader and even cause him or her to wonder about the writer's professionalism.

There are other comma rules, though, that the average reader will not know, and he or she will not notice whether they are applied correctly. Still these rules are helpful to writers who not only care about writing correctly but also recognize that knowing the more esoteric comma rules allows them to add to their repertoire those sentence structures that require using these rules.

Finally, the last group of comma rules includes those situations in which commas are inserted unnecessarily. Please notice, too, that some of the last rules are marked with an asterisk (*). The asterisk indicates those few comma rules about which some authorities disagree. See Chart 28.1.

Exhibit 28.1	Overview of the Comma Rules

Critical Commas: Those That Affect Meaning and Clarity

Rule 1:   **Use a comma before a coordinating conjunction joining two main clauses.**

The prosecutor spoke about the defendant's motive, and the jury listened carefully.

Rule 2:   **Use a comma to set off long introductory phrases or clauses from the main clause.**

Using their overhead lights and sirens, the police followed the defendant out of the area.

Rule 3:   **Use a comma to prevent a possible misreading.**

At the time, the prosecution informed Jones that it would recommend a sentence of eighteen months.

Rule 4:   **Use a comma to set off nonrestrictive phrases or clauses.**

Officer Bates, acting as a decoy, remained outside on the sidewalk.

Basic Commas: Those That Educated Readers Expect

Rule 5:   **Set off nonrestrictive appositives with commas.**

A corrections officer called Diane Cummins, the defendant's girlfriend.

Rule 6:   **Set off nonrestrictive participial phrases with a comma or commas.**

The trial court denied the motion, finding that the seizure fell under the plain view doctrine.

Rule 7:   **Use a comma or commas to set off transitional or interrupting words and phrases.**

The trial court, however, imposed an exceptional sentence of thirty months.

Rule 8:   **Use commas according to convention with quotation marks.**

Corbin said, "I never saw the other car."

Rule 9:   **Use a comma or commas to set off phrases of contrast.**

Adams initially indicated that he, not Wilson, was involved in the robbery.

Rule 10:   **Use commas between items in a series.**

Wong had no money, identification, or jewelry.

Rule 11:   Use a comma between coordinate adjectives not joined by a conjunction.

The contract was written in concise, precise language.

Rule 12:   Use commas according to convention with dates, addresses, and names of geographical locations.

The land in Roswell, New Mexico, was surveyed on October 4, 2001, and purchased less than a month later.

<u>Esoteric Commas: Those That Are Required in Sophisticated Sentence Structures</u>

Rule 13:   Use commas to set off absolutes.

His career destroyed, Williams lapsed into a state of depression.

Rule 14:   Use a comma to indicate an omission of a word or words that can be understood from the context.

The first witness said the attacker was "hairy"; the second, bald.

Rule 15:   Use commas to set off expressions that introduce examples or explanations.

Collins testified that Adams had participated in the robbery and had fenced some of the items, namely, a camera, stereo, and silver.

<u>Unnecessary Commas: Those That Should Be Omitted</u>

Rule 16:   Do not use a comma to set off restrictive adverbial clauses that follow the main clause.
Complicity may be found if a defendant participates in the early stages of an activity that results in the attack on the victim.

Rule 17:   Do not use a comma to separate a subject from its verb or a verb from its object.

The idea that an individual can obtain another person's property through adverse possession is difficult for many people to accept.

Rule 18:   Do not use a comma to separate correlative pairs unless the correlatives introduce main clauses.

Neither the United States Supreme Court nor this Court has ever ruled that a defendant has a due process right to an instruction on lesser included offenses.

*Rule 19:   Do not use a comma between a conjunction and introductory modifiers or clauses.

The fire had completely destroyed the trailer, and according to the fire chief, there was some concern that the overhead structure of the barn would collapse.

*Rule 20:   Do not use a comma between "that" and introductory modifiers or clauses.

He testified that when they returned to his hotel room, Wells demanded a $150 fee.

* Some authorities disagree on these comma rules.

§ 28.1.1 Critical Commas: Those That Affect Meaning and Clarity

Commas are like the signs along the highway. They signal, usually subtly, how the sentence structure will unfold. The correct use of commas, like the correct highway sign, will prepare the reader for what's to come, whether it be another main clause, an explanatory appositive, or a shift from an introductory element to the main clause. Seasoned readers absorb the information they get from commas in much the same way seasoned drivers absorb the information they get from highway signs. Sometimes it grabs their attention; more often than not, it works almost subconsciously. The comma rules that follow are the ones that affect meaning and clarity. If they are used incorrectly, they will miscue the reader in much the same way that an incorrect highway sign would miscue a driver.

Rule 1	Use a Comma Before a Coordinating Conjunction Joining Two Main, or Independent, Clauses

Reminder

There are seven coordinating conjunctions: "and," "but," "or," "for," "nor," "yet," and "so."[1]

Reminder

A main, or independent, clause has its own subject and verb, and it can stand alone as a sentence. The diagram below represents a sentence with a Rule 1 comma.

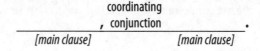

Brackets mark the main clauses in the following examples.

EXAMPLE 1	Comma + Conjunction Joining Main Clauses

[The prosecutor spoke about the defendant's motive], and [the jury listened carefully.]

[The corrections officer contacted several other persons], but [none knew of Wilson's disappearance.]

When applying Rule 1, be sure that you are not mistakenly assuming that a comma must precede every coordinating conjunction. It precedes those coordinating conjunctions that join two main clauses.

In addition, be sure to distinguish between sentences with two main clauses (subject-verb, and subject-verb), which require a comma before the conjunc-

---

1. Some writers prefer to use a semicolon before "yet" and "so." The semicolon signals a longer pause.

tion, and sentences with compound verbs (subject-verb and verb), which do not require a comma before the conjunction.

EXAMPLE 2   **Joining Main Clauses vs. Joining Verbs**

Two Main Clauses

The defendant's girlfriend denied that she knew where he was, and she refused to answer any more questions.

Compound Verbs

The defendant's girlfriend denied that she knew where he was and refused to answer any more questions.

If writers omit the comma before a coordinating conjunction joining two main clauses, they miscue their readers. No comma before a coordinating conjunction signals the second half of a pair of structures other than main clauses. This error is often labeled a fused sentence or run-on sentence. When the main clauses are short and closely related, however, the comma before the coordinating conjunction may be omitted.

EXAMPLE 3   **Omitting Comma for Short Main Clauses**

The prosecutor spoke and the jury listened.

Exception to Rule 1

When the main clauses are long or when they have internal punctuation, use a semicolon before the coordinating conjunction.

EXAMPLE 4   **Semicolon Between Main Clauses**

After analyzing the defendant's claim under ER 401, the court rejected it, explaining that the evidence at issue was relevant to the question of falsity; and because falsity was an element to be proved by the plaintiff, the evidence met the ER 401 requirements of probative value and materiality.

Rule 2   **Use a Comma to Set Off Long Introductory Clauses or Phrases from the Main, or Independent, Clause**

If a main, or independent, clause is preceded by introductory material, the reader needs a comma to signal where the introductory material ends and where the main clause begins. The diagram below represents a sentence with a Rule 2 comma.

_____, _____.

*[long introductory   [main clause]
clause or phrase]*

Long introductory clauses that must be set off with a comma are easy to spot. Because they are clauses, they will have a subject and a verb. Because they are subordinate, not main, clauses, they will also begin with a subordinating conjunction such as "after," "although," "as," "because," "before," "if," "unless," "until," "when," or "where." (See section 27.1 for more on subordinate clauses and subordinating conjunctions.)

EXAMPLE 5   **Setting Off Long Introductory Clauses**

If the accident were unavoidable, Smith's intoxication was not "a cause . . . without which the death would not have occurred."

When Abbott failed to return to the work release facility, a corrections officer called his mother's home.

Of the many kinds of introductory phrases used in legal writing, the most common are prepositional phrases, infinitive phrases, and participial phrases. (Section 27.1 defines and explains prepositions, infinitives, and participles. It is not critical, however, to be able to identify the types of introductory phrases to punctuate them correctly.)

EXAMPLE 6   **Setting Off Phrases**

Introductory Prepositional Phrase

In the present case, the record shows that Thompson initially assaulted Blevins.

Introductory Infinitive Phrase

To support an argument that the trial court abused its discretion, a defendant must point to specific prejudice.

Introductory Participial Phrase

Using their overhead lights and sirens, the police followed the defendant out of the area.

Notice that long introductory phrases are often made up of several prepositional phrases or a combination of prepositional, infinitive, and participial phrases.

EXAMPLE 7   **Setting Off Phrases**

Two Introductory Prepositional Phrases

[On the evening] [of August 13, 2012], Larry Utter was robbed at gunpoint while making a deposit at a local bank.

Introductory Prepositional and Infinitive Phrases

[At the hearing] [on McDonald's motion] [to dismiss], the parties stipulated to the admission of an incident report prepared by McDonald's probation officer.

Furthermore, there is no specific rule for what constitutes a "long" phrase or clause. An introductory phrase or clause of four or more words is usually set off with a comma, but writers have some discretion, particularly with introductory phrases.

Short prepositional phrases, for example, are often set off by a comma, especially when the writer wants to emphasize the information in the phrase, as with dates or case names.

EXAMPLE 8   **Setting Off Dates and Case Names**

In 2007, the Oltmans removed the fence separating their property from the farm.

In *Harris*, the defendant was charged with first degree robbery.

Short, introductory transitional expressions, such as "consequently," "for example," "therefore," "in addition," and "on the other hand," are almost always set off by a comma.

EXAMPLE 9   **Setting Off Transitions**

Consequently, unlawful restraint is invariably an element of the greater offense of attempted kidnapping.

Note that "although" is a subordinating conjunction, not a transitional expression, so it should not be set off by a comma.

EXAMPLE 10   **No Comma After "Although"**

Although the Dicksons purchased the home in 2006, they did not move in until fall of 2007.

Rule 3   Use a Comma to Prevent a Possible Misreading

A reader should be able to read a sentence correctly the first time. If a comma can prevent a possible misreading, it should be included.

EXAMPLE 11   **Comma to Prevent Misreading**

Confusing

People who can usually hire their own lawyer.

Edited

People who can, usually hire their own lawyer.

Rule 4	**Use a Comma to Set Off Nonrestrictive Phrases or Clauses**

Nonrestrictive phrases or clauses do not restrict or limit the words they modify. They give additional information.

Restrictive phrases or clauses restrict or limit the words they modify. They add essential information.

EXAMPLE 12	**Setting Off Nonrestrictive Phrases and Clauses**

Nonrestrictive Phrase

Officer Bates, <u>acting as a decoy</u>, remained outside on the sidewalk.

Nonrestrictive Clause

Officer Bates, <u>who acted as a decoy</u>, remained outside on the sidewalk.

In both of the examples above, "Officer Bates" is completely identified by her name. "Acting as a decoy" or "who acted as a decoy" does not give restricting or limiting information, so both are set off by commas.

If the name of the officer were unknown, the writer may need to use the phrase or clause as a way to identify the officer. The phrase or clause would then be restrictive because it would limit the meaning of "officer." When used as a restrictive phrase or clause, the same words are not set off by commas.

EXAMPLE 13	**No Commas with Restrictive Phrases and Clauses**

Restrictive Phrase

An officer acting as a decoy remained outside on the sidewalk.

Restrictive Clause

An officer who acted as a decoy remained outside on the sidewalk.

A few more examples may be helpful in learning to distinguish which phrases and clauses are nonrestrictive and therefore set off by commas.

EXAMPLE 14	**Example 14**	**Nonrestrictive Clause**

The child's father, who is six months behind in his child support payments, has fled the state.

"The child's father" clearly identifies the individual in question; "who is six months behind in his child support payments" does not restrict or limit the meaning of "the child's father," even though it is important information for understanding the sentence.

EXAMPLE 15   **Restrictive Clause**

The uncle who lives in Oklahoma has agreed to care for the child until an appropriate foster home is found.

This sentence suggests that the child has more than one uncle. "Who lives in Oklahoma" restricts or limits the meaning of "the uncle." It is the uncle in Oklahoma, not the one in Arkansas, who has agreed to care for the child.

Notice that whether a phrase or clause is punctuated as restrictive or nonrestrictive can significantly change the meaning of a sentence.

EXAMPLE 16   **Restrictive Clause**

Attorneys who intentionally prolong litigation for personal gain misuse the legal system.

The preceding sentence says that there is a restricted or limited group of attorneys — those who intentionally prolong litigation for personal gain — who misuse the legal system.

EXAMPLE 17   **Nonrestrictive Clauses**

Attorneys, who intentionally prolong litigation for personal gain, misuse the legal system.

The preceding sentence does not refer to a restricted or limited group of attorneys. It says that all attorneys misuse the legal system and that all attorneys intentionally prolong litigation for personal gain.

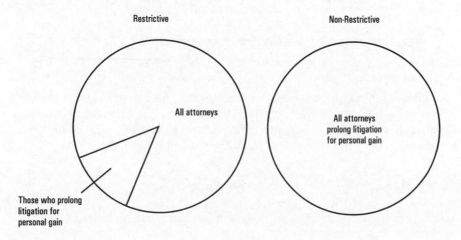

Restrictive and nonrestrictive clauses that modify people begin with "who" or "whom." Careful writers still observe the usage rule that restrictive clauses that modify things or objects use "that" and nonrestrictive clauses that modify things or objects use "which."

EXAMPLE 18   Using "Which" and "That" Correctly

Incorrect Usage

The instruction which is unchallenged is an accomplice instruction that includes the "ready to assist" language.

Corrected

The instruction that is unchallenged is an accomplice instruction that includes the "ready to assist" language. *OR*

Instruction 21, which is unchallenged, is an accomplice instruction that includes the "ready to assist" language.

---

§ 28.1.2 Basic Commas: Those That Educated Readers Expect

Rule 5   Set Off Nonrestrictive Appositives with Commas

Reminder

Appositives are nouns or noun substitutes that follow another noun to identify it or further describe it.

EXAMPLE 19   Appositive Set Off by Comma

A corrections officer called <u>Diane Cummins</u>, the <u>defendant's girlfriend</u>.
              (noun)   *(appositive)*

Because most appositives are nonrestrictive, they need to be set off with commas. However, restrictive appositives, like the restrictive phrases and clauses in Rule 4, add information that restricts or limits the preceding noun; therefore, restrictive appositives are not set off with commas.

EXAMPLE 20   Nonrestrictive Appositive

The court sentenced the defendant, a juvenile, to a term outside the standard range.

There is only one defendant; "a juvenile" adds information, but it does not restrict or limit the meaning of "defendant."

EXAMPLE 21   **Restrictive Appositive**

The defendant's brother Joseph contradicted the story another brother Daniel told to the police.

The defendant has more than one brother, so the noun phrases "defendant's brother" and "another brother" must be restricted or limited by the brothers' names.

Some appositives are introduced by the word "or." Be sure to distinguish between the appositional "or," which is a restatement of or explanation for the preceding noun, and the disjunctive "or," which introduces an alternative to the preceding noun.

EXAMPLE 22   **Appositional "Or" vs. Disjunctive "Or"**

Appositional "Or"

You may designate an attorney-in-fact, or agent, to make your health care decisions in the event you are unable to do so. *("Attorney-in-fact" and "agent" are the same thing.)*

Disjunctive "Or"

The girl's father or uncle always accompanied her on dates. *("Father" and "uncle" are alternatives.)*

Rule 6   **Set Off Nonrestrictive Participial Phrases with a Comma or Commas**

Reminder

Participles, which are formed from verbs, can serve as adjectives. Present participles have an "-ing" ending; past participles have a variety of endings, depending on whether the verb is regular or irregular. Common past participle endings include "-d," "-ed," "-t," "-n," and "-en."

verb	present participle	past participle
reason	reasoning	reasoned
find	finding	found

Many sentences in legal writing use a beginning or an ending participial phrase to describe the rationale for the action expressed in the main verb. Such participial phrases are not dangling or misplaced (see sections 27.6.1 and 27.6.2) if, as in the following examples, they modify the subject of the sentence.

EXAMPLE 23   **Setting Off Participial Phrases**

Reasoning that the sentence imposed was disproportionate to the gravity of the offense, the State Supreme Court reversed and remanded for resentencing.

The State Supreme Court reversed and remanded for resentencing, reasoning that the sentence imposed was disproportionate to the gravity of the offense.

Finding that the seizure fell under the plain view doctrine, the trial court denied the motion.

The trial court denied the motion, finding that the seizure fell under the plain view doctrine.

Rule 7   **Use a Comma or Commas to Set Off Transitional or Interrupting Words and Phrases**

Legal writers frequently break the flow of a sentence intentionally by inserting a word or phrase in the middle of a main clause. Readers have no trouble understanding what the main clause is and what the transitional or interrupting word or phrase is as long as those transitions or interrupters are set off with commas. The diagram below represents a sentence with an interrupter.

$$\underline{\hspace{3cm}}, \text{interrupter}, \underline{\hspace{3cm}}.$$
              (main)   *(clause)*

EXAMPLE 24   **Commas with Interrupting Words or Phrases**

The trial court, however, imposed an exceptional sentence of thirty months.

The Court of Appeals held that Wells, through her own fault and connivance, caused the delay between the time the State filed the information and the time of Wells's arraignment.

Note, however, that many of the same transitional words and phrases ("however," "therefore," "on the other hand") that interrupt a main clause can also be used between two main clauses. Be sure to distinguish between the two and punctuate accordingly.

EXAMPLE 25   **Punctuation and Transitions**

Interrupter

His vision, therefore, was blurred.

Transition Between Two Main Clauses

The driver lost his contact lenses; therefore, his vision was blurred.

| Rule 8 | Use Commas According to Convention with Quotation Marks |

Commas are frequently used to separate short or informal quotations from words in the same sentence that introduce, interrupt, or follow the quotation.

| EXAMPLE 26 | Commas with Quotation Marks |

Corbin said, "I never saw the other car."

"I never saw the other car," Corbin said, "until it was right on top of me."

"I never saw the other car," said Corbin.

Commas are placed inside closing quotation marks[2] and outside closing parentheses or brackets.

| EXAMPLE 27 | Commas with Other Marks of Punctuation |

Inside Closing Quotation Marks

Identification searches are valid if limited to wallets or other "common repositories of identification papers," and the examination is confined to locating a driver's license or similar document. 4 Wayne LaFave, *Search and Seizure* § 9.6(g), at 695 (4th ed. 2004).

A 24-month sentence does not appear to be "clearly excessive," especially when the presumptive range of 12-14 months could have been increased by 12 months under RCW 9.94A.310.

Outside Closing Parentheses

Both of the defendants are young (nineteen and twenty), and both of them are first-time offenders.

Quotations that are immediately preceded by "that" do not have a comma between the quotation and "that."

| EXAMPLE 28 | No Comma When "That" Precedes Quote |

In *Herron v. King*, the court stated that "actual malice can be inferred from circumstantial evidence including . . . the reporter's knowledge that his sources are hostile to the plaintiff . . . ." *Id.*

---

2. Some countries apply a different rule. For example, in the United Kingdom, India, Australia, and South Africa, the comma goes outside the quotation marks unless it is part of the quotation, in which case, it goes inside the closing quotation mark,

Rule 9   Use a Comma or Commas to Set Off Phrases of Contrast

Phrases of contrast usually begin with "not," "but," or "yet."

EXAMPLE 29   Commas Setting Off Contrasting Phrases

Adams initially indicated that he, not Wilson, was involved in the robbery.

Some writers occasionally omit commas with phrases of contrast that begin with "but." Either way is correct. In addition, commas are usually omitted between elements joined by the paired conjunctions "not only . . . but also . . . ."

EXAMPLE 30   Omitted Commas with Paired Conjunctions

The trial court not only overruled defense counsel's repeated objections but also accused the defendant's attorney of intentionally delaying the proceedings.

Rule 10   Use Commas Between Items in a Series

Reminder

A series is three or more items that are grouped together and that are in the same grammatical form. Each item may be as short as one word or as long as a clause.

EXAMPLE 31   Commas Separating Items in a Series

Series of Single Words

Wong had no money, identification, or jewelry.

Series of Verb Phrases

Mason moved at least twice during the period of his escape, changed his name and his appearance, and held four or five jobs.

Series of Clauses

Koenig could not remember who he was, where he lived, what he did for a living, or what he had done during the last two weeks.

Even a series composed of short main clauses can use commas to separate the items.

| EXAMPLE 32 | Commas with a Series of Main Clauses |

Matthews pulled a knife on O'Hara, she screamed, and he turned and ran away.

Although the comma before the final "and" in a series is sometimes described as "optional,"[3] legal writers should make it a habit to include it because some sentences become ambiguous when that comma is omitted.

| EXAMPLE 33 | Ambiguous Meaning |

Mrs. Corsini wants her property divided equally among the following relatives: Michael Corsini, Glenda Corsini, Ralph Meyers, Joanna Mitchem, Louis Mitchem, Donna Mitchem and Donald Mitchem.

Should the property be divided six or seven ways? Assume Donna Mitchem and Donald Mitchem are married. Did Grandmother Corsini intend for the couple to get one-sixth of her property, or did she intend for each of them to receive one-seventh?

Adding a comma before the final "and" tells the reader that the property should be divided seven ways. Adding another "and" before "Donna Mitchem" says that it should be divided six ways and that Donna and Donald should, as a couple, receive a one-sixth share.

Remember that the rule to add the comma applies to a <u>series</u>, which is <u>three</u> or more items. Ordinarily, commas are not used to separate <u>pairs</u> of words, phrases, or clauses that are joined by coordinating conjunctions.

| EXAMPLE 34 | No Comma with Pairs |

Pair of Words

Lundquist was <u>arrested</u> and <u>charged</u> with negligent homicide.

Pair of Phrases

The Supreme Court is remarkably free <u>to emphasize certain issues of the case over others</u> or <u>to stress completely new issues</u>.

Pair of Clauses

The trial court asked the defendant <u>whether he understood his right to a jury trial</u> and <u>whether he received any promises of better treatment if he waived that right</u>.

Commas are not used between items in a series when all the items are joined by coordinating conjunctions. As a stylistic technique, joining all the

---

3. In journalism, and therefore in most newspapers and popular magazines, the comma before the final "and" or "or" is omitted. Likewise, in many English-speaking countries outside of the United States, the comma before the final "and" or "or" is also omitted.

items in a series with conjunctions has the effect of slowing down a series, which may be desirable on rare occasions when the writer wants the reader to focus special attention on each of the individual items in the series. (See section 26.2.2 on cadence.)

EXAMPLE 35   **No Commas for Items in Series Joined by Conjunctions**

There is no indication that the delay was negligent or deliberate or unusual.

Rule 11   Use a Comma Between Coordinate Adjectives Not Joined by a Conjunction

Coordinate adjectives are two or more adjectives that independently modify the same noun.

concise,   precise   language
(adjective)   *(adjective)*   *(noun)*

The test for whether adjectives are coordinate is simple: (1) reverse the order of the adjectives; or (2) add an "and" between the adjectives. If the adjectives are modifying the noun independently, then changing their order or adding an "and" will not change the meaning.

1. precise, concise language
2. concise, precise language
3. precise and concise language

The following example does not have a comma because it does not contain coordinate adjectives. Instead, "black" modifies "leather" and "leather" modifies "briefcase." Notice that you can tell that the adjectives are not coordinate by applying either part of the test. Both create awkward constructions.

EXAMPLE 36   **No Comma When Adjectives Are Not Coordinate**

black leather briefcase

Reverse Order

leather, black briefcase

Add "and"

black and leather briefcase

Rule 12   Use Commas According to Convention with Dates, Addresses, and Names of Geographical Locations

When a full date is written out in the month-day-year order, use a comma after the day.

July 4, 1776

Dates in this order also require a comma (or other punctuation) after the year when the sentence continues after the date.

EXAMPLE 37   Comma After Year in Full Date

The land was surveyed on October 4, 2001, and purchased less than a month later.

If the day is omitted or if the full date has the month and date reversed, omit commas because there are no adjacent groupings of digits.

July 1776   4 July 1776

Use commas to set off individual elements in addresses and geographical names. Note that the state and zip code are considered one element and therefore are not separated by a comma. When addresses or geographical names are followed by the remainder of a sentence, they should be followed by a comma.

Chicago, Illinois   Ontario, Canada

EXAMPLE 38   Commas with Geographical Locations

The string of robberies began in San Diego, California, and ended in Oakland, California, after the police arrested the defendant.

When possible, rephrase a date or geographical name used as a modifier when the date or geographical name will have to be followed by a comma.

EXAMPLE 39   Editing When Comma After Full Date Is Awkward

Awkward

the June 21, 2004, meeting

Edited

the meeting on June 21, 2004

| **Rule 13** | **Use Commas to Set Off Absolutes** |

Reminder

Absolutes are made up of either a noun or pronoun followed by a participle. They modify an entire sentence or main clause and can appear at the beginning, at the end, or within a sentence.

his <u>career</u> <u>destroyed</u>   their <u>lights</u> <u>flashing</u>
 (noun) (participle)   *(noun)(participle)*

his <u>gun</u> <u>drawn and loaded</u>   the <u>last</u> <u>being</u> a year ago
 (noun)   (participles)   *(noun)(participle)*

| **EXAMPLE 40** | **Commas with Absolutes** |

His career destroyed, Williams lapsed into a state of depression.

The police followed the defendant for less than one mile, their lights flashing.

The defendant reentered the tavern, his gun drawn and loaded, and proceeded to order the tavern's patrons to line up against the wall.

She testified that on four or five occasions, the last being a year ago, he demanded that she rewrite her will.

| **Rule 14** | **Use a comma to indicate an omission of a word or words that can be understood from the context** |

| **EXAMPLE 41** | **Comma to Show Omission** |

The first witness said the attacker was "hairy"; the second, bald.

In Texas there are five elements to the crime; in Delaware, four.

| **Rule 15** | **Use commas to set off expressions that introduce examples or explanations** |

"For example," "for instance," "that is," "namely," "*i.e.*," "*e.g.*," and "*viz.*" are usually followed by a comma. A comma can also be used before these expressions if the break in the flow of the sentence is slight. Dashes or semicolons are used before these expressions if the break is substantial.

EXAMPLE 42   Punctuation with Examples

Collins testified that Adams had participated in the robbery and had fenced some of the items, namely, a camera, stereo, and silver.

The State must prove that the defendant acted by color or aid of deception—that is, that he operated to bring about the acquisition of the property or services by either creating or confirming another's false impression, which he knew to be false, or by failing to correct another's impression, which he had previously created.

Crestwood Elementary accepted all standard forms of identification, e.g., birth certificate, driver's license, or military identification.

Some authorities suggest that writers avoid the abbreviations "*i.e.*," "*e.g.*," and "*viz.*" in the text of their writing and use their English equivalents instead ("that is," "for example," and "namely" respectively). The rationale for this suggestion is that many readers misunderstand the abbreviations. If you decide to use the abbreviations, remember to italicize or underline them.

§ 28.1.4   Unnecessary Commas: Those That Should Be Omitted

Rule 16   Do not use a comma to set off restrictive adverbial clauses that follow the main clause

Reminder

Adverbial clauses have their own subject and verb, and they are introduced by an adverb such as "although," "because," "before," "when," and "while."

A restrictive adverbial clause restricts or limits the action of the verb to a time, manner, or circumstance. Nonrestrictive adverbial clauses give additional information.

Clauses introduced by the adverb "if" are always restrictive, so they are not set off by commas.

EXAMPLE 43   No Comma with "If" Clause

Complicity may be found if a defendant participates in the early stages of an activity that results in the attack on the victim.

Clauses introduced by the adverbs "because" and "unless" are usually restrictive, although they can be nonrestrictive.

EXAMPLE 44   No Comma with "Because"/"Unless" Clauses

Summary judgment was granted because the plaintiff failed to establish the *prima facie* elements.

Special damages may not be presumed without proof unless actual malice is proved.

When clauses beginning with "after," "as," "before," "since," "when," and "while" restrict the time of the main verb, they should not be set off with commas.

EXAMPLE 45   No Comma with Clauses That Restrict Time of Verb

The tractor trailer entered the parking lot as the game was ending and the crowd was beginning to leave the stadium.

Morton was drinking beer while he was driving the boat.

When adverbial clauses beginning with "as," "since," or "while" do not restrict the time of the verb but rather express cause or condition, they are nonrestrictive and should be set off by commas.

EXAMPLE 46   Comma with Clause Expressing Cause or Condition

Southworth returned to the scene of the assault, as he feared that he had lost his neck chain in the scuffle.

Clauses introduced by the adverbs "although" and "though" are always nonrestrictive, so they must be set off with commas.

EXAMPLE 47   Commas with "Although" and "Though"

Del Barker admits that he received his 2008 tax statement, although he claims that the only notice he received of the filing requirements was from general news articles in the newspaper.

Each physician received compensation and paid expenses in direct proportion to his or her production of the gross income of the partnership, even though the partnership was an equal partnership.

Rule 17   Do not use a comma to separate a subject from its verb or a verb from its object

Legal writers are often inclined to write long subjects. When they do, it is tempting to insert a comma after the subject and before the verb because the reader will need a pause. The comma is the wrong solution; instead, the writer should revise the sentence.

In Example 48, the subject is enclosed in brackets.

EXAMPLE 48   **No Comma Between Subject and Verb**

Incorrect

[The idea that an individual can obtain another person's property through adverse possession], is difficult for many people to accept.

Edited

Many people find it difficult to accept the idea that an individual can obtain another person's property through adverse possession.

In Example 49, the verb "received" is incorrectly separated from its object, "the note," by a comma.

EXAMPLE 49   **No Comma Between Verb and Its Object**

Incorrect

Bloomquist had received from a fellow employee at Landover Mills, a note describing where the "crack house" was located.

Edited

A fellow employee at Landover Mills sent Bloomquist a note describing where the "crack house" was located.

Exception

Nonrestrictive modifiers and interrupters that separate a subject from its verb should be preceded and followed by commas, even though the commas separate the subject from its verb. See Rules 4, 5, and 7 in this section.

Rule 18   **Do not use a comma to separate correlative pairs unless the correlatives introduce main clauses**

> **Reminder**
>
> Correlative pairs include "either . . . or," "neither . . . nor," "both . . . and," and "not only . . . but also."

EXAMPLE 50   No Comma with Correlative Pair

Incorrect

> Neither the United States Supreme Court, nor this Court has ever ruled that a defendant has a due process right to an instruction on lesser included offenses.

Edited

> Neither the United States Supreme Court nor this Court has ever ruled that a defendant has a due process right to an instruction on lesser included offenses.

EXAMPLE 51   Comma When Correlative Pair Introduces Main Clauses

> Either the manager will have to describe the damage done to the apartment, or he will have to return the deposit.

The correlative pair "not only . . . but also" connects two elements, so a separating comma is inappropriate. Some authorities, however, do recommend a comma to separate the "not . . . but" pair because it is used to contrast elements.

Rule 19   Do not use a comma between a conjunction and introductory modifiers or clauses

When a coordinating conjunction joins two main clauses, the second main clause frequently begins with introductory modifiers or its own subordinate clause. Although some writers add a comma after the conjunction and before the introductory modifier or clause, this extra comma is needless; it merely slows the sentence down.

$$\underline{\hspace{3cm}}, and \quad \underline{\hspace{5cm}}, \quad \underline{\hspace{4cm}}.$$
[main clause]   *[introductory modifiers/clause]*   *[main clause]*

EXAMPLE 52   No Comma Between Conjunction and Introductory Modifier

Incorrect

> The fire had completely destroyed the trailer, and, according to the fire chief, there was some concern that the overhead structure of the barn would collapse.

Edited

> The fire had completely destroyed the trailer, and according to the fire chief, there was some concern that the overhead structure of the barn would collapse.

EXAMPLE 53	**No Comma Between Conjunction and Introductory Modifier**

Incorrect

The woman demanded that Thomas hand over his wallet, but, when Thomas replied that he did not have his wallet, the woman shot him in the chest.

Edited

The woman demanded that Thomas hand over his wallet, but when Thomas replied that he did not have his wallet, the woman shot him in the chest.

Rule 20	**Do not use a comma between "that" and introductory modifiers or clauses**

EXAMPLE 54	**No Comma Between "That" and Introductory Modifier**

Incorrect

He testified that, when they returned to his hotel room, Wells demanded a $150 fee.

Edited

He testified that when they returned to his hotel room, Wells demanded a $150 fee.

Chapter 28 Quiz No. 1

Draft answers for each of the following questions. Make your points clearly and concisely, and write sentences that are easy to read and that are grammatical and correctly punctuated.

1. Comma rule 1 applies only when a coordinating conjunction joins two main clauses. What is a main clause, and what are the coordinating conjunctions?
2. What is the difference between nonrestrictive and restrictive phrases and clauses?
3. What are appositives?
4. What is a series?
5. What is the test for determining coordinate adjectives?

§ 28.2   The Semicolon

The semicolon is one of the easiest punctuation marks to learn how to use. Unfortunately, some legal writers avoid using semicolons because they believe semicolons are quite complicated and will require learning numerous rules. Exactly the opposite is true. There are only two general rules for using semicolons; all other uses are variations or exceptions to these two rules.

Rule 1	**Use a Semicolon to Separate Main, or Independent, Clauses Not Joined by a Coordinating Conjunction**

The diagram below represents a sentence with a Rule 1 semicolon.

<u>main clause   ;   main clause</u>   .

Reminder

Main clauses contain a subject and verb. They can stand alone as a sentence. There are only seven coordinating conjunctions: "and," "but," "or," "for," "nor," "yet," and "so."

EXAMPLE 1	**Semicolons Between Main Clauses**

Officer Thompson administered the breathalyzer test; the results showed that the defendant's blood alcohol level was over the maximum allowed by the state.

The plaintiff is a Nevada resident; the defendant is a California resident.

If you use a comma or no punctuation between main clauses, you will produce a comma splice or run-on sentence. (See section 28.6.)

Main clauses joined by a semicolon should be closely related in meaning. Often the semicolon suggests that the ideas in the connected main clauses work together as a larger idea. (See the first sentence in Example 1.) The semicolon can also be used to balance one idea against another. (See the second sentence in Example 1.) In all cases, the semicolon signals to the reader to pause slightly longer than a comma but shorter than a period.

Variation on Rule 1

To show the relationship between the main clauses, a conjunctive adverb frequently follows the semicolon separating main clauses. The conjunctive adverb is usually followed by a comma. The most commonly used conjunctive adverbs are "accordingly," "also," "besides," "consequently," "furthermore," "hence," "however," "indeed," "instead," "likewise," "meanwhile," "moreover," "nevertheless," "still," "then," "therefore," and "thus." (See section 27.1.) The diagram below represents a sentence with a Rule 1 semicolon followed by a conjunctive adverb.

<u>main clause   ; *therefore,*   main clause</u>   .
                  [conjunctive
                      adverb]

EXAMPLE 2   **Semicolons Between Main Clauses**

The summons was not delivered to his usual place of abode; therefore, service was not effected in the manner prescribed by law.

The elements of the test have not been completely defined; however, the court has clarified the policies underlying the rule.

Conjunctive adverbs may also occur in the middle of main clauses. In such cases, they are preceded and followed by a comma, and no semicolon is used. (See comma Rule 7.)

<u>main   *, therefore,*   clause   </u>.

EXAMPLE 3   **Commas with Interrupting Conjunctive Adverbs**

The motor was not running, however, because of a problem with the distributor cap.

Compare the preceding example and the following example.

EXAMPLE 4   **Semicolon with Conjunctive Adverbs**

The motor was not running because of a problem with the distributor cap; however, the inoperability of the vehicle was irrelevant.

Rule 2   **Use Semicolons to Separate Items in a Series if the Items Are Long or if One or More of the Items Has Internal Commas**

Reminder

A series is three or more items of equal importance. If the items in a series are relatively short or if they do not have internal commas, then the items can be separated by commas.

<u>item 1, item 2, and item 3</u>
Typical series with items separated by commas

<u>item 1   ;   item 2   ;   and item 3</u>
Long items separated by semicolons

<u>item 1   ,   ; item 2   ,   ; and item 3</u>
Internal commas in one or more items separated by semicolons

| **EXAMPLE 5** | **Semicolons with Items in a Series** |

Long Items

The Montana court has applied these definitions to cases with the following fact patterns: the driver was asleep and intoxicated; the driver was positioned behind the steering wheel; the vehicle's motor was running; and the vehicle was parked.

Long Items

The court must determine the following issues to resolve your claim:

1. whether your ex-landlord sent you a written statement within thirty days of termination;
2. whether your ex-landlord withheld your deposit in bad faith; and
3. whether the court wishes to include attorneys' fees as part of a possible damage award.

Internal Commas

The prosecutor called the following witnesses: Linda Hastings, an advertising executive; Samuel Hedges, an accountant; and Timothy Lessor, president of the company.

Internal Commas

The defendant claims to reside in Maryland, even though (1) his car is registered in California; (2) he is registered to vote in California; and (3) all of his financial assets, including stocks, bonds, and a savings and checking account, are in a California bank.

Note that if the individual items are numbered, the items are invariably separated by semicolons.

§ 28.2.1   Use of the Semicolon with "Yet" or "So"

Some writers prefer to use a semicolon rather than a comma before the coordinating conjunctions "yet" and "so" when they join two main clauses. Either the comma or the semicolon is correct in the following examples, but note that the longer pause suggested by the semicolon adds a bit more emphasis to the conjunction and to the words that immediately follow the semicolon.

| **EXAMPLE 6** | **Comma or Semicolon with "So"** |

Our client was legally intoxicated at the time of the arrest, so being asleep or unconscious is not a defense.

Our client was legally intoxicated at the time of the arrest; so being asleep or unconscious is not a defense.

---

§ 28.2.2   Use of the Semicolon with Coordinating Conjunctions

Usually main clauses joined by a coordinating conjunction require only a comma before the conjunction. (See section 28.1, Rule 1.) However, when the main clauses are long and grammatically complicated or when they have internal commas, it is helpful for the reader if a semicolon rather than a comma precedes the coordinating conjunction. The semicolon makes it easier to spot the break between the main clauses.

$$\underline{\hspace{3cm}} ; but \hspace{1cm} , \hspace{1cm} , \hspace{0.5cm} , \underline{\hspace{2cm}} .$$
$$\textit{main clause} \hspace{4cm} \textit{main clause}$$

EXAMPLE 7   **Semicolon When Main Clause Has Internal Commas**

Your landlord can withhold a reasonable amount to cover the cost of repairing the window; but if he failed to send you a check for the remainder of the deposit, or if he failed to state why he withheld the deposit, or if he failed to do both within thirty days of termination of the lease, then he forfeited his right to withhold any part of the deposit.

---

§ 28.3   The Colon

Colons are useful to legal writers for a number of reasons. They are regularly used to introduce quotations or lists, and they are often the best way to set up explanations or elaborations.

EXAMPLE 1   **Colon to Introduce Quote, List, Explanation**

Quotation

In support of this result, the court noted that the limitation on the use of the *corpus delicti* rule is based on the "suspect nature" of out-of-court confessions: "Corroboration of the confession is required as a safeguard against the conviction of the innocent persons through the use of a false confession of guilt." *Id.* at 419.

List

There are three ways to measure a plaintiff's recovery for personal property damage: (1) if the destroyed personal property has a market value, the measure is that market value; (2) if the destroyed property has no market value but can be replaced, then the measure is the replacement cost; or (3) if the destroyed property has no market value and cannot be replaced, then the measure is the property's intrinsic value.

Explanation/Elaboration

The periodic polygraph examinations are arguably connected logically to the ultimate goal of Nyles's rehabilitation: to deter him from molesting children.

Mr. Baker has sustained personal property damage: his picture windows and valuable vase were smashed.

The main function of a colon is to introduce what will follow. For this reason, a colon requires a lead-in main clause that is grammatically complete. The following diagram represents a sentence with a colon.

grammatically complete main clause: _____ .

In the example that follows, "the subsections that do not apply are" is not grammatically complete; therefore, the colon is used incorrectly.

EXAMPLE 2   **Incorrect**

The subsections that do not apply are: 201-1(3)(a), 201-1(3)(b), and 201-1(3)(c).

One way to correct the example above is to omit the colon.

EXAMPLE 3   **Corrected**

The subsections that do not apply are 201-1(3)(a), 201-1(3)(b), and 201-1(3)(c).

Another option is to add filler expressions, such as "the following" or "as follows," to make the lead-in main clause grammatically complete.

EXAMPLE 4   **Corrected**

The subsections that do not apply are the following: 201-1(3)(a), 201-1(3)(b), and 201-1(3)(c).

What follows the colon may or may not be a main clause. If a complete sentence follows a colon, the writer has the option of capitalizing the first word of that sentence.

Quotations that are integrated into the writer's own sentences are not introduced by a colon.

EXAMPLE 5   **No Colon for Integrated Quotation**

The first letter the Guptas received stated that "permits are issued subject to existing water rights."

Because colons set up the endings of sentences, they can be used effectively to create emphasis. (See section 24.6.4.)

EXAMPLE 6   **Colons to Create Emphasis**

Orlando's trial was originally scheduled for May 15, 2012: ninety-three days after his arraignment.

Gibson claimed that his intent was to do a lawful act: administer parental discipline.

Traditionally colons were followed by two spaces, but in typeset material, one space is often used after colons.

§ 28.4   The Apostrophe

Apostrophes determine who owns what. If you and your clients care about whether ownership is stated correctly, then apostrophes are worth the few minutes it takes to learn how to use them correctly.

All the apostrophe rules are important, but take special note of Rules 5 and 6. Misusing these two rules can create either ambiguity or the appearance of incompetence.

Rule 1	**Use "'s" to Form the Possessive of Singular or Plural Nouns or Indefinite Pronouns Not Ending in "-s"**

defendant's alibi   children's guardian
a day's wages   everyone's concern

Rule 2	**Use "'s" to Form the Possessive of Singular Nouns Ending in "-s"[4] as Long as the Resulting Word Is Not Difficult to Pronounce**

James's contract   Congress's authority
business's license   witness's testimony

Three or more "s" sounds together are difficult to pronounce. When necessary, avoid three "s" sounds together by dropping the "s" after the apostrophe.

In the examples above, the double "s" ending in "business" or "witness" makes only one "s" sound, so when the "'s" is added, as in "business's" and "witness's," only two "s" sounds are required. However, when these same words are followed by words that begin with "s," then the "s" after the apostrophe is dropped for ease in pronunciation.

business' sales   witness' signature

For the same reason, many idioms that include the word "sake" drop the "s" after the apostrophe.

for goodness' sake   for appearance' sake

Although almost all singular proper names follow the standard rule and form their possessive by adding "'s," those few proper names with internal and ending "s" sounds also drop the "s" after the apostrophe for ease in pronunciation. Note that the "s" sound may be made by a "z" or an "x" as well as an "s."

---

4. A few recognized authorities, including *The Associated Press Stylebook and Libel Manual*, recommend using only an apostrophe with singular proper names.

Jesus' teaching	Alexis' prior conviction
Velasquez' hearing	Kansas' case law

But   Arkansas's case law (because the final "s" in Arkansas is silent)

Rule 3	**Use Only an Apostrophe to Form the Possessive of Plural Nouns Ending in "-s"**

framers' intent	workers' rights
ten dollars' worth	thirty days' notice

Plural proper nouns follow the same rule.

the Smiths' attorney	the Thomases' dog

It is easier to form plural possessives correctly if you form the plural first and then apply the rules for possessives.

Singular	*Plural*	*Plural Possessive*
day →	days →	two days' labor
family →	families →	families' petition
Jones →	Joneses →	Joneses' prenuptial agreement

Occasionally a singular idea is expressed in words that are technically plural, for example, "United States," or "General Motors." In such cases, apply the rule for forming plural possessives and add just an apostrophe.

United States' commitment	General Motors' lobbyists

Rule 4	**Use "'s" After the Last Word to Form the Possessive of a Compound Word or Word Group**

mother-in-law's statement	district manager's idea
attorney general's office	somebody else's problem
the Governor of Florida's recommendation	

Rule 5	**To Show Joint Possession, Use "'s" Only After the Last Noun in a Group of Two or More Nouns; to Show Individual Possession, Use "'s" After Each of the Nouns in a Group of Two or More Nouns**

John and Mary's stocks →	stocks are jointly owned
John's and Mary's stocks →	some stocks are owned by John; some are owned by Mary

Rule 6	To Form the Possessive of Personal Pronouns, Do Not Use the Apostrophe

> hers   its   ours   theirs   yours

Many writers confuse the contractions "it's," "they're," and "who's" with the possessive of the personal pronouns "its," "their," and "whose."

> it's = it is   its = possessive of "it"
> they're = they are   their = possessive of "they"
> who's = who is   whose = possessive of "who"

Besides showing possession, the apostrophe has a few other uses, including the formation of contractions and some plurals.

Rule 7	To Form Contractions, Use the Apostrophe to Substitute for One or More Omitted Letters or Numbers

> it's = it is   ma'am = madam
> they're = they are   class of '98 = class of 1998

Note that contractions are used rarely in formal writing, including most legal writing.

Rule 8	To Form the Plural of Numbers, Letters, or Words Referred to as Words, Add "'s"

> seven 0's   cross all the t's and dot all the i's
> 1950's   replace all the and's with or's
> two Boeing 767's

Some authorities recommend adding just "s" to make numbers plural: 1950s, two Boeing 767s.

Chapter 28 Quiz No. 2

Draft answers for each of the following questions. Make your points clearly and concisely, and write sentences that are easy to read and that are grammatical and correctly punctuated.

1. A semicolon without a coordinating conjunction can be used to join two main clauses. In what situations might a writer use a semicolon rather than a period between two main clauses?
2. When is a semicolon rather than a comma used between items in a series?
3. What types of information can a colon be used to introduce?

4. What does a colon require before it introduces a quotation, list, explanation, or elaboration?
5. Should a colon be used when a quotation is integrated into a sentence (usually with the word "that")?

§ 28.5   Other Marks of Punctuation

§ 28.5.1 Quotation Marks

a.   Identification of Another's Written or Spoken Words

There is nothing mysterious about quotation marks; they do just what their name suggests: They mark where something is quoted.

Although many legal writers have a problem with excessive quoting (see section 25.2.3), there are still several occasions, most notably statutes and memorable phrasing, where quoting is necessary or appropriate. For these occasions, use quotation marks around those words that are not your own and that you have taken from the cited source.

EXAMPLE 1   **Quotation Marks to Show Another's Words**

The relationship between Southwestern Insurers and each of its agents is governed by an agreement that includes the following statement: "The location of the agent's office cannot unduly interfere with the business established by another agent."

EXAMPLE 2   **Quotation Marks to Show Another's Words**

In Ryan, the Court of Appeals ruled that the plaintiff's choice in not swerving was "prudent under the circumstances." *Id.* at 508.

Take care to quote the source's words exactly; use the ellipsis (see section 28.5.2) to indicate any omissions you have made to the wording, and use brackets (see section 28.5.3) to indicate changes in capitalization and additions for clarity and readability.

EXAMPLE 3   **Brackets and Ellipsis to Show Changes to Quotation**

In his *Roviaro* dissent, Justice Clark observed that "[e]xperience teaches that once this policy [of confidentiality] is relaxed . . . its effectiveness is destroyed. Once an informant is known, the drug traffickers are quick to retaliate." *Id.* at 67.

Notice that in Examples 2 and 3, the quotation is integrated into the writer's own sentence. When you integrate a quotation into one of your own sentences, be sure that the parts fit. The grammar of your sentence must be compatible with the grammar of the quotation.

EXAMPLE 4	**Integrating a Quotation into a Sentence**

Incorrect

An actionable nuisance is "an obstruction to the free use of property, so as to essentially interfere with the comfortable enjoyment of life and property, is a nuisance and the subject of an action for damages and other further relief." RCW 7.48.010.

Revised

An actionable nuisance is "an obstruction to the free use of property, so as to essentially interfere with the comfortable enjoyment of life and property . . . ." RCW 7.48.010.

b.　Block Quotations

Do not use quotation marks around quotations of fifty words or more. A quotation of this length should be set up as a block quotation, that is, single-spaced, indented left and right, and without quotation marks.

Unfortunately, some court rules require quotation marks for block quotations. As a writer, then, determine which method your reader prefers and then apply it. Know too that the trend seems to be toward using block quotations for long quotations that are not quite fifty words. The rationale seems to be that it is easier for the reader to see where the quotation begins and ends.

EXAMPLE 5	**Omitting Quotation Marks for Block Quotations**

Davis argues that the trial court erred in giving instruction 19, which reads as follows:

> Evidence has been introduced in this case regarding the fact that stop signs were installed in the neighborhood of Ohio and Texas Streets approximately one and one-half years after the accident of December 24, 2006. You are not to consider this evidence as proof of negligence nor as an admission of negligence on the part of the City.

Block quotations also tend to highlight the quoted material; consequently, some writers use them for persuasive reasons even when the quotation is fairly short.

c.　Effective Lead-Ins for Quotations

In Examples 1 and 5 above, the quotations are not integrated into the writer's own sentences; instead, they are formally introduced and set up as separate statements. Notice that the language in the lead-ins prepares the reader for the quotation, sometimes by summarizing or paraphrasing the quotation, sometimes by explaining in advance why the quotation is significant.

Compare the lead-ins in the following pairs of examples. The ineffective lead-ins do little more than indicate that a quotation will follow; the effective lead-ins guide the reader into the quotation and suggest what the reader should look for in it.

EXAMPLE 6	Writing Effective Lead-ins to Quotations

Ineffective Lead-In

The court found the following:

> The juvenile has an extensive record of adjudications and diversions for a variety of criminal offenses. . . . The court concludes that a sentence within the standard range would constitute a manifest injustice. . . . [C]ommitment . . . for a period of fifty-two (52) weeks is a more appropriate and reasonable sentence, taking into consideration the age of the defendant, his level of criminal sophistication and lack of success in rehabilitation . . . .

Effective Lead-In

The court found a "manifest injustice" and increased Boyd's sentence because of his criminal history:

> The juvenile has an extensive record of adjudications and diversions for a variety of criminal offenses. . . . The court concludes that a sentence within the standard range would constitute a manifest injustice. . . . [C]ommitment . . . for a period of fifty-two (52) weeks is a more appropriate and reasonable sentence, taking into consideration the age of the defendant, his level of criminal sophistication and lack of success in rehabilitation . . . .

Ineffective Lead-In

In *Curtis v. Blacklaw*, the court said the following:

Effective Lead-In

In *Curtis v. Blacklaw*, the court explained the relationship between the standard of ordinary care and the emergency doctrine:

> [T]he existence of a legally defined emergency does not alter or diminish the standards of care imposed by law upon the actors. . . . With or without an emergency instruction, the jury must determine what choice a reasonably prudent and careful person would have made in the same situation.

Id. at 363.

Notice too that when a quotation is formally introduced and preceded by a colon, the portion of the sentence before the colon—the lead-in—should be grammatically complete. (See section 28.3.)

d.   Quotations Within Quotations

Occasionally, something you want to quote will already have quotation marks in it, either because your source quoted someone else or because your source used a term in a special way. For a quotation within a quotation, use single quotation marks (an apostrophe on most keyboards).

EXAMPLE 7	**Single Quotation Marks for Quotations Within Quotations**

"Police must discover incriminating evidence 'inadvertently,' which is to say, they may not 'know in advance the location of [certain] evidence and intend to seize it,' relying on the plain view doctrine as a pretext." *Texas v. Brown*, 460 U.S. 730, 743 (1983) (quoting *Coolidge*, 403 U.S. at 370).

e.   Quotation Marks with Other Marks of Punctuation

Periods and commas go inside closing quotation marks; semicolons and colons go outside closing quotation marks. Dashes, question marks, and exclamation points go inside closing quotation marks when they are part of the quotation and outside closing quotation marks when they are part of the larger sentence.

EXAMPLE 8	**Placement of Other Punctuation with Quotation Marks**

Davis's employer described him as a "street-smart youngster who knew what not to get involved with."

The jury could have arguably considered Wilson's insulting remarks to Harris as "unlawful," thereby depriving Harris of her self-defense claim.

Parole is a "variation on imprisonment"; therefore, parole and its possible revocation are a continuing form of custody relating back to the criminal act.

f.   Other Uses for Quotation Marks

Quotation marks may also indicate that a word is being used in some special way.

EXAMPLE 9	**Quotation Marks Around Special Words and Phrases**

Mrs. Hartley claims that her husband played "mind games" with her to get her to sign the agreement.

The Court of Appeals held that the attorney's phrasing was calculated to imply that Morris was a "hired gun" for insurance carriers.

Special terms are often introduced by phrases such as "the word" or "the term." Put the words that follow these phrases in quotation marks, but do not use quotation marks around words that follow "so-called."

EXAMPLE 10   Quotation Marks Around Special Terms

The words "beyond a reasonable doubt" in the constitutional error test created confusion in the Arizona courts for some time.

Quotation marks should also be used around words that follow the terms "signed," "endorsed," or "entitled."

EXAMPLE 11   Quotation Marks Around Signing Terms

The contract was signed "Miss Cathryn Smith," not "Ms. Kathryn Smith."

Do not use quotation marks around the single words "yes" and "no"; do not use quotation marks around a paraphrase.

EXAMPLE 12   No Quotation Marks with Yes and No

When the officer asked her if she needed a ride home, she said yes.

§ 28.5.2 Ellipses

Use the ellipsis (three spaced periods) to indicate an omission in a quotation. The ellipsis allows you to trim quotations down and focus the reader's attention on the parts of the quotation that are relevant to your case.

EXAMPLE 13   Ellipsis to Show Omission in Quotation

Helen signed a quitclaim deed to Richard, disclaiming "an interest in the . . . property."

Retain the space before the first period and after the last period in an ellipsis.

When the omission occurs in the middle of a quoted sentence, retain any necessary punctuation. Notice, for example, that the comma after "union" is retained in the following quotation because it is necessary punctuation for the sentence as it is quoted.

EXAMPLE 14   Retaining Other Punctuation with Ellipsis

"We the people of the United States, in order to form a more perfect union, . . . do ordain and establish this Constitution for the United States of America."

When the omission occurs at the end of a quoted sentence, use the ellipsis (three spaced periods) to indicate that omission and then space and add a fourth period for the punctuation to end the sentence.

EXAMPLE 15   Fourth Period After Ellipsis to End Sentence

"We the people of the United States, in order to form a more perfect union, . . . do ordain and establish this Constitution . . . ."

When the omission occurs after the end of a quoted sentence, punctuate the quoted sentence and then insert the ellipsis. In such a case, the sentence period is closed up to the last word in the sentence.

This is demonstrated in the next two examples, both of which are quotations from the following original material.

EXAMPLE 16   Omission at End of Quoted Sentence

Original Material

The hostility/claim of right element of adverse possession requires only that the claimant treat the land as his own as against the world throughout the statutory period. The nature of his possession will be determined solely on the basis of the manner in which he treats the property. His subjective belief regarding his true interest in the land and his intent to dispossess or not dispossess another is irrelevant to this determination.

Id. at 860-61.

Quotation from the Original Material

The hostility/claim of right element of adverse possession requires only that the claimant treat the land as his own as against the world throughout the statutory period. . . . His subjective belief regarding his true interest in the land and his intent to dispossess or not dispossess another is irrelevant to this determination.

Id. at 860-61.

Another Quotation from the Same Original

"The hostility/claim of right element of adverse possession requires only that the claimant treat the land as his own as against the world throughout the statutory period. . . . [H]is intent to dispossess or not dispossess another is irrelevant to this determination." *Id.* at 860-61.

When the omission occurs at the beginning of the quotation, do not use an ellipsis. The reader will be able to tell that the original quotation did not begin at that point because the quotation begins with a lowercase letter.

EXAMPLE 17   Omitting Ellipsis at the Beginning of a Quotation

Incorrect

In 1995, King granted to the State a ". . . permanent easement assignable in whole or in part" over King's property. CP 106.

Correct

> In 1995, King granted to the State a "permanent easement assignable in whole or in part" over King's property. CP 106.

When the quoted material is just a phrase or clause, no ellipsis is needed before or after the quoted material.

EXAMPLE 18   **No Ellipsis for Phrases**

Courts weigh the cost against the need of the other party, which must be "substantial" in order to prevail. *Doe*, 232 F.3d at 1267.

When a paragraph or more is omitted, indent and use the ellipsis plus the fourth period for the end punctuation.

EXAMPLE 19   **Ellipsis to Show Omitted Paragraph(s)**

The Safe Drivers' Insurance policy contains the following relevant provisions:

Definitions

> ....
> A car is a 4-wheel motor vehicle licensed for use on public roads. It includes any motor home that is not used for business purposes and any utility trailer.
> ....
> A motor vehicle is a land motor vehicle designed for use on public roads. It includes cars and trailers. It also includes any other land motor vehicle while used on public roads.

Like all good things, ellipses can be misused. Never use the ellipsis to change the original intent in the quotation. Also, take care not to overuse the ellipsis in any one quotation. Too many omissions make the quotation difficult to read.

§ 28.5.3   Brackets

Brackets are used to show changes in quotations. The most common are additions of clarifying material and changes in capitalization and verb tense.

EXAMPLE 20   **Brackets to Show Changes to Quotations**

Addition of Clarifying Material

The defendant can emphasize that asylum seekers are in a unique position of desperate need for relief, that denial of her claim is "replete with danger . . . that [she] will be subject to death or persecution if forced to return to [her] home country." *I.N.S. v. Cardoza-Fonseca*, 480 U.S. at 449.

Capitalization Change

The Fifth Amendment states that "[n]o person . . . shall be compelled in any criminal case to be a witness against himself." U.S. Const. amend. V.

Change in Verb Tense

The Council authorized the construction of a twelve-story tower, finding that reducing the tower to this height "substantially mitigate[s] adverse impacts on the land use pattern in the vicinity."

Use empty brackets ("[ ]") to indicate that a single letter has been omitted.

In some cases, a pronoun in a quotation may be ambiguous in the new context, so for clarity the writer substitutes the appropriate noun in brackets. In such cases, the omission of the pronoun does not need to be indicated.

EXAMPLE 21   Brackets to Add Clarifying Substitute

At the time of her medical release, Wainwright made the following admission: "I did continue to have some pain and discomfort in my back, neck, and arms, but [Dr. Rodgers] felt this was normal pain and discomfort and that it would go away."

Occasionally, something that you want to quote has a significant error in it. In such cases, use a bracketed "sic" immediately after the error to indicate that the error was in the original and not inadvertently added.

EXAMPLE 22   Bracketed SIC to Show Error in Original

On the day after the union vote was held, the shop foreman issued a memo to all machinists stating that how they voted "would not effect [*sic*] their performance reviews."

§ 28.5.4   Parentheses

In everyday writing, parentheses are used to add additional information to sentences. They are one way to signal that that information is of lesser importance.

EXAMPLE 23   Parentheses Around Additional Information

Newcombe wrested one-eighth ounce of marijuana (worth $40) from Tyson's pocket.

Because conciseness is a cardinal virtue in legal writing, legal writers usually edit out any information that is of lesser importance. Consequently, parenthetical inserts are not common in legal writing.

This does not mean that parentheses themselves do not appear anywhere in legal documents. They are frequently used in the following ways.

a.   To Enclose Short Explanations of Cases Within Citations

EXAMPLE 24   **Parentheses Around Cases Explanations in Citations**

Washington courts have held the emergency doctrine inapplicable when the actor is already in a position of peril. *Mills v. Park*, 409 P.2d 646 (Wash. 1966) (where the defendant's vision in a snowstorm was already obscured and a snowplow throwing snow on defendant's car did not constitute a sudden emergency); *see also Hinkel v. Weyerhaeuser Co.*, 494 P.2d 1008 (Wash. Ct. App. 1972) (where dense smoke did not constitute application of the emergency doctrine because the defendant was warned of the smoke ahead).

The costs of asserting one's Fifth Amendment right against self-incrimination that are held to be too high are often economic or proprietary costs. *See, e.g., Slochower v. Bd. of Higher Educ. of N.Y.C.*, 350 U.S. 551, 559 (1956) (holding termination of state-employed professor based on adverse inference of guilt from refusal to answer violated due process); *Spevak v. Klein*, 385 U.S. 511, 518 (1967) (holding disbarment of lawyer for asserting the privilege violated Fifth Amendment).

---

b.   To Refer Readers to Attached or Appended Documents

EXAMPLE 25   **Parentheses for Attachments**

Before signing the agreement, Miller crossed out the language "at time of closing" in paragraph 12 and inserted the language "pro ratio as received by sellers" in paragraph 24. (See appendix 1.)

---

c.   To Confirm Numbers

EXAMPLE 26   **Parentheses Confirming Numbers**

In 2007, Patrick and Rose Milton borrowed five thousand dollars ($5,000) from Southern Security Company.

---

d.   To Enclose Numerals That Introduce the Individual Items in a List

---

EXAMPLE 27   **Parentheses Enclosing Numerals**

The company's regulations list seven circumstances under which an employee may be separated from his or her job: (1) resignation, (2) release, (3) death, (4) retirement, (5) failure to return from a leave of absence, (6) failure to return from a layoff, and (7) discharge or suspension for cause.

---

e.   To Announce Changes to a Quotation That Cannot Be Shown by Ellipses or Brackets

---

EXAMPLE 28   **Parentheses in Citations to Show Changes to Quotations**

"[I]solated incidents are normally insufficient to establish supervisory inaction upon which to predicate § 1983 liability.", 717 F.2d at 936 (footnote omitted).

The court held that "[a]n instruction, *when requested,* defining intent is required when intent is an element of the crime charged." *Id.* (emphasis added).

---

f.   To Introduce Abbreviations After a Full Name Is Given

EXAMPLE 29   **Parentheses Around Abbreviations**

Beaver Custom Carpets (BCC) has been in business for one year.

---

§ 28.5.5   The Hyphen

Hyphens combine words to form compound modifiers or compound nouns. The trick is knowing when a pair or grouping of modifiers or nouns should be joined by hyphens to show that they are acting as one unit.

For modifiers, the first step is a simple one: If the modifiers do not precede the noun they modify, then they are usually not hyphenated.

EXAMPLE 30   **Hyphen with Modifiers**

Owens's argument ignores other rules of statutory construction that are <u>well established</u>.

Owens's argument ignores other <u>well-established</u> rules of statutory construction.

Notice that legal writers use many compound modifiers that begin with "well." As long as these modifiers precede the noun they modify, they are hyphenated.

> a well-reasoned opinion   a well-defined test
> a well-known fact   a well-founded argument

Obviously, though, not all compound modifiers begin with "well," and, unfortunately, often the only way to know whether to hyphenate is to consult a good dictionary with a recent publication date. The recent publication date is important because our language changes: What was once two or more separate words may later be hyphenated and eventually combined into one word.

air plane → air-plane → airplane

Separate

trier of fact	*prima facie* case
leave of absence	

Hyphenated

price-fixing contract	take-home pay
out-of-pocket expenses	stop-limit order
sudden-emergency doctrine	court-martial
cross-examination	hit-and-run accident
family-car doctrine	

Combined

wraparound mortgage	quitclaim deed
counterclaim	online
ongoing	layoffs

Our changing language also gives us new hyphenated nouns.

frame-up   split-off   squeeze-out

Many words are in transition. For example, you may notice that "line-up" is spelled with a hyphen in some cases and as the combined word "lineup" in others. The same is true for "pre-trial" and "pretrial" and "e-mail" and "email." In such instances, consult your most recent authority and try to be consistent within the document you are writing.

In addition to using the dictionary as a guide to hyphen use, there are a few general rules about when to use hyphens.

1. Always hyphenate modifiers and nouns that begin with the prefixes "all," "ex," and "self."

all-American	all-purpose
ex-partner	ex-employee
self-defense	self-incrimination

2. Other prefixes, including "anti," "co," "de," "inter," "intra," "multi," "non," "para," "pro," "re," "semi," and "super," generally should not be used with a hyphen.

antitrust	nonpayment
codefendant	paralegal
degenerate	prorate
interagency	reallocate
intrastate	semiannual
multinational	supersede

Unfortunately, however, there are enough exceptions to this general rule that you may often have to look up the word you need. The following exceptions apply to larger categories of words:

a. Use the hyphen when it is needed for clarity ("re-create," not "recreate");
b. Use the hyphen when it is needed to prevent a doubled vowel ("re-enact," "de-emphasize") or a tripled consonant;
c. Use the hyphen when it is needed because the second element is capitalized ("post-World War II," "un-American," or "anti-Semitic").

3. "Elcct" is the one suffix that usually requires a hyphen.

> governor-elect   president-elect

4. Hyphens are used to form compound numbers from twenty-one to ninety-nine. Hyphens are also used with fractions functioning as adjectives, but not with fractions functioning as nouns.

> the seventy-second Congress
> one-half acre *but*
>   one half of the employees
> two-thirds majority *but*
>   two thirds of the board

5. Hyphens are often used to join a number and a noun to make a compound modifier.

> twenty-year-old appellant   ten-year lease
> three-mile limit   ten-acre tract
> nine-year-old conviction   first-year student

6. Do not use a hyphen in the following instances:

a. when the first word in a two-word modifier is an adverb ending in "-ly" ("previously taxed income," "jointly acquired property");
b. when the compound modifier contains a foreign phrase ("bona fide purchaser," "per se violation");
c. when a civil or military title denotes one office ("justice of the peace" but "secretary-treasurer").

Sometimes two or more compound modifiers share the same second element. In such cases, use hyphens after each first element and do not use the second element twice.

> high- and low-test gasoline
> nine- and ten-acre parcels

7. Hyphens are also frequently used to combine two parties into one modifier.

> attorney-client privilege   husband-wife tort actions

8. Initially hyphens were common in terms such as "Mexican-American" and "Asian-American." Recently, however, the trend seems to be to drop the hyphen. The exception is "Afro-American." (See section 25.5.2.)

9. Most new words that have abbreviated "electronic" with an "e" before another word retain the hyphen, but both "e-mail" and "email" are now common usage.

e-book   e-commerce

§ 28.5.6   The Dash

The traditional dash, now known as the em dash, is rarely used in legal writing. The consensus seems to be that dashes are too informal for the serious work of law.

Still, there are a few occasions when the dash is useful. For example, in sentences in which a list is an appositive, a pair of dashes can be used to signal the beginning and end of the list.

EXAMPLE 31   **Em Dashes with Internal Lists**

By 1996, the defendant had opened up bank accounts in several foreign countries—Switzerland, Brazil, South Africa, and Spain—all under different names.

The conservative bloc—Rehnquist, O'Connor, Scalia, and Kennedy—controlled the major cases of the 1988-1989 term.

Similarly, a dash is needed to set off an introductory list containing commas.

EXAMPLE 32   **Em Dash with Introductory List**

Name-calling, threats, and repeated beatings—these were the ways Wilson gave attention to his son.

When used with discretion, dashes can also be an effective way to create emphasis. Notice how in the following sentences, the dashes do more than the commas to highlight what they enclose.

EXAMPLE 33   **Em Dashes to Create Emphasis**

Commas

The victim's age, eighteen months, made him particularly vulnerable.

Dashes

The victim's age—eighteen months—made him particularly vulnerable.

Dashes can also be used to show abrupt shifts or to cue the reader that the words that follow are shocking or surprising.

| EXAMPLE 34 | **Em Dashes to Indicate Surprise** |

Several witnesses—including the defendant's mother—testified that they believed Willie was capable of committing such a heinous crime.

With typesetting and increasingly sophisticated software programs, writers should distinguish between the en dash ("–"), which is slightly longer than a hyphen and found in the "symbol" or "special characters" pull-down menus, and the em dash ("—"), which is longer than an en dash.

The en dash means "to" and is used to connect numbers and occasionally words.

| EXAMPLE 35 | **En Dash to Connect Numbers or Other Words** |

The advertised salary, $120,000–$140,000, was significantly more than her previous salary.

The Dallas–Chicago flight was cancelled.

Note that the en dash should not be used if the word "from" or "between" precedes the first number or word. In such instances, "to" should be used instead of the en dash.

| EXAMPLE 36 | **No En Dash with "From" or "Between"** |

The advertised salary range from $120,000 to $140,000 was significantly more than her previous salary.

The flight between Dallas and Chicago was cancelled.

Chapter 28 Quiz No. 3

Draft answers for each of the following questions. Make your points clearly and concisely, and write sentences that are easy to read and that are grammatical and correctly punctuated.

1. Usually "'s" is used to form the possessive of singular nouns. When a singular noun ends in "-s," what is the rule for whether to use an apostrophe?
2. What is the rule for creating the possessive form of plural nouns ending in "-s"?
3. What is the difference between "it's" and "its"? Which is the possessive form of "it"?
4. What are the rules about setting up a block quotation?
5. What punctuation mark indicates a quotation within a quotation?
6. What is the rule in the United States for commas, periods, semicolons, colons, and other punctuation marks with closing quotation marks?
7. What does an ellipsis (three spaced periods) indicate in a quotation?
8. What does a fourth period after the three spaced periods in an ellipsis indicate?

9. What does a pair of brackets indicate in a quotation?

10. What does the word "sic" in brackets in a quotation mean?

§ 28.6   Comma Splices and Fused Sentences

§ 28.6.1 Comma Splices

Perhaps the most common punctuation error in all writing, not just legal writing, is the comma splice. Simply put, a comma splice is the joining of two main, or independent, clauses with just a comma. The following diagram represents a sentence that incorrectly joins two main clauses with a comma.

<u>   main clause   </u>   ,   <u>   main clause   </u>   .

Reminder

A main clause has both a subject and verb and can stand alone as a sentence.

EXAMPLE 1   **Comma Splices**

The prosecutor spoke about the defendant's motive, the jury listened carefully.

The corrections officer contacted several other persons, none knew of Wilson's disappearance.

Mr. Baker sustained personal property damage, his picture windows and valuable vase were smashed.

There are five simple methods for correcting a comma splice. Use the method that best suits the context.

1. Make each main clause a separate sentence.

EXAMPLE 2   **Comma Splice Corrected**

The prosecutor spoke about the defendant's motive. The jury listened carefully.

---

2. Add a coordinating conjunction ("and," "but," "or," "for," "nor," "yet," "so") after the comma separating the two main clauses. (See Rule 1 in section 28.1.)

EXAMPLE 3   **Comma Splice Corrected**

The corrections officer contacted several other persons, but none knew of Wilson's disappearance.

---

3. Change the comma separating the two main clauses to a semicolon. (See section 28.2.)

EXAMPLE 4   **Comma Splice Corrected**

The corrections officer contacted several other persons; none knew of Wilson's disappearance.

---

4. Change one of the main clauses to a subordinate clause.

EXAMPLE 5   **Comma Splices Corrected**

While the prosecutor spoke about the defendant's motive, the jury listened carefully.

Although the corrections officer contacted several other persons, none knew of Wilson's disappearance.

---

5. If the second main clause is an explanation or illustration of the first main clause, use a colon to separate the two main clauses. (See section 28.3.)

EXAMPLE 6   **Comma Splice Corrected**

Mr. Baker sustained personal property damage: His picture windows and valuable vase were smashed.

Comma splices often occur in sentences that have two main clauses and a conjunctive adverb introducing the second main clause. The following diagram represents a sentence that incorrectly joins two main clauses with a comma.

    _____ main clause _____ , therefore, _____ main clause _____ .

Reminder

The most commonly used conjunctive adverbs are "accordingly," "also," "besides," "consequently," "furthermore," "hence," "however," "indeed," "instead," "likewise," "meanwhile," "moreover," "nevertheless," "still," "then," "therefore," and "thus."

EXAMPLE 7   **Incorrect**

The summons was not delivered to his usual place of abode, therefore, service was not effected in the manner prescribed by law.

Such comma splices are corrected by changing the comma to a semicolon or a period.

| **EXAMPLE 8** | **Corrected** |

The summons was not delivered to his usual place of abode; therefore, service was not effected in the manner prescribed by law.

The summons was not delivered to his usual place of abode. Therefore, service was not effected in the manner prescribed by law.

---

§ 28.6.2   Fused Sentences

Fused sentences, also known as run-on sentences, are a less frequent but even more serious writing error than comma splices. A fused sentence has no punctuation or coordinating conjunction between two main clauses. The following diagram represents a fused sentence, which is incorrect.

<u>   main clause   main clause   </u>.

| **EXAMPLE 9** | **Fused Sentence** |

The prosecutor spoke about the defendant's motive the jury listened carefully.

Fused sentences can be corrected using the same methods for correcting comma splices.

Chapter 28 Quiz No. 4

Draft answers for each of the following questions. Make your points clearly and concisely, and write sentences that are easy to read and that are grammatical and correctly punctuated.

1. What is the punctuation error known as the comma splice?
2. What are the five methods for correcting a comma splice?
3. What is a fused, or run-on, sentence?

Mechanics

§ 29.1   Spelling

With the advent of Spellcheck on everyone's computer, it might seem as though misspelled words are no longer an issue in legal writing. Spellcheckers have been a godsend, but they have not solved all the problems related to spelling in legal writing.

First, spellcheckers still do not have many commonly used legal words in their dictionaries. For example, "articulable," as in the phrase "articulable suspicion" may show up as a misspelling. The way to solve this problem is to add the word to your computer's dictionary. You may also find it useful to add other common abbreviations like those that appear in many citations to your computer's dictionary.

Second, most spellcheckers accept secondary spellings that many legal readers dislike. For example, most legal readers consider "judgment" without the "e," a misspelling; in fact, a court judgment must be spelled without the "e," but the computer dictionary may accept "judgement" without comment.

Third, computer spelling programs check spelling by making a blind match between the words you have typed and the words in the dictionary. The program does not consider context. Consequently, it will read "torte" as spelled correctly without knowing whether the writer intended a wrongful act or a cake with rich frosting.

Fourth, the autocorrect function in some word processing programs may make changes that you did not intend and actually insert spelling or other errors into your writing. For example, if you haven't added "tortious" to your dictionary, it may automatically change it to "tortuous." It may also set ordinals in superscript, changing "4th" to "4th" in your citations. It may automatically insert a space after a period or capitalize the next word. You may decide that the solution is to turn the autocorrect feature off. If you keep the autocorrect on, you may want to modify the words it corrects and disable features like superscript.[1]

Finally, spelling programs do not include most proper names. This means that writers have to be particularly careful proofreading names and not just click "ignore" or "ignore all" too quickly. Make a point of checking whether it is Stephen with a "ph" or Steven with a "v," Schmitt with a "t" or Schmidt with a "d." There is no quicker way to alienate someone than to misspell his or her name.

§ 29.2   Capitalization

§ 29.2.1   General Rules

In English, there are two general rules for capitalization: (1) to mark the beginning of a sentence, and (2) to signal a proper name or adjective. Unfortunately, however, there is occasional disagreement about what is a proper name or adjective.

Two additional principles can serve as useful guides: First, be consistent. Once you have decided that a word or type of word is capitalized or lowercased, apply that decision consistently throughout the document you are writing. Second, note that the tendency in English now is toward what is called the "down" style,[2] which is a lowercase rather than an uppercase style.

a. Beginning of a Sentence

The first word of a sentence is always capitalized. Even sentence fragments such as those that begin brief answers in legal memoranda have their first word capitalized.

A complete sentence enclosed in parentheses starts with a capital letter, unless the parenthetical sentence occurs within another sentence.

EXAMPLE 1   **Capitalization with Parenthetical Sentences**

The Wilsons extended their garden beyond the property line and onto the disputed strip. (See Attachment A.)

The Wilsons extended their garden beyond the property line (see Attachment A) and onto the disputed strip.

---

1. Section 1D in the *ALWD Citation Manual* has an excellent discussion of the problems default settings create in citations and how to disable AutoCorrect in Word or QuickCorrect in WordPerfect.

2. *See The Chicago Manual of Style* 387 (16th ed. U. of Chicago Press 2010).

1. *Quotations*

Capitalize the first word of a direct quotation when the quotation is formally introduced and set up as a separate sentence.

EXAMPLE 2   **Capitalization with Formally Introduced Quotations**

The Supreme Court unanimously struck down a policy banning women of child-bearing age from hazardous but top-paying jobs: "Decisions about the welfare of future children must be left to the parents who conceive, bear, support, and raise them rather than to the employers who hire those parents." *Int'l Union, United Auto., Aerospace & Agric. Implement Workers of Am., UAW v. Johnson Controls, Inc.*, 499 U.S. 187, 206 (1991).

Do not capitalize the first word of a direct quotation when the quotation is integrated into the writer's sentence. See section 28.5.3 for discussion of the use of brackets when making a change to a quotation.

EXAMPLE 3   **No Capitalization with Integrated Quotations**

The Supreme Court unanimously struck down a policy banning women of child-bearing age from hazardous but top-paying jobs, stating that "[d]ecisions about the welfare of future children must be left to the parents who conceive, bear, support, and raise them rather than to the employers who hire those parents." *Int'l Union, United Auto., Aerospace & Agric. Implement Workers of Am., UAW v. Johnson Controls, Inc.*, 499 U.S. 187, 206 (1991).

Do not capitalize the beginning of the second segment of a split direct quotation.

EXAMPLE 4   **No Capitalization with Second Half of Split Quote**

"Concern for a woman's existing or potential offspring," wrote Justice Blackmun for the majority, "historically has been the excuse for denying women equal employment opportunities." *Id.* at 210.

---

2. *Sentences Following a Colon*

When a colon introduces two or more full sentences, capitalize the first word of each of those sentences.[3] When a colon introduces a single full sentence, that sentence does not begin with a capital letter.

---

3. Not all authorities agree on this rule. For example, the *AP Style Manual* recommends capitalizing the first word after a colon if the colon introduces a single full sentence.

| EXAMPLE 5 | Capitalize After Colon That Introduces Two Sentences |

The company has evidence that Mrs. McKibbin accepted the written proposal: She made a telephone call to place the order for the rugs. She sent an email that included the rugs' measurements.

| EXAMPLE 6 | No Capitalization After Colon That Introduces a Single Sentence |

The company has evidence that Mrs. McKibbin accepted the written proposal: she made a telephone call to place the order for the rugs.

Do not capitalize the first word after the colon if what follows the colon is less than a complete sentence.

| EXAMPLE 7 | No Capitalization After Colon |

In *Traweek*, the court found that the appearance of the defendants differed from the witness's description in just one detail: the color of the shirts worn by the defendants.

If the items in a series following a colon are not complete sentences, do not capitalize the first word in each item.

| EXAMPLE 8 | No Capitalization After Colon Introducing Series of Dependent Clauses |

The parties will dispute whether three of the four elements of the sudden emergency doctrine are met: (1) whether Mr. Odoki was confronted by a sudden and unexpected emergency, (2) whether his own negligence created or contributed to that emergency, and (3) whether he made a choice such as a reasonable person placed in the same situation might make.

b. Proper Nouns and Adjectives

As a general rule, capitalize a word used to name someone or something specific; use a lowercase letter when the same word is used as a general reference.

the President of Shell Oil
a president of a company

Stanford Law School
a law school

Environmental Protection Agency
an agency of the federal government

Note that nationalities and ethnic groups are treated as proper nouns and capitalized, but racial groups defined by color are not.

> Italian
> Chinese
> *but*
> black
> white

Traditionally, the short forms of proper nouns were also capitalized. If, for example, the defendant in a lawsuit was the "Green River Community College," after the first reference the writer then used the short form "the College," and "College" was capitalized. Rule 8 in the 19th edition of *The Bluebook* seems to suggest a similar approach. Unfortunately, there is also disagreement about whether to capitalize the words "defendant" and "plaintiff" (and similar terms such as "appellant," "appellee," "respondent," and "petitioner"). Some authorities capitalize these words only when they refer to the parties in the matter that is the subject of the document.[4] Others simply say not to capitalize the terms at all[5] or not to capitalize them when they are descriptive titles that describe a person's role,[6] as in the example "defendant Smith." All agree that these words should be capitalized on cover sheets for briefs. Once you have started capitalizing (or not capitalizing) a particular term, be consistent throughout that document.

Particularly difficult for legal writers is determining when to capitalize certain words that commonly occur in legal writing ("act," "amendment," "bill," "circuit," "code," "congressional," "constitution," "court," "federal," "legislature," "national," "statute," and "the"). Use the following list as a quick reference.

"Act"

Capitalize the word "act" when it is part of a full title.

> the Clean Air Act
> the Controlled Substance Act of 1970
> but
> an act passed by the legislature

"Act" is also capitalized when it is used as the short form of a proper name.

> the Clean Air Act → the Act

---

4. *See The Bluebook* B7.3.2 (19th ed. 2010).

5. *See Texas Law Review Manual on Usage, Style & Editing* 36 (11th ed. 2008) (stating that common names for litigants are not capitalized unless they refer to a governmental party, such as "State" or "Government").

6. *See The Chicago Manual of Style* 398 (16th ed. 2010).

"Amendment"

Most authorities capitalize "amendment" when referring to amendments of the U.S. Constitution.

> Fifth Amendment
> A general reference to an amendment should not be capitalized.
> an amendment to the tax laws

Notice that when referring to one of the amendments to the Constitution, most writers spell out ordinals through the Ninth Amendment and use figures for the 10th Amendment and above.

> Fifth Amendment   14th Amendment

When two or more amendments are mentioned together, use figures if either is for the 10th Amendment or above.

> the 5th Amendment and the 14th Amendment

"Bill"

With the exception of the Bill of Rights, "bill" should be written in lowercase. This practice does seem to be an exception to the general rule of capitalizing words that are part of a full title.

> Senate bill 47   House bill 11

"Circuit"

Capitalize "circuit" when it is used as part of a full title or with a circuit number. Use lowercase when "circuit" is part of a general reference.

> United States Court of Appeals for the Second Circuit
> the Second Circuit
> but
> circuit courts

"Code"

Capitalize "code" when it is part of a full title or when it refers to a specific code. Use lowercase for all general references.

> the *United States Internal Revenue Code*
> *United States Code*
> but
> the tax code
> state codes
> unofficial code

"Congress"

Capitalize "Congress" when it is part of the full title of the United States Congress or the short form "the Congress." The adjective "congressional," on the other hand, is usually lowercase unless it is part of a full title such as the *Congressional Record*.

"Constitution"

Capitalize "constitution" when used as part of the full title of any constitution or when used as a short form reference to the United States Constitution. Do not capitalize the adjective "constitutional" unless it is part of a title.

> the United States Constitution
> the Constitution (short for United States Constitution)
> *but*
> a new state constitution
> a constitutional issue

"Court"

Probably the most common capitalization question in legal writing is when "court" should be capitalized.

1. The official and full names of all international and higher courts are capitalized.

> International Court of Justice
> United States Court of Appeals for the Third Circuit
> Texas Court of Appeals
> Arizona Supreme Court

2. Always capitalize "court" when referring to the United States Supreme Court. Note that even the short forms for referring to the United States Supreme Court are capitalized.

> the Supreme Court of the United States
> the United States Supreme Court
> the Supreme Court
> the Court (short form for Supreme Court)

3. Do not capitalize "court" if it is part of the name of a city or county court.

> the Phoenix night court
> juvenile court

Despite the agreement among the authorities about not capitalizing "court" if it is part of the name of a city or county court, most practitioners seem to ignore the rule and capitalize "court" in such instances.

4. Capitalize "court" in a document when referring to the very court that will receive that document.

5. Capitalize "court" when the term specifically refers to the judge or presiding officer.

It is the opinion of this Court . . . .

Other personifications such as "Your Honor" and "the Bench" are also capitalized.

"Federal"

The word "federal" is capitalized only when it is part of a specific name or when the word it modifies is capitalized.

Federal Bureau of Investigation
Federal Deposit Insurance Corporation
Federal Energy Regulatory Commission
but
federal government
federal agents
federal court

"Legislature"

Capitalize "legislature" only when it refers to the branch of the national government of the United States. Otherwise, "legislature" should be lowercase. Note that the same rule applies to other branches of government: capitalize "executive branch" and "judicial branch" only when they apply to the U.S. national government.

the Legislature (when referring to the U.S. Congress)
the state legislature

"National"

The word "national" is capitalized only when it is part of a specific name or when the word it modifies is capitalized.

National Security Council
but
national security interests

Another test for whether to capitalize "federal" or "national" is whether the word following those terms is capitalized. If it is, then capitalize "federal" or "national" because it is part of a specific name.

"State"

Capitalize when "state" is part of the full title for a state or when referring to the governmental actor or party to a suit.

> State of Washington
> The State will argue that the evidence should be admitted.

"Statute"

Use lowercase for "statute," unless it is part of a title.

> federal statutes
> state statutes
> statute of limitations

"The"

In names and titles, capitalize "the" only if it is part of an official name.

> The Hague
> *The Bluebook*
> *but*
> the United States Supreme Court
> the American Bar Association

§ 29.2.2 Miscellaneous Rules for Capitalization

Academic Degrees

Academic degrees are capitalized, but some have lowercase internal letters.

> J.D.   LL.M.   M.D.   Ph.D.

Acronyms

Most acronyms are written in all capitals (CEO, OPEC, NASA, CERCLA). Abbreviations of government agencies, corporations, and military organizations are also all capital letters (EEOC, FCC, IBM, USMC).

Compass Points, Geographical Names, and Topographical Names

Compass points are capitalized when they refer to a geographical region; adjectives derived from compass points are also capitalized. The compass points themselves are lowercased if they just name a direction.

the Middle West
the Northeast
Southern hospitality
Southwestern cuisine
but
the car was heading west
the fence runs along the northern boundary

Topographical Names

Capitalize topographical names when they are part of a proper name.

Lake Superior	*but*	a lake
the Mississippi River		the river
the Rocky Mountains		those mountains

In legal documents, words such as "state," "county," or "city" are capitalized when they are part of a specific name.

Washington State
Chaves County
the City of Spokane
the State of Florida
Commonwealth of Virginia

Similarly, capitalize words such as "bridge," "square," "building," "park," and "hotel" when they are part of a place name.

Brooklyn Bridge	Central Park
Transamerica Building	Tiananmen Square

Rules of Law

Despite efforts at uniformity, several rules of law are known by several versions of their name, all with differing capitalization. The common issue is whether a certain phrase is part of the title of the rule. The general guideline is to capitalize the words that are essential to the rule's name. Another reasonable guideline is to use the most common form of the rule's name.

Is it, for example, "the rule in Shelley's case," "the Rule in Shelley's case," "the Rule in Shelley's Case," or "The Rule in Shelley's Case"? Using the guideline of capitalizing those words that are essential to the rule's name, "rule" and "case" should be capitalized because they are commonly treated as part of the name. "The," on the other hand, should probably be lowercase to avoid making the phrase look like a book title.

Is it the "rule against perpetuities," the "Rule against Perpetuities," or the "Rule Against Perpetuities"? Professor Dukeminier asked this question in his article Perpetuities: Contagious Capitalization[7] and determined that "Rule

---

7. Jesse Dukeminier, Perpetuities: Contagious Capitalization, 20 J. Legal Educ. 341 (1968).

against Perpetuities" and "rule against perpetuities" were both commonly used and therefore acceptable.

What should a legal writer do, then, when faced with a similar question? One easy suggestion is to go online and do a quick search to see what the courts do. If that does not solve the problem, consider the following factors:

1. What words are essential to the rule's name?
2. What capitalization is most common?
3. Is there a historical reason for preferring one version over another?

The most important consideration of all, though, is consistency. Once you have determined which version you will use, use it consistently throughout the document.

Titles

Capitalize titles of court documents. Use all capitals for titles on the documents themselves.

Titles are capitalized when they precede a personal name and are treated as part of that name. Titles are also capitalized when they immediately follow a name as an appositive. The same titles are then normally lowercased when they follow a personal name or when they are used as a short form for the name.

Governor Rick Perry
Rick Perry, Governor of the State of Texas
the governor

Trademarks

Use all capitals to distinguish a trademark from the name of a company or corporation.

XEROX (trademark)   Xerox (corporation)

Vessels

Although one occasionally sees all capitals used for the name of a vessel, capitalizing only the first letter is preferred.

Titanic   Valdez

§ 29.3   Abbreviations and Symbols

§ 29.3.1   General Rules for Abbreviations

Abbreviations, or shortened forms, should be used primarily for the convenience of the reader. Properly used, an abbreviation saves the reader time and energy. It gets across the same message in less space.

The temptation for writers, of course, is to use abbreviations that are convenient for them. A writer who fails to adopt the reader's perspective may use an abbreviation to save the writer time and energy only to find that the reader is unsure, confused, or even frustrated by the abbreviation.

One source of abbreviation confusion is the sheer number of specialized abbreviations used in some legal documents.[8] The result of such overuse is obvious: the harried reader has to keep turning back in the document to keep the abbreviations straight. The solution to the problem is equally obvious: avoid using numerous specialized abbreviations in the same document.

All of the abbreviation rules that follow apply to abbreviations in textual sentences, not in citations.

Rule 1	**Abbreviate only when the abbreviation will be clear to the reader**

Rule 2	**If an abbreviation will be initially unfamiliar to the reader, use the full form first and then follow with the abbreviation in parentheses**

EXAMPLE 1   **Full Form Followed by Abbreviation**

Mrs. Kearney telephoned Beaver Custom Carpets (BCC) and asked if it manufactured custom-made carpets. BCC's representative took down a description of the carpets she wanted made.

Mr. Washburn wants to know whether the Oregon Wilderness Watchers (OWW) can create a prescriptive easement across his land. OWW has been using a path across Washburn's property to reach its property.

Abbreviations created for a specific document, such as BCC and OWW in Example 1, are usually written in all capitals. Notice that common abbreviations that are acronyms (ERIC, SARA, ERISTA) are also written in all capitals, unless they have been fully incorporated into the language ("radar," "sonar," "scuba," and "zip code").

§ 29.3.2   Miscellaneous Rules for Abbreviation

Geographical Names

United States Postal Service abbreviations are acceptable when used on envelopes and in other situations when an address is written in block form. Note that state abbreviations are all capitalized without end periods. (This rule does not apply to states in case citations.)

---

8. Writing about a case in which no fewer than seven different groups of initials were used, Justice Rehnquist complained that "the 'alphabet soup' of the New Deal era was, by comparison, a clear broth." *Chrysler Corp. v. Brown*, 441 U.S. 281, 284, 286-87 (1979).

Professor Mary Brown
8990 6th Ave. NE
Tacoma, WA 98498

The same words (avenue, street, northeast, Washington) should be spelled out when they appear in text. Note that all compass points (northeast, southwest) are also lowercase, unless they are used as the name of a region (the Pacific Northwest, the South).

"Saint" may be abbreviated when it is part of the name of a city (St. Louis); follow the bearer's preference when it is part of a person's name (David Saint-Johns, Ruth St. Denis).

Foreign Phrases

Some Latin words commonly used in legal texts and citations are abbreviations, so they should be followed by periods (*id.*, *i.e.*, *e.g.*). Others are complete words (the *ex* in *ex parte* or *re*), so a period should not be used.

Names of Laws

The first time a law is mentioned in text, its title should be typed out in full; thereafter, abbreviations may be used. (*See The Bluebook* or *ALWD Citation Manual* for how to write the names of laws in citations.)

> first mention: Article II, Section 3
> later references: Art. II, Sec. 3

Academic Degrees

Academic degrees are abbreviated. Note that capitalization should be checked in a dictionary.

> Ph.D.   LL.D.   M.B.A.   C.P.A.
> J.D.   LL.B.   LL.M.   M.D.

Time

The abbreviations for ante meridiem and post meridiem are most commonly written as unspaced, lowercase letters with periods.

> 9:00 a.m.

Measures and Weights

When the numeral is written out,[9] the unit must also be written out. When the figure is used, the unit may be abbreviated.

---

9. According to *The Bluebook* Rule 6.2(a), numbers from zero to ninety-nine are written out and larger numbers use numerals, unless the number begins a sentence. Numbers used at the beginning of a sentence must be written out.

| one hundred square miles | or | 100 sq. mi. |
| one hundred eighty pounds | or | 180 lbs. |

Double Punctuation

Occasionally, an abbreviation will be the last word in a sentence. In such cases, do not add an additional period after the period for the abbreviation.

The officer had checked in at 8:00 p.m.
Clark claimed she had a Ph.D.

A period for an abbreviation is used with a question mark or an exclamation point.

Did the officer check in at 8:00 p.m.?

§ 29.3.3 Inappropriate Abbreviations

Informal Abbreviations

Avoid informal abbreviations such as "ad," "cite," "exam," "memo," "quote" (as a noun), and "&" in formal legal writing. Use the more formal, full name: "advertisement," "citation," "examination," "memorandum," "quotation," and "and."

Dates

Do not abbreviate dates. Write them out in full.

Monday, February 13, 2009
not
Mon. Feb. 13, '09

Abbreviations Between Lines or Pages

Do not separate parts of an abbreviation. The full abbreviation should be on one line on one page.

Beginnings of Sentences

Avoid beginning a sentence with an abbreviation unless the abbreviation is a courtesy title (Mr., Mrs., Ms., Dr., Messrs.).

Titles

Most titles other than Mr., Mrs., Ms., Dr., and Messrs. are not abbreviated.

Professor Mary Bowman
General Martin Dempsey

When "Honorable" and "Reverend" are preceded by "The," then "Honorable" and "Reverend" are spelled out; when used without "The," they can be abbreviated.

The Reverend James P. Coyne	*but*	Rev. James P. Coyne
The Honorable Walter Jackson	*but*	Hon. Walter Jackson

§ 29.3.4 General Rules for Symbols

Rule 1   Do not begin a sentence with a symbol

"Section" and "paragraph" are always spelled out at the beginning of a sentence.

Section 289 was amended in 2008.
not
§ 289 was amended in 2008.

The symbol for "section," §, or §§ for "sections," must be used in footnotes or citations as long as the symbol does not begin a sentence. Be sure to separate the symbol from the number following it with a space.

Rule 2   Use the symbol for dollar ($) and percent (%) with numerals. Spell out the words if the numbers are spelled out

fifteen dollars	*or*	$15.00
sixty percent	*or*	60%

There is no space between $ or % and their accompanying numerals.

§ 29.4   Italics

In legal writing, italics are most commonly used for case names, titles of publications, foreign phrases, introductory signals, and, occasionally, emphasis. In some jurisdictions, underlining is an acceptable substitute; other jurisdictions, such as Washington State, explicitly state in their style sheet that case names must be italicized. What is not acceptable is mixing italicizing with underlining.

Rule 1   All case names, including the v.,[10] should be in italics

Smith v. Jones
United States v. Foster

---

10. Some attorneys do not italicize the v., presumably because the Supreme Court of the United States does not. *The Bluebook* and the *ALWD Citation Manual* rules, however, require that the v. be italicized.

If underlining is used, underline the blank spaces between the words.

<u>Smith v. Jones</u>
<u>United States v. Foster</u>

Rule 2   Italicize (or underline) all introductory signals, phrases introducing related authority, and explanatory phrases in citations (See *The Bluebook* or the *ALWD Citation Manual* for a complete list.)

Accord	*See also*	*Cf.*	*E.g.,*
aff'd	*cert. denied*	*rev'd*	*but see*
cited with approval in	*construed in*		

"See" is not italicized when it is used in text, rather than as part of the citation, to introduce an authority.

Rule 3   Italicize all titles of publications when they appear in text (See *The Bluebook* or the *ALWD Citation Manual* for titles in citations.)

Titles of books, reports, periodicals, newspapers, and plays are all italicized when they appear in textual sentences. Even titles of nonprint media, such as television and radio programs, musical works, and works of visual art are italicized.

Handbook of Federal Indian Law
Index to Legal Periodicals
Yale Law Review
New York Times
Presumed Innocent
Law and Order

The Bible, however, is not italicized.

Rule 4   Italicize names of aircraft, ships, and trains

Hindenburg   *Nimitz*   *Orient Express*

Rule 5   Italicize foreign words that are not incorporated into the English language

carpe diem
qua
infra
supra

Rule 6   **Italics may be used to indicate that a word is being used as a word**

EXAMPLE 1   **Italics for a Word Used as a Word**

Article 6 is silent about what constitutes service as opposed to *merchandise.*

Rule 7   **If used sparingly, italics may be used for emphasis**

EXAMPLE 2   **Example 2**   **Italics for Emphasis**

Fremont's coach insists that he asked *all* of his players to participate in the drug-testing program.

Use of italics or underlining for emphasis occurs most commonly in long quotations. In such cases, the writer must indicate whether the emphasis was added or whether it was part of the original quotation.

EXAMPLE 3   **Italics for Emphasis Added**

The relevant portion of § 2339B reads as follows:

> § 2339B. Providing material support or resources to designated foreign terrorist organizations
>> (a) Prohibited activities.
>>> (1) Unlawful conduct. Whoever knowingly provides material support or resources to a foreign terrorist organization, or attempts or conspires to do so, shall be fined under this title or imprisoned not more than 15 years, or both, and, if the death of any person results, shall be imprisoned for any term of years or for life. *To violate this paragraph, a person must have knowledge that the organization is a designated terrorist organization . . . , that the organization has engaged or engages in terrorist activity . . . , or that the organization has engaged or engages in terrorism. . . .*
>>> . . . .
>> (g) Definitions. As used in this section—
>> . . . .
>>> (4) the term "material support or resources" has the same meaning given that term in section 2339A (including the definitions of "training" and "expert advice or assistance" in that section);
>>> . . . .
>>> (i) Rule of construction. *Nothing in this section shall be construed or applied so as to abridge the exercise of rights guaranteed under the First Amendment to the Constitution of the United States.*

18 U.S.C. § 2339B (2012) (emphasis added).

§ 29.5   Conventions of Formal Writing

The conventions of formal writing apply to legal writing, particularly briefs and memoranda. Consequently, some practices that are acceptable in informal writing or oral language are generally considered inappropriate in formal legal documents.

§ 29.5.1   Use of First-Person Pronouns

Although in recent years there has been a bit more acceptance of first-person pronouns (I, me, my, we, our, us) in legal writing, most legal writers still use only third person in legal memoranda and briefs.

"Our" is fairly well accepted when used in office memos to refer to the client's case ("in our case"), although purists still prefer that the client's name be used ("in Brown's case"). "My" is well accepted in client letters ("in my opinion"), and many attorneys use other first-person pronouns throughout client letters ("I received your letter"; "please call me if you have any questions").

§ 29.5.2   Use of Contractions

Contractions are closely associated with the informality of most oral language. For this reason, there has been strong resistance to the use of contractions in legal writing. Occasionally, you will see a contraction used in a client letter, but these instances are not the norm. As a general rule, avoid contractions in all legal writing.

§ 29.5.3   Use of Numbers

The Bluebook sets the standard for what is the acceptable way to write numbers in legal writing. In a nutshell, the rule is to spell out numbers from zero to ninety-nine in text and from zero to nine in the content of a footnote. For larger numbers, use numerals unless the number begins a sentence or the number is a round number (hundred, thousand).

If a series of numbers includes one or more numbers that should be written with numerals, then numerals should be used for the entire series.

EXAMPLE 1   **Numerals for an Entire Series**

The dispatch operator received 104 calls on Friday, 72 calls on Saturday, and 11 calls on Sunday.

Numerals should be used with numbers that contain a decimal point, with numbers used for sections or subdivisions, and in contexts in which numbers are used frequently to refer to percentages and dollar amounts.

§ 29.5.4   Use of Questions and Exclamations

As a general rule, avoid questions in legal writing. With the exception of the question presented, or issue statement, sentences in legal writing are almost always statements, not questions or exclamations.

When you want to use a question, revise the question into a statement that says, in effect, this question exists.

EXAMPLE 2   **Revising a Question into a Statement**

Draft

Will the court apply the center of activity test or the nerve center test?

Edited

The question is whether the court will apply the center of activity test or the nerve center test.

When you are tempted to use a rhetorical question, revise that point into a positive assertion or statement.

EXAMPLE 3   **Revising a Rhetorical Question into an Assertion**

Rhetorical Question

How can the police do their job if they are not allowed to stop suspects who match an eyewitness's description?

Revised

The police will be unable to do their job if they are not allowed to stop suspects who match an eyewitness's description.

Exclamatory statements may appear to be forceful and therefore persuasive, but they often achieve the opposite effect. Instead of strengthening a position, exclamatory statements may weaken it because they make the writer appear unsophisticated, immature, or inflammatory. As a general rule, then, unless you are quoting another person, do not use exclamatory sentences.

Chapter 29 Quiz

Draft answers for each of the following questions. Make your points clearly and concisely, and write sentences that are easy to read and that are grammatical and correctly punctuated.

1. When should a writer capitalize the first word of a direct quotation?
2. When is the word "state" capitalized in legal writing?
3. What is the standard capitalization for acronyms?
4. Which foreign words should be italicized?
5. What are some of the conventions of formal writing that have been incorporated into legal writing?

Before You Practice

Before you know it, you will have graduated from law school and be starting your first job as a practicing attorney. Your exciting career in law will provide many opportunities for growth, not least of all in the area of legal writing. Before you start that first job, take one last look at the writing basics discussed in this chapter. From your very first day as an attorney, these tips will help you master effective legal writing.

Exhibit 30.1 gives you a quick overview of your "day one" list of things to know.

§ 30.1   Usage

Affect vs. Effect

The primary use of **affect** is as a <u>verb</u> meaning "to influence" or "to produce a change."

Examples:

Crying on the witness stand will not **affect** the judge's ruling.
Smoking **affects** a person's overall health.

The primary use of **effect** is as a <u>noun</u> meaning "a result" or "an outcome."

Examples:

The witness's tears did not have the desired **effect** on the judge.
The **effect** of smoking on a person's health is common knowledge.

Exhibit 30.1	Writing Basics for Day One

Usage
Affect vs. Effect
Council vs. Counsel
Its vs. It's
Principal vs. Principle
That vs. Which

Punctuation
Apostrophes (forming the possessive)
Comma splices (how to recognize and correct them)
Commas with dates
Commas with items in a series

Grammar
Pronoun Agreement

Writing Style and Editing
Conciseness (in sentence openers)
Conciseness (needless repetition)
Conciseness (strong verbs)
Problem sentences (All I'm trying to say is . . .)
Transitions (placement of generic transitions)
Transitions (selection for exact meaning)

Proofreading

Defeating Procrastination

Affect can also be used as a <u>verb</u> meaning "to pretend" or "to feign." (This verb comes from the noun "affectation," meaning "a pretense" or "artificial behavior.")

Example:

The defendant **affected** indifference when the verdict was read.

So the most reliable way to determine whether to use **affect** or **effect** is to figure out whether you need a verb or a noun in the sentence.

affect — usually a verb
effect — usually a noun

Unfortunately, however, both words also have less common uses that don't match the uses of **affect** as a <u>verb</u> and **effect** as a <u>noun</u>.

A less common use of **affect** is as a <u>noun</u> meaning "a disposition," "feeling," or "emotion." You sometimes hear someone described as having a "low **affect**," meaning that the person's demeanor is rather emotionless.

A less common use of **effect** is as a <u>verb</u> meaning "to bring about."

Examples:

The doctor **effected** a cure by ordering the treatment.

By passing the bill, the legislature hoped to **effect** a change in our marriage laws.

To sum up:

- **Affect** usually is a <u>verb</u> meaning "to influence"
- **Affect** can be a <u>verb</u> meaning "to pretend"
- **Affect** can be a <u>noun</u> meaning "a disposition"
- **Effect** usually is a <u>noun</u> meaning "a result" or "outcome"
- **Effect** can be a <u>verb</u> meaning "to bring about"

Council vs. Counsel

1. **Council** is a <u>noun</u> meaning "an assembly of persons called together" or "a body of people elected or appointed."

Examples:

The union **council** recommended that the workers reject the contract.
New members of the Lakewood City **Council** were elected on November 4.

2. **Counsel** as a <u>noun</u> means a lawyer or a group of lawyers.

Example:

Counsel for the defense asked the court if she could withdraw from the case.

3. **Counsel** as a <u>noun</u> can also mean "advice," "opinion," or "guidance."

Example:

Many clients depend heavily on the **counsel** of their attorneys.

4. **Counsel** as a <u>verb</u> means "to advise."

Example:

His attorney **counseled** him to plead guilty by reason of insanity.

Remember: When you become an attorney, you will be a **counselor**. The short form of that is **counsel**.

Its vs. It's

This pair of words causes some needless confusion. Here's a quick way to remember which is which.

It's is always a contraction

Use **it's** only when you can substitute in the words "it is" or "it has."

Examples:

It's raining. → It is raining.
It's been difficult representing this client. → It has been difficult representing this client.

Note: As a general rule we do not use contractions in legal writing (unless the contraction is in a direct quote) because legal writing requires a more formal and professional tone; consequently, you will probably not be using **it's** in your legal writing.

Its is the possessive form of "it"

Examples:

The dog bit **its** owner.
Boeing is laying off some of **its** employees.

Why do people find "**it's**" and "**its**" confusing? With nouns, we are used to forming the possessive by adding "'s" (*e.g.,* defendant's attorney), but notice that with pronouns (hers, ours, theirs, yours) we just add "s."

One final point: There is no word "its'."

Principal vs. Principle

Principal has several different meanings, and it can be both a <u>noun</u> and an <u>adjective</u>.

Principal can be a <u>noun</u> meaning "the head administrator of a school." (One way many of us were taught to remember which ending to use for this definition is "the princi<u>pal</u> is your pal.") This memory clue can be helpful with other meanings if you remember that a **principal** is often a person who holds the top position or plays an important role.

For example, in criminal law, the <u>noun</u> **principal** means "one who commits or participates in a crime."[1] In the law of agency, a **principal** is "one who

---

1. *Black's Law Dictionary* 1230 (Bryan A. Garner ed., 8th ed. 2004).

authorizes another to act on his or her behalf."[2] The agent is acting for the **principal**. In the law of guaranty, the **principal** is the person primarily liable.

Principal can also be a <u>noun</u> meaning "the capital or main body of an estate or financial holding, not including the interest or revenue from it."[3]

Example:

The school's endowment requires that scholarship funding come from the interest earned on it; the school is not allowed to touch the **principal**.

Principal can also be an <u>adjective</u> meaning "main," "chief," or "most important."

Examples:

The **principal** reason why Jones was fired was his lack of computer skills.

A court's **principal** objective in interpreting a statute is to ascertain the legislative intent.

Principle is *only* a <u>noun</u>, meaning "a fundamental truth," "doctrine," "established rule," or "moral and ethical standards."

Examples:

The **principle** of equal treatment under the law is well established in our legal system.

Nothing in *Jones* undermines these **principles**.

To sum up:

- **Principal** can be used as a <u>noun</u> meaning "a person who holds the top position or plays an important role."
- **Principal** can be used as a <u>noun</u> meaning "an amount of money other than the interest earned from that money."
- **Principal** can be an <u>adjective</u> meaning "main" or "most important."
- **Principle** can be used *only* as a <u>noun</u> meaning "truth," "doctrine," or "moral standards."

That vs. Which

Assume a context in which a writer is writing about a defendant being charged with stealing two cars. At the time they were stolen, both cars were parked in front of a motel; one car had the keys in the ignition.

---

2. *Id.*

3. *The American Heritage Dictionary of the English Language* 1394 (4th ed., Houghton Mifflin Co. 2000).

Should a writer use "**that**" or "**which**" in the following sentence?

The car (**that/which**) had the keys in the ignition was found in the defendant's garage.

If you said "**that**," you are correct. Next question: Should commas be added to the sentence? If you said "no," you're on a roll.

Why is "**that**" with no commas correct? Because the clause "**that** had the keys in the ignition" restricts the meaning of "the car." It tells the reader which one of the two cars was found in the defendant's garage.

Assume the same context. Should a writer use "**that**" or "**which**" in the following sentence, and does the sentence require commas?

Both cars (**that/which**) were parked in front of a motel were owned by a motel guest.

If you said "**which**" and added commas before "**which**" and after "motel," you are correct.

Both cars, **which** were parked in front of a motel, were owned by a motel guest.

Why? Because *in our context* "both cars" completely identifies the cars the writer means. The clause "**which** were parked in front of a motel" gives additional information, but that information does not restrict the meaning of "both cars."

Consider this pair of sentences, both of which are correct:

1. Signs **that** are posted in the parking lot state that the motel is not responsible for cars parked there.
2. Signs, **which** may be torn down by vandals, are ineffective deterrents.

In sentence 1, "**that**" is correct because the clause "**that** are posted in the parking lot" restricts the meaning of "signs." The writer does not mean all signs—just those signs **that** are posted in the parking lot.

In sentence 2, "**which**" with the commas is correct because the clause "**which** may be torn down by vandals" does not restrict the meaning of "signs." The writer means all signs are ineffective deterrents. Even though the point "**which** may be torn down by vandals" may be an important one to understanding why signs are ineffective deterrents, that clause does not restrict the group of signs to which the sentence refers.

What is the difference between sentence 2 and the following sentence?

3. Signs that may be torn down by vandals are ineffective deterrents.

Unlike sentence 2, sentence 3 does not mean all signs are ineffective deterrents. By changing the "**which**" to "**that**" and omitting the commas, the writer is now restricting the point to only those signs that may be torn down. (Presumably, indestructible signs might still be a deterrent.)

Two final points: First, if you are debating between using "**that**" or "**which**" and the clause follows a proper noun (one that is capitalized) naming a specific thing, you can pretty much count on using "**which**" and commas. Why? Because if the writer has already used the specific proper name, then it is unlikely that the clause will restrict the meaning any further.

Example:

The Industrial Insurance Act, **which** does not cover stress-related occupational diseases, does cover occupational diseases that arise naturally out of employment.

Because "the Industrial Insurance Act" is named, the clause "**which** does not cover stress-related occupational diseases" does not restrict or further limit its meaning. Note, however, that "occupational diseases" is a broad general category that is then restricted later in the sentence by "**that** arise naturally out of employment."

Second, the more common mistake in legal writing is to use "**which**" when you need to use "**that**." It may be helpful to remember that the comma precedes the "**which**," so if you are using "**which**" without a comma, check to see if you should be using "**that**."[4]

To sum up:

"**that**" without commas   →   restricts meaning of the word it modifies
"**which**" with commas   →   does not restrict the meaning of the word it modifies
Proper names (capitalized) will be followed by "**which**" with commas.

§ 30.2   Punctuation

Apostrophes (Forming the Possessive)

The best way to ensure that you form the possessive correctly is to start by simply writing the word without the apostrophe.

Examples:

defendant (one)
defendants (more than one)

one parent
two parents

Then use the following to make the word you have written possessive.

1. In most cases, if the word is singular, add **'s**
2. If the word is plural and ends in s, just add an apostrophe (**'**)

---

4. Obviously, the words "that" and "which" are used in numerous other ways in sentences that do not set up restrictive or nonrestrictive clauses and that do not involve this comma rule.

one defendant's attorney
two defendants' attorney

one parent's house
two parents' house

Singular nouns that end in s can be made possessive in one of two ways:

1. by adding "'s" or
2. by adding just the apostrophe (').

Example:

one witness's testimony **OR**
one witness' testimony

The first method is preferred in legal writing; the second method is commonly used in journalistic writing.[5]

Plural words that do not end in "s" (e.g., children) form the possessive with "'s."

Example:

children's mother

Why take the time to (1) write the word as singular or plural and then (2) add the possessive? Things can get a bit confusing with names that end in "s."

Example:

Jones (singular)
Jones's house (singular possessive—preferred form)
Joneses (plural)
Joneses' house (plural possessive)

Comma Splices (How to Recognize and Correct Them)

What does your legal writing professor mean when he or she says a sentence has a "comma splice"?

A comma splice occurs when a writer joins (or splices) two main clauses together with just a comma. Remember that a main clause (sometimes called an independent clause) has a subject and verb and that it could stand alone as a sentence.

---

5. A few recognized authorities, including *The Associated Press Stylebook and Libel Manual*, recommend using only an apostrophe with singular proper names.

Incorrect Example of a Comma Splice:

The defendant is from North Carolina, the plaintiff is from New Mexico.

<u>The defendant is from North Carolina,</u>	<u>the plaintiff is from New Mexico.</u>
main clause	*main clause*
(could be a sentence)	*(could be a sentence)*

A comma by itself is not enough to hold two main clauses together. You can correct the **comma splice** error in one of four ways:

1. Change the comma to a period:

    The defendant is from North Carolina. The plaintiff is from New Mexico.

2. Change the comma to a semicolon:

    The defendant is from North Carolina; the plaintiff is from New Mexico.

3. Add a coordinating conjunction (for, and, nor, but, or, yet, so) after the comma:

    The defendant is from North Carolina, **and** the plaintiff is from New Mexico.

    The defendant is from North Carolina, **but** the plaintiff is from New Mexico.

4. Change one of the two main clauses to a dependent clause:

    Although the defendant is from North Carolina, the plaintiff is from New Mexico.

Commas with Dates

In legal writing, you will be writing many sentences with dates. More often than not, the date will appear at the beginning of a sentence. In this position, the date provides a context for the information that follows.

Example:

On June 12, 2012, a process server appeared at a halfway house and asked if Elaine still lived there.

Notice that full dates written in the order of month, day, year (e.g., June 12, 2012) have a comma after the day. If the sentence continues after a full date, add a comma after the year. The comma after the year will look a little strange to you at first, but now that it has been pointed out to you, you'll notice it in newspapers, magazines, and the like. It has been there all along.

Example:

A process server appeared at a halfway house on June 12, 2012, and asked if Elaine still lived there.

When there is not a day in the date (e.g., March 2011), there is no comma between the month and year.

Example:

Elaine began using drugs in March 2011.

When a partial date (e.g., March 2011) appears in the middle of a sentence, it is not followed by a comma, unless there is another rule requiring a comma.

Examples:

Elaine began using drugs in March 2011 after Marci kicked her out of the house.

(No comma after 2011.)

But:

In March 2011, Elaine began using drugs again.

(The comma is included after 2011 in the preceding example because the phrase is an introductory element.)

Commas with Items in a Series

In legal writing you will often group a number of items and write them as a series. (A series is three or more items in a group.[6]) Sometimes the items are only one word long, sometimes they are short phrases, and sometimes they are longer clauses. In the examples below, each item is underlined separately.

Examples:

red, white, and blue
(one word items)

out of the house, through the backyard, over the fence, and into the alley
(short phrase items)

who he was, where he lived, what he did for a living, or what he had done during the last two weeks
(longer clause items)

Depending on your major as an undergraduate or your employment before law school, you may have learned that with a series

---

6. With a pair (two items) do not use a comma before the conjunction (ex. "red and white" or "out of the house and through the backyard" or "who he was and where he lived"); the one exception is that you should use a comma before a conjunction joining two main clauses. (See Rule 1, commas in Chapter 28.)

a. you do not need a comma before the conjunction "and" or "or";

b. you need a comma before the conjunction "and" or "or"; or

c. the serial comma before "and" or "or" is optional.

For some types of writing the correct answer is **c**. In newspapers and in informal writing, the tendency is to omit the serial comma, but in more formal writing such as legal writing, the serial comma is included to prevent ambiguity.

Notice the ambiguity if you omit the comma before "and" in the following series:

> The safety deposit box contained five gold coins, the decedent's last will and testament, two small knives, a Swiss army knife and a paring knife.

Does the safety deposit box contain four knives, or did the writer mean that the two small knives were a Swiss army knife and paring knife? Adding a comma before the "and" means that there were four knives. If the writer meant there were just two knives, he or she could have made that clear in the following way:

> The safety deposit box contained five gold coins, the decedent's last will and testament, two small knives, one of which was a Swiss army knife and the other a paring knife.

To sum up:

In legal writing, **use the serial comma**.

§ 30.3   Grammar

Pronoun Agreement

Pronouns (I, me, he, him, she, her, they, them, their, it, its, etc.) are substitutes for nouns. Consequently, they must match the noun they substitute for in number. A singular noun requires a singular pronoun; a plural noun requires a plural pronoun.

There are two situations in which this becomes a little tricky. The first is with collective nouns, which are those nouns that have a number of people working together as one unit. For example, a team may be made up of many players, but it still functions as one unit, so "team" is an "it," not a "they." Other common collective nouns include "court," "legislature," "jury," "family," and any company or corporation (Microsoft, Boeing).

Examples:

The **court** ruled that a person can have more than one usual place of abode, and **it** concluded that Ms. Fettig had two centers of domestic activity.

Mr. Holguerra could argue that if the **legislature** wanted to suggest that a defendant could have more than one usual place of abode, **it** could have left the word "usual" out of the statute.

The second tricky situation occurs when a pronoun substitutes for a generic noun. For example, when a sentence includes a general reference to singular nouns such as "a defendant" or "a plaintiff," it may be tempting to use a plural pronoun later in the sentence, but the correct pronoun form must be singular.

Incorrect:

If **a defendant** has two houses of usual abode, **they** may be served at either house.

Corrected:

If **a defendant** has two houses of usual abode, **he or she** may be served at either house.

You can also correct this error by revising the sentence so that it does not require a pronoun.

Another correct version (no pronoun):

If **a defendant** has two houses of usual abode, a summons can be left at either house.

Reminder: The court is an "**it**," not a "they."

§ 30.4   Revising, Editing, and Proofreading

Conciseness (Strong Verbs)

If you've read the materials on conciseness in sentence openers (a.k.a. avoiding throat-clearing expressions), you may remember a related point in the tip about making sure the real action is in the verb slot. A big key to writing crisp, concise sentences is finding the real action in a sentence and making it the verb. Consider the examples below.

Example:

The landlord <u>made</u> a decision to delay replacement of the heating units. **(12 words)**

The verb in this sentence is "made," but is the real action expressed in the word "made"? What exactly is it that the landlord did? If the real action is trapped in a noun such as "decision," use the verb form of that noun in the verb slot.

Revision 1:

The landlord <u>decided</u> to delay replacement of the heating units. **(10 words)**

If the real action is in "to delay," then revise so that "delay" is the main verb.

Revision 2:

The landlord <u>delayed</u> replacing the heating units. (**7 words**)

Note that 12 words have been cut back to 7, resulting not only in a shorter sentence but in a better sentence.

Although "to be" verbs are useful when the point of a sentence is that something exists, they often take up the verb slot when the real action is buried in a noun or adjective elsewhere in the sentence.

Examples:

Smith's case <u>is</u> an illustration of this point. (**8 words** — action buried in noun "illustration")
Smith's case <u>is</u> illustrative of this point. (**7 words** — action buried in adjective "illustrative")

Revised:

Smith's case <u>illustrates</u> this point. (**5 words**)

One final point: Another way to spot these wordy constructions is to look for "of" prepositional phrases. Some are necessary, but many are clutter that can be cut.

Example:

The prosecutor <u>is</u> in the process **of** making a determination **of** whether to charge Greene.

Revised:

The prosecutor <u>is deciding</u> whether to charge Greene.

Conciseness (in Sentence Openers)

Many of us waste a few words at the beginning of some of our sentences because we use what are called "throat-clearing expressions" to get the sentence started.

Example:

<u>It is important to note that</u> the defendant lied.

The throat-clearing expression, "<u>it is important to note that</u>," conveys little if any information. After all, in legal writing you are not going to bother telling your reader anything that is not important to note. The real message in this sentence is "the defendant lied."

Revised:

The defendant lied.

Notice that in the revised version, the real actor (the defendant) is in the subject position and the real action (lied) fills the verb position. In the wordy original sentence, the subject and verb positions were filled with words that conveyed no meaning (it is).

Other favorite throat-clearing expressions include the following:

It is significant that
It is clear that
It is noteworthy that
It must be remembered that
It is generally recognized that
It is interesting to note that

Notice that all of these constructions waste the subject and verb slots and wait until after "that" for the real point of the sentence.

So when you are editing your writing for conciseness, consider omitting throat-clearing expressions and starting your sentence with the word or words that follow "that."

Examples:

~~It is clear that~~ the prosecutor's peremptory strike was racially motivated.
~~It must be remembered that~~ Brambo hit Layton after the referee blew his whistle.

One final thought: Throat-clearing expressions can be useful when you are writing rough drafts. They can help you keep some momentum in your writing during those early stages in a writing project. If you notice that you include a throat-clearing expression in a rough draft, don't worry about it. Just remember to cut it out when you are editing your writing.

Conciseness (Needless Repetition)

"It's like déjà vu all over again."
"Ninety percent of all mental errors are in your head."

As delightful as these Yogi Berra quotes are when they appear in Aflac commercials, the same kind of needless repetition is not likely to delight legal readers. Most of us believe we would never write something as obvious as "You can observe a lot by watching" (another Yogi-ism), but check out the sentences below to see some examples that often appear in legal writing. The word or words in parentheses should be omitted.

Jones parked her car at 10:00 p.m. (at night) and did not return for it until 7:00 a.m. (in the morning).

Ferguson described the car as an older model sedan that was green (in color).

For (a period of) three years, Bowman worked as a grocery checker, but during (the year of) 2009, she was promoted to store manager.

Her coworkers were surprised by her (sudden) outburst. They had never (before) seen her angry or upset.

Have fun editing your writing for needless repetition, and remember, if Yogi had been a lawyer rather than a baseball player and coach, he probably would have said, "If you edit your writing for conciseness, you'll probably omit needless words."

Problem Sentences ("All I'm Trying to Say Is . . . .")

Has this ever happened to you? You are in the midst of writing something, and you find that you've written a sentence that's just not working. Maybe you've tried to pack too much into it, or maybe the sentence structure has taken on a life of its own and the pieces are not working together.

You tried revising it, but the sentence is still "off" somehow. It's late and you're tired, but you keep trying. And trying. And trying. Now, when you look at the mangled sentence you doubt whether you've improved it much. In fact, you may be afraid that you've actually made matters worse.

Been there? If so, try this. Push back from the computer and say aloud in the room, **"All I'm trying to say is** . . ." What comes out to fill in that blank is often a nice, clean, simple expression of the point you've been laboring to express. Quickly jot down what was in the blank and then work it right into what you were writing. *Voilà!* Problem solved.

Here are three more small suggestions about using the "all I'm trying to say is" technique. First, once you've captured your point in oral language, jot it down before returning to the computer. If you don't, when you are back at the computer, you'll spot the original problem sentence and get drawn right back into its clutches. Second, realize that the oral language version may be expressed a bit more informally than is appropriate for the writing you are doing, so be willing to tune it up a notch if needed. Third, as with any addition that you insert into a piece of writing, read it with the sentences before it and after it and revise so that they flow together.

Transitions (Placement of Generic Transitions)

When you are driving down a road, it is helpful to have highway signs to indicate where you are going and what is coming. If you spot an arrow curving to the right, you anticipate that the road will, fairly soon, begin a curve to the right. It would not be helpful to have the curved arrow sign after the road started the right-hand bend. The same is true for transitions. Place them right at the point where the reader needs them, which is right before "the bend," or shift, in the line of reasoning.

Examples:

(poor placement)

In Washington, courts have consistently found that a defendant's license to enter public premises was properly revoked when the defendant was disruptive or engaging in criminal behavior. In *Kutch*, the defendant was caught shoplifting at a mall, **for example**. 90 Wn. App. at 246.

(good placement)

In Washington, courts have consistently found that a defendant's license to enter public premises was properly revoked when the defendant was disruptive or engaging in criminal behavior. **For example**, in *Kutch*, the defendant was caught shoplifting at a mall. 90 Wn. App. at 246.

(also good placement)

In Washington, courts have consistently found that a defendant's license to enter public premises was properly revoked when the defendant was disruptive or engaging in criminal behavior. In *Kutch*, **for example**, the defendant was caught shoplifting at a mall. 90 Wn. App. at 246.

(poor placement)

The defendant has a possible defense to criminal trespass if "[t]he premises were at the time open to members of the public and the actor complied with all lawful conditions imposed on access to or remaining on the premises." RCW 9A.52.090(2). It is undisputed that at least portions of the restaurant's premises were open to members of the public at the time of Mr. Deyoung's alleged trespass. It will be disputed whether Mr. Deyoung complied with the lawful conditions imposed on entry to the Grand Illusion, **however**.

(good placement)

The defendant has a possible defense to criminal trespass if "[t]he premises were at the time open to members of the public and the actor complied with all lawful conditions imposed on access to or remaining on the premises." RCW 9A.52.090(2). It is undisputed that at least portions of the restaurant's premises were open to members of the public at the time of Mr. Deyoung's alleged trespass. It will be disputed, **however**, whether Mr. Deyoung complied with the lawful conditions imposed on entry to the Grand Illusion.

Some writers may prefer to open the third sentence with the transition "however," but there is lingering insistence by some grammarians that "however" should not be used to begin a sentence.

Transitions (Selection for Exact Meaning)

Learning to use transitions effectively starts with selecting a transition with the exact meaning you want. The Generic Transitions chart in Chapter 23 groups transitions by category. The difference in meaning between categories is obvious: a transition **For Restatement**, such as "in other words," sets up a completely different connection between points than say a transition **For**

Examples, such as "for instance." Note too that even within the same category, there are differences in meaning for the transitions listed there. In the **For Conclusion** category, for example, "finally" means that you will now address your last point, but "to sum up" means you will conclude by summarizing all the main points.

Careful writers will want to attend to these subtle differences in meaning and learn which transitions work in different contexts. For example, both "also" and "moreover" are in the category **For Addition**, but "also" suggests that whatever has been added is of equal weight to what has come before, whereas "moreover" means something beyond what has already been said. "Moreover" tends to stress the importance of the additional element. Notice too that "also" placed at the beginning of a sentence makes the writing seem less sophisticated.

Examples:

(unsophisticated use of "also")
The court will probably find that Mr. Healy had implied permission to use the warehouse. The owner, Ms. Canaveral, knew that a homeless man was living there and did nothing to evict him. **Also**, she admits that she failed to evict him because she felt sorry for him.

("also" used here to suggest the reasons in the first and second sentences are of equal weight)
The court will probably find that Mr. Healy had implied permission to use the warehouse. The owner, Ms. Canaveral, knew that a homeless man was living there and did nothing to evict him. She **also** admits that she failed to evict him because she felt sorry for him.

("moreover" used here to suggest the reason in sentence 3 is more important than the reason in sentence 2)
The court will probably find that Mr. Healy had implied permission to use the warehouse. The owner, Ms. Canaveral, knew that a homeless man was living there and did nothing to evict him. **Moreover**, she admits that she failed to evict him because she felt sorry for him.

Proofreading Tips

1. While you are still at the computer, get the computer to do as many of the mindless proofreading tasks as possible. In addition to using your word processor's spell check and grammar check tools, use the "Find" function to search for predictable problems. For example, if you've noticed that you sometimes type "statue" when you mean "statute," use "Find and Replace" to hunt out and correct those errors. If you've just learned that periods always go inside closing quotation marks, use Find to locate ". and replace it with ."

2. Manage your time so that you can proofread at a completely different time from writing time. In other words, don't go straight

from writing your conclusion to proofreading the whole document. You need to be fresh to proofread effectively, and you need some "distance" from the words so that you can see what is really there, not just what you think should be there.

3. **Print out a hard copy and do at least one proofread on the hard copy**. You will see things on hard copy that you might miss on the computer screen.

4. Realize that proofreading is not reading; it is looking for errors. Go SLOWLY and look at individual words.

5. Proofreading is not revising and editing. You need to do all of those writing tasks, but they are not the same thing as looking for errors. If you try to revise, edit, and proofread all at the same time, chances are that you will really just be editing.

6. To make yourself go slowly and focus on the words that are really there, consider using a blank sheet of paper to cover up all but the line you are proofreading.

7. Consider reading your writing aloud as you proofread. This strategy is particularly helpful for catching omitted words or additional words that should not be there.

8. Consider proofreading your citations at a separate sitting.

9. If you have limited proofreading time, spend it proofreading
   a. the last things you wrote and
   b. the most complicated portions of the document.
   It does not make sense to spend your best and freshest proofreading time on the part of the document that has been extensively reworked and massaged. Use your best proofreading time on the parts of the document where you are likely to have the most errors.

§ 30.5   Defeating Procrastination

Defeating procrastination is a two-step process. First, determine why you procrastinate about writing. Second, select strategies for defeating procrastination that are directed at the reasons why you procrastinate.

Some writers procrastinate because they are overly optimistic about how much time they have and they underestimate how much the writing project will take. The experts call this type the "relaxed procrastinators"; they don't start working until they feel deadline pressure, and they often believe that they "do their best work under pressure."

If you are a relaxed procrastinator, your best strategy may be to develop a writing schedule with mini-deadlines for completing your research, preparing an outline, completing a draft, doing an after-the-fact outline, editing, proofreading, and so on. If you are a "hardened" relaxed procrastinator, you may need to report in to someone who will hold you to those mini-deadlines.

Other people procrastinate because they lack confidence in their ability to do the project well. They don't believe that they are good writers, and they are anxious about whether their work will be good enough. Experts label these folks the "anxious, tense procrastinators."

If you are an anxious, tense procrastinator, you are more likely to respond to strategies that build your confidence about writing. It might be helpful to review any past written project that was a success. How did you go about getting it done? Can that process be replicated for the current project? Simply re-reading a successful piece can help a person start a new project with a more positive frame of mind. In building a positive frame of mind, check the "self talk" you are engaging in related to the current project. Instead of "There's no way I can get this assignment done" try "Where should I start?" Instead of "I'll probably do this the wrong way" try "I'm likely to succeed if I . . ."

Related to the anxious, tense procrastinator is the "perfectionist procrastinator." Perfectionists may feel they must research exhaustively before beginning to write; they may want the first sentence to be perfect before proceeding to the second sentence; if they are having trouble with one section, that problem may bring a whole project to a halt.

If you are a perfectionist procrastinator, good strategies are ones that help you keep perspective. Real clients can rarely pay for exhaustive research. It is important to know when you have done enough research and are ready to write. Once you start writing the first draft, try to focus on just a few big tasks, such as getting your ideas down and organizing them. Realize that you can come back to a less-than-perfect sentence and revise it in later drafts. Giving yourself permission to skip over a problem area for the time being and let your subconscious work on the problem while you keep writing another part can be key to maintaining some writing momentum.

A Guide to Legal Writing for English-as-a-Second-Language Writers

Legal writing courses are challenging for native speakers of English who have spent their lives immersed in a culture heavily influenced by the United States legal system. Even for these law students, some of the terminology of legal prose is new, and many of the conventions are unfamiliar.

If you are an English-as-a-second-language (ESL) law student,[1] you have two additional language-related challenges. First, there are numerous grammatical rules that native speakers have internalized but that non-native speakers must still learn. The first half of Chapter 31 focuses on three grammatical areas that many ESL law students find difficult: articles, verbs, and prepositions.

Second, if you are an ESL law student who was raised in a different culture, you will have naturally internalized your native culture's approach to writing. Consequently, as an ESL law student, you will face a second challenge: learning how native speakers of English, particularly those in the United States legal culture, approach writing. These different approaches to writing, or what we will call "rhetorical preferences," tend to affect the whole piece of writing and include such things as what is assumed about the writer-reader relationship, how direct and explicit writers are when they explain and support their arguments,

---

1. In this chapter we use the term "English-as-a-Second-Language" and the acronym "ESL" to apply to persons who are living in the United States but whose first language is not English, as well as to persons who studied English as a foreign language when living in their home countries.

and what writing patterns are commonplace and expected. The second half of Chapter 31 addresses how the rhetorical preferences in the United States and particularly in the legal culture may differ from the rhetorical preferences of other cultures.

Legal Writing for English-as-a-Second-Language Writers

§ 31.1 Grammar Rules for Non-Native Speakers of English

§ 31.1.1 Articles

Errors in the use of articles ("a," "an," and "the") are distracting to many readers. Too many missing or incorrect articles draw attention away from content and toward the errors. Consequently, most ESL law students find that if they want their writing to be considered professional, they must devote time and energy to mastering the use of articles in English.

One of the simplest and most effective strategies for learning the correct use of articles is to note how they are used in judicial opinions and other writing about law. Many ESL law students simply memorize phrases and law terminology, including how articles are used in these phrases and with these terms, from the writing of capable native speakers.

A second strategy is to learn the rules governing the use of articles in English. Unfortunately for most ESL law students, many of their native languages do not use articles, and others use articles in ways that are different from English. As a result, most ESL law students cannot rely on their native languages to help them with the rules of English articles. Instead they must learn the general rules and then be aware that there are still many exceptions.

Exhibit 31.1, following section 31.1.1, is a *decision tree* that summarizes the discussion about how to use articles with common nouns in English.

a.   "A" and "An"

Rule 1	Use the indefinite articles "a" and "an"[1] with count nouns when the noun is singular and when the reader does not know the specific identity of the noun

Count nouns[2] refer to persons, places, or things that can be counted. Count nouns have both a singular and plural form.

EXAMPLE 1   **Some Count and Non-Count Nouns**

Singular form of count nouns

   a contract   an easement   a trial court   an appellate court
   one juror

Plural form of count nouns

   contracts   easements   trial courts   appellate courts
   twelve jurors

Non-Count nouns

   anger   equipment   pollution   science   testimony[3]   wealth

---

Remember that "a" and "an" are used only (1) with the singular form of a count noun (2) when the reader does not know the specific identity of that noun. The second part of the rule usually applies when a particular noun is mentioned for the first time in the writing because at that point the reader does not know the specific identity of the noun.

EXAMPLE 2   **"A" with Singular Count Noun**

(Assume "truck" is being mentioned for the first time.)
<u>A</u> truck slowly approached.

---

1. "A" is used before consonant sounds; "an" is used before vowel sounds. Examples: "A jury," "a contract," "an assault," "an incident," "an unusual request," "an alleged victim," "an hour," "an honest man," ("h" is silent in "hour" and "honest") "a unique opportunity," "a university," "a unit," "a unanimous jury," ("u" has consonant "y" sound in "unique," "university," "unit," and "unanimous") and "a one-hour delay" ("o" has "w" sound in "one"). See *A/An* in the Glossary of Usage.

2. Many nouns such as "paper" can be used as count or non-count nouns depending upon the particular sense in which they are used. Most ESL dictionaries indicate whether a noun is a count or non-count noun and, for nouns that can be both, under which meanings the noun is a count or non-count noun.

3. Although the online *Merriam Webster* dictionary (http://www.merriam-webster.com/diction ary/testimony) includes a plural form of "testimony," United States attorneys and judges continue to treat it as a non-count noun.

Rule 1 also applies when the specific identity of the noun is unknown to the writer or when the writer intends to name a general member of a class or group.

EXAMPLE 3   "A" and "An" with Unknown Specific Identity or General Member

(The writer does not know the specific identity of the officer.)
<u>An</u> officer observed a truck slowly approach.

(The writer intends a general member of the class of cell phones.)
A cell phone is often a good safety precaution.

Exception to Rule 1. Do not use "a" or "an" with a singular count noun that is preceded by another noun marker.

Noun markers include possessive nouns such as "Kelly's" or "Florida's," numbers, and pronouns such as "his," "her," "its," "their," "this," "that," "these," "those," "every," "few," "many," "more," "most," "much," "either," "neither," "each," "any," "all," "no," "several," and "some."

EXAMPLE 4   No Article When Noun Marker Precedes Singular Noun

Incorrect examples:

A this officer observed a truck slowly approach.
("This" is a noun marker, so "a" should be omitted.)

An one officer observed a truck slowly approach.
("One" is a noun marker, so "an" should be omitted.)

Corrected examples:

This officer observed a truck slowly approach.

One officer observed a truck slowly approach.

Other common exceptions to Rule 1 include many prepositional phrases that are idiomatic expressions.

on vacation	by plane	by car	at home	in school
to bed	to college	in class	at night	at school
in bed				

EXAMPLE 5   No Article in Some Idioms

The defendant testified that he was <u>at home</u> by 8:00 p.m. and <u>in bed</u> by 8:30 p.m.

| Rule 2 | Do not use "a" or "an" with non-count nouns |

Non-count nouns refer to abstractions that cannot be counted. Non-count nouns do not have a plural form.

| EXAMPLE 6 | Common Non-Count Nouns in Law |

negligence   evidence   violence   arson   discretion

However, if an amount of a non-count noun is expressed by adding a quantifier, then an article is used before the quantifier.

a piece of evidence   an act of violence

In most instances, the following words are non-count nouns.

Nouns naming drinks and food:

water, milk, coffee, tea, wine, juice,
fruit, fish, beef, chicken, meat

Nouns naming generalized objects:

ammunition, clothing, equipment, freight, furniture, jewelry, luggage, lumber, machinery, mail, money, propaganda, scenery, stationery, traffic, vegetation

Nouns naming substances, matter, or material:

(Asterisks indicate the substance, not an object.)
air, coal, dirt, electricity, gasoline, gold, grass, hair, ice, iron*, oil, oxygen, paper*, plastic, steel, wood

Nouns related to weather:

fog, ice, rain, snow

Nouns naming subject matter:

architecture, art, chemistry, civics, economics, engineering, geology, grammar, history, literature, mathematics, music, philosophy, physics, science, and all names of languages (*Arabic, Chinese, English, French, German, Italian, Japanese, etc.*) when they are used as nouns

Nouns related to games, sports, and recreation:

(Asterisks indicate the game, not an object.)
baseball*, basketball*, bowling, bridge, camping, chess, dancing, football*, golf, hiking, hockey, hunting, opera, sailing, singing, soccer, swimming, tennis, television*, volleyball*

Abstract nouns:

> advice, anger, beauty, capitalism, communism, confidence, democracy, education, employment, energy, fun, happiness, health, help, homework, honesty, ignorance, information, intelligence, justice, kindness, knowledge, laughter, liberty, life, love, merchandise, nature, news, pollution, poverty, recreation, research, satisfaction, society *(in the sense of people in general)*, strength, technology, transportation, trouble, truth, violence, virtue, wealth, wisdom, work

Law-related nouns:

> abandonment, abatement, access, acquiescence, adultery, alimony, arson, authentication, capital (in the sense of money or property), commerce, conduct, depreciation, discretion, duress, evidence, extortion, harassment, housing, insolvency, insurance, intent, land, malice, negligence, privacy, real estate, testimony

---

EXAMPLE 7   **No Article with Non-Count Nouns**

The detective found a weapon and ammunition in the defendant's trunk.
(No article before non-count noun "ammunition.")

Magistrates must exercise discretion when determining whether to authorize hidden recording devices.
(No article before non-count noun "discretion.")

Gerunds[4] and gerund phrases are non-count nouns and therefore do not require "a" or "an."

EXAMPLE 8   **Gerunds as Non-Count Nouns**

<u>Drowning</u> was the cause of death.
(gerund)

Most attorneys enjoy <u>making arguments</u>.
                    (gerund phrase)

---

4. Gerunds are verbals that end in "-ing" and that function as nouns. Gerunds with modifying phrases fall under Rule 3 and are preceded by "the." Example: "The drowning of her second child raised the prosecutor's suspicions."

b. "The"

> **Rule 3**   **Use the definite article "the" with count[5] and non-count nouns when the specific identity of the noun is clear to the reader**

The specific identity of a noun can be clear to the reader for a number of reasons.

Reason #1: Readers know the specific identity of a noun after it has already been used once in a given context.

EXAMPLE 9   Switch from "A" to "The"

A truck slowly approached. An officer noticed <u>the</u> truck contained several garbage cans.
(Use "a" before "truck" when it is first mentioned; use "the" before "truck" for subsequent references.)

Reason #2: Readers know the specific identity of a noun when it is followed by a phrase or clause that restricts or limits its identity.

EXAMPLE 10   "The" When Phrase Restricts Meaning

<u>The</u> driver of the truck appeared nervous.
(Use "the" before "driver" because "of the truck" is a phrase that restricts or limits the meaning of "driver.")

Many but not all modifying phrases and clauses that follow a noun restrict or limit the noun's identity, thereby making it specific. You can determine which "of" prepositional phrases restrict or limit the identity of a noun by testing to see if they can be changed to the possessive form. If they can be changed to the possessive form, they are restricting or limiting the noun, so "the" should precede the noun.

EXAMPLE 11   Restricting "Of" Phrases Can Be Possessive

the driver of the truck → the truck's driver
the cost of a trial → a trial's cost
the length of the skidmarks → the skidmarks' length

Other "of" phrases, however, do not restrict or limit the identity of a noun; they show that only a part or a measured amount of the noun is intended.

---

5. Notice that this rule applies to both singular and plural count nouns.

These "of" phrases cannot be changed to the possessive form. Use "a" or "an" before these nouns.

EXAMPLE 12   **"Of" Phrases That Show a Part**

a pound of marijuana   a third of her salary
a slice of bread   a gallon of gasoline

Similarly, when a noun is followed by a phrase or clause that defines rather than restricts or limits, use "a" or "an" before the noun.

EXAMPLE 13   **"A" with Clause That Defines**

A contract that has all of its terms in writing is a formal contract.
(An "a" is used before "contract" because "that has all of its terms in writing" defines it.)

Reason #3: Readers know the specific identity of a noun when it is preceded by a superlative[6] or ranking adjective.[7]

EXAMPLE 14   **"The" with Superlatives and Ranking Adjectives**

The best example of a public figure is a film star.
(Use "the" because "example" is preceded by the superlative "best.")

The defendant was the tallest man in the line-up.
(Use "the" because "man" is preceded by the superlative "tallest.")

The plaintiff will be unable to satisfy the third element.
(Use "the" before the ranking adjective "third.")

Reason #4: Readers know the specific identity of a noun when both the writer and the reader have shared knowledge about the identity of the noun. Shared knowledge can be universal, such as knowledge of the sun, and it can be local, such as knowledge of a local landmark.

---

6. Superlatives compare the thing modified with two or more things. Superlatives include "best," "worst," words ending in "est" ("biggest," "smallest," "tallest," "shortest," "wisest," "fastest," "slowest," "luckiest," "loudest"), and comparisons that use "most" or "least" ("the most beautiful," "the most egregious," "the least responsible," "the least humiliating"). Be sure not to use comparative or superlative forms with things that cannot be compared ("perfect," "unique," "pregnant," "dead," "impossible," and "infinite").

7. Ranking adjectives include sequential adjectives such as "first," "second," "third," and "next" and adjectives that show the noun is one of a kind ("unique").

| EXAMPLE 15 | "The" with Shared Knowledge About a Noun |

The moon provided enough light for the officers to see the defendant open his trunk.
(Use "the" before "moon" because the writer and the reader have shared knowledge about its identity.)

Numerous gang-related activities have occurred at the shopping mall.
(Use "the" before "shopping mall" if the writer and reader have shared knowledge about its identity as a local landmark.)

One way to determine whether a noun is specific is to ask "which one (or ones)?" For specific nouns, you will have a specific answer. When you have a specific answer, use "the." For example, if the test is applied to some of the earlier example sentences, the questions and answers are as follows:

Question: Which driver?   Answer: The driver of the truck
Question: Which example?   Answer: The best example
Question: Which element?   Answer: The third element
Question: Which moon?   Answer: The moon we all know about
Question: Which shopping   Answer: The shopping mall that is a
   mall?   local landmark

If the answer to the "which one (or ones)?" question is "any one" or "all" or "I don't know which one" or "one that has not been mentioned before," then the noun is general.

| Rule 4 | Do not use "the" before plural nouns meaning all in a class, all of a group, or "in general" |

| EXAMPLE 16 | Omit "The" Before General Plural Nouns |

Defendants have the right to an attorney.
(No "the" before "defendants" because it is plural and all defendants are intended, but "an" before "attorney" because it is singular and no specific attorney is intended.)

Appellate courts do not re-try the facts of a case.
(No "the" before "appellate courts" because it is plural and the intended meaning is appellate courts "in general"; "the" before "facts" because the restricting phrase "of a case" makes it specific, and "a" before "case" because it is singular and no specific case is intended.)

| Rule 5 | Do not use "the" before most singular proper nouns, including names of persons, streets, parks, cities, states, continents, and most countries |

EXAMPLE 17   Omit "The" Before Singular Proper Nouns

Navarro was last seen in Yellowstone National Park.

Tam offered trips to New York City, Florida, Germany, and Africa as sales incentives.

The possessive form of a singular name is also not preceded by "the."

EXAMPLE 18   Omit "The" Before Possessive

Mr. Hempstead learned of the affair by reading Carol's email.
(No "the" before possessive "Carol's.")

Notice, however, that the plural form of proper nouns that are family names is preceded by "the." (See Rule 7.)

EXAMPLE 19   "The" Before Plural Family Names

The Navarros were last seen in Yellowstone National Park.

Rule 6   **Use "the" with proper nouns containing the word "of"; a political word such as "kingdom," "union," or "republic"; or organizational words such as "institute," "foundation," or "corporation"**

EXAMPLE 20   "The" Before Political/Organizational Proper Nouns

the city[8] of Los Angeles	the Republic of Korea
the University of Notre Dame	the Ford Foundation
the Intel Corporation	the Commonwealth of Virginia

Notice that many things have two proper noun names and that "the" is only used with the form containing "of" or the political or organizational word.

the city of Los Angeles	*but*	Los Angeles
the Republic of Korea	*but*	Korea
the University of Notre Dame	*but*	Notre Dame
the Ford Foundation	*but*	Ford
the Intel Corporation	*but*	Intel
the Commonwealth of Virginia	*but*	Virginia

---

8. Words such as "city" are usually, but not always, written in lowercase when they precede the noun and when they appear in text. In citations, however, capitalize geographic terms such as "city." See Rule 10.2.1(f) in *The Bluebook*.

Do not use "the" with names of universities, colleges, or schools unless the name is written with an "of."

| EXAMPLE 21 | When to Use "The" with Schools |

Harvard University Law School   the School of Law
Smith College   the College of Engineering

| Rule 7 | Use "the" before most plural proper nouns, including the plural form of a family name |

| EXAMPLE 22 | "The" with Plural Proper Nouns |

the United States	the United Nations	the Bahamas
the Rockies	the Philippines	the Cayman Islands
the Smiths	the Joneses	the Nguyens

| Rule 8 | Use "the" before the names of most bodies of water and the names of specific geographic regions |

| EXAMPLE 23 | "The" with Geographic Terms |

| the Atlantic Ocean | the Mississippi River | the Persian Gulf |
| the Southwest | the Midwest | the Middle East |

c.   No Article

| Rule 9 | Do not use "a," "an," or "the" before non-count nouns used in a general sense or plural common nouns used in a general sense |

| EXAMPLE 24 | No Article with General or Plural Non-Count Nouns |

Information can lead to justice.
(No article before non-count nouns "information" and "justice" when used in a general sense.)

Expert witnesses have become common in courtrooms.
(No article before plural nouns "expert witnesses" or "courtrooms" when used in a general sense.)

Exhibit 31.1	**Decision Tree and General Definitions for Articles in English**

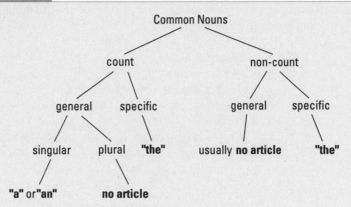

Step 1:   Decide if the noun is a count or non-count noun.

Step 2:   If the noun is a count noun, decide if the use of the noun is general or specific. If the use is specific, usually "the" is the correct article. Rule 3.

Step 3:   If the use of a count noun is general, decide if the noun is singular or plural. If the noun is singular, usually "a" or "an" is the correct article. If the noun is plural, usually no article is needed. Rule 4.

Step 4:   If the noun is a non-count noun, decide if its use is general or specific. If the use is general, usually no article is needed. If the use is specific, use "the." Rule 3.

Count nouns refer to persons, places, or things that can be counted. Count nouns have both a singular and plural form.

a contract	contracts	an appellate court	appellate courts
an easement	easements	one juror	twelve jurors
a trial court	trial courts		

Non-count nouns refer to entities or abstractions that cannot be counted.

negligence   evidence   violence   arson   discretion   harassment

General use of a noun usually occurs the first time a noun is used in a given context. General use of a noun also occurs when the writer intends any one of a group or class.

Specific use of a noun usually occurs for any one of the following reasons:

1.   The noun has already been used once in a given context;
2.   The noun is followed by a phrase or clause that restricts its identity;
3.   The noun is preceded by a superlative or a ranking adjective;
4.   The writer and the reader have shared knowledge about the identity of the noun.

Specific nouns will have a specific answer to the question "which one (or ones)?"

Chapter 31 Quiz No. 1

Draft answers for each of the following questions. Make your points clearly and concisely, and write sentences that are easy to read and that are grammatical and correctly punctuated.

1. What are count nouns?
2. When should a writer use "a" or "an" with a count noun?
3. "A" or "an" are not used with singular count nouns when they are preceded by another noun marker. What are some examples of noun markers?
4. "A" and "an" are not used with non-count nouns. Give some examples of non-count nouns that are common words used in law.
5. When should a writer use the definite article "the"?

§ 31.1.2 Verbs

Verbs present many challenges to both native and non-native speakers of English. Some of these challenges are addressed in other chapters. (Sections 27.3.1 and 27.3.2 discuss verb tense and mood, section 27.4.1 discusses subject-verb agreement, section 24.1 discusses active and passive voice, and sections 24.3 and 24.4 discuss action verbs and the distance between subjects and verbs.)

As an ESL law student, you also need to pay special attention to verb phrases that contain auxiliary, or helping, verbs and verb tenses in conditional and speculative sentences. In addition, you will need to learn which verbs commonly used in legal writing are followed by gerunds, infinitives, and objects.

a. Verbs with Auxiliary, or Helping, Verbs

Unlike article errors, errors in verbs often change the meaning and are therefore much more serious. Fortunately, few ESL law students have difficulty with the main verbs in English verb phrases. The challenge is to learn the subtle yet often significant differences in meanings that auxiliary, or helping, verbs add to the main part of the verb phrase.

For example, "can" (or "cannot") before a verb shows ability or knowledge.

EXAMPLE 1   **"Can" Shows Ability**

Despite his back injury, the plaintiff can still drive a semi-truck.
("Can" indicates the ability to drive.)

"Can" is also used to suggest that the action is a possibility or an option.

EXAMPLE 2   **"Can" Shows Possibility**

The defendant can argue that *Smith* applies.
("Can" indicates the possibility of the defendant arguing that Smith applies.)

Exhibit 31.2 lists the most common meanings for many auxiliary, or helping, verbs.

Exhibit 31.2	**Common Meanings for Auxiliary, or Helping, Verbs**	
Auxiliary Verb	**Meanings**	**Example Sentences**
can	shows ability or knowledge	Despite his back injury, the plaintiff can still drive a semi-truck.
	suggests possibility	The defendant can argue that *Smith* applies.
	gives an option	The prosecutor can charge the defendant with first- or second-degree murder.
could	shows past ability	Before his back injury, the plaintiff could drive a semi-truck.
	shows possibility	The defendant could argue that *Smith* applies.
could have	suggests past opportunity that was missed	The plaintiff could have learned to drive a semi-truck, but he cannot now because of his back injury.
may	asks or gives permission	Students may leave the campus during the lunch hour.
	shows possibility	The court may grant a motion to dismiss.
might	shows possibility	The court might grant a motion to dismiss.
must	shows requirement	The court must ask the defendant how she pleads.
	shows probability	The defendant must be considering a plea bargain.
must not	shows prohibition	The prosecution must not suggest that the defendant's post-arrest silence implies guilt.
should	shows advisability or expectation	The court should grant a motion to continue when the State amends a charge the day before trial.
	shows obligation	The court should instruct the jury to disregard that remark.
	shows expectation	You should receive the signed agreement in tomorrow's mail.
should have	shows obligation that was not met	The court should have instructed the jury to disregard that remark, but it failed to do so.
	shows expectation that was not met	You should have already received the signed agreement in the mail; I do not know why it is late.
	shows advisability after the fact	The officer should have handcuffed the suspect, but he did not.

Auxiliary Verb	Meanings	Example Sentences
ought to	shows advisability or expectation	The court ought to grant a motion to continue when the State amends a charge the day before trial.
	shows obligation	The court ought to instruct the jury to disregard that remark.
	shows expectation	You ought to receive the signed agreement in tomorrow's mail.
ought to have	shows obligation that was not met	The court ought to have instructed the jury to disregard that remark, but it failed to do so.
	shows expectation that was not met	You ought to have received the signed agreement in yesterday's mail; I do not know why it is late.
	shows advisability after the fact	The officer ought to have handcuffed the suspect, but he did not.
will	shows future time	The verdict will be announced after the parties return to the courtroom.
	shows a promise or willingness	Acme will clean up the toxic waste site.
would	indicates a repeated past action	The arsonist would often warn his victims.
	indicates a future act in a past tense sentence	The arsonist warned his victims that he would set fire to the building.

In addition to learning how meanings change based on auxiliary, or helping, verbs, ESL law students have to master which form of the verb is used with various helping verbs.

Auxiliary, or helping, verbs that are followed by the base form

Use the base form of a verb after the following auxiliary, or helping, verbs: "can," "could," "did," "do," "does," "may," "might," "must," "shall," "should," "will," and "would."

EXAMPLE 3   Helping Verbs + Base Form

can argue	could deny	did object	may plead
might consider	must rely	should admit	will determine

<u>Auxiliary, or helping, verbs that are followed by objects and then the base form</u>

A few verbs ("make," "let," and "have") must be followed by a noun or pronoun object and then by the base form of a verb.

EXAMPLE 4   **Verbs + Objects + Base Form**

The children's father lets <u>them</u> <u>leave</u> for school without eating breakfast.
                    (pronoun)(base form)

The mother makes the <u>children</u> <u>do</u> their homework.
                    (noun) (base form)

The verb "help" can be followed by a noun or pronoun and then a base form or the infinitive form of a verb.

EXAMPLE 5   **"Help" + Object + Base Form**

Both parents helped the children <u>learn</u> different sports.
                        (base form)

Both parents helped the children <u>to</u> <u>learn</u> different sports.
                        (infinitive)

<u>Auxiliary, or helping, verbs that are followed by the past participle of the verb</u>

Use the past participle of a verb with "have," "has," or "had."

EXAMPLE 6   **"Have," "Has," "Had" + Past Participle**

have determined   has begun   had stolen   has written

<u>Auxiliary, or helping, verbs that are followed by the present participle of the verb</u>

Use the present participle of a verb after forms of "be," including "am," "are," "is," "was," "were," "have been," and "had been."

EXAMPLE 7   **Helping Verbs + Present Participle**

are relying   is considering   was driving

---

b.   Verb Tense in Conditional Sentences

Lawyers frequently use conditional sentences to express possibilities or to suggest what might happen in the future. "If" and "unless" clauses are commonly used either before or after the main clause. Use present tense in the "if" or "unless" clause and future tense in the main clause.

EXAMPLE 8   **Conditional Sentences**

If the court <u>applies</u> the *Reed* test, it <u>will find</u> that the element is met.
  (present tense)   *(future tense)*

The prosecutor <u>will charge</u> the defendant with arson unless she <u>has</u> an alibi.
    (future tense)   *(present tense)*

---

c. Verb Tense in Speculative Sentences

To show that an outcome is possible but unlikely, use past tense in an "if" clause and "would," "could," or "might" as the auxiliary, or helping, verb in the main clause.

EXAMPLE 9   **Speculative Sentences**

If the witness <u>saw</u> the defendant's car at the accident scene, he would have also seen
  (past tense)
the defendant.

The jury might ignore its instructions if it <u>believed</u> the police fabricated the evidence.
        (past tense)

To speculate about something that did not happen, use the past perfect tense in an "if" clause and "would have," "could have," or "might have" as auxiliary, or helping, verbs with the past participle. Remember that "had" is the helping verb that creates the past perfect tense.

EXAMPLE 10   **Speculative Sentences**

If the defendant <u>had spoken</u> to Mr. Torres, he would have apologized to him, not threatened him.

The tenants could have complained to the building superintendent if he <u>had been</u> available.

To express conditions that are contrary to fact, use "were" in an "if" clause and "would," "could," or "might" in the main clause.

EXAMPLE 11   **Verb Tense with Contrary to Fact Conditions**

If I <u>were</u> you, I might try apologizing to the plaintiff.

If Mrs. Henderson <u>were</u> alive, she would not want the jury to find the defendant guilty of manslaughter.

---

d. Verbs + Gerunds, Infinitives, or Objects

Some verbs should be followed by gerunds (a verb form ending in "-ing" and used as a noun); other verbs should be followed by infinitives (a verb form made up of "to" plus the base form of the verb); others require objects (nouns or pronouns); and some verbs can be followed by either a gerund or an infinitive.[9] Some ESL law students may find that the most effective strategy for determining whether to use an infinitive or gerund after a certain verb is to apply the "Bolinger principle," which is to use infinitives to express something "hypothetical, future, unfulfilled" and to use gerunds to express something "real, vivid, fulfilled." (Bolinger, 1968)

EXAMPLE 12   **Bolinger Principle**

The defendant wants <u>to enter</u> a plea of not guilty.
(The sentence expresses an as yet unfulfilled action so the infinitive is used.)

The defendant admits <u>hitting</u> the pedestrian.
(The sentence expresses a past action so the gerund is used.)

The neighbors hope <u>to obtain</u> an easement.
(The sentence expresses a future action so the infinitive is used.)

His responsibilities include <u>hiring</u> employees.
(The sentence expresses a real, not a hypothetical action.)

Exceptions

Unfortunately, the Bolinger principle does not apply to approximately one-fourth of the verbs in question, including the following verbs:

<u>Verbs that are exceptions to the Bolinger principle and use gerunds:</u>

anticipate, consider, delay, envision, imagine, keep, mind, postpone, recommend, risk, suggest, understand

<u>Verbs that are exceptions to the Bolinger principle and use infinitives:</u>

claim, continue, fail, get, have, hire, manage, teach, tell

EXAMPLE 13   **Exceptions to the Bolinger Principle**

Her attorney will recommend <u>accepting</u> the offer.
         (gerund)
(The sentence expresses a future action but still uses a gerund after the verb.)

The officer managed <u>to distract</u> the gunman.
         (infinitive)
(The sentence expresses a past action but still uses an infinitive after the verb.)

Consequently, many ESL law students may prefer using lists that group verbs according to what must follow them. Below are lists of verbs commonly

---

9. Most verbs can also be followed by "that" clauses.

used in law grouped by what follows them. The patterns for each combination are in boldface type.

<u>Verbs that are usually followed by a gerund rather than an infinitive</u>[10]

(<u>verb</u>+_____-ing)

acknowledge	justify
admit	keep
advocate	keep on
anticipate	mention
appreciate	mind
approve	miss
avoid	necessitate
begrudge	postpone
cannot help	practice
complete	put off
condemn	quit
consider	recall
contemplate	recollect
defend	recommend
defer	relinquish
delay	relish
deny	renounce
detest	report
disclaim	resent
discuss	resist
dislike	resume
enjoy	risk
entail	sanction
escape	shirk
evade	suggest
facilitate	tolerate
finish	understand
get through	visualize
give up	withhold
imagine	witness
involve	

EXAMPLE 14   **Verb + Gerund**

The defendant admits <u>knowing</u> the victim, but he denies <u>killing</u> him.
            (gerund)   *(gerund)*

---

10. Although gerunds rather than infinitives often follow these verbs, using a gerund is not required. Many of these verbs are often followed by "that" clauses.

Some verbs can be immediately followed by an infinitive; others are followed by an object and then an infinitive; still other verbs can be followed by either an object or an infinitive. When an object is between the verb and the infinitive, the object performs the action of the infinitive.

Verbs that can be followed by either an infinitive or a "that" clause with little or no change in meaning are indicated by an asterisk below.

Verbs that are usually followed by an infinitive rather than a gerund

(**verb**+to _____)

agree*	know how
appear	learn
arrange	manage
ask	need
attempt	offer
bother	plan
care	prepare
claim	pretend*
condescend	promise*
consent	refuse
decide*	say
demand	seem
deserve	struggle
desire	swear
endeavor	tend
expect	threaten
fall	venture
happen	volunteer
have	want
hesitate	wait
hope*	wish

EXAMPLE 15   **Verb + Infinitive**

The workers expect <u>to reconcile</u> their differences with management.
            (infinitive)

Management plans <u>to offer</u> them a contract with a 5 percent salary increase.
            (infinitive)

The mediator <u>hoped to extend</u> the negotiation deadline.
      (verb followed by infinitive "to extend")

The mediator <u>hoped that</u> the negotiation deadline would be extended.
      (verb followed by "that" clause)

Verbs that can be followed by either a gerund or an infinitive

A few verbs can be followed by either a gerund or infinitive with little change in meaning.

(verb+_____-ing OR verb+to _____)

abhor	disdain
afford	dread
attempt	endure
bear	go
begin	hate
cannot bear	intend
cannot stand	like
cease	love
choose	neglect
commence	propose
continue	scorn
decline	start

EXAMPLE 16   **Verb + Infinitive or Gerund**

Landowners continue <u>to assert</u> their rights.
            (infinitive)

Landowners continue <u>asserting</u> their rights.
            (gerund)

A few verbs can be followed by a gerund or infinitive but with a significant change in meaning. One common pattern, which is supported by the Bolinger principle (infinitive expresses unfulfilled action, gerund expresses fulfilled action), is that when the verb is followed by a gerund, past time is indicated; when the verb is followed by an infinitive, future time is indicated.

forget   prefer   regret   remember   sense   stop   try

EXAMPLE 17   **Changing from Gerund to Infinitive Changes Meaning**

Mrs. Warren remembered <u>locking</u> the safe.
            (gerund)
(She has a past memory of locking the safe.)

Mrs. Warren remembered <u>to lock</u> the safe.
            (infinitive)
(She did not forget to lock the safe.)

Mrs. Warren must remember <u>to lock</u> the safe.
                (infinitive)
(She must remember this for the future.)

<u>Verbs usually followed by objects, then infinitives (except in the passive[11] voice)</u>

(<u>verb</u>+(object)+to _____)

advise	oblige
allow	order
appoint	permit
authorize	persuade
cause	remind
challenge	request
command	require
convince	select
encourage	teach
forbid	tell
force	tempt
get	train
hire	trust
instruct	urge
invite	warn

EXAMPLE 18   **Verb + Object + Infinitive**

Opposing counsel <u>will advise</u> her <u>client to settle</u>.
                (verb)   (object)(infinitive)

The judge <u>permitted</u> the <u>prosecutor to ask</u> questions about prior convictions.
             (verb)   (object) (infinitive)

Acme <u>encouraged</u> its <u>employees to participate</u> in the political campaign.
        (verb)   (object)   (infinitive)

Acme <u>instructed them to use</u> their lunch hour stuffing envelopes.
        (verb) (object)(infinitive)

Employees <u>were permitted to attend</u> the rally.
              (passive verb)   (infinitive)
(No noun or pronoun before infinitive because verb is in passive voice.)

---

11. In the passive voice the action of the verb is done to the subject. Example: "The motion was denied." In the example, "was denied" is done to "the motion." In active voice, the subject performs the action in the verb. Example: "The judge denied the motion." In this example, the judge is doing the denying. See section 24.1 for an extensive discussion of passive and active voice.

<u>Verbs that can be followed by either an object or an infinitive</u>

(verb+(object)) OR (<u>verb</u>+to _____)

ask	need
beg	prefer
choose	prepare
dare	promise
expect	want
help	wish
intend	would like
like	

EXAMPLE 19   **Verb + Object or Infinitive**

The landlord expected the <u>tenants to check</u> the batteries in the smoke detectors.
(Object "the tenants" follows "expected.")

The landlord <u>expected to hear</u> tenants complain about the rent increase.
(Infinitive "to hear" follows "expected.")

<u>Verbs followed by "too," "enough," and "how" expressions and an infinitive</u>

Use infinitives when expressions with "too," "enough," or "how" follow a verb.

EXAMPLE 20   **"Too," Enough," "How" + Infinitive**

The police arrived <u>too</u> late <u>to apprehend</u> the burglar.
("too" expression followed by infinitive "to apprehend")

The defendant is not strong <u>enough to kick</u> that door down.
("enough" expression followed by infinitive "to kick")

A 20-year-old woman knows <u>how to protect</u> herself.
("how" expression followed by infinitive "to protect")

---

e.   Two- or Three-Word Verbs

Learning which prepositions[12] to use in two- or three-word verbs, or phrasal verbs, is crucial because the prepositions in these verbs often completely change the meaning of the verb.

---

12. The prepositions in phrasal verbs are often called "particles."

EXAMPLE 21	**Phrasal Verbs**

One-Word Verb	*Meaning of One-Word Verb*
catch	find and stop

Two-Word Verb	*Meaning of Two-Word Verb*
catch up	to improve and reach the same standard

Three-Word Verb	*Meaning of Three-Word Verb*
catch up with	to come from behind and reach OR to find someone doing something illegal and punish that person

Because there are so many two- or three-word verbs in English and because several of them (such as "catch up with") have different meanings for different contexts, the best strategy for learning them is to note how they are used in native speakers' oral and written language. In addition, note that most of these verbs have more formal synonyms that are preferred in legal writing.

EXAMPLE 22	**Synonyms for Phrasal Verbs**

The brief must be *turned in* by 5:00 p.m. → The brief must be *submitted* by 5:00 p.m.
The protester *handed out* leaflets. → The protester *distributed* leaflets.
The attorney *put off* the meeting. → The attorney *postponed* the meeting.
Firefighters *put out* the blaze. → Firefighters *extinguished* the blaze.

§ 31.1.3   Prepositions

The preceding section discussed two- or three-word verbs in which the addition of one or more prepositions made a significant change to the base verb's meaning. Other English verbs, adjectives, and nouns must also be followed by specific prepositions. Unfortunately, the use of prepositions is idiomatic; it is not based on rules. Consequently, we have resorted to alphabetical lists of verbs, adjectives, and nouns commonly used in legal writing and their correct prepositions. When more than one preposition can be used with a given verb, adjective, or noun, the different preposition choices are separated by slash (/) marks. Parentheses show the types of words that may follow a given preposition. Brackets indicate meaning. Some verbs are in their present tense form; others are in their past tense form.

a.   Prepositions That Follow Verbs Commonly Used in Law

absolved from (wrongdoing)

absolved of (financial liability)

accompanied by

accused of

acquainted with

acquiesced in/to

adhered to

affected by

agree on (a contract, a date)

agree to [means "to acquiesce"]

agree with [means "to be in accord with" or "have the same opinion"]

allude to

appeal from

apply for (a position)

apply to

approve of [means to "find something good or suitable"]

attribute to

based on/upon

blamed for

caused by

charge at/into/toward

charge with (murder)

comment on

commit to

communicate to [means "to express thoughts or feelings"]

communicate with [used when two people understand thoughts or feelings]

compare to [used with similarities]

compare with [used with similarities and differences]

compensate for

compete against/for

compete with

composed of

confined to

consent to

contrast with [used with differences]

convicted of (crimes)

convicted on (counts)

cooperate with

covered with

decide against/for (the plaintiff)

decide in favor of (the plaintiff)

decide on (a date)

derived from

discriminate against

distinguish between/from

divided into

divorced from

experiment with (drugs)

fill in (a crack or hole)

filled out (an application)

filled up (a tank)

filled with (emotion, light, sound)

finished with

founded by (a person)

founded in (a date)

founded on [means the main idea that something else develops from]

free from/to

gain access to

impressed by/with

informed about/of [means to give information]

informed on [used when information is given to police or an enemy]

interfere with

object to

participate in

prevent from

prohibit from

protect against/from

questioned about/concerning

reach (a conclusion) about

reach for (a gun)

recover from

refer to

rely on/upon

rescue from

resigned from

respond to

save for [means "to keep money to use for a specific purpose"]

save from (harm or danger)

steal from

suffer from

suspected of

worry about

b.   Prepositions That Follow Adjectives Commonly Used in Law

accustomed to
afraid of
amazed at
angry about/at/over/with
anxious about
appreciative of
appropriate for
ashamed of
averse to
aware of
bad at
bored with
capable of
careful about/with
certain about/of
clever at
comparable to/with
concerned about/with
confident about
confused about
conscious of
consistent with
critical of/to
dedicated to
delighted at/by/with
dependent on/upon
different from
eager for/to
enthusiastic about
excited about/by
experienced in
familiar to/with
famous for
far above/below/from
fearful of

fond of
glad about
good at/for
grateful for
guilty of
happy about/with
hopeful about/of
inconsistent with
innocent of
interested in
jealous of
known for
liable for (damages) [means "to be legally responsible for"]
liable to [means "to be likely to"]
married to
nervous about
oblivious of/to (danger)
opposed to
proud of
qualified for
quick to
regardless of
related to
responsible for
satisfied with
sensitive about/to
similar to
sorry about/for
suitable for
tired of
tolerant of
upset about/by/over
used to

c.   Prepositions That Follow Nouns Commonly Used in Law

access to
amendment to
approval of
attempt at
authority on (area of expertise)
belief in
choice between/of
commitment to
complaint about/against
concern about/for/over

confidence in
confusion about/as to/over
dedication of/to
difference among (three or more)
difference between (two)
division between/of
doubt about/as to
effect of/on
experience in/of/with
explanation for/of

fear for/of
idea about/for/of
knowledge about/of
liability for
means of
need for
in need of
objection to
opposition to
participation in
possibility for/of
preference for
prevention of

process of
protection against/from
reason for
reference to
reliance on
respect for/of
response to
responsibility for
satisfaction from/in/of
search for
skill at/in
success as/in

d.   Prepositions in Idioms

during the course of (his employment)
in circumstances like (those in this case)
in contrast
in favor of
in light of
on the contrary

Chapter 31 Quiz No. 2

Draft answers for each of the following questions. Make your points clearly and concisely, and write sentences that are easy to read and that are grammatical and correctly punctuated.

1. What auxiliary, or helping, verb is used to show ability or knowledge or possibility?
2. In conditional sentences, what verb tenses are used?
3. In speculative sentences, what verb tense and auxiliary verbs are used?
4. The Bolinger principle helps writers determine whether a gerund or infinitive should be used with a particular verb. In a nutshell, what is the Bolinger principle?

§ 31.2   Rhetorical Preferences in Writing

Discourse patterns vary from language to language and from culture to culture. The way an expert writer makes a point in one culture is often quite different from the way an expert writer in another culture would make the same point. Indeed, what one culture may consider a good point in a given context, another culture might consider irrelevant in the same context.

What is particularly fascinating about this phenomenon, though, is that it often goes unnoticed. In fact, most writers have internalized their own culture's rhetorical preferences to the point that these preferences are subconscious choices. Most people seem to assume that their culture's world view and how it is expressed in writing is the way all human beings "naturally" think and write.

Because these cultural differences in discourse are so deeply embedded in language and in our subconscious, they are rarely taught to students. Most ESL law students report that their foreign language classes concentrated only on vocabulary and sentence grammar; they stopped short of addressing the larger cultural issues that affect the overall approach to writing. If this was true of your language classes, you may be unconsciously assuming that what was appropriate and conventional when writing in your native language is also appropriate and conventional when writing in English.

This section examines the rhetorical preferences in expository and argumentative writing in the United States culture, with a particular emphasis on how those preferences are manifested in legal writing. The section also compares and contrasts these preferences with some of the more common rhetorical preferences from other cultures in hopes of giving ESL law students insights about writing in English.

Remember, however, that this is a discussion of what is generally true about writing in the discourse community of United States lawyers and judges, and that in certain instances, the generalizations will not apply. For example, while it is generally true that writing that is direct is preferred in the United States legal culture, there are occasions when vagueness or indirection better serves the writer's purposes. The discussion makes similar generalizations about writing preferences in other cultures based on the research done by contrastive rhetoricians.[13] Again, like all generalizations, they may not be true in every instance, and unfortunately, the research available on rhetorical preferences in other cultures is somewhat incomplete. Even more important to remember is that language, including rhetorical preferences, does not stand still. The information that follows will need constant updating as the rhetorical preferences of various cultures evolve.

§ 31.2.1 Cultural Assumptions About Readers and the Purposes for Writing

All cultures treat writing as an act of communication, but they differ widely in their assumptions about that communication. Some operate under the assumption that the reader bears the heavier responsibility; it is the reader who must strive to understand the writer. Other cultures operate under the assumption that the writer has the heavier responsibility; it is the writer who must strive to be understood by the reader.[14] In reader-responsible cultures, writers may intentionally obscure meaning. Good writing often has an element of mystery to it. Readers are expected to work at understanding what is written. If they fail to understand, it is their fault.

In writer-responsible cultures, writers are expected to work at being clear. Good writing is not mysterious. Writers are expected to present their ideas in

---

13. The sources for the information in the following section are in the Bibliography for ESL Law Students, which appears at the end of this chapter, and one for legal writing professors at the end of the Teaching Notes for Chapter 31 in the Teacher's Manual. Students who are interested in reading the source material that applies to their specific native language and culture should consult the Bibliography for ESL Law Students.

14. John Hinds, *Reader versus Writer Responsibility: A New Typology in Writing Across Languages: Analysis of 2L Text* (Ulla Connor & Robert B. Kaplan eds., 1987).

ways that can be easily understood. If the reader has trouble understanding, it is the writer's fault.

a.   Assumptions and Expectations in the United States and in the United States Legal Culture

Because English is a writer-responsible language, the primary responsibility for successful communication lies with the writer. Writing clear sentences that can be understood the first time they are read is expected.[15] Being able to make a complicated topic easy for a reader to understand is admired.

The Reader's Time Is Valuable

An underlying assumption of the United States legal culture is that the reader's time is more valuable than the writer's time. Legal readers — including judges and partners in law firms — tend to have positions of power over the writers of legal prose: lawyers writing briefs for the court; interns and associates writing memoranda for supervising attorneys. Consequently, writers are expected to expend their time and energy writing clearly so that readers do not have to spend extra time and energy understanding.

In addition, United States readers tend to be far less patient than readers from other cultures. Consequently, the beginning of a piece of writing in the United States tends to get to the point quickly. It answers the question, "What is this about?"

Legal readers in the United States tend to expect a quick overview at the beginning of a piece of writing that sets out its content and structure. Many prefer statements of facts with an overview paragraph that introduces the parties, the legal problem, and the source of the facts. Discussion sections in legal memoranda are almost always begun by giving an overview of the law and a roadmap to its application. Even when a writer must describe how the law developed over a period of time, such historical discussion tends to be brief. The writer hits only the high points and moves rapidly toward the current state of the law. Giving some background and context for understanding the policy underlying the law is also common, but these discussions tend to be short and to the point. In general, United States legal readers want only enough background and context for the law to deal with the case before them.

As a rule, judges are even more impatient than other United States legal readers. They are eager for brief writers to get to the application of the law to the facts. Long-winded introductions or treatises on the applicable law are likely to irritate judges who are already knowledgeable about the law and who are reading the brief with the primary purpose of thinking through how that law applies to the case before them.

Introductory paragraphs in letters to clients also tend to have some features of an overview. They may include a short, polite beginning that helps establish or reinforce the relationship between the writer and reader, but then they usually move rather quickly to stating the purpose of the letter. In many cases that means stating the legal question the client brought to the attorney

---

15. Clarity has not always been a top priority in legal writing. In the past, consumer contracts and statutes were often written in long, complex sentences that were difficult to understand because they were filled with abstractions and other legalese. See section 24.3.

and, particularly when the answer to that question is one the client will like, introducing the answer the attorney found after researching the problem.

The Reader Wants to Know What You Are Thinking; Be Direct and Explicit

To ensure that their meaning is clearly conveyed to their readers throughout a document, attorneys use two common features of the prose style used in the United States: directness and explicitness. For example, in office memoranda, which are typically in-house documents that are read only by members of the firm, writers are expected to be direct and candid with their readers. Writers should lay out the facts, the rules, the relevant cases, and the arguments each side is likely to make. Writers should tell their readers when, in the writer's opinion, the court will probably find an argument weak or persuasive. Unfavorable facts, rules, analogous cases, and weaknesses in the client's case are dealt with openly. A key objective of the office memorandum is a frank and honest assessment of the case. Some firms also want office memoranda to include some candid strategic advice, such as whether the firm should take the case or whether settling out of court might be the client's best option.

Directness manifests itself in a brief when the writer tells the court exactly what he or she wants from the court (for example, denial of summary judgment or admission of some evidence). Directness may lead a brief writer to concede a point, but it does not mean that a brief writer should be neutral or lay out the opponent's arguments in a favorable light.

It is possible, of course, to be too direct with a court. Some judges and justices admit that they do not like being told by an attorney that they "must" do something even when that something is required by law. Using "should" rather than "must" in sentences such as "The court should grant the motion to suppress . . ." or "This court should find that the trial court abused its discretion . . ." allows the writer to be direct without seeming to be ordering the court around. Passive voice is another way to avoid sounding like the writer is bossing the court around. Revising "The court must grant the motion . . ." to "The motion should be granted . . ." is less likely to elicit a negative reaction from a judge. Yet another way of being direct without seeming to boss the court is to make the law the subject of the sentence — "Section 409 requires that . . ."

In letters to clients, directness tends to be most obvious when an attorney writer is telling the client about his or her options. Attorneys writing to clients also find that it is effective to be direct about any instructions or deadlines they must convey to the client, even though these instructions and deadlines may be softened a bit with a word such as "please" (for example, "Please sign and return the enclosed documents to my office by Tuesday, December 17, 2013."). Attorney writers are also invariably direct in pointing out that their predictions are their professional opinions and not guarantees of a certain outcome. On the other hand, attorneys writing to clients tend to be slightly less direct about conveying bad or disappointing news. While the writer may save unhappy news for the end of a letter or soften the blow with an empathetic word like "unfortunately," the attorney writer will still be clear about what the bad news is.

Despite the preference for directness, most attorneys avoid first and second person references ("I" and "you") in both legal memoranda and briefs. Rather than write "I think the court will find the first element is met" in an office memorandum, most attorneys write "the court will probably find that the first element is met." Rather than write "you should consider" when addressing the court, virtually all attorneys write "the court should consider." Use of "I" and "you" is more common in letters to clients, but even there many attorneys prefer "in my opinion" to "I think" or "I believe." Even though the use of "you" is commonplace in letters to clients, indiscriminate use of "you" can make a letter seem bossy or too informal. Many attorneys prefer using "we" in letters to clients to mean both the client and the attorney. "We" conveys the impression that the two are or will be working together as a team.

Explicitness is most evident when legal memorandum and brief writers construct their arguments. Facts are analogized and distinguished explicitly. Little is left to the imagination as the writer makes explicit connections between points and draws explicit conclusions from the points he or she has made. Summaries that synthesize and repeat earlier points are admired. Indeed, explicitly drawn conclusions are hallmarks of United States legal writing.

The Writing Has to Get a Job Done

Another assumption of the United States legal culture is that writing is primarily functional; it has a job to do — explain, persuade, or both — and its value is judged almost exclusively by whether it accomplishes its purpose. Legal writers would not create prose that is aesthetically pleasing for its own sake. Eloquence is admired only when it serves the underlying purposes of explaining or persuading. Further, excessive elaboration is not considered eloquent writing; rather, it is treated as unwanted fluff or padding.

The Writer Should State and Support a Position

Writing is assumed to be the writer's own view or opinion. Readers in the United States expect writers to state a position and then defend it. Other people's writing is considered "fair game" — that is, it is completely acceptable to challenge, disagree with, or criticize the writing and analysis of another, including an expert in the field or even a court, as long as the challenge, disagreement, or criticism is well supported and directed at the ideas and arguments and not at the individual. Attacking the arguments of one's opponents is expected, but once again the criticism should address the weaknesses in the arguments and not become personal.

Support for one's ideas can take a number of forms. In United States writing in general, facts, statistics, and other "hard data" are favorite forms of support. Readers expect concrete support for most of a writer's points. The use of detail as evidence supporting one's position is considered persuasive. Simple assertions that are not backed up by supporting evidence are widely criticized as unpersuasive.

In the United States legal culture, support for one's ideas or arguments generally falls into three categories: plain language arguments, analogous case arguments, and policy arguments. United States legal readers expect that most of a legal writer's points will be supported by cited authority. A plain language argument relies on the authority of the law and a common sense reading of it. An analogous case argument relies on the authority of another court and how it ruled in a similar case. Policy arguments often cite legislative history as the authority for statements about the policy underlying a rule. Citing to the record and using detailed facts from the case to support one's arguments are all considered effective advocacy. Conversely, assertions without support are considered poor advocacy.

When an attorney uses facts and cases to support an argument, the expectation is that attorneys will be meticulously accurate. If an attorney is caught misrepresenting a fact or a case, he or she loses credibility. Legal readers would become suspicious of that attorney's other representations of fact and law. What is also expected in the United States legal culture, however, is that attorneys writing as advocates will "characterize" the facts and case law in a light that is favorable to their client. Attorneys disagree about where the line is drawn between characterizing and misstating facts. Most agree that characterization includes emphasis. For example, favorable facts are highlighted and discussed in detail; unfavorable facts are downplayed and only mentioned briefly. Most agree that omitting key facts or cases that are unfavorable is not only dishonest and ineffective advocacy, but also a probable violation of the rules. Virtually all agree that misstating key facts or cases is totally unacceptable and possibly even malpractice.

One way to determine whether a given way of expressing a fact or discussing a case is just a favorable characterization or an outright misstatement is to ask what the opponent would say in response. If an opponent would be inclined to say something like "I wouldn't put it that way," then the attorney can assume he or she has stayed within the legitimate boundaries of characterization. If an opponent would say "that's not true," then the attorney can assume he or she has stepped over the line into misstatement.

Assuming then that misstatement is not an option, what is still confusing is whether it is better to err on the side of understatement or on the side of overstatement. Many lawyers would argue that understatement is safer and better for building one's reputation with other attorneys and judges. Even so, a quick survey of writing in the profession would probably show that, if an attorney is erring on one side or the other, most err on the side of overstatement.

Writing Is Like Personal Property; Avoid Plagiarism

An added complication to the United States culture's views about writing and support for ideas is its notion of plagiarism. Because people in the United States place a high value on originality, an original idea or an original expression in words is considered a valuable possession. Consequently, people in the United States culture tend to think that a writer's ideas, and especially the words a writer uses to express those ideas, are that writer's personal property. Using someone's ideas or words *without attribution* is treated like stealing that person's ideas or words. Using someone's ideas or words *with attribution*,[16] however, is a commonplace and respectable form of supporting one's own points. In fact, use of attributed quotations from experts and other authorities is considered effective support as long as the writer is selective about what he or she quotes. Overquoting, while not nearly as serious a mistake as plagiarism, is frowned upon because it suggests the writer has borrowed too heavily from other sources and has not contributed any original thinking.

---

16. In some instances, writers also need the original author's express permission.

Exhibit 31.3	United States Concept of Plagiarism

- People in the United States culture tend to think that a writer's ideas, and especially the words a writer uses to express those ideas, are that writer's personal property.
- Using someone's ideas or words without attribution is treated like stealing that person's ideas or words.
- When using someone else's ideas, include citations to the source; when using someone else's words, include citations to the source and use quotation marks around that person's words.

Concerns about plagiarism also appear in legal writing, but they are somewhat overshadowed by the heavy emphasis on having authority for one's arguments. Citing cases, statutes, books, law review articles, and other secondary sources is considered of paramount importance. These citations show that the writer has the support of the law, other courts, and other legal minds behind his or her arguments. There is universal agreement about not only the need for citations to authority but also the use of quotation marks[17] to show that a writer has set out the exact language of a rule.[18]

There is a difference of opinion, however, in the United States legal culture about whether legal writers need to use quotation marks as well as the citation when they are using the exact language of a court. Some legal writers and readers seem to feel that court opinions are almost like public property. Others continue to be careful to use quotation marks around exact language from another court. The safe choice is to apply the same standards in legal writing as in other writing in the United States and use quotation marks around another's words.

An additional important point concerns plagiarism in law school settings: In all United States law schools, plagiarizing is considered a serious ethical offense. Despite the recent shift to encouraging some limited collaboration in legal writing classes, virtually every United States law school has a student code of conduct that strictly forbids copying another student's work and representing it as one's own. Plagiarizing the words, ideas, or even the key organizational features of another student's writing has serious consequences, often including expulsion from law school. Similarly, law students writing seminar papers and law review articles must be conscientious about citing their sources and using quotation marks when they are using the language of an authority. The penalties for plagiarizing the work of a published author are usually identical to the penalties for plagiarizing the work of another student.

In United States law firms, however, very different standards apply. Attorneys who are members of the same firm often share sample forms, in-house memoranda, and even rule sections from briefs. Using the writing of another member of the firm as a model is common. Some firms even have memorandum and brief "banks," which are copies of office memoranda and briefs written by firm members that other firm members can use when they are writing about

---

17. Long quotations of fifty words or more are written as block quotations. No quotation marks are used with block quotations even though the wording is exactly the same as the original. See section 28.5.1b in this book, Rule 48.5(a) in the *ALWD Citation Manual*, and Rule 5.1 in *The Bluebook*.

18. Using ellipses to omit parts of the rule that are not applicable to the matter at hand is completely acceptable.

Exhibit 31.4	Writer-Responsible versus Reader-Responsible Languages and Cultures

English ↓ Writer-Responsible	Most East Asian and Middle Eastern Languages ↓ Reader-Responsible
▪ Primary responsibility for successful communication lies with the writer.	▪ Primary responsibility for successful communication lies with the reader.
▪ If the reader has trouble understanding, it is the writer's fault.	▪ If the reader has trouble understanding, it is the reader's fault.
▪ Writers are expected to work at being clear.	▪ Writers may intentionally obscure meaning; good writing often has an element of mystery to it.
▪ Writers are expected to present their ideas in ways that can be easily understood.	▪ Readers are expected to work at understanding what is written.
▪ Writing clear sentences that can be understood the first time they are read is expected.	▪ Readers do not expect sentences that can be readily understood the first time they are read.
▪ Being able to make a complicated topic easy for a reader to understand is admired.	▪ Not fully grasping a writer's intended meaning does not frustrate these readers.

similar legal problems. This sharing within a firm is not considered plagiarism; rather, it is considered a practical way to save time and resources.

b. Assumptions and Expectations in Other Cultures

Most East Asian and Middle Eastern languages are reader-responsible languages. Consequently, not fully grasping a writer's intended meaning does not frustrate these readers. They do not expect sentences that can be automatically understood the first time they are read. Japanese readers, for example, assume that the writer may have deliberately hidden some of the meaning. Even though a Japanese writer may continually return to the theme of an article, the theme may not be stated explicitly. Similarly, Hebrew and Arabic readers expect to "read between the lines" and draw the appropriate conclusion on their own.

The tradition in Russian academic writing is for writers to show their intelligence and the importance of their ideas by being intentionally complex. Long sentences, long paragraphs, and even long paragraphs that are made up of one long sentence are admired. Writers achieve some of the complexity by using subordination, parallelism, and parenthetical comments. Using technical terms, sometimes without even defining them, adds to the complexity.

A few cultures and their written languages seem to be in a transition period. Experts in contrastive rhetoric believe, for example, that modern Chinese (Mandarin) is in the process of changing from a reader-responsible to a writer-responsible approach.

In some cultures, the best way to begin a piece of expository writing is with an appropriate proverb, parable, or anecdote. This sets a tone for the discussion that follows and also underscores the "truth" of what will be said. Thai writing, for example, tends to begin with an anecdote, is followed by specific detail, and then ends with an overall statement of the main point in the very last sentence. In Haitian Creole, or Kreyòl, essays begin with flowery and philosophical introductions and then may go on to include numerous proverbs. In Japanese prose, *ki*, which is comparable to the introduction, does not include the thesis. German writers are also taught not to state a thesis before they have set out the evidence that supports it. Other cultures favor a personal approach to beginnings. Relating how the topic is connected to the writer is a common way to introduce a topic. Still others rely heavily on beginnings that develop a historical context. Arabic speakers tend to set the stage for their topics by broad statements about the general state of affairs.

The length of the introduction or how much of the total piece of writing should be taken up by the introduction also varies greatly from culture to culture. Lengthy introductions are a noteworthy feature of Spanish writing. An introduction that takes up to a third of the total pages would not be uncommon.

Rather than introducing the main point quickly, Chinese writers use a "brush clearing" or "clearing the terrain" approach. In this approach, the writer begins by discussing all the ideas related to his or her main idea. Once this is done (the brush is cleared), the main idea is ready to be explored.

As a general rule, writers in East Asian languages prefer indirectness to directness and inferring meaning rather than writing explicitly. Stating one's point baldly is equated with a lack of sophistication. Chinese writers, for example, may give concrete examples, but the cultural preference is to stop after listing the examples and allow the reader to make the connections and draw the inevitable conclusion. Explicit conclusions are considered repetitious and possibly even insulting to educated readers.

Japanese writers may, as a general rule, be even more indirect than Chinese writers. Good Japanese writing implies or alludes to rather than explicitly states its points. Making a point indirectly, or hinting at meaning is regarded as a sign of intelligence and sensitivity. Directness is equated with brashness. Korean writers rarely use direct persuasion and explicit description. Arguing directly or explicitly is apt to have a negative effect on readers. The more common approach is to hide criticisms in metaphors. The preference to be indirect is not limited, however, to writers of Asian languages. Finnish writers also tend to leave unsaid things that seem obvious.

In many cultures, writing is treated as received wisdom. Writers strive to pass along the insights of the past; consequently, readers do not assume that a writer is expressing his or her own opinion. Instead, students are encouraged first to memorize and later to repeat in their own writing the words of the respected authorities from the past. The purpose of writing in these cultures is to create harmony between writer and reader, not to debate or explicate a point of view. In China, for example, being a writer is equated with being a scholar and therefore one who knows and writes the truth.

Other cultures, by contrast, have developed a long history of skepticism about their governments and the so-called expert opinion that may be based on officially sanctioned "truth." As a result, writers in these cultures tend not to support their arguments by quoting other authorities, citing statistics that come from governmental agencies, or offering concrete proof. Polish writers, for example, tend not to refer to the work of others; instead, the dominant rhetorical techniques in their tradition are comparing and contrasting and defining and redefining.

In Japanese writing, there is a tendency to use a mix of arguments for and against a position. Japanese writers also may end an argument by taking a different position from their beginning position. Even in argumentative essays, Japanese writers tend to be somewhat tentative and use more hedges and qualifiers than do writers from other cultures.

Korean writers may use a formulaic expression like "some people say" as a way to introduce their own point of view, particularly when the position they are taking is a controversial one. The formulaic expression allows the writer to avoid being too direct and to suggest that there is other support for the position the writer states.

Other cultures treat writing more as an art than as a functional skill. Japanese writers, for example, tend to be very concerned about the aesthetics of their writing. Writers of Romance languages like Spanish or French pride themselves in using the language beautifully. Writers in Arabic also tend to place a stronger emphasis on the form of language. They prefer richness in language, particularly in the form of metaphors and other figurative language, over conciseness.

The best support for one's points varies from culture to culture. Some cultures support points through analogies, appeals to intuition, beautiful language, or references to sages from the past. Chinese writers prefer elaborate metaphors and literary references. They also use numerous references to historical events. Rather than using different pieces of evidence as support, some cultures prefer to argue the same point in many different ways. Different cultures also disagree about what is understatement and overstatement. Middle Eastern law students, particularly those who were educated in classical Arabic, may consider a supporting statement as neutral that a typical person from the United States would consider an exaggeration. What native speakers of English would consider neutral, a classical Arabic speaker would tend to view as examples of understatement.

§ 31.2.2   Culturally Determined Patterns in Writing

a.   Preferences in the United States

As a general rule, students in the United States receive more direct instruction in rhetorical patterns in writing than do students in most other school systems. Composition textbooks stress paragraphs that use a general topic sentence, specific supporting sentences, and a general concluding sentence. The five-paragraph essay taught in junior high and high school expands this same general → specific → general structure over a slightly longer piece of prose. The typical term paper or research paper with its thesis statement expands the structure over a still longer piece of writing.

In other words, United States students internalize a hierarchical approach with numerous levels of subordination as the appropriate way to present ideas. In fact, the degree to which a writer uses a hierarchical approach to writing is often the basis for judging whether that writer's work is mature. Conversely, frequent use of coordination (this point "and" this point "and" this point "and" this point) is considered a sign of an immature prose style. One-sentence paragraphs are also generally frowned upon and thought to be the mark of undeveloped ideas.

Writing in the United States legal culture emulates this same hierarchical approach. An effective prose style in law typically uses an overview → analysis → synthesis organizational strategy. In fact, successful attorney writers deliberately use topic sentences, signposts, and enumeration to reveal the hierarchical organization of their line of reasoning.

Writing that is deemed "coherent" prose in the United States usually has very explicit language links to guide readers across the levels of generality and specificity. Indeed, lexical ties are the primary ways native speakers of English create coherence in their prose. These sentence-to-sentence connections result in a linear prose style. Narratives in English also tend to be linear because speakers of English perceive time as linear. Temporal-causal sequencing is typical.

English sentences tend to be written in an old information → new information pattern. Topics tend to be in the first half of sentences.

b.   Preferences in Other Cultures

The traditional United States formula for writing (introduction, body, conclusion) with roadmaps and signposts along the way is considered mechanical, unsophisticated, and even childish in many other cultures. French writing, for example, uses more of a meandering approach. The writer might touch on the topic initially and then circle back to it later in the writing. Topic sentences are not part of the French writing tradition, primarily because they are deemed too obvious and condescending to readers. Contrary to the English tradition of conclusions simply summarizing what has already been said, French writers often conclude an essay by introducing a new but related topic.

The Japanese formula for prose, *ki-shoo-ten-ketsu*, is as predictable as the traditional United States structure of introduction, body, and conclusion, but the Japanese version has distinct differences. *Ki*, which is roughly comparable to the introduction, will not typically include the thesis; *shoo* will develop the argument; *ten* will abruptly shift and introduce a new sub-theme, which is often an examination of the thesis from a new angle; and *ketsu*, which is the conclusion, may state the thesis, but rather than just summarize the earlier ideas, *ketsu* may introduce some new ideas. *Ketsu* need not have the closure expected from a United States conclusion. It may end with a question or otherwise express some lingering doubt.

Korean expository essays also tend to be organized from specific to general. Like the Japanese *ketsu*, Korean conclusions may contain the thesis but only in an indirect form.

The Slavic countries such as Poland use yet another form of organization known as "circumvoluted discourse."[19] In this approach, the writer tackles a point from numerous perspectives and works toward a thesis, which is finally revealed near the end. Like the Japanese *ten*, the circumvoluted approach may seem to English readers to take the writing off course when in fact the technique is more about tackling a topic from many points of view.

Several cultures, particularly Arabic-speaking cultures, do not particularly value hierarchy and subordination in ideas. As a rule, Arabic writers are inclined to restate their positions, often with warnings, rather than support them with examples. In fact, most Arabic languages have relatively few markers for sub-

---

19. Leslie Kosel Eckstein et al., *Understanding Your International Students: An Educational, Cultural, and Linguistic Guide* (Jeffra Flaitz ed., 2003).

ordination. Instead, parallelism is a key ingredient in Arabic for conveying a rich array of parallel ideas. Coordination and balance are the hallmarks of sophisticated Arabic prose. Unlike in English, where excessive coordination is treated as "unsophisticated," mature Arabic writers tend to join many of their ideas together with "*wa*," the Arabic word for "and." Writers in many other languages, including Chinese, also favor additive conjunctions to connect ideas.

Unlike United States writers, who tend to move from the general to the specific, Japanese writers prefer to move from the specific to the general. This tradition is reinforced in Japanese journalistic writing, which begins with details and saves the lead until much later in the story. Chinese writers also tend to use an inductive approach.

Many other cultures prefer to hide the underlying organization of a piece of writing. Numbering one's points or reasons is not favored. In general, writers in most other cultures use fewer language links than do their United States counterparts. In a few languages, most notably Puerto Rican Spanish, one- or two-sentence paragraphs are common.

Native speakers of Chinese tend to use centrifugal organizational patterns, and native speakers of Spanish tend to use linear organizational patterns but with tangential breaks. Spanish writers do not tend to use signposts or transitional words and phrases to guide readers through the text.

Because both Chinese and Japanese are languages that rely heavily on the concept of topic, the typical sentence structure in these languages is a topic-comment structure. Consequently, ESL law students who have Chinese or Japanese as their first language may be inclined to replicate this sentence structure preference in English and produce what native speakers of English would consider too many sentences that begin with "as for," "in regard to," "there is," or "there are."

§ 31.2.3 Conciseness vs. Repetition

a. Preferences in the United States

In all types of expository prose in the United States, conciseness is heralded as a writing virtue. Saying a great deal in a few words is considered a sign of the writer's intelligence and respect for his or her readers. In the United States legal culture, conciseness is even more highly prized as lawyers fight to keep their heads about the paper blizzard created by complex litigation. Courts require lawyers to write within page limits. Judges admonish attorneys "to be brief." Supervising attorneys chastise young lawyers to "get to the point."

In the United States legal culture, writers are expected to be concise in two different ways: They are expected to edit their sentences of all excess verbiage (see section 25.2), and they are expected to stay on track and focused on points that are central to developing a line of reasoning. Straying, even slightly, from the point puzzles and irritates legal readers in the United States, who are likely to view writing with digressions as disorganized, unfocused, and a waste of their time. In fact, one of the strongest condemnations of any part of a piece of legal writing is to label it "irrelevant."

Only in law review articles is exploration of a related side issue encouraged, and even in law review articles, this type of digression must be done in footnotes and not in the main body of the text. A few writers have borrowed the law review footnote system as a means for exploring tangential points in memoranda and briefs, but this practice is the exception, not the norm. Many more memoranda and brief writers use appendices when they believe that some but not all of their readers might appreciate extensive supporting, background, or related information. In any case, the virtually unanimous view is that anything in the body of the text of any memorandum or brief must be directly "on point."

Although writing textbooks, including legal writing textbooks, often advise writers to be concise and denounce "needless" repetition, at least two kinds of repetition are favored in legal prose style. First, legal writers tend to repeat their conclusions. In legal memoranda, the overall conclusion may appear in both the brief answer and in the separate conclusion section. In addition, legal writers often state mini-conclusions after an extended discussion of a significant point and then draw these mini-conclusions together into an overall conclusion.

Second, when writing as advocates, lawyers tend to repeat points, albeit subtly, that are favorable to their case. In fact, many effective advocates expend a great deal of effort finding slightly different ways to emphasize essentially the same point. Brief writers who write an argumentative point heading and then open the next section with a positive assertion are often making exactly the same point but choosing a different sentence structure and slightly different words. The net effect of deliberate but subtle repetition is to create an overall theme, or theory of the case, that the writer hopes the reader will adopt. Lawyers in the United States who use subtle repetition as a form of advocacy generally know that they must use this technique selectively and carefully because they are aware that they risk annoying legal readers, particularly judges, if the repetition becomes too obvious.

b.   Preferences in Other Cultures

In many other cultures, elaborate and extended prose is greatly admired. In most Romance languages, for example, sophisticated writers use frills and flourishes to embellish their points. The very kinds of digressions that United States legal readers find irritating and irrelevant are admired in many other cultures. Spanish readers, for example, consider the exploration of side points a sign that the writer is highly intelligent and well versed in the topic. French writers also have much more freedom to digress and introduce related material. Earlier we saw how Japanese writers use an organizational framework called *ki-shoo-ten-ketsu*. They shift the topic and look at it from a new angle when they are in the *ten* element.

Many cultures prefer to argue the same point in many different ways. Paragraph after paragraph says essentially the same thing with only modest additions or changes. Arabic writers, for example, pride themselves in saying the same thing in many different ways. Polish writers have a tradition of restating the same idea. Chinese writers return several times to a main idea before moving on. Their readers expect repetition; indeed, they expect Chinese writers to use and re-use stock phrases. Naturally, the repetition in all these rhetorical traditions lengthens a typical piece of writing.

Exhibit 31.5   Contrasting Rhetorical Preferences*

	U.S. Legal Writing	Chinese	Japanese	Korean	French	Spanish	Arabic	Russian
Introductions	▪ U.S. legal writers tend to give a quick overview at the beginning of a piece of writing that sets out its content and structure. ▪ Beginnings in writing tend to get to the point quickly, answering the question, "What is this about?"	▪ Chinese writers often use a "clearing the terrain" approach, discussing all of the ideas related to the main idea before exploring the main idea.	▪ Japanese writers using the organizational framework called *ki-shoo-ten-ketsu*, do not typically include the thesis in *ki*, which is roughly comparable to the introduction.			▪ Spanish writers tend to compose lengthy introductions that may take up to a third of the total pages.	▪ Arabic writers tend to set the stage for topics by broad statements about the general state of affairs.	
Conciseness	▪ Conciseness—saying a great deal in a few words—is considered a sign of the writer's intelligence and respect for his or her readers. Writers are expected to be concise by (1) editing their sentences of all excess verbiage and (2) staying on track and focusing on points that are central to developing a line of reasoning.	▪ Chinese writers return several times to the main idea before moving on. ▪ Chinese readers expect repetition. ▪ Chinese readers expect writers to use and re-use stock phrases.					▪ Arabic writers prefer richness in language, particularly in the form of metaphors and other figurative language, over conciseness. ▪ Arabic writers pride themselves in making the same point in many different ways.	

(continues)

* The many empty spots in the chart highlight the point that the work of contrastive rhetoricians is far from complete. We still have much to learn about the rhetorical preferences of many cultures.

Exhibit 31.5 Contrasting Rhetorical Preferences* (continued)

	U.S. Legal Writing	Chinese	Japanese	Korean	French	Spanish	Arabic	Russian
Directness	■ Writers are generally expected to be direct and candid with their readers. ■ Writers should lay out the facts, the rules, the relevant cases, and the arguments each side is likely to make. ■ Unfavorable facts, rules, analogous cases, and weaknesses in the client's case are dealt with openly. ■ Although brief writers should be direct by telling a court exactly what they want, writers do not want to sound like they are ordering the court around. ■ Despite the preference for directness, most attorneys avoid first and second person references ("I" and "you") in both legal memoranda and briefs.	■ Chinese writers may give concrete examples, but the cultural preference is to stop after listing the examples and allow the reader to make the connection and draw the inevitable conclusion.	■ Japanese writers may continually return to the theme of an article, although the theme may not be stated explicitly. ■ Making a point indirectly or hinting at meaning is regarded as a sign of intelligence and sensitivity. ■ Good writing implies or alludes to rather than explicitly states its points. ■ Directness is equated with brashness.	■ Korean writers rarely use direct persuasion and explicit description. ■ Arguing directly or explicitly is apt to have a negative effect on Korean readers. ■ It is common to hide criticisms in metaphors.			■ Arabic writers expect readers to "read between the lines" and draw appropriate conclusions on their own.	■ Russian writers tend to show their intelligence and the importance of their ideas by being intentionally complex.

	U.S. Legal Writing	Chinese	Japanese	Korean	French	Spanish	Arabic	Russian
Digressions	▪ U.S. legal readers are likely to view writing with digressions as disorganized, unfocused, and a waste of their time. ▪ Only in law review articles is exploration of a related side issue encouraged, and even in law review articles, this type of digression must be done in footnotes, not in the main body of the text.	▪ Chinese writers have much more freedom to digress and introduce related material.	▪ Japanese writers, using the organizational framework called *ki-shoo-ten-ketsu*, shift the topic and look at it from a new angle when they are in the *ten* element.		▪ French writers have much more freedom to digress and introduce related material.	▪ Spanish readers consider the exploration of side points a sign that the writer is highly intelligent and well versed in the topic.		

(continues)

Exhibit 31.5 — Contrasting Rhetorical Preferences* (continued)

	U.S. Legal Writing	Chinese	Japanese	Korean	French	Spanish	Arabic	Russian
Writer's Opinion	▪ Writers are assumed to be expressing their own view or opinion. ▪ Readers in the U.S. expect writers to state a position and stick to it. It is acceptable to challenge, disagree with, or criticize the writing of another, including an expert in the field or even a court, as long as the challenge, disagreement, or criticism is well supported and directed at the ideas and arguments and not at the individual.	▪ Writers are equated with scholars and therefore people who know and write the truth.	▪ Japanese writers tend to be more tentative and use more qualifiers than writers from other cultures.	▪ Korean writers may use a formulaic expression like "some people say" as a way to introduce their view, particularly when they are taking a controversial position.				

	U.S. Legal Writing	Chinese	Japanese	Korean	French	Spanish	Arabic	Russian
Support	▪ Writers use facts, statistics, and other "hard data" as forms of support. ▪ Legal writers are expected to be meticulously accurate when using facts and cases to support an argument. ▪ In the U.S. legal culture, it is also expected that attorneys, writing as advocates, will "characterize" the facts and case law in a light that is favorable to their client. ▪ Citing cases, statutes, books, law review articles, and other secondary sources is important to show that the writer has the support of the law, other courts, and other legal minds behind his or her arguments.	▪ Chinese writers prefer to support their points through elaborate metaphors and literary references. ▪ Chinese writers also use numerous references to historical events.	▪ Japanese writers tend to use a mix of arguments for and against a position. ▪ Japanese writers may also end an argument by taking a different position from their beginning position.				▪ Arabic writers are inclined to restate their positions, often with warnings, rather than support them with examples.	

(continues)

Exhibit 31.5 Contrasting Rhetorical Preferences* (continued)

Rhetorical Patterns/Organizational Strategies

U.S. Legal Writing	Chinese	Japanese	Korean	French	Spanish	Arabic	Russian
▪ U.S. writers use a linear prose style that moves from the general to the specific. ▪ Writers generally use a hierarchical approach with numerous levels of subordination to express their ideas. ▪ Frequent use of coordination is considered a sign of an immature prose style. ▪ One-sentence paragraphs are generally disfavored. ▪ An effective prose style in law typically uses an overview → analysis → synthesis organizational strategy. Successful writers use topic sentences, signposts, and enumeration to reveal the hierarchical organization of their line of reasoning.	▪ Chinese writers tend to use an inductive approach, moving from the specific to the general. ▪ Native Chinese speakers tend to use centrifugal rather than linear organizational patterns. ▪ Chinese writers favor additive conjunctions to connect ideas. ▪ The typical sentence structure in Chinese is a topic-comment structure.	▪ Japanese writers move from the specific to the general. ▪ The Japanese formula for prose, *ki-shoo-ten-ketsu*, is as predictable as the traditional American structure of introduction, body, and conclusion, but the Japanese version has distinct differences. ▪ The typical sentence structure in Japanese is a topic-comment structure. ▪ Japanese writers tend to be very concerned about the aesthetics of their writing.	▪ Korean expository essays tend to be organized from specific to general.	▪ French writing uses more of a meandering approach; the writer might touch on the topic initially and then circle back to it later in the writing. ▪ Topic sentences are not used because they are deemed too obvious and condescending to readers. ▪ Writers of Romance languages, like French, pride themselves in using the language beautifully.	▪ Spanish writers tend to use linear organizational patterns but with tangential breaks. ▪ Spanish writers do not tend to use signposts or transitional words and phrases to guide readers through the text. ▪ One- or two-sentence paragraphs are common. ▪ Writers of Romance languages, like Spanish, pride themselves in using the language beautifully.	▪ Arabic writers do not particularly value hierarchy and subordination in ideas. ▪ Parallelism is a key ingredient for conveying a rich array of parallel ideas. ▪ Coordination and balance are signs of sophisticated Arabic prose. ▪ Arabic writers tend to join many of their ideas together with *"wa,"* the Arabic word for *"and."* ▪ Arabic writers tend to place a strong emphasis on the form of language.	▪ Writers are intentionally complex, using subordination, parallelism, parenthetical comments, and technical terms, sometimes without defining them. ▪ Long sentences, long paragraphs, and even long paragraphs that are made up of one long sentence are admired.

	U.S. Legal Writing	Chinese	Japanese	Korean	French	Spanish	Arabic	Russian
Conclusions	■ Summaries that synthesize and repeat earlier points are admired. ■ Explicitly drawn conclusions are hallmarks of U.S. legal writing. ■ Legal writers tend to repeat their conclusions. ■ The overall conclusion may appear in more than one place, such as in office memoranda, where the overall conclusion may appear in both the brief answer and in the separate conclusion section.	■ Explicit conclusions are considered repetitious and possibly even insulting to educated readers.	■ *Ketsu*, which is roughly comparable to the conclusion, may state the thesis, but rather than just summarize the earlier ideas, *ketsu* may introduce some new ideas. ■ *Ketsu* need not have the closure expected from an American English conclusion. ■ It may end with a question or otherwise express some lingering doubt.	■ Korean conclusions may contain the thesis but only in an indirect form.	■ French writers often conclude an essay by introducing a new but related topic.			

§ 31.2.4 Some Final Thoughts

The work of contrastive rhetoricians is far from complete. As a result, readers of this chapter may be somewhat disappointed that their country or culture is not represented in the examples or that the examples do not cover every point that they would like to see made. Admittedly, more work must be done before we have a complete picture of the rhetorical preferences of various cultures.

In the meantime, our hope is that by being more explicit about some of the preferences of the United States legal culture and comparing those preferences with those of some non-United States and non-legal cultures, ESL writers can more easily adapt to writing for the United States legal culture. After all, being explicit is one of the valued characteristics of legal writing in the United States!

Chapter 31 Quiz No. 3

Draft answers for each of the following questions. Make your points clearly and concisely, and write sentences that are easy to read and that are grammatical and correctly punctuated.

1. What does it mean to say that English is a "writer-responsible" language?
2. In the United States legal culture, writers are expected to support their points with specific types of arguments. What are the three types of arguments that are considered effective support?
3. What is plagiarism?
4. What are the two main ways writers in United States legal culture are expected to be concise?

BIBLIOGRAPHY FOR ESL LAW STUDENTS

For more information on reader-responsible and writer-responsible languages

John Hinds, *Reader Versus Writer Responsibility: A New Typology in* WRITING ACROSS LANGUAGES: ANALYSIS OF 2L TEXT (Ulla Connor & Robert B. Kaplan eds., 1987).

For an excellent synthesis of the differences between the rhetorical preferences in the United States and many other cultures

Ilona Leki, UNDERSTANDING ESL WRITERS: A GUIDE FOR TEACHERS (1992).

Gayle L. Nelson, How Cultural Differences Affect Written and Oral Communication: The Case of Peer Response Groups, 1997 NEW DIRECTIONS FOR TEACHING & LEARNING 77 (Summer).

Richard E. Nisbett, THE GEOGRAPHY OF THOUGHT: HOW ASIANS AND WESTERNERS THINK DIFFERENTLY . . . AND WHY (2003).

Jill J. Ramsfield, CULTURE TO CULTURE: A GUIDE TO U.S. LEGAL WRITING (2005).

Jill J. Ramsfield, *Is "Logic" Culturally Based? A Contrastive, International Approach to the U.S. Law Classroom*, 47 J. Legal Educ. 157 (1997).

Julie M. Spanbauer, *Lost in Translation in the Law School Classroom: Assessing Required Coursework in LL.M. Programs for International Students*, 35 Int'l J. Legal Info. 396 (Winter 2007).

Jiang Xueqin, *Thinking Right*, Chron. Higher Educ., July 19, 2011.

For other common problem areas that appear in ESL students' writing

Raymond C. Clark et al., The ESL Miscellany: A Treasury of Cultural and Linguistic Information (2d ed. 1991).

Diana Hacker & Nancy Sommers, *ESL Trouble Spots, in* A Writer's Reference (7th ed. 2010).

The remaining sources are grouped by country or language.

Arabic:

English for Specific Purposes in the Arab World (John Swales & Hassan Mustafa eds., 1984).

Shirley E. Ostler, *English in Parallels: A Comparison of English and Arabic Prose* in Writing Across Languages: Analysis of 2L Text (Ulla Connor & Robert B. Kaplan eds., 1987). (Note that Ostler's research has subsequently been criticized by John Swales because Ostler compared student essays written in Arabic with published texts in English. Swales believes that contrastive rhetoricians must compare writing in the same genre.)

Terry Prothro, *Arab-American Differences in the Judgment of Written Messages*, 42 J. Soc. Psychol. 3 (1955).

Richard Yorkey, *Practical EFL Techniques for Teaching Arabic-Speaking Students* in The Human Factors in ESL (J. Alatis & R. Crymes eds., 1977).

Japan:

John Hinds, *Japanese Expository Prose*, 13 Papers in Linguistics: Int'l J. Human Comm. 158 (1980).

John Hinds, *Linguistics and Written Discourse in Particular Languages: Contrastive Studies: English and Japanese*, in Ann. Rev. Applied Linguistics (Robert B. Kaplan et al. eds., 1979).

H. Kobayashi, *Rhetorical Patterns in English and Japanese*, Dissertation Abstracts Int'l 45(8):2425A.

Hebrew:

Michael Zellermayer, *An Analysis of Oral and Literate Texts: Two Types of Reader-Writer Relationships in Hebrew and English* in The Social Construction of Written Communication (Bennett A. Rafoth & Donald L. Rubin eds., 1988).

China:

Carolyn Matalene, *Contrastive Rhetoric: An American Writing Teacher in China*, 47 COLL. ENG. 789 (1985).

Patricia Ross McCubbin, Malinda L. Seymore, Andrea Curcio & Llewellyn Joseph Gibbons, *China's Future Lawyers: Some Differences in Education and Outlook*, 7 ASPER REV. INT'L BUS. & TRADE L. 293 (2007).

B. A. Mohan & A. Y. Lo, *Academic Writing and Chinese Students: Transfer and Developmental Factors*, TESOL Q. 19:515-534.

Robert T. Oliver, COMMUNICATION AND CULTURE IN ANCIENT INDIA AND CHINA (1971).

Shelley D. Wong, *Contrastive Rhetoric: An Exploration of Proverbial References in Chinese Student L1 and L2 Writing*, 6 J. INTENSIVE ENG. STUD. 71 (1992).

India:

Robert T. Oliver, COMMUNICATION AND CULTURE IN ANCIENT INDIA AND CHINA (1971).

Korea:

William G. Eggington, *Written Academic Discourse in Korean: Implications for Effective Communication* in WRITING ACROSS LANGUAGES: ANALYSIS OF L2 TEXT (Ulla Connor & Robert B. Kaplan eds., 1987).

Thai:

Indrasuta Chantanee, *Narrative Styles in the Writing of Thai and American Students,* in WRITING ACROSS LANGUAGES AND CULTURES: ISSUES IN CONTRASTIVE RHETORIC 6 (Alan C. Purves ed., 1988).

Glossary of Usage

In grammar, "usage" simply means what word or phrase a speaker whose first language is English would use in certain situations. In legal writing, appropriate usage will typically be that of the educated professional. Choices will usually reflect a conservative, more traditional view of language.

Even in law, though, usage is not static. The language of law may be traditional and formal, but it is still living and changing. As a consequence, "correct" usage varies from time to time. What was once unacceptable may, in a decade, become the appropriate choice. For this reason, astute legal writers should consider the date of publication for any authority they consult about usage and, as always, they should consider the reader and purposes of the document they are producing.

In addition, all usage errors are not created equal. Some are egregious errors; others, more forgivable. While it is certainly best to master all the usage questions in the following glossary, those marked with an asterisk (*) are important to learn first either because they appear frequently in legal writing or because they represent an error that would distract most readers.

*A/An. Use "a" before words that begin with a consonant sound, and use "an" before words that begin with a vowel sound. Notice that some words begin with a vowel but still use "a" because the initial sound in the word is a consonant sound. This situation occurs when the word begins with a long "u" or "eu" and before the word "one" (a university, a one-hour delay). A few words (usually silent "h" words) begin with a consonant but still use "an" because the initial sound in the word is a vowel sound (an honor, an heir).

*A lot. "A lot" as in the expression "a lot of time" is always spelled as two words. "Alot" as one word is never correct. Notice, however, that "a lot" tends to sound rather informal and may also be imprecise. For these reasons, "a lot" is often not the best choice in legal writing ("a lot of time" → "a great deal of time"; "a lot of prior convictions" → "numerous prior convictions"; "a lot of experience" → "considerable experience").

*Adverse/Averse. "Adverse" means "unfavorable," "opposed," or "hostile." One can get an "adverse verdict" or "adverse criticism." "Averse" means "disinclined" or "reluctant." Use "averse" to show a distaste for something or a tendency to avoid something. One may be averse to representing certain types of clients.

*Advice/Advise. "Advice" is the noun; "advise" is the verb. One can advise a client, or one can give advice to a client.

*Affect/Effect. Generally, "affect" is used as a verb meaning "to influence, impress, or sway": "The jury did not seem to be affected by the defendant's emotional appeal for mercy." "Affect" may also be used as a verb meaning "to pretend or feign": "The witness affected surprise when she was told that the signature was forged." Less common is "affect" used as a noun in psychology meaning "emotion."

The most common use of "effect" is as a noun meaning "the result, consequence, or outcome." "Effect" is also used to mean "goods," as in "one's personal effects," and "impression" as in "done for effect."

"Effect" is used as a verb meaning "to bring about or accomplish": "The mediator successfully effected an agreement between labor and management." Had the preceding example been "the mediator affected an agreement between labor and management" the meaning would have been significantly different. "Effected an agreement" means the agreement was reached; "affected an agreement" means the mediator had some influence on the agreement.

Study Aid

Part of what seems to confuse writers about "affect" and "effect" is that "affect" as a verb means "to have an effect on." For this reason, it may be helpful to analyze the grammar of a sentence in which "affect" or "effect" would appear. If the sentence needs a verb and you cannot substitute "to bring about," then use "affect." If the choice requires a noun, use "effect."

*Among/Between. Use "among" when discussing three or more objects or people; use "between" when discussing two objects or people: "The members of the Board of Directors could not agree among themselves." "Attorney-client privilege refers to those confidential communications that occur between a client and her attorney."

Amount/Number. Use "amount" with nouns that cannot be counted and "number" with nouns that can be counted: "The amount of grief this mother has suffered cannot be measured by the number of dollars a jury awards her."

And/or. Although this usage is gaining in popularity, many authorities consider it cumbersome; others point out that it can be ambiguous, unless you use "and/or" to show that three possibilities exist (for example, husband

and/or wife can mean (1) husband, (2) wife, or (3) both). Consequently, because the reader has to stop and sort through the three possibilities, it is easier on the reader to present each of the three possibilities separately (for example, "husband or wife or both").

Anxious/Eager. "Anxious" comes from the root word "anxiety." Consequently, if one is "anxious," one is "concerned or worried": "I feel anxious about the interview." "Eager," on the other hand, means "looking forward to": "When asked what happened, the defendant was eager to talk to the police." Opposition to the use of "anxious to" to mean "eager to" is abating, but careful writers still observe the distinction.

Study Aid

Use "anxious about," but "eager to." A defendant may be "anxious about" (worried about) testifying or "eager to" (looking forward to) testify.

As/Like. "Like" can be used as a preposition, not just as a conjunction. Consequently, if a full clause follows, use "as" or "as if": "The defendant looked as if she were lying."

A While/Awhile. "A while" is an article plus a noun; "awhile" is an adverb. Use "awhile" only when it modifies a verb, not as an object of a preposition: "The shopkeeper waited awhile before answering the officer's question; then he paused for a while before showing the officer the safe."

But however/But yet. These phrases are redundant; avoid them. Use just "but" or just "however" or just "yet" alone.

Compare to/Compare with/Contrast. Use "compare to" when pointing out only similarities; use "compare with" when pointing out similarities and differences; use "contrast" when pointing out only differences.

Complement/Compliment. A complement completes something: "Ajax, Inc. considered Lee to be the perfect complement to its sales department." A compliment is a flattering remark.

Comprise/Compose/Include. "Comprise" means "to contain": "The panel comprises three judges." Notice that "is composed of" can substitute for "comprise." For precision's sake, do not substitute "include" for "comprise." "Comprise" denotes a complete listing; "include" may mean a partial listing or complete listing.

Study Aid

The whole comprises all the parts. The whole is composed of all the parts. The whole includes some or all of the parts.

Continual/Continuous. "Continual" means "frequently repeated"; "continuous" means "unceasing": "His clients' continual complaint was that he never returned telephone calls." "Continuous water flow cools the reactor."

Criteria/Criterion. "Criteria" is the plural form; "criterion" is the singular form. "Acme published the following criteria for the new position: a four-year college degree, experience in sales, and willingness to travel. It waived the first criterion for applicants who had completed Acme's own in-house training program."

Different from/Different than. Use "different from" when comparing two things; use "different than" when the usage is followed by a clause. "The new contract is different from the old one." "The court's reasoning in this case is different than it was ten years ago."

Disinterested/Uninterested. "Disinterested" means "neutral, unbiased"; "uninterested" means "bored": "We want judges to be disinterested, not uninterested, in the cases before them."

e.g./i.e. In textual sentences, the English equivalents for "*e.g.*" (for example) and "*i.e.*" (that is, or namely) are generally preferable to the Latin abbreviations, although "*i.e.*" and "*e.g.*" are appropriate in footnotes and parenthetical matter. When the Latin abbreviations are used, they should be italicized and followed by a comma. Some writers mistakenly use "*i.e.*" to mean "for example." In citations, use the signal "*e.g.*" according to Rule 1.2(a) in *The Bluebook* or 45.3 in the *ALWD Citation Manual*.

Eminent/Imminent. "Eminent" means "distinguished," "prominent," or "high ranking." An expert witness may be an "eminent scholar." "Imminent" means "about to happen" or "impending." "Imminent" is often used with danger or misfortune as in the phrases "imminent attack," "imminent disaster," or "imminent harm."

Etc. Avoid using "etc." in legal writing. Whenever possible, replace "etc." with specifics, or use the appropriate English equivalent ("and so forth" or "and others") instead. Never use "and etc." This phrase is redundant; it means "and and so forth."

Farther/Further. Use "farther" for geographical distances and "further" for showing other additions: "The placement of the fence suggested that the property line was farther north." "We can discuss this matter further after we have more facts."

Fewer/Less. Use "fewer" for objects that can be counted; use "less" for generalized quantities or sums that cannot be counted: "Elaine used fewer sick days than any other employee. She also had less work." "Less than" can be used with plural nouns of time, amount, or distance. "Less than four weeks."

***Good/Well.** Use "good" as an adjective and "well" as an adverb, except when referring to health: "The prosecutor is a good lawyer who prepares well for trial." "Will the witness be well enough to testify in court?"

Hanged/Hung. Use "hung" as the past tense for "hang" in all situations except executions: "The counterfeit bill was framed and hung in the lobby." "The whistleblower was hanged by the members as a warning to others."

***Have/Of.** "Have," not "of," should be used after the auxiliary verbs "could," "should," and "would": "The plaintiff could have offered a compromise before initiating the lawsuit."

*Imply/Infer. "To imply" means "to indicate, suggest, or express indirectly": "At the show-up, the police officer implied that the defendant was the assailant when he said, 'Don't you think that's him?'" "To infer" means "to deduce, conclude, or gather": "The jury may infer that the defendant is guilty if it hears about her prior convictions."

Study Aid

Use "infer" when the actors in the sentence are drawing inferences from something.

Is when/Is where. Do not use these constructions in sentences that are definitions. A well-crafted definition should have a noun following "is": "An endowment is the transfer of money or property to an institution." Not: "An endowment is when someone transfers money or property to an institution."

*Its/It's. "Its" is the possessive form of "it." Like many other pronouns, "it" forms the possessive by simply adding "s," not " 's" (hers, yours, ours). "It's" is a contraction for "it is" or sometimes "it has." Because contractions are generally avoided in legal writing, "its" or spelling out the words "it is" will be the correct choice in most legal writing.

Lay/Lie. "Lay" is a transitive verb, which means it must have an object. "Lay" means to "put, place, or set down": "Just lay the file on my desk." "Lie" is an intransitive verb, which means it does not have an object. "To lie" means "to recline or remain": "The file will lie unopened on my desk until the bill is paid."

Study Aid

The confusion over "lay/lie" stems from the conjugation of these verbs. "Lay" is a regular verb (lay, laid, laid), but "lie" is an irregular verb (lie, lay, lain) with a past tense that matches the present tense of "lay." The simplest way to determine which word to use is to (1) decide which verb you need ("lay" or "lie") and then (2) decide which tense is required.

Literally. "Literally" is not an all-purpose intensifier. It has a specific meaning: "exactly what the words say." The sentence "The defendant was literally on pins and needles waiting to hear the verdict" means that somehow the defendant was positioned atop pins and needles.

*Loose/Lose. "Lose" is the opposite of "win": "I am afraid you will lose in court." It can also mean "to mislay." "Loose" is the opposite of "tight": "The victim described his attacker as wearing loose clothing."

*Principal/Principle. "Principle" is a noun meaning a "rule, truth, or doctrine": "The principle of negligence per se may make the plaintiff's evidentiary burden easier." "Principal" can be a noun meaning "the head person or official." In finance, "principal" also means "the capital sum," as distinguished from interest: "The principal of Lincoln High School authorized an investment that earned less than one percent on the principal." In criminal law, a principal is the chief actor or perpetrator or aider and abettor present at the commission of the crime. In real estate, a principal is a person who empowers another to act as his or her representative: "The broker owes his principal, the seller, loyalty and good faith."

"Principal" as an adjective means "main" or "chief": "The principal question before the jury is whether the eyewitness is credible."

Supposed to/Used to. Be sure to include the final "d" in both expressions.
Sure and/Sure to. Always use "be sure to."

*Than/Then. Use "than" for comparisons, such as "taller than," "greater than," "more than," and "rather than." Use "then" to denote a time.

That. (When it cannot be omitted). Do not omit the subordinate conjunction "that" when it will prevent a possible misreading. This problem occurs when a noun clause is used as the direct object. In such cases, the subject of the noun clause alone can be misread as the direct object. Incorrect: "Florida courts found a woman who had attempted three suicides and had been committed to a state mental hospital was an unfit and improper person." Corrected: "Florida courts found that a woman who had attempted three suicides and had been committed to a state mental hospital was an unfit and improper person."

That/Which/Who. Use "that" and "which" for things; use "who" for people. Use "that" for restrictive clauses and "which" for nonrestrictive clauses: "The defendant's truck, which does not have oversized tires, was identified by the victim as the vehicle that hit him." The clause "which does not have oversized tires" is nonrestrictive because it does not restrict or limit the meaning of "defendant's truck." Unless the defendant has more than one truck and the reader needs the clause to determine which truck is meant, the phrase "defendant's truck" is already clearly identified. The clause "that hit him," on the other hand, restricts or limits the meaning of the noun "vehicle.

Exception: "Which" is used in restrictive clauses that use the constructions "that which," "of which," or "in which."

*Their/There/They're. "Their" is the possessive form of "they." "There" denotes a place ("stay there"), or it can be used as an expletive ("There is one last point I want to make"). "They're" is a contraction for "they are."

Through/Thru. Always use "through."

Thus/Thusly. Always use "thus."

*To/Too/Two. "To" is a preposition with a great number of functional and idiomatic uses: "The defendant drove back to the city. To his surprise, the police had set up a roadblock. Ultimately, he was sentenced to death." "Too" is an adverb meaning "also," "very," or "excessively": "His story was too implausible." "Two" is the number.

Toward/Towards. Both are acceptable; "toward" is preferred in the United States because it is shorter.

Try and/Try to. Always use "try to."

When/Where. "When" denotes a time; "where" denotes a place. When indicating a particular situation, choose "when" or "in which," not "where." Avoid the expression "a case where . . . ." A case is not a place. Replace with "a case in which . . . ." Common practice, however, seems to be to use "where" in parentheticals after citations.

Which/Who. "Which" should not be used to refer to people.

Who/Whom. Use "who" in most subject positions and "whom" in most object positions. (See below for the exception.)

This general rule means, however, that you will have to analyze a sentence before you can determine whether "who" or "whom" is correct. One easy way to analyze question sentences is to answer the question. If in the answer you use the subjective form ("I," "we," "he," "she," or "they"), then use "who" in the question. If in the answer you use the objective form ("me," "us," "him," "her," or "them"), then use "whom" in the question.

> Who is calling? (He is calling.)
> (*subject*)
>
> To whom does the clerk report? (The clerk reports to her.)
> (*object*)

For some questions, you may find it easier to determine whether to use "who" or "whom" if you recast the sentence in normal subject/verb/object order.

> Whom should I pay?
> (*object*)
>
> I should pay whom? (I should pay them.)

The greatest confusion concerning "who/whom" occurs in sentences in which the same pronoun appears to be the object of one part of the sentence and the subject of another part of the sentence.

> The police questioned a woman who they thought matched the victim's description.

The sentence above is correct. Although "who" may appear to be the object of "they thought," it is actually the subject of "matched the victim's description." A simple way to determine which form of the pronoun is correct in such situations is to mentally delete the subject/verb immediately after the "who" or "whom." If the sentence still makes sense, use "who"; if not, use "whom."

> The police questioned a woman who ~~they thought~~ matched the victim's description.

Use the same method to determine that "whom" is the correct choice in the following example.

> The man whom the police questioned matched the victim's description of her assailant.
>
> The man whom ~~the police questioned~~ matched the victim's description of her assailant.

When the subject and verb following the "who/whom" slot are deleted, the sentence no longer makes sense. Notice too that you can isolate the clause "whom the police questioned," put it in normal order, "the police questioned whom," and answer the question ("the police questioned him") to determine that "whom" is the correct form.

Exception: The one exception to the rule is that "whom" is used for subjects of infinitives.

Whom does our client want to represent him?

Our client wants whom to represent him? (normal word order)

Our client wants her to represent him. (Answer the question or substitute another pronoun.)

Your/You're. "Your" is the possessive form of "you." "You're" is the contraction for "you are."

Glossary of Terms

Active voice. Active voice is the quality of a transitive verb in which the action of the verb is performed by the subject: "Judges decide cases." (Compare with Passive voice.)

Advance Sheets. Advance sheets are paperback pamphlets that contain copies of recent published decisions. They are usually filed at the end of a set of reporters and are used to keep the print version of the reporter up to date.

Alliteration. Alliteration is the repetition of consonant sounds as in "Peter Piper picked a peck of pickled peppers."

ALWD Citation Manual. The *ALWD Citation Manual*, which is published by Wolters Kluwer Law & Business, is a manual that sets out rules for citing to constitutions, statutes, cases, secondary sources, and other materials in legal memos and briefs.

American Jurisprudence (Am. Jur.). *American Jurisprudence* (Am. Jur.) is a comprehensive multi-volume legal encyclopedia that is available both in book form and on Lexis.coms®, Lexis®Advance, Westlaw® Classic, and WestlawNext™. Am. Jur. has over 440 articles, covering a wide range of legal topics. The topics are set out in alphabetical order and include references to selected cases and to A.L.R. annotations. Am. Jur. is not jurisdiction specific: Instead of setting out federal law or a particular state's law, it discusses the law in general terms. Most attorneys use Am. Jur. as a finding tool to obtain an overview of an area of law.

American Law Reports (A.L.R.). *American Law Reports* collects and summarizes cases that relate to a particular topic or issue. A.L.R. Fed. and A.L.R. Fed. 2d collect and summarize cases that discuss federal issues, and A.L.R., A.L.R.2d, A.L.R.3d, A.L.R.4th, A.L.R.5th, and A.L.R.6th collect and summarize state law issues. A.L.R. is available in book form and on Lexis.com, LexisAdvance, Westlaw Classic, and WestlawNext.

Analogous case. An analogous case is a case that is similar to the client's case. An analogous case argument is an argument in which the attorney compares and contrasts the facts in analogous cases to the facts in the client's case and explains why those similarities or differences are legally significant.

Analysis. When you analyze something, you examine it closely, identifying each part and determining how the parts are related. In law, there are two types of analysis: statutory analysis, which involves the close examination of a statute, and case analysis, which involves the close examination of a case.

Annotated codes. An annotated code is a code that contains not only the text of the statutes but also historical notes, cross-references to other sources published by the same publisher, and notes of decision. Thus, an annotated code is a primary authority because it sets out the law itself and a finding tool because you can use it to find other primary authorities (cases that have interpreted and applied the statute) and secondary authorities (for example, practice books and treatises that discuss the statute.)

Assonance. Assonance is the repetition of vowel sounds.

Atlantic Reporter (A., A.2d). The *Atlantic Reporter* and the *Atlantic Reporter, Second Series*, set out the published decisions of the highest court and intermediate courts of appeals in the following states: Connecticut, Delaware, District of Columbia, Maine, Maryland, New Hampshire, New Jersey, Pennsylvania, Rhode Island, and Vermont. The decisions are organized by date and not by jurisdiction.

Attorney general opinions. The United States Attorney General is the attorney for the federal government's executive branch, and a state attorney general is the attorney for a state's executive branch. Some of the opinion letters that attorney generals write answering their clients' questions are made available to the public in the form of attorney general opinions. The opinions that are made available to the public are persuasive authority and are usually available in both book and electronic formats.

Background fact. A background fact, while not necessary to decide the legal issue, is a fact that helps put the legally significant facts in context to tell a clear story. (Compare with Emotionally significant fact and Legally significant fact.)

BCite. BCite the citatory that is on Bloomberg Law.

Bias-free language. Bias-free language is language that suggests that persons from minority racial, religious, and ethnic groups are valued members of society. The term is also used to refer to language that is sensitive to perceptions about people who are poor, people who are elderly, people who are disabled, or people who are homosexual or transsexual.

Bing.com. Bing.com is one of a number of search engines that can be used to locate websites on the Internet. Some other commonly used search engines are Google, Yahoo, and MSN.

Black's Legal Dictionary. *Black's Legal Dictionary* is a popular legal dictionary that is available in hardbound form, in paperback form, and on Westlaw Classic and WestlawNext™.

Bloomberg Law. Bloomberg Law is a fee-based, computer-assisted research service.

The Bluebook: A Uniform System of Citation. Because *The Bluebook* was originally written as a guide to citing authorities in law review footnotes, most of the text and examples describe how to cite material in footnotes. There is, however, a section that describes how to modify the rules and examples for citations in memos and briefs. Although The Bluebook can be difficult to use, many courts base their citation systems on it.

Boolean searching. Boolean searches are named after George Boole, the British mathematician who developed the set of "connectors" that carry his name and that describe the logical relationships among search terms. When you do Boolean or "terms and connectors" searching, you search for documents using "search terms" and "connectors" that describe the relationship among terms. Some of the more common connectors are "and," which retrieves only those documents that contain both search terms; "or," which retrieves documents that contain at least one of the search terms; but not," which retrieves documents that contain the first search term but not the second search term; "/s," which retrieves documents that contain both search terms in the same sentence; and "/50," which retrieves documents in which the search terms are within 50 words of each other ("noise" words may not be counted.) Because the connectors may vary from service to service, check the service's documentation to see what connectors are available and what they mean.

Briefs. A brief is a document submitted to the court by a party or interested individual in which the party or individual argues that the court should or should not take a particular action. Some briefs are now available online. For example, Lexis.com, LexisAdvance, Westlaw Classic, and WestlawNext have databases containing briefs.

Case briefing. Case briefing is a technique used to analyze a court's written opinion. A case brief usually contains a summary of the facts, a statement of the issue(s), the court's holding, and the court's rationale.

Case law. Case law includes both those cases that set out the common law and those cases that interpret and apply enacted law.

Chronological organization. A writer using chronological organization for the facts in a memo or brief sets the facts out in the order in which the related events occurred. (Compare with Topical organization.)

Citation. A typical legal citation identifies an authority and gives readers the information needed to locate that authority. In addition, many citations give readers information that they can use to determine how much weight to give to the authority. The two most frequently used citation manuals are the *ALWD Citation Manual* and *The Bluebook: A Uniform System of Citation*. In addition, many states and courts have their own citation manuals or rules.

Citators. Citators serve two purposes. First, they are used to determine whether a particular authority — for example a case — is still good law. Second, they are used to find other authorities that have cited to a particular case, statute, regulation, law review article, or other authority. Today, the two most commonly used citators are KeyCite®, which is available on Westlaw Classic and WestlawNext and *Shepard's*®, which is available on Lexis.com and LexisAdvance. Bloomberg Law also has a citatory: BCite.

Cite checking. Cite checking is the process used to determine the current status of an authority and to locate sources that have cited that authority. The two most common systems for cite checking an authority are *Shepard's®*, which is available on Lexis.com and Lexis Advance; KeyCite®, an online service available on Westlaw Classic and WestlawNext; and BCite, an online service available on Bloomberg Law.

Code. A code sets out statutes and regulations not in the order in which they were enacted but by topic. Accordingly, in a code, all of the statutes or regulations relating to a particular topic are placed under a single title. For instance, in the United States Code, all of the federal statutes relating to interstate highways are placed under one title, all of the statutes relating to endangered species are placed under a different title, and all of the statutes relating to Social Security benefits are placed under yet a different title.

***Code of Federal Regulations* (C.F.R.).** The *Code of Federal Regulations* contains federal regulations currently in effect. These regulations are set out not in the order in which they were promulgated but by topic. For example, all of the federal regulations relating to income tax are set out under one title, and all of the federal regulations relating to the Americans with Disabilities Act are set out under another title. The Code of Federal Regulations is published in book form and is available on both free Internet sites and on fee-based websites like Lexis.com, LexisAdvance, Westlaw Classic, and WestlawNext.

Common law. The common law is a system of law that is derived from judges' decisions rather than statutes or constitutions.

***Congressional Information Service* (CIS).** The Congressional Information Service is a fee-based service that collects and provides access to congressional materials. The bound volumes have a wide range of indexes and abstracts summarizing bills, committee reports, and hearings.

Congressional Record. The *Congressional Record* is the official record of the proceedings and debates of the United States Congress and is available both as print and electronically. In print, the daily version is published at the end of each day that Congress is in session, and the multi-volume version is published at the end of each Congressional session. One of the best online sources is www.gpoaccess.gov/crecord/index.html. Its databases are updated daily, and, at the back of each daily issue, is the "Daily Digest," which summarizes the day's floor and committee activities.

Connotation. The connotation of a word is all the associations the word carries with it. For example, the word "lawyer" may have positive connotations for individuals who respect lawyers or who aspire to be lawyers, but it may have negative connotations for people who have had bad experiences with lawyers. (Compare with Denotation.)

***Corpus Juris Secundum* (C.J.S.).** *Corpus Juris Secundum* (C.J.S.) is a multi-volume legal encyclopedia that is available both as a book and on Lexis.com, LexisAdvance, Westlaw Classic, and WestlawNext. Like Am. Jur., C.J.S. has more than four hundred articles, covering a wide range of legal topics set out in alphabetical order. C.J.S. is not jurisdiction specific: Instead of setting out federal law or a particular state's law, it discusses the law in general terms. Most attorneys use C.J.S. as a finding tool to obtain an overview of an area of law. C.J.S. uses West's Key Number System®.

Denotation. The denotation of a word is its dictionary definition. (Compare with Connotation.)

Dicta. Comments made by a court that are not directly related to the issue before it or that are not necessary to its holding are dicta. Such comments are often preceded by the word "if"" If the evidence had established . . . ." Although in some cases dicta are easily identifiable, in other cases they may not be. When the issue is broadly defined, the statement may be part of the court's holding; when the issue is narrowly defined, the statement is dicta. (Compare with Holding.)

Digests. Digests are a finding tool that is used to find cases. Each digest contains a number of topics, for example, criminal law, evidence, and real estate. Under each of these topics are a series of subtopics and under these subtopics are annotations describing cases that have discussed those subtopics. Most states have state digests, which list cases from that state, and Thomson West publishes a series of regional digests and federal digests. Most digests also have descriptive word indexes and other finding aids. Although historically digests were available in only book form, some digest information is now available online. For example, West's Key Number Digest is on Westlaw.

Dovetailing. Dovetailing is the overlap of language between two sentences that creates a bridge between those two sentences. Dovetails are often created by moving the connecting idea to the end of the first sentence and the beginning of the second sentence, repeating key words, using pronouns to refer back to nouns in an earlier sentence, and using "hook words" (this, that, these, such) and a summarizing noun.

Elements analysis. When you do an elements analysis, you systematically analyze the requirements set out either in a statute or as part of a common law doctrine by determining whether, given a particular set of facts, each requirement is met.

Emotionally significant fact. An emotionally significant fact is one that, while not legally significant, may affect the way the judge or jury decides the case. (Compare with Background fact and Legally significant fact.)

Enacted law. Enacted law is a system of law created by the legislative and executive branches. For example, statutes and regulations are enacted law.

ESL. The acronym "ESL" stands for "English as a second language."

Federal Civil Rules Handbook. The *Federal Civil Rules Handbook* sets out the text of each Federal Rule of Civil Procedure; the authors' commentary, which includes a description of the rule; and citations to key cases.

Federal legislative histories. Federal legislative histories contain some or all of the documents that were created during the process of enacting or amending a federal statute. For example, a federal legislative history might contain the text of the bill as it was originally submitted, transcripts from committee hearings, committee reports, and transcripts from any floor debates. While some judges use legislative histories as a tool for determining what Congress intended when it enacted or amended a particular statute, other judges give such histories little weight. As a legal researcher, look first for a compiled legislative history.

Federal Practice and Procedure **(Second Edition).** *Federal Practice and Procedure* is a multivolume treatise that sets out and discusses the Federal Rules of Civil Procedure, the Federal Rules of Criminal Procedure, the Federal Rules of Evidence, and other federal rules in detail.

Federal Register. The *Federal Register* publishes copies of proposed federal regulations, copies of proposed changes to existing federal regulations, and the final version of the regulations that are ultimately promulgated. In addition, the *Federal Register* also publishes notices of hearings, responses to public comments on proposed regulations, and helpful tables and indexes. It is published almost every weekday, with continuous pagination throughout the year. Because the *Federal Register* uses continuous pagination, page numbers in the thousands are common. An online version of the Federal Register is available on the FDsys website (www.gpo.gov/fdsys/) and on Lexis.com, LexisAdvance, Westlaw Classic, and WestlawNext.

Federal Reporter; Federal Reporter, Second Series; Federal Reporter, Third Series. The decisions of the United States Court of Appeals are published in the *Federal Reporter* (F.), *Federal Reporter, Second Series* (F.2d), or *Federal Reporter, Third Series* (F.3d). The *Federal Reporter* has decisions issued between 1889 and 1924; the *Federal Reporter, Second Series*, has decisions issued between 1924 and 1993; and Federal Reporter, Third Series, has decisions issued since 1993. Decisions are set out not by topic or by circuit but in chronological order.

Federal Rules of Evidence Manual **(9th ed.).** The *Federal Rules of Evidence Manual* is a multivolume treatise that sets out the text of each federal rule of evidence along with commentary and an annotated list of cases

Federal Supplement, Federal Supplement, Second Series. While most United States District Court decisions are not published, some are published in the *Federal Supplement, Federal Supplement, Second Series*, or in another specialized reporter, for example the *Federal Rules Decisions* or the *Bankruptcy Reporter*. The *Federal Supplement* has decisions issued between 1932 and 1998 and the *Federal Supplement, Second Series*, has decisions issued after 1998.

Finding. A finding is a decision on a question of fact. For example, a trial court judge may find a defendant incompetent to stand trial, or a jury may find that a police officer acted in good faith. (Compare with Holding.)

Finding tools. Finding tools are what the name suggests: They are tools that help you locate primary and secondary authority. Some examples of finding tools are digests, annotated codes, and search engines. While digests serve only as finding tools, annotated codes contain both the primary authority (the statutes) and finding tools (notes of decision/case notes, which are one-paragraph summaries of a point of law set out in a case, and cross-references to other primary and secondary authorities.)

FindLaw.com. FindLaw.com is a website sponsored by Thomson West that either sets out or has links to the electronic version of federal and state statutes and regulations, selected cases, court rules, and other legal materials.

Gender-neutral language. Gender-neutral language is language that treats males and females as having equal value. It does not assume being male is the norm or that certain jobs or positions are primarily filled by males or females.

Generic transition. Generic transitions are those transitions that are commonly used in writing to describe standard mental moves, such as "consequently" to show cause/effect or "however" to show contrast.

Google.com. Google.com is one of a number of search engines that can be used to locate websites on the Internet. Some other commonly used search engines are Bing, Yahoo, and MSN.

Google™ Scholar. Google Scholar is a searchable database that provides free access to the text of federal and state court opinions. To access Google Scholar, go to www.scholar.google.com

Harmless error. An error is harmless when an appellate court determines that an error occurred at trial but that the error does not require reversal because the outcome would likely have been the same absent the error. The test the court applies in deciding if reversal is required turns on whether the error was a constitutional or non-constitutional error. (Compare with Reversible error.)

Headnotes. A headnote is a one-sentence summary of a rule of law found at the beginning of a court's opinion. Because headnotes are written by an attorney employed by the company publishing the reporter in which the opinion appears and not the court, they cannot be cited as authority.

Holding. A holding is the court's decision in a particular case. "When the court applied the rule to the facts of the case, it held that . . . ." Thus, a holding has two components: a reference to the applicable rule of law and a reference to the specific facts to which that rule was applied. Because the holding is the answer to the legal question, it can be formulated by turning the issue (a question) into a statement. (Compare with Dicta.)

Hornbooks. Hornbooks are books written for law students that summarize an area of law and provide citations to key constitutional provisions, statutes, cases, and regulations. Legal researchers use a hornbook to obtain an overview of a particular area of law or issue.

Integrated format. The phrase "integrated format" refers to a method of organizing the discussion section of an objective memorandum. Instead of using the "script format," in which the discussion section is organized around the arguments that each side makes, the writer organizes the discussion around legal principles or points. (Compare with Script format.)

Jump cite. A jump, or pinpoint, cite tells you the specific page on which a particular quote, rule, or statement appears.

KeyCite. KeyCite is Westlaw's cite checking system. You can use it to determine if a case, statute, or regulation is still good law and to find other authorities that have cited to that case, statute, or regulation.

Key Numbers. Key Numbers are part of West's Key Number System. West has divided the law into more than four hundred topics. Under these topics, each point of law is assigned a Key Number. Once you identify the topic and Key Number for a particular point of law, you can use that topic and Key Number to locate information related to that point of law in almost all of West's publications. For example, you can use the topic and Key Number to locate information in C.J.S.; in West's state, regional, and general digests; in secondary sources published by West; and on Westlaw Classic and WestlawNext.

Law reviews and journals. Law reviews and journals are periodicals that contain articles written by law school professors, law students, judges, and attorneys. Law reviews and journals published by law schools are edited by students: Second- and third-year law students select and edit the articles that are published in these journals. Law reviews and journals published by other groups are usually edited by members of that group. For instance, *Legal Writing: The Journal of the Legal Writing Institute* is edited by law school professors who teach legal writing.

Legalese. Legalese is a broad term used to describe several common features of legal writing such as the use of archaic language Latin terms, boiler plate language, and long and convoluted sentences. "Legalese" is usually a pejorative term.

Legally significant fact. A legally significant fact is a fact that a court would consider significant either in deciding that a statute or rule is applicable or in applying that statute or rule. (Compare with Background fact and Emotionally significant fact.)

Legislative history. Legislative histories are a tool that attorneys and courts use to determine what Congress or a state legislature intended when it enacted a particular statute. In general, a legislative history consists of the original and amended texts of the bills, transcripts of committee hearings, committee reports, and transcripts of floor debates.

Legislative intent. Legislative intent is what a legislative body intended when it enacted a particular statute. Attorneys and courts use legislative histories to determine what a state legislature or Congress intended in enacting a statute. In addition, some statutes include a purpose section setting out the underlying intent of the statute.

Lexis.com. Lexis.com is LexisNexis's older fee-based service. It is being replaced with Lexis Advance.

Looseleaf Services. Historically, looseleaf services were what their name suggests: a service that provided information in "looseleaf" notebooks, which were updated by removing outdated pages and replacing them with new pages. Today, most looseleaf services are available both in book form and on fee-based services like Lexis.com, Lexis Advance, Westlaw Classic, and WestlawNext Although each looseleaf service is different, most deal with specialized areas of law. For example, there are looseleaf services that deal with federal tax issues, with federal benefits issues (for example, Social Security), and with many other federal issues (for example, environmental issues). Most loose-leaf services provide a wide range of up-to-date information about these specialized areas. For instance, many of them set out the text of the applicable statutes and regulations, the text of proposed legislation and regulations, and summaries of relevant court and administrative decisions.

Main clause. A clause is a group of related words that has both a subject and a verb. A main clause is a clause that can stand alone as a sentence. (Compare with Subordinate clause.)

Mandatory authority. Mandatory authority is law that is binding on the court deciding the case. The court must apply that law. In contrast, persuasive authority is law that is not binding. Although the court may look to that law for guidance, it need not apply it. Determining whether a particular statute or case is mandatory or persuasive authority is a two-step process. You must first determine which jurisdiction's law applies (that is, whether federal or state law applies and, if state law applies, which state's law); you must then determine which of that jurisdiction's statutes and cases are binding on the court that will be deciding the case.

Metaphor. A metaphor is a direct comparison. For example, a journey is often a metaphor for life.

***Moore's Federal Practice* (Third Edition).** *Moore's Federal Practice* is a multi-volume treatise that sets out and discusses in detail the Rules of Civil Procedure, the Rules of Criminal Procedure, and the United States Court of Appeals and Supreme Court rules.

Natural language searching. Unlike Boolean or terms and connectors searching, which allows you to determine the logical relationships between your search terms, natural language searching uses an algorithm that weighs each search term based on its "rareness" and on its proximity to other search terms. In addition, unlike Boolean searching, which lists your results by date, natural language searches list your results based on their "relevance" scores. Both Lexis Advance and WestlawNext use natural language searching.

***New York Supplement* (N.Y.S.2d).** The *New York Supplement* sets out the published decisions of the New York Court of Appeals. The decisions are set out in date order.

Nominalization. Nominalization is the process of converting verbs into nouns (determine → determination).

***Northeastern Reporter* (N.E., N.E.2d).** The *Northeastern Reporter* sets out the published decisions of the highest court and intermediate courts of appeals in the following states: Illinois, Indiana, Massachusetts, and Ohio, The decisions are organized by date and not by jurisdiction.

***Northwestern Reporter* (N.W., N.W.2d).** The *Northwestern Reporter* sets out the published decisions of the highest court and intermediate courts of appeals in the following states: Iowa, Michigan, Minnesota, Nebraska, South Dakota, and Wisconsin. The decisions are organized by date and not by jurisdiction.

Notes of Decisions/Case Notes. A Note of Decision is a one-sentence summary of a point of law set out in a case. Because Notes of Decisions are written by the attorneys who work for West, a Thomson Reuters business, you cannot cite them as authority. Instead, you must read and cite the cases from which they were drawn.

Nutshells. *Nutshells* are one-volume books written for students summarizing an area of law. The books are written by an expert in the area of law and are published by Thomson West.

Onomatopoeia. Onomatopoeia is the quality some words have when they sound like what they mean. For example, both "plop" and "slap" tend to sound like what they mean.

Orienting transitions. Orienting transitions are transitions that provide a context for the information that follows. They locate the reader physically, logically, or chronologically.

Overruled. A case is overruled when, in a different case, a court determines that, in an earlier decision, the court applied the wrong rule of law. In contrast, a decision is reversed when, in the same case, a higher court reverses the decision of a lower court.

Pacific Reporter **(P., P.2d, P.3d).** The *Pacific Reporter* sets out the published decisions of the highest court and intermediate courts of appeals in the following states: Alaska, Arizona, California, Hawaii, Idaho, Kansas, Nevada, New Mexico, Oklahoma, Oregon, Utah, Washington, and Wyoming. The decisions are organized by date and not by jurisdiction.

Paragraph block. A paragraph block is a group of two or more paragraphs that together develop a point within a larger document.

Paragraph coherence. A paragraph has coherence when the various points raised in the paragraph are connected to each other. Common connecting devices include repetition of key words, transitional phrases, parallelism, and pronouns.

Paragraph unity. A paragraph has unity when all the points raised in the paragraph are related to one larger point, the paragraph's topic.

Parallel citation. If a case is published in more than one reporter, the citation to that case may include references to more than one reporter. The first reference will be to the official reporter. Any other references are called parallel citations. For example, the United States Supreme Court's decision in *Terry v. Ohio* is published in three reporters: *United States Reports*, *Supreme Court Reporter*, and *United States Supreme Court Reports, Lawyers' Edition, 2d.* The first reference is to the official reporter, and the second and third references are parallel cites to unofficial reporters.

Parallelism. Parallel construction is the use of the same part of speech or similar grammatical structures in a pair or series of related words, phrases, or clauses. In other words, a noun is matched to a noun, a verb is matched to a verb, a phrase to a phrase, etc. Parallel construction is also required with correlative conjunctions such as either/or, neither/nor, and not only/but also.

Parenthetical case description. A parenthetical case description can be used when a full description of the case is not required, for example when the case is being used to illustrate a specific point, or when one or two cases have already been described in full in the text and the writer wants to alert the reader to additional case law.

Passive voice. Passive voice is the quality of a transitive verb in which the subject receives rather than performs the action of the verb: "Cases are decided by judges." (Compare with Active voice.)

Personification. Personification is the attribution of human qualities or characteristics to abstractions or inanimate objects.

Persuasive authority. Persuasive authorities are cases, statutes, regulations, and secondary authorities that a court may consider, but is not required to follow, in deciding a case.

Pinpoint cite. A pinpoint, or jump, cite tells you the specific page on which a particular quote, rule, or statement appears.

Plain English. Plain English is the term used to describe a movement to encourage the use of simple, straightforward language (in professions such as law) that is readily understandable by lay people. In other countries, the same movement is referred to as the "Plain Language Movement."

Policy argument. A policy argument is one in which the attorney argues that a particular interpretation of a statute, regulation, or common law rule is (or is not) consistent with public policy, that is, the objective underlying a particular law. For example, child custody laws usually seek to provide stability for children, and environmental laws usually try to balance the interests of developers and preservationists.

Primary authority. Primary authority is the law. For example, constitutions, statutes, regulations, and cases are primary authorities. Some primary authorities are mandatory authority, and some are only persuasive authority. For example, while a decision of the California Supreme Court is always primary authority, the only courts that are bound by that decision are California state courts. Thus, California Supreme Court decisions are mandatory authority in California but only persuasive authority in other states. (Compare with Secondary authority.)

Published case. A published case is a case that the court determines is part of the legal precedent in a jurisdiction. While the highest court in each jurisdiction publishes all of its opinions, intermediate courts of appeal (and district courts in the federal system) look to specified criteria to determine whether a case should be published based on whether it adds to the body of law. Generally, the decision to publish a case is made when the case is filed and is not related to whether the case has yet been included in a reporter's advance sheet or bound volume.

Purple prose. Purple prose is the overuse of flowery language that draws attention to itself.

Raise and dismiss. You can raise and dismiss issues, elements, and arguments. In each case, both sides will agree on the point; therefore, extensive analysis is not necessary. However, a writer goes through the raise-and-dismiss process to assure the reader that the point was considered.

Record. An appeal is based on the record created in the trial court. The record generally consists of documents filed, exhibits admitted, and transcripts of testimony.

Regulation. Regulations are promulgated by the executive branch under authority granted to it by the legislative branch. Regulations are similar in form and substance to statutes and are usually compiled into codes. For example, regulations promulgated by federal agencies are compiled and published in the *Code of Federal Regulations*.

Reporters. Reporters are sets of books that set out the published decisions of one or more courts in the order in which the decisions were issued. For example, *United States Reports* has the decisions of the United States Supreme Court set out in date order, the *Pacific Reporter* has decisions from the state courts in the Pacific region set out in date order, and *Nebraska Reports* has decisions of the Nebraska Supreme Court set out in date order.

Reversed. A decision is reversed when, in the same case, a higher court reverses the decision of a lower court. In contrast, a case is overruled when, in a different case, a court determines that in an earlier decision the court applied the wrong rule of law.

Reversible error. Reversible error occurs when an appellate court determines that an error occurred at trial and the error affected the outcome of the trial. The test the court applies in deciding if reversal is required turns on whether the error was a constitutional error or a non-constitutional error (Compare with Harmless error.)

Roadmap. Roadmaps are paragraphs that give readers an overview of an entire document or a section of a document.

Rule. The rule is the legal standard that the court applies in deciding the issue before it. In some cases, the rule will be enacted law (a statute or regulation); in other cases, it will be a court rule (for example, one of the Federal Rules of Civil Procedure); and in still other cases, it will be a common law rule or doctrine. Although in the latter case the rule may be announced in the context of a particular case, rules are not case-specific. They are the general standards that are applied in all cases. (Compare with Test.)

Script format. When you use the "script format" to organize the arguments in an objective memo, you set out all of the plaintiff's or moving party's arguments, all of the defendant's or responding party's arguments, the plaintiff's or moving party's rebuttal, and then a mini-conclusion in which you predict how the court will decide that element or issue. Thus, while the "integrated format" used a form of deductive reasoning (conclusion and then reasons supporting that conclusion), the script format uses a form of inductive reasoning (arguments and then conclusion). (Compare with Integrated format.)

Search engine. Search engines allow you to search for and retrieve websites. Some examples of search engines are Google and Bing.

Secondary authority. A secondary authority is an authority that explains or comments on the law. For example, practice books, treatises, and law reviews are secondary authority. A court is never bound by a secondary authority. (Compare with Primary authority.)

Session laws. Session laws are the laws enacted during a particular legislative session arranged in date order. The federal session laws are set out in the *Statutes at Large*.

Shepardize. When you *shepardize* a case, you cite check the case to determine whether it is still good law and to identify other authorities that have cited that case. This is a generic term for cite checking a case, and can be done using *Shepard's*, which is on Lexis.com and LexisAdvance; KeyCite, which is on Westlaw Classic and WestlawNext™; or BCite, which is on Bloomberg Law.

Shepard's. *Shepard's* is a system that you can use to cite check cases, statutes, and regulations. Although it is still available in book form, most attorneys now use the version that is on LexisAdvance. You can use Shepard's to determine whether a case, statute, or regulation is still good law and to find other authorities that have cited to that case, statute, or regulation.

Signposts. Signposts are words and phrases that keep readers oriented as they move through a document. Transitional phrases, particularly ones like "first," "second," and "third," are the most common signposts. Topic sentences can also be considered a type of signpost.

Simile. Similes are indirect comparisons that use "like" or "as," such as "his mind is like a steel trap."

Slip opinion. The phrase "slip opinion" refers to the court's opinion in the form that it is initially released by the court. Slip opinions do not have volume numbers, page numbers, or editorial features, for example, headnotes.

South Eastern Reporter **(S.E., S.E.2d).** The *South Eastern Reporter* sets out the published decisions of the highest court and intermediate courts of appeals in the following states: Georgia, North Carolina, South Carolina, Virginia, and West Virginia. The decisions are organized by date and not by jurisdiction.

Southern Reporter **(So., So. 2d).** The *Southern Reporter* sets out the published decisions of the highest court and intermediate courts of appeals in the following states: Alabama, Florida, Louisiana, Mississippi. The decisions are organized by date and not by jurisdiction.

South Western **(S.W., S.W.2d).** The *South Western Reporter* sets out the published decisions of the highest court and intermediate courts of appeals in the following states: Arkansas, Kentucky, Missouri, Tennessee, and Texas. The decisions are organized by date and not by jurisdiction.

Standard of review. "Standard of review" refers to the level of scrutiny an appellate court will use to review a trial court's decision. For example, in de novo review the appellate court does not give any deference to the decision of the trial court; it decides the issue independently. In contrast, when the standard of review is abuse of discretion, the appellate court defers to the trial court, reversing its decision only when a reasonable judge would not have reached the same decision.

Statute. A statute is a law enacted by the legislative branch of fedcral and state governments (municipal and county enactments are called ordinances). Statutes can be contrasted with common law (or case law), which is made by the judicial branch.

Statutes at Large. *Statutes at Large* contains the session laws enacted by Congress during a particular congressional session. You may use the *Statutes at Large* when doing a legislative history for a federal statute.

Subordinate clause. A clause is a group of related words that has both a subject and a verb. A subordinate clause cannot stand alone as a sentence because it is introduced by a subordinating conjunction (for example, "although") or relative pronoun (for example, "which"). (Compare with Main clause.)

Substantive transitions. Substantive transitions are connecting words and phrases that also add content. Unlike generic transitions, which signal standard mental moves, substantive transitions tend to be document-specific. (Compare with Dovetailing.)

Synthesis. When you synthesize, you bring the pieces together into a coherent whole. For example, when you synthesize a series of cases, you identify the unifying principle or principles.

Term of art. Although sometimes used to describe any word or phrase that has a "legal ring" to it, "term of art" means a technical word or phrase with a specific meaning. "Certiorari" is a true term of art.

Test. Although the words "rule" and "test" are sometimes used interchangeably, they are not the same. A test is used to determine whether a rule is met. (Compare with Rule.)

Theory of the case. The theory of the case is the "theme" created for the case. A good theory of the case appeals both to the head and to the heart; it combines the law and the facts in a way that is legally sound and that produces a result the court sees as just.

Topic sentence. A topic sentence is the sentence in a paragraph that introduces the key point in the paragraph or that states the topic of the paragraph. Topic sentences are often the first sentence in a paragraph.

Topical organization. A writer using topical organization groups facts by topics. Topical organization generally works best when there are a number of facts not related by dates (for example, the description of several pieces of property), or a number of events that occurred during the same time period (for example, four unrelated crimes committed by the same defendant over the same time period). (Compare with Chronological organization.)

Unannotated codes. An unannotated code has the text of statutes currently in effect. It does not, however, have cross-references to other sources or notes of decision/case notes describing cases that have discussed a particular statutory section.

United States Code (U.S.C.). The *United States Code* is the official source for United States statutes. Although the *United States Code* sets out the text of all of the federal statutes currently in effect and historical notes, it does not have cross-references to other sources or notes of decision/case notes.

United States Code Annotated (U.S.C.A.). The *United States Code Annotated* (U.S.C.A.) is an unofficial version of the United States Code published by Thomson West. In addition to setting out the current version of the federal statutes, the U.S.C.A. has historical notes, which summarize amendments; cross-references to other materials published by Thomson West; and notes of decisions/case notes that describe cases that have interpreted and applied the statute. The U.S.C.A. is available in book form and on Westlaw Classic and WestlawNext.

United States Code Service (U.S.C.S.). The *United States Code Service* is an unofficial version of the United States Code published by LexisNexis. In addition to setting out the current version of the federal statutes, the U.S.C.S. has historical notes, which summarize amendments; cross-references to other materials published by LexisNexis; and case notes, which quote key language from cases that have interpreted and applied the statute. U.S.C.S. is available in book form and on Lexis.com and LexisAdvance.

United States Constitution. The easiest place to find a copy of the United States Constitution is the Internet. There are copies on the Cornell website (http://www.law.cornell.edu/constitution/constitution.overview.html) and on FindLaw.com (http://www.findlaw.com/casecode/constitution/). Use the search function on the FindLaw site to search for particular words or phrases. You can also find the text of the United States Constitution in the first volume of the United States Code, the United States Code Annotated, and the United States Code Service, and in most state codes.

Unpublished case. An unpublished case is a case filed for public record that the issuing court has determined has no precedential value. An unpublished case decides the issue for the parties involved, but does not become part of the body of law in a jurisdiction. While unpublished opinions are not included in reporters, they are often available on electronic databases (with a notation if the jurisdiction prohibits citation to unpublished decisions). Some jurisdictions prohibit citations to unpublished cases.

Voice. Voice is the active or passive quality of a transitive verb.

West's Key Number System. West's Key Number System is a system developed by Thomson West. The system works as follows. Through the years, West has created a series of topics and within those topics, Key Numbers for each point of law. This set of topics and Key Numbers is West's Key Number System. When a court publishes an opinion, it sends a copy of its opinion to West, which assigns the case to an editor. The editor identifies each point of law set out in the court opinion, writes a single sentence summarizing that point of law, and assigns that summary a topic and Key Number. These summaries are used in two ways. First, West uses these summaries as headnotes for the case. In West publications, these headnotes are placed at the beginning of the case, after the name of the case but before the court's opinion. Second, these summaries are placed the appropriate digests under their assigned topic and Key Number.

Westlaw Classic. Westlaw Classic is a fee-based, computer-assisted research service. It is being replaced by WestlawNext.

WestlawNext. WestlawNext is a fee-based service for legal research that allows for "Google"-like searching: Users do not need to select a database or construct terms and connectors searches.

West's Key Number System®. West's Key Number System® is a system developed by West, a Thomson Reuters business. Through the years, West has created a series of topics and within those topics, Key Numbers for each point of law. This set of topics and Key Numbers is West's Key Number System®. When a court publishes an opinion, it sends a copy of its opinion to West, which assigns the case to an editor, who is an attorney. The editor identifies each point of law set out in the court opinion, writes a single sentence summarizing that point of law, and then assigns that summary a topic and Key Number. These summaries are used in two ways. First, West uses these summaries as headnotes for the case. In West publications, these headnotes are placed at the beginning of the case, after the name of the case but before the court's opinion. Second, these summaries are placed in the appropriate digests under their assigned topic and Key Number.

WEX. Wex is a free legal dictionary and encyclopedia sponsored and hosted by the Legal Information Institute at the Cornell Law School. Wex entries are collaboratively created and edited by legal experts.

Index

"A" and "an," 812–815
Abbreviations, 779–783
   academic degrees, 781
   foreign phrases, 781
   geographical names, 780–781
   inappropriate, 782–783
   measures and weights, 781–782
   names of laws, 781
   parentheses, 761
   time, 781
Absolute phrases, 684, 738
Academic degrees, style for, 777, 781
Acronyms, 777
"Act," capitalization of, 773
Active voice, 589–593
   effective use, 590–592
   identifying, 589–590
   mixing with passive voice, 593
   in persuasive writing, 314, 428
   sentences, 199–201
Adjectives, 682
Adverbs, 682
   adverb clutter, 637
   conjunctive, 687
"Affect/effect," 789–791
After-the-fact outlines, 195, 543

Agency decisions, arguments based
   on, 260–261
Agreement, 697–706
   pronoun, 703–706
   subject-verb, 698–703
"Airtime," 311, 422–423
Alliteration, 665–667
Ambiguity, grammatical, 626
"Amendment," capitalization of, 774
American Jurisprudence, 60, 82
American Law Reports, 53–54, 67,
   85–86
Analogous cases
   arguments, 180
   descriptions of analogous cases,
     168–178
   introducing cases, 173–176
   using parentheticals, 178
Analysis of research results, 137–140,
   211–217
"And," to start sentence, 547
Annotated codes, 48, 62
Apostrophes, 749–752, 795–796
Appellate briefs. *See also* Sample
   briefs
   appendix, 462–463

Appellate briefs *(continued)*
  argument, 431–438. *See also*
    Arguments in appellate brief
  argumentative headings, 431–438
  audience, 385–386
  conclusion, 461–462
  conventions, 387–391
  court rules governing, 381–382,
    387–391
  cover, 408
  editing, 463–464
  ends-means analysis, 400
  facts, selection of, 416–417
  issues presented for review,
    409–415
  jurisdictional statement, 409
  notice for discretionary review,
    383–384
  notice of appeal, 383–384
  organizational scheme, 417
  organizing the argument,
    439–443
  petition for review, 383
  planning, 400–408
  prayer for relief, 461–462
  proofreading, 463–464
  purpose, 387
  question presented, 409–415
  record on appeal, 384–385, 399
  reviewing record for error,
    393–394
  revising, 463–464
  sample briefs, 464–507
  scope of review, 384
  selecting and ordering arguments,
    403–408
  selecting issues on appeal,
    395–398
  signature, 462
  statement of the case, 415–430
  statement of the facts, 416–417
  statement of the issue, 409–415
  summary of the argument,
    430–431
  table of authorities, 408–409
  table of contents, 408
  theory of the case, 400, 402–403
  time limits for filing notice of
    appeal, 383
  types of appellate review, 382–383
  types of briefs, 385
Appendix, in appellate brief,
    462–463
Appositives, 685–686
Archaic language, 644–645
Argot, 647–648
Arguing the application of the law
  analogous case arguments, 180
  plain language arguments,
    179–180
  policy arguments, 181–182
Argumentative headings checklist
  conventions, 325, 437–438
  functions, 322–325, 431–438
  motion briefs, 322–326
  persuasive techniques, 431–437
  positive assertion, 432–433
Arguments in appellate brief
  connections within argument,
    458–459
  constructing arguments, 451–453
  good arguments, 460–461
  presenting arguments, 451–453
  quotations, use of, 453–455
  responding to arguments of other
    side, 455–458
  selecting and ordering arguments,
    403–408
  summary of the argument,
    430–431
  weaknesses, dealing with,
    459–460
Articles
  correct use of, 811–822
  decision tree, 821
  no article, 820–821
Assonance, 665–667
Attorney general opinions, 53
Authority. *See also* Types of
    authority
  binding, 26–28
  jurisdiction, 26
  weight of, 25–28

Background facts, 143, 217–218, 307,
    417
Background reading
  Google, 47, 59, 80, 91
  hornbooks, 46, 60, 81–82, 90
  Internet, 46–47, 58–59, 80

law reviews and journals, 54, 67, 86, 90

legal encyclopedias, 60, 82

Nutshells, 46, 60, 81–82

practice books and manuals, 45–46, 60, 80–81

BCite (Bloomberg Law), 106–107

"Because," to start sentence, 548

Bias-free language, 655–662

accurate terms, 658–659

changes in terminology and connotation, 656, 660

emphasis on person, 660

euphemistic terms, avoiding, 661

irrelevant references, 656

patronizing terms, avoiding, 661

precise terms, 659

preferred terms, 656–661

self-chosen labels, 657–658

specific terms over general terms, 659–660

victimization, avoiding, 661

Bibliography for ESL students, 856–858

"Bill," capitalization of, 774

Bing, 47, 59, 73, 80, 91, 92

Block of paragraphs, 569–571

Block quotations, 753

Bloomberg Law (BCite), 106–107

Bolinger principle, 830

Brackets, 758–759

Branches of government

generally, 16–23

executive branch, 16

judicial branch, 17–23

legislative branch, 16–17

Brief answer

checklist, 155, 225

content, 153–155, 224

format, 153, 224–225

purpose, 153, 224

Broad pronoun reference, 707–709

"But," to start sentence, 547

Cadence, 667–669

Capitalization, 770–779

academic degrees, 777

acronyms, 777

compass points, 777–778

following colon, 748, 771–772

geographical names, 777–778

proper nouns and adjectives, 772–777

quotations, 771

rules of law, 778–779

titles, 779

topographical names, 778

trademarks, 779

vessels, 779

Cases

analysis of, 31–39, 138–140, 211–217

in common law research, 84

context, 36

find by citation, 52–53

find using LexisNexis, Westlaw, or WestlawNext, 50, 52–53, 66, 82–83, 93–94

headnotes, 50, 64

Internet sites, 65–66, 84

locating, 49–53

presenting persuasively, 336–337, 445–451

reading, 31–39, 138–140, 215–217

reporters, 51–53, 65–66, 85

selecting, 176

in statutory research, 49–53

synthesis, 138–140, 169–173, 215–217

unpublished, 65

Charters, 73–74

Checklists

argumentative headings in briefs, 326

argument section in briefs, 339–340

brief answer in memos, 155

conclusion in memos, 193–194

discussion section in memos, 190–191, 237–238

e-memos, 270–271

issue statements in briefs, 320

issue statements in memos, 153, 224

opinion letter, 291–292

oral argument, 523–524

revision, 544

statement of facts in briefs, 316

statement of facts in memos, 147–148, 220–221

Chevron analysis, 260–261

Circuit courts
    "circuit," capitalization of, 774
    map of, 20
Circuit split, 258–260
    Chevron analysis, 260–261
    templates for organizing
        discussion, 259–260
Citations
    editing and proofreading of, 206
    placement of, 206
Citators, 104–108
    BCite (Bloomberg Law), 106–107
    KeyCite, 106–107
    Shepard's, 106–107
    types, 106–107
Clauses, 684–685
"Clearly," overuse of, 608
Client letters. *See* Opinion letters
Clustering, as drafting method,
    533–534
"Code," capitalization of, 774
Code of Federal Regulations, 58, 59,
    63
Coherence in paragraphs, 560–562
Collective nouns, 706
Colloquial language, 617
Colons, 747–748
Commas, 721–743
    with addresses, 737
    conjunctions and introductory
        modifiers or clauses,
        742–743
    between coordinate adjectives,
        736
    before coordinating conjunction,
        724–725
    correlative pair separation,
        741–742
    with dates, 737, 797–798
    with geographical locations, 737
    to introduce examples, 738–739
    between items in a series, 734–
        736, 798–799
    with long introductory clauses or
        phrases, 725–727
    overview of the rules, 722–723
    with phrases of contrast, 734
    to prevent misreading, 727
    with quotation marks, 733
    to set off absolutes, 738

    to set off nonrestrictive
        appositives, 730–731
    to set off nonrestrictive participial
        phrases, 731–732
    to set off nonrestrictive phrases or
        clauses, 728–730
    to show omission, 738
    subject/verb separation, 740–741
    "that" and introductory modifiers
        or clauses, 743
    with transitions and interrupters,
        732
    unnecessary, 739–740
Comma splices, 766–768, 796–797
Common law
    background reading, 81–82
    description, 77–79
    research plan, 79–80
Comparisons, imprecise, 620–621
Compass points, 777–778
Competing interests, balancing of,
    254–257
    organizational schemes, 253–254
    templates, 254–255
Compound modifiers, 761–764
Compound nouns, 761–764
Conciseness, 626–641
    clutter, 636–637
    combining sentences, 637–640
    editing, 241–242
    excessive, 641
    overuse of quotations, 628–630
    repetition, 634–636, 802–803
    revising, 241–242
    sentence openers, 801–802
    starting too far back, 628
    stating the obvious, 627
    strong verbs, 800–801
    throat-clearing expressions,
        631–633
Concluding sentences, 567–569
Conclusion in memos, 191–194,
    239–240
Confidential information
    e-mail, 276
    e-memos, 270
    text messaging, 280
"Congress," capitalization of, 775
Conjunctions
    coordinating, 686, 724–725

correlative, 687, 718
subordinating, 684
Conjunctive adverbs, 687
Connections in writing, 551–556,
    573–587. *See also*
    Roadmaps; Signposts;
    Transitions
Consistent terminology, 620
Constitutional issues
    background reading, 90–92
    briefs, 95
    federal cases, 92–93
    federal constitutional law, 90–92
    finding tools, 94–95
    primary authority, 92–93
    research plan, 89–90
    sources, 90–95
    state cases, 93
    state constitutional law, 90–92
    state constitutions, 93
    United States Constitution, 92
"Constitution," capitalization of, 775
Constructing arguments, 178–189,
    326–329, 451–453
Contractions, 786
Conventions of formal writing,
    10–11, 786–787
Corpus Juris Secundum, 60, 82
Correlative conjunctions
    fragments, 687
    parallelism for, 718
"Council/counsel," 791
County and city charters, 73–74
County and city ordinances
    introduction to county and city
        government, 72
    research plan, 72–73, 75
    sources, 74
"Court"
    capitalization of, 775–776
    as collective noun, 701, 706
Court rules
    federal, sources for, 99–101
    governing appellate briefs,
        381–382, 387–391
    local, sources for, 102–103
    research plans, 98
    state, sources for, 101–102
Court system, 17–23
    federal courts, 19–21

hierarchical nature, 17–19
    map of circuits, 20
    state courts, 22–23
Cover for appellate brief, 408
Cultural assumptions about writing,
    837–856

Dangling modifiers, 202–203,
    712–714
Dashes, use of, 764–766
Decision tree for articles, 821
De novo, defined, 36
Detail, effective use of in persuasive
    writing, 311–312, 423–424
Determining issues on appeal,
    395–398
    abstract of the record, 398–399
    harmless error, 397–398
    preserving errors, 395–396
    reviewing the record, 393–394
    standard of review, 396
Diction, 615–626
Differences, using sentence
    structure to highlight,
    610–614
Digests, 83
Direct object, 680
Discussion section in memos
    generally, 156–191, 225–238
    arguments, 178–189, 232–237
    checklist, 190–191, 237–238
    circuit split, 258–260
    competing interests, balancing of,
        254–257
    descriptions of analogous cases,
        176–178, 229–230
    disputed elements, 167–168
    disputed factors, 252–253
    elements analysis, 137–138,
        156–159, 214, 248–251
    factor analysis, 247–254
    format, 225–238
    general rules, 160–164, 251–252
    inductive vs. deductive reasoning,
        226
    integrated format, 225–238, 253,
        254–257, 259–260, 262
    introductory section, 251–252, 256
    issue of first impression, 257–262
    mini-conclusions, 189, 230–232

Discussion section in memos
    (continued)
    organizing, 156–159, 259–260
    script format, 179, 225–234,
        248–251, 253–257, 259–260,
        262
    specific rules, 167–168, 228
    templates, 157–159
    undisputed elements, 164–167
    undisputed factors, 252
Disputed elements, 167–168
Disputed factors, 252–253
Distance between subject and verb,
    597–598
Double punctuation, 782
Dovetailing, 197–199, 561, 580–584
Drafting a document, 535–542

Editing, 199–205, 240–246, 289–
    292, 544–545
Elements
    disputed, 167–168
    undisputed, 164–167
Ellipses, 629, 756–758, 761
Eloquence, 663–676
E-mail tips, 275–279
    attaching files, 278
    confidential information, 276
    court rules, 103
    "flaming," 277
    forwarding without permission,
        279
    inappropriate language, 276
    proofreading, 278
    subject line, 278
    tone, 277
E-memos
    audience, 264–265
    checklists, 270–271
    confidentiality, 270
    conventions, 264–269
    introductory paragraph,
        265–266
    key facts, 268–269
    law, summary of, 266–268
    samples, 271–275
    tone of, 269
    writing style, 269
Emotionally significant facts, 143,
    217–218, 307, 416–417

Emphasis, 602–610
    positions of, 312–313, 425–426,
        604–606
    punctuating for, 606–607
    single-word, 607–608
Enacted law, 77–79
Encyclopedias
    American Jurisprudence, 60, 82
    Corpus Juris Secundum, 60, 82
    as federal law source, 60
    secondary authorities, 82
English-as-a-second language,
    811–858
    advice for specific groups of
        writers, 14
    bibliography, 856–858
    correct use of articles, 811–822
    cultural assumptions about
        writing, 837–856
    prepositions in idioms, 836
    prepositions that follow
        adjectives, 835
    prepositions that follow nouns,
        835–836
    prepositions that follow verbs,
        834
    rhetorical preferences, 836–856
    two- or three-word verbs, 832–833
    verbs generally, 822–833
    verbs with gerunds, 826–832
    verbs with infinitives, 826–832
    verbs with objects and infinitives,
        826–832
English majors, as writers, 11–12
Ethnic bias in language, 655–662
Exclamatory sentences, 691,
    786–787
Executive branch, 16
Expectations of readers, 617–618
Expletive constructions, 201–202,
    631

Factor analysis, 247–254
    disputed factors, 252–253
    integrated format, 253
    organizational schemes, 253
    script format, 253
    templates, 248–251
    undisputed factors, 252
    weighing the factors, 253–254

Facts, identifying legally and emotionally significant, 141–143, 150–152, 217–218
"Federal," capitalization of, 776
Federal cases, 59, 92–93
Federal Civil Rules Booklet, 99
Federal Civil Rules Handbook, 100
Federal courts, 19–21
Federal law, sources of statutory research, 58–62
  annotated codes, 62
  session laws, 61
  unannotated codes, 61–62
Federal Local Courts Rules, 102
Federal Ninth Circuit Civil Appellate Practice, 102
Federal Practice and Procedure, 100
Federal Register, 63
Federal regulations, 62–63
Federal Reporter, 59
Federal Rules of Criminal Procedure, 100
Federal Rules of Evidence, 100
Federal Rules of Evidence Manual, 100
Federal statutes
  finding, 62
  research plan, 58, 68
  sources for research, 58–61
Federal Supplement, 59
Finding tools
  American Jurisprudence, 60, 82
  American Law Reports, 53–54, 67, 85–86
  for cases applying common law, 82–84
  for constitutional issues, 94–95
  digests, 83
  for federal cases, 63–64
  notes of decision, 50, 64
  practice manuals and books, 45–46, 60, 82
FindLaw
  state regulations, 49
  using to find cases, 63, 93
First impression, issue of. *See* Issue of first impression
First-person pronouns, 649–651, 786
Foreign phrases, 645–647

Formal writing, conventions of, 10–11, 786–787
Fractions, 763
Fragments, 687–691
  permissible uses of, 690–691
Fused sentences, 768

Gender-neutral language, 651–655, 705
General rule, presenting, 160–164
Generic transitions, 573–578, 584–585
Geographical names, 777–778, 780–781
Gerunds, 826–832
  articles with, 815
  phrases, 683
  verbs with, 826–832
Google
  for United States Constitution, 92
  using for background reading, 47, 59, 73–74, 80, 91
Google Scholar, 54
Grammar, basic, 679–687

Harmless error, 397–398
Headings
  generally, 551–553
  argumentative, 322–326, 431–438
  in memos, 140–141, 217
Headnotes, 50, 64
"He," generic use of, 652–653, 705
"Herein," use of, 644
"Herewith," use of, 644
"Hook" words, 581, 584
Hornbooks, 46, 60, 81–82
"However," to start sentence, 548
Hyphen, use of, 761–764

Idioms
  with prepositions, 836
  reader expectations, 617–618
Indirect objects, 681
Infinitives, 546–547, 684
Informal language, 617
Integrated format for discussion section, 225–238, 253, 254–257, 259–260, 262

Internet
    background reading, 46–47,
        58–59, 80
    free sites, 84, 93, 100–102
    state codes, 48
    state regulations, 49
IRAC, 544, 560
Issue of first impression, 257–262
    agency decisions, arguments
        based on, 260–261
    Chevron analysis, 260–261
    circuit split, 258–260
    legislative history arguments,
        261–262
    policy arguments, 261–262
    statute, ambiguity of, 260
    templates for organizing
        discussion, 259–260
Issues on appeal, 395–398, 399–400,
    409–415
Issue statements in briefs
    checklist, 320
    format, 317–318, 410–411
    making the question persuasive,
        318–320, 411–414
    readability, 414–415
Issue statements in memos
    checklist, 153, 224
    format, 149–152, 221–222
    number and order, 148
    readability, 152–153
    readability, ease of, 222–223
    under-does-when format, 149–
        152, 221–222
    whether format, 221–222
Italics, use of, 783–785
"Its/it's," 751, 792
"I," use of, 649–650, 786

Job titles, gender-neutral, 653–654
Journalism majors, as writers, 12–13
Journalists, as writers, 12–13
Journals, 54, 67, 86
Judicial branch, 17–23
    federal courts, 19–21
    hierarchical nature, 17–19
    map of circuits, 20
    state courts, 22–23
Jurisdictional statement, in appellate
    brief, 409

Jurisdiction and authority, 26
"Jury"
    as collective noun, 701
    pronoun for, 706

KeyCite, 105–107
Key terms, for coherence, 242–243,
    561, 609, 620

Latin words and phrases, 645–647
Law reviews and journals, 54, 67, 86
Lead-ins for quotations, 753–754
Legal encyclopedias
    American Jurisprudence, 60, 82
    Corpus Juris Secundum, 60, 82
Legalese, 642–651
Legal Information Institute website,
    93
Legally significant facts
    statement of facts, 141–143,
        217–218, 307
    statement of the case, 416
Legal writing in general, 3–14
    advice for specific groups of
        writers, 11–14
    conventions of legal writing,
        10–11
    goals of legal writing, 4–6
    readers of legal writing, 6–9
    role of legal writer, 9–10
    writers from specific groups,
        11–14
Legislative branch, 16–17
Legislative history, arguments based
    on, 262
"Legislature," capitalization of,
    776
LexisNexis
    federal law source, 60
    multi-tasking, 538
    primary authority, 93
    secondary authorities, 82
    Shepard's, 106–107
    using to find annotated codes,
        48
    using to find briefs, 95
    using to find cases, 50, 52–53, 64,
        67, 77, 83, 93–94
    using to find law reviews, 54, 86
Looseleaf services, 67–68

Mandatory authority, 25
"Man," generic use of, 651
Memos
    analogous cases, 168–178,
        229–230
    analyzing statutes and cases,
        138–140, 211–217
    audience, 112
    brief answer, 153–155, 224–225
    citations, editing and
        proofreading of, 205–206
    competing interests, balancing of,
        254–257
    conclusion, 191–194, 239–240
    conventions, 112
    discussion section, 156–191,
        225–238, 253. *See also*
        Discussion section in
        memos
    editing, 199–205, 240–246
    elements analysis. *See* Elements
    e-memos, 125–129, 263–275
    factor analysis. *See* Factor
        analysis
    headings, 140–141, 217
    integrated format, 225–238, 253,
        254–257, 259–260, 262
    issue statements, 148–153,
        221–224
    organizing research notes,
        211–214
    proofreading, 205–206, 245–246
    purpose, 112
    researching, 133–137, 211
    revising, 194–199, 240–246
    sample memos, 113–129
    script format, 156–191, 225–234,
        248–251, 253–257, 259–260,
        262
    statement of facts, 141–148,
        217–221
    synthesizing cases, 169–173
Metaphor, 674–675
Mini-conclusions in memos
    integrated format, 230–232
    script format, 189, 230–232
Mismatch, subject-verb-object,
    621–626
Modifiers, 710–714
    dangling, 202–203, 651, 712–714
    misplaced, 651, 710–712
    sexist, 654–655
    single-word, 682
    squinting, 714
Mood, 692–697
Moore's Federal Practice, 100
Motion briefs, 301–379
    argumentative headings,
        322–326
    arguments, 326–340
    assertions, 327–329
    audience, 301–302
    caption, 305
    conventions, 302
    deductive reasoning, 329–330
    example case, 302–304
    inductive reasoning, 329–331
    introductory paragraph, 305–306
    issue statements, 317–321
    motion briefs, 301–302
    ordering the arguments, 321
    organizational scheme, 329–332
    prayer for relief, 340–341
    purpose, 302
    sample briefs, 342–380
    signing the brief, 341
    statement of facts, 306–316
    templates, 330–331
    theory of the case, 304–305
Multi-tasking, 538–542
    billing issues, 542
    parallel processing, 539, 541
    task switching, 539
    toggling, 539
Myths about writing, 546–548

"National," capitalization of, 776
Nominalizations, 201, 597, 630–631
Nonrestrictive constructions
    appositives, 730–731
    phrases and clauses, 728–730
Notes of decision, 50, 64
Nouns
    with "a" and "an," 812–815
    count nouns, 812, 816–818
    with no article, 820–821
    non-count nouns, 814–818
    with "the," 816–820
Numbers, 760, 786
Nutshells, 46, 60, 81–82

Objective complements, 682
Objective memoranda. *See* Memos
One-sentence paragraphs, 548,
    562–563
Onomatopoeia, 673–674
Opinion letters
    advice in, 289
    audience, 284–285
    checklist, 291–292
    concluding paragraph, 289
    conventions, 285
    explanation of law, 288–289
    facts, summary of, 288
    introductory paragraph, 286–287
    issue, statement of, 287
    opinion in, 287–288
    purpose, 264, 284–285
    samples, 292–297
    tone of, 289–291
    warnings, 289
Oral argument
    argument, 513–518
    audience, 509–510
    checklist, 523–524
    closing, 518
    courtroom procedures and
        etiquette, 512–513
    delivery, 519–520
    dress, 513
    eye contact, 519
    facts, summary of, 515–516
    gestures, 520
    introductions, 514
    issues, statement of, 514–515
    opening, 514
    persuasiveness, 520
    posture, 519
    preparation for, 510–512
    problems, 520–522
    purpose, 510
    questions, answering, 517–518
    rebuttal, 518
    references to the record, 516
Organizing writing, 531–535
Orienting transitions, 578–579
"Or," to start sentence, 547
Outlines
    generally, 543
    after-the-fact, 195, 543
Overuse of quotations, 569, 628–630

Paragraph block, 569–571
Paragraphs
    coherence, 560–562
    function of, 557–558
    length, 562–563
    one-sentence, 548, 562–563
    patterns, 558–559
    unity, 559–560
Parallelism, 601, 671–673, 714–719
Parentheses, 759–761
Parenthetical explanations, 178
Participles, 683, 712–714
Passive voice, 589–593
    conciseness, 631
    effective use, 592–593
    persuasive writing, 314, 428
Patterns in sentences, 679–682
Personification, 675
Persuasive authority, 25
Persuasive writing
    active and passive voice, 314, 428,
        589–593
    airtime, 311, 422–423
    constructing arguments, 451–453
    context, creating, 308–309,
        418–420
    detail, 311–312, 423–424
    point of view, 310, 420–422
    positions of emphasis, 312–313,
        425–426, 604–606
    presenting arguments, 337–339,
        451–453
    presenting cases, 336–337,
        445–451
    presenting rules, 332–336,
        443–445
    sentence construction, 314–315,
        427
    sentence length, 313–314,
        426–427
    word choice, 315, 428–429
Philosophy majors, as writers, 12
Phrases, 682–684
    absolute, 684
    participial, 683
    prepositional, 682–683
Plagiarism, 841–843
"Plain English," 642–651
Plain language arguments, 179–180
Point of view, 310, 420–422

Policy arguments, 181–182, 262
Pompous language, 633
Positions of emphasis, 312–313,
    425–426, 604–606
Possessive, correct use of, 749–752,
    795–796
Practice books, 45–46, 60, 80–81, 82
Practice manuals, 45–46, 60, 80–81,
    82
Precision, 242–245, 615–626
Predicates, 679–682
Prepositions
    at end of sentence, 548
    in idioms, 836
    that follow adjectives, 835
    that follow nouns, 835–836
    that follow verbs, 834
Primary authority, 92–94
"Principal/principle," 792–793
Procrastination, 537–538, 806–807
Pronouns
    agreement, 799–800
    broad reference, 707–709
    as devices for achieving
        coherence, 561–562
    first-person, 649–651, 786
    indefinite, 705–706
    reference, 706–710
    relative, 685
    second-person, 649–651
    in substantive transitions, 581
Proofreading, 205–206, 245–246,
    545–546, 805–806
Prosecutors, 25
Psychology of writing, 529–531
Punctuation. *See specific
    punctuation mark (e.g.,
    Commas)*
Punctuation for emphasis, 606–607
Purple prose, 664–665
"Pursuant to," usage of, 645

Questions in text, 786–787
Quotation marks, 752–756
    with other marks of punctuation,
        733, 755
    other uses, 755–756
Quotations
    in appellate brief, 453–455
    block, 753

lead-ins for, 753–754
overuse of, 569, 628–630
within quotations, 754–755

Racial bias in language, 656–661
Raise and dismiss, 165
Readers
    expectations, 617–618
    sentence length determined by
        audience, 599–601
Reading cases, 31–39, 138–140,
    215–217
Record on appeal, 384–385
Redundancy, 634–636
Regulations, 49, 62–63
Relationship between federal and
    state governments, 23–25
Relationship between state and
    federal courts, 24
Relative pronouns, 685
Repetition
    of key words, 242–243, 561, 609,
        620
    needless, 634–636, 847–848
    in persuasive writing, 847–848
Reporters
    generally, 51–53, 65–66, 85
    Federal Reporter, 59
    federal reporters, 59, 65–66
    Federal Supplement, 59
    state reporters, 51–53, 85
    Supreme Court Reporter, 59,
        66
    *Supreme Court Reporter, Lawyers'
        Edition*, 59, 66
    United States Reports, 59, 66
Research plans
    city ordinances, 72–73, 75
    common law, 79–80
    county ordinances, 72–73, 75
    court rules, 98
    federal statutes, 58, 68
    state statutes, 43–44
Research templates
    common law, 212–214
    completed, 212–214
Restrictive phrases or clauses,
    728–730
Reviewing the record for error,
    393–394

Revising
    in general, 542–544
    memos, 194–199, 240–246
Rhetorical preferences, 836–856
Rhetorical questions, 786–787
Roadmaps, 195–196, 553–555
Rule section in memos
    citations, 164
    general rules, 160–164
        content, 160–164
        order of information, 160–161
    specific rules, 167–168
Rules of law
    capitalization rules, 778–779
    understanding, 138–140
Run-on sentences, 768

"Said," as an adjective, 648
Sample briefs
    appellate briefs, 464–507
    motion briefs, 342–380
Sample memoranda, 113–129
Schedules for writing, 530
Science majors, as writers, 13–14
Scientists, as writers, 13–14
Scope of review, 384
Script format, 156–191, 225–234,
        248–251, 253–257, 259–260,
        262
Secondary authorities
    American Law Reports, 53–54, 67,
        85–86
    Google, 59, 80
    hornbooks, 46, 60, 81–82
    law reviews and journals, 54, 67,
        86
    looseleaf services, 67–68
    Nutshells, 46, 60, 81–82
    practice books and manuals,
        45–46, 60, 80–81, 82
    state attorney general opinions,
        53
Second-person pronouns, 649–651
Selecting cases, 176
Semicolons, 743–747
    with coordinating conjunctions,
        746–747
    main clauses not joined by
        coordinating conjunctions,
        744

    to separate items in a series,
        745–746
    with "yet" or "so," 746
Sentence openers
    conciseness, 801–802
    throat-clearing expressions,
        631–633
    variety in, 670–671
    weak, 595
Sentence patterns, 679–682
Sentences
    active and passive voice, 199–201,
        314, 428, 589–593
    concluding, 567–569
    editing techniques, 199–205
    emphasis in, 602–610
    length, 599–602
        variety in, 204–205, 669–670
    new information at end, 203–204
    old information at beginning,
        203–204
    patterns within, 679–682
    persuasive writing, 313–314,
        426–427
    problem sentences, 803
    short, 602
    similarities or differences,
        highlighting with sentence
        structure, 610–614
    subject-verb distance, 203,
        597–598
    topic, 563–567
Session laws, 47, 61
Sexist modifiers, 654–655
Shepard's, 105
Short sentences, 602
Signing a brief, 341, 462
Signposts, 196–197, 555–556
Similarities, using sentence structure
        to highlight, 610–614
Simile, 674–675
Single tasking, 542
Single-word emphasizers, 607–608
Spelling, 769–770
Split infinitives, 546–547
Standard of review, 396
State attorney general opinions, 53
"State," capitalization of, 777
State cases, 51–53, 86
State courts, 22–23

State law, sources of, 44–54, 81,
    101–102
Statement of facts in memos
    checklist, 147–148, 220–221
    fact selection, 141–144, 217–218
    organizational patterns, 144–146,
        218–220
    presentation of facts, 146–147,
        220
Statement of facts in motion brief,
    306–316
    active and passive voice, 314
    airtime, 311
    checklist, 316
    context, favorable, 308–309
    dependent and main clauses,
        314–315
    detail, 311–312
    point of view, 310
    positions of emphasis, 312–313
    presentation of facts, 308–316
    selecting an organizational
        scheme, 307–308
    selecting the facts, 307
    sentence length, 313–314
    word choice, 315–316
Statement of the case in appellate
    brief, 415–430
    active and passive voice, 428
    airtime, 422–423
    context, favorable, 418–420
    detail, 423–424
    facts, selection of, 416–417
    main and dependent clauses, 427
    organizational scheme, 417
    paragraph length, 426–427
    point of view, 420–422
    positions of emphasis, 425–426
    references to the record, 417
    rules governing, 415
    selecting an organizational
        scheme, 417
    sentence construction, 427
    sentence length, 426–427
    word choice, 428–429
State regulations, 49
State statutes
    annotated codes, 48
    background reading, 44–47
    hornbooks and Nutshells, 46

practice manuals and practice
    books, 45–46
research plans, 43–44
session laws, 47
sources, 44–54
unannotated codes, 47–48
State websites, 47
"Statute," capitalization of, 777
Statutes
    ambiguity of, 260
    analysis, 137–138
    annotated codes, 48, 62
    notes of decision, 50, 64
    session laws, 47, 61
    unannotated codes, 47–48,
        61–62
    understanding, 137–138
Subject complements, 682, 701
Subjects
    active voice, 589–590
    concrete, 593–595
    distance from, 203, 597–598
    sentence patterns, 679–682
Subject-verb agreement, 698–703
Subject-verb-object combinations,
    630–631
Subject-verb-object mismatch,
    621–626
Subjunctive mood, 696–697
Subordinating conjunctions, 684
Substantive transitions, 580–587
"Such," as an adjective, 648
Summary of argument in appellate
    brief, 430–431
Supreme Court Reporter, 66
Supreme Court Reporter, Lawyers'
    Edition, 66
Symbols, 783
Synonyms, 618–620
Synthesis, 169–173, 214–217

Table of authorities for appellate
    brief, 408–409
Table of contents for appellate brief,
    408
Templates
    for memorandum discussion
        section
        Chevron analysis, 261
        circuit split, 259–260

Templates (*continued*)
    competing interests, balancing
       of, 254–255
    issue of first impression,
       259–260
    statutory question, 157–159
    for research
       common law, 212–214
       completed, 212–214
Tense, 692–697
Terms of art, 647–648
Text messaging, 279–281
"That" vs. "which," 730, 793–795
"The"
    capitalization of, 777
    correct use of, 816–820
    omission of, 648–649
"The fact that," 639
Theory of the case, 304–305, 400
Three-column chart, 532
Throat-clearing expressions, 631–633
Time management, 529–531,
    538–542
Titles of works, 702, 779
Tone
    in e-mail, 277
    in e-memos, 269
    in opinion letter, 289–291
    pompous language, 633
Topic sentences, 563–567
    analogous case, 230
    implied, 567
    revising, 196–197
    stated, 564–566
Topographical names, 778
Trademarks, capitalization rule, 779
Transitions, 573–587
    exact meaning, 804–805
    generic, 573–578, 803–804
    imprecise, 577
    late, 577
    missing, 576
    orienting, 578–579
    revising, 196–197
    substantive, 580–587
Types of authority
    citators, 106–107
    finding tools. *See* Finding tools
    mandatory, 25
    persuasive, 25

    primary, 92–94
    secondary. *See* Secondary
      authorities

Unannotated codes, 47–48, 61–62
Underlining, 604
Undisputed elements, 164–167
Undisputed factors, 252
United States Code, 59, 62, 99
United States Code Annotated, 59,
    62, 99
United States Code Service, 59, 62,
    99
United States Reports, 66
Unity in paragraphs, 544, 559–560
Unknown facts, 144, 217–218

Variety
    in sentence length, 204–205,
      669–670
    in sentence openers, 670–671
Verbs, 822–833
    action, 595–597
    auxiliary, 680, 822–825
    auxiliary or helping verb chart,
      822–824
    distance from subject, 203,
      597–598
    with gerunds, 826–832
    helping, 680, 822–825
    with infinitives, 826–832
    linking, 681
    mixing active and passive, 593
    with objects and infinitives,
      826–832
    with prepositions, 834
    sentence patterns, 680–682
Verb tense, 692–697, 825–826
Vessels, capitalization rule, 779
Voice, 589–593
    effective use of active voice,
      590–592
    effective use of passive voice,
      592–593

Westlaw
    KeyCite, 106–107
    multi-tasking, 538
    primary authority, 93
    using to find briefs, 95

using to find cases, 50, 66, 94
using to find law review and
    journal articles, 54, 67, 86
using to find statutes, 48, 62
WestlawNext, 48, 54, 60, 82, 86
using to find cases, 52–53, 64, 77,
    83, 93
"Whereas," 644
"Which" vs. "that," 730, 793–795
"Who/whom," 685, 689
Word choice, 428–429, 449,
    615–626
Wordiness, 626–641, 838–840,
    847–848
Word order, changing, 608–609
Writers. *See also* Legal writing in
    general

advice for specific groups, 11–14
English majors, 11–12
journalism majors, 12–13
journalists, 12–13
other cultures, 14
philosophy majors, 12
role of, 9–10
science majors, 13–14
scientists, 13–14
Writer's block, 529, 535, 536
Writing lists, 531–535
Writing plans, 531–535

"You," use of, 649–651